Liquidity and Crises

Liquidity and Crises

EDITED BY
Franklin Allen
Elena Carletti
Jan Pieter Krahnen
Marcel Tyrell

OXFORD
UNIVERSITY PRESS
2011

OXFORD
UNIVERSITY PRESS

Oxford University Press, Inc., publishes works that further
Oxford University's objective of excellence
in research, scholarship, and education.

Oxford New York
Auckland Cape Town Dar es Salaam Hong Kong Karachi
Kuala Lumpur Madrid Melbourne Mexico City Nairobi
New Delhi Shanghai Taipei Toronto

With offices in
Argentina Austria Brazil Chile Czech Republic France Greece
Guatemala Hungary Italy Japan Poland Portugal Singapore
South Korea Switzerland Thailand Turkey Ukraine Vietnam

Published by Oxford University Press, Inc.
198 Madison Avenue, New York, New York 10016
www.oup.com

Library of Congress Cataloging-in-Publication Data
Liquidity and crises / edited by Franklin Allen . . . [et al.].
p. cm.
Includes bibliographical references and index.
ISBN 978-0-19-539070-4 (cloth) –
ISBN 978-0-19-539071-1 (pbk.)
1. Liquidity (Economics) 2. Financial crises.
I. Allen, Franklin, 1956–
HG178.L568 2010
338.5′42–dc22 2009049205

Contents

Contributors

Viral V. Acharya, New York University

Franklin Allen, University of Pennsylvania

Sudipto Bhattacharya, London School of Economics

Ricardo Caballero, Massachusetts Institute of Technology

Elena Carletti, European University Institute

Juan Carlos Cordoba, Rice University

Amil Dasgupta, London School of Economics

Giovanni Dell'Ariccia, International Monetary Fund

Casper de Vries, Erasmus University Rotterdam

Douglas W. Diamond, University of Chicago

Andrea L. Eisfeldt, Northwestern University

Mark J. Flannery, University of Florida

Xavier Freixas, Universitat Pompeu Fabra

Craig H. Furfine, Northwestern University

Douglas Gale, New York University

Itay Goldstein, University of Pennsylvania

Gary Gorton, Yale University

Philipp Hartmann, European Central Bank

Bengt Holmström, Massachusetts Institute of Technology

Cornelia Holthausen, European Central Bank

Lixin Huang, Georgia State University

Nobuhiro Kiyotaki, Princeton University

Jan Pieter Krahnen, Goethe University Frankfurt

Arvind Krishnamurthy, Northwestern University

Guido Lorenzoni, Massachusetts Institute of Technology

Robert Marquez, Boston University

John Moore, University of Edinburgh

Raghuram G. Rajan, University of Chicago

Rafael Repullo, The Center for Monetary and Financial Studies

Marla Ripoll, University of Pittsburgh

Jean-Charles Rochet, Swiss Banking Institute

Stefan Straetmans, Maastricht University

Jean Tirole, Toulouse School of Economics

Marcel Tyrell, Goethe University Frankfurt

Christian Upper, Bank for International Settlements

Xavier Vives, IESE Business School, University of Navarra

Andrea Worms, Deutsche Bundesbank

Tanju Yorulmazer, Federal Reserve Bank of New York

Liquidity and Crises

1 An Introduction to Liquidity and Crises

Franklin Allen, Elena Carletti, Jan Pieter Krahnen, and Marcel Tyrell

Introduction

Financial crises have occurred for hundreds of years. However, the fact that they often appear without warning is something that most people have apparently forgotten in the recent past. Hence the financial crisis that started in the summer of 2007 came as a surprise to many observers. In particular, it was astonishing to see that a breakdown in just one part of the housing market, i.e. the US subprime mortgage market, did lead to a systemic crisis that escalated and spilled over to financial markets all over the world. Thus, the financial crisis, that began in the US, did not only spread to Europe but became global, even affecting emerging markets and less developed countries that resisted the bad lending practices, did not purchase toxic assets, and did not allow their banks to engage in excessive risk taking through derivatives.

One important reason for the global impact of the 2007 financial crisis is massive illiquidity in combination with an extreme exposure of economically and politically relevant parties to liquidity needs and market conditions. As a consequence, many financial instruments could not be traded anymore, investors ran on a variety of financial institutions particularly in wholesale markets, financial institutions and industrial firms started to sell assets at fire sale prices to raise cash, and central banks all over the world injected huge amounts of liquidity into financial systems.

But what is liquidity and why is it so important for firms and financial institutions to command enough liquidity? This handbook brings together classic articles and recent contributions to this important field of research. In this introduction we will provide an overview of the book and review each section in turn, thereby drawing connections to some of the most recent academic literature on liquidity and crises.

We start in Section 1 with a discussion of liquidity and interbank markets. Section 2 considers the public provision of liquidity and regulation. Money, liquidity and asset prices are covered in Section 3. Section 4 is concerned with contagion effects in financial crises. Section 5 considers financial crises and currency crises. Finally, Section 6 concludes.

1. Liquidity and Interbank Markets

Interbank markets play a key role for the functioning of financial systems. They should ensure an efficient liquidity transfer between surplus and needy banks. They are the focus of central banks' implementation of monetary policy and a smooth functioning of interbank markets is essential for maintaining the financial stability of the overall financial system. Despite this key role they play and despite the potentially significant effect their functioning has on the whole economy, there was, at least in the past, relatively little work studying interbank markets. That might be related to the fact that until Bryant (1980) and Diamond and Dybvig (1983) developed a consistent framework with banks performing an important role in terms of maturity transformation, i.e. collecting demand deposits and raising funds in the short-term capital market and investing them in long-term assets, there was no theory in which interbank markets could be an important part of an optimal financial arrangement.

The seminal paper by Bhattacharya and Gale (1987, reprinted in this handbook) is the pioneering theoretical study in this area. In the spirit of the Diamond-Dybvig model, where consumers, who are subject to privately observed preference shocks, put their money in the bank in exchange for a deposit, they analyze a setting in which individual banks face privately observed liquidity shocks due to the proportion of depositors wishing to make early withdrawals. In addition to this liquidity demand shift, each bank has private information about the fraction of its portfolio of liquid assets. Since the liquidity shocks are imperfectly correlated across intermediaries, banks coinsure each other against liquidity shocks through an interbank lending market. Bhattacharya and Gale show that even in the absence of an aggregate liquidity shock over the intermediary sector as a whole, banks are induced to under-invest in liquid assets and free-ride on the common pool of liquidity. The main reason is the lower return which liquid assets yield. Therefore, one can have aggregate liquidity shortages notwithstanding the presence of an interbank market. Hence, as Bhattacharya and Gale suggest, a central bank can mitigate this problem by (even imperfectly) monitoring banks' asset choices. However, they argue one would not expect to achieve the first-best, as in such an asymmetric information setting it seems unrealistic to assume that a central bank can elicit perfect knowledge of the quality of the assets in overall bank portfolios. In addition, in such a framework pumping liquidity into the banking sector at large does not guarantee it will end up at the banks which need it most.

It is fair to say that the Bhattacharya-Gale model provided an extremely promising start to a research program, one that seriously examined the implications of microeconomically founded financial intermediation theory for the functioning of financial markets and financial intermediaries, optimal liquidity provision and financial fragility. First of all, it appears to be the case that market liquidity varies with the state of the economy. Thus, one can observe countercyclical variations in spreads between liquid and illiquid assets over the business cycle, liquidity crises being released by economic downturns, and in cross-sectional studies a positive relationship between industrial productivity and the liquidity of the respective asset markets. Eisfeldt (2004) (reprinted in this handbook), develops an interesting model to understand these features of liquidity in asset markets. She analyzes an economy with long-term risky assets that vary in quality. Illiquidity is a consequence of adverse selection as investors want to realize part of the value of the long-term assets early on by issuing claims against the assets in a pooled market. It follows that the equilibrium price is given by the average quality of the claims sold. Hence, the term "liquidity" refers here to the cost of transferring expected future payoffs into current income. This framework allows her to draw a connection from the degree of adverse selection to market liquidity. As the claim price is an increasing function of the portion of high-quality assets sold in the market, it is the case that the higher the fraction of high-quality claims traded, the less adverse selection there is in the market and the more liquid is the asset market.

However, what basically determines the degree of adverse selection and hence the liquidity of the asset markets? In principle, in a market setting it is the amount of trade for reasons other than private information, such as consumption, investment, or portfolio rebalancing motives, which can ameliorate adverse selection. Eisfeldt finds that, in particular, a higher productivity of the economy increases liquidity. High productivity leads to a high relative return on risky assets, and this induces more investment in large-scale risky projects at all income levels. Investors then self-insure less with riskless assets, the outcome of risky projects has a higher impact on the income of investors, and more claims to high quality projects are sold in the market because of motives such as consumption and new investment. Essentially, a high productivity does increase the fraction of high quality assets traded and the amount of trade for reasons other than private information. Both factors reduce adverse selection problems and cause liquidity to increase.

In addition, there is an interesting feedback mechanism at work: liquidity enlarges the impact of productivity on investment. Of course, investment increases with productivity, but liquidity amplifies this effect since higher liquidity makes long-term risky investment even more attractive. Of course, we should observe the opposite effects in economic downturns. Even though literally taken the framework provided by Eisfeldt was not developed to analyze banking markets and financial crises, the basic mechanisms she studies have a more general appeal. It appears quite natural to interpret the liquidity squeeze in the interbank market in terms of the mechanics of her model.

Another very prominent line of research followed in the literature is to develop a deeper and more general understanding of the interaction of financial markets and financial intermediaries. For instance in the Bhattacharya-Gale setup, the characterisation of interbank markets is quite rudimentary and, in addition, interbank markets are not part of an optimal arrangement in their framework. Thus, it is essential to have a framework with both a role for financial intermediaries and for markets modelled from first principles. Allen and Gale (2004a, 2004b, both reprinted in this handbook, 2010), among others such as Diamond (1997) and Fecht (2004), developed such an approach. They argue that in modern financial systems financial markets and financial intermediaries are complementary. Following the argument in Diamond and Dybvig (1983), intermediaries provide an insurance function to consumers against their individual liquidity shocks in their framework. However, individual investors cannot trade directly in the full range of markets since due to information and transaction costs it is too costly for them. That is the reason why markets also play an important role in this environment. Markets allow financial intermediaries (and hence their depositors) to share risk. Intermediaries such as banks and mutual funds can invest in financial markets. They are providing risk-sharing services by packaging existing claims on behalf of investors who do not have access to markets and, of course, are trading these claims on markets. Such a general equilibrium framework allows Allen and Gale a normative analysis of liquidity provision by the financial system.

Consumers deposit funds into banks which provide liquidity insurance such that depositors can withdraw whenever they have liquidity needs. Banks accumulate the funds and lend them to firms to fund long-term investments. There are two types of uncertainty concerning liquidity needs which makes liquidity management on the part of banks quite difficult. The first is that each bank is exposed to idiosyncratic liquidity risk. At any given date its customers may have more or less liquidity needs. The second type of uncertainty is aggregate liquidity risk which banks have to face. In some periods liquidity demand is high while in others it is low, thereby exposing all banks to the same shock at the same time.

What Allen and Gale analyze in such a framework is the ability of banks to hedge themselves against these liquidity shocks. They show in Allen and Gale (2004a) that this crucially depends on the completeness of financial markets. If markets are complete in the sense that for each aggregate state an Arrow security can be traded, then the financial system provides liquidity efficiently as it ensures that banks' liquidity shocks are hedged. In particular, they show that in an environment with complete markets and in which intermediaries can offer complete contingent contracts, the resulting allocation is incentive-efficient. With complete contracts, the consequences of default will be anticipated and therefore included in the contract, so default and financial crises do not occur. If intermediaries can only offer incomplete contracts, a case in point is where banks only offer deposit contracts, default can improve welfare by improving the contingency of contracts. Thus, financial crises do occur in such a model, but are not necessarily a source of market failure. Hence, even in this case with incomplete contracts, the financial system provides optimal liquidity and risk sharing if markets for aggregate risks are complete. A set of complete and perfect financial markets, which includes of course interbank markets, is necessary for an efficient functioning of the financial system. Only missing markets may provide a role for government intervention. If markets are incomplete, then there may be too much or too little liquidity, and government regulation may be welfare-improving.

Allen and Gale (2004b) explore in further detail interesting ramifications of this framework. By using a simplified version of the general equilibrium model introduced in Allen and Gale (2004a), they investigate the role of liquidity in determining asset prices. The incompleteness of markets leads to an inefficient provision of liquidity by the financial system. This can generate cash-in-the-market pricing, which implies that the prices of long-term safe assets can fall below their fundamental value, and leads to financial fragility, which means that even small shocks can have large price effects.

The intuition for this result is as follows. When markets are incomplete, liquidity provision is achieved by selling assets when liquidity is required. That implies, asset prices are determined by the available liquidity or in other words by the cash in the market in case liquidity is scarce. Due to the incompleteness of markets, liquidity cannot be traded in a state-contingent manner and hence suppliers of liquidity can no longer be compensated for the cost of providing liquidity state by state. Instead they must be compensated on average across all states and that causes inefficiency. Providers of liquidity have the alternative of investing in a productive long-term asset. Therefore holding liquidity is associated with an opportunity cost as this has a lower return than the productive long-term asset. Hence, providers of liquidity must be able to make a profit in some states in order to get compensated for holding the liquidity. However, in equilibrium they can only make a profit in those states where liquidity is scarce. In states of abundant liquidity where banks do not need liquidity, liquidity suppliers have to bear the opportunity cost of holding liquidity. Accordingly it must be the case that in states where banks face high liquidity demand, the equilibrium price of the long-term asset is low enough to compensate the liquidity providers for all the other states where they do not make any profit. Otherwise, they will not hold the liquidity in the first place. Hence, prices are low in states where banks need more liquidity. Asset price volatility is a consequence of compensating liquidity suppliers. But from an efficiency point of view there is a transfer from the banks who need liquidity to the providers of liquidity. Negative insurance and suboptimal risk sharing will be the result. Allen and Gale (2004b) show that the only equilibria that are robust in such a setting involve stochastic consumption as well as volatile asset prices.

This framework also builds the cornerstone of further analysis on the structure and behaviour of financial systems in crisis situations. In Allen and Gale (2006) and Allen and Carletti (2006, reprinted in Section 4 of this handbook, 2010) the standard model of intermediation is extended by adding an insurance sector, where banks and insurance companies do different things. Banks provide liquidity insurance to depositors, and insurance companies pool risks. Again with complete markets and contracts for aggregate risks intersectoral transfers are desirable. They allow risks to be shared efficiently between different industries. However, with incomplete markets and contracts for aggregate risks, Allen and Gale (2006) show how inefficient capital regulation can lead to credit risk transfer as a result of regulatory arbitrage and this in turn can increase systemic risk. Allen and Carletti (2006) analyze how financial innovation can create contagion across sectors and lower welfare relative to the autarky situation where banks face idiosyncratic liquidity risk and hedge this risk in the interbank market. Credit risk transfer can lead to contagion between sectors and increase the risk of financial crises. Allen and Carletti (2008) analyze the effects of mark-to-market accounting when financial markets are incomplete. They emphasize the point made above that in times of financial crisis the interaction of institutions and markets can cause prices in markets to reflect the amount of cash or liquidity available to buyers in the market rather than reflecting future payoffs. However, with mark-to-market accounting the asset price volatility directly affects the value of banks' assets. This can lead to contagion and force banks into insolvency even though they would be fully able to cover their commitments if they were allowed to continue until the assets mature.

Also cross-country bank lending appears to be affected by market imperfections. Freixas and Holthausen (2004, reprinted in this handbook) investigate the scope for interbank market integration across countries when there is better information about the solvency of domestic banks than of foreign banks. In a Diamond-Dybvig type of framework, where consumers want to insure themselves against uncertainty about the timing of their consumption needs by depositing in banks, they analyze the scope for international interbank market integration when cross-country information is noisy.

The timing of consumption needs generates liquidity shocks for the banks, which are present both at the individual and at the aggregate level. Banks can cope with these shocks by investing in a storage technology. However, as this technology yields a lower return than alternative investments, it is efficient for banks to use the interbank market for channelling liquidity. This reduces the amount of liquidity needed in the economy. Because banks are assumed to have some risk of failure, "peer monitoring" is important in improving the efficiency of the interbank market. Banks monitor each other in the interbank market to obtain a signal on the solvency probability of each of their peers. But cross-border information about banks is less precise than home country information.

Freixas and Holthausen analyze different interbank lending scenarios. They look at secured repo and unsecured interbank lending markets since both allow banks to cope with liquidity shocks, and they consider under which conditions segmented integrated international interbank markets (co-)exist. They show that a segmented interbank market is always an equilibrium, while the emergence of an integrated international market depends on the quality of cross-border information. Only if cross-border information is sufficiently precise, is integration of markets possible. However, the integration does not always lead to a more efficient outcome. The existence of repo markets appears to be a mixed blessing. On the one hand, a repo market is a perfect medium to channel funds between banks and countries, on the other hand, the secured nature of repo markets reduces the incentives for peer monitoring. Hence, a repo market reduces interest rate spreads and improves upon the segmentation equilibrium, but it can lead to a collapse of the unsecured integrated market, thereby reducing overall welfare.

A similar argument is suggested by Fecht and Grüner (2007) and Leitner (2005). Fecht and Grüner (2007) study the role of secured versus unsecured lending on the interbank market and show that only in states of abundant liquidity, secured interbank lending dominates unsecured lending. However, when aggregate liquidity is scarce, only unsecured lending delivers proper incentive effects. They argue that unsecured lending induces banks with excess liquidity to internalize, at least in part, the costs which their withdrawal decision in the interbank market inflicts on their counterparty. This is in particular the case when withdrawal raises the default risk of the respective counterparty and the counterparty's bankruptcy is costly for the withdrawer. Therefore, in a situation of expected aggregate liquidity shortage, unsecured interbank lending provides stronger incentives not to misreport excess liquidity to the market. Banks are able to mutually insure each other against regional liquidity shocks, however, this comes at the cost of creating stronger contagion risks.

Leitner (2005) also refers to the disciplinary effect of unsecured interbank deposits. He argues that banks intentionally choose fragile or incomplete interbank structures to expose themselves to the risk of contagion in order to credibly commit to bail each other out in the event of an individual crisis. In a related paper, Kahn and Santos (2008) investigate whether banks choose the optimal degree of mutual insurance against liquidity shocks. They show that when there is a shortage of exogenously supplied liquidity, which can be supplemented by bank liquidity creation, the banks generally fail to find the correct degree of interdependence. In aggregate, they become too risky.

There are in addition some very interesting recent contributions to this line of literature that are spurred by the turbulence in the interbank markets in the 2007/2008 financial crisis. These include Allen, Carletti and Gale (2009), Acharya, Gromb and Yorulmazer (2008), Heider, Hoerova and Holthausen (2009), Freixas and Jorge (2008), Freixas, Martin and Skeie (2009), Diamond and Rajan (2009), and Acharya, Gale and Yorulmazer (2009).

Allen, Carletti and Gale (2009) show that the interbank market is characterized by excessive price volatility when there is a lack of opportunities for banks to hedge aggregate and idiosyncratic liquidity shocks. They analyze how the central bank should intervene to restore efficiency. By using open market operations to fix the short-term interest rate, the central bank can prevent price volatility and implement the constrained efficient solution. Thus, the central bank effectively completes the market, a result in line with the argument of Goodfriend and King (1988) that open market operations are sufficient to address pure liquidity risk on the interbank markets. Interestingly, one implication of the model is that situations where banks stop trading with each other can be a feature of the constrained efficient solution implemented by central bank policy if aggregate uncertainty is high. Banks may hoard liquidity because they may need it to meet high aggregate demand. When aggregate demand is low, however, they have enough liquidity to meet idiosyncratic shocks and accordingly do not need the interbank market. As a result the volume in the market falls to zero, but there is no need for central banks to intervene since the freeze is consistent with constrained efficiency.

Acharya, Gromb and Yorulmazer (2008) model the interbank markets as being characterized by moral hazard, asymmetric information, and monopoly power in times of crisis. They show that in such a situation a bank with surplus liquidity has bargaining power vis-à-vis deficit banks which are in need of liquidity to keep funding projects. Surplus banks may strategically provide insufficient lending in the interbank market in order to induce inefficient sales of bank-specific assets by the needy banks, which results in an inefficient allocation of resources. The role of the central bank is to provide an outside option to the deficit bank for acquiring the needed liquidity.

Freixas and Jorge (2008) examine how financial imperfections in the interbank market affect the monetary policy transmission mechanism. In their model, firms face liquidity shocks and rely on bank credit to raise external finance. Through this channel, firms' shocks will result in a demand for credit and a liquidity shock for the banks. As a buffer against liquidity shocks banks hold assets and liquid securities. Since banks hold different amounts of securities and face different liquidity shocks, there is a role for an interbank market to trade reserves. However, asymmetric information in the interbank market induces an equilibrium with quantity rationing in the bank loan market since the interbank market is unable to efficiently channel liquidity to solvent illiquid banks. As a consequence, monetary transmission might have a strong effect because by tightening monetary policy banks with less liquidity are forced to cut down on their lending. In addition, liquidity reserves condition the banks' reaction to monetary policy.

In a similar vein, Heider, Hoerova and Holthausen (2009) analyze the functioning of interbank markets. They build a model in the spirit of Diamond and Dybvig (1983). As banks face individual liquidity shocks, there is a role for an interbank market in which banks with surplus liquidity can lend to those with a liquidity shortage. An interbank loan may not be repaid, however, because the long-term investment is risky, thus, giving rise to counterparty risk. Asymmetric information about counterparty risk can elevate the interbank market spreads and in extreme situations lead to a total interbank market break down. In case of such severe adverse selection problems, either all the lenders in the market prefer to hoard liquidity despite high interest rates or all the borrowers drop out because they find the interest rates too high.

Both, Freixas and Jorge (2008) and Heider, Hoerova and Holthausen (2009), assume the existence of an interbank market despite the fact that in their setting interbank markets are not part of an optimal financial arrangement. This is different in the model of Freixas, Martin and Skeie (2009) where, similar in spirit to the model of Allen, Carletti and Gale (2009), interbank markets are efficient. They suggest that inducing low interbank market rates in states of financial disruptions is an optimal policy response of the central bank. As they argue, a primary role for banks under incomplete markets is to provide better risk-sharing possibilities and more liquidity than markets. Yet during financial disruption, the banks themselves face considerable uncertainty regarding their own idiosyncratic liquidity needs. Hence, they may have large borrowing needs in the interbank market. They show that an interbank market can achieve the optimal allocation, which implies efficient risk sharing to consumers and insuring banks against idiosyncratic liquidity shocks. Though, in the optimum the interest rate on this market must be state-contingent and low in states of financial disruption. This suggests a role for the central bank which in their model can implement the efficient allocation by setting the interest rates in the interbank market.

Diamond and Rajan (2009) relate the seizing up of term credit with the overhang of illiquid securities. When banks have a significant quantity of assets with a limited set of potential buyers, shocks in future liquidity demands may trigger sales at fire sale prices. The prospect of a future fire sale of the bank's assets depresses their current value. In these conditions, banks prefer holding on to the illiquid assets and risking a fire sale and insolvency than selling the asset and ensuring its own stability in the future, since the states in which the depressed asset value recovers are precisely the states in which the bank survives. In turn, this creates high expected returns to holding cash or liquid securities across the financial system and an aversion to locking up money in term loans.

Acharya, Gale and Yorulmazer (2009) show that freezes in markets for rollover debt, such as asset-backed commercial paper, depend on how information about the quality of the asset is revealed. When there is a constant probability that "bad news" is revealed each period and, in the absence of bad news, the value of the assets is high. By contrast, when there is a constant probability that "good news" is revealed each period and, in the absence of good news, the value of the assets is low. In the latter scenario, the debt capacity of the assets is below the fundamental value and is decreasing in the liquidation cost and frequency of rollovers. In the limit, as the number of rollovers becomes unbounded, the debt capacity goes to zero even for an arbitrarily small default risk.

A closely related literature focuses on the operation of markets when agents have liquidity shocks and trade in markets. The difference is that there are no banks or other intermediaries. A number of interesting results are derived. Huang and Wang (2008a, b) show that purely idiosyncratic and non-fundamental shocks can cause market crashes if capital flow is costly. Agents trade to smooth out idiosyncratic shocks to their wealth. Since there is no aggregate uncertainty, their trades will be perfectly synchronized and matched, and there will be no need for liquidity if market presence is costless. In this case, the market-clearing price always reflects the fundamental value of the asset, and idiosyncratic shocks generate trading but have no impact on prices. In contrast, when market presence is costly, the need for liquidity arises endogenously and idiosyncratic shocks can affect prices via two channels: first trading becomes infrequent which makes traders more risk averse, and second the gains from trading for potential sellers are always larger than the gains from trading for potential buyers. The asymmetry in their appetite to trade leads to order imbalances in the form of excess supply, and the price has to decrease in response.

Two studies isolate illiquidity risk from other confounding effects. Morris and Shin (2009) define "illiquidity risk" the probability of a default due to a run when the institution would otherwise have been solvent. They show that there is a difference between "asset insolvency risk," as the conditional probability of default due to deterioration of asset quality if there is no run by short term creditors, and "total credit risk," as the unconditional probability of default, either because of a (short term) creditor run or (long run) asset insolvency.

Brunnermeier and Pedersen (2009) distinguish between market liquidity and funding liquidity. Market liquidity reflects how difficult is to raise money by selling the asset, instead of by borrowing against it. Traders provide market liquidity, and their ability to do so depends on their availability of funding. Conversely, traders' funding, i.e., their capital and margin requirements, depends on the assets' market liquidity. They show that, under certain conditions, margins are destabilizing and market liquidity and funding liquidity are mutually reinforcing, leading to liquidity spirals.

There is some interesting empirical research on the functioning of interbank markets. One of the first studies was conducted by Furfine (2001, reprinted in this handbook). In the paper it will be investigated by examining the pricing of interbank lending agreements whether banks are really monitoring other banks. The main empirical finding is that the interest rate charged on federal funds transactions reflects, at least in part, the credit risk of the borrowing institution in the sense that borrowing institutions with higher profitability, higher capital ratios, and fewer problem loans pay lower rates. Furthermore, the size and relative importance of the trading institution has a negative impact on the interest rate charged for overnight borrowing. Both results suggest that banks can distinguish credit risk among peers and price it in accordance, therefore effectively monitoring other banks.

In a recent study conducted by Fecht, Nyborg and Rocholl (2008) which is based on 78 consecutive repo auctions by the Eurosystem between June 2000 and December 2001, the authors confirm the result that the price of liquidity systematically depends on bank characteristics such as size and liquidity position and on market conditions. They find that a greater imbalance in liquidity positions across banks is associated with a rise in the price of liquidity. In particular, banks which are in need of liquidity are affected by the need to pay a higher price in times of overall greater imbalances in liquidity positions. This suggests that even in relatively normal times in the interbank market, liquidity squeezes occur and needy banks are most affected by the potential for a squeeze. Imperfections in the market for liquidity appear to be an enduring and pertinent feature of modem financial systems.

2. Public Provision of Liquidity and Regulation

Liquidity problems, among others, have played a crucial role in several financial crises of the past. But in particular the credit crisis that began in the summer of 2007 reminds us how important it is in particular for macroeconomic stability to have sufficient financial market liquidity. In addition, as ample evidence from the recent crisis shows, liquidity can suddenly dry up with disastrous consequences for the real economy. This raises many interesting questions. However, among the most important ones are the following. When is the corporate sector of an economy in fact liquidity constrained? How should we define liquidity shortage? Is there a role for governments and international financial markets in providing liquidity?

Holmström and Tirole (1998, reprinted in this handbook) provide an answer to these questions. They offer an explanation of the demand for and supply of liquid assets based on the insight from modern corporate finance that, in general, some part of a firm's income stream cannot be pledged to investors. Several reasons can be given for why part of the income from investment would be non-pledgeable, for instance it might be due to the missing participation of investors in certain markets or due to imperfect information which reduces the potential set of financial claims. However, one key implication of non-pledgeability is that firms as well as consumers can rely on liquidating only part of their wealth whenever they need funds. Hence, to cope with negative financial shocks, they must hoard liquid assets or contract in other ways for the provision of liquidity. Accordingly, they are willing to pay a premium for financial services. As the supply of liquid assets is constrained by the fact that only part of the return from productive assets can be pledged, non-pledgeability also reduces the amount of wealth in the economy which investors could use to promise future financing of firms. In sum, non-pledgeability gives rise to a demand for stores of value across periods as well as across future states of nature. Based on this framework, Holmström and Tirole investigate three ways by which the private sector can meet future liquidity needs on its own: by issuing new claims, by obtaining a credit line from a financial intermediary and by holding claims on other firms. They show that the private sector provides enough liquidity if the corporate sector is a net borrower and there is no aggregate shock. However, even without aggregate uncertainty, financial intermediaries that hoard financial assets and allocate liquidity to firms in need are required to support such a second-best plan. They have to coordinate the use of scarce liquidity by creating a sufficiently rich set of contingent claims, a function which a stock and bond market in general cannot fulfil. The reason is that, because of limited commitment possibilities, there is not a rich enough set of financial instruments and therefore liquidity is wasted. If all firms are hit by the same macroeconomic shock or more generally if there is sufficient aggregate uncertainty, the private sector cannot provide enough liquidity on its own.

Holmstöm and Tirole show that in such a situation financial instruments that originate outside the private sector can improve productive efficiency by facilitating access to liquidity and by lowering the cost of it. They argue that a government can provide these instruments by issuing bonds that commit future consumer income. Since the government has the power to enforce tax payments, it can commit funds on behalf of consumers who are unable to commit their future endowments, unless these endowments are backed up by marketable assets. Through its taxation power, governments can issue securities at a premium, thereby creating liquidity for the corporate sector. They show that the government should loosen liquidity when the economy is hit by a high negative aggregate liquidity shock, and should tighten liquidity when the shock is low.

The setup by Holmström-Tirole proved to be extremely useful for analyzing a broad range of questions. For instance, Holmström and Tirole (2008) study how such a theory can explain the pricing of assets, the role of liquidity management, real investment and how this theory relates to some classic issues in macroeconomics and international finance, such as the questions why international markets cannot meet a country's liquidity needs even though there are more than enough financial instruments for saving and insurance and why inefficiencies arise when firms do not coordinate either the use or the acquisition of international liquidity.

In our discussion of liquidity provision so far, asymmetric information has played a relatively small role. In particular, the assets that are traded are not characterized by asymmetric information. In the current crisis many people believe that asymmetric information has played an important role. In the context of banks there exists surprisingly little theoretical research about this aspect. However, Bolton, Santos and Scheinkman (2008, 2009) have provided an interesting theory of liquidity provision with asymmetric information. In their model there are three sets of agents. These are investors with a short horizon, intermediaries and investors with a long horizon. The basic source of inefficiency is asymmetric information about asset values between long-horizon investors and financial intermediaries. Long-horizon investors cannot distinguish between an asset sale that is due to a liquidity need and an asset sale to offload low quality securities. This leads to an adverse selection problem and consequently to a price discount. Furthermore, they assume that as time passes, the intermediary earns more about the assets it holds, and, therefore, the adverse selection problem gets worse and the price discount if the intermediary sells increases.

If now an intermediary is hit by a liquidity shock it has to decide whether to sell its asset immediately at a discount or to try to ride out the crisis. By riding out the crisis, however, the intermediary risks that it has to sell the assets at even higher discount if the crisis lasts longer than expected. It is shown that two types of rational expectations equilibrium exists. In what they call the immediate trading equilibrium, intermediaries sell assets immediately to ensure they have enough liquidity. In the delayed trading equilibrium intermediaries try to ride out the crisis and only sell if they are forced to. Surprisingly, Bolton, Santos and Scheinkman show that for some parameter values both equilibria exist, and, furthermore, that the delayed trading equilibrium is Pareto superior when both exist. The reason is that short-horizon investors undervalue long-term assets while long-horizon investors undervalue cash. There is a gain from inducing short-horizon investors to hold more long-term assets and long-horizon investors more cash. This is what the delayed equilibrium does. Likewise, a potentially beneficial intervention is a policy of public provision of liquidity by a central bank, which guarantees a minimum price for assets by lending against collateral. An interesting aspect is also the notion of liquidity used in their paper. What they call inside liquidity refers to the cash holdings of the intermediaries while the term outside liquidity refers to the proceeds from asset sales to long-horizon investors. That draws a connection to the paper by Brunnermeier and Pedersen (2009) discussed above, which in the context of a market microstructure model also focus on the spillover effects of inside and outside liquidity, or what they refer to as funding and market liquidity.

Gorton and Huang (2004, reprinted in this handbook) also analyze the conditions under which there is a role for the government to supply liquidity by issuing securities. However, they use a framework which is remarkably different from Holmström and Tirole and, therefore leads to a different notion of liquidity as well. In their general equilibrium model, the focus is on the transferability of distressed projects which is the motivation for immediate selling and borrowing. While in Holmström and Tirole, Bolton, Santos and Scheinkman, and, for instance, Diamond and Rajan (2001, 2005, 2006 reprinted in this handbook), a liquidity shock is typically modelled as a sudden need for funds, here a shock means that long-term projects have a low value, i.e. are distressed, which may induce owners of these projects to engage in value destroying activities – in other words, there is moral hazard. Such a negative shock to the value of assets in the hands of an entrepreneur creates a potential need to sell the control rights to the project. Only a recapitalization of such a project by selling it in a "liquidation" market to agents with enough available liquid capital, leads to a situation where the new owners will not engage in value destroying activities. In anticipation of these opportunities on the market for liquidation, entrepreneurs choose at the first date whether to be buyers or sellers in the secondary market. As buyers they invest at the first date in short-term projects with the only purpose of obtaining liquid assets to possibly buy a distressed long-term project at a later date. As sellers they invest in a risky long-term project which is socially more efficient, but illiquid. In that way, the supply of liquidity is endogenized. Gorton and Huang argue, however, that the private provision of liquidity is typically costly for a society. It would be better if instead of projects being sold in the liquidation market, original lenders are willing to forgive debt of borrowers with low-value projects. But, debt forgiveness is not always in the interest of lenders. If it is not in their interest, liquidity will, even though socially inefficient, be hoarded because this is the only way to recapitalize projects. Therefore, they suggest one should analyze whether the government can improve welfare by supplying liquidity. Similarly to Holmström and Tirole (1998), they show that the government can use its taxation power on the owners of illiquid high value projects to recapitalize owners of low-value projects. The state can issue securities backed by tax revenue collected from these entrepreneurs at a later time, to subsidize low-value projects. By extending this analysis to consider possible systemic risk in the banking system, they investigate whether bank bail outs are efficient. Building on the same argument, they provide conditions under which the government can improve welfare by bailing out banks. This is the case, if when banks suffer a negative shock to their capital they are subject to moral hazard by not being interested in recapitalizing their borrowers' projects. Anticipating this, too much liquidity will be privately supplied and that reduces welfare. The papers by Holmström and Tirole (1998) and Gorton and Huang (2004) complement each other. While the first one analyze why it is important to have a stock of government-supplied liquidity in the economy and why this liquidity should be actively managed, Gorton and Huang in addition offer a rationale for bank bailouts done by the government. They show that this type of intervention can improve efficiency whenever there is the potential problem of banks engaging in moral hazard. However, since both settings are quite general, they offer, at least in their original formulation, no detailed answers to the questions of which instruments the government or a central bank as lender of last resort should use in a financial crisis and what the "microstructure" of a lender of last resort policy should look like.

Flannery (1996, reprinted in this handbook) provides a partial answer to these questions. He starts his analysis by suggesting that for every developed economy a cheap, reliable payment system is crucial because it facilitates mutually profitable exchanges and allows agents to exploit economies of specialization. Hence, a proper role of a government lender of last resort (LLOR) should lie in producing payment stability. In particular, he investigates in the context of payment stability the question whether and how the provision of liquidity by a government LLOR should be "fine-tuned". The answer to this question is not clear-cut. Direct government lending (by providing, for example, daylight overdrafts) subsidizes payments made via a central banks' payment system, blunting initiatives by the private sector to produce safer payment arrangements. In this context, Flannery evaluates whether one can rely on private credit markets to channel liquidity to the appropriate banks in a financial crisis. He shows that in a payment system crisis information costs are too high for private lenders, preventing them from redistributing aggregate liquidity to the banks that need it most. Therefore, open market operations which just provide liquidity to the system cannot replace direct LLOR lending to specific institutions. In this sense, there may be a positive role for the government in assuring payment system stability. Under certain circumstances direct LLOR lending can supplement open market operations as a means of enhancing social welfare during a crisis.

In the papers by Repullo (2005, reprinted in this handbook) and Rochet and Vives (2004, reprinted in this handbook) the optimal LLOR framework is also analyzed. Repullo investigates the claim that LLOR lending creates a moral hazard problem in the sense of increasing the incentives of banks to increase risk, a proposition on which the contemporary literature on LLOR policy, irrespective of whether they are proponents of an open market policy or of individual liquidity assistance, seems to agree. By modelling the strategic interaction between a bank and a LLOR, he shows that in general this proposition is not true.

He assumes a bank which is funded with insured deposits and equity capital, is subject to capital requirements and can invest, like in a Diamond-Dybvig framework, in two assets: a safe liquid asset and an illiquid asset, whose risk will also be privately chosen by the bank. Since deposits are randomly withdrawn, the bank is subject to liquidity shocks. Because the bank optimally will not invest all its endowment in liquidity, in case of a large negative withdrawal shock it has to rely on emergency lending from a LLOR. Otherwise the bank will be forced into liquidation. In this setting, Repullo shows that in equilibrium the bank chooses a risk level that is decreasing in the capital requirement and increasing in the penalty rate charged by the LLOR. However, in the case where the LLOR does not charge the penalty rate, we get an irrelevance result regarding the risk choice. Irrespective of the existence of a LLOR, the bank chooses the same level of risk, but the liquidity buffer chosen is lower when a LLOR exists.

The intuition for this result is the following. It is assumed that the LLOR, who decides whether to provide emergency funding, observes a noisy signal of the final return by supervising the bank. This signal indicates whether the return is low or high, but not the particular value taken by the high return, which depends on the risk chosen by the bank. Though such a signal does not distort the decision to provide emergency funding in a direction that higher risk taking will be compensated, one can conclude that the introduction of deposit withdrawals and a LLOR does not affect the bank's incentives to take risk, unless the LLOR charges penalty rates. Since penalty rates increase the expected interest rate payments in the high-return state, this will induce banks to undertake projects with lower success probabilities but higher returns in case of success. The bank is pushed toward a riskier strategy. In this sense, the classical doctrine on the lender of last resort policy put forward by Bagehot (1873) that the LLOR should lend freely against good collateral, valued at pre-crisis levels, and at a penalty rate must be put into perspective.

Rochet and Vives (2004) also examine the Bagehot doctrine. In particular, they focus on Bagehot's assertion that the LOLR should lend to solvent but illiquid banks. In the past several authors have dismissed this view as obsolete since in modern interbank markets it cannot be the case that a solvent bank is illiquid. Of course, in light of the recent crisis, one can have serious doubts whether such an argument is true. For that reason, it is even more interesting that the Rochet-Vives paper provides a theoretical foundation supporting Bagehot's doctrine regarding this dimension. An important problem in the banking literature in the spirit of Diamond and Dybvig (1983) and Bryant (1980) is that the fragility of banks depends crucially on possible coordination failures between depositors which can provoke bank runs. Given the assumption of first-come, first-served, and costly liquidation of long-term assets there are multiple equilibria. However it is hard to base any policy recommendations on such a framework, since it systematically possesses multiple equilibria. Therefore by using the global games approach, Rochet and Vives develop a theory which does not rely on multiple equilibria. Instead, in their model of banks' liquidity crises a unique Bayesian equilibrium will result. This equilibrium is characterized by a positive probability that a solvent bank cannot get enough liquidity assistance in the market. Hence, in this respect the Bagehot doctrine still has a solid theoretical foundation.

To elaborate on the argument, it is important that one grasp a basic understanding of the underlying modelling approach. Carlsson and van Damme (1993), who also coined the term "global games", showed that incorporating a small amount of asymmetric information regarding fundamentals into an otherwise standard coordination game eliminates the multiplicity of equilibria that are otherwise typical for this type of game. The reason why in games where it is in the interest of the players to coordinate their actions, multiplicity arises is that common knowledge about fundamentals allows all players to coordinate their behaviour, which in turn naturally leads to multiple equilibria. If one introduces individual noise into the knowledge function of the agents, the fundamentals are no longer common knowledge and, accordingly, the coordination that is essential for the multiplicity can be prevented. However, a unique equilibrium only emerges if the noisy private information of investors about the payoff fundamentals is sufficiently precise relative to the public common knowledge information about the fundamentals. Only then is it in the interest of the players to rely heavily on their private signal and not to coordinate on the public information.

In the tradition of this setup, Rochet and Vives assume that the economy is characterized by uncertainty about the fundamental value of the banks' assets and the investors in a bank have private noisy information regarding this value. If the private information of the investors is precise enough, the game among them has a unique equilibrium whose characteristics depend on the bank's asset returns. Their main finding is that for an intermediate interval of values of the bank's assets, the unique equilibrium is characterized by the feature that the bank is solvent but can still fail if the proportion of investors who withdraw their money is too large. Thus if the fundamentals of the banks are in an intermediate range, the potential for a coordination failure exists. Interestingly, the better the bank is in terms of its ex ante strengths of fundamentals, the smaller is the range where such a coordination failure can occur. Hence, in order to avoid such failures, they analyze the effectiveness of certain policy instruments. In particular, Rochet and Vives discuss the interaction of ex ante solvency and liquidity regulation and ex post provision of emergency liquidity assistance. It is found that both types of instruments are complementary to each other. The ex ante regulation can solve the coordination problem, however, since this is costly for the banks in terms of foregone returns, the prudential measures should be combined with an ex post discount window emergency facility in order to optimize the costs. Lastly, they endogenize banks' short-term debt structure so as to mitigate a moral hazard problem on the side of bank managers, and in this richer environment derive a similar result regarding the complementarity of policy instruments. Public involvement through a LLOR and other regulatory measures and private market involvement should be combined to resolve crisis situations.

Coordination problems are prominent not only as a trigger of banking crises but also on the level of regulatory institutions. Hence, the accelerated integration of international financial markets and the increasing importance of banks' cross-border activities made it even more crucial to think twice about the appropriate regulatory structure. Is it still adequate that the regulators remain nationally bounded or is an international regulatory agency necessary or desirable? For example, Boot and Marinc (2008) discuss some of these key issues related to supervisory arrangements in the Euro-system countries.

To gain a better understanding of these issues, Dell'Ariccia and Marquez (2006, reprinted in this handbook) analyze the incentives for independent bank regulators with financially integrated jurisdictions to form a regulatory union. Integration allows the internalization of interdependencies that may exist across countries due to the integration of their financial system, but it limits the flexibility in the design of policy rules since a centralized regulator typically imposes a uniform standard across all the countries under its jurisdiction. To model this trade-off, Dell'Ariccia and Marquez assume that banks compete across countries in the loan market. They grant risky loans to borrowers, but can reduce the default risk of these loans through monitoring. However, the level of loan monitoring is socially inefficiently low since the banks are protected by limited liability and deposit insurance. Regulators can increase the monitoring incentives by imposing minimum capital requirements. That will potentially increase the stability and profitability of the banking system, but is costly to the (owners of the) banks.

Dell'Ariccia and Marquez compare a setting in which national regulators act only in the interest of their respective country and, accordingly, set policies noncooperatively to one in which an international regulator sets uniform standards for all banks. What they find is that externalities lead competing regulators to choose suboptimally low regulatory standards. They do not internalize the effect that stricter capital requirements not only increase the stability of the domestic banking system but also the stability of these foreign banks that compete with the domestic ones.

The intuition is as follows. Higher capital requirements in one country have a negative effect on the lending volume granted by domestic banks, which increases the stability of the domestic banking system but also reduces the competitive pressure in the loan market. Since therefore the return to monitoring for foreign banks increases, their probability of bank failure in foreign markets will be reduced. Accordingly, the stability of foreign banks will be enhanced. But national regulators do not internalize this positive spillover effect and impose regulatory requirements that are in comparison to the one chosen by a unified regulatory body too low. In addition, to the extent that regulators act in the interest of the shareholders of their domestic banks, they might be induced to lower their banks' regulatory requirements in order to give them a competitive advantage vis-a-vis their foreign competitors. Both reasons point in the same direction: National regulators set regulatory standards that are too low.

Based on this result, Dell'Ariccia and Marquez explore the conditions under which a centralized regulator emerges. They find that among relatively homogenous jurisdictions/countries centralized regulation will likely emerge. Furthermore, a centralized regulator will be unanimously preferred to independence only if such a regulator sets regulatory standards that are significantly tighter than the strictest country-specific regulatory requirements. Only then will all the banks in the different countries accept the regulation. Because tighter regulation in each country hurts domestic banks, they must be compensated by also raising standards for foreign banks. Since this is true for all countries, regulatory requirements must increase above the level of individual standards when the countries switch to a uniform standard.

The Dell'Ariccia-Marquez paper represents one of the first fully-fledged models of competition among regulators. However, the setting could be beneficially extended in several directions. In particular, contagion effects among banks must be integrated into the analysis, an issue we will take up in Section 5.

3. Money, Financial Crises and Asset Prices

Fiat money does not play a role in most models of banking crises. Typically, banks contract with depositors in real terms, and if government injected liquidity is essential in preventing a crisis or alleviating an aggregate liquidity shortage, it will be done using appropriate financial and fiscal instruments. In addition, it is quite obvious from many crisis experiences in the past that monetary policy also seems important in crisis situations. Hence, money appears to play an ambivalent role in financial crises. However, what is the connection between money, banks, and aggregate credit volume? When has expansionary monetary policy an expansive effect on bank credit and what are the circumstances under which monetary policy can help to alleviate the effects of banking crises or prevent failures altogether?

Smith (2002) was one of first to start addressing these questions. He considers a model in which spatial separation and limited communication introduce a role for money into a standard banking model with early and late consumers. He shows that the lower the inflation rate and the nominal interest rate, the lower is the probability of a banking crisis. Reducing the inflation rate to zero, in line with the Friedman rule, eliminates banking crises. However, this solution is inefficient as it causes banks to hold excess cash reserves at the expense of investment in higher yielding assets.

Diamond and Rajan (2006, reprinted in this handbook) start with a "real" model borrowed from Diamond and Rajan (2001) in which banks have special skills to ensure that loans are repaid. By issuing real demand deposits, banks create a fragile capital structure that enables them to commit to repay whatever the bank collects to depositors. This allows long-term projects to be funded and depositors to consume when they have liquidity needs. However, this arrangement leads to the possibility of a liquidity shortage in which banks curtail credit when there is real shock.

Diamond and Rajan (2006) augment this model by introducing money and nominal deposit contracts. Money commands value because it can be used to pay taxes (the fiscal demand) and because it must be used in facilitating certain transactions (the transaction demand). They show that the use of money can improve risk sharing, since price adjustments introduce a form of state-contingency in contracts. However, this is not the only possibility. Since money is used for an array of transactions, the transactions value of money may show oscillations which are quite independent of aggregate production. If this is the case, banks that issue nominal demandable claims are particularly vulnerable to withdrawal. For instance, if so called cash goods, i.e. goods that may be sold only for cash, are temporarily cheap (for example, because the supply of money is low relative to cash goods), depositors have strong incentives to withdraw their demand deposits to gain from such an opportunity. However, this is not in the interest of banks. To keep depositors from withdrawing, they must, accordingly, increase the interest rate they pay on deposits. But this, in turn, will increase the real repayment obligations of the banks. As a result, bank failures can occur.

More generally, suppose that for whatever reason the value of money is not well behaved, in such a situation it can be the case that nominal deposits may actually increase aggregate real liquidity demand when aggregate supply falls instead of decreasing it. As a consequence, real liquidity shocks will be amplified and credit will be reduced. Hence, variations in the transaction value of money can lead to bank failure. Monetary intervention can help to solve this problem. The intervention should have the objective to achieve a better correspondence of value for money and aggregate liquidity conditions. For instance, if in such a situation of real liquidity shortages the central bank buys bonds with money, this will increase the money supply available for transactions when the transaction demand is high. That changes the liquidity conditions in the market and keeps the price level stable. The incentives of depositors to withdraw are limited and the future repayment obligations of banks reduced. This will allow banks to fund more long-term projects than in the absence of intervention.

The model thus provides a different perspective on the operation of monetary policy through bank lending. In two recent papers by Diamond and Rajan (2005, 2008), the setup is applied to analyze the optimal interest policy in episodes of illiquidity and financial fragility. Fecht and Tyrell (2009) apply the framework to analyze different crisis resolution policies.

Also Kiyotaki and Moore (2005, reprinted in this handbook) examine the interaction between liquidity, asset prices, and aggregate economic activity. However, in their model they do not consider, as Diamond and Rajan (2006) do, the specific characteristics of banks and monetary policy in transmitting or alleviating economic shocks. Instead they investigate in a general equilibrium framework the role of liquid assets for resource allocation. They define liquid assets, which they also call monetary assets, as any asset class that can be readily sold in the market and, therefore, serve as a medium of exchange since it circulates among many agents as a means of short-term saving. This allows Kiyotaki and Moore to analyze the conditions under which the circulation of liquid assets is essential for the smooth running of the economy. The terms liquid assets and monetary assets will be used interchangeably since all assets are real and not denominated in cash. In contrast to Diamond and Rajan (2006), there is no issue of fiat money and also no inflationary effect in the model.

Output is produced from two types of assets, capital and land, with the usual assumption that the capital stock can be built up through investment, whereas the supply of land is fixed. They, however, depart from the usual representative agent framework in assuming that at each point in time only a fraction of agents has access to productive investment opportunities, even though agents are equally likely to find investment opportunities in the future, and in assuming incomplete markets in the sense that the agents have no possibilities to buy ex ante insurance contingent on the arrival of investment opportunities. Furthermore, the capital stock is an asset with limited liquidity as, at the time of investment, agents can sell only a fraction of their capital stock. This type of financial friction is in its impact similar to the non-pledgeability assumption in Holmström and Tirole (1998) or to the limited commitment assumption in Diamond and Rajan (2001). Therefore, investing agents may face binding liquidity constraints. Only land is a liquid or monetary asset in the sense that agents can pledge the full value of their land holdings at the time of investment.

They show that in such an economy the circulation of monetary assets is essential for resource allocation since only this allows a smooth transfer of purchasing power from those who do not have an investment opportunity to those who do. Second, this circulation of liquid assets is even more important if each agent rarely has an investment opportunity, if investing agents can only pledge a small fraction of their capital, and if the income share of land is small relative to capital.

The model delivers an explanation of the liquidity premium that liquid assets typically command. If investing agents anticipate liquidity constraints at the time of investment, they have strong incentives to hold the liquid assets in their portfolios even if the return on the liquid assets is lower than the time preference rate. Furthermore, the model generates an interesting feedback mechanism between asset prices and aggregate economic activity. As in the standard framework, higher future expected dividends translate into higher asset prices, but here higher asset prices also leads to higher liquidity, which eases the transfer of resources from savers to investors, thus encouraging aggregate investment and production. Thus, the model can explain the interaction between asset prices, liquidity, and economic activity, in particular, it delivers an account of the large fluctuations in asset prices and aggregate output which are typically observable in financial crisis, even though to a smaller extent also in "normal" times. However, since fiat money has no particular role in the framework, it is, at least in the specific setting developed in Kiyotaki and Moore (2005), not possible to analyze the impact of monetary shocks or monetary instruments. However, Kiyotaki and Moore (2008) provide an interesting extension of the model. They study how aggregate production and asset prices fluctuate with shocks to productivity and liquidity. Thereby, they also examine the role of government policy, which basically through open market operations, changes the mix of assets held by the private sector.

The Cordoba and Ripoll (2004, reprinted in this handbook) paper also takes up this aspect by analyzing in detail the role of financial constraints in transforming small monetary shocks into large persistent aggregate output fluctuations. They introduce money in a Kiyotaki and Moore (1997) economy, a setting which also forms the basis of the Kiyotaki and Moore (2005) paper. Money enters, similarly to Diamond and Rajan (2006), in a cash-in-advance constraint and monetary policy is conducted via open-market operations. As agents face endogenous credit limits, which are in the end determined by the value of the collateralized assets, collateral constraints are a powerful mechanism of amplification and persistence of shocks.

Cordoba and Ripoll show that monetary shocks generate persistent movements in output. However, the quantitative and structural impact of a certain shock depends on which contracts are allowed in the economy. If only nominal contracts are traded, a money shock can trigger large output fluctuations in the usual sense that a monetary easing triggers a boom and a contraction a recession. If indexed contracts are allowed, amplification is smaller and under certain conditions, the structural relationship is the other way around. The intuition for this main result is easy to understand: An unanticipated money shock will ease collateral constraints if indexed contracts are not possible since the monetary expansion redistributes resources from lenders to borrowers, who have productive investments at hand. This will trigger a boom. A money contraction, however, can trigger depressions since now the basic Fisher effect is at work, according to which an unexpected debt deflation redistributes resources the other way around. In contrast, the indexation of contracts has the effect that redistribution of resources will be prevented. It is no surprise that unanticipated shocks trigger much smaller and less pertinent fluctuations. Money expansion can generate downturns in such an environment, since now the inflationary tax can reduce borrowers' net worth which has negative output consequences.

The authors also analyze what happens if in default borrowers and lenders are allowed to renegotiate their debt contracts. Since renegotiation will typically benefit borrowers, the negative impact of default will be dampened and that means, unanticipated shocks have a smaller impact on the collateral constraints even if contracts are nonindexed. Hence, renegotiation reduces the responses of aggregate output to shocks, an effect which is in particular relevant in downturns since default probability is higher in times of monetary contractions. Therefore the model can generate asymmetric business cycles with recessions milder than booms.

Generally speaking, what the model of Cordoba and Ripoll, and many other similar models developed in the literature, shows is that the interaction of monetary policy and aggregate output depends in a fundamental way on the "microstructure" of the financial friction in the economy. It is extremely difficult to come up with general results. This is true in economically "normal" times but even more in crisis situations where we typically know even less about the prevailing structural relationships in the financial sector.

An interesting example of inefficiencies created by the working of the financial system is analyzed in the paper by Lorenzoni (2008, reprinted in this handbook) where the question is raised why inefficient credit booms can emerge. Financial frictions, both on the borrowers' (entrepreneurs) and on the lenders' (consumers) side, are the fundamental source of inefficiency. Both have limited ability to commit to future repayments which implies that entrepreneurs face (external) financial constraints and consumers cannot fully insure ex ante entrepreneurs against aggregate liquidity shocks, as in Holmström and Tirole (1998). Lorenzoni motivates his analysis about the (in-)efficiency of credit booms with the observation that in particular in the last two decades, many developed and emerging countries have experienced episodes of credit expansion which were typically followed by a financial crisis with a collapse in asset prices. He analyzes the conditions under which a credit boom arises, why the credit boom may be inefficient from an ex ante perspective, and whether any intervention is warranted. He shows that excessive borrowing activity by entrepreneurs can arise in equilibrium which, in turn, leads to an excessive contraction in investment activity and asset prices if the crisis takes place, even though all entrepreneurs are rational and correctly perceive the risks and rewards associated with different financial decisions. Key to the result is a pecuniary externality which arises from the combination of the financial constraints mentioned above with a competitive market for real assets.

The model uses a three-period framework where in the first period entrepreneurs have to borrow funds for productive investment. In the second period, the investment returns are subject to an aggregate shock. When a bad shock hits, entrepreneurs face operational losses, which means that they have to sell part of the assets to finance these losses. Assets are sold in a competitive market where they are bought by a traditional sector, i.e. other entrepreneurs which are less productive. In essence, this setup is closely related to Gorton and Huang (2005). In the third period consumption takes place and capital fully depreciates.

Though the entrepreneurs have access to state-contingent contracts in the sense that they can ex ante decide how much to borrow in the first period and how much to repay in different states of the world in the following periods, an inefficiency will arise. Basically, entrepreneurs face the following trade-off: if they invest more in the first period, they can earn higher returns if the good shock is realized but incur larger losses if the bad shock hits. However, even with these state-contingent contracts and being fully rational, the entrepreneurs do not take into account the general equilibrium effect of asset sales on asset prices, since they are atomistic. They do not internalize this pecuniary externality. Therefore, from a social efficiency viewpoint, they invest too much. Accordingly, a social planner should reduce aggregate investment ex ante, because this reduces the amount of asset sales in the bad state. This has a positive effect on asset prices and leads to a reallocation of funds to more productive uses, i.e. from the traditional sector to the entrepreneurial sector which due to the presence of financial frictions leads to a welfare gain. In essence, the paper formalizes the notion that credit booms might be inefficient because they lead to higher systemic risk in the economy. Here systemic risk is increased because more individual borrowing by the entrepreneurs creates a pecuniary externality which results in higher fluctuation of asset prices. Again, we have a general equilibrium feedback mechanism between financial distress and asset prices that drives the results.

One important empirical question which arises out of all these theoretical studies is how should the liquidity of the financial system, in particular of financial institutions as banks, be measured? Berger and Bouwman (2008a) have suggested a method for measuring liquidity created by the banking system and have applied it to the US. They start by classifying all bank liabilities together with off-balance sheet items as liquid, semi-liquid and illiquid. By assessing weights for these threes categories, they calculate the amount of liquidity created by the banking system. They show that liquidity increased every year between 1993 and 2003, almost doubling during the period. By applying this measure, similar results are found by Rauch, Steffen, Hackethal and Tyrell (2009) for the German savings bank sector.

In a subsequent paper Berger and Bouwman (2008b) use their measure of liquidity to examine the relationship between liquidity and crises by focussing on the sample period from 1984 until 2008. They find that banking crises were preceded by abnormal high liquidity creation. Hence, it is important to understand how liquidity is created and how this relates to crisis.

4. Contagion Effects in Financial Crises

Financial contagion refers to the process by which a shock in one part of the financial system spreads to other parts through a series of "interlinkages". In principle, there are many kinds of inter-linkages in the financial systems. "Informational" inter-linkages belong to a class of explanations for contagion effects that posits that the adverse information that triggers a crisis in one institution also implies adverse information about the other. Hence, correlations in underlying value across institutions and Bayesian learning by rational agents are typically emphasized by this view. A second type of explanation begins with the observation that financial institutions are often linked to each other in a more direct way, for instance through portfolio or balance sheet connections. Such balance sheet connections might be for whatever reasons desirable ex ante, however, during a crisis the failure of one institution can have direct negative payoff consequences for the stakeholders of institutions with which it is linked.

The model of contagion effects provided by Dasgupta (2004, reprinted in this handbook) belongs to this second class. It focuses on banks that have cross-held deposits (for clearance, regulatory or insurance reasons), so that the failure of one bank has direct consequences on others through capital linkages in the same way as in Allen and Gale (2000). However, the analysis of contagious bank failure is particularly complex. While the existence of multiple equilibria makes it difficult to examine even individual bank failures, these difficulties are compounded in many a bank setting if one has to isolate contagious effects.

Therefore Dasgupta (2004) applies the global games framework to present a model of an economy with multiple banks where the probability of individual bank failures, and of systemic crises, is uniquely determined. He develops a model of two regions with one representative bank in each region. Each bank can invest in liquidity and a local illiquid risky asset whose expected return is higher than the return of the riskless asset. The return realizations are determined by regional economic fundamentals. The cross-holding of deposits is motivated by negatively correlated liquidity shocks in each region. However, the aggregate liquidity demand in the economy is fixed. Banks want to insure against such regional shocks by exchanging deposits in the initial period. Since regional liquidity shocks are realized first and become public information, interbank deposits will be withdrawn by the bank which faces the high liquidity demand. This creates an asymmetry between the two banks: one bank becomes a net debtor to the other. In addition, depositors also have to take into account the information they get about the fundamentals in both regions. Since the return of the risky asset depends on the regional fundamentals, information about fundamentals helps them to determine whether they want to withdraw early. Typically, the choices made by depositors at each bank involve a coordination problem: they wish to withdraw if they believe that enough other depositors withdraw, leading to a run on the bank. However, the information available about economic fundamentals in either region is imperfect. This implies that depositors receive private but correlated signals about the potential future return on their deposits. This, in turn, creates substantial strategic uncertainty about the actions of other depositors and prevents the depositors from coordinating their actions.

In the end, the game between the depositors is characterized by a unique threshold in regional economic fundamentals below which each bank will fail due to a run by depositors. Hence, bank failure depends upon the release of adverse information about local asset returns. However, the emergence of adverse information about asset returns in one region can cause instability in the other region. Contagion arises in equilibrium. Conditional on the failure of a debtor bank, a creditor bank fails with higher probability, i.e. for a wider range of its own fundamentals, than if the debtor bank survives. In addition, the incidence of contagion is increasing in the size of interbank deposit holdings. This brings up the question whether one should hold interbank deposits at all. Dasgupta (2004) shows that only partial cross-holdings are optimal when the probability of a bank run is relatively high. Contagion risk prevents banks from perfectly insuring each other against liquidity shocks.

Brusco and Castiglionesi (2007) develop a model with negatively correlated liquidity shocks for banks in different regions. Opening links between the regions thus has the potential to improve welfare. However, they show that there is a positive probability of bankruptcy and propagation of a crisis across regions when banks keep interbank deposits and may engage in excessive risk taking if they do not have sufficient capital. Nevertheless opening interbank markets is Pareto improving.

The effects of information contagion are investigated in an interesting paper by Acharya and Yorulmazer (2008, reprinted in this handbook). They show that banks engage in herding behaviour in order to minimize the information spillover from bad information about other banks on their own financing costs. In an otherwise standard banking model with two banks which have access to risky loans and get their funding from risk-averse depositors, the return on each bank's loans is determined by a common systematic component, say an industry effect, and an idiosyncratic component. The exposure of each bank's loan return to the systematic and to the idiosyncratic factor is common knowledge and also the ex post performance of each bank's loan portfolio is observed by the public. However, what is not observed by the economic agents is the exact realization of the systematic and idiosyncratic factors. The banks can choose their lending structure, in particular whether they want to lend to similar industries which implies a high level of interbank correlation. However, lending to similar industries has a negative impact on the margin since in that case competition in the loan market increases.

Given this structure, Acharya and Yorulmazer (2008) show that the cost of borrowing for a bank increases when the depositors can observe bad news about another bank, since such news conveys bad information about the common factor. In particular, the increase in a bank's borrowing costs relative to a situation where one can observe good news about other banks is greater when bank loans have less commonality. Therefore, banks have incentives to herd and undertake similar investment in order to minimize the expected costs of borrowing. Only the erosion of lending margins if banks lend into similar industries counteracts this herding force. However, as long as the competitive effect is not too large, banks will herd even if this leads to productive inefficiency since they do not invest in profitable projects in other industries of the economy.

Since herding behaviour and contagion effects lead to a higher number of systemic banking crises, an interesting issue is how one should design the resolution of bank failures when many banks fail. This question is taken up by Acharya and Yorulmazer (2009, reprinted in this handbook) in their analysis of systemic banking crises. They argue that during systemic banking crises, a private sector resolution for bank failures does no good since it leads to allocation inefficiency. The reason is "cash-in-the-market-pricing" for bank assets in liquidation. The acquisition of bank assets in liquidation is no problem if only a few banks fail since then these banks can be acquired by the surviving banks. However, in the case of a larger banking crisis with a high number of bank failures, the liquidity of the surviving banks is typically quite scarce. This implies that they can acquire all the assets of the failed banks only at fire-sale prices. There are too many banks to liquidate. However, the resulting "cash-in-the-market" pricing attracts liquidity-endowed investors from outside the banking sector. Since these investors are quite often not the most efficient users of these assets, the wrong agents end up purchasing failed banks' assets.

Acharya and Yorulmazer (2009) also analyze which type of regulatory intervention might be optimal to avoid allocation inefficiencies. An ex post optimal bailout policy is typically suboptimal from an ex ante viewpoint since it induces banks to herd, as in Acharya and Yorulmazer (2008). Anticipating such a policy, banks have incentives to lend funds to similar industries or to bet on common risks in order to increase the likelihood of being bailed out. In turn, such behaviour just increases the probability of experiencing systemic crises. However, there is a solution to this time-inconsistency problem. The government should provide liquidity by subsidizing surviving banks for the purchase of failed banks. This liquidity provision policy gives banks incentives to differentiate ex ante, yet can be designed to be ex-post equivalent to the bailout policy.

Allen and Carletti (2006, reprinted in this handbook) also rely on "cash-in-the-market" pricing in their analysis of contagion effects. They are in particular interested in answering the question whether the introduction of certain financial innovations, such as credit risk transfer instruments, creates inter-linkages between different financial sectors that increase the danger of contagion. They focus on the structure of liquidity shocks that hit the banking sector in order to determine whether contagion results. When banks are not hit by a liquidity shock and therefore face a uniform demand for liquidity, they keep a sufficient amount of the short-term asset and do not need to raise additional liquidity in the market. In this case credit risk transfer is beneficial as it improves risk sharing across different sectors in the finance industry. However, when banks face idiosyncratic shocks, a negative spillover effect can arise because of credit risk transfer.

The intuition is as follows. Banks now invest into a long-term riskless asset, for instance government bonds, to hedge the idiosyncratic risk. If it is the case that the bank has a large number of early consumers who want to withdraw, it can sell the long-term asset in the market to other banks who have a demand for such assets because they have a high fraction of late consumers. Since there is assumed to be no aggregate risk, the hedging of banks is perfect in the autarkic equilibrium and only insurance companies face systemic risk. However, the introduction of credit risk transfer can be damaging, as it makes contagion possible. As the insurance sector uses the long-term asset to undertake its credit risk transfer effectively, insurance companies will be forced to liquidate that asset if they are hit by a negative systemic shock. This puts downward pressure on the price for the long-term asset because there is a “cash-in-the-market” pricing. This implies that the price must go down if the quantity sold goes up since only the available liquidity can be used to buy assets. However, this fall now also affects negatively the banking industry as banks are using the long-term assets to hedge their idiosyncratic liquidity risks. Banks who must sell the long-term asset in the market to repay withdrawing depositors receive now a lower amount of liquidity with the consequence that they are unable to pay their depositors. Hence, there is the possibility of damaging contagion of systemic risk to the banking sector. The systemic risk is costly since banks' loans cannot be liquidated on short notice without serious welfare consequences, and the contagion interferes with the risk sharing between banks through the interbank market.

In an interesting paper, Cerasi and Rochet (2008) analyze the optimality of credit risk transfer between banks. They show that in a model where banks' main activity is to monitor loans, a combination of credit risk transfer instruments, i.e. loan sales and credit derivatives, might be optimal while preserving monitoring incentives. However, the model does not capture potential spillover effects resulting from the interlinkages of financial institutions. A broad perspective on the cost and benefits of securitization is taken by Franke and Krahnen (2008). They analyze possible reasons for the breakdown of primary and secondary securitization markets and argue that misaligned incentives along the value chain are the primary cause of the problems. Hence, illiquidity of asset and interbank markets are a consequence of a market failure derived from bad-designed mechanisms.

What the web of claims and obligations which links financial institutions together in a tightly knit system implies for the pricing of debt, is analyzed by Shin (2008). He shows that it is extremely important to assess the financial claims in a system context in order to capture features such as liquidity spillovers across financial institutions resulting from expansions and contractions of balance sheets.

A number of recent theories of contagion have applied the tools of the network literature in economics to study the endogenous formation of links between banks and the contagion that can occur as a result. Babus (2007) proposes a model where banks form links with each other as an insurance mechanism to reduce the risk of contagion. At the base of the link formation process lies the intuition that better connected networks are more resilient to contagion. The model predicts a connectivity threshold above which contagion does not occur, and banks form links to reach this threshold. However, an implicit cost associated with being involved in a link prevents banks from forming more connections than required by the connectivity threshold. Banks manage to form networks where contagion rarely occurs.

Castiglionesi and Navarro (2007) are also interested in decentralizing the network of banks that is optimal from a social planner perspective. In a setting where banks invest on behalf of depositors and there are positive network externalities on the investment returns, fragility arises when banks that are not sufficiently capitalized gamble with depositors' money. When the probability of bankruptcy is low, the decentralized solution approximates the first best. For surveys of the network literature in finance see Allen and Babus (2009) and Allen, Babus and Carletti (2009).

Besides the theoretical investigations, there has been a substantial interest in looking for evidence of contagious failures of financial institutions. Most of these papers use balance sheet information to estimate bilateral credit relationships. Based on these estimates, the stability of the banking system is tested by simulating the breakdown of a single bank. Upper and Worms (2004, reprinted in this handbook) use this methodology. They estimate a matrix of bilateral credit relationships for the German banking system and then simulate the failure of a single bank. They find broad scope for contagion. However, the prevailing financial safety net in Germany, that is, institutional guarantees for savings banks and cooperative banks, reduces the danger of contagion considerably. But even so, the failure of a single bank could lead to a breakdown of up to 15% in terms of bank assets.

There are many other empirical studies to assess the danger of contagion in interbank markets (see Upper (2007) for a survey). For most countries, the simulations suggest that contagious defaults are unlikely, but at least in some countries they cannot be fully ruled out. If contagion does take place, then the simulations indicate typically a breakdown of a substantial part of the banking system. But one should be cautious in accepting this result that contagion is unlikely. First, since most of the studies have focussed on simulating the failure of a single bank for idiosyncratic reasons, this is not the scenario most relevant for supervisors. The analysis of the effects of shocks that affect several banks simultaneously on the stability has more relevance and should be explored in future work. First studies in this direction are conducted by Elsinger, Lehar and Summer (2006a, 2006b). Second, the simulations conducted typically do not model the price effects of bank failures. However, as argued by Cifuentes, Ferrucci and Shin (2004) and others, these price effects are the main transmission mechanism for contagion. In addition having the cases of Bear Stearns and AIG and, for example, the model results of Allen and Carletti (2006) in mind, one should examine in future work to what extent the failure of a big player in the derivatives markets leads to contagious effects in the finance industry.

5. Financial Crises and Currency Crises

The increasing occurrence of twin crises in the last three decades also points to the direction that contagion effects are a prominent force in today's financial systems. As a case in point, Kaminsky and Reinhart (1999) show in their research that following the liberalization of financial markets across many parts of the world, banking and currency crises became closely intertwined. Furthermore, there is a growing literature on contagious currency crises and international contagion, which is surveyed by Masson (1999). An example of a more recent study is the paper by Hartmann, Straetmans and de Vries (2004, reprinted in this handbook) which assesses the contagion effects resulting from asset market interlinkages in periods of crises.

The study by Hartmann, Straetmans and de Vries differs in two aspects from most of the existing literature in this area. First, they apply a novel methodology in analyzing asset market interlinkages. While typically in this type of study conditional correlation analysis based on multivariate normal distribution is used to analyze the likelihood of crash spillover, Hartmann, Stratmans and de Vries characterize the return linkages between markets by employing a measure from statistical extreme-value analysis. By capturing the dependence structure of multivariate distributions far away from the center, this measure is particularly suitable for analyzing the economic interdependence between markets during times of stress. As they show in their empirical analysis, using the multivariate normal instead dramatically underestimates the frequency of extreme market spillovers. Second, they study the comovements between different asset classes. In contrast to most other studies that analyze the linkage between different stock markets during crisis periods, Hartmann, Straetmans and de Vries focus on the connection between stock and government bond markets. This allows them to capture phenomena such as "flight to quality" which we typically observe during crisis periods: A crash in stock markets accompanied by a boom in government bond markets.

To be more precise, they use the extreme-value methodology to analyze linkages within and between equity and bond markets in the G-5 industrial countries during episodes of market turmoil by looking at the weekly stock and government bond returns for the G-5 market indices over the period 1987 to 1999. They find small but nonnegligible cross-asset market linkages in crisis periods. However, the strongest extreme linkages seem to be between different national equity markets. The flight-to-quality phenomenon is about as common as a simultaneous crash of stock and bond markets which highlights that there should be some limits to the propagation of shocks across different asset classes. Overall, the results imply that in line with free capital flows and financial integration between G-5 countries, national borders do not seem to matter much and therefore surveillance of financial stability also should not stop at national borders. Extreme cross-border linkages are similar to national linkages indicating that spillover effects are a pervasive phenomenon in financial markets.

Despite convincing evidence regarding the existence of an intimate connection between banking crises and currency crises, the theoretical literatures on the two topics have, for the most part, developed independently. To date, few models have addressed the relationship between banking and currency crises. The paper by Goldstein (2005, reprinted in this handbook) is an interesting example of this literature strand. The paper starts with the observation that, as shown by Diamond and Dybvig (1983) and many others, strategic complementarities among economic agents may cause financial crises. However, it asks the question under what conditions the incentive of depositors to run on a bank increases, not only with the number of depositors that run on the bank, but also with the number of speculators that attack the currency of the country the bank is located in. Similarly, there is the reverse causation of the incentives of speculators to attack the currency depending on what depositors do.

Such a pattern of strategic complementarities seems quite realistic, as ample evidence from crisis episodes in the last three decades shows. The two features that typically describe these crises are, first, governments try to maintain fixed exchange rate regimes, which of course makes them vulnerable to speculative attacks, and, second, domestic banks that had a mismatch between foreign liabilities and domestic assets, which expose them to exchange rate risks. Goldstein takes up these features and shows in his model that they account for strategic complementarities. A successful attack that leads to a currency depreciation reduces the value of the banks' assets relative to the value of their liabilities. Knowing that, foreign creditors to the bank expect that banks will have fewer resources at hand to repay them and thus find it more profitable to withdraw their money immediately, with the consequence that a run on the bank emerges. In turn, that makes it more difficult for the government to maintain the exchange rate since the foreign creditors, who run on the bank, pull the money out of the economy and this indirectly reduces the amount of reserves held by the government. Accordingly the government faces a higher cost of defending the currency which implies that they have to abandon the exchange rate regime in more circumstances. This will increase the incentives of speculators to attack, as they know that the attack is more likely to succeed. As a result there are strategic complementarities between foreign creditors and speculators.

Goldstein shows that due to these complementarities, a vicious cycle between banking crises and currency crises will be generated. This magnifies the correlation of these crises and destabilizes the economy. Goldstein gets this clear-cut result because his model, unlike most models of self-fulfilling beliefs, has a unique equilibrium. This enables him to characterize endogenous probabilities of both types of crisis. As usual in the global games literature, the uniqueness result stems from the assumption that agents do not have common knowledge about fundamentals but observe a noisy signal.

At least two policy implications follow from the model. First, a useful way to reduce the probability of one crisis is to prevent the other crisis. For instance, an increase in the transaction costs that speculators have to bear when they attack reduces also indirectly the probability of a bank run. Second, a lender of last resort might not be able to prevent bank runs since in an attack the government loses even more reserves because of the complementarities between both crises. Anticipating the existence of a lender of last resort, speculators do have more incentives to attack which, in turn, increases the probability of a banking crisis. Other policy measures, such as an international lender of last resort, may be preferable in the presence of contagion between the banking sector and the currency market.

At least two interesting questions arise out of this analysis. First, why do agents in these countries borrow so much from foreign investors, and, second, what would an adequate monetary policy regime for (emerging) countries look like? The first issue is taken up by Tirole (2003, reprinted in this handbook), the second one by Caballero and Krishnamurthy (2005, reprinted in this handbook). More specifically, the Tirole (2003) paper starts with an analysis of the incentives of countries for borrowing too much. It then investigates which factors do enhance borrowing countries' access to international lending, thereby relating the level and quality of access to certain institutional factors such as the level of domestic savings, the extent of control rights held by political authorities, and the interest of the dominant domestic political party.

It is argued that foreign borrowing relationships are typically characterized by a dual- and common-agency problem, which is the source of the market failure. Dual agency, also called "moral hazard in teams", means that the investor's prospect of recouping his investment depends not only on the behaviour of the specific borrower, with whom he contracts, but also on the behaviour of the borrower's government, with whom he has not a written contract. Hence, we have two agents involved whose combined actions affect the welfare of a principal, here the investor. Furthermore, the government is a common agent of all dual agency relationships, which constitutes a common agency relationship. The problem is that pairwise optimal contracts, written between borrowers and investors, exert externalities on each other through their impact on the behaviour of the government. Since the government is a common agent of all borrower-investor pairs, its policy choice depends on a representative financial contract, but not on each individual written financial contract between investor and borrower.

The model has three dates. At date 0, the financing stage, pairwise optimal contracts between foreign and domestic lenders and private sector companies, which also includes banks, will be written. Since domestic capital is limited, firms benefit, in principle, from access to foreign capital and therefore from capital account liberalization. At date 2, the proceeds from investments accrue and are distributed according to contractual commitments. However, the date 2 outcome also depends on the policy choice by the government at date 1. As is usually assumed in the international economics literature, the government favors domestic interests over foreign ones and, of course, has a quite a few possibilities of affecting foreign investors' returns. This could happen through changes in corporate governance and bankruptcy laws or a change in tax and labor laws, but also by more subtle means of affecting the tradeable-nontradeable mix of the economy and reducing the amount of assets that can serve as international collateral respectively, such as encouraging excessive investments in the nontradeable sector, for example in real estate. All these measures can be used to reduce the return to foreign investors. As these mechanisms are, subsequent to the contracting stage, employed at date 1, a time inconsistency problem emerges. The favoritism of domestic interests could, if anticipated, result in scarce or more expensive foreign borrowing, and the ex post optimal date-1 policy would no longer internalize the possibility that an investor-friendly course of action mitigates credit rationing and attracts foreign capital, when domestic firms are subject to agency costs.

Three broad conclusion emerge from the analysis of Tirole (2003). No strong case can be built on a priori grounds that countries over- or underborrow. However, capital controls impose a substantial cost to the extent that firms are subject to credit rationing and therefore short of access to productive capital. Second, so called "dangerous forms of debts", such as short maturities and foreign currency denomination, may very well be the optimal financing instrument for those who issue them because they are "policy resistant" in the sense of making the government more accountable. In a similar vein, this argument can also be found in Diamond and Rajan (2001), where it is argued that demandable debt makes bankers more accountable. Third, a country's ability to borrow and its terms of borrowing can only be assessed if one also takes into account the internal politics of the respective country. In particular, one needs a guess to what extent the interests of foreigners are aligned or not with those of dominant interest groups.

But what happens if, for whatever reason, the capital inflows to emerging countries suddenly reverse ("sudden stop")? How should monetary policy react? What is the right response to this event? These issues are analyzed by Caballero and Krishnamurthy (2005, reprinted in this handbook). They show that it is extremely difficult for monetary policy to offset the credit squeeze that local firms, who are already in normal times exposed to severe financial frictions and credit constraints, experience during crises. Even though an expansionary monetary policy might succeed in offsetting the effect of a credit squeeze during mild downturns, the expansionary effect vanishes during severe external crises. The starting point of their analysis is the observation that credit constraints in emerging markets exist not only at the firm level, but also at the country level. As Caballero and Krishnamurthy (2001) emphasize, in the context of emerging economies it is typically the case that the country as a whole has limited international collateral, a feature absent in developed economies where the credit constraint plausibly exist only at the firm level. This distinction is important because it helps for thinking about the effect of monetary policy in downturns.

Caballero and Krishnamurthy (2005) argue that the distinction between domestic and international constraints is only immaterial during mild crises. In such a scenario, the typical monetary policy response, as stressed in the credit channel literature, should be to increase the net worth of the borrowers. However, the recipe of using monetary policy fails when the credit constraints exist at the country level since the monetary policy only regulates the borrowing of a domestic agent from a domestic lender. As monetary policy does not alter the international collateral or liquidity of the country, monetary policy is ineffective when the marginal lender is a foreign investor.

Even though a monetary expansion has little effect on output during a severe crisis caused by a sudden stop, Caballero and Krishnamurthy (2005) show it has important general equilibrium effects on asset prices. It is the case that a monetary expansion increases domestic liquidity since it raises firms' borrowing capacity. But, as it does not lead to an expansion in international liquidity, the relative price of domestic liquidity must react in the sense that it falls in relation to the price of international liquidity. However, the fall in the price of domestic liquidity can only imply that the exchange rate has to depreciate, in fact, a temporary currency depreciation which is beyond the one commanded by the interest rate parity condition in order to reduce the dollar value of domestic collateral until equilibrium in domestic markets is consistent with the external constraint. Hence, general equilibrium effects imply that in emerging markets monetary policy is impotent during severe crises caused by a sudden stop of capital inflow, as it does not loosen the international collateral constraints. A monetary expansion will just induce a depreciation of the exchange rate. Certainly, the depreciation can weaken firms' balance sheets, as argued in the standard credit channel literature, but this is an indirect consequence of the monetary policy.

But what do these considerations imply for the incentives of the private sector agents to insure themselves against a crisis? Despite the fact that monetary policy is ineffective during sudden stop, expectations regarding the prevailing monetary rule have important effects on the private sector's ex ante decisions. A central bank that is expected to contract money in the event of a severe crisis actually causes the private sector to alter its ex ante decisions so as to arrive later on with a smaller amount of international liquidity. Precisely while such a policy supports the currency, ex ante the private sector overborrows and underinsures against the crisis. Conversely, the expectation of an expansionary monetary policy induces the private sector to insure itself more against a crisis and to reduce ex ante borrowing. This, in turn, may reduce the incidence of a severe crisis. More generally, monetary policies and its constraints have important (unintended) consequences for the private sector's insurance decisions with respect to sudden stops.

The term "flight to quality" is used to describe a situation where investors seek to sell assets perceived as risky and instead purchase safe liquid assets. This is what typically happens in financial and currency crises, as the behavior of the private sector leads to widening risk premia and severe disruptions in credit in other financial markets. At least, two amplification mechanisms operate during these liquidity crises. The first mechanism, which works through asset prices and balance sheets, has already been quite accurately described. A negative shock to the balance sheet of asset holders, i.e. banks and other financial institutions and/or firms, causes them to liquidate assets, lowering prices, further deteriorating balance sheets, culminating in a crisis. But there is also a second mechanism at work: Knightian uncertainty. Unusual shocks to untested financial innovations lead agents to become in a fundamental sense more uncertain about their investments. Market participants face risk they don't understand, and treat these risks as Knightian (Knight, 1921). Accordingly, they try to disengage from risk and seek liquid investments, which can lead to a liquidity crisis dynamic.

Caballero and Krishnamurthy (2008) analyze this dynamic in a very interesting contribution. Furthermore, one can make quite convincingly the argument that this flight to quality is also at the root of our global turbulences. For instance, Caballero, Farhi and Gourinchas (2008) argue that the persistent global imbalances, the subprime crisis, and the volatile oil and asset prices are tightly connected. They all stem from a global environment where sound and liquid assets are in scarce supply.

6. Concluding Remarks

This introductory chapter has sampled the rich and varied literature on liquidity and financial crises. The articles we have selected provide important insights into the relationship of liquidity and crises, emphasizing in particular the implications for the functioning of the interbank market, the public provision of liquidity, the role of money in financial crises, and the risk of contagion. However, there is obviously still much that we do not know. But at least in one respect there is hope: The recent financial crisis will guide us into fascinating new research directions that will surely deepen our knowledge of the mechanisms of financial crises.

References

Acharya, V., D. Gale and T. Yorulmazer (2009), "Rollover Risk and Market Freezes," working paper, New York University.

Acharya, V., D. Gromb and T. Yorulmazer (2008), "Imperfect Competition in the Interbank Market for Liquidity as a Rationale for Central Banking," working paper, London Business School.

Acharya, V., and T. Yorulmazer (2008): "Information Contagion and Bank Herding," *Journal of Money, Credit and Banking* 40, 215–231.

Acharya, V. and T. Yorulmazer (2009): "Cash-in-the-Market Pricing and Optimal Bank Resolution," *Review of Financial Studies*, (forthcoming).

Allen, F. and A. Babus (2009): "Networks in Finance," in *The Network Challenge: Strategy, Profit, and Risk in an Interlinked World* edited by P. Kleindorfer and J. Wind with R. Gunther, Upper Saddle River, NJ: Wharton School Publishing/Pearson, pp. 367–382.

Allen, F., A. Babus, and E. Carletti (2009): "Financial Crises: Theory and Evidence," *Annual Review of Financial Economics* 1, forthcoming.

Allen, F. and E. Carletti (2006): "Credit Risk Transfer and Contagion," *Journal of Monetary Economics* 53, 89–111.

Allen, F. and E. Carletti (2008): "Mark-to-Market Accounting and Cash-in-the-Market Pricing," *Journal of Accounting and Economics* 45, 358–373.

Allen, F., E. Carletti and D. Gale (2009): "Interbank Market Liquidity and Central Bank Intervention," *Journal of Monetary Economics* 56, 639–652.

Allen, F. and D. Gale (2000): "Financial Contagion," *Journal of Political Economy* 108, 1–33.

Allen, F. and D. Gale (2004a): "Financial Intermediaries and Markets," *Econometrica* 72, 1023–1061.

Allen, F. and D. Gale (2004b): "Financial Fragility, Liquidity, and Asset Prices," *Journal of the European Economic Association* 2, 1015–1048.

Allen, F. and D. Gale (2006): "Systemic Risk and Regulation", in M. Carey and Rene Stulz (eds.), *The Risks of Financial Institutions*, Chicago: Chicago University Press, 341–375.

Allen, F. and D. Gale (2007): *Understanding Financial Crises*, Clarendon Lectures in Finance, Oxford and New York: Oxford University Press.

Babus, A. (2007): "The Formation of Financial Networks," Discussion Paper 06–093, Tinbergen Institute.

Berger, A. and C. Bouwman (2008a): "Bank Liquidity Creation," *Review of Financial Studies*, (forthcoming).

Berger, A. and C. Bouwman (2008b): "Financial Crises and Bank Liquidity Creation," working paper, University of South Carolina.

Bhattacharya, S. and D. Gale (1987): "Preference Shocks, Liquidity and Central Bank Policy," in W. Barnett and K. Singleton (eds.), *New Approaches to Monetary Economics*, Cambridge: Cambridge University Press, 69–88.

Bolton, P., T. Santos and J. Scheinkman (2008): "Inside and Outside Liquidity," working paper, Columbia University.

Bolton, P., T. Santos and J. Scheinkman (2009): "Market and Public Liquidity," *American Economic Review* 99, 594–599.

Boot, A. and M. Marinc (2008): "Crisis Management and Lender of Last Resort in the European Banking Market," working paper, University of Amsterdam.

Brunnermeier, M. and L. Pedersen (2009): "Market Liquidity and Funding Liquidity," *Review of Financial Studies* 22(6), 2201–2238.

Brusco S. and F. Castiglionesi (2007). "Liquidity Coinsurance, Moral Hazard and Financial Contagion," *Journal of Finance* 62, 2275–2302.

Bryant, J. (1980): "A Model of Reserves, Bank Runs, and Deposit Insurance," *Journal of Banking and Finance* 4, 335–344.

Caballero, R. and A. Krishnamurthy (2001): "International and Domestic Collateral Constraints in a Model of Emerging Market Crises," *Journal of Monetary Economics* 48, 513–548.

Caballero, R. and A. Krishnamurthy (2005): "Exchange Rate Volatility and the Credit Channel in Emerging Markets: A "Vertical" Analysis," *International Journal of Central Banking* 1, 207–245.

Caballero, R. and A. Krishnamurthy (2008): "Collective Risk Management in a Flight to Quality Episode," *Journal of Finance* 63, 2195–2230.

Caballero, R., E. Farhi and P.-O. Gourinchas (2008): "Financial Crash, Commodity Prices and Global Imbalances," *Brooking Papers on Economic Activity*, forthcoming.

Carlsson, H. and E. van Damme (1993): "Global Games and Equilibrium Selection," *Econometrica* 61, 989–1018.

Castiglionesi, F., and N. Navarro (2007): "Optimal Fragile Financial Networks," working paper, Tilburg University.

Cerasi, V. and J.-C. Rochet (2008): "Solveny Regulation and Credit Risk Transfer," "Paolo Baffi" Centre Research Paper No. 2008–21, Milano.

Cifuentes, R., G. Ferrucci and H. Shin: "Liquidity Risk and Contagion," *Journal of the European Economic Association* 3, 556–566.

Cordoba, J. and M. Ripoll (2004): "Collateral Constraints in a Monetary Economy," *Journal of the European Economic Association* 2, 1172–1205.

Dasgupta, A. (2004): "Financial Contagion through Capital Connections: A Model of the Origin and Spread of Bank Panics," *Journal of the European Economic Association* 2, 1049–1084.

Dell'Ariccia, G. and R. Marquez (2006): "Competition among Regulators and Credit Market Integration," *Journal of Financial Economics* 79, 401–430.

Diamond D. (1997): "Liquidity, Banks, and Markets," *Journal of Political Economy* 105, 928–956.

Diamond, D. and P. Dybvig (1983): "Bank Runs, Deposit Insurance, and Liquidity," *Journal of Political Economy* 91, 401–419.

Diamond, D. and R. Rajan (2001): "Liquidity Risk, Liquidity Creation and Financial Fragility," *Journal of Political Economy* 109, 2431–2465.

Diamond, D. and R. Rajan (2005): "Liquidity Shortages and Banking Crises," *Journal of Finance* 60, 615–647.

Diamond, D. and R. Rajan (2006): "Money in a Theory of Banking," *American Economic Review* 96, 30–53.

Diamond, D. and R. Rajan (2008): "Illiquidity and Interest Rate Policy," working paper, University of Chicago.

Diamond, D. and R. Rajan (2009): "Fear of Fire sales and the Credit Freeze," working paper University of Chicago.

Eisfeldt, A. (2004): "Endogeneous Liquidity in Asset Markets", *Journal of Finance* 59, 1–30.

Elsinger, H., A. Lehar and M. Summer (2006a): "Risk Assessment to Banking Systems," *Management Science* 52, 1301–1314.

Elsinger, H., A. Lehar and M. Summer (2006b): "Using Market Information for Banking System Risk Assessment," *International Journal of Central Banking* 2, 137–185.

Fecht, F. (2004): "On the Stability of Different Financial Systems," *Journal of the European Economic Association* 2, 960–1014.

Fecht, F. and H.P. Grüner (2007): "Systemic Risk and the Incentive Effects of Secured Interbank Lending," working paper, University of Mannheim.

Fecht, F., K. Nyborg and J. Rocholl (2008): "The Price of Liquidity: Bank Characteristics and Market Conditions," Discussion Paper Series 1: Economic Studies No 30/2008, Deutsche Bundesbank Frankfurt.

Fecht, F. and M. Tyrell (2009): "Crisis Resolution: Asset Purchase Programs versus Individual Bailout Plans," working paper, European Business School and Zeppelin University Friedrichshafen.

Flannery, M. (1996): "Financial Crises, Payment System Problem and Discount Window Lending," *Journal of Money, Credit and Banking* 28, 804–824.

Franke, G. and J.P. Krahnen (2008): "The Future of Securitization," Center for Financial Studies Working Paper 2008/31, Frankfurt.

Freixas, X. and C. Holthausen (2005): "Interbank Market Integration under Asymmetric Information", *Review of Financial Studies* 18, 459–490.

Freixas, X. and J. Jorge (2008): "The Role of Interbank Markets in Monetary Policy: A Model with Rationing," *Journal of Money, Credit and Banking* 40, 1151–1176.

Freixas, X., A. Martin and D. Skeie (2009): "Bank Liquidity, Interbank Markets and Monetary Policy," working paper, Federal Reserve Bank of New York.
Furfine, C. (2001): "Banks as Monitors of Other Banks: Evidence from the Overnight Federal Funds Market," *Journal of Business* 74, 33–57.
Goldstein, I. (2005): "Strategic Complementarities and the Twin Crises," *Economic Journal* 115, 368–390.
Goodfriend, M. and R. King (1988): "Financial Deregulation, Monetary Policy and Central Banking," *Federal Reserve Bank of Richmond Economic Review* 74, 3–22.
Gorton, G. and L. Huang (2004): "Liquidity, Efficiency, and Bank Bailouts," *American Economic Review* 94, 455–483.
Hartmann, P., S. Straetmans and C. de Vries (2004): "Asset Market Interlinkages," *Review of Economics and Statistics* 86, 313–326.
Heider, F., M. Hoerova and C. Holthausen (2009): "Liquidity Hoarding and Interbank Market Spreads: The Role of Counterparty Risk," mimeo European Central Bank, Frankfurt.
Holmström, B. and J. Tirole (1998): "Private and Public Supply of Liquidity," *Journal of Political Economy* 106, 1–40.
Holmström, B. and J. Tirole (2008): "Wicksell Lectures: Inside and Outside Liquidity," mimeo, Toulouse School of Economics, forthcoming as a book by Princeton University Press.
Huang, J., and J. Wang (2008a): "Liquidity and Market Crashes," *Review of Financial Studies*, forthcoming.
Huang, J., and J. Wang (2008b): "Market Liquidity, Asset Prices and Welfare," *Journal of Financial Economics*, forthcoming.
Kahn, C., and J. Santos (2008): "Liquidity, Payment and Endogenous Financial Fragility," working paper, Federal Reserve Bank of New York.
Kaminsky, G. and C. Reinhart (1999): The Twin Crises: The Causes of Banking and Balance-of-Payments Problems, *American Economic Review* 89, 473–500.
Kiyotaki, N. and J. Moore (1997): "Credit Cycles," *Journal of Political Economy* 105, 211–248.
Kiyotaki, N. and J. Moore (2005): "Liquidity and Asset Prices," *International Economic Review* 46, 317–349.
Kiyotaki, N. and J. Moore (2008): "Liquidity, Business Cycles, and Monetary Policy," working paper, Princeton University.
Knight, F. (1921): "*Risk, Uncertainty, and Profit*," Boston: Houghton Miffin.
Morris, S. and H. Shin (2009): "Illiquidity Component of Credit Risk," working paper Princeton University.
Leitner, Y. (2005): "Financial Networks: Contagion, Commitment, and Private Sector Bailouts," *Journal of Finance* 60, 2925–2953.
Lorenzoni, G. (2008): "Inefficient Credit Booms," *Review of Economic Studies* 75, 809–833.
Masson, P. (1999): "Contagion: Monsoonal Effects, Spillovers and Jumps between Multiple Equilibria," Chapter 8 in P Agénor, M. Miller, D. Vines and A. Weber Eds., *The Asian Financial Crisis: Causes, Contagion and Consequences*, Cambridge, U.K.: Cambridge University Press.
Rauch, C., S. Steffen, A. Hackethal and M. Tyrell (2009): "Savings Banks, Liquidity Creation and Monetary Policy," working paper, Goethe University Frankfurt.
Repullo, R. (2005): "Liquidity, Risk Taking, and the Lender of Last Resort," *International Journal of Central Banking* 1, 47–80.
Rochet, J.-C. and X. Vives (2004): "Coordination Failures and the Lender of Last Resort: Was Bagehot Right after all?," *Journal of the European Economic Association* 2, 1116–1147.
Shin, H. (2008): "Risk and Liquidity in a System Context," *Journal of Financial Intermediation* 17, 315–329.
Smith, B. (2002): "Monetary Policy, Banking Crises, and the Friedman Rule," *American Economic Review* 92, 128–134.
Tirole, J. (2003): "Inefficient Foreign Borrowing: A Dual- and Common-Agency Perspective," *American Economic Review* 93, 1678–1702.
Upper, C. and A. Worms (2004): "Estimating Bilateral Exposures in the German Interbank Market: Is there a Danger of Contagion?," *European Economic Review* 48, 827–849.
Upper, C. (2007): "Using Counterfactual Simulations to Assess the Danger of Contagion in Interbank Markets," BIS Working Papers No. 234, Basel.

I LIQUIDITY AND INTERBANK MARKETS

2 Preference Shocks, Liquidity, and Central Bank Policy

Sudipto Bhattacharya and Douglas Gale

1. Introduction

Several recent papers have examined the micro-theoretic foundations for a theory of financial intermediation. The role of intermediaries as agents who provide delegated monitoring services has been developed in Leland and Pyle (1977) and Diamond (1984). More recently, Bryant (1980) and Diamond and Dybvig (1983) have considered issues pertaining to the optimal form of intermediary (deposit) contracts. They examine intertemporal models in which depositors are subject to privately observed preference shocks and the returns to investments depend on their time to maturity (liquidity). Within this framework, Bryant, Diamond–Dybvig and Jacklin (1986) have demonstrated the superiority of deposit contracts over Walrasian (mutual fund) trading mechanisms in providing agents with insurance for risks connected with preference shocks.[1]

The work on banking contracts has also served to focus attention on problems of coordination across agents who have private information on (risky) investments undertaken by the depository intermediaries or mutual funds. The pioneering study of Bryant (1980) considered the instabilities (panics) and imperfect risk-sharing that would arise if bank depositors (with fixed commitment contracts) make earlier withdrawals based on information about asset returns. Jacklin and Bhattacharya (1985) have analyzed the implications of such phenomena for the welfare-optimal choice over depository and mutual-fund (Walrasian) intermediation mechanisms. Diamond and Dybvig (1983) have shown that, even in the absence of private information about asset returns, deposit contracts are subject to a coordination problem across agents (multiple Pareto-ordered Nash equilibria). In essence, the insurance aspect of deposit contracts leads to the possibility of panics. Agents who conjecture that other agents will panic and make early withdrawals are then led to make early withdrawals themselves because excessive early withdrawals make their promised second-period payoffs infeasible.

While the Diamond–Dybvig analysis of "banking panics" provides a useful starting point, its implications for optimal policies to improve coordination are somewhat sparse.

[1] As Jacklin (1986) has noted, with the specific "corner" parameterization employed in Diamond and Dybvig (1983) – and given the socially optimal production decision – their optimal (first-best) allocation is indeed achievable through a mutual-fund trading mechanism. However, this is not true with more general smooth preferences.

As noted in their paper, when (privately observed) preference shocks are statistically independent across a large number of agents, panics are easily eliminated by a policy of precommitment not to liquidate more than a certain proportion of investments early. Such a policy, which they term "suspension of convertibility," serves to ensure that agents who conjecture that others might withdraw early nevertheless perceive no impact on the feasibility of their later contractual payoffs. Thus, no agent who truly wishes to consume later is induced to join the panic; that is, the Pareto-superior Nash equilibrium is uniquely attained. Diamond and Dybvig also consider the case in which the proportion of agents who (truly) wish to consume early is stochastic in aggregate, owing to correlations among agents' preference shocks. In this case, suspension of convertibility is an imperfect measure which leads to second-best distortions in optimal risk-sharing, unless intermediary contracts can respond to the realized proportion of early diers.

Diamond and Dybvig consider a role for central bank policy, in the case of aggregate preference shocks, arising from the central bank's assumed superior ability to make payoffs to depositors contingent on realized aggregate outcomes. But we find this explanation less than compelling (cf. Section 5). Instead, we focus on a setting in which individual intermediaries are subject to privately observed shocks affecting the proportion of their depositors wishing to make early withdrawals. In addition to these shifts in their demand for liquidity, intermediaries have private information about the mix of liquid (short-term) and illiquid (longer-term) investments in their portfolios. The liquidity shocks, which may be regional in nature, are imperfectly correlated across intermediaries. Thus there is a need for a borrowing–lending mechanism across banks to insure depositors partially against variations in their liquidity requirements.

By developing a model of such an interbank coordination problem, we are able to show that the optimal mechanism design problem is subject to inherent second-best distortions, even in the absence of aggregate liquidity shocks over (a large number of) intermediaries as a whole. In addition, we are able to provide fairly sharp characterizations of the extent and terms of the optimal quantity-constrained borrowing-lending program across banks. We also show that, in many cases involving plausible restrictions on preferences, banks are induced to underinvest in liquid assets at the second-best optimum, relative to a setting with representative intermediaries or (equivalently) informationally unconstrained coordination across banks. Our results here provide a promising start to a research program, one that seriously examines the implications of the recent micro-theoretic modeling of intermediation for detailed and realistic aspects of optimal (governmental) policy.

This paper is organized as follows. In Section 2, we first discuss the underlying framework developed in Diamond and Dybvig (1983), and then proceed to the detailed development of our model of interbank coordination. The characteristics of our second-best optimal interbank contract are analyzed in Section 3, and further interpreted in terms of the role and function of a central bank in Section 4. In Section 5, which concludes the paper, we suggest avenues for further research and integration with related literature, particularly on models with aggregate shocks and fiat money.

2. The Model of Interbank Coordination

Since the Diamond–Dybvig framework is used as a basis for the subsequent analysis, it is worth sketching the outlines here. There are three dates indexed $T = 0, 1, 2$ and a single commodity at each date. Agents are identical ex ante and observe (privately) an idiosyncratic preference shock at date 1. Their preferences are given by

$$U(C_0, C_1, C_2) = \begin{cases} U(C_1) & \text{with probability } t, \\ U(C_2) & \text{with probability } (1-t), \end{cases} \tag{2.1}$$

where U is a von Neumann–Morgenstern utility function and C_T denotes consumption at date $T = 0, 1, 2$. Agents who realize the utility function $U(C_1)$ [respectively, $U(C_2)$] at date 1 are called early [late] diers.

Each agent has an initial endowment of one unit of the consumption good at date 0 and none at subsequent dates. The agent deposits this endowment with the intermediary at date 0 in return for consumption at dates 1 and 2. The intermediary has access to two investment technologies. The first, corresponding to investment in the short-term asset, yields one unit of consumption at date 1 for every unit of investment at the beginning of that period. The second, corresponding to investment in the long-term asset, yields $R > 1$ units of consumption at date 2 for every unit of investment at date 1. Individuals are also able to store consumption between date 1 and date 2.

It is assumed that the number of agents is large and that there is no aggregate uncertainty. The cross-sectional distribution of preference shocks realized at date 1 is the same as the probability distribution of these shocks for an individual agent at date 0. Thus t is the proportion of early diers realized at date 1 and $(1 - t)$ the proportion of late diers. A representative intermediary accepts a deposit of one unit from each depositor and knows that a fraction t of them will be early diers. In exchange for the deposit, the intermediary offers each agent a contract which allows him to withdraw either C_1 units of consumption at date 1 or C_2 units at date 2. In order to finance withdrawals, the intermediary liquidates L units per capita at date 1 and hence receives $R(1 - L)$ units per capita at date 2.

The intermediary chooses (C_1, C_2, L) to maximize the ex ante expected utility of individual agents. Then it solves the problem:

$$\underset{(C_1, C_2, L)}{\text{Max}} \{tU(C_1) + (1-t)U(C_2)\} \tag{2.2}$$

$$\text{subject to} \quad t_1 C_1 = L, \tag{2.3a}$$

$$(1-t)C_2 = R(1-L). \tag{2.3b}$$

Assuming U is differentiable, strictly increasing, and strictly concave, any interior optimum must satisfy:

$$\begin{aligned} &U'(C_1^*) = RU'(C_2^*), \\ &C_1^* = L^*/t \quad \text{and} \quad C_2^* = (1-L^*)R/(1-t). \end{aligned} \tag{2.4}$$

Clearly $C_2^* > C_1^*$ is implied by (2.4) and the condition $R > 1$. A sufficient condition for C_2^*/C_1^* to be less than R is that $CU'(C)$ be decreasing in C. Thus if U has a coefficient of relative risk aversion greater than unity, early diers will share in the higher returns on illiquid assets. In what follows it will always be assumed that this condition holds.[2]

[2]This assumption about the Arrow–Pratt relative risk-aversion coefficient of the "representative investor" is an empirically plausible one, in the light of recent (and past) studies [e.g., Hansen and Singleton (1983)].

In attempting to implement the first-best allocation (C_1^*, C_2^*, L^*) defined by (2.4), the intermediary faces a coordination problem. In defining the first-best allocation problem above, it was assumed that only early diers consumed C_1 and only late diers consumed C_2. Since preference shocks are privately observed the intermediary may not be able to guarantee this. In fact, the late dier's decision whether to withdraw C_1 at date 1 and store it or to withdraw C_2 at date 2 is a strategic one, depending on what other agents do. Diamond and Dybvig find that there are two, Pareto-ranked, Nash equilibria. In the first (Pareto-dominant) equilibrium, only those agents who have a genuine preference for early consumption choose to make an early withdrawal. In the second (Pareto-dominated) equilibrium, agents who actually prefer late consumption, fearing withdrawal by others of the same type, also choose to withdraw early. The inefficiency of these "bank runs" arises directly from the premature and unnecessary disinvestment of the higher yielding assets.

Another way to solve the problem of bank runs is to treat the intermediary as a mutual fund. That is, the intermediary chooses L^* as its investment in short-term assets and provides each depositor with an income stream $(L^*, (1 - L^*)R)$ over the remaining two periods. At date 1 a market opens on which agents can trade shares in these income streams. The optimal consumption plan (C_1^*, C_2^*) can be implemented through such a market, but the resulting share price does not make L^* a value-maximizing decision for the intermediary. To see this, note that the ex dividend share price at date 1 is $(1 - t)L^*/t$. Each shareholder receives a dividend of L^* at the beginning of date 1. Early diers supply their shares inelastically and late diers supply consumption goods inelastically. The supply of shares is t and the supply of consumption is $(1 - t)L^*$, so the market-clearing price is $(1 - t)L^*/t$. Then the share price at date 1 *per unit of period 2 payoff* R is $(1 - t)L^*/t(1 - L^*)$. At this price, an intermediary choosing L to maximize its own realizable value at date 1 would solve

$$\operatorname*{Max}_L [L + (1 - L)P[R]],$$

where $P[R] \equiv (1 - t)L^*/t(1 - L^*) = RC_1^*/C_2^* > 1$. The solution is $L = 0$. The apparent liquidity created by the market in shares leads to underinvestment in the short-term asset.

In this paper we have tried to shift the focus away from the Diamond–Dybvig coordination problem. Instead we focus on the problems faced by the intermediaries themselves when their demand for liquidity is uncertain. We make three basic changes in the Diamond–Dybvig model. First, we assume that while there is no aggregate uncertainty, individual intermediaries are uncertain at date 0 about what proportion of their depositors will be early diers at date 1. Second, we assume that the intermediary's investment decision is made (irrevocably) at date 0.[3] Third, we assume that the intermediaries have incomplete information. Each intermediary observes its own investment decision and the proportion of early diers among its own depositors but not those of the other intermediaries.

Under these assumptions there is clearly scope for intermediaries to provide themselves with insurance against unexpected liquidity needs. Because L is fixed at date 0, an intermediary cannot provide itself with extra liquidity by changing L once the demand

[3]It should be noted that this irreversibility of investment allocations, where illiquid assets cannot be realized earlier, removes the Diamond–Dybvig bank runs problem. This assumption is also more consistent with a context where intermediaries can signal the value of their well-diversified *aggregate* portfolios, but are subject to a Lemons problem [Akerlof (1970)] in liquidating individual elements (loans) in their portfolios.

for liquidity is realized. On the other hand, the intermediaries can collectively provide extra liquidity by borrowing and lending after their liquidity needs are known. In other words, they have an incentive to set up an interbank market at date 1. However, setting up a Walrasian interbank market creates a free-rider problem. Individual intermediaries will rely on the ex post market to provide them with liquidity and will underinvest in the liquid asset. In the aggregate however, the liquidity of the market is limited by the investments of individual intermediaries in the liquid asset. For this reason we should not expect an interbank market to perform very well. We are thus led to consider the design of an optimal insurance scheme and the distortions that result from its implementation.

In our model, as in the Diamond–Dybvig model, depositors have one unit of the good at date 0 and none at subsequent dates. They are identical ex ante, but ex post discover themselves to be early or late diers. Their preferences are given by (2.1). Intermediaries are also assumed to be identical ex ante, discovering ex post that they are one of two types. These types are distinguished by the proportion of early diers. Let t_i denote the proportion of early diers in the ith type of intermediary ($i = 1, 2$) and assume $0 < t_1 < t_2 < 1$. Intermediaries have probability p_i of being type i and, in the aggregate, the proportion of intermediaries of type i is $p_i(p_1 + p_2 = 1)$. The aggregate proportion of early diers is constant and equal to $t = \sum p_i t_i$.

What we have in mind is that the intermediaries are banks, distinguished by geographical location. Depositors attach themselves to particular banks by locational proximity. Then local economic conditions in the area where the bank operates will have a marked impact on the demand for liquidity. For example, when unemployment is high (the proportion of early diers is high), the demand for liquidity is high also as the unemployed draw down their savings.

We can represent the choice of an optimal insurance contract among the banks as a planning problem. The hypothetical planner chooses an allocation to maximize the ex ante expected utility of the representative bank/depositor. The planner, like the typical intermediary, knows the stochastic structure of the model but cannot observe either the type or the investment decision of an intermediary.[4] He therefore relies on the individual bank to choose the correct level of investment in the liquid asset at date 0 and to reveal his true type (demand for liquidity) at date. The planner is therefore constrained to choose an *incentive-compatible* allocation. It must not give the bank an incentive to lie or deviate from the correct investment decision.

The choice variables for the planner are the per capita investment in the liquid asset (L), and the consumption of early diers (C_{1i}) and of late diers (C_{2i}) in type-i banks[5]

[4]This assumption is the most extreme form of allowing intermediaries to have superior ex ante information about their withdrawal pattern and liquidity needs. We also do not allow interbank contracts to respond to public information, if any, about realized preference shocks. Considerations outside our model (e.g., the effect of enhanced liquidity on the elimination of panics by depositors) provide additional justification for this assumption. Although it is not clear that our qualitative results would be affected by altering this assumption (when banks have imperfect private information about their local liquidity shocks), it would be interesting to consider extensions in which there are other liquidity effects, such as timing effects in liquid asset returns when intermediaries have asymmetric information about realized returns.

[5]This dependence on payments of early and later diers on the realized $[t_i]$ may to some extent be viewed as an adjustment of "implicit interest" paid to depositors, as documented by Startz (1979). More realistically, such adjustments should probably be viewed as emersions/additions to the shareholder equity in a bank. Under the latter interpretation, questions of aggregation of preferences across depositors and shareholders (in each bank) arise quite naturally, if simplicity in modeling preference shocks is to be preserved. Our two-point support assumption about $[t_i]$ may allow for some sort of Chipman aggregation if $U(\cdot)$ is homothetic (but

($i = 1, 2$). The expected utility of a representative depositor at date 0, given the choice of $\{C_{1i}, C_{2i}\}_{i=1}^{2}$, is

$$V = \sum_{i=1}^{2} p_i\{t_i U(C_{1i}) + (1 - t_i)U(C_{2i})\}. \tag{2.5}$$

With probability p_i the depositor is in a type-i bank and, given that he finds himself in a type-i bank, the probability that he receives C_{1i} [respectively, C_{2i}] is t_i [$(1 - t_i)$].

The resource-balance constraints for the first period are implicit in the assumption that investment in the longer-term asset equals $(1 - L)$. The resource-balance constraints for the second and third periods are respectively,

$$\sum_{i=1}^{2} p_i t_i C_{1i} = L, \tag{2.6a}$$

$$\sum_{i=1}^{2} p_i(1 - t_i)C_{2i} = (1 - L)R. \tag{2.6b}$$

The total per capita supply of goods is L at date 1 and $(1 - L)R$ at date 2. A fraction p_i of the banks are in state i and the per capita demand for consumption in a type-i bank is $t_i C_{1i}$ at date 1 and $(1 - t_i)C_{2i}$ at date 2. So the aggregate requirement for goods is $\sum p_i t_i C_{1i}$ at date 1 and $\sum p_i(1 - t_i)C_{2i}$ at date 2.

The incentive-compatibility constraints are complicated by the mixture of moral hazard and adverse selection problems implicit in the model. An intermediary that wishes to deviate from the plan laid down by the planner can do so in two different ways. It can choose an investment in the liquid asset $\ell \neq L$ or it can report a realized state $s(i) \neq i$. Thus the action of a deviant intermediary can be represented by an ordered pair (ℓ, s), where ℓ is the choice of investment in the liquid asset and s is a signalling strategy. A type-i bank receives a net transfer of $(t_i C_{1i} - L)$ at date 1 and $((1 - t_i)C_{2i} - (1 - L)R)$ at date 2. These transfers are simply the difference between the per capita consumption level chosen by the planner and the per capita supply of goods available to the bank from its own investments. A deviant bank that chooses (ℓ, s) will therefore be able to give every early dier

$$\frac{t_{s(i)}C_{1s(i)} - L + \ell}{t_i}$$

units of consumption in state i. Similarly, in state i it can give every late dier

$$\frac{(1 - t_{s(i)})C_{2s(i)} - (1 - L)R + (1 - \ell)R}{1 - t_i}.$$

In order for the plan to be implemented there must be no incentive for any intermediary to deviate. That means that for any deviant action (s, ℓ) the expected utility of the representative depositor in the deviating intermediary must not exceed the expected utility of the

possibly different across depositors and shareholders because income-expansion paths are necessarily linear in this case.

representative depositor in an intermediary that does not deviate. Incentive-compatibility requires that, for any (ℓ, s),

$$\sum_{i=1}^{2} p_i\{t_i U(C_{1t}) + (1-t_i)U(C_{2i})\}$$
$$\geq \sum_{i=1}^{2} p_i \left\{ t_i U\left[\frac{t_{s(i)}C_{1s(i)} + \ell - L}{t_i}\right] \right.$$
$$\left. + (1-t_i)U\left[\frac{(1-t_{s(i)})C_{2s(i)} + (L-\ell)R}{1-t_i}\right]\right\}. \tag{2.7}$$

Definition 2.1: The second-best optimal risk-sharing problem is solved by choosing $\{L, (C_{1i}, C_{2i})_{i=1}^{2}\}$ to maximize (2.5) subject to (2.6) and (2.7).

It is helpful, for analytical purposes as well as for the interpretation of the problem, to reformulate (2.5), (2.6), and (2.7) in terms of borrowing and lending. Let

$$B \equiv t_2 C_{12} - L \tag{2.8}$$

denote the net transfer to a type-2 bank at date 1. Resource balance (2.6a) implies that the net transfer to a type-1 bank is $-Bp_2/p_1$. We can interpret B as the net amount borrowed by a type-2 bank or lent by a type-1 bank. Of course, B may be positive or negative. Next let

$$DB \equiv R(1-L) - (1-t_2)C_{22} \tag{2.9}$$

denote the amount repaid by a type-2 bank at date 2, that is, the net transfer from the bank to the insurance system. Again, resource balance (2.6b) implies that the net transfer to a type-2 bank at date 2 is $-DBp_2/p_1$. The variable D implicitly defined by equation (2.9) can be interpreted as the (gross) borrowing (lending) rate. To simplify notation we deal explicitly only with the case $p_1 = p_2$. However, *all propositions are valid for the more general case* $p_1 \neq p_2$. Using equations (2.8) and (2.9), the planner's problem can be equivalently expressed as

$$V^* = \underset{|B,D,L|}{\text{Max}} \sum_{i=1}^{2} \left\{ t_i U\left[\frac{(-1)^i B + L}{t_i}\right] + (1-t_i)U\left[\frac{(-1)^{i+1}DB + (1-L)R}{1-t_i}\right]\right\} \tag{2.10}$$

subject to:

$$V^* \geq \sum_{i=1}^{2} \left\{ t_i U\left[\frac{(-1)^{s(i)} B + \ell}{t_i}\right] + (1-t_i)U\left[\frac{(-1)^{s(i)+1}DB + (1-\ell)R}{1-t_i}\right]\right\}$$
$$\text{for any } (s, \ell). \tag{2.11}$$

The resource-balance constraints (2.6a) and (2.6b) have been subsumed in (2.10) using (2.8) and (2.9); (2.11) is the reformulated incentive-compatibility constraint.

3. Analysis of the Optimal Interbank Contract

In this section we wish to examine the qualitative properties of the second-best optimal contract. We focus on the relationship between the return on interbank lending D and the return on the illiquid asset R, as well as on the relationship between the second-best optimal investment in liquid assets (reserves) L and the first-best investment L^*.

The constrained maximization problem stated in (2.10) and (2.11) is a rather complicated one. The incentive-compatibility constraint (2.11) does not lend itself to ordinary Lagrangean techniques because it contains a discrete variable s. One way to deal with the problem would be to replace (2.11) with four separate constraints, one corresponding to each possible choice of s. Fortunately, there is an easier way: The problem can be further simplified so that it reduces to a standard Lagrangean problem. The successive steps in this reduction are presented as a sequence of propositions. The proofs that are not given here can be found in the Appendix to Bhattacharya and Gale (1986). The first thing to note is that, under the maintained assumptions, we have the following.

Proposition 1: *The first-best optimum is not attainable as a solution to the second-best risk-sharing problem defined by* (2.10) *and* (2.11) *when* $(t_2 - t_1)$ *is not too large.*

The next step is to note that the second-best optimum involves giving a net transfer (loan) to the intermediaries with a higher proportion of early diers at date 1.

Proposition 2: *If* (B, D, L) *is the second-best optimum contract, then* $B > 0$.

The next result shows that we do not need to consider all possible signaling strategies. Strictly speaking, incentive compatibility requires that (2.11) is satisfied for all possible deviations (s, ℓ). What matters, however, is the deviations for which (2.11) is binding – that is, values of (s, ℓ) such that (2.11) is satisfied as an equation. Let $V(B, D, s, \ell)$ denote the expected utility ex ante of an intermediary who plans to use the deviation (s, ℓ). $V(B, D, s, \ell)$ is just the right-hand side of (2.11). We are concerned, therefore, with deviations that satisfy $V^* = V(B, D, s, \ell)$; these deviations are called *optimal* deviations. The next result tells us that we need not consider all possible signaling strategies. If (s, ℓ) is an optimal deviation then the signaling strategy s makes the same report in both states.

Proposition 3: *If* (s, ℓ) *is an optimal deviation – that is,* $V^* = V(B, D, s, \ell)$ *– then* $s(1) = s(2)$.

Thus, in considering deviations from the social optimum, one need only consider two possible signaling strategies: either the deviant always claims to be in type 1 or he always claims to be in type 2. Let j denote the reported type, now known to be independent of the true type. The incentive-compatibility constraint (2.11) can be written, without loss of generality, as

$$V^* \geq \sum_{i=1}^{2} \left\{ t_i U \left[\frac{(-1)^j B + \ell}{t_i} \right] + (1 - t_i) U \left[\frac{(-1)^{j+1} DB + R(1 - \ell)}{1 - t_i} \right] \right\} \tag{3.1}$$

for any (ℓ, j). Note that since the right-hand side of (3.1) is strictly concave in ℓ, there is a unique optimal deviation corresponding to each choice of $j = 1, 2$.

Proposition 4: *Suppose that* $V(B, D, j, \ell) = V^*$. *Then* $D < R$ *implies* $j = 2$ *and* $D > R$ *implies* $j = 1$.

If the interbank rate is less than the rate of return of illiquid assets, deviant bank will always claim to have a high proportion of early diers. It will borrow at date 1 whether it actually has a high proportion or a low proportion of early diers. Conversely, if the interbank rate is greater than the return on illiquid assets, a deviant bank will always lend to the system. These results are quite intuitive and, in fact, the proof follows from a straightforward dominance argument.

Proposition 4 does not tell us what happens when $D = R$. One might expect this to be a boundary case at which two constraints, corresponding to two optimal deviations, were just binding. In fact, there is no binding incentive-compatibility constraint in this case.

Proposition 5: *If* (B, D, L) *is an optimal contract and* $D = R$, *then there is no binding incentive-compatibility constraint; that is, the first-best is achieved.*

Thus, in the cases of interest, Proposition 4 applies and there is a unique optimal deviation for any optimal contract (B, D, L). [The value of j is given by Proposition 4 and, given j, there is a unique ℓ such that $V^* = V(B, D, j, \ell)$.] This means that there is a single incentive-compatibility constraint of the standard form, from which we can form a standard Lagrangean.

Proposition 6: *Let* (B, D, L) *be a second-best optimal contract that does not implement the first best. Then there is a Lagrangean multiplier* λ *and an optimal deviation* (j, ℓ) *such that* (B, D, L, ℓ, λ) *is an extreme point c of the Lagrangean:*

$$\sum_{i=1}^{2}\left\{t_iU\left[\frac{(-1)^iB+L}{t_i}\right]+(1-t_i)U\left[\frac{(-1)^{i+1}DB+(1-L)R}{1-t_i}\right]\right\}$$
$$+\lambda\left\{V^*-\sum_{i=1}^{2}\left\{t_iU\left[\frac{(-1)^jB+\ell}{t_i}\right]+(1-t_i)U\left[\frac{(-1)^{j+1}DB+(1-\ell)R}{1-t_i}\right]\right\}\right\}$$

where $j = 1, 2$ *as* $D \gtrless R$.

The analysis of this Lagrangean leads immediately to a characterization of the optimal consumption allocation $\{(C_{1i}, C_{2i})_{i=1}^{2}\}$.

Proposition 7: *Let* (B, D, L) *be a second-best optimal contract that does not implement the first best. Let* $\{(C_{1i}, C_{2i})\}$ *be the corresponding consumption allocation. Then*

$$U'(C_{1i}) = RU'(C_{2i}) \quad (i = 1, 2)$$

and

$$C_{11} \gtrless C_{12} \quad as\ D \lessgtr R.$$

There is a partial decentralization of the optimal consumption allocation, according to Proposition 7. For each $i = 1, 2$, the consumption pattern (C_{1i}, C_{2i}) solves the problem

$$\text{Max } t_i U(C_{1i}) + (1 - t_i)U(C_{2i}) \tag{3.2a}$$

$$\text{Subject to} \quad t_{i1} C_{1i} + (1 - t_i)C_{2i}/R = W_i. \tag{3.2b}$$

It is as if the type-i bank were given a shadow income and allowed to allocate it, at the shadow prices $(1, R^{-1})$, to maximize the ex ante expected utility of its members conditional on the bank's type. Furthermore, the shadow income of a type-1 bank is greater (respectively, less) than that of a type-2 bank as D is less (greater) than R. The intuition behind this is quite straightforward. Suppose that $D > R$. Then Proposition 4 tells us that the optimal deviation from truth-telling always involves claiming to be a type-1 bank. In order to discourage deviations and hence relax the incentive-compatibility constraint, the planner reduces the planned utility of a type-1 bank and increases the planned utility of a type-2 bank. If $D < R$ the situation is simply reversed.[6]

The preceding discussion leaves open the question of whether D is greater than or less than R at the second-best optimum. Our intuition about the free-rider problem, presented in Section 2, suggests that deviant banks will want to borrow too much and invest too little in the liquid asset. In other words, $D < R$ so that $j = 2$ and $L < L^*$. The next proposition shows that this intuition is indeed justified when the preference shocks (t_1, t_2) do not differ very greatly.

Proposition 8: *Let (B, D, L) be a second-best optimal contract. Then $D < R$ if $t_2 - t_1$ is not too large.*

The proposition follows from an application of the envelope theorem at the point where $t_2 = t_1$. It can be shown that if t_2 rises slightly relative to t_1, the ex ante expected utility of type-2 banks falls relative to that of type-1 banks. From Proposition 7 it follows that $D < R$. Thus, within some region next to the diagonal $\{t_1 = t_2\}$, the free-rider problem determines the outcome. Farther from the diagonal, the case $D > R$ may conceivably arise. It is worth noting that Proposition 8 does depend on the assumption that $U'(C)C$ is decreasing. If $U'(C)C$ were assumed increasing then the result could be reversed. For a particular class of utility functions the result in Proposition 8 can be shown to hold globally.

Proposition 8A: *Let $U(C) = (1/a)C^a$ $(a < 1)$ and let (B, D, L) be an optimal, second-best contract. Then $D \lesseqgtr R$ as $a \lesseqgtr 0$.*

Note that the limiting case $a = 0$ corresponds to the logarithmic utility function, for which the first best is attainable and $D = R$.

Proposition 8B: *Let $U(C) = (1/a)\exp(aC)$ and let (B, D, L) be an optimal, second-best contract (i.e., not the first best). Then $D < R$ as $a < 0$.*

Finally we come to the question of how much investment in the liquid asset takes place at the second-best optimum. Is it greater or less than L^*? Here again the relationship between

[6]Thus, our results generalize to situations in which banks can locally reverse their two-period investment decisions at date 1, as in Diamond and Dybvig (1983), provided that mechanisms for dealing with coordination problems across depositors are in place in each bank.

D and R appears to be crucial. In order to obtain a determinate result we have had to restrict our attention to a special class of utility functions. We assume that, for some constants α and β which depend on the utility function U,

$$RU'(\alpha + \beta x) = U'(x) \tag{3.3}$$

for all $x \geq 0$. Strictly speaking, (3.3) need only hold for $x \in \{C_{11}, C_{12}\}$, but we cannot guarantee this without assuming that (3.3) holds globally. Note that (3.3) is satisfied by such familiar examples as the quadratic utility function, logarithmic and power utility functions, and the exponential utility function.[7]

Proposition 9: *Let* (B, D, L) *be an optimal, second-best contract and suppose that* U *satisfies* (3.3). *Then* $L \lesseqgtr L^*$ *as* $D \lesseqgtr R$.

To summarize, we have shown that when the "normal case" (which arises in the neighborhood of the first-best solution) holds, $D < R$. Furthermore, when $D < R$, $L < L^*$. The optimal mechanism thus involves banks borrowing (and being forced to lend) at a subsidized rate, but results in underinvestment in reserves relative to the first-best level that obtains in the absence of asymmetric information.

4. Preference Shocks, Adverse Selection, and Central Banks

Our model with heterogeneous intermediaries above suggests a multiplicity of roles for a centralized institution, with respect to monitoring the values of key economic variables as well as permitting the date-0 commitment that our mechanism design formulation assumed. The first, and most obvious, role for a centralized (unduplicated) entity in our setting is that of improving the external observability of the date-0 investment allocation. Given our underinvestment (relative to the first-best) results above, even noisy imperfect monitoring is likely to be welfare-improving.[8] Of course, if $L = L^*$ could be perfectly enforced (i.e., "moving-support" monitoring) then free trading across intermediaries ex post would implement the first-best in our simple setup, along the lines of Section 2. This is unrealistic, however, given that the abstractions of asymmetric observability of L, as well as the illiquidity of longer-term investments, represent in reality asymmetric knowledge of the quality of a continuum of assets in overall bank portfolios.

Our results for borrowing/lending at $D < R$ (Proposition 8) may be combined with the above observation to yield a date-0 *reserve requirement* on which the full rate of interest is not paid, coupled with date-1 access to a "discount-window" (at a subsidized interest rate) that is made use of to a greater extent by type-2 banks. Note, however, that the right comparison to a market rate of interest is unclear, since free trading of intermediary claims to date-2 payoffs at date 1 may produce an interest rate that is strictly lower than R, as in the representative intermediary case of Section 2. In addition, our model does not account for voluntary reserves that are maintained because of risky loan assets (i.e., portfolio choice), nor for ongoing liquid reserve requirements (mandated or otherwise)

[7]Equation (3.3) is satisfied by all utility functions in the Hyperbolic Absolute Risk-Aversion (HARA) class, functions satisfying $U'(C)/U''(C) = a + bC$ for all C and for some a and b.

[8]The proof of such a result will differ from that of Shavell (1979), given the essential interaction between heterogeneity and moral hazard in our model, where the first-best is achieved if either problem is absent.

beyond date 1. Making realistic connections to existing institutions and policies requires, in our opinion, further enrichment of (our type of) modeling to incorporate intertemporal and portfolio tradeoffs, as well as the juxtaposition of market versus nonmarket contracting in assets and liabilities.

Even within our simplified framework, however, it is possible to make the case for a nonmarket entity which acts as the planner (mechanism designer) that solves the second-best risk-sharing problem. This is the case because both the problems of ex post state revelation and ex ante moral hazard must be dealt with.[9] As a result, while intermediaries which are ex ante identical may themselves design the allocation process analyzed above, at $T = 1$ there may be incentives for some to reverse themselves and propose alternative allocations. Knowing that such proposals might arise would, in turn, dilute the (second-best) optimal ex ante incentives. For example, given $D < R$ and the characterization in Proposition 7, type-1 intermediaries would not wish to lend as much at date 1 as the ex ante optimal mechanism calls for because $[-U'(C_{11}) + DU'(C_{21})] < 0$.

Some (limited) analyses of such "durability" problems have been carried out in the literature, in a market context by Rothschild and Stigiltz (1976) and Miyazaki (1977), and in a more explicitly strategic setting by Myerson (1983). Their results suggest that, in general, the ex ante optimum we have characterized cannot be attained by unfettered strategic interactions across privately motivated agents. Only a welfare-maximizing agent (such as a central bank), acting subject to resource and ineffective constraints but with ex ante commitment, will suffice.

5. Concluding Remarks

In contrast to our focus on central bank policy as a cross-sectional coordination device, several recent models have focused on the implication of aggregate shocks for various aspects of banking and monetary policy. Diamond and Dybvig (1983) have suggested that when the aggregate proportion of early-diers t is stochastic, central bank or governmental policy is (more) able to make depositors' real consumption payoff responsive to the realized value of t, even though individual (representative) banks are unable to do so. While their claim lacks a sound foundation in the form of an explicit model of fiscal or monetary allocation mechanisms, it is possible that further refinement of themes such as those developed in Bhattacharya (1982) – which suggest that monetary mechanisms for risk-sharing may be able to elicit information regarding heterogeneous agents with lower communication costs – may provide some justification for such a role for policy in an intertemporal overlapping-generations setting. Other models of banking with more explicit aggregate shocks, in the form of depositors' information about banks' asset return have been analyzed by Bryant (1980) and by Jacklin and Bhattacharya (1985). These models suggest that governmental deposit insurance, possibly backed by powers of intergenerational taxation, may improve ex ante welfare by discouraging agents from collecting information about asset returns.

Without an explicit incorporation of fiat money into models of banking, it is clearly difficult to provide detailed monetary interpretations of results such as ours on underinvestment

[9] Essentially, agents' preference functionals are defined over a larger-dimensional commodity space than what is commonly observable – e.g., $(L^* - B)/t_1$ versus B. Given this and a more general support for the distribution of the preference shock variable $\tilde{t}$, non-linear loan contracts across intermediaries (with some centralized monitoring of quantities) may be required.

in liquid assets by banks and the resulting need for central-bank reserve requirements. Recently, Siegel (1981) has considered the role of optimal monetary reserve requirements in a model of banks which postulates demand and supply functions for banks' and depositors' portfolio choices across different classes of assets and liabilities. By considering exogenously given (aggregate) shocks to these functions, Siegel is able to develop a theory of price-level fluctuations and show that there exists an optimal reserve requirement that minimizes price-level variability. Furthermore, such an optimal reserve requirement does not minimize the variability of the usual ad hoc "money stock" measures aggregated across currency and deposits. These results are related to those of Weiss (1980), who shows that an active monetary policy responsive to realized investment return shocks may improve the information content of nominal prices by removing the portfolio reactions of agents who have superior information about asset returns.

The lines of enquiry pursued in the work of Siegel and Weiss ought to be incorporated in greater detail in richer models of banking, models that incorporate the roles of interbank coordination as well as aggregate shocks. In particular, the explicit modeling of preference-shocks in agents' objective functions – characteristic of the latter type of models – should be preserved. As Polemarchakis and Weiss (1977) and Muench (1977) have noted in the context of the Lucas (1972) model, plausible derivative goals such as those optimized in the models of Siegel and Weiss may not be welfare-optimal in models that explicitly incorporate (market incompleteness arising from) privately observed preference shocks. Our understanding of the role of and interactions among contractual and market-mediated allocation processes (e.g., banks and mutual funds), and the resulting implications for government policy, is likely to be greatly enhanced by the process of integrating these diverse types of models.

Appendix

Proof of Proposition 7: Differentiate the Lagrangean in Proposition 6 with respect to B, D, L, and ℓ and set the partial derivatives equal to zero. Using the notation $U'_{Ti} \equiv U'(C_{Ti})$ for $T, i = 1, 2$ and

$$\hat{U}'_{1i} \equiv U'\left[\frac{(-1)^j B + \ell}{t_i}\right], \quad \hat{U}'_{2i} \equiv U'\left[\frac{(-1)^{j+1} DB + (1-\ell)R}{1-t_i}\right]$$

for $i = 1, 2$, this gives us the following equations:

$$\sum_{i=1}^{2} [U'_{1i}(-1)^i + U'_{2i}(-1)^{i+1}D] - \lambda \sum_{i=1}^{2} \{\hat{U}'_{1i}(-1)^j + \hat{U}'_{2i}(-1)^{j+1}D\} = 0, \tag{A.1}$$

$$\sum_{i=1}^{2} \{U'_{2i}(-1)^{i+1}B - \lambda \hat{U}'_{2i}(-1)^{j+1}B\} = 0, \tag{A.2}$$

$$\sum_{i=1}^{2} \{U'_{1i} - U'_{2i}R\} = 0, \tag{A.3}$$

$$\sum_{i=1}^{2} \lambda\{\hat{U}'_{1i} - \hat{U}'_{2i}R\} = 0. \tag{A.4}$$

Because $B > 0$, equation (A.2) implies that

$$\sum_{i=1}^{2} \{U'_{2i}(-1)^{i+1}D - \lambda \hat{U}'_{2i}(-1)^{j+1}D\} = 0, \tag{A.5}$$

and substituting this equation into (A.1) gives

$$\sum_{i=1}^{2} U'_{1i}(-1)^{i} - \lambda \sum_{i=1}^{2} \hat{U}'_{1i}(-1)^{j} = 0. \tag{A.6}$$

From (A.4) and (A.2) (recalling $B > 0$) we obtain

$$\sum_{i=1}^{2} \{\lambda \hat{U}'_{1i}(-1)^{j} - U'_{2i}(-1)^{i}R\} = 0. \tag{A.7}$$

Substituting (A.7) into (A.6) gives us

$$\sum_{i=1}^{2} \{U'_{1i}(-1)^{i} - U'_{2i}(-1)^{i}R\} = 0. \tag{A.8}$$

But (A.3) and (A.8) together imply that

$$U'_{1i} - RU'_{2i} = 0 \tag{A.9}$$

for $i = 1, 2$.

From (A.6) it is clear that

$$\sum_{i=1}^{2} U'_{1i}(-1)^{i} \lessgtr 0 \quad \text{as} \quad j = 1, 2.$$

Thus $j = 2$ implies $U'_{12} > U'_{11}$ and $j = 1$ implies $U'_{11} > U'_{12}$. In view of (A.9) this means that $(C_{12}, C_{22}) \ll (C_{11}, C_{21})$ if $j = 2$ and $(C_{11}, C_{21}) \ll (C_{12}, C_{22})$ if $j = 1$. Q.E.D.

Proof of Proposition 8A: We give the proof when $a < 0$. The other case is similar. From Proposition 7,

$$\left(\frac{L-B}{t_1}\right)^{a-1} = R\left(\frac{R(1-L)+DB}{1-t_1}\right)^{a-1} \tag{A.10}$$

and

$$\left(\frac{L+B}{t_2}\right)^{a-1} = R\left(\frac{R(1-L)-DB}{1-t_2}\right)^{a-1} \tag{A.11}$$

Rearranging (A.10) and (A.11), we obtain

$$\left(\frac{L-B}{t_1}\right) = R^{\gamma}(R(1-L)+DB)+(L-B), \qquad \text{(A.12)}$$

$$\left(\frac{L+B}{t_2}\right) = R^{\gamma}(R(1-L)-DB)+(L+B), \qquad \text{(A.13)}$$

where $\gamma = 1/(a-1)$. Subtracting (A.13) from (A.12) gives

$$\left(\frac{L-B}{t_1}\right) - \left(\frac{L+B}{t_2}\right) = (R^{\gamma}D-1)2B.$$

If (contrary to what we wish to prove) $D \geq R$ then $R^{\gamma}D > 1$, contradicting Proposition 7. So $D < R$ as required. Q.E.D.

Proof of Proposition 8B: From (A.9) we have

$$\exp[-a(L-B)/t_1] = R\exp[-a\{R(1-L)+DB\}/(1-t_1)].$$

Taking logarithms and rearranging gives us:

$$C_{11} = (L-B)/t_1 = -(\ln R)/a + [R(1-L)+DB+L-B]. \qquad \text{(A.14)}$$

Similarly, it can be shown that

$$C_{12} = (L+B)/t_2 = -(\ln\ R)/a + \{R(1-L)-DB+L+B\}. \qquad \text{(A.15)}$$

Subtracting (A.16) from (A.15) yields:

$$C_{11} - C_{12} = 2B(D-1).$$

If $D > R > 1$ then $C_{11} - C_{12} > 0$, contradicting Proposition 7, so we must have $D < R$. Q.E.D.

Proof of Proposition 9: From Proposition 7 and condition (13), $C_{1i} = \alpha + \beta C_{2i}$ for $i = 1, 2$. Then

$$\tfrac{1}{2}(t_1C_{11}+t_2C_{12}) = \alpha t + \beta(\tfrac{1}{2}t_1C_{21}+\tfrac{1}{2}t_2C_{22}). \qquad \text{(A.16)}$$

Because $t_1 < t_2$ and $C_{21} \lesseqgtr C_{22}$ as $D \gtreqless R$ (Proposition 7), it follows that

$$\frac{t_1C_{21}+t_2C_{22}}{t_1+t_2} \gtreqless \frac{(1-t_1)C_{21}+(1-t_2)C_{22}}{(1-t_1)+(1-t_2)} \quad \text{as } D \gtreqless R. \qquad \text{(A.17)}$$

From the feasibility conditions (2.6a) and (2.6b), the left-hand side of (A.16) is L and the right-hand side of (A.17) is $R(1-L)/(1-t)$. Then (A.16) and (A.17) together imply that

$$L/t \gtreqless \alpha + \beta R(1-L)/(1-t) \quad \text{as } D \gtreqless R. \qquad \text{(A.18)}$$

Now condition (3.3) and the first-best optimal condition (2.4) imply that L^* satisfies $L^*/t = \alpha + \beta R(1-L^*)/(1-t)$. Comparison with (A.18) yields the desired result. Q.E.D.

References

Akerlof, George. 1970. "The Market for Lemons: Quality Uncertainty and the Market Mechanism." *Quarterly Journal of Economics* 84: 488–500.
Bhattacharya, S. 1982. "Aspects of Monetary and Banking Theory and Moral Hazard." *Journal of Finance* 37: 371–84.
Bhattacharya, S., and D. Gale. 1986. "Preference Shocks, Liquidity, and Central Bank Policy." CARESS Working Paper #86-01, University of Pennsylvania.
Bryant, J. 1980. "A Model of Reserves, Bank Runs and Deposit Insurance." *Journal of Banking and Finance* 4: 335–44.
Diamond, D. W. 1984. "Financial Intermediation and Delegated Monitoring." *Review of Economic Studies* 51: 393–414.
Diamond, D. W., and P. H. Dybvig. 1983. "Bank Runs, Deposit Insurance, and Liquidity." *Journal of Political Economy* 91: 401–19.
Hansen, L. P., and K. J. Singleton. 1983. "Stochastic Consumption, Risk Aversion, and the Temporal Behavior of Asset Returns." *Journal of Political Economy* 91: 249–65.
Holmstrom, B. 1979. "Moral Hazard and Observability." *Bell Journal of Economics* 10: 74–91.
Jacklin, C. 1986. "Demand Deposits, Trading Restrictions and Risk Sharing." In E. C. Prescott and N. Wallace (eds.), *Contractual Arrangements for Intertemporal Trade*, University of Minnesota Press.
Jacklin, C., and S. Bhattacharya. 1985. "Distinguishing Panics and Information-Based Bank Runs: Welfare and Policy Implications." Unpublished manuscript, University of Chicago.
Leland, H., and D. Pyle. 1977. "Informational Asymmetries, Financial Structure and Financial Intermediation." *Journal of Finance* 32: 371–87.
Lucas, R. E., Jr. 1972. "Expectations and the Neutrality of Money." *Journal of Economic Theory* 4: 103–24.
Miyazaki, H. 1977. "The Rat Race and Internal Labor Markets." *Bell Journal of Economics* 8: 394–418.
Muench, T. 1977. "Optimality, the Interaction of Spot and Futures Markets, and the Nonneutrality of Money in the Lucas Model." *Journal of Economic Theory* 15: 325–44.
Myerson, R. B. 1983. "Mechanism Design by an Informed Principal." *Econometrica* 51: 1767–97.
Polemarchakis, H. M., and L. Weiss. 1977. "On the Desirability of a Totally Random Monetary Policy." *Journal of Economic Theory* 15: 345–50.
Rothschild, M., and J. E. Stiglitz. 1976. "Equilibrium in Competitive Insurance Markets." *Quarterly Journal of Economics* 90: 629–49.
Shavell, S. 1979. "Risk Sharing and Incentives in the Principal-Agent Model." *Bell Journal of Economics* 10: 55–73.
Siegel, J. J. 1981. "Bank Reserves and Financial Stability." *Journal of Finance* 36: 1073–84.
Startz, R. 1979. "Implicit Interest on Demand Deposits." *Journal of Monetary Economics* 5: 515–34.
Weiss, L. M. 1980. "The Role for Active Monetary Policy in a Rational Expectations Model." *Journal of Political Economy* 88: 221–33.

3 Endogenous Liquidity in Asset Markets

Andrea L. Eisfeldt

Market liquidity appears to vary with the state of the economy. This is evident in the variation in spreads between liquid and illiquid assets over the business cycle and in the fact that liquidity crises are associated with economic downturns.[1] Moreover, in the cross section highly productive industries and economies are associated with more liquid asset markets.

This paper analyzes a model economy in which long-term risky assets vary in quality and are illiquid due to adverse selection. Investors can realize part of the value of payoffs from long-term assets early by issuing claims against the assets in a pooled market. The equilibrium claims price is determined by the average quality of claims sold. I use "liquidity" to describe the cost of transferring the value of expected future payoffs from long-term assets into current income. A lower cost implies higher liquidity. The claims price is increasing in the fraction of high-quality claims traded thus the market is more liquid when there is less adverse selection.

Adverse selection causes markets to be illiquid because claims sold are likely to be of low quality. However, trade for other reasons, such as consumption, investment, or portfolio rebalancing, can mitigate the adverse selection problem. How should we expect the relative fraction of adverse selection motivated trades to vary with the state of the economy? Is adverse selection driven liquidity consistent with procyclical liquidity? The answer is not obvious. Consider an environment where assets are sold either if they are of low quality or if the owner of the asset has an exogenous negative income shock. If more investors received the negative income shock in bad times then more high-quality assets would trade in bad times, making liquidity countercyclical.[2]

Instead, in this paper the state of the economy is determined by the standard business cycle fundamental, productivity. Liquidity is endogenously determined as a function of productivity in the following way: When productivity is high the relative return on risky investment is high and investors initiate larger scale risky projects at all income levels.

[1] See Chordia, Roll, and Subrahmanyam (2001), Huberman and Halka (2001), and Longstaff (2001) for evidence of a systematic time varying component of liquidity. See also Pulvino (1998) and Eisfeldt and Rampini (2003) for evidence that real assets are less liquid in recessions.

[2] Gibbons and Katz (1991) study this type of effect on labor markets noting that workers displaced by plant closings should be less affected by adverse selection. Thus, if there were more plant closings in bad times adverse selection would have a smoothing effect on wages.

Investors also self insure less with riskless assets. Consequently, the outcome of risky projects has a larger impact on investors' income and more claims to high-quality projects are sold in order to supplement current income for use in consumption and new investment. The claims price, and hence market liquidity, increases.

Liquidity also magnifies the effect of changes in productivity on investment and volume. We expect investment to increase with productivity, but investment increases by more when liquidity also improves since higher liquidity makes long-term risky investment even more attractive. Similarly, liquidity magnifies the effect of higher productivity on volume. Higher productivity and investment alone can lead to a larger claims market but a correspondingly more liquid claims market (a higher claims price) further increases the number of claims issued.

Why is it important to study endogenous liquidity? Empirically, there seem to be states of the world in which "too few" trades occur. These are states of the world in which the popular press reports that "liquidity dries up" – sellers cannot find buyers at what they believe to be fair (risk adjusted) prices. Too few trades implies that there is a market friction. Too few trades only in some states implies that this friction varies with the state of the economy. Moreover, from a quantitative theoretical standpoint, if we calibrate the level of asset illiquidity to what we think is a reasonable unconditional level it is difficult to get liquidity to matter much for equilibrium asset prices and quantities.[3] In particular, we seem to observe a larger demand for liquid assets than our models predict. However, if liquidity in fact varies positively with fundamentals and assets are less liquid in bad times, liquidity can have a much larger effect.[4]

Much work has been devoted to understanding the role of liquidity in asset markets. A large literature beginning with Diamond and Dybvig (1983) and including Diamond (1997) and Holmström and Tirole (1996, 1998, 2001) studies how institutions may improve upon markets for liquidity provision when there are information asymmetries. Related work on the financial accelerator by Bernanke, Gertler, and Gilchrist (1996, 1999) and others studies the effects of agency costs on the availability of external financing. Illiquidity is often motivated by adverse selection. Myers and Majluf (1984), Lucas and McDonald (1990), and Korajczyk, Lucas, and McDonald (1992) study the effect of adverse selection on equity issues, focusing on separating equilibria. Stiglitz and Weiss (1981) study a model in which the intensity of the adverse selection problem in loan markets varies with the interest rate, holding investment constant. Hendel and Lizzeri (1999) and House and Leahy (2000) study the effects of adverse selection in dynamic durable goods markets. Finally, Shleifer and Vishny (1992) show that liquidity can vary with whether the average purchaser is an industry insider or outsider; in contrast this model focuses on the average seller's reason for trading.

Market liquidity is also a central focus of the market microstructure literature. In the model presented here claims risk is idiosyncratic and agents trade simultaneously in a competitive market taking prices as given. This is in contrast to microstructure models where sellers have private information about a common payoff and agents trade sequentially, sometimes in an imperfectly competitive market. See, for example, Glosten and Milgrom (1985) for a model of a competitive market with sequential trade, or Kyle (1985) for a model

[3]For the effects of a fixed level of illiquidity (i.e., transactions costs) on asset prices and turnover, see, for example, Constantinides (1986), Vayanos (1998), and the introduction to Huang (1999). For a quantitative analysis of the demand for liquid assets in this context, see Aiyagari and Gertler (1991) and Eisfeldt (2003).

[4]Accordingly, Pàstor and Stambaugh (2003) construct liquidity betas and find liquidity to be a significant factor for asset pricing.

with imperfect competition. Sequential trade and imperfect competition allow for a price impact dimension of liquidity not featured here. In this model investors in long-term assets expect to incur a cost if they sell the asset early. Claims purchasers, however, do not incur a cost. They diversify claims risk away and purchase a risk-free claims portfolio which earns a risk-free return. Sellers of high-quality assets in this model are like the liquidity traders of the microstructure literature in that they bear the cost of the asymmetric information and it is their trades which improve liquidity. In this model, the amount of such liquidity enhancing trades is endogenous.

The paper is organized as follows. In Section I, I describe the model economy, the claims market, and the problem faced by an investor in this economy. Section II defines the stationary equilibrium of the model and discusses how to solve for such an equilibrium. Section III describes the stationary equilibrium of a particular economy. In Section IV, I describe the effects of changes in productivity on liquidity through comparative statics across economies with varying productivities of the risky asset. Section V discusses results for aggregate fluctuations and Section VI concludes.

I. Model

A. The Model Economy

There is measure one of identical investors with preferences over consumption ordered by

$$E\left[\sum_{t=\tau}^{\infty}\beta^t(1-\delta)^t\frac{c_t^{(1-\sigma)}}{1-\sigma}\right], \tag{3.1}$$

where β is the discount factor and δ is the probability that an investor dies in any given period t. Each period a fraction of investors dies and the same measure of investors are born.[5]Investors have a constant endowment stream and access to a riskless storage technology and a long-term risky technology. The riskless storage technology has a zero depreciation rate and thus bears a risk-free rate of return equal to one.

The risky technology has an initial investment cost of I per unit. Risky projects pay off only after two periods and have a payoff $Y \in \{0, 1\}$ per unit invested. In the period following investment, investors receive a signal which indicates the conditional probability $q \in \{q_L, q_H\}$, where $q_H > q_L$, that the project will succeed (i.e., that the payoff will be one). The signal is common to all ongoing projects an investor owns and therefore we can think of investors owning one project, of variable scale. The probability of receiving the high signal, q_H, is q_0 and hence the unconditional expected payoff of a risky project is $(q_0q_H + (1 - q_0)q_L)$. The timeline for a risky project is illustrated in Figure 3.1. Since the risky technology is linear, productivity is measured by the ratio of the expected payoff relative to the initial investment.

Since agents are long lived they hold overlapping projects. Investors begin each period with both projects that are ongoing (corresponding to the $t + 1$ node) and completed (corresponding to the $t + 2$ node). Investors are ex ante identical, but differ in terms of their current income realization (from storage and completed projects), the scale of their

[5]Death is used both to ensure the existence of a unique stationary distribution for a given claims price (see, for example, Stokey and Lucas (1989) Theorem 11.2) and to prevent investors from reaching the upper bound of the state space in the numerical solution discussed below.

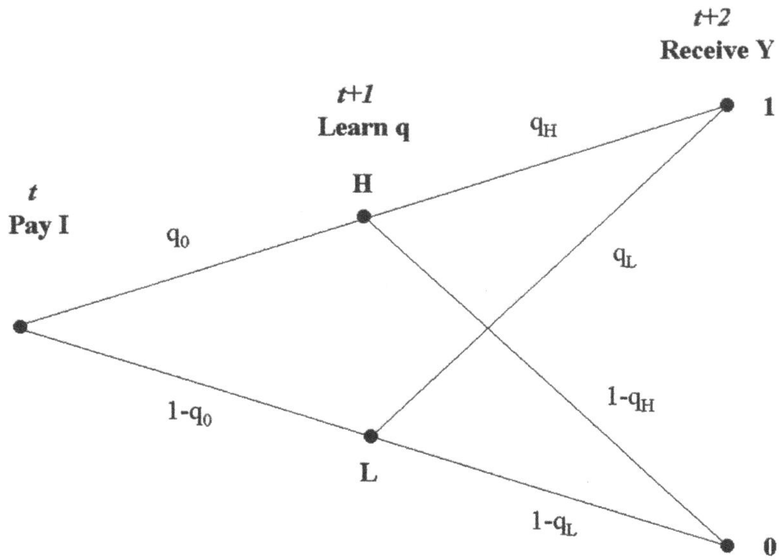

Figure 3.1. Timeline of a risky project.

ongoing projects, and the quality of those projects, due to idiosyncratic shocks to their risky investments. The interaction of shocks to and decisions about projects at different horizons is a crucial feature of the infinite horizon model. In particular, the decision to issue claims to ongoing projects depends on the scale and quality of those projects relative to the success of completed projects and the prospects for new projects.

B. The Claims Market

In addition to access to the riskless and risky technologies, each period investors also have access to an anonymous competitive market in which they can sell claims to their ongoing risky projects. In terms of Figure 3.1, each period investors can sell claims to the $t + 2$ output of ongoing projects at the $t + 1$ node for a price of P. Hence, investors can supplement their current period income by selling claims to the future output of their ongoing projects. The claims price is equal to the price of the average claim sold and is discussed further in Section II. Since the quality of ongoing projects is private information, the claims market is illiquid due to adverse selection.

The information structure in the model is as follows: Investors have private information about the quality of their ongoing projects. In Figure 3.1 this corresponds to private information at the $t + 1$ node. Project qualities are independent across investors and over time for any particular investor. Moreover, and importantly, the claims market is anonymous. The decision to sell claims to a project of a particular quality depends on the investor's income and project scale so that knowledge of these quantities along with the investor's selling decision could potentially reveal the quality of their ongoing projects.[6]

[6]See Leland and Pyle (1977) for a model where agents can signal quality by retaining partial ownership in their project.

Payments on claims to future output are enforceable.[7] While investors do not know who the owner of any particular project is and moreover they cannot keep track of other investors over time, investors can keep track of individual projects on which they have claims. An alternative assumption is that investors in fact sell fractions of projects instead of claims on their output in which case there is no question of enforcement. Note that, since the low payoff is zero, enforceability rules out claims which promise a positive amount with certainty.

Although reputation and some knowledge of an investor's other decisions are certainly mitigating factors, in practice some degree of information asymmetry remains. However, there is clearly pressure in this economy with exogenously incomplete markets to develop mechanisms or institutions to alleviate the information asymmetries.[8] The simplest way for investors to alleviate the adverse selection problem would be to develop a market for claims to initiated projects. In such a market, investors could diversify away all idiosyncratic risk since there is no private information upon initiation. One way to justify the fact that these claims are ruled out is to assume that there is no way for buyers of such claims to ensure investment.

The cost of an equilibrium framework is that market incompleteness is exogenously imposed. The benefit of an equilibrium as opposed to an optimal contracting approach is that we are able to study a market where investors can trade any number of claims at the equilibrium price instead of essentially treating each size contract as a unique asset. Clearly, the optimal contract would insure investors against some of the idiosyncratic risk they face; how much would depend on the specific assumptions about the information structure. Note that here the secondary market provides partial insurance since the distortion of the claims price by adverse selection implies that investors are ex ante partially insured against the low-quality realization. In fact, pooling in the claims market provides some insurance that a market with known qualities could not provide.

C. The Individual's Problem

Each period investors allocate funds to consumption and to investments in the riskless and risky technology, and choose how many claims to their ongoing project to issue. The optimization problem for an individual investor is:

$$\max_{\{c_t, x_{t+1}, y_{o,t+1}\} \in \Re^3_+, y_{s,t} \in [0, y_{o,t}]} E_\tau \left[\sum_{t=\tau}^{\infty} \beta^t (1-\delta)^t \frac{c_t^{(1-\sigma)}}{1-\sigma} \right] \tag{3.2}$$

subject to

$$c_t + x_{t+1} + y_{o,t+1} I \leq e + x_t + (y_{o,t-1} - y_{s,t-1}) Y_t + y_{s,t} P \tag{3.3}$$

given initial ongoing projects $y_{o,\tau}$, an associated quality signal q_τ, and initial income from riskless assets and projects, $x_\tau + (y_{o,\tau-1} - y_{s,\tau-1})Y_\tau$. Consumption in period t is denoted by c_t, x_{t+1} is riskless storage for next period, $y_{o,t+1}$ is the number of risky projects initiated this period, that is, the number of ongoing projects for next period, and $y_{s,t}$ is the number of

[7]The mortgage market, for example, has similar features to this market. Banks securitize mortgage loans and sell them to a pool of agents. The market is anonymous, with claims enforced by the bank.

[8]See, for example, Nachman and Noe (1994) and DeMarzo and Duffie (1999) for how optimal security design can alleviate ex ante information asymmetries.

claims to ongoing projects sold. For reasons discussed in Section II.A, it is not necessary to distinguish investment in riskless storage from investment in claims to other investors' ongoing projects. Intuitively, since investors can diversify away the risk from these claims by holding a perfectly diversified portfolio, they will do so. The initial investment cost for risky projects is I, $Y_t \in \{0, 1\}$ is the payoff of projects completed at time t, and P is the price of claims to the future output of ongoing projects.

The expectation is over the pair (Y, q) which follows a Markov chain. The univariate processes $\{Y_t\}$ and $\{q_t\}$ are independently distributed across investors and over time. Furthermore, Y_t and q_t are independently distributed. However the current period signal q_t is the conditional probability that next period output Y_t equals one.

In words, each period the investor chooses that period's consumption, how much storage and ongoing projects to initiate, and how many claims against the future output of currently ongoing projects to sell, to maximize expected discounted utility subject to the per period budget constraint, a constraint that prevents investors from selling unbacked claims, and nonnegativity constraints on storage, ongoing projects, and claims sold. The nonnegativity constraint on claims sold is crucial because it prevents investors from creating ongoing projects, that is, it makes the risky technology a long-term technology. The budget constraint in words states that an investor's consumption, plus the amount of storage for next period, plus the number of projects initiated times the cost of new projects, must be less than the income from storage from last period, ongoing projects from last period to which claims were not sold, and income from claims sold against currently ongoing projects plus the investor's endowment.

The optimization problem for an individual investor can be stated in recursive form by defining the individual state vector as (w, y_o, q). Using minus to denote previous period values, $w = e + x + (y_0^- - y_s^-)Y$, that is, an investor's current period income is their endowment plus storage from the previous period plus income from completed projects; y_o is the number of ongoing projects in the investor's portfolio (projects initiated in the previous period); and q is the signal about the quality of those projects.

The Bellman equation for an individual investor's problem is:

$$v(w, y_o, q) = \max_{\{c, x', y_o'\}, \in \Re^3_+, y_s \in [0, y_o]} \frac{c^{(1-\sigma)}}{1-\sigma}$$

$$+ \beta(1-\delta)E[v(e + x' + (y_o - y_s)Y', y_o', q')|q] \tag{3.4}$$

subject to

$$c \leq w + y_s p - y_o' I - x'. \tag{3.5}$$

The budget constraint holds with equality because of nonsatiation. We can verify the following properties of the function v which solves the problem in equations (4) and (5).

Proposition 1: *There exists a unique fixed point v to the functional equation in (4). This function v is increasing in each of its arguments, w, y_o, and q. In addition, v is concave and the associated policy functions are continuous and single valued.*

The proof is standard and is hence omitted.[9]

[9]The standard proof (see, for example, Stokey and Lucas (1987)) that v is increasing in the state variable q needs to be modified slightly since q does not enter the one-period return function directly, but instead affects

Taking first-order and envelope conditions and combining equations, we find the Euler equations for storage, new investment, and claims sold. These are just the familiar equilibrium asset pricing Euler equations, modified by the multipliers on the constraints:

$$u'(c) = \beta(1-\delta)E[u'(c')|q] + v_x \tag{3.6}$$

$$Iu'(c) = \beta^2(1-\delta)^2 E[Y''u'(c'') + v_s^{y_o'}|q] + v_o \tag{3.7}$$

$$Pu'(c) = \beta(1-\delta)E[Y'u'(c')|q] + v_s^{y_o} - v_s^0. \tag{3.8}$$

In words, equation (6) states that the cost of storing one more unit equals the return next period. If the cost exceeds the return then $x' = 0$. Equation (7) states that the cost of investing in an additional unit of the risky technology equals the return on the investment. This return can be decomposed into two parts: first, the return from having the option to sell claims to that project next period (thereby relaxing the multiplier, $v_s^{y_o'}$, on the constraint that $y_s' \leq y_o'$) and the return from receiving the payoff of the project after two periods. If the cost exceeds the return then $y_o' = 0$. Finally, equation (8) states that the return from selling an additional claim equals the cost in foregone payoffs tomorrow. If the return is less than the cost then $y_s = 0$, and if the return is greater than the cost then $y_s = y_o$.

The Euler equations illustrate the magnification effect liquidity has on investment and volume. Market liquidity feeds back on the investment decision by making the option of selling claims to the long-term technology more valuable and thereby increasing the return to investing an additional unit. Liquidity feeds back on the selling decision by increasing the return to selling, thereby increasing volume.

II. Stationary Equilibrium

Solving the general equilibrium problem amounts to finding the endogenous distribution over the individual state vector and the associated policy functions for storage, new investment, and claims sold as a function of the state. Given this distribution and the policy functions we can compute all endogenous prices and quantities. In particular we can compute P, the claims price to ongoing projects, and determine the level of liquidity in the stationary equilibrium. Before defining the stationary equilibrium of the model described above, I first discuss how P is determined in equilibrium.

A. Equilibrium Claims Price

The following argument establishes that the market claims price P is equal to the price of the average claim sold. Define the "no adverse selection" price of a quality q_i claim to be p_i. One can think of this price as the "true value" of a claim of quality q_i. The expected payoff of a claim to a particular project is $\kappa p_H + (1-\kappa)p_L$, where κ is the fraction of claims on the market which are of high quality. The certain payoff of a diversified portfolio of claims is $\kappa p_H + (1-\kappa)p_L$, or the same as the expected payoff of any one claim. Since investors are

value by determining the expectation over payoffs in the following period. The fact that v is increasing in w along with the fact that $q > \hat{q}$ implies that $E[w'|q] > E[w'|\hat{q}]$ for all policies for storage, initiated projects and claims sold, replaces the condition in the standard proof that the one-period return function is increasing in q.

risk averse, they prefer the certain payoff of the diversified portfolio. The return on storage is one, thus the claims price is equal to the payoff of a diversified portfolio of claims, that is,

$$P = \kappa p_H + (1 - \kappa) p_L, \tag{3.9}$$

and there is no need to distinguish storage from claims to risky projects. Investors take the equilibrium price P as given, that is, they know the average quality of claims on the market.

To ensure that the market for risk-free assets clears at a risk-free rate of one, the equilibrium per capita quantity of riskless assets, which is the sum of per capita storage plus per capita claims sold, must be greater than or equal to the per capita number of claims sold. Since this is not always the case for storage held by investors who have access to the risky technology, I use a second class of "buffer stock" agents to clear this market at a risk-free rate of one. These agents also have measure one and preferences described by (1). We can think of these agents as young agents who become investors with probability δ each period. They bear idiosyncratic risk in their endowment streams and have access to the storage technology and the claims market. They use these riskless assets to insure their endowment streams through buffer stocks. Alternatively, one can view the model as representing a small open economy which takes the risk-free rate as given.

Thus, the equilibrium claims price will be a weighted average of the "no adverse selection" prices of high and low-quality claims. In an economy with only diversifiable idiosyncratic risk, if there were no private information and if pooling risk were costless, claims would sell for their expected value and all projects would be sold off in their entirety. In other words, the entire return from long-term risky investment would accrue to the investor during the first period, and at the end of the first period ownership of risky assets would be sold off as riskless pooled claims.

I define the "no adverse selection" price of a quality q_i claim to be a fraction ϕ of the conditional expected payoff of a quality i project. Thus $p_i = \phi E[Y'|q_i]$, where $\phi \in (0, 1)$. The parameter ϕ is a reduced form representation of the fact that even without adverse selection, perfect risk sharing is not costless. One can think of ϕ as the result of the following informational friction: If claims to a project are sold, the project must be monitored at a proportional cost of $1 - \phi$. Claims to projects which are not monitored have a zero payoff and thus all projects which are sold are monitored. Thus, the conditional expected payoff net of monitoring costs of a claim to a project of quality i is $\phi E[Y'|q_i]$, which is the price specified above.

The parameter ϕ captures the fact that pooling risk is not costless even in the absence of adverse selection, and has the realistic effect in the economy with adverse selection that low-quality projects are not all immediately sold off to outsiders. Note also that investors who die do not complete their projects, and setting $(1 - \phi) \geq \delta$ accounts for the fact that these projects "fail" with certainty. The qualitative results of the model carry over to the case where $\phi = 1$; however, I will focus on the case where $\phi < 1$ throughout the paper since it allows for more robust numerical examples. A detailed discussion of this and the effect of the parameter ϕ on the equilibrium in the model appears in Section III.D.

B. Definition of a Stationary Equilibrium

Denote the individual state vector (w, y_o, q) by z. An economy $\mathcal{E}$ is described by the risk aversion parameter, discount factor, death rate, constant endowment, initial investment cost for risky projects, probability of receiving the high and low signals, the conditional probabilities of success given the high and low signals, prices at which claims to high and low projects could be issued in an economy with no adverse selection, and risky endowment processes for the second class of agents $\{\hat{e}\}$. Thus, an economy $\mathcal{E}$ is defined as: $\mathcal{E} \equiv \{\sigma, \beta, \delta, e, I, q_0, q_H, q_L, p_H, p_L, \{\hat{e}\}\}$. Define a stationary equilibrium of this economy as:

Definition 1: *A stationary equilibrium for an economy $\mathcal{E}$ consists of: Policy functions $\{c(z), x'(z), y_o'(z), y_s(z)\}$, a price P, quantities $\bar{x}, \bar{y}_o$, and $\bar{y}_s$, and a probability distribution $\lambda(z)$, such that:*

1. *The policy functions $\{c(z), x'(z), y_o'(z), y_s(z)\}$ solve the investor's optimization problem given P.*
2. *The probability distribution $\lambda(z)$ is the stationary distribution of the transition matrix $\Lambda(z'|z)$ induced by investors' policy functions and the Markov process for payoffs and signals, $(\{c(z), x'(z), y_o'(z), y_s(z)\}, \Pi(Y, q))$.*[10]
3. *The per capita quantities of storage, ongoing projects, and claims to projects sold $\bar{x}, \bar{y}_o$, and $\bar{y}_s$ are implied by the average consumer behavior given the policy functions and the stationary distribution.*
4. *The per capita quantity of claims to projects sold $\bar{y}_s$ is less than or equal to the per capita quantity of storage $\bar{x}$ plus the per capita quantity of storage $\hat{x}$ demanded by the buffer stock agents.*[11]
5. *P is consistent with the quality distribution of claims sold, that is, $P = \kappa p_H + (1-\kappa)p_L$, where κ is the endogenous fraction of claims sold which correspond to high-quality projects.*

C. Solving for a Stationary Equilibrium

To solve for a stationary equilibrium, we need to find a fixed point in P, where the price of claims is consistent with the quality distribution. I solve for the equilibrium numerically using discrete state space dynamic programming and the following algorithm:[12]

1. Fix the parameters for an economy, $\mathcal{E}$, that is, fix preference (σ, β, δ), endowment (e) and technology $(I, q_0, q_H, q_L, p_H, p_L)$ parameters.
2. Initialize κ, the fraction of projects sold which are of high quality. Then, $P = \kappa p_H + (1-\kappa)p_L$.
3. Solve the investors' maximization problem. Find the policy functions and calculate the implied stationary distribution over individual states, $\lambda(z)$.
4. Update κ and P by finding the fraction of claims sold which are of high quality. In other words, compute $\kappa^+ = \frac{\sum_{(W \times Y_O)} \lambda(w, y_o, q_H) y_s(w, y_o, q_H)}{\sum_Z \lambda(z) y_s(z)}$, where $\lambda(z)$ is the measure of investors in state z. Then, $P^+ = \kappa^+ p_H + (1-\kappa^+)p_L$.
5. Iterate on steps (3) to (4) to convergence.

[10] The transition matrix $\Lambda(z'|z)$ is formed by setting $\Lambda(w', y_o', q'|z) = \Pr(q')\Pr(Y'|q)$ if the policy functions for x, y_o, and y_s imply that tomorrow's state will be (w', y_o', q') when Y' is the payoff realization. Otherwise, $\Lambda(z'|z) = 0$.

[11] I assume that the risky endowment stream of the buffer stock agents ensures that this is the case, and do not explicitly consider these agents further, here or below.

[12] See, for example, Lungqvist and Sargent (2000). It is straightforward to show that the problem here satisfies the properties necessary for value function iteration to work, that is, standard proofs for convergence of the value function v and the policy functions $\{c(z), x'(z), y_o'(z), y_s(z)\}$ apply (see Stokey and Lucas (1989)). Moreover, as noted above, the existence and uniqueness of the stationary distribution for a given claims price are guaranteed by the fact that all investors face a positive probability of dying and being reborn into a common state.

6. Use the implied stationary distribution $\lambda(z)$ and the policy functions $\{c(z), x'(z), y_o'(z), y_s(z)\}$ to find the equilibrium per capita quantities $\bar{x}$, $\bar{y}_o$, $\bar{y}_s$, and $\bar{c}$. The equilibrium claims price is the price P from the last iteration.

The problem defined by equations (4) and (5) in Section I is difficult to solve analytically. As in models with transaction costs, the solution is characterized by action (selling) and inaction (not selling) regions.[13] Moreover, the investment choice problem involves allocating funds between two risky investments (new and ongoing projects) with different horizons and different payoff distributions.

I provide an analytical characterization of the solution to a finite horizon analogue to this model in the Appendix. However, the finite horizon analogue cannot deliver on the following dimensions: First, finite versions which accommodate analytical solutions must leave out the crucial interaction between projects of different vintages which arises in the infinite horizon case from having long-lived investors with overlapping projects.[14] It is important to include the effect of the risky income from completed projects on the selling decision. Part of the reason liquidity increases with productivity is precisely that when risky investment increases, pre-trade income streams are riskier. It is also important to include the effect of the demand for income for new investment on the selling decision. Liquidity increases with productivity partly because the optimal scale for new investment in the issuing period is larger. Second, solving for the stationary equilibrium of the infinite-horizon model endogenizes the distribution over income and project scale as a function of productivity. With other modeling strategies this distribution would be a free parameter, and one with important implications for liquidity since conditional on project quality these variables exactly determine how many claims are issued. Finally, solving the infinite horizon problem shows that long-lived consumers do not circumvent the liquidity problem by saving in the riskless asset.[15]

III. Characterization of a Stationary Equilibrium

In this section, I present the parameterization and results for what I will refer to as the "baseline" economy. I use these results to discuss the numerical solution to the individual's problem, paying particular attention to the policy function determining claims sold.

A. Parameterization

Table 3.1 summarizes the preference, endowment, and technology parameter values for the baseline economy. The analysis here is intended to provide insight into the qualitative properties of endogenous liquidity due to adverse selection and though most parameters are assigned standard values, they are not based on data from specific markets.

The value of the risk aversion parameter σ is 2. The discount rate $\beta = 0.99$ and the death rate $\delta = 0.03$ together imply an effective rate of time preference of 0.9603, thus a time

[13] See, for example, Constantinides (1986).

[14] See also Hendel and Lizzeri (1999) for a model of adverse selection in the used car market where the interaction between the market for new and used goods is key to their results.

[15] This is in contrast to the standard result in the literature on consumption and savings behavior with liquidity constraints starting with Deaton (1991). This literature finds that long-lived agents display "buffer stock" behavior and self insure shocks through savings in the riskless asset. Here, although investors are long lived and have access to a riskless liquid asset, they also use the claims market to insure shocks.

Table 3.1 Parameterization of the Baseline Economy
This table presents the values for the risk aversion parameter σ, discount factor β, death rate δ, constant endowment e, initial investment cost for risky projects I, probability of receiving the high and low signals q_0, conditional probabilities of success q_H and q_L, prices at which claims to high and low projects could be issued in an economy with no adverse selection p_H and p_L, and the discretized state space for storage x, ongoing risky projects y_o, and claims sold y_s used in the baseline economy.

Preferences	Endowment	Technology	Grid
σ 2	e 0.2	I 0.4167	ystep 0.05
β 0.99		q_0 0.5	xstep 0.1
δ 0.03		q_L 0.45	x^{UB} 1.5
		q_H 0.55	y_o^{UB} 0.75
		p_L 0.405	y_s^{UB} 0.75
		p_H 0.495	

period is taken to be one year. The death rate is used to ensure that few investors will be at the upper bounds of the discretized state space. The projects of an investor who dies are not completed; as discussed in Section II.A this loss is accounted for by setting $(1-\phi) \geq \delta$. When investors are born they are initialized with the smallest scale ongoing project and income equal to endowment. This slightly positive scale initial project ensures that positive investment occurs even in economies with low productivity.[16] The endowment e=0.2 is chosen relative to the technology input and output parameters for the same reason, that is, to ensure that positive investment occurs in equilibrium.

The conditional probabilities that a project succeeds are centered around 0.5. The low-quality signal $q_L = 0.45$ and high-quality signal $q_H = 0.55$ are equally likely so $q_0 = 0.5$. The timing of uncertainty resolution for the risky project is important. If too much information about quality is revealed by the signal, the market with adverse selection breaks down and only low-quality claims are sold or in extreme cases no investment is undertaken, similar to the standard result of Akerlof (1970). Therefore, I focus on parameters which load the risk of the risky technology toward the second period of the project.

The unconditional expected payoff of the risky technology is $E[Y] = q_0 q_H + (1-q_0)q_L$. The net return on investment in the risky technology is $E[Y/I] - 1 \equiv r_2$. The choice for the required input to the technology, $I = 0.4167$, relative to its output, $Y \in \{0, 1\}$ implies a two-period expected net return of 20 percent, or a one-period expected return of 9.5 percent on projects held to maturity. The one-period return on projects to which claims are sold $P/I \equiv r_1$ is determined by the equilibrium claims price. The fraction of expected payoffs which yields the "no adverse selection" prices of high- and low-quality claims is $\phi = 0.9$, which implies that $p_H = 0.495$ and $p_L = 0.405$.

To discretize the state space for income w, storage x, and risky projects y_o, I first choose an upper bound for y_o. I set the upper bound on risky projects to 0.75, and allow investors to initiate risky projects in increments of 0.05 up to a maximum scale of 0.75. I set the grid for x such that the upper bound is not binding in states with significant mass in the stationary equilibrium.

[16]Alternatively I could use a finer grid and give investors no initial project, or a slightly positive initial income. I have verified that the results do not change using either specification. Moreover, in all of the examples studied here, only investors with the low-quality signal sell claims to their initial projects.

Table 3.2 Results for the Baseline Economy
This table presents the price and quantity results for the baseline economy. Prices: Two-period expected returns $E[r_2]$, one-period return on projects to which claims are sold r_1, fraction of claims which are high-quality κ, claims price P, discount from true value at which claims are sold, $\frac{p_H-P}{p_H}$. Quantities: Per capita quantities of storage $\bar{x}$, ongoing projects $\bar{y}_o$, projects to which claims are sold $\bar{y}_s$, projects to which claims are sold as a fraction of total projects $\frac{\bar{y}_s}{\bar{y}_o}$, and storage as a fraction of total investment $\frac{\bar{x}}{\bar{x}+\bar{y}_o}$.

Prices		Quantities	
$E[r_2]$	20%	$\bar{x}$	0.0623
r_1	−1.5%	$\bar{y}_o$	0.2552
κ	0.0605	$\bar{y}_s$	0.0787
P	0.4104	$\bar{y}_s/\bar{y}_o$	30.82%
$(p_H - P)/p_H$	17%	$\bar{x}/(\bar{x}+\bar{y}_o)$	19.61%

B. Equilibrium Level of Liquidity

The results for the baseline economy are shown in Table 3.2. The fraction of claims sold which are of high quality, κ, is 6.05 percent in this example, which implies that the claims price, P, is slightly higher than the no adverse selection value of low-quality claims. I define liquidity as the cost of transferring the value of expected future payoffs from long-term assets into current income and measure this cost in two ways. First, liquidity can be measured by the tradeoff between the timing of income ("maturity") and expected return.[17] Investors who sell claims to their ongoing projects realize a one-period return of about −1.5 percent on those projects, whereas they earn a one-period expected return of 9.5 percent on projects to which they retain ownership. Alternatively, liquidity can be measured by the discount incurred by extracting income early. Claims to high-quality projects sell at a discount of about 17 percent from their true value. In terms of quantities, investment in the risky project is about four times the amount of storage, and claims are sold to 30 percent of all ongoing projects.

C. Equilibrium Policy Function for Claims Sold

The equilibrium policy function for claims sold as a function of individual state, $y_s(w, y_o, q)$, along with the stationary distribution over individual states is all we need to determine the equilibrium claims price. The policy function tells us how many claims are issued by investors with each combination of current income, ongoing project scale, and project quality. The distribution over individual investors tells us how many of each of these "types" of investors there are. The claims price is simply determined by computing how many claims are issued by investors with high-quality projects relative to the total number of claims issued and taking the implied weighted average of the no adverse selection prices.

Investors sell claims to their ongoing projects the lower is their current income, the larger is the scale of their ongoing projects, and the lower is the quality of those projects. Thus, we can use standard portfolio intuition to understand the selling decision. Loosely, there are two reasons investors issue claims to their ongoing projects: (1) the adverse selection reason

[17] See Hirshleifer (1971, p. 2) for a similar description of liquidity: "Illiquid assets are those characterized by a relatively large discount for "premature" realization; this corresponds to a relatively high time-rate of return if the asset is held rather than so realized."

and (2) a rebalancing reason. First, investors issue more claims to projects if they are of low quality. Second, investors issue claims even to high-quality projects if there is an imbalance in the scale of their ongoing project relative to their current income realization. Investors want both to smooth consumption and to smooth and diversify investment across vintages. Issuing claims to their ongoing projects supplements their current income for use in consumption and new investment, and reduces their exposure to risky project income.

The fact that ongoing projects are illiquid implies that the policy function will be characterized by two regions, an inaction region and a selling region. I will characterize the decision to sell by first characterizing the boundary to the selling/not selling regions, and then showing that conditional on selling claims, the number of claims sold y_s is decreasing in income w and quality q and increasing in project scale y_o. In the Appendix, I characterize the boundary to the selling region for the finite horizon analogue in terms of the scale of the ongoing project that an investor owns analytically. This boundary is given by a linear function of current income, with a slope and intercept which are increasing in project quality. Simple comparative statics show that in this case, conditional on selling claims, the number of claims sold y_s is indeed decreasing in current income and project quality and increasing in the scale of the ongoing project. The finite horizon eliminates the investment allocation decision between projects of different vintages which allows for analytical characterization, but has several drawbacks as discussed in Section II.C.

I present numerical results for the policy functions and selling regions for the infinite horizon problem here. Figure 3.2 graphs the selling regions for the infinite horizon problem with the base case parameterization. White cells denote states in which no claims are sold and cells are darker as more claims get sold; a black cell denotes the maximum amount of claims (0.75) is sold, which can only occur when $y_o = 0.75$, and gray cells darken in increments of 0.05. The boundary of the selling region appears to be almost linear in current income with a slope and intercept which are increasing in project quality.[18] Moreover, conditional on being inside the selling region, the number of claims sold is decreasing in income and project quality and increasing in the scale of the ongoing project.

The policy functions at the upper tail of income for investors who hold the maximum scale project are affected by the binding upper bound on the grid for storage.[19] However, we do not need to concern ourselves with this region as long as there are few investors in the affected region of the state space and their contribution to the equilibrium variables of interest is economically insignificant. This is the case in this economy, 99.6 percent of investors have incomes w less than or equal to two, and holds for all of the economies discussed in Section IV. Accordingly, Figure 3.3 shows that this upper bound does not affect the equilibrium per capita quantities of high- and low-quality claims sold. Figure 3.3 shows the contribution of claims sold by investors in a specific state to the total amount of claims sold. White denotes states where no claims are sold or where there is no mass in the stationary equilibrium, the lightest shade of gray corresponds to a fraction of 0.1 percent of claims sold, and black denotes states in which at least one percent of sales occur. Essentially, only sales by low income investors get positive weight in the stationary equilibrium; investors

[18] Note also that for the case $e = 0$ the problem for a given q is homogenous in the pair (w, y_o) and the boundary is again exactly linear.

[19] The policy functions for investors with very high wealth and the maximum scale project will be affected by the binding upper bound on storage no matter how high this upper bound is, but as long as few investors are affected this does not matter. Investors sell projects here because they have reached the upper bound on the amount of storage and new projects they can initiate and expect to be constrained in the next period as well.

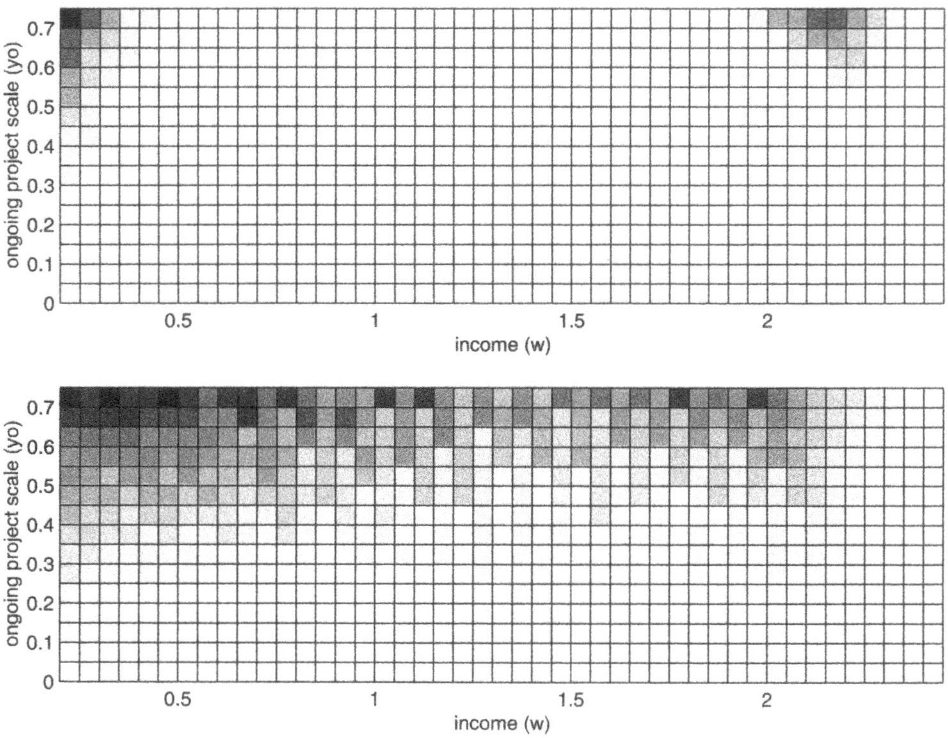

Figure 3.2. **Selling regions**. Claims sold y_s as a function of income w and ongoing project scale y_o for investors with high (top) and low (bottom) quality signal. White is 0, black is 0.75, and gray cells darken in increments of 0.05 claims.

with current income realizations smaller than two contribute 96.2 percent of high-quality claims sold.

D. Comments on the Equilibrium

In constructing the examples in this paper, I looked for economies with equilibria in which some high-quality sales occur, but not all high-quality projects are sold, and for economies which seemed to have a unique interior equilibrium for a broad range of parameters. This facilitates the numerical comparative statics which are the focus of this paper. Such examples require parameterizations which rule out the $\kappa = 0$ (no high-quality sales) and the $\kappa = q_0$ (all high-quality projects are sold in their entirety) equilibria.

To illustrate, consider the mapping which describes for any given initial value of κ and implied price of claims the resulting fraction of high-quality claims on the market for a single iteration of the solution algorithm described in Section II.C. Figure 3.4 graphs this mapping $f : \kappa \rightarrow \kappa^+$ for the baseline economy as well as the economies studied in Section IV.A. The equilibrium claims price satisfies $f(\kappa^*) = \kappa^*$. Economies in which some high-quality sales occur, but not all high-quality projects are sold have mappings with $f(0) > 0$ and $f(q_0) < q_0$, where $q_0 = 0.5$ in the examples presented. For $f(0) > 0$, it must be the case that some high-quality projects are sold even when the claims price equals the price of low-quality claims. This can be achieved, for example, by narrowing the spread between high- and low-quality claims, by making agents more risk averse, or by decreasing

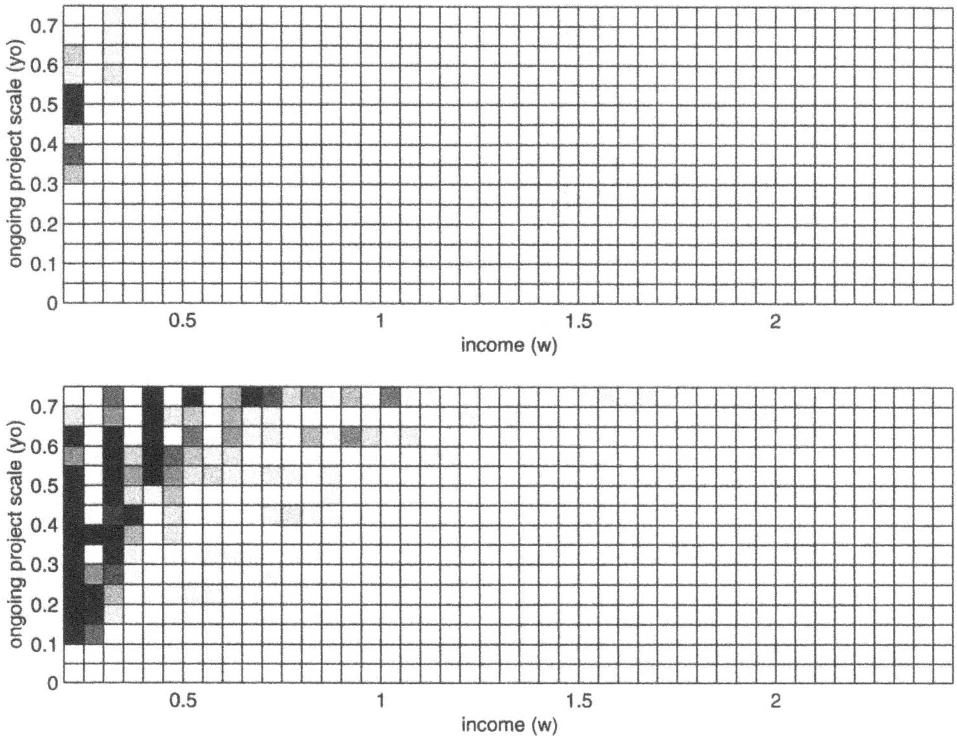

Figure 3.3. **Weighted sales.** Claims sold by state weighted by the weight on that state in the stationary equilibrium as a fraction of total claims sold by investors with high (top) and low (bottom) quality projects $\frac{y_s|_{(w,y_O,q)}\lambda(w,y_o,q)}{\bar{y}_s}$. White is 0, black is $\geq 1\%$ and gray cells darken in increments of 0.1%.

agents' endowment. For $f(q_0) < q_0$, it must be the case that even if the price of claims is $q_0 p_H + (1 - q_0)p_L$, not all high-quality projects are sold off in their entirety. This can be achieved, for example, by lowering ϕ, or by increasing q_H, both of which make selling more costly relative to holding on to a high-quality project.

The parameter ϕ turns out to allow a useful degree of freedom in parameterizing the expected return on risky projects from initiation to the intermediate stage relative to the expected return from the intermediate stage to completion. In particular, ϕ directly decreases the portion of the expected return which accrues over the first period of investment since it lowers the maximum possible equilibrium claims price for a given q_0, q_H, and q_L. This makes selling more costly, which in turn makes the $f(q_0) = q_0$ equilibrium where all high-quality projects are sold in their entirety unlikely. It allows for numerical examples which are robust over a larger parameter range because it does this without affecting either the amount of information asymmetry at the intermediate stage, or the two-period return on risky projects held to completion. For the examples presented in the paper, I chose values for q_H and q_L symmetric around 0.5, let q_0 be 0.5, and set $\phi = 0.9$ to ensure that $f(0.5) < 0.5$.[20]

[20]Qualitatively very similar results arise from choosing, for example, $\phi = 1$, $q_L = 0.4$, $q_H = 0.7$ and $e = 0.05$, with all other parameters unchanged.

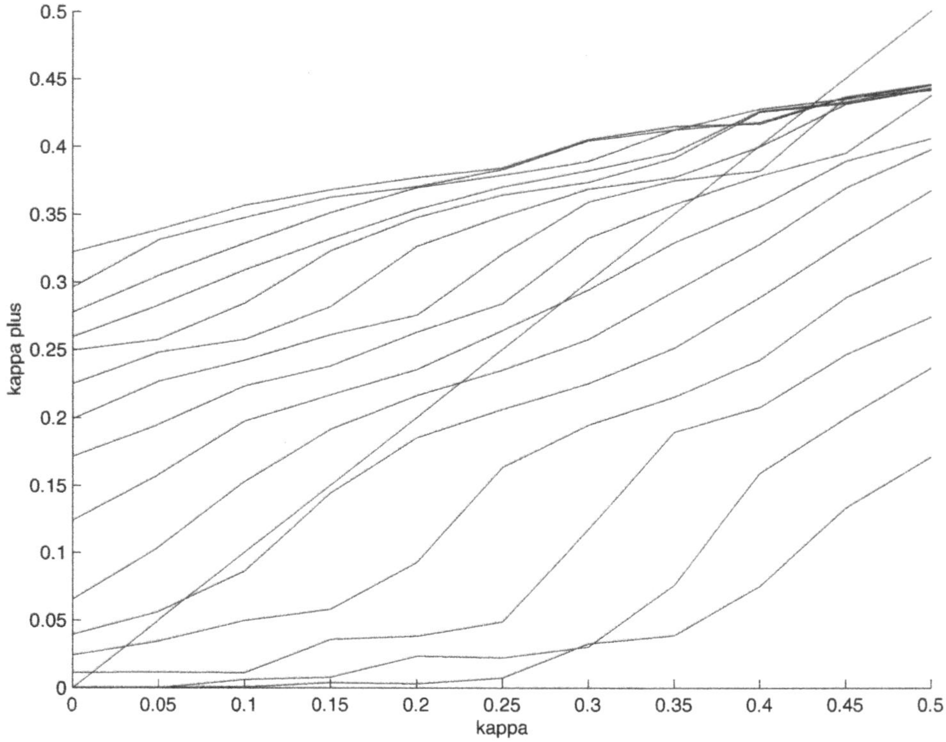

Figure 3.4. $f: \kappa \to \kappa^+$ Each line shows the mapping from κ into κ^+ for a single economy from Section IV.A. For each economy, the mapping is plotted for $\kappa \in \{0, 0.05, 0.10, \ldots, 0.5\}$. The intersection of the mapping with the 45° line is the equilibrium fraction of high-quality claims for that particular economy. The bottom mapping is for the economy with the lowest productivity, where $E[r_2] = 12\%$, the one above it is for the $E[r_2] = 14\%$ economy, and so on.

The example economies constructed in this way typically have unique equilibria; they are characterized by $\kappa \to \kappa^+$ mappings which cross the 45° line once from above. However, as is common in economies with adverse selection, there are certain parameterizations of this economy which display multiple equilibria (at least numerically).[21] If adverse selection is present there are externalities from selling—when other high-quality sellers participate in the pooled market each investor faces a smaller discount for selling high-quality assets and may choose to sell, and vice versa if there are few other high-quality sellers.

To see this, consider again the mapping in Figure 3.4. For each of the economies studied here there is a unique fixed point where $f(\kappa^*) = \kappa^*$; this is the equilibrium discussed above. For any initial κ below this fixed point, for example $\kappa = 0$, the solution algorithm converges to the equilibrium κ^* from below and vice versa for initial values above the fixed point, for example $\kappa = q_0$, without finding any other equilibrium points. It is possible, however, to construct economies with mappings with multiple fixed points, for example by constructing economies with mappings exhibiting a slope which exceeds one in the relevant range. Notice, though, that in all of the examples I computed, up to numerical precision, the mapping f shifted up as productivity increased. This suggests that

[21] See, for example, Azariadis and Smith (1998). I thank Beatrix Paal for comments on this section.

even in economies with multiple equilibria, given an appropriate equilibrium selection mechanism, the comparative statics results from the examples presented here would carry over.

IV. Comparative Statics

For liquidity to be increasing in the state of the economy, high-quality claims must constitute a larger fraction of the claims market (κ should increase) the more productive the risky technology is. The intuition for why liquidity increases with productivity is as follows: As the technology gets more productive, risky investment opportunities improve and investors optimally initiate larger scale projects at all income levels each period. Investors also store less and hence carry less insurance against low payoffs to their risky projects.[22] This implies that the risky payoff has a larger impact on investors' current income; pre-trade income streams are more risky.[23] Moreover, when productivity increases it becomes more costly for investors to have an imbalance between ongoing and newly initiated risky projects. Risk-averse investors want to smooth both their consumption and their level of investment in the risky technology across vintages and when the risky investment is more productive the optimal investment level is higher. Thus, more claims are sold to high-quality projects to supplement current income for use in consumption and new investment when the risky technology is more productive. The claims price, and hence market liquidity, increases. Furthermore, at the higher claims price investors with higher current income realizations and smaller scale ongoing projects issue claims to high-quality projects. The claims price in the stationary equilibrium is the "fixed point" of these effects, where the quality distribution of claims sold is consistent with the claims price.

More claims issued for non-adverse selection reasons leads to a more liquid market when the risky asset is more productive. This seems intuitive—investors infer the reason assets are on the market from the state of the economy. In good times, it is likely assets are sold because of temporarily low cash flows or to raise money for high productivity new projects. Conversely, in bad times more claims are sold due to projects turning sour rather than to these "course of business" shocks.[24] Since investors with low-quality projects sell claims mainly due to the low-quality realization, the selling decision for these investors is less sensitive to changes in productivity and the state sensitive volume is of high quality.

A. Varying Productivity

The productivity of the risky linear technology is given by the slope of the expected payoff $E[Y]$ relative to the initial investment cost I and can be summarized by the two-period expected net return $E[Y/I] - 1 \equiv E[r_2]$. The simplest way to model increases in productivity without affecting conditional variances and while holding the low payoff

[22] Policy functions for storage (shown in the working paper version of this paper, Eisfeldt (2000a)), reveal that investors store a smaller fraction of their income when the risky asset is more productive.

[23] It is precisely the increased pre-trade riskiness of income that induces better post-trade risk sharing through the more liquid claims market. Interestingly, post-trade income can actually be less risky (i.e., we can observe counter cyclical income variation) even as risky investment increases since liquidity enables better income smoothing.

[24] Accordingly, Pilotte (1992) finds that the stock price response to new financing is less adverse when growth opportunities are better.

constant at zero is by decreasing the initial investment cost. Comparative statics are over changes in I implied by two percent changes in the two-period expected net return holding the expected payoff constant at 0.5. The initial investment cost I is such that the implied two-period expected return $E[r_2]$ is 40 percent in the most productive economy and 12 percent in the least productive economy.

Figure 3.5 graphs the increase in liquidity as a function of increases in productivity. The top left panel shows how the quality distribution of claims sold shifts toward high-quality projects as the initial investment cost decreases relative to the expected output. The top right panel plots the resulting claims price. In the least productive economy the fraction of claims which are high-quality κ is small and hence the market claims price $P = \kappa p_H + (1 - \kappa)p_L$ is very close to the true value of low-quality claims p_L. As productivity increases, the claims price increases to a value close to the no-adverse selection price, $P = q_0 p_H + (1 - q_0)p_L$.

Between $E[r_2] = 20\%$ and $E[r_2] = 22\%$, the claims price P overtakes the initial investment cost I. At this point, the endogenous one-period return from projects to which

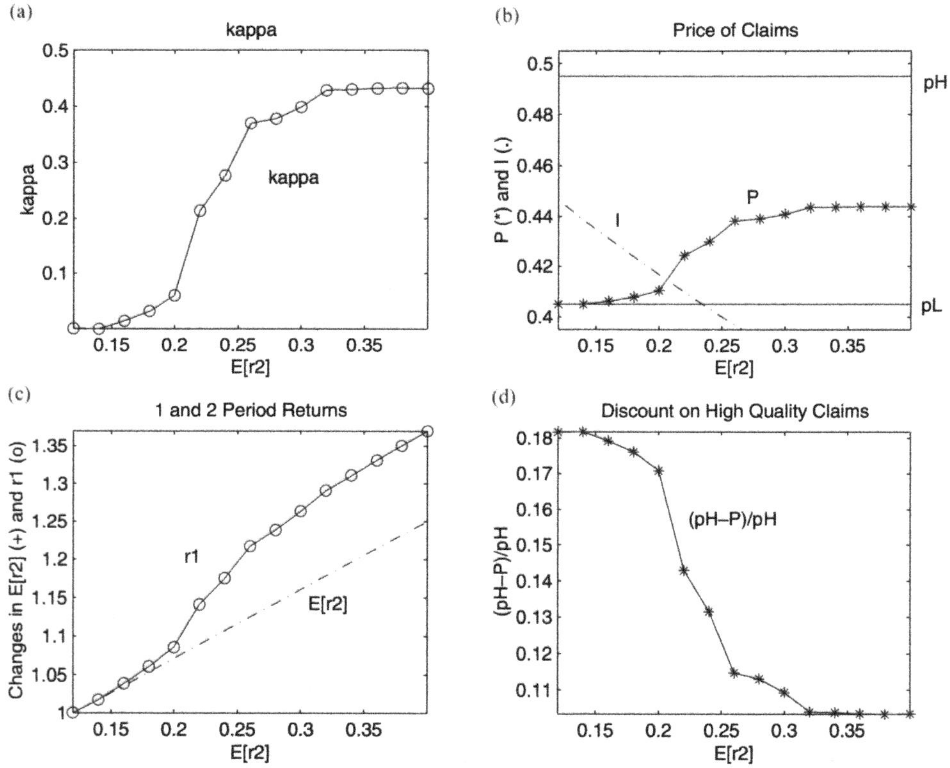

Figure 3.5. **Effects of changing the initial investment cost I on liquidity.** (a) Fraction of claims which are high quality, κ, as a function of the expected two-period return, $E[r_2]$. (b) Claims price P and initial investment cost I as a function of the expected two-period return, $E[r_2]$. True values of claims p_H and p_L are plotted as horizontal lines at 0.405 and 0.495, respectively, (c) Tradeoff between maturity and expected return as a function of the expected two-period return, $E[r_2]$: Endogenous one-period return r_1 and exogenous two-period expected return normalized by their $E[r_2] = 12\%$ values. (d) Cost of transferring future into current income as a function of the expected two-period return $E[r_2]$: Equilibrium discount from true value at which claims to high-quality projects sell, $\frac{p_H - P}{p_H}$, as a function of the expected two-period return $E[r_2]$.

claims are sold $P/I - 1 \equiv r_1$ becomes positive and it becomes better to invest in risky projects to which one can sell claims after one period than to invest in storage. Accordingly, the model economy is very sensitive to changes in productivity in this region.

The bottom panels of Figure 3.5 show that the tradeoff between the timing of income and expected return improves and that the cost of supplementing current income by selling claims to future output decreases. The left panel shows that the endogenous one-period return increases faster with productivity than the exogenous two-period return. The right panel graphs the discount from "true value" at which high-quality claims sell. This discount decreases from about 18 percent to just over 10 percent.

Three effects on the high-quality selling region drive the changes in liquidity. First, since risky investment increases, more investors realize individual states with large scale ongoing projects and low current income; states in the selling region. This effect alone drives the claims price up. Second, at the higher claims price agents within the selling region sell weakly more. Finally, the selling region grows; investors with smaller scale ongoing projects or higher current income realizations become willing to sell claims to high-quality projects at the higher claims price. Figure 3.6 verifies that the selling region for high-quality projects indeed increases with productivity. From top to bottom, the figure displays the selling region for investors with high-quality projects when $E[r_2] = 18\%$, 20%, and 22%.[25] The selling region for low-quality projects also increases, however the amount of high-quality claims sold is much more sensitive to changes in productivity.

Liquidity magnifies the effects of changes in productivity on investment and volume. Figure 3.7 graphs the decomposition of the effects of increases in productivity and liquidity compared to increases in productivity alone. The top line shows investment and volume as a function of the two-period expected return when liquidity effects are accounted for. The bottom line nets out liquidity effects by holding the claims price for all economies constant at the equilibrium price of the least productive economy. Since κ is bounded between zero and one, magnification is necessarily local. For intermediate levels of productivity, liquidity is very sensitive to changes in productivity and in this region liquidity magnifies the effect of higher productivity on investment and volume. Moreover, investment and volume are always strictly greater when liquidity effects are included. Note also that in this model market breakdown works through investment. At low levels of productivity and hence liquidity (e.g., when $E[r_2] = 12\%$), investment which would occur if there were no adverse selection is not undertaken. Investment (and volume) is nearly zero.

We can further measure the quantitative effect of liquidity by determining the amount of consumption an investor would be willing to forego to obtain an increase in liquidity alone, netting out the effect of productivity increases.

To compute the welfare cost of illiquidity, let $v(w, y_0, q)$ solve the problem in (4) and (5) for economy $\mathcal{E}$. Define the average value for an investor in this economy as $\hat{v}$. This average value satisfies

$$\hat{v} \equiv \sum_{(W \times Y_o \times Q)} \lambda(w, y_o, q) v(w, y_o, q) = \sum_{t=0}^{\infty} \beta^t (1-\delta)^t \frac{\hat{c}^{(1-\sigma)}}{1-\sigma}, \tag{3.10}$$

[25] Again, there are almost no investors in the upper tail of the income distribution (with incomes larger than 1.8). For clarity I do not graph this region here.

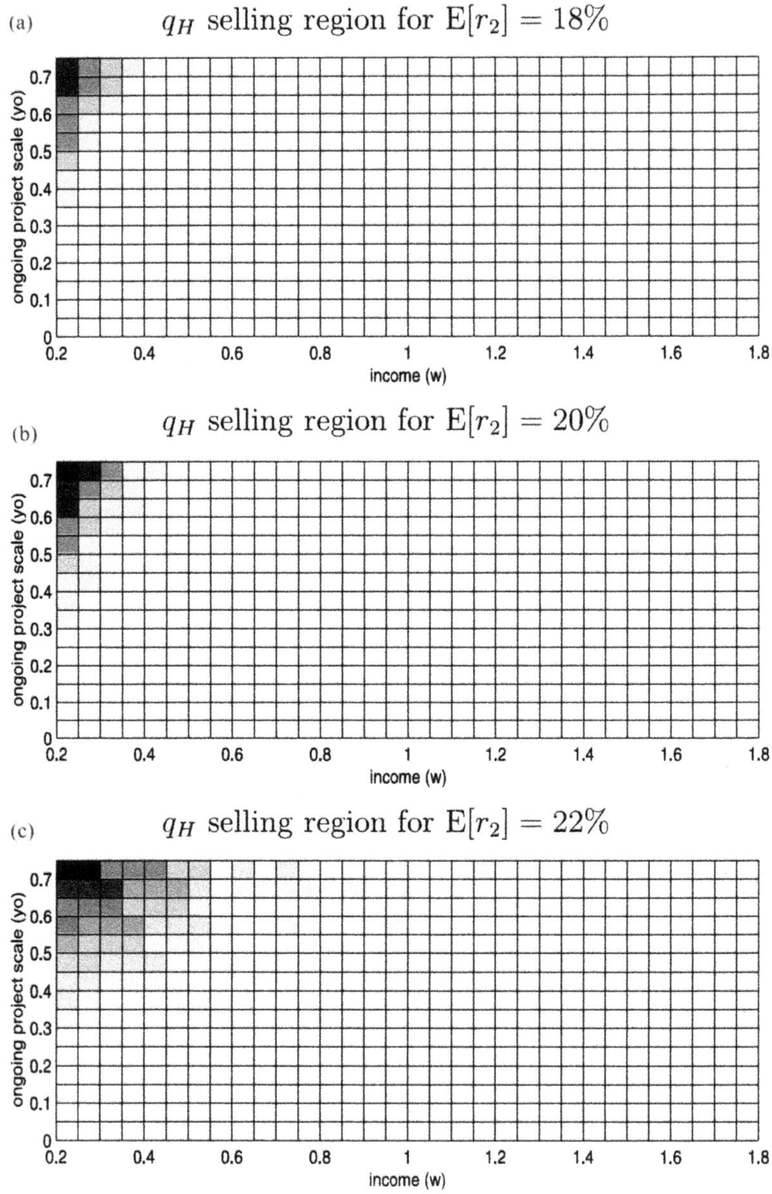

Figure 3.6. **Selling regions increase as productivity increases.** Claims sold y_s as a function of income w and ongoing project scale y_o for investors with the high-quality signal. White is 0, black is 0.75 and gray cells darken in increments of 0.05 claims. The expected two-period return $E[r_2]$ is 18% (a), 20% (b), 22% (c). For clarity I do not graph incomes greater than 1.8 where upper bounds on the state space may be binding. Investors with incomes over 1.8 contribute less to high-quality claims volume as productivity increases and constitute less than 5% of high-quality claims sold in all cases.

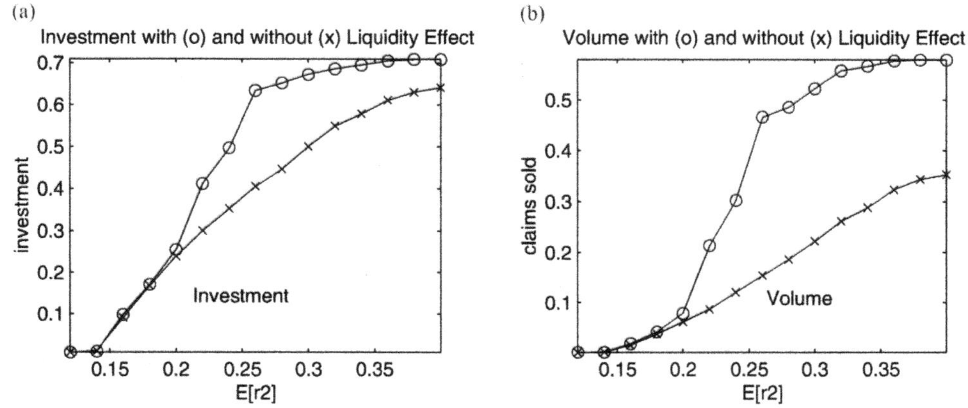

Figure 3.7. **Liquidity magnifies the effects of changing the initial investment cost, *I*, on investment and volume.** (a) Investment with and without liquidity effects. Liquidity is held constant by holding the claims price P constant at the level of the lowest productivity ($E[r_2] = 12\%$) economy. (b) Volume (size of claims market) with and without liquidity effects. Liquidity is held constant by holding the claims price P constant at the level of the lowest productivity ($E[r_2] = 12\%$) economy.

where $\lambda(w, y_o, q)$ is the measure of investors in state (w, y_o, q) in the stationary equilibrium. The constant consumption stream $\hat{c}$ associated with this value can be found by inverting equation (10).

The fraction of consumption an investor with the average value of utility would be willing to forego to move from an economy with low productivity to an economy with high productivity is

$$\theta_{(r_2^L,p^L)\to(r_2^H,p^H)} \equiv \frac{\hat{c}_{(r_2^H,p^H)} - \hat{c}_{(r_2^L,p^L)}}{\hat{c}_{(r_2^L,p^L)}}, \tag{3.11}$$

where the subscripts on $\hat{c}$ give the productivity and liquidity of the associated economies. Part of this fraction is due to the change in productivity, and part is due to the higher liquidity of the economy with high productivity. To decompose this fraction, let $\hat{c}_{(r_2^L,p^H)}$ be the constant consumption stream associated with the average value of an investor who lives in an economy with low productivity but high liquidity. Define $\theta_{(r_2^L,p^L)\to(r_2^L,p^H)}$ analogously to equation (11), replacing $\hat{c}_{(r_2^H,p^H)}$ with $\hat{c}_{(r_2^L,p^H)}$. The fraction $\theta_{(r_2^L,p^L)\to(r_2^L,p^H)}$ determines how much consumption an investor in the low-productivity low-liquidity economy would forego in order to move to the economy with higher liquidity but the same low productivity. The contribution of liquidity to the fraction of consumption an investor would give up to move from the low-productivity low-liquidity to the high-productivity high-liquidity economy is given by $\theta_{(r_2^L,p^L)\to(r_2^L,p^H)}/\theta_{(r_2^L p^L)\to(r_2^H,p^H)}$.

For example, we can compare the economies from Figure 3.6. Investors would forego about 3.7 percent of consumption to move from the economy with $E[r_2] = 18\%$ to the economy with $E[r_2] = 20\%$, about 43 percent of which is due to the change in liquidity. The effect of liquidity varies. When liquidity has a larger effect, the difference in welfare across economies is magnified. Investors would forego about 2.2 percent of their consumption to move from the economy with $E[r_2] = 20\%$ to the economy with $E[r_2] = 22\%$, about 27% of which is due to the change in liquidity.

B. Varying the Ex Ante Quality Distribution

The intuition from the comparative statics in Section IV.A applies to changes in other model parameters which essentially affect the relative productivity of the risky asset. This is because the key to higher liquidity in this model is more investment in the risky asset. For example, increasing productivity by increasing the exogenous fraction of high-quality projects, q_0, also leads to higher liquidity. The endogenous fraction of high-quality claims sold moves in the same direction as and by more than changes in the exogenous fraction of high-quality projects initiated. The results of comparative statics over q_0 mimic those of Section IV.A almost exactly.[26] Notice that in this experiment all changes in the return on projects to which claims are sold are due to changes in the claims price alone since the initial investment cost is held constant.

V. Cycles

This section extends the comparative statics to aggregate fluctuations of a single economy over time. An explicit extension is important since some of the results for comparisons across stationary equilibria discussed in Section IV may not carry over to an economy with fluctuations since investors can smooth cyclical shocks over time. The aggregate fluctuations I study here are deterministic cycles. In a model with stochastic aggregate fluctuations, distributions emerge as state variables, which makes solving the model intractable due to the "curse of dimensionality" Thus, to illustrate, I study the effect of deterministic cycles.

The length of the cycles plays an important role in the effect of productivity on liquidity. As discussed above, the fact that investors initiate larger scale risky projects at all income levels when productivity increases drives the rebalancing sales which increase liquidity. If cycles are only two periods long, the high productivity period is also the period when investors have few ongoing projects (since the low-productivity period always precedes the high-productivity period). As a result, even though the investment opportunity for risky projects is good in periods of high productivity (as measured by the two-period return) and the income from risky projects (initiated two periods prior, in the last high-productivity period) has a large impact on current income, investors have few ongoing projects and thus sell few claims (and even fewer high-quality ones). Thus, I study an economy with four-period cycles consisting of two periods of low productivity followed by two periods of high productivity.

Clearly, the exact specification of the productivity process is important for the economy to exhibit procyclical liquidity. As argued above, the "persistence" of the deterministic productivity changes is a crucial determinant of the results. A quantitative stochastic business-cycle study would require calibrating this persistence and the magnitude of the productivity shocks, as well as the timing of project payoffs. Similarly, as in the comparison across stationary equilibria, we would expect different effects from positive shocks to income vs. productivity. Positive income shocks might reduce contemporaneous high-quality sales, whereas a positive productivity shock would increase risky investment and hence lead to more rebalancing sales in the future. In the light of these comments, the results of the example with deterministic cycles must be viewed as illustrative.

Figure 3.8 plots productivity, the claims price (which determines the level of liquidity), investment, and volume over a four-period cycle. The cycle consists of two periods where

[26]The complete results appear in the working paper version of this paper, Eisfeldt (2000).

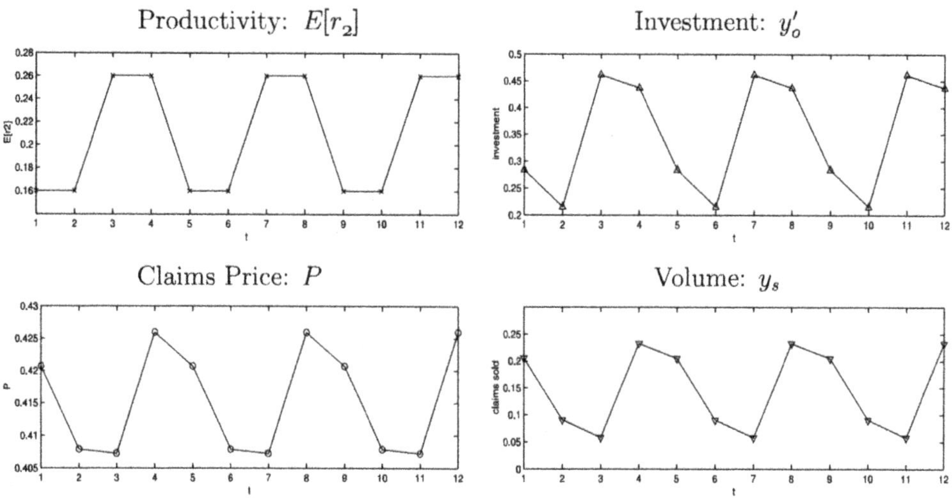

Figure 3.8. **Aggregate fluctuations.** Productivity, claims price, investment and volume over the cycle.

the two-period return to risky projects is 16 percent followed by two periods where the two-period return to risky projects is 26 percent. The pattern of investment closely follows that of the productivity level; when productivity is high investors invest more in the risky asset. Liquidity and volume lag productivity and investment by one period. As discussed in Section IV, investors issue claims when they have large scale ongoing projects relative to their current income from storage and past investments. In periods of high productivity investors of all income levels invest more in the risky asset and insure less through storage. The higher the investment in the risky asset relative to storage, the more likely it is that in the following period investors realize a state in which their exposure to the risky asset is too large relative to their current income. Thus liquidity and volume follow the cyclical pattern of productivity and investment, lagged by one period. Intuitively, participants in the claims market expect to see more sales of high-quality claims and a higher claims price when investment was high in the previous period, since a high investment level leads to rebalancing sales.

I conclude this section with a conjecture about the results of an extension to stochastic productivity shocks. Since the productivity changes in this model are deterministic, investors do not need to rebalance to take advantage of investment opportunities; the only shocks are to their current income. If productivity was stochastic, more rebalancing might occur in order to take advantage of productivity increases. In this case, liquidity would still be procyclical, but might not lag productivity as pronouncedly because the productivity shock itself would lead investors to rebalance their holdings between old (ongoing) and new (highly productive) projects.

VI. Conclusions

This paper studies a dynamic economy in which high productivity leads to higher investment in risky assets and hence more rebalancing trades, mitigating the adverse selection problem and improving liquidity. State dependent liquidity is important for understanding the following two features of asset market data: First, liquidity spreads vary both cross sectionally and in the time series in a way which suggests that markets are more liquid in good times. Second, the unconditional level of illiquidity in most long-term asset markets (as measured, for example, by transactions costs) is too low to explain the observed demand for liquid assets.

Two aspects of the model are worth noting here. First, there is more heterogeneity than just across project quality in the economy studied here. The idea is to model the reasons why investors sell claims explicitly, and then to determine how many investors sell claims for each reason. It turns out that more investors sell claims for reasons other than a low-quality realization when productivity is high. Second, the level of liquidity depends on the interaction between investment at different vintages. Increased risky investment at higher productivity levels leads to riskier pre-trade income streams from past investments. Moreover, when productivity is high the optimal new project scale is larger thus more current income is necessary to start it. As a result, more rebalancing sales occur and the volume of high-quality sales is procyclical.

Appendix

The regions where investors sell or do not sell claims to their ongoing projects can be characterized analytically in a simplified two-period analogue to the infinite horizon problem. The crucial simplification is that this finite-horizon problem eliminates the interaction between projects of different vintages. Consider the following finite-horizon version of the model with two dates 0 and 1. At time 0, an investor is born with income w_0, ongoing projects $y_{o,0}$, and a signal for ongoing projects q. The investor chooses how much storage x_1 to carry over to date 1 and the number of claims to ongoing projects to sell $y_{s,0}$. At time 1 the investor simply consumes the endowment and any income from risky projects and storage. Due to the finite horizon the investor does not initiate any new projects, which simplifies the analysis.

Formally, at dates 0 and 1 the investor solves the following problems, respectively:

$$[t=0] \quad v_0(w_0, y_{o,0}, q) = \max_{\{c_0, x_1\}\in\Re^2_+, y_{s,0}\in[0, y_{o,0}]} \{u(c_0) + \beta E[v_1(w_1)|q]\}$$

$$\text{s.t. } c_0 \leq w_0 + y_{s,0}P - x_1$$

$$w_1 \leq x_1 + (y_{o,0} - y_{s,0})Y_1$$

$$[t=1] \quad v_1(w_1) = \max_{c_1} u(c_1)$$

$$\text{s.t. } c_1 \leq e + w_1$$

given w_0, $y_{o,0}$, and q, where $u(c) = \frac{c^{(1-\sigma)}}{1-\sigma}$.

The first-order conditions for this problem are:

$$\begin{aligned} 0 = &-u'(w_0 + y_{s,0}P - x_1) \\ &+ \beta[qu'(e + y_{o,0} + y_{s,0} + x_1) + (1-q)u'(e + x_1)] \end{aligned} \qquad (3.A1)$$

$$0 = Pu'(w_0 + y_{s,0}P - x_1) - \beta qu'(e + y_{o,0} - y_{s,0} + x_1) + v_s^0, \qquad (3.A2)$$

where v_s^0 is the multiplier on the constraint that ongoing projects cannot be created. Here, I ignore the constraint that investors cannot sell unbacked claims since I am focusing on the boundary of the selling region, where $y_{s,0} = 0$.

Comparative statics for claims sold $y_{s,0}$ with respect to income w_0, number of ongoing projects $y_{o,0}$ and project quality q show that the number of claims investors issue is decreasing in w_0, increasing in $y_{o,0}$, and decreasing in q. Investors sell more ongoing projects the lower their income, the more ongoing projects they have, and the lower the quality of those projects.

Moreover, we can explicitly characterize the regions in which claims to projects are sold by characterizing the boundary to the regions (where $y_{s,0} = 0$) as follows. Assume that $x_1 > 0$. At $x_1 = 0$, a similar argument, using only equation (3.A2), applies. If the investor is indifferent between selling and not selling, at $y_{s,0} = 0$, equations (3.A1) and (3.A2) reduce to

$$0 = -u'(w_0 - x_1) + \beta[qu'(e + y_{o,0} + x_1) + (1 - q)u'(e + x_1)] \tag{3.A3}$$

$$0 = Pu'(w_0 - x_1) - \beta qu'(e + y_{o,0} + x_1). \tag{3.A4}$$

It is straightforward to solve equations (3.A3) and (3.A4) for $y^*_{o,0}$, the critical level of ongoing projects at which investors begin to sell claims to their projects, in terms of parameters. One can easily verify that $y^*_{o,0}$ is an increasing linear function of w_0, with an intercept and slope which are increasing in q. Figure 3.Al describes the selling regions as a function of w_0, $y_{o,0}$, and q.

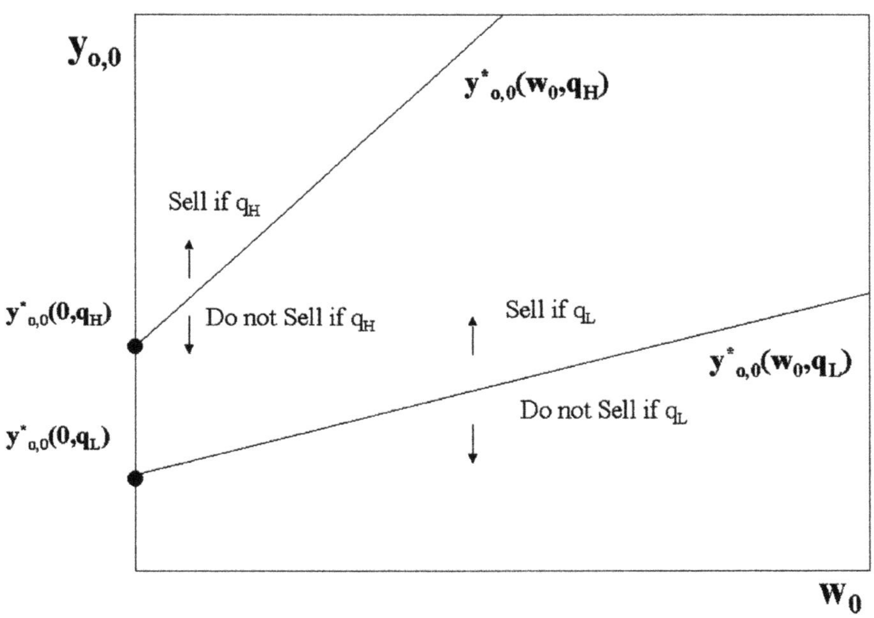

Figure 3.A1. **Selling regions.** Finite horizon problem.

References

Aiyagari, S. Rao, and Mark Gertler, 1991, Asset returns with transactions costs and uninsured individual risk, *Journal of Monetary Economics* 27, 311–331.

Akerlof, George A., 1970, The market for lemons: Qualitative uncertainty and the market mechanism, *Quarterly Journal of Economics* 84, 488–500.

Azariadis, Costas, and Bruce Smith, 1998, Financial intermediation and regime switching in business cycles, *American Economic Review* 88, 516–536.

Bernanke, Ben, Mark Gertler, and Simon Gilchrist, 1996, The financial accelerator and the flight to quality, *Review of Economics and Statistics* 78, 1–15.

Bernanke, Ben, Mark Gertler, and Simon Gilchrist, 1999, The financial accelerator in a quantitative business cycle framework, in John Taylor and Michael Woodford, eds.: *Handbook of Macroeconomics* (North Holland, Amsterdam).

Chordia, Tarun, Richard Roll, and Avanidhar Subrahmanyam, 2001, Market liquidity and trading activity, *Journal of Finance* 56, 501–530.

Constantinides, George M., 1986, Capital market equilibrium with transaction costs, *Journal of Political Economy* 94, 842–862.

Deaton, Angus, 1991, Saving and liquidity constraints, *Econometrica* 59, 1221–1248.

DeMarzo, Peter, and Darrell Duffie, 1999, A liquidity-based model of security design, *Econometrica* 67, 65–99.

Diamond, Douglas W., 1997, Liquidity, banks and markets, *Journal of Political Economy* 105, 928–956.

Diamond, Douglas W., and Philip H. Dybvig, 1983, Bank runs, deposit insurance, and liquidity, *Journal of Political Economy* 91, 401–419.

Eisfeldt, Andrea L., 2000, Endogenous liquidity in asset markets, Working paper, Northwestern University.

Eisfeldt, Andrea L., 2003, Smoothing with liquid and illiquid assets, Working paper, Northwestern University.

Eisfeldt, Andrea L., and Adriano A. Rampini, 2003, Capital reallocation and liquidity, Working paper, Northwestern University.

Gibbons, Robert, and Lawrence F. Katz, 1991, Layoffs and lemons, *Journal of Labor Economics* 9, 351–380.

Glosten, Lawrence, and Paul Milgrom, 1985, Bid, ask, and transaction prices in a specialist market with heterogeneously informed traders, *Journal of Financial Economics* 13, 71–100.

Hendel, Igal, and Alessandro Lizzeri, 1999, Adverse selection in durable goods markets, *American Economic Review* 89, 1097–1115.

Hirshleifer, Jack, 1971, Liquidity, uncertainty, and the accumulation of information, Western Management Science Institute, UCLA, Working paper No. 168.

Holmström, Bengt, and Jean Tirole, 1996, Modeling aggregate liquidity, *AEA Papers and Proceedings* 86, 187–191.

Holmström, Bengt, and Jean Tirole, 1998, Private and public supply of liquidity, *Journal of Political Economy* 106, 1–40.

Holmström, Bengt, and Jean Tirole, 2001, LAPM: A liquidity-based asset pricing model, *Journal of Finance* 56, 1837–1867.

House, Christopher L., and John V. Leahy, 2000, An *s*, *S* model with adverse selection, Working paper, Boston University.

Huang, Ming, 1999, Liquidity shocks and equilibrium liquidity premia, Working paper, Stanford University.

Huberman, Gur, and Dominika Halka, 2001, Systematic liquidity, *Journal of Financial Research* 24, 161–178.

Korajczyk, Robert A., Deborah J. Lucas, and Robert L. McDonald, 1992, Equity issues with time-varying asymmetric information, *Journal of Financial and Quantitative Analysis* 27, 397–417.

Kyle, Albert S., 1985, Continuous auctions and insider trading, *Econometrica* 53, 1315–1335.

Leland, Hayne E., and David H. Pyle, 1977, Informational asymmetries, financial structure, and financial intermediation, *Journal of Finance* 32, 371–387.

Longstaff, Francis A., 2001, The flight-to-liquidity premium in U.S. Treasury Bond prices, Working paper, UCLA.

Lucas, Deborah J., and Robert L. McDonald, 1990, Equity issues and stock price dynamics, *Journal of Finance* 45, 1019–1043.
Lungqvist, Lars, and Thomas J. Sargent, 2000, *Recursive Macroeconomic Theory* (MIT Press, Cambridge, MA).
Myers, Stewart C., and Nicholas S. Majluf, 1984, Corporate financing and investment decisions when firms have information that investors do not have, *Journal of Financial Economics* 13, 187–221.
Nachman, David C, and Thomas H. Noe, 1994, optimal design of securities under asymmetric information, *Review of Financial Studies* 7, 1–44.
Pàstor, Ľuboš, and Robert F. Stambaugh, 2003, Liquidity risk and expected stock returns, *Journal of Political Economy* 11, 642–685.
Pilotte, Eugene, 1992, Growth opportunities and the stock price response to new financing, *Journal of Business* 65, 371–394.
Pulvino, Todd C., 1998, Do asset fire sales exist? An empirical investigation of commercial aircraft transactions, *Journal of Finance* 53, 939–978.
Shleifer, Andrei, and Robert W. Vishny, 1992, Liquidation values and debt capacity: A market equilibrium approach, *Journal of Finance* 47, 1343–1366.
Stiglitz, Joseph E., and Andrew Weiss, 1981, Credit rationing in markets with imperfect information, *American Economic Review* 71, 393–410.
Stokey, Nancy L., and Robert E. Lucas, Jr. with Edward C. Prescott, 1989, *Recursive Methods in Economic Dynamics* (Harvard University Press, Cambridge, MA).
Vayanos, Dimitri, 1998, Transactions costs and asset prices: A dynamic equilibrium model, *Review of Financial Studies* 11, 1–58.

4 Financial Intermediaries and Markets

Franklin Allen And Douglas Gale

1. Markets, Intermediaries, and Crises

For a long time, it has been taken as axiomatic that financial crises are best avoided. We confront this conventional wisdom by showing that, under certain conditions, a laisser-faire financial system achieves the incentive-efficient or constrained-efficient allocation.[1] Furthermore, constrained efficiency may require financial crises in equilibrium. The assumptions needed to achieve these efficiency results are restrictive, but no more so than the assumptions normally required to ensure Pareto-efficiency of Walrasian equilibrium. The important point is that optimality of avoiding crises should not be taken as axiomatic. If regulation is required to minimize or obviate the costs of financial crises, it should be justified by a microeconomic welfare analysis based on standard assumptions. Furthermore, the form of the intervention should be derived from microeconomic principles. Financial institutions and financial markets exist to facilitate the efficient allocation of risks and resources. Any government intervention will have an impact on the normal functioning of the financial system. A policy of preventing financial crises will inevitably create distortions. One of the advantages of a microeconomic analysis of financial crises is that it clarifies the costs and benefits of these distortions.

Policy analyses of banking and securities markets tend to be based on very specific models.[2] In the absence of a general equilibrium framework, it is hard to evaluate the robustness of the results and, ultimately, to answer the question: What precisely are the market failures associated with financial crises? In this paper, we take a step toward developing a general model to analyze market failures in the financial sector and study a complex, decentralized, financial system comprising both financial markets and financial intermediaries.[3] For the most part, the seminal models of bank runs, such as Bryant

[1] Wallace (1990) suggests that bank runs might be efficient. Examples of efficient bank runs were provided by Alonso (1996) and Allen and Gale (1998). Here we provide general sufficient conditions for the efficiency of financial crises.

[2] See Bhattacharya and Thakor (1993) for a survey. For examples of more recent work that stresses the analysis of welfare, see Matutes and Vives (1996, 2000).

[3] In this paper we use the term "financial markets" narrowly to denote markets for securities. Other authors have allowed for markets in which mechanisms are traded (e.g., Bisin and Gottardi (2000)). We prefer to call

(1980) and Diamond and Dybvig (1983), analyze the behavior of a single bank and consist of a contracting problem followed by a coordination problem.[4] We combine recent developments in the theory of banking with further innovations to model a complex financial system. The model has several interesting features: it introduces markets into a general-equilibrium theory of institutions; it endogenizes the cost of forced liquidation;[5] it allows for a fairly general specification of the economic environment; it allows for interaction between liquidity and asset pricing;[6] and it allows us to analyze the regulation of the financial system using the standard tools of welfare economics.

In our model, intermediaries have two functions. Following Diamond and Dybvig (1983), intermediaries are providers of insurance services. By pooling the assets of individuals with uncertain preference for liquidity they can provide a higher degree of liquidity for any given level of returns on the portfolio. Their second function is to provide risk sharing services by packaging existing claims on behalf of investors who do not have access to markets. In this respect the intermediary operates more like a mutual fund, but both functions are essential to the operation of an optimal intermediary. Financial intermediaries have many other functions, of course, including payments, information gathering, lending, and underwriting, but we ignore these for the purpose of focusing on risk sharing and macroeconomic stability.

We distinguish between intermediaries that can offer *complete* contingent contracts and intermediaries that can only offer *incomplete* contracts. An example of the latter would be banks that can only offer deposit contracts. With complete contracts, the consequences of default can be anticipated and included in the contract, so without loss of generality we can assume default does not occur. With incomplete contracts, however, default can improve welfare by increasing the contingency of the contract (see, e.g., Zame (1993)).

Aggregate risk in our model takes the form of shocks to asset returns and preferences. Formally, there is a finite set of *aggregate* states of nature that determines asset returns and preferences. We contrast economies with *complete* markets, in which there is a complete set of Arrow securities, one for each aggregate state, from economies with *incomplete* markets, in which the set of Arrow securities is less than the number of aggregate states.

this intermediation. Formally, the two activities are similar, but in practice the economic institutions are quite different.

[4]Early models of financial crises were developed in the 1980's by Bryant (1980) and Diamond and Dybvig (1983). Important contributions were also made by Chari and Jagannathan (1988), Chari (1989), Champ, Smith, and Williamson (1996), Jacklin (1986), Jacklin and Bhattacharya (1988), Postlewaite and Vives (1987), Wallace (1988, 1990), and others. Theoretical research on speculative currency attacks, banking panics, the role of liquidity and contagion have taken a number of approaches. One is built on the foundations provided by early research on bank runs (e.g., Hellwig (1994, 1998), Diamond (1997), Allen and Gale (1998, 1999, 2000a, 2000b), Peck and Shell (1999), Chang and Velasco (2000, 2001), and Diamond and Rajan (2001)). Other approaches include those based on macroeconomic models of currency crises that developed from the insights of Krugman (1979), Obstfeld (1986), and Calvo (1988) (see, e.g., Corsetti, Pesenti, and Roubini (1999) for a recent contribution and Flood and Marion (1999) for a survey), game theoretic models (see Morris and Shin (1998), Morris (2000), and Morris and Shin (2000) for an overview), amplification mechanisms (e.g., Cole and Kehoe (2000) and Chari and Kehoe (2000)), and the borrowing of foreign currency by firms (e.g., Aghion, Bacchetta, and Banerjee (2000)).

[5]Most of the literature, following Diamond and Dybvig (1983), assumes the existence of a technology for liquidating projects. Here we assume that a financially distressed institution sells assets to other institutions. This realistic feature of the model has important implications for welfare analysis. Ex post, liquidation does not entail a deadweight cost because assets are merely transferred from one owner to another. Ex ante, liquidation can result in inefficient risk sharing, but only if markets for hedging the risk are incomplete.

[6]In particular, there is a role for cash-in-the-market pricing (Allen and Gale (1994)).

This produces a 2 × 2 classification of models, according to the completeness of contracts and markets:

	Complete markets	Incomplete markets
Complete contracts	incentive-efficient	not efficient
Incomplete contracts	constrained-efficient	not efficient

Financial crises do occur in our model, but are not necessarily a source of market failure. A sophisticated financial system provides optimal liquidity and risk sharing, where a financial system is "sophisticated" if markets for aggregate risks are complete and market participation is incomplete. Efficiency depends on the completeness of markets but does not depend on whether contracts are complete or incomplete.

These results provide a benchmark for evaluating government intervention and regulation. If a sophisticated financial system leads to an incentive-efficient or constrained-efficient allocation, what precisely is the role of the government or central bank in intervening in the financial system? What can the government or central bank do that private institutions and the market cannot do? Our efficiency theorems assume that markets for aggregate risk are complete. Missing markets may provide a role for government intervention.

In addition, the model provides some important insights into the working of complex financial systems. We include a series of examples to illustrate the properties of the model. In particular, we show that, in some cases, (a) existence and optimality require that equilibria be "mixed," that is, identical banks choose very different risk strategies; (b) default and crises are optimal when markets are complete and contracts incomplete; (c) asset pricing in a crisis is determined by the amount of liquidity in the market as well as by the asset returns; and (d) risk sharing is suboptimal with incomplete markets.

Our results are related to a small but important literature that seeks to extend the traditional intermediation literature in a more general equilibrium direction, von Thadden (1999) also studies an integrated model of demand deposits and anonymous markets. Martin (2000) addresses the question of whether liquidity provision by the central bank can prevent crises without creating a moral hazard problem. Gromb and Vayanos (2001) study asset pricing in a model of collateralized arbitrage.

The rest of the paper is organized as follows. Section 2 describes the primitives of the model. Section 3 explores the welfare properties of liquidity provision and risk sharing in the context of an economy with a sophisticated financial system in which institutions take the form of general intermediaries. Section 4 shows that incomplete participation is critical for the optimality results achieved in the previous two sections. Section 5 extends this analysis to an economy with a sophisticated financial system in which institutions use incomplete contracts. In Section 6, we consider an economy with incomplete markets and characterize the conditions under which welfare can be increased by in some cases increasing and in some cases decreasing liquidity. Section 7 contains some final remarks and some of the proofs are gathered together in the Appendix.

2. The Basic Economy

There are three dates $t = 0, 1, 2$ and a single good at each date. The good is used for consumption and investment.

The economy is subject to two kinds of uncertainty. First, individual agents are subject to idiosyncratic preference shocks, which affect their demand for liquidity (these will be described later). Second, the entire economy is subject to aggregate shocks that affect asset returns and the cross-sectional distribution of preferences. The aggregate shocks are represented by a finite number of states of nature, indexed by $\eta \in H$. At date 0, all agents have a common prior probability density $\nu(\eta)$ over the states of nature. All uncertainty is resolved at the beginning of date 1, when the state η is revealed and each agent discovers his individual preference shock.

Each agent has an endowment of one unit of the good at date 0 and no endowment at dates 1 and 2. So, in order to provide consumption at dates 1 and 2, they need to invest.

There are two assets distinguished by their returns and liquidity structure. One is a short-term asset (the *short asset*), and the other is a long-term asset (the *long asset*). The short asset is represented by a storage technology: one unit invested in the short asset at date $t = 0, 1$ yields a return of one unit at date $t + 1$. The long asset yields a return after two periods. One unit of the good invested in the long asset at date 0 yields a random return of $R(\eta) > 1$ units of the good at date 2 if state η is realized.

Investors' preferences are distinguished ex ante and ex post. At date 0 there is a finite number n of types of investors, indexed by $i = 1, \ldots, n$. We call i an investor's ex ante type. An investor's ex ante type is common knowledge and hence contractible. The measure of investors of type i is denoted by $\mu_i > 0$. The total measure of investors is normalized to one so that $\sum_i \mu_i = 1$.

While investors of a given ex ante type are identical at date 0, they receive a private, idiosyncratic, preference shock at the beginning of date 1. The date 1 preference shock is denoted by $\theta_i \in \Theta_i$, where Θ_i is a finite set. We call θ_i the investor's ex post type. Because θ_i is private information, contracts cannot be explicitly contingent on θ_i.

Investors only value consumption at dates 1 and 2. An investor's preferences are represented by a von Neumann–Morgenstern utility function, $u_i(c_1, c_2; \theta_i)$, where c_1 denotes consumption at date $t = 1, 2$. The utility function $u_i\ (\cdot; \theta_i)$ is assumed to be concave, increasing, and continuous for every type θ_i. Diamond and Dybvig (1983) assumed that consumers were one of two ex post types, either early diers who valued consumption at date 1 or late diers who valued consumption at date 2. This is a special case of the preference shock θ_i. The present framework allows for much more general preference uncertainty.

The probability of being an investor of type (i, θ_i) conditional on state η is denoted by $\lambda_i(\theta_i, \eta) > 0$. The probability of being an agent of type i is μ_i. Consistency therefore requires that

$$\sum_{\theta_i} \lambda_i(\theta_i, \eta) = \mu_i, \quad \forall \eta \in H.$$

By the usual "law of large numbers" convention, the cross-sectional distribution of types is assumed to be the same as the probability distribution λ. We can therefore interpret $\lambda_i(\theta_i, \eta)$ as the number of agents of type (i, θ_i) in state η.

3. Optimal Intermediation

Intermediaries have two broad functions in this model. First, because individual investors do not have access to markets for sharing aggregate risk, intermediaries trade existing claims on their behalf to produce a synthetic risk-sharing contract for the investors. In this respect, they are like mutual funds. Secondly, as in the Diamond–Dybvig model, intermediaries provide investors with insurance against the preference shocks. One difference from the Diamond–Dybvig model is that intermediaries cannot physically liquidate projects when they need liquidity. Instead, they sell assets on the capital market at date 1. Because there is no physical cost of liquidating assets, liquidation is ex post efficient: the buyer's loss is the seller's gain and vice versa.

In this section we assume that financial institutions take the form of general intermediaries. Each intermediary offers a single contract and each ex ante type is attracted to a different intermediary. Contracts are contingent on the aggregate states η and individuals' reports of their ex post types, subject to incentive compatibility constraints.

One can, of course, imagine a world in which a single "universal" intermediary offers contracts to all ex ante types of investors. A universal intermediary could act as a central planner and implement the first-best allocation of risk. There would be no reason to resort to markets at all. Our world view is based on the assumption that transaction costs preclude this kind of centralized solution and that decentralized intermediaries are restricted in the number of different contracts they can offer. This assumption provides a role for financial markets in which financial intermediaries can share risk and obtain liquidity.

At the same time, financial markets alone will not suffice to achieve optimal risk sharing. Because individual economic agents have private information, markets for individual risks are incomplete. The markets that are available will not achieve an incentive-efficient allocation of risk. Intermediaries, by contrast, can offer individuals incentive-compatible contracts and improve on the risk sharing provided by the market.

In the Diamond–Dybvig (Diamond and Dybvig (1983)) model, all investors are ex ante identical. Consequently, a single representative bank can provide complete risk sharing and there is no need for markets to provide cross-sectional risk sharing across banks. Allen and Gale (1994) showed that differences in risk and liquidity preferences can be crucial in explaining asset prices. This is another reason for allowing for ex ante heterogeneity.

3.1 Markets

At date 0 investors deposit their endowments with an intermediary in exchange for a general risk sharing contract. The intermediaries have access to a complete set of Arrow security markets at date 0. For each aggregate state η there is a security traded at date 0 that promises one unit of the good at date 1 if state η is observed and nothing otherwise. Let $q(\eta)$ denote the price of one unit of the Arrow security corresponding to state η, that is, the number of units of the good at date 0 needed to buy one unit of the good in state η at date 1.

All uncertainty is resolved at the beginning of date 1. Consequently there is no need to trade contingent securities at date 1. Instead, we assume there is a spot market and a forward market for the good at date 1. The good at date 1 is the numeraire so $p_1(\eta) = 1$; the price of the good at date 2 for sale at date 1 is denoted by $p_2(\eta)$, i.e., $p_2(\eta)$ is the number of units of the good at date 1 needed to purchase one unit of the good at date 2 in state η. Let $p(\eta) = (p_1(\eta), p_2(\eta)) = (1, p_2(\eta))$ denote the vector of goods prices at date 1 in state η.

Note that we do not assume the existence of a technology for physically liquidating projects. Instead, we follow Allen and Gale (1998, 2000b) in assuming that an institution in distress sells long-term assets to other institutions. From the point of view of the economy as a whole, the long-term assets cannot be liquidated—someone has to hold them.

3.2 Intermediation Mechanisms

Investors participate in markets indirectly, through intermediaries. An intermediary is a risk-sharing institution that invests in the short and long assets on behalf of investors and provides them with consumption at dates 1 and 2. Intermediaries use markets to hedge the risks that they manage for investors.

Each investor of type i gives his endowment (one unit of the good) to an intermediary of type i at date 0. In exchange, he gets a bundle of goods $x_i(\theta_i, \eta) \in \mathbf{R}^2_+$ at dates 1 and 2 in state η if he reports the ex post type θ_i. In effect, the function $x_i = \{x_i(\theta_i, \eta)\}$ is a *direct mechanism* that maps agents' reports into feasible consumption allocations.[7]

A feasible mechanism is incentive-compatible. The appropriate definition of the incentive-compatibility constraint must take into account the fact that agents can use the short asset to store the good from date 1 to date 2. Suppose that the agent receives a consumption bundle $x_i(\theta_i, \eta)$ from the intermediary. By saving, he can obtain any consumption bundle $c \in \mathbf{R}^2_+$ such that

$$c_1 \leq x_{i1}(\theta_i, \eta), \quad \sum_{t=1}^{2} c_t \leq \sum_{t=1}^{2} x_{it}(\theta_i, \eta). \tag{4.1}$$

Let $C(x_i(\theta_i, \eta))$ denote the set of consumption bundles satisfying (1). The maximum utility that can be obtained from the consumption bundle $x_i(\theta_i, \eta)$ by saving is denoted by $u_i^*(x_i(\theta_i, \eta), \theta_i)$ and defined by

$$u_i^*(x_i(\theta_i, \eta), \theta_i) = \sup\{u_i(c, \theta_i) : c \in C(x_i(\theta_i, \eta))\}.$$

Then the incentive constraint with saving can be written as:

$$u_i(x_i(\theta_i, \eta), \theta_i) \geq u_i^*(x_i(\hat{\theta}_i, \eta), \theta_i), \quad \forall \theta_i, \hat{\theta}_i \in \Theta_i, \forall \eta \in H. \tag{4.2}$$

Notice that by placing $u_i(\cdot)$ on the left-hand side of (2), we ensure that even a truth-telling agent will not want to save outside of the intermediary. There is no loss of generality in this restriction, since the intermediary can tailor the timing of consumption to the agent's needs. Let X_i denote the set of incentive-compatible mechanisms when the depositor has access to the storage technology.

3.3 Equilibrium

Recall that each intermediary issues a single contract and serves a single ex ante type of investor. We denote by i the representative intermediary that trades with the ex ante investor type i. The representative intermediary i takes in deposits of μ_i units of the good at date 0 and invests in $y_i \geq 0$ units of the short asset and $\mu_i - y_i \geq 0$ units of the long asset. In exchange it offers depositors an incentive-compatible mechanism x_i. Given the prevailing

[7]A direct mechanism is normally a function that assigns a unique outcome to each profile of types chosen by the investors. In a symmetric direct mechanism, the outcome for a single investor depends only on the individual's report and the distribution of reports by other investors. In a truth-telling equilibrium, the reports of other investors are given by the distribution $\lambda(\cdot, \eta)$ so a symmetric direct mechanism should properly be written $x_i(\theta_i, \lambda(\cdot, \eta), \eta)$ but since $\lambda(\cdot, \eta)$ is given as a function of η there is no loss of generality in suppressing the reference to $\lambda(\cdot, \eta)$.

prices (p, q), a mechanism x_i and investment portfolio y_i yield nonnegative profits for the intermediary if it satisfies the following "budget constraint:"

$$\sum_{\eta} q(\eta) \sum_{\theta_i} \lambda_i(\theta_i, \eta) p(\eta) \cdot x_i(\theta_i, \eta)$$
$$\leq \sum_{\eta} q(\eta) p(\eta) \cdot (y_i, (\mu_i - y_i) R(\eta)). \tag{4.3}$$

(In equilibrium, free entry will drive the value of profits to zero.) In state η, the cost of goods given to investors who report θ_i, is $p(\eta) \cdot x_i(\theta_i, \eta)$ and there are $\lambda(\theta_i, \eta)$ such agents, so summing across ex post types θ_i we get the total cost of the mechanism in state η as $\sum_{\theta_i} \lambda(\theta_i, \eta) p(\eta) \cdot x_i(\theta_i, \eta)$. Multiplying by the cost of one unit of the good at date 1 in state η and summing over states η gives the total cost of the mechanism, in terms of units of the good at date 0, as the left-hand side of (3). The right-hand side is the total value of investments by the intermediary. In state η the short asset yields y_i units of the good at date 1 and the long asset yields $(\mu_i - y_i)R(\eta)$ units of the good at date 2 so the total value of the portfolio is $p(\eta) \cdot (y_i, (\mu_i - y_i)R(\eta))$. Multiplying by the price of a unit of the good at date 1 in state η and summing across states gives the total value of the investments by the intermediary, in terms of units of the good at date 0.

An *intermediated allocation* specifies an incentive-compatible mechanism x_i and a feasible portfolio y_i for each representative intermediary $i = 1, \ldots, n$. An intermediated allocation $\{(x_i, y_i)\}$ is *attainable* if it satisfies the market-clearing conditions at dates 1 and 2, that is,

$$\sum_{i} \sum_{\theta_i} \lambda_i(\theta_i, \eta) x_{i1}(\theta_i, \eta) \leq \sum_{i} y_i, \quad \forall \eta \tag{4.4}$$

and

$$\sum_{i} \sum_{\theta_i} \lambda_i(\theta_i, \eta) \left(x_{i1}(\theta_i, \eta) + x_{i2}(\theta_i, \eta)\right)$$
$$= \sum_{i} y_i + (\mu_i - y_i) R(\eta), \quad \forall \eta. \tag{4.5}$$

Condition (4) says that the total consumption at date 1 in each state η must be less than or equal to the supply of the good (equal to the amount of the short asset). Condition (4) is an inequality because it is possible to transform an excess of the short asset at date 1 into consumption at date 2. Condition (5) says that the sum of consumption over the two periods is equal to the total returns from the two assets. Alternatively, we can read this as saying that consumption at date 2 is equal to the return on the long asset *plus* whatever is left over from date 1.

An intermediary offers a contract $x_i \in X_i$ that maximizes the profit per contract, subject to a participation constraint

$$\sum_{\eta} \sum_{\theta_i} \lambda(\theta_i, \eta) u_i(x_i(\theta_i, \eta), \theta_i) \geq \bar{u}_i,$$

where $\bar{u}_i$ is the maximum expected utility the ith type can obtain from any other contract in the market. Hence, a *pure intermediated equilibrium* consists of a price system (p^*, q^*)

and an attainable allocation $\{(x_i^*, y_i^*)\}$ such that, for every intermediary i, the choice of mechanism x_i^* and portfolio y_i^* solves the decision problem

$$\max \sum_\eta q^*(\eta)p^*(\eta) \cdot ((y_i, (\mu_i - y_i)R(\eta))$$
$$- \sum_\eta q^*(\eta) \sum_{\theta_i} \lambda_i(\theta_i, \eta)p^*(\eta) \cdot x_i(\theta_i, \eta) \quad \text{subject to}$$
$$x_i \in X_i,$$
$$\sum_\eta \sum_{\theta_i} \lambda(\theta_i, \eta)u_i(x_i(\theta_i, \eta), \theta_i) \geq \sum_\eta \sum_{\theta_i} \lambda(\theta_i, \eta)u_i(x_i^*(\theta_i, \eta), \theta_i),$$

and equilibrium profits are zero:

$$\sum_\eta q^*(\eta) \sum_{\theta_i} \lambda_i(\theta_i, \eta)p^*(\eta) \cdot x_i(\theta_i, \eta)$$
$$= \sum_\eta q^*(\eta)p^*(\eta) \cdot (y_i, (\mu_i - y_i)R(\eta)).$$

Competition and free entry force the intermediaries to undercut one another by offering more attractive contracts to the investors. In equilibrium, the contract chosen maximizes the welfare of the typical depositor subject to a zero-profit constraint. (On the one hand, no intermediary will offer a contract that earns negative profits and, on the other, if the contract earns positive profits or fails to maximize the investor's expected utility, an entrant can steal customers and still make positive profits.) Hence, the intermediary's decision problem is equivalent to the following:

$$\max \sum_\eta \sum_{\theta_i} \lambda(\theta_i, \eta)u_i(x_i(\theta_i, \eta), \theta_i) \quad \text{subject to}$$
$$x_i \in X_i,$$
$$\sum_\eta q(\eta) \sum_{\theta_i} \lambda_i(\theta_i, \eta)p(\eta) \cdot x_i(\theta_i, \eta)$$
$$\leq \sum_\eta q(\eta)p(\eta) \cdot (y_i, (\mu_i - y_i)R(\eta)). \tag{4.6}$$

In a pure equilibrium, we assume that all intermediaries serving type i choose the same portfolio and contract. To ensure the existence of equilibrium, we need to allow for the possibility that intermediaries of type i make different choices. A *mixed allocation* is defined by a finite set of numbers $\{p^j\}$ and allocations $\{(x_i^j, y_i^j)\}$ such that $p^j \geq 0$ and $\sum_j p^j = 1$. A mixed allocation represents the following situation. The population is divided into groups. Each group j is a representative sample of size p^j, that is, the relative frequency of ex ante types in group j is the same as in the population at large. Each ex ante type i in group j is served by an intermediary that offers a contract x_i^j and chooses a portfolio y_i^j. In a sense, we can think of (x_i^j, y_i^j) as a pure allocation for group j, except that there is no requirement for group j to be self-sufficient (there can be trade among groups) and each type i must be indifferent among the different groups in equilibrium.

A mixed allocation is *attainable* if the mean $\{(x_i, y_i)\} = \sum_j p^j\{(x_i^j, y_i^j)\}$ satisfies the market-clearing conditions (4) and (5). Note that $\{(x_i, y_i)\}$ may not be an allocation: even if each (x_i^j, y_i^j) belongs to X_i the mean (x_i, y_i) may not, because the set X_i is not convex.

A *mixed intermediated equilibrium* consists of a price system (p, q) and a mixed attainable allocation $\{(p^j, x_i^j, y_i^j)\}$ such that for every intermediary i, and every subgroup j, the choice (x_i^j, y_i^j) solves the decision problem (6).

Assumption 1 (Nonempty Interior): *For any ex ante type $i = 1, \ldots, n$, for any consumption bundle $x_i \in X_i$ and price system $p \in P$, and for any $\varepsilon > 0$, either*

$$\sum_{\eta} p(\eta) \cdot \left(\sum_{\theta_i} \lambda(\theta_i, \eta) x_i(\theta_i, \eta) \right) = 0$$

or there exists a bundle x_i' within a distance ε of x_i such that

$$\sum_{\eta} p(\eta) \cdot \left(\sum_{\theta_i} \lambda(\theta_i, \eta) x_i'(\theta_i, \eta) \right) < \sum_{\eta} p(\eta) \cdot \left(\sum_{\theta_i} \lambda(\theta_i, \eta) x_i(\theta_i, \eta) \right).$$

Theorem 1: *Under the maintained assumptions, there exists a mixed intermediated equilibrium, if Assumption 1 is satisfied.*

For the proof see "Existence of Equilibrium: An Addendum to 'Financial Intermediaries and Markets'" at http://www.nyu.edu/econ/user/galed/papers.html.

A pure equilibrium is a special case of a mixed equilibrium, but there is no guarantee that pure equilibria exist. In fact, we show in Section 5.1 that pure equilibria fail to exist in straightforward cases.

For some purposes it is useful to interpret a mixed intermediated equilibrium as a pure intermediated equilibrium with a different set of ex ante types. Let (i, j) denote the new ex ante subtype consisting of investors in the subgroup j of ex ante type i and let $\mu_{ij} = p^j \mu_i$ denote the measure of investors in the new ex ante type (i, j). Notice that we have to define a distinct economy for every mixed intermediated equilibrium. This is because the weights μ_{ij} depend on the endogenous variables p^j. In a mixed equilibrium, all agents of given ex ante type i receive the same expected utility. Thus, the expected utility of subtype (i, j) is the same as the expected utility of type (i, j') for any given type i. Taking the weights $\{\mu_{ij}\}$ as given, we might be able to find other pure equilibria of the artificial economy, but they would not necessarily be mixed equilibria of the original economy, because they would not necessarily satisfy this equilibrium condition. For most purposes, this is not an issue, so without loss of generality we can restrict attention to pure equilibria.

3.4 Efficiency

Under mild assumptions, we can show that the equilibrium allocation is incentive-efficient. An attainable allocation $(x, y) = \{(x_i, y_i)\}$ is *incentive efficient* if there does not exist an attainable mixed allocation $\{(p^j, x_i^j, y_i^j)\}$ such that

$$\sum_{\eta} \sum_{\theta_i} \lambda(\theta_i, \eta) u_i(x_i^j(\theta_i, \eta), \theta_i) \geq \sum_{\eta} \sum_{\theta_i} \lambda(\theta_i, \eta) u_i(x_i(\theta_i, \eta), \theta_i)$$

for every (i, j) with strict inequality for some (i, j). (This definition differs from Pareto efficiency only to the extent that we restrict attention to the incentive-compatible mechanisms $x_i \in X_i$.)

In order to prove the incentive-efficiency of equilibrium, we need an additional regularity condition:

Assumption 2 (Local Nonsatiation): *For any ex ante type* $i = 1, \ldots, n$, *for any mechanism* $x_i \in X_i$, *and for any* $\varepsilon > 0$, *there exists a mechanism* $x_i' \in X_i$ *within a distance* ε *of* x_i *such that*

$$\sum_{\eta} \sum_{\theta_i} \lambda(\theta_i, \eta) u_i(x_i'(\theta_i, \eta), \theta_i) > \sum_{\eta} \sum_{\theta_i} \lambda(\theta_i, \eta) u_i(x_i(\theta_i, \eta), \theta_i).$$

Remark 1: This assumption is the counterpart of the nonsatiability assumptions used in the classical theorems of welfare economics. It requires more than the nonsatiability of each ex post type's utility function, $u_i(\cdot, \theta_i)$, however, because the incentive constraints must be satisfied also. To illustrate the meaning of Assumption 2, consider the following example. There are two ex post types, $\theta_i = 1, 2$, with utility functions $u_i(c, 1)$ and $u_i(c, 2)$. The utility functions are defined as follows:

$$u_i(c, 1) = c_1 + c_2,$$
$$u_i(c, 2) = c_1 + c_2 \quad \text{if} \quad c_1 + c_2 \leq 1,$$

and for any utility level $\bar{u} > 1$, we denote the indifference curve consisting of the locus of consumption bundles yielding $\bar{u}$ to an agent of type $\theta_i = 2$ by $I_i(\bar{u}, 2)$ and define it by putting

$$I_i(\bar{u}, 2) = \left\{(c_1, c_2) = \left((1 - \alpha)\frac{\bar{u} + 1}{2}, \alpha \bar{u}\right) : 0 \leq \alpha \leq 1\right\}.$$

Notice that both types have linear indifference curves, but their indifference curves have different slopes at consumption bundles $c = (c_1, c_2)$ such that $c_1 + c_2 > 1$. Now consider an incentive-compatible mechanism x_i satisfying $x_i(1, \eta) = (1, 0)$ and $x_i(2, \eta) = (0, 1)$. Both incentive constraints (2) are just satisfied. Any mechanism x_i' that is ε-close to x_i and makes type i better off ex ante must make at least one of the ex post types better off and the incentive constraint then requires that the other ex post type be better off too. In other words, both of the consumption bundles $x_i'(1, \eta)$ and $x_i'(2, \eta)$ must lie above the line $c_1 + c_2 = 1$. Above the line $c_1 + c_2 = 1$, the two ex post types have linear indifference curves and the indifference curve of type 2 is steeper than that of ex post type 1. Since $x_i'(\theta_i, \eta)$ is very close to $x_i(\theta_i, \eta)$ for $\theta_i = 1, 2$, at least one type θ_i must envy the other. Thus, local nonsatiation is not satisfied.

This example turns on the difference between lower hemi-continuity and upper hemi-continuity. A convergent sequence of incentive-compatible allocations will have an incentive-compatible limit, but it may not be possible to approximate a given incentive-compatible allocation by a sequence of incentive-compatible allocations *from certain directions*. The line $c_1 + c_2 = 1$ contains many incentive-compatible allocations but most of these cannot be approximated from above by a sequence of incentive-compatible allocations.

Theorem 2: *Under the maintained assumptions, if (p, q, x, y) is an intermediated equilibrium and Assumption 2 is satisfied, then the allocation (x, y) is incentive-efficient.*

For the proof see the Appendix.

Theorem 2 is in the spirit of Prescott and Townsend (1984a, 1984b), but the present model takes the decentralization of the incentive-efficient allocation a step further. Markets are used in Prescott and Townsend (1984a, 1984b) to allocate mechanisms to agents at the first date. After the first date all trade is intermediated by the mechanism. Here, markets are also used for sharing risk and for intertemporal smoothing and intermediaries are active participants in markets at each date. In Section 4 we show that efficiency requires that individuals do not have access to financial markets. To this extent, we follow Prescott–Townsend in assuming that individuals' trade is intermediated by the mechanism. In Section 5, we consider incomplete contracts and the possibility of default. In the event of default, individuals' trade is no longer intermediated by the mechanism.

Remark 2: An important qualification to the incentive-efficiency of the intermediated equilibrium is the "equilibrium selection" implicit in the definition of equilibrium. Following the standard principal-agent approach (see, e.g., Grossman and Hart (1983)), we allow the principal (the intermediary), to choose the actions of the agents (the investors), subject to an incentive-compatibility constraint.

Remark 3: The incentive-efficiency of equilibrium is in marked contrast to the results in Bhattacharya and Gale (1987). The difference is explained by the informational assumptions. In the model above, there is no asymmetry of information in the markets for Arrow securities. Once the state η is observed, all aggregate uncertainty is resolved. The distribution of ex post types in each intermediary is a function of η and hence becomes common knowledge once η is revealed. Trading Arrow securities at date 0 is sufficient to provide optimal insurance against all aggregate shocks at date 1. In Bhattacharya and Gale (1987), by contrast, an intermediary's true demand for liquidity is private information at date 1. Markets for Arrow securities cannot provide incentive-efficient insurance against private shocks.

While symmetry of information in financial markets is a useful benchmark, one can easily imagine circumstances in which intermediaries have private information, for example, the intermediary knows the distribution of ex post types among its depositors, but outsiders do not. In that case, providing incentive-efficient insurance to the intermediaries would require us to supplement markets for Arrow securities with an incentive-compatible insurance mechanism, as in Bhattacharya and Gale (1987).

3.5 Examples

In this section we consider a series of numerical examples with complete markets and complete contracts with respect to aggregate states. These provide an efficient benchmark for subsequent examples with incomplete markets and/or contracts. We look first at an example of asset-return shocks and then look at an example with liquidity shocks.

Return Shocks

Example 1: We assume there is a single ex ante type of investor with Diamond–Dybvig preferences. There are two ex post types, early consumers ($\theta = 1$) and late consumers ($\theta = 2$). The utility function is

$$u(c_1, c_2, \theta) = \begin{cases} \log c_1, & \theta = 1, \\ \log c_2, & \theta = 2. \end{cases}$$

The probability of being an early consumer is one half, independently of the aggregate state η. There are two equally likely aggregate states $\eta = 1, 2$ and the return on the long asset at date 2 is contingent on the state:

$$R(1) = r; \quad R(2) = 2.$$

Different equilibria are generated by varying r.

Since investors are ex ante identical, the open interest in Arrow securities will be 0 in equilibrium.

Since the investors are either early or late consumers, the optimal bundles will be of the form $x(\theta, \eta) = \{(c_1(\eta), 0), (0, c_2(\eta))\}$ with early consumers consuming $c_1(\eta)$ at date 1 and late consumers consuming $c_2(\eta)$ at date 2. The market-clearing conditions are

$$.5c_1(\eta) \leq y, \tag{4.7}$$

$$.5c_1(\eta) + .5c_2(\eta) = y + (1 - y)R(\eta), \tag{4.8}$$

for $\eta = 1, 2$.

The form of the equilibrium depends on whether (7) is binding. In the first type of equilibrium, it binds in both states; in the second, it only binds in state 2; in the third, it does not bind in either state.

Example 1A: For $R(1) = r > 1$, equilibrium is unique and $.5c_1(\eta) = y$ in both states. A typical equilibrium with $r = 1.5$ is shown in Table 4.1. The intermediary puts .5 in the safe asset and .5 in the risky asset. The early consumers receive 1 at date 1 irrespective of the state, and late consumers receive 1.5 in state 1 and 2 in state 2. With these allocations it is clear that the incentive constraint does not bind. No late consumer would choose 1 at date 1 rather than 1.5 or 2 at date 2. The Arrow securities are priced at .5 for both states. The date 1 spot price of consumption is higher in state 1 than state 2 because date 2 consumption is lower and marginal utility is higher in state 1.

Table 4.1 Examples

Example	r	y	$(q(1), p_2(1))$	$(q(2), p_2(2))$	$(c_1(1), c_2(1))$	$(c_1(2), c_2(2))$	$E[U]$
1A	1.5	.5	(.5, .67)	(.5, .5)	(1, 1.5)	(1, 2)	.275
1B	.5	.64	(.61, 1)	(.39, .89)	(.82, .82)	(1.28, 1.44)	.054
1C	.3	.79	(.59, 1)	(.41, 1)	(.85, .85)	(1.21, 1.21)	.016
2 *A*:	.5	.5	(.5, .8)	(.5, .8)	(1, 1.25)	(1, 1.25)	.112
2 *N*:		1.0			(0, .25)	(0, 4.75)	1.250
3	1.6	.5	(.4, .94)	(.6, .42)	(1.25, 1.33)	(.83, 2)	.213
4A	1.5	.5	(.33–.75, .25–1)	(.25–.67, .38–1)	(1, 1.5)	(1, 2)	.275
4B	.95	.49	(.55–.77, .70–.98)	(.45–.33, .53–.73)	(.97, .97)	(.97, 2.05)	.157
4C *S*:	.5	.67	(.65, .90)	(.35, 1)	(.95, .95)	(.95, 1.41)	.045
4C *B*:		0			(.77, .77)	(1.41, 1.41)	.045

Example 1B: For $.4 \leq r < 1$, the unique pure intermediated equilibrium is such that the consumption profile satisfies $.5c_1(1) < y$ and $.5c_1(2) = y$. In state 1, the returns to the long asset are so low that some of the short asset must be saved to provide consumption at date 2; in state 2, all of the short asset is consumed at date 1. In order for the intermediaries to be willing to hold the short asset between date 1 and date 2 in state 1, the price must be equal to 1. Thus, consumption is equalized across time in state 1. The amount invested in the short asset rises as the expected payoff on the long asset falls. Table 4.1 illustrates the equilibrium values for the case where $r = .5$. The amount invested in the safe asset has moved up to .64, in state 1 $p_2(1) = 1$, and consumption is the same at both dates.

Example 1C: It remains to consider the case $0 \leq r \leq .4$. As r continues to fall the intermediary invests more in the short asset and less in the long asset. The total output and consumption in state 2 are also falling and for $r < .4$ the consumption at date 1 is less than the holding of the short asset in both states: $.5c_1(\eta) < y$. Consumption is equalized across time in both states. The equilibrium values corresponding to $r = .3$ are given in Table 4.1. Here $y = .78$, $p_1(1) = p_2(1) = 1$, and in both states consumptions are equated at each date.

The next example introduces a second ex ante type consisting of risk neutral investors. The purpose of this example is to illustrate how the Arrow securities allow cross-sectional risk sharing and to show their role in ensuring an incentive-efficient allocation.

Example 2: There are two ex ante types of investors, the risk averse investors, denoted by A, and the risk neutral investors denoted by N. The period utility functions are $U_A(c) = \log(c)$ and $U_N(c) = c$, respectively. The measure of each type is normalized to 1 and each type has a probability .5 of being an early or late consumer. Otherwise things are the same as in Example 1.

As in Example 1, the qualitative features of the equilibrium depend on whether some of the short asset is carried over from date 1 to date 2. One case is sufficient to illustrate how the Arrow securities allow risk to be shared. For $r \geq .4$ the allocation is the same as in Example 1A, except that all uncertainty is absorbed by the risk neutral type. The equilibrium portfolios are $y_A = .5$ and $y_N = 0$, for the representative intermediaries of type A and type N, respectively.

Table 4.1 gives the equilibrium values for the case where $r = .5$. The market-clearing prices are $q(1) = .5$, $q(2) = .5$, $p_2(1) = .8$, $p_2(2) = .8$. The portfolio returns (receipts) of each intermediary and consumption of each type are given as follows:

	State 1	State 2
$(y_A, R(\eta)(1 - y_A))$	(.5, .25)	(.5, 1)
$(y_N, R(\eta)(1 - y_N))$	(0, .5)	(0, 2)
$(c_{A1}(\eta), c_{A2}(\eta))$	(1, 1.25)	(1, 1.25)
$(c_{N1}(\eta), c_{N2}(\eta))$	(0, .25)	(0, 4.75)

Risk sharing between the intermediaries for the two groups is achieved through trading in the Arrow security markets at date 0 and the spot consumption markets at date 1. In state 1 the type A intermediaries have .5 of the good from their short asset holdings. They have promised each of their .5 early consumers 1 unit of the good each so they can simply pay out what they receive from the short asset to meet their obligations. At date 2 they receive .25 from their holdings of the long asset. They have promised their .5 late consumers 1.25 each. The deficit is $.5 \times 1.25 - .25 = .375$. To ensure that they have this, they need to use the $\eta = 1$ Arrow security and the spot market at date 1. They purchase .3 units of the $\eta = 1$ Arrow security at date 0 for $q(1) \times .3 = .5 \times .3 = .15$ and then use the .3 they receive at date 1 in state 1 to purchase $.3/p_2(1) = .3/.8 = .375$ of the date 2 good in the date 1 spot market. At date 0 they finance the . 15 needed to purchase the $\eta = 1$ Arrow security by selling .375 of the good at date 2 in state 2 and .3 of the $\eta = 2$ Arrow security. Since they have 1 unit of output from their long asset at date 2, this will leave them with .625 of the good to pay out to their .5 late consumers who receive 1.25 each. The type N's are willing to take the other side of these trades since they are risk neutral. It can be seen that this improvement in risk sharing increases the expected utility of type A's from .054 in Example 1B to .112 here.

There are other intermediated equilibria corresponding to these parameter values. In particular, the portfolio holdings of the type-A intermediaries are not uniquely determined. For example, the type-A intermediaries could hold less of the short term asset and more of the long term asset, as long as this is offset by changes in the holdings of the type-N intermediaries. As long as the aggregate portfolio remains the same, investors' consumption and welfare is unchanged.

Liquidity Shocks The uncertainty in Examples 1 and 2 is generated by shocks to asset returns. Similar results can be obtained by assuming aggregate uncertainty about the demand for liquidity.

Example 3: This example is similar to Example 1. There are two main differences. First, it is assumed that there is no uncertainty about the return to the long asset:

$$R(1) = R(2) = r.$$

Second, there is aggregate uncertainty about the demand for liquidity. The states $\eta = 1, 2$ are equally likely but now the proportions of early and late consumers differ across states:

Proportion	State 1	State 2
Early consumers	.4	.6
Late consumers	.6	.4

By varying r we can generate the same phenomena as in the case of return shocks. Rather than go through all the different cases, we illustrate a pure intermediated equilibrium for the case $r = 1.6$. The equilibrium values are shown in Table 4.1. For this case the aggregate liquidity constraint binds in both states because the return on the long asset is high. At date 1 all the proceeds from the short asset are used for consumption. In state 1 aggregate liquidity needs are low at date 1. Since consumption is split evenly among early consumers, per capita consumption is high compared to state 2 where aggregate liquidity needs are high at date 1. At date 2 there are many late consumers in state 1, so consumption per capita is lower than in state 2 where there are relatively few late consumers.

4. Complete Participation and Redundancy

Cone (1983) and Jacklin (1986) have pointed out that the beneficial effects of banks in the Diamond–Dybvig (Diamond and Dybvig (1983)) model depend on the assumption that individuals are not allowed to trade assets at the intermediate date. Increasing access to financial markets actually lowers welfare. If investors are allowed to participate in asset markets, then the market allocation weakly dominates the allocation implemented by the banks.

In this section, we show that with complete markets and complete market participation, banks are redundant in the sense that they cannot improve on the risk sharing achieved by markets alone. The ability of intermediaries to provide insurance against shocks to liquidity preference depends crucially on the assumption that investors cannot participate directly in asset markets. To show this, we first characterize an equilibrium with markets but without intermediaries. Then we show that the introduction of intermediaries is redundant.

The market data is the same as in Section 2. Investors are allowed to trade in markets for Arrow securities at date 0 and can trade in the spot markets for the good at date 1. Let y_i denote the portfolio chosen by a representative investor of type i and let $x_i(\theta_i, \eta)$ denote the consumption bundle chosen by an investor of type θ_i in state η. The investor's choice of (x_i, y_i) must solve the decision problem:

$$\max \sum_{\eta} \sum_{\theta_i} \lambda(\theta_i, \eta) u_i(x_i(\theta_i, \eta), \theta_i) \quad \text{subject to}$$

$$\sum_{\eta} q(\eta) \cdot x_i(\theta_i, \eta) \leq \sum_{\eta} q(\eta) p(\eta) \cdot (y_i, (1 - y_i) R(\eta)), \quad \forall \theta_i.$$

The maximization problem for the individual is similar to that of an intermediary of type i except for two things. First, there is no explicit incentive constraint $x_i \in X_i$. Second, there is no insurance provided against the realization of θ_i. This is reflected in the fact that, instead of summing the budget constraint over η and θ_i, it is summed over η only and must be satisfied for each θ_i. The ex ante type i can redistribute wealth across states η in any way he likes, but each type θ_i, will get the same amount to spend in state η. As a result, for each realization of θ_i in a given state η, the choice of $x_i(\theta_i, \eta)$ must maximize the utility function $u_i(x_i(\theta_i, \eta), \theta_i)$ subject to a budget constraint that depends on η but not on θ_i. This ensures that incentive compatibility is satisfied.

An equilibrium for this economy consists of a price system $\{p, q\}$ and an attainable allocation $\{(x_i, y_i)\}$ such that, for every type i, (x_i, y_i) solves the individual investor's problem above.

Comparing this definition of equilibrium with the intermediary equilibrium, it is clear that an equilibrium with complete market participation cannot implement the incentive-efficient equilibrium except in the special case where there are no gains from sharing risk against liquidity preference shocks.

The more interesting question is whether introducing intermediaries in this context can make investors any better off. The answer, as we have suggested, is negative. To see this, note first of all that in an equilibrium with complete participation, all that investors care about in each state is the market value of the bundle they receive from the intermediary. If an intermediary offers a mechanism x_i, the investors of type θ_i will report the ex post type $\hat{\theta}_i$ that maximizes $p(\eta) \cdot x_i(\hat{\theta}_i, \eta)$ in state η. Using the Revelation Principle, there is no loss of generality in assuming that the value of consumption $p(\eta) \cdot x_i(\theta_i, \eta) = w_i(\eta)$ is independent of θ_i. But this means that the intermediary can do nothing more than replicate the effect of the markets for Arrow securities. More precisely, the intermediary is offering a security that pays $w_i(\eta)$ in state η and the intermediary's budget constraint

$$\sum_{\eta} q(\eta)w_i(\eta) \leq \sum_{\eta} q(\eta)p(\eta) \cdot (y_i, (\mu_i - y_i)R(\eta))$$

ensures that $\{w_i(\eta)\}$ can be reproduced as a portfolio of Arrow securities at the same cost.

Theorem 3: *In an equilibrium with complete market participation, the introduction of intermediaries is redundant in the sense that an equilibrium allocation in an economy with intermediaries is payoff-equivalent to (i.e., yields the same expected utilities as) an equilibrium allocation of the corresponding economy without intermediaries.*

This is, essentially, a "Modigliani–Miller" result, saying that whatever an intermediary can do can be done (and undone) by individuals trading on their own in the financial markets.

Theorem 2 provides conditions under which an equilibrium will be incentive-efficient. However, the equilibrium described in Theorem 2 does not necessarily Pareto-dominate the equilibrium described in Theorem 3: with many ex ante types, it is possible that one type i will be worse off in the incentive-efficient equilibrium. In the special case where there is a single ex ante type, complete participation makes everyone worse off. The results of Cone (1983) and Jacklin (1986) to which we referred earlier assume a single ex ante type of investor.

5. Incomplete Contracts and Default

In the benchmark model defined in Section 3, intermediaries use general, incentive-compatible contracts. In reality, we do not observe such complex contracts. There are many reasons for this, which are well documented in the literature. These include transaction costs, asymmetric information, and the nature of the legal system. These kinds of assumptions can justify the use of debt and many other kinds of contracts that intermediaries use in practice. Since we are interested in developing a general framework, we do not model any specific justification for incomplete contracts. Instead we assume that the contract incompleteness can take any form and prove results that hold for any type of incomplete contract.

With complete contracts, intermediaries can always meet their commitments. Default cannot occur. Once contracts are constrained to be incomplete, then it may be optimal for the intermediary to default in some states. In the event of default, it is assumed that the intermediary's assets, including the Arrow securities it holds, are liquidated and the proceeds distributed among the intermediary's investors. For markets to be complete, which is an assumption we maintain for the moment, the Arrow securities that the bank issues must be default-free. Hence, we assume that these securities are collateralized and their holders have priority. Anything that is left after the Arrow securityholders have been paid off is paid out pro rata to the depositors.

An intermediary of type i chooses a formal contract $x_i \in X_i^1$ and an indicator function $B\colon H \to \{0, 1\}$, where $B(\eta) = 1$ means that the intermediary defaults on the formal contract. There is also a "default contract," which describes what happens when the intermediary defaults. The "default contract" $\bar{x}_i$ is defined by $x(\theta_i, \eta) = (w_i(\eta), 0)$, where $w_i(\eta)$ is the liquidated value of assets in state η. The "default contract" is not part of the formal contract;

it is determined by the institution of bankruptcy (the nexus of law, courts, creditors, and debtors) when the contract has been breached. Formally, it is possible to describe all this as a single mechanism, which is what we do, but conceptually there is an important difference between what the formal contract says and what happens if the formal contract is breached. The institution of bankruptcy is exogenous to the model, something the intermediary takes as given when writing the contract.

Given this bankruptcy procedure, an intermediary has to choose two contracts for individuals, a formal contract $x_i \in X_i^1$ and a default contract $\bar{x}_i$, and a decision rule $B: H \rightarrow \{0, 1\}$ that indicates when the bank defaults. Then the effective contract $\hat{x}_i$ is defined by

$$(1 - B(\eta))x_i(\theta_i, \eta) + B(\eta)\bar{x}_i(\theta_i, \eta)$$

for every (θ_i, η). Since everything is paid out at date 1 in the event of default, investors use the short asset to provide consumption at date 2. Then the utility of a contract x_i generated in this way is given by $u_i^*(x_i(\theta_i, \eta), \theta_i)$ in the state (θ_i, η) and the incentive constraint is

$$u_i^*(x_i(\theta_i, \eta), \theta_i) \geq u_i^*(x_i(\hat{\theta}_i, \eta), \theta_i), \quad \forall \theta_i, \hat{\theta}_i \in \Theta_i.$$

Let $\hat{X}_i$ denote the set of incentive-compatible contracts generated in this way.

To demonstrate how default works, consider the following simple illustration.

Example: Suppose that intermediaries are restricted to offering noncontingent contracts. Then $x_i \in X^1$ if and only if

$$x_i(\theta_i, \eta) = x_i(\theta_i, \eta')$$

for any $\eta, \eta' \in H$. If we assumed further that agents are either early consumers, who value consumption at date 1, or late consumers who value consumption at date 2, we could without loss of generality write the contract as

$$x_i(\theta_i, \eta) = \begin{cases} (c_1, 0) & \text{if } \theta_i = 0, \\ (0, c_2) & \text{if } \theta_i = 1. \end{cases}$$

This contract is highly inflexible because it does not allow the intermediary to adjust the payment across states in response to changing demands for liquidity or changing asset returns. If default is not allowed, the intermediary is forced to distort the contract. Default allows the intermediary to replace this inflexible contract with the following:

$$\hat{x}_i(\theta_i, \eta) = \begin{cases} (c_1, 0) & \text{if } \theta_i = 0, B_i(\eta) = 0, \\ (0, c_2) & \text{if } \theta_i = 1, B_i(\eta) = 0, \\ (w_i(\eta), 0) & \text{if } B_i(\eta) = 1. \end{cases}$$

The possibility of *incomplete* contracts is represented by restricting the choice of contract to a subset $\hat{X}_i \subset X_i$. The theory developed in Section 3 is essentially the same, but with X_i replaced by $\hat{X}_i$. With this substitution, an intermediated equilibrium becomes an *intermediated equilibrium with incomplete contracts*, an incentive-efficient allocation becomes a *constrained-efficient* equilibrium, and Assumption 2 becomes Assumption 2′.

Then Theorem 2 can be interpreted as a theorem about constrained-efficiency of equilibrium with incomplete contracts but complete markets.

Theorem 4: *Under the maintained assumptions, if* (p, q, x, y) *is an intermediated equilibrium with incomplete contracts and Assumption 2′ is satisfied, then the allocation* (x, y) *is constrained-efficient.*

Although this result is a direct corollary of Theorem 2, it is substantively the most important result of the paper, for it shows that, in the presence of complete markets, the incidence of default is optimal in a laisser-faire equilibrium. For example, consider the case where banks are restricted to using demand deposits that promise a fixed payment at date 1. A bank may default in some states because its assets are insufficient to meet its noncontingent commitments. Default allows the bank to make its risk-sharing contract more contingent, that is, more complete. But if several banks default in the same state, this may cause a financial crisis, as the simultaneous liquidation of several banks forces down asset prices, which may in turn cause distress in other banks. Nonetheless, the theorem shows that, given complete markets for insuring against aggregate shocks, the occurrence of these crises is optimal and not a market failure. There is no scope for *welfare-improving* government intervention to prevent financial crises.

Remark 4: The definition of constrained efficiency is *formally* similar to the definition of incentive-efficiency—we simply substitute $\hat{X}_i$ for X_i in the latter—but there are important substantive differences. The definition of $\hat{X}$ implicitly incorporates the "bankruptcy code" and requires consumers to be autarkic once the intermediary defaults. Allowing trade after default would complicate the theory but should not change the basic result as long as markets for aggregate risk are complete.

Remark 5: Alonso (1996) and Allen and Gale (1998) have argued that financial crises can sometimes be optimal, or at least Pareto-preferred to government intervention to suppress crises entirely. While these arguments have a similar flavor to the present results, they are substantially different. Both Alonso (1996) and Allen and Gale (1998) rely on very special examples to show that laisser faire may be preferred to a policy of preventing financial crises. There is no general efficiency result. In fact, Allen and Gale (1998) show that even within the context of their example, the efficiency of financial crises is not robust.

More importantly, there is no role for Arrow securities in the examples provided by Alonso (1996) and Allen and Gale (1998). In their models, a representative bank chooses a portfolio and deposit contract to maximize the expected utility of the representative agent. Because of the representative agent assumption, banks are autarkic and complete markets are irrelevant. So the results presented here are based on a different argument and apply to a much broader class of economies.

Remark 6: The role of Arrow securities deserves further attention in a model with default. An Arrow security is a promise to deliver one unit of the good in some state at date 1. It is assumed, crucially, that Arrow securities are fully collateralized so there is no risk of default on these promises. Equivalently, traders in Arrow securities can anticipate each intermediary's ability to repay borrowing through Arrow securities in each state and Arrow securities take priority over other claims on the intermediary's assets. This means that, at date 0, the intermediary will not be allowed to execute trades that cannot be fulfilled at date 1 and that the intermediary's position in Arrow securities is settled at the beginning of date 1 before anything else happens, in particular, before the default decision is made and before investors receive any payments. These assumptions are restrictive but they are essential to the definition of Arrow security markets.

Remark 7: Default is completely voluntary in the sense that the intermediary chooses at date 0 those states in which it wishes to default. Default is not forced on the intermediary by the budget constraint; in fact, in the presence of complete markets it is not clear what this would mean. Because Arrow security markets are complete, there is a single budget constraint and the intermediary chooses the amount of wealth allocated to each state. We do however assume that the intermediary is committed to his default decision at date 0 and further, that he makes the default decision in the ex ante interest of the representative investor. These assumptions are restrictive but interesting insofar as they are required for efficiency. We can interpret them as a description of an optimal bankruptcy institution.

5.1 Examples

In this section we demonstrate a number of results using examples. These results include the following:

(1) the existence (indeed necessity) of mixed equilibria;
(2) the optimality of default and crises;
(3) cash-in-the-market pricing when there is a crisis;
(4) suboptimal risk sharing with incomplete markets.

There are many examples of intermediaries that use incomplete contracts with their depositors. As we have seen, as soon as incomplete contracts are introduced the possibility of default must be allowed. This in turn introduces the possibility of financial crises. In practice crises can be precipitated by a wide array of intermediaries. Historically, however, it has been banks that have caused most crises. In order to illustrate the model with incomplete contracts and default we consider examples where the intermediaries are banks, that is, they are restricted to issuing deposit contracts. A deposit contract promises a fixed payment at date 1. If the bank is unable to meet its commitment to its depositors, then it is liquidated and all its assets are sold. If it can meet its commitment, depositors can keep their funds in the bank until date 2.

Example 4: To illustrate the properties of a banking equilibrium, we revert to the parameters from Example 1.

Example 4A: For $r \geq 1$ the first best can again be implemented as a banking equilibrium. The first-best allocation requires that consumption at date 1 be the same in both states, so the optimal incentive-compatible contract is in fact a deposit contract. Moreover, bankruptcy does not occur in equilibrium. The allocation corresponding to a pure banking equilibrium is exactly the same as the allocation corresponding to a pure intermediated equilibrium, which as we have seen is the same as the first best. For $r = 1.5$, for example, the equilibrium values will be the same as for Example 1A, as shown in Table 4.1.

The main difference between Examples 1A and 4A is that the prices supporting the first best allocation are unique in Example 1A but are not in Example 4A. In Example 1A the general intermediaries can freely vary payoffs across states and dates so only one set of prices can support the optimal allocation. Because the banks are restricted to using deposit contracts in Example 4A, consumption at date 1 is independent of the state as long as there is no bankruptcy. This prevents the banks from arbitraging between the states at date 1. In effect, we have lost one equilibrium condition compared with the intermediated equilibrium. Any vector of prices $(q(1), q(2), p_2(1), p_2(2))$ that supports the equilibrium allocation at date 2 is consistent with a banking equilibrium. The following no-arbitrage conditions are satisfied:

$$q(1)p_2(1) = .33, \tag{4.9}$$

$$q(2)p_2(2) = .25, \tag{4.10}$$

$$q(1) + q(2) = 1, \tag{4.11}$$

and the existence of the short asset implies that

$$p_2(1) \leq 1, \quad p_2(2) \leq 1.$$

Combining these conditions, it follows that the range of possible prices for $q(1)$ is

$$.33 \leq q(1) \leq .75.$$

The other prices are determined by (9)–(11).

For $r < 1$ deposit contracts cannot be used to implement the first best or incentive-efficient allocation. In particular, a deposit contract that is consistent with the incentive-efficient consumption in state 2 would imply bankruptcy in state 1 (see, e.g., Example 1B). If all banks were to offer a contract that allowed bankruptcy in state 1, they would all be forced to liquidate their assets. If they all do this, there is no bank on the other side of the market to buy the assets and the price of future consumption, $p_2(1)$, falls to 0. This cannot be an equilibrium because it would be worthwhile for an individual bank to offer a contract that did not involve bankruptcy. This bank could then buy up all the long term assets in state 1 at date 1 for $p_2(1) = 0$ and make a large profit.

This argument indicates that for $r < 1$ there cannot be a pure banking equilibrium with bankruptcy. There are two other possibilities. One is that there is a pure equilibrium in which all banks remain solvent. The other is that there is a mixed equilibrium in which banks choose different contracts and portfolios. In particular, a group of banks with measure ρ makes choices that allow it to remain solvent in state 1 while the remaining $1 - \rho$ banks go bankrupt. The banks that are ensured of solvency are denoted type S while those that can go bankrupt are denoted type B. It turns out that both the pure equilibrium with all banks remaining solvent and the mixed equilibrium can occur when $r < 1$.

Example 4B: For $.90 \leq r < 1$ there is a pure banking equilibrium in which all the banks choose to remain solvent ($\rho = 1$). There is again a range of prices that can support the allocation. Type-S banks stay solvent by lowering the amount promised at date 1, lowering their investment in the short asset and increasing their investment in the long asset. The equilibrium values for the case where $r = .95$ are shown in Table 4.1. The range of $q(1)$ that will support the allocation and prevent entry by type B banks is $.55 < q(1) < .77$. The other prices are determined by the equilibrium conditions:

$$q(1)p_2(1) = .54,$$

$$q(2)p_2(2) = .24,$$

$$q(1) + q(2) = 1.$$

Example 4C: For $0 < r < .90$ there exists a mixed banking equilibrium. At the boundary $r = .90$, the set of prices that will support the equilibrium of the type shown in Example 4B shrinks to a singleton: $(q(1) = 2/3, q(2) = 1/3)$. For values of $r < .90$ but close to .90 the proportion of type-S banks is large ($\rho \approx 1$). As r falls, the proportion of type-B banks rises until as r goes to 0 the proportion of type-B banks $1 - \rho$ approaches 1. The mixed banking equilibrium corresponding to $r = .5$ is shown in Table 4.1. The proportion of type-S banks is $\rho = .35$. As in the earlier examples, the portfolios of individual banks are indeterminate. It is only the aggregate portfolio that is determined by the equilibrium conditions.

The pricing of assets in state 1 in Example 4C illustrates the principle of "cash-in-the-market pricing." When the type-B banks go bankrupt in state 1 they have to liquidate all their holdings of the long asset. These are purchased by the type-S banks who use all of their spare liquidity to do so. In making the decision on how much of the short asset to hold they trade off the benefits of liquidity in the low output state with the cost of holding idle funds in the high output state.

The effect of cash-in-the-market pricing can be seen if we compare this example with Example 1B. The price of the long asset is $.5 \times 1 = .5$ in Example 1B and $.5 \times .9 = .45$ in the present example. It can easily be shown that the price of the long asset could be depressed further by changing the parameters. For example, the lower the probability of the low-output state, the less liquidity the type-S bank will hold and the lower the price of the long asset will be in the low-output state.

The mixed equilibrium in Example 4C illustrates a number of interesting phenomena. First, banks serving identical depositors may do quite different things in equilibrium. One subset will find it optimal to follow a safe strategy and avoid the risk of bankruptcy. Another subset will follow a risky strategy that makes bankruptcy inevitable in state 1. As a result, even when all investors are identical ex ante, there can be a financial crisis in which some banks remain solvent while others go under. In the context of the example, the crisis is more severe when the state-1 return r is lower. However, the results in Section 5 show that these crises are consistent with the constrained efficiency of equilibrium. There is no justification for intervention or regulation of the financial system. A planner could not do better.

Many analyses of banking assume that there is a technology for early liquidation of the long term asset. The resulting equilibria are typically symmetric. This example illustrates that this assumption materially changes the form of the equilibrium. With endogenous liquidation one group of banks must provide liquidity to the market and this results in mixed equilibria.

A comparison of Example 4C with Example 1 shows the importance of non-contingent contracts in causing financial crises. In Example 1 the ability to use state contingent contracts with investors means that bankruptcy never occurs and as a result there is never a crisis. However, with deposit contracts crises of varying severity always occur in the low output state.

There are a number of other types of equilibrium, depending on whether the short asset is held between date 1 and date 2 and the number of ex ante groups. The properties of these equilibria are similar to those illustrated in Examples 1 and 2 and will not be repeated here.

In Example 4 it was assumed that markets are complete. However, it can straightforwardly be seen that with incomplete markets the allocation in each case would be the same. In Examples 4A and 4B there is only one ex ante type in equilibrium and they all do the same thing so the open interest in Arrow securities is zero and there is no role for risk sharing. In the mixed equilibrium of Example 4C there are two types of banks providing different allocations even though ex ante all investors are identical. Complete markets do not help risk sharing, however. The reason is that the contract forms restrict the amounts that can be paid out and the trade-offs given these mean that no improvement can be made. The only difference in Example 4C if markets are incomplete is the equilibrium holdings of assets of the two banks are now unique. The type-S banks hold .82 of the short asset and the type-B banks hold .59 of it. This fact that complete markets does not make a difference here is clearly a special case as the next example, which mixes Example 2 and Example 4C, demonstrates.

Example 5A: The example is the same as Example 2 except that contracts are incomplete. There are risk averse type-A investors and risk neutral type-N investors, $r = .5$, and there are complete Arrow security markets. It can straightforwardly be seen that the equilibrium is exactly the same as that shown in Table 4.1 for Example 2. The type-A banks can use a deposit contract promising 1 at date 1 to implement the optimal allocation. Similarly the type-N banks can use a deposit contract promising 0 at date 1.

Example 5B: This example is the same as Example 5A except now there are no Arrow securities so markets are incomplete. Here it can be seen that the equilibrium is essentially the same as in Example 4C. The banks for the type-A investors behave exactly as in Example 4C. The banks for the *type-N* investors do not find it worthwhile to enter the markets that do exist. They simply put all their customers' endowment in the long asset and pay out 0 at date 1 and whatever is produced at date 2.

A comparison of Examples 5A and 5B demonstrates the crucial role that complete markets can play. With complete markets the financial system produces the first best allocation. However, with incomplete markets the allocation is much worse. Moreover the incompleteness of markets leads to default and crises in equilibrium.

In conclusion, the examples in this section have demonstrated the results mentioned initially. First, Example 4C has shown that a mixed equilibrium can exist. When there is only one type of bank they cannot all go bankrupt at the same time. If they did there would be nobody to buy their assets and the assets' price would fall to 0. This cannot be an equilibrium though since it would be worthwhile for a bank to stay solvent and buy up all the assets at the 0 price. As a result the equilibrium must be mixed.

Second, Example 4C shows that default can be optimal for the banks. Theorem 4 shows that the crises that result from banks' defaulting are also socially optimal. In fact crises are necessary for the constrained-efficient allocation to be achieved.

Third, the logic demonstrating the existence of mixed equilibria shows how cash-in-the-market pricing occurs. In making their decision on how much of the short asset to hold, the solvent banks take into account the fact that if there is a crisis they can buy up the long asset cheaply and trade this off against the cost of not investing in the long asset at date 0 and rolling over the liquidity in state 2.

Fourth, Example 5 demonstrates the important role of complete markets. With incomplete markets the equilibrium is completely different from the one with complete markets. Not only is risk sharing much better with complete markets but also there are no crises.

6. Incomplete Markets and Liquidity Regulation

The absence of markets for insuring individual liquidity shocks does not by itself lead to market failure. As we showed in Section 3, intermediaries with complete contracts can achieve an *incentive-efficient* allocation of risk under certain conditions. We showed in

Section 5, under the same conditions, that intermediaries with incomplete contracts can achieve a *constrained-efficient* allocation of risk. Two assumptions are crucial for these results: markets for aggregate uncertainty are complete (there is an Arrow security for each state η) and market participation is limited. Markets for aggregate risk allow intermediaries to share risk among different ex ante types of investor and limited participation allows intermediaries to offer insurance against the realization of ex post types.

In order to generate a market failure and provide some role for government intervention, an additional friction must be introduced. Here we assume that it comes in the form of *incomplete markets for aggregate risk.* There are two sources of aggregate risk in this model. One is the return to the risky asset $R(\eta)$; the other is the distribution of investors' liquidity preferences $\lambda(\theta_i, \eta)$. Although there is a continuum of investors, correlated liquidity shocks give rise to aggregate fluctuations in the demand for liquidity.

Market incompleteness may be expected to vary according to the source of the risk. On the one hand, asset returns can be hedged using markets for stock and interest rate options and futures. For example, financial markets allow intermediaries to take hedging positions on future asset prices and interest rates. Additional hedges can be synthesized using dynamic trading strategies. On the other hand, liquidity shocks seem harder to hedge. Asset prices and interest rates are functions of the *aggregate* distribution of liquidity shocks in the economy. Inverting this relationship, we can use asset prices and interest rates to infer the average demand for liquidity, but not the liquidity shock experienced by a particular intermediary. Hence, trading options and futures will not allow intermediaries to provide insurance against their own liquidity shocks. So markets for hedging liquidity shocks are likely to be more incomplete than the markets for hedging asset returns.

We analyze a polar case below: we assume that there exist complete markets for hedging asset return shocks, but no markets for hedging liquidity shocks. Since complete markets for asset-return shocks permit efficient sharing of that risk, we might as well assume that asset returns are nonstochastic. In what follows, we adopt the simplifying assumption that the return to the long asset is a constant $r > 1$ and the only aggregate uncertainty comes from liquidity shocks.

We continue to assume that each intermediary serves a single type of investor. Let x_i denote the mechanism and y_i the portfolio chosen by the representative intermediary of type i. The problem faced by the intermediary is to choose (x_i, y_i) to maximize the expected utility of the representative depositor subject to multiple, state-contingent budget constraints:

$$\max \sum_{\eta} \sum_{\theta_i} \lambda(\theta_i, \eta) u_i(x_i(\theta_i, \eta), \theta_i) \quad \text{subject to}$$

$$x_i \in X_i,$$

$$\sum_{\theta_i} \lambda(\theta_i, \eta) p(\eta) \cdot x_i(\theta_i, \eta) \leq p(\eta) \cdot (y_i, (\mu_i - y_i) R(\eta)), \quad \forall \eta.$$

The incompleteness of markets is reflected in the fact that there is a separate budget constraint for each aggregate state of nature η, rather than a single budget constraint that integrates surpluses and deficits across all states.

With incomplete markets, the existence of welfare-improving interventions is well known in many contexts (cf. Geanakoplos and Polemarchakis (1986)). Rather than pursuing general inefficiency results, we investigate a more specific policy intervention: Is there too much or too little liquidity in a laisser-faire equilibrium? The interest of the results follows not from the *existence* of a policy that increases welfare, but rather from the precise characterization of the optimal (small) intervention to regulate liquidity. Our intuition suggests that market provision of liquidity will be too low when markets are incomplete. However, even in an equilibrium with a lot of structure, our analysis shows that whether there is too much or too little liquidity depends crucially on the degree of relative risk aversion.

We identify *liquidity regulation* with manipulation of portfolio choices at the first date. For example, a lower bound on the amount of the short asset held by intermediaries can be interpreted as a reserve requirement. We examine regulation in the context of an economy with Diamond–Dybvig preferences.

As usual, there are n ex ante types of investors $i = 1, \ldots, n$. The ex ante types are symmetric and the size of each type is normalized to $\mu_i = 1$. There are two ex post types, called early consumers and late consumers. Early consumers only value consumption at date 1, while late consumers only value consumption at date 2. The ex ante utility function of type i is defined by

$$u_i(c_1, c_2, \theta_i) = (1 - \theta_i)U(c_1) + \theta_i U(c_2),$$

Where $\theta_i \in \{0, 1\}$. The period utility function U: $\mathbf{R}_+ \to \mathbf{R}$ is twice continuously differentiable and satisfies the usual neoclassical properties, $U'(c) > 0$, $U''(c) < 0$, and $\lim_{c \searrow 0} U'(c) = \infty$.

Each intermediary is characterized at date 1 by the proportions of early and late consumers among its customers. Call these proportions the intermediary's type. Then aggregate risk is characterized by the distribution of types of intermediary at date 1. We assume that the cross-sectional distribution of types is constant and that there is no variation in the total demand for liquidity. In this sense there is no aggregate uncertainty. However, individual intermediaries receive different liquidity shocks: some intermediaries will have high demand for liquidity and some will have low demand for liquidity. The asset market is used to reallocate liquidity from intermediaries with a surplus of liquidity to intermediaries with a deficit of liquidity. It is only the cross-sectional distribution of liquidity shocks that does not vary. To make this precise, we need additional notation. We identify the state η with the n-tuple $(\eta_1, \ldots, \eta_n)$, where η_i, is the fraction of investors of type i who are early consumers in state η. The fraction of early consumers takes a finite number of values, denoted by $0 < \sigma_k < 1$, where $k = 1, \ldots, K$. We assume that the marginal distribution of η_i, is the same for every type i and that the cross-sectional distribution is the same for every state η. Formally, let λ_k denote the ex ante probability that the proportion of early consumers is σ_k. Let $H_{ik} = \{\eta \in H : \eta_i = \sigma_k\}$. Then $\lambda_k = \sum_{\eta \in H_{ik}} \lambda_i(0, \eta)$, for every k and every type i. Ex post, λ_k equals the fraction of ex ante types with a proportion σ_k of early consumers. Then $\lambda_k = n^{-1}\#\{i\colon \eta_i = \sigma_k\}$, for every k and every state η.

The return on the long asset is nonstochastic,

$$R(\eta) = r > 1, \quad \forall \eta.$$

The only aggregate uncertainty in the model relates to the distribution of liquidity shocks across the different ex ante types i.

In what follows, we focus on symmetric equilibrium, in which the prices at dates 1 and 2 are independent of the realized state η and the choices of the intermediaries at date 0 are independent of the ex ante type i. Let the good at date 1 be the numeraire and let p denote the price of the good at date 2 in terms of the good at date 1. At date 0 the representative intermediary of type i chooses a portfolio $y_i = y$ and a consumption mechanism $x_i(\eta) = x(\eta_i)$ to solve the following problem:

$$\max \sum_k \lambda_k \{\sigma_k U(x_1(\sigma_k)) + (1 - \sigma_k) U(x_2(\sigma_k))\} \quad \text{subject to}$$

$$\sigma_k x_1(\sigma_k) + (1 - \sigma_k) p x_2(\sigma_k) \leq y + pr(1 - y), \quad \forall k,$$
$$x_1(\sigma_k) \leq x_2(\sigma_k), \quad \forall k. \tag{4.12}$$

The incentive constraint $x_1(\sigma_k) \leq x_2(\sigma_k)$ is never binding. To see this, drop the incentive constraint and solve the relaxed problem. The special early-consumer, late-consumer structure of preferences and the assumption $r > 1$ imply that the incentive constraint is automatically satisfied by the solution to the relaxed problem.

A symmetric equilibrium consists of an array (p, x, y) such that (x, y) solves the problem (12) for the equilibrium price p and the market-clearing conditions

$$\sum_{k=1}^{k} \lambda_k \sigma_k x_1(\sigma_k) \leq y,$$

$$\sum_{k=1}^{k} \lambda_k \{\sigma_k x_1(\sigma_k) + (1 - \sigma_k) x_2(\sigma_k)\} = y + r(1 - y),$$

are satisfied.

To study the effect of regulation of intermediaries, we take as given the choice of portfolio y at date 0 and consider the determination of the consumption mechanism x and the market-clearing price p. Call (p, x, y) a *regulated equilibrium* if x solves the problem (12) for the given values of p and y, and (x, y) satisfies the market-clearing conditions (15).

Suppose that (p, x, y) is a regulated equilibrium and $p > p^* = 1/r$. Then the short asset is dominated by the long asset between dates 0 and 1 and no one will want to hold the short asset. If the regulator requires intermediaries to hold a minimum amount of the short asset, then each intermediary will want to hold the minimum. In that case, (x, y) solves the maximization problem (12) subject to the additional constraint $y \geq \bar{y}$ for an appropriately chosen value of $\bar{y}$. Similarly, if $p < p^*$, then the long asset is dominated and (x, y) solves the maximization problem subject to an additional constraint $y \leq \bar{y}$. Thus, any regulated equilibrium can be interpreted as an equilibrium in which the intermediaries choose the mechanism x and the portfolio y to maximize the expected utility of the depositors subject to a constraint that requires them to hold a minimum amount of the short asset in the case $p > p^*$ or of the long asset in the case $p < p^*$. In this sense, the regulator can implement the regulated equilibrium (p, x, y) by imposing an appropriate constraint $\bar{y}$ on the intermediaries' portfolio choice.

By manipulating the intermediaries' portfolio choice, the regulator is able to manipulate the equilibrium price p. The welfare effect of this change in price depends on the degree of risk aversion. We can state a positive result for regulatory policy as follows: it is possible to increase welfare by imposing a lower bound on intermediaries' holdings of the short asset if the degree of relative risk aversion is greater than one. More precisely, let $W(p)$ denote the expected utility of the typical depositor in the regulated equilibrium (p, x, y).

Theorem 5: *If* (p^*, x^*, y^*) *is a symmetric equilibrium and* $-U''(c)c/U'(c) > 1$, *then for some* $\bar{y} > y^*$ *there is a regulated equilibrium* (p, x, y) *in which intermediaries are required to hold at least* $\bar{y}$ *units of the short asset and* $W(p) > W(p^*)$.

The proof of this result is in the Appendix. The key step in the argument is provided by the following lemma, which shows how the degree of risk aversion determines the welfare effect of a change in the regulated equilibrium price.

Lemma 6: *For any* $p > p^*$ *sufficiently close to* p^*, $W(p) > W(p^*)$ *if*

$$-\frac{U''(c)c}{U'(c)} > 1. \tag{4.13}$$

For any $p < p^*$ *sufficiently close to* p^*, $W(p) > W(p^*)$ *if*

$$-\frac{U''(c)c}{U'(c)} < 1.$$

For the proof see the Appendix.

So an increase in liquidity (increase in the price of the long asset) may increase or decrease welfare, depending on the degree of risk aversion.

The intuition behind this result is the following. When relative risk aversion is high, optimal risk sharing requires that consumption at date 1 be higher than the present value of consumption at date 2, that is, $c_1 > pc_2$. An increase in the fraction of early consumers σ, ceteris paribus, implies an increase in the present value of total consumption $\sigma c_1 + (1 - \sigma)pc_2$. In order to satisfy the budget constraint,

$$\sigma c_1 + (1 - \sigma)pc_2 = y + pr(1 - y),$$

both c_1 and c_2 must fall (efficient risk-sharing implies that c_1 and c_2 always rise and fall together). Then $(1 - \sigma)c_2$, the total consumption at date 2, falls and the budget constraint implies that σc_1 the total demand for liquidity at date 1, rises. So per capita consumption at dates 1 and 2 and demand for liquidity go in opposite directions. From this it follows that, when σ is high, $\sigma c_1 > y$ and $(1 - \sigma)c_2 < r(1 - y)$, so an increase in liquidity (increase in p), has a positive income effect and raises consumption and, when σ is low, an increase in liquidity has the opposite effect. Thus, an increase in liquidity lowers consumption in good states (where per capita consumption is high) and raises it in bad states (where per capita consumption is low). This transfer from high-consumption states to low-consumption states raises welfare. When relative risk aversion is low, the argument works in the opposite direction. The welfare effect depends on the correlation between equilibrium consumption and the liquidity shocks.

The preceding analysis assumes intermediaries offer complete contracts. A parallel analysis with incomplete (deposit) contracts reaches similar conclusions (Allen and Gale (2000c)).

7. Concluding Remarks

We have argued that, contrary to the conventional wisdom, it is not axiomatic that financial crises are bad from a welfare point of view. In fact, we have presented conditions under which they are essential for constrained efficiency. This should give economists pause for thought. Although the conditions for efficiency are restrictive, they are no more so than the conditions usually required for efficiency of general equilibrium. We should also note that, while the focus of this paper is on a rudimentary model of banks and financial intermediaries, the basic ideas have a wider application. Wherever incompletely contingent contracts, such as debt contracts, are used, there is the possibility of default. In the absence of complete markets for the aggregate risks involved, financial crises in the form of widespread default may constitute a market failure requiring some form of intervention by the financial regulator.

The model we have used is special in several respects. For example, we have assumed that investors are condemned to autarky after a default. A more realistic model would allow intermediaries to enter and offer deposit contracts to investors whose intermediaries have defaulted at date 1. We have seen, in Section 4, that incentive-efficient risk sharing requires limited participation in markets. In particular, we cannot allow investors to deal with more than one bank at a time. If investors could deal with a second bank ex post, this could undermine the incentive constraints in the original contract and result in lower welfare. However, once an intermediary has defaulted, there is no reason to prevent investors from accepting contracts with the surviving intermediaries and thus avoiding the inefficiency that arises from being excluded from asset markets. This would be more complicated, but would not fundamentally alter the results, as long as entry occurs after the original intermediary has defaulted and liquidated its assets.

Although we have tried to lay the groundwork for a welfare analysis of financial crises, we have only scratched the surface as far as the study of optimal regulation of the financial system is concerned. In particular, the role of central banking requires a much richer model of the monetary system and monetary policy. We have also avoided analyzing aggregate uncertainty in the context of incomplete markets and the possible role this provides for the central bank as a lender of last resort. We have not explored the interaction of the financial sector and the real sector, which is where the impact of financial crises is largely felt (Bernanke and Gertler (1989)).

These are all clearly subjects for future work.

Appendix: Proofs

A.1. *Proof of Theorem 2*: The argument follows the lines of the familiar proof of the first fundamental theorem of welfare economics. Let (x, y, p, q) be an equilibrium and suppose, contrary to what we want to show, that there is an attainable mixed allocation $\{(p^j, x_i^j, y_i^j)\}$ that makes some ex ante types better off and none worse off. If type (i, j) is (strictly) better off under the new allocation, then clearly

$$\sum_{\eta} q(\eta) \sum_{\theta_i} \lambda(\theta_i, \eta) p(\eta) \cdot x_i^j(\theta_i, \eta) > \sum_{\eta} q(\eta) p(\eta) \cdot \left(y_i^j, (\mu_i - y_i^j) R(\eta)\right),$$

or x_i^j, y_i^j would have been chosen. The next thing to show is that for every ex ante type (i, j)

$$\sum_{\eta} q(\eta) \sum_{\theta_i} \lambda(\theta_i, \eta) p(\eta) \cdot x_i^j(\theta_i, \eta) \geq \sum_{\eta} q(\eta) p(\eta) \cdot \left(y_i^j, (\mu_i - y_i^j) R(\eta)\right)$$

If not, then by Assumption 2 it is possible to find a feasible mechanism x_i' such that (x_i', y_i^j) satisfies the budget constraint and makes type i (strictly) better off than (x_i, y_i), contradicting the definition of equilibrium. Then summing the budget constraints for all types (i, j) we have

$$\sum_{i,j} \rho^j \sum_{\eta} q(\eta) \sum_{\theta_i} \lambda(\theta_i, \eta) p(\eta) \cdot x_i^j(\theta_i, \eta)$$
$$> \sum_{i,j} \rho^j \sum_{\eta} q(\eta) p(\eta) \cdot \left(y_i^j, (\mu_i - y_i^j) R(\eta)\right),$$

or

$$\sum_{\eta} q(\eta) p(\eta) \cdot \sum_{i,j} \sum_{\theta_i} \lambda(\theta_i, \eta) \rho^j x_i^j(\theta_i, \eta) > \sum_{\eta} q(\eta) p(\eta) \cdot \sum_{i,j} \rho^j \left(y_i^j, (\mu_i - y_i^j) R(\eta)\right). \tag{4.14}$$

The market-clearing conditions imply that, for each state η, either

$$\sum_{i} \sum_{\theta_i} \lambda(\theta_i, \eta) \sum_{j} \rho^j x_i^j(\theta_i, \eta) = \sum_{i} \sum_{j} \rho^j \left(y_i^j, (\mu_i - y_i^j) R(\eta)\right)$$

if all the good is consumed at date 1, or $p_1(\eta) = p_2(\eta)$ and

$$\sum_{i,j} \sum_{\theta_i} \lambda(\theta_i, \eta) \rho^j \left(x_{i1}^j(\theta_i, \eta) + x_{i2}^j(\theta_i, \eta)\right) = \sum_{i,j} \rho^j \left(y_i^j + (\mu_i - y_i^j) R(\eta)\right),$$

if some of the good is stored until date 2. In either case,

$$p(\eta) \cdot \sum_{i,j} \sum_{\theta_i} \lambda(\theta_i, \eta) \rho^j x^j(\theta_i, \eta) = p(\eta) \cdot \sum_{i,j} \rho^j \left(y_i^j, (\mu_i - y_i^j) R(\eta)\right)$$

Multiplying this equation by $q(\eta)$ and summing over η yields

$$\sum_{\eta} q(\eta) p(\eta) \cdot \sum_{i,j} \sum_{\theta_i} \lambda(\theta_i, \eta) \rho^j x^j(\theta_i, \eta)$$
$$= \sum_{\eta} q(\eta) p(\eta) \cdot \sum_{i,j} \rho^j \left(y_i^j, (\mu_i - y_i^j) R(\eta)\right),$$

in contradiction of the inequality (14). This completes the proof.

A.2. *Proof of Lemma 6*:

Proposition 7: *There exists a unique symmetric equilibrium* (p^*, x^*, y^*).

Proof: *Uniqueness*. The Inada conditions imply that the optimal mechanism will provide positive consumption at both dates, so both assets are held in equilibrium. Both assets will be held between date 0 and date 1 only if the returns on the two assets are equal. If $pr > 1$, then the return on the long asset is greater than the return on the short asset between dates 0 and 1 and no one will hold the latter; if $pr < 1$, then the return on the short asset is greater than the return on the long asset between dates 0 and 1 and no one will hold the long asset. Then equilibrium requires that $p = 1/r$ at date 1 (Allen and Gale (1994)).

At the price $p = 1/r$, the short asset is dominated between dates 1 and 2 so no one will hold it. It follows that all consumption at date 1 is provided by the short asset and all consumption at date 2 is provided by the long asset. Then the market-clearing conditions are

$$\sum_{k=1}^{K} \lambda_k \sigma_k x_1(\sigma_k) = ny,$$

$$\sum_{k=1}^{K} \lambda_k (1 - \sigma_k) x_2(\sigma_k) = nr(1 - y). \tag{4.15}$$

At the price $p = 1/r$, intermediaries are indifferent between the two assets at date 0. Thus, the quantities of the assets held in equilibrium are determined by the market-clearing conditions.

Finally, note that at the price $p = 1/r$, the right-hand side of the budget constraint in (12) is equal to 1 for all k, so the choice of x is independent of y. Strict concavity implies that there is at most one solution to the maximization problem. Hence, the equilibrium values are uniquely determined.

Existence. The existence of a symmetric equilibrium follows directly from the existence of a solution of the intermediary's decision problem (12). A solution exists because the choice set is compact and the objective function is continuous. The objective function is increasing, so the budget constraint holds as an equation for each k. Summing the budget constraint over k we get

$$\sum_{k} \lambda_k \{\sigma_k x_1(\sigma_k) + (1 - \sigma_k) p x_2(\sigma_k)\} = n,$$

where $p = 1/r$. Clearly, there exists a value of $0 \leq y \leq 1$ such that the market-clearing conditions (15) are satisfied. Then (p, x, y) constitutes a symmetric equilibrium. Q.E.D.

To study the effect of regulation of intermediaries, we take as given the choice of portfolio y at date 0 and consider the determination of the consumption mechanism x and the market-clearing price p. Call (p, x, y) a regulated equilibrium if x solves the problem (12) for the given values of p and y, and (x, y) satisfies the market-clearing conditions (15).

Proposition 8: *For any p sufficiently close to* p^*, *there exists a unique regulated equilibrium* (p, x, y).

Proof: *Uniqueness.* At any price p close to p^*, the short asset is dominated between dates 1 and 2 so no one will hold it. It follows that all consumption at date 1 is provided by the short asset and all consumption at date 2 is provided by the long asset. Then the market-clearing conditions are

$$\sum_{k=1}^{K} \lambda_k \sigma_k x_1(\sigma_k) = ny, \quad \sum_{k=1}^{K} \lambda_k (1-\sigma_k) x_2(\sigma_k) = nr(1-y).$$

The budget constraints are

$$\sigma_k x_1(\sigma_k) + (1-\sigma_k) p x_2(\sigma_k) = y + pr(1-y),$$

for each k. For the given (p, y), strict concavity implies that there is at most one solution to the maximization problem. Hence, the equilibrium values are uniquely determined. If there exist two, distinct, regulated equilibria (p, x, y) and (p, x', y'), say, then from the budget constraints and the fact that consumption at each date is a normal good, consumption must be uniformly higher at each date in one regulated equilibrium. But this is clearly impossible from the market-clearing conditions. Hence, there is at most one regulated equilibrium.

Existence. Similar to the proof of Proposition 7. Q.E.D.

A.2.1. *Proof of the Lemma*: Let $X(\sigma_k, p, y) = (X_1(\sigma_k, p, y), X_2(\sigma_k, p, y))$ denote the optimal mechanism for each value of (p, y). An optimal mechanism is one that solves the problem:

$$\max \sigma_k U(x_1(\sigma_k)) + (1-\sigma_k) U(x_2(\sigma_k)) \quad \text{subject to}$$
$$\sigma_k x_1(\sigma_k) + (1-\sigma_k) x_2(\sigma_k)/r \leq y + pr(1-y)$$

for each k. The necessary and sufficient conditions for this are

$$U'(X_1(\sigma_k; p, y)) = rU'(X_2(\sigma_k; p, y)) \tag{4.16}$$

and

$$\sigma_k X_1(\sigma_k; p, y) + (1-\sigma_k) p X_2(\sigma_k; p, y) = y + pr(1-y), \tag{4.17}$$

for every k.

The function $X(\sigma_k, p, y)$ is well defined and continuously differentiable for every (p, y) in a sufficiently small neighborhood of (p^*, y^*). This follows from the implicit function theorem and the regularity of the system (16)–(17) at (p^*, y^*):

$$\det \begin{bmatrix} U''(X_1(\sigma_k; p^*, y^*)) & -rU''(X_2(\sigma_k; p^*, y^*)) \\ \sigma_k & (1-\sigma_k)p^* \end{bmatrix} \neq 0.$$

The market-clearing condition can be written as

$$\sum_{k=1}^{K} \lambda_k \sigma_k X_1(\sigma_k; p, y) = y,$$

since the other market-clearing condition is automatically satisfied by Walras' law. To show the existence of a regulated equilibrium for each p sufficiently close to p^* we can use the implicit function theorem again, noting that

$$\frac{\partial}{\partial y}\left(\sum_{k=1}^{K}\lambda_k\sigma_k X_1(\sigma_k;p,y)-y\right)=\sum_{k=1}^{K}\lambda_k\sigma_k\frac{\partial X_1(\sigma_k;p^*,y^*)}{\partial y}-1$$
$$=-1,$$

because $y+p^*r(1-y)=1$ is independent of y.

We next calculate the change in expected utility caused by a small change in p at p^*:

$$\frac{d}{dp}\sum_k \lambda_k\{\sigma_k U(X_1(\sigma_k;p,y))+(1-\sigma_k)U(X_2(\sigma_k;p,y))\}$$
$$=\sum_k \lambda_k\left\{\sigma_k U'(X_1(\sigma_k;p,y))\frac{\partial X_1}{\partial p}(\sigma_k;p,y)\right.$$
$$\left.+(1-\sigma_k)U'(X_2(\sigma_k;p,y))\frac{\partial X_2}{\partial p}(\sigma_k;p,y)\right\}$$
$$=\sum_k \lambda_k U'(X_2(\sigma_k;p,y))\left\{r\sigma_k\frac{\partial X_1}{\partial p}(\sigma_k;p,y)+(1-\sigma_k)\frac{\partial X_2}{\partial p}(\sigma_k;p,y)\right\}$$
$$=\sum_k \lambda_k U'(X_2(\sigma_k;p,y))\{r(1-y)-(1-\sigma_k)X_2(\sigma_k;p,y)\}.$$

Now suppose that the degree of relative risk aversion is less than one (the other case can be dealt with in exactly the same way). Then (16) implies that

$$rx_1(\sigma_k)<x_2(\sigma_k),\quad \forall\sigma_k.$$

This in turn implies that $x_1(\sigma_k)$ and $(1-\sigma_k)x_2(\sigma_k)$ move in opposite directions. To see this, note that, within a fixed equilibrium, an increase in $(1-\sigma_k)$ must lead to a decrease in consumption at both dates (this follows directly from the fact that $x_1(\sigma_k)<x_2(\sigma_k)/r$). Then $\sigma_k x_1(\sigma_k)$ falls as $(1-\sigma_k)$ increases and so in order to satisfy the budget constraint it must be the case that $(1-\sigma_k)x_2(\sigma_k)/r$ increases. Assuming the distributions are not degenerate, it must be the case that

$$\sum_k \lambda_k U'(X_2(\sigma_k;p,y))\{r(1-y)-(1-\sigma_k)X_2(\sigma_k;p,y)\}$$
$$>\sum_k \lambda_k U'(X_2(\sigma_k;p,y))\sum_k \lambda_k\{r(1-y)-(1-\sigma_k)X_2(\sigma_k;p,y)\}$$
$$=0,$$

where the last equation follows from the market-clearing condition,

$$\sum_k \lambda_k(1-\sigma_k)X_2(\sigma_k;p,y)=r(1-y). \qquad Q.E.D.$$

References

AGHION, P., P. BACCHETTA, AND A. BANERJEE (2000): "Currency Crises and Monetary Policy in an Economy with Credit Constraints," Working Paper, University College, London.

ALLEN, F., AND D. GALE (1994): "Liquidity Preference, Market Participation and Asset Price Volatility," *American Economic Review*, 84, 933–955.

—— (1998): "Optimal Financial Crises," *Journal of Finance*, 53, 1245–1284.

—— (1999): *Comparing Financial Systems*. Cambridge: MIT Press.

—— (2000a): "Financial Contagion," *Journal of Political Economy*, 108, 1–33.

—— (2000b): "Optimal Currency Crises," *Carnegie-Rochester Conference Series on Public Policy*, 53, 177–230.

—— (2000c): "Financial Intermediaries and Markets Addendum: Prudential Regulation of Banks," http://www.nyu.edu/econ/user/galed/papers.html.

ALONSO, I. (1996): "On Avoiding Bank Runs," *Journal of Monetary Economics*, 37, 73–87.

BERNANKE, B., AND M. GERTLER (1989): "Agency Costs, Net Worth, and Business Fluctuations," *American Economic Review*, 79, 14–31.

BHATTACHARYA, S., AND D. GALE (1987): "Preference Shocks, Liquidity and Central Bank Policy," in *New Approaches to Monetary Economics*, ed. by W. Barnett and K. Singleton. New York: Cambridge University Press.

BHATTACHARYA, S., AND A. THAKOR (1993): "Contemporary Banking Theory," *Journal of Financial Intermediation*, 3, 2–50.

BISIN, A., AND P. GOTTARDI (2000): "Decentralizing Incentive-Compatible Allocations in Adverse Selection Economies," Working Paper, New York University.

BRYANT, J. (1980): "A Model of Reserves, Bank Runs, and Deposit Insurance," *Journal of Banking and Finance*, 4, 335–344.

CALVO, G. (1988): "Servicing the Public Debt: The Role of Expectations," *American Economic Review*, 78, 1411–1428.

CHAMP, B., B. SMITH, AND S. WILLIAMSON (1996): "Currency Elasticity and Banking Panics: Theory and Evidence," *Canadian Journal of Economics*, 29, 828–864.

CHANG, R., AND A. VELASCO (2000): "Financial Fragility and the Exchange Rate Regime," *Journal of Economic Theory*, 92, 1–34.

—— (2001): "A Model of Financial Crises in Emerging Markets," *Quarterly Journal of Economics*, 116, 489–517.

CHARI, V. (1989): "Banking Without Deposit Insurance or Bank Panics: Lessons from a Model of the U.S. National Banking System," *Federal Reserve Bank of Minneapolis Quarterly Review*, 13 (Summer), 3–19.

CHARI, V., AND R. JAGANNATHAN (1988): "Banking Panics, Information, and Rational Expectations Equilibrium," *Journal of Finance*, 43, 749–760.

CHARI, V., AND P. KEHOE (2000): "Financial Crises as Herds," Working Paper, Federal Reserve Bank of Minneapolis.

COLE, H., AND T. KEHOE (2000): "Self-Fulfilling Debt Crises," *Review of Economic Studies*, 67, 91–116.

CONE, K. (1983): "Regulation of Depository Institutions," Stanford University Ph.D. dissertation.

CORSETTI, G., P. PESENTI, AND N. ROUBINI (1999): "Paper Tigers? A Model of the Asian Crisis," *European Economic Review*, 43, 1211–1236.

DIAMOND, D. (1997): "Liquidity, Banks and Markets," *Journal of Political Economy*, 105, 928–956.

DIAMOND, D., AND P. DYBVIG (1983): "Bank Runs, Liquidity, and Deposit Insurance," *Journal of Political Economy*, 91, 401–419.

DIAMOND, D., AND R. RAJAN (2001): "Liquidity Risk, Liquidity Creation and Financial Fragility: A Theory of Banking," *Journal of Political Economy*, 109, 287–327.

FLOOD, R., AND N. MARION (1999): "Perspectives on Recent Currency Crises Literature," *International Journal of Finance and Economics*, 4, 1–26.

GEANAKOPLOS, J., AND H. POLEMARCHAKIS (1986): "Existence, Regularity, and Constrained Suboptimality of Competitive Allocations when the Asset Market Is Incomplete," in *Essays in Honor of Kenneth J. Arrow: Volume 3, Uncertainty, Information, and Communication*, ed. by W. Heller, R. Starr, and D. Starrett. Cambridge, New York and Sydney: Cambridge University Press, 65–95. Also reprinted in *General Equilibrium Theory*, Vol. 2, Elgar Reference Collection,

International Library of Critical Writings in Economics, No. 67, ed. by G. Debreu. Cheltenham, U.K.: Elgar, 1996, 67–97; distributed by Ashgate, Brookfield, Vt.

GROMB, D., AND D. VAYANOS (2001): "Equilibrium and Welfare in Markets with Financially Constrained Abitrageurs," Working Paper, MIT Sloan School of Management.

GROSSMAN, S., AND O. HART (1983): "An Analysis of the Principal-Agent Problem," *Econometrica*, 51, 7–45.

HELLWIG, M. (1994): "Liquidity Provision, Banking, and the Allocation of Interest Rate Risk," *European Economic Review*, 38, 1363–1389.

—— (1998): "Banks, Markets, and the Allocation of Risks in an Economy," *Journal of Institutional and Theoretical Economics*, 154, 328–345.

JACKLIN, C. (1986): "Demand Deposits, Trading Restrictions, and Risk Sharing," in *Contractual Arrangements for Intertemporal Trade*, ed. by E. Prescott and N. Wallace. Minneapolis, MN: University of Minnesota Press.

JACKLIN, C., AND S. BHATTACHARYA (1988): "Distinguishing Panics and Information-Based Bank Runs: Welfare and Policy Implications," *Journal of Political Economy*, 96, 568–592.

KRUGMAN, P. (1979): "A Model of Balance-of-Payments Crises," *Journal of Money Credit and Banking*, 11, 311–325.

MARTIN, A. (2000): "Liquidity Provision vs. Deposit Insurance: Preventing Bank Panics Without Moral Hazard," Working Paper, Federal Reserve Bank of Minneapolis.

MATUTES, C., AND X. VIVES (1996): "Competition for Deposits, Fragility, and Insurance," *Journal of Financial Intermediation*, 5, 184–216.

—— (2000): "Imperfect Competition, Risk Taking, and Regulation in Banking," *European Economic Review*, 44, 1–34.

MORRIS, S. (2000): "Contagion," *Review of Economic Studies*, 67, 57–78.

MORRIS, S., AND H. S. SHIN (1998): "Unique Equilibrium in a Model of Self-Fulfilling Currency Attacks," *American Economic Review*, 88, 587–597.

—— (2000): "Global Games: Theory and Applications," Working Paper, Yale University.

OBSTFELD, M. (1986): "Rational and Self-Fulfilling Balance of Payments Crises," *American Economic Review*, 76, 72–81.

PECK, J., AND K. SHELL (1999): "Bank Portfolio Restrictions and Equilibrium Bank Runs," Working Paper, Cornell University.

POSTLEWAITE, A., AND X. VIVES (1987): "Bank Runs as an Equilibrium Phenomenon," *Journal of Political Economy*, 95, 485–491.

PRESCOTT, E., AND R. TOWNSEND (1984a): "Pareto Optima and Competitive Equilibria with Adverse Selection and Moral Hazard, *Econometrica*, 52, 21–45.

—— (1984b): "General Competitive Analysis in an Economy with Private Information," *International Economic Review*, 25, 1–20.

VON THADDEN, E.-L. (1999): "Liquidity Creation through Banks and Markets: Multiple Insurance and Limited Market Access," *European Economic Review*, 43, 991–1006.

WALLACE, N. (1988): "Another Attempt to Explain an Illiquid Banking System: The Diamond and Dybvig Model with Sequential Service Taken Seriously," *Federal Reserve Bank of Minneapolis Quarterly Review*, 12 (Fall), 3–16.

—— (1990): "A Banking Model in Which Partial Suspension Is Best," *Federal Reserve Bank of Minneapolis Quarterly Review*, 14(Fall), 11–23.

ZAME, W. (1993): "Efficiency and the Role of Default when Security Markets are Incomplete," *American Economic Review*, 83, 1142–1164.

5 Financial Fragility, Liquidity, and Asset Prices

Franklin Allen and Douglas Gale

1. Excess Sensitivity and Sunspots

There are numerous historical examples of financial fragility, where shocks that are small in relation to the economy as a whole have a significant impact on the financial system. For example, Kindleberger (1978, pp. 107–108) argues that the immediate cause of a financial crisis

> may be trivial, a bankruptcy, a suicide, a flight, a revelation, a refusal of credit to some borrower, some change of view which leads a significant actor to unload. Prices fall. Expectations are reversed. The movement picks up speed. To the extent that speculators are leveraged with borrowed money, the decline in prices leads to further calls on them for margin or cash, and to further liquidation. As prices fall further, bank loans turn sour, and one or more mercantile houses, banks, discount houses, or brokerages fail. The credit system itself appears shaky and the race for liquidity is on.

Schnabel and Shin (2004) document one such example, the financial crisis of 1763. They argue that the bankruptcy of the de Neufville brothers' banking house forced them to sell their stocks of commodities. In the short run, the liquidity of the market was limited and the commodity sales resulted in lower prices. The fall in prices, in turn, put other intermediaries under strain and forced them to sell. A collapse in commodity prices and a financial crisis followed. Schnabel and Shin draw a parallel between the 1763 crisis and the Long Term Capital Management (LTCM) episode in 1998. They suggest that, without the rescue coordinated by the Federal Reserve Bank of New York, there might have been a collapse in asset prices and a widespread financial crisis.

In this paper, we use the term crisis to mean a profound drop in the value of asset prices that affects the solvency of a large number of banks and their ability to meet their commitments to depositors. If the price movement is large enough, some banks are forced into liquidation; but there may also be crises in which banks avoid default, although their balance sheet is under extreme pressure. It is well known that sufficiently large exogenous shocks can cause a crisis. For example, Allen and Gale (1998) describe a model in which financial crises are caused by exogenous asset-return shocks. Following a large (negative) shock to asset returns, banks are unable to meet their commitments and are forced to default and liquidate assets. In the current paper we investigate endogenous crises, where small or negligible shocks set off self-reinforcing and self-amplifying price changes. We use a simple version of the general equilibrium model introduced in Allen and Gale (2004; henceforth AG). The key element of the model is the role of liquidity in determining asset prices. The supply of liquidity is determined by the banks' initial portfolio choices. Subsequently, small shocks to the demand for liquidity, interacting with the fixed supply, cause a collapse in asset prices.

We model liquidity preference in the standard way by assuming that consumers have stochastic time preferences. There are three dates, $t = 0, 1, 2$; contracts are drawn up at Date 0, and all consumption occurs at Dates 1 and 2. There are two types of consumers: early consumers, who only value consumption at Date 1; and late consumers, who only value consumption at Date 2. Consumers are identical at Date 0 and learn their true type, early or late, at the beginning of Date 1.

There are two types of investments in this economy: short-term investments, which yield a return after one period; and long-term investments, which take two periods to mature. There is a trade-off between liquidity and returns: long-term investments have higher returns but take longer to mature (are less liquid). By contrast, there is no risk-return trade-off: We assume that asset returns are nonstochastic in order to emphasize that, in the present model, financial crises are not driven by shocks to asset returns. For an example of a more general model of financial crises, including a risk-return trade-off, see AG.

Banks are modeled as risk-sharing institutions that pool consumers' endowments and invest them in a portfolio of long- and short-term investments. In exchange for their endowments, banks give consumers a deposit contract, which is an option to receive either a fixed amount of consumption at Date 1 or a fixed amount of consumption at Date 2. The deposit contract provides consumers with insurance against liquidity shocks by intertemporally smoothing the returns paid on deposits. There is free entry into the banking sector: In a competitive equilibrium, banks must maximize the expected utility of depositors to attract customers.

Once the supply of liquidity is fixed by the banks' portfolio decisions, shocks to the demand for liquidity can cause substantial asset-price volatility and/or default. The supply of liquidity is fixed in the short run by the banks' portfolio decisions at Date 0. In the absence of default, the demand for liquidity is perfectly inelastic in the short run. If the banks' supply of liquidity is sufficient to meet the depositors' demand when liquidity preference is high, there must be an excess supply of liquidity when liquidity preference is low. The banks will be willing to hold this excess liquidity between Dates 1 and 2 only if the interest rate is zero (the price of Date-2 consumption in terms of Date-1 consumption is 1). A low interest rate implies that asset prices are correspondingly high. However, asset prices cannot be high in all states for then the short asset would be dominated at Date 0 and no one would be willing to hold it. So, in the absence of default, there will be substantial price volatility. Note that this argument does not require large shocks to liquidity demand.

We define a financial system to be *fragile* if a small aggregate shock in the demand for liquidity leads to disproportionately large effects in terms of default or asset-price volatility. One test for financial fragility is to allow the shocks to become vanishingly small and see whether the effects disappear in the limit. If they do not, we can say that the system is fragile because the shocks are infinitesimal relative to the consequences. As we have argued so far, there must be either substantial asset-price volatility or default (or both), regardless of the size of the shocks. In fact, we can show that we must have positive asset-price volatility even in the case of default. Further, we can show that this volatility is bounded away from zero as the variance of the shocks becomes vanishingly small. In the limit, the volatility of asset prices is disproportionately large relative to the shocks—that is, the financial system is fragile.

In the limit, when the shocks become vanishingly small, there is no aggregate exogenous uncertainty, but this does not mean that there is no endogenous uncertainty. We distinguish two kinds of uncertainty. Intrinsic uncertainty is caused by stochastic fluctuations in the primitives or fundamentals of the economy. Examples would be exogenous shocks that effect liquidity preferences or asset returns. Extrinsic uncertainty by definition has no effect on the fundamentals of the economy. An equilibrium with no extrinsic uncertainty is called a fundamental equilibrium, because the endogenous variables are functions of the exogenous primitives or fundamentals of the model (endowments, preferences, technologies). An equilibrium with extrinsic uncertainty is called a sunspot equilibrium,[1] because endogenous variables may be influenced by extraneous variables (sunspots) that have no direct impact on fundamentals. A crisis cannot occur in a fundamental equilibrium in the absence of exogenous shocks to fundamentals, such as asset returns or liquidity demands. In a sunspot equilibrium, by contrast, asset prices fluctuate in the absence of aggregate exogenous shocks, and crises appear to occur spontaneously.

There are multiple equilibria in the limit economy with no aggregate exogenous uncertainty. Some of these equilibria are characterized by financial crises and some are not. Which type of equilibrium is most likely to be observed? To test the robustness of a given equilibrium in the limit economy, we perturb the economy by introducing a small amount of aggregate uncertainty and ask whether there exists an equilibrium of the perturbed economy that is close to the given equilibrium. If the answer is yes, then we describe the equilibrium as robust. Equivalently, we say that an equilibrium is robust if it is the limit of a sequence of equilibria, corresponding to a sequence of perturbed economies, as the shocks become vanishingly small. We already know which equilibria are robust in this sense. We have seen that any equilibrium of the perturbed economy is characterized by asset-price volatility that is bounded away from zero as the aggregate liquidity shocks converge to zero. Thus, a robust equilibrium of the limit economy must have extrinsic uncertainty. Conversely, the fundamental equilibrium of the limit economy is not robust.[2]

These results help us understand the relationship between two traditional views of financial crises. One view is that they are spontaneous events, unrelated to changes in the real economy. Historically, banking panics were attributed to "mob psychology" or "mass hysteria" (see e.g., Kindleberger 1978). The modern version of this theory explains banking panics as equilibrium coordination failures (Bryant 1980; Diamond and Dybvig 1983). An alternative view is that financial crises are a natural outgrowth of the business cycle (Gorton 1988; Calomiris and Gorton 1991; Calomiris and Mason 2000; Allen and Gale 1998, 2000a, 2000b, 2000c, 2004). Our model combines the most attractive features of both traditional approaches. Like the sunspot approach, it produces large effects from

[1]The theoretical analysis of sunspot equilibria began with the seminal work of Azariadis (1981) and Cass and Shell (1983), which gave rise to two streams of literature. The Cass and Shell paper is most closely related to work in a Walrasian, general equilibrium framework; the Azariadis paper is most closely related to the macroeconomic dynamics literature. For a useful survey of applications in macroeconomics, see Farmer (1999); for an example of the current literature in the general equilibrium framework, see Gottardi and Kajii (1995, 1999).

[2]The limit economy has two types of equilibria with extrinsic uncertainty. In a trivial sunspot equilibrium, prices are random but the allocation is essentially the same as in the fundamental equilibrium and no banks default. In a nontrivial sunspot equilibrium, the prices and the equilibrium allocation are random.

small shocks.[3] Like the real business cycle approach, it makes a firm prediction about the conditions under which crises will occur.[4]

There are important differences between the present model of systemic or economy wide crises and models of individual bank runs or panics (Bryant 1980; Diamond and Dybvig 1983). In our model a crisis is a systemic event. It occurs only if the number of defaulting banks is large enough to affect the equilibrium asset price. In the panic model, by contrast, bank runs are an idiosyncratic phenomenon. Whether a run occurs at a particular bank depends on the decisions taken by the bank's depositors, independently of what happens at other banks. It is only by coincidence that runs are experienced by several banks at the same time.

Another difference between panics and crises concerns the reasons for the default. In the Bryant–Diamond–Dybvig story, bank runs are spontaneous events that depend on the decisions of late consumers to withdraw early. Given that almost all agents withdraw at Date 1, early withdrawal is a best response for every agent; but if late consumers were to withdraw at Date 2, then late withdrawal is a best response for every late consumer. So there are two "equilibria" of the coordination game played by agents at Date 1, one with a bank run and one without. This kind of coordination failure plays no role in the present model. In fact, coordination failure is explicitly ruled out: a bank run occurs only if the bank cannot simultaneously satisfy its budget constraint and its incentive constraint.[5] From the point of view of a single, price-taking bank, default results from an exogenous shock. When bankruptcy does occur, it is the result of low asset prices. Asset prices are endogenous, of course, and there is a "self-fulfilling" element in the relationship between asset prices and crises. Banks are forced to default and liquidate assets because asset prices are low, and asset prices are low as a result of mass bankruptcy and the associated liquidation of bank assets.

An interesting feature of the model is the role of mixed equilibria, in which ex ante identical banks must choose different strategies. For some parameter specifications, we can show that one group of banks will follow a risky strategy by investing almost all of their funds in the long asset. They meet their demands for liquidity by selling the asset in the market. Another group of banks follow a safe strategy and hold a large amount of the short asset. The safe banks provide liquidity to the risky banks by purchasing the risky banks' long-term assets. Safe banks also provide liquidity to each other: because there are idiosyncratic shocks to liquidity demand, the safe banks with a high demand for liquidity sell long-term assets to those with a low demand.

Our work is related to the wider literature on general equilibrium with incomplete markets (GEI). As is well known, sunspots do not matter when markets are complete (for a precise statement, see Shell and Goenka 1997). The incompleteness in our model reveals itself in two ways. First, sunspots are assumed to be noncontractible—that is, the

[3]Strictly speaking, much of the banking literature exploits multiple equilibria without addressing the issue of sunspots. We adopt the sunspots framework here because it encompasses the standard notion of equilibrium and allows us to address the issue of equilibrium selection.

[4]Models of sunspot phenomena typically have many equilibria, including as a special case the fundamental equilibria in which extrinsic uncertainly has no effect on endogenous variables. Thus, financial fragility remains a possibility but not a necessity.

[5]This is a refinement of the equilibrium concept. We assume that late consumers withdraw at the last date whenever it is incentive-compatible for them to do so. Bank runs occur only when it is impossible for the bank to meet its obligations in an incentive-compatible way. Such runs are called "essential" in AG to distinguish them from the coordination failures in Diamond and Dybvig (1983).

deposit contract is not explicitly contingent on the sunspot variable. In this respect we are simply following the incomplete contracts literature (see e.g., Hart 1995). Second, there are no markets for Arrow securities contingent on the sunspot variable, so financial institutions cannot insure themselves against asset-price fluctuations associated with the sunspot variable. This is the standard assumption of the GEI literature (see, e.g., Geanakoplos 1990 or Magill and Quinzii 1996).

There is a small but growing literature related to financial fragility. Financial multipliers were introduced by Bernanke and Gertler (1989). In the model of Kiyotaki and Moore (1997), the impact of illiquidity at one link in the credit chain has a large impact further down the chain. Chari and Kehoe (2000) show that herding behavior can cause a small information shock to have a large effect on capital flows. Lagunoff and Schreft (2001) show how overlapping claims on firms can cause small shocks to lead to widespread bankruptcy. Bernardo and Welch (2004) develop a model of runs on financial markets and asset-price collapses based on the anticipation of liquidity needs.

Postlewaite, Mailath, and Samuelson (2003) study a model in which transactions in a competitive market are preceded by fixed investments. They show that, in the absence of forward contracts, equilibrium spot prices are highly volatile even when the degree of uncertainty is very small.

In AG, the authors provide a more general model of which the present model is a very special case. The focus of that paper is on the welfare properties of equilibrium rather than financial fragility. For example, it is shown that, with complete markets for aggregate risks, the laissez-faire equilibrium is either incentive-efficient or constrained-efficient—depending on whether intermediaries can use general incentive-compatible contracts or incomplete contracts. By contrast, if markets are incomplete, then there may be too much or too little liquidity, and government regulation may be welfare-improving. There is no discussion of the sensitivity of equilibrium to small shocks, which is the central point of the present paper.

The rest of this paper is organized as follows. Section 2 establishes the basic assumptions of the model. Section 3 describes the optimal contracts offered by banks and the rules governing default and liquidation. Section 4 defines equilibrium. A special case of the model and a numerical example are considered in Section 5. Section 6 contains a full analysis of the equilibria of the economy. We first consider the limit economy with no aggregate uncertainty and then perturb the economy by introducing aggregate uncertainty. We show that, in any equilibrium of the economy with aggregate uncertainty, crises occur with positive probability. We also show that the limit of a sequence of equilibria corresponding to a sequence of perturbed economies is an equilibrium in the limit economy, and we characterize these limit equilibria. Section 7 contains a discussion. Proofs are gathered in the Appendix.

2. Assets and Preferences

The model we use is a special case of that in AG.

2.1 Dates

There are three dates ($t = 0, 1, 2$) and a single good at each date. The good can be used for consumption or investment.

2.2 Assets

There are two assets, a short-term asset (the short asset) and a long-term asset (the long asset).

1. The short asset is represented by a storage technology. Investment in the short asset can take place at Date 1 or Date 2. One unit of the good invested at Date t yields one unit at Date $t+1$ for $t = 0, 1$.
2. The long asset takes two periods to mature and is more productive than the short asset. Investment in the long asset can take place only at Date 0. One unit invested at Date 0 produces $r > 1$ units at Date 2.

2.3 Consumers

There is a continuum of ex ante identical consumers, whose measure is normalized to unity. Each consumer has an endowment (1, 0, 0) consisting of one unit of the good at Date 0 and nothing at subsequent dates. There are two (ex post) types of consumers at Date 1: early consumers, who value consumption only at Date 1; and late consumers, who value consumption only at Date 2. If η denotes the probability of being an early consumer and c_t denotes consumption at Date $t = 1, 2$, then the consumer's ex ante utility is

$$u(c_1, c_2; \eta) = \eta U(c_1) + (1 - \eta)U(c_2).$$

The period utility function $U : \mathbb{R}_+ \to \mathbb{R}$ is twice continuously differentiable and satisfies the usual neoclassical properties: $U'(c) > 0$, $U''(c) < 0$, and $\lim_{c \searrow 0} U'(c) = \infty$.

2.4 Uncertainty

There are three sources of intrinsic uncertainty in the model. First, each individual consumer faces idiosyncratic uncertainty about her preference type (early or late consumer). Second, each bank faces idiosyncratic uncertainty about the number of early consumers among the bank's depositors. For example, different banks could be located in regions subject to independent liquidity shocks. Third, there is aggregate uncertainty about the fraction of early consumers in the economy. Aggregate uncertainty is represented by a state of nature θ, a nondegenerate random variable with finite support and density function $f(\theta)$. The bank's idiosyncratic shock is represented by a random variable α, with finite support and density function $g(\alpha)$. The probability of being an early consumer at a bank in state (α, θ) is denoted by $\eta(\alpha, \theta)$, where

$$\eta(\alpha, \theta) \equiv \alpha + \varepsilon\theta$$

and $\varepsilon \geq 0$ is a constant. We adopt the usual "law of large numbers" convention and assume that the fraction of early consumers at a bank in State (α, θ) is identically equal to the probability $\eta(\alpha, \theta)$. The economywide average of α is assumed to be constant and equal to the mean $\bar{\alpha} = \sum \alpha g(\alpha)$. Thus, there is aggregate intrinsic uncertainty only if $\varepsilon > 0$.

2.5 Information

All uncertainty is resolved at Date 1. The true value of θ is publicly observed,[6] the true value of α for each bank is publicly observed, and each consumer learns his type—that is, whether he is an early consumer or a late consumer.

2.6 Asset Markets

There are no asset markets for hedging against aggregate uncertainty at Date 0; for example, there are no Arrow securities contingent on the state of nature θ. At Date 1, there is a market in which future (Date-2) consumption can be exchanged for present (Date-1) consumption. If $p(\theta)$ denotes the price of future consumption in terms of present consumption at Date 1, then one unit of the long asset is worth $p(\theta)r$ at Date 1 in State θ.

Markets are incomplete at Date 0 but complete at Date 1. We assume that market participation is incomplete: financial institutions such as banks can participate in the asset market at Date 1, but individual consumers cannot.[7]

3. Banking

Banks are financial institutions that provide investment and liquidity services to consumers. They do this by pooling the consumers' resources, investing them in a portfolio of short- and long-term assets, and offering consumers future consumption streams with a better combination of asset returns and liquidity than individual consumers could achieve by themselves. Banks also have access to the interbank capital market, where they can buy or sell the long asset at Date 1 and from which consumers are excluded.

As noted in AG, one could imagine a world in which a single "universal" intermediary offering contingent contracts could act as a central planner and implement the first-best allocation of risk. There would be no reason to resort to markets at all. Our worldview is based on the assumption that transaction costs preclude this kind of centralized solution and that decentralized intermediaries are restricted in the number of different contracts they can offer. Here we further assume that intermediaries are restricted to offering deposit contracts.

Banks compete by offering deposit contracts to consumers in exchange for their endowments, and consumers respond by choosing the most attractive of the contracts offered. Free entry ensures that banks earn zero profits in equilibrium. The deposit contracts offered in equilibrium must maximize consumers' welfare subject to the zero-profit constraint. Otherwise, a bank could enter and make a positive profit by offering a more attractive contract.

Anything a consumer can do, the bank can do. So there is no loss of generality in assuming that consumers deposit their entire endowment in a bank at Date 0.[8] Consumers cannot

[6] It is not strictly necessary to assume that θ is observed. In equilibrium, all that, agents need to know is the equilibrium price $p(\theta)$, which may or may not reveal θ.

[7] As Cone (1983) and Jacklin (1986) showed, if consumers have access to the capital market then it is impossible for banks to offer risk-sharing that is superior to the market.

[8] This is not simply an application of the Modigliani–Miller theorem. The consumer may do strictly better by putting all his "eggs" in the bank's "basket." Suppose that the deposit contract allows the individual to hold m units in the short asset and deposit $1 - m$ units in the bank. The bank invests y in the short asset and $1 - m - y$

diversify by spreading their money across more than one bank.[9] The bank invests y units per capita in the short asset and $1 - y$ units per capita in the long asset and offers each consumer a deposit contract, which allows the consumer to withdraw either d_1 units at Date 1 or d_2 units at Date 2. Without loss of generality, we set $d_2 = \infty$. This ensures that consumers receive the residue of the bank's assets at Date 2. Then the deposit contract is characterized by the middle-period payment $d_1 \equiv d$.

If $p(\theta)$ denotes the price of future consumption at Date 1 in state θ, then the value of the bank's assets at Date 1 is $y + p(\theta)r(1 - y)$.

A consumer's type is private information. An early consumer cannot misrepresent his type because he needs to consume at Date 1; but a late consumer can claim to be an early consumer, withdraw d at Date 1, store it until Date 2, and then consume it. The deposit contract is incentive-compatible if and only if the residual payment to late consumers at Date 2 is at least d. Because the late consumers are residual claimants at Date 2, it is possible to give them at least d units of consumption if and only if

$$\eta(\alpha, \theta)d + (1 - \eta(\alpha, \theta))p(\theta)d \leq y + p(\theta)r(1 - y) \tag{5.1}$$

The left-hand side is a lower bound for the present value of consumption when early consumers are given d and late consumers are given at least d. The right-hand side is the value of the portfolio. Thus, condition (1) is necessary and sufficient for the deposit contract d to satisfy incentive compatibility and the budget constraint simultaneously. We often refer to the inequality in (1) as the incentive constraint, for short.

In what follows, we assume that bank runs occur only if they are unavoidable. In other words, late consumers will withdraw at Date 2 as long as the bank can satisfy the incentive constraint. If (1) is violated, then all consumers will want to withdraw at Date 1. In the event of bankruptcy, the bank is required to liquidate its assets in an attempt to provide the promised amount d to the consumers who withdraw at Date 1. Whatever withdrawal decisions consumers make, those who withdraw at Date 2 will receive less than those who

in the long asset. If the bank does not default at Date 1, then early consumers receive $d + m$ and late consumers receive

$$\frac{p(\theta)r(1 - m - y) + y - \eta(\theta)d}{(1 - \eta(\theta))p(\theta)} + m.$$

If the bank defaults, both early and late consumers receive

$$p(\theta)r(1 - m - y) + y + m.$$

Suppose that $m > 0$ and consider a reduction in m and an increase in y and d of the same amount. It is clear that early consumers' consumption is unchanged. So is late consumers' consumption if the bank defaults. The change in the late consumers' consumption when the bank does not default is

$$\frac{\Delta y - \eta(\theta)\Delta d}{(1 - \eta(\theta))p(\theta)} + \Delta m = \frac{-\Delta m}{p(\theta)} + \Delta m \geq 0$$

because $p(\theta) \leq 1$ and $\Delta m < 0$. Thus, it is optimal for the bank (and for the consumer) to choose $m = 0$.

[9]Note that an investor would like to diversify his holdings across intermediaries if, for example, there is a positive risk of default, so the assumption of no diversification does have bite. However, the equilibrium implications of allowing diversification are unclear because the objective function of the intermediary will change as a result of changing the composition of its customers, and so the behavior of the intermediary will also change. This remains an interesting question for future research.

withdraw at Date 1. Hence, in equilibrium, all consumers must withdraw at Date 1. Then each consumer receives the liquidated value of the portfolio $y + p(\theta)r(1 - y)$.

Let $x_t(d, y, \alpha, \theta)$ denote the consumption at Date t if the bank chooses (d, y) and the bank is in state (α, θ) at Date 1. Let $x = (x_1, x_2)$, where:

$$x_1(d, y, \alpha, \theta) = \begin{cases} d & \text{if (1) is satisfied,} \\ y + p(\theta)r(1 - y) & \text{otherwise;} \end{cases}$$

$$x_2(d, y, \alpha, \theta) = \begin{cases} \frac{y+p(\theta)r(1-y)-\eta d}{(1-\eta)p(\theta)} & \text{if (1) is satisfied;} \\ y + p(\theta)r(1 - y) & \text{otherwise.} \end{cases}$$

Here $\eta = \eta(\alpha, \theta)$. Using this notation, the bank's decision problem can be written as

$$\begin{aligned} \max \quad & E\left[u(x(d, y, \alpha, \theta), \eta(\alpha, \theta))\right] \\ \text{subject to.} \quad & 0 \leq d, 0 \leq y \leq 1 \end{aligned} \qquad \text{(DP1)}$$

An ordered pair (d, y) is *optimal* for the given price function $p(\bullet)$ if it solves (DP1).

4. Equilibrium

The bank's decision problem is nonconvex. To ensure the existence of equilibrium, we take advantage of the convexifying effect of large numbers and allow for the possibility that ex ante identical banks will choose different deposit contracts d and portfolios y. Each consumer is assumed to deal with a single bank, and each bank offers a single contract. In equilibrium, consumers will be indifferent between banks offering different contracts. Consumers allocate themselves to different banks in proportions consistent with equilibrium.

To describe an equilibrium, we need some additional notation. A partition of consumers at date 0 is defined by an integer $m < \infty$ and an array $\rho = (\rho_1, \ldots, \rho_m)$ of numbers $\rho_i \geq 0$ such that $\sum_{i=1}^{m} \rho_i = 1$. Consumers are divided into m groups, and each group i contains a measure ρ_i of consumers. We impose an arbitrary bound m on the number of groups to rule out pathological cases.[10] The banks associated with group i offer a deposit contract d_i and a portfolio y_i, both expressed in per-capita terms. An allocation consists of a partition (m, ρ) and an array $\{(d, y) = \{(d_i, y_i)\}_{i=1}^{m}$ such that $d_i \geq 0$ and $0 \leq y_i \leq 1$ for $i = 1, \ldots, m$.

To define the market-clearing conditions we need some additional notation. Let $\bar{x}(d_i, y_i, \alpha, \theta) = (\bar{x}_1(d_i, y_i, \alpha, \theta), \bar{x}_2(d_i, y_i, \alpha, \theta))$ denote the bank's demand for goods. If the bank is solvent then a fraction $\eta(\alpha, \theta)$ of consumers are paid $x_1(d_i, y_i, \alpha, \theta)$ at Date 1 and a fraction $(1 - \eta(d_i, y_i, \alpha, \theta))$ are paid $x_2(d_i, y_i, \alpha, \theta))$ at Date 2. Then the bank's total demand for goods is given by

$$\bar{x}(d_i, y_i, \alpha, \theta) = (\eta(\alpha, \theta)x_1(d_i, y_i, \alpha, \theta), (1 - \eta(d_i, y_i, \alpha, \theta))x_2(d_i, y_i, \alpha, \theta)).$$

[10] In general, two groups are sufficient for existence of equilibrium.

If the bank is bankrupt, on the other hand, then everyone gets paid $x_1(d_i, y_i, \alpha, \theta) = x_2(d_i, y_i, \alpha, \theta)$ at Date 1 and the bank's total demand for goods is

$$\bar{x}(d_i, y_i, \alpha, \theta) = (x_1(d_i, y_i, \alpha, \theta), 0).$$

An allocation (m, ρ, d, y) is attainable if it satisfies the market-clearing conditions

$$\sum_i \rho_i E[\bar{x}_1(d_i, y_i, \alpha, \theta)] \leq \sum_i \rho_i y_i \tag{5.2}$$

and

$$\sum_i \rho_i \{E[\bar{x}_1(d_i, y_i, \alpha, \theta) + \bar{x}_2(d_i, y_i, \alpha, \theta)]\} = \sum_i \rho_i \{y_i + r(1 - y_i)\}$$

for any State θ. In the market-clearing conditions, we take expectations with respect to α because the cross-sectional distribution of idiosyncratic shocks is assumed to be the same as the probability distribution. The first inequality says that the total demand for consumption at Date 1 is less than or equal to the supply of the short asset. The inequality may be strict, because an excess supply of liquidity can be reinvested in the short asset and consumed at Date 2. The second condition states that total consumption at Date 2 is equal to the return from the investment in the long asset plus the amount invested in the short asset at Date 1, which is the difference between the left- and right-hand sides of (2).

In equilibrium, it must be the case that $p(\theta) \leq 1$. Otherwise banks could make an arbitrage profit at Date 1 by selling goods forward and investing the proceeds in the short asset. If $p(\theta) < 1$, then no one is willing to invest in the short asset at Date 1 and so (2) must hold as an equation. A price function $p(\cdot)$ is admissible (for the given allocation) if it satisfies the following complementary slackness condition:

For any State θ, $p(\theta) < 1$ and $p(\theta) \leq 1$ imply that (2) holds as an equation.

Now we are ready to define an equilibrium.

An equilibrium consists of an attainable allocation (m, ρ, d, y) and an admissible price function $p(\cdot)$ such that, for every group $i = 1, \ldots, m$, (d_i, y_i) is optimal given the price function $p(\cdot)$.

5. A First Look at Equilibrium

In this section we use a simple parametric example to illustrate the properties of the model. We will see that relatively small shocks to liquidity demand have substantial effects on asset-price volatility and the possibility of default. Asset-price volatility and bank defaults have real effects on the equilibrium allocations and the welfare of individuals. Furthermore, these real effects remain substantial even as the liquidity shocks that cause them become vanishing small. This is a clear example of financial fragility, defined as excess sensitivity to small shocks (and, in the limit, to no shocks at all).

Recall that the fraction of early consumers in any bank is $\eta(\alpha, \theta) = \alpha + \varepsilon\theta$, where α is an idiosyncratic (bank-specific) shock and θ is an aggregate shock. For simplicity, we assume that the random variables α and θ have two-point supports. That is:

$$\alpha = \begin{cases} \alpha_H & \text{with prob. } 0.5, \\ \alpha_L & \text{with prob. } 0.5, \end{cases}$$

where $0 < \alpha_L < \alpha_H < 1$; and

$$\theta = \begin{cases} 0 & \text{with prob. } \pi, \\ 1 & \text{with prob. } (1-\pi), \end{cases}$$

where $0 < \pi < 1$. Because there are only two values of θ, the price of future consumption at Date 1 takes at most two values, $p(0)$ and $p(1)$.

5.1 Safe Banks

Suppose that a bank chooses a deposit contract d and a portfolio y such that it never has to default in equilibrium. Then, in each State θ, the early consumers will receive the promised payment $c_1(\alpha,\theta) = d$ at Date 1 and the late consumers will receive the residue of the bank's portfolio at Date 2. The budget constraint implies that the consumption of the late consumers is

$$c_2(\alpha,\theta) = \frac{y + p(\theta)r(1-y) - \eta(\alpha,\theta)d}{p(\theta)(1-\eta(\alpha,\theta))}.$$

By assumption, the incentive constraint $c_2(\alpha,\theta) \geq d$ is satisfied in every State (α,θ). Thus, the bank's decision problem is to choose the ordered pair (d, y) so as to

$$\begin{array}{rl} \max & E[\eta U(d) + (1-\eta)U(c_2(\alpha,\theta))] \\ \text{subject to} & c_2(\alpha,\theta) \geq d\forall(\alpha,\theta). \end{array}$$

In the sequel, we call a bank that never defaults a safe bank and denote the safe strategy it chooses by (d_S, y_S).

5.2 Equilibrium Without Default

One of our objectives is to show that even a small amount of aggregate uncertainty, as represented by a small but positive value of ε_g can have large effects on equilibrium values. Specifically, it can cause either high volatility of asset prices or a nonnegligible probability of default (or both). We begin by assuming that there is no default in equilibrium and show that this implies a high volatility of asset prices.

Examining the decision problem of the safe bank (just described), it is clear that this is a convex programming problem. Since the utility functions are strictly concave, the decision problem has a unique solution and so there is no loss of generality in assuming that all banks choose the same contract (d_S, y_S).

Since α represents purely idiosyncratic risk, the fraction of early consumers in the economy is $\eta(\bar{\alpha},\theta)$, where $\bar{\alpha} = (\alpha_H + \alpha_L)/2$. Then, at Date 1, the total demand for consumption is $\eta(\bar{\alpha},\theta)d$, the total supply is y, and the market-clearing condition requires that

$$\eta(\bar{\alpha},\theta)d \leq y\forall\theta,$$

with the complementary slackness condition

$$\eta(\bar{\alpha},\theta)d < 1 \Rightarrow p(\theta) = 1.$$

By definition, $\eta(\bar{\alpha}, 0) < \eta(\bar{\alpha}, 1)$, so clearly the market-clearing condition $\eta(\bar{\alpha}, 1)d \leq y$ implies that $\eta(\bar{\alpha}, 0)d < y$. Then the complementary slackness condition implies that $p(0) = 1$.

Equilibrium requires that the short asset must be held at Date 0; otherwise, there can be no consumption at Date 1. But since $p(0) = 1$, the short asset will be dominated by the long asset at Date 0 unless $p(1) < 1/r$. This shows that, in the absence of default, asset-price volatility is unavoidable in equilibrium. Furthermore, asset-price volatility is bounded away from zero for any value of $\varepsilon > 0$ however small. Thus, only a very small amount of aggregate uncertainty is needed to generate substantial price volatility.

The fact that all banks choose the same behavior is not essential to this argument. As long as there is no default, the same argument applies when there are multiple groups of banks. The essential feature of an equilibrium with no default is that demand for and supply of liquidity are both inelastic. Then a small shift in demand or supply can require a large change in the market-clearing price.

We may summarize the discussion so far as follows.

Default or Volatility. In equilibrium with $\varepsilon > 0$, there must be either default or substantial asset-price volatility (or both).

5.3 Risky Banks

Avoiding default is costly. To satisfy the incentive constraint $c_2(\alpha, \theta) \geq d$ means either choosing a small value of d, which distorts the intertemporal consumption stream, or choosing a high value of y, which means foregoing the higher returns on the long-term asset. If the costs of avoiding default are too great, it will be optimal for the bank to choose a policy (d, y) that results in default with positive probability. So in practice, there may also be some banks that choose to default.

A bank defaults only if it violates the incentive constraint $c_2(\alpha, \theta) \geq d$ in some state. Since there are four possible combinations of the variables (α, θ), there are several possible states in which a bank may default. We must consider all the possible combinations of default states in order to figure out which is the optimal contract for the bank. For the sake of illustration, suppose that (a) the dominant factor in the bank's decision is the variation in asset prices and (b) a bank finds it optimal to default if and only if $\theta = 1$ regardless of the value of α. Then, if $\theta = 0$, the consumption of early consumers is d and the consumption of late consumers is $c_2(\alpha, 0)$. If $\theta = 1$, then the bank defaults and everyone receives the liquidated value of the bank's portfolio $w(1) = y + p(1)r(1 - y)$. Thus, the decision problem of a bank anticipating default when $\theta = 1$ is to maximize

$$\pi E[\alpha U(d) + (1 - \alpha)U(c_2(\alpha, 0))] + (1 - \pi)U(y + p(1)r(1 - y)),$$

subject to the incentive constraint

$$c_2(\alpha, 0) \geq d, \quad \alpha = \alpha_H, \alpha_L.$$

We call this bank a "risky bank" and denote the risky strategy by (d_R, y_R).

5.4 Equilibrium with Default

Given the assumption that the risky banks default in State $\theta = 1$ regardless of the value of α, there must be some banks that choose the safe strategy in equilibrium. Otherwise, all the banks in the economy will default when $\theta = 1$ and all will have to liquidate their assets. There will be no solvent banks left to purchase assets and the asset price $p(1)$ will fall to zero. Clearly, this cannot be an equilibrium because, anticipating the price $p(1) = 0$, the banks would find it more profitable at Date 0 to choose the safe strategy and make an unboundedly large arbitrage profit at Date 1. So, under our assumption that all risky banks default in State $\theta = 1$, any equilibrium with default is of necessity a *mixed* equilibrium—that is, one with positive proportions of safe and risky banks.

To illustrate the possibility of a mixed equilibrium with two types of banks, one safe and the other risky, we consider a numerical example with the following parameters:

$$U(c) = \log_e c, \quad \varepsilon = 0.1, \quad \pi = 0.65, \quad (\alpha_H, \alpha_L) = (0.85, 0.75), \quad r = 1.5.$$

The equilibrium values are listed in Table 5.1.

Depositors must be indifferent between the safe and the risky bank in equilibrium. The first column of Table 1 shows that the two types of banks yield the same expected utility, as required. The second column shows that the safe bank holds a large amount of liquidity in the form of the short asset, whereas the risky bank goes to the other extreme and holds no liquidity at all.

The safe bank gives early consumers the same consumption d_S in all states; late consumers face risk. When the idiosyncratic shock is low ($\alpha = \alpha_L$), the safe bank has excess liquidity and can make profits buying up the long asset at a low price in state $\theta = 0$. Hence late consumers do better when the price is low ($\theta = 1$) than when it is high ($\theta = 0$). When the idiosyncratic shock is high ($\alpha = \alpha_H$), the safe bank has insufficient liquidity and must sell the long asset to meet the demands of early consumers. So the late consumers in the safe bank do better when the price is high ($\theta = 0$) than when it is low ($\theta = 1$).

Depositors in the risky bank generally do well when the price is high ($\theta = 0$). The early consumers receive the constant amount d_R and the late consumers bear the risk of variations in α. When the price is low ($\theta = 1$), the bank defaults and all depositors receive the liquidated value of the bank's portfolio, which is low because of the fall in the asset price.

Notice that, although the price is high when $\theta = 0$, it does not equal unity—as it would if there were no default in $\theta = 1$. Default introduces some elasticity into the demand for liquidity, so the quantity of liquidity demanded can be the same in both states.

Table 5.1 Equilibrium values

$$\begin{bmatrix} E[U_S] \\ E[U_R] \end{bmatrix} \quad \begin{bmatrix} y_S \\ y_R \end{bmatrix} \quad \begin{bmatrix} (d_S, c_2^S(\alpha_L, 0), c_2^S(\alpha_H, 0)) \\ (d_S, c_2^S(\alpha_L, 1), c_2^S(\alpha_H, 1)) \\ (d_R, c_2^R(\alpha_L, 0), c_2^R(\alpha_H, 0)) \\ (w_R(1), w_R(1), (w_R(1)) \end{bmatrix} \quad \begin{bmatrix} p(0) \\ p(1) \end{bmatrix}$$

$$\begin{bmatrix} 0.077 \\ 0.077 \end{bmatrix} \quad \begin{bmatrix} 0.809 \\ 0 \end{bmatrix} \quad \begin{bmatrix} (0.995,\ 1.414,\ 1.624) \\ (0.995,\ 1.700,\ 1.366) \\ (1.360,\ 1.502,\ 1.502) \\ (0.678,\ 0.678,\ 0.678) \end{bmatrix} \quad \begin{bmatrix} 0.940 \\ 0.430 \end{bmatrix}$$

5.5 Financial Fragility

So far, we have illustrated an equilibrium in which there is high asset-price volatility and a high probability of default. Is this the same thing as "financial fragility"? We think of financial fragility as meaning that small shocks can produce a large effect on the system. If it takes very large shocks to produce these effects, the financial system would be robust rather than fragile. But what is large? And what is small? The usual way to establish that small shocks have large consequences is to let ε become vanishingly small and then show that the impact of aggregate uncertainty does not disappear in the limit.

We have already shown that, in the absence of default, there must be high asset-price volatility for any value of $\varepsilon > 0$. Thus, we must have either high asset-price volatility or default (or both) when $\varepsilon > 0$. We can use this fact to demonstrate that the asset-price volatility does not disappear as $\varepsilon \to 0$. Therefore, in the limit as $\varepsilon \to 0$, the consequences of small shocks become disproportionately large and we have an example of financial fragility. The proof of this result is by contradiction. Suppose, contrary to what we want to prove, that asset-price volatility becomes vanishingly small as $\varepsilon \to 0$. By our earlier result (default or volatility), this implies that there must be default in equilibrium for arbitrarily small values of $\varepsilon \to 0$. Then we can find a subsequence of equilibria, corresponding to values of $\varepsilon \to 0$, such that (i) asset prices converge to a constant and (ii) it is optimal to choose default in each of the equilibria in the sequence. In Section 6 we show that the limit of equilibria as $\varepsilon \to 0$ is an equilibrium of the limit economy. We will also show that $p(0) = p(1) = 1/r$ if there is no volatility in the limit equilibrium. Note that, if it is optimal for a bank to choose default when $\varepsilon \to 0$, it will be optimal in the limit. However, if there is no asset-price volatility, then the only reason for defaulting is because α is too high. Comparing the utility of the safe and the risky bank, we can check that the risky bank's strategy is not optimal. This contradicts our claim that default is optimal as $\varepsilon \to 0$, and this contradiction forces us to conclude that asset-price volatility does not disappear in the limit.

The financial fragility of equilibrium as $\varepsilon \to 0$ is really the central result of this paper, but the interpretation of this result requires some care. What we have established so far is that small liquidity shocks cause a large amount of asset-price volatility. This does not necessarily imply that small liquidity shocks have a large impact on the allocation of consumption and risk and hence on expected utility. In fact, the impact of price variations on consumption and risk depends on the idiosyncratic shocks α. Examining the bank's budget constraints (above), it is clear that a change in asset prices has a wealth effect if and only if there is an imbalance between the bank's supply of liquidity y and the depositors' demand for liquidity $\eta(\alpha, \theta)d$. If α is random, then for any choice of d and y there is a positive probability that $\alpha d \neq y$ and prices have a wealth effect.

By contrast, if α is a nonstochastic constant then, in the limit as $\varepsilon \to 0$, the bank can achieve the optimal expected utility while remaining autarkic. Price changes have no effect because the bank does not have a net excess demand for liquidity at Date 1.

Another point to note about equilibrium in the limit as $\varepsilon \to 0$ is that, although it is optimal for banks to default, none of the banks chooses to do so. In other words: when α is nonstochastic, the proportion of risky banks converges to zero. This is a very special case, but it warns us against jumping to conclusions about the incidence of default in equilibrium.

The following result sums up our discussion.

Financial Fragility. Asset-price volatility is bounded away from zero in the limit as $\varepsilon \to 0$. The effect of volatility depends on the presence of idiosyncratic risk: This asset price volatility has an effect on the allocation of consumption and risk in the limit if and only if α is stochastic.

5.6 Robustness of Financial Fragility

In addition to showing that small shocks can have large consequences, we can use the analysis of the limiting behavior of equilibria to test the robustness of certain other kinds of equilibria.

In the limit economy, where $\varepsilon = 0$, there is no aggregate uncertainty and yet the endogenous variables such as prices exhibit aggregate (extrinsic) uncertainty. This is nothing but a sunspot equilibrium of the limit economy. We can therefore think of our analysis of what happens in the limit as providing some justification for sunspot equilibria. The limit economy has other kinds of equilibria, but these are not the limit of equilibria as $\varepsilon \to 0$. In other words, financial fragility is a robust phenomenon.

The presence of multiple equilibria of different types makes the analysis of what happens in the limit technically difficult. We offer a classification of these equilibria in the following section.

6. Analysis

In this section we proceed to characterize the set of equilibria of the model by considering several different cases. We begin by analyzing the equilibria of the limit economy with no aggregate uncertainty ($\varepsilon = 0$), and here we distinguish two subcases. In Section 6.2, we consider the economy in which there are no idiosyncratic or bank-specific shocks to liquidity demand. This is the case where α is nonstochastic. Then, in Section 6.3, we consider the case where banks are subject to idiosyncratic shocks to liquidity demand. This is the case where α is stochastic. The difference between these two cases is that asset-price fluctuations necessarily have real effects if and only if α is stochastic. Then we consider economies with aggregate uncertainty ($\varepsilon > 0$). Our two main results, default or volatility (Theorem 3) and financial fragility (Theorem 5), are contained in Section 6.4.

6.1 Equilibria with $\varepsilon = 0$

In this section we first characterize the equilibria of the limit economy in which $\varepsilon = 0$. There is no aggregate intrinsic uncertainty in the model, but there may still be aggregate extrinsic uncertainty (sunspots). We first classify equilibria in the limit economy according to the impact of extrinsic uncertainty. An equilibrium (m, ρ, d, y, p) in the limit economy is a fundamental equilibrium (F) if $x(d_i, y_i, \alpha, \theta)$ is constant for each i and α and if $p(0)$ is constant. In that case, the sunspot variable θ has no influence on the equilibrium values. An equilibrium (m, ρ, d, y, p) of the limit economy is a trivial sunspot equilibrium (T) if $x(d_i, y_i, \alpha, \theta)$ is constant for each i and α and if $p(\theta)$ is not constant. In this case, the sunspot variable θ has no effect on the allocation of consumption, but it does affect the equilibrium price $p(\theta)$. An equilibrium (m, ρ, d, y, p) that is neither an F nor a T is called a nontrivial sunspot equilibrium (N); that is, an N is an equilibrium in which the sunspot variable has some nontrivial impact on the allocation of consumption.

We can also classify equilibria according to the variety of choices made by different groups of banks. An equilibrium (m, ρ, d, y, p) is pure if each group of banks makes the same choice:

$$(d_i, y_i) = (d_j, y_j) \quad \forall i, j = 1, \ldots, m.$$

An equilibrium (m, ρ, d, y, p) is semipure if the consumption allocations are the same for each group of banks:

$$x(d_i, y_i, \alpha, \theta) = x(d_j, y_j, \alpha, \theta) \quad \forall i, j = 1, \ldots, m.$$

Otherwise, (m, ρ, d, y, p) is a mixed equilibrium where different types of banks provide different allocations (but the same ex ante expected utility). The role of mixed equilibria is to ensure the existence of equilibrium in the presence of nonconvexities.

6.2 Equilibrium with $\varepsilon = 0$ and Nonstochastic α

In the special case with α constant, the following theorem partitions the equilibrium set into two cases with distinctive properties.

Theorem 1: *Suppose that α is constant, and let (ρ, m, x, y, p) be an equilibrium of the limit economy in which $\varepsilon = 0$. There are two possibilities:*

(i) (ρ, m, x, y, p) is a semipure, fundamental equilibrium F *in which the probability of default is zero; or*
(ii) (ρ, m, x, y, p) is a pure, trivial sunspot equilibrium T *in which the probability of default is zero.*

Proof: See the Appendix. □

By definition, an equilibrium must be either an F, T, or N. What Theorem 1 shows is that an N does not occur, and each of the remaining cases is associated with distinctive properties in terms of symmetry and probability of default.

Because the incentive constraint is not binding in either the F or T, both achieve the first-best or Pareto-efficient allocation. No equilibrium can do better, Any bank can guarantee this level of utility by choosing $\alpha d_i = y_i$, where d_i is the deposit contract chosen in the F. For this choice of (d_i, y_i), prices have no effect on the bank's budget constraint and the depositors will receive the first-best consumption. In an N, by contrast, agents receive noisy consumption allocations. Because these agents are risk-averse, the noise in their consumption allocations is inefficient. The equilibrium condition that depositors must be indifferent between the two types of banks is violated, since an individual bank can choose an allocation with the same mean consumption and no risk.

6.3 Equilibrium with $\varepsilon = 0$ and Stochastic α

In economies with stochastic α, individual banks face idiosyncratic risk. For some choices of (d_i, y_i) a bank may be forced to default in some states. More importantly, the bank may find it optimal to choose (d_i, y_i) so that default occurs with positive probability, because the costs of avoiding default are greater than the benefits. In order to distinguish crises caused by aggregate extrinsic uncertainty from defaults caused by idiosyncratic shocks, in the sequel we assume that the parameters of the model are such that default is never optimal in the F. In that case, the bank's optimal choice of (d_i, y_i) must satisfy the incentive constraint, so the bank's optimal decision problem can be written as follows. At the equilibrium price $\bar{p} = 1/r$, the value of the bank's assets at Date 1 is $y_i + \bar{p}r(1 - y_i) = 1$, independently of the choice of y_i. In the absence of default, the budget constraint implies that the consumption at Date 2 is given by $r(1-\alpha d_i)/(1-\alpha)$. The incentive constraint requires that $r(1-\alpha d_i)/(1-\alpha) \geq d_i$. Thus, the decision problem can be written as:

$$\begin{array}{rl} \max & E[\alpha U(d_i) + (1-\alpha)U(r(l-\alpha d_i)/(l-\alpha))] \\ \text{subject to} & r(l-\alpha d_i)/(l-\alpha) \geq d_i, \forall \alpha. \end{array}$$

This is a convex programming problem that has a unique solution for d_i. As noted, y_i is indeterminate, but the equilibrium allocation must satisfy the market-clearing condition

$$\sum_i \rho_i \bar{\alpha} d_i = \sum_i \rho_i y_i,$$

where $\bar{\alpha} = E[\alpha]$. Note that there is a single pure F $(\rho, m, d, y, \bar{p})$, in which $y_i = E[\alpha d_i]$ for every $i = 1, \ldots, m$.

In the case of idiosyncratic shocks, the following theorem partitions the equilibrium set into two cases, F and N.

Theorem 2: *Let (ρ, m, d, y, p) be an equilibrium of the limit economy, in which α is stochastic and $\varepsilon = 0$. There are two possibilities:*

(i) (ρ, m, d, y, p) is a semipure, fundamental equilibrium F in which the probability of default is zero; or

(ii) (ρ, m, d, y, p) is a nontrivial sunspot equilibrium N that, is pure if the probability of default is zero.

Proof: See the Appendix. □

The fundamental equilibrium is semipure for the usual reasons, and there is no default by assumption. Unlike the case with no idiosyncratic shocks (nonstochastic α), there can be no trivial sunspot equilibrium. To see this, suppose that some bank group i with measure ρ_i chooses (d_i, y_i) and that default occurs with positive probability. Then consumption for both early and late consumers is equal to $y_i + p(\theta)r(1-y_i)$, which is independent of $p(\theta)$ only if $y_i = 1$. In that case, there is no point in choosing $d > 1$ and hence no need for default. If there is no probability of default, then the consumption of the late consumers is

$$\frac{y_i + p(\theta)r(1-y_i) - \alpha d_i}{(1-\alpha)p(\theta)}.$$

This is independent of $p(\theta)$ only if $y_i = \alpha d_i$, which cannot hold unless α is a constant. Thus, there can be no T.

The only remaining possibility is an N. If the probability of default is zero, then the bank's decision problem is a convex programming problem and the usual methods suffice to show uniqueness of the optimum choice of (d, y) under the maintained assumptions.

The properties of equilibria in the limit economy when α is stochastic are summarized in the following table.

Symmetry	Type	Default
Semipure	F	No
Pure	T	No
Mixed or pure	N	Possible

6.4 The Limit of Equilibria as $\varepsilon \searrow 0$

According to the definition of equilibrium in Section 4, prices $p(\theta)$ and consumption $x(\cdot,\theta)$ are functions of θ. When $\varepsilon = 0$, a change in θ has no effect on preferences, so any dependence of $p(\theta)$ or $x(\cdot,\theta)$ on θ represents extrinsic uncertainty. When $\varepsilon > 0$, on the other hand, a change in θ has an effect on preference, so any dependence on θ of either $p(\theta)$ or $x(\cdot,\theta)$ represents intrinsic uncertainty. Thus, an equilibrium for an economy with aggregate uncertainty, $\varepsilon > 0$, is by definition "fundamental" in the sense that endogenous variables depend only on real exogenous shocks. To avoid confusion with the fundamental equilibrium in the limit economy with $\varepsilon = 0$, we use the letter A to denote equilibria with aggregate uncertainty.

The next theorem characterizes the properties of equilibria in perturbed economies.

Theorem 3: *(Default or Volatility). Let (m, ρ, d, y, p) denote an A. Then either there is a positive probability of default or there is nontrivial price volatility; that is, $p(\theta) = 1$ with positive probability and $p(\theta) < 1/r$ with positive probability.*

Proof: See the Appendix. □

We note several other properties of equilibrium with $\varepsilon > 0$. First, there cannot be a state in which all banks are in default, for this would imply $p(\theta) = 0$, which is inconsistent with equilibrium. Hence, any equilibrium with default must be mixed. Second, as we have seen, if there is no default then there must be a positive probability that $p(\theta) = 1$. Finally, in the absence of default: For any value of $\varepsilon > 0$, the volatility of asset prices, as measured by the variance of $p(\cdot)$, is bounded away from zero. Both assets are held at date 0 in equilibrium and this requires that the high returns to the long asset, associated with $p(\theta) = 1$, must be balanced by low returns associated with $p(\theta) < 1/r$. These properties are all preserved in the limit as $\varepsilon \to 0$.

The next result shows that the limit of a sequence of equilibria is an equilibrium in the limit.

Theorem 4: *Consider a sequence of perturbed economies corresponding to $\varepsilon = 1/q$, where q is a positive integer, and let $(m^q, \rho^q, d^q, y^q, p^q)$ be the corresponding As. For some convergent subsequence $q \in Q$, let*

$$(m^0, \rho^0, d^0, y^0, p^0) = \lim_{q \in Q} (m^q, \rho^q, d^q, y^q, p^q).$$

If $d_i^0 > 0$ and $0 < y_i^0 < 1$ for $i = 1, \ldots, m^0$, then $(m^0, \rho^0, x^0, y^0, p^0)$ is an equilibrium of the limit economy.

Proof: See the Appendix. □

Theorem 4 shows that, under certain conditions, the limit of a sequence of equilibria as $\varepsilon \to 0$ is an equilibrium of the limit economy where $\varepsilon = 0$. We are also interested in the opposite question—namely, which equilibria of the limit economy in which $\varepsilon = 0$ are limits of equilibria from the perturbed economy in which $\varepsilon > 0$? This requirement of lower hemi-continuity is a test of robustness: if a small perturbation of the limit economy causes an equilibrium to disappear, we argue that the equilibrium is not robust. Since there are many equilibria of the limit economy, it is of interest to see whether any of these equilibria can be eliminated by being shown to be nonrobust.

We have shown in Theorem 3 that equilibria of the perturbed economy are characterized by default or nontrivial asset-price uncertainty. Furthermore, because the random variable θ has a finite support, the probability of these events is bounded away from zero, uniformly in ε. The fundamental equilibrium of the limit economy with $\varepsilon = 0$ has none of these properties. However, this does not by itself prove that the fundamental equilibrium is not robust. It could be the limit of a sequence of equilibria of the perturbed economy if the fraction of banks that defaults in equilibrium converges to zero as $q \to \infty$. However, if the fundamental equilibrium were the limit referred to in Theorem 4, then it must be the case that (a) default is optimal in the limit and (b) there is no price volatility in the limit. These two properties can be shown to be inconsistent. This contradiction shows that asset-price volatility is bounded away from zero in the limit as the shocks become vanishingly small. In other words, the model exhibits financial fragility. As we have seen already, this asset-price volatility has real effects if and only if there is idiosyncratic risk (iff α is stochastic).

Theorem 5: *(Financial Fragility). If $(m^0, \rho^0, x^0, y^0, p^0)$ is the equilibrium of the limit economy mentioned in Theorem 4, then $(m^0, \rho^0, x^0, y^0, p^0)$ is not an F of the limit economy. In fact, the limiting equilibrium $(m^0, \rho^0, x^0, y^0, p^0)$ will be a T if α is a constant or an N if α is a nondegenerate random variable.*

Proof: Suppose that, contrary to what we wish to prove, $(m^0, \rho^0, x^0, y^0, p^0)$ is the fundamental equilibrium. Then $p^0(\theta) = 1/r < 1$ with probability 1 and hence $p^q(\theta) < 1$ for all θ and all q sufficiently large. From Theorem 3 we know that this implies some group i defaults with positive probability for all sufficiently large q. Thus, in the limit, default must be optimal for group i and $p_i^q \to p_i^0 = 0$. However, we assumed in Section 6.3 that default is not optimal for stochastic α, and it is clear that it is not optimal with nonstochastic α because

$$U(1) < \max_{\alpha c_1 + (1-\alpha)c_2/r = 1} \{\alpha U(c_1) + (1-\alpha)U(c_2)\}.$$

This contradiction proves that $(m^0, \rho^0, x^0, y^0, p^0)$ is not an F, i.e., the F is not robust. This implies that the limiting equilibrium is either an N or a T. Which case obtains depends on the idiosyncratic shocks α.

If α is a constant, the first best can be achieved by an autarkic bank when $\varepsilon = 0$, and this implies that the equilibrium allocation must be nonstochastic in the limit, So $(m^0, \rho^0, x^0, y^0, p^0)$ is a T if α is a constant.

Consider then the case where α is a nondegenerate random variable. For each n, either asset-price volatility is bounded away from zero (uniformly in n) or default is optimal.

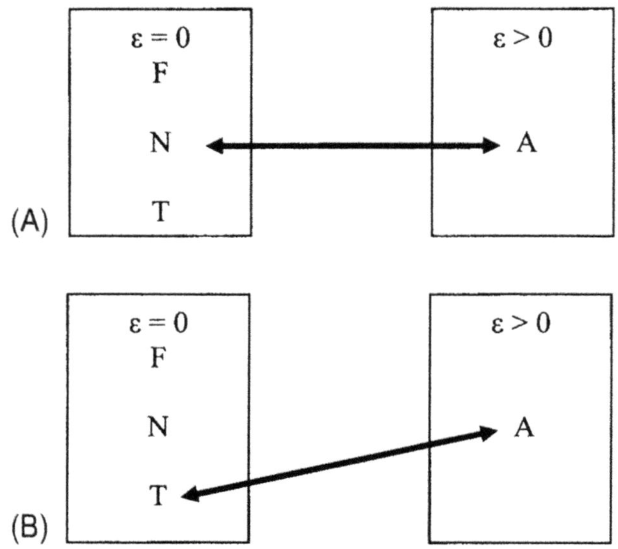

Figure 5.1. A Equilibrium correspondence; stochastic α; (B) Equilibrium correspondence; nonstochastic α.

Suppose, contrary to what we want to prove, that $(m^0, \rho^0, x^0, y^0, p^0)$ is a T. Then the limiting allocation is nonstochastic. This implies that $p^0(\theta) = 1/r$ with probability 1 and that default is optimal in the limit. But we have assumed that variations in α are not sufficient to make default optimal at this price. This contradiction implies that p^0 is not a constant. When α is random, any changes in prices have real effects so the equilibrium $(m^0, \rho^0, x^0, y^0, p^0)$ cannot be a T—that is, it must be an N. □

Thus, we have shown that F is not robust (not the limit of a sequence of equilibria of the perturbed economy) and so conversely, there must be uncertainty in any robust equilibrium. Hence this approach of regarding sunspot equilibria as a limiting case selects the sunspot equilibria as the only robust equilibria. Furthermore, the intrinsic uncertainty is nontrivial (i.e., has real effects) except in the special case where α is a constant.

Figure 5.1 illustrates these results. The key issue is whether banks face idiosyncratic liquidity risk. If they do, then α is stochastic and, as shown in Figure 5.1A, the only robust equilibria in the limit are nontrivial sunspot equilibria N, where the allocation of consumption is random. The reason for this is that prices have a volatility that is bounded away from zero and banks must trade at these prices if they face idiosyncratic liquidity risk. As a result, the extrinsic aggregate uncertainty has a real effect. In contrast, if banks do not face idiosyncratic liquidity risk so α is nonstochastic, then the banks can be autarkic and do not need to trade. In the limit, as shown in Figure 5.1B, the equilibrium is a T and has a nonrandom consumption allocation even though prices are varying.

7. Discussion

In this paper, we have defined financial fragility in terms of excess sensitivity to small shocks. We showed that small shocks can have large effects on prices and that this may lead banks to default. How small can the shocks be? This question led us to investigate the relationship between intrinsic and extrinsic uncertainty. Our general approach is to regard extrinsic uncertainty as a limiting case of intrinsic uncertainty. In our model, small shocks to the demand for liquidity are always associated with large fluctuations in asset prices. In this sense, the system is financially fragile. In the limit, as the liquidity shocks become vanishingly small, the model converges to one with extrinsic uncertainty.

The limit economy has three kinds of equilibria:

1. Fundamental equilibria F, in which there is neither aggregate uncertainty nor a positive probability of crisis;
2. Trivial sunspot equilibria T, in which prices fluctuate but the real allocation is the same as in the fundamental equilibrium; and
3. Nontrivial sunspot equilibria N, in which prices fluctuate and financial crises can occur with positive probability.

Introducing small shocks into the limit economy destabilizes the first type of equilibrium, leaving the second and third as possible limits of equilibria of the perturbed economy. If α is a constant, then the limiting equilibrium as $\varepsilon \to 0$ is a trivial sunspot equilibrium in which price fluctuations have no real effects. If α is random, the limiting equilibrium as $\varepsilon \to 0$ is a nontrivial sunspot equilibrium, in which price fluctuations have a real effect on consumption and expected utility. We argue that only the sunspot equilibria are robust, in the sense that a small perturbation of the model causes a small change in these equilibria. This selection criterion provides an argument for the relevance of extrinsic uncertainty and the necessity of financial crises.

At the heart of our theory is a pecuniary externality: When one group of banks defaults and liquidates its assets, it forces down the price of assets and this may cause another group of banks to default. This pecuniary externality may be interpreted as a form of contagion that operates through the interbank asset market. Allen and Gale (2000a) describes a model of contagion in a multiregion economy where the nature of the contagion is rather different. Bankruptcy is assumed to be costly: long-term projects can be liquidated prematurely, but a fraction of the returns are lost. This deadweight loss from liquidation creates a spillover effect in the adjacent regions where the claims on the bankrupt banks are held. If the spillover effect is large enough, the banks in the adjacent regions will also be forced into default and liquidation. Each successive wave of bankruptcies increases the loss of value and strengthens the impact of the spillover effect on the next region. Under certain conditions, a shock to one small region can propagate throughout the economy. By contrast, in the present model, a bank's assets are always marked to market. Given the equilibrium asset price p, bankruptcy does not change the value of the bank's portfolio. However, if a group of banks defaults, the resulting change in the price p may cause other banks to default, which will cause further changes in p, and so on. The "contagion" in both models is instantaneous.

Several features of the model are special and deserve further consideration. Pecuniary externalities "matter" in our model because markets are incomplete: if banks could trade Arrow securities contingent on the states θ, they would be able to insure themselves against changes in asset values (AG). With a complete set of Arrow securities, risk-sharing must be efficient, so in the absence of intrinsic uncertainty ($\varepsilon = 0$) the only possible equilibrium is the one we have called the fundamental equilibrium F. The equilibrium allocation is incentive-efficient, sunspots have no real impact, and there are no crises. Note that, although the existence of the markets for Arrow securities has an effect (by eliminating the other equilibria), there is no trade in Arrow securities in the fundamental equilibrium. Arrow securities are, of course, a convenient fiction that do not exist in reality, but it may be that other derivatives, such as options, would serve as well. However, derivatives are conditional on $p(\theta)$ rather than directly on θ, so it is not obvious how many derivatives or what kind would be required. This is an interesting topic for future research.

We have noted the importance of inelastic demand for liquidity in generating large fluctuations in asset prices from small demand shocks. The inelasticity of demand follows two assumptions. The first is the assumption that banks use demand deposits, which do not allow the payment at Date 1 to be contingent on demand (or anything else). The second is the assumption of the Diamond and Dybvig preferences, which rule out intertemporal substitution of consumption. We see both the Diamond and Dybvig preferences and the use of demand deposits as a counterpart to the empirical fact that financial contracts are typically written in a "hard" way that requires strict performance of precisely defined acts, independently of many apparently relevant contingencies. These hard contracts may be motivated by enforcement and incentive problems, but it would be too difficult to include them explicitly in the model. There seems little doubt that such factors are relevant in real markets and should be taken into account here.

An alternative justification for incomplete contracts is that they provide a way of modeling—within the standard, Walrasian, auction-market framework—some realistic features of alternative market-clearing mechanisms. In an auction market, prices and quantities adjust simultaneously in a tatonnement process until a full equilibrium is achieved. An alternative mechanism is one in which quantities are chosen before prices are allowed to adjust. An example is the use of market orders in markets for company stocks. In the banking context, if depositors were required to make a withdrawal decision before the asset price was determined in the interbank market, then the same inelasticity of demand would be observed even if depositors had preferences that allowed for intertemporal substitution. There may be other institutional structures that have the qualitative features of our example. An investigation of these issues goes far beyond the scope of the present paper, but it is undoubtedly one of the most important topics for future research.

Our theory of banking is also rather special. Two assumptions should be noted. We have assumed that each bank offers a single type of contract and that each consumer can deal with only one bank. These assumptions are restrictive because they prevent banks and consumers from taking advantage of opportunities for diversification. For example, a consumer would like to hedge some of the idiosyncratic risk associated with a deposit contract by spreading his claims across several banks. As we have already noted, the pecuniary externalities associated with asset-price volatility have an impact on welfare only if there is some friction that prevents Pareto-efficient sharing of risk. Just as we assumed incomplete markets (no Arrow securities) in order to ensure that risk-sharing was not efficient, we need to assume some limits on the ability of consumers and banks to contract and hedge risks. The assumptions adopted here can probably be relaxed somewhat, but if we want nontrivial crises then there must be some friction that prevents the economy from achieving the first-best outcome.

In this paper we have ignored the possibility of intervention by the central bank or government. A full understanding of the laissez-faire case should be seen as a prelude to the analysis of optimal intervention. In the same way, the analysis of a "real" model is a prelude to the introduction of fiat money into the model. These are both important topics for future research.

Appendix: Proofs

Proof of Theorem 1: By definition, an equilibrium (ρ, m, d, y, p) must be either an F, T, or N. The theorem is proved by considering each case in turn.

Case (i): If (ρ, m, d, y, p) is an F then by definition the price $p(\theta)$ is constant and, for each group i, the consumption allocation $x(d_i, y_i, \alpha, \theta)$ is constant. In particular. $x_1(d_i, y_i, \alpha, \theta) = d_i$ with probability 1 so there is no default in equilibrium.

Let $\bar{p}$ denote the constant price and let $c_i = (c_{i1}, c_{i2})$ be the consumption allocation chosen by banks in group i. The decision problem of a bank in Group i is

$$\begin{aligned} \max \quad & [\alpha U(c_{i1}) + (1-\alpha)U(c_{i2})] \\ \text{subject to} \quad & c_{i1} \le c_{i2}, 0 \le y_i \le 1, \\ & \alpha c_{i1} + (1-\alpha)\bar{p}c_{i2} \le y_i + \bar{p}r(1-y_i). \end{aligned}$$

Clearly, y_i will be chosen to maximize $y_i + \bar{p}r(1-y_i)$. Then the strict concavity of $U(\cdot)$ implies that c_i is uniquely determined and independent of i. Thus, the equilibrium is semipure: $c_i = c_j$ for any i and j.

Case (ii): Suppose that (ρ, m, d, y, p) is a T. Then by definition $p(\theta)$ is not constant and, for each Group i, the consumption allocation $x(d_i, y_i, \alpha, \theta)$ is constant. In particular, $x_1(d_i, y_i, \alpha, \theta) = d_i$ with probability 1 and so there is no default in equilibrium.

Let c_i denote the consumption allocation chosen by banks in Group i. The budget constraint at Date 1 reduces to

$$\alpha c_{i1} - y_i = -p(\theta)((1-\alpha)\alpha c_{i2} - r(1-y_i)) \text{ a.s.}$$

Since $p(\theta)$ is not constant, this equation can be satisfied only if

$$\alpha c_{i1} - y_i = (1-\alpha)c_{i2} - r(1-y_i) = 0.$$

Then the choice of (c_i, y_i) must solve the problem

$$\begin{aligned} \max \quad & E[\alpha U(c_{i1}) + (1-\alpha)U(c_{i2})] \\ \text{subject to} \quad & c_{i1} \le c_{i2}, 0 \le y_i \le 1, \\ & \alpha c_{i1} = y_i, (1-\alpha)c_{i2} = r(1-y_i). \end{aligned}$$

The strict concavity of $U(\cdot)$ implies that this problem uniquely determines the value of c_i and hence y_i, independently of i. Consequently, the equilibrium is pure.

Case (iii): Suppose that (ρ, m, d, y, p) is an N. Then the allocation of consumption for Group i is $x(d_i, y_i, \alpha, \theta)$, and the expected utility of each group is the same

$$E[u(x(d_i, y_i, \alpha, \theta), \alpha)] = E[u(x(d_j, y_j, \alpha, \theta), \alpha)] \forall i, j.$$

The mean allocation $\sum_i \rho_i x(d_i, y_i, \alpha, \theta)$ satisfies the market-clearing conditions for every θ so consumption bundle $E\left[\sum_i \rho_i x(d_i, y_i, \alpha, \theta)\right]$ is feasible for the planner. Since agents are strictly risk-averse, it follows that

$$u\left(E\left[\sum_i \rho_i x(d_i, y_i, \alpha, \theta)\right], \alpha\right) > \sum_i \rho_i E[u(x(d_i, y_i, \alpha, \theta), \alpha)].$$

This contradicts the equilibrium conditions, since the individual bank could choose

$$y_0 = \alpha d_0 = \alpha E\left[\sum_i \rho_i x(d_i, y_i, \alpha, \theta)\right]$$

and achieve a higher utility.

Proof of Theorem 2: Again we let (ρ, m, d, y, p) be a fixed but arbitrary equilibrium and consider each of three cases in turn.

Case (i): If (ρ, m, d, y, p) is an F then $p(\theta)$ is constant and, for each Group i and each α, the consumption allocation $x(d_i, y_i, \alpha, \theta)$ is constant. In particular, $x_1(d_i, y_i, \alpha, \theta) = d_i$ with probability 1, so there is no default in equilibrium.

Let $\bar{p}$ denote the constant price and let $c_i(\alpha) = (c_{i1}(\alpha), c_{i2}(\alpha))$ be the consumption allocation chosen by banks in Group i. The decision problem of a bank in Group i is

$$\begin{aligned} \max \quad & E(\alpha U(c_{i1}(\alpha)) + (1-\alpha)U(c_{i2}(\alpha))] \\ \text{subject to} \quad & c_{i1}(\alpha) \leq c_{i2}(\alpha), 0 \leq y_i \leq 1, \\ & \alpha c_{i1}(\alpha) + (1-\alpha)\bar{p}c_{i2}(\alpha) \leq y_i + \bar{p}r(1-y_i). \end{aligned}$$

Clearly, y_i will be chosen to maximize $y_i + \bar{p}r(1-y_i)$. Then the strict concavity of $U(\cdot)$ implies that $c_i(\alpha)$ is uniquely determined and independent of i (but not of α). Thus, the equilibrium is semipure: $c_i = c_j$ for any i and j.

Case (ii): Suppose that (ρ, m, d, y, p) is a T. Then by definition $p(\theta)$ is not constant and, for each Group i and α, the consumption allocation $x(d_i, y_i, \alpha, \theta)$ is constant. In particular, $x_i(d_i, y_i, \alpha, \theta) = d_i$ with probability 1 and so there is no default in equilibrium.

Let $c_i(\alpha)$ denote the consumption allocation chosen by banks in Group i. The budget constraint at Date 1 reduces to

$$\alpha c_{i1}(\alpha) - y_i = -p(\theta)((1-\alpha)\alpha c_{i2}(\alpha) - r(1-y_i)) \text{ a.s.}$$

Since $p(\theta)$ is not constant, this equation can be satisfied only if

$$\alpha c_{i1}(\alpha) - y_i = (1-\alpha)c_{i2}(\alpha) - r(l-y_i) = 0.$$

Since α is not constant, this can only be true if $c_{i1}(\alpha) = c_{i2}(\alpha) = 0$—a contradiction. Thus, there cannot be a T when α is not constant.

Case (iii): The only remaining possibility is that (ρ, m, d, y, p) is an N. If there is no default in this equilibrium, then each bank in Group i solves the problem

$$\begin{aligned}\max \quad & E\left[\alpha U(d_i) + (1-\alpha)U\left(\frac{y_i + p(\theta)r(1-y_i) - \alpha d_i}{(1-\alpha)p(\theta)}\right)\right] \\ \text{subject to} \quad & \frac{y_i + p(\theta)r(1-y_i)}{(1-\alpha)p(\theta)} \geq d_i.\end{aligned}$$

This is a convex programming problem, and it is easy to show that the strict concavity of $U(\cdot)$ uniquely determines (d_i, y_i). Thus, an N without default is pure.

Proof of Theorem 3: Suppose that the probability of default in (ρ, m, d, y, p) is zero. Then, for each group i, $x_1(d_i, y_i, \alpha, \theta) = d_i$ and the market-clearing condition (2) implies

$$\sum_i E[\rho_i \eta(\alpha, \theta) d_i] \leq \sum_i \rho_i y_i. \tag{5.3}$$

There are two cases to consider. In the first case, $\sum_i \rho_i y_i = 0$. Then $d_i = 0$ for every i, and the utility achieved in equilibrium is

$$E\left[\eta(\alpha, \theta)U(0) + (1 - \eta(\alpha, \theta))U\left(\frac{r}{1 - \eta(\alpha, \theta)}\right)\right].$$

By holding a small amount $\delta > 0$ of the short asset, positive consumption could be guaranteed at the first date. Optimality requires that

$$\begin{aligned}& E\left[\eta(\alpha, \theta)U\left(\frac{\delta}{\eta(\alpha, \theta)}\right)\right] + E\left[(1 - \eta(\alpha, \theta))U\left(\frac{r(1-\delta)}{1 - \eta(\alpha, \theta)}\right)\right] \\ & \leq E\left[\eta(\alpha, \theta)U(0) + (1 - \eta(\alpha, \theta))U\left(\frac{r}{1 - \eta(\alpha, \theta)}\right)\right]\end{aligned}$$

for any $\delta > 0$. In the limit as $\delta \to 0$ we have

$$E[U'(0)] - E\left[U'\left(\frac{r}{1 - \eta(\alpha, \theta)}\right)\right] \leq 0,$$

which contradicts the assumption that $U'(G) = \infty$.

In the second case, $\sum_i \rho_i y_i > 0$. Then the market-clearing condition (3) and the fact that $\eta(\alpha, \theta) = \alpha + \varepsilon\theta$ together imply that

$$\sum_i \rho_i \eta(\alpha, \theta) d_i < \sum_i \rho_i y_i$$

with positive probability. The complementary slackness condition implies that $p(\theta) = 1$ with positive probability, and the short asset will be dominated by the long asset at Date 0 unless $p(\theta) < 1/r$ with positive probability. Thus, the price volatility is nontrivial if the probability of default is zero.

Proof of Theorem 4: Continuity and the convergence of $\{(\rho^q, m, d^q, y^q, p^q)\}$ immediately imply the following properties of the limit point $(\rho^0, m, d^0, y^0, p^0)$.

(i) $\sum_i \rho_i^0 = 1$ and $\rho_i^0 \geq 0$ for, every i, so (ρ^0, m) is a partition.
(ii) For every i, $(d_i^0, y_i^0) \in \mathbb{R}_+ \times [0, 1]$. The market-clearing conditions

$$\sum_i \rho_i^0 E[\alpha \bar{x}_1(d_i^0, y_i^0, \alpha, \theta)|\theta] \leq \sum_i \rho_i^0 y_i^0$$

and

$$\sum_i \rho_i^0 E\{\alpha \bar{x}_1(d_i^0, y_i^0, \alpha, \theta) + (1-\alpha)\bar{x}_2(d_i^0, y_i^0, \alpha, \theta)|\theta\}$$
$$= \sum_i \rho_i^0 \{y_i^0 + r(1 - y_i^0)\}$$

are satisfied in the limit, and the complementary slackness condition holds. Thus (d^0, y^0) is an attainable allocation.

It remains to show that (d_i^0, y_i^0) is optimal for each i. Let $W^q(d_i, y_i, \alpha, \theta)$ denote the utility associated with the pair (d_i, y_i) in the perturbed economy corresponding to $\varepsilon = 1/q$ when the price function is p^q and let $W^0(d_i, y_i, \alpha, \theta)$ denote the utility associated with the pair (d_i, y_i) in the limit economy corresponding to $\varepsilon = 0$, where the price function is p^0. The function $W_i^0(\cdot)$ is discontinuous at the bankruptcy point, defined implicitly by the condition

$$(\alpha + (1-\alpha)p^0(\theta))d_i = y_i + p^0(\theta)r(1 - y_i). \tag{5.4}$$

If (4) occurs with probability zero in the limit, then it is easy to see from the assumed convergence properties that

$$W^q(d_i, y_i, \alpha, \theta) \to W^0(d_i, y_i, \alpha, \theta) \text{ a.s.;}$$

hence

$$\lim_{q\to\infty} E[W^q(d_i, y_i, \alpha, \theta)] = E[W^0(d_i, y_i, \alpha, \theta)].$$

Let (d_i^0, y_i^0) denote the pair corresponding to the limiting consumption allocation x_i^0, and let $\{(d_i^q, y_i^q)\}$ denote the sequence of equilibrium choices converging to (d_i^0, y_i^0). There may exist a set of states (α, θ) with positive measure such that (d_i^q, y_i^q) implies default in state (α, θ) for arbitrarily large q but that (d_i^0, y_i^0) does not imply default in state (α, θ). Then at least we can say that

$$\liminf_q W^q(d_i^q, y_i^q, \alpha, \theta) \leq W^0(d_i^0, y_i^0, \alpha, \theta) \text{ a.s.}$$

and this implies that

$$\liminf_q E[W^q(d_i^q, y_i^q, \alpha, \theta)] \leq E[W^0(d_i^0, y_i^0, \alpha, \theta)].$$

Now suppose, contrary to what we want to prove, that (d_i^0, y_i^0) is not optimal. Then there exists a pair (d_i, y_i) such that $E[W^0(d_i, y_i, \alpha, \theta)] > E[W^0(d_i^0, y_i^0, \alpha, \theta)]$. If $d_i = 0$ then

(4) holds with probability zero and it is clear that, for some sufficiently large value of q, $E[W^0(d_i, y_i, \alpha, \theta)] > E[W^q(d_i^q, y_i^q, \alpha, \theta)]$, contradicting the equilibrium conditions. If $d_i > 0$, then either the critical condition (4) holds with probability zero or we can find a slightly lower value $d' < d$ that does satisfy the critical condition. To see this, note first that the critical condition uniquely determines the value of $p^0(\theta)$ as long as

$$(1 - \alpha)d \neq r(1 - y),$$

which is true for almost every value of d. Second, if the value of $p^0(\theta)$ for which the critical condition is satisfied is an atom, then we can always find a slightly smaller value $d_i' < d_i$ such that the value of $p^0(\theta)$ for which the critical condition is satisfied is not an atom. Furthermore, reducing d slightly will at most reduce the payoff by a small amount, so for $d_i' < d_i$ and close enough to d_i we still have $E[W^0(d_i', y_i, \alpha, \theta)] > E[W^0(d_i^0, y_i^0, \alpha, \theta)]$. This then leads to a contradiction in the usual way.

References

Allen, Franklin and Douglas Gale (1998). "Optimal Financial Crises." *Journal of Finance*, 53, 1245–1284.

Allen, Franklin and Douglas Gale (2000a). "Financial Contagion." *Journal of Political Economy*, 108, 1–33.

Allen, Franklin and Douglas Gale (2000b). "Optimal Currency Crises." *Carnegie Rochester Series on Public Policy*, 53, 177–230.

Allen, Franklin and Douglas Gale (2000c). "Bubbles and Crises." *The Economic Journal*, 110, 236–256.

Allen, Franklin and Douglas Gale (2004). "Financial Intermediaries and Markets." *Econometrica*, 72, 1023–1061.

Azariadis, Costas (1981). "Self-Fulfilling Prophecies." *Journal of Economic Theory*, 25, 380–396.

Bernanke, Ben and Mark Gertler (1989). "Agency Costs, Net Worth, and Business Fluctuations." American *Economic Review*, 79, 14–31.

Bernardo, Antonio and Ivo Welch (2004). "Financial Market Runs." *Quarterly Journal of Economics*, 119, 135–158.

Bryant, John (1980). "A Model of Reserves, Bank Runs, and Deposit Insurance." *Journal of Banking and Finance*, 4, 335–344.

Calomiris, Charles and Gary Gorton (1991). "The Origins of Banking Panics, Models, Facts, and Bank Regulation." In *Financial Markets and Financial Crises*, edited by Glenn Hubbard. University of Chicago Press.

Calomiris, Charles and Joseph Mason (2000). "Causes of U.S. Bank Distress During the Depression." NBER Working Paper No. W7919.

Cass, David and Karl Shell (1983). "Do Sunspots Matter?" *Journal of Political Economy*, 91, 193–227.

Chari, Varadarajan and Patrick Kehoe (2000). "Financial Crises as Herds." Federal Reserve Bank of Minneapolis Working Paper.

Cone, Kenneth (1983). "Regulation of Depository Institutions." Ph.D. dissertation, Stanford University.

Diamond, Douglas and Philip Dybvig (1983). "Bank Runs, Deposit Insurance, and Liquidity." *Journal of Political Economy*, 91, 401–419.

Farmer, Roger (1999). *The Macroeconomics of Self-Fulfilling Prophecies*. MIT Press.

Geanakoplos, John (1990). "An Introduction to General Equilibrium with Incomplete Asset Markets." *Journal of Mathematical Economics*, 19, 1–38.

Gorton, Gary (1988). "Banking Panics and Business Cycles." *Oxford Economic Papers*, 40, 751–781.

Gottardi, Piero and Atsushi Kajii (1995). "Generic Existence of Sunspot Equilibria: The Real Asset Case." CARESS Working Paper 95/12, University of Pennsylvania.

Gottardi, Piero and Atsushi Kajii (1999). "The Structure of Sunspot Equilibria: The Role of Multiplicity." *Review of Economic Studies*, 66, 713–732.
Hart, Oliver (1995). *Firms, Contracts and Financial Structure*. Oxford University Press.
Jacklin, Charles (1986). "Demand Deposits, Trading Restrictions, and Risk Sharing." In *Contractual Arrangements for Intertemporal Trade*, edited by Edward Prescott and Neil Wallace. University of Minnesota Press.
Kindleberger, Charles (1978). *Manias, Panics, and Crashes: A History of Financial Crises*. Basic Books.
Kiyotaki, Nobu and John Moore (1997). "Credit Chains." *Journal of Political Economy*, 99, 220–264.
Lagunoff, Roger and Stacey Schreft (2001). "A Model of Financial Fragility." *Journal of Economic Theory*, 99, 220–264.
Magill, Michael and Martine Quinzii (1996). *Theory of Incomplete Markets, Volume I*. MIT Press.
Postlewaite, Andrew, George Mailath, and Larry Samuelson (2003). "Sunk Investments Lead to Unpredictable Prices." University of Pennsylvania. <http://www.ssc.upenn.edu/~apostlew>.
Schnabel, Isabel and Hyun Song Shin (2004). "Liquidity and Contagion: The Crisis of 1763." *Journal of the European Economic Association*, 2, 929–968.
Shell, Karl and Aditya Goenka (1997). "When Sunspots Don't Matter." *Economic Theory*, 9, 169–178.

6 Interbank Market Integration under Asymmetric Information

Xavier Freixas and Cornelia Holthausen

The objective of this article is to study the effects of cross-country asymmetric information on the structure of financial markets. Our main concern is the design of money markets and the role of repo and (unsecured) interbank markets in an international framework, but our results carry over to a more general framework of the analysis of cross-country direct investment, covering the cross-country market both for bonds and equity. The creation of an integrated interbank market is particularly relevant in order for banks to cope efficiently with liquidity shocks. Interbank markets are instrumental in allowing for a smooth working of the payment systems (so that a bank that is lacking liquidity in the payment system is able to borrow from another bank), and in channeling liquidity to the banks and countries that need it most. Both repo and unsecured interbank lending allow banks to cope with liquidity shocks. Still, because unsecured markets are based on peer monitoring, they introduce market discipline, thus playing the role unsecured deposits may play when depositors receive information [Calomiris and Kahn (1991)].

The collapse of a well-functioning unsecured interbank market proved to be crucial in the context of Eastern Asia financial crises where interbank lending by foreign countries had played a key role in these countries' funding structure. It also sheds light on the construction of a European interbank market after the creation of the European Monetary Union. Finally, the issue has direct policy implications since, if the interbank market's provision of liquidity is inefficient, this calls for regulatory intervention.

The role of the interbank market to cope with bank specific liquidity shocks and avoid unnecessary liquidation of long-term investments was first acknowledged in Bhattacharya and Gale (1987). Later contributions built upon this role while introducing either moral hazard [Rochet and Tirole (1996)], aggregated liquidity risk [Allen and Gale (2000)], or else by introducing credit risk [Freixas, Parigi, and Rochet (2000)]. These studies yield similar results pointing at the potential contagion provided by an interbank market as well as the effect the network of interbank lending may have on financial fragility. Furthermore, Bhattacharya and Fulghieri (1994) analyze the efficiency of an interbank market in a framework where banks face uncertain timing of liquidity returns, and Holmström and Tirole (1998) discuss the role of liquidity provision by the public sector.

Although our article does not focus on financial crises, we also consider two different interbank lending networks, segmentation versus integration, where the collapse of integration may be interpreted as a financial crisis.

As in Rochet and Tirole, we consider "peer monitoring" as a key factor in improving the efficiency of the interbank market; still we are concerned with asymmetric information and therefore about the quality of signals rather than about moral hazard and the way to discipline borrowers. From that perspective, our work is related to Broecker (1990) and to Flannery (1996) who consider models of asymmetric information and credit risk. An important difference to their work is that the value of a signal is given exogenously in their model, while in our model it is endogenous, as it results from the equilibrium behavior of borrowers.

Our model uses a Diamond and Dybvig type of framework, where consumers are uncertain about the timing of their consumption needs. This generates liquidity shocks, which we assume are present both at the individual and at the aggregate level. To be able to cope with these shocks, banks can invest in a storage technology. Because this technology has a lower return than alternative investment opportunities, it is efficient for banks to use the interbank market. We consider both an unsecured interbank market and a repo market where government bills are traded. In order to introduce credit risk, the model assumes that banks have some risk of failure. As in Rochet and Tirole (1996), banks monitor each other in the interbank market, thus obtaining a signal on the solvency probability of each of their peers. The key assumption of our model is that cross-border information about banks is less precise than home country information. Hence, when a bank tries to borrow from a foreign bank, it does so either because it belongs to a liquidity-short country or else because it has generated a "bad" signal at a domestic level and is therefore unable to borrow in his home country. As it is intuitive, depending on the equilibrium probability distribution of the two types of motivations for borrowing abroad, an integrated interbank market may or may not exist.

Our contribution is to show, using this framework, that having a single currency is no guarantee for having a single uninsured interbank market. Namely, a segmented interbank market is *always* an equilibrium, while the emergence of an integrated international market is only possible when the quality of cross-border information is sufficiently good. A further result is that the integration of markets does not always yield a more efficient outcome.

On the other hand, the repo market provides a perfect medium to channel liquidity between banks and across countries. However, the secured nature of the repo reduces banks' incentives for peer monitoring. As a result, banks with a low probability of solvency are able to obtain liquidity via the repo market and to avoid liquidation, although their liquidation value might exceed their expected continuation value. Surprisingly, we also establish that the combination of both types of markets need not yield a more efficient allocation, as it may lead to the collapse of the unsecured integrated market.

This article is organized as follows. In Section 1 we set up the basic model of interbank credit and the structure of signals. Section 2 analyzes the unsecured interbank market in a two country setting, while Section 3 is devoted to the general and more complex case when the two markets — unsecured and repo — are coexistent. Section 4 extends the analysis by allowing for the introduction of correspondent banking, transnational banking, and too-big-to-fail banks. Section 5 offers some concluding remarks on the policy implications of our results. All proofs are in the Appendix.

1. The Model

We consider an economy with two countries.

Consumers. In each country, there is a continuum of consumers of a total measure of one, who possess one unit of endowment each at time 0. Consumers are risk averse with twice differentiable concave utility functions and face liquidity shocks as in a Diamond and Dybvig (1983) type of model: they need to consume either at time 1 or at time 2. At time 0, consumers deposit their endowments in a bank, and can withdraw funds at the time they need to consume. Deposits are fully insured by a deposit insurance, so no bank runs occur.[1] We assume that the demand-deposit contract promises them a consumption c_1 in period 1 or c_2 in period 2.

Banks' investment. There is an infinite number of risk neutral, profit-maximizing banks.[2] We assume the population of banks to be exogenously given. In the baseline model, banks are ex ante equal, however, in Section 4 we consider different types of cross-border cooperation in the form of correspondent banking and transnational banks (we do not analyze the free entry equilibrium as this would depend trivially on the sunk cost of setting up a bank domestically and abroad).

Banks receive the consumers' endowments at time 0, and invest them either in a risky technology or in reserves (storage technology). Furthermore, a bank can buy government Treasury bills, which are issued at price B_0, and yield 1 in the second period with certainty. Denote the investment in the risky technology I, the one in Treasury bills $T_0 B_0$ and the one in reserves $s_0 \equiv I - T_0 B_0$.

Each unit invested in the risky technology yields an uncertain payoff $\tilde{R}$ at time 2, where $\tilde{R} = R$ (solvency) with probability $p \geq \frac{1}{2}$, and $\tilde{R} = 0$ (insolvency) with probability $1 - p$. Investment in the technology is assumed to be ex ante efficient in that $pR > 1$. This risky asset can also be (partially) liquidated at time 1, with the following technology: liquidation of ΔI units gives a liquidation value of $l(\Delta I)$, where $l(\Delta I)$ is increasing and concave. For simplicity we use a logarithmic liquidation function $l(\Delta I) = \ln(\Delta I + 1)$.

Because banks have limited liability they have incentives to forbear no matter how bad the prospects of the risky technology are. As a consequence, in our model bank closure will only occur if it is triggered by a liquidity shock.

Liquidity shocks. Our model combines bank-specific liquidity shocks with countrywide ones. Banks are uncertain about the liquidity demand they face at time 1. For a fraction q of all banks, a high fraction of consumers π_H is impatient and wishes to withdraw at time 1. A fraction $1 - q$, on the other hand, faces a low liquidity demand π_L, $\pi_L < \pi_H$. The remaining consumers are patient and withdraw at time 2.

The variable q reflects the countrywide aggregate demand for liquidity and is uncertain as well. We assume aggregate liquidity shocks to occur with probability $\frac{1}{2}$ and restrict our comparative statics analysis to changes in the probability of solvency. Thus, with probability $\frac{1}{2}$, $q = q_B$, in which case a country is in a state of high aggregate liquidity demand, because many banks face high time-1 withdrawals (π_H). On the other hand, with probability $\frac{1}{2}$ the country faces a low liquidity demand with $q = q_A$, where $q_A < q_B$, so that fewer banks face a high amount of withdrawals. For the sake of simplicity we assume

[1]The deposit insurance company is assumed to raise funds at unit cost. The deposit insurance is fair in that banks have to bear the expected cost of their failures.

[2]Because of perfect competition in the market for deposits, the banks' optimal deposit contract maximizes depositors' welfare, and bank equilibrium profits are driven to zero.

$q_A + q_B$ constant, so that there is no liquidity shock for the two countries taken together. The probability of solvency and liquidity are uncorrelated.

Banks can manage their liquidity needs at time 1 by borrowing or lending in the interbank market, by buying or selling Treasury bills on the repo market, by liquidating assets, and by storing reserves until the next period. If illiquid banks fail to meet their creditors' demand, they are forced into bankruptcy, liquidating all assets. In this case, the proceeds are absorbed by the deposit insurance company.

The timing of the model is the following:

$t = 0$	$t = 1$	$t = 2$
– consumers deposit – banks invest	– q, π and signals observed – liquidation takes place – repo and interbank market operations realized – impatient consumers withdraw	– returns $\tilde{R}$ realized – patient consumers withdraw – interbank loans repaid

Information. At time 0, the ex ante probability of being solvent, p, is common knowledge. At time 1, all banks in a given country receive a common, nonverifiable signal s_D about the solvency of each domestic counterpart. The signal can either be good ($\bar{s}$) or bad ($\underline{s}$), it is defined as

$$\text{prob}(s_D = \bar{s} | \tilde{R} = R) = \text{prob}(s_D = \underline{s} | \tilde{R} = 0) = \alpha,$$

where we assume that the signal is informative, that is, $\alpha \in (\frac{1}{2}, 1]$. Our setting thus reflects the existence of "soft" domestic information regarding the individual banks' strategies, their risk-taking behavior, and their accounting strategy (loan-loss provisions, window dressing, and so on). This information is not directly observable by foreign banks, even at a cost.

Denote $\theta \equiv p\alpha + (1 - p)(1 - \alpha)$, the ex ante probability that the good signal is received about a bank.[3] The above expressions allow us to compute the probability $\bar{p}$ of success, conditional on the bank having produced the signal $s_D = \bar{s}$. It is given by $\bar{p} \equiv \text{prob}(\tilde{R} = R | s_D = \bar{s}) = p\alpha/\theta$ and we denote, symmetrically, $\underline{p} \equiv \text{prob}(\tilde{R} = R | s_D = \underline{s}) = \frac{p(1-\alpha)}{(1-\theta)}$.

The signals received in the foreign country can only be observed with some noise. We make the following assumption, which holds regardless of the bank's solvency.

Assumption 1: *(Noisy cross-country information)*

$$\text{prob}(s_F = \bar{s} | s_D = \bar{s}) = \text{prob}(s_F = \underline{s} | s_D = \underline{s}) = 1 - \beta,$$

where $\beta \in (0, \frac{1}{2})$ denotes the probability that the domestic signal is received wrongly in the foreign country. Again, the signal is a common one, that is, all foreign banks receive the same signal about a particular bank.

The lower the value of β, the better is the information flow between countries. Each bank is then characterized by a pair (s_D, s_F), denoting the signals that have been received

[3] Because we are dealing with a continuum of banks, the ex ante probability is equal to the ex post fraction of banks of this type.

by domestic and foreign banks about this particular bank. Assumption 1 implies that s_D is a sufficient statistics for (s_D, s_F).[4]

Since this assumption plays a crucial role in the whole analysis, it is worth fully developing its implications. To begin with, we think of our assumption as applied to *soft*, not to *hard*, information. Obtaining a balance sheet of a foreign bank is obviously as easy as obtaining it for a domestic one. Our assumption is that a balance sheet interpretation draws on the "cultural" context that is not exportable. To take a few examples, the level of derivatives operations and the way in which they are used to hedge or to speculate could be known domestically but not cross border. Rumors about a banks' financial distress could also be local. Similarly, the level of window dressing that the regulators allow for may be country-specific unwritten information. Whether a bank will be bailed out or not in case of failure is also soft information. These examples seem to indicate that a bank operating in another country (i.e., operating under different supervision and different regulatory rules) is culturally different, an explanation for why we observe so often the lack of success of cost-efficient foreign banks trying to enter another country.

Note that a bank cannot observe its own solvency, but only the signal. Therefore, it has no informational advantage over the other market participants regarding its own solvency. This assumption is required in order to leave aside additional moral hazard problems.

The second assumption we make regarding the signal structure is that when a bad signal is observed it is efficient to close down the bank. That is, we assume that the parameters are such that in equilibrium, the following condition holds:

Assumption 2: *(Efficient closure of bad-signal banks)*

$$\text{prob}(\tilde{R} = R | s_F = \underline{s})R \leq l'(I).$$

Because of concavity of $l(\cdot)$, this assumption implies that it is efficient to liquidate the entire risky technology of a bank when the bad signal has been received in the foreign country. Assumption 2 obviously implies that it is also efficient to close down this bank with better quality of information, for example, after observing the domestic bad signal $(pR \leq l'(I))$.

On the other hand, from the assumption $pR > 1$ it follows that $\bar{p}R > 1$, so that (partial) liquidation of a high-signal bank is never efficient.

2. Cross-country Unsecured Interbank Market Integration

This section focuses on the emergence of unsecured markets for liquidity, leaving aside the repo market. For simplicity, we assume that banks hold no Treasury bills. These will be reintroduced in Section 3. As usual, we start by analyzing banks' time-1 problem of liquidity management, which is the focus of our analysis. In Section 2.3, we will turn to their time-0 investment decision.

We regard two countries with different aggregate liquidity demands. For $q = q_A$, there is excess liquidity, while for $q = q_B$, the liquidity shortage is so high that both lenders and

[4] It can easily be checked that for any signal combination, for example, for $(\bar{s}, \bar{s})$, we have

$$p(\tilde{R} = R|(\bar{s}, \bar{s}) = \frac{p\alpha(1-\beta)}{p\alpha(1-\beta) + (1-p)(1-\alpha)(1-\beta)} = p(\tilde{R} = R|s_D = \bar{s}).$$

borrowers liquidate. It will be verified later on (Lemma 6) that this is consistent with the optimal investment strategy.

Let us denote A as the country with excess liquidity, and B as the one with a liquidity deficit. We assume that there are no legal or infrastructural barriers to the emergence of an international money market.

2.1 Equilibrium Structure

Our assumptions imply that each bank is characterized by a pair (s_D, s_F) consisting of the signals observed about this particular bank in the home country and abroad: Banks with liquidity needs can find themselves with one of the four pairs of signals: $(s_D, s_F) = (\bar{s}, \bar{s}), (\bar{s}, \underline{s}), (\underline{s}, \bar{s})$, or $(\underline{s}, \underline{s})$. The individual signal pair will determine the ability of a bank to borrow in the interbank markets. An interbank market is modeled as an anonymous competitive market where all agents are price takers. The anonymity assumption is justified in our context as there is no cost in diversifying the portfolio of interbank loans, so lenders are exposed to the average credit risk of the interbank market. Equilibrium interest rates are those for which the markets clear. Participating agents know the structure of the equilibrium including the proportion of agents affected by each type of domestic and foreign signal, the bank specific liquidity shocks, and the aggregate liquidity shocks. As a consequence, observing the equilibrium interest rates does not allow to infer any additional information, in particular not about specific banks. Domestic lenders know they are endowed with a superior information structure while foreign borrowers know they face a worse population of borrowers and this is reflected in the equilibrium interest rates. It is crucial that foreign lenders do not have access to the information available to domestic lenders, since otherwise, our source of asymmetric information disappears.

Assumption 2 implies that lending to banks about which the low signal $\underline{s}$ has been obtained has a negative net present value. Consequently, only banks with the signal pair $(\bar{s}, \bar{s})$ are able to choose in which country to borrow. The other banks are constrained to using either the domestic market if they are $(\bar{s}, \underline{s})$, or the foreign market if they are $(\underline{s}, \bar{s})$. Banks of type $(\underline{s}, \underline{s})$ are not able to borrow at all. It is important to realize that in equilibrium, banks with $s_F = \underline{s}$ will not ask for a loan abroad since this loan will always be denied by the foreign lender. This is because if all banks from a country — with a good or a bad foreign signal — ask for a foreign loan, it is impossible for the foreign lender to infer any (domestic) information from this strategy. Hence he has to rely on his own signal and does not lend to the bad-signal bank. On the other hand, when only banks with a good foreign signal $s_F = \bar{s}$ ask for a loan, in equilibrium lenders will be able to update their information on foreign borrowers' solvency on the basis of their strategic behavior and on equilibrium interest rates: When facing the demand for a loan from a foreign bank, lenders know that the bank wishes to borrow abroad for one of the two reasons: either it is of the type $(\underline{s}, \bar{s})$ and thus not able to obtain a domestic loan, or it is of the type $(\bar{s}, \bar{s})$ and chooses to borrow abroad because of a better interest rate. While a lender does not know of which type a particular bank is, he can observe the proportion of each type and thus infer the corresponding probability of solvency of the foreign bank, which we will denote as p_F. A lender's decision whether to lend at all to foreign banks and if so, at which interest rate, therefore depends on the proportion of each type of foreign borrower.

Because of the limited access of $(\bar{s}, \underline{s})$ banks to the foreign interbank market and of $(\underline{s}, \bar{s})$ to the local interbank market, insurance against liquidity shocks is only partial. This is illustrated in Figure 6.1.

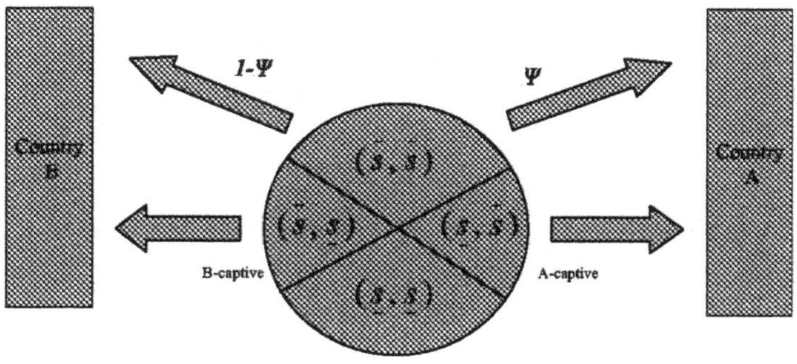

Figure 6.1. **Borrowing choices for country-B banks**
Banks can only obtain a loan in the country where the good signal $\underline{s}$ has been obtained about them. In equilibrium, a fraction $1 - \psi$ of $(\bar{s}, \bar{s})$ banks borrows domestically while ψ borrow abroad.

All in all, there are four credit markets, for each country $i = A, B$ a market that clears domestic demand for loans at interest rate r_i, and one for the foreign demand for domestic loans at rate r_{iF}. Naturally, liquidity supply in the market for domestic and foreign loans is interdependent. For expositional reasons, we add supply and demand for these two markets in the following way: Liquidity demand in country i, Ω_i, is the sum of time-1 withdrawals of all agents active in the markets, that is, domestic borrowers and lenders as well as foreign borrowers. Liquidity supply Λ_i is the sum of these agents' reserve holdings plus any liquidity they obtain by liquidation. These are given by the following expressions:

$$\Omega_i \equiv \left(\sigma_L^i \pi_L + \sum_{k=D,F} \sigma_k^i \pi_H \right) c_1 \tag{6.1}$$

$$\Lambda_i \equiv \sum_{k=L,D,F} \sigma_k^i [s_0 + l(\Delta I_k^i)], \tag{6.2}$$

where the subindex k denotes the different agents active in the local interbank market, $k = L, D, F$. Here, L denotes lenders, D refers to domestic borrowers, and F to foreign borrowers, and σ_k^i is the (equilibrium) measure of each type of bank in country i. Here, interbank interest rates are crucial in determining how much of the long run technology the banks will liquidate. Using the banks' first-order conditions, we can establish the following lemma:

Lemma 1: *The supply of liquidity in country i, Λ_i, is nondecreasing in the domestic interbank interest rate r_i.*

Proof: See Appendix.

For low levels of interbank interest rates, only reserves are used and the credit market does not develop. For larger levels of interest rates, a market begins to develop where lending banks do not liquidate, but lend out their reserves and have a zero expected yield. When we consider higher interest rates, both borrowing and lending banks liquidate their long-term assets and the expected yield for the lending banks is strictly positive.

Unsurprisingly, the interbank interest rate is an increasing function of the net aggregate demand for liquidity. However, markets do not provide for a perfect smoothing of liquidity shocks: Lending banks liquidate less than borrowing banks. The reason is that the expected cost of borrowing is higher than the expected return from lending. This can be seen by computing the expected return on lending and the expected cost of borrowing conditional on the banks' survival: Lenders obtain an expected return of $\bar{p}(1 + r)$ on loans, while borrowers pay $(1 + r)$ on each unit borrowed. Notice that this discrepancy on the valuation of the returns has its origin on the *lender's* limited liability: Lenders' probability of default plays no role in the calculation of borrowers, while lenders do care about the possibility that borrowers default. The lender undervalues the return on a loan because with some probability it will accrue to the deposit insurance authority.

It is quite intuitive that the equilibrium will be characterized by a unilateral flow of borrowers from the country with high liquidity needs and high interest rates to the country with excess liquidity and low interest rates. The following lemma establishes this point. Denoting by ψ_i the fraction of $(\bar{s}, \bar{s})$ banks in country i that choose to borrow abroad, we prove that $\psi_A = 0$.

Lemma 2: *Borrowers from the excess liquidity country A borrow only in country* $A(\psi_A = 0)$. *In addition, in the case of segmented markets* $(\psi_B = \psi_A = 0)$, *interest rates in country B are higher than in country* $A(r_A < r_B)$.

Proof: See Appendix.

This will reduce the number of markets to three, and moreover simplify our notations, since it implies having only one foreign market, the one for borrowers of country B that wish to borrow in country A. Thus, denote $\psi \equiv \psi_B$, and $r_F \equiv r_{AF}$ the rate for foreign borrowers in country A. A perfect Bayesian equilibrium in the interbank market is a quintuple $(\psi^*, r_A^*, r_B^*, r_F^*, p_F^*)$, specifying the fraction ψ^* of $(\bar{s}, \bar{s})$ banks from country B borrowing abroad as well as the interest rates demanded and the corresponding rationally updated probability $p_F^*(\psi)$. The variable ψ is crucial for the following analysis, since it describes the behavior of the only types of borrowers that are free to choose in which country to borrow. Accordingly, it characterizes the type of equilibrium that prevails: *Integration*[5] will be defined as the case where in equilibrium $\psi^* > 0$, while *segmentation* is defined as the opposite case where $\psi^* = 0$.

In an integrated equilibrium, with $0 < \psi^* < 1$, two conditions need to be satisfied: on the one hand, lenders in country A should be indifferent between lending to either country:

$$\bar{p}(1 + r_A) = p_F(\psi)(1 + r_F). \tag{6.3}$$

Also, borrowers able to borrow at home or abroad should be indifferent where to borrow, thus

$$r_B = r_F \tag{6.4}$$

while in an integrated equilibrium with $\Psi^* = 1$, Equation (4) holds as an inequality: $r_B \geq r_F$.

[5]The case $\Psi^* = 1$ is theoretically possible and corresponds to the (exceptional) case where all banks having a choice as where to borrow prefer to borrow abroad. For the sake of completeness we have chosen to consider this case, and to include it as a form of integration, since indeed, the borrowers are able to use either of the two markets.

Equation (3) allows us to derive r_F as a function of r_A. Then, we have two market clearing conditions, Equations (5) and (6), one for each country, to determine the remaining two interest rates r_A and r_B.

$$F_A \equiv \Omega_A - \Lambda_A = 0 \tag{6.5}$$

$$F_B \equiv \Omega_B - \Lambda_B = 0. \tag{6.6}$$

In the segmented equilibrium, $\psi^* = 0, p_F(0) = \text{prob}(\tilde{R} = R|\underline{s}) = p$, and r_F is indeterminate. The equilibrium with integration is characterized by the following proposition:

Proposition 1: *Under integration we have* $r_B(\psi^*) \geq r_F(\psi^*) > r_A(\psi^*), p_F(\psi)(1 + r_F^*) = \bar{p}(1 + r_A^*)$. *Under segmentation we have* $r_F(0) > r_B(0), p_F(0) = \text{prob}(\tilde{R} = R|\underline{s}) = \underline{p}$.

Proof: See Appendix.

Notice that in our terminology, integration includes the corner solution where $\psi = 1$, and $r_B(1) > r_F(1)$: the interest rate charged abroad is still lower than the domestic one, and all banks who are able to, will borrow abroad.[6] Only "captive" $(\bar{s}, \underline{s})$ banks will be forced to borrow domestically at the higher rate $r_B(1)$.

Even in the equilibrium with integration, this integration is only partial as long as there is noise in the flow of information across borders. This implies that first, lenders in country *B* draw an informational rent from the liquidity shortage. Second, lending banks in country *A* finance a heterogenous population of foreign banks, consisting of all the high risk banks $(\underline{s}, \bar{s})$, and a fraction ψ of the low risk ones $(\bar{s}, \bar{s})$.

2.2 Integration versus Segmentation

We will now proceed to establish under what conditions segmentation and integration occur, that is, to determine the equilibrium values of ψ. We will define all variables as functions of ψ. A crucial element in the analysis is the information updating of foreign lenders. Observing the measure of banks trying to borrow abroad, lenders can infer ψ and therefore the fraction of $(\bar{s}, \bar{s})$ and $(\underline{s}, \bar{s})$ banks among the foreign borrowers. As is intuitive, a higher fraction of $(\bar{s}, \bar{s})$ banks implies a higher updated probability of solvency $p_F(\psi)$. Moreover, from Equation (3) it follows that the premium on foreign loans, $r_F(\psi) - r_A(\psi)$, is decreasing in ψ.

Lemma 3: *A foreign bank's updated probability of solvency* $p_F(\psi)$ *is increasing in* ψ. *For* $\psi > 0$, *the premium charged to foreign borrowers* $r_F(\psi) - r_A(\psi)$ *is decreasing in* ψ.

Proof: See Appendix.

In order to obtain ψ^*, we first derive the demand and supply of liquidity in the domestic and foreign markets for given values of ψ. Market clearing then allows us to characterize interest rates in both markets as functions of ψ. As a final step, we need to compare interest rates r_B and r_F because these are the ones that $(\bar{s}, \bar{s})$ banks would need to pay in their home

[6]Notice that Equation (4) was stated for the opposite case that $\psi < 1$.

respective in the foreign country. A fixed-point argument then determines how many of these banks will choose to borrow in which country, that is, the equilibrium value of ψ. As a first result, we have

Lemma 4: *The domestic interest rate in country B, r_B, is decreasing in ψ.*

Proof: See Appendix.

Unsurprisingly, a higher level of cross-country borrowing eases the liquidity shortage in country *B* and leads to a lower interest rate r_B. Regarding interest rates charged in country *A*, the results are not so clear-cut, because two factors influence the interest rate r_F: On the one hand, a higher ψ implies a higher demand for liquidity in the local market, hence r_A is nondecreasing in ψ.[7] On the other hand, the results from Lemma 3 apply, that is, the quality of foreign borrowers is increasing in ψ, which implies a downward tendency for foreign interest rates. As a result, r_F may be in — or decreasing in — ψ.

This, together with the results from Lemma 4, has two implications: First, it might be the case that $r_F(\psi) > r_B(\psi)$ for all values of ψ. In this case, borrowing abroad is never an equilibrium strategy. Second, if $r_F(\psi) < r_B(\psi)$ for some ψ, an equilibrium with integration exists. However, nothing precludes the segmentation equilibrium to be obtained as well so that multiple equilibria are possible.

To illustrate these different possible scenarios, Figure 6.2 shows the interest rates $1 + r_B$ and $1 + r_F$ as functions of ψ for different parameter constellations. In constructing the figure, all equilibrium conditions except Equation (4) are taken into account. The first graph corresponds to a case where interest rates in country *B* are moderate compared to r_F, while in cases (ii) and (iii), r_B is higher relative to r_A, and thus to r_F.

In all cases, a segmented equilibrium with separated interbank markets (point A) is possible. In case (i), it is the only equilibrium because for all values of ψ, the rate charged abroad is strictly higher than the one in country *B*. In this situation, banks of the $(\bar{s}, \bar{s})$-type prefer to borrow domestically in country *B*, so $\psi^* = 0$. Any bank trying to borrow abroad will be denied a loan because it reveals being of the bad type.

In cases (ii) and (iii), the curves $1 + r_B(\psi)$ and $1 + r_F(\psi)$ cross for some $\psi > 0$ so there are values of ψ for which $r_B \geq r_F$. In case (ii), three equilibria coexist, two of them with

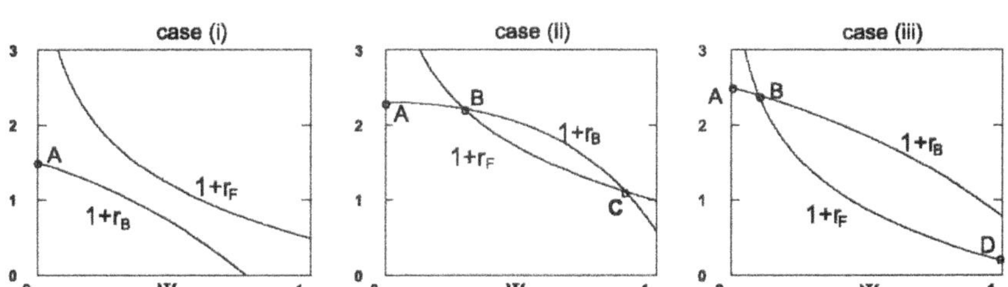

Figure 6.2. **Interest rates for country-*B* borrowers as functions of ψ**
Liquidity-short banks in country *B* can either borrow domestically at rate r_B, or in the foreign market at rate r_F. Both rates depend on the fraction of $(\bar{s}, \bar{s})$-banks borrowing abroad, ψ. The existence of an integrated equilibrium depends on the relative location of both rates.

[7]The proof is analogous to the one of Lemma 4.

an active international market (at the crossing points B and C): borrowers face the same interest rates in both countries, and they are indifferent as to where to demand a loan. Still, C implies a higher level of integration than B. Finally, in case (iii), there is an equilibrium with integration at point D, where all banks prefer to borrow abroad ($\psi = 1$) and the only banks in country B to borrow domestically are the $(\bar{s}, \underline{s})$ ones.

Figure 2 illustrates under which circumstances an equilibrium with an integrated market can be obtained. Since the foreign interest rate is increasing in the informational premium, integration becomes impossible for very high β [case (i)]. Another important parameter is the difference in liquidity needs across countries, $\Delta q \equiv q_B - q_A$: Only when Δq is sufficiently large [cases (ii) and (iii)], integration is possible.

The following proposition outlines the results of this market imperfection.

Proposition 2: *(Multiple equilibria). If the difference in aggregate liquidity demand in the two countries is large enough, both the integrated and segmented market equilibrium exist. Otherwise, only the segmented market equilibrium exists.*

Proof: See Appendix.

Proposition 2 implies, first that there is a threshold $\overline{\Delta q}$ (which depends on the exogenous parameters α, β, and $\bar{p}$) such that only for $\Delta q \geq \overline{\Delta q}$ an integrated equilibrium exists. Second, and more important for its policy implications, it implies that whenever an integrated market exists the segmented market also exists. So even if integration is possible it is not necessarily reached, and even if integration is reached, the possibility to revert to the segmentation equilibrium is always present. This possible collapse of the integrated equilibrium is somewhat reminiscent of Flannery's (1996) argument for the collapse of a domestic interbank market. In both cases it is the existence of excessively noisy information that drives the collapse of the market.

In this model, segmentation is quite a "robust" equilibrium because there exist self-fulfilling beliefs that support it, independently of the existence of an integrated interbank market equilibrium. This is of concern because usually, but not necessarily, integration will Pareto dominate segmentation, a point that the following proposition establishes.

Proposition 3: *For a given investment portfolio, the integrated equilibrium does not always dominate the segmented equilibrium, but it does so for sufficiently small β.*

Proof: See Appendix.

As is intuitive, for most parameter constellations integration leads to a higher expected welfare than segmentation because of higher cross-country interest rate smoothing. However, if the signals in the foreign country are sufficiently imprecise, foreign lenders make more "mistakes" in granting loans to insolvent banks, which decreases welfare. Still, parameter values for which this effect dominates are hard to find since the integrated equilibrium exists only for small β.

The analysis shows that a high level of cross-border information (i.e. low β) is essential for an integrated interbank market to exist. However, even when the difference in information across borders is sufficiently low, there is no guarantee that private market forces reach the most efficient equilibrium.

Furthermore, in all possible equilibria, an inefficiency remains that is due to the informational asymmetry between countries. Because of the concavity of the liquidation technology, the most efficient outcome would involve all banks with the domestic good signal to liquidate the same amount. However, since borrowers from country B pay a premium that reflects the asymmetry in information, they liquidate more than banks in country A in both equilibria.

Proposition 3 was stated for a given investment decision by banks. Obviously, banks may choose a different portfolio depending on the type of equilibrium they expect at time 1. This will have a further impact on welfare. To complete the analysis, we now turn to banks' time-0 investment decision.

2.3 The Investment Decision

At time 0, banks choose how much to invest in reserves or in the risky asset in order to maximize ex ante expected profits Π. For an interior equilibrium to exist, the following condition is required: $\frac{\partial \Pi}{\partial I} = \frac{\partial \Pi}{\partial s_0}$. While the expected return on the risky asset, pR, is exogenously given, the return on reserves depends on the continuation equilibrium at time 1, which reflects the prevailing liquidity conditions.

Without loss of generality, we assume in the following that in the integrated equilibrium, there is still excess liquidity after interbank transactions have taken place, that is, $\bar{p}(1+r_A) = 1$ (the other case is derived analogously). Denoting $\mu = \{q_A, q_B, \pi_L, \pi_H, \alpha, \beta\}$ the set of model parameters, this equilibrium requires the following:

Lemma 5: *(Continuation equilibrium). For every μ and s_0, there exists a time $t = 1$ continuation equilibrium characterized by an equilibrium interbank interest rate in the liquidity-short country, $r_B(\mu, s_0)$, which satisfies the equilibrium condition $\Omega_B = \Lambda_B$, that is:*

$$1 + r_B(\mu, s_0) = R \exp\left\{ \frac{(\sigma_L^R \pi_L + \sigma_D^B(\psi)\pi_H)c_1}{\sigma_L^B + \sigma_D^B(\psi)} - s_0 \right\}. \tag{6.7}$$

Proof: See Appendix.

Lemma 5 is derived for an equilibrium with an integrated market, however, by setting $\psi = 0$ it applies also to the case of segmented markets.

Now, because of rational expectations on the lottery $r_k(\mu, s_0)$ where the randomness comes from $k = A, B$ (i.e., the aggregate liquidity shock), we have the following lemma:

Lemma 6: *An equilibrium at time $t = 0$ always exists. The interior solution is characterized by an equilibrium interest rate in country B satisfying*

$$E\{\bar{p}(1 + r(\mu, s_0))\} = \frac{\sigma_L^A p(R-1) + \sigma_B^A(\bar{p}R - 1) + (\sigma_L^B p + \sigma_B^B \bar{p})R}{\sigma_L^B p + \sigma_B^B}. \tag{6.8}$$

Proof: See Appendix.

In order for an integrated equilibrium to exist, notice that it is not possible that $\bar{p}(1 + r_A) > R$, because $r_A < r_B$ implies that $\frac{\partial \Pi}{\partial s_0} > \frac{\partial \Pi}{\partial I}$ so that investment in reserves would always dominate. On the other hand, $1 + r_B < R$ implies $\frac{\partial \Pi}{\partial s_0} < \frac{\partial \Pi}{\partial I}$ in which case banks would invest all in the risky asset. In other words, for an interior equilibrium, it needs to be the case that some agents liquidate positive amounts at time 1, while others do not. This is always possible, as $q_A < q_B$.

From Lemmas 5 and 6, we can derive the optimal investment in reserves s_0^* that is consistent with rational expectations. It is easy to see that

$$\frac{\partial s_0}{\partial \psi} < 0,$$

that is, the investment in reserves is decreasing in the "degree of integration", measured by ψ. This result is intuitive, because more integration implies that there is less need for banks to insure themselves against the possibility of being in the liquidity-short country. In particular, this implies that, for the same parameter constellations, if banks expect a segmentation of markets, they will invest more in reserves then they would if the integrated equilibrium was expected. This makes expected welfare in the integrated equilibrium comparatively higher, because investment in reserves is ex ante less efficient than investment in the risky asset, since $pR > 1$. Nevertheless, this result does not allow us to go beyond Proposition 3 and to obtain a general result ranking the two types of equilibria in terms of welfare.

3. Coexistence of Unsecured and Repo Markets in an International Setting

Finally, we discuss the general case where both types of markets, repo and unsecured, coexist. In the analysis, the difference between reserves and Treasury bills is crucial. Reserves allow agents to consume at time $t = 1$, while Treasury bills entitle the bearer to liquidity at time $t = 2$. Still, since there is a market for Treasury bills that opens at time $t = 1$, Treasury bills are a close substitute for reserves at the individual level. Nevertheless, at the aggregate level only reserves can be used as consumption at time $t = 1$. For a bank, a unit invested in reserves, that is, in the storage technology, will yield 1; a unit invested in Treasury bills that is sold at time 1 will yield B_1/B_0. In equilibrium, banks will have to hold both reserves and Treasury bills and therefore the equilibrium price B_0 will have to adjust accordingly.

We assume that the supply of Treasury bills is exogenously given by the government, and that they are issued at a price T_0 that induces banks to include them in their equilibrium portfolio. We focus on the more interesting case where the supply of Treasury bills is small so that borrowers cannot rely on the repo market alone to obtain liquidity, and liquidity-short banks without access to unsecured markets have to close down (the opposite case where banks are able to cope with liquidity shocks by selling Treasury bills is trivial). In this way we are able to examine the combined effect of integration through the repo market and market discipline by peer monitoring. The role of Treasury bills in the model will be to allow the transfer of reserves from the liquidity-long country to the liquidity-short one without any risk, at the cost of a lower return.

In this context, as it is intuitive, it is possible to show that the excess liquidity banks of the liquidity-short country will never hold Treasury bills until time 2. This is in line with the fact that these lenders have an informational rent from lending to the interbank market because of more accurate information, so that they can lend the liquidity they obtain through the sale of Treasury bills. Therefore, equilibrium is now obtained with a transfer of liquidity equal to Δs_0 through the sale of Treasury bills. That is, time-1 equilibrium in the interbank markets requires

$$\Omega_A = \Lambda_A - \Delta s_0 \tag{6.9}$$

$$\Omega_B = \Lambda_B + \Delta s_0. \tag{6.10}$$

The following proposition extends Proposition 1 and characterizes equilibrium in the two countries:

Proposition 4: *The continuation equilibrium in the interbank market is characterized by* $r_B^* \geq r_F^* > r_A^*$ and either

1. *Integration if* $0 < \psi^* \leq 1$, $r_B(\psi^*) \geq r_F(\psi^*)$, $p_F(1+r_F^*) = \bar{p}(1+r_A^*) = (\frac{1}{B_1}) < \bar{p}(1+r_B^*)$, *and country-B banks will sell all their Treasury bills to the country-A ones.*
2. *Integration with unsecured markets segmentation if* $r_B^* = r_A^*$ and $\psi^* = 0$ *in which case* $p_F = \text{prob}(\tilde{R} = R|\underline{s})$. *This will occur when the aggregate liquidity shocks are small with regard to the Treasury bill market.*
3. *Segmentation if* $\psi^* = 0$ *and* $r_B^* > r_A^*$, *in which case* $p_F = \text{prob}(\tilde{R} = R|\underline{s})$, *and country-B banks will sell all their Treasury bills.*

Proof: See Appendix.

Proposition 4 considers a situation where banks with excess liquidity are willing to both buy repos and lend in the unsecured market. Therefore, the price for liquidity on both markets is the same one for lenders in country A, that is, $\bar{p}(1 + r_A) = \frac{1}{B_1}$. This implies that for borrowers in both countries, the cost of obtaining liquidity through the repo market, $\frac{1}{B_1}$, is smaller than the cost it faces in the unsecured market, which is $1 + r_s$, $s = A, B$.[8] The borrowing banks will resort to the unsecured market only after having sold all their Treasury bills. Thus, in an international framework, the repo facility will be used to transfer liquidity from the excess liquidity country to the liquidity-short one, while the unsecured market will be used to provide liquidity to domestic and foreign borrowers, with foreign borrowers paying an imperfect information premium $r_F - r_A$.

This immediate effect from the introduction of a repo market is therefore that the liquidity spread between countries is reduced. However, from Proposition 2 we know that a large difference in liquidity needs is essential for the emergence of an integrated equilibrium. The repo market may thus crowd out the integrated unsecured market. This is stated in the following proposition:

Proposition 5: *The introduction of a cross-border repo market implies*

- *for a segmented equilibrium,* $(\psi^* = 0)$, $r_B - r_A$ *is reduced*
- *the integrated equilibrium* $(\psi^* > 0)$ *collapses for sufficiently high* Δs_0.

Proof: See Appendix.

The possible equilibria in the unsecured market are illustrated in Figure 3. The left graph illustrates the case where Δs_0 is relatively low. Here, equilibria with both separated and

[8] See the discussion on Lemma 1.

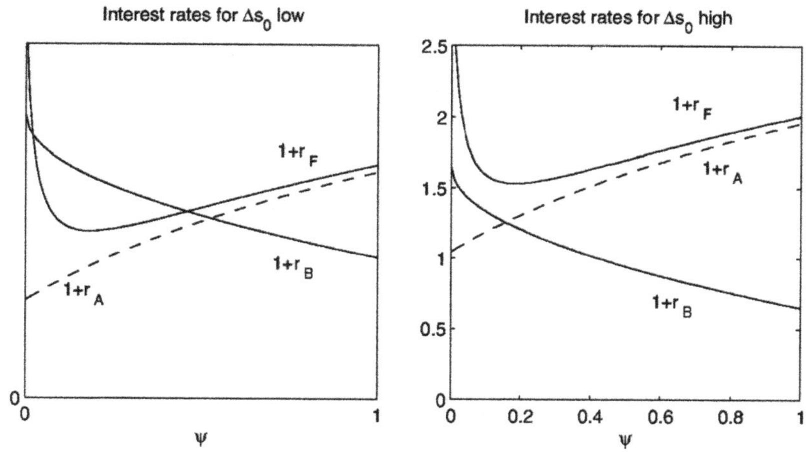

Figure 6.3. **Equilibria with different levels of Treasury bill holdings**

integrated unsecured markets exist. In the right graph, on the other hand, Δs_0 is so high that integration in the unsecured market is not possible any longer.

Finally, let us turn to the welfare effects of the introduction of a repo market. First, as long as the nature of the integrated equilibrium is not altered by the introduction (i.e., the market remains integrated, or remains segmented), a repo market leads to an increase in welfare, because the transfer of liquidity smoothes interest rates across countries.[9]

However, if the integrated unsecured market breaks down, the degree of integration will be reduced again. It would be tempting to jump to the conclusion that the collapse of the integrated equilibrium resulting from an infinitesimal increase in Treasury bills decreases welfare. Still, in the light of Proposition 3, we know that the analysis is more involved. Indeed, the next proposition establishes that the collapse of an integrated equilibrium need not be welfare decreasing.

Proposition 6: *The introduction of a repo market is welfare improving*

- *if the equilibrium type is unchanged (either integrated or segmented), or*
- *if the integrated equilibrium collapses, provided that β is sufficiently large.*

Proof: See Appendix.

To sum up, for a given investment, the establishment of a repo market is unambiguously welfare improving as long as it does not lead to the collapse of the integrated unsecured market for liquidity. Should this happen, however, the direction of the welfare effects is inconclusive and will depend on the model parameters.

However, we have to again consider the banks' time-0 investment decision to completely assess the welfare effects. The following lemmas are equivalent to Lemmas 5 and 6 from Section 2.3.

[9]If the amount of Treasury bills were sufficient for liquidity-short banks to survive, the repo market would enable some banks to survive (those with a $\underline{s}$-signal), even though from an efficiency point of view, they should close down. This negative effect of a repo market is ruled out, however, under our model assumptions.

Lemma 7: *(Continuation equilibrium). For every μ and s_0, there exists a time $t = 1$ continuation equilibrium characterized by an equilibrium interbank interest rate $r_B(\mu, s_0)$ and an equilibrium price for bonds $B_1(\mu, s_0)$ that satisfy the equilibrium condition $\Omega_B = \Lambda_B$, that is:*

$$s_0 = \frac{[\sigma_L^B \pi_L + \sigma_D^B(\psi)\pi_H]}{\sigma_L^B + \sigma_D^B(\psi)} c_1 - \ln\left(\frac{1 + r_B(\mu, s_0)}{R}\right) - T_0 B_1(\mu, s_0) \tag{6.11}$$

and

$$\frac{1}{B_1(\mu, s_0)} = \bar{p}(1 + r_A(\mu, s_0)). \tag{6.12}$$

Lemma 8: *An equilibrium at time $t = 0$ always exists. The equilibrium interest rate in country B satisfies*

$$E\{1 + r(\mu, s_0)\} = \frac{1}{B_0} = \frac{\sigma_L^A p(R-1) + \sigma_B^A(\bar{p}R - 1) + \sigma_L^B p + \sigma_B^B \tilde{p}}{\sigma_L^B p\bar{p} + \sigma_B^B \tilde{p}} \tag{6.13}$$

Proof: See Appendix.

Equations (11) through (13) determine the optimal investment in reserves, s_0. Similar to Section 2, we find that s_0 is decreasing in ψ so that more reserves are held in a segmented than in an integrated equilibrium. Again, this makes the integrated one relatively more appealing from a welfare point of view.

Notice that banks are indifferent between investing in the risky asset or reserves, so the optimal T_0 is determined by the exogenously given supply of Treasury bills. Investment in the risky asset can then be derived as the residual.

4. Extensions

Till now we have restricted our focus to a simplified world where banks were either domestic or foreign, correspondent banking services were excluded and the population of banks was homogeneous in regard of their credit risk. In the following three subsections we consider these extensions, starting with correspondent banking, then turning to transnational banks and concluding with the introduction of safe banks.

4.1 Correspondent Banking

Correspondent banking will develop when some banks are able to borrow from the liquid country and lend to the illiquid one. These are liquidity-long banks from country B with a $\bar{s}$ foreign signal that will borrow at the rate r_F, and lend at the domestic rate r_B. As correspondent banking develops, some aggregate amount of liquidity Z is channeled into the illiquid country and this will result in new equilibrium interest rates $r_B(Z)$ and $r_F(Z)$.

For correspondent banking to be profitable, the cost of borrowing in country A, $1 + r_F(Z)$, cannot exceed the average return from lending to borrowers in country B, $\bar{p}(1 + r_{CB}(Z))$, where $r_{CB}(Z)$ represents the interest rate charged by correspondent banks. Therefore, it is required that

$$1 + r_F(Z) \leq \bar{p}(1 + r_B(Z)). \tag{6.14}$$

Condition (14) implies that $r_F(Z) < r_B(Z)$, requiring that the equilibrium is of the $\psi = 1$ type, which corresponds to the case where all $(\bar{s}, \bar{s})$ banks of country B borrow abroad. In addition, corresponding banking is unable to reduce the spread $r_B - r_F$ to zero as the following proposition establishes.

Proposition 7: *Correspondent banking will develop only in the $\psi = 1$ equilibrium provided that the interest rate wedge $r_B(0) - r_F(0)$ is sufficiently large, and in equilibrium the wedge $r_B(Z^*) - r_F(Z^*)$ is strictly positive.*

Proof: See Appendix.

This interest rate differential will trigger the arbitrage operated by correspondent banking: Those banks able to borrow abroad would do so, even if they are liquidity long, and then use the liquidity obtained to lend it to those banks in their home country.

At best, the interbank market equilibrium will be such that competition among correspondent banks will lead to the limit point Z^* where there are no more gains from correspondent banking:

$$1 + r_F(Z^*) = \bar{p}(1 + r_{CB}(Z^*)) = \bar{p}(1 + r_B(Z^*)). \tag{6.15}$$

From this discussion it is clear that correspondent banking has a positive effect on welfare, since it helps channeling liquidity to where it is most needed: It is efficient that banks with the signals $(\bar{s}, \underline{s})$ liquidate as little as possible. This fact together with a concave liquidation technology implies that having correspondent banking is welfare-improving. The difference with respect to the introduction of a repo market is that there is no possible switch to another equilibrium, as correspondent banking requires $\psi = 1$. The inefficiency due to the asymmetry of information across countries is not completely removed since an interest rate differential continues to remain.

4.2 Transnational Banks

We will define a transnational bank as one which is part of the financial systems in the two countries and thus issues the same domestic signal in both countries. Therefore, there is no cross-country information asymmetry for transnational banks, so that they are able to operate in both markets when the signal they receive is good, and in none when it is bad. This implies that transnational banks borrow from the country with lower interest rates and lend in the country with the higher ones. Contrasting with the corresponding banking case that emerged only for $\psi = 1$, a transnational bank will operate whenever there is an interest rate differential, including the case of $\psi = 0$.

Because in our model there is no limit to the amount a bank can borrow other than its credit appraisal, transnational banks will borrow from country A and lend to country B, as correspondent banks do.

The difference with respect to correspondent banking is that in the correspondent banking case, when arbitraging interest rate differentials is not profitable because condition (14) is not met, transnational banks will still choose to borrow from the cheapest source, in country A, if they are liquidity-short (π_H), and to lend at the best rates, in country B, if they are liquidity long (π_L). Consequently, we will have a "variable size market", as transnational banks will choose the market they enter. If we assume there is a measure μ of transnational banks in each country, the effect we will have is an increase in the supply of loans in the country with a liquidity shortage, and an increase in the demand for loans in the excess liquidity country. Equilibrium will occur with

$$\widehat{\Omega}_B = \Lambda_B \tag{6.16}$$

$$\widehat{\Omega}_A = \Lambda_A, \tag{6.17}$$

where the expression for $\widehat{\Omega}_B$ and $\widehat{\Omega}_A$ are given by:

$$\widehat{\Omega}_B = (1-\mu)\Omega_B(\psi) + \mu(\sigma_L^A + \sigma_L^B)\pi_L$$

$$\widehat{\Omega}_A = (1-\mu)\Omega_A(\psi) + \mu(\sigma_D^A + \sigma_F^A + \sigma_D^B)\pi_H.$$

As a consequence, the effect of transnational banks is, even in the absence of cross-country arbitrage, to diminish the liquidity shocks by allowing a fraction of banks to choose the best rates without facing any information asymmetries.

It is also worth noticing that whenever transnational banks are present, correspondent banking is not profitable. This means that obviously, all transnational banks are able to act as correspondent banks. Still, if the amount of transnational banks is sufficiently large, banks with a good foreign signal will be indifferent between borrowing at home or borrowing abroad, as an integrated market with $r_B = r_F$ can be achieved. This is in contrast to the result we obtain with correspondent banking (Proposition 7). If the amount of transnational banks is even larger, then the spread between $r_B = r_F$ and r_A diminishes and the informational rents in the illiquid country begin to be eroded. This is so as a transnational bank is able to obtain liquidity in the country with excess liquidity at interest rate r_A (while a correspondent bank would borrow at r_F).

Notice that the presence of transnational banks is similar to an economy with a cross-border repo market: In both cases, the transfer of liquidity is facilitated and this is efficient provided there is no switch to an inferior equilibrium, as established in Proposition 5.

4.3 Heterogeneous Default Risk Levels

Assume now that banks are not homogeneous anymore, and that some banks in each country have a lower probability of failure which is common knowledge. For the sake of simplicity we take the extreme case where some banks are perfectly safe while others are risky. We consider this case to be particularly meaningful, as the too-big-to-fail argument implies that some banks have the unlimited support of the regulatory authority, while others face default with a nonzero probability.

The assumption $\bar{p} = 1$ immediately implies that such a bank is able to borrow freely from any market, as a transnational bank. But in addition, Equation (15) implies a complete integration of the markets. The existence of noisy information for foreign banks will imply that lending unsecured to banks abroad is not profitable, as there is no spread to compensate for the risk. In equilibrium, liquidity is transferred from the excess liquidity country to the one experiencing the liquidity shortage by the safe banks at no cost. This equilibrium is efficient, (independently of the existence of an implicit transfer from the government to the too-big-to-fail bank that is out of the focus of our analysis).

This type of equilibrium seems to describe rather well the current situation in the European Monetary Union. While interest rates in the different member states have converged rapidly [see ECB (2000)], the interbank market seems to be characterized by a two-tier structure: In a recent study, Ciampolini and Rhode (2000) report the results of a survey conducted among European Banks according to which only a few large banks are active in the international market while smaller ones are confined to domestic sources for liquidity.

The implications of this finding are far reaching. It implies that a country that lacks the resources (or the credibility) to back up its major banks in case of distress will be at a disadvantage in obtaining liquidity in the international interbank market. For developed countries that are able to bail-out their banks, it may also imply that there is an interest on behalf of the country to build strong "too-big-to-fail" banks in order to compete in the international arena. If this was so, governments might have an interest in promoting national mergers by creating national banks rather than allowing for the creation of transnational banks that they would not be able to support.

5. Conclusion

In this article, we analyzed a model of interbank markets in an international context. We focused on the respective roles played by an unsecured money market and a repo market on the domestic and international levels, and developed their welfare properties.

In an economy with unsecured markets, lending takes place on the basis of peer monitoring. This is shown to be efficient, as funds are channeled to the most efficient projects. In repo markets, on the other hand, monitoring plays no role because all loans are collateralized. Therefore, markets are unable to achieve efficient liquidation of unprofitable projects, and insolvent banks forebear. Still, contrary to unsecured markets, a repo market is able to achieve liquidity smoothing across solvent market participants.

In an international context, interbank markets seem to work less efficiently, leading to market imperfections such as liquidity shortages or interest rate differentials. Although these differences could be attributed to exchange rate risk, we argue that the main barrier to an integrated international market is the existence of asymmetric information between different countries.

We have shown that as long as peer monitoring across borders is less efficient than on a domestic level, the integration of unsecured markets can never be perfect. In particular, cross-border lending involves the payment of interest rate premia which reflect the adverse selection of borrowers in the international market. This implies that a perfect liquidity smoothing across borders cannot take place. As a consequence, we show, first, that an equilibrium with an integrated interbank market does not always exist. Second, even if it does exist, at the same time market segmentation is always an equilibrium. Therefore, even with monetary integration or currency pegging, market integration is not necessarily achieved. Interestingly, we also found that in an integrated equilibrium, welfare is not necessarily higher than in the segmented one.

A repo market, on the other hand, is always able to function on an international basis, since it overcomes the problem of asymmetric information. Thus, it is able to achieve liquidity smoothing at least to some degree that is ex ante beneficial to both countries. Still, the welfare effects from a repo facility remain ambiguous: Our analysis shows that a repo market reduces the benefits from peer monitoring and might even impede the integration of markets. Furthermore, even the combination of both types of markets is not necessarily beneficial since integration comes at the cost of a higher degree of inefficient forbearance.

Finally, the effects of correspondent banks, transnational banks with varying degrees of riskiness are analyzed. We show that these institutions can play, in varying degrees, a crucial role in the cross-border liquidity transfer.

Appendix: Proof of Lemmas and Propositions

Proof of Lemma 1: Without loss of generality (w.l.o.g.), assume that $T_0 = 0$, as the repo market is inactive and Treasury bills play no role. For a bank of type k, $k = L, D, F$, denote ΔI_k as the amount liquidated, $L_k^S(L_k^D)$ as the loan given to (demanded by) a bank of type k, and s_k^1 as the storage of reserves. Country indices are dropped. The time-1 optimization problem for a bank facing withdrawals π_L is:

$$\max_{\{\Delta I_L, s_L^1, L_D^S, L_F^S\}} p\{R(I - \Delta I_L) + \bar{p}(1 + r_D)L_D^S + p_F(1 + r_F)L_F^S + s_L^1 - (1 - \pi_L)c_2\}$$

$$\text{s.t. } s_0 + l(\Delta I_L) \geq \pi_L c_1 + s_L^1 + L_D^S + L_F^S,$$

as well as the appropriate nonnegativity constraints. Here, r_D and r_F denote the domestic and foreign interbank market rates, and p_F refers to the expected probability of solvency of foreign banks. Notice that we have assumed that the investment in the risky technology I is so large that the bank fails whenever the risky project is not successful. Similarly, a bank of type $k = D, F$ with withdrawals π_H faces the problem

$$\max_{\{\Delta I_k, s_k^1, L_k^D\}} p\{R(I - \Delta I_k) + (1 + r_k)L_k^D + s_k^l - (1 - \pi_H)c_2\}$$

$$\text{s.t. } s_0 + L_k^D + l(\Delta I_k) \geq \pi_H c_1 + s_k^1.$$

The first-order conditions for the Lagrangian for an L-bank, with the multiplier $p\lambda$ for the liquidity constraint are the following:

$$\begin{aligned} \bar{p}(1 + r_D) - \lambda &\leq 0 \\ p_F(1 + r_F) - \lambda &\leq 0 \\ -R + \lambda l'(\Delta I_L) &\leq 0 \\ 1 - \lambda &\leq 0, \end{aligned} \tag{6.18}$$

while in a state of nature $k = D, F$ (and multiplier $p\mu$) they are characterized by:

$$\begin{aligned} -(1 + r_k) + \mu &\leq 0 \\ -R + \mu l'(\Delta I_k) &\leq 0 \\ 1 - \mu &\leq 0 \end{aligned} \tag{6.19}$$

In order for L-banks to lend to liquidity-short banks from both countries, we need $\bar{p}(1 + r_D) = p_F(1 + r_F)$. If $\bar{p}(1 + r_D) \leq 1$, only reserves are used, $\Delta I_k = 0$ for every k, and the interbank markets are inactive. Banks with a liquidity shortage liquidate positive amounts only for $1 + r_k > 1/R$, while excess liquidity banks offer loans for $\bar{p}(1 + r_D) > 1$, and liquidate for $\bar{p}(1 + r_D) > 1/R$. The optimal liquidation decisions are

$$l(\Delta I_L) = \max\left\{0, \ln\left(\frac{\bar{p}(1 + r_D)}{R}\right)\right\}$$

$$l(\Delta I_D) = \max\left\{0, \ln\left(\frac{(1 + r_D)}{R}\right)\right\}$$

$$l(\Delta I_F) = \max\left\{0, \ln\left(\frac{(1 + r_F)}{R}\right)\right\} = \max\left\{0, \ln\left(\frac{\bar{p}(1 + r_D)}{{}_{PF}R}\right)\right\}.$$

From Equation (2), it follows that Λ_i is nondecreasing in the local interest rate. ∎

Proof of Lemma 2: We will prove the lemma in two steps. First we prove that only one ψ_i can be nonzero, the one corresponding to the country with high interest rates. Second, we prove that if $\psi_A > 0$, the interest rates differentials between the two countries would imply a contradiction.

1. Assume by way of contradiction that $r_i \geq r_j$ and $\psi_j > 0$. Because country i banks have access to coarser information on foreign borrowers, we have $r_i < r_{iF}$, for $i = A, B$.

   On the other hand, a necessary condition for $\psi_j > 0$ is that $r_{iF} \leq r_j$ (borrowing in country i is attractive for $(\bar{s}, \bar{s})$ borrowers in country j) but this would imply $r_j > r_i$, a contradiction, so that $r_i \geq r_j$, implies $\psi_j = 0$.
2. To prove this second point, consider first the interest rates when $\psi_A = \psi_B = 0$. Equilibrium demands $\Omega_i = \Lambda_i(r_j)$ for $i = A, B$. Since the liquidation technology is the same in the two countries, so is the supply function, and as we have $\Omega_A < \Omega_B$ and the supply is increasing in r_j, we obtain $r_A < r_B$.

Consider now the case $\psi_A > 0$ and $\psi_B = 0$. In this case, the demand Ω'_B in country B is larger than in the $\psi_A = \psi_B = 0$ case, while the demand for Ω'_A is lower than before. This would imply therefore that the market clearing interest rates satisfy again $r_A < r_B$. But then, using the argument in (1), yields a contradiction, since we have proved in (1) that in order to have $\psi_A > 0$ we need $r_A > r_B$. ∎

Proof of Proposition 1: A necessary condition for $\psi > 0$ is that borrowing abroad is no more expensive than borrowing domestically, so that $r_B \geq r_F$, with $\psi = 1$ in case of strict inequality. On the other hand, Equation (3) implies $r_F \geq r_A$.

If $\psi = 0$, there is segmentation, since any potential borrower is identified as a $(\underline{s}, \bar{s})$-type and therefore, $p_F = \underline{p}$. But, if $r_F < r_B$, we would have $\psi > 0$, a contradiction. ∎

Proof of Lemma 3: The updated probability of solvency of a foreign borrower is

$$p_F(\psi) = \frac{\psi \text{prob}(\tilde{R} = R \text{ and } (\bar{s}, \bar{s})) + \text{prob}(\tilde{R} = R \text{ and } (\underline{s}, \bar{s}))}{\psi \text{prob}(\bar{s}, \bar{s}) + \text{prob}(\underline{s}, \bar{s})}$$

$$= \frac{\psi p\alpha(1 - \beta) + p(1 - \alpha)\beta}{\psi(1 - \beta)\theta + (1 - \theta)\beta}.$$

Taking into account that $\theta = \alpha p + (1 - \alpha)(1 - p)$, it is easy to see that $p'_F(\psi) > 0$.

From Equation (3), the foreign premium is given by $r_F - r_A = (1 + r_A)\left(\frac{\bar{p}}{p_F(\psi)} - 1\right)$. Because $p'_F(\psi) > 0$, it is decreasing in ψ. ■

Proof of Lemma 4: In country B, there are $\sigma_A^B = 1 - q_B$ lenders, $\sigma_D^B(\psi) = q_B\theta[1 - \psi(1 - \beta)] \equiv q_B\xi^B$ domestic borrowers, and no foreign borrowers, $\sigma_F^B = 0$. Using the first-order conditions (20), we can express liquidity demand and supply, Equations (1) and (2), as functions of ψ,

$$\Omega_B(\psi) = (\sigma_L^B\pi_L + \sigma_D^B(\psi)\pi_H)c_1$$

$$\Lambda_B(\psi) = \sigma_L^B\left[s_0 + \ln\left(\frac{\bar{p}(1 + r_B)}{R}\right)\right] + \sigma_D^B(\psi)\left[s_0 + \ln\left(\frac{1 + r_B}{R}\right)\right].$$

Since $\bar{p}R > 1$, it is never efficient to choose s_0 so that $\Omega_B(\psi) > s_0(\sigma_L + \sigma_D^B(\psi))$. This implies that some banks (i.e., domestic borrowers) will always liquidate positive amounts. The interest rate r_B adjusts so that

$$F_B \equiv \Lambda_B(\psi) - \Omega_B(\psi) = 0. \tag{6.22}$$

Then, $\frac{\partial F_B}{\partial r_B} = \frac{\sigma_L^B + \sigma_D^B}{1+r_B} > 0$ (respectively $\frac{\partial F_B}{\partial r_B} = \frac{\sigma_D^B}{1+r_B} > 0$ if lenders do not liquidate) and $\frac{\partial F_B}{\partial \sigma_D^B(\psi)} = l(\Delta I_D^B) - (\pi_H c_1 - s_0) \equiv X_D^B$ which is negative because π_H-banks borrow. Then, the Implicit Function Theorem implies $\frac{dr_B}{d\sigma_D^B(\psi)} > 0$, and together with $\frac{d\sigma_D^B(\psi)}{d(\psi)} < 0$, we obtain

$$\frac{dr_B}{d\psi} = \frac{dr_B}{d\sigma_D^B(\psi)}\frac{d\sigma_D^B(\psi)}{d\psi} < 0.$$ ■

Proof of Proposition 2: The segmented equilibrium exists since for $\psi = 0$, any $(\bar{s}, \bar{s})$ bank would prefer to borrow at rate r_B rather than not obtaining any credit. Therefore, $\psi = 0$ is consistent with their behavior, $F_A = 0$ and $F_B = 0$ determine r_A and r_B, respectively, while r_F is indeterminate since there is no cross-border interbank lending.

An integrated equilibrium does not exist if and only if

$$\min_{\psi} r_F(\psi) - r_B(\psi) > 0. \tag{6.23}$$

Let $\psi^*(\Delta q)$ be the solution to Equation (23) with equality. We will show that if Δq satisfies

$$\min_{\psi^*(\Delta q)} r_F(\psi^*(\Delta q)) - r_B(\psi^*(\Delta q)) = 0,$$

then for any $\Delta q'$ such that $\Delta q' \leq \Delta q$, condition (23) holds, that is, the integrated equilibrium does not exist. We only have to prove that $\frac{d(r_F - r_B)}{d\Delta q} < 0$.

Since $q_B + q_A = \bar{Q}$, we have $dq_A = -dq_B$, so that $d\Delta q = 2dq_B$. Consider first $\frac{dr_B}{d\Delta q}$. In country B, r_B solves $\Lambda_B = \Omega_B$ (as in the proof of Lemma 4). From Equation (22), denote

$F_B \equiv \Lambda_B - \Omega_B = (1 - q_B)X_L^B + q_B\xi^B X_D^B = 0$ where $X_L^B \geq 0$ and $X_D^B \leq 0$. From the proof of Lemma 4, we have $\frac{\partial F_B}{\partial r_B} = \frac{1}{1+r_B}(\sigma_L^B + \sigma_D^B)$. On the other hand,

$$\frac{\partial F_B}{\partial \Delta q} = 2\frac{\partial F_B}{\partial q_B} = 2\{-X_L^B + \xi^B X_D^B\} = -\frac{2}{q_B}X_L^B \leq 0$$

where the last equality follows from Equation (22).

Next, consider $\frac{dr_F}{d\Delta q}$. Liquidity demand and supply in country A are

$$\Omega_A = (\sigma_L^A \pi_L + \sigma_D^A(\psi)\pi_H + \sigma_F^A(\psi)\pi_H)c_1$$

$$\Lambda_A = \sigma_L^A\left[s_0 + \ln\frac{p_F(1+r_F)}{R}\right] + \sigma_D^A\left[s_0 + \ln\frac{p_F(1+r_F)}{\bar{p}R}\right] + \sigma_F^A\left[s_0 + \ln\frac{1+r_F}{R}\right]$$

with $\sigma_L^A = 1 - q_A, \sigma_D^A = 1 - q_A\theta$, and $\sigma_F^A = q_B[\psi(1-\beta)\theta + \beta(1-\theta)] \equiv q_B\xi^A$, and where we have used Equation (3). Denote

$$F_A = \Lambda_A - \Omega_A \equiv (1 - q_A)X_L^A + q_A\theta X_D^A + q_B\xi^A X_F^A = 0 \tag{6.24}$$

with $X_L^A \geq 0$, $X_D^A \leq 0$ and $X_F^A \leq 0$. Then, $\frac{\partial F_A}{\partial r_F} = \frac{\sigma_L^B + \sigma_D^A + \sigma_F^A}{1+r_F}$ and

$$\frac{\partial F_A}{\partial \Delta q} = 2\frac{\partial F_A}{\partial q_B} = 2\left\{[-X_L^A + \theta X_D^A]\frac{dq_A}{dq_B} + \xi^A X_F^A\right\} = \frac{2}{q_B}\{[X_L^A - \theta X_D^A](q_B + q_A) - X_L^A\}$$

where the last equality follows from Equation (24).

Using the Implicit Function Theorem and that $r_F = r_B$ for Δq belonging to F, we find

$$\begin{aligned}\frac{d(r_F - r_B)}{d\Delta q} &= -\frac{\partial F_A/\partial \Delta q}{\partial F_A/\partial r_F} + \frac{\partial F_B/\partial \Delta q}{\partial F_B/\partial r_B}\\ &= -\frac{2(1+r_F)}{q_B}\left\{\frac{(X_L^A - \theta X_D^A)(q_B + q_A)}{\sigma_L^A + \sigma_D^A + \sigma_F^A} + \frac{X_L^B}{\sigma_L^B + \sigma_D^B} - \frac{X_L^A}{\sigma_L^A + \sigma_D^A + \sigma_F^A}\right\}\end{aligned}$$

The first term is positive. Furthermore, the second term exceeds the third term: first, $X_L^B > X_L^A$ because $r_B > r_A$ implies $l(\Delta I_L^B) > l(\Delta I_L^A)$. Second, it is easy to show that $\sigma_L^B + \sigma_D^B < \sigma_L^B + \sigma_D^A + \sigma_F^A$, as it is equivalent to $(q_B - q_A)(1-\theta) + q_A\psi(1-\beta) + q_B\xi^A \geq 0$. Hence, $\frac{d(r_F - r_B)}{d\Delta q} < 0$. ■

Proof of Proposition 3: Suppose that the integrated equilibrium exists. Denoting by index $i = A, B$ the country, and k the bank type. Expected welfare is equal to the expected returns on total assets in the economy (notice that the distribution of assets among banks, depositors, and the deposit insurance company is irrelevant because the latter raises funds at unit cost). Expected welfare is

$$W = I(pR - 1) - \frac{1}{2}\sum_{i=A,B}\sum_{k}\sigma_k^i[p_k R\Delta I_k^i - l(\Delta I_k^i)], \tag{6.25}$$

where p_k denotes the expected probability of solvency for a given type k, i.e. $p_k \in \{p, \bar{p}, \underline{p}\}$.

Denote the integrated equilibrium I and the separated one S. W.l.o.g. suppose that in country A, even in the integrated equilibrium $\bar{p}(1+r_A)=1$. This implies that country-A banks liquidate the same amount in both equilibria, so we can neglect them in the welfare comparison. For country B, denote interest rates in the segmented equilibrium $r_B(S)$ and those in the integrated one $r_B(I)=r_F(I)$, where $r_B(S)>r_B(I)$. A change from a separated to an integrated equilibrium then affects the following banks in country B: $\sigma_L^B \equiv 1-q_B$ lenders and $\sigma_D^B \equiv q_B\theta$ borrowers with the good domestic signal will face higher interest rates $1+r_B$. Thus, $\Delta I_k^B(S)>\Delta I_k^B(I)$, $k=L,D$. Furthermore, $\sigma_C^B \equiv q_B(1-\theta)\beta$ borrowers with the signal pair $(\underline{s},\bar{s})$ will go bankrupt in the equilibrium with separation, having to liquidate $\Delta I_C^B(S)\geq \Delta I_D^B(S)$, but obtain a foreign loan with integration and liquidate $\Delta I_D^B(I)$.

For $p_L=p, p_D=\bar{p}$, and $p_C=\underline{p}$, we can manipulate the change in welfare from Equation (25) so that

$$\begin{aligned}
\Delta W &\equiv W(S)-W(I)\\
&=\sum_{k=L,D,C}\sigma_k^B\{[p_kR\Delta I_k^B(S)-l(\Delta I_k^B(S))]-[p_kR\Delta I_k^B(I)-l(\Delta I_k^B(I))]\}\\
&=\sum_{k=L,D,C}\sigma_k^B\left\{\int_{\Delta I_k^B(I)}^{\Delta I_k^B(S)} l'(\Delta I)d\Delta I-\int_{\Delta I_k^B(I)}^{\Delta I_k^B(S)} p_kRd\Delta I\right\}\\
&=\sum_{k=L,D,C}\sigma_k^B\left\{\int_{\Delta I_k^B(I)}^{\Delta I_k^B(S)} [l'(\Delta I)-p_kR]d\Delta I\right\}. \qquad (6.26)
\end{aligned}$$

Our model assumptions imply $\bar{p}R\geq pR\geq l'(\Delta I)$ and hence that the terms corresponding to $k=L,D$ are negative, while Assumption 2 implies $\underline{p}R\leq l'(\Delta I)$ so that the term for $k=C$ is positive.

The sign of ΔW depends therefore on parameters. Suppose first that $\beta\to 0$, so that $\sigma_C^B\to 0$. Then, $\Delta W<0$, and the break down of the integrated equilibrium decreases welfare.

On the other hand, consider the following set of parameters: $R=2$, $p=0.8$, $\alpha=0.9$, $\beta=0.45$, $I=0.5$, $T_0=0$, $q_B=0.55$, $q_A=0.425$, $\pi_H=0.8$, and $\pi_L=0.3$. Calculations show that expected welfare [Equation (25)] is $W^{\text{seg}}=0.2968$ in the segmented equilibrium. Furthermore, an integrated equilibrium exists for $\psi\approx 0.77$, leading to expected welfare of $W^{\text{int}}=0.2964<W^{\text{seg}}$. ∎

Proof of Lemma 5: From the proof of Lemma 1, we know that in the liquidity-short country, $l(\Delta I_L^B)=\ln(\frac{\bar{p}(1+r_B)}{R})$ and $l(\Delta I_D^B)=\ln(\frac{1+r_B}{R})$. At time 1, liquidity demand and supply in country B are then given as

$$\begin{aligned}
\Omega^B(\mu)&=[\sigma_L^B\pi_L+\sigma_D^B(\psi)\pi_H]c_1\\
\Lambda^B(\mu,s_0)&=\sigma_L^B\left[s_0+\ln\left(\tfrac{\bar{p}(1+r)}{R}\right)\right]+\sigma_D^B(\psi)\left[s_0+\ln\left(\tfrac{1+r}{R}\right)\right].
\end{aligned}$$

Market clearing demands $\Omega^B(\mu)=\Lambda^B(\mu,s_0)$, which yields Equation (7). ∎

Proof of Lemma 6: Existence of the time-0 equilibrium follows from the fact that we are maximizing a continuous function on a compact set. The time-0 maximization problem is

$$\max_{\{I,s_0\}} \Pi = \frac{1}{2}(\sigma_L^A \Pi_L^A + \sigma_B^A \Pi_B^A + \sigma_L^B \Pi_L^B + \sigma_B^B \Pi_B^B)$$

such that $I + s_0 = 1$, where Π_k^i, $i = A, B$, $k = L, B$ denote time-1 expected profits and are defined as

$$\Pi_L^i = \max_{\Delta I_L^i} p\{R(I - \Delta I_L^i) + \bar{p}(1 + r_i)L_L^i + s_L^{i1} - (1 - \pi_L)c_2\}$$
$$\text{s.t. } L_L^i = s_0 + l(\Delta I_L^i) - \pi_L c_1 - s_L^{i1}$$

for a lender (L), or

$$\Pi_B^i = \max_{\Delta I_B^i} \bar{p}\{R(I - \Delta I_B^i) - (1 + r_i)L_B^i + s_B^{i1} - (1 - \pi_B)c_2\}$$
$$\text{s.t. } L_B^i = \pi_H c_1 + s_B^{i1} - s_0 - l(\Delta I_B^i)$$

for a borrower (B), or zero if the bank needs liquidity but has a bad signal. The first-order conditions for the time-0 problem are

$$2\frac{\partial \Pi}{\partial I} = \sigma_L^A pR + \sigma_B^A \bar{p}R + \sigma_L^B pR + \sigma_B^B \bar{p}R$$
$$2\frac{\partial \Pi}{\partial s_0} = \bar{p}(1 + r_A)[\sigma_L^A p + \sigma_B^A] + \bar{p}(1 + r_B)[\sigma_L^B p + \sigma_B^B]. \tag{6.28}$$

Without loss of generality, we focus on the case $\bar{p}(1 + r_A) = 1$, that is, that there is excess liquidity in country A even after the interbank market has taken place. For an interior solution, $\frac{\partial \Pi}{\partial I} = \frac{\partial \Pi}{\partial s_0}$ requires Equation (8). ■

Proof of Proposition 4: We know that $p_F(1 + r_F^*) = \bar{p}(1 + r_A^*) < \bar{p}(1 + r_B^*) < 1 + r_B^*$. Now, depending on the Treasury bills yield $\frac{1}{B_1}$, banks will be willing to buy and sell Treasury bills rather than making loans. Notice first that if $\frac{1}{B_1} > 1 + r_B^*$ there is an excess demand in the Treasury bill market as no agent wants to sell Treasury bills, and if $\frac{1}{B_1} < \bar{p}(1 + r_A^*)$ there is an excess supply as no one wants to buy them. As a consequence, for possible equilibria we have to focus on the following cases:

1. $p_F(1 + r_F^*) = \bar{p}(1 + r_A^*) = \frac{1}{B_1} < \bar{p}(1 + r_B^*)$
2. $\bar{p}(1 + r_A^*) = \frac{1}{B_1} < \bar{p}(1 + r_B^*)$
3. $\bar{p}(1 + r_A^*) < \frac{1}{B_1} = \bar{p}(1 + r_B^*)$
4. $\bar{p}(1 + r_A^*) = \frac{1}{B_1} = \bar{p}(1 + r_B^*)$

Case 1 corresponds to integration. Country-B banks will all prefer to sell their Treasury bills and use the liquidity thus obtained either to borrow less or to lend more in the interbank market. Case 2 corresponds to segmentation. For a higher Treasury bill yield, we would reach case 3. This, however, cannot be sustained as an equilibrium as we have assumed that the Treasury bill holdings are insufficient to guarantee survival by borrowing on the

Treasury bills market only. Consequently, liquidity-short banks from country A will bid higher interest rates rather than being liquidated. If this occurs, the interest rate hike either restores the case 1–2 type of equilibrium or else it involves only the domestic interbank market. In the latter case, we reach case 4 which corresponds to the case where unsecured interbank market segmentation occurs so that there is no strict inequality between r_A^* and r_B^*. In case 4, the Treasury bill market leads to interest rate equalization without any cross-country unsecured borrowing. If the yield on interest rates is higher, then only liquidity-short country-B banks will sell Treasury bills. Competition among buyers will then restore the equality of either 1, 2, or 4. ■

Proof of Proposition 5: Suppose the cross-country trading of Treasury bills leads to a transfer of liquidity of Δs_0 as in Equations (10) and (9). It is sufficient to show that $\frac{\partial (r_B - r_A)}{\partial \Delta s_0} < 0$. Consider country A. From Equation (9), equilibrium with the market now requires a lower supply of liquidity Λ_A. Lemma 1 implies that $\frac{\partial r_A}{\partial \Delta s_0} \geq 0$. Consider now country B. Notice first that without the Treasury bill market, there is a liquidity shortage in B so that in equilibrium, a positive measure of banks need to liquidate positive amounts. W.l.o.g. assume that $\Delta I_L^B = 0$. From Equations (1), (10), and (20) it follows $1 + r_B = R\ \exp\{\frac{\Omega_B - \Delta s_0}{\sigma_D^B}\}$ so that $\frac{\partial r_B}{\partial \Delta s_0} < 0$. This proves the first part of the proposition.

To establish the second part, suppose that T_0 is so high that an equilibrium of the second type in Proposition 4 is obtained, where $r_A(\psi = 0) = r_B(\psi = 0)$. Since $r_F \geq r_A$, r_A is nondecreasing and r_B nonincreasing in ψ (see Lemma 4), if follows that $r_F(\psi) > r_B(\psi)$ for all ψ. ■

Proof of Proposition 6: Part 1: Suppose that prior to the establishment of the repo market, the economy is in the segmented equilibrium. Welfare is defined in Equation (25). We need to show that $\frac{\partial W}{\partial \Delta s_0} > 0$. Notice first that for the segmented equilibrium, the equilibrium conditions Equation (9) and (10) can be rewritten

$$l(\Delta I^A) \equiv \sum_{k=L,D} \sigma_k^A l(\Delta I_k^A) = \Omega_A - s_0(\sigma_L^A + \sigma_D^A) + \Delta s_0 \tag{6.29}$$

$$l(\Delta I^B) \equiv \sum_{k=L,D} \sigma_k^B l(\Delta I_k^B) = \Omega_B - s_0(\sigma_L^B + \sigma_D^B) - \Delta s_0. \tag{6.30}$$

This implies that

$$\sum_{i=A,B} l(\Delta I^i) = \Omega_A + \Omega_B - \sum_{i=A,B} \sum_{k=L,D} \sigma_k^i s_0$$

is independent of Δs_0. Therefore, from Equation (25), $\frac{\partial W}{\partial \Delta s_0}$ reduces to

$$\frac{\partial W}{\partial \Delta s_0} = -\frac{1}{2} \sum_{i=A,B} \sum_{k=L,D} \sigma_k^i p_k R \frac{\partial \Delta I_k^i}{\partial \Delta s_0}.$$

Consider first a situation in which there is no repo market, that is, $\Delta s_0 = 0$. Because $\Omega_B > \Omega_A$ by assumption, and $\sigma_L^A + \sigma_D^A - (\sigma_L^B + \sigma_D^B) = (q_B - q_A)(1 - \theta) > 0$, we have $l(\Delta I^B) > l(\Delta I^A)$, that is, in a situation without an active repo market, aggregate liquidation is higher in country B than in country A.

Now consider an increase in Δs_0:

$$\sigma_k^i \frac{\partial \Delta I_k^i}{\partial \Delta s_0} = \sigma_k^i \exp(l(\Delta I_k^i)) \frac{\partial l(\Delta I_k^i)}{\partial \Delta s_0} = (\Delta I_k^i + 1)\sigma_k^i \frac{\partial l(\Delta I_k^i)}{\partial \Delta s_0},$$

which implies, using Equations (29) and (30),

$$\sum_{k=L,D} \sigma_k^A \frac{\partial \Delta I_k^A}{\partial \Delta s_0} = - \sum_{k=L,D} (\Delta I_k^A + 1)$$

$$\sum_{k=L,D} \sigma_k^B \frac{\partial \Delta I_k^B}{\partial \Delta s_0} = \sum_{k=L,D} (\Delta I_k^B + 1).$$

Therefore, and since $r_A < r_B$ implies $\Delta I_k^B > \Delta I_k^A$ for $k = L, D$,

$$\frac{\partial W}{\partial \Delta s_0} = -\frac{1}{2} \sum_{k=L,D} p_k R[\Delta I_k^B - \Delta I_k^A] > 0,$$

as was to be proved. The case of the integrated equilibrium is derived analogously.

Part 2: An integrated equilibrium does not exist if and only if Equation (23) holds. Suppose that the size of the repo market, Δs_0, is such that the equilibrium value of ψ just satisfies

$$\min_{\psi(\Delta s_0)} r_F(\psi(\Delta s_0)) - r_B(\psi(\Delta s_0)) = 0. \tag{6.31}$$

We first show that if Δs_0 satisfies Equation (31), then for any $\Delta s_0'$ such that $\Delta s_0' > \Delta s_0$, condition Equation (23) holds, that is, the integrated equilibrium does not exist. For this, we have to prove that $\frac{d(r_F - r_B)}{d\Delta s_0} > 0$. From Equations (10) and (9), define $\hat{F}_A \equiv F_A - \Delta s_0$ and $\hat{F}_B \equiv F_B - \Delta s_0$ with F_B and F_A as defined in Equations (22) and (24). From the proof of Lemma 4 and Proposition 2, we have $\frac{\partial F_B}{\partial r_B} > 0$ and $\frac{\partial F_A}{\partial r_A} < 0$. The Implicit Function Theorem then indeed yields

$$\frac{dr_B}{d\Delta s_0} = -\frac{\partial \hat{F}_B / \partial \Delta s_0}{\partial \hat{F}_B / \partial r_B} > 0$$

and

$$\frac{dr_F}{d\Delta s_0} = -\frac{\partial \hat{F}_A / \partial \Delta s_0}{\partial \hat{F}_A / \partial r_F} < 0.$$

As a second step, we show under which circumstances welfare is decreased. For Δs_0 satisfying (31), consider an infinitesimal increase in Δs_0, $\Delta s_0' = \Delta s_0 + \varepsilon$. The direct effect of this ε-change on welfare will be negligible compared to the effect of the equilibrium switch, since the latter implies a discrete jump in welfare. This change in welfare resulting from the equilibrium switch is given by Equation (26), which holds also for the case that banks hold a small amount of Treasury bills before and after the change (this can be checked easily). It follows that for β sufficiently small, the switch to a segmented equilibrium reduces welfare. ■

Proof of Lemma 7: At time 1, liquidity demand and supply in country B, Ω_B and Λ_B, are as in the case without a repo market, and given by Equation (27). However, because banks can obtain liquidity from abroad by selling Treasury bills, equilibrium on the interbank market now requires

$$\Omega_B = \Lambda_B + \Delta s_0, \tag{6.32}$$

where Δs_0 denotes the liquidity obtained from selling all Treasury bills, $\Delta s_0 = (\sigma_L^B + \sigma_D^B(\psi))T_0 B_1$. Notice here that because B_1 is a function of $1 + r_B$, we cannot find a closed-form solution for the interest rate because the expression is nonlinear in $1 + r_B$. Instead solving Equation (32) for s_0, we obtain Equation (11) which defines the equilibrium interest rate implicitly. Finally, Equation (12) results from the discussion on Proposition 4. ■

Proof of Lemma 8: The time-0 maximization problem is

$$\max_{\{I,s_0\}} \Pi = \frac{1}{2}(\sigma_L^A \Pi_L^A + \sigma_B^A \Pi_B^A + \sigma_L^B \Pi_L^B + \sigma_B^B \Pi_B^B)$$
$$\text{s.t. } 1 = I + s_0 + T_0 B_0$$

where

$$\sigma_L^A = 1 - q_A \quad \sigma_L^B = 1 - q_B$$
$$\sigma_B^A = q_A \theta \qquad \sigma_B^B = q_B[\theta + (1-\theta)\beta]$$

Time-1 profits for lenders in country i, $i = A, B$ are

$$\Pi_L^i = \max_{\Delta I_L^i} p\{R(I - \Delta I_L^i) - \bar{p}(1 + r_i)L_L^i + s_L^{i1} - (1 - \pi_L)c_2 + T_L^{i1}\}$$
$$\text{s.t. } L_L^i = s_0 + l(\Delta I_L^i) - \pi_L c_1 + s_L^{i1} - B_1 \Delta T_L^i$$

where we have defined $\Delta T_L^i \equiv T_L^{i1} = T_0$ – notice that L_L^A denotes the total loans given to domestic and foreign banks: they have the same expected return since $\bar{p}(1 + r_A) = p_F(1 + r_F)$. For a borrower in country A:

$$\Pi_B^A = \max_{\Delta I_B^A} \bar{p}\{R(I - \Delta I_B^A) - (1 + r_A)L_B^A + s_B^{A1} - (1 - \pi_B)c_2 + T_B^{A1}\}$$
$$\text{s.t. } L_B^A = \pi_H c_1 + s_B^1 - s_0 - l(\Delta I_B^A) - B_1 \Delta T_B^A.$$

For banks in country B, these terms are equivalent with one exception: because the population of borrowers in country B is different, its rate of solvency is different. Denote it $\tilde{p} \equiv \left(\frac{\theta\bar{p} + (1-\theta)\beta p)}{(\theta + (1-\theta)\beta}\right)$. The time-0 first-order conditions are

$$2\frac{\partial \Pi}{\partial I} = \sigma_L^A pR + \sigma_B^A \bar{p}R + \sigma_L^B pR + \sigma_B^B \tilde{p}R - \lambda$$
$$2\frac{\partial \Pi}{\partial s_0} = \bar{p}(1 + r_A)[\sigma_L^A p + \sigma_B^A] + (1 + r_B)[\sigma_L^B p\bar{p} + \sigma_B^B \tilde{p}] - \lambda$$
$$2\frac{\partial \Pi}{\partial T_0} = \bar{p}(1 + r_A)B_1[\sigma_L^A p + \sigma_B^A] + (1 + r_B)B_1[\sigma_L^B p\bar{p} + \sigma_B^B \tilde{p}] - \lambda B_0.$$

We focus again on the case $\bar{p}(1+r_A)=1$. Setting $\frac{\partial \Pi}{\partial I}=\frac{\partial \Pi}{\partial s_0}=\frac{\partial \Pi}{\partial T_0}$ yields Equation (13).■

Proof of Proposition 7: Using the fact that $r_F'(Z) \geq 0$ and $r_B'(Z) \leq 0$, condition (14) for $Z=0$ implies

$$\frac{1-\bar{p}}{\bar{p}}(1+r_F(0)) \leq r_B(0)-r_F(0).$$

On the other hand, the same inequality will hold in equilibrium replacing 0 by Z, so that the wedge $r_B(Z)-r_F(Z)$ has a lower bound. ■

References

Allen, F., and D. Gale, 2000, "Financial Contagion," *Journal of Political Economy*, 108, 1–33.

Bhattacharya, S., and P. Fulghieri, 1994, "Uncertain Liquidity and Interbank Contracting," *Economics Letters*, 44, 287–294.

Bhattacharya, S., and D. Gale, 1987, "Preference Shocks, Liquidity, and Central Bank Policy," in W. Barnett and K. Singleton (eds.) *New Approaches to Monetary Economics*, Cambridge University Press, Cambridge.

Broecker, T., 1990, "Credit-Worthiness Tests and Interbank Competition," *Econometrica*, 58(2), 429–452.

Calomiris, C., and C. Kahn, 1991, "The Role of Demandable Debt in Structuring Optimal Banking Arrangements," *American Economic Review*, 81(3), 497–513.

Ciampolini, M., and B. Rhode, 2000, "Money Market Integration: A Market Perspective," paper presented at the ECB Conference on *The Operational Framework of the Eurosystem and Financial Markets*, Frankfurt.

Diamond, D., and P. Dybvig, 1983, "Bank Runs, Deposit Insurance, and Liquidity," *Journal of Political Economy*, 91, 401–419.

ECB (European Central Bank), 2000, "The Euro Area One Year After the Introduction of the Euro: Key Characteristics and Changes in the Financial Structure," *ECB Monthly Bulletin*, January, pp. 35–50.

Flannery, M., 1996, "Financial Crises, Payment System Problems and Discount Window Lending," *Journal of Money Credit and Banking*, 28, pt. 2, 804–824.

Freixas, X., B. Parigi, and J. C. Rochet, 2000, "Systemic Risk, Interbank Relations, and Liquidity Provision by the Central Bank," *Journal of Money Credit and Banking*, 32(3), pt. 2, 611–638.

Holmström, B., and J. Tirole, 1998, "Private and Public Supply of Liquidity," *Journal of Political Economy*, 106, 1–40.

Rochet, J. C., and J. Tirole, 1996, "Interbank Lending and Systemic Risk," *Journal of Money Credit and Banking*, 28, pt. 2, 733–762.

7 Banks as Monitors of Other Banks: Evidence from the Overnight Federal Funds Market

Craig H. Furfine

I. Introduction

Banks have traditionally been both regulated and supervised in order to protect them from failure and to maintain the safety and viability of the financial system. Recently, however, rapid developments in technology and increased financial sophistication have challenged the ability of traditional regulation and supervision to foster a safe and sound banking system (see Jones 1998). As banks continue to become more adept at innovating beyond the borders of existing regulation, policy makers have begun to look to the marketplace as a potential additional monitor of the risk-taking of banks (see Flannery 1998).

Although many ways to incorporate the marketplace into prudential supervision of banks can be imagined, one currently popular proposal envisages using banks themselves as monitors of other banks (see Calomiris 1998). The attraction of such an idea is readily apparent; who better to identify a risky bank than another bank? Nevertheless, the ability of banks to identify the risk of other banks has never been documented.

This research investigates whether banks could effectively be employed as monitors of their peers by providing the first empirical examination of the pricing of interbank lending agreements. Banks lend significant amounts of money to one another every day in the federal funds market, the market where reserves are both bought and sold. These loans are both large and uncollateralized, and thus expose lending institutions to significant credit risk. Lending banks therefore have an incentive to monitor their counterparties and to price these loans as a function of, among other things, the credit risk of the borrowing bank.

The main empirical finding of this article is that the interest rate charged on federal funds transactions reflects, in part, the credit risk of the borrowing institution. In particular, borrowing banks with higher profitability, higher capital ratios, and fewer problem loans pay lower interest rates on federal funds loans. Thus, the empirical evidence suggests that banks identify risk in their peers and effectively monitor other banks.

The remainder of the article is organized as follows. Section II reviews previous work that examines the effectiveness of market participants to monitor bank risk. Section III summarizes the limited information that has been previously documented regarding pricing in the federal funds market. Section IV describes the source, strengths, and weaknesses of the transaction-level data used in the analysis. Section V presents the empirical findings. Section VI concludes.

II. Market Monitoring of Banks

Preliminary research examining whether market information could be a useful part of bank regulation and supervision has found that in many circumstances, supervisors and markets are often complementary sources of information regarding bank health (Berger, Davies, and Flannery 1998; De Young et al. 1998; Peek, Rosengren, and Tootell 1999). These studies conclude, therefore, that market information could be a useful supplement to traditional regulation. Nevertheless, banks do appear to have some ability to thwart market-based monitoring by shifting their liabilities away from claim holders (uninsured depositors) with a great incentive to monitor to those (insured depositors) with little incentive to monitor (Billet, Garfinkel, and O'Neal 1998).

Although market information has been shown to be potentially useful, deciding how best to incorporate this information into traditional regulation is difficult in practice. In particular, policy makers must decide *which market participants* holding *what financial claims* would make the best monitors of bank risk-taking. The most obvious monitors for a bank would be depositors. As is well known, however, deposit insurance has the consequence of eliminating the incentive for insured depositors to monitor their banks (White 1989). Uninsured depositors may be able to fill this role. Evidence provided by Baer and Brewer (1986), Hannan and Hanweck (1988), and Ellis and Flannery (1992) demonstrates that rates paid on wholesale (uninsured) CDs can be partially explained by proxies for bank risk.

Bank equity holders, too, impose discipline on bank management. Extensive evidence suggests that following the failure of a bank, the stock price of surviving institutions reacts negatively when the surviving institution shares common portfolio characteristics with the failing institution (Cornell and Shapiro 1986; Swary 1986; Musumeci and Sinkey, Jr. 1990; Wall and Peterson 1990; Karafiath, Mynatt, and Smith 1991; and Jayanti and Whyte 1996). This finding suggests that equity holders can act in a way that distinguishes banks according to their risk. The ability of stockholders to discipline banks, however, may not be a useful complement to regulation and supervision because of the different incentives that stockholders and supervisors face when a bank nears insolvency. Because stockholders have limited liability, they have the incentive to gamble for resurrection by increasing risk, whereas supervisors wish to minimize losses and therefore want to restrict risk-taking.

It has long been understood that holders of banks' subordinated debt, because other lenders have higher priority in case of insolvency, have incentives similar to supervisors and thus might be a useful complement to current supervisory practice (Keehn 1989; and Wall 1989). Although Avery, Belton, and Goldberg (1988) and Gorton and Santomero (1990) raise doubts about whether subordinated debt yields provide information on bank risk, Flannery and Sorescu (1996) do find that such yields provide evidence of market discipline during periods when holders of subordinated debt were not implicitly insured.

Recent thinking on the benefits of using market-based information to complement banking supervision has addressed the question of not only the type of financial instrument that would be the most appropriate indicator of bank risk but also the type of investors who would be the most effective monitors. In particular, it has been suggested that banks might be particularly effective monitors of other banks because similar institutions might be expected to identify a peer's risk best. In one example of using interbank monitoring as a supplement to current regulation, Calomiris (1998, p. 6) proposes that banks be required to issue subordinated debt that must be held by "reputable foreign financial institutions."[1] According to the plan, a bank would be required to issue subordinated debt equal to a fraction of its assets. Further, the debenture interest rate would not be allowed to exceed some given ceiling. Thus, whenever the issuing bank's creditors perceived a bank to be sufficiently risky, the bank would find itself unable to issue subordinated debt at a rate below the ceiling. The bank would then be forced to contract in order to maintain the required subordinated-debt-to-asset ratio.

Rochet and Tirole (1996) provide theoretical support for the notion that banks would be particularly good monitors of other banks. They argue that interbank relationships established through federal funds transactions or similar interdependencies generate powerful incentives for banks to monitor each other. Unfortunately, Rochet and Tirole (1996) also point out that the effectiveness of banks as monitors of other banks is influenced by other existing policies, most notably the "too big to fail" policy. In particular, if the largest banks were viewed as immune from failure, then these banks' creditors, including other banks, would have little incentive to monitor their exposures.

The arguments of Rochet and Tirole (1996) suggest that the effectiveness of banks as monitors of their peers depends on whether lenders believe that an interbank transaction exposes them to potential losses. If so, then the pricing of such transactions should reflect differences in borrower risk. Whether, and to what extent, the credit risk of a borrowing institution is priced into interbank lending agreements is the important empirical question addressed in this article.

This article examines the pricing of individual federal funds transactions. The federal funds market is a particularly attractive place to examine the pricing of interbank lending because funds transactions are largely free of complicating factors present in other interbank contracts that would typically make gleaning the "price" of the loan difficult. In particular, federal funds transactions are uncollateralized, have an overnight maturity, have maturity equal to duration, and are free from unusual payment schedules or covenants. Thus, differential pricing should readily appear in a funds transaction's interest rate. By examining the determinants of the interest rate on federal funds transactions, one can directly test whether credit risk is priced into interbank lending agreements. Anticipating the results, the article concludes that differences in borrower credit risk are reflected in the interest rate charged.

III. Pricing in the Market for Federal Funds

To date, the literature has only provided anecdotal evidence regarding the pricing of individual federal funds transactions. Stigum (1990) discusses tiering in the funds market by which large institutions generally get better terms than smaller institutions. Allen and Saunders (1986) report in a footnote that, based on conversations with market participants, non-money-center banks generally pay between 1/8% and 1/4% above the rate of their

[1] Calomiris (1998) argues that the requirement that the institutions holding subordinated debt be foreign ensures that they will not be bailed out in a crisis.

money-center counterparts. In contrast, this article provides an in-depth empirical analysis of the pricing of individual federal funds transactions. In particular, the credit quality of the borrowing bank is shown to influence the price paid on a federal funds loan.

Before describing the data used in this article, it is worthwhile to dispel a common misperception that the Federal Reserve sets the rate at which financial institutions trade reserves. As part of its implementation of monetary policy, the Fed announces a "target" for "the" funds rate. For example, throughout the entire sample period studied in this article, the first quarter of 1998, the Fed had an announced "target" of 5.5%. The Fed, however, is not concerned about determining the rate for individual federal funds transactions. Rather, the Fed summarizes the cross-sectional variation in transaction interest rates by surveying five leading federal funds brokers about the total value of federal funds trades conducted at different interest rates. These totals are then aggregated across brokers for each interest rate, and a value-weighted average is then taken. This resulting daily average rate is published with the name "effective federal funds rate." To implement monetary policy, the Fed conducts daily open market operations in an attempt to bring the effective federal funds rate to or near its stated target. Thus, although Fed action largely influences the effective federal funds rate, it is bank credit quality and other market factors that ultimately influence the cross-sectional differences in actual rates paid.

IV. Identification and Validation of Federal Funds Transactions

Both large and small institutions wish to trade in the federal funds market. This is because all institutions face some degree of unexpected inflows and outflows of reserves that they may wish to counteract through overnight borrowing or lending. In general, a bank looking to sell funds and an institution wishing to buy funds agree on a mutually acceptable quantity, term (typically overnight), and interest rate.[2] The lender (seller) of funds transfers the funds on the day of the sale to the borrower, and the borrower (buyer) of funds returns the borrowed amount plus interest to the lender the following business day. These two payments typically occur over Fedwire, the large-value transfer system operated by the Fed.[3]

These Fedwire payments allow the identification of federal funds transactions analyzed in this study.[4] For business reasons, the Fed temporarily maintains a record of each payment transaction sent over Fedwire and, from this record, every Fedwire funds transfer made during the first quarter of 1998 was collected. Of the several hundred thousand transactions recorded each day, only a relatively small number are related to the federal funds market. Stigum (1990) argues that federal funds transactions are usually made in round lots of over $1 million. Based on this anecdotal evidence, the sample of transactions was searched, and payments whose amounts were greater than $1 million, ended in five zeros, and had a payment the following business day in the opposite direction in an amount that could reasonably be construed as the initial payment plus interest were identified as federal funds transactions. As interest rates charged vary across transactions, a range of values for valid rates of interest was allowed. For the results below, a window of interest rates was allowed, ranging from 50 basis points below the minimum to 50 basis points above the maximum of six publicly available measures of a day's federal funds rate: the 11:00 A.M. rate, the high,

[2] Brokers sometimes facilitate this process.

[3] Small federal funds transactions between banks that have correspondent relationships may be arranged through book transfers (accounting entries) and may not require any Fedwire payments.

[4] A more detailed description of the transaction-identification process can be found in Furfine (1999).

low, and closing rates reported by the surveyed brokers, the effective rate, and the Fed's target rate.[5]

Potentially the greatest weakness of this approach to identifying federal funds transactions is that the sending and receiving banks identified in the data need not be the actual parties to the transaction. These banks could be acting as dealers for the funds transactions of others, or the transactions may represent overnight lending arrangements between nonfinancial firms operating through different banks. It is also possible that there are transactions struck at a rate outside the selection window, and of course these will be missed.[6] Finally, this approach will fail to capture the small number of federal funds loans that do not have an overnight maturity.[7]

Before turning to the formal analysis, it is useful to consider whether the identification procedure correctly identifies federal funds transactions. The most reliable information available on true federal funds transactions is the effective federal funds rate, the weighted average interest rate of transactions conducted by five leading funds brokers. As a comparison, a weighted average interest rate for the sample of transactions identified in the data was calculated for each day and compared with the published effective federal funds rate. These two series are plotted in figure 7.1. As is evident from the figure, the interest rate series calculated from the sample of transactions replicates the published series quite well. The average daily interest rate in the sample is 5.529%, whereas the average

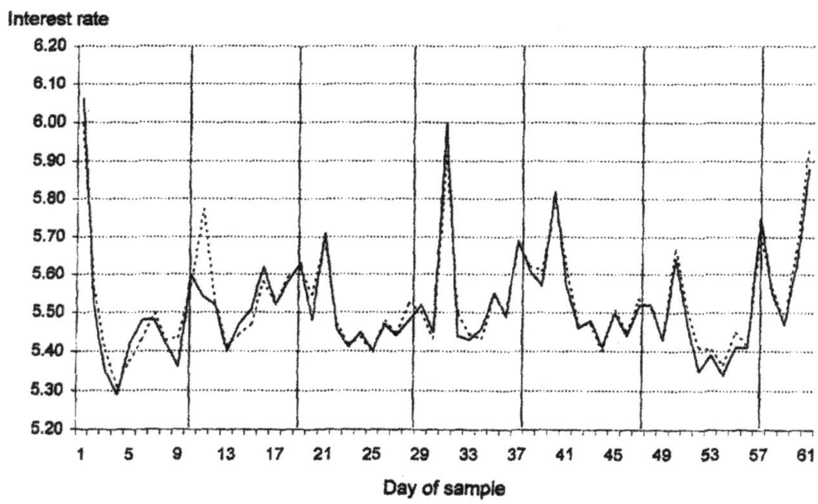

Figure 7.1. Sample and published effective funds rate. Solid line, published series; dashed line, sample. Vertical lines indicate reserve settlement days.

[5]The 11:00 A.M. rate is the weighted average interest rate derived from summaries of transactions that have already occurred that morning when the Fed conducts its daily (morning) survey of the five leading funds brokers. The high and low rates report the highest and lowest rates observed by any of the five brokers for the day. The closing rate is the rate on the last transaction conducted by the surveyed brokers.

[6]Enlarging the window had a negligible effect on the number of payments identified as federal funds transactions.

[7]According to a Federal Reserve Bank of New York (1987) survey, 96% of federal funds loans were for an overnight maturity.

effective federal funds rate during the first quarter of 1998 was 5.520%, a difference of less than 1 basis point. The standard deviation of the sample daily rate is 0.139, slightly below the published value of 0.147. Finally, the two series have a correlation of 0.95. Thus, the sample appears to reflect the federal funds market accurately.[8]

V. Empirical Results

The empirical analysis estimates the importance of various factors in determining the interest rate paid on a federal funds transaction. Because the focus of this study is on the effectiveness of banks as monitors of other banks, the sample of transactions was limited to those between U.S. commercial banks with call report data available for December 31, 1997. Because of the importance of government-sponsored agencies, foreign institutions, and federal home loan banks, this criterion reduced the sample of transactions from 190,439 to 117,756. An additional 729 (0.62%) observations were deleted because of extreme outliers in the borrowing bank's call report data, leaving a final sample of 117,027 transactions.

The dependent variable for the analysis is the interest rate on the given federal funds transaction, measured at an annual rate.[9]

Table 7.1 reports some simple statistics about the data that validate the anecdotal evidence about interest rate setting in the funds market presented in Allen and Saunders (1986) and Stigum (1990). Larger institutions tend to get more favorable rates, regardless of which side of the transaction they are on. For example, institutions with over $10 billion in assets, on average, receive 12 basis points more than a smaller institution when lending to a small institution and 8 basis points more when lending to another large institution. When borrowing, institutions with over $10 billion in assets save 3 basis points when borrowing from a small institution and 7 basis points when borrowing from a large institution.

Table 7.1 Interest Rates Paid by Size of Institution

	Average Interest Rate (SD)		
	Lender < $10 Billion in Assets (1)	Lender > $10 Billion in Assets (2)	Difference between Cols. 1 and 2 (3)
Borrower < $10 billion in assets	5.50%	5.62%	.12%
	(.001%)	(.003%)	(.003%)
Borrower > $10 billion in assets	5.47%	5.55%	.08%
	(.001%)	(.002%)	(.002%)
Difference between rows A and B	−.03%	−.07%	
	(.002%)	(.003%)	

NOTE.—Standard errors given in parentheses.

[8]The underestimation of the variability of daily interest rates is partially explained by reserve settlement days. For the 55 days that were not reserve settlement days, the sample standard deviation (SD) is 0.142 versus 0.148 for the published series. On the 6 reserve settlement days, the sample SD is 0.101, as opposed to 0.142 for the published series.

[9]Transactions that extend over holidays or weekends require more than 1 day of interest. Thus, the calculated interest rates account for the number of calendar days that pass between delivery and repayment of the loan.

Differences of means tests are all highly significant. These simple statistics suggest that, at a minimum, one would need to control for the size of the participating institutions when trying to explain the cross-sectional variation in interest rates. The next subsection systematically reviews the different determinants of pricing that are examined.

Determinants of Transaction Interest Rates

Borrower credit risk. As federal funds transactions are a type of bank loan, one would expect that the borrower's credit risk would be an important determinant of a transaction's interest rate. Although the short-term nature of the loan suggests limited scope for credit risk, these loans are large and also uncollateralized.[10] Several proxies for the borrower's credit risk were considered. First, a bank's profitability, measured by its return on assets, is included. A bank's profitability should be positively correlated with its ability to repay its federal funds transactions and so this measure is expected to be negatively related to the transaction interest rate. A bank's loan quality may also partially capture a bank's ability to service its debts. A bank's loans past due more than 90 days and its nonaccruing loans as a proportion of total loans were included to account for this possibility. If these variables were proxies for credit risk, one would expect them to be positively related to the transaction interest rate. Ultimately, a bank's capitalization reflects its ability to repay, and therefore the regressions include the ratio of a bank's total capital to risk-weighted assets. Banks with higher capital ratios might be expected to pay lower interest rates. In addition, the ratio of the transaction size to the borrower's capital was included to account for the possibility that relative capitalization may be a more relevant proxy for borrower credit risk than the previous absolute measure.[11]

As a check on the robustness of the findings, the above measures of borrower risk were also constructed at the holding-company level. Measuring risk at the holding-company level might be justified in light of the Fed's source-of-strength doctrine as modified by the Federal Deposit Insurance Corporation Improvement Act (FDICIA) of 1991. The FDICIA requires capital infusions on the part of the bank holding company as part of a voluntary capital restoration plan to aid a troubled bank subsidiary (Schinski and Mullineaux 1995). Thus, the financial strength of a bank's holding company might be the relevant measure of counterparty risk.

Borrower and lender characteristics. To measure the importance of borrower credit risk accurately, one must adequately control for other factors that influence the observed interest rate. The first set of controls represents other characteristics of the borrowing bank. The estimation includes a variable that measures the market share of the particular borrowing bank. That is, for institution X, this variable would be the amount borrowed by institution X on day Y divided by aggregate borrowing on day Y.

A small number of banks may actually be borrowing in the funds market on behalf of others. To account for the possibility that these institutions may generally pay a different interest rate, the regressions include a dummy variable indicating whether or not the borrowing bank is a dealer in the funds market, defined as an indicator for one of the five institutions in the sample that both bought and sold at least $1 billion in funds on each

[10]Even for loans of an overnight maturity, the interest rate charged must be a markup over a risk-free rate to compensate the lender for the possibility of losing the entire principal (Merton 1974). For example, if a federal funds loan had a 0.1% (1 in 1000) chance of default, a risk-neutral investor would require a markup of approximately 10 basis points.

[11]The distribution of this variable was highly skewed, and therefore the log of this ratio was used.

day of the sample. The analysis also includes a variable indicating whether the borrowing bank was a net seller of funds, on average, during the quarter ending December 31, 1997. This variable controls for the possibility that a bank transacting differently from its typical requirements might pay a different interest rate.[12]

As documented by the simple statistics in table 7.1, the size of the borrower likely influences the interest rate paid. Dummy variables denoting five different size categories of borrowers attempted to account for this. Size is defined as the borrower's total assets as of December 31, 1997.

The second set of control variables accounts for characteristics of the lending institution. An identical set of variables measuring the lending institution's lending share, dealer status, typical net position, and size was included in the regressions.

Transaction characteristics. The third set of control variables measures the characteristics of the transaction. The first such variable proxies for the funds market's liquidity at the time of the transaction. The relationship between liquidity and pricing in the funds market may be like that found in stock- and foreign-exchange markets.[13] However, the data here do not allow for a traditional volume-liquidity-pricing study because the information available on timing relates to the time that the payments were transferred over Fedwire and not to the time that the original trade was made. Anywhere from a few minutes to several hours may elapse between the execution of a federal funds trade and the flow of money over Fedwire. Nevertheless, one should expect payment times to be positively correlated with trading times simply because the payments necessarily follow the underlying trade. Thus, one might use the timing of payment flows to proxy for market liquidity. To explore this possibility, the analysis includes a variable measuring the share of federal funds value that was delivered over Fedwire during the half-hour period of the given transaction.

Liquidity may also be affected by the size of the transaction. For example, very large loans may have both a limited supply and a limited demand. Dummy variables denoting transactions less than or equal to \$10 million, between \$10 million and \$100 million, and over \$100 million were included in the estimation. These categories identify 38.7%, 55.1%, and 6.2% of the transactions, respectively.

The final transaction characteristic examined is the duration of the federal funds loan. The duration of a loan may affect pricing because it affects the intraday balances of the participating institutions. These balances are important to a bank because the Fed charges banks that have a negative balance, a "daylight overdraft," interest at an annualized rate of 27 basis points (Richards 1995).[14] Because overdraft charges are applied to a bank's *average* overdraft during the 18 hours that Fedwire operates, an earlier delivery or a delayed repayment of a federal funds loan will affect a bank's interest charges in the same proportion that it affects the magnitude of a bank's average overdraft. For example, extending the duration of a federal funds loan for 1 hour would save a borrowing bank running a daylight overdraft one-eighteenth of 27 basis points, or 1.5 basis points.

[12]The call report does not distinguish between federal funds and repo transactions, and so the indicator for "net selling" behavior is not strictly comparable to the transactions used in this study. Quarterly average values were used to construct this measure to account for the possibility of bank window dressing as documented by Allen and Saunders (1992).

[13]Bollerslev, Domowitz, and Wang (1997), Peiers (1997), and Huang and Masulis (1999) study this relationship in foreign exchange markets. Stephan and Whaley (1990) and French and Roll (1986) examine the same in equity markets.

[14]This discussion abstracts from a bank's allowable deductible.

For many reasons, however, one would expect that extending the duration of a federal funds loan by 1 hour would correlate with an increase in the interest rate observed of less man 1.5 basis points. First, since both the borrower and the lender are aware that the timing of payments influences the fees charged by the Fed, the two counterparties may agree to share the 1.5 basis point benefit. Second, the borrowing bank may not necessarily be running an overdraft at the time of repayment and so would be unwilling to pay for an extended duration. Third, the Fed's treatment of intraday reserve balances is asymmetric. Although the Fed charges 27 basis points for overdrafts, it does not pay anything to a bank that holds a positive intraday balance. Overall, therefore, the value of extending a federal funds loan by 1 hour is an empirical question. For this reason, a variable measuring the number of operating hours that the loan was outstanding has been included in the analysis.

Borrower and lender relationships. The fourth set of controls proxies for the relationship that may exist between the borrower and seller of funds. The relationship-banking literature finds empirical evidence that small borrowers (presumed to be nonfinancial firms) benefit by maintaining a relationship with a single bank or a small number of banks (see, e.g., Petersen and Rajan 1994; and Berger and Udell 1995). In the case of the federal funds market, both the borrower and the lender are financial institutions. Borrowing institutions may build relationships with particular institutions to establish that they are a good credit risk. By so doing, they may get a more attractive interest rate.

Relationships were measured in two ways: by the number of transactions between the given pair of banks and by the number of days on which the given pair of banks transacted.[15] These measures of relationships implicitly assume that the patterns observed during this quarter are indicative of the relationship between the counterparties in the past. As the theories of relationship banking focus on small borrowers, the above measures were also interacted with a dummy variable indicating whether the borrowing institution has less than $250 million in assets.[16] Such small financial institutions may have a particularly difficult time conveying to potential lenders that they are a good credit risk, and thus they may especially benefit from establishing a relationship.

Day of the sample. Finally, dummy variables for each of the 61 business days in the sample were included. As documented in Hamilton (1996), Spindt and Hoffmeister (1988), and Furfine (2000), the effective federal funds rate follows patterns during the 2-week reserve maintenance period as well as around holidays and ends of quarters. To isolate the cross-sectional variation in loan pricing, a complete set of dummy variables was used rather than attempting to measure each calendar-related effect separately. To save space, the results for these variables are not reported but are available separately. These dummy variables capture the daily variation in interest rates found in the effective funds rate, differing only slightly because of the weighting that occurs in the published series.

Before turning to the empirical results, table 7.2 reviews the definitions of the various variables, and table 7.3 presents some summary statistics. As mentioned, the interest rate data replicate the effective funds rate quite well, and it is therefore no surprise that the transaction-level average interest rate of 5.504% is so close to the target funds rate of 5.5%. The summary statistics also indicate a fair degree of skewness in the distribution of many variables. In banking, a small number of institutions typically have characteristics quite different from most other institutions, and this sample is no different. Whereas the

[15]These variables were entered in log form to account for the highly skewed nature of their distribution.

[16]A smaller cutoff of $100 million delivered similar results.

Table 7.2 Definitions of Variables Used in This Study

Variable	Definition
Borrower's credit risk (from December 31, 1997, call report):	
Return on assets	Net income divided by total assets
Loans 90 or more days past due	Total loans 90 or more days past due as a fraction of total loans
Nonaccruing loans	Nonaccruing loans as a fraction of total loans
Risk-based capital ratio	Total (tier 1 and tier 2) capital as a fraction of risk-weighted assets
Log (transaction-size-to-capital ratio)	Log of transaction size as a fraction of total (tier 1 and tier 2) capital
Other institution characteristics (for both borrowing and lending bank):	
Daily borrower (lender) share	Share of the day's total borrowing (lending) of the given institution
Assets $<$ \$250 million	
Assets between \$250 million and \$1 billion	
Assets between \$1 billion and \$10 billion	Indicator variables reflecting the borrower's or lender's total assets
Assets between \$10 billion and \$100 billion	
Assets $>$ \$100 billion	
Dealer bank	Indicator variable representing a bank that bought and sold at least \$1 billion of federal funds during each of the 61 days of the sample period
Quarter-end net seller	Indicator variable representing a bank that reported more "federal funds sold and securities purchased with intent to resell" than "federal funds purchased and securities sold with intent to repurchase," reported as quarterly averages on the December 31, 1997, call report
Transaction characteristics:	
Transaction $\leq$ \$10 million	
Transaction between \$10 million and \$100 million	Indicator variables reflecting the size of the federal funds transaction
Transaction over \$100 million	
Business hours duration	Number of Fedwire operating hours between delivery of the federal funds sold and return of the funds with interest
Liquidity	Share of the day's total federal funds value that was delivered during the given transaction's half-hour interval
Relationship characteristics:	
Log (no. of transaction pair)	Log of the number of transactions involving the sale of funds by the given lender to the given borrower during the entire sample period
Log (no. of days pair)	Log of the number of days on which funds were sold by the given lender to the given borrower during the entire sample period

Table 7.3 Summary of Transaction Data

	Mean	SD	Median	Minimum	Maximum
Interest rate	5.504	.349	5.469	.585	19.950
Borrower's credit risk:					
Return on assets	.011	.004	.011	−.001	.030
Loans 90 or more days past due	.002	.003	.002	0	.047
Nonaccruing loans	.005	.003	.005	0	.015
Risk-based capital ratio	.113	.014	.109	.091	.231
Transaction-size-to-capital ratio	.018	.053	.005	.000	3.534
Other borrower characteristics:					
Daily borrower share	.039	.057	.014	.000	.214
Asset size (millions of $)	89,900	104,000	38,800	40	297,000
Dealer bank	.300	.458	0	0	1
Quarter-end net seller	.142	.349	0	0	1
Lender characteristics:					
Daily lender share	.027	0.045	.003	.000	.214
Asset size (millions of $)	52,400	93,300	3,880	10	297,000
Dealer bank	.219	.413	0	0	1
Quarter-end net seller	.783	.412	1	0	1
Transaction characteristics:					
Transaction size (millions of $)	37.7	68.9	18.0	1	990
Business hours duration	15.31	2.79	15.73	1.17	34.66
Liquidity	.107	.065	.103	.000	0.274
Relationship characteristics:					
No. of transaction pair	215.58	457.32	51	1	2, 007
No. of days pair	40.98	19.23	47	1	61

NOTE.—Summary statistics in the federal funds transaction data containing 117,027 observations over 61 business days between January 2, 1998, and March 31, 1998.

median observation on the borrowing share variable is 1.4%, its mean is 3.9%. This is reflective of a small number of institutions with significant market share. For example, one institution bought 21.4% of a day's total funds exchanged. A similar skewness is apparent in the size of the institutions. The participating institutions have a size ranging from a low of only $10 million in assets to a high of $297 billion. Transaction size and measures of relationships are also skewed. For instance, the mean transaction size is just under $38 million, but the median is only $18 million. With regard to proxies for relationships, some banks sell funds to a given institution only once during the entire quarter. The median number of transactions for a given pair of institutions is 51, although as many as 2,007 transactions occurred between a given buyer and seller.

Regression Results for the Full Sample

Table 7.4 presents the output from three regression specifications for the complete sample of 117,027 observations. The first three columns report the results when borrower risk is measured at the bank level and the last three columns report the results when borrower risk is measured at the holding-company level. The different specifications utilized two different proxies for the quality of the borrower's loan portfolio and two ways of measuring bank relationships. Overall, the variables included in the regression explain 20% of the variation in interest rates charged, although time dummies alone explain 16%.

Table 7.4 Parameter Estimates—All Transactions

	Bank Level			Holding-Company Level		
	(1)	(2)	(3)	(4)	(5)	(6)
Borrower's credit risk:						
Return on assets	−1.2004	−1.9145	−1.9282	−1.0314	−.6579	−.6683
	(.2843)**	(.2782)**	(.2793)**	(.2722)**	(.2800)*	(.2798)*
Loans 90 or more days past due	−2.6482			.6684		
	(.2510)**			(.1547)**		
Nonaccruing loans		.7087	.7053		.0942	.1027
		(.3551)*	(.3556)*		(.0385)*	(.0386)**
Risk-based capital ratio	−.6339	−.6793	−.6703	−.7644	−.7513	−.7516
	(.0496)**	(.0501)**	(.0503)**	(.0585)**	(.0597)**	(.0599)**
Log(Transaction-size-to-capital ratio)	.0082	.0085	.0088	.0086	.0085	.0090
	(.0015)**	(.0016)**	(.0016)**	(.0006)**	(.0006)**	(.0006)**
Other borrower characteristics:						
Daily borrower share	.0646	.0884	.0727	.1254	.1298	.1145
	(.0362)	(.0358)*	(.0371)*	(.0384)**	(.0384)**	(.0391)**
Assets < $250 million	.2206	.2288	.2515	.1815	.1820	.1980
	(.0675)**	(.0673)**	(.0673)**	(.0671)**	(.0671)**	(.0672)**
Assets between $250 million and $ 1 billion	.1004	.1048	.1051	.0705	.0706	.0681
	(.0079)**	(.0079)**	(.0079)**	(.0060)**	(.0060)**	(.0061)**
Assets between $1 billion and $10 billion	−.0030	−.0004	−.0007	−.0146	−.0150	−.0162
	(.0052)	(.0052)	(.0052)	(.0034)**	(.0035)**	(.0035)**
Assets between $10 billion and $100 billion	−.0243	−.0227	−.0230	−.0298	−.0308	−.0314
	(.0039)**	(.0039)**	(.0039)**	(.0032)**	(.0033)**	(.0033)**
Assets over $100 billion	Baseline					
Dealer bank	−.0012	−.0019	−.0041	.0058	.0050	.0027
	(.0036)	(.0037)	(.0036)	(.0039)	(.0039)	(.0038)
Net seller on average	.0054	.0046	.0045	.0047	.0050	.0050
	(.0033)	(.0033)	(.0033)	(.0034)	(.0034)	(.0034)
Lender characteristics:						
Daily lender share	−.2393	−.2442	−.2848	−.2420	−.2415	−.2898
	(.0414)**	(.0413)**	(.0427)**	(.0412)**	(.0412)**	(.0425)**
Assets < $250 million	−.0943	−.0950	−.0990	−.0972	−.0968	−.1000
	(.0080)**	(.0080)**	(.0079)**	(.0079)**	(.0079)**	(.0078)**

Continued

Table 7.4 Cont'd

	Bank Level			Holding-Company Level		
	(1)	(2)	(3)	(4)	(5)	(6)
Assets between $250 million and $1 billion	−.1069	−.1080	−.1116	−.1085	−.1080	−.1108
	(.0079)**	(.0079)**	(.0078)**	(.0079)**	(.0079)**	(.0078)**
Assets between $1 billion and $10 billion	−.0827	−.0831	−.0843	−.0848	−.0844	−.0851
	(.0078)**	(.0078)**	(.0078)**	(.0078)**	(.0078)**	(.0078)**
Assets between $10 billion and $100 billion	−.0155	−.0165	−.0167	−.0167	−.0165	−.0166
	(.0070)*	(.0070)*	(.0070)*	(.0070)*	(.0070)*	(.0070)*
Assets over $100 billion			Baseline			
Dealer bank	.0236	.0233	.0199	.0215	.0215	.0179
	(.0066)**	(.0067)**	(.0066)**	(.0067)**	(.0067)**	(.0066)**
Net seller on average	−.0185	−.0185	−.0186	−.0170	−.0170	−.0169
	(.0022)**	(.0022)**	(.0021)**	(.0022)**	(.0022)**	(.0021)**
Transaction characteristics:						
Transaction $\leq$ $10 million			Baseline			
Transaction between $10 million and $100 million	−.0031	−.0036	−.0040	−.0059	−.0054	−.0062
	(.0027)	(.0027)	(.0027)	(.0028)*	(.0028)	(.0029)*
Transaction over $100 million	−.0506	−.0523	−.0541	−.0535	−.0527	−.0552
	(.0056)**	(.0056)**	(.0056)**	(.0052)**	(.0052)**	(.0053)**
Business hours duration	.0090	.0090	.0089	.0090	.0090	.0089
	(.0006)**	(.0006)**	(.0006)**	(.0006)**	(.0006)**	(.0006)**
Liquidity	−.0085	−.0072	−.0040	−.0045	−.0046	−.0020
	(.0154)	(.0154)	(.0154)	(.0153)	(.0153)	(.0153)
Relationship characteristics:						
Log (no. of transaction pair)			.0014			.0026
			(.0012)			(.0012)*
Log (no. of transaction pair) (small borrower)			−.0442			−.0362
			(.0227)			(.0229)
Log (no. of days pair)	−.0064	−.0062		−.0041	−.0041	
	(.0015)**	(.0015)**		(.0015)**	(.0015)**	
Log (no. of days pair) (small borrower)	−.0342	−.0367		−.0308	−.0298	
	(.0229)	(.0227)		(.0229)	(.0229)	
Observations	117,027	117,027	117,027	117,027	117,027	117,027
R^2	.20	.20	.20	.20	.20	.20
R^2 with only time dummies	.16					

NOTE.—Mean of dependent variable = 5.50432. SD of dependent variable = .3493963. Robust standard errors given in parentheses.
* Significant at 5% level.
** Significant at 1% level.

Looking across columns, it is clear that the different specifications are not particularly influential.[17] For ease of exposition, therefore, the description of the results will focus on the coefficients reported in column 2.

A 1 SD increase in the borrower's return on assets correlates with a reduction in the loan rate of approximately 0.75 basis points. A similar increase in nonaccruing loans tends to relate to a rise in interest rates of around 0.2 basis points. A 1 SD increase in a borrowing bank's capital ratio correlates with nearly a full basis-point reduction in interest rates. The most economically significant variable regarding borrower credit risk appears to be the transaction-size-to-capital ratio. A 1 SD increase in this variable correlates with a 1.5 basis point increase in the transaction interest rate.

Turning to the variables representing other characteristics of the borrower, estimates suggest an increase in the share of overall borrowing tends to increase the transaction interest rate. This is consistent with movement along a supply curve. A 1 SD increase in the market share of the borrowing bank correlates with a 0.5 basis point increase in the transaction interest rate.

Asset size is an extremely important determinant of transaction interest rates. As the size of the borrowing bank increases, transaction interest rates generally fall. The smallest institutions pay nearly a quarter of a percentage point more for overnight funds than institutions with over $1 billion in assets. Dealing in funds does not affect the rate at which one can borrow, nor does the typical net funds position.

For the lending institution, higher lending shares correlate with lower interest rates, consistent with movement along a demand curve. A 1 SD increase in a bank's lending share correlates with a transaction interest rate 1 basis point lower. As was the case for the borrowing bank, greater size improves the terms of the loan, although to a lesser extent than was true for borrowers. The smallest institutions receive around 10 basis points less than the largest institutions receive when lending. Being a dealer seems to improve the terms of lending, with such institutions receiving about 2 basis points more for funds sold. The coefficient on the net selling indicator suggests that institutions that on balance sell funds actually receive less for their money when they sell. Since net selling institutions are generally small, this may reflect the fact that the size dummies are underestimating the pricing advantage of large institutions.

With regard to transaction-specific variables, the results suggest that the largest transactions generally trade around 5 basis points below smaller transactions. As transactions over $100 million are generally between very large institutions, this coefficient may partly be capturing the pricing of transactions between money-center banks described by Allen and Saunders (1986). The coefficient on the duration of the federal funds loan provides evidence of an intraday market for funds. Each hour of additional duration is correlated with a 0.9-basis-point increase in the transaction interest rate. This estimate is consistent with the prior expectation of getting a positive coefficient of less than 1.5 basis points. Such pricing is quite significant economically given that banks have an 18-hour window in which to return funds that are borrowed. The coefficient on the proxy for market liquidity is not statistically different from zero. However, as mentioned, the timing of federal funds payments is not equivalent to the timing of federal funds trades. It may be the case that this error in measurement is sufficient to mask a true liquidity effect, or it may be that

[17]With the exception of loans past due in specification 1, all of the variables that proxy for the credit risk of the borrowing institution enter significantly and with the correct sign. The only other significant difference across specifications is that relationship proxies only enter significantly when they are measured by days rather than by the number of transactions.

there is not a relationship between price and volume in the funds market as has been found elsewhere.

Results for the relationship proxies are consistent with the notion that banking relationships are important in the funds market when relationships are measured in days. A 1 SD increase in the number of days that the two banks have transacted correlates with a 0.5 basis point reduction in the transaction interest rate. For the smallest borrowers, the effects are much larger, although these estimates are not significant at traditional levels.

Regression Results for Subsamples

Table 7.5 reports the output from the same specification as in the second column of table 7.4, except that the sample of transactions has been limited.[18] For ease of comparison, the first column of table 7.5 replicates the second column of table 7.4. The second column of table 7.5 includes only transactions less than or equal to $10 million in the regression. For such transactions, borrower credit risk appears far more important than for the sample as a whole. Although nonaccruing loans no longer enter significantly, the other coefficients on proxies for credit risk enter with noticeably higher absolute values. For instance, a 1 SD increase in the borrower's return on assets now correlates with a decline in the interest rate of around 1.1 basis points. The coefficient on relative transaction size is nearly double that estimated from the entire sample. With regard to other variables, the size of the lending institution is correlated with about twice the change in interest rates as was true for the entire sample, but the size of the borrowing institution is correlated with a noticeably smaller change. Relationships also appear more significant in the sample of smaller transactions. A 1 SD increase in the length of an interbank relationship correlates with a 1.2 basis point decline in transaction interest rates, over twice that found in the full sample.

The third column of table 7.5 presents the results for the subsample of transactions involving at least one dealer bank. Because a dealer is involved with these transactions, it is more likely that they do not represent transactions undertaken for the account of the sending and receiving bank. Thus, one might expect it would be more difficult to explain pricing for this subset of transactions. Consistent with this prior belief, the results show that proxies for credit risk generally fail to correlate with pricing in a manner consistent with theory. The coefficient on return on assets is insignificant, and the coefficients on nonaccruing loans and relative transaction size are significant but of the wrong sign. The only credit risk variable entering with the proper sign is the borrower's capital level, but this enters with a smaller magnitude than it did for the whole sample. Overall, the regression explains 0.16 of the variation in transaction interest rates, but 0.14 of this is due to the time dummies.

The last column of table 7.5 explores whether pricing in the federal funds market is noticeably different on the 6 reserve settlement days covered by the sample. As described in Hamilton (1996), Spindt and Hoffmeister (1988), and Furfine (2000), such days typically witness a higher than average effective funds rate. The results suggest that there are many noteworthy differences in the way transactions are priced on these days. First, the relative transaction size variable enters with a coefficient nearly three times the magnitude of that found in the complete sample. Second, the largest borrowers actually tend to pay significantly *higher* interest rates than banks of a moderate size. According to the estimates, banks with over $100 billion in assets pay around 5 basis points more than banks with

[18]As reported at the bottom of table 7.5, F-tests reject the hypothesis that (*a*) the four borrower risk coefficients and (*b*) all the coefficients from each subsample are the same as those reported for the full sample.

Table 7.5 Parameter Estimates—Various Samples

	All Transactions (from Table 4, Col. 2)	Transactions ≤ $10 Million	Transactions Involving a Dealer Bank	Transactions on Settlement Days
Borrower's credit risk:				
Return on assets	−1.9145	−2.8684	−.2856	−1.1643
	(.2782)**	(.4856)**	(1.0553)	(.5901)*
Nonaccruing loans	.7087	−.0282	−4.1361	.2647
	(.3551)*	(.7429)	(.9462)**	(.8246)
Risk-based capital ratio	−.6793	−.9925	−.5144	−.5579
	(.0501)**	(.1008)**	(.1517)**	(.1309)**
Log (transaction-size-to-capital ratio)	.0085	.0155	−.0124	.0233
	(.0016)**	(.0027)**	(.0036)**	(.0029)**
Other borrower characteristics:				
Daily borrower share	.0884	.2262	−.2423	.0747
	(.0358)*	(.0723)**	(.0594)**	(.0638)
Assets < $250 million	.2288	.1481	.8391	.0894
	(.0673)**	(.0680)*	(.5934)	(.0526)
Assets between $250 million and $1 billion	.1048	.0382	.0936	.0750
	(.0079)**	(.0137)**	(.0236)**	(.0183)**
Assets between $1 billion and $10 billion	−.0004	−.0157	.0171	−.0398
	(.0052)	(.0093)	(.0158)	(.0113)**
Assets between $10 billion and $100 billion	−.0227	−.0283	−.0315	−.0546
	(.0039)**	(.0077)**	(.0106)**	(.0082)**
Assets over $100 billion			Baseline	
Dealer bank	−.0019	−.0017	.0496	−.0189
	(.0037)	(.0067)	(.0095)**	(.0068)**
Net seller on average	.0046	.0074	−.0137	.0050
	(.0033)	(.0067)	(.0062)*	(.0060)
Lender characteristics:				
Daily lender share	−.2442	−.5192	−.1944	−.0987
	(.0413)**	(.1944)**	(.0548)**	(.0666)
Assets < $250 million	−.0950	−.1930	−.1321	−.0333
	(.0080)**	(.0245)**	(.0125)**	(.0150)*
Assets between $250 million and $1 billion	−.1080	−.2095	−.1358	−.0563
	(.0079)**	(.0244)**	(.0115)**	(.0149)**
Assets between $1 billion and $10 billion	−.0831	−.1890	−.0838	−.0402
	(.0078)**	(.0241)**	(.0109)**	(.0151)**

Continued

Table 7.5 Cont'd

	All Transactions (from Table 4, Col. 2)	Transactions ≤ \$10 Million	Transactions Involving a Dealer Bank	Transactions on Settlement Days
Assets between \$10 billion and \$100 billion	−.0165	−.0412	−.0023	−.0064
	(.0070)*	(.0220)	(.0075)	(.0124)
Assets over \$100 billion			Baseline	
Dealer bank	.0233	.0254	.0426	.0095
	(.0067)**	(.0207)	(.0100)**	(.0110)
Net seller on average	−.0185	−.0192	−.0146	−.0109
	(.0022)**	(.0046)**	(.0051)**	(.0039)**
Transaction characteristics:				
Transaction < \$10 million			Baseline	
Transaction between \$10 million and \$100 million	−.0036		−.0079	.0063
	(.0027)		(.0072)	(.0054)
Transaction over \$100 million	−.0523		−.0136	−.0407
	(.0056)**		(.0120)	(.0119)**
Business hours duration	.0090	.0107	.0088	.0090
	(.0006)**	(.0013)**	(.0011)**	(.0012)**
Liquidity	−.0072	.0192	.0375	.0575
	(.0154)	(.0338)	(.0368)	(.0239)*
Relationship characteristics:				
Log (no. of days pair)	−.0062	−.0134	−.0085	.0022
	(.0015)**	(.0035)**	(.0039)*	(.0040)
Log (no. of days pair) (small borrower)	−.0367	−.0130	−.3397	−.0151
	(.0227)	(.0231)	(.2862)	(.0159)
Observations	117,027	45,278	48,483	11,617
R^2	.20	.18	.16	.24
R^2 with only time dummies	.16	.12	.14	.16
Mean of dependent variable	5.50432	5.475114	5.531565	5.545332
SD of dependent variable	.349	.442	.473	.228
Joint test of significance of 4 borrower risk measures	$F(4, 116, 942) = 77.16$	$F(4, 45, 195) = 55.38$	$F(4, 48, 398) = 11.72$	$F(4, 11, 587) = 23.45$
	Prob > F = .0000	Prob > F = .0000	Prob > F = .0000	Prob > F = .0000
Joint test of significant difference from col. 1 coefficients of 4 borrower risk measures		$F(4, 116, 921) = 18.72$	$F(4, 116, 920) = 26.85$	$F(4, 116, 918) = 7.35$
		Prob > F = .0000	Prob > F = .0000	Prob > F = .0000
Joint test of significant difference from col. 1 coefficients of all variables		$F(21, 116, 921) = 36.09$	$F(22, 116, 920) = 13.31$	$F(24, 116, 918) = 6.17$
		Prob > F = .0000	Prob > F = .0000	Prob > F = .0000

NOTE.—Robust standard errors given in parentheses. Prob = probability.
* Significant at 5% level.
** Significant at 1% level.

between \$1 and \$100 billion in assets on settlement days. Third, the size of the lending institution, while still generally positively correlated with interest rates, reveals only a difference of around 5 basis points between the biggest and smallest institutions, around half that of the full sample. Fourth, the liquidity variable is significant for the first time. This likely captures the fact that most federal funds value is delivered in the afternoon and that the funds rate on settlement days tends to increase more noticeably in the afternoon. Finally, relationships do not appear to influence pricing on settlement days.

Because the behavior of the funds rate on settlement days has attracted so much attention, it is perhaps worthwhile to question to what extent the different behavior of the effective rate can be attributed to the differences uncovered in the cross-sectional pricing of transactions on those days. During the first quarter of 1998, the weighted average funds rate calculated from my sample was 7 basis points above target, averaged across the 6 settlement days. To try to explain this fact, fitted values were calculated from the full-sample coefficients and the settlement-day coefficients. The predicted weighted average rate was then calculated for the settlement days and compared across the two estimates. The estimates for the settlement day coefficients were, on average, about 1 basis point higher. Thus, changes in the pricing behavior of institutions can only explain 1 point of the 7-basis-point increase in the funds rate occurring on the settlement days in my sample. The time dummies captured the remainder of the effect. Thus, factors outside of those examined here explain most of the unusual settlement-day behavior of interest rates.

VI. Implications and Conclusions

The price of a federal funds loan reflects, in part, the credit risk of the borrowing institution. In particular, banks with higher profitability, fewer problem loans, and higher capital ratios pay lower interest rates when they borrow overnight. This suggests that banks can distinguish credit risk among their peers and price loan contracts accordingly.

Being able to distinguish credit risk, however, does not imply that interest rates on federal funds transactions would be able to price credit risk adequately when counterparty default became likely. For instance, a risk premium of 300 basis points would only compensate a risk-neutral lender for a 3% probability of default *within the next year*. Put another way, a 300 basis point additional spread on a \$1 million overnight loan generates an additional \$83.33 in revenue each day for the lending institution, a negligible amount when the bank could conceivably lose its entire principal. Thus, access to federal funds borrowing dries up for a bank with a significant perceived possibility of default.[19] Further, this decline in borrowing is generally not accompanied by exceptionally high risk premiums because, as argued by Benston et al. (1986), a bank wishes to avoid giving the market a signal that it is having difficulty attracting funds.[20]

[19]When such drying up of liquidity occurs depends largely on when financial markets realize a bank is in trouble. The uninsured depositor run on Continental Illinois first began on May 8, 1984, a relatively short time before the FDIC's resolution plan was approved by Congress on September 26 of that same year (Wall and Peterson 1990). In contrast, Peek and Rosengren (1998) report that the closure of the Bank of New England Corporation (BNEC) on January 7, 1991, followed almost 2 years of declines in overnight depositors. By the end of 1989, the BNEC had lost over half its overnight funding (both secured and unsecured) and by June of 1990, BNEC's overnight borrowing stood at roughly 3% of its early 1989 levels.

[20]Consistent with this proposition, Ellis and Flannery (1992) note that Continental Illinois failed to report offering rates for its uninsured CDs between May 16 and October 3, 1984. Between May 9 and May 15, 1984,

For good reason, therefore, discipline of very risky institutions in the federal funds market takes the form of quantity rationing rather than higher interest rates on transactions. That is, a bank with a high perceived probability of failure generally cannot attract overnight unsecured funds, regardless of price. Nevertheless, the finding that banks do charge interest rates that distinguish the risk of their generally healthy peers does have at least three implications. First, banks can and do monitor the risk present in their interbank transactions. Thus, proposals to incorporate some sort of interbank monitoring into traditional regulation and supervision have been given some empirical credibility. Second, the magnitude of the differential pricing found in the overnight funds market is economically significant. Consider two hypothetical banks, one of which has values for the four risk variables equal to the tenth percentile in the sample while the other has values equal to the ninetieth percentile. That is, one bank is constructed to be "risky" and the other to be "safe." Holding all other variables constant, the coefficient estimates from the first column of table 7.5 predict an interest rate differential between these two banks of 18.4 basis points. Considering only banks with assets greater than $10 billion, the interest rate differential between the two similarly defined hypothetical banks is still over 11 basis points. Third, this pricing of credit risk found at an overnight maturity suggests that if something like the Calomiris (1998) plan were implemented using 10-year subordinated debt, a fairly wide range of allowable debenture interest rates might be required if risk and maturity have a significantly positive correlation.

References

Allen, Linda, and Saunders, Anthony. 1986. The large-small bank dichotomy in the federal funds market. *Journal of Banking and Finance* 10, no. 2:219–30.

Allen, Linda, and Saunders, Anthony. 1992. Bank window dressing: Theory and evidence. *Journal of Banking and Finance* 16, no. 3:585–623.

Avery, Robert B.; Belton, Terrence M.; and Goldberg, Michael A. 1988. Market discipline in regulating bank risk: New evidence from the capital markets. *Journal of Money, Credit, and Banking* 20, no. 4:597–610.

Baer, Herbert, and Brewer, Elijah. 1986. Uninsured deposits as a source of market discipline: Some new evidence. *Federal Reserve Bank of Chicago Economic Perspectives* 10, no. 5(September–October):23–31.

Benston, George J.; Eisenbeis, Robert A.; Horvitz, Paul M.; Kane, Edward J.; and Kaufman, George G. 1986. *Safe and Sound Banking*. Cambridge, Mass.: MIT Press.

Berger, Allen N.; Davies, Sally M.; and Flannery, Mark J. 1998. Comparing market and supervisory assessments of bank performance: Who knows what when? Finance and Economics Discussion Series no. 1998–32. Washington, D.C.: Federal Reserve Board of Governors.

Berger, Allen N., and Udell, Gregory F. 1995. Relationship lending and lines of credit in small firm finance. *Journal of Business* 68, no. 3:351–81.

Billet, Matthew T.; Garfinkel, Jon A.; and O'Neal, Edward S. 1998. The cost of market versus regulatory discipline in banking. *Journal of Financial Economics* 48, no. 3:333–58.

Bollerslev, Tim; Domowitz, Ian; and Wang, Jianxin. 1997. Order flow and the bid-ask spread: An empirical probability model of screen-based trading. *Journal of Economic Dynamics and Control* 21, nos. 8–9:1471–91.

Calomiris, Charles W. 1998. Blueprints for a new global financial architecture. Text of speech available on www.aei.org. American Enterprise Institute for Public Policy Research, Washington, D.C.

Continental's offer rates on 3-month CDs were only 30–40 basis points above the rates offered by First Chicago and Chase Manhattan.

Cornell, Bradford, and Shapiro, Alan C. 1986. The reaction of bank stock prices to the international debt crisis. *Journal of Banking and Finance* 10, no. 1:55–73.

De Young, Robert; Flannery, Mark J.; Lang, William W.; and Sorescu, Sorin M. 1998. The informational advantage of specialized monitors: The case of bank examiners. Working paper. Gainesville: University of Florida, College of Business Administration.

Ellis, David M., and Flannery, Mark J. 1992. Does the debt market assess large banks' risk? Time series evidence from money center CDs. *Journal of Monetary Economics* 30, no. 3: 481–502.

Federal Reserve Bank of New York. 1987. A study of large-dollar payment flows through CHIPS and Fedwire. New York: Federal Reserve Bank of New York.

Flannery, Mark J. 1998. Using market information in prudential bank supervision: A review of the U.S. empirical evidence. *Journal of Money, Credit, and Banking* 30, no. 3:273–305.

Flannery, Mark J., and Sorescu, Sorin M. 1996. Evidence of bank market discipline in subordinated debenture yields: 1983–1991. *Journal of Finance* 51, no. 4:1347–77.

French, Kenneth R., and Roll, Richard. 1986. Stock return variances: The arrival of information and the reaction of traders. *Journal of Financial Economics* 17, no. 1:5–26.

Furfine, Craig H. 1999. The microstructure of the federal funds market. *Financial Markets, Institutions, and Instruments* 8, no. 5:24–44.

Furfine, Craig H. 2000. Interbank payments and the daily federal funds rate. *Journal of Monetary Economics* 46, no. 2:535–53.

Gorton, Gary, and Santomero, Anthony M. 1990. Market discipline and bank subordinated debt. *Journal of Money, Credit, and Banking* 22, no. 1:119–28.

Hamilton, James D. 1996. The daily market for federal funds. *Journal of Political Economy* 104, no. 1:26–56.

Hannan, Timothy H., and Hanweck, Gerald A. 1988. Bank insolvency risk and the market for large certificates of deposit. *Journal of Money, Credit, and Banking* 20, no. 2:203–12.

Huang, Roger D., and Masulis, Ronald W. 1999. FX spreads and dealer competition across the 24-hour trading day. *Review of Financial Studies* 12, no. 1:61–93.

Jayanti, S. V., and Whyte, Ann Marie. 1996. Global contagion effects of the Continental Illinois failure. *Journal of International Financial Markets, Institutions and Money* 6, no. 1: 87–99.

Jones, David. 1998. Emerging problems with the accord: Regulatory capital arbitrage and related issues. Working paper. Washington, D.C.: Federal Reserve Board of Governors.

Karafiath, Imre; Mynatt, Ross; and Smith, Kenneth L. 1991. The Brazilian default announcement and the contagion effect hypothesis. *Journal of Banking and Finance* 15, no. 3:699–716.

Keehn, Silas. 1989. Banking on the balance: Powers and the safety net. Unpublished manuscript. Chicago: Federal Reserve Bank of Chicago.

Merton, Robert C. 1974. On the pricing of corporate debt: The risk structure of interest rates. *Journal of Finance* 29, no. 2:449–70.

Musumeci, James J., and Sinkey, Joseph F., Jr. 1990. The international debt crisis, investor contagion, and bank security returns in 1987: The Brazilian experience. *Journal of Money, Credit, and Banking* 22, no. 2:209–20.

Peek, Joe, and Rosengren, Eric S. 1998. The dissemination of adverse information prior to the Bank of New England failure: "What we have here is a failure to communicate." Unpublished manuscript. Boston: Federal Reserve Bank of Boston.

Peek, Joe; Rosengren, Eric S.; and Tootell, Geoffrey M. B. 1999. Is bank supervision central to central banking? *Quarterly Journal of Economics* 114, no. 2:629–53.

Peiers, Bettina. 1997. Informed traders, intervention, and price leadership: A deeper view of the microstructure of the foreign exchange market. *Journal of Finance* 52. no. 4: 1589–1614.

Petersen, Mitchell A., and Rajan, Raghuram G. 1994. The benefits of lending relationships: Evidence from small business data. *Journal of Finance* 49, no. 1:3–37.

Richards, Heidi W. 1995. Daylight overdraft fees and the Federal Reserve's payment system risk policy. *Federal Reserve Bulletin* 81, no. 12:1065–77.

Rochet, Jean-Charles, and Tirole, Jean. 1996. Interbank lending and systemic risk. *Journal of Money, Credit, and Banking* 28, no. 4:733–62.

Schinski, Michael, and Mullineaux, Donald. 1995. The impact of the Federal Reserve's source of strength policy on bank holding companies. *Quarterly Review of Economics and Finance* (special issue) 35:483–96.

Spindt, Paul A., and Hoffmeister, J. Ronald. 1988. The micromechanics of the federal funds market: Implications for day-of-the-week effects in funds rate variability. *Journal of Financial and Quantitative Analysis* 23, no. 4:401–16.

Stephan, Jens A., and Whaley, Robert E. 1990. Intraday price change and trading volume relations in the stock and stock option markets. *Journal of Finance* 45, no. 1:191–220.

Stigum, Marcia. 1990. *The Money Market*. 3d ed. Homewood, Ill.: Dow Jones-Irwin.

Swary, Itzhak. 1986. Stock market reaction to regulatory action in the Continental Illinois crisis. *Journal of Business* 59, no. 3:451–73.

Wall, Larry D. 1989. A plan for reducing future deposit insurance losses: Puttable subordinated debt. *Federal Reserve Bank of Atlanta Economic Review* 74, no. 4:2–17.

Wall, Larry D., and Peterson, David R. 1990. The effect of Continental Illinois' failure on the financial performance of other banks. *Journal of Monetary Economics* 26, no. 1:77–99.

White, Lawrence J. 1989. The reform of federal deposit insurance. *Journal of Economic Perspectives* 3, no. 4:11–29.

II PUBLIC PROVISION OF LIQUIDITY AND REGULATION

8 Private and Public Supply of Liquidity

Bengt Holmström and Jean Tirole

I. Introduction

This paper addresses a basic, yet unresolved, question: Do private assets provide sufficient liquidity for the efficient functioning of the productive sector? Or does the state have a role in supplying additional liquidity and regulating it through adjustments in the stock of government securities or by other means?

These questions presume a demand for liquidity, where liquidity refers to the availability of instruments (market and nonmarket) that can be used to transfer wealth across periods.[1] Part of this demand will, of course, come from consumers who want to implement their optimal intertemporal consumption plans. Indeed, papers that have addressed the sufficiency of liquidity have typically focused on the consumer sector (see Sec. V). We are interested in the production side of the economy. Theoretically, it is less clear why producers demand liquidity. Indeed, in the standard theory of finance (based on the Arrow-Debreu model of general equilibrium) there is no such demand. Since at any time firms can issue claims up to the full value of their expected returns, they have no reason to hold liquid reserves in order to meet future financing needs. As long as firms use their funds to finance positive net present value projects, they will never encounter liquidity problems.

The first step in our analysis then is to build a model in which firms have a demand for liquidity; that is, they need advance financing. For this purpose we use an entrepreneurial model of moral hazard in which the value of external claims on the firm is strictly less than the full value of the firm for the standard reason that the entrepreneur must be given a minimum share in order to be motivated. The wedge between the full value of the firm and the external value of the firm prevents it from financing all projects that have positive net present value. In a dynamic setting, this feature implies that liquidity shocks could force the firm to terminate a project midstream even though the project has a positive continuation value. To protect itself against such risks, the firm wants to hold liquid reserves in the form of marketed assets that can be readily sold or by arranging in advance for a line of credit (a long-term loan).

[1] Liquidity can be given many other interpretations. For instance, the liquidity of an asset is often measured by how quickly it can be sold without a price discount. The role of liquidity in atemporal exchange leads to an entirely different set of issues that our model does not address (see, e.g., Banerjee and Maskin 1996).

The second step in our analysis links the firm's financing problem with the market supply of liquidity. The key observation here is that the same agency problem that limits the amount of financing that firms can raise ex post also limits the amount of liquid assets that are available in the market to back up long-term financial commitments by outside investors. When firms can sell outsiders only a small fraction of their expected returns, the security market as a whole has a very limited capacity to transfer wealth from one period to the next. It is this interplay between the ex post agency problem of the individual firm and the ex ante commitment problem of the market investor that is the central and novel feature of our analysis.

After this brief tour of the main plot, let us describe the paper in some more detail.

We study the determinants of the firm's liquidity demand in a simple, dynamic moral hazard model. There are three periods. At date 0, the firm raises funds to invest in a variable-sized project that pays off at date 2. At date 1, the firm experiences a liquidity shock. The shock is a random fraction of the date 0 investment and represents the amount of additional investment that must be made to continue the project.[2] If the necessary funds can be raised, the project proceeds, delivering a stochastic date 2 return that depends on the entrepreneur's effort.

We show that the optimal date 0 contract between the firm and the outside investors limits both the initial investment level and the amount that the firm is allowed to spend on the liquidity shock, both constraints being proportional to the firm's initial assets. Because the firm is credit-constrained, the second-best solution trades off the benefits of a higher initial investment against the increased likelihood of having to terminate the project early and see it all go to waste. This solution can be implemented in several ways. One is to give the firm all the necessary funds in advance but add a *liquidity covenant* in which the firm promises to set aside a certain amount of funds to cover future liquidity needs. Alternatively, intermediaries could fund future liquidity needs via a *credit line*.[3]

Having established a demand for liquidity, we move on to study its supply by embedding the model of the firm in a general equilibrium setting with a large number of similar firms. Each firm (or intermediary) can issue arbitrary claims contingent on its date 2 financial position, and these claims can be freely traded in the market.[4] The government can also supply liquidity by selling securities such as Treasury bonds. There are no other assets that firms and intermediaries can use to transfer wealth from one period to the next.[5] Thus a firm can meet liquidity needs in four ways: by issuing claims on its own productive assets, by holding claims on other firms, by holding government-issued claims, or by using a credit line.

We are mainly interested in understanding the government's role in supplying and managing liquidity as a function of the severity and nature of the liquidity shocks. We consider two polar cases: one in which the firms' liquidity shocks are independent, so that

[2]The liquidity shock admits several interpretations. It can be a cost overrun on the initial investment. Alternatively, it can represent a shortfall in the date 1 revenue, which could have been used to finance date 1 operating expenses. Or the shock might simply be information about the firm's date 2 returns. The central feature in all these cases is that the shock affects the firm's net worth, which determines its financing capacity.

[3]Our theory is too sparse to distinguish between different financial institutions. When we use language that suggests an institutional interpretation (intermediary, bank, etc.), it should be interpreted merely as illustrative of many similar arrangements.

[4]In contrast to much of the literature, we do not restrict the set of claims that firms can issue. This is to avoid a spurious demand for publicly supplied liquidity.

[5]We can allow other assets, such as real estate, as long as their value does not fulfill the private sector's liquidity needs. See Sec. VI.

there is no aggregate uncertainty; and the opposite case in which the firms' liquidity shocks are identical.

In the absence of aggregate uncertainty, we show that government securities do not add useful liquidity beyond that provided by private claims; nor does the government have any role in managing aggregate liquidity.[6] There is a simple intuition behind the self-sufficiency of the private sector: The date 1 continuation value of the private sector, which is deterministic, must exceed its date 0 value; else it could not have invested at date 0. Therefore, the private sector can raise sufficient funds at date 1 by diluting its shareholdings or, equivalently, by leveraging itself up with new debt.

However, even though the private sector is self-sufficient in the aggregate, we show that individual firms will in general be unable to satisfy their liquidity needs by holding only private market instruments. One might have thought that it would suffice for each firm to hold a share of the market portfolio, which it could sell when the liquidity shock hits. But this market solution is, in general, not efficient because lucky firms with low liquidity shocks end up holding excess liquidity. Thus scarce liquidity is wasted.

We show that an optimal allocation can be achieved by introducing intermediaries that hold all corporate claims and simultaneously grant credit lines to firms. These intermediaries take into account the fact that some firms (namely, those with low liquidity needs) will not exhaust their credit lines at date 1. Intermediaries can therefore redistribute excess liquidity to firms that do need extra funds. They act like *liquidity pools* or insurers in preventing a wasteful accumulation of liquidity in the firms that end up being lucky at date 1. Thus *intermediation may strictly dominate financial markets that trade in individually issued claims.*[7]

In the presence of pure aggregate uncertainty, the preceding argument for self-sufficiency breaks down. Now there can be no cross-subsidization, because each firm faces trouble exactly when the other firms do. As the private sector is unable to provide insurance, there will be a liquidity shortage whenever the reinvestment need exceeds the date 1 value of corporate claims. This creates a potential demand for government-provided liquidity. We show that the government can achieve a Pareto improvement by issuing Treasury bonds and that these bonds can be sold at a *liquidity premium*. The productive sector is willing to purchase low-yielding securities because they serve as an input into the production process. Despite identical, risk-neutral consumers, securities with different rates of return can coexist in equilibrium.

It is important to point out what the government can achieve that the private sector cannot. In our model, investors are assumed unable to commit their future endowments, unless these commitments are backed up by marketable assets (wealth). Unsecured credit, including short selling, is not available to individuals. This assumption is both theoretically and empirically reasonable. In practice, individuals can borrow very limited amounts without pledging collateral (as in the case of a mortgage). Because the private sector has no power to audit income and levy taxes, it is unable to check who is lying about endowments at date 1. By contrast, the government has the power to audit incomes and impose nonfinancial penalties (such as jail) to enforce tax payments. It can therefore commit funds on behalf of the consumers at date 1.[8] This is what Treasury bonds issued at date 0 achieve.

[6] If issued, government securities will carry no liquidity premium.

[7] The critical feature of the credit line that yields a productive optimum is that it allows negative net present value investments at date 1. Such commitments may be possible in markets as well if we allow put options on mutual funds. We shall discuss this in more detail later.

[8] If our model included overlapping generations, the government could commit the incomes of future consumers as well.

When the government issues securities at a premium and when firms are constrained to issue a single security (equity), a problem of free-riding emerges. Firms can get liquidity more cheaply by buying shares of those firms that purchase government securities. We show that firms have an incentive to eliminate free-riding by issuing multiple securities in order to price-discriminate between the investors who value liquidity services (producers) and those who do not (consumers). Corporate debt then sells at a premium relative to equity.

Issuing multiple securities is better than issuing single securities, but the solution still falls short of achieving the socially efficient outcome. Since bonds sell at a premium, the productive sector will try to economize on their use by distorting its investment policy. In particular, firms (or intermediaries) will resort to partial liquidations at date 1, a practice that is socially inefficient. The source of the problem is that the private sector often ends up paying for bonds that it does not need ex post. We show that it is more efficient to have the government issue state-contingent bonds, which supply liquidity only as needed by the private sector. Such bonds have a high value when liquidity needs are high and a low (zero) value when liquidity needs are low. We interpret state-contingent bonds as a metaphor for an active government policy in which liquidity is tightened when the aggregate liquidity shock is favorable (low) and loosened when the aggregate shock is unfavorable (high). Thus the model offers a potential rationale not only for government-supplied liquidity but also for the active management of liquidity by the government.

The paper is organized as follows. Section II studies the partial equilibrium problem of a single firm. Section III analyzes the general equilibrium model under the assumption of independent liquidity shocks. Section IV considers the case of aggregate uncertainty and analyzes the demand for and supply of government securities, including the optimal use of state-contingent bonds. Section V relates our results to the literatures on credit rationing, intermediation, and government debt. Section VI discusses the robustness of the results and potential extensions.

II. Exogenous Liquidity Supply

A. The Model

This section studies the investment decision of an individual firm.

There are three periods, $t = 0, 1, 2$, and two types of agents, firms (entrepreneurs) and investors (consumers). There is one (universal) good used for both consumption and investment. All agents are risk-neutral with an additively separable utility function over undiscounted consumption streams: $u(c_0, c_1, c_2) = c_0 + c_1 + c_2$. For the moment we assume that the good can be stored at a zero rate of return and simply refer to it as "cash." This guarantees that there is no shortage of liquidity. In later sections we shall drop this assumption since we are interested in the endogenous supply of liquidity, that is, in how well financial assets can service the liquidity needs of firms.

The firm has access to a stochastic constant-returns-to-scale technology, which for an initial investment I returns RI if the project succeeds and zero if it fails. The scale of the investment I can be varied freely, subject only to financial constraints. The investment is made at date 0. At date 1, an additional, uncertain amount $\rho I > 0$ of financing is needed to cover operating expenditures and other cash needs. The liquidity shock ρ is distributed according to the cumulative distribution function F, with a density function f. If ρI is paid, the project continues and a final payoff is realized at date 2. If ρI is not paid, the project terminates and yields nothing (partial liquidation will be considered later).

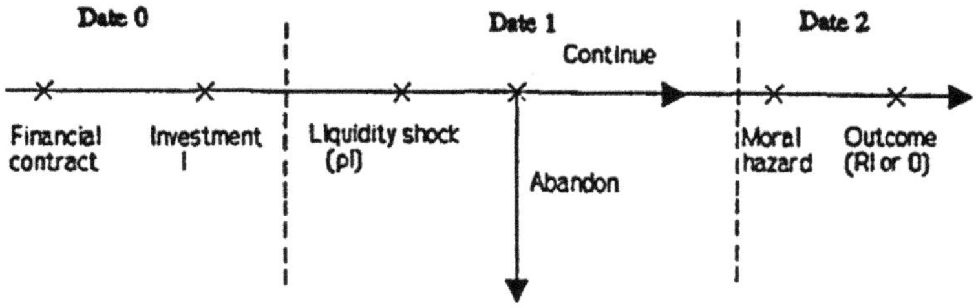

Figure 8.1.

Investment is subject to moral hazard in that the firm (entrepreneur) privately chooses the probability p that the project succeeds. The firm can either "behave" or "shirk." If the firm behaves, the probability of success is p_H (high); if it shirks, the probability of success is p_L (low), where $p_H - p_L \equiv \Delta p > 0$. If the firm shirks, it enjoys a private benefit, $BI > 0$, proportional to the level of its investment I. The firm makes the decision on p after the continuation decision. The timing of events is described in figure 8.1.

The firm has a date 0 endowment of cash, $A > 0$, and no endowments at dates 1 and 2.[9] It can raise additional funds from outside investors. For the moment, we assume that the initial investment level, the project outcome, and the liquidity shock are all verifiable (as we shall see, nothing changes if only the entrepreneur observes the liquidity shock). A contract with outside investors specifies the amount that the investors will contribute, the initial scale of the project, the contingencies in which the project is continued at date 1, and the distribution of the proceeds from the investment. The contract has to offer the investors a nonnegative expected return. A key constraint is that the firm cannot pay out more funds than it has: there is *limited liability*.

The net present value of the investment is maximized by continuing the project if and only if $\rho \leq \rho_1 \equiv p_H R$, that is, whenever the expected return $p_H R$ from continuation exceeds the cost ρ. We shall refer to ρ_1 as the *first-best cutoff*. To make the problem interesting, we assume that the project's net present value is positive if the firm is diligent (chooses p_H) but not if it shirks (chooses p_L):

$$\int \max\{p_H R - \rho, 0\} f(\rho)\, d\rho - 1 > 0$$

$$> \int \max\{p_L R + B - \rho, 0\} f(\rho)\, d\rho - 1. \tag{8.1}$$

Given (1), we need to consider only contracts that implement the action p_H. Let $C = \{I, \lambda(\rho), R_f(\rho)\}$ be a generic contract, where I is the level of investment, $\lambda(\rho)$ is a state-contingent continuation policy (1 = continue, 0 = abandon), and $R_f(\rho)$ is the amount the firm is paid if the project succeeds (given a liquidity shock ρ). Investors are left with $R - R_f(\rho)$. If the project fails or is abandoned, we assume that both sides receive zero. This assumption is made without loss of generality since any feasible contract in which transfers are made despite a zero outcome can be replaced by a payoff-equivalent (or superior) contract in

[9]There is no loss of generality in assuming zero endowments as long as cash is available. In the presence of a random date 1 revenue stream, the liquidity shock should be thought of as the *net* cash flow at date 1.

which payments are made only when the project succeeds. An optimal contract can be found by choosing $\{I, \lambda(\rho), R_f(\rho)\}$ to solve the following *second-best program:*

$$\max I \int p_H R_f(\rho)\,\lambda(\rho) f(\rho)\,d\rho - A \tag{8.2a}$$

subject to

$$I \int \{p_H[R - R_f(\rho)] - \rho\}\,\lambda(\rho) f(\rho)\,d\rho \geq I - A \tag{8.2b}$$

and

$$R_f(\rho)\Delta p \geq B \quad \text{for every}\,\rho. \tag{8.2c}$$

Program (2) maximizes the firm's net return subject to the investors' break-even constraint (2b) and the firm's incentive compatibility constraint (2c).

Program (2) is linear in I, so it will have a finite solution only if constraint (2b) binds. For the moment, assume that this is the case; we shall provide precise conditions below. Solving (2), one finds that the optimal continuation policy is a cutoff rule of the form "continue if and only if $\rho \leq \hat{\rho}$." Substituting (2b) into (2a), we can then write the firm's objective in the form

$$U_f(\hat{\rho}) = m(\hat{\rho})I, \tag{8.3}$$

where

$$m(\hat{\rho}) = \int_0^{\hat{\rho}} (\rho_1 - \rho) f(\rho)\,d\rho - 1 \tag{8.4}$$

is the *marginal net social return* on investment. Writing the firm's payoff in the form (3) underscores the fact that, as a residual claimant, the firm receives the full social surplus.

It is easily verified that $m(\hat{\rho})$ is quasi-concave and achieves its maximum at the first-best cutoff $\hat{\rho} = \rho_1$. Because the net present value of the project is positive by assumption (1), we have $m(\rho_1) > 0$. But then the marginal return $m(\hat{\rho})$ for the second-best policy must also be strictly positive because the first-best cutoff rule $\hat{\rho} = \rho_1$ is feasible in (2) (for small enough I). Given $m(\hat{\rho}) > 0$, it follows from (3) that the firm will choose payments $R_f(\rho)$ to maximize I. This is achieved by setting $R_f(\rho) = R_b \equiv B/\Delta p$, the minimum payment necessary to keep the entrepreneur diligent.[10] By taking out as little as possible, the firm maximizes the amount that it can pay to outside investors, which (per unit invested) is $p_0 \equiv p_H[R - (B/\Delta p)]$. We shall refer to ρ_0 as the *date 1 pledgeable unit return* from investment.

The fact that outside investors can be promised only an expected return $\rho_0 I$ at date 1 rather than the full social value $\rho_1 I$ plays a key role in our analysis.[11] Without a positive

[10]The minimum payment to the entrepreneur can more broadly be interpreted as a rent shared by all employees of the firm. Without such rents, employees will not work as efficiently.

[11]We could have created a wedge between the social value ρ_1 and the pledgeable value ρ_0 more expediently, but less realistically, by assuming that the entrepreneur can steal the difference.

wedge $\rho_1 - \rho_0 > 0$, investments would be self-financing and there would be no demand for liquidity (as will become clear later). In fact, the firm would be free to invest arbitrary large amounts at date 0, making the second-best problem unconstrained. To see this, return to the break-even constraint (2b). The left-hand side is maximized by following the cutoff policy $\hat{\rho} = \rho_0$ and promising investors ρ_0 in each contingency ρ. To eliminate self-financing, we must assume that such a policy does not provide investors an expected marginal return that is larger than the marginal cost of their date 0 investment, which means that

$$\int_0^{\rho_0} (\rho_0 - \rho) f(\rho)\, d\rho < 1. \tag{8.5}$$

Note that if $\rho_0 = \rho_1(B = 0)$, assumption (5) is inconsistent with assumption (1). A positive wedge $\rho_1 - \rho_0 > 0$ is therefore essential for ruling out self-financing.

Condition (5) is necessary and sufficient for the break-even constraint (2b) to be binding and for the second-best solution to be finite. It follows from (2b) that the firm's *investment capacity*, the maximum amount it can invest at date 0 given the cutoff rule $\hat{\rho}$, is

$$I = k(\hat{\rho})A, \tag{8.6}$$

where

$$k(\hat{\rho}) \equiv \frac{1}{1 + \int_0^{\hat{\rho}} \rho f(\rho)\, d\rho - F(\hat{\rho})\rho_0} \tag{8.7}$$

is the *equity multiplier*. The denominator of the equity multiplier specifies the amount of internal funds that the firm has to put in per unit invested in order to make up for the shortfall implied by (5).

It is easy to verify that $k(\hat{\rho})$ is quasi-concave, achieves its maximum at $\hat{\rho} = \rho_0$, and has $k(\rho_0) > 1$. The equity multiplier can be less than one if the cutoff $\hat{\rho}$ is set sufficiently high. This may be optimal if the expected liquidity demand at date 1 is large. In that case $I - A < 0$. (The total investment, the initial investment plus the expected liquidity payments, will of course exceed the firm's initial cash A; else the firm would not go outside for funding.) Unless otherwise specified, we shall assume that $I - A > 0$, since it seems natural to have the firm a net borrower at date 0.[12]

It remains to determine the second-best continuation threshold ρ^*. If we substitute (6) into (3), the firm's net payoff becomes

$$U_f(\hat{\rho}) = m(\hat{\rho})\, k(\hat{\rho})A. \tag{8.8}$$

The second-best threshold is chosen to maximize (8). Because m and k are both quasi-concave functions, with m reaching a maximum at ρ_1 and k reaching a maximum at ρ_0, the second-best threshold ρ^* must fall in the interval $[\rho_0, \rho_1]$. Economically, this can be understood by noting that if $\rho < \rho_0$, both the firm and the investors prefer to continue ex post; if $\rho > \rho_1$, the net present value of continuing is negative, and hence it is Pareto-optimal to abandon the project. (Since transfers from investors to the firm are not constrained by incentive compatibility, investors can always pay the firm to abandon an inefficient project.)

[12]A sufficient condition for $I - A > 0$ is that $k(\rho_1) > 1$.

Within the interval $[\rho_0, \rho_1]$ the firm faces a trade-off. It can raise $\hat{\rho}$ in order to be able to withstand higher liquidity shocks, thereby raising the marginal return $m(\hat{\rho})$ on its date 0 investment, or it can lower $\hat{\rho}$ to expand on the date 0 level of investment $k(\hat{\rho})A$. It cannot do both, because the investors' break-even constraint places a limit on its overall spending. Because m is strictly increasing at ρ_0 and k is strictly decreasing at p_1, the firm resolves this trade-off by choosing ρ^* so that

$$\rho_0 < \rho^* < \rho_1. \tag{8.9}$$

Faced with credit rationing, the firm lets itself be rationed both ex ante and ex post.

This choice of ρ^* can also be interpreted as the outcome of (second-best) risk sharing. Because the firm cannot raise more than $\rho_0 I$ at date 1 even though the social value of continuation is $\rho_1 I$, it purchases insurance from investors at date 0. If the liquidity shock ρ falls below ρ_0, the investors win (the firm would not have needed insurance). If ρ falls above ρ_0, the firm wins (the investors participate in a deal that gives them a negative expected return). With limited resources the second-best policy is to buy some, but not full, insurance.

To characterize ρ^*, we can write out the firm's net payoff $U_f(\hat{\rho})$ using (4) and (7) and then divide through by $F(\hat{\rho})$. This shows that

$$\rho^* \text{minimizes} \frac{1 + \int_0^{\hat{\rho}} \rho f(\rho)\, d\rho}{F(\hat{\rho})}. \tag{8.10}$$

Stated verbally, the second-best threshold minimizes the expected unit cost of total expected investment. The first-order condition for (10) is simply

$$\int_0^{\rho^*} F(\rho)\, d\rho = 1. \tag{8.11}$$

It is a bit surprising that the second-best cutoff ρ^* does not depend either on ρ_0 or on ρ_1 as long as it falls between these two values.[13] Thus the additional funding that becomes available when ρ_0 goes up will all be used to expand scale rather than to add liquidity. The result is driven by the linear structure, which implies that marginal rates of substitution across states and periods are independent of the level of investment.

With (11), the firm's net return can be written in the compact form

$$U_f(\rho^*) = \frac{\rho_1 - \rho^*}{\rho^* - \rho_0} A. \tag{8.12}$$

Equations (11) and (12) have the following interesting consequence. Suppose that the liquidity shock becomes riskier in the sense of a mean-preserving spread in the distribution F. Then (11) shows that the cutoff ρ^* goes down; the firm buys less insurance, because it costs more in reduced date 0 investment. At the same time, (12) shows that the firm's net return $U_f(\rho^*)$ is higher when the liquidity shock has a riskier distribution. The explanation for this slightly counterintuitive result is that the option to terminate the project

[13] If ρ^*, as determined by (11), falls below ρ_0, the firm's investment capacity is infinite. If it falls above ρ_1, the firm cannot profitably raise external funds.

makes a riskier distribution more valuable. Indeed, if the liquidity shock had a degenerate distribution, assumption (5) would imply that the firm could never invest.

We close this subsection with two remarks.

Remark 1: The results above are unaffected if we allow for partial liquidation. This can be seen by letting $\lambda(\rho)$ vary freely between zero and one in program (2). The second-best $\lambda(\rho)$ would still be zero or one, with no change in the optimal cutoff. As we shall see later, this result will not hold when the firm has to pay a premium for liquidity services.

Remark 2: For future reference we note that the firm's expected output, $F(\hat{\rho})\rho_1 k(\hat{\rho})A$, and the value of the investors' claims on this output, $F(\hat{\rho})\rho_0 k(\hat{\rho})A$, are quasi-concave in $\hat{\rho}$ and reach their maximum at the second-best optimum $\hat{\rho} = \rho^*$.

B. Implementation of the Optimal Policy

Suppose that the decision to continue the project is left to be negotiated at date 1. In that case, investors would be willing to inject more cash into the project if $\rho \leq \rho_0$, but not if $\rho > \rho_0$. In the latter case, even if the firm were allowed to dilute the claims of the initial investors by issuing senior securities at date 1, it could not raise enough cash because the most the firm can promise outside investors at date 1 is $\rho_0 I$. Thus, to cover liquidity shocks up to the second-best cutoff $\rho^* > \rho_0$, one must find a way for outside investors to commit funds at date 0.

One solution is to give the firm $I - A$ at date 0 and extend it an *irrevocable line of credit* in the amount $\rho^* I$, which the firm can use to meet liquidity needs at date 1. Since the firm cannot consume funds and since it always prefers to continue the project whenever it can, this credit line will implement the second-best soludon.[14] Equivalently, the investors can extend an irrevocable credit line in the amount $(\rho^* - \rho_0)I$ and grant the firm the right to dilute outside claims as needed to cover the liquidity shock.

In practice, individuals do not grant credit lines to firms. One reason is that individuals have difficulties committing their future income or endowments. They can too easily avoid payment by claiming that they have no funds. The limited amount of nonsecured, personal borrowing that takes place testifies to these problems. In practice, credit lines are granted by intermediaries such as banks, which can make commitments, assuming of course that they have enough funds to meet later credit needs. This raises the question, How do intermediaries guarantee that their own liquidity needs can be met? In the next section, we show that they can do so by issuing shares that pay off only at date 2.

An alternative solution is to give the firm $I(1 + \rho^*) - A$ at date 0 and require that $\rho^* I$ of this amount is kept in liquid assets. In other words, investors demand that the firm maintains a *liquidity ratio* equal to $\rho^*/(1 + \rho^*)$, at least up to date 1. Indeed, a minimum liquidity ratio is a commonly observed debt covenant. As in the case of credit lines, an intermediary is the natural party for overseeing the compliance of such a covenant. It is worth stressing that the partial equilibrium model with "cash" does not distinguish between a credit line and the hoarding of liquid assets by the firm. But as the next section shows, these two methods

[14]Could the line of credit be renegotiated for mutual advantage once ρ is realized? The answer is no. If $\rho \leq \rho^*$, then $\rho < p_H R$ and it is ex post efficient to continue, so there is no scope for renegotiation. Nor can both parties benefit from an increase in the line of credit when $\rho^* < \rho \leq p_H R$. Even though this increase raises total surplus, there is no way to distribute the surplus in a manner that satisfies the investors.

of providing reserves are no longer equivalent once general equilibrium aspects (implying that liquid assets sell at a premium) are brought into consideration.

Remark 1: We assumed that the liquidity shock is verifiable. Nothing is altered if only the firm observes the liquidity shock as long as the firm cannot use part of the credit line or its financial assets for consumption at date 1. Given the firm's reserves, it can continue whenever $\rho < \rho^*$. If $\rho > \rho^*$, it cannot continue, since no outsider can be induced to invest in the firm. A rational investor would infer that a firm that tries to raise new funds does so because it has exceeded its reserves and therefore has experienced a shock $\rho > \rho^* > \rho_0$.

Remark 2: If investors cannot control the firm's initial allocation of funds, one can show that the firm does not want to distribute the funds between date 0 investment and date 1 investment in accordance with the second-best solution. Either the firm wants to invest less initially in order to be able to continue in more states at date 1; or the firm wants to invest excessively at date 0, relying partly on being bailed out by the investors when $\rho < \rho_0$ and there is a cash shortfall. To illustrate the latter possibility, suppose that the firm invests the full amount $I(1 + \rho^*) \equiv I^*$ at date 0 rather than saving $\rho^* I$ for date 1. Despite no cash for reinvestment, the project will often be continued since the investors have an incentive to rescue the firm whenever $\rho \leq \rho_0$. Of course, the investors might want to claim initially that they will not put any more money into the venture, but this is not a credible commitment. Anticipating a "soft budget constraint," the firm may overinvest. Indeed the firm prefers investing I^* rather than I if $F(\rho^*) p_H R_b I < F(\rho_0) p_H R_b I^*$, or $F(\rho^*) < F(\rho_0)(1 + \rho^*)$. This condition can be satisfied by adjusting B so that ρ_0 falls just below ρ^*.

We summarize the results of this section in the following proposition.

Proposition 1: In the second-best allocation, the following are true: (i) A firm with initial capital A invests $I = k(\rho^*)A$, where the equity multiplier $k(\cdot)$ is given by (7). (ii) The project is continued if and only if the liquidity shock falls below the cutoff ρ^*. The cutoff ρ^* lies strictly between the (per unit of investment) pledgeable expected return $\rho_0 = p_H[R - (B/\Delta p)]$ and the expected return $\rho_1 = P_H R$. (iii) Neither party is paid anything if the project is terminated or fails. If the project succeeds, the firm is paid $(B/\Delta p)I$ and the investors $[R - (B/\Delta p)]I$. (iv) The second-best allocation can be implemented by raising $I - A$ in external funds for the initial investment and by extending the firm a line of credit in the amount $\rho^* I$ to be used for reinvestment. Alternatively, the firm can be given $(1 + \rho^*)I$ at date 0 with the covenant that it keeps $\rho^* I$ in reserve for reinvestments.

III. Endogenous Liquidity Supply without Aggregate Uncertainty

A. The Economy

Next we embed our model in a general equilibrium framework. Our objective is to analyze the endogenous supply of liquidity. To focus on the problem of creating assets that can meet the demand for liquidity at date 1, we drop the assumption that there is an exogenously given storage technology. The single consumption good cannot be stored (there is no longer cash), nor are there any other private assets (such as real estate) that can be used to transfer wealth from one period to the next. The only way to transfer wealth across periods is to buy claims issued by firms. Later on, we shall introduce government bonds.

There is a continuum of firms with unit mass. Each firm is endowed with the stochastic technology described in Section II. Because of constant returns to scale, there is no loss in assuming that firms have identical endowments; the representative firm is endowed with A units of the good at date 0 and none at dates 1 and 2.

As before, consumers and entrepreneurs are risk-neutral and do not care about the timing of consumption. Consumers receive endowments per period that collectively are large enough to finance all required investments and taxes that may be levied. Consumers cannot sell claims on (or borrow against) their future endowments because they can default with impunity. Only promises that are backed up by marketable assets (claims on firms) can be made. This is a key assumption. Without it, there would be no shortage of liquid instruments, nor any role for government intervention.

Any assets purchased by the consumers must yield a zero expected return given that their collective endowments exceed investment demand. By contrast, firms may be willing to purchase assets at a premium (a negative return) as long as those assets help them to meet their liquidity needs. Thus rates of return, to the extent that they deviate from zero, will be entirely determined by the productive sector. This is the convenience afforded by a linear preference structure.

In this section we shall consider the case in which liquidity shocks are independent. Because there is a continuum of firms, there is no aggregate uncertainty; and $F(\rho)$ denotes both the ex ante probability that a given firm faces a liquidity shock below ρ and the realized fraction of firms with liquidity shock below ρ. The independence assumption and the analysis in Section II imply that the date 1 funds needed by the productive sector to achieve the productive optimum are the deterministic amount

$$D \equiv I \int_0^{\rho^*} \rho f(\rho)\, d\rho, \tag{8.13}$$

where I is the representative firm's investment.

The two ways of implementing the productive optimum discussed in Section II, an irrevocable credit line and a liquidity requirement, both relied on an exogenously supplied liquid asset, cash. With cash no longer available, we are led to investigate whether firms can finance their liquidity needs D by using available market instruments, that is, by issuing additional claims at date 1 or by holding stakes in other firms.

B. Financial Markets

For the time being, assume that there are no intermediaries. There is only a financial market for individual claims issued by firms or composite securities such as mutual funds. We exclude put options. In our interpretation, puts on mutual funds fall in the category of intermediation.

We first compute the maximum amount that a firm can raise by selling new (senior) securities at date 1. If the firm is able to continue with the amount thus raised, its market value at date 1 is $p_H(R - R_b)I = \rho_0 I$. This value reflects the fact that the firm must retain a minimum stake $R_b I$ as an inside claim in order to behave. Since date 0 investors, those who bought the firm's initial securities, get nothing if the firm cannot meet its liquidity needs, they are willing (ex post) to dilute their claims up to the full amount $\rho_0 I$ in order to salvage some of their initial investment. Of course, initial investors take the possibility of dilution into account in the pricing of initial claims.

A firm is unable to meet its liquidity needs by issuing new claims whenever the realized liquidity shock ρ falls in the interval $(\rho_0, \rho^*]$. Can a firm cover the potential shortfall by buying, at date 0, claims issued by other firms and selling these claims at date 1? That is, can the firm assure itself enough liquidity through the financial market? The answer is, in general, negative.

To develop an intuition for why the financial market may be unable to serve the firms' liquidity needs efficiently, let us assume (for illustration only) that all external claims are equity claims and that, to the extent that firms buy these claims to meet liquidity needs, they all end up with the same share of the market portfolio (because firms are identical).[15] The absence of aggregate shocks implies that S_1, the value of the market portfolio at date 1, is deterministic. Suppose that the productive optimum of Section II obtains: a firm with liquidity shock ρ continues if and only if $\rho \leq \rho^*$. Then a fraction $F(\rho^*)$ of firms will continue at date 1. The total value of external claims on the productive sector at date 1 is therefore

$$V_1 = F(\rho^*)\,\rho_0 I. \tag{8.14}$$

In the absence of credit lines, these external claims need to be diluted by the amount D defined in (13), so the value S_1 of the market portfolio at date 1 is

$$\begin{aligned} S_1 &= V_1 - D \\ &= \left[F(\rho^*)\,\rho_0 - \int_0^{\rho^*} \rho f(\rho)\,d\rho \right] I = I - A. \end{aligned} \tag{8.15}$$

The value of the market portfolio is positive, since we assumed that $I - A > 0$.

Let us conduct the following thought experiment: Suppose that a fraction $\alpha \in (0, 1)$ of the market portfolio is held by the firms. At date 1, each firm can then withstand liquidity shocks ρ satisfying

$$\rho I \leq \rho_0 I + \alpha S_1. \tag{8.16}$$

For the right-hand side of (16) to equal $\rho^* I$ for some $\alpha < 1$, one must have

$$\rho^* + \int_0^{\rho^*} \rho f(\rho)\,d\rho < [1 + F(\rho^*)]\,\rho_0. \tag{8.17}$$

Recalling that ρ^* is independent of the extent of moral hazard as measured by B (see [11]), we conclude that, for B large enough, ρ_0 is so small that condition (17) is violated. In that case, firms are unable to withstand liquidity shocks up to ρ^* by holding a share of the market portfolio. Intuitively, when B is large, the firm's minimum inside share R_b must be large, and therefore the firm cannot raise much capital by diluting claims at date 1. Concurrently, and for the same reason, the market portfolio has a low value, so the firm cannot raise much by selling its shares in the other firms.

Actually, as the next section demonstrates, the issue is not that the stock market delivers too little liquidity *in the aggregate*. Rather, the ex post *distribution* of liquid assets is

[15] Assuming that firms are identical is not significant for the argument.

inefficient. Lucky firms (those with liquidity shocks $\rho < \rho_0$) end up holding shares they do not need, whereas unlucky firms with large liquidity shocks cannot continue because the average share of the market portfolio offers insufficient liquidity.

It is clear that the previous reasoning does not rely on the particular securities issued by individual firms. The difference between the total value of external claims and the aggregate reinvestment cost when the threshold is ρ^*, S_1, is an upper bound on the combined value of *all* external date 0 claims on the productive sector. Hence, in the aggregate, the value of the financial claims held by the firms cannot exceed S_1. Given that dilution cannot raise more than $\rho_0 I$ per firm, some firms (all firms, if financial claims are uniformly distributed among firms) cannot withstand shocks exceeding $\rho_0 I + S_1$.

To conclude, financial markets in which only "pure plays" (claims on individual firms) are traded cannot in general implement the productive optimum.

C. Intermediation

When the financial market fails to supply enough liquidity, the productive optimum can be implemented by introducing an intermediary that offers insurance against liquidity needs by pooling firm risks. In accordance with Section II, optimal insurance entails subsidizing firms with a high liquidity demand by allowing them to draw on the market value of firms that experience a low liquidity demand.

We first check that there is enough liquidity in the aggregate to implement the second-best policy. Let all individual firms be pooled together into a single firm, an economywide conglomerate. If the conglomerate follows the second-best policy, where individual firms continue if and only if $\rho \leq \rho^*$, the conglomerate can be sold at date 1 (gross of reinvestments) for the value $F(\rho^*)\rho_0 I$. The conglomerate needs to raise D (see [13]) to cover its liquidity needs. Since $F(\rho^*)\rho_0 I - D = S_1$, which is positive, the conglomerate can raise the necessary funds to implement the second-best policy.

It remains to show that an intermediary can make full use of the potential market value of the private sector. There are many ways in which this can be done. The simplest is to let the intermediary replicate the conglomerate solution as follows.[16] At date 0, it issues shares to investors. These shares are claims on the intermediary's financial position at date 2.[17] The intermediary uses the proceeds from its share issue to buy up all the external claims on firms. Firms are priced so that the intermediary breaks even on each firm issue (ex ante). Similarly, the shares of the intermediary are so priced that investors break even. If the intermediary succeeds in implementing the second-best policy, its shares will now sell for the amount S_1, since its market value equals the value of its investment portfolio. The intermediary's net "cash flow" at date 0 is zero, guaranteeing that the arrangement is financially feasible.

The intermediary proceeds to grant each firm a credit line equal to $\rho^* I$. Attached to the credit line is the covenant that a firm cannot issue new claims at date 1. A firm can use all or just a portion of its credit line at date 1. There is no charge for using credit (we shall return to this point below). However, the firm has no use for excess credit since the entrepreneur cannot consume funds, and any returns from market assets that the firm might purchase at

[16] In our model, the number of intermediaries is indeterminate. We shall describe the implementation of the second-best solution as though there were a single intermediary.

[17] As in Jacklin (1987), it is important to avoid claims that can be redeemed at date 1, since such claims can lead to "bank runs."

date 1 will go to the intermediary (except for the portion $R_b I$, which goes to the entrepreneur if the project succeeds). Given the credit line, a firm can continue whenever $\rho \le \rho^*$.

The only remaining issue is whether the intermediary can raise enough funds at date 1 to meet its (deterministic) credit obligations D. But this follows immediately from the fact, argued above, that the private sector in the aggregate can raise $S_1 + D = (I - A) + D > D$. Since we assumed that firms raise a positive amount ex ante ($I - A > 0$) and the ex ante calculation includes the expected cost of covering the liquidity shock, firms must be able to raise a positive amount also ex post when the liquidity shock is not part of the valuation.

Remark 1: There are many variations on intermediation that are equivalent to the one described above. For instance, the intermediary could be made to resemble a bank by letting firms issue shares directly to investors and having the intermediary hold only firm debt (claims senior to equity). The intermediary could also charge the firm according to the amount of credit used rather than just an upfront fixed fee. To illustrate, a credit arrangement could call for a repayment of $(\rho/\rho^*)\ (R - R_b)I$ at date 2 (which can be met, of course, only if the project succeeds) if the firm uses $\rho I (\le \rho^* I)$ of credit at date 1. Note that the implied price for credit is below par since the expected repayment equals $(\rho\rho_0/\rho^*)I$, which is less than ρI, the amount of credit used. In fact, because firms are fully diluted when $\rho > \rho_0$, there is no credit contract that charges an actuarially fair price for all realizations of ρ. An additional up-front fee must be imposed to cover the intermediary's expected loss. In reality, such fees are common, suggesting that use of credit is indeed underpriced ex post.

Variations like these influence only how surplus is redistributed among external claim holders and how initial claims are priced, but they have no effect on real outcomes. Therefore, we can proceed without pinning down these contractual details.[18]

Remark 2: One may wonder what it is that an intermediary can do that the financial market cannot do. We argued in Section III*A* that the financial market fails to provide adequate liquidity because the value of the market claims that the firm holds cannot be made contingent on the firm's idiosyncratic liquidity shock. By contrast, the value of the credit line does depend on the firm's realized need for liquidity. Even when the intermediary is unable to observe ρ, the firm reveals the liquidity shock voluntarily. Thus intermediation does not necessarily require more information than the market has. This feature is of course quite dependent on our assumption that the firm cannot spend credit on anything other than the liquidity shock. Without that assumption, the self-revelation mechanism implied by the credit line would break down.

If the intermediary is just a passive coordinator of contracts, one would think that a complex market instrument could replace it. Indeed, we could interpret our intermediary solution as a put option on a mutual fund that holds the market portfolio. Puts would function just like credit lines, assuming that the firms could not use the puts for anything other than to cover their liquidity shocks. On the other hand, if one assumes that anonymous markets cannot impose constraints on how investors use the proceeds from their market trades, then an intermediary that can put such constraints on firms will dominate the market. To the

[18] Monitoring and control right considerations could be introduced to reduce contractual ambiguity, but the implications of such embellishments must await further research.

extent that such constraints require monitoring, our intermediary solution does require more information than the market has.

Proposition 2: In the absence of aggregate uncertainty, the following are true: (i) The productive optimum cannot always be achieved through an (anonymous) financial market. Ex post, liquidity may be misallocated. (ii) The productive optimum can be implemented (if $I - A > 0$) by relying on private intermediation of credit. Intermediaries act like insurers against liquidity shocks, cross-subsidizing firms. Intermediaries need not observe individual liquidity shocks in order to implement the optimum. (iii) There is no liquidity role for government securities. If issued, such securities must be offered at par (yielding zero interest) and do not affect real allocations.

IV. Endogenous Liquidity Supply with Pure Aggregate Uncertainty

A. The Demand for Government Bonds

In the previous section liquidity shocks were independent. We now shift to the other extreme, the case in which there is only aggregate uncertainty. All firms experience the same liquidity shock.

It is clear that in this case the private sector cannot be self-sufficient. With pure aggregate uncertainty, every firm needs to raise ρI at the same time. Since a firm is worth at most $\rho_0 I$ to outsiders at date 1, the aggregate demand for liquidity will exceed the aggregate value of the private sector whenever $\rho_0 < \rho \leq \rho^*$. Intermediation cannot overcome the problem, because at best it can realize the net ex post value of the productive sector, which in this event is zero.

This creates a demand for government-supplied liquidity. The government can meet the demand thanks to its assumed ability to commit future consumer endowments via taxation. Suppose that the government issues one-period bonds in the amount $(\rho^* - \rho_0)I$ at date 0 and sells them at par. We are then back to the environment analyzed in Section II, with government bonds providing a storage facility equivalent to cash. The productive optimum can be achieved by having investors invest $(1 + \rho^*)I - A$ in each firm at date 0, with the requirement that firms spend $(\rho^* - \rho_0)I$ of this amount on the purchase of bonds.[19]

Since government bonds, issued at par, lead to the productive optimum, we know from the analysis in Section II that the introduction of bonds raises total output and expected aggregate investment (the date 0 investment plus the expected value of date 1 reinvestments). Recall, however, that the initial level of investment I decreases as firms save more of their resources to cover date 1 liquidity needs. Thus issuing government bonds crowds out productive investments at date 0 but increases (expected) reinvestments at date 1.

Proposition 3: In the presence of aggregate uncertainty, the following are true: (i) The private sector is not self-sufficient with regard to the supply of liquidity. (ii) If the net social cost of taxation is zero, the government can ensure the productive optimum by issuing enough bonds at the market rate of interest (here, zero), in which case there is

[19] Alternatively, an intermediary can offer each firm a credit line $(\rho^* - \rho_0)I$, backed by the purchase of an equal amount of government bonds. Firms can raise the missing $\rho_0 I$ by issuing new shares.

no demand for intermediation. (iii) The introduction of government bonds reduces date 0 investments and increases date 1 reinvestments (reduces liquidations). Expected output, aggregate investment, and the value of firms all increase.

B. The Government's Objective and Liquidity Premia

By restricting attention to government securities that yield the market rate of interest, Section IV*A* made two implicit assumptions. First, there is no deadweight loss of taxation.[20] Otherwise, the gain in productive efficiency brought about by the bond issue must be traded off against the change in the deadweight loss of taxation. Second, the government maximizes the firms' profit subject to the consumers' breaking even. If either assumption is violated, the government may want to issue securities at a price q above par ($q > 1$) per unit of expected return. We refer to $q - 1$ as the *liquidity premium*. Note that since consumers have no liquidity needs, they will not buy bonds (or any other assets) that sell at a premium. They would like to go short on bonds, but this is excluded by our assumption that individual consumers cannot make financial commitments without backing them up with marketable assets.[21] For small premia, there is still a demand for government securities since the private sector uses them as complementary inputs into the production process.

As is well known, credit rationing models raise some conceptual difficulties for a welfare analysis. A government that aims at maximizing total surplus (consumers' plus producers') would redistribute all endowments to entrepreneurs since one unit of net worth creates more than one unit of output. On the other hand, a government that represents only consumers might confiscate some or all of the entrepreneurs' initial wealth A. Because these conceptual problems are not specific to our model and lie beyond the limited scope of this paper, we shall not investigate the effects of alternative assumptions on the government's objective function. Instead, we simply assume that the government arranges the financing of bonds so that firms bear the net cost of supplying liquidity, leaving consumers as well off as without government intervention (see, however, the upcoming remark on seigniorage). The overall tax effect includes the benefit of distributing the proceeds from the bond issue at date 0 (or reducing date 0 taxes) and the deadweight loss from taxing consumers to redeem the bonds at date 1. It is apparent that at the social optimum the marginal deadweight loss of taxation must be time-increasing. Suppose that the marginal deadweight loss were higher at date 0 than at date 1, say. The government could then issue at date 0 additional one-period bonds at par (at a zero rate of interest). Taxpayers would strictly gain and firms would be made (at least weakly) better off by the increased supply of liquidity. We conclude that, for the optimal debt policy, $q \geq 1$.[22]

C. The Demand for Government Bonds

Let us temporarily rule out cross-shareholdings and intermediation, and run through the analysis of Section II*A* to see how firms respond to the presence of a liquidity premium $q - 1 > 0$. We continue to assume that a firm cannot partially liquidate its investment.

[20] Or, more generally, the marginal deadweight loss of taxation is the same at all dates; so the date 0 deadweight loss due to the income received by issuing government securities is equal to the date 1 (or date 2) deadweight loss associated with the reimbursement of the public debt.

[21] Claims on firms will not do as collateral because they do not span the bond return.

[22] The government cannot gain by reimbursing public debt at date 2 because the deadweight loss of taxation is higher at date 2 than at date 1 by the same reasoning.

Given a cutoff $\hat{\rho}$, the investors' participation constraint becomes

$$F(\hat{\rho})\,\rho_0 I \geq I - A + \left[\int_0^{\hat{\rho}} \rho f(\rho)\,d\rho\right] I + (q-1)(\hat{\rho} - \rho_0)I, \tag{8.18}$$

where use is made of the fact that the maximum dilution at date 1 is $\rho_0 I$, so that $(\hat{\rho} - \rho_0)I$ in government securities is needed to reach the threshold $\hat{\rho}$.

The firm's net utility is now

$$U_f(\hat{\rho}, q) \equiv m(\hat{\rho}, q)\,k(\hat{\rho}, q)A,$$

where

$$m(\hat{\rho}, q) \equiv F(\hat{\rho})\,\rho_1 - 1 - \int_0^{\hat{\rho}} \rho f(\rho)\,d\rho - (q-1)(\hat{\rho} - \rho_0)$$

is the modified margin per unit of investment profit, and

$$k(\hat{\rho}, q) \equiv \frac{1}{1 + \int_0^{\hat{\rho}} \rho f(\rho)\,d\rho + (q-1)(\hat{\rho} - \rho_0) - F(\hat{\rho})\rho_0} \tag{8.19}$$

is the modified equity multiplier. The firm chooses the threshold $\rho^*(q)$ to minimize the expected unit cost of effective investment:

$$\rho^*(q)\ \text{minimizes}\ \frac{1 + \int_0^{\hat{\rho}} \rho f(\rho)\,d\rho + (q-1)(\hat{\rho} - \rho_0)}{F(\hat{\rho})}$$

over $\hat{\rho} > \rho_0$. As a generalization of condition (9) we get

$$\rho_0 < \rho^*(q) + \frac{q-1}{f(\rho^*(q))} < \rho_1.$$

We next ask whether this allocation remains an equilibrium when firms are allowed to issue and trade claims in a financial market. First we argue that if firms are constrained to issue a *single security* (equity), the equilibrium described above unravels because of free-riding. Suppose that all firms issue shares at date 0. Suppose to the contrary that the opening of the financial market does not affect the equilibrium. Shares must then trade at par; else investors would not want to buy them. But then an individual firm could satisfy its liquidity needs more cheaply by buying shares rather than government bonds. To see this, note that the representative firm in the equilibrium without a financial market has an ex post value equal to $[\rho^*(q) - \rho]I > 0$ when the liquidity shock ρ falls in the interval $(\rho_0, \rho^*(q))$. This value stems from the excess amount of bonds it holds. Hence, by holding enough shares in the other firms, an individual firm can accommodate shocks arbitrarily close to $\rho^*(q)$ without paying any liquidity premium. Thus the equilibrium without cross-shareholdings must unravel once firms are allowed to buy each other's shares.

The intuition why the equilibrium breaks down is clear: *Liquidity is a public good if the government charges a premium.* Each firm therefore wants to free-ride on those firms that purchase government bonds. Of course, all firms cannot follow the free-rider strategy, since then no firm would buy government bonds and there would be no protection at all against liquidity shocks above ρ_0.

D. An Analysis of the Private Sector's Optimal Policy

This subsection derives the private sector's optimal policy when the government charges a premium. The next subsection will analyze the implementation of this policy, in particular the private sector's response to the possibility of free-riding.

Suppose that the private sector buys $(\hat{\rho} - \rho_0)I$ bonds (where I is the investment level of the representative firm) and allocates the funds efficiently at date 1. All firms can withstand the liquidity shock if $\rho \leq \hat{\rho}$; but if $\rho > \hat{\rho}$, some firms must shut down. Instead of shutting down all firms, however, the private sector can resort to *partial liquidation* at the industry level, allowing a fraction $(\hat{\rho} - \rho_0)/(\rho - \rho_0)$ of firms to continue (we can assume that firms that continue are drawn randomly). Whether this is optimal depends on how high the liquidity shock is. If ρ is high enough, it may be better to return the bonds to the investors rather than to use the funds for reinvestment.

To determine the private sector's optimal policy, let zI be the face value of the bonds that the private sector buys and let $\lambda(\rho, z)$ be the fraction of firms allowed to continue when the aggregate shock is ρ. Since entrepreneurs get paid $p_H R_b = \rho_1 - \rho_0$ per unit invested if the project continues, an optimal strategy can be found by solving the following program:

$$\max_{I,\lambda(\cdot)} I \int_0^\infty \lambda(\rho, z)(\rho_1 - \rho_0) f(\rho) d\rho$$

$$\text{subject to (i)} \quad I \int_0^\infty \lambda(\rho, z)(\rho_0 - \rho) f(\rho) d\rho - I(q-1)z \geq I - A, \tag{8.20}$$

$$\text{(ii)} \quad 0 \leq \lambda(\rho, z) \leq \min\left\{1, \frac{z}{\rho - \rho_0}\right\}.$$

Let δ be the Lagrangian multiplier for the budget constraint. Then the optimal choice of λ is

$$\lambda(\rho, z) = \begin{cases} \min\left\{1, \frac{z}{\rho - \rho_0}\right\} & \text{if } \rho \leq \bar{\rho} \equiv \frac{\rho_1 + (\delta - 1)\rho_0}{\delta} \\ 0 & \text{if } \rho > \bar{\rho}. \end{cases} \tag{8.21}$$

The choice of z is governed by the first-order condition

$$\int_{\rho_0 + z}^{\hat{\rho}} \frac{\partial \lambda(\rho, z)}{\partial z} [(\rho_1 - \rho_0) + \delta(\rho_0 - \rho)] \; f(\rho) d\rho - \delta(q - 1) = 0. \tag{8.22}$$

Note that the lower integration bound is $\rho_0 + z$ because of (21). Also, by (21), the term in brackets in the integrand is nonnegative. Therefore, (22) implies that $\partial\lambda(\delta, z)/\partial z > 0$ for some values of ρ as δ and $q - 1 > 0$. In particular, $z < \bar{\rho} - \rho_0$, so that whenever $z + \rho_0 \equiv \hat{\rho} < \rho \leq \bar{\rho}$, we have $0 < \lambda(\rho, z) < 1$, implying that the private sector uses the option of partial liquidation for these ρ-values.

The reason the private sector resorts to partial liquidation is suggested by this analysis. If the private sector bought enough bonds to allow all firms to continue whenever $\rho \leq \bar{\rho}$, the choice of λ would be unconstrained (λ would equal zero or one). The first-order cost of a reduction in z would then be zero, whereas the first-order benefit would be $q - 1 > 0$; it would be better to reduce z. Partial liquidation allows the private sector to economize on the use of bonds. Only when bonds carry no opportunity cost ex post ($q = 1$) will the private sector buy full coverage against liquidity shocks.

Proposition 4: If $q > 1$, that is, if the net deadweight loss of taxation (which must be nonnegative) is strictly positive, the private sector's optimal solution is characterized by two thresholds, $\hat{\rho}$ and $\bar{\rho}$, such that (i) $\rho_0 < \hat{\rho} < \bar{\rho} < \rho_1$; (ii) the private sector buys $zI = (\hat{\rho} - \rho_0)I > 0$ government bonds; and (iii) all firms continue if $\rho \leq \hat{\rho}$; the fraction $(\hat{\rho} - \rho_0)/(\rho - \rho_0) < 1$ of firms continue if $\hat{\rho} < \rho \leq \bar{\rho}$, and no firms continue if $\rho \geq \bar{\rho}$. This solution is more efficient, privately and socially, than when firms act independently.

The last inequality in part i follows because δ represents the marginal value of firm wealth and therefore must be greater than one. The integrated solution of proposition 4 is better than what individual firms could obtain on their own (as described in Sec. IV*C*) because partial liquidation is feasible at the aggregate level, but not at the firm level. The outcome is also socially more efficient because consumers are as well off whether firms act alone or collectively. In both cases, all the social surplus goes to the entrepreneurs.[23] If partial liquidation at the firm level were feasible, the analysis of Section IV*C* would of course coincide with the analysis in this subsection.

E. Implementing the Optimal Policy: A Rationale for Multiple Securities

We turn to the implementation of the optimal policy described in proposition 4. There are two issues to discuss.

The first one concerns the role of intermediation in coordinating the use of liquidity. If partial liquidation is impossible at the firm level, it must be carried out by intermediaries operating on an industry or economy level. Intermediation reduces the cost of liquidity by allowing firms to economize on the purchase of expensive government bonds. Intermediaries can buy fewer bonds without increasing the average extent of liquidation. This function of intermediation is closely related to, though distinct from, the insurance role that intermediation played in an environment without aggregate shocks. In the independent risk case, liquid claims command no premium, and the function of intermediation is to dispatch liquidity efficiently across a heterogeneous set of firms. This function remains even if firms could liquidate partially. By contrast, *with purely aggregate risk, intermediation is unnecessary if partial liquidation at the firm level is feasible.* As we mentioned earlier, firms then solve the same program and achieve the same outcome as in proposition 4.

The second, and more interesting, implementation issue to discuss is free-riding. We argued earlier that if bonds sell at a premium and if firms that buy bonds issue a single type of security (equity), there will be an opportunity to free-ride. Equity will provide valuable liquidity without charge because it has to be priced to attract consumers, who do not care about liquidity. Free-riding becomes an issue whether intermediation is used or not. We conclude that if firms or intermediaries issue only one kind of security, the optimum in Section IV*D* cannot be achieved.

[23]It is worth noting that the established social value of the private optimum depends on the government's objective function. If the government, instead of letting all the surplus go to the entrepreneurs, chose to maximize its net revenue from selling bonds (i.e., consumer surplus), it might well be that restrictions on private arrangements would lead to a higher social utility. The private sector's optimal policy just described has two effects. On the one hand, it makes bonds more valuable to firms, increasing their demand; on the other hand, it allows firms to bypass the government's markup, reducing the demand for bonds. This situation is reminiscent of a government trying to maximize seigniorage in a monetary model. Seigniorage may be higher if private liquidity creation by way of intermediation and cross-shareholdings is restricted.

The problem has a simple solution. Firms can issue multiple securities, allowing them to price-discriminate among investors who value liquidity services differently.[24] To illustrate this idea in the simplest way, let us eliminate the role of intermediation by allowing *partial liquidation at the firm level*. We shall construct an industry equilibrium that implements the allocation described in proposition 4. In this equilibrium, all firms invest I (the level given in proposition 4) and all have a capital structure designed to withstand liquidity shocks up to $\bar{\rho}$. A fraction α of the firms, the *type 1 firms*, purchase $(\bar{\rho} - \rho_0)I$ bonds at price q and hold no shares in other firms. At date 0 they issue two kinds of claims: (i) equity, sold at par, and (ii) short-term debt (maturing at date 1) with face value $(\bar{\rho} - \rho_0)I$, sold at price q'. The debt issue comes with the covenant that the firm will dilute its equity before selling any bonds. This implies that equity in type 1 firms carries no liquidity premium, since it becomes valueless when the aggregate shock exceeds ρ_0. Once the liquidity shock exceeds ρ_0, the firm is allowed to sell up to $(\rho - \rho_0)I$ of bonds before servicing its short-term debt. This covenant makes the short-term debt worth $(\bar{\rho} - \rho)I$ at date 1 if the liquidity shock ρ belongs to the interval $[\rho_0, \bar{\rho}]$.

The remaining fraction $1 - \alpha$ of the firms, the *type 2 firms*, do not purchase bonds, but buy all the short-term debt of type 1 firms. Let α be given by

$$\alpha(\bar{\rho} - \hat{\rho}) = (1 - \alpha)(\hat{\rho} - \rho_0). \tag{8.23}$$

There is no liquidation in either type of firm when $\rho \leq \hat{\rho}$. Suppose that $\rho_0 \leq \rho \leq \hat{\rho}$. Then the value of short-term debt (of a type 1 firm) held by a representative type 2 firm is equal to $\alpha(\bar{\rho} - \rho)I/(1 - \alpha) \geq (\rho - \rho_0)I$; thus by selling these debt claims and by diluting their initial equity (to obtain $\rho_0 I$), type 2 firms can withstand their liquidity shock, ρI. On the other hand, when $\rho \in [\hat{\rho}, \bar{\rho}]$, type 2 firms will partially liquidate but type 1 firms will not. Type 2 firms can continue to operate a fraction λ_2 of their assets, where

$$\lambda_2 \rho I = \lambda_2 \rho_0 I + \frac{\alpha}{1 - \alpha}(\bar{\rho} - \rho)I.$$

That is, they can pledge $\lambda_2 \rho_0$ to new investors in addition to the income from their short-term debt in type 1 firms. The aggregate fraction λ of assets (from both types of firms) that are not liquidated is therefore

$$\begin{aligned}\lambda &= \alpha + (1 - \alpha)\lambda_2 = \alpha + (1 - \alpha)\left(\frac{\alpha}{1 - \alpha}\frac{\bar{\rho} - \rho_0}{\rho - \rho_0}\right) \\ &= \frac{\hat{\rho} - \rho_0}{\rho - \rho_0}\end{aligned}$$

and coincides with the fraction specified in proposition 4. Note also that the aggregate demand for bonds is the same as in part ii of proposition 4, because (23) implies that

$$\alpha(\bar{\rho} - \rho_0)I = (\hat{\rho} - \rho_0)I.$$

Finally, set the price of short-term senior debt, q', so that firms are indifferent between being a type 1 and a type 2 firm. Then α can be chosen as specified in (23).

[24] This clientele rationale is reminiscent of, but distinct from, the argument in Gorton and Pennacchi (1990).

We conclude that the optimal policy can be implemented by issuing multiple corporate securities in the case in which partial liquidation at the firm level is feasible. When it is infeasible, the optimal policy can be implemented by intermediaries that act like the firms described above, issuing multiple securities in order to price-discriminate and avoid free-riding.

F. State-Contingent Bonds

While partial liquidation reduces the deadweight loss of taxation and is efficient for the private sector given that the government issues noncontingent bonds at a premium, this is not the socially most efficient solution. In this subsection we show how the government can achieve a better outcome by issuing state-contingent bonds. We begin by characterizing the social optimum when general state-contingent transfers between consumers and producers are allowed.

A social plan is defined by (i) the initial level of investment I per firm and (ii) a state-contingent continuation policy $\lambda(\rho) \in [0, 1]$ that determines the fraction of firms that continue when the aggregate liquidity shock is ρ.

The social program is identical to the program studied in Section IV*D*, with the exception that the transfers are not constrained by an initial purchase of bonds. Formally, the social program solves

$$\max_{I,\lambda(\cdot)} I \int_0^\infty \lambda(\rho)\,(\rho_1 - \rho_0)f(\rho)d\rho$$

$$\text{subject to} \quad \text{(i)} \quad Iq \int_0^\infty \lambda(\rho)\,(\rho_0 - \rho)f(\rho)d\rho \geq I - A, \qquad (8.24)$$

$$\text{(ii)} \quad 0 \leq \lambda(\rho) \leq 1.$$

The budget constraint takes into account that the consumer cost of date 1 tax transfers expressed in date 0 units is $q > 1$. Let δ be the Lagrangian multiplier of the budget constraint. Then the solution to this program is

$$\lambda^*(\rho) = \begin{cases} 1 & \text{if } \rho \leq \rho^\# \\ 0 & \text{if } \rho > \rho^\#, \end{cases}$$

where $\rho^\#$ is defined by

$$\rho^\# - \rho_0 = \frac{\rho_1 - \rho_0}{\delta q}. \qquad (8.25)$$

In contrast to the solution in Section IV*D*, the social optimum specifies either that all firms continue or that no firm continues; there is never partial liquidation. The explanation for this is that in the social program bonds do not have to be purchased in advance to guarantee liquidity; rather, ex post transfers can be provided as needed.[25] Furthermore, since $q > 1$ and $\delta > 1$ (it is the shadow price on entrepreneurial wealth), we see that the socially optimal cutoff $\rho^\#$ satisfies $\rho_0 < \rho^\#\, \rho_1$.

[25] Partial liquidation would become relevant only if investors or entrepreneurs were risk-averse or if the government could not use state-contingent transfers.

The social optimum $\lambda^*(\rho)$ can be implemented using state-contingent bonds, which pay the holder an amount $x(\rho)$ as a function of the aggregate shock ρ. Let the bonds have the following date 1 payoff:

$$x(\rho) = \begin{cases} 0 & \text{if } \rho \leq \rho_0 \text{ or } \rho > \rho^{\#} \\ \rho - \rho_0 & \text{if } \rho_0 < \rho \leq \rho^{\#}. \end{cases}$$

Set their date 0 price equal to

$$\int_{\rho_0}^{\rho^{\#}} q(\rho - \rho_0) f(\rho) d\rho.$$

Priced this way, bond revenues exactly compensate consumers for the deadweight loss of taxation associated with the policy $\lambda^*(\rho)$.

It is straightforward to check that with these payoffs and prices, firms can replicate the social optimum, if they so desire, by buying I bonds, where I is the socially optimal level of investment. This amount of bonds enables a firm to continue exactly when the social plan calls for continuation. Also, the firm's budget constraint coincides with the social budget constraint so that the firm can attract the required funds from investors at date 0.

Can the firm do better by deviating from the socially optimal plan? Suppose that there is a better plan for the firm. In this plan, let $\bar{I}$ be the date 0 investment level, let $\bar{z}\bar{I}$ be the amount of state-contingent bonds the firm purchases, and let $\bar{\lambda}(\rho)$ be the continuation policy. To be feasible, the plan must satisfy both an ex ante and an ex post budget constraint. The ex ante constraint is

$$\begin{aligned} &\bar{I} \int_0^\infty \bar{\lambda}(\rho)\,(\rho_0 - \rho) f(\rho) d\rho \\ &\quad - \bar{I}\bar{z} \int_0^\infty \lambda^*(\rho)\,(q-1)\,(\rho - \rho_0) f(\rho) d\rho \geq \bar{I} - A. \end{aligned} \tag{8.26}$$

The ex post constraint is

$$0 \leq \bar{\lambda}(\rho) \leq \min\{1,\ \bar{z}\lambda^*(\rho)\}. \tag{8.27}$$

Substituting the ex post constraint into the ex ante constraint, we see that it would be feasible for a social planner to replicate the firm's plan. Given that the social objective function coincides with the firm's, the firm's plan cannot be better than the social optimum.

Finally, note that the government need not concern itself with the possibility of free-riding because, used correctly, state-contingent bonds never leave any extra liquidity in firms.

Remark on seigniorage: As an alternative objective, suppose that the government aims at maximizing net revenue from issuing government securities, ignoring costs of taxation. Let us compute an upper bound R on the government's net revenue. Let $\overline{U}(= m(\rho_0)k(\rho_0)A)$ denote the "autarky utility" of an entrepreneur with assets A, that is, the utility she gets when holding no reserves. Clearly, $\overline{U}$ is a lower bound on entrepreneurial utility. Consider the following program:

$$\max_{I,\lambda(\cdot)} R$$

$$\begin{aligned} \text{subject to} \quad &\text{(i)} \quad I\int_0^\infty \lambda(\rho)\,(\rho_1 - \rho_0)f(\rho)d\rho \geq \overline{U}, \\ &\text{(ii)} \quad -R + I\int_0^\infty \lambda(\rho)\,(\rho_0 - \rho)f(\rho)d\rho \geq I - A, \\ &\text{(iii)} \quad 0 \leq \lambda(\rho) \leq 1. \end{aligned} \tag{8.28}$$

Constraint ii reflects the fact that investors must break even. Substituting constraint ii (which obviously holds with equality) into the objective function, we see that program (28) is the dual of program (24). That is, the social optimum has the same characterization whether the government maximizes entrepreneurial welfare subject to a deadweight loss of taxation or maximizes seigniorage.

G. An Interpretation of State-Contingent Bonds

The economic rationale for using state-contingent bonds is simple. Bonds that pay a fixed amount will provide excess liquidity in most states at date 1. Firms (or intermediaries) will cash in the bonds that they do not need for reinvestment, forcing the government to tax consumers and implement a wealth transfer that is unnecessary and socially costly (in the interpretation of the deadweight loss of taxation). While partial liquidation reduces the tax burden, it still leaves slack and also distorts investment and liquidation decisions. The solution that attacks the root cause of the problem is a state-contingent bond, which dispenses liquidity exactly as needed and eliminates all wasteful wealth transfers.

Of course, this solution works ideally only in our idealized model. In reality, state-contingent bonds are not used. The most obvious reason why such bonds are not used is that there is no aggregate, measurable state that unequivocally identifies times when firms should be provided more liquidity. Rather than the use of bonds that are contingent on a few foreseeable and verifiable variables, a discretionary policy may be more effective (when commitment and credibility problems associated with such a policy are ignored). Thus we view the use of state-contingent bonds as a metaphor for an active government policy rather than as a serious policy instrument in its own right.[26] Their value shows that, besides *creating* liquidity, the government has a potential role in actively *managing* liquidity. This is true even if private contracts could be indexed on government actions or on the aggregate shock. However, it is important to recognize that our model does not rationalize continuous intervention and fine tuning in the bond market. Quite the opposite. In our model, *optimal liquidity management entails increasing the value of government bonds only in times when liquidity needs are high.*

Since we have assumed that bonds mature at date 1, redemption of bonds is accompanied by a corresponding immediate increase in taxes. It may seem odd that taxes are being raised in adverse liquidity states (recessions), as consumers could simultaneously be experiencing negative demand shocks. But this just underscores the importance of considering multiple shocks, as mentioned above. Our specific result is clearly sensitive to the assumption that

[26] Pagano (1988) and Gale (1990) offer the same interpretation in their analysis of state-contingent bonds.

there is a single liquidity shock with consumers experiencing no shocks at all. If consumers experience an adverse demand shock that requires resources to be shifted to consumption, then taxation might need to be shifted to date 2 or reduced overall rather than increased. This does not negate the general logic that an active policy can improve the allocation of resources through wealth transfers between consumers and producers.

We cannot associate state-contingent bonds with monetary policy, since our model does not distinguish between nominal and real claims. But certain analogies can be drawn between the effects of state-contingent bonds in the model and the alleged effects of monetary policy in reality. One aspect of monetary policy suggested by our analysis is that the government should attempt to inflate the value of the corporate sector's liquid claims in recessions.[27] In particular, in a more realistic model in which there is still a demand for liquid assets at date 1, the government can control the date 1 price of long-term bonds issued at date 0 by early redemptions (purchases) of these bonds or by issuing new bonds. For instance, purchases raise the price of existing bonds (lower the rate of interest) at date 1 and help the corporate sector to withstand the liquidity shock at date 1. Such state-contingent debt management is akin to our state-contingent bonds.

Of course, one should endogenize the date 1 demand for bonds. So, imagine a second generation of entrepreneurs entering at date 1, facing liquidity shocks at date 2, and producing at date 3. Then tighter liquidity (lower bond prices) at date 1 would *decrease* date 1 investments and increase date 2 reinvestments (proposition 3), since the cost of carrying liquidity into date 2 would become relatively less expensive. In other words, tighter liquidity at date 1 reduces both reinvestments (of date 0 entrepreneurs) and initial investments (of date 1 entrepreneurs), moving aggregate investment unambiguously down at date 1. Again, this conforms with standard views on policy effects.

V. Relationship to the Literature

Several papers have relevance for our work, although they do not address in a unified way the main questions we are interested in, namely corporate liquidity needs, the partial self-sufficiency of the private sector, and the foundations for liquidity supply and management by the government. Let us take up these themes in order.

A. Corporate Liquidity Demand

By now, there is a very large literature on credit rationing, making the point that investment will be constrained by the firm's net worth. Much of this literature is focused on the implications of credit rationing on aggregate investment, consumption, and other macroeconomic phenomena (for a survey, see Bernanke, Gertler, and Gilchrist [1994]). These models rarely address the demand for liquidity because they work out of a single-period agency framework. The demand for liquidity is inherently tied to the need for long-term financing. Recently, there has been a surge of multiperiod agency models in corporate

[27] For instance, consider the recent collapse of the Eastern Bloc. In several European countries no attempt was initially made to accommodate this shock (or, if one wants to interpret the central banks' stubborn stance on exchange rates as an active policy, money was made very tight). The result was a big reduction in entrepreneurial wealth as interest rates soared and asset values plunged. Our analysis supports those who argued that governments should have responded to the shock with looser money that would have transferred some wealth back to the entrepreneurs.

finance in which long-term contracts are essential for implementing second-best investment plans (see, e.g., Hart and Moore 1989; Diamond 1991; Berglof and von Thadden 1994). Any one of these models could have been used as the basic building block for our analysis. The virtue of our model is that it is very simple and lends itself readily to a characterization of the second-best solution. For this reason, it has some independent interest. Also, the result that the implementation of the optimal contract limits the firm to maintain a minimum liquidity ratio and a maximum leverage is, to the best of our knowledge, new.[28]

That real assets serve a dual purpose, as productive inputs as well as collateral for debt, has been exploited in recent papers by Shleifer and Vishny (1992) and Kiyotaki and Moore (1997). Both models are concerned with the general equilibrium implications of wealth-constrained financing. Shleifer and Vishny's model, in particular, shares some features with our model. It has two firms, each facing an idiosyncratic demand shock. If the demand shocks are not perfectly correlated (so that firms are not in default simultaneously), the firms can offer each other partial insurance, not directly through security purchases, as we have it, but rather by offering a viable resale market for liquidated assets. In effect, the model describes a market mediated (albeit imperfect) way of enhancing firm liquidity.

B. Private Liquidity Supply and Intermediation

The study of the demand for consumer liquidity was originated by Bryant (1980) and Diamond and Dybvig (1983); see also Ramakrishnan and Thakor (1984), Williamson (1986), and von Thadden (1994). Diamond and Dybvig demonstrate that intermediaries can provide limited insurance by subsidizing consumers that are experiencing high liquidity needs. Jacklin (1987), however, shows that the associated cross-subsidy is infeasible in the presence of financial markets, since those consumers with low liquidity needs can pretend to have high liquidity needs, pocket the subsidy, and reinvest it in financial markets.[29] Thus financial markets in the Diamond-Dybvig framework are detrimental to welfare since they undermine the insurance role of intermediation. In our model, intermediaries bring strict improvements despite the existence of financial markets; indeed, the ability to issue and sell securities in the date 1 market is essential for implementing the second-best outcome. One reason for the difference in conclusions is that our firms cannot abuse credit lines. Entrepreneurs cannot divert corporate funds for their own use other than in the limited fashion captured by the opportunity cost B (the alternative project).

The prescription in Section IV on how the government should manage liquidity is also quite different from that in Diamond and Dybvig. In their model, government policy can be made contingent on the macroeconomic shock (the number of withdrawing depositors), whereas bank contracts with depositors cannot be made contingent on this macroeconomic shock.[30]In our model, government policies do not use more aggregate information than private contracts.

[28]Our model is also related to a smaller literature that focuses specifically on loan commitments and how they can be kept in light of the temptation to renege on promises to finance projects with a negative ex post value (see, e.g., Boot, Thakor, and Udell 1991). The suggested solutions to these commitment problems are much more elaborate than what we offer.

[29]Diamond (1997) shows that intermediaries have a role to play as long as some consumers have imperfect access to financial markets.

[30]The subsequent literature on bank runs for the most part assumes independent shocks, as we do in Sec. III. Hellwig (1994) introduces macroeconomic uncertainty through a date 1 shock on the short-term interest rate between date 1 and date 2 and shows that depositors who withdraw at date 1 must bear some of the aggregate risk.

Boyd and Prescott (1986), in a related effort to understand the role of intermediation, construct a model in which financial markets cannot duplicate the services provided by intermediaries. Their model is not about the provision of liquidity as such but rather about the efficient organization of monitoring. Financial markets are inefficient relative to intermediation because financial contracts are assumed to be contingent on whether projects are evaluated and also on the outcome of the evaluation. Intermediaries, on the other hand, can offer contracts before an evaluation is made, avoiding the problem of premature information revelation. This seems to be an ad hoc limitation in favor of intermediation.

Bhattacharya and Gale (1987) look at a variation of the Diamond-Dybvig model that is closer in structure to ours. In their model there are several banks (corresponding to our firms), which experience idiosyncratic, sectoral liquidity shocks that cancel out in the aggregate. The paper characterizes the socially optimal mechanism for sharing risks across banks, noting that this mechanism cannot be implemented through an interbank lending market. Whether a market in bank shares or some other institution could implement the social optimum is left open. The authors suggest that a central bank might be the right institution for carrying out interbank risk sharing.

C. Government-Supplied Liquidity

The first paper to argue that government debt can improve the intertemporal allocation of investment is Diamond (1965). In an overlapping generations model, he showed that government debt can improve welfare by crowding out real investments that in the absence of government debt may be excessive. In our model, public debt facilitates private investment. Another difference is that in Diamond's model, government bonds provide no liquidity services and are sold at par. Models of intergenerational insurance (Fischer 1983; Pagano 1988; Gale 1990) and of asynchronized investment opportunities (Woodford 1990) are expressly concerned with the role of government debt as a medium of transfer across periods. Woodford's paper is perhaps closest to ours. In one version of his model, individuals periodically receive investment opportunities, which they cannot take advantage of without storing wealth from one period to the next. Government debt is a vehicle for storing wealth. He shows that in a stationary state, the optimal level of government debt should be positive. He interprets government debt as a liquidity-enhancing instrument the way we do and shows that bonds will sell at a premium. However, he does not consider the possibility that a private market in claims on output could accomplish the same as government debt, something it may well do, since there are no agency costs to limit how much can be pledged to outsiders.

Gale (1990) studies the efficient design of public debt, using various overlapping generations models in which asset markets are incomplete. In his models, the purpose of government debt is to improve intergenerational risk sharing. He shows that noncontingent debt can enhance welfare if the asset market is sufficiently sparse and that debt of longer maturity can be particularly valuable when productivity shocks are serially correlated, since then bond prices will vary negatively with asset returns. Gale also considers contingent debt, concluding that this instrument, while valuable as a mechanism for transferring wealth between generations, cannot in general implement the optimal state-contingent transfer policy. These results resemble ours, but it is difficult to draw exact parallels since the style of modeling is quite different. A key distinction is that Gale, following the tradition of a large literature on incomplete markets, simply takes the imperfect market structure as exogenously given (something he fully recognizes and discusses at length).[31] In principle, the government or even a private, long-lived institution could complete the market and get to the first-best. In our model the informational constraints that limit first-best are explicitly spelled out.

Finally, there are some points of contact with the literature on money. The most closely connected may be the paper by Williamson (1992), who demonstrates the benefits of fiat money in a model in which adverse selection prevents entrepreneurs from pledging their entire future income.[32] Fiat money plays the role of a store of value (which is the counterpart of government securities in our model and may have value because Williamson's model is one of overlapping generations). Williamson's focus is distinct from ours: he argues in favor of government securities (in the form of fiat money) and against the trading of private claims. Indeed, Williamson concludes that fiat money has no value if private claims are traded and that there exists an equilibrium with fiat money that Pareto-dominates the purely private equilibrium as long as agents are prevented from trading private claims.

VI. Concluding Remarks

We view our model as a preliminary investigation into the logical link between wealth-constrained financing and the liquidity services offered by financial markets. A large literature has emphasized the importance of an individual firm's or an entrepreneur's net worth for the ability to invest and grow, but little attention has been paid to the fact that, to the extent that net worth constrains capital formation, it will also reduce market liquidity and restrict the financing options for all market participants. Highlighting the close connection between liquidity and capital formation has been one of the main objectives of this paper.

How significant this connection is depends, as we have emphasized, on how correlated the firms' liquidity needs are. If the shocks are independent, wealth constraints do not limit aggregate liquidity; if the shocks are identical, the market offers no additional liquidity support. While we have not analyzed the case extensively, it is evident that a shortage of liquidity will lead firms to invest in technologies that place lesser demands on long-term financing. Firms will move in the direction of self-supplied liquidity by investing in self-financing projects. A proper welfare analysis of the government's role in managing liquidity would have to assess the costs of distorted investments in the private sector with the costs associated with distortionary consumer taxes. Liquidity premia on government debt should provide the right starting point for such calculations.

In our model, the only source of private liquidity is the very projects that seek financing and demand liquidity. One may wonder how the analysis would change if we were to introduce real estate or other real assets, which could be used to transfer wealth from one period to the next.[33] Our initial investigations suggest the following conclusions. If there are enough real assets and the values of these assets are constant, then liquidity problems

[31] Elul (1995) has recently shown that generically one can add an asset to such a market structure and make everyone better off.

[32] On the adverse selection problem and related issues, see also Banerjee and Maskin (1996) and the references in Williamson (1992). For other models on money and government debt, see, e.g., Bewley (1980) and Levine (1991).

[33] A reduction in the net funding needs of a firm at date 1 corresponds to adding real assets to the model. Note that the value of an additional unit of funds at date 1 is higher than the value of a unit of funds at date 0, if there is a liquidity premium.

would disappear and with them the need to issue government bonds. But there is reason to believe that neither assumption holds. First, the empirical evidence suggests that there are liquidity premia. Such premia can emerge only when there is a shortage of liquid instruments. Second, if real estate and other similar assets are held for liquidity purposes, then their prices are likely to be negatively correlated with liquidity shocks, because the assets will be sold off when firms need liquidity and bought when firms want to store liquidity. The negative correlation will make the assets less desirable as sources of liquidity (see Holmström and Tirole 1997*b*). A potential role for government-supplied liquidity will remain, and part of that role may entail maintaining stable asset prices.

A related question concerns the realism of the investment/capital ratio. Our model implies that government intervention is needed only when the aggregate demand for liquidity exceeds the value of the private sector. This seems grossly at odds with the empirical fact that the market value of the corporate sector is large relative to investment. Part of the explanation has to do with the interpretation of investment. In our model, reinvestments include all the cash outlays (wages and working capital, for instance) needed to continue the firm, not just investments in physical capital. This figure is surely an order of magnitude larger than measured aggregate investment.

Nevertheless, it remains true that the private sector can continue on its own as long as $\rho \leq \rho_0$, that is, as long as the value of the initial claim holders' investment has not been driven down to zero. Only when their investment has lost all its value need the government step in. This is an unrealistic feature of the model. It is driven by the equally unrealistic feature that external claims are fully liquid. To the extent that new issues of equity and debt are costly, because of difficulties in valuing these claims correctly, the private sector will run into reinvestment problems before the initial claim holders have lost all their investment. Similarly, the holdings of monitors (large shareholder, bank, venture capitalist, etc.) cannot be diluted without generating further incentive problems.[34] Thus we think of ρ_0 as the point at which the private sector hits a serious debt capacity constraint, a point that is likely to be encountered well before the initial investors have been cleaned out.

Finally, let us suggest some extensions of our model. The presence of liquidity constraints suggests that this type of analysis can be used to develop a model of asset pricing based on liquidity premia. In Holmström and Tirole (1997*b*), we describe a simple version of such a liquidity-based asset pricing model. There are several reasons for our interest in this model. One is that the demand for assets is not uniform across agents; rather, different groups demand different types of assets. Such heterogeneity has implications for the empirical evaluation and estimation of Euler equations and may help to explain such phenomena as the equity premium puzzle. A second potential application is the term structure of interest rates. It is often suggested that the term structure is driven in part by the "preferred habitats" of institutional investors. Such preferences are hard to explain without reference to liquidity constraints that vary depending on the nature of investments in the corporate sector.

Currently, the link between the producer and the consumer sector is very stark and uninteresting. In reality, consumer and producer shocks affect the overall economy and feed back on each other. A general equilibrium extension provides a more realistic picture of the need for transferring wealth in one direction or the other and therefore on how the government should manage liquidity. In this context, one would also want to be more careful about the deadweight losses caused by taxation and the role played by individual time preferences and risk aversion. A related extension would introduce more periods into

[34]It is straightforward to add monitors into our model, along the lines of Holmström and Tirole (1997a).

our model. The government could then issue long-term as well as short-term bonds, which would allow one to address questions about the optimal maturity structure of government debt.

While intermediaries play a role in our model, it is a passive one. Intermediaries are merely conduits for forming contracts that are unavailable in the financial market. This is an artifact of assuming that firms have no use for extra credit and therefore never abuse their credit lines. In reality, intermediaries play a more active role, monitoring investments and liquidity needs. A more advanced model of liquidity would recognize the importance of intermediaries in generating information and in creating local pools of liquidity. How these pools should be linked to each other and what effect this information hierarchy has on the management of liquidity are among the most interesting research questions that lie ahead.

References

Banerjee, Abhijit V., and Maskin, Eric S. "A Walrasian Theory of Money and Barter." *Q.J.E.* 111 (November 1996): 955–1005.

Berglof, Erik, and von Thadden, Ernst-Ludwig. "Short-Term versus Long-Term Interests: Capital Structure with Multiple Investors." *Q.J.E.* 109 (November 1994): 1055–84.

Bernanke, Ben; Gertler, Mark; and Gilchrist, Simon. "The Financial Accelerator and the Flight to Quality." Working Paper no. 4789. Cambridge, Mass.: NBER, July 1994.

Bewley, Truman. "The Optimum Quantity of Money." In *Models of Monetary Economies*, edited by John H. Kareken and Neil Wallace. Minneapolis: Fed. Reserve Bank, 1980.

Bhattacharya, Sudipto, and Gale, Douglas. "Preference Shocks, Liquidity, and Central Bank Policy." In *New Approaches to Monetary Economics*, edited by William A. Barnett and Kenneth J. Singleton. Cambridge: Cambridge Univ. Press, 1987.

Boot, Arnoud W. A.; Thakor, Anjan V.; and Udell, Gregory F. "Credible Commitments, Contract Enforcement Problems and Banks: Intermediation as Credibility Assurance." *J. Banking and Finance* 15 (June 1991): 605–32.

Boyd, John H., and Prescott, Edward C. "Financial Intermediary-Coalitions." *J. Econ. Theory* 38 (April 1986): 211–32.

Bryant, John. "A Model of Reserves, Bank Runs, and Deposit Insurance." *J. Banking and Finance* 4 (December 1980): 335–44.

Diamond, Douglas W. "Debt Maturity Structure and Liquidity Risk." *Q.J.E.* 106 (August 1991): 709–37.

——. "Liquidity, Banks, and Markets." *J.P.E.* 105 (October 1997): 928–56.

Diamond, Douglas W., and Dybvig, Philip H. "Bank Runs, Deposit Insurance, and Liquidity." *J.P.E.* 91 (June 1983): 401–19.

Diamond, Peter A. "National Debt in a Neoclassical Growth Model." *A.E.R.* 55 (December 1965): 1126–50.

Elul, Ronel. "Welfare Effects of Financial Innovation in Incomplete Markets Economies with Several Consumption Goods." *J. Econ. Theory* 65 (February 1995): 43–78.

Fischer, Stanley. "Welfare Aspects of Government Issue of Indexed Bonds." In *Inflation, Debt, and Indexation*, edited by Rudiger Dornbusch and Mario H. Simonsen. Cambridge, Mass.: MIT Press, 1983.

Gale, Douglas. "The Efficient Design of Public Debt." In *Public Debt Management: Theory and History*, edited by Rudiger Dornbusch and Mario Draghi. Cambridge: Cambridge Univ. Press, 1990.

Gorton, Gary, and Pennacchi, George. "Financial Intermediaries and Liquidity Creation." *J. Finance.* 45 (March 1990): 49–71.

Hart, Oliver D., and Moore, John. "Default and Renegotiation: A Dynamic Model of Debt." Working Paper no. 89-069. Boston: Harvard Bus. School, 1989.

Hellwig, Martin. "Liquidity Provision, Banking, and the Allocation of Interest Rate Risk." *European Econ. Rev.* 38 (August 1994): 1363–89.

Holmström, Bengt, and Tirole, Jean. "Financial Intermediation, Loanable Funds, and the Real Sector." *Q.J.E.* 112 (August 1997): 663–92. (*a*)

——. "LAPM: A Liquidity-Based Asset Pricing Model." Manuscript. Cambridge: Massachusetts Inst. Tech., March 1997. (*b*)

Jacklin, Charles J. "Demand Deposits, Trading Restrictions, and Risk Sharing." In *Contractual Arrangements for Intertemporal Trade*, edited by Edward C. Prescott and Neil Wallace. Minneapolis: Univ. Minnesota Press, 1987.

Kiyotaki, Nobuhiro, and Moore, John. "Credit Cycles." *J.P.E.* 105 (April 1997): 211–48.

Levine, David K. "Asset Trading Mechanisms and Expansionary Policy." *J. Econ. Theory* 54 (June 1991): 148–64.

Pagano, Marco. "The Management of Public Debt and Financial Markets." In *High Public Debt: The Italian Experience*, edited by Francesco Giavazzi and Luigi Spaventa. Cambridge: Cambridge Univ. Press, 1988.

Ramakrishnan, Ram T. S., and Thakor, Anjan V. "Information Reliability and a Theory of Financial Intermediation." *Rev. Econ. Studies* 51 (July 1984): 415–32.

Shleifer, Andrei, and Vishny, Robert W. "Liquidation Values and Debt Capacity: A Market Equilibrium Approach." *J. Finance* 47 (September 1992): 1343–66.

von Thadden, Ernst-Ludwig. "Optimal Liquidity Provision and Dynamic Incentive Compatibility." Manuscript. Basel: Univ. Basel, 1994.

Williamson, Stephen D. "Costly Monitoring, Financial Intermediation, and Equilibrium Credit Rationing." *J. Monetary Econ.* 18 (September 1986): 159–79.

——. "Laissez-Faire Banking and Circulating Media of Exchange." *J. Financial Intermediation* 2 (June 1992): 134–67.

Woodford, Michael. "Public Debt as Private Liquidity." *A.E.R. Papers and Proc.* 80 (May 1990): 382–88.

9 Liquidity, Efficiency, and Bank Bailouts

Gary Gorton and Lixin Huang

In the early 1980's high interest rates caused many U.S. savings and loan institutions to become economically distressed. At the height of the crisis, the period 1988–1992, an average of one bank or S&L was closed every day (Mary L. Bean et al., 1998).[1] But, what was to become the thrift crisis in the late 1980's has, in large part, been attributed to the fact that insolvent institutions were allowed to remain open, mostly due to the depleted resources of the Federal Savings and Loan Insurance Corporation. Insolvent thrifts were not promptly closed and their assets sold to new investors. The policy of allowing insolvent institutions to remain open was labeled a policy of "forbearance" and Edward J. Kane deemed the insolvent thrifts "zombies."[2] Eventually, the Resolution Trust Corporation was established to liquidate the assets of insolvent thrifts.[3] The bailout of the thrift industry ultimately cost $180 billion (3.2 percent of GDP); see Gerard Caprio and Daniela Klingebiel (1996).[4]

Prolonged and expensive government bailouts of financial intermediaries following banking crises have recently proliferated around the world, and it is not only transitional

[1]During the period 1980–1994, 1,617 banks with $302.6 billion in assets were closed or received assistance from the Federal Deposit Insurance Corporation. During the same period, 1,295 savings and loans, with $621 billion in assets, were closed by the Federal Savings and Loan Insurance Corporation (FSLIC) or the Resolution Trust Corporation, or received assistance from FSLIC; see Bean et al. (1998). On the thrift crisis generally, see R. Dan Brumbaugh, Jr. (1988), Edward Kane (1989), James Barth (1991), and Lawrence White (1991).

[2]The term "zombie thrifts" became widely used and is now applied to similar banking situations. In a private communication, Ed Kane recalls having first used this term in a speech to the American Bar Association in 1986. It first appeared in published work in Kane (1987), a paper that was presented at the Western Economics Association in 1986.

[3]The 1989 Financial Institutions Recovery, Reform and Enforcement Act (FIRREA) substantially changed the regulatory structure of the thrift industry. The Resolution Trust Corporation (RTC) was part of the 1989 law. The RTC was the government vehicle for selling the assets of closed thrifts.

[4]According to Barth and Bartholomew (1992), as of 1992: "More than 500 institutions were closed at an estimated present-value cost in excess of $50 billion. Still another 500 or more institutions were open but insolvent at the end of the decade. These remaining candidates for closure will cost an estimated $100 billion or more . . . " (p. 37). Other estimates are considerably higher. For example, the *Wall Street Journal*, April 6, 1990, cites a Congressional Budget Office and General Accounting Office projection of a cost of $300 to $350 billion. See Kane and Min-Teh Yu (1996) for market value estimates.

and emerging economies that have had such experiences.[5] As in the U.S. thrift crisis, the resolution of these crises typically involves the use of public money to subsidize the restructuring or disposal of impaired loans, a "bailout." In a survey of 120 banks in 24 developed countries in the 1980's and 1990's, Charles A. E. Goodhart (1995) found that two out of three failed banks were bailed out. These bailouts are expensive. In a sample of 40 such episodes, Patrick Honohan and Klingebiel (2000) found that, on average, countries spend 12.8 percent of their GDP cleaning up their banking systems. Stijn Claessens et al. (1999) set the costs at 15–50 percent of GNP. To emphasize, even developed economies other than the United States have faced large costs of bank bailouts. For example, Spain is estimated to have spent 16.8 percent of GNP on bailouts; Sweden, 6.4 percent of GDP; Finland, 8 percent of GDP. See Caprio and Klingebiel (1996).

In bank bailouts the government directly aids banks by buying equity, extending long-term loan guarantees to the banks, or buying bank loans at favorable prices. [Usually, nonperforming loans are purchased by the government at face value (see Daniel, 1997).] Sometimes government bonds are exchanged for bad bank loans. Often a public centralized asset management company is set up that uses government funds to lend to troubled banks against specific loan collateral or that buys the loans from the banks (e.g., see John Hawkins and Philip Turner, 1999; David Woo, 2000). For example, in the Asian crisis, government-owned asset management companies in Indonesia, Malaysia, Korea, and Thailand had, by April 1999, taken over bank assets with face values equivalent to 20, 17, 10, and 17.5 percent of the GDP of these respective countries (Lindgren et al., 1999).[6] An early, and influential, example of such a vehicle was the Reconstruction Finance Corporation (RFC) that President Herbert Hoover initiated during the onset of the Great Depression in the United States (see James Stuart Olson, 1977; Joseph Mason, 2001). The RFC is the (implicit or explicit) model for a large number of such vehicles in countries around the world, including the Resolution Trust Corporation, founded to use federal money to buy and then sell assets of insolvent U.S. savings and loans institutions (see Walker Todd, 1992). As we discuss later, government bank restructuring agencies are now commonplace.[7]

Why do government bailouts occur? Why does the government engage in forbearance, rather than simply closing insolvent banks and selling their assets to private investors immediately?[8] Are government bailouts efficient? The basic idea developed in

[5] Caprio and Klingebiel (1999) count 112 episodes of systemic banking crises in 93 countries since the late 1970's. Since 1980, at least two-thirds of International Monetary Fund member countries have experienced problems with their banking systems (see James A. Daniel, 1997). Also, see Carl-Johan Lindgren et al. (1999).

[6] Hawkins and Turner (1999) list 15 countries that have recently restructured their banking systems and corporate sector with asset management companies; see their Table 12.

[7] It is not only financial institutions that are bailed out. Nonfinancial firms are also sometimes bailed out directly. Nonfinancial firm bailout examples include firms that had outstanding commercial paper during the Penn Central crisis (see Charles Calomiris, 1994), the Chrysler Corporation (see Lee Iacocca and William Novak, 1986), and the airlines industry following the terrorist attacks of September 11, 2001. In these cases, the government provided loan guarantees to a syndicate of banks and, in the case of Penn Central crises, provided liquidity through the Federal Reserve's discount window lending. A related example is the case of the hedge fund Long Term Capital Management (LTCM), where the lenders in effect purchased the assets at the government's instigation (see Lowenstein, 2000). But, in most countries corporate restructuring is intimately related with bank restructuring because of the prevalence of bank loans; most of the nonperforming loans of a banking system are the obligations of nonfinancial firms that are no longer able to meet their debt payments (see Hawkins and Turner, 1999, and Mark Stone, 2002).

[8] We do not address the issue of why banking systems come to be distressed. See Gorton and Andrew Winton (2003) for a survey of the literature on banking crises and banking panics.

this paper is that it is costly for private agents to be prepared to purchase substantial amounts of assets on short notice, such as the assets of the banking system (or a large part of the banking system), because liquidity is socially costly. Simply put, the sheer volume of the assets that need to be sold can be too large for private agents to absorb quickly. The resources of private agents are "illiquid." In order to make this point, we first must address the issue of "liquidity." What is "liquidity" and where does it come from? And, how does "liquidity" relate to "market efficiency"? The first part of the paper addresses these questions. The second part of the paper demonstrates how these answers are useful in understanding government bailouts. We show how the government can create liquidity and improve welfare. We go on to address the issue of whether the government has the resources to bail out the banking system. Perhaps a policy of "forbearance" is optimal. We provide conditions under which this is the case.

We start with a general setting in which agents who have invested in securities or projects sometimes need to sell them later. The price the projects fetch at that time depends upon the "liquidity" of the market. We present a general-equilibrium model in which not all assets can be used to purchase all other assets at every date. "Liquid" assets are the only readily available funds that can be used to purchase projects/securities from other agents. "Liquidity" then refers to the extent to which liquidity supply can meet liquidity demand. If insufficient liquid funds are available, then claims on projects cannot be subsequently transferred, because potential new owners have no way to buy them. Projects that cannot be transferred may decline in value. Recognizing that there may be opportunities at future dates to buy, some agents initially choose to invest in "liquid" assets. So, liquidity provision can be socially efficient.

There are two requirements for a model of liquidity. First, there must be a need to trade: at some dates there must be agents seeking to sell assets and there must be other agents who are willing to buy. Second, there is a restriction needed, namely, not all assets can be used to purchase all other assets at every date. Buyers must be restricted to making purchases only with certain assets, "liquid" assets. This restriction is akin to a cash-in-advance constraint. The constraint arises from the fact that other assets are not liquid; they cannot be used to trade at some dates. In the model here agents make investment choices at the initial date, choosing a long-term investment project or choosing a short-term investment project. The only purpose of selecting a short-term project is to get "liquid" assets to possibly buy a troubled long-term project at a later date. Long-term projects are financed by borrowing from lenders. Subsequently, long-term project borrowers learn whether their projects are high value or low value. Owners of low-value projects are "distressed" and may engage in moral hazard. But low-value projects may be recapitalized by being sold in the "liquidation" market to agents with available liquid capital. The only buyers available are agents who initially chose short-term projects for exactly this purpose ("vulture" investors).

It is costly for a society to always have liquid funds stand by in large amounts, as alternative investments (long-term projects) are (socially) more attractive, but "illiquid." The private provision of liquidity can be avoided, if, instead of projects being sold in the liquidation market, the original lenders are willing to forgive debt of borrowers with low-value projects. Such forgiveness dominates the private provision of liquidity since it does not involve inefficient "hoarding," i.e., investing in the short-term project to get liquid funds. But, forgiveness is not always in the interests of lenders. If forgiveness is not in their interests, then privately supplied liquidity is the only way to recapitalize projects. Since this is socially costly, perhaps the government can improve welfare by supplying liquidity. We show what it means for the government to supply liquidity.

Owners of long-term projects that had a high value realization are privately illiquid because they cannot monetize their gains, i.e., their assets are illiquid. But, the government can monetize their gains by issuing securities backed by tax revenue collected from these agents later. The government securities are used to subsidize owners of low-value projects, while owners of high-value projects are taxed later. Low-value projects are recapitalized by the subsidies.

We then extend the analysis to consider possible systematic risk in the banking system and to investigate the phenomena of bank bailouts. As above, investment in projects at the initial date is financed through borrowing. Subsequently, long-term project owners learn the value of their projects and may desire to sell their projects in the liquidation market in order to obtain the recapitalization. But, the lending banks may also want to engage in moral hazard for the same reasons that their borrowers might engage in moral hazard. If banks suffer a negative shock to their capital (from other asset-side activities), then they may acquiesce in allowing their borrowers to engage in moral hazard rather than seeking to recapitalize them. In this case, banks are not interested in liquidating their borrowers' projects. Anticipating that this may occur affects the initial choice of investments, in particular the supply of liquidity, and can reduce social welfare. We provide conditions under which the government can improve welfare by bailing out banks.

There are many different notions of "liquidity" and "illiquidity" in the literature.[9] In the finance literature, liquidity is not explicitly modeled. Rather there are "noise traders" or "liquidity traders," modeled as exogenous random amounts of buy and sell orders. The other side of the market is the "market maker" who has an inventory that potentially can be long or short an infinite amount (see Albert S. Kyle, 1985). Because the market maker's inventory is infinite, the price set is equal to expected value of the payoff (conditional on available information). That is, the supply curve of liquidity is infinitely elastic so the price is not influenced by the size of the market maker's inventory. The model here obviously differs in important respects. Because the model is one of general equilibrium, the supply of liquidity will be determined endogenously and will not be infinitely elastic. Because we explicitly model liquidity provision we can conduct welfare analysis.

Often, "liquidation" of projects is modeled in partial equilibrium as an exogenous value, interpreted as the value of the project in its next best alternative use. In reality, the next best alternative use is the value of the project to another agent, so the "liquidation value" of a project depends on the price that the project fetches in the market when it is sold to the other agent. And that price, in turn, depends on the supply of liquidity, that is, on the aggregate resources of those agents who can feasibly bid at that date. Andrei Shleifer and Robert Vishny (1992) observe that when a distressed firm needs to sell assets, the natural buyers are other firms in the same industry. The other firms may also be distressed, leading to the conclusion that the price of the assets being liquidated is partly a function of the available supply of liquidity, not just information about payoffs. We formalize this by showing how it can occur that liquidity is not in perfectly elastic supply; in that case,

[9]Douglas W. Diamond and Philip H. Dybvig (1983) view consumption smoothing as liquidity. Hugo A. Hopenhayn and Ingrid M. Werner (1996) develop a notion of liquidity based on search. In Gorton and George Pennacchi (1990) liquid assets are assets that minimize trading losses to uninformed traders when they trade in markets with privately informed traders. "Liquid assets" are not sensitive to private information because they are relatively riskless, like bank deposits. Andrea Eisfeldt (2002) presents a general-equilibrium model of liquidity based on adverse selection. Agents are motivated to trade by changes in productivity and this interacts with desires to self-insure.

a project's "fundamental value" may be different from the price it trades for in the market, a price that depends upon the amount of liquidity available, or the market "depth." Thus, the notion of "market efficiency," i.e., the idea that prices are conditional expectations of project payoffs, requires perfectly liquid markets. Otherwise, markets are not price efficient, but there is no arbitrage possible because of the lack of liquid assets to conduct such a trade. We provide a model of this.

Intimately related to any notion of "liquidity" is an assumption of a shock that is the motivation for immediate selling or borrowing. Our focus on the transferability of distressed projects, or more specifically on the transferability of control rights to such projects, is quite different from the notion of liquidity in Bengt Holmström and Jean Tirole (1998) and Diamond and Raghuram G. Rajan (2001, 2002). In those papers, a "liquidity shock" is an event that causes firms to need to borrow extra funds from other firms or from consumers. This idea has its origin in Diamond and Dybvig (1983), although in that instance the shock was to consumers' consumption timing rather than to firms' investment opportunities. In our paper there is no investment boom-type shock (where firms suddenly need resources), but there is a shock to the value of assets in the hands of an entrepreneur for a given level of liabilities—a "capitalization shock." Then there is a potential need to sell the control rights to the project. Anticipating that this market may be open at the interim date, entrepreneurs choose at the first date whether to be either buyers or sellers in the secondary market. Thus, we endogenize the supply of liquidity.

The choice of shock, Diamond-Dybvig-type "liquidity shocks" versus "capitalization shocks" is important for policy results. For example, Diamond and Rajan (2001, 2002) also discuss recapitalization by the government, observing that it may be counterproductive because it increases the demand for liquidity without increasing the supply of liquidity. As a result, the interest rate rises and banks may be forced into insolvency. Such distortionary government intervention should not occur in equilibrium. Our model is very different, partly because the shock is different. Unlike Diamond and Rajan, no firm is forced to liquidate; firms may choose to liquidate. Government intervention in our model is not distortionary because the price in the liquidation market adjusts so that good projects will never be liquidated. In addition, in their model government intervention only affects the market for liquidity, but not the investment choice. In our model, in contrast, government intervention corrects investment inefficiency through its impact on the liquidation price. While ultimately an empirical matter, our view is that "capitalization shocks" are more important.[10]

Also, the notion of liquidity we develop is intuitive. It refers to the amount of resources standing ready to purchase the claims on projects should there be a desire to sell the projects at some date between initiation and final payoff. The motivation for projects to be sold is financial distress. As in Sanford J. Grossman (1988), some agents must commit at the initial date to have certain resources available at an interim date, should opportunities arise. We provide a model of this "liquidity-in-advance" constraint. Our focus enables us to extend the analysis to banking crises and bank bailouts. Since the model is one of general equilibrium, we can conduct welfare analysis.

[10]There are many other papers that make use of Diamond-Dybvig-type shocks, e.g., Sudipto Bhattacharya and Douglas Gale (1987), Diamond (1997), and Franklin Allen and Gale (1998), among others. These papers examine the consequences of an aggregate shortage of liquidity. Not only is our shock different, but also in our model the liquidity problem is generated by incentives to add risk when capital is inefficient. The moral hazard not only generates a demand for liquidity, but also restricts the supply of liquid.

The paper proceeds as follows. In Section I the model is presented and the assumptions discussed. In Section II we show that there is no need for liquidity, in the sense of agents standing ready to buy projects, if lenders are willing to forgive the debt of distressed borrowers. Debt forgiveness is a kind of liquidity provision on the part of the lender, and it can implement the first-best allocation. If debt forgiveness is not optimal for lenders, then there is a need for private agents to provide liquidity. This is studied in Section III. The equilibrium in which liquidity is provided privately is analyzed. This allocation is not first best, but the government via bailouts may be able to improve welfare and achieve first best. A system of taxing and subsidizing amounts to liquidity creation, and we provide a condition under which first best can be achieved. It is studied in Section IV. Section V considers the extended case where bank lenders themselves may seek to engage in moral hazard, by acquiescing in allowing their distressed borrowers to engage in moral hazard. This results in an even less efficient outcome. However, under certain conditions, a government bailout can achieve first best. Section VI concludes.

I. The Model

In this section we present the model and discuss the important assumptions.

There is a continuum of depositors, a continuum of entrepreneurs, and a continuum of banks in the economy. There are three dates: 0, 1, and 2. At date 0 entrepreneurs must choose one of two possible investment projects, either a long-term project or a short-term project. The long-term project requires an investment of \$1 at date 0. The short-term project only needs the entrepreneurs' human capital. The cash flow of the long-term project is realized at date 2. It can be high (H) with probability π or low (L) with probability $1 - \pi$. Information about the date 2 cash flow arrives at date 1. The cash flow of the short-term project is realized at date 1, which is a random variable equal to r, where r is uniformly distributed on the interval $[0, R]$. For simplicity, there is no available short-term project between dates 1 and 2.

A. Assumptions

We make the following assumptions on cash flows from the projects, operation of the projects, and how the projects can be financed.

Assumption 1: $\pi H + (1 - \pi)L > 1 + R/2$. *That is, the long-term project has a higher expected cash flow than the short-term project.*

Because the long-term project offers superior returns, we refer to investing in the short-term project as "hoarding." As we will see, the only reason any entrepreneur will invest in the short-term project is that it enables him to purchase a long-term project in the low state at date 1.

Assumption 2: *Each entrepreneur can only manage one project at a time. Projects are not divisible.*

Assumption 3: *Neither the date 1 states (H or L), nor the cash flows realized at date 2, are contractible. Therefore, outside equity financing is not feasible.*

Entrepreneurs have no resources at date 0, so they need to borrow from banks. The credit market is competitive at date 0. Therefore, entrepreneurs receive the entire expected surplus and lenders earn zero expected profits. For simplicity, all agents are risk neutral and the risk-less interest rate is zero.

At date 0 investment decisions are taken and entrepreneurs who choose long-term projects borrow from the lenders. Because states and cash flows are not verifiable, we only allow debt contracts. Gorton and James Kahn (2000) rationalize the use of a debt contract in this setting, where there is no interim cash flow from the project, but where there is a moral hazard problem. They show the optimality of bank debt, where the debt can be renegotiated at the interim date. Initial terms are not set to price default risk but rather are set to efficiently balance bargaining power in later renegotiation, and renegotiated interest rates may not be monotonic in firm risk.

At date 1 entrepreneurs operating short-term projects receive the realization of the projects' cash flows. Entrepreneurs operating the long-term project receive no cash flows at date 1, but they learn the realization of the state, H or L. This information is also observable by the lenders, but by Assumption 3 it is not contractible. Other agents, in particular the government, do not observe the realized project states at date 1.

Denote by α the fraction of entrepreneurs that take the long-term project at date 0; the fraction of the entrepreneurs that take the short-term project at date 0 is $1 - \alpha$. After each entrepreneur chooses a project type, those choosing the long-term project sign a debt contract with one of the lenders. The face value of the debt contract, F, will be determined in equilibrium.

There is a potential moral hazard problem because the entrepreneurs may engage in asset substitution at date 1. Each entrepreneur, regardless of which project has been selected at date 0, has access to a constant returns to scale risk-adding technology. By adding risk, one unit of certain value generates either a very large value, T, with probability δ or a value of zero with probability $1 - \delta$.

Assumption 4: $\delta T < 1$. *That is, adding risk to the project is inefficient.* $1 - \delta T$ *is the expected loss per unit from asset substitution.*

Suppose an entrepreneur owes an amount f and he learns that his cash flow at date 2 will be v. If he does not add risk, his payoff is: $\max[v - f, 0]$. If he adds risk, his expected payoff is: $\max[\delta(vT - f), 0]$. Suppose vT is greater than f. The entrepreneur is not going to add risk if and only if $\delta(vT - f) \leq v - f$. That is, the face value of the debt, f, cannot exceed γv, where $\gamma \equiv \frac{1-\delta T}{1-\delta}$.

Assumption 5: $\gamma L < 1$. *Since the debt face value is at least \$1, this assumption says that in the low state, the cash flow to the long-term project is not large enough to prevent entrepreneurs from adding risk. Thus, there is a moral hazard problem at date 1.*

Although entrepreneurs may have incentives to engage in moral hazard at date 1, *ex ante* they want to prevent it because they get the entire expected surplus and bear the entire potential loss caused by risk-adding. There are two possible ways to prevent the moral hazard problem. First, the contract between the lender and an entrepreneur can be renegotiated at date 1 to remove the entrepreneur's incentive to engage in asset substitution. In particular, the lender can forgive some of the debt, by lowering the face value of the (pure discount) debt, and thus increase the entrepreneur's equity to eliminate his incentive to add risk. But this depends on whether the lender is willing to forgive debt. It can happen that the lender finds forgiveness unprofitable and renegotiation breaks down.

Secondly, the project may be "liquidated." "Liquidation" means that the "troubled" project, i.e., the project of an entrepreneur who will otherwise add risk, is sold to a new owner at date 1. It is better to sell the troubled project if the liquidation value is higher than the continuation value of the project with risk being added. On the other hand, selling the project to a new owner means that the assets are redeployed, but does not necessarily mean that the new owner will add no risk. If the new owner has to borrow at date 1 to buy the project, then the lender will have to ensure that the new owner has enough equity in the project so that they do not have an incentive to add risk upon buying the project.

A central question is: Who will buy troubled projects at date 1? Because each entrepreneur can only manage one project at a time, buyers of projects at date 1 can only be entrepreneurs who undertook the short-term project at date 0. We will call them "liquidity suppliers" since it is the availability of their resources at date 1 that can allow project ownership to be transferred. Clearly, the price at which a troubled project can be sold at date 1 will depend on the demand and supply of liquidity and this price will be determined in equilibrium. In addition to the assumptions we have made, we make the following assumptions about the cash flows from the long- and short-term projects to make our model more interesting.

Assumption 6: $(\pi + \delta(1 - \pi))\gamma H \geq 1$. *Due to the possible moral hazard problem, the face value of the debt cannot exceed γH. Otherwise entrepreneurs will add risk even in the high state. This assumption guarantees that the cash flow in the high state is large enough that the bank is willing to lend at date 1, even though entrepreneurs might engage in risk-adding when they are in the low state.*

Assumption 7: $TL > \gamma H$. *That is, if an entrepreneur engaging in moral hazard is lucky, there is a chance that risk-adding can produce a cash flow high enough that his equity value is positive after repaying the face value of the debt.*

Assumption 8: $\delta T > \gamma$. *This assumption is equivalent to $\delta TL > \gamma L$. δTL is the expected date 1 value of a long-term project in the low state when risk has been added. γL is the maximum of the face value that a bank can charge (possibly after forgiveness) such that the entrepreneur has no incentive to add risk. By assuming $\delta TL > \gamma L$, we make it possible that forgiveness is not in the interests of the lenders.*

Assumption 9: $R > L - \gamma TL$. *R is the maximum payoff from the short-term project. This assumption implies that if there is an excess supply of liquidity, the liquidation price can be as large as the "fundamental" value of the asset. This will become clear when we analyze the liquidation market in Section III.*

To summarize, the sequence of events at date 1 is as follows.

(i) An entrepreneur who invested in the short-term project at date 0 receives a cash flow of r at date 1.
(ii) News arrives about whether the date 2 cash flow of each long-term project will be high (H) or low (L).

(iii) Owners of troubled long-term projects renegotiate with their lenders to try to reduce their debt burden.

(iv) Depending on the outcome of the renegotiation, an entrepreneur may "liquidate" his project, i.e., sell it in the market, or he may continue until date 2 (possibly adding risk) to receive the final cash flow. If the project is sold in the liquidation market, then the new owner operates the project (possibly adding risk), and receives the final cash flow at date 2.

(v) If the project is liquidated, then a final payment (that was previously renegotiated) is made (at date 1 or possibly at date 2) to the lender to settle the outstanding loan. The new owner then operates the project.

At date 2, the cash flows of the long-term projects are realized and lenders are repaid.

By Assumption 1, the first-best outcome would be for all the entrepreneurs to invest in the long-term project. But, because of the moral hazard problem, this may not be the outcome of private decisions. Some entrepreneurs may choose to invest in the short-term project, in order to act as liquidity providers at date 1. The date 1 opportunity may be sufficiently valuable to make "hoarding" at date 0 attractive.

B. Discussion of Assumptions

Assumption 2 (projects are indivisible and entrepreneurs can only run one project at a time) means that markets are incomplete. Note that some entrepreneurs who chose the long-term project at date 0 receive good news at date 1 so they have projects worth H. In other words, at date 1 they have a capital gain relative to the expected value of the project as of date 0. If their equity is high enough, they could issue subordinated debt to buy another troubled project. But, since projects are indivisible, their equity value has to be high enough to buy an entire firm. Whether this can happen or not depends on parameter values. For simplicity, we just assume that their limited human capital only allows them to manage one project at a time.[11] Alternatively, the long-term projects of different borrowers can be interpreted to be different (say, different industries), and entrepreneurs in the high state in one industry do not have the expertise to manage the projects in the low state, implicitly in another industry.[12]

There are several interpretations of the random cash flow return to the short-term project, r, realized at date 1. A straightforward interpretation is that the short-term projects literally are a technology with some uncertainty. Alternatively, one can think of the short-term projects as producing R, but entrepreneurs have a random consumption need or production cost uniformly distributed in $[0, R]$ which is subtracted from R, leaving r. As a practical matter we have in mind agents who hoard cash, government securities, short-term commercial paper, and so on—securities with low yields—in order to be able to buy distressed projects. We assume that the new owner generates the same cash flow. Cases of higher or lower cash flow can easily be solved with slight modification.

[11] Alternatively, one can imagine more complicated explanations for why entrepreneurs who have realized H cannot credibly issue securities to buy projects at date 1, e.g., asymmetric information could be introduced.

[12] Holmström and Tirole (1998) have a similar assumption. Lucky firms (with additional liquidity) are not allowed to take over unlucky firms (short of liquidity). In Diamond and Rajan (2002) banks find out at an interim date whether their loan maturities are long or short; banks cannot insure against the risk of having a long maturity portfolio realization at this date.

A model of liquidity needs a motive for some agents to sell assets. Here moral hazard provides the motivation for selling projects at date 1. The "capitalization shock" generates liquidity demand from the asset side, which differs from liability side shocks, such as random preferences over the timing of consumption. The specific motivation of moral hazard is important in Section V, when we consider the banking system.

Another issue concerns the shocks to the long-term projects. They are idiosyncratic and independent of the random payoffs to the short-term projects. However, we could have systematic shocks and idiosyncratic shocks, plus correlation between the cash flows from the long-term and short-term projects without changing the main results. For simplicity, we do not include systematic shocks and correlation in the model.

II. Debt Forgiveness

To avoid the moral hazard problem, borrowers need an equity injection at date 1 if their projects are in the low state. If the project is sold in the liquidation market, then a new owner injects equity. But, the lender is an alternative source of equity, in the sense that debt forgiveness creates equity for the original owner. To begin the analysis, we analyze the case where equity is injected via the lender forgiving some of the debt. In this case, all entrepreneurs will invest in the long-term project at date 0, which is the first-best outcome, as there is no need for private liquidity provision at date 1. Investment in the short-term project is dominated.

We start by solving for the subgame equilibrium at date 1. At date 1, if a long-term project is in the high state, then nothing happens (by Assumption 6, there exists a face value of the debt, F, such that an entrepreneur has no incentive to add risk in the high state.) However, if a long-term project is in the low state, L, then the project is worth L if no risk as added and is worth δTL if risk is added. By Assumption 5 borrowers will add risk if they retain ownership of the project without any new equity.

Renegotiation between the borrower and the lender has three possible outcomes. First, the original owner may continue until date 2 without adding risk if the lender forgives some debt. Second, the project may be sold or liquidated, in which case the original owner receives the price Q (the liquidation value). However, this entrepreneur owes the lender F, which must be paid at date 1 if the debt is short term or at date 2 if the debt is long term. Renegotiation must allocate Q between the borrower and the lender. Finally, the project may remain in the original owner's hands with risk being added. Equilibrium at date 1 involves determining which of these outcomes is the result of renegotiation between borrowers and lenders.

In order for the first possibility to occur, the lender must forgive part of the debt. This is an equity injection, a subsidy granted to the entrepreneur by the lender, to induce the entrepreneur not to add risk. By the analysis above (just before Assumption 5), the lender must agree to lower the face value of the debt to γL to remove the entrepreneur's incentive to add risk. The lender is willing to forgive debt, that is, reduce the face value from F to γL, if and only if γL is greater than δF, the expected payoff to the lender when risk will be added. The following lemma provides the condition under which debt forgiveness is feasible.

Lemma 1: *Debt forgiveness is feasible if and only if* $\gamma L \geq \frac{\delta}{\pi+\delta(1-\pi)}$.

Proof: See Appendix.

If debt forgiveness is feasible, then there will be no need for liquidity provision at date 1.[13] Since, *ex ante*, the long-term project is more efficient than the short-term project, no entrepreneur will choose the short-term project at date 0; all entrepreneurs will choose the long-term project. Lenders only receive the face value of the debt, F, in the high state, which happens with probability π. In order to make lenders break even, F has to satisfy the following condition: $\pi F + (1-\pi)\gamma L \geq 1$, or $F \geq \frac{1-(1-\pi)\gamma L}{\pi}$. Proposition 1 summarizes the above analysis:

Proposition 1: *If* $\gamma L \geq \frac{\delta}{\pi+\delta(1-\pi)}$, *then all entrepreneurs choose the long-term project at date* 0. *The face value of the debt is* $\frac{1-(1-\pi)\gamma L}{\pi}$. *This is the first-best outcome.*

The proposition says that as long as debt forgiveness at date 1 is feasible, it will occur. The details of the division of the surplus between the lender and the borrower do not matter. Whatever the division, based on relative bargaining power, the equilibrium will be the same, as the entrepreneurs price this in getting the entire expected surplus at date 0.

Debt forgiveness by the lender is a kind of liquidity provision because the lender is essentially refinancing the project, taking into account the new information, namely the state L, and the problem of moral hazard.[14] Liquidity provision is an important function of banks.[15] If forgiveness by the lender is feasible, then there is no need for a secondary market to refinance the project (by selling it to another party). Proposition 1 allows us to identify the condition under which the provision of liquidity (by agents other than the lenders, i.e., by entrepreneurs who hoard liquid assets) is socially valuable. According to the proposition, debt forgiveness solves the moral hazard problem, and there is no need for liquidity provision, so long as $\gamma L \geq \frac{\delta}{\pi+\delta(1-\pi)}$. If this is not the case, then there is a need for the liquidation market. *Ex ante*, the owners of long-term projects get a surplus if the liquidation price prevailing in the secondary market is higher than the value of project with risk being added. The liquidity suppliers gain a profit if the liquidation price is less than the value of the project free from added risk. At date 0 entrepreneurs make project choices and at the same time choose to be liquidity demanders or liquidity suppliers. At date 1, a secondary market will arise endogenously. This is analyzed in the next section with the assumption that $\gamma L \leq \frac{\delta}{\pi+\delta(1-\pi)}$, i.e., debt forgiveness is not feasible.

III. The Market for Liquidity

If lenders are unwilling to forgive debt, then equity will have to be created in some other way as a solution to the moral hazard problem. The alternative is to sell the project to another, better capitalized, entrepreneur at date 1. We refer to this secondary market as the "liquidation market." In other words, at date 1 there is a market in which owners of long-term projects can sell their projects to other entrepreneurs with available resources to purchase the project.

[13]Later we will show that the liquidation price cannot exceed L. Therefore, the entrepreneurs who choose the long-term project at date 0 also choose debt contracts under which renegotiation results in forgiveness of debt.

[14]The case of the hedge fund Long Term Capital Management (LTCM) is a recent example of forgiveness by lenders (see Roger Lowenstein, 2000).

[15]The empirical results of Scott Lummer and John McConnell (1989) suggest the positive announcement effect associated with bank loans is due to loan renewals, rather than the initial loan, consistent with bank debt forgiveness being important. See Gorton and Winton (2003) for a survey of the related literature.

A. Preliminaries

Because we are assuming that debt forgiveness is not feasible, the project can either be liquidated at price Q, or can be continued with risk being added, in which case it has an expected cash flow of δTL. Actually, whether the project will be liquidated only depends on the liquidation price Q. It does not depend on the maturity of debt contracts and the assignment of bargaining power when renegotiation occurs at date 1. So long as Q is greater than δTL, the lender and the borrower can always reach an agreement to liquidate the project and split the surplus. For simplicity, we assume that the debt contracts are long-term and the borrower has all the bargaining power. When renegotiation occurs at date 1, he makes a take-it-or-leave-it offer to the lender. The lender gets δF (the lender's expected payoff if the project continues with risk being added) and the borrower gets $Q - \delta F$.

B. The Liquidation Market and Liquidation Prices

Potential liquidity suppliers at date 1 are those entrepreneurs who invested in the short-term project at date 0. At date 1, each of them has realized a cash flow of r, drawn from a uniform distribution on $[0, R]$. If r is small, then the entrepreneur will not have enough to afford the liquidation price. Therefore, some of the entrepreneurs may have to borrow in order to buy a troubled project. Buyers themselves also face the moral hazard problem since they too have access to the risk-adding technology. Although the realized r is not publicly observable, we assume that if a project buyer borrows from a lender to buy a project, how the loan is used is verifiable. In other words, the amount borrowed can only be used to buy the project. In this way, if a buyer borrows B and buys a project at price Q, the lender knows the borrower's realized r is at least $Q - B$. Therefore, it can be determined whether potential buyers have incentives to add risk to the project and whether the loan to the buyer is safe.

A buyer has no incentive to add risk if and only if the face value of the debt B is small enough such that $L - B \geq \delta(TL - B)$, i.e., $B \leq \gamma L$. Therefore, the buyers who have a realized $r \geq Q - \gamma L$ are not going to engage in moral hazard and loans to them are safe. Other buyers do not have enough equity and have incentives to add risk once they get the control of the projects.

Because of the buyers' potential moral hazard problems, not every entrepreneur who hoarded liquid assets can be a liquidity supplier. Liquidity supply at date 1 depends on the buyers' ability to buy. "Ability" means how much equity they have, that is, the size of the realized return from their short-term project. The next lemma characterizes their ability to supply liquidity at a given price.

Lemma 2: *Suppose the liquidation price of a project is Q. Then:*

(i) If $Q > L$, then there will be no liquidity supply in the liquidation market.
(ii) If $\delta TL < Q \leq L$, then only those buyers with realized cash flows $r \geq Q - \gamma L$ are able to supply liquidity.
(iii) If $Q < \delta TL$, then all buyers can be liquidity suppliers.

Proof: See Appendix.

We know that a troubled project is liquidated if and only if the liquidation price Q is greater than or equal to δTL. So, the liquidity demand curve (or the project supply curve) is perfectly elastic at price δTL. By Lemma 2, we know that no entrepreneur is willing to pay more than L to buy a project. Moreover, as the liquidation price declines from L to δTL, more and more entrepreneurs are willing to buy the projects. Thus, there is a downward-sloped liquidity supply curve (or a downward-sloped project demand curve). Combining liquidity demand with liquidity supply determines the liquidation price in the secondary market, which depends on the fraction of entrepreneurs taking the long-term project at date 0.

Lemma 3: *At date* 1, *the price in the liquidation market, Q, will be:*

$$Q = \delta TL \quad \textit{if } (1-\alpha)\left(1 - \frac{\delta TL - \gamma L}{R}\right) \leq \alpha(1-\pi)$$

$$Q = \gamma L + R\left(1 - \frac{\alpha(1-\pi)}{1-\alpha}\right) \quad \textit{if } (1-\alpha)\left(1 - \frac{L - \gamma L}{R}\right)$$

$$< \alpha(1-\pi) < (1-\alpha)\left(1 - \frac{\delta LT - \gamma L}{R}\right)$$

$$Q = L \quad \textit{if } \alpha(1-\pi) \leq (1-\alpha)\left(1 - \frac{L - \gamma L}{R}\right).$$

Proof: See Appendix.

We define the "liquidity discount" to be the difference between the "fundamental" value of the project, namely L, and the liquidation price Q. Lemma 3 shows that a liquidity discount can arise in equilibrium. That is, the equilibrium price in the liquidation market, Q, can be *below* the value of the project if risk is not added, L. This discount is necessary to entice liquidity suppliers to invest in the short-term project in order to buy the projects.

To emphasize that the market price of the equity sold in the liquidation market has a price that depends on liquidity, we further examine the relationship between the price and the supply of liquidity with a figure. Figure 9.1 shows the secondary market equilibrium with respect to different levels of α, the fraction of entrepreneurs taking the long-term project. (So, $1-\alpha$ is the fraction that has chosen short-term projects in order to later be liquidity suppliers.) When α is very small, liquidity demand is small while liquidity supply is large, and the liquidation price is at its maximum L. In this case, the liquidity discount is equal to zero (the vertical part of the liquidity demand curve intersects the supply curve at L). When α is very large, liquidity demand is large while liquidity supply is small, and the liquidation price is at its minimum δTL (the vertical part of the liquidity demand curve shifts right and intersects the supply curve at δTL). The liquidity discount is at its maximum $L - \delta TL = L(1-\delta T)$. When α is in the medium range, there is an interior equilibrium

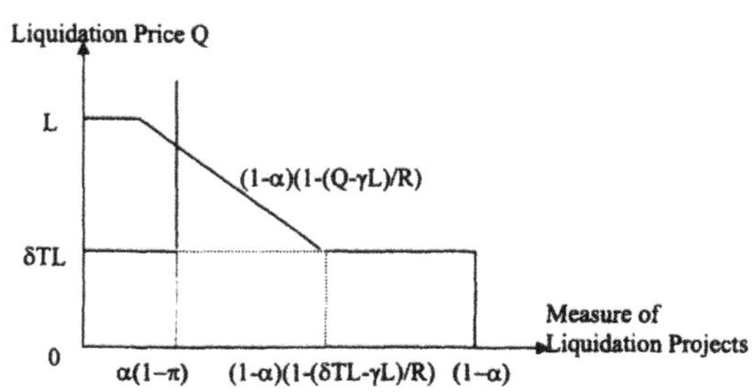

Figure 9.1 Liquidation Market Equilibrium
Notes: When α is in the intermediate range, liquidity demand curve intersects liquidity supply curve when it is still sloped down. The liquidation price is between δTL and L; the liquidity premium is between zero and $L - \delta TL$.

liquidation price, Q, at which all the liquidity demand can be satisfied while liquidity supply is downward sloped. In this case the liquidity discount is between zero and $L(1 - \delta T)$, as shown in the figure.

In the liquidation market, ownership claims, i.e., equity claims, to the project are sold and a new entrepreneur acquires control rights. The new entrepreneur has the right to choose whether to add risk or not. In equilibrium no risk is added. In the finance literature, when "market efficiency" is mentioned, the transfer of control rights, which usually results in a change of the asset value, is typically not considered. Moreover, the supply of liquidity is perfectly elastic. Here, due to the moral hazard problem and the limited liquidity supply, the notion of "market efficiency" is altered. Although, in equilibrium, risk will not be added and the continuation value of the project is L, there is a liquidity discount. *Ex post*, the liquidity discount reflects insufficient liquid assets in the market. *Ex ante*, the liquidity discount is necessary to compensate the liquidity suppliers because there is a cost associated with supplying liquidity. We next solve the entrepreneur's date 0 decision problem.

C. Initial Investment Choices

At date 0, entrepreneurs have rational expectations about how the liquidation price is formed in the secondary or liquidation market of date 1. An entrepreneur makes his project choice, taking other entrepreneurs' choices as given. We solve for the date 0 equilibrium in the following proposition (under the maintained assumption that debt forgiveness is not feasible at date 1).

Proposition 2: *Suppose that* $\gamma L < \frac{\delta}{\pi+\delta(1-\pi)}$, *i.e., debt forgiveness is not feasible at date* 1. *Then:*

(i) If $\pi H + (1-\pi)\delta TL > 1 + \frac{R}{2} + (L - \delta TL) \times \left(1 - \frac{\delta TL - \gamma L}{R}, \right)$ *then all the entrepreneurs choose the long-term project at date* 0. *In this case, there will be no liquidity supplied at date* 1, *and risk will be added to all projects realizing the low state at date* 1.

(ii) If $\pi H + (1-\pi)\delta TL \leq 1 + \frac{R}{2} + (L - \delta TL) \times \left(1 - \frac{\delta TL - \gamma L}{R}\right)$, *then there is a fraction* $\alpha^* \in (0, 1)$ *of entrepreneurs who choose the long-term project, and a fraction* $(1 - \alpha^*)$ *of entrepreneurs who choose the short-term project at date* 0. $\alpha^* = \frac{R+\gamma L - Q^*}{(2-\pi)R+\gamma L - Q^*}$, *where* $Q^* \in [\delta TL, L]$, *defined in the Appendix, is the liquidation price at date* 1.

Proof: See Appendix.

Proposition 2 relates the primitives of the economy to the incidence of liquidation. Entrepreneurs compare the expected payoffs on the two projects available to them at date 0, taking into account the possible transactions in the liquidation market. The short-term project has a return of r over the first period and a return over the second period that depends on the profitability of buying a distressed project at date 1 and operating it until date 2. If these returns are too low, compared to the long-term project (when risk is added in case L is realized), then all entrepreneurs will still take the long-term project. Otherwise there is an active secondary market and some entrepreneurs engage in each activity. In that case, supplying liquidity is both privately profitable and socially efficient.

D. Comparative Statics

Proposition 2 provides the solution to the initial general-equilibrium investment problem. In equilibrium, entrepreneurs are indifferent between investing in the long-term project or in the short-term project at date 0; they get the same expected payoff *ex ante*. By assumption, entrepreneurs get the entire expected surplus, thus their expected payoff is a measure of social welfare. The expected payoff to entrepreneurs who take the long-term project is $\pi H + (1 - \pi)Q^*$, and the expected payoff to entrepreneurs who take the short-term project is $1 + \frac{R}{2} + (L - Q^*)\left(1 - \frac{Q^* - \gamma L}{R}\right)$. Social welfare, the liquidation price, Q^*, and thus the liquidity discount, $L - Q^*$, all depend on the parameter values: π, R, and δ. π measures the quality of the long-term project; R measures the quality of the short-term project; and δ measures the severity of the moral hazard problem. Proposition 3 and Corollary 1 show the comparative statics:

Proposition 3: *Social welfare is increasing in π and R, and decreasing in δ.*

Corollary 1: *The liquidation price Q^* (the liquidity discount, $L - Q^*$) is increasing (decreasing) in R and decreasing (increasing) in π and δ.*

Proof: See Appendix.

$L - Q^*$ is the equilibrium liquidity discount, which is a measure of how profitable it is to hoard assets by investing in the short-term project. It is also the necessary compensation a liquidity provider requires to sacrifice the long-term project. The larger the difference between the expected payoff from a long-term project (in the absence of the moral hazard problem) and that from a short-term project, the higher the required liquidity discount. When δ increases, γ increases, and thus the threshold to be a liquidity supplier is increased. The liquidity discount has to be increased to compensate for the decrease in the probability of being a liquidity supplier (a lower Q^*). A larger π increases the expected payoff of the long-term project and decreases liquidity demand, thereby resulting in a higher liquidity discount (a lower Q^*). On the other hand, a higher R increases the expected return of the short-term project and also increases the potential to become a liquidity supplier; therefore it results in a lower liquidity discount (a higher Q^*).

The effects of R, π, and δ on welfare are quite intuitive. When R and π increases, the overall investment quality in the economy is improved. Hence, welfare increases. When δ increases, the reservation price δTL is higher and more short-term investors are needed to purchase the distressed long-term projects. More investment in dominated short-term projects results in lower welfare.

E. Summary

Entrepreneurs cannot buy insurance at date 0 against declines in the value of their equity at date 1. Nor can entrepreneurs with high-value projects at date 1 use that value to inject equity into the low-value projects. These markets do not exist and as a result of these missing markets, private liquidity provision can be efficient. The existence of a liquidity discount is a measure of the shadow price of the liquidity-in-advance constraint. To the extent that this constraint binds, the market price of project equity at date 1 reflects this constraint, not just the expected payoff on the project.

However, the government may be able to improve upon the private allocation because hoarding by investing in the short-term project is dominated by investment in the long-term project. We now analyze the role of the government.

IV. Government Bailouts

Because of the moral hazard problem, the first-best outcome cannot be reached in the equilibrium studied above. The private supply of liquidity is inefficient since some investments are made in short-term projects, which are *ex ante* dominated by long-term projects. Can the government improve the efficiency of the economy? If the entrepreneurs had enough capital at date 0, then there would be no need for them to borrow, and the first-best outcome could be reached. Suppose the lenders are banks.[16] If the government has the power to tax bank depositors and subsidize the entrepreneurs at date 0 then they would have enough equity to avoid borrowing and the moral hazard problem would never arise. But, such transfers require that date 0 endowments be verifiable. In our model, entrepreneurs get the entire surplus. Depositors will not save their endowments in the bank if they anticipate the government is going to tax their savings. Therefore the subsidies have to be financed via taxing entrepreneurs in high states at the final date.

If the government can tax entrepreneurs with high returns and subsidize entrepreneurs with low returns, the government can at least partially improve efficiency by eliminating the incentives to add risk from some of the entrepreneurs in the low state. Unfortunately, the states of the long-term projects are only observable by banks and entrepreneurs and they are not verifiable. If the government cannot observe the states of projects at date 1, it has to design a screening mechanism to determine entrepreneurs are in the high state and which entrepreneurs are in the low state. We will show that the government can screen the banks by offering to buy the loans. In this section we examine such government bailouts.

A. Government Liquidity Provision

The government bailout mechanism works as follows. At date 1, the government offers to buy loans from banks. Each bank can either sell its loans to the government at a specified price P, or pay a tax, t, at date 2 if it does not sell its loans to the government at date 1. Once the government holds the loans, it can forgive a fraction of the liabilities of the troubled projects to remove the entrepreneurs' incentives to engage in moral hazard.

Alternatively, the government can offer subsidies to the banks (e.g., loan guarantees). To receive a subsidy, the bank has to lower the face value of its troubled loans. In equilibrium, only the banks with troubled loans will accept the offer from the government. In this way, the government can distinguish the high state projects from the low state projects and make transfers to improve efficiency. Whether government intervention can generate the first-best outcome depends on how much tax revenue it can collect from projects in the high state. The government certainly does not want the high-value projects to suffer from moral hazard problems and thus it must ensure that the owners of high-value projects pay less than γH at date 2 (i.e., the face value of the debt cannot exceed γH). If government intervention alone cannot generate the first-best outcome, there may still be a need for private liquidity to be supplied at date 1.

Proposition 4: *If* $\gamma(\pi H + (1-\pi)L) \geq 1$, *then a government bailout can generate the first-best outcome as of date 0. At date 0, entrepreneurs and banks sign debt contracts with a face value of* $F = \frac{1-(1-\pi)\gamma L}{\pi}$. *At date* 1, *the government offers to buy the loan at*

[16] At this point, we assume lenders are banks, to foreshadow the analysis of bank bailouts in Section V.

price $P = \frac{\delta}{\pi+\delta(1-\pi)}$. *Banks with troubled projects sell their loans to the government and banks with high state projects retain their loans and pay a tax of* $t = \frac{1-(1-\pi)\gamma L}{\pi} - \frac{1}{\pi+\delta(1-\pi)}$ *at date* 2.

Proof: See Appendix.

If $\gamma(\pi H + (1-\pi)L) < 1$, then government intervention cannot produce the first-best outcome because the government cannot levy enough taxes on the entrepreneurs in high states. Since the government cannot subsidize (or bail out) all the troubled projects at date 1, some of the troubled projects will suffer from the moral hazard problem if there is no private liquidation market. Whether there are entrepreneurs willing to take the short-term project and supply liquidity depends on the expected payoffs from the short-term project and the long-term project. We assume the government randomly chooses which projects to bail out when it does not have enough resources. The government determines the optimal bailout policy to maximize social welfare by choosing the loan price, P, tax on high state projects, t, and the fraction, ω, of projects to bail out. So, the government's objective function is as follows:

$$\text{Max}_{\omega,P,t}\ \pi H + (1-\pi)(\omega L + (1-\omega)Q)$$

s.t. (1) $F \leq \gamma H$

(2) $P \geq \delta(F-t)$

(3) $\pi(F-t) + (1-\pi)(\omega P + (1-\omega)\delta(F-t)) = 1$

(4) $\pi t \geq (1-\pi)\omega(P - \gamma L)$

(5) $Q = \delta TL$ if $\pi H + (1-\pi)(\omega L + (1-\omega)\delta TL) > 1 + \frac{R}{2} + (L - \delta TL)\left(1 - \frac{\delta TL - \gamma L}{R}\right)$

(6) Q solves $\pi H + (1-\pi)(\omega L + (1-\omega)Q) = 1 + \frac{R}{2} + (L - Q)\left(1 - \frac{Q-\gamma L}{R}\right)$

if $\pi H + (1-\pi)(\omega L + (1-\omega)\delta TL) \leq 1 + \frac{R}{2} + (L - \delta TL)\left(1 - \frac{\delta TL - \gamma L}{R}\right)$.

Constraint (1) says that F must be less than γH, to prevent entrepreneurs in the high state from engaging in moral hazard. Constraint (2) says that banks are willing to sell loans at a price no lower than $\delta(F-t)$, which is the amount they can receive if low state projects are liquidated or risk is added to them. Constraint (3) says that banks must break even. Constraint (4) is the government budget constraint: tax revenue collected from the measure of projects with the high value, πt, must be enough to cover the fraction of projects that the government chooses to subsidize. Each troubled project is subsidized by the amount $P - \gamma L$, and $(1-\pi)\omega$ is the measure of low state projects subsidized. The final two constraints, (5) and (6), are participation constraints for private agents to supply liquidity. These are functions of the equilibrium price of projects at date 1, Q, which in turn depends upon the fraction of projects that the government subsidizes.

The following proposition characterizes the situations in which the liquidation market coexists with a government bailout at date 1.

Proposition 5: *Suppose* $\gamma(\pi H + (1-\pi)L) < 1$. *Define* $\omega^* \equiv \frac{\pi((\pi+(1-\pi)\delta)\gamma H - 1)}{(1-\pi)(\delta - (\pi+(1-\pi)\delta)\gamma L)}$. *Then:*

(i) *If* $\pi H + (1-\pi)[\omega^* L + (1-\omega^*)\delta TL] \geq 1 + \frac{R}{2} + (L - \delta TL)\left(1 - \frac{\delta TL - \gamma L}{R}\right)$, *then all the entrepreneurs choose the long-term project at date* 0. *In this case, there will be no liquidity supplied at date* 1. *The government subsidizes a fraction* ω^* *of the troubled* *long-term projects and the remaining fraction* $1 - \omega^*$ *of the troubled long-term projects will suffer from the moral hazard problem.*

(ii) *If* $\pi H + (1-\pi)[\omega^* L + (1-\omega^*)\delta TL] < 1 + \frac{R}{2} + (L - \delta TL)\left(1 - \frac{\delta TL - \gamma L}{R}\right)$, *then there is a fraction* α^* *of entrepreneurs choosing the long-term project, and a fraction* $(1-\alpha^*)$ *entrepreneurs choosing the short-term project at date* 0. $\alpha^* = \frac{R+\gamma L - Q^*}{(1+(1-\pi)(1-\omega^*))R + \gamma L - Q^*}$, *where* $Q^* \in [\delta TL, L]$, *defined in the Appendix, is the liquidation price at date* 1.

Proof: See Appendix.

Depending on the parameters, there may or may not be private liquidity provision. In either instance, not all entrepreneurs with troubled projects can be bailed out. The government cannot afford that, as there are not enough resources that can be taxed to subsidize the troubled entrepreneurs. The government randomly bails out the maximum number of troubled bank projects that it can afford, and in the remainder either risk is added or they go to the liquidation market. This may be viewed as a type of "forbearance," that is, the government policy results in some borrowers engaging in moral hazard. But, this is the socially optimal second-best policy.

B. Taxes and Government Bonds

The government can improve matters because it has the power to overcome the market incompleteness. Entrepreneurs who invested in long-term projects at date 0, and then saw their prospects brighten because they realized H on their project, have valuable resources, the capital gains on their project. But, they have no way to monetize these gains to create "liquidity" and provide equity to the troubled projects. The government, however, can monetize these gains by issuing government bonds, as follows. The government buys troubled projects from banks, paying with the newly created bonds. The government then forgives some of the debt of the entrepreneurs, to prevent them from engaging in moral hazard. The newly created bonds, held by the banks, are paid off at date 2 with the tax revenues raised from the lucky entrepreneurs who realized H.

Alternatively, the government can tax banks that make loans to long-term projects at date 0. The government then hoards the tax revenue and uses it to finance the bailouts at date 1. Since the burden has to be borne by the entrepreneurs, banks will raise the face value of the debt to cover the tax they pay at date 0. This would generate the same outcome as the government issuing bonds and tax at date 2.

The fact that the government maximizes social welfare is also important for the argument. Suppose there is a private insurer who signs a contract with the bank and the entrepreneur at date 0. The contract specifies that the bank has the right to sell the loan to the insurer at (pre-specified) price $P = \delta(F - t)$ at date 1 (a put option). However, contingent on the sale of the loan, the insurer must lower the face value of the debt to γL. If the bank does not sell the loan to the insurer at date 1, it has to pay the insurer t at date 2. The problem with this contract is that it is subject to collusion between the profit-maximizing insurer and the bank. At date 1 the insurer can bribe the bank not to force the insurer to buy the loan, according to the contract. The insurer gives the bank $t + \varepsilon$(ε is a very small number) at date 1 if the bank agrees not to sell the loan; the bank accepts. Thus the insurer avoids losing $P - \gamma L$. Therefore no bank sells loans and if entrepreneurs anticipate the collusion, they will not purchase insurance at date 0. The government scheme works because the government is concerned with social welfare and does not want the entrepreneurs to add risk. The private insurer maximizes profits not social welfare.

C. Discussion

There is a long history to government bailouts of banking systems, either directly or via an asset management company, which is set up for the purpose of relieving banks of bad loans by buying loans at a price that implicitly subsidizes the banks. The Reconstruction Finance Corporation loans to railroads during the Great Depression, the examples of Chrysler, Penn Central Railroad, and the current (post-September 11) bailouts of the airlines in the United States are examples of government liquidity provision, as described above. Claessens et al. (1999) describe corporate-sector bailouts in Indonesia, Korea, Malaysia, and Thailand. In the aftermath of the Asian Crisis, Indonesia, Korea, Malaysia, and Thailand established centralized asset management companies. As a percent of GDP, the amounts of bank assets purchased by these asset management companies were: Indonesia, 20 percent; Korea, 10 percent; Malaysia, 17 percent; and Thailand, 17.5 percent. See Lindgren et al. (1999) for details of the bailouts resulting from the Asian Crisis. There is, however, a range of ways in which the bailouts are accomplished. Surveying the experiences of 24 countries in the 1980's and early 1990's, Claudia Dziobek and Ceyla Pazarbasioglu (1998) write:

> Removing nonperforming loans from the banks' balance sheets and transferring them to a separate recovery agency can be an effective way of addressing the banks' solvency problems. ... Loan workouts can be done by a central organization, usually operated by the state, or by special loan collection agencies tied to individual banks, an approach Sweden used successfully in 1991. The survey results suggest that the institutional setting does not matter. Some countries, including Chile, the Philippines, and the transition countries, approached the loan workout indirectly by providing debt relief to borrowers by engaging simultaneously in the restructuring of borrowing enterprises themselves (p. 7).

(Also see Dziobek and Pazarbasioglu, 1997). Whether the debt relief came in the form of forgiveness, subsidized loans, or loan guarantees, the government provided equity injections to these firms.

From the viewpoint of the analysis above, bailouts occur when there is not enough private liquidity available to implement transfers of ownership quickly. Private agents anticipate that the government will supply liquidity, as indeed it does. The above examples of large-scale corporate distress—including the transition economies, Latin American economies such as Mexico, as well as Scandinavian countries—are often related to a banking crisis. This situation is analyzed next.

V. Bank Capital, Banking Crises, and Bailouts

We now turn to the analysis of bailouts of banking systems. In the above equilibrium, we assumed that banks were always solvent. However, there is the possibility that a troubled project could turn a solvent bank into an insolvent bank. In this section, we provide more detail about the situation of the bank. We introduce a measure of the amount of equity in a bank. As a function of how well capitalized a bank is, it may or may not behave as in the above equilibrium. In particular, a weakly capitalized bank, faced with troubled projects, may itself face the moral hazard problem of seeking to add inefficient risk. That is, there will be no incentive to liquidate projects. This means that when projects are troubled, weak banks cause a knock-on effect, where banks and entrepreneurs find it in their joint interests to engage in moral hazard.

A. Bank Capital Ratios and Bank Moral Hazard Problems

Suppose a representative bank lends to a single entrepreneur at date 0, and owes depositors an amount D at date 2. Imagine that the bank has some assets other than the projects discussed so far. These other assets have a payoff of V, where V is a random variable that will be realized at date 2. The date 2 realization will be V_H with probability θ and V_L with probability $1-\theta$. However, nonverifiable information about the realization of V becomes known to the banks at date 1.

We assume the risk associated with V is systematic and independent of the states of the long-term projects. In addition, we assume:

Assumption 10: $V_H > D$, and $V_L + 1 > D$, *but* $V_L + L < D$. *That is, when the bank receives a negative shock and the project it lent to is also in trouble, the bank is insolvent even if it receives the entire cash flow from the troubled project, L.*

Now, even though it is efficient to forgive part of the debt or to liquidate troubled projects, it can happen that the bank has a moral hazard problem itself and prefers not to liquidate troubled projects.

Lemma 4: *If, at date* 1, *a bank learns that the realization of V is* V_L, *then the bank will not agree to renegotiate the debt contract or to liquidate a troubled project.*

Proof: See Appendix.

Previously, successful renegotiation resulted because the bank was willing to forgive some debt or to share the proceeds of liquidation with the entrepreneur. Here, by refusing to share the benefits of liquidation with the entrepreneur (via debt forgiveness), the bank removes any incentive for the entrepreneur to liquidate the project. If the entrepreneur cannot benefit by selling the project, then there is no reason to sell; adding risk is the entrepreneur's optimal strategy when the state is L. The bank engages in moral hazard by refusing to renegotiate with the borrower, thereby enticing the entrepreneur to add risk. As a result, there is a chance, δ, that the entrepreneur will be able to repay F at date 2. In that case, the bank will be able to honor its date 2 obligations to repay D to depositors.[17]

Forgiveness or liquidation is now possible only if the bank's cash flow from its other business is V_H. The bank's moral hazard problem causes an additional inefficiency in the economy. If the realization of the systematic shock is V_L, then the liquidity demand at date 1 is zero. This happens with probability $1-\theta$. Now, the equilibrium project choices at date 0

[17] If depositors can observe which entrepreneurs are in the low state, they can run on the banks and withdraw their deposits forcing the banks to "liquidate" (that is, the bank assets would have to be sold to the liquidity suppliers). Once they run the banks, both the bank's equity and the entrepreneur's equity are zero. Projects will be sold in the liquidation market, and the proceeds will be used to honor deposit contracts. If depositors cannot observe which entrepreneurs are in the low state, they might mistakenly run the banks with healthy projects. If depositors anticipate they might run the good banks, it may be better for them not to run any banks. These issues are discussed at length in Gorton and Huang (2001) and, for the sake of brevity, are avoided here. Here, imagine that there is deposit insurance in place (though the reasons for this are not modeled).

depend on θ. We first examine the case when debt forgiveness would be feasible without the bank moral hazard problem.

Proposition 6: *Suppose that* $\gamma L \geq \frac{\delta}{\pi+\delta(1-\pi)}$, *i.e., debt forgiveness is feasible at date* 1. *Then:*

(i) *If* $\pi H+(1-\pi)[\theta L+(1-\theta)\delta TL] \geq 1+\frac{R}{2}$, *then all entrepreneurs choose the long-term project at date* 0.
(ii) *If* $\pi H+(1-\pi)[\theta L+(1-\theta)\delta TL] < 1+\frac{R}{2}$, *then all entrepreneurs choose the short-term project at date* 0.

Proof: See Appendix.

Because of the bank's moral hazard problem, renegotiation fails when the bank's state is V_L. *Ex ante*, the value of the long-term project decreases. The above proposition shows that the problem can be so severe that the long-term project can even be dominated by the short-term project. Investment in the long-term projects is then abandoned.

Next, we study how the bank moral hazard problem affects the equilibrium in the case where debt forgiveness is not feasible.

Proposition 7: *Suppose that* $\gamma L < \frac{\delta}{\pi+\delta(1-\pi)}$, *i.e., debt forgiveness is not feasible at date* 1. *Then*:

(i) *If* $\pi H + (1-\pi)\delta TL > 1 + \frac{R}{2} + \theta(L-\delta TL)\left(1-\frac{\delta TL-\gamma L}{R}\right)$, *then all entrepreneurs choose the long-term project at date* 0. *In this case, there will be no liquidity supply at date* 1, *and risk will be added for projects realizing the low state at date* 1.
(ii) *If* $\pi H+(1-\pi)[\theta L+(1-\theta)\delta TL] < 1+\frac{R}{2}$, *then all entrepreneurs choose the short-term project at date* 0.
(iii) *If* $\pi H + (1-\pi)\delta TL \leq 1 + \frac{R}{2} + \theta(L-\delta TL)\left(1-\frac{\delta TL-\gamma L}{R}\right)$ *and* $\pi H + (1-\pi)[\theta L + (1-\theta)\delta TL] \geq 1+\frac{R}{2}$, *then there exists a measure,* α^*, *of entrepreneurs that choose the long-term project at date* 0, *and a measure,* $(1-\alpha^*)$, *of entrepreneurs that choose the short-term project at date* 0. *At date* 1 *the liquidation price is* $Q^* \in [\delta TL, L]$. α^* *and* Q^* *are defined in the Appendix.*

Proof: See Appendix.

The moral hazard problem with banks can result in troubled projects not being sold in the liquidation market at date 1. This is a kind of market failure and adds inefficiency to the economy. Recall that θ is the chance of V_H occurring. We can view θ as a measure of this additional inefficiency.

Corollary 2: *Social welfare is increasing in* θ.

Proof: See Appendix.

The intuition is straightforward. Higher θ means banks have more capital and are less likely to want to engage in moral hazard. Consequently, by increasing θ, the chance that a troubled project receives equity either from the lender by forgiveness or via the liquidation market is increased, and so efficiency in the economy is improved. If banks are weaker, however, then inefficiency increases.

B. Government Bank Bailouts

Government intervention can improve efficiency when there is the potential problem of banks engaging in moral hazard. When the state is low and banks have V_L, the government has to consider not only the entrepreneurs' moral hazard problem but also the banks' moral hazard problem. Therefore the government has to offer banks a larger amount to induce banks to sell their projects to the government. The next lemma shows how much the government needs to pay the banks to bail out the troubled projects.

Lemma 5: *Suppose the face value of the debt is F, and the government's tax is t at date 2. The government has to pay banks at least $P' \equiv \delta(F-t)+(1-\delta)(D-V_L)$ to remove banks' moral hazard problem.*

Proof: See Appendix.

Although it seems that the banks' moral hazard problem will make government intervention less efficient, the first-best outcome can still be reached so long as the condition $\gamma(\pi H+(1-\pi)L)\geq 1$ is satisfied. The intuition is as follows. Anticipating that banks will get a higher price, P', at date 1, the net interest, $(F-t)$, paid to banks can be lowered and thus the government can tax more (increase t) at date 2 to finance the subsidy at date 1. In other words, the bank moral hazard problem requires more public liquidity at date 1. However, due to the decrease in the interest paid to banks, the government has more liquidity available at date 1. So long as we have $\gamma(\pi H+(1-\pi)L)\geq 1$, the government has enough public liquidity to bail out all troubled projects. The first-best outcome can be attained.

If $\gamma(\pi H+(1-\pi)L)<1$, government intervention cannot produce the first-best outcome because the government cannot levy enough taxes on entrepreneurs in high states. As in the case without the banks' moral hazard problem, it is possible that a liquidation market at date 1 is desirable. The following proposition characterizes the situations in which the liquidation market exists. If some projects are allowed to continue, because the government only bails out a fraction of them, then we may say that "forbearance" occurs.

Proposition 8: *If $\gamma(\pi H+(1-\pi)L)\geq 1$, then government intervention can still generate the first-best outcome even if the potential banks' moral hazard problem exists. Entrepreneurs and banks sign debt contracts with a face value of $F=\frac{1-(1-\pi)\gamma L}{\pi}$. At date 1, the government offers to buy the loan at price $P=\frac{\delta+\pi(1-\delta)(D-V_L)}{\pi+\delta(1-\pi)}$. Banks with troubled projects sell their loans to the government and banks with high state projects retain their loans and pay a tax of $t=\frac{1-(1-\pi)\gamma L}{\pi}-\frac{1-(1-\pi)(1-\delta)(D-V_L)}{\pi+\delta(1-\pi)}$ at date 2. If $\gamma(\pi H+(1-\pi)L)<1$, then the government can only bail out a fraction $\omega\equiv\frac{\pi((\pi+(1-\pi)\delta)\gamma H+(1-\pi)(1-\delta)(D-V_L)-1)}{(1-\pi)(\delta+\pi(1-\delta)(D-V_L)-(\pi+(1-\pi)\delta)\gamma L)}$ of the troubled long-term projects and the remaining $1-\omega$ fraction of the troubled long-term projects will either suffer from the moral hazard problem or be liquidated.*

Proof: See Appendix.

The government may not be able to bail out all the low-value projects because of limited resources. Limited resources seems like a realistic assumption because of political constraints or because taxes are distortionary, so that in a larger model the social welfare-maximizing government would choose not to bail out all the low-value projects.

C. Discussion

As mentioned in the introduction, government bailouts of banking systems have recently become very common. Modern versions of the U.S. Reconstruction Finance Corporation have been used in many countries. In Mexico, for example, the Tequila crisis of 1994–1995 resulted in massive losses for Mexican banks. A public restructuring vehicle, the Trust Fund for the Protection of Bank Savings [the Fondo Bancario de Proteccion al Ahorro (FOBAPROA)], was initially used to (in part) buy loans from banks [see Honohan (no date) and Jose De Luna Martinez (2000)]. The FOBAPROA purchased nonperforming loans in an amount equal to twice the private contribution to capital, including subordinated debt, made by existing and new shareholders. The loans were purchased at book value (net of provisions) with ten-year zero coupon bonds. As Woo (2000) observes: "By purchasing the nonperforming loans from banks at book value, the FOBAPROA was essentially offering the banks free capital or a subsidy" (p. 11, footnote 14).

Argentinean banks also suffered during the Tequila crisis and the subsequent bank restructuring also involved public assistance from newly established public entities (see Augusto De la Torre, 2000). In Thailand, the Financial Institutions Development Fund—a distinct public entity—was established following the crisis of 1997. In Bulgaria, the government issued "Zunk" bond, government bonds that it used to substitute for unrecoverable bank loans. Cameroon also established a public vehicle, the Société de Recouvrement des Créances that replaced bad loans with government obligations on bank balance sheets. In Japan, there is the Financial Reconstruction Commission (see Hiroshi Nakaso, 1999). And there are many other examples (see Andrew Sheng, 1996; William Alexander et al., 1997; Charles Enoch et al., 1999; Lindgren et al., 1999; Klingebiel, 2000).

Bailouts are not without controversy. One issue concerns whether such government safety nets generate incentive problems that we have not included in the model. For example, in our model, entrepreneurs do not have an effort choice that determines the probability of the high and low state. If they had such a choice, anticipating that the government will bail them out in the low state, entrepreneurs would shirk and free ride on other entrepreneurs' efforts (those who work hard and pay taxes to finance the bailouts). Then the *ex post* efficient government bailouts may cause an *ex ante* efficiency loss. And consequently, governments would like to commit to only bailout entrepreneurs under certain circumstances. This is an interesting and important topic, which we are pursuing.[18]

VI. Conclusion

Bailouts by the government occur when the amount of the assets to be sold is so large that it would be inefficient for private agents to have hoarded liquid resources to purchase these assets in a short period of time. When the banking system is insolvent, private agents cannot readily buy the assets of the banks; it is simply not feasible since private agents lack liquidity. The government can improve welfare by creating this liquidity. However, forbearance occurs when the government cannot bail out all banks, corresponding to a situation where the government's tax capacity in the short run is too small.[19] These arguments stem from the basic idea that not all assets can be used to purchase other assets at every date.

[18]The obvious moral hazard problem seems to be hard to detect in empirical work, suggesting that the situation is more complicated. See Gorton and Winton (2003) for a survey of the literature.

[19]In our model, the constraint on the government is the amount that can be taxed at date 2. If this is too low, then not all banks can be bailed out. In reality, there may also be political constraints that prevent the government

"Liquidity" refers to the amount of readily available resources that can be used to purchase claims on projects when they are offered for sale at later dates. Not all resources can be used to buy projects. When there is a "liquidity-in-advance" constraint, the price at which claims can be sold is not just determined by the available information on their payoffs. Liquidity considerations result in prices that deviate from "efficient" market prices (i.e., the conditional expectation of the payoffs on the claim). A "liquidity discount" can arise.

At the root of the problem is the inability of private agents to buy insurance against declines in the value of their equity. Equity insurance is not available at date 0. Such insurance would have entrepreneurs with high-value projects insure entrepreneurs with low-value projects. But, this cannot occur. The incompleteness in markets raises the possibility that investment in the short-term project, what we have called hoarding, can be a desirable investment. Such investors commit to stand ready at subsequent dates to buy claims should they be offered for sale. These liquidity suppliers provide a valuable service when lender forgiveness is not optimal. But, from society's point of view it is costly to have agents engage in this activity. The government can overcome the lack of an equity insurance market by subsidizing either distressed firms or banks.

Empirically studying bailouts, and testing the model, seems like an interesting, but difficult, agenda. In reality, the issues we have discussed are complicated by the nature of the country's bankruptcy code, or lack of bankruptcy code, as well as fiscal and political considerations. Some progress is being made, however, in the form of interesting case studies. For example, in addition to the studies of bailouts and restructuring mentioned above, Enoch et al. (2002) study the transition economies, Guonan Ma and Ben S. C. Fung (2002) study China, and Mari Pangestu and Manggi Habir (2002) study Indonesia.

Appendix

Proof of Lemma 1: If the bank forgives the debt at date 1, the maximum the bank can get in the low state is $f = \gamma L$. The face value of the debt, F, that was set at date 0, must be high enough such that $\pi F + (1-\pi)\gamma L \geq 1$, or $F \geq \frac{1-(1-\pi)\gamma L}{\pi}$. But, in order for the bank to be willing to forgive debt, it must be the case that $\gamma L \geq \delta F$. Combining these two conditions, we get that $\gamma L \geq \frac{\delta}{\pi + \delta(1-\pi)}$.

Proof of Lemma 2: Suppose the liquidation price is Q and an entrepreneur who took the short-term project has realized a cash flow of r. If $r \geq Q$, then he can afford to buy a troubled project by using his own money and no risk will be added. If $r < Q$, then he will have to borrow $Q - r$ to buy the project. He adds risk if and only if $Q - r > \gamma L$. The payoff to buying a project is $L - Q$ if risk is not added, and is $\delta TL - Q$ if risk is added.

If $Q > L$, the liquidation price is greater than the continuation value of the troubled project even if risk is not added. Therefore, no one will buy. If $Q \leq \delta TL$, buying a troubled project is profitable even if risk is added and all liquidity suppliers want to buy. If $\delta TL < Q \leq L$, then buying a troubled project is profitable only if risk is not added. Therefore, only those liquidity suppliers with $r \geq Q - \gamma L$ will buy troubled projects.

from raising taxes. For example, see Thomas Romer and Barry Weingast (1992) with regard to the U.S. thrift crisis.

Proof of Lemma 3: At date 1, the total measure of troubled projects is $\alpha(1-\pi)$. The total measure of liquidity at a price $Q \in [\delta TL, L]$ is $(1-\alpha)\left(1-\frac{Q-\gamma L}{R}\right)$.

If $(1-\alpha)\left(1-\frac{\delta TL-\gamma L}{R}\right) \le \alpha(1-\pi)$, then liquidity demand is so high that there is no liquidation price, Q, with $Q > \delta TL$, that clears the liquidation market. Bertrand competition then drives the price down to the reservation value of δTL.

If $\alpha(1-\pi) \le (1-\alpha)\left(1-\frac{L-\gamma L}{R}\right)$, then there is an excess supply of liquidity at date 1. The price is at its highest level, L.

Finally, if $(1-\alpha)\left(1-\frac{L-\gamma L}{R}\right) < \alpha(1-\pi) < (1-\alpha)\left(1-\frac{\delta LT-\gamma L}{R}\right)$, then there exists a $Q \in (\delta TL, L)$ that clears the market. Equating liquidity demand to liquidity supply: $(1-\alpha)\left(1-\frac{Q-\gamma L}{R}\right) = \alpha(1-\pi)$, results in $Q = \gamma L + R\left(1-\frac{\alpha(1-\pi)}{1-\alpha}\right)$. All those entrepreneurs with $r \ge \delta TL - \gamma L$ get projects and will not add risk.

Proof of Proposition 2: Suppose the liquidation price is Q. We know that Q must be in the interval $[\delta TL, L]$. At date 0, the expected payoff to the long-term project is $\pi H + (1-\pi)Q$, which is increasing in Q; the expected payoff to the short-term project is $1 + \frac{R}{2} + (L - Q)\left(1-\frac{Q-\gamma L}{R}\right)$, which is decreasing in Q. When liquidation price Q is δTL, the value of the long-term project reaches its minimum $\pi H + (1-\pi)\delta TL$, and the value of the short-term project reaches its maximum $1 + \frac{R}{2} + (L-\delta TL) \times \left(1-\frac{\delta TL-\gamma L}{R}\right)$. *If* $\pi H + (1-\pi)\delta TL > 1 + \frac{R}{2} + (L-\delta TL)\left(1-\frac{\delta TL-\gamma L}{R}\right)$, then taking the long-term project dominates taking the short-term project. In that case, all entrepreneurs choose the long-term project at date 0. Suppose $\pi H + (1-\pi)\delta TL \le 1 + \frac{R}{2} + (L-\delta TL) \times \left(1-\frac{\delta TL-\gamma L}{R}\right)$. Recall that we have assumed that $\pi H + (1-\pi)L > 1 + R/2$. Therefore, there exists a unique $Q^* \in [\delta TL, L]$ such that $\pi H + (1-\pi)Q^* = 1 + \frac{R}{2} + (L-Q^*) \times \left(1-\frac{Q^*-\gamma L}{R}\right)$. Solving for Q^*, we get:

$$Q^* = \frac{(2-\pi)R+(1+\gamma)L-\sqrt{((2-\pi)R+(1+\gamma)L)^2-4\left(R\left(1+\frac{R}{2}-\pi H+L\right)+\gamma L^2\right)}}{2}.$$

To obtain α^*, the secondary liquidation market must be cleared at date 1, i.e., $(1-\alpha) \times \left(1-\frac{Q^*-\gamma L}{R}\right) = \alpha(1-\pi)$. Solving this equation gives: $\alpha^* = \frac{R+\gamma L-Q^*}{(2-\pi)R+\gamma L-Q^*}$.

Proof of Proposition 3 and Corollary 1:

(1) Define:

$$G(\pi, \delta, R, Q^*) = \pi H + (1-\pi)Q^* - 1 - \frac{R}{2} - (L-Q^*)\left(1-\frac{Q^*-\gamma L}{R}\right).$$

$$\frac{\partial Q^*}{\partial R} = -\frac{\partial G/\partial R}{\partial G/\partial Q^*} = \frac{\frac{1}{2}+\frac{(L-Q^*)(Q^*-\gamma L)}{R^2}}{(1-\pi)+\left(1-\frac{Q^*-\gamma L}{R}\right)+\frac{L-Q^*}{R}} > 0;$$

$$\frac{\partial Q^*}{\partial \pi} = -\frac{\partial G/\partial \pi}{\partial G/\partial Q^*} = \frac{H-Q^*}{(1-\pi)+\left(1-\frac{Q^*-\gamma L}{R}\right)+\frac{L-Q^*}{R}} < 0;$$

$$\frac{\partial Q^*}{\partial \delta} = -\frac{\partial G/\partial \delta}{\partial G/\partial Q^*} = \frac{\frac{(L-Q^*)L(T-1)}{R(1-\delta)^2}}{(1-\pi)+\left(1-\frac{Q^*-\gamma L}{R}\right)+\frac{L-Q^*}{R}} < 0.$$

(2) To prove that social welfare is increasing in R and decreasing in δ, we use the expected payoff to entrepreneurs who take the long-term project. Define $W = \pi H + (1-\pi)Q^*$. Then: $\frac{\partial W}{\partial R} = (1-\pi)\frac{\partial Q^*}{\partial R} > 0$, and $\frac{\partial W}{\partial \delta} = (1-\pi)\frac{\partial Q^*}{\partial \delta} < 0$. To prove that social welfare is increasing in π, we use the expected payoff to entrepreneurs who take the short-term project. Define $W = 1 + \frac{R}{2} + (L-Q^*)\left(1-\frac{Q^*-\gamma L}{R}\right)$. Then, $\frac{\partial W}{\partial \pi} = -\left(\frac{(L-Q^*)}{R} + 1 - \frac{Q^*-\gamma L}{R}\right)\frac{\partial Q^*}{\partial \pi} > 0.$

Proof of Proposition 4: Suppose the face value of the debt is F and the government levies t on each bank at date 2. $F - t$ is the net payment a bank receives from a loan in the high state. When the government buys the loans from banks at date 1, the minimum price it has to pay to the banks is $\delta(F-t)$, which is the payoff banks with low-state projects can get if risk is added. And, in order to remove the incentive to engage in moral hazard, the government has to forgive the face value of the debt to less than or equal to γL. Therefore, $\delta(F-t) - \gamma L$ is the necessary subsidy to bail out a troubled project. The government has a budget constraint condition: $\pi t \geq (1-\pi)(\delta(F-t) - \gamma L)$. Banks have to break even, so we have $\pi(F-t) + (1-\pi)\delta(F-t) \geq 1$. Finally, the face value of the debt cannot be too high; otherwise even entrepreneurs in the high state will add risk. So, we must have $F \leq \gamma H$. Combining these conditions, we obtain $\gamma(\pi H + (1-\pi)L) \geq 1$. The equilibrium is the solution to the following system of equations: $P = \delta(F-t), \pi t = (1-\pi)(P - \gamma L), \pi(F-t) + (1-\pi)P = 1$. Solving for the equilibrium gives us: $F = \frac{1-(1-\pi)\gamma L}{\pi}$, $P = \frac{\delta}{\pi+\delta(1-\pi)}$, and $t = \frac{1-(1-\pi)\gamma L}{\pi} - \frac{1}{\pi+\delta(1-\pi)}$.

Proof of Proposition 5: When $\gamma(\pi H + (1-\pi)L) < 1$, the first-best outcome characterized in Proposition 4 is not feasible because the government lacks enough resources to bail out all distressed long-term projects. The government chooses the loan price, P, tax on high projects, t, and bails out a fraction, ω, of the low state projects. We first suppose that there is private liquidity supply [i.e., Q solves $\pi H + (1-\pi)[\omega L + (1-\omega)Q] = 1 + \frac{R}{2} + (L-Q)\left(1-\frac{Q-\gamma L}{R}\right)$] and show that the government's optimal choice is to maximize ω.

Define $J(\pi,\delta,R,Q) = \pi H + (1-\pi)[\omega L + (1-\omega)Q] = 1 + \frac{R}{2} + (L-Q)\left(1-\frac{Q-\gamma L}{R}\right)$.

$$\frac{\partial Q}{\partial \omega} = -\frac{\partial J/\partial \omega}{\partial J/\partial Q} = -\frac{(1-\pi)(L-Q)}{(1-\pi)(1-\omega)+\left(1-\frac{Q-\gamma L}{R}\right)+\frac{L-Q}{R}} < 0.$$

In equilibrium the expected payoff to entrepreneurs who take the long-term project and the expected payoff to entrepreneurs who take the short-term project are the same, which is equal to $\pi H + (1-\pi)[\omega L + (1-\omega)Q]$. We show it is increasing in ω.

Define $W = \pi H + (1-\pi)[\omega L + (1-\omega)Q]$.

$$\frac{\partial W}{\partial R} = (1-\pi)\left[(L-Q) + (1-\omega)\frac{\partial Q}{\partial \omega}\right] = (1-\pi)(L-Q)\frac{\left(1-\frac{Q-\gamma L}{R}\right)+\frac{L-Q}{R}}{(1-\pi)(1-\omega)+\left(1-\frac{Q-\gamma L}{R}\right)+\frac{L-Q}{R}} > 0.$$

By constraint (4), in order to maximize ω, the government needs to minimize P. To satisfy constraint (2), P will be set to equal $\delta(F-t)$, which is the expected payoff banks receive if risk is added to low state projects, and is also the expected payoff banks receive in case the projects are sold because the bargaining power is in the hands of entrepreneurs. Substituting $P = \delta(F - t)$ into constraint (3), we get $\pi(F - t) + (1 - \pi)\delta(F - t) = 1$, or $t = F - \frac{1}{\pi + (1-\pi)\delta}$.

Since the government has to subsidize each troubled project by the amount $\delta(F - t) - \gamma L$, the fraction of troubled projects that can be subsidized is equal to $\frac{(\pi+(1-\pi)\delta)F-1}{(1-\pi)(\delta F-\gamma L)}$. This fraction is maximized when F is equal to γH. The maximum is equal to $\omega^* \equiv \frac{\pi((\pi+(1-\pi)\delta)\gamma H-1)}{(1-\pi)(\delta-(\pi+(1-\pi)\delta)\gamma L)}$. Note that ω is always less than one because we have $\gamma(\pi H + (1 - \pi)L) < 1$. The remaining $(1 - \omega)$ projects cannot be bailed out by the government. Risk will be added to these projects if they are not liquidated. Then the question is whether there are liquidity suppliers in the secondary market. We need to check whether a deviation to the short-term project is profitable if all other entrepreneurs take the long-term project.

Suppose $\pi H + (1 - \pi)[\omega^* L + (1 - \omega^*)\delta TL] > 1 + \frac{R}{2} + (L - \delta TL)$, i.e., there is no entrepreneur willing to supply liquidity. Can the government lower ω to improve welfare? The answer is no. Suppose the government lowers ω to a certain level such that some entrepreneurs are willing to invest in the short-term project. According to the proof above, the governments will set ω as high as possible, so the maximum point is reached when $Q = \delta TL$. But when $Q = \delta TL$, welfare must be less than $\pi H + (1 - \pi)[\omega^* L + (1 - \omega^*)\delta TL]$ because ω cannot be larger than ω^*.

Similar to the proof of Proposition 2, we can solve for Q^* and α^*. Since entrepreneurs must be indifferent between taking the short-term project and taking the long-term project at date 1, the liquidation price Q^* must satisfy $\pi H + (1 - \pi)[\omega L + (1 - \omega)Q] = 1 + \frac{R}{2} + (L - Q)\left(1 - \frac{Q-\gamma L}{R}\right)$. Solving for Q^*, we get:

$$Q^* = \frac{(1+(1-\omega)(1-\pi))R+(1+\gamma)L-\sqrt{((1+(1-\omega)(1-\pi))R+(1+\gamma)L)^2-4\left(R\left(1+\frac{R}{2}-\pi H+L(1-\omega(1-\pi))\right)+\gamma L^2\right)}}{2}$$

Finally, substituting Q^* into the market-clearing condition at date 1 gives: $\alpha(1 - \pi)(1 - \omega) = (1 - \alpha)\left(1 - \frac{Q^*-\gamma L}{R}\right)$. Solving this equation gives us $\alpha^* = \frac{R+\gamma L-Q^*}{(1+(1-\pi)(1-\omega))R+\gamma L-Q^*}$.

Proof of Lemma 4: The bank can get at most L from forgiveness or liquidation. In these cases, its equity is negative. Therefore, the bank will not forgive debt or sell the project, forcing continuation with risk added. In that case, there is still some hope that the bank will be solvent at date 2.

Proof of Proposition 6: If the systematic shock turns out to be high, i.e., V is equal to V_H, then there will be debt forgiveness and the value of the project is L in the low state. If the systematic shock turns out to be low, i.e., V is equal to V_L, then there will be no debt forgiveness by Lemma 4 and the value of the project is δTL in the low state. Therefore the expected payoff from taking the long-term project is $\pi H + (1 - \pi)[(1 - \theta)\delta TL + \theta L]$. On the other hand, if an entrepreneur takes a short-term project, there is no chance for him to buy a troubled project and hence the expected payoff is $1 + \frac{R}{2}$. At date 0 entrepreneurs make investment decisions by comparing these two expected values.

Proof of Proposition 7: If $\pi H + (1 - \pi)\delta TL > 1 + \frac{R}{2} + \theta(L - \delta TL)\left(1 - \frac{\delta TL-\gamma L}{R}\right)$, then the return to the long-term project dominates that of the short-term project even if the date 1 liquidation price is at its reservation value δTL. Therefore, no entrepreneur invests in the short-term project at date 0. If $\pi H + (1-\pi)[(1-\theta)\delta TL + \theta L] \leq 1 + \frac{R}{2}$, then even if the troubled project can be sold for its maximum value of L in the liquidation market, θ is so low that, *ex ante*, the payoff from a long-term project is less than the payoff from a short-term project. No entrepreneur chooses the long-term project at date 0. Suppose $\pi H + (1-\pi)\delta TL \leq 1 + \frac{R}{2} + \theta(L - \delta TL)\left(1 - \frac{\delta TL - \gamma L}{R}\right)$ and $\pi H + (1-\pi) \times [(1-\theta)\delta TL + \theta L] > 1 + \frac{R}{2}$. Then there is a unique liquidation price, Q^*, that solves the equation: $\pi H + (1-\pi)[(1-\theta)\delta TL + \theta Q] = 1 + \frac{R}{2} + \theta(L-Q)\left(1 - \frac{Q-\gamma L}{R}\right)$. Solving this equation, we get

$$Q^* = \frac{(2-\pi)R+(1+\gamma)L-\sqrt{((2-\pi)R+(1+\gamma)L)^2-4\left(\frac{R}{\theta}\left(1+\frac{R}{2}-\pi H-(1-\pi)(1-\theta)\delta TL+\theta L\right)+\gamma L^2\right)}}{2}.$$

At Q^* an individual entrepreneur is indifferent between choosing the long-term project or the short-term project at date 0. Equilibrium project choice must be consistent with Q^* , so α^* is the solution to the equation: $(1-\alpha)\left(1 - \frac{Q^*-\gamma L}{R}\right) = \alpha(1-\pi)$. Solving for α^*, we get $\alpha^* = \frac{R+\gamma L - Q^*}{(2-\pi)R + \gamma L - Q^*}$.

Proof of Corollary 2: When debt forgiveness is feasible, social welfare is equal to

$$\max\left\{\pi H + (1-\pi)[\theta L + (1-\theta)\delta TL], 1 + \frac{R}{2}\right\},$$

which is increasing in θ. Suppose debt forgiveness is not feasible. If all entrepreneurs take the short-term project or all entrepreneurs take the long-term project, there is no liquidation market. Social welfare is either $\pi H + (1-\pi)\delta TL$ or $1 + \frac{R}{2}$. If entrepreneurs choose different projects and there is a liquidation market at date 1, social welfare is equal to $\pi H + (1-\pi)[\theta Q + (1-\theta)\delta TL]$. Let $W(\theta) \equiv \pi H + (1-\pi)[\theta Q + (1-\theta)\delta TL$. We have $W'(\theta) = (1-\pi)[Q - \delta TL + \theta\frac{\partial Q}{\partial \theta} > 0$.

Proof of Lemma 5: To make V_L banks sell the troubled projects, the government has to pay a price, P', such that $V_L + P' - D \geq \delta(V_L + F - t - D)$. Rearranging the terms, we get $P' \geq \delta(F-t) + (1-\delta)(D - V_L)$.

Proof of Proposition 8: Suppose the face value of the debt is F and the government levies tax t on each bank at date 2. By Lemma 5, when the government buys the claims from banks at date 1, the minimum price it has to pay to the banks is $\delta(F-t) + (1-\delta)(D-V_L)$. And in order to remove the entrepreneurs' incentives to engage in moral hazard, the government has to forgive the face value of the debt to less than or equal to γL. The government has a budget constraint: $\pi t \geq (1-\pi)(\delta(F-t) + (1-\delta)(D-V_L) - \gamma L)$. Banks have to break even, so we have $\pi(F-t) + (1-\pi)(\delta(F-t) + (1-\delta)(D-V_L)) \geq 1$. Finally, the face value of the debt cannot be too high because otherwise even entrepreneurs in the high state will add risk. So, we must have $F \leq \gamma H$. Combining these conditions, we obtain $\gamma(\pi H + (1-\pi)L) \geq 1$. The equilibrium is the solution to the following system of equations: $P = \delta(F-t) + (1-\delta)(D-V_L)$, $\pi t = (1-\pi)(P - \gamma L)$, $\pi(F-t) + (1-\pi)P = 1$. Solving for the equilibrium gives us: $F = \frac{1-(1-\pi)\gamma L}{\pi}$, $P = \frac{\delta + \pi(1-\delta)(D-V_L)}{\pi + \delta(1-\pi)}$, and $t = \frac{1-(1-\pi)\gamma L}{\pi} - \frac{1-(1-\pi)(1-\delta)(D-V_L)}{\pi+\delta(1-\pi)}$.

Now suppose $\gamma(\pi H + (1-\pi)L) < 1$. Similar to the Proof of Proposition 5, the government chooses the largest possible ω to maximize its objective function. This is achieved by setting: $\pi(F-t) + (1-\pi)(\delta(F-t) + (1-\delta)(D-V_L)) = 1$, $P = \delta(F-t) + (1-\delta)(D-V_L)$, and $\pi t = (1-\pi)\omega(P-\gamma L)$, which correspond to the banks' break-even condition, incentive compatibility condition, and the government's budget constraint, respectively. Moreover, F takes its highest possible value, γH. The maximum fraction is equal to $\omega \equiv \frac{\pi((\pi+(1-\pi)\delta)\gamma H+(1-\pi)(1-\delta)(D-V_L)-1)}{(1-\pi)(\delta+\pi(1-\delta)(D-V_L)-(\pi+(1-\pi)\delta)\gamma L)}$. Note that ω is always less than one because we have $\gamma(\pi H + (1-\pi)L) < 1$. The remaining $(1-\omega)$ projects cannot be bailed out by the government and risk will be added to these projects if they are not liquidated.

The next question is whether there are liquidity suppliers in the secondary market. We need to check whether deviation to the short-term project is profitable if all other entrepreneurs take the long-term project. If all other entrepreneurs take the long-term project, and one entrepreneur takes the short-term project, then this entrepreneur is the sole liquidity supplier at date 1 and he can buy a troubled project at price δTL. His expected payoff from taking the short-term project is: If this entrepreneur does not deviate, his expected payoff is: $1 + \frac{R}{2} + \theta(L - \delta TL)\left(1 - \frac{\delta TL - \gamma L}{R}\right)$. If this entrepreneur does not deviate, his expected payoff is: $\pi H + (1-\pi)[\omega L + (1-\omega)\delta TL]$. Therefore, there are liquidity suppliers if and only if $\pi H + (1-\pi)[\omega L + (1-\omega)\delta TL] \leq 1 + \frac{R}{2} + \theta(L - \delta TL)\left(1 - \frac{\delta TL - \gamma L}{R}\right)$.

The remainder of the proof is similar to the Proof of Proposition 2. Since entrepreneurs must be indifferent between taking the short-term project and taking the long-term project at date 1, the liquidation price Q^* must satisfy:

$$\pi H + (1-\pi)[\omega L + (1-\omega)(\theta Q + (1-\theta)\delta TL)] = 1 + \frac{R}{2} + \theta(L-Q)\left(1 - \frac{Q-\gamma L}{R}\right).$$

Solving for Q^*, we get:

$$Q^* = \frac{(1+(1-\omega)(1-\pi))R+(1+\gamma)L-\sqrt{((1+(1-\omega)(1-\pi))R+(1+\gamma)L)^2-4\left(\frac{R}{\theta}\left(1+\frac{R}{2}-\pi H+L(\theta-\omega(1-\pi))-(1-\pi)(1-\omega)(1-\theta)\delta TL\right)+\gamma L^2\right)}}{2}.$$

Once we get Q^*, we plug Q^* into the market-clearing condition at date 1: $\alpha(1-\pi)(1-\omega) = (1-\alpha)\left(1 - \frac{Q-\gamma L}{R}\right)$. Solving this equation gives us: $\alpha^* = \frac{R+\gamma L-Q^*}{(1+(1-\pi)(1-\omega))R+\gamma L-Q^*}$.

References

Alexander, William; Davis, Jeffrey; Ebrill, Liam and Lindgren, Carl-John. *Systemic bank restructuring and macroeconomic policy*. Washington, DC: International Monetary Fund, 1997.

Allen, Franklin and Gale, Douglas. "Optimal Financial Crises." *Journal of Finance*, August 1998, *53*(4), pp. 1245–84.

Barth, James. *The great savings and loan debacle*. Washington, DC: AEI Press, 1991.

Barth, James and Bartholomew, Philip. "The Thrift Industry Crisis: Revealed Weaknesses in the Federal Deposit Insurance System," in James Barth and R. Dan Brumbaugh, Jr., eds., *The reform of federal deposit insurance: Disciplining the government and protecting taxpayers*. New York: HarperBusiness, 1992, pp. 36–116.

Bean, Mary L.; Hodge, Martha; Ostermiller, William; Spaid, Mike and Stockton, Steve. "Executive Summary: Resolution and Asset Disposition Practices in Federal Deposit Insurance

Corporation," in *Managing the crisis: The FDIC and RTC experience, 1980–1994*. Washington, DC: FDIC, 1998, pp. 3-52.

Bhattacharya, Sudipto and Gale, Douglas M. "Preference Shocks, Liquidity, and Central Bank Policy," in William A. Barnett and Kenneth J. Singleton, eds., *New approaches to monetary economics: Proceedings of the second international symposium in economic theory and econometrics*. Cambridge, MA: Cambridge University Press, 1987, pp. 69–88.

Brumbaugh, R. Dan, Jr. *Thrifts under siege*. Cambridge, MA: Ballinger Publishing Company, 1988.

Calomiris, Charles. "Is the Discount Window Necessary? A Penn Central Perspective" *Federal Reserve Bank of St. Louis Review*, May/June 1994, pp. 31–55.

Caprio, Gerard and Klingebiel, Daniela. "Bank Insolvencies: Cross Country Experience." World Bank Policy Research Working Paper No. 1620, 1996.

——. "Episodes of Systemic and Borderline Financial Crises." Mimeo, World Bank, 1999.

Claessens, Stijn; Djankov, Simeon and Klingebiel, Daniela. "Financial Restructuring in East Asia: Halfway There?" World Bank Financial Sector Discussion Paper No. 3, 1999.

Daniel, James A. "Fiscal Aspects of Bank Restructuring." Working paper, International Monetary Fund, 1997.

De la Torre, Augusto. "Resolving Bank Failures in Argentina: Recent Developments and Issues." World Bank Policy Research Working Paper No. 2295, 2000.

De Luna Martinez, Jose. "Management and Resolution of Banking Crises: Lessons from the Republic of Korea and Mexico." World Bank Discussion Paper No. 413, 2000.

Diamond, Douglas W. "Liquidity, Banks, and Markets." *Journal of Political Economy*, October 1997, *105*(5), pp. 928–56.

Diamond, Douglas W. and Dybvig, Philip H. "Bank Runs, Deposit Insurance, and Liquidity." *Journal of Political Economy*, June 1983, *91*(3), pp. 401–19.

Diamond, Douglas W. and Rajan, Raghuram. "Liquidity Risk, Liquidity Creation, and Financial Fragility: A Theory of Banking." *Journal of Political Economy*, April 2001, *109*(2), pp. 287–327.

——. "Bank Bailouts and Aggregate Liquidity." Unpublished manuscript, University of Chicago, 2002.

Dziobek, Claudia and Pazarbasioglu, Ceyla. "Lessons from Systemic Bank Restructuring: A Survey of 24 Countries." International Monetary Fund Working Paper No. 97/161, December 1997.

——. "Lessons From Systemic Bank Restructuring." International Monetary Fund *Economic Issues*, No. 14, 1998.

Eisfeldt, Andrea. "Endogenous Liquidity in Asset Markets." Unpublished manuscript, Kellogg School, Northwestern University, 2002.

Enoch, Charles; Garcia, Gillian and Sundararajan, V. "Recapitalizing Banks with Public Funds: Selected Issues." International Monetary Fund Working Paper No. 99/139, 1999.

Enoch, Charles; Gulde, Anne-Marie and Hardy, Daniel. "Banking Crises and Bank Resolution: Experiences in Some Transition Economies." International Monetary Fund Working Paper No. 02/56, 2002.

Goodhart, Charles A. E. *The central bank and the financial system*. London: Macmillan, 1995.

Gorton, Gary and Huang, Lixin. "Bank Panics and the Endogeneity of Central Banking." Working paper, Wharton School, 2001.

Gorton, Gary and Kahn, James. "The Design of Bank Loan Contracts." *Review of Financial Studies*, Summer 2000, *13*(2), pp. 331–54.

Gorton, Gary and Pennacchi, George. "Financial Intermediaries and Liquidity Creation." *Journal of Finance*, March 1990, *45*(1), pp. 49–71.

Gorton, Gary and Winton, Andrew. "Financial Intermediation," in George Constantinides, Milton Harris, and René Stulz, eds., *Handbook of the economics of finance*. Amsterdam: North-Holland, 2003, pp. 431–552.

Grossman, Sanford J. "An Analysis of the Implications for Stock and Futures Price Volatility of Program Trading and Dynamic Hedging Strategies." *Journal of Business*, July 1988, *61*(3), pp. 275–98.

Hawkins, John and Turner, Philip. "Bank Restructuring in Practice: An Overview." Bank for International Settlements Policy Paper No. 6, 1999.

Holmström, Bengt and Tirole, Jean. "Private and Public Supply of Liquidity." *Journal of Political Economy*, February 1998, *106*(1), pp. 1–40.

Honohan, Patrick. "Recapitalizing Banking Systems: Implications for Incentives and Fiscal and Monetary Policy." World Bank Working Paper No. 2540 (no date).
Honohan, Patrick and Klingebiel, Daniela. "Controlling Fiscal Costs of Bank Crises." World Bank Working Paper No. 2441, 2000.
Hopenhayn, Hugo A. and Werner, Ingrid M. "Information, Liquidity, and Asset Trading in a Random Matching Game." *Journal of Economic Theory*, February 1996, *68*(2), pp. 349–79.
Iacocca, Lee and Novak, William. *Iacoca: An autobiography*. New York: Bantam Books, 1986.
Kane, Edward. "Dangers of Capital Forbearance: The Case of the FSLIC and 'Zombie' S&Ls." *Contemporary Policy Issues*, January 1987, *5*(1), pp. 77–83.
——. *The S&L mess: How did it happen?* Washington, DC: Urban Institute Press, 1989.
Kane, Edward J. and Yu, Min-Teh. "Opportunity Cost of Capital Forbearance during the Final Years of the FSLIC Mess." *Quarterly Review of Economics and Finance*, Fall 1996, *36*(3), pp. 271–90.
Klingebiel, Daniela. "The Use of Asset Management Companies in the Resolution of Banking Crises: Cross-Country Experience." World Bank Policy Research Working Paper No. 2284, 2000.
Kyle, Albert S. "Continuous Auctions and Insider Trading." *Econometrica*, November 1985, *53*(6), pp. 1335–55.
Lindgren, Carl-Johan; Baliño, Toniás J. T.; Enoch, Charles; Gulde, Anne-Marie; Quintyn, Marc and Teo, Leslie. "Financial Sector Crisis and Restructuring: Lessons From Asia." International Monetary Fund Occasional Paper No. 188, 1999.
Lowenstein, Roger. *When genius failed*. New York: Random House, 2000.
Lummer, Scott and McConnell, John. "Further Evidence on the Bank Lending Process and the Capital-Market-Responses to Bank Loan Agreements." *Journal of Financial Economics*, November 1989, *25*(1), pp. 99–122.
Ma, Guonan and Fung, Ben S. C. "China's Asset Management Corporations." Bank for International Settlements Working Paper No. 115, 2002.
Mason, Joseph. "Reconstruction Finance Corporation Assistance to Financial Institutions and Commercial & Industrial Enterprise in the U.S. Great Depression, 1932–1937," in Stijn Claessens, Simeon Djankov, and Ashoka Mody, eds., *Resolution of financial distress*. Washington, DC: World Bank Press, 2001, pp. 167–204.
Nakaso, Hiroshi. "Recent Banking Sector Reforms in Japan." *Economic Policy Review*, Federal Reserve Bank of New York, July 1999, *5*(2), pp. 1–7.
Olson, James Stuart. *Herbert Hoover and the Reconstruction Finance Corporation, 1931–1933*. Ames, LA: Iowa State University Press, 1977.
Pangestu, Mari and Habir, Manggi. "The Boom, Bust, and Restructuring of Indonesian Banks." International Monetary Fund Working Paper No. 02/66, 2002.
Romer, Thomas and Weingast, Barry. "Political Foundations of the Thrift Debacle," in James Barth and R. Dan Brumbaugh, Jr., eds., *The reform of federal deposit insurance: Disciplining the government and protecting tax payers*. New York: HarperBusiness, 1992, pp. 167–202.
Sheng, Andrew. *Bank restructuring: Lessons from the 1980s*. Washington, DC: World Bank, 1996.
Shleifer, Andrei and Vishny, Robert. "Liquidation Values and Debt Capacity: A Market Equilibrium Approach." *Journal of Finance*, September 1992, *47*(4), pp. 1343–66.
Stone, Mark. "Corporate Sector Restructuring: The Role of Government in Times of Crisis." *Economic Issues*, International Monetary Fund, June 2002, *31*.
Todd, Walker. "History of and Rationales for the Reconstruction Finance Corporation." Federal Reserve Bank of Cleveland. *Economic Review*, Quarter 4, 1992, pp. 22–35.
White, Lawrence. *The S&L debacle: Public policy lessons for bank and thrift regulation*.New York: Oxford University Press, 1991.
Woo, David. "Two Approaches to Resolving Nonperforming Assets During Financial Crises." International Monetary Fund Working Paper No. 00/03, 2000.

10 Financial Crises, Payment System Problems, and Discount Window Lending

Mark J. Flannery

A developed economy's basic infrastructure must include a cheap, reliable payment system to facilitate the mutually profitable exchanges required for agents to exploit economies of specialization. A better payment system permits risks to be spread more efficiently, makes prices more informative, and enhances the allocation of real resources. If payments cannot be effected cheaply and reliably, social welfare is constrained to a lower level. Modern economies possess complex payment systems that successfully transmit numerous daily payments, totaling a large fraction of the typical country's GDP. A staggering velocity of monetary claims can be attained in these systems, largely because institutional arrangements have evolved that substitute credit exposures for the immediate payment of "good money" (Goodfriend 1991).[1] The payment system's credit component constitutes its (potential) Achilles' heel: if traders lose faith in their counterparties' abilities to pay as promised, the costs of transacting within a credit-based system can rise dramatically. The close interconnection of many financial institutions through the payment system has raised public concerns that one firm's failure could jeopardize the solvency of many others.[2] Because the payment system is so crucial to a modem economy's functioning, its potential failure—"payment system risk"—elicits great concern: "without doubt the most important public policy issue of global application is the containment or elimination of payment system risk" (Morris 1994, p. 18). The proper role of a government lender of last resort (LLR) in producing payment system stability has become an increasingly relevant and important question in recent years.

Many writers contend that the government or central bank must sometimes act as a lender of last resort (LLR), standing ready to provide liquidity to individual banks which cannot fund themselves in private markets. Goodhart (1988, ch. 7) bases this conclusion on the fact that banking firms specialize in financing assets which are intrinsically hard to value. An illiquid bank may have trouble convincing private lenders of its solvency, giving rise to the common prescription that the LLR should lend to "solvent, but illiquid" banks. The difficulty, of course, lies in determining which illiquid banks are solvent. If the government has better information about banks' solvency than market investors do, the optimal social policy might be for the central bank to lend directly to illiquid institutions.

[1]The annual transactions velocity of demand deposit balances in major NYC banks has risen from 503 in 1977 to 4,481 in 1995 (Federal Reserve *Bulletin*, various issues).

[2]McAndrews and Wasilyew (1995) provide a recent example.

However, if private lenders possess (or, absent a government LLR, *could* possess) more accurate estimates of bank solvency, the argument for direct LLR loans becomes less tenable.

Open market operations can always provide liquidity to the financial system, but how should that liquidity be allocated to individual firms in a crisis? Goodfriend and King (1988) contend that the monetary authority *should never lend to individual banks* because private lenders can best identify solvent-but-illiquid institutions. Kaufman (1991) and Schwartz (1992) enthusiastically endorse this view that a central bank should limit its "lender of last resort" activities to providing general market liquidity through open market operations. According to these authors, the main danger (social cost) of extending LLR credit to individual banks is that the central bank will be inclined to support insolvent institutions, thus blunting market discipline and producing riskier, less-efficient banks. [Rochet and Tirole (1996) evaluate a similar problem.] In the context of payment system stability, direct government lending (for example, daylight overdrafts) subsidizes payments made via the central bank's large-dollar payment system, blunting private initiatives to produce safer payment arrangements.

This paper evaluates whether private credit markets can, in fact, be relied upon to channel liquidity to the appropriate banking firms during a "financial crisis." I begin by defining two main features of a "financial crisis" in a developed economy. First, at least a few large banks (and/or perhaps many small ones) experience a liquidity shock, most likely because bank creditors suddenly become concerned that some banks may be insolvent. Aharoney and Swary (1983), Swary (1986), and Musumeci and Sinkey (1990) demonstrate that a negative surprise about one bank's condition depresses equity prices at other banks with similar credit risk exposures.[3] Informed depositors should similarly revise their assessments of the same banks, and a sufficiently large shock could set off substantial withdrawals from the exposed banks. The second essential feature of a financial crisis is that the initial liquidity shock makes private lenders uncertain about the accuracy (appropriateness) of their traditional underwriting techniques and judgments. Just when some banks require credit from new sources on short notice, potential lenders become uncertain about how to identify borrower solvency. Section 2 presents a simple model in which information costs during a "financial crisis" prevent private lenders from redistributing aggregate liquidity to firms that truly deserve it. *In this model open market operations cannot replace direct LLR lending to specific institutions.*

Although my model could be applied to any type of firm, I evaluate the efficacy of direct discount window lending in the context of a payment system crisis because private credit arrangements seem most likely to falter in this situation. During a payment system crisis, troubled institutions' liquidity problems must be resolved within (at most) a few hours. Arguably, many private lenders will be unable to gather and evaluate appropriate credit information in such a short interval. If the payment problems occur in the context of a financial crisis, aggregate liquidity may not flow to the appropriate banks—even if it would do so in "normal" times. Confronted with a private credit market failure, there may be a positive role for government in assuring payment system stability.[4]

[3]In Flannery (1994), I argue that these findings support the market's rational ability to separate banks that are affected by the news from those that are not. Such discrimination bodes well for the market's ability to evaluate and discipline risky banks during "normal" times.

[4]The primary motive for government interventions in the private sector should be that intervention improves on market solution.

The paper proceeds as follows. Section 1 describes the economic value of a cheap, safe payment system, and discusses the alternative means of organizing payments among numerous counterparties. From the variety of possible payment methods, almost all modern payment systems have chosen arrangements that include credit extensions as an integral component. While this reliance on credit can be extremely efficient and appropriate in "normal" times, the emergence of a financial crisis can render a credit-based payment system unstable. Section 2 presents a simple model of private credit extensions under asymmetric information. The model is applied to a payment system liquidity crisis in the following section, which develops policies to govern the Federal Reserve's discount window operations. Section 4 concludes by summarizing the paper's main points.

1. Organizing Reliable Exchange

The economic effects of payment system transaction costs are illustrated in Figure 10.1, which describes investors' aggregate desire to trade a particular security.[5] The horizontal axis measures quantity traded, while the vertical axis measures price (for example, the sterling price of deutsche marks or the dollar price of DRAM chips). In a frictionless world, the equilibrium market price would be P^*, at a traded volume of Q^*. This equilibrium constitutes a social optimum because all traders who value the good at P^* or higher will actually own it, while those who value it at P^* or lower will be able to sell it.[6]

Transaction costs reduce the social welfare produced in this market by imposing a wedge between the seller's and buyer's prices. The transaction cost c_1 reduces the equilibrium quantity traded to Q_1, depriving traders of the welfare triangle ABC. If c_1 is indeed the irreducible cost of transacting, Q_1 represents the socially optimal level of trading in this commodity.

Transaction costs include both real resource costs and the counterparty risks generated by the trade's settlement procedure. Counterparty credit risks can be substantial for some transactions, such as a dollar-yen FX trade. Because FX trades require that payment be made in each currency's "home country," a dollar buyer may not be paid dollars even after delivering the promised yen. Hence, the dollar buyer's transaction costs include an expected credit cost ("Herstatt risk") equal to the counterparty's probability of default during the interval between Tokyo's and New York's close of business, multiplied by the trade's principal amount. The magnitude of this transaction cost component depends on the counterparty's creditworthiness, collateral, or netting arrangements, and the time lag between payment in one currency and receipt of the other. The higher is the expected default cost of an FX trade, the fewer trades will occur—and hence the worse will FX risks be distributed throughout the society.

Figure 10.1 clearly illustrates that private traders have a shared incentive to minimize the welfare loss ABC by minimizing the sum of expected counterparty default losses and

[5]The institutional complexities associated with modern payment systems and their risks are described in many places, including Humphrey (1987), Flannery (1988), Gilbert (1989, 1992), Borio and Van den Bergh (1993), or Van den Bergh (1994).

[6]When the "commodity" being traded is a FX or swap contract, the value to each party can depend in part on his own endowments. The ability to trade risks increases the efficiency of risk-bearing, which can have important effects on real savings/investment decisions. Merton (1995) therefore argues that extensive derivatives trading enhances social welfare.

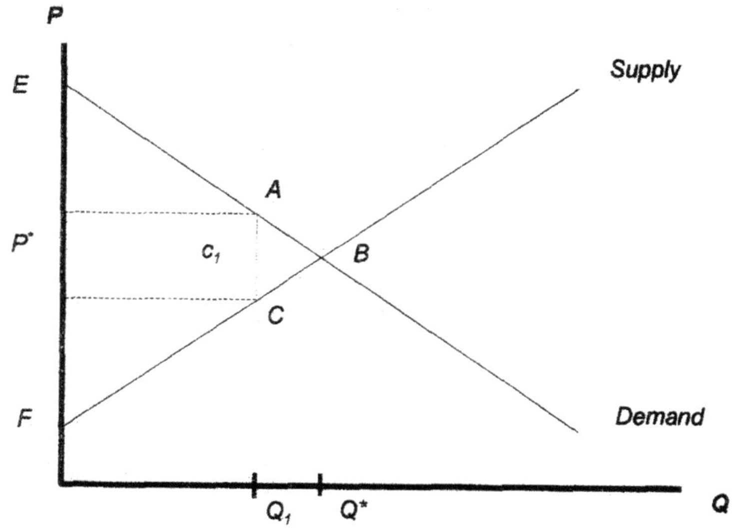

Figure 10.1.

the operational cost of settling trades in a particular manner. If government could lower the true social cost of transactions below what private parties can accomplish by themselves, social welfare would increase with government intervention. However, simply subsidizing transaction costs will *reduce* social welfare, despite the fact that it increases the amount of trading (hedging, risk-spreading). To see this, suppose the government paid all transaction costs, either by subsidizing operational costs or by absorbing counterparty risk (for example, through daylight overdrafts or cheap discount window lending). With zero transaction costs in Figure 10.2, traders would earn a surplus of EBF, while the government bears transaction

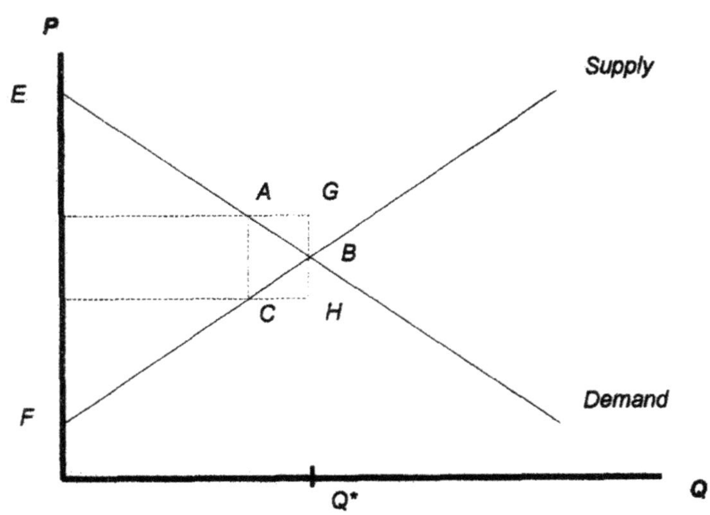

Figure 10.2.

costs c_1Q^*. The *net* surplus in this market is smaller than in Figure 10.1.[7] When traders needn't bear their own transaction costs, they trade too much.

Hanley, McCann, and Moser (1995) and Baer, France, and Moser (1994) model the costs and benefits of settling trades in different ways, and evaluate the optimal combination of credit and collateral to employ in a payments settlement system. Goodfriend (1991) argues that historical payment innovations have generally involved the substitution of credit for the need to hold sterile base money. As a consequence, "the drive for greater efficiency ... has brought with it a need to make arrangements to protect the payments system" (Goodfriend 1991, p. 10). The remainder of this section surveys alternative means of organizing payments in a developed economy. The available evidence casts doubt on the proposition that the most efficient system would exclude private credit as an integral component. In other words, we should not expect the market to produce a payment system that is devoid of systemic risk potential.

A. Payments Without Credit: Delivery Versus Payment

Cash transactions (such as purchasing one's morning coffee on the way from the Metro) occur with negligible payments risk because they involve the simultaneous exchange of a commodity and good funds. The same "delivery versus payment" (DVP) procedure could eliminate payments-related credit extensions from any transaction. No payment would be made unless the deliverable good or security were simultaneously provided; and all payers would deliver "good funds."[8] Some central banks have revised payment procedures to eliminate public credit entirely from the payment system, though this is not equivalent to a pure DVP system. For example, since January 1989 the Swiss National Bank's (SNB) Swiss Interbank Clearing (SIC) system has operated on a real-time gross settlement (RTGS) basis with zero overdrafts (BIS 1993, pp. 351–84).[9] If a Swiss bank submits a payment order that would overdraw its SNB account, the order is queued until the bank's account balance becomes sufficient to cover the payment.[10] Late in the business day the SNB may extend "lombard loans" to banks with queued payments in excess of their available SNB balances. (These loans are always secured and carry a rate 2 percent above the current money market rate.) At day's end, any payment orders still in the queue are canceled. The SIC specifies substantial penalties for canceling payments that have been entered into the system,[11] but "queued payment

[7] To see this, note that the additional consumer surplus generated by the government's absorption of transaction costs (ABC) is smaller than society's additional transaction costs (AGHC).

[8] The Bank of Japan was reportedly planning to introduce a DVP settlement system for government bonds, linking its BOJ-NET funds transfer system with the BOJ-NET government bond delivery system. (BIS 1993, p. 277).

[9] Other examples include the Bank of Japan, which rejects any transaction that would generate a daylight overdraft on its BOJ-NET payment system (BIS 1993, p. 268), and the reported intention of the British Clearing House Automated Payment System (CHAPS) to undertake real-time gross settlements by the end of 1995 (George 1994).

[10] Critics frequently contend that a real-time gross settlement system would be subject to "gridlock" unless the central bank stands ready to provide credit to temporarily illiquid firms. Although the SIC initially experienced some of this tendency, the problems appear to be largely manageable. Bono and Van den Bergh (1993) report that "[p]articipants ... have adjusted to the system by spreading payment orders over the day and by splitting up large payments" (p. 46).

[11] Specifically, any payment orders canceled after 3:00 P.M. "without the consent of the receiving bank or which are deleted during day-end processing are subject to a penalty of 3 percent p.a. of the amount of the payment for the duration of the delay. The receiving bank is entitled to claim this penalty from the bank which issued

orders are regularly deleted during processing at the end of the day" (Borio and Van den Bergh 1993, p. 46).

The SNB's RTGS system frees the central bank from payments-related credit exposures, but it does not necessarily eliminate *private* credit from the payment system. Payees still have the option to deliver a good or security against a promise of future payment. During "normal" times, the cost of effecting DVP may exceed the perceived benefits and traders will therefore rely on credit as part of their transactions settlement procedures. Accordingly, one troubled institution could still impose large illiquidity costs on its counterparties at day's end, because private credit exposures remain possible in the Swiss payment system.

B. Collateral and Netting Reduce the Payment System's Credit Components

Traders' counterparty credit risks can also be controlled via collateral or netting procedures. Consider the case of futures, where a reliable clearinghouse takes the opposite side of each trader's transactions. The futures contract's economic value can thus be separated from the risk that one's counterparty will not perform. But how does the clearinghouse assure *its* ability to perform? It must impose capital and collateral standards on clearinghouse members, who in turn require collateral (margin accounts) of their customers. A similar arrangement has evolved for equity trading, via the Depository Trust Corporation and the National Securities Clearing Corporation (NSCC) (see Stigum 1988, ch. 16), and for GNMA certificates, via the Participants Trust Corporation (Stehm 1992). Finally, the Chicago Mercantile Exchange has recently announced plans to form a swap settlement and clearing corporation, applying the credit controls of futures settlement to idiosyncratic OTC swap contracts (Petzel 1995).

Netting arrangements provide another mechanism for reducing the amount of credit risk associated with a fixed set of trades. Suppose two parties engage in multiple trades with one another over the day. In the absence of an enforceable netting agreement, each party must make full payment for all its purchases, *regardless* of whether the counterparty makes payment for its purchases (McAndrews and Roberds 1994; Mengle 1990; Cody 1990; Gilbert 1992; Cohen and Roberds 1993; Emmons 1994; Schoenmaker 1994). Rather than exchanging gross payments which largely offset one another, the trade partners could agree to transmit only the *net* value due from one to the other.[12] Netting could greatly reduce credit risk exposures in certain types of dealer markets. Within a clearinghouse, netting can be expanded to incorporate all of a trader's obligations to other clearinghouse members. Such "multilateral netting" can further reduce the credit components of transaction costs, although at the cost of involving unrelated parties in each trade's potential defaults.[13]

As Rochet and Tirole (1996) make clear in their analysis, this mutualization of credit generates deadweight costs by shifting bilateral risks to a multilateral organization.[14]

the payment instruction ... irrespective of any further claims [for damages] by the receiving bank" (BIS 1993, p. 365).

[12]This arrangement effectively provides trade counterparties a senior claim on the assets of an insolvent firm. Netting therefore has implications beyond payment system stability, which must be balanced against its advantages in this arena.

[13]Netting can involve either a single type of financial security (for example, provide for the net payment of FX or equity or check-clearing amounts due, or the net payment on interest rate swap payments), or can offset payments due across a range of financial contract types.

[14]Gorton (1985), Calomiris and Kahn (1996), and others argue that nineteenth-century U.S. bank clearinghouses provided valuable, collective monitoring and regulation of individual clearinghouse members, which was more efficient than requiring each bank's depositors to undertake their own monitoring.

Mutualized credit extensions may generate greater payments defaults than if each trader were fully responsible for his own counterparty performance. In place of the individual traders' responsibility for assessing counterparties' credit risks, the settlement organization must assess and monitor each member's ability to perform as promised. "Prudential" capital standards and collateral play prominent roles in this monitoring, but they impose costs on the clearinghouse's members (Baer, France, and Moser 1994). The application of netting arrangements to all large transactions is complicated by the fact that many such transactions occur across national borders. Unless all the legal jurisdictions treat netting contracts similarly, traders cannot be certain that netting will survive subsequent legal challenges that may arise (see Guynn 1995). In summary, netting can reduce or eliminate private credit exposures in trading goods or financial instruments, but private netting agreements may be expensive to design and maintain.

C. Private and Public Credit in the U.S. Payment System

Most of the payments, by dollar volume, undertaken daily in the United States occur over one of the two large-dollar transfer systems, Fedwire or the New York Clearinghouse Association's Clearinghouse Interbank Payments System (CHIPS).

On Fedwire, all payments are guaranteed by the Federal Reserve (under the Board's Regulation J). The central bank permits limited daylight overdrafts (DO), and hence provides at least some of the credit required to effect timely payments (Hancock and Wilcox 1996). DO exposures have aggregated very large amounts (relative to total bank equity or reserves), and tend to be concentrated at a relatively small number of banks with extensive securities, derivatives, interbank, or FX trading activities. In an effort to limit its (unpriced) credit risk exposure, the Fed introduced a system of self-administered DO caps in 1986. Cap levels were made more restrictive in subsequent years, and an explicit charge for overdrafts was introduced on April 14, 1994. Hancock and Wilcox (1996) estimate that the introduction of explicit fees for DO substantially reduced their average volume.[15]

Private credit occupies a central place in CHIPS, because all CHIPS payments are provisional until day's end. Until fairly recently, paying banks did not routinely recognize their CHIPS intraday positions as credit risk exposures (Flannery 1988, pp. 268–69), but CHIPS has recently moved to control the credit dimensions of its payment arrangements (Federal Reserve Bank of New York 1991). Each CHIPS member now maintains a bilateral exposure limit for every other clearinghouse member, and the central CHIPS computer will not process payments that violate these bilateral limits. Each participant is also subject to a *net* debit cap, which limits its aggregate net obligations to clearinghouse members. In October 1990, CHIPS moved from simply monitoring net debit positions to collateralizing them. Each CHIPS participant is now assessed an "additional settlement obligation" (ASO) for which it would be liable if any member failed to settle at day's end. Members post marketable collateral which the Clearinghouse can sell or pledge in order to obtain the funds required to satisfy a failed member's settlement obligations. While ASOs can surely prevent some failures from spreading to other clearinghouse members, there can be no guarantee that total settlement failures will never exceed the amount of posted collateral.

[15]Much of the DO activity in U.S. banks reflected the simple fact that there was no economic reason to avoid Fedwire overdrafts (Flannery 1988). Any positive price for DO would therefore reduce their use quite sharply, consistent with the conclusions of Hancock and Wilcox (1996).

The ASO mechanism has undoubtedly improved CHIPS' reliability, but potential private credit risk exposures remain in this private payment system.[16]

D. Optimal Payment Arrangements Vary Across Counterparties—and Across Time

Optimal payment arrangements differ across transaction types. For example, the ease and security of cash make it a natural choice for small purchases, while the risk of loss or theft makes cash needlessly expensive for larger transactions or those undertaken at a distance. Checks address these problems, but introduce private credit risk to the system.[17] Credit cards can satisfy a merchant's need for safe payment, but only because the issuing bank accepts credit risk in the merchant's stead. Finally, large-dollar payments involve time value and credit risks that are best addressed by a quick (that is, electronic) payment system.

Large-dollar payments can be arranged in a variety of ways along a cost-credit risk continuum (Berger, Hancock, and Marquardt 1996). Market participants rationally trade off the added costs of more secure transactions (via collateral, netting, etc.) against the expected default risk savings. If bankruptcy risks vary across (actual or potential) counterparties, traders may prefer different payment procedures with different counterparties. In some cases, trade with an unusually risky counterparty may require such costly security measures that traders choose to avoid them entirely. This is a form of market discipline.

Just as the optimal payments arrangement need not be the same for all transactions, neither need it be uniform across time. [18] A system that relies heavily on private credit may function well in "normal" times, when institutions are known to be well capitalized and hence likely to fulfill their payment obligations. Under these circumstances, the additional costs of queuing payments (in an RTGS) or posting collateral might be unwarranted, compared to the relatively low level of perceived credit risk in the transaction cost c_1 in Figure 10.1. However, a "financial crisis" could alter this cost-benefit analysis. If many payment system participants are poorly capitalized (due to recent large changes in asset values, for example, or unknown credit risk exposures), the credit risk component of c_1 rises and may become larger than the cost of implementing alternative payment techniques.[19] The crucial question is whether, how, and at what cost payment arrangements can be revised to suit current conditions.

[16]Humphrey (1987) and McAndrews and Wasilyew (1995) simulate the effects of a settlement failure on CHIPS, and find that the potential effects are large: one bank's failure to settle could render a number of other institutions illiquid or insolvent.

[17]The check may bounce, or the seller may not deliver the goods once the check has cleared.

[18]An analogy with daily life may help here. High-rise buildings would be unworkable without rapid elevators, which reduce the transaction costs of reaching the upper floors during normal times. In the event of a fire, however, building occupants are advised to switch to an alternative method of descent—the stairs—that become optimal because elevators tend to migrate toward the hottest floors. The fact that elevators can sometimes do much harm does not detract from their value in normal times. However, building occupants must be prepared to switch systems when circumstances dictate.

[19]No discussion of a credit-based payment system's stability would be complete without the observation that such a system can be reliable so long as all participants are sound. If regulators assure that banks always maintain adequate capital—by quickly closing an institution whose capital remains too low—the costs of a bank's insolvency will be borne entirely by its own shareholders. [Such a process of "structured early intervention and resolution" (SEIR), first proposed by Benston and Kaufman (1988), was incorporated into FDICIA.] While SEIR has many merits, its implementation will surely be imperfect. So long as a firm's failure *could* impose losses on payments counterparties, we need a policy response appropriate to the situation. (Of course, the proper government policy may be to do nothing!)

The following section presents a model of private lending under asymmetric information, in which sudden changes in economic conditions discontinuously affect the private market's willingness to lend, even to firms that appear to be solvent. In this framework, a payment system that relies on private credit exposures will tend to collapse, and alternative payment arrangements must emerge to prevent a consequent collapse in trade. Section 3 then argues that the substitution of government discount window advances for private credit can mitigate the impact of financial problems on the payment system.

2. A Model of Competitive Lending With Information Asymmetry

Open market operations constitute a sufficient policy response to all instances of financial illiquidity (Goodfriend and King 1988; Kaufman 1991; Schwartz 1992) *only if* private loan markets continue to function well, even during a crisis. But the assertion that private credit markets function better at some times than others is quite common:

> Financial markets function most efficiently when market participants have sufficient information about risks and returns to make informed investment and trading decisions. However, the evolution of financial trading and risk management practices has moved ahead of the public disclosures that most firms make of information that is relevant for such decisions. ... This asymmetry of information can cause a misallocation of capital among firms and *can also amplify market disturbances. During episodes of market stress, this lack of transparency can contribute to an environment in which rumours alone can cause a firm's market access and funding to be impaired.* (BIS 1994, p. 1, emphasis added)

> Even though the interbank market operates quite well during normal times among most banks, it cannot necessarily be relied upon to protect the banking system from panics. (Calomiris 1994, p. 34)

> The August 1995 paralysis of the banking system was caused by the practices of Russian bankers, likely aggravated by a change in monetary policy in early 1995. ... A lack of truthful, publicly available information made it impossible to tell strong banks from weak. The banks themselves became nervous about their large exposures in the interbank market; the crisis erupted as banks, with no good way to judge counterparty risk, reacted to mild signs of illiquidity by simply refusing to transact. (Jaffee and Levonian 1995, p. 3)

The necessary condition for government intervention in credit markets is not that private markets are doing a poor job, but that the government could do better. Unless the government possesses superior information about individual banks' solvency, it is difficult to defend the proposition that a government LLR should displace private credit decisions and assessments during a crisis. Indeed, many critics of direct LLR loans contend that the advantages of private lending are greatest when lenders must make informed judgments about illiquid firms' solvency during turbulent times. Justification for direct government lending to illiquid banks must therefore rest on an argument that the government can sometimes lend on more socially appropriate terms than the private sector would. This section presents a model of private lending that illustrates one mechanism by which asymmetric information can "amplify market disturbances" and prevent legitimate credit needs from being fulfilled.[20]

[20]This model was inspired by Calomiris' (1994) intriguing (but nontechnical) analysis of the Fed's discount window response to the Penn Central crisis.

Consider a one-period economy with many potential borrowers, of whom some are "Good" and others are "Bad." At the end of the period, Good loan applicants will be worth V_G, which is sufficient to repay loans *provided* that the contract rate is not too high. Bad applicants will be worth only $V_B 0(<< V_G)$ and will be unable to repay any loans they may obtain. The number of borrowers and their quality are fixed exogenously: the proportion of Good firms is δ_G, while the proportion of Bad firms is $\delta_B(= (1 - \delta_G))$.[21] There are two lenders, each of which has a costless [22] technology for assessing the creditworthiness of loan applicants. Specifically, the lender i observes a signal of the kth borrower's quality such that

$$\begin{aligned} \text{if } \hat{V}_k = 1 \text{ then } & \Pr(V_k = V_G) = p_i \text{ and} \\ & \Pr(V_k = V_B) = (1 - p_i) \\ \text{and if } \hat{V}_k = 0 \text{ then } & \Pr(V_k = V_B) = p_i \text{ and} \\ & \Pr(V_k = V_G) = (1 - p_i). \end{aligned}$$

Informative credit quality signals increase the probability of identifying an applicant's true quality. Credit signals used to make loan decisions must therefore have $pi >$ max $[\delta_B, \delta_G]$. Within this range, a higher p_i is preferred. For simplicity, assume that a borrower who cannot repay in full repays nothing, that the riskless market rate of interest is zero, and that the loan signals obtained for the same applicant by competing lenders are independent of one another.

Suppose that $p_1 > p_2$, and that each lender knows its relative underwriting accuracy. Then the loan pricing problem is simple if applicants randomly apply to only one lender. The ith lender will charge a Good-looking applicant a loan rate (R_i) given by

$$1 \leq (1 + R_i)p_i + 0(1 - p_i)$$

The contract rate, which will be paid with probability p_i, must compensate for the probability $(1 - p_i)$ that nothing will be repaid. A lender therefore charges

$$R_i \geq \frac{1}{p_i} - 1. \tag{10.1}$$

Analogously, an applicant who appears to be Bad will be charged a loan rate that reflects the possibility that the credit quality signal is incorrect:

$$1 \leq (1 + R_i)(1 - p_i) + 0(p_i)$$

or

$$R_i \geq \frac{1}{(1 - p_i)} - 1 \tag{10.2}$$

[21] I conjecture that an endogenous supply of Bad applicants would make it more difficult for the LLR to add value to the private sector's allocational equilibrium, unless the government were at least as good an underwriter as the private sector is.

[22] One could imagine that a costly test of creditworthiness could generate private credit market failures similar to those derived below.

For simplicity, I assume that the loan rate implied by (2) is so large that even a Good firm could not repay the loan, and subsequently ignore the possibility that any lender would extend credit to a firm showing a Bad credit signal.

If borrowers can apply to *both* lenders and accept the lowest available rate, the less-accurate lender cannot price according to (1) and expect to break even. [Broecker (1990) presents a related model.] If a borrower is truly Good, the more-accurate lender is likely to have offered her a loan. Lender 2 will be repaid only if the borrower is truly Good (which happens with probability p_2) *and* the more accurate lender has mistakenly assessed the borrower's quality as Bad (which happens with probability $(1-p_1)$ if the borrower is truly Good). Accordingly, the less-accurate lender's break-even loan rate satisfies

$$1 \leq (1+R_2)p_2(1-p_1)+0$$

or

$$R_2 \geq \frac{1}{p_2(1-p_1)} - 1 \qquad (10.3)$$

Equation (3) illustrates three important features of the less-accurate lender's pricing and portfolio risk exposure. First, competing with a stronger underwriter (that is, one with a larger p_1) raises a lender's break-even loan rate. Second, the value of the less-accurate lender's loan portfolio depends on the *accuracy* of its assessment about the competitor's underwriting ability. If Lender 2 underestimates p_1, its loan contract rates will be too low. Finally, and most important, this competitive risk is *not* diversifiable across loans. Regardless of the number of individual loans in its portfolio, Lender 2 bears more portfolio risk the greater is its uncertainty about Lender 1's underwriting ability.

That private financial markets function well in normal times strongly implies that the winner's curse in (3) is generally manageable. Perhaps lenders know enough about their usual customers that another lender's opinion does not materially influence their probability of securing the loan business. [See, for example, Nakamura (1995).] However, when a large shock impacts the financial system, normal lending relationships may become insufficient to provide all the funds required for an illiquid firm's continued operations. If banks must turn to new potential lenders at just the time when it is feared (or known) that many have been substantially weakened, a lender's assessment of its own underwriting abilities *and that of its competitors* may become much less certain. Lenders must innovate new information evaluation systems to interpret credit quality. Even banks that are normally the most accurate lenders could become uncertain about their relative underwriting ability during a crisis. The winner's curse has a more substantial effect on break-even loan rates when lenders are uncertain about their relative underwriting abilities.

To see this effect, assume that in a financial crisis each lender believes that there is a fifty-fifty chance that it is the more accurate underwriter. While each lender is confident about the quality (p_i) of its own creditworthiness test, it is unsure about the rival's test quality (p_j). For Lender i (who competes only with Lender j), the break-even loan rate is then given by

$$1 \leq (1+R_i)[0.5(p_i)+0.5(p_i(1-p_j))].$$

Lender i believes that it is the better underwriter with probability 0.5, in which case it would get the loan business of any applicant who appears to be Good, and p_i of these borrowers will repay. But there is also 50 percent chance that Lender i is the *less*-accurate underwriter, in which case it will attract a truly Good loan applicant only if Lender j mistakenly believes the borrower is Bad. Solving for the break-even loan rate yields

$$R_i \geq \frac{1}{p_i(1 - 0.5p_j)} - 1. \tag{10.4}$$

Both lenders now confront the *non-diversifiable* risk that their loan offers will be subject to a winner's curse. By contrast, this risk was absent (or, at least, smaller) during "normal" times, when relative underwriting abilities were better understood.[23]

The model thus implies that equilibrium loan rates will rise during a financial crisis, as documented by Mishkin (1991).[24] If the winner's curse effect is sufficiently large, the break-even loan rate (4) might become so high that even Good borrowers cannot repay the promised amount and the private loan market would collapse as in Akerlof (1970). The interbank loan market may also fail if aversion to the nondiversifiable winner's curse causes lenders to withdraw from the new loan market. This could occur for either (or both) of two reasons. First, if a lender's solvency depends on the repayment of new loans made during a financial crisis, a poor outcome would expose the firm to financial distress costs.[25] Less-confident underwriters may rationally confine their investments to the Treasury market, in which they have no information disadvantage. Second, if obtaining an applicant's quality signal is costly, lenders will incur the cost only if there is a reasonable chance of obtaining an apparently Good borrower's loan business. When a lender is unsure of its relative underwriting ability, it may choose to forego investing in credit quality signals until the crisis has passed.

To summarize, the model implies that private loan markets can fail not because the average borrower's credit quality deteriorates, but because lenders become less certain about how to identify risks. When lenders become uncertain about the accuracy of their own or competitors' underwriting abilities, break-even loan rates can rise sharply and the loan market can fail. In addition, lenders must accept nondiversifiable risk exposures in order to satisfy new loan demands. Rather than bear these risks, lenders may decide to protect their charter value by withdrawing from the interbank market during a crisis. If so, some illiquid banks will be unable to obtain funds, regardless of their solvency or of the aggregate state of financial sector liquidity. This private market equilibrium entails socially wasteful distress costs for the illiquid-but-solvent banks.

I now consider whether a government lender of last resort can mitigate the deadweight costs of a financial crisis.

[23]My model generates a discrete shift in loan-pricing behavior in response to an exogenous credit quality shock. Romer (1993) presents a related model in which equity prices change discretely when traders learn something about other traders' beliefs.

[24]The model's loan rates rise even if the underlying distribution of borrower qualities remain unchanged. A deterioration in average borrower quality during a crisis would raise equilibrium loan rates even further.

[25]This loss of value could arise from a nonmarketable charter value [as in Marcus (1984) or if large fluctuations in the lender's cash flows reduce its ability to finance attractive investment projects [as in Froot, Sharfstein, and Stein (1993)].

3. Model Implications: How can the Discount Window Support a Stable Payment System?

When a bank encounters settlement difficulties near the end of a business day, it must either borrow or convert assets to good funds in order to make settlement. The salient question is how a needy bank can obtain other banks' excess funds, on short notice. In normal times, the banks with excess funds may confidently lend to the needy banks. If the liquid banks are unfamiliar with the needy bank, they can lend to other (familiar) banks which are, in turn, willing to lend to the illiquid institution. During a financial crisis, however, the banks with excess funds may not be confident that they properly understand the condition of other banks in the system. The situation may be exacerbated by the fact that illiquid banks tend to approach new potential lenders in a crisis because their usual loan providers are also short of funds. Given the time pressures associated with settlement, it might be rational for banks with excess liquidity to seek refuge in riskless investments rather than extending loans to distressed firms. This market equilibrium would entail deadweight bankruptcy costs for the illiquid banks, and perhaps also for their counterparties.

The "winner's curse" equilibrium occurs because no bank has sufficient resources to lend to *all* the illiquid banks. If the banks with excess liquidity could form a consortium or mutual fund, however, they could lend to all troubled banks knowing that δ_G are Good and $(1 - \delta_G)$ are Bad (Calomiris 1994). The break-even loan rate (R^*) would be

$$1 = (1 + R^*)\delta_G + 0(1 - \delta_G)$$

or

$$R^* = \frac{1}{\delta_G}.$$

Is this sort of cooperative private solution likely to suffice? Three problems seem obvious. First, private-sector coordination costs may prevent formation of the loan consortium. Second, even if a consortium were formed in anticipation of a crisis, individual members may refuse to perform. (Sometimes, it seems cheaper to take one's chances in the courts than to lay out large amounts in an uncertain environment.) Finally, a payments problem requires action within a very short time frame, and coordinated action may not occur quickly enough to avert a settlement failure.

Another potential solution to the private lending problem described in section 2 would be for illiquid banks to provide security for new loans. Goodfriend (1991, p. 16 and footnote 37) explains that banks may not pledge any assets, except Treasury and agency bonds, as security for loans. This restriction means that most private loans to distressed banks must be made on an unsecured basis, though the Federal Reserve may accept any marketable collateral as security for its advances. Under present federal statutes, the discount window therefore constitutes a unique mechanism for providing secured funding to a distressed institution on short notice. Should we protect payment system stability by revising these statutes to permit secured interbank lending? This is a complex issue. A banking firm's decision to pledge collateral or sell assets can materially affect its *unsecured* creditors' ability to obtain repayment if the firm defaults. Attaining payment system stability through this mechanism would therefore generate higher unsecured debt rates, which may depress banking firms' values in other ways. We cannot discuss pledging or discount window collateralization without regard for the impact of these devices on banks' other credit arrangements. It seems unlikely that a general equilibrium analysis would imply that banks should be permitted to pledge assets without limit in order to render the payment system more secure.

What, then, can a government LLR do to ameliorate a payment system crisis? Putting aside the (unlikely?) possibility that the government's supervisory responsibilities provide it with better information about illiquid banks' true condition, the government has two advantages over private lenders: its size and its immunity to bankruptcy. A government LLR can (uniquely) finance the entire banking sector's liquidity needs, and it can do so quickly, with no coordination problems. Moreover, in order to protect itself against adverse selection, the government can afford to lend at a rate below any (potential) private lender's. If all private lenders withdraw from the market, the Fed simply charges R^* and breaks even on its advances. However, if some private lenders remain sufficiently confident of their underwriting abilities that they "skim off" a disproportionate share of Good borrowers, the Fed's break-even loan rate may exceed the rate which Good banks could afford to repay. The Fed should therefore evaluate whether lending at a loss entails lower social costs than those associated with letting Good firms bear distress costs.

It is very important to contrast this view of the appropriate Fed discount rate with Bagehot's classical view that in a crisis the central bank should lend *freely, but at a penalty rate*. If the Fed sets a penalty rate on loans during my type of financial crisis, it may suffer a winner's curse vis-à-vis private lenders, potentially increasing its cost of intervention. In a crisis, the Federal Reserve must stand ready to *subsidize* credit in order to avoid the winner's curse that governs private loan pricing decisions.[26]

A. Discount Window Loans during "Normal" Times

My model provides no justification for LLR advances to an *individual* firm with an *idiosyncratic* liquidity problem. Indeed, during normal times there are several reasons for the Fed to avoid all loans:

(1) If private lenders are better underwriters, the Fed will tend to attract the weaker credits, imposing losses on taxpayers.
(2) Access to cheap Fed credit will subsidize bank risk-taking, contributing to riskier payment and financial systems.
(3) Cheap Fed credit will inhibit the development of private mechanisms for providing quick access to liquidity.

During normal times, private markets should be able to assess the distressed firm's condition at least as well as the LLR can. Once the Fed has provided sufficient aggregate liquidity through open market operations, it should rely on private lending to channel funds to solvent but illiquid firms.

Some will argue that the Fed should support a troubled institution if its failure would impose large credit losses on other banks. Rochet and Tirole (1996) point out that the bad incentive effects of this "too big to fail" policy can be avoided by subsidizing the troubled institution's counterparties instead of bailing out the troubled firm itself.

[26] In an important sense, this is a tautology: if the Fed lent only on the same terms which the market would set, it cannot improve upon private market outcomes.

B. Collateral and Discount Window Lending

The Fed presently lends on both secured and unsecured bases. Regulation A requires that overnight discount window advances be fully collateralized, while Fedwire DO are generally unsecured. Unsubsidized, collateralized discount window loans can add no social value except to the extent that they constitute a means of circumventing securities trading deadlines or statutory restrictions on pledging assets to private lenders.[27] Without meaning to minimize the value of these services, I wish to concentrate on unsecured lending—where the Fed can most dramatically influence social allocations. The model in section 2 implies that the Fed can best mitigate social deadweight costs by lending on an unsecured basis to any illiquid bank, perhaps at a subsidized rate.

C. Discount Loans' Maturity

I have discussed discount window lending in the context of a payment system crisis because such crises must be resolved within a very short time. Private efforts to coordinate emergency lending cannot be relied upon to occur quickly enough to avoid an important settlement failure. At the same time, my confidence in private investors' ingenuity suggests that discount window loans should be very short term, *even* in a financial crisis. The Fed's value lies in carrying banks over the period of market uncertainty, until they can sell securities (which should be possible on the next business day) or demonstrate their solvency to liquid outsiders (which may take longer when asset prices are more volatile). It is hard to imagine situations in which widespread Fed lending would be appropriate for more than a few business days.

D. Comparing the Costs and Benefits of Discount Window Lending

So far, I have tried to define the circumstances under which direct LLR lending *could* supplement open market operations as a means of enhancing social welfare during a crisis. While these circumstances are quite limited, we should not dismiss the discount window as obviously unnecessary. At the same time, however, almost any government activity entails inefficiencies and costs as well as the benefits identified here. Assessing whether such lending *is truly* appropriate requires a comparison between the deadweight costs of a settlement failure and the (ex ante and ex post) costs of inefficient risk bearing in the financial system. These latter social costs *do not* include the Fed's direct credit losses (which are only a transfer payment), but rather the effects of distorted risk-taking incentives induced by a policy of lending broadly to banks, regardless of their credit condition. Provided that very short-term discount window loans are extended only during a broad financial crisis, the potential benefits of LLR loans far outweigh the likely damage to the banking system's risk-taking incentives.

4. Summary and Conclusions

Substantial amounts of public and private credit underlie modern large-dollar payment systems. A number of institutional arrangements make it possible to reduce the amount of

[27]The Fed's current practice, making *secured* loans to individual firms in normal times, tends to reduce the value of unsecured creditors' claims, should the bank eventually go bankrupt. No strong justification for this type of loan springs immediately to mind.

credit required to effect payments, but each has costs as well as benefits. During "normal" times, in which private lenders can assess one another's financial conditions with reasonable accuracy, a payment system that entails substantial private credit exposures is efficient and appropriate. However, any credit-based payment system incorporates the potential for "systemic risk," by which one firm's failure to settle can make other firms also unable to settle. We must consider the appropriate role for a government LLR when one or more banks cannot fulfill their payment system obligations.

Unless we believe that private banks and investors routinely make poor credit quality evaluations, there is little need for unsecured discount window loans during "normal" times. When credit markets are functioning well, the LLR's only advantage lies in its ability to provide good funds more quickly than the distressed bank could raise them by asset sales or private borrowing. However, such advances must be kept very short term (perhaps extending no longer than a single business day), after which a solvent bank should be able to sell assets or secure funding from private lenders. Unless the discount window administrator is assumed to know more about a bank's true condition than the market does, there is no reason to extend loans for very long.

The discount window's unique value arises when disarray strikes private financial markets. If lenders cannot confidently assess other firms' conditions, they may rationally withdraw from the interbank loan market, leaving solvent but illiquid firms unable to fund themselves. Private lenders seeking to fill this gap would confront a nondiversifiable adverse selection bias (winner's curse), which the discount window need not experience. In response to this sort of financial crisis, government may need to do more than assure adequate aggregate liquidity through open market operations. Broad, short-term discount window lending, unsecured and at (perhaps) subsidized rates, may constitute the least-cost means of resolving some types of widespread financial uncertainties, including those affecting payment systems settlement.

Literature Cited

Aharoney, J., and I. Swary. "Contagion Effects of Bank Failures: Evidence from Capital Markets." *Journal of Business* 56 (3:1983), 305–22.

Akerlof, George. "The Market for Lemons: Qualitative Uncertainty and the Market Mechanism." *Quarterly Journal of Economics* 84 (1970), 488–500.

Baer, Herbert L., Virginia G. France, and James T. Moser. "Opportunity Cost and Prudentiality: An Analysis of Futures Clearinghouse Behavior." The World Bank, Policy Research Working paper 1340, August 1994.

Bank for International Settlements. *Payments Systems in the Group of Ten Countries*. Basle, December 1993.

——. "Public Disclosure of Market and Credit Risks by Financial Intermediaries." Mimeo, September 1994.

——. "Prudential Supervision of Banks' Derivatives Activities." Mimeo, December 1994.

——. "Public Disclosure of the Trading and Derivatives Activities of Banks and Securities Firms." Mimeo, November 1995.

Benston, George J., and George C. Kaufman. *Risk and Solvency Regulation of Depository Institutions: Past Policies and Current Options*. Salomon Brothers Center, Graduate School of Business, New York University, 1988.

Berger, Allen N., Diana Hancock, and Jeffrey Marquardt. "Introduction." *Journal of Money, Credit and Banking* 28 (November 1996, Part 2).

Borio, C.E.V., and P. Van den Bergh. "The Nature and Management of Payment System Risks: An International Perspective." *BIS Economic Paper*, no. 35, February 1993.

Broecker, Thorsten. "Creditworthiness Tests and Interbank Competition." *Econometrica* 58(2) (March 1990), 429–52.

Calomiris, Charles W. "Is the Discount Window Necessary? A Penn Central Perspective." Federal Reserve Bank of St. Louis *Review* (May/June 1994), 31–56.
Calomiris, Charles W., and Charles M. Kahn, "The Efficiency of Self-Regulated Payment Systems: Learning from the Suffolk System." *Journal of Money, Credit, and Banking* 28 (November 1996, Part 2).
Cody, Brian J. "Reducing the Costs and Risks of Trading Foreign Exchange." Federal Reserve Bank of Philadelphia *Business Review* (November/December 1990), 13–23.
Cohen, Hugh, and William Roberds. "Toward the Systematic Measurement of Systemic Risk." Federal Reserve Bank of Atlanta Working Paper Series, WP-93–14, October 1993.
Emmons, William R. "The Payments System, Delegated Monitoring, and Banking Safety Nets." Working paper, Dartmouth College, November 1994.
Federal Reserve Bank of New York. "The Clearinghouse Interbank Payments System." January 1991.
Flannery, Mark J. "Payments System Risk and Public Policy." In *Restructuring Banking and Financial Services in America*, edited by William S. Haraf and Rose Marie Kushmeider, pp. 261–87. Washington, D.C.: American Enterprise Institute for Public Policy Research, 1988.
——. "Corporate Finance, Market Discipline, and Bank Supervision." In *Proceedings* of the Conference on Bank Structure and Competition, pp. 313–30. Federal Reserve Bank of Chicago, 1994.
——. "Regulatory Responses to the Potential for Systemic Risk in the Financial Sector." In *Research in Financial Services: Private and Public Policy*, edited by George G. Kaufman, pp. 323–36. Greenwich: JAI Press, 1995.
Froot, Kenneth A., David S. Scharfstein, and Jeremy C. Stein. "Risk Management: Coordinating Corporate Investment and Financing Policies." *Journal of Finance* (December 1993), 1629–58.
George, Eddie. "International Banking, Payment Systems, and Financial Crises." In *Symposium Proceedings: International Symposium on Banking and Payment Services*, Board of Governors of the Federal Reserve System, December 1994.
Gilbert, R. Alton. "Payments System Risk: What Is It and What Will Happen If We Try to Reduce It?" Federal Reserve Bank of St. Louis *Review* (January/February 1989), 3–17.
——. "Implications of Netting Arrangements for Bank Risk in Foreign Exchange Transactions." Federal Reserve Bank of St. Louis *Review* (January /February 1992), 3–16.
Goldstein, Morris. "International Aspects of Systemic Risk." Working paper, Office of the Comptroller of the Currency, December 1994.
Goodfriend, Marvin. "Money, Credit, Banking, and Payment System Policy." Federal Reserve Bank of Richmond *Economic Review* 77 (January/February 1991), 7–23.
Goodfriend, Marvin, and Robert G. King. "Financial Deregulation, Monetary Policy, and Central Banking." In *Restructuring Banking and Financial Services in America*, edited by William S. Haraf and Rose Marie Kushmeider, pp. 216–53. Washington, D.C.: American Enterprise Institute for Public Policy Research, 1988.
Goodhart, Charles. *The Evolution of Central Banks*. Cambridge: The MIT Press, 1988.
Gorton, Gary. "Clearing Houses and the Origin of Central Banking in the U.S." *Economic History* 45(2) (1985), 277–83.
Guynn, Randall D. "Modernizing Securities Ownership, Transfer and Pledging Laws: A Discussion Paper on the Need for International Harmonization." Mimeo, May 1995.
Jaffee, Dwight, and Mark Levonian. "Russian Banking." FRBSF Weekly Letter, Number 95–35, October 20, 1995.
Hancock, Diana, and James A. Wilcox. "Intraday Bank Reserve Management: The Effects of Caps and Fees on Daylight Overdrafts." *Journal of Money, Credit, and Banking* 28 (November 1996, Part 2).
Hanley, William J., Karen McCann, and James T. Moser. "Public Benefits and Public Concerns: An Economic Analysis of Regulatory Standards for Clearing Facilities." Federal Reserve Bank of Chicago Working Paper Series (WP-95-12), September 1995.
Humphrey, David B. "Payments System Risk, Market Failure, and Public Policy." In *Electronic Funds Transfers and Payments: The Public Policy Issues*, edited by Elinor Harris Solomon, pp. 83–110. Boston: Kluwer-Nijhoff Publishing, 1987.
Kaufman, George G. "The Lender of Last Resort: A Contemporary Perspective." *Journal of Financial Services Research* 5(2) (October 1991), 95–110.
Marcus, Alan J. "Regulation and Bank Financial Policy." *Journal of Banking and Finance* 8 (1984), 557–65.

McAndrews, James, and William Roberds. "Banks, Payments, and Coordination." Working paper, Federal Reserve Banks of Philadelphia and Atlanta, August 1994.

McAndrews, James J., and George Wasilyew. "Simulations of Failure in a Payment System." Federal Reserve Bank of Philadelphia Working Papers, June 1995.

Mengle, David L. "Legal and Regulatory Reform in Electronic Payments: An Evaluation of Payment Finality Rules." In *The U.S. Payment System: Efficiency, Risk and the Role of the Federal Reserve*, edited by David B. Humphrey, pp. 145–95. Boston: Kluwer Academic Publishers, 1990.

Merton, Robert C. "Financial Innovation and the Management and Regulation of Financial Institutions." *Journal of Banking and Finance* (July 1995), 461–82.

Mishkin, Frederic S. "Asymmetric Information and Financial Crises: A Historical Perspective." In *Financial Markets and Financial Crises*, edited by R. Glenn Hubbard, pp. 69–108. Chicago: The University of Chicago Press, 1991.

Morris, Bert. "Changes in Payment and Settlement Systems around the World." In *Symposium Proceedings: International Symposium on Banking and Payment Services*, pp. 15–26. Board of Governors of the Federal Reserve System, December 1994.

Musumeci, J. J., and J. F. Sinkey, Jr. "The International Debt Crisis, Investor Contagion, and Bank Security Returns in 1987: The Brazilian Experience." *Journal of Money, Credit, and Banking* 22 (May 1990), 209–20.

Nakamura, Leonard I. "The Informational Impact of Competition on Loan Screening." Mimeo, Federal Reserve Bank of Philadelphia, November 1995.

Petzel, Todd E. "Managing Collateral On Exchanges and Off: A New Perspective." *The Journal of Derivatives* (Spring 1995), 64–72.

Rochet, Jean Charles, and Jean Tirole. "Interbank Lending and Systemic Risk." *Journal of Money, Credit, and Banking* 28 (November 1996, Part 2).

Romer, David. "Rational Asset-Price Movements without News." *American Economic Review* 83(5) (December 1993), 1112–30.

Schoenmaker, Dirk. "A Comparison of Net and Gross Settlement." London School of Economics Financial Markets Group Special Paper, May 1994.

Schwartz, Anna. "The Misuse of the Fed's Discount Window." Federal Reserve Bank of St. Louis *Review* (September/October 1992), 58–69.

Stehm, Jeff. "Clearance and Settlement of Mortgage-Backed Securities through the Participants Trust Company." Finance and Economic Discussion Series #214, Board of Governors of the Federal Reserve System, November 1992.

Stigum, Marcia. *After the Trade*. Homewood: Dow Jones-Irwin, 1988.

Swary, I. "Stock Market Reaction to Regulatory Action in the Continental Illinois Crisis." *Journal of Business* 59 (3:1986), 451–73.

Van den Bergh, Paul. "Operational and Financial Structure of the Payment System." In *The Payment System: Design, Management and Supervision*, edited by Bruce J. Summers. Washington: The International Monetary Fund, 1994.

11 Liquidity, Risk Taking, and the Lender of Last Resort

Rafael Repullo

From their inception, central banks have assumed as one of their key responsibilities the provision of liquidity to banks unable to find it elsewhere. The classical doctrine on the lender of last resort (LLR) was put forward by Bagehot (1873, 96–7): "Nothing, therefore, can be more certain than that the Bank of England ... must in time of panic do what all other similar banks must do.... And for this purpose there are two rules: First. That these loans should only be made at a very high rate of interest.... Secondly. That at this rate these advances should be made on all good banking securities, and as largely as the public ask for them." The contemporary literature on the LLR has disagreed on whether the aim of "staying the panic" may be achieved by open market operations (see, for example, Goodfriend and King [1988] or Kaufman [1991]) or whether it requires lending to individual banks (see, for example, Flannery [1996] or Goodhart [1999]).[1] However, both sides seem to agree on the proposition that such lending creates a moral hazard problem. As argued by Solow (1982, 242): "The existence of a credible LLR must reduce the private cost of risk taking. It can hardly be doubted that, in consequence, more risk will be taken."

The purpose of this paper is to show that this proposition is not generally true. Specifically, we model the strategic interaction between a bank and an LLR. The bank is funded with insured deposits and equity capital, is subject to a minimum capital requirement, and can invest in two assets: a safe and perfectly liquid asset, and a risky and illiquid asset, whose risk is privately chosen by the bank. Deposits are randomly withdrawn. If the withdrawal is larger than the funds invested in the safe asset (the liquidity buffer), the bank will be forced into liquidation unless it can secure emergency lending from the LLR. In this setting, we show that when the LLR does not charge penalty rates, the bank chooses the same level of risk and a smaller liquidity buffer than in the absence of an LLR. Moreover, the equilibrium choice of risk is increasing in the penalty rate.

To explain the basic intuition for these results, consider a setup in which a risk-neutral bank raises a unit of insured deposits at an interest rate that is normalized to zero, and invests all these funds in an illiquid asset that yields a gross return $R_1 = R(p)$ with probability p, and $R_0 = 0$ otherwise. Moreover, suppose that p is chosen by the bank at the time of investment, and that the success return $R(p)$ is decreasing in p, so safer investments yield a lower success return.

[1] All these references (and more) are usefully collected in Goodhart and Illing (2002).

Without deposit withdrawals, and hence without the need for an LLR, with probability p the bank gets the return $R(p)$ of its investment in the risky asset minus the amount due to the depositors, that is, $R(p) - 1$, and with probability $1 - p$ the bank fails. Under limited liability, the bank then maximizes $p[R(p) - 1]$, which gives $p^* = \arg\max p[R(p) - 1]$.

Suppose now that a certain fraction of the deposits are withdrawn, and that there is an LLR that only provides the required funding if its supervisory information on the quality of the bank's asset is good. Specifically, let s_1 denote the good supervisory signal, and let $q = \Pr(s_1|R_1)$ denote the quality of the supervisory information. If the LLR only charges the zero deposit rate, the bank will get $R(p) - 1$ with probability $\Pr(s_1, R_1) = \Pr(s_1|R_1)\Pr(R_1) = qp$. Since the constant q factors out of the maximization problem, we get the same $p^* = \arg\max p[R(p) - 1]$. Hence we conclude that the introduction of deposit withdrawals and an LLR does not affect the bank's incentives to take risk.

As for the result on penalty rates, the intuition is that they increase the expected interest payments in the high-return state and, consequently, push the bank toward choosing higher risk and higher return strategies (i.e., a lower p). This positive relationship between the bank's (expected) funding costs and its portfolio risk is not new, since it is a simple implication of the analysis in the classical paper on credit rationing of Stiglitz and Weiss (1981). In particular, they show (p. 393) how "higher interest rates induce firms to undertake projects with lower probabilities of success but higher payoffs when successful." Applying the same argument to banks instead of firms gives the key result.

To endogenize the decision of the LLR, we adopt a political economy perspective according to which government agencies have objectives that need not correspond with the maximization of social welfare. In particular, following Repullo (2000) and Kahn and Santos (2001), we assume that the LLR cares about (1) the revenues and costs associated with its lending activity and (2) whether the bank fails. This may be justified by relating the payoff of the officials in charge of LLR decisions with the surpluses or deficits of the agency, as well as with the possible reputation costs associated with a bank failure.

Specifying an objective function for the LLR would not be needed if the supervisory information were verifiable, because then the intervention rule could be specified ex-ante, possibly in order to implement a socially optimal decision. However, the information coming from bank examinations is likely to contain many subjective elements that are difficult to describe ex-ante, so it seems reasonable to assume that it is nonverifiable. In this case, the decision will have to be delegated to the LLR, which will simply compare its conditional expected payoff of supporting and not supporting the bank.

To facilitate the presentation, the analysis starts with a basic model in which the bank is fully funded with deposits and can only invest in the risky asset. Then the model is extended to the case where the bank can invest in a safe and perfectly liquid asset and can raise equity capital. In the general model, we also assume that the bank is subject to a minimum capital requirement, and that (in line with Basel bank capital regulation) investment in the safe asset does not carry a capital charge.

We characterize the Nash equilibrium of the game between the bank and the LLR, where the former chooses the level of risk (and, in the general model, its capital and liquidity buffer) and the latter its contingent lending policy. The LLR's equilibrium strategy is straightforward: it will support the bank if and only if the liquidity shortfall is smaller than or equal to a critical value that is decreasing in the ex-post (i.e., conditional on the supervisory signal) probability of bank failure. The bank's equilibrium strategy is, however, more difficult to characterize. The reason is that its objective function is likely to be convex in the capital decision, which leads to a corner solution where the bank's capital is equal to the minimum required by regulation. In this case, the equilibrium level of risk only depends on the capital requirement, with higher capital increasing the bank shareholders' losses in case of default and reducing their incentives for risk taking. We complete the analysis by deriving numerically, for a simple parameterization of the model, the bank's equilibrium liquidity. We show that in equilibrium, the bank chooses the same level of risk of its illiquid portfolio and a lower liquidity buffer than in the absence of an LLR.

Four extensions are then discussed. First, we derive the result that penalty rates increase the equilibrium choice of risk. Next, we examine the second of Bagehot's rules—namely, that last-resort lending be collateralized—and show that this protection translates into a lower liquidity buffer and therefore a higher probability that the bank will require emergency liquidity assistance, but without any effect on risk taking. Third, we consider the effects of introducing a higher discount rate for the LLR, which yields a forbearance result: in equilibrium, the bank is more likely to receive support from the LLR, and hence it will hold a lower liquidity buffer. Finally, we look at the case where the LLR shares a fraction of the deposit insurance payouts (which includes, in the limit, the case where the LLR is the deposit insurer) and show that in this case the LLR's decision becomes more sensitive to the supervisory information.

It is important to stress that the key result on the zero effect on risk taking of having an LLR crucially depends on the specification of the order of moves, in particular the fact that the bank cannot modify the level of risk after receiving the support of the LLR (or cannot borrow from the LLR to undertake new investments). But in such a situation, the LLR is likely to carefully monitor the bank, preventing it from engaging in any significant risk shifting, so this seems a reasonable assumption.

Although the literature on the LLR is extensive (see Freixas et al. [2000] for a recent survey), somewhat surprisingly there has been little formal modeling of the issues discussed in this paper. Most of the relevant papers invoke general results on the link between any form of insurance and moral hazard. Moreover, liquidity support is not always distinguished from capital support, which clearly has bad incentive effects whenever it translates into rescuing the shareholders of a distressed bank. This paper restricts attention to liquidity support based on supervisory information on the quality of the bank's assets, and shows that under fairly general conditions this support does not encourage risk taking.

The paper is organized as follows. Section 1 presents the basic model of the game between the bank and the LLR. Section 2 introduces equity capital and a minimum capital requirement, and allows the bank to invest in a safe asset, characterizing the equilibrium with and without an LLR and discussing its comparative statics properties. Section 3 analyzes the effects of Bagehot's rules of charging penalty rates and requiring collateral, as well as changing the objective function of the LLR to allow for higher discounting of future payouts and sharing deposit insurance payouts. Section 4 offers some concluding remarks.

1. The Basic Model

Consider an economy with three dates ($t = 0, 1, 2$) and two risk-neutral agents: a *bank* and a *lender of last resort* (LLR). At date 0 the bank raises one unit of deposits at an interest rate that is normalized to zero, and invests these funds in an asset that yields a random *return* R at date 2. The probability distribution of R is described by

$$R = \begin{cases} R_0, & \text{with probability } 1-p, \\ R_1, & \text{with probability } p, \end{cases} \tag{11.1}$$

where $p \in [0, 1]$ is a parameter chosen by the bank at date 0. We assume that $R_0 < 1 < R_1$, so $1 - p$ measures the riskiness of the bank's portfolio. The risky asset is illiquid in that there is no secondary market where it can be traded at date 1. However, the asset can be fully liquidated at this date, which yields a *liquidation value* $L \in (0, 1)$.[2] Deposits are fully insured and can be withdrawn at either date 1 or date 2. To simplify the presentation, deposit insurance premia are set equal to zero.

At date 1 a fraction $v \in [0, 1]$ of the deposits are withdrawn. Since the bank's asset is illiquid, if $v > 0$ the bank faces a liquidity problem that can only be solved by borrowing from the LLR. If such funding is not provided, the bank is liquidated at date 1. Otherwise, the bank stays open until the final date 2. The liquidity shock v is observable, and we initially suppose that the LLR only charges the deposit rate, which has been normalized to zero.

In order to decide whether to provide this emergency funding, the LLR supervises the bank, which yields a *signal* $s \in \{s_0, s_1\}$ on the return of the bank's risky asset. Signal s is assumed to be nonverifiable, so the LLR's decision rule cannot be designed ex-ante, but will be chosen ex-post by the LLR in order to maximize an objective function that will be specified below.

We introduce the following assumptions.

Assumption 1: $R_0 = 0$ and $R_1 = R(p)$, where $R(p)$ is decreasing and concave, with $R(1) \geq 1$ and $R(1) + R'(1) < 0$.

Assumption 2: $\Pr(s_0|R_0) = \Pr(s_1|R_1) = q \in [\frac{1}{2}, 1]$.

Assumption 1, together with (1), implies that the expected final return of the risky asset, $E(R) = pR(p)$, reaches a maximum at $\widehat{p} \in (0, 1)$, which is characterized by the first-order condition

$$R(\widehat{p}) + \widehat{p}R'(\widehat{p}) = 0. \tag{11.2}$$

To see this, notice that the first derivative of $pR(p)$ with respect to p equals $R(0) > 0$ for $p = 0$ and $R(1) + R'(1) < 0$ for $p = 1$, and the second derivative satisfies $2R'(p) + pR''(p) < 0$. Thus, increases in p below (above) $\widehat{p}$ increase (decrease) the expected final return of the risky asset. Moreover, we have $\widehat{p}R(\widehat{p}) > R(1) \geq 1$. Assumption 1 is borrowed from Allen and Gale (2000, chap. 8) and allows us to analyze in a continuous manner the risk-shifting effects of different institutional settings.[3]

Assumption 2 introduces a parameter q that describes the quality of the supervisory information.[4] This information is only about whether the final return of the risky asset will be low (R_0) or high (R_1), and not about the particular value $R(p)$ taken by the high return. By Bayes' law, it is immediate to show that

$$\Pr(R_1|s_0) = \frac{p(1-q)}{p(1-q) + (1-p)q}, \tag{11.3}$$

[2]The liquidation value L could be correlated with the final return R, but this would not change the results.
[3]This assumption has also been used by Cordella and Levy-Yeyati (2003) and Repullo (2005).
[4]More generally, we could have $\Pr(s_0|R_0) \neq \Pr(s_1|R_1)$, but this would not change the results.

and

$$\Pr(R_1|s_1) = \frac{pq}{pq + (1-p)(1-q)}. \tag{11.4}$$

Hence when $q = \frac{1}{2}$ we have $\Pr(R_1|s_0) = \Pr(R_1|s_1) = p$, so the supervisory signal is uninformative, while when $q = 1$ we have $\Pr(R_1|s_0) = 0$ and $\Pr(R_1|s_1) = 1$, so the signal completely reveals whether the final return will be low or high. Since $\Pr(R_1|s_0) < p < \Pr(R_1|s_1)$ for $p < 1$ and $q > \frac{1}{2}$, s_0 and s_1 will be called the bad and the good signal, respectively.

From the point of view of the initial date 0, the deposit withdrawal v is a continuous random variable with support [0, 1] and cumulative distribution function $F(v)$.[5] Since deposits are fully insured, it is natural to assume that the withdrawal v is independent of the final return R. Also, v is assumed to be independent of the supervisory signal s.

The bank and the LLR play a sequential game in which the bank chooses at date 0 the riskiness of its portfolio p, and if $v > 0$, the LLR decides at date 1 whether to support the bank based on two pieces of information: the size of the liquidity shock v, and the supervisory signal s. Importantly, the LLR does not observe the bank's choice of p, so we have a game of complete but imperfect information.

In this game, the LLR is assumed to care about the expected value of its final wealth net of a share α of the *social cost* c incurred in the event of a bank failure. Such cost comprises the administrative costs of closing the bank and paying back depositors and the negative externalities associated with the failure (contagion to other banks, breakup of lending relationships, distortions in the monetary transmission mechanism, etc.). As noted above, the LLR's objective function may be justified by relating the payoff of the officials in charge of its decisions with the income generated or lost through its lending activity and the social cost associated with a bank failure. To simplify the presentation, we assume that $\alpha = 1$, so the LLR fully internalizes the social cost of bank failure.[6]

Consider a situation in which $v > 0$, and let s be the signal observed by the LLR. The payoff of the LLR if it supports the bank is computed as follows. With probability $\Pr(R_1|s)$ the bank will be solvent at date 2 and the LLR will recover its loan v, while with probability $\Pr(R_0|s)$ the bank will fail and the LLR will lose v and incur the cost c, so the LLR's expected payoff is $-(v + c)\Pr(R_0|s)$. On the other hand, if the LLR does not provide the liquidity support, the bank will be liquidated at date 1, and the LLR's payoff will be $-c$. Hence the LLR will support the bank if

$$-(v + c)\Pr(R_0|s) \geq -c.$$

Using the fact that $\Pr(R_1|s) = 1 - \Pr(R_0|s)$, this condition simplifies to

$$v \leq \frac{c\Pr(R_1|s)}{\Pr(R_0|s)}.$$

[5]The distribution function $F(v)$ could have a mass point at $v = 0$, in which case $F(0) > 0$ would be the probability that the bank does not suffer a liquidity shock at date 1.

[6]Clearly, this assumption does not affect the characterization of the equilibrium of the game, since it is equivalent to a change in the cost c. Interestingly, Repullo (2000) assumes $\alpha < 1$, while Kahn and Santos (2001) assume $\alpha > 1$.

Substituting (3) and (4) into this expression, it follows that when the LLR observes the bad signal s_0, it will support the bank if

$$v \leq v_0 \equiv \frac{cp(1-q)}{(1-p)q}, \tag{11.5}$$

and when the LLR observes the good signal s_1, it will support the bank if

$$v \leq v_1 \equiv \frac{cpq}{(1-p)(1-q)}. \tag{11.6}$$

The critical values v_0 and v_1 defined in (5) and (6) satisfy

$$v_1 = \left(\frac{q}{1-q}\right)^2 v_0,$$

which implies $v_1 > v_0$ whenever $q > \frac{1}{2}$. Hence if the signal is informative, the LLR is more likely to provide support to the bank when it observes the good signal s_1 than when it observes the bad signal s_0. Moreover, the critical value v_0 is decreasing in the quality q of the supervisory information, with $\lim_{q \to 1} v_0 = 0$, and the critical value v_1 is increasing in q, with $\lim_{q \to 1} v_1 = \infty$.[7] Thus, when the signal is perfectly informative, the bank will never be supported if the signal is bad, and will always be supported if it is good.

The critical values v_0 and v_1 are increasing in the social cost of bank failure c, because when this cost is high, the LLR has a stronger incentive to lend to the bank in order to save c when the high return R_1 obtains. They are also increasing in $p = \Pr(R_1)$, because when this probability is high, the LLR is more likely to recover its loan v and save the cost c.

By limited liability, the bank gets a zero payoff if it is liquidated at date 1 or fails at date 2, and gets $R(p) - 1$ if it succeeds at date 2. This event happens when the high return R_1 obtains and either the LLR observes the bad signal so and the liquidity shock satisfies $v \leq v_0$, or it observes the good signal s_1 and the liquidity shock satisfies $v \leq v_1$. By assumption 2 and the independence of v we have

$$\begin{aligned}\Pr(R_1, s_0, \text{ and } v \leq v_0) &= \Pr(R_1)\Pr(s_0|R_1)\Pr(v \leq v_0)\\ &= p(1-q)F(v_0),\\ \Pr(R_1, s_1, \text{ and } v \leq v_1) &= \Pr(R_1)\Pr(s_1|R_1)\Pr(v \leq v_1)\\ &= pqF(v_1).\end{aligned}$$

Hence, the bank's objective function is

$$U_B = p[(1-q)F(v_0) + qF(v_1)][R(p) - 1]. \tag{11.7}$$

A Nash equilibrium of the game between the bank and the LLR is a choice of risk p^* by the bank, and a choice of maximum liquidity support by the LLR contingent on the bad

[7]The fact that v_1 may be greater than one is not a problem, because since the support of v is [0, 1], we have $\Pr(v \leq v_1) = F(v_1) = 1$, so in this case the bank would be supported with probability one.

and the good signal, v_0^* and v_1^*, such that p^* maximizes

$$p[(1-q)F(v_0^*)+qF(v_1^*)][R(p)-1],$$

and

$$v_0^* = \frac{cp^*(1-q)}{(1-p^*)q} \quad \text{and} \quad v_1^* = \frac{cp^*q}{(1-p^*)(1-q)}.$$

In this definition, it is important to realize that since the LLR does not observe the bank's choice of risk, the critical values v_0^* and v_1^* only depend on the equilibrium p^*. This in turn implies that the term $[(1-q)F(v_0^*)+qF(v_1^*)]$ factors out in the bank's objective function, so its problem reduces to maximize $p[R(p)-1]$.[8]

The first-order condition that characterizes the equilibrium choice of risk p^* is

$$R(p^*)+p^*(R)'(p^*)=1. \tag{11.8}$$

Since, by assumption 1, $R(p)+pR'(p)$ is decreasing in p, conditions (2) and (8) imply that p^* is strictly below the first-best $\widehat{p}$, so the bank will be choosing too much risk. This is just the standard risk-shifting effect that follows from debt financing under limited liability.

It should be noted that the bank's choice of p changes the probability distribution of the signals, increasing $\Pr(s_1)=pq+(1-p)(1-q)$ and decreasing $\Pr(s_0)=1-\Pr(s_1)$ (as long as $q>\frac{1}{2}$). However, by assumption 2, p does not affect the distribution of the signals conditional on the realization of the high return R_1, which implies that the bank's probability of getting $R(p)-1$ is linear in $p=\Pr(R_1)$.

To sum up, we have set up a model of a bank and an LLR in which the former chooses the riskiness of its portfolio and the latter chooses whether to lend to the bank to cover random deposit withdrawals, a decision that depends on a signal on the ex-post quality of the portfolio. We have shown that the bank's equilibrium choice of risk is independent of the distribution of the liquidity shocks and the other parameters that determine the LLR's decision, such as the quality of the supervisory information or the social cost of bank failure.

2. The General Model

We now introduce in our basic model two features of banking in the real world that are relevant to the problem under discussion. First, on the asset side of the bank's balance sheet, we suppose that, apart from the risky asset, the bank can invest in a safe and perfectly liquid asset that can be used as a buffer against liquidity shocks. Second, on the liability side, we suppose that the bank can be funded with both deposits and equity capital, and that the bank is subject to a minimum capital requirement. The LLR observes both the bank's equity capital and its investment in the liquid asset. We characterize the equilibrium of the new game between the bank and the LLR, compare it with that of a model without an LLR, and examine its comparative statics properties.

[8] In a sequential game of complete information, the characterization of equilibrium would be more complicated, since the critical values v_0^* and v_1^* would depend on the bank's choice of p.

Specifically, suppose that at date 0 the bank raises k equity capital and 1-k deposits, and invests λ in the safe asset and $1 - \lambda$ in the risky asset, so the size of its balance sheet is normalized to one.[9] Bank capital has to satisfy the constraint $k \geq \kappa(1-\lambda)$, where $\kappa \in (0, 1)$. Thus, the capital requirement depends on the (observable) bank's investment in the risky asset, but not on the (unobservable) bank's choice of risk.

We assume that the return of the safe asset is equal to the deposit rate, which has been normalized to zero, and that bank capital is provided by a special class of agents, called bankers, who require an expected rate of return $\delta \geq 0$ on their investment. A strictly positive value of δ captures either the scarcity of bankers' wealth or, perhaps more realistically, the existence of a premium for the agency and asymmetric information problems faced by the bank shareholders.[10]

2.1 Characterization of Equilibrium

At date 1 a fraction $v \in [0, 1]$ of the deposits are withdrawn. Since the bank has $1 - k$ deposits, then $v(1 - k)$ deposits are withdrawn at this date. There are two cases to consider. First, if $v(1 - k) \leq \lambda$, the bank can repay the depositors by selling the required amount of the safe asset, so it keeps $\lambda - v(1 - k)$ invested in the safe asset. In this case the bank's payoff in the high-return state equals the return of its investment in the safe asset, $\lambda - v(1 - k)$, plus the return of its investment in the risky asset, $(1 - \lambda)R(p)$, minus the amount paid to the remaining depositors, $(1 - v)(1 - k)$, that is,

$$\lambda - v(1-k) + (1-\lambda)R(p) - (1-v)(1-k) = (1-\lambda)[R(p) - 1] + k.$$

Second, if $v(1 - k) > \lambda$, the bank needs to borrow $v(1 - k) - \lambda$ from the LLR in order to avoid liquidation. If such funding is obtained, the bank's payoff in the high-return state equals the return of its investment in the risky asset, $(1 - \lambda)R(p)$, minus the amount paid to the remaining depositors, $(1 - v)(1 - k)$, minus the amount paid to the LLR, $v(1 - k) - \lambda$, that is,

$$(1-\lambda)R(p) - (1-v)\,(1-k) - [v(1-k) - \lambda] = (1-\lambda)\,[R(p) - 1] + k.$$

In both cases, if the low-return state obtains, the bank's net worth is $\lambda - (1 - k)$, which will be negative as long as the bank's investment in the liquid asset, λ, does not exceed its deposits, $1 - k$, which will generally obtain in equilibrium.[11] Hence, by limited liability, the bank's payoff in the low-return state will be zero. Obviously, its payoff will also be zero when $v(1 - k) > \lambda$ and the LLR does not support the bank.

The decision of the LLR in the case in which the bank requires emergency lending, $v(1 - k) > \lambda$, is characterized as follows. If the LLR observes signal s and decides to support the bank, with probability $\Pr(R_1|s)$ the bank will be solvent at date 2 and the LLR will recover its loan $v(1 - k) - \lambda$, while with probability $\Pr(R_0|s)$ the bank will fail and the

[9] This assumption is made without loss of generality. The same results would obtain if, for example, the bank raised one unit of deposits and k units of capital, and invested λ in the safe asset and $1 + k - \lambda$ in the risky asset.

[10] See Holmström and Tirole (1997) and Diamond and Rajan (2000) for explicit models of why δ might be positive. The same assumption is made by Bolton and Freixas (2000), Hellmann, Murdock, and Stiglitz (2000), and Repullo and Suarez (2004), among others.

[11] In particular, we show below that under plausible conditions the capital requirement will be binding, so $k = \kappa(1 - \lambda)$, which implies $\lambda - (1 - k) = -(1 - \kappa)(1 - \lambda) < 0$.

LLR will lose $v(1-k)-\lambda$ and incur the cost c. If, on the other hand, the LLR does not provide the liquidity support, the bank will be liquidated at date 1, and the LLR's payoff will be $-c$. Hence the LLR will support the bank if

$$-[v(1-k)-\lambda+c]\Pr(R_0|s) \geq -c.$$

As before, substituting (3) and (4) into this expression, it follows that when the LLR observes the bad signal s_0, it will support the bank if the liquidity shortfall, $v(1-k)-\lambda$, is smaller than or equal to the critical value v_0 given by (5), that is, if

$$v \leq \frac{v_0+\lambda}{1-k}, \tag{11.9}$$

and when it observes the good signal s_1, it will support the bank if the liquidity shortfall, $v(1-k)-\lambda$, is smaller than or equal to the critical value v_1 given by (6), that is, if

$$v \leq \frac{v_1+\lambda}{1-k}. \tag{11.10}$$

Thus, the probability that the bank will reach the final date 2 is increasing in its investment in the safe asset λ and its equity capital k. This is explained by the role of the safe asset as a buffer against liquidity shocks, and by the fact that the higher the bank capital, the lower its deposits and hence the size of the liquidity shocks.

The bank's objective function is to maximize the expected value of the shareholders' payoff net of the opportunity cost of their initial infusion of capital. The latter is simply $(1+\delta)k$. To compute the former, notice that bank shareholders get a zero payoff if the bank is liquidated at date 1 or fails at date 2, and they get $(1-\lambda)(R(p)-1)+k$ if it succeeds at date 2. This event happens when the high return R_1 obtains and either the LLR observes the bad signal s_0 and the liquidity shock v satisfies (9), or it observes the good signal s_1 and the liquidity shock v satisfies (10). As before, we have

$$\Pr\left(R_1, s_0, \text{ and } v \leq \frac{v_0+\lambda}{1-k}\right) = p(1-q)F\left(\frac{v_0+\lambda}{1-k}\right),$$
$$\Pr\left(R_1, s_1, \text{ and } v \leq \frac{v_1+\lambda}{1-k}\right) = pqF\left(\frac{v_1+\lambda}{1-k}\right).$$

Hence, the bank's objective function in the general model is

$$U_B = p\left[(1-q)F\left(\frac{v_0+\lambda}{1-k}\right) + qF\left(\frac{v_1+\lambda}{1-k}\right)\right] \times [(1-\lambda)(R(p)-1)+k] - (1+\delta)k. \tag{11.11}$$

Obviously, U_B coincides with the objective function (7) in the previous section when $\lambda = 0$ and $k = 0$.

A Nash equilibrium of the game between the bank and the LLR is a choice of liquidity λ^*, capital k^*, and risk p^* by the bank, and a choice of maximum liquidity support by the LLR contingent on the bad and the good signal, v_0^* and v_1^*, such that (λ^*, k^*, p^*) maximizes

$$p\left[(1-q)F\left(\frac{v_0^*+\lambda}{1-k}\right)+qF\left(\frac{v_1^*+\lambda}{1-k}\right)\right] \times [(1-\lambda)(R(p)-1)+k]-(1+\delta)k, \qquad (11.12)$$

subject to the capital requirement $k \geq \kappa(1\text{-}\lambda)$, and

$$v_0^* = \frac{cp^*(1-q)}{(1-p^*)q} \quad \text{and} \quad v_1^* = \frac{cp^*q}{(1-p^*)(1-q)}. \qquad (11.13)$$

As in the basic model, it is important to note that since the LLR does not observe the bank's choice of risk, the critical values v_0^* and v_1^* only depend on the equilibrium p^*. This in turn implies that the bank's problem reduces to maximize $p[(1-\lambda)(R(p)-1)+k]$. Thus, the bank's choice of risk is characterized by the first-order condition

$$(1-\lambda^*)[R(p^*)-1]+k^*+p^*(1-\lambda^*)R'(p^*)=0,$$

which simplifies to

$$R(p^*)+p^*R'(p^*)=1-\frac{k^*}{1-\lambda^*}. \qquad (11.14)$$

Comparing this expression with (2) and (8), and taking into account that, by assumption 1, $R(p)+pR'(p)$ is decreasing in p, it follows that the bank's equilibrium choice of risk p^* will be closer to the first-best $\widehat{p}$ than in the model without the capital requirement. This is just the standard *capital-at-risk effect*: higher capital implies higher losses for the bank's shareholders in case of default and hence lower incentives for risk taking.[12]

If the bank's equilibrium choice of capital k^* is at the corner $\kappa(1-\lambda^*)$, then the first-order condition (14) further simplifies to

$$R(p^*)+p^*R'(p^*)=1-\kappa. \qquad (11.15)$$

In this case, the equilibrium p^* only depends on the capital requirement κ. Moreover, assumption 1 implies that $R(p)+pR'(p)$ is decreasing in p, which gives $dp^*/d\kappa > 0$. Hence, the higher the capital requirement, the lower the risk chosen by the bank.[13]

In general, it is difficult to prove that this corner solution will obtain, since the properties of the bank's objective function (12) depend on the shape of the distribution function of the liquidity shock $F(v)$.[14] For this reason, in what follows we work with a specific parameterization of $F(v)$, namely $F(v)=v^{\eta}$, where $\eta \in (0,1)$.[15] In this case it can be

[12] See Hellmann, Murdock, and Stiglitz (2000) and Repullo (2004) for a recent discussion of this effect.

[13] Notice that for $\kappa = 1$, that is, a 100% capital requirement, (2) and (15) imply $p^* = \widehat{p}$.

[14] However, finding that k is at the minimum required by regulation is standard in both static and dynamic models of banking; see, for example, Repullo and Suarez (2004) and Repullo (2004).

[15] Notice that this is a simple special case of a beta distribution for which the density function $F'(v)=\eta v^{\eta-1}$ is decreasing in v, so small liquidity shocks are more likely than large shocks.

checked that the bank's objective function (12) is convex in k, so we can only have either $k^* = \kappa(1-\lambda^*)$ or $k^* = 1$. But for large k we have

$$F\left(\frac{v_0^* + \lambda}{1-k}\right) = F\left(\frac{v_1^* + \lambda}{1-k}\right) = 1,$$

so the derivative of (12) with respect to k is $p - (1+\delta) < 0$. Hence $k = 1$ cannot be a solution, which gives $k^* = \kappa(1-\lambda^*)$.

This result implies that the equilibrium of the game between the bank and the LLR is easy to characterize. The risk p^* chosen by the bank is the unique solution of the first-order condition (15). This in turn determines the critical values v_0^* and v_1^* that characterize the behavior of the LLR. Substituting $p = p^*$ and $F(v) = v^n$ into the bank's objective function (12), we then find the value of λ^* by maximizing

$$p^*\left[(1-q)\left(\frac{v_0^*+\lambda}{1-k}\right)^{\eta} + q\left(\frac{v_1^*+\lambda}{1-k}\right)^{\eta}\right] \times [(1-\lambda)(R(p^*)-1)+k] - (1+\delta)k, \qquad (11.16)$$

subject to $k = \kappa(1-\lambda)$. Finally, we get $k^* = \kappa(1-\lambda^*)$.

Going analytically beyond this point is, however, complicated, because although the bank's objective function (16) is concave in λ, this is in general no longer the case once we substitute the constraint $k = \kappa(1-\lambda)$ into (16), since this function is convex in k. For this reason, our results on equilibrium liquidity and capital will be derived from numerical solutions.

2.2 Equilibrium Without an LLR

We now compare the equilibrium behavior of the bank when there is an LLR with its behavior when there is no LLR. The objective function of the bank in such a model is a special case of (11) when we set $v_0 = v_1 = 0$ (i.e., no last-resort lending), which gives

$$U_B = pF\left(\frac{\lambda}{1-k}\right)[(1-\lambda)(R(p)-1)+k] - (1+\delta)k.$$

Thus, the bank gets $(1-\lambda)(R(p)-1)+k$ in the high-return state, which obtains with probability p, but only if it has sufficient liquidity to cover the deposit withdrawals at date 1—that is, if $v(1-k) \leq \lambda$, an event that happens with probability $F(\lambda/(1-k))$.

From here we can follow our previous steps to conclude that when the bank's capital k is at the corner $\kappa(1-\lambda^*)$, its choice of risk is characterized by the first-order condition (15), so we get exactly the same p^* as in the model with the LLR. In other words, contrary to what has been taken for granted in the banking literature, our model predicts that *the existence of an LLR does not have any effect on the bank's incentives to take risk.*

Computation of the effects of having an LLR on the liquidity decision of the bank requires us to specify the functional forms of the high return of the risky asset, $R(p)$, and the cumulative distribution function of the liquidity shock, $F(v)$, as well as the parameter values of the capital requirement κ, the cost of capital δ, the informativeness of the supervisory signal q, and the social cost of bank failure c. Since our focus is on qualitative results, we will not calibrate the model to obtain plausible numerical results, but instead choose simple functional forms and parameter values. Specifically, the functional forms $R(p) = 3 - 2p^2$

Table 11.1 Equilibria with and without an LLR

	With LLR	Without LLR
λ^*	0.11	0.23
k^*	0.09	0.08
p^*	0.59	0.59
v_0^*	0.10	–
v_1^*	0.22	–

and $F(v) = v^\eta$, with $\eta = 0.25$, will be maintained in all our simulations,[16] and our baseline parameter values are $L = 0.50$, $\kappa = \delta = c = 0.10$, and $q = 0.60$.

The corresponding equilibria with and without an LLR are shown in table 11.1. As noted above, the level of risk p^* chosen by the bank is the same in both models, and may be obtained by substituting $R(p) = 3 - 2p^2$ into (15), which gives $p^* = \sqrt{(2+\kappa)/6} = 0.59$. Not surprisingly, the results in table 11.1 show that the liquidity buffer λ^* is much larger in the absence of an LLR.[17] Given that $k^* = \kappa(1 - \lambda^*)$, this in turn implies a lower level of capital.

When the deposit withdrawal $v(1 - k^*)$ is below the bank's liquidity λ^* (an event that happens with probability 0.58 in the model with the LLR, and with probability 0.71 in the model without it), the bank will be able to repay the depositors by selling the required amount of the safe asset. Moreover, in the first model, when $v(1 - k^*) > \lambda^*$, the LLR will provide liquidity up to $v_0^* = 0.10$ when it observes the bad signal s_0, and up to $v_1^* = 0.22$ when it observes the good signal s_1.

The probability that the bank gets a positive payoff in the model with an LLR is

$$p^* \left[(1-q)F\left(\frac{v_0^* + \lambda^*}{1-k^*}\right) + qF\left(\frac{v_1^* + \lambda^*}{1-k^*}\right) \right] = 0.44,$$

while the corresponding probability in the model without an LLR is

$$p^* F\left(\frac{\lambda^*}{1-k^*}\right) = 0.42.$$

Since in the first model the bank is investing a higher proportion of its portfolio in the risky asset, its equilibrium expected payoff is significantly higher with an LLR (0.45 against 0.37).

2.3 Comparative Statics

We next analyze the effect on the equilibrium of the game between the bank and the LLR of changes in the capital requirement κ, the cost of capital δ, the informativeness of the

[16]Observe that $R(p) = 3 - 2p^2$ is decreasing and concave, with $R(1) = 1$ and $R(1) + R'(1) = -3 < 0$, so assumption 1 is satisfied. Also, the median liquidity shock is $F^{-1}(0.5) = 0.0625$.

[17]Gonzalez-Eiras (2003) provides some interesting empirical evidence on this result. He shows that the contingent credit line agreement signed by the Central Bank of Argentina with a group of international banks in December 1996 enhanced that central bank's ability to act as an LLR and led to a significant decrease in the liquidity holdings of domestic Argentinian banks.

Table 11.2 Equilibrium Effects of Changes in the Capital Requirement κ, the Cost of Capital δ, the Informativeness of the Supervisory Signal q, and the Social Cost of Bank Failure c

x	$\frac{dp^*}{dx}$	$\frac{d\lambda^*}{dx}$	$\frac{dk^*}{dx}$	$\frac{dv_0^*}{dx}$	$\frac{dv_1^*}{dx}$
κ	+	+	+	+	+
δ	0	+	−	0	0
q	0	−	+	−	+
c	0	−	+	+	+

supervisory signal q, and the social cost of bank failure c. The results summarized in table 11.2 are derived by computing the equilibrium corresponding to deviations in κ, δ, q, and c from the baseline case.

As noted above, an increase in the capital requirement κ leads to an increase in p^*, which by (13) increases the maximum support provided by the LLR contingent on the bad and the good signal, $v_0^*$and v_1^*. The effect on λ^* is also positive. Two reasons explain this result. First, the higher capital requirement makes investment in the risky asset, which does not carry a capital charge, relatively less attractive for the bank than investing in the safe asset. Second, the higher p^* reduces the success payoff of the risky asset, $R(p^*)$, and also makes it relatively less attractive for the bank than the safe asset. On the other hand, the higher liquidity support offered by the LLR reduces the bank's incentives to invest in the safe asset, but the numerical results show that this effect is dominated by the other two.

With regard to the other comparative statics results, note first that, as shown analytically, the value of p^* chosen by the bank only depends on the capital requirement κ, so the effect of the other three parameters is zero.

Since the cost of capital δ does not affect p^*, it does not have any effect either on the maximum liquidity support provided by the LLR contingent on the bad and the good signal, v_0^* and v_1^*. The cost of capital δ has a positive effect on equilibrium liquidity λ^*, because when capital is more expensive, investing in the safe asset (which does not carry a capital charge) is relatively more attractive than investing in the risky asset. Since $k^* = \kappa(1 - \lambda^*)$, this also explains why an increase in δ has a negative effect on k^*.

As noted in section 1, the critical value v_0^* is decreasing in the quality q of the supervisory information, while the critical value v_1^* is increasing in q, so with better information the bank is less (more) likely to be supported by the LLR when the signal is bad (good). The sign of the derivative of λ^* with respect to q is negative, which means that the positive effect of having less support when the signal is bad is dominated by the negative effect of having more support when the signal is good. Since $k^* = \kappa(1 - \lambda^*)$, this in turn explains why an increase in q has a positive effect on k^*. However, when q is sufficiently large, we may get to the corner $\lambda^* = 0$ and $k^* = \kappa$, where these derivatives become zero.

As also noted in section 1, the critical values v_0^* and v_1^* are increasing in the social cost of bank failure c, because when this cost is high, the LLR has a stronger incentive to lend to the bank in order to save c when the higher return state obtains. This explains why the bank wants to hold a lower liquidity buffer λ^*, so $k^* = \kappa(1 - \lambda^*)$ will be higher. However, as in the case of parameter q, when c is sufficiently large, we may get to the corner $\lambda^* = 0$ and $k^* = \kappa$, where these derivatives become zero.

If we consider that the social cost of failure increases more than proportionately with the size of the bank's balance sheet (which we have normalized to one), c will be higher for large banks, which implies a "too big to fail" result: large banks are more likely to be supported by the LLR, and consequently they will hold smaller liquidity buffers.

3. Extensions

3.1 Penalty Rates

The classical doctrine on the LLR put forward by Bagehot (1873) required "that these loans should only be made at a very high rate of interest." We now examine how the results in section 2 are modified when the LLR charges a penalty rate $r > 0$. Importantly, we assume that r is exogenously given ex-ante, and not chosen by the LLR ex-post.

To characterize the equilibrium of the new game between the bank and the LLR, suppose that $v(1-k)$ deposits are withdrawn at date 1. If $v(1-k) \leq \lambda$, the bank can repay the depositors by selling the required amount of the safe asset, so there is no change with respect to our previous analysis. If, on the other hand, $v(1-k) > \lambda$, the bank needs to borrow $v(1-k) - \lambda$ from the LLR. If such funding is obtained, the bank's payoff in the high-return state equals the return of its investment in the risky asset, $(1-\lambda)R(p)$, minus the amount paid to the remaining depositors, $(1-v)(1-k)$, minus the amount paid to the LLR, $(1+r)[v(1-k)-\lambda]$, that is,

$$(1-\lambda)R(p) - (1-v)(1-k) - (1+r)[v(1-k)-\lambda]$$
$$= (1-\lambda)[R(p)-1] + k - r[v(1-k)-\lambda].$$

The last term in this expression accounts for the interest payments to the LLR.

The decision of the LLR in the case when $v(1-k) > \lambda$ is now characterized as follows. If the LLR observes signal s and decides to support the bank, with probability $\Pr(R_1|s)$ the bank will be solvent at date 2 and the LLR will recover its loan $v(1-k)-\lambda$ and net $r[v(1-k)-\lambda]$ in interest payments, while with probability $\Pr(R_0|s)$ the bank will fail and the LLR will lose $v(1-k)-\lambda$ and incur the cost c, so the LLR's expected payoff is

$$r[v(1-k)-\lambda]\Pr(R_1|s) - [v(1-k)-\lambda+c]\Pr(R_0|s).$$

On the other hand, if the LLR does not provide the liquidity support, the bank will be liquidated at date 1, and the LLR's payoff will be $-c$. Hence the LLR will support the bank if

$$r[v(1-k)-\lambda]\Pr(R_1|s) - [v(1-k)-\lambda+c]\Pr(R_0|s) \geq -c.$$

Substituting (3) and (4) into this expression, it follows that when the LLR observes the bad signal s_0, it will support the bank if the liquidity shortfall, $v(1-k)-\lambda$, is smaller than or equal to the critical value

$$v_0 \equiv \frac{c\Pr(R_1|s_0)}{\Pr(R_0|s_0) - r\Pr(R_1|s_0)} = \frac{cp(1-q)}{(1-p)q - rp(1-q)},$$

and when the LLR observes the good signal s_1 it will support the bank if the liquidity shortfall, $v(1-k)-\lambda$, is smaller than or equal to the critical value

$$v_1 \equiv \frac{c\Pr(R_1|s_1)}{\Pr(R_0|s_1) - r\Pr(R_1|s_1)} = \frac{cpq}{(1-p)(1-q) - rpq}.$$

As before, it is easy to check that $v_1 > v_0$ whenever $q > \frac{1}{2}$. Also, notice that both v_0 and v_1 are increasing in r, so with penalty rates the LLR will be softer with the bank, providing emergency funding for a larger range of liquidity shocks.

To compute the bank's new objective function, we have to subtract from U_B in (11) the expected interest payments to the LLR. If the LLR observes the bad signal s_0, the bank borrows from the LLR when $0 < v(1-k) - \lambda \leq v_0$, that is, when

$$\frac{\lambda}{1-k} < v \leq \frac{v_0 + \lambda}{1-k},$$

so the conditional expected cost of this borrowing is

$$r\left[\int_{\frac{\lambda}{1-k}}^{\frac{v_0+\lambda}{1-k}} [v(1-k) - \lambda]\, dF(v)\right] \Pr(s_0|R_1).$$

Similarly, if the LLR observes the good signal s_1, the conditional expected cost of the bank's borrowing is

$$r\left[\int_{\frac{\lambda}{1-k}}^{\frac{v_1+\lambda}{1-k}} [v(1-k) - \lambda]\, dF(v)\right] \Pr(s_1|R_1).$$

Hence the bank's new objective function is

$$\begin{aligned} U_B = {} & p\left[(1-q)F\left(\frac{v_0+\lambda}{1-k}\right) + qF\left(\frac{v_1+\lambda}{1-k}\right)\right] \\ & \times\ [(1-\lambda)(R(p) - 1 + k] - (1+\delta)k \\ & - rp\left[(1-q)\int_{\frac{\lambda}{1-k}}^{\frac{v_0+\lambda}{1-k}} [v(1-k) - \lambda]\, dF(v)\right. \\ & \left. + q\int_{\frac{\lambda}{1-k}}^{\frac{v_1+\lambda}{1-k}} [v(1-k) - \lambda]\, dF(v)\right]. \end{aligned}$$

Assuming that $F(v) = v^\eta$, the integrals in this expression can be easily solved, and we can compute for the baseline parameters the equilibrium effects of charging a penalty rate r.[18] The results are presented in table 11.3.

Thus, an increase in the penalty rate r leads to a reduction in p^*, so the bank's portfolio becomes riskier. The reason for this result is that penalty rates increase the expected interest

Table 11.3 Equilibrium Effects of Changes in the Penalty Rate r

x	$\frac{dp^*}{dx}$	$\frac{d\lambda^*}{dx}$	$\frac{dk^*}{dx}$	$\frac{dv_0^*}{dx}$	$\frac{dv_1^*}{dx}$
r	−	−	+	+	+

[18] It should be noted that this computation is complicated because now p^* depends on r, and cannot be directly solved from the first-order condition (15). The equilibrium is obtained by numerical iteration of the best response functions of the two players.

payments in the high-return state and, consequently, the bank tries to compensate for this effect by choosing a higher risk and higher return portfolio (recall that by assumption 1, a decrease in p increases $R(p)$). The reduction in p^* would ceteris paribus lead to a decrease in both v_0^* and v_1^*, but this is more than compensated by the positive effect of the interest payments on the LLR's willingness to lend. The increase in v_0^* and v_1^* in turn explains why the bank chooses a lower liquidity buffer λ^*, so $k^* = \kappa(1 - \lambda^*)$ will be higher.

3.2 Collateralized Lending

The classical doctrine on the LLR put forward by Bagehot (1873) not only required charging "a very high rate of interest," but also "that at this rate these advances should be made on all good banking securities." We now examine how the results in section 2 are modified when last-resort lending is collateralized, so the LLR becomes a senior claimant when it provides the liquidity support and the bank subsequently fails.[19] Obviously, for this to make any difference the failure return should be positive, so in this subsection we assume that $R_0 = l \in (0, L)$.[20]

To analyze the effect of this change, consider a situation in which $v(1-k) > \lambda$, and let s be the signal observed by the LLR. There are two cases to consider. First, if the liquidity shortfall, $v(1-k) - \lambda$, is smaller than or equal to the collateral l, the LLR is fully covered, so its expected payoff if it supports the bank, $-c\Pr(R_0|s)$, is greater than the payoff if it does not, $-c$, so the bank will always be supported. Second, if the liquidity shortfall, $v(1-k) - \lambda$, is greater than the collateral l, the expected payoff of the LLR if it supports the bank is

$$-[v(1-k) - \lambda - l + c]\Pr(R_0|s),$$

since with probability $\Pr(R_0|s)$ the bank will fail at date 2 and the LLR will lose $v(1-k) - \lambda - l$ and incur the cost c. On the other hand, if the LLR does not provide the liquidity support, the bank will be liquidated at date 1, and the LLR's payoff will be $-c$. Hence the LLR will support the bank if

$$-[v(1-k) - \lambda - l + c]\Pr(R_0|s) \geq -c.$$

Substituting (3) and (4) into this expression, it follows that when the LLR observes the bad signal s_0, it will support the bank if the liquidity shortfall, $v(1-k) - \lambda$, is smaller than or equal to the critical value $v_0 + l$, where v_0 is given by (5); when the LLR observes the good signal s_1, it will support the bank if the liquidity shortfall, $v(1-k) - \lambda$, is smaller than or equal to the critical value $v_1 + l$, where v_1 is given by (6).

[19] The referee criticized this interpretation, noting that "if we follow Bagehot's second rule and only provide liquidity backed by 'good banking securities,' it is not clear why the central bank will end up underwriting risky investments." In the referee's view, in the present model, "a fairer interpretation of Bagehot might imply no lending by the central bank at all." However, as noted by Goodhart (1999, 343), "Bagehot's proposal related simply to the collateral that the applicant could offer, and the effect of this rule in practice was to distinguish, in part, between those loans on which the central bank might expect with some considerable probability to make a loss and those on which little, or no, loss should eventuate."

[20] The assumption that the failure return l at date 2 is smaller than the liquidation value L at date 1 is not required for our analysis, but makes a lot of sense in the context of the model.

Table 11.4 Equilibrium Effects of Collateralization

x	$\frac{dp^*}{dx}$	$\frac{d\lambda^*}{dx}$	$\frac{dk^*}{dx}$	$\frac{d(v_0^*+l)}{dx}$	$\frac{d(v_1^*+l)}{dx}$
l	0	$-$	$+$	1	1

Hence the bank's objective function becomes

$$U_B = p\left[(1-q)F\left(\frac{v_0+l+\lambda}{1-k}\right)+qF\left(\frac{v_1+l+\lambda}{1-k}\right)\right]$$
$$\times\,[(1-\lambda)(R(p)-1)+k]-(1+\delta)k.$$

Using the same arguments as in section 2, it follows that the bank's choice of risk p^* will also be characterized by the first-order condition (15), so it only depends on the capital requirement κ.

As for the effect of collateralization on the bank's liquidity and capital decisions, note that the case in which the LLR's loan is not collateralized (and it is junior to the claim of the deposit insurer) is equivalent to the case $l = 0$ analyzed in section 2, so the signs of derivatives with respect to l in table 11.4 indicate the effect of collateralization on λ^* and k^*.

Thus, collateralization of last-resort lending does not have any effect on the bank's incentives to take risk, but increases the maximum support that the LLR is willing to provide contingent on the bad and the good signal, $v_0^* + l$ and $v_1^* + l$. This explains why the bank wants to hold a lower liquidity buffer λ^*, so $k^* = \kappa(1\text{-}\lambda^*)$ will be higher. In other words, the protection for the LLR advocated by Bagehot translates into a lower liquidity buffer and hence a higher probability that the bank will require emergency liquidity assistance, but without any effect on risk taking.

3.3 Discounting of Future Payoffs

The LLR is a public institution that is run by officials that may have fixed terms of office. If these terms are short or the officials are close to finishing their terms, the officials may have an incentive to avoid current costs possibly at the expense of some larger future costs that would be assumed by their successors. Formally, we can incorporate this possibility into our model by introducing a discount factor $\beta < 1$ for the LLR.[21]

To analyze the effect of such discounting, consider a situation in which $v(1-k) > \lambda$, and let s be the signal observed by the LLR. The expected discounted payoff of the LLR if it supports the bank is now

$$-\beta[v(1-k)-\lambda+c]\Pr(R_0|s),$$

since with probability $\Pr(R_0|s)$ the bank will fail at date 2 and the LLR will lose $v(1-k)-\lambda$ and incur the cost c. On the other hand, if the LLR does not provide the liquidity support,

[21] This assumption is justified by Kaufman (1991) in the following terms: "The discount rate used by policy makers, who are under considerable political pressure to optimize economic performance in the short-term and whose terms of office are relatively short and not guaranteed to last until the next crisis, is likely to be overestimated."

the bank will be liquidated at date 1, and the LLR's payoff will be $-c$. Hence the LLR will support the bank if

$$-\beta[v(1-k)-\lambda+c]\Pr(R_0|s)\geq -c.$$

Substituting (3) and (4) into this expression, it follows that when the LLR observes the bad signal s_0, it will support the bank if the liquidity shortfall, $v(1-k)-\lambda$, is smaller than or equal to the critical value

$$v_0 \equiv \frac{c[1-\beta\Pr(R_0|s_0)]}{\beta\Pr(R_0|s_0)} = \frac{c[p(1-q)+(1-\beta)(1-p)q]}{\beta(1-p)q},$$

and when the LLR observes the good signal s_1, it will support the bank if the liquidity shortfall, $v(1-k)-\lambda$, is smaller than or equal to the critical value

$$v_1 \equiv \frac{c[1-\beta\Pr(R_0|s_1)]}{\beta\Pr(R_0|s_1)} = \frac{c[pq+(1-\beta)(1-p)(1-q)]}{\beta(1-p)(1-q)}.$$

As before, it is easy to check that $v_1 > v_0$ whenever $q > \frac{1}{2}$. Also, notice that both v_0 and v_1 are decreasing in the discount factor β. This means that an LLR with $\beta < 1$ will be softer with the bank, providing funding for a larger range of liquidity shocks.

We can now compute for the baseline parameters the equilibrium effects of introducing a discount factor $\beta < 1$ for the LLR. As in the model in section 2, the bank's choice of risk p^* is again characterized by the first-order condition (15), so the discount factor β does not have any effect on the bank's incentives to take risk. The full comparative statics results are presented in table 11.5.

As expected, an increase in the discount factor β (that is, a decrease in the corresponding discount rate) makes the LLR more willing to incur the current costs of not supporting the bank in order to save some larger future costs, so the derivative of v_0^* and v_1^* with respect to β is negative. The reduction in v_0^* and v_1^* in turn explains why the bank chooses a higher liquidity buffer λ^*, so $k^* = \kappa(1-\lambda^*)$ will be lower.

Thus we conclude that a high LLR discount rate leads to forbearance, but in line with our previous results, this only translates into a lower liquidity buffer, without any effect on risk taking.

3.4 Internalizing Deposit Insurance Payouts

We have assumed so far that the LLR is institutionally separated from the deposit insurer, so the former does not take into account deposit insurance payouts in deciding whether to support the bank. We now consider a situation in which the LLR either internalizes or assumes a fraction $\gamma \in [0, 1]$ of these payouts. When $\gamma = 0$, the LLR is completely

Table 11.5 Equilibrium Effects of Changes in the LLR's Discount Factor β

x	$\frac{dp^*}{dx}$	$\frac{d\lambda^*}{dx}$	$\frac{dk^*}{dx}$	$\frac{dv_0^*}{dx}$	$\frac{dv_1^*}{dx}$
β	0	+	−	−	−

independent from the deposit insurer (e.g., a central bank with no deposit insurance role), whereas when $\gamma = 1$, the LLR also acts as deposit insurer.[22]

To analyze the effect of such possible connection between the LLR and the deposit insurer, consider a situation in which $v(1\text{-}k) > \lambda$, and let s be the signal observed by the LLR. The expected payoff of the LLR if it supports the bank is now

$$-[v(1-k) - \lambda + c + \gamma(1-v)(1-k)]\,\Pr(R_0|s),$$

since with probability $\Pr(R_0|s)$ the bank will fail at date 2 and the LLR will lose $v(1-k)-\lambda$, incur the cost c, and assume a fraction γ of the deposit insurance payouts that are given by $(1-v)(1-k)$. On the other hand, if the LLR does not provide the liquidity support, the bank will be liquidated at date 1, and the LLR will incur the cost c and assume a fraction γ of the deposit insurance payouts that are given by $(1-k) - \lambda - (1-\lambda)L$, where $(1-\lambda)L$ is the liquidation value of the bank's risky asset.[23] Hence the LLR will support the bank if

$$\begin{aligned} &-[v(1-k) - \lambda + c + \gamma(1-v)(1-k)]\,\Pr(R_0|s) \\ &\geq -[c + \gamma[(1-k) - \lambda - (1-\lambda)L]]. \end{aligned}$$

Substituting (3) and (4) into this expression, it follows that when the LLR observes the bad signal s_0, it will support the bank if the liquidity shortfall, $v(1-k) - \lambda$, is smaller than or equal to the critical value

$$\begin{aligned} v_0 &\equiv \frac{[c + \gamma(1-k-\lambda)]\,\Pr(R_1|s_0) - \gamma(1-\lambda)L}{(1-\gamma)\,\Pr(R_0|s_0)} \\ &= \frac{[c + \gamma(1-k-\lambda)]\,p(1-q) - \gamma(1-\lambda)L[p(1-q) + (1-p)q]}{(1-\gamma)(1-p)q}, \end{aligned}$$

and when the LLR observes the good signal s_1, it will support the bank if the liquidity shortfall, $v(1-k) - \lambda$, is smaller than or equal to the critical value

$$\begin{aligned} v_1 &\equiv \frac{[c + \gamma(1-k-\lambda)]\,\Pr(R_1|s_1) - \gamma(1-\lambda)L}{(1-\gamma)\,\Pr(R_0|s_1)} \\ &= \frac{[c + \gamma(1-k-\lambda)]\,pq - \gamma(1-\lambda)L[pq + (1-p)(1-q)]}{(1-\gamma)(1-p)(1-q)}. \end{aligned}$$

As before, one can check that $v_1 > v_0$ whenever $q > \frac{1}{2}$.

We can now compute for the baseline parameters the equilibrium effects of internalizing a fraction γ of the deposit insurance payouts. As before, the bank's choice of risk p^* is again characterized by the first-order condition (15), so the share γ does not have any effect on the bank's incentives to take risk. The full comparative statics results are presented in table 11.6.

[22]Intermediate cases are also relevant. For example, until 1998 the Bank of Spain matched the contribution of the Spanish banks to the deposit insurance fund, so γ was $\frac{1}{2}$.

[23]We are implicitly assuming that the amount of deposits is greater than or equal to the liquidation value of the bank at date 1, that is, $1 - k \geq \lambda + (1-\lambda)L$. Notice that if k is at the corner $\kappa(1-\lambda)$, this condition reduces to $(1-\lambda)(1-\kappa-L) \geq 0$. In our numerical analysis we take $\kappa = 0.10$ and $L = 0.50$, so it holds.

Table 11.6 Equilibrium Effects of Changes in the LLR's Share of Deposit Insurance Payouts γ

x	$\frac{dp^*}{dx}$	$\frac{d\lambda^*}{dx}$	$\frac{dk^*}{dx}$	$\frac{dv_0^*}{dx}$	$\frac{dv_1^*}{dx}$
γ	0	$-/+$	$+/-$	$-$	$+$

An increase in the share γ makes the LLR tougher when it observes the bad signal s_0 (since the critical value v_0^* is decreasing in γ), and makes it softer when it observes the good signal s_1 (since the critical value v_1^* is increasing in γ). The sign of the derivative of λ^* with respect to γ is negative for small values of γ, for which the positive effect of having less support when the signal is bad is dominated by the negative effect of having more support when the signal is good. However, for sufficiently high values of γ, the critical value v_1^* reaches the value of 1, which means that the bank will always be supported when the signal is good, and so the only remaining effect will be the positive one associated with further reductions in v_0^*. Since $k^* = \kappa(1\text{-}\lambda^*)$, this explains the two possible signs of the effect of γ on k^*.

4. Concluding Remarks

Goodhart (1999, 339–40) has argued that "there are few issues so subject to myth, sometimes unhelpful myths that tend to obscure rather than illuminate real issues, as is the subject of whether a central bank ... should act as a lender of last resort." The third myth in his list is that "moral hazard is everywhere and at all times a major consideration."[24] This paper provides a rationale for the claim that this is indeed a myth. Specifically, it shows that the existence of a lender of last resort does not have any effect on the risk of the banks' illiquid portfolios, but simply reduces their incentives to hold liquid assets.

Although our model is special in a number of respects, we believe that the results are fairly robust. In particular, neither full deposit insurance nor the assumption that deposit withdrawals are purely random is essential. To see this, suppose that in the context of our basic model (without liquidity λ and capital k) there is an exogenous fraction $u \in (0, L)$ of junior uninsured deposits that require an expected return equal to zero,[25] and let d denote the corresponding interest rate. We assume that uninsured depositors observe the same signal $s \in \{s_0, s_1\}$ as the LLR,[26] and run on the bank at date 1 if and only if they observe the bad signal s_0.

In this situation, the LLR will support the bank if the withdrawal u is smaller than the critical value v_0 given by (5), so the bank's objective function (7) becomes

$$U_B = p[(1-q)1(u \leq v_0) + q][R(p) - 1 - ud],$$

[24] The other myths are that it is generally possible to distinguish between illiquidity and insolvency, that national central bank LLR capabilities are unrestricted whereas international bodies cannot function as LLRs, and that it is possible to dispense with an LLR altogether.

[25] The assumption that $u \leq L$ is made for simplicity, in order to ensure that the junior uninsured depositors get zero when the bank is liquidated at date 1.

[26] This assumption is also made for simplicity. See Repullo (2005) for a model where the depositors' signal is different (but coarser) than that of the LLR.

where $1(u \leq v_0)$ is an indicator function that takes the value 1 if $u \leq v_0$, and 0 otherwise. From here it follows that the first-order condition that characterizes the equilibrium choice of risk p^* is

$$R(p^*) + p^*R'(p^*) = 1 + ud^*, \tag{11.17}$$

where d^* is the equilibrium deposit rate. Assuming that uninsured depositors can only claim at date 1 the principal (and not the interest), they receive $1(u \leq v_0^*)u$ at date 1 with probability $\Pr(s_0) = q + (1-2q)p^*$, and $u(1+d^*)$ at date 2 with probability $\Pr(R_1, s_1) = qp^*$. Hence their participation constraint is

$$[q + (1-2q)p^*]1(u \leq v_0^*) + qp^*(1+d^*) = 1. \tag{11.18}$$

Solving equations (17) and (18) gives the equilibrium values of p^* and d^*.[27]

On the other hand, in the absence of an LLR, the bank's objective function becomes $U_B = pq[R(p) - 1 - ud]$, so the first-order condition (17) does not change, while the participation constraint (18) simplifies to $qp^*(1+d^*) = 1$. Hence we conclude that when $u > v_0^*$ the existence of an LLR does not have any effect on the bank's incentives to take risk. Moreover, when $u \leq v_0^*$, the existence of an LLR reduces the deposit rate that satisfies the participation constraint (18), which in turn, by the Stiglitz and Weiss (1981) argument noted in the introductory paragraphs of this paper, increases the equilibrium value of p^*. Hence having an LLR may actually reduce the bank's incentives to take risk.

The stark contrast between our results and the extant literature deserves further discussion. It is true that in general any form of insurance (e.g., against liquidity shocks) has the potential to create a moral hazard problem. In the context of our model, this clearly shows in the effect on the holding of liquid assets. But to have an effect on risk taking, something else is needed. One such case would be the following. Suppose that instead of observing a signal s on the return of the bank's risky asset, the uninsured depositors observe the bank's choice of p. Furthermore, suppose that, in the absence of an LLR, they can make the deposit rate d contingent on the choice of p (for example, by threatening to withdraw their funds). In this case, the bank would maximize $U_B = p[R(p) - 1 - ud(p)]$ subject to the uninsured depositors' participation constraint $p[1 + d(p)] = 1$. Substituting the constraint into the bank's objective function and maximizing the resulting expression with respect to p gives the first-order condition

$$R(\tilde{p}) + \tilde{p}R'(\tilde{p}) = 1 - u. \tag{11.19}$$

Since $R(p) + pR'(p)$ is decreasing, the bank's choice of risk $\tilde{p}$ is increasing in the proportion u of uninsured deposits, and converges to the first-best $\widehat{p}$ when u tends to 1. So we conclude that the existence of uninsured depositors that observe the bank's choice of risk and use this information to renegotiate the terms of their contract ameliorates the bank's risk-shifting incentives. Moreover, the introduction of an LLR that facilitates the withdrawal of the funds at date 1 may upset this disciplining mechanism, bringing us back to the $p^* < \tilde{p}$ characterized above.

[27] Since the relationship between p^* and d^* in both the first-order condition (17) and the participation constraint (18) is decreasing, we may have multiple equilibria, in which case we focus on the one that is closest to the first-best $\widehat{p}$—that is, the one with the highest p^*.

Two objections can be made to this argument. The standard one is that small depositors do not have the ability or the incentives to monitor banks.[28] The nonstandard one that we are putting forward here is that one should distinguish between the *monitoring of actions* and the *monitoring of the consequences of those actions*.[29] In the absence of an LLR, the former ameliorates the moral hazard problem, but the latter does not, because it simply changes the bank's objective function from $p[R(p) - 1 - ud]$ to $pq[R(p) - 1 - ud]$. Clearly, multiplying the function by a constant does not have any effect on the first-order condition that characterizes the bank's choice of risk. And the same result obtains when there is an LLR. Since arguably the second is the most plausible type of monitoring,[30] we conclude that there should be no presumption that the existence of an LLR worsens the bank's risk-shifting incentives—except, as shown in section 3.1, when it charges penalty rates.

Finally, it is worth noting that our model also provides a rationale for a standard feature of LLR policy, namely the principle of "constructive ambiguity." This is taken to mean that LLRs do not typically spell out beforehand the procedural and practical details of their policy. One possible rationalization of this principle is based on the idea of the LLR committing to a mixed strategy; see Freixas (1999). Our model supports a different story, suggested by Goodfriend and Lacker (1999), according to which the policy is not random from the perspective of the LLR, but it is perceived as such by outsiders that cannot observe the supervisory information on the basis of which decisions are made. Thus, the randomness lies in the supervisory information, not in the policy rule.

References

Allen, Franklin, and Douglas Gale. 2000. *Comparing Financial Systems.* Cambridge, MA: MIT Press.

Bagehot, Walter. 1873. *Lombard Street. A Description of the Money Market.* References from the 1962 edition. Homewood, IL: Richard D. Irwin.

Bolton, Patrick, and Xavier Freixas. 2000. "Equity, Bonds, and Bank Debt: Capital Structure and Financial Market Equilibrium under Asymmetric Information." *Journal of Political Economy* 108:324–51.

Cordella, Tito, and Eduardo Levy-Yeyati. 2003. "Bank Bailouts: Moral Hazard vs. Value Effect." *Journal of Financial Intermediation* 12:300–30.

Corrigan, E. Gerald. 1991. "The Risks of Financial Crises." In *The Risk of Economic Crisis*, ed. Martin Feldstein, 44–53. Chicago: University of Chicago Press.

Diamond, Douglas W., and Raghuram G. Rajan. 2000. "A Theory of Bank Capital." *Journal of Finance* 55:2431–65.

Flannery, Mark. 1996. "Financial Crises, Payment System Problems, and Discount Window Lending." *Journal of Money, Credit, and Banking* 28:804–24.

Freixas, Xavier. 1999. "Optimal Bail-Out, Conditionality and Constructive Ambiguity." CEPR Discussion Paper No. 2238.

Freixas, Xavier, Curzio Giannini, Glenn Hoggarth, and Farouk Soussa. 2000. "Lender of Last Resort: What Have We Learned Since Bagehot?" *Journal of Financial Services Research* 18:63–84.

[28]As forcefully argued by Corrigan (1991, 49–50), "I think it is sheer fantasy to assume that individual investors and depositors—and perhaps even large and relatively sophisticated investors and depositors—can make truly informed credit judgements about highly complex financial instruments and institutions."

[29]See Prat (2003) for a detailed discussion of the related distinction between signals on actions and signals on the consequences of actions.

[30]This is, for example, the assumption made in the recent work of Rochet and Vives (2004) on the LLR.

Gonzalez-Eiras, Martin. 2003. "Bank's Liquidity Demand in the Presence of a Lender of Last Resort." Working Paper No. 61, Universidad de San Andrés.
Goodfriend, Marvin, and Robert G. King. 1988. "Financial Deregulation, Monetary Policy, and Central Banking." Federal Reserve Bank of Richmond, *Economic Review* 74:3–22.
Goodfriend, Marvin, and Jeffrey M. Lacker. 1999. "Limited Commitment and Central Bank Lending." Federal Reserve Bank of Richmond, *Economic Quarterly* 85:1–27.
Goodhart, Charles. 1999. "Myths about the Lender of Last Resort." *International Finance* 2:339–60.
Goodhart, Charles, and Gerhard Illing. 2002. *Financial Crises, Contagion, and the Lender of Last Resort.* Oxford: Oxford University Press.
Hellmann, Thomas F., Kevin C. Murdock, and Joseph E. Stiglitz. 2000. "Liberalization, Moral Hazard in Banking, and Prudential Regulation: Are Capital Requirements Enough?" *American Economic Review* 90:147–65.
Holmström, Bengt, and Jean Tirole. 1997. "Financial Intermediation, Loanable Funds, and the Real Sector." *Quarterly Journal of Economics* 112:663–91.
Kahn, Charles M., and Joao A.C. Santos. 2001. "Allocating Bank Regulatory Powers: Lender of Last Resort, Deposit Insurance and Supervision." BIS Working Paper No. 102.
Kaufman, George G. 1991. "Lender of Last Resort: A Contemporary Perspective." *Journal of Financial Services Research* 5:95–110.
Prat, Andrea. 2003. "The Wrong Kind of Transparency." CEPR Discussion Paper No. 3859.
Repullo, Rafael. 2000. "Who Should Act as Lender of Last Resort? An Incomplete Contracts Model." *Journal of Money, Credit, and Banking* 32:580–605.
——. 2004. "Capital Requirements, Market Power, and Risk-Taking in Banking." *Journal of Financial Intermediation* 13:156–82.
——. 2005. "Policies for Banking Crises: A Theoretical Framework." In *Systemic Financial Crises: Containment and Resolution*, ed. Patrick Honohan and Luc Laeven. Cambridge: Cambridge University Press.
Repullo, Rafael, and Javier Suarez. 2004. "Loan Pricing under Basel Capital Requirements." *Journal of Financial Intermediation* 13:496–521.
Rochet, Jean-Charles, and Xavier Vives. 2004. "Coordination Failures and the Lender of Last Resort: Was Bagehot Right After All?" *Journal of the European Economic Association* 2:1116–47.
Solow, Robert M. 1982. "On the Lender of Last Resort." In *Financial Crisis: Theory, History, and Policy*, ed. Charles P. Kindleberger and Jean-Pierre Laffargue, 237–48. Cambridge: Cambridge University Press.
Stiglitz, Joseph E., and Andrew Weiss. 1981. "Credit Rationing in Markets with Imperfect Information." *American Economic Review* 71:393–410.

12 Coordination Failures and the Lender of Last Resort: Was Bagehot Right After All?

Jean-Charles Rochet and Xavier Vives

1. Introduction

There have been several recent controversies about the need for a Lender of Last Resort (LOLR) both within national banking systems (central bank) and at an international level (International Monetary Fund, IMF).[1] The concept of a LOLR was elaborated in the nineteenth century by Thornton (1802) and Bagehot (1873). An essential point of the 'classical' doctrine associated with Bagehot asserts that the LOLR role is to lend to "solvent but illiquid" banks under certain conditions.[2]

Banking crises have been recurrent in most financial systems. The LOLR facility and deposit insurance were instituted precisely to provide stability to the banking system and avoid unfavorable consequences for the real sector. Indeed, financial distress may cause important damage to the economy, as the example of the Great Depression makes clear.[3] Traditional banking panics were eliminated with the LOLR facility and deposit insurance by the end of the nineteenth century in Europe, after the crisis of the 1930s in the United States and, by now, also mostly in emerging economies, which have suffered numerous crises until today.[4] Modern liquidity crises associated with securitized money or capital markets have also required the intervention of the LOLR. Indeed, the Federal Reserve intervened in the crises provoked by the failure of Penn Central in the U.S. commercial paper market in 1970, by the stock market crash of October 1987, and by Russia's default in 1997, and subsequent collapse of LTCM (in the latter case a "lifeboat" was arranged by the New York Fed). For example, in October 1987 the Federal Reserve supplied liquidity to banks through the discount window.[5]

[1] See for instance Calomiris (1998a, 1998b), Kaufman (1991), Fischer (1999), Mishkin (1998), and Goodhart and Huang (1999, 2000).

[2] The LOLR should lend freely against good collateral, valued at precrisis levels, and at a penalty rate. These conditions are due to Bagehot (1873) and are also presented, for instance, in Humphrey (1975) and Freixas et al. (1999).

[3] See Bernanke (1983) and Bernanke and Gertler (1989).

[4] See Gorton (1988) for U.S. evidence and Lindgren, García, and Saal (1996) for evidence on other IMF member countries.

[5] See Folkerts-Landau and Garber (1992). See also Freixas, Parigi, and Rochet (2004) for a modeling of the interactions between the discount window and the interbank market.

The LOLR's function of providing emergency liquidity assistance has been criticized for provoking moral hazard on the banks' side. Perhaps more importantly, Goodfriend and King (1988) (see also Bordo 1990; Kaufman 1991; and Schwartz 1992) remark that Bagehot's doctrine was elaborated at a time when financial markets were underdeveloped. They argue that, whereas central bank intervention on aggregate liquidity (monetary policy) is still warranted, individual interventions (banking policy) are not anymore: with sophisticated interbank markets, banking policy has become redundant. Open-market operations can provide sufficient liquidity, which is then allocated by the interbank market. The discount window is not needed. In other words, Goodfriend and King argue that, when financial markets function well, a solvent institution cannot be illiquid. Banks can finance their assets with interbank funds, negotiable certificates of deposit (CDs), and repurchase agreements (repos). Well-informed participants in this interbank market will distinguish liquidity from solvency problems.This view has consequences also for the debate about the need for an international LOLR. Indeed, Chari and Kehoe (1998) claim, for example, that such an international LOLR is not needed because joint action by the Federal Reserve, the European Central Bank, and the Bank of Japan can take care of any international liquidity problem.[6]

Those developments have led qualified observers to dismiss bank panics as a phenomenon of the past and to express confidence in the efficiency of financial markets—especially the interbank market—for resolving liquidity problems of financial intermediaries. This is based on the view that participants in the interbank market are the best-informed agents to ascertain the solvency of an institution with liquidity problems.[7]

The main objective of this article is to provide a theoretical foundation for Bagehot's doctrine in a model that fits the modern context of sophisticated and presumably efficient financial markets. We are thinking of a short time horizon that corresponds to liquidity crises. We shift emphasis from maturity transformation and liquidity insurance of small depositors to the 'modern' form of bank runs, where large well-informed investors refuse to renew their credit (CDs for example) on the interbank market. The decision not to renew credit may arise as a result on an event (e.g., failure of Penn Central, October 1987 crash, LTCM failure) that puts in doubt the repayment capacity of an intermediary or a number of intermediaries. The central bank may then decide to provide liquidity to those troubled institutions. The question arises of whether such intervention is warranted.

Since Diamond and Dybvig (1983) and Bryant (1980), banking theory has insisted on the fragility of banks due to possible coordination failures between depositors (bank runs). However it is hard to base any policy recommendation on their model, since it systematically possesses multiple equilibria. Furthermore, a run equilibrium needs to be justified with the presence of sunspots that coordinate the behavior of investors. Indeed, otherwise no one would deposit in a bank that would be subject to run. This view of banking

[6]Jeanne and Wyplosz (2003) compare the required size of an international LOLR under the "open market monetary policy" and the "discount window banking policy" views.

[7]For example, Tommaso Padoa-Schioppa, member of the European Central Bank's executive committee in charge of banking supervision, has gone as far as saying that classical bank runs may occur only in textbooks, precisely because measures like deposit insurance and capital adequacy requirements have been put in place. Furthermore, despite recognizing that "rapid outflows of uninsured interbank liabilities" are more likely, Padoa-Schioppa (1999) states: "However, since interbank counterparties are much better informed than depositors, this event would typically require the market to have a strong suspicion that the bank is actually insolvent. If such a suspicion were to be unfounded and not generalized, the width and depth of today's interbank market is such that other institutions would probably replace (possibly with the encouragement of the public authorities as described previously) those which withdraw their funds."

instability has been disputed by Gorton (1985) and others who argue that crises are related to fundamentals and not to self-fulfilling panics. In this view, crises are triggered by bad news about the returns to be obtained by the bank. Gorton (1988) studies panics in the U.S. National Banking Era and concludes that crises were predictable by indicators of the business cycle. The phenomenon has been theorized in the literature on information-based bank runs; see Chari and Jagannathan (1988), Jacklin and Bhattacharya (1988), and Allen and Gale (1998). There is an ongoing empirical debate about whether crises are predictable and their relation to fundamentals.[8]

Our approach is inspired by Postlewaite and Vives (1987), who present an incomplete information model featuring a unique Bayesian equilibrium with a positive probability of bank runs. However, the model of Postlewaite and Vives (1987) differs from our model here in several respects. In particular, in Postlewaite and Vives there is no uncertainty about the fundamental value of the banks' assets (no solvency problems) but incomplete information about the liquidity shocks suffered by depositors. The uniqueness of equilibrium in their case comes from a more complex specification of technology and liquidity shocks for depositors than in Diamond and Dybvig (1983). The present model is instead adapted from the "global game" analysis of Carlsson and Van Damme (1993) and Morris and Shin (1998).[9] This approach builds a bridge between the "panic" and "fundamentals" views of crises by linking the probability of occurrence of a crisis to the fundamentals. A crucial property of the model is that, when the private information of investors is precise enough, the game among them has a unique equilibrium. Moreover, at this unique equilibrium there is an intermediate interval of values of the bank's assets for which, in the absence of intervention by the central bank, the bank is solvent but still can fail if too large a proportion of investors withdraw their money. In other words, in this intermediate range for the fundamentals there exists a potential for coordination failure. Furthermore, the range in which such a coordination failure occurs diminishes with the ex ante strength of fundamentals.

Given that this equilibrium is unique and is based on the fundamentals of the bank, we are able to provide some policy recommendations on how to avoid such failures. More specifically, we discuss the interaction between ex ante regulation of solvency and liquidity ratios and ex post provision of emergency liquidity assistance. It is found that liquidity and solvency regulation can solve the coordination problem, but typically the cost is too high in terms of foregone returns. This means that prudential measures must be complemented with emergency discount-window loans.

To complete the policy discussion we introduce moral hazard and endogenize banks' short-term debt structure as a way to discipline bank managers. This framework allows us to discuss early closure policies of banks as well as the interaction of the LOLR, prompt corrective action, and orderly resolution of failures. We can then study the adequacy of Bagehot's doctrine in a richer environment and derive the complementarity between public (LOLR and other facilities) and private (market) involvement in crisis resolution.

Finally, we provide a reinterpretation of the model in terms of the banking sector of a small open economy and derive lessons for a international LOLR facility.

The rest of the paper is organized as follows. Section 2 presents the model. Section 3 discusses runs and solvency. Section 4 characterizes the equilibrium of the game between investors. Section 5 studies the properties of this equilibrium and the effect of prudential regulation on coordination failure. Section 6 makes a first pass at the LOLR policy

[8] See also Kaminsky and Reinhart (1999) and Radelet and Sachs (1998) for perspectives on international crises.

[9] See also Goldstein and Pauzner (2003), Heinemann and Illing (2000), and Corsetti et al. (2004).

implications of our model and its relation to Bagehot's doctrine. Section 7 shows how to endogenize the liability structure and proposes a welfare-based LOLR facility with attention to crisis resolution. Section 8 provides the international reinterpretation of the model and discusses the role of an international LOLR and associated facilities. Concluding remarks end the paper in Section 9.

2. The Model

Consider a market with three dates: $\tau = 0, 1, 2$. At date $\tau = 0$ the bank possesses its own funds E and collects uninsured wholesale deposits (CDs for example) for some amount D_0 that is normalized to unity. These funds are used in part to finance some investment I in risky assets (loans), the rest being held in cash reserves M. Under normal circumstances, the returns RI on these assets are collected at date τ=2, the CDs are repaid, and the stockholders of the bank receive the difference (when it is positive). However, early withdrawals may occur at an interim date $\tau = 1$, following the observation of private signals on the future realization of R. If the proportion x of these withdrawals exceeds the cash reserves M of the bank then the bank is forced to sell some of its assets. To summarize our notation, the bank's balance sheet at $\tau = 0$ is represented as:

I	$D_0 = 1$
M	E

The terms in this representation are defined as follows.

1. $D_0(= 1)$ is the volume of uninsured wholesale deposits that are normally repaid at $\tau = 2$ but can also be withdrawn at $\tau = 1$. The nominal value of deposits upon withdrawal is $D \geq 1$ independently of the withdrawal date. Thus, early withdrawal entails no cost for the depositors themselves (when the bank is not liquidated prematurely).
2. E represents the value of equity (or, more generally, long-term debt; it may also include insured deposits)[10]
3. I denotes the volume of investment in risky assets, which have a random return R at $\tau = 2$.
4. M is the amount of cash reserves (money) held by the bank.

We assume that the withdrawal decision is delegated to fund managers who typically prefer to renew the deposits (i.e., not to withdraw early) but are penalized by the investors if the bank fails. This is consistent with the fact that the vast majority of wholesale deposits are held by collective investment funds and the empirical evidence on the remuneration of fund managers (see, for example, Chevalier and Ellison 1997, 1999). Indeed, the salaries of fund managers depend on the size of their funds and are not directly indexed on the returns on these funds. Instead, managers are promoted (i.e., get more funds to manage) if they build a good reputation, and demoted otherwise. Accordingly, we suppose that fund managers payoffs depend on whether they take the "right decision." When the bank does not fail the differential payoff of withdrawing with respect to rolling over the CD, is negative and equal to $-C < 0$. When the bank does fail the differential payoff of withdrawing with respect to rolling over the CD, is positive and equal to $B > 0$. Therefore, fund managers adopt the

[10] If they are fully insured, these deposits have no reason to be withdrawn early and can therefore be assimilated into stable resources.

following behavioral rule: withdraw if and only if they anticipate $PB - (1 - P)C > 0$ or $P > \gamma = C/(B + C)$, where P is the probability that the bank fails.

This payoff structure is obtained, for example, if fund managers obtain a benefit $B > 0$ if they get the money back or if they withdraw and the bank fails. They get nothing otherwise. However, to withdraw involves a cost $C > 0$ for the managers (for example because their reputation suffers if they have to recognize that they have made a bad investment) as well as not withdrawing and the bank failing.

At $\tau = 1$, fund manager i privately observes a signal $s_i = R + \varepsilon_i$, where the ε_i are i.i.d. and also independent of R. As a result, a proportion x of them decides to "withdraw" (i.e., not to renew their CDs). By assumption there is no other source of financing for the bank (except perhaps the central bank, see next), so if $x > M/D$ then the bank is forced to sell a volume y of assets.[11] If the needed volume of sales y is greater than the total of available assets I, the bank fails at $\tau = 1$; if not, the bank continues until Date 2. Failure occurs at $\tau = 2$ whenever

$$R(I - y) < (1 - x)D. \qquad (12.1)$$

Our modeling tries to capture, in the simplest possible way, the main institutional features of modern interbank markets. In our model, banks essentially finance themselves by two complementary sources: stable resources (equity and long-term debt) and uninsured short-term deposits (or CDs), which are uncollateralized and involve fixed repayments. However, in case of a liquidity shortage at Date 1, banks may also sell some of their assets (or equivalently borrow against collateral) on the repo market. This secondary market for bank assets is assumed to be informationally efficient in the sense that the secondary price aggregates the decentralized information of investors about the quality of the bank's assets.[12] Therefore, we assume that the resale value of the bank's assets depends on R. However, banks cannot obtain the full value of these assets but only a fraction $1/(1+\lambda)$ of this value, with $\lambda > 0$. Accordingly, the volume of sales needed to face withdrawals x is given by

$$y = (1 + \lambda)\frac{[xD - M]_+}{R}, \qquad (12.1)$$

where $[xD - M]_+ = \max(0, xD - M)$. The parameter λ measures the cost of "fire sales" in the secondary market for bank assets. It is crucial for our analysis and can be explained via considerations of asymmetric information or liquidity problems.[13]

Indeed, asymmetric information problems may translate into either limited commitment of future cash flows (as in Hart and Moore 1994 or Diamond and Rajan 2001), or moral hazard (as in Holmstrom and Tirole 1997), or adverse selection (as in Flannery 1996). We have chosen to stress the last explanation because it gives a simple justification for the superiority of the central bank over financial markets in the provision of liquidity to banks in trouble. This adverse selection premium comes from the fact that a bank may want to sell its assets for two reasons: because it needs liquidity or because it wants to get rid of its bad loans (with a value normalized to zero). Investors only accept to pay $R/(1 + \lambda)$ because

[11] These sales are typically accompanied with a repurchase agreement (or repo). They are thus equivalent to a collateralized loan.

[12] We can imagine, for instance, that the bank organizes an auction for the sale of its assets. If there is a large number of bidders and their signals are (conditionally) independent, then the equilibrium price p of this auction will be a deterministic function of R.

[13] For a similar assumption in a model of an international lender of last resort, see Goodhart and Huang (1999).

they assess a probability $1/(1+\lambda)$ to the former case. The superiority of the central bank comes from its supervisory knowledge of banks.[14] The presence of an adverse selection discount in credit markets is well established (see, e.g., Broecker 1990; Riordan 1993). Flannery (1996) presents a specific mechanism that explains why the secondary market for bank assets may be plagued by a winner's curse, inducing a fire-sale premium. He argues, furthermore, that this fire-sale premium is likely to be higher during crises, given that investors are then probably more uncertain about the precision of their signals. This makes the winner's curse more severe because it is then more difficult to distinguish good from bad risks.

The parameter λ can also be interpreted as a liquidity premium—that is, the interest margin that the market requires for lending on short notice. (See Allen and Gale (1998) for a model in which costly asset sales arise due to the presence of liquidity-constrained speculators in the resale market.) In a generalized banking crisis we would have a liquidity shortage, implying a large λ. Interpreting it as a market rate, λ can also spike temporarily in response to exogenous events, such as September 11.

In our model we will be thinking mostly of the financial distress of an individual bank (a bank is close to insolvency when R is small), although—for sufficiently correlated portfolio returns of the banks—the interpretation could be broadened (see also the interpretation in an international context in Section 8).

Operations on interbank markets do not involve any physical liquidation of bank assets. However, we will show that, when a bank is close to insolvency (R small) or when there is a liquidity shortage (λ large), the interbank markets do not suffice to prevent early closure of the bank. Early closure involves the physical liquidation of assets, and this is costly. We model this liquidation cost (not to be confused with the fire-sale premium λ) as being proportional to the future returns on the bank's portfolio. If the bank is closed at $\tau = 1$ then the (per-unit) liquidation value of its assets is νR, with $\nu \ll 1/(1+\lambda)$.

3. Runs and Solvency

We focus in this section on some features of banks' liquidity crises that cannot be properly taken into account within the classical Bryant–Diamond–Dybvig (BDD) framework. In doing so we take the banks' liability structure (and, in particular, the fact that an important fraction of these liabilities can be withdrawn on demand) as exogenous. A possible way to endogenize the bank's liability structure is to introduce a disciplining role for liquid deposits. In Section 7 we explore such an extension.

We adopt explicitly the short time horizon (say, two days) that corresponds to liquidity crises. This means that we shift the emphasis from maturity transformation and liquidity insurance of small depositors to the "modern" form of bank runs—that is, large investors refusing to renew their CDs on the interbank market.

A second element that differentiates our model from BDD is that our bank is not a mutual bank but rather a corporation that acts in the best interest of its stockholders. This allows us to discuss the role of equity as well as the articulation between solvency requirements and provision of emergency liquidity assistance. In Section 7 we endogenize the choice of assets by the bank through the monitoring effort of its managers (first-order stochastic

[14]The empirical evidence points at the superiority of the central bank information because of its access to supervisory data (Peek, Rosengren, and Tootell 1999, for example). Similarly, Romer and Romer (2000) find evidence of a superiority of the Federal Reserve over commercial forecasters in forecasting inflation.

dominance), but we take as given the amount of equity E. It would be interesting to extend our model by endogenizing the level of equity to capture the impact of leverage on the riskiness of assets chosen by banks (second-order stochastic dominance). In this model, however, both the amount of equity and the riskiness of assets are taken as given.

As a consequence of our assumptions, the relation between the proportion x of early withdrawals and the failure of the bank is different from that in BDD. To see this, let us recapitulate the different cases.

1. $xD \leq M$: there is no sale of assets at $\tau = 1$. In this case, there is failure at $\tau = 2$ if and only if

$$RI + M < D \Leftrightarrow R < R_s = \frac{D - M}{I} = 1 - \frac{1 + E - D}{I}.$$

Here R_s can be interpreted as the solvency threshold of the bank. Indeed, if there are no withdrawals at $\tau = 1$ ($x = 0$) then the bank fails at $\tau = 2$ if and only if $R < R_s$. The threshold R_s is a decreasing function of the solvency ratio E/I.

2. $M < xD \leq M + RI/(1 + \lambda)$: there is a partial sale of assets at $\tau = 1$. Failure occurs at $\tau = 2$ if and only if

$$RI - (1 + \lambda)(xD - M) < (1 - x)D \Leftrightarrow R < R_s + \lambda\frac{xD - M}{I} = R_s\left[1 + \lambda\frac{xD - M}{D - M}\right].$$

This formula illustrates how, because of the premium λ, solvent banks can fail when the proportion x of early withdrawals is too large.[15] Note, however, an important difference with BDD: when the bank is "supersolvent" ($R > (1 + \lambda)R_s$) it can never fail, even if everybody withdraws ($x = 1$).

3. $xD > M + RI/(1 + \lambda)$, the bank is closed at $\tau = 1$ (early closure).

The failure thresholds are summarized in Figure 12.1.

A few comments are in order. In our model, early closure is never ex post efficient because physically liquidating assets is costly. However, as discussed in Section 7, early closure may be ex ante efficient for disciplining bank managers and inducing them to exert effort. The perfect information benchmark of our model (where R is common knowledge at $\tau = 1$) has different properties than in BDD: here, the multiplicity of equilibria arises only in the median range $R_s \leq R \leq (1 + \lambda)R_s$. When $R < R_s$ everybody runs ($x = 1$), when $R > (1 + \lambda)R_s$ nobody runs ($x = 0$), and only in the intermediate region do both

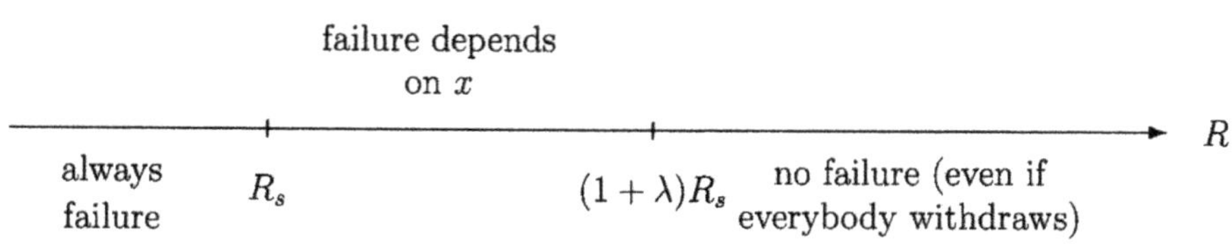

Figure 12.1. The failure thresholds.

[15]We may infer that to obtain resources $xD - M > 0$ we must liquidate a fraction $\mu = [(xD - M)/(RI)](1 + \lambda)$ of the portfolio; hence, $\tau = 2$ we have $R(1 - \mu)I = RI - (1 + \lambda)(xD - M)$ remaining.

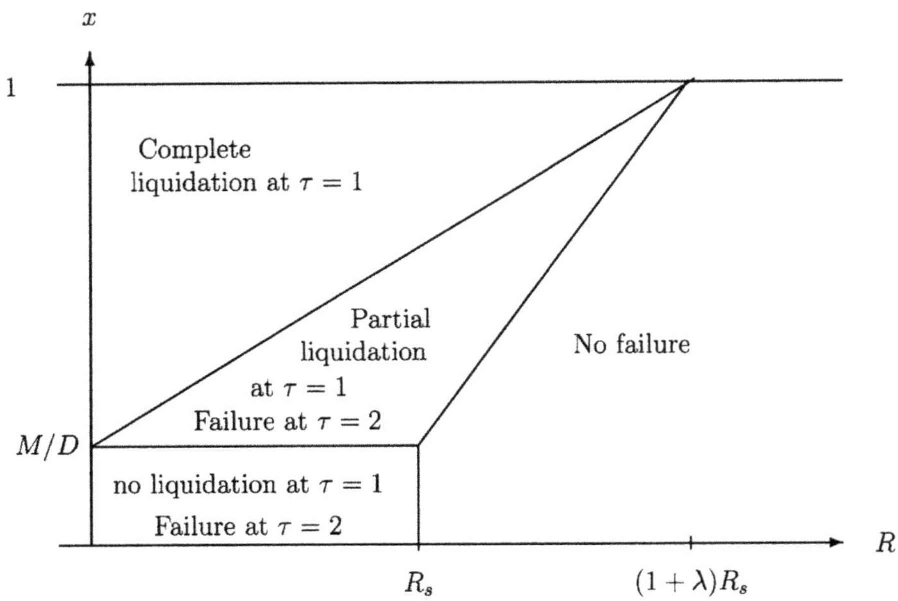

Figure 12.2. The different regimes in the (R, x) plane.

equilibria coexist.[16] This pattern is crucial for being able to select a unique equilibrium via the introduction of private noisy signals (when noise is not too important, as in Morris and Shin (1998)).[17]

The different regimes of the bank are represented in Figure 12.2 as a function of R and x. The critical value of R below which the bank is closed early (early closure threshold R_{ec}) is given by

$$R_{ec}(x) = (1+\lambda)\frac{[xD - M]_+}{I},$$

and the critical value of R below which the bank fails (failure threshold R_f) is given by

$$R_f(x) = R_s + \lambda\frac{[xD - M]_+}{I}. \tag{12.2}$$

The parameters R_s, M, and I are not independent. Since we want to study the impact of prudential regulation on the need for central bank intervention, we will focus on R_s

[16]When $R < R_s$ the differential payoff of withdrawing for fund managers is B. When $R > (1+\lambda)R_s$ the differential payoff of withdrawing is $-C$.

[17]Goldstein and Pauzner (2003) adapt the same methodology to the BDD model, in which the perfect information game always has two equilibria, even for very large R. Accordingly, they have to make an extra assumption, namely that short-term returns are high when the value of the bank's assets is large, or that there exists a potential lender who can cover the liquidity needs of the bank, to get an upper dominance region. Goldstein and Pauzner (2003) provides a very useful extension of the methodology of global games to cases where strategic complementarity is not satisfied. See also Morris and Shin (2000).

(a decreasing function of the solvency ratio E/I) and $m = M/D$ (the liquidity ratio). Replacing I by its value $(D - M)/R_s$, we obtain:

$$R_{ec}(x) = R_s(1+\lambda)\frac{[x-m]_+}{1-m}; \text{ and}$$

$$R_f(x) = R_s\left(1+\lambda\frac{[x-m]_+}{1-m}\right).$$

It should be obvious that $R_{ec}(x) < R_f(x)$, since early closure implies failure whereas the converse is not true (see Figure 12.2).

4. Equilibrium of the Investors' Game

To simplify the presentation we concentrate on "threshold" strategies, in which each fund manager decides to withdraw if and only if his signal is below some threshold, t.[18] As we shall see, this is without loss of generality. For a given R, a fund manager withdraws with probability

$$\Pr[R + \varepsilon < t] = G(t - R),$$

where G is the c.d.f. of the random variable ε. Given our assumptions, this probability also equals the proportion of withdrawals $x(R, t)$.

A fund manager withdraws if and only if the probability of failure of the bank (conditional on the signal s received by the manager and the threshold t used by other managers) is large enough. That is, $P(s, t) > \gamma$, where

$$\begin{aligned} P(s,t) &= \Pr[\text{failure}|s,t] \\ &= \Pr[R < R_f(x(R,t))|s]. \end{aligned}$$

Before we analyze the equilibrium of the investor's game, let us look at the region of the plane (t, R) where failure occurs. For this, transform Figure 12.2 by replacing x by $x(R, t) = G(t - R)$; this yields Figure 12.3. Notice that $R_F(t)$, the critical R that triggers failure, is equal to the solvency threshold R_s when t is low and fund managers are confident about the strength of fundamentals:

$$R_F(t) = R_s \quad \text{if} \quad t \le t_0 = R_s + G^{-1}(m).$$

For $t > t_0$, however $R_F(t)$ is an increasing function of t and is defined implicitly by

$$R = R_s\left(1+\lambda\left[\frac{G(t-R)-m}{1-m}\right]\right).$$

[18] It is assumed that the decision on whether to withdraw is taken before the secondary market is organized and thus before fund managers have the opportunity to learn about R from the secondary price. (On this issue see Atkeson's comments on Morris and Shin (2000).)

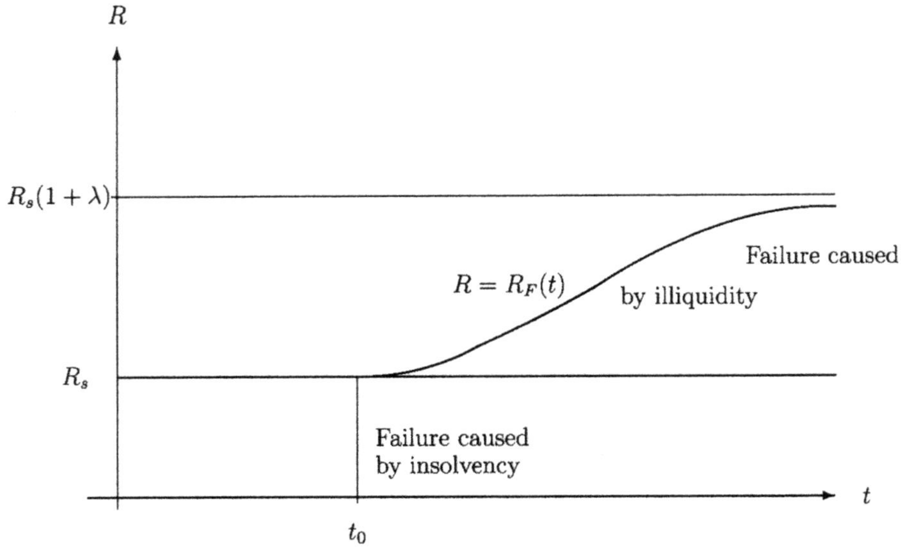

Figure 12.3. The different regimes in the (R, t) plane.

Let us denote by $G(\cdot|s)$ the c.d.f. of R conditional on signal s:

$$G(r|s) = \Pr[R < r|s].$$

Then, given the definition of $R_F(t)$,

$$P(s, t) = \Pr[R < R_F(t)|s] = G(R_F(t)|s) \tag{12.3}$$

It is natural to assume that $G(r|s)$ is decreasing in s: the higher s, the lower the probability that R lies below any given threshold r. Then it is immediate that P is decreasing in s and nondecreasing in t: $\partial P/\partial s < 0$ and $\partial P/\partial t \geq 0$. This means that the depositors' game is one of strategic complementarities. Indeed, given that other fund managers use the strategy with threshold t, the best response of a manager is to use a strategy with threshold $\bar{s}$: withdraw if and only if $P(s, t) > \gamma$ or (equivalently) if and only if $s < \bar{s}$, where $P(\bar{s}, t) = \gamma$. Let $\bar{s} = S(t)$. Now we have that $S' = -(\partial P/\partial t)/(\partial P/\partial s) \geq 0$: a higher threshold t by others induces a manager to use a higher threshold also.

The strategic complementarity property holds for general strategies. For a fund manager, all that matters is the conditional probability of failure for a given signal, and this depends only on aggregate withdrawals. Recall that the differential payoff to a fund manager for withdrawing versus not withdrawing is given by $PB - (1 - P)C$. A strategy for a fund manager is a function $a(s) \in \{\text{not withdraw, withdraw}\}$. If more managers withdraw, then the probability of failure conditional on receiving signal s increases. This just means that the payoff to a fund manager displays increasing differences with respect to the actions of others. The depositor's game is a supermodular game that has a largest and a smallest equilibrium. In fact, the game is symmetric (i.e., exchangeable against permutations of the players) and hence the largest and smallest equilibria are symmetric.[19] At the largest equilibrium, every fund manager withdraws on the largest number of occasions; at the smallest equilibrium, withdrawal is on the smallest number of occasions. The largest (smallest) equilibrium can be identified then with the highest (lowest) threshold strategy, $\bar{t}(\underline{t})$.[20] These extremal equilibria bound the set of rationalizable outcomes. That is, strategies outside this set can be eliminated by iterated deletion of dominated strategies.[21] We will make assumptions so that $\bar{t} = \underline{t}$ and equilibrium will be unique.

The threshold $t = t^*$ corresponds to a (symmetric) Bayesian–Nash equilibrium if and only if $P(t^*, t^*) = \gamma$. Indeed, suppose that funds managers use the threshold strategy t^*. Then for $s = t^*$ we have $P = \gamma$ and, since P is decreasing in s for $s < t^*$, it follows that $P(s, t^*) > \gamma$ and the manager withdraws. Conversely, if t^* is a (symmetric) equilibrium then, for $s = t^*$, there is no withdrawal and hence $P(t^*, t^*) \leq \gamma$. If $P(t^*, t^*) < \gamma$ then, by continuity, for s close to but less than t^* we would have $P(s, t^*) < \gamma$ a contradiction. It is clear then that the largest and smallest solutions to $P(t^*, t^*) = \gamma$ correspond respectively to the largest and smallest equilibrium.

An equilibrium can also be characterized by a couple of equations in two unknowns (a withdrawal threshold t^* and a failure threshold R^*):

$$G(R^* | t^*) = \gamma; \tag{12.4}$$

$$R^* = R_s \left(1 + \lambda \left[\frac{G(t^* - R^*) - m}{1 - m}\right]_+\right). \tag{12.5}$$

Equation (4) states that, conditional on observing a signal $s = t^*$, the probability that $R < R^*$ is γ. Equation (5) states that, given a withdrawal threshold t^*, R^* is the critical return (i.e., the one below which failure occurs). Equation (5) implies that R^* belongs to $[R_s, (1 + \lambda)R_s]$. Notice that early closure occurs whenever $x(R, t^*)D > M + IR/(1 + \lambda)$, where $x(R, t^*) = G(t^* - R)$. This happens if and only if R is smaller than some threshold $R_{EC}(t^*)$. We will have that $R_{EC}(t^*) < R^*$, because early closure implies failure whereas the converse is not true, as remarked before.

To simplify the analysis of this system, we shall make distributional assumptions on returns and signals. More specifically, we will assume that the distributions of R and ϵ are normal, with respective means $\bar{R}$ and 0 and respective precisions (i.e., inverse variances) α and β. Denoting by Φ the c.d.f. of a standard normal distribution allows us to characterize the equilibrium by a pair (t^*, R^*) such that

$$\Phi\left(\sqrt{\alpha + \beta} R^* - \frac{\alpha \bar{R} + \beta t^*}{\sqrt{\alpha + \beta}}\right) = \gamma \tag{12.6}$$

[19] See Remark 15, in Vives (1999, p. 34). See also Chapter 2 in the same reference for an exposition of the theory of supermodular games.

[20] The extremal equilibria can be found with the usual algorithm in a supermodular game (Vives 1990), starting at the extremal points of the strategy sets of players and iterating using the best responses. For example, to obtain $\bar{t}$, let all investors withdraw for any signal received (i.e., start from $\bar{t}_0 = +\infty$ and $x = 1$) and apply iteratively the best response $S(\cdot)$ of a player to obtain a decreasing sequence $\bar{t}_k$ that converges to t. Note that $S(+\infty) = t_1 < +\infty$, where $\bar{t}_1$ is the unique solution to $P(t, +\infty) = G(R_s(1 + \lambda)|t) = \gamma$ given that G is (strictly) decreasing in t. The extremal equilibria are in strategies that are monotone in type, which with two actions means that the strategies are of the threshold type. The game among mutual fund managers is an example of a "monotone supermodular game" for which, according to Van Zandt and Vives (2003), extremal equilibria are monotone in type.

[21] See Morris and Shin (2000) for an explicit demonstration of the outcome of iterative elimination of dominated strategies in a similar model.

and

$$R^* = R_s \left(1 + \lambda \left[\frac{\Phi(\sqrt{\beta}(t^* - R^*)) - m}{1 - m}\right]_+\right). \tag{12.7}$$

We now can now state our first result.

Proposition 1: *When β (the precision of the private signal of investors) is large enough relative to α (prior precision), there is a unique t^* such that $P(t^*, t^*) = \gamma$. The investor's game then has a unique (Bayesian) equilibrium. In this equilibrium, fund managers use a strategy with threshold t^*.*

Proof: We show that $\varphi(s) \stackrel{\text{def}}{=} P(s, s)$ is decreasing for

$$\beta \geq \beta_0 \stackrel{\text{def}}{=} \frac{1}{2\pi}\left(\frac{\lambda \alpha D}{I}\right)^2$$

with $I = D - M/R_s$. Under our assumptions, R conditional on signal realization s follows a normal distribution

$$N\left(\frac{\alpha \overline{R} + \beta s}{\alpha + \beta}, \frac{1}{\alpha + \beta}\right).$$

Denoting by Φ the c.d.f. of a standard normal distribution, it follows that

$$\begin{aligned} \varphi(s) = P(s, s) &= \Pr[R < R_F(s) | s] \\ &= \Phi\left[\sqrt{\alpha + \beta} R_F(s) - \frac{\alpha \overline{R} + \beta s}{\sqrt{\alpha + \beta}}\right]. \end{aligned} \tag{12.8}$$

This function is clearly decreasing for $s < t_0$ since, in this region, we have $R_F(s) \equiv R_s$. Now, if $s > t_0$ then $R_F(s)$ is increasing and its inverse is given by

$$t_F(R) = R + \frac{1}{\sqrt{\beta}} \Phi^{-1}\left(\frac{I}{\lambda D}(R - R_s) + m\right).$$

The derivative of t_F is

$$t_F'(R) = 1 + \frac{1}{\sqrt{\beta}} \frac{I}{\lambda D}\left[\Phi'\left(\Phi^{-1}\left(\frac{I}{\lambda D}(R - R_s) + m\right)\right)\right]^{-1}.$$

Since Φ' is bounded above by $1/\sqrt{2\pi}$, it follows that t_F' is bounded below:

$$t_F'(R) \geq 1 + \sqrt{\frac{2\pi}{\beta}} \frac{I}{\lambda D}.$$

Thus

$$R'_F(s) \leq \left[1 + \sqrt{\frac{2\pi}{\beta}\frac{I}{\lambda D}}\right]^{-1}.$$

Given formula (8), $\varphi(s)$ will be decreasing provided that

$$\sqrt{\alpha+\beta}\left(1 + \sqrt{\frac{2\pi}{\beta}\frac{I}{\lambda D}}\right)^{-1} \leq \frac{\beta}{\sqrt{\alpha+\beta}},$$

which (after simplification) yields:

$$\beta \geq \frac{1}{2\pi}\left(\frac{\lambda \alpha D}{I}\right)^2.$$

If this condition is satisfied then there is at most one equilibrium. Existence is easily shown. When s is small, $R_F(s) = R_s$ and formula (8) implies that $\lim_{s\to-\infty} \varphi(s) = 1$. On the other hand, if $s \to +\infty$ then $R_F(s) \to (1+\lambda)R_s$ and $\varphi(s) \to 0$. □

The limit equilibrium when β tends to infinity can be characterized as follows: From equation (6) we have that $\lim_{\beta\to+\infty} \sqrt{\beta}(R^* - t^*) = \Phi^{-1}(\gamma)$. Given that $\Phi\{-z\} = 1 - \Phi\{z\}$, we obtain from formula (7) that, in the limit,

$$t^* = R^* = R_s\left(1 + \frac{\lambda}{1-m}[\max\{1-\gamma-m, 0\}]\right).$$

The critical cutoff R^* is decreasing with γ and ranges from R_s for $\gamma \geq 1-m$ to $(1+\lambda)R_s$ for $\gamma = 0$. It is also nonincreasing in m. As we establish in the next section, these features of the limit equilibrium are also valid for $\beta \geq \beta_0$.

It is worth noting also that, with a diffuse prior ($\alpha = 0$), the equilibrium is unique for any private precision of investors (indeed, we have that $\beta_0 = 0$). From (6) and (7) we obtain immediately that

$$R^* = R_s\left(1 + \frac{\lambda}{1-m}[\max\{1-\gamma-m, 0\}]\right)$$

and $t^* = R^* - \Phi^{-1}(\gamma)/\sqrt{\beta}$. Both the cases $\beta \to +\infty$ and $\alpha = 0$ have in common that each investor faces maximal uncertainty about the behavior of other investors at the switching point $s_i = t^*$. Indeed, it can be easily checked that in either case the distribution of the proportion $x(R, t^*) = \Phi(\sqrt{\beta}(t^* - R))$ of investors withdrawing is uniformly distributed over $[0, 1]$ conditional on $s_i = t^*$. This contrasts with the certainty case with multiple equilibria when $R \in (R_s, (1+\lambda)R_s)$, where (for example) in a run equilibrium an investor thinks that with probability one all other investors will withdraw. It is precisely the need to entertain a wider range of behavior of other investors in the incomplete information game that pins down a unique equilibrium, as in Carlsson and Van Damme (1993) or Postlewaite and Vives (1987).

The analysis could be easily extended to allow for fund managers to have access to a public signal $y = R + \eta$, where $\eta \sim N(0, 1/\beta_p)$ is independent from R and from the error terms ε_i of the private signals. The only impact of the public signal is to replace the unconditional moments $\overline{R}$ and $1/\alpha$ of R by its conditional moments, taking into account the public signal, v. A disclosure of a signal of high enough precision will imply the existence of multiple equilibria—much in the same manner as a sufficiently precise prior.

The public signal could be provided by the central bank. Indeed, the central bank typically has information about banks that the market does not have (and, conversely, market participants also have information that is unknown to the central bank).[22] The model allows for the information structures of the central bank and investors to be nonnested. Our discussion then has a bearing on the slippery issue of the optimal degree of transparency of central bank announcements. Indeed, Alan Greenspan has become famous for his oblique way of saying things, fostering an industry of "Greenspanology" or interpretation of his statements. Our model may rationalize oblique statements by central bankers that seem to add noise to a basic message. Precisely because the central bank may be in a unique position to provide information that becomes common knowledge, it has the capacity to destabilize expectations in the market (which in our context means to move the interbank market to a regime of multiple equilibria). By fudging the disclosure of information, the central bank makes sure that somewhat different interpretations of the release will be made, preventing destabilization.[23] Indeed, in the initial game (without a public signal) we may well be in the uniqueness region, but adding a precise enough public signal will mean we have three equilibria. At the interior equilibrium we have a result similar to that with no public information, but run and no-run equilibria also exist. We may therefore end up in an "always run" situation when disclosing (or increasing the precision of) the public signal while the economy is in the interior equilibrium without public disclosure. In other words, public disclosure of a precise enough signal may be destabilizing. This means that a central bank that wants to avoid entering in the "unstable" region may have to add noise to its signal if that signal is otherwise too precise.[24]

5. Coordination Failure and Prudential Regulation

For β large enough, we have just seen that there exists a unique equilibrium whereby investors adopt a threshold t^* characterized by

$$\Phi\left(\sqrt{\alpha+\beta}R_F(t^*) - \frac{\alpha\overline{R}+\beta t^*}{\sqrt{\alpha+\beta}}\right) = \gamma,$$

or

$$R_F(t^*) = \frac{1}{\sqrt{\alpha+\beta}}\left(\Phi^{-1}(\gamma) + \frac{\alpha\overline{R}+\beta t^*}{\sqrt{\alpha+\beta}}\right). \tag{12.9}$$

For this equilibrium threshold, the failure of the bank will occur if and only if

$$R < R_F(t^*) = R^*.$$

This means that the bank fails if and only if fundamentals are weak, $R < R^*$. When $R^* > R_s$ we have an intermediate interval of fundamentals $R \in [R_s, R^*)$ where there is a coordination

[22] See Peek, Rosengren, and Tootell (1999), DeYoung et al. (1998), and Berger, Davies, and Flannery (2000).
[23] The potential damaging effects of public information is a theme also developed in Morris and Shin (2001).
[24] See Hellwig (2002) for a treatment of the multiplicity issue.

failure: the bank is solvent but illiquid. The occurrence of a coordination failure can be controlled by the level of the liquidity ratio m, as the following proposition shows.

Proposition 2: *There is a critical liquidity ratio $\bar{m}$ of the bank such that, for $m \geq \bar{m}$, we have $R^* = R_s$; this means that only insolvent banks fail (there is no coordination failure). Conversely, for $m < \bar{m}$ we have $R^* > R_s$; this means that, for $R \in [R_s, R^*)$, the bank is solvent but illiquid (there is a coordination failure).*

Proof: For $t^* \leq t_0 = R_s + 1/(\sqrt{\beta})\Phi^{-1}(m)$, the equilibrium occurs for $R^* = R_s$. By replacing in formula (6) we obtain

$$(\alpha + \beta)R_s \leq \sqrt{\alpha + \beta}\Phi^{-1}(\gamma) + \alpha\bar{R} + \beta R_s + \sqrt{\beta}\Phi^{-1}(m),$$

which is equivalent to:

$$\Phi^{-1}(m) \geq \frac{\alpha}{\sqrt{\beta}}(R_s - \bar{R}) - \sqrt{1 + \frac{\alpha}{\beta}}\Phi^{-1}(\gamma). \tag{12.10}$$

Therefore, the coordination failure disappears when $m \geq \bar{m}$, where

$$\bar{m} = \Phi\left(\frac{\alpha}{\sqrt{\beta}}(R_s - \bar{R}) - \sqrt{1 + \frac{\alpha}{\beta}}\Phi^{-1}(\gamma)\right).$$

□

Observe that, since R_s is a decreasing function of E/I, the critical liquidity ratio $\bar{m}$ decreases when the solvency ratio E/I increases.[25]

The equilibrium threshold return R^* is determined (when (10) is not satisfied) by the solution to

$$\phi(R) \equiv \alpha(R - \bar{R}) - \sqrt{\beta}\Phi^{-1}\left(\frac{1-m}{\lambda R_s}(R - R_s) + m\right) - \sqrt{\alpha + \beta}\Phi^{-1}(\gamma) = 0. \tag{12.11}$$

When $\beta \geq \beta_0$ we have $\phi'(R) < 0$ and the comparative statics properties of the equilibrium threshold R^* are straightforward. Indeed, it follows that $\partial\phi/\partial m < 0$, $\partial\phi/\partial R_s > 0$, $\partial\phi/\partial\lambda > 0$, $\partial\phi/\partial\gamma < 0$, and $\partial\phi/\partial\bar{R} < 0$. The following proposition states the results.

Proposition 3: *The comparative statics of R^* (and of the probability of failure) can be summarized as follows:*

1. *R^* is a decreasing function of the liquidity ratio m and the solvency (E/I) of the bank, of the critical withdrawal probability γ, and of the expected return on the bank's assets $\bar{R}$.*
2. *R^* is an increasing function of the fire-sale premium λ and of the face value of debt D.*

[25] More generally, it is easy to see that the regulator in our model can control the probabilities of illiquidity $(Pr(R < R^*))$ and insolvency $(Pr(R < R_s))$ of the bank by imposing appropriately high ratios of minimum liquidity and solvency.

We have thus that stronger fundamentals, as indicated by a higher prior mean $\overline{R}$, also imply a lower likelihood of failure. In contrast, a higher fire-sale premium λ increases the incidence of failure. Indeed, for a higher λ, a larger portion of the portfolio must be liquidated in order to meet the requirements of withdrawals. We also have that R^* is decreasing with the critical withdrawal probability γ and that $R^* \to (1+\lambda)R_s$ as $\gamma \to 0$.

A similar analysis applies to changes in the precision of the prior α and the private information of investors β. Assume that $\gamma = C/B < 1/2$. Indeed, we should expect that the cost C of withdrawal is small in relation to the continuation benefit B for the fund managers. If $\gamma < 1/2$ then it is easy to see that:

1. For large β and bad prior fundamentals ($\overline{R}$ low), increasing α increases R^* (more precise prior information about a bad outcome worsens the coordination problem).
2. Increasing β decreases R^*.

6. Coordination Failure and LOLR Policy

The main contribution of our paper so far has been to show the theoretical possibility of a solvent bank being illiquid as a result of coordination failure on the interbank market. We shall now explore the Lender of Last Resort (LOLR) policy of the central bank and present a scenario where it is possible to give a theoretical justification for Bagehot's doctrine.

We start by considering a simple central bank objective: eliminate the coordination failure with minimal involvement. The instruments at the disposal of the central bank are the liquidity ratio m and intervention in the form of open-market or discount-window operations.[26]

We have shown in Section 5 that a high enough liquidity ratio m eliminates the coordination failure altogether by inducing $R^* = R_s$. This is so for $m \geq \bar{m}$. However, it is likely that imposing $m \geq \bar{m}$ might be too costly in terms of foregone returns (recall that $I + M = 1 + E$, where I is the investment in the risky asset). In Section 7 we analyze a more elaborate welfare-oriented objective and endogenize the choice of m. We look now at forms of central bank intervention that can eliminate the coordination failure when $m < \bar{m}$.

Let us see how central bank liquidity support can eliminate the coordination failure. Suppose the central bank announces it will lend at rate $r \in (0, \lambda)$—and without limits—but only to solvent banks. The central bank is not allowed to subsidize banks and is assumed to observe R. The knowledge of R may come from the supervisory knowledge of the central bank or perhaps by observing the amount of withdrawals of the bank. Then the optimal strategy of a (solvent) commercial bank will be to borrow exactly the liquidity it needs, that is, $D[x-m]_+$. Whenever $x - m > 0$, failure will occur at Date 2 if and only if

$$\frac{RI}{D} < (1-x) + (1+r)(x-m).$$

Given that $D/I = R_s/1 - m$, we obtain that failure at $t = 2$ will occur if and only if

$$R < R_s\left(1 + r\frac{[x-m]_+}{1-m}\right).$$

[26]Open-market operations typically involve performing a repo operation with primary security dealers. The Federal Reserve auctions a fixed amount of liquidity (reserves) and, in general, does not accept bids by dealers below the Federal Funds rate target.

This is exactly analogous to our previous formula giving the critical return of the bank, except here the interest rate r replaces the liquidation premium λ. As a result, this type of intervention will be fully effective (yielding $R^* = R_s$) only when r is arbitrarily close to zero. It is worth remarking that central bank help in the amount $D[x - m]_+$ whenever the bank is solvent ($R > R_s$), and at a very low rate, avoids early closure, and the central bank loses no money because the loan can be repaid at $\tau = 2$. Note also that, whenever the central bank lends at a very low rate, the collateral of the bank is evaluated under "normal circumstances"—that is, as if there were no coordination failure. Consider as an example the limit case of β tending to infinity. The equilibrium with no central bank help is then

$$t^* = R^* = R_s\left(1 + \frac{\lambda}{1-m}[\max\{1 - \gamma - m, 0\}]\right).$$

Suppose that $1 - \gamma > m$ so that $R^* > R_s$. Then withdrawals are $x = 0$ for $R > R^*, x = 1 - \gamma$ for $R = R^*$, and $x = 1$ for $R < R^*$. Whenever $R > R_s$, the central bank will help to avoid failure and will evaluate the collateral as if $x = 0$. This effectively changes the failure point to $R^* = R_s$.

Central bank intervention can take the form of open-market operations that reduce the fire-sale premium or of discount-window lending at a very low rate. The intervention with open-market operations makes sense if a high λ is due to a temporary spike of the market rate (i.e., a liquidity crunch). In this situation, a liquidity injection by the central bank will reduce the fire-sale premium. After September 11, for example, open-market operations by the Federal Reserve accepted dealers' bids at levels well below the Federal Funds Rate target and pushed the effective lending rate to lows of zero in several days.[27]

Intervention via the discount window—perhaps more in the spirit of Bagehot—makes sense when λ is interpreted as an adverse selection premium. The situation when a large number of banks is in trouble displays both liquidity and adverse selection components. In any case, the central bank intervention should be a very low rate, in contrast with Bagehot's doctrine of lending at a penalty rate.[28] This type of intervention may provide a rationale for the Fed's apparently strange behavior of lending below the market rate (but with a "stigma" associated to it, so that banks borrow there only when they cannot find liquidity in the market).[29] In Section 7 we provide a welfare objective for this discount-window policy.

In some circumstances the central bank may not be able to infer R exactly because of noise (in the supervisory process or in the observation of withdrawals). Then the central bank will obtain only an imperfect signal of R. In this case, the central bank will not be able to distinguish perfectly between illiquid and insolvent banks (as in Goodhart and Huang 1999) and so, whatever the lending policy chosen, taxpayers' money may be involved with some

[27] See Markets Group of the Federal Reserve Bank of New York (2002). Martin (2002) contrasts the classical prescription of lending at a penalty rate with the Fed's response to September 11—namely, to lend at a very low interest rate. He argues that penalty rates were needed in Bagehot's view because the gold standard implied limited reserves for the central bank.

[28] Typically, the lending rate is kept at a penalty level to discourage arbitrage and perverse incentives. Those considerations lie outside the present model. For example, in a repo operation the penalty for not returning the cash on loan is to keep paying the lending rate. If this lending rate is very low then the incentive to return the loan is small. See Fischer (1999) for a discussion of why lending should be at a penalty rate.

[29] The discount-window policy of the Federal Reserve is to lend at 50 basis points below the target Federal Funds Rate.

probability. This situation is realistic given the difficulty in distinguishing between solvency and liquidity problems.[30]

It may be argued also that our LOLR function could be performed by private banks through credit lines. Banks that provide a line of credit to another bank would then have an incentive to monitor the borrowing institution and reduce the fire-sale premium. The need for a LOLR remains, but it may be privately provided. Goodfriend and Lacker (1999) draw a parallel between central bank lending and private lines of credit, putting emphasis on the commitment problem of the central bank to limit lending.[31] However, the central bank typically acts as LOLR in most economies, presumably because it has a natural superiority in terms of financial capacity and supervisory knowledge.[32] For example, in the LTCM case it may be argued that the New York Fed had access to information that the private sector—even the members of the lifeboat operation—did not. This unique capacity to inspect a financial institution might have made possible the lifeboat operation orchestrated by the New York Fed. An open issue is whether this superior knowledge continues to hold in countries where the supervision of banks is basically in the hands of independent regulators like the Financial Services Authority of the United Kingdom.[33]

7. Endogenizing the Liability Structure and Crisis Resolution

In this section we endogenize the short-term debt contract assumed in our model, according to which depositors can withdraw at $\tau = 1$ or otherwise wait until $\tau = 2$. We have seen that the ability of investors to withdraw at $\tau = 1$ creates a coordination problem. We argue here that this potentially inefficient debt structure may be the only way that investors can discipline a bank manager subject to a moral hazard problem.

Suppose, as seems reasonable, that investment in risky assets requires the supervision of a bank manager and that the distribution of returns of the risky assets depends on the effort undertaken by the manager. For example, the manager can either exert or not exert effort, $e \in \{0, 1\}$; then $R \sim N(\overline{R}_0, \alpha^{-1})$ when $e = 0$, and $R \sim N(\overline{R}, \alpha^{-1})$ when $e = 1$, where $\overline{R} > \overline{R}_0$. That is, exerting effort yields a return distribution that first-order stochastically dominates the one obtained by not exerting effort. The bank manager incurs a cost if he chooses $e = 1$; if he chooses $e = 0$, the cost is 0. The manager also receives a benefit from continuing the project until Date 2. Assume for simplicity that the manager does not care about monetary incentives. The manager's effort cannot be observed, so his willingness to undertake effort will depend on the relationship between his effort and the probability that

[30]We may even think that the central bank cannot help ex post once withdrawals have materialized but that it receives a noisy signal s_{CB} about R at the same time as investors. The central bank then can act preventively and inject liquidity into the bank contingent on the received signal $L(s_{CB})$. In this case, also the risk exists that an insolvent bank ends up being helped. The game played by the fund managers changes, obviously, after liquidity injection by a large actor like the central bank.

[31]If this commitment problem is acute then the private solution may be superior. However, Goodfriend and Lacker (1999) do not take a position on this issue. They state: "We are agnostic about the ultimate role of CB lending in a welfare-maximizing steady state."

[32]One of the few exceptions is the Liquidity Consortium in Germany, in which private banks and the central bank both participate.

[33]See Vives (2001) for the workings of the Financial Services Authority and its relation with the Bank of England.

the bank continues at Date 1. Thus, withdrawals may enforce the early closure of the bank and so provide incentives to the bank manager.[34]

In the banking contract, short-term debt/demandable deposits can improve upon long-term debt/nondemandable deposits. With-long term debt, incentives cannot be provided to the manager because liquidation never occurs; therefore, the manager does not exert effort. Furthermore, neither can incentives be provided with renegotiable short-term debt, because early liquidation is ex post inefficient. Dispersed short-term debt (i.e., uninsured deposits) is what is needed.

Let us assume that it is worthwhile to induce the manager to exert effort. This will be true if $\overline{R} - \overline{R}_0$ is large enough and the (physical) cost of asset liquidation is not too large. Recall that the (per-unit) liquidation value of its assets is vR, with $v \ll 1/(1+\lambda)$, whenever the bank is closed at $\tau = 1$. We assume, as in previous sections, that the face value of the debt contract is the same in periods $\tau = 1, 2$ (equal to D), and we suppose also that investors—in order to trust their money to fund managers—must be guaranteed a minimum expected return, which we set equal to zero without loss of generality.

The banking contract will have short-term debt and will maximize the expected profits of the bank by choosing to invest in risky and safe assets and deposit returns subject to: the resource constraint $1 + E = I + Dm$ (where $Dm = M$ is the amount of liquid reserves held by the bank); the incentive compatibility constraint of the bank manager; and the (early) closure rule associated with the (unique) equilibrium in the investors' game. This early closure rule is defined by the property $x(R, t^*)D > M + IR/(1 + \lambda)$, which is satisfied if and only if $R < R_{EC}(t^*)$. As stated before, $R_{EC}(t^*) < R^*$, because early closure implies failure whereas the converse is not true. Let R^o be the smallest R that fulfills the incentive compatibility constraint of the bank manager. We thus have $R_{EC}(t^*) \geq R^o$. The banking program will maximize the expected value of the bank assets which consists of two terms: (i) the product of the size $I = 1 + E - Dm$ of the bank's investments by the net expected return on these investments, taking into account expected liquidation costs; and (ii) the value of liquid reserves Dm. Hence the optimal banking contract will solve

$$\max_m\{(1 + E - Dm)(\overline{R} - (1 - v)\, E(R|R < R_{EC}(t^*(m))) \times \Pr(R < R_{EC}(t^*(m))) + Dm\}$$

subject to:

1. $t^*(m)$ is the unique equilibrium of the fund managers' game; and
2. $R_{EC}(t^*(m)) \geq R^o$.

Given that $t^*(m)$, and thus $R_{EC}(t^*(m))$, decrease with m, the optimal banking contract is easy to characterize. If the net return on banks' assets is always larger than the opportunity cost of liquidity (even when the banks have no liquidity at all)—that is, when

$$\overline{R} - (1 - v)\, E(R|R < R_{EC}(t^*(0))\Pr(R < R_{EC}(t^*(0))) > 1$$

then it is clear that $m = 0$ at the optimal point. If, on the contrary,

$$\overline{R} - (1 - v)\, E(R|R < R_{EC}(t^*(0))\Pr(R < R_{EC}(t^*(0))) < 1,$$

then there is an interior optimum. An interesting question is how the banking contract compares with the incentive efficient solution, which we now describe.

[34]This approach is based on Grossman and Hart (1982) and is followed in Gale and Vives (2002). See also Calomiris and Kahn (1991) and Carletti (1999).

Given that the pooled signals of investors reveal R, we can define the incentive-efficient solution as the choice of investment in liquid and risky assets and probability of continuation at $\tau = 1$ (as a function of R) that maximizes expected surplus subject to the resource constraint and the incentive compatibility constraint of the bank manager. [35] Furthermore, given the monotonicity of the likelihood ratio $\phi(R|e=0)/\phi(R|e=1)$, the optimal region of continuation is of the cutoff form. More specifically, the optimal cutoff will be R^o, the smallest R that fulfills the incentive compatibility constraint of the bank manager. The cutoff R^o will be (weakly) increasing with the extent of the moral hazard problem that bank managers face.

The incentive-efficient solution solves

$$\max_m\{(1+E-Dm)(\overline{R}-(1-v)E(R|R<R^o))\Pr(R<R^o)+Dm\},$$

where R^o is the minimal return cutoff that motivates the bank manager. If

$$\overline{R}-(1-v)E(R|R<R^o)\Pr(R<R^o)>1$$

then $m^o = 0$. Thus, at the incentive-efficient solution it is optimal not to hold any reserves. This should come as no surprise, since we assume there is no cost of liquidity provision by the central bank. A more complete analysis would include such a cost and lead to an optimal combination of LOLR policy with ex ante regulation of a minimum liquidity ratio.

Since $R_{EC}(t^*)$ must also fulfill the incentive compatibility constraint of the bank manager, it follows that, at the optimal banking contract with no LOLR, $R_{EC}(t^*) \geq R^o$. In fact, we will typically have a strict inequality, because there is no reason for the equilibrium threshold t^* to satisfy $R_{EC}(t^*) = R^o$. This means that the market solution will entail too many early closures of banks, since the banking contract with no LOLR intervention uses an inefficient instrument (the liquidity ratio) to provide indirect incentives for bankers through the threat of early liquidation.

The role of a modified LOLR can be viewed, in this context, as correcting these market inefficiencies while maintaining the incentives of bank managers. By announcing its commitment to provide liquidity assistance (at a zero rate) in order to avoid inefficient liquidation at $\tau = 1$ (i.e., for $R > R^o$), the LOLR can implement the incentive-efficient solution. When offered help, the bank will borrow the liquidity it needs, $D[x-m]_+$.[36]

To implement the incentive-efficient solution, the modified LOLR must be more concerned with avoiding inefficient liquidation at $\tau = 1$ in the range (R^o, R_{EC}) than about avoiding failure of the bank. Now the solvency threshold R_s has no special meaning. Indeed, R^o will typically be different from R_s. The reason is that R_s is determined by the promised payments to investors, cash reserves, and investment in the risky asset, whereas R^o is just the

[35] We disregard here the welfare of the bank manager and that of the funds' managers.

[36] We could also envision help by the central bank in an ongoing crisis to implement the incentive-efficient closure rule. The central bank would then lend at a very low interest rate to illiquid banks for the amount that they could not borrow in the interbank market in order to meet their payment obligations at $\tau = 1$. It is easy to see that in this case the equilibrium between fund managers is not modified. This is so because central bank intervention does not change the instances of failure of the bank (indeed, when a bank is helped at $\tau = 1$ because $x(R, t^*)D > M + IR/(1+\lambda)$, it will fail at $\tau = 2$). In this case the coordination failure is not eliminated, but its effects (on early closure) are neutralized by the intervention of the central bank. The modified LOLR helps the bank in the range $(R^o, R_{EC}(t^*))$ in the amount $Dx(t^*, R) - (M + IR/(1+\lambda)) > 0$. Thus LOLR help (bailout) complements the money raised in the interbank market $IR/(1+\lambda)$(bail-in).

minimum threshold that motivates the banker to behave. We will have that $R^o > R_s$ when the moral hazard problem for bank managers is severe and $R^o < R_s$ when it is moderate.

This modified LOLR facility leads to a view on the LOLR that differs from Bagehot's doctrine and introduces interesting policy questions. Whenever $R^o > R_s$ there is a region (specifically, for R in (R_s, R^o)) where there should be early intervention (or "prompt corrective action", to use the terminology of banking regulators). Indeed, in this region the bank is solvent but intervention is needed to control moral hazard of the banker. On the other hand, in the range (R^o, R_{EC}) a LOLR policy is efficient if the central bank can commit. If it cannot and instead optimizes ex post (whether because building a reputation is not possible or because of weakness in the presence of lobbying), it will intervene too often. Some additional institutional arrangement is needed in the range (R_s, R^o) in order to implement prompt corrective action (i.e., early closure of banks that are still solvent).

When $R^o < R_s$, there is a range (R^o, R_{EC}) where the bank should be helped even though it might be insolvent (and in this case money is lost). More precisely, for R in the range $(R^o, \min\{R_s, R_{EC}\})$, the bank is insolvent and should be helped. If the central bank's charter specifies that it cannot lend to insolvent banks, then another institution (deposit insurance fund, regulatory agency, treasury) financed by other means (insurance premiums or taxation) is needed to provide an "orderly resolution of failure" when R is in the range $(R^o, \min\{R_s, R_{EC}\})$. This could be interpreted, as in corporate bankruptcy practice, as a way to preserve the going-concern value of the institution and to allow its owners and managers a fresh start after the crisis.

An important implication of our analysis is the complementarity between bail-ins (interbank market) and bailouts (LOLR) as well as other regulatory facilities (prompt corrective action, orderly resolution of failure) in crisis management. We can summarize by comparing different organizations as follows.

1. With neither a LOLR nor an interbank market, liquidation takes place whenever $x > mD$, which inefficiently limits investment I.
2. With an interbank market but no LOLR (as advocated by Goodfriend and King), the closure threshold is R_{EC} and there is excessive failure whenever $R_{EC} > R^o$.
3. With both a LOLR facility and an interbank market:
   (i) If $R^o > R_s$ (severe moral hazard problem for the banker) then the incentive-efficient solution can be implemented, complementing the LOLR with a policy of prompt corrective action in the range (R_s, R^o);
   (ii) If $R^o < R_s$ (moderate moral hazard problem for the banker), then a different institution (financed by taxation or by insurance premiums) is needed to complement the central bank and implement the incentive-efficient solution. The central bank helps whenever the bank is solvent, and the other institution provides an "orderly resolution of failure" in the range $(R^o, \min\{R_s, R_{EC}\})$.

8. An International Lender of Last Resort (ILOLR)

In this section we reinterpret the model in an international setting and provide a potential rationale for an international lender of last resort (ILOLR) à la Bagehot. Financial and banking crises, usually coupled with currency crises, have been common in emerging economies in Asia (Thailand, Indonesia, Korea), Latin America (Mexico, Brazil, Ecuador, Argentina) and in the periphery of Europe (Turkey). These crisis have proved costly in terms of output. The question is whether an ILOLR can help alleviate, or even avoid, such crises.

An ILOLR could follow a policy of injecting liquidity in international financial markets—by actions that range from establishing the proposed global central bank that issues an international currency to merely coordinating the intervention of the three major central banks[37]—or could act to help countries in trouble, much like a central bank acts to help individual banking institutions. The latter approach is developed in several proposals that adapt Bagehot's doctrine to international lending; see, for example, the Meltzer Report (IFIAC 2000) and Fischer (1999). As pointed out by Jeanne and Wyplosz (2003), a major difference between the approaches concerns the required size of the ILOLR. The former (global CB) approach requires an issuer of international currency; in the latter, the intervention is bounded by the difference between the short-term foreign exchange liabilities of the banking sector and the foreign reserves of the country in question. We will look here at the second approach. The main tension identified in the debate is between those who emphasize the effect of liquidity support on crisis prevention (Fischer 1999) and those who are worried about generating moral hazard in the country being helped (IFIAC 2000).

8.1 A Reinterpretation of the Model

Suppose now that the balance sheet of Section 2 corresponds to a small open economy for which D_0 is the foreign-denominated short-term debt, M is the amount of foreign reserves, I is the investment in risky local entrepreneurial projects, E, equity and long-term debt (or local resources available for investment), and D is the face value of the foreign-denominated short-term debt.[38] Our fund managers are now international fund managers operating in the international interbank market. The liquidity ratio $m = M/D$ is now the ratio of foreign reserves to foreign short-term debt—a crucial ratio, according to empirical work, in determining the probability of a crisis in the country.[39] The parameter λ now represents the fire-sale premium associated with early sales of domestic bank assets in the secondary market. Furthermore, for a given amount of withdrawals by fund managers $x > m$ at $\tau = 1$, there are critical thresholds for the return R of investment below which the country is bankrupt ($R_f(x)$) or will default at $\tau = 1$ ($R_{ec}(x) < R_f(x)$). The effort e necessary to improve returns could be understood to be exerted by bank managers, entrepreneurs, or even the government. According to Section 7, effort has a cost and the actors exerting effort are interested in continuing in their job. Default by the country at $\tau = 1$ deprives those actors from their continuation benefits (for example, because of restructuring of the banking and/or private sectors or because the government is removed from office), and consequently "default" at $\tau = 1$ for some region of realized returns is the only disciplining device.

8.2 Results

(i) There is a range or realizations of the return R, (R_s, R^*) for which a coordination failure occurs. This happens when the amount of withdrawals by foreign fund managers is so large that the country is bankrupt even though it is (in principle) solvent.

[37] See Eichengreen (1999) for a survey of the different proposals.

[38] The balance sheet corresponds to the consolidated private sector of the country. In some countries, local firms borrow from local banks and then the latter borrow in international currency.

[39] Indeed, Radelet and Sachs (1998) as well as Rodrik and Velasco (1999) find that the ratio of short-term debt to reserves is a robust predictor of financial crisis (in the sense of a sharp reversal of capital flows). The latter also find that a greater short-term exposure aggravates the crisis once capital flows reverse.

(ii) For a high enough foreign reserve ratio m, the range (R_s, R^*) collapses and there is no coordination failure of international investors.

(iii) The probability of bankruptcy of the banking sector is:

- decreasing in the foreign reserve ratio, the solvency ratio, the critical withdrawal probability γ, and the expected mean return of the country investment;
- increasing in the fire-sale premium and the face value of foreign short-term debt; and
- increasing in the precision of public information about R when public news is bad and decreasing in the precision of private information (both provided $\gamma < 1/2$).

(iv) An ILOLR that follows Bagehot's prescription can minimize the incidence of coordination failure among international fund managers—provided it is well informed about R. One possibility is that the ILOLR performs in-depth country research and has supervisory knowledge of the banking system of the country where the crisis occurs.[40]

(v) The disclosure of a public signal about country return prospects may introduce multiple equilibria. A well-informed international agency may want to be cautious and not publicly disclose too precise information in order to avoid a rally of expectations in a run equilibrium.

(vi) In the presence of the moral hazard problem associated with eliciting high returns, foreign short-term debt serves the purpose of disciplining whoever must exert effort to improve returns. Note that domestic currency–denominated short-term debt will not have a disciplining effect because it can be inflated away. There will be an optimal cutoff point R^o below which restructuring (of either the private sector or government) must occur in order to provide incentives to exert effort.

The following scenarios can be considered.

No Bail-In and No Bailout. With no ILOLR and no access to the international interbank market, country projects are liquidated whenever withdrawals by foreign fund managers are larger than foreign reserves. This inefficiently limits investment.

Bail-In but No Bailout. With no ILOLR but with access to the international interbank market, some costly project liquidation is avoided by having fire sales of assets, but still there will be excessive liquidation of entrepreneurial projects.

Bail-In and Bailout. With ILOLR and access to the international interbank market, we have two cases as follows:

- The moral hazard problem in the country is severe ($R^o > R_s$). In this case a policy of prompt corrective action in the range (R_s, R^o) is needed to complement the ILOLR facility. A solvent country may need to 'restructure' when returns are close to the solvency threshold.
- The moral hazard problem in the country is moderate ($R^o < R_s$). Then, in addition to the ILOLR help for a solvent country, an orderly "resolution of failure" process is needed in the range $(R^o, \min\{R_s, R_{EC}\})$. An insolvent country should be helped when it is not too far away from the solvency threshold. This may be interpreted as a mechanism similar to the sovereign debt restructuring mechanism (SDRM) of the sort currently studied by the IMF with the objective of restructuring unsustainable debt.[41] In our case, this would be the foreign short-term debt. In the range $(R^o, \min\{R_s, R_{EC}\})$, an institution like an international bankruptcy court could help.

[40] Although this seems more far-fetched than in the case of a domestic LOLR, the IMF (for example) is trying to enhance its monitoring capabilities by way of "financial sector assessment" programs.

[41] See Bolton (2003) for a discussion of SDRM-type facilities from the perspective of corporate bankruptcy theory and practice.

As before, an important insight from the analysis is the complementarity between the market (bail-ins) and an ILOLR facility (bailout)—together with other regulatory facilities—can provide for prompt corrective action and orderly failure resolution. Our conclusion is that an ILOLR facility à la Bagehot can help to implement the incentive-efficient solution, provided that it is complemented with provisions of prompt corrective action and orderly resolution of failure.

9. Concluding Remarks

In this paper we have provided a rationale—in the context of modern interbank markets—for Bagehot's doctrine of helping illiquid but solvent banks. Indeed, investors in the interbank market may face a coordination failure and so intervention may be desirable. We have examined the impact of public intervention along the following three dimensions:

(i) solvency and liquidity requirements (at $\tau = 0$);
(ii) lender-of-last-resort policy (at the interim date $\tau = 1$); and
(iii) closure rules, which can consist of two types of policy: prompt corrective action or the orderly resolution of bank failures.

The coordination failure can be avoided by appropriate solvency and liquidity requirements. However, the cost of doing so will typically be too large in terms of foregone returns, and ex ante measures will only help partially. This means that prudential regulation needs to be complemented by a LOLR policy. The paper shows how discount-window loans can eliminate the coordination failure (or alleviate it, if for incentive reasons some degree of coordination failure is optimal). It also sheds light on when open-market operations will be appropriate.

A main insight of the analysis is that public and private involvement are both necessary in implementing the incentive-efficient solution. Furthermore, implementation of this solution may also require complementing Bagehot's LOLR facility with prompt corrective action (intervention on a solvent bank) or orderly failure resolution (help to an insolvent bank).

The model, when given an interpretation in an international context, provides a rationale for an international LOLR à la Bagehot, complemented with prompt corrective action and provisions for orderly resolution of failures, and it points to the complementarity between bail-ins and bailouts in crisis resolution.

References

Allen, Franklin and Douglas Gale (1998). "Optimal Financial Crises." *Journal of Finance*, 53, 1245–1284.

Bagehot, Walter (1873). *Lombard Street*. H.S. King, London.

Berger, Allen, Sally Davies, and Mark Flannery (2000). "Comparing Market and Supervisory Assessments on Bank Performances: Who Knows What When?" *Journal of Money, Credit and Banking*, 32(2), 641–667.

Bernanke, Ben (1983). "Nonmonetary Effects of the Financial Crisis in the Propagation of the Great Depression." *American Economic Review*, 73, 257–263.

Bernanke, Ben and Mark Gertler (1989). "Agency Costs, Net Worth, and Business Fluctuations." *American Economic Review*, 79, 14–31.

Bolton, Patrick (2003). "Toward a Statutory Approach to Sovereign Debt Restructuring: Lessons from Corporate Bankruptcy Practice Around the World." Mimeo, Princeton University and IMF Working Paper.

Bordo, Michael D. (1990). "The Lender of Last Resort: Alternative Views and Historical Experience." *Federal Reserve Bank of Richmond, Economic Review*, 18–29.
Broecker, Thoersten (1990). "Credit-Worthiness Tests and Interbank Competition." *Econometrica*, 58(2), 429–452.
Bryant, James (1980). "A Model of Reserves, Bank Runs and Deposit Insurance." *Journal of Banking and Finance*, 4, 335–344.
Calomiris, Charles (1998a). "The IMF's Imprudent Role as a Lender of Last Resort." *Cato Journal*, 17(3), 275–294.
Calomiris, Charles (1998b). "Blueprints for a New Global Financial Architecture." Joint Economics Committee, United States Congress, Washington, DC.
Calomiris, Charles and Charles Kahn (1991). "The Role of Demandable Debt in Structuring Optimal Banking Arrangements." *American Economic Review*, 81(3), 497–513.
Carletti, Elena (1999). "Bank Moral Hazard and Market Discipline." FMG Discussion Paper, London School of Economics.
Carlsson, Hans and Eric Van Damme (1993). "Global Games and Equilibrium Selection." *Econometrica*, 61(5), 989–1018.
Chari, Varadarajan V. and Ravi Jagannathan (1988). "Banking Panics, Information, and Rational Expectations Equilibrium." *Journal of Finance*, 43(3), 749–761.
Chari, Varadarajan V and Patrick Kehoe (1998). "Asking the Right Questions about the IMF." *Public Affairs*, 13, 3–26.
Chevalier, Judy and Glenn Ellison (1997), "Risk Taking by Mutual Funds as a Response to Incentives." *Journal of Political Economy*, 105, 1167–1200.
Chevalier, Judy and Glenn Ellison (1999), "Are Some Mutual Funds Managers Better than Others?" *Journal of Finance*, 54(2), 875–899.
Corsetti, Giancarlo, Amil Dasgupta, Stephen Morris, and Hyun S. Shin (2004). "Does One Soros Make a Difference? The Role of a Large Trader in Currency Crises." *Review of Economic Studies*, 71(1), 87–113.
DeYoung, Robert, Mark J. Flannery, Walter W. Lans, and Sorin M. Sorescu (1998). "The Informational Advantage of Specialized Monitors: The Case of Bank Examiners." Working paper, Federal Reserve Bank of Chicago.
Diamond, Douglas and Phil Dybvig (1983). "Bank Runs, Deposit Insurance and Liquidity." *Journal of Political Economy*, 91(3), 401–419.
Diamond, Douglas and Ragu Rajan (2001). "Liquidity Risk, Liquidity Creation and Financial Fragility: A Theory of Banking." *Journal of Political Economy*, 109(2), 287–327.
Eichengreen, Barry (1999). *Toward a New International Financial Architecture: A Practical Post-Asia Agenda*. Institute for International Economics.
Fischer, Stanley (1999). "On the Need for an International Lender of Last Resort." *Journal of Economic Perspectives*, 13, 85–104.
Flannery, Mark J. (1996). "Financial Crises, Payment Systems Problems, and Discount Window Lending." *Journal of Money, Credit and Banking* 28(4), 804–824.
Folkerts-Landau, Dieter and Peter Garber (1992). "The ECB: A Bank or a Monetary Policy Rule?" In *Establishing a Central Bank: Issues in Europe and Lessons from the US*, Chapter 4, edited by Matthew B. Canzoneri, Vittoria Grilland, Paul R. Masson. CEPR Cambridge University Press.
Freixas, Xavier, Curzio Giannini, Glenn Hoggarth, and Farouk Soussa (1999). "Lender of Last Resort-A Review of the Literature." *Financial Stability Review, Bank of England*, 7, 151–167.
Freixas, Xavier, Bruno Parigi, and Jean-Charles Rochet (2004). "The Lender of Last Resort: A 21st Century Approach." *Journal of the European Economic Association*, 2: 1085–1115.
Gale, Douglas and Xavier Vives (2002). "Dollarization, Bailouts, and the Stability of the Banking System." *Quarterly Journal of Economics*, 117(2), 467–502.
Goldstein, Itay and Ari Pauzner (2003). "Demand Deposit Contracts and the Probability of Bank Runs." Discussion paper, Tel-Aviv University.
Goodfriend, Marvin and Robert King (1988). "Financial Deregulation, Monetary Policy and Central Banking." In *Restructuring Banking and Financial Services in America*, edited by Williams Haraf and Rose Marie Kushmeider. *AEI Studies*, 481, Lanham, MD.
Goodfriend, Marvin and Jeff Lacker (1999). "Limited Commitment and Central Bank Lending." Working Paper 99-2, Federal Reserve Bank of Richmond.
Goodhart, Charles and Haizhou Huang (1999). "A Model of the Lender of Last Resort." FMG, LSE Discussion Paper 313, London, U.K.

Goodhart, Charles and Haizhou Huang (2000). "A Simple Model of an International Lender of Last Resort." *Economic Notes*, 29(1), 1–11.
Gorton, Gary (1985). "Bank Suspension of Convertibility." *Journal of Monetary Economics*, 15, 177–193.
Gorton, Gary (1988). "Banking Panics and Business Cycles." *Oxford Economic Papers*, 40, 751–781.
Grossman, Sandy and Oliver Hart (1982). "Corporate Financial Structure and Managerial Incentives." In *The Economics of Information and Uncertainty*, edited by John J. McCall. University of Chicago Press.
Hart, Oliver and John Moore (1994). "A Theory of Debt Based on the Inalienability of Human Capital." *Quarterly Journal of Economics*, 109(4), 841–879.
Heinemann, Frank and Gerhard Illing (2002). "Speculative Attacks: Unique Sunspot Equilibrium and Transparency." *Journal of International Economics*, 58(2), 429–450.
Hellwig, Christian (2002). "Public Information, Private Information and the Multiplicity of Equilibria in Coordination Games." *Journal of Economic Theory*, 107, 191–222.
Holmstrom, Bengt and Jean Tirole (1997). "Financial Intermediation, Loanable Funds, and the Real Sector." *Quarterly Journal of Economics*, 112(3), 663–691.
Humphrey, Thomas (1975). "The Classical Concept of the Lender of Last Resort." *Economic Review*, 61, 2–9.
IFIAC (2000). *Report of the International Financial Institution Advisory Commission*, Allan H. Meltzer, Chairman, Washington, DC.
Jacklin, Charles and Sudipto Bhattacharya (1988). "Distinguishing Panics and Information-Based Bank Runs: Welfare and Policy Implications." *Journal of Political Economy* 96(3), 568–592.
Jeanne, Olivier and Charles Wyplosz (2003). "The International Lender of Last Resort: How Large is Large Enough?" In *Managing Currency Crisis in Emerging Markets*, edited by Michael P. Dooley and Jeffrey A. Frankel. University of Chicago Press.
Kaminsky, Graciela L. and Carmen Reinhart (1999). "The Twin Crises: The Causes of Banking and Balance-of-Payments Problems." *American Economic Review*, 89, 473–500.
Kaufman, George (1991). "Lender of Last Resort: A Contemporary Perspective." *Journal of Financial Services Research*, 5, 95–110.
Lindgren, Carl-Johan, Gillian Garcia, and Matthew Saal (1996). *Bank Soundness and Macroeconomic Policy*. IMF, Washington, DC.
Markets Group of the Federal Reserve Bank of New York (2002). "Domestic Open Market Operations During 2001." Federal Reserve Bank of New York.
Martin, Antoine (2002). "Reconciling Bagehot with the Fed's response to Sept. 11." FRB of Kansas City, October.
Mishkin, Frederick (1998). "Systemic Risk, Moral Hazard and the International Lender of Last Resort." NBER and Columbia University, April.
Morris, Stephen and Hyun S. Shin (1998). "Unique Equilibrium in a Model of Self-Fulfilling Currency Attacks." *American Economic Review*, 88, 587–597.
Morris, Stephen and Hyun S. Shin (2000). "Rethinking Multiple Equilibria in Macroeconomic Modelling." NBER *Macroeconomics Annual* 2000, MIT Press, Cambridge.
Morris, Stephen and Hyun S. Shin (2001). "The CNBC Effect: Welfare Effects of Public Information." Yale Cowles Foundation Discussion Paper 1312.
Padoa-Schioppa, Tomaso (1999). "EMU and Banking Supervision." Lecture at the London School of Economics, Financial Market Group.
Peek, Joe, Eric Rosengren, and Geoffrey Tootell (1999). "Is Bank Supervision Central to Central Banking?" *Quarterly Journal of Economics*, 114(2), 629–653.
Postlewaite, Andy and Xavier Vives (1987). "Bank Runs as an Equilibrium Phenomenon." *Journal of Political Economy*, 95(3), 485–491.
Radelet, Steven and Jeffrey Sachs (1998). "The Onset of the Asian Financial Crisis." Mimeo, Harvard Institute for International Development.
Riordan, Mike (1993). "Competition and Bank Performance: A Theoretical Perspective." In *Capital Markets and Financial Intermediation*, edited by Colin Mayer and Xavier Vives. Cambridge University Press.
Rodrik, Dani and Andres Velasco (1999). "Short-Term Capital Flows." World Bank 1999 ABCDE Conference.

Romer, Christina and David Romer (2000). "Federal Reserve Information and the Behavior of Interest Rates." *American Economic Review*, 90(3), 429–453.
Schwartz, Anna J. (1992). "The Misuse of the Fed's Discount Window." *Federal Reserve Bank of St. Louis Review*, September/October, 58–69.
Thornton, Henry (1802). *An Enquiry into the Nature and Effects of Paper Credit of Great Britain.* Hatchard, London.
Van Zandt, Timothy and Xavier Vives (2003). "Monotone Equilibria in Bayesian Games of Strategic Complementarities." INSEAD Working Paper.
Vives, Xavier (1990). "Nash Equilibrium with Strategic Complementarities." *Journal of Mathematical Economics*, 19(3), 305–321.
Vives, Xavier (1999). *Oligopoly Pricing: Old Ideas and New Tools.* MIT Press.
Vives, Xavier (2001). "Restructuring Financial Regulation in the European Monetary Union." *Journal of Financial Services Research*, 19(1), 57–82.

13 Competition among Regulators and Credit Market Integration

Giovanni Dell'Ariccia and Robert Marquez

1. Introduction

In recent years, technological progress and regulatory changes have led to the progressive integration of international financial markets. As a result, banks' cross-border activities have become increasingly important, raising new challenges for regulators that have remained nationally bounded. This trend has spurred a debate on the costs and benefits of the international harmonization of bank regulation. As a specific example, in the E.U. the introduction of the Euro and the single market has raised the question of whether a continental regulatory agency is necessary or desirable.

In this paper, we compare the costs and benefits of centralized and decentralized banking regulation. The benefit of centralizing regulation is that it internalizes any interdependencies that may exist across countries due to the integration of their financial systems. The cost is that it limits flexibility in the design of policy to the extent that a centralized regulator would be forced to impose uniform standards across all the countries under its jurisdiction. We develop a model that incorporates this trade-off to address three main issues. First, we examine how competition among regulators affects regulatory standards. Second, we analyze countries' incentives to form bilateral "regulatory unions." Finally, we study how those incentives are affected by the existence of financial integration among multiple countries.

In our model, banks compete across countries to extend risky loans to borrowers. Banks can reduce the default risk of these loans through monitoring. However, limited liability and the existence of deposit insurance keep loan monitoring at a socially inefficient level. Regulators concerned with the stability as well as the profitability of the banking system can increase banks' incentives to monitor by imposing minimum capital adequacy standards – standards that are costly to the banks, however. We compare a setup in which national regulators concerned solely with their respective domestic banking system set policies noncooperatively to one in which an international regulator sets uniform standards for all banks.

We start by focusing on a situation with two symmetric countries and show that competition among regulators leads to lower capital adequacy standards than under a unified regulator. This occurs for two reasons. First, in financially integrated economies, banking regulation introduces an externality: higher capital adequacy standards in one country not only enhance the stability of the domestic banking system, but also the stability of foreign banks that compete with domestic banks. This benefit results from the fact that tighter capital requirements constrain lending by domestic banks. In turn, this reduces competition and increases the return to monitoring for foreign banks, thereby lowering the probability of bank failure in foreign markets. Independent regulators do not internalize this positive spillover and thus impose standards that are too low relative to those that would be chosen by a unified regulatory agency. Second, to the extent that regulators are concerned about the shareholders of their domestic banks, they may lower their banks' capital adequacy standards in order to provide them with an advantage over foreign banks and increase their profitability. In other words, in addition to the externality raised above, there can also be "competition in laxity" as regulators attempt to promote their domestically chartered banks.[1]

We use this basic result for the subsequent analysis of the conditions under which a centralized international regulator is likely to emerge. That is, we ask when would domestic regulators find it preferable to surrender their authority to a supranational agency in order to reap the benefits from centralization. Toward this end, we drop the symmetry assumption and allow country-level regulators to have different needs or tastes for regulation. Here, we find two of the main results in our paper. First, with asymmetric countries, a centralized regulator will be unanimously preferred to independence only if such a regulator were to choose capital adequacy standards higher than those of the country with the highest set of individual standards. Second, independent domestic regulators will endogenously agree to merge into a centralized agency only if the countries are not too dissimilar in their individual regulatory standards or objectives.

The intuition for these results is as follows. While large benefits may derive from coordinating regulatory policies and internalizing the externalities generated by regulation, there are also costs associated with forming a regulatory union. These costs stem from the loss of flexibility associated with uniform standards if, as we assume, a central regulator finds it politically difficult, if not impossible, to impose different standards across countries. These costs are therefore higher for more asymmetric countries. Hence, more similar countries are more likely to opt for a centralized solution, while more asymmetric countries will generally choose to maintain independent regulators. However, even if countries are similar, we find that regulatory standards still have to increase relative to the highest standards under independent regulation in order for both countries to be better off. This occurs because tighter standards in each country hurt domestic banks. To compensate for this effect, it must be that standards are also raised for foreign banks. Since this is true for all countries, regulatory requirements must increase across the board when switching to a common standard.

Extending the analysis beyond the case of two countries illustrates a series of new trade-offs. First, we find that, with multiple financially integrated countries, regulatory unions among a subset of countries may fail to emerge if the number of countries that remain independent is sufficiently large, even when these partial unions would have emerged in the absence of the other countries. This occurs because the tighter standards that stem from coordinating regulation puts the merged banking systems at a significant disadvantage relative to banks in the countries that remain outside the union. Related, we also show that partial integration may not be a good avenue for achieving full integration, as countries

[1] This latter effect has been studied in the literature on environmental regulation. See Oates (1996) for a discussion of these and other issues.

outside the regulatory union may find it preferable to free-ride off the increased regulation in member countries of the union rather than to join the union.

Most of the insights and implications of this paper can be applied to the broad issue of bank regulation in a financially integrated international economy or to a single economy with competing regulatory agencies, such as the U.S. In the U.S., banks are faced with the choice of chartering at the state versus national level, and of being regulated by different supervisory agencies. The recent deregulation of interstate branching restrictions and lowering of legal barriers to entry into other banking activities raise the question of whether a unified regulatory body would be desirable for the U.S. This analysis is also relevant to the European case for a number of reasons. First, the Single Market Act has created an environment in which banks chartered in any E.U. member country are allowed to open branches anywhere in the Union while remaining under the supervisory authority of their country of origin. Second, the introduction of the Euro has intensified the linkages among financial markets. Finally, Euroland is characterized by a separation between the geographic domain of monetary and regulatory authorities. Indeed, since the inception of the Euro, the European Central Bank (ECB) has assumed full authority over monetary policy, while bank regulation and supervision has remained in the hands of independent national agencies.

The framework just described has allowed regulatory and supervisory practices to vary across countries. Although the Basel Accord has gone a long way towards harmonizing capital standards at an international level, individual countries have maintained a large degree of discretion in the determination of which assets can be used to meet capital requirements.[2] Information disclosure, inspection procedures, accounting systems, and limits on the scope of banks' activities are also heterogeneous across countries, as well as rescue policies designed to manage banking crises. For example, Wagster (1996) finds that despite the Basel Accord's purported intent of "leveling the playing field" for banks across countries, it does not appear that the accord went very far in eliminating the pricing advantage of Japanese banks. In this paper, we work on the basis of the view that even in the presence of international agreements, countries maintain sufficient autonomy to compete over regulatory standards (see White, 1993, for a discussion of this issue).

This paper proceeds as follows. Section 2 briefly reviews some related literature. Section 3 describes the model. Section 4 provides a preliminary analysis. Section 5 contains the central issues of the paper, analyzing both the incentives for a regulatory union to form between two countries as well as the effects introduced by the existence of multiple countries. Section 6 discusses robustness of the model. Section 7 concludes.

2. Related Literature

Traditionally, bank regulation has been justified as providing protection for depositors from the risk of failure of their bank. However, bank failures also create negative externalities that can adversely affect the economy, hurting not only their customers, both depositors and borrowers, but also possibly spreading to other banks (see Bhattacharya and Thakor, 1993, for a survey of these issues). Therefore, regulation has focused primarily on promoting the safety and soundness of the banking system.

[2] Gorton and Winton (2000) discuss how this issue has led to significant heterogeneity in the definition of Tier 1 capital across countries. Also see Prati and Schinasi (1999) for a detailed examination of the differences across European countries.

To promote this stability, a number of regulatory instruments have been identified, ranging from portfolio restrictions to capital adequacy standards. Moreover, while some policies, such as deposit insurance, have been instituted in order to benefit depositors directly, others, such as deposit interest rate ceilings, are believed to benefit depositors only indirectly by increasing bank profits and thus strengthening the system. Much of the recent literature has focused on the optimal assignment of these instruments to address the concerns highlighted above (see Santos, 2001, for a recent survey). For example, regulators have instituted capital requirements in response to increased risk-taking by banks resulting from deposit insurance.[3] From this perspective, a closely related paper is that by Acharya (2003), who focuses on how coordinating on only one regulatory dimension, such as capital adequacy ratios, can generate detrimental effects when other instruments, such as closure policies, are allowed to differ. Acharya does not consider, however, the incentives to form a regulatory union from the regulator's perspective, an issue that is central to this paper.

There are a number of models in the literature on banking regulation that share many of the features of our model. For example, recent work by John et al. (2000) illustrates the classic result that bank capital regulation, or bank portfolio restrictions, may help reduce banks' risk-shifting incentives, but constrain banks' activities and profits. There is also a vast literature on prudential regulation of banks with features similar to those in this paper (see Dewatripont and Tirole, 1994, for a survey). Hellmann et al. (2000), Matutes and Vives (2000), and Repullo (2004) show that regulatory instruments (capital requirements coupled with deposit rate controls) can increase efficiency and facilitate prudent investment, but may be costly to the banks. Our contribution is to model the interaction between credit market integration and the objectives of regulators in providing for a sound banking system.

The notion of competition among regulators has been analyzed recently in a context in which multiple regulators have authority over the same group of agents. Kane (1984) argues that competition among financial regulators is beneficial as it fosters the production of more efficient regulatory services. Similarly, Dermine (1991) argues that competition among exchanges would improve their quality if participants were able to choose the market in which to operate and investors were able to judge the quality of regulation. Laffont and Martimort (1999) demonstrate that, in the presence of self-interested regulators, splitting authority among different regulatory bodies limits their discretion in engaging in socially wasteful activities by making collusion between regulators and regulated firms more difficult. Here, we focus on an alternative situation whereby multiple regulators have authority over different groups of agents that in turn compete with each other over common markets. Our paper is closer to White (1994), who argues that cooperation among independent regulators may not be sustainable by drawing a parallel with the well-known problems of cartel stability. Santos and Scheinkman (2000) also analyze a similar issue by examining whether competing exchanges have incentives to lower their standards and demand fewer contractual guarantees to their traders (see also Gehrig, 1998, for an analysis of competing stock exchanges). They do not, however, endogenize regulators' decisions to coordinate actions. Finally, Vives (2000, 2001) discusses challenges associated with the regulation of financial services firms in the E.U. following monetary unification, and some of the arguments for and against centralizing regulation.

[3]There is some debate as to the ultimate effect of many of these instruments. In particular, much focus has been placed on the role of capital adequacy ratios in curbing risk-taking behavior. For example, see the discussion in Rochet (1992) or more recently in Besanko and Kanatas (1996), Calem and Rob (1999), and Hellmann et al. (2000).

3. Model

We present a simple model of bank regulation and lending competition. There are two countries, indexed by $i = 1, 2$. In each country, a single domestic bank with limited liability operates under the authority of a local regulator.[4] The two economies are financially integrated in that banks can extend loans to borrowers in either country. For simplicity, we abstract from issues related to exchange rate risk and implicitly assume fixed exchange rates or a common currency. These loans are risky, but can be made safer through monitoring. Regulators can provide banks with incentives to increase the level of loan monitoring. The resulting allocation of bank credit together with monitoring will determine the gross return on banks' portfolios. We discuss this specification in detail in what follows.

Bank lending: In each country, the domestic bank has access to a fixed amount of equity E at an average cost of ρ, and to an unlimited amount of domestically raised insured deposits at an average cost of δ. In order to maintain some degree of symmetry across countries, we assume that the level of capital available to each country's bank is the same, E.[5] We capture the idea that bank capital is a particularly costly form of financing by assuming that $\rho \geq \delta$ (see Gorton and Winton, 2000, for a formalization of this issue; Hellmann et al., 2000; Repullo, 2004, make similar assumptions.). The fixed supply of bank equity, E, represents the notion that bank capital is not only costly but also difficult to raise, at least on short notice (see also Stein, 1998; Almazan, 2002).

Given its level of equity, each bank i chooses how much to lend on aggregate, L_i, and what fraction of that amount to lend at home, γ_i, versus abroad, $1 - \gamma_i$. We assume lending markets are imperfectly competitive, so each bank faces demands for loans at home and abroad that reflect some degree of market power, as summarized by the following inverse demand curves that give the price of loans made by bank i (the superscripts h and f refer to its demand at home and abroad, respectively):[6]

$$P_i^h = A - \gamma_i L_i - \theta(1 - \gamma_j)L_j, \tag{13.1}$$

$$P_i^f = A - (1 - \gamma_i)L_i - \theta\gamma_j L_j, \tag{13.2}$$

where $\gamma_i L_i$ is the amount bank i lends in its domestic market, and $(1 - \gamma_i)L_i$ is the amount lent abroad (similar terms hold for the bank in country j). We assume throughout that A is large relative to E, so that the demand for loans is large enough that a duopoly is viable.

[4] This particular market structure simplifies notation. The results in this paper would hold even if there were multiple banks in each country.

[5] While issues related to competition between large and small countries are clearly important in the design of policy related to integration, they lie somewhat outside the current focus of this paper on the behavior of competing regulators. The assumption of the exogeneity of the deposit rate, as well as the ability of banks to also raise deposits abroad, is discussed in Section 6.

[6] These inverse demand curves can be obtained by inverting the demand curves for a model of price competition with differentiated products. Specifically, the demand curve for bank i at home is $Q_i^h = a - P_i^h + \lambda P_j^f$, while the demand for bank j abroad is $Q_j^f = a - P_j^f + \lambda P_i^h$. Substituting the second equation into the first and solving for the price obtained by bank i yields

$$P_i^h = \frac{1}{1 - \lambda^2}((1 + \lambda)a - Q_i^h - \lambda Q_j^f),$$

which corresponds to the inverse demand function above, with $A = (1 + \lambda)a$ and $\theta = \lambda(1/(1 - \lambda^2))$ is just a scaling factor). Analogous results obtain for the price obtained by bank i in country j.

The parameter θ represents the extent to which products offered by either the domestic or the foreign bank are substitutes for domestic customers. In fully integrated markets the law of one price should apply (see Chen and Knez, 1995). In this model, this corresponds to a situation in which $\theta = 1$. An increase in θ therefore makes the markets more competitive and reduces each bank's profit.

Bank monitoring: Banks extend risky loans, but can increase the probability of success of their portfolios by monitoring their borrowers. When the borrowers' projects are successful, bank revenue is the product of the total amount lent and the average interest rate (i.e., price) charged on each loan, which can be expressed for bank i as

$$\Phi_i = L_i(\gamma_i P_i^h + (1 - \gamma_i)P_i^f). \tag{13.3}$$

When unsuccessful, however, the projects fail and the loan portfolio has a zero return. Each bank can choose a monitoring effort q_i (per dollar lent), which for simplicity also represents the probability of success of its portfolio. The role of bank monitoring in this model is thus analogous to that in Besanko and Kanatas (1993) in that it increases the expected return on the project and reduces the probability of failure (see also Dewatripont and Tirole, 1994). This monitoring effort carries a cost cq_i^2 per dollar. As a bank's objective is to maximize profits, banks choose the level of monitoring, q_i, that maximizes their expected return given their loan allocations, and choose the loan allocation γ_i that maximizes Φ_i.

Regulatory standards: Bank regulators care about the safety and soundness ("stability") of the banking sector, which in this model is just the probability that the banks under their jurisdiction do not fail. Further, our requirement for the regulator's objective function is that it internalize the benefits of intermediation to the bank's constituents in some way. We therefore also allow for the possibility that regulators care about the well-being of bank shareholders who, together with depositors, represent the main stakeholders of the bank. We do this by assuming that the regulator in each country i puts weights α_i on bank profits directly and $1 - \alpha_i$ on banking system stability. Therefore, the overall utility of the regulator in country i can be expressed as

$$U^i = \alpha_i \Pi_i + (1 - \alpha_i)\xi q_i, \tag{13.4}$$

where Π_i represents bank profits in country i, and ξ is a scaling factor to take into account the fact that $q_i \in [0, 1]$.The regulator maximizes U^i by setting a capital requirement, k_i, for the bank under its jurisdiction. This capital standard forces the bank to hold equity at least equal to a fraction k_i of the loans it grants. We later show that these capital standards act in the usual way to constrain banks' lending and to decrease portfolio risk.

We will consider two separate cases, one of independent national regulators, where each bank is regulated only by its home country, and the other of a central regulator that sets regulatory standards for all banks in the system. We assume that each independent national regulator can set capital adequacy standards only for the banks chartered in that country, and so can only control k_i. In the case of a centralized regulator, we assume that this regulator sets both k_i and k_j, but must treat all banks equally, so it must set both to be the same ($k = k_i = k_j$). Indeed, it seems reasonable to assume that a centralized regulator would find it politically infeasible to impose different regulatory standards for each country.

We model asymmetry between countries by allowing the weights each regulator places on bank profits versus stability, α_i, to differ. This setup allows us to analyze situations in which regulators from different jurisdictions have different tastes or needs for regulation and place greater or less emphasis on bank profits versus financial system stability. In some contexts, this has been referred to as the degree to which regulators are captured by the financial institutions under their control.[7] A further reason why each country might treat its banks differently is that in some countries there may be greater foreign ownership of domestic banks. Indeed, we would expect domestic regulators to be relatively less concerned about bank shareholders if a significant fraction of them are foreigners. Though we do not focus explicitly on this issue, for countries with highly captured regulators, centralizing bank regulation could be a way of decreasing the influence banks yield over their regulators, as it is likely to be more difficult for local banks to exert influence on a central regulator.

Timing: We divide the model into three stages. In stage one each regulator chooses the capital adequacy standard, k_i. In stage two, banks simultaneously choose how much to lend in each country. In stage three, banks choose how much effort to put into monitoring their portfolios.

4. Preliminary Analysis

As a preliminary step, we briefly illustrate the impact of the lack of coordination on regulators' optimal choices. Then, we turn to the main focus of the paper and analyze the incentives to form a regulatory union. As usual, we solve the model by backwards induction.

Stage 3: By stage 3, banks have already chosen how much to lend in each country. Conditional on project success, this allocation determines the gross return for each bank on its aggregate portfolio, which for each bank i can be defined on a per-dollar basis as $R_i = \Phi_i(\widehat{\gamma}_i, \widehat{\gamma}_j)/L_i$, where $\widehat{\gamma}_i$ and $\widehat{\gamma}_j$ represent the optimal allocations for banks i and j, respectively. Each bank i now chooses a monitoring effort so as to maximize expected profits, which can be expressed as

$$\max_{q_i} q_i L_i (R_i - (1 - k_i)\delta) - k_i \rho L_i - c q_i^2 L_i. \tag{13.5}$$

The profit-maximizing monitoring effort (per-dollar) is thus given by

$$\widehat{q}_i = \min \left\{ \frac{R_i - (1 - k_i)\delta}{2c}, \ 1 \right\}. \tag{13.6}$$

Note that $\widehat{q}_i$ is increasing in bank i's return, R_i, as well as in the level of bank capital, k_i.

In this framework, moral hazard associated with limited liability biases bank monitoring downward. If instead banks fully internalized the cost associated with defaulting on depositors, they would choose

$$\bar{q}_i = \min \left\{ \frac{R_i}{2c}, \ 1 \right\} \geq \widehat{q}_i, \tag{13.7}$$

with the inequality strict whenever $\widehat{q}_i < 1$. Therefore, a rationale for regulation is to limit bank moral hazard and raise the level of monitoring.

[7] An example of this issue is discussed in Kane (1990), who argues that regulatory capture in the Resolution Trust Corporation may have led to inefficiencies in closure policies for U.S. savings and loans corporations during the 1980s.

Stage 2: In this stage banks choose how much to lend in each country. In our model, the assumption that the banks' cost of capital, ρ, is greater than the cost of deposits, δ, implies that banks never choose to hold excess capital. This together with the assumption that bank capital is in short supply yields the standard result that banks will choose to leverage themselves as much as possible (see Repullo, 2004). Given the available capital E and the capital requirement k_i, the total loan amount for bank i will be $\widehat{L}_i = \frac{E}{k_i}$.

Consider now the goal of the bank in country i to maximize its revenue with respect to its loan allocation γ_i, given its loan quantity $\widehat{L}_i$,

$$\max_{\gamma_i} \Phi_i = \widehat{L}_i(\gamma_i P_i^h + (1-\gamma_i)P_i^f), \tag{13.8}$$

with a similar maximization problem for the bank in country j. Since loan markets in the two countries are symmetrical, the solutions to these maximization problems yield the equilibrium allocation of each bank as

$$\widehat{\gamma}_i = \frac{1}{2}; \quad \widehat{\gamma}_j = \frac{1}{2}. \tag{13.9}$$

These allocations determine the pricing of loans and the gross return on each bank's aggregate portfolio. Substituting these equilibrium values into the per-dollar gross return defined above, we have $R_i(\widehat{\gamma}_i, \widehat{\gamma}_j) = A - \frac{1}{2}L_i - \frac{1}{2}\theta L_j$. From this it is clear that $\partial R_i/\partial L_i < 0$ and $\partial R_i/\partial L_j < 0$, or, in other words, that the per-dollar return to the bank is decreasing in the amount lent by either bank. Moreover, since $\widehat{L}_i = E/k_i, \widehat{L}_j = E/k_j$, and $\partial^2 R_i/\partial L_i^2 = 0$, together these imply that $\partial R_i/\partial k_i > 0$, $\partial R_i/\partial k_j > 0$, and $\partial^2 R_i/\partial k_i^2 \leq 0$, so that average revenue for bank i is increasing in both banks' capital requirements, and is concave in its own capital requirement. An important implication of this discussion is that, since bank lending is a decreasing function of the capital requirement, the level of monitoring per dollar, q_i, will be increasing not only in the regulatory variable k_i but also in the competing country's capital requirement, k_j.[8] It is also worth noting that even though average revenue is increasing in k_i, in equilibrium total bank profits will be decreasing in the capital requirement.

Stage 1: We can now solve the first stage of the model, in which each regulator chooses the capital adequacy standard for the bank in its country. Assume for now that both countries are symmetric, so that $\alpha_i = \alpha_j = \alpha$. In this case, the maximization problem for each independent regulator is

$$\max_{k_i} U^i(k_i, k_j) = \max_{k_i}\{\alpha\widehat{\Pi}_i(k_i, k_j) + (1-\alpha)\xi\widehat{q}_i(k_i, k_j)\}, \tag{13.10}$$

where $\widehat{\Pi}_i(k_i, k_j) = \Pi_i(\widehat{q}_i, \widehat{L}_i, \widehat{L}_j)$ represents the equilibrium (maximized) profits of the bank in country i, obtained by substituting the equilibrium allocations and monitoring choices into Eq. (5) above. In what follows we restrict our analysis to values of $\alpha \in [\alpha, \bar{\alpha}]$ such that the regulator's maximization problem admits an interior solution.

We compare this problem to the case of a centralized regulator who is able to choose capital adequacy standards for both banks. Since the countries are symmetric, we can

[8]There is widespread empirical evidence suggesting that increases in capital requirements have a significantly negative effect on aggregate lending. See, for instance, Peek and Rosengren (1997, 2000). From a theoretical perspective, Thakor (1996) presents a model in which capital requirements increase credit rationing and lower aggregate lending.

assume that the central regulator's objective function is the sum of the objective functions of the national regulators, and we drop the subscripts i and j from the objective function. The central regulator would therefore maximize

$$\max_{\mathbf{k}} U(\mathbf{k}) = \max_{\mathbf{k}} \{2\alpha\widehat{\Pi}(\mathbf{k}) + 2(1-\alpha)\xi\widehat{q}(\mathbf{k})\}, \tag{13.11}$$

where $\mathbf{k} = (k, k)$, so that the central regulator must choose the same capital requirement for both countries. For these two maximization problems, we have the following result.

Proposition 1: *Two independent symmetric regulators, with $\alpha_i = \alpha$ for $i = 1, 2$, will choose a lower capital requirement than what would be chosen by a centralized regulator who puts the same weight α on bank profits relative to stability.*

Proof: See the appendix.

The proposition holds for two reasons. First, independent regulators fail to internalize the positive spillover to other countries caused by the regulation of their banks. By tightening the regulatory standard (e.g., setting a higher capital requirement), a regulator restricts its banks' lending activities. This implies that the residual demand for loans a foreign bank faces will be higher, allowing it to charge a higher price (i.e., higher interest rate). This yields an increase in the foreign bank's revenue, Φ_j, with the net effect that its average return to lending rises, increasing the return to monitoring and thus improving stability in the foreign country. Second, to the extent that national regulators care about all of their banks' claimants, including bank shareholders ($\alpha > 0$), they will have an incentive to lower capital adequacy standards in order to provide their banks an advantage over foreign institutions. In other words, tight capital standards put a country's banks at a competitive disadvantage vis-a-vis banks subject to looser standards, and thus able to make loans more freely. The optimal response of regulators is to loosen their own standards in order to reduce the harm to the profitability of their banks.

It is worth pointing out that some of the literature on both bank and environmental regulation has discussed the possibility that independent regulators would choose a sub-optimal level of regulation. In particular, some authors have focused on the second effect that we identify, namely, the "race to the bottom" effect: the risk that national regulators, in an attempt to favor their own banks vis-a-vis foreign institutions, will have an incentive to reduce regulatory standards and increase forbearance (see, e.g., White, 1993, and more formally in the literature on environmental regulation, Oates, 1996). Our model formalizes this result in the context of banking regulation, and argues that to the extent that there are international spillovers in banking regulation, national regulators are unlikely to internalize such externalities and, hence, will underegulate relative to a centralized solution. We note, however, that this laxity in regulation is measured only relative to the optimal regulatory standard that would be imposed if regulation were instead coordinated across countries. We take no stance on whether regulation should optimally be lax or tight, assuming that any incentive to loosen or tighten regulations will be reflected in the regulator's objective function. For example, one reason to want regulation to be lax may be to promote financial innovation.

Denote by (k_i^*, k_j^*) the solution to Eq. (10) for countries i and j, and (k^*, k^*) the solution to the centralized regulator's problem, Eq. (11). From the proposition, it follows directly that $U^i(k^*, k^*) > U^i(k_i^*, k_j^*)$ for $i, j = 1, 2$. In other words, symmetric national regulators will always have an incentive to surrender their authority to a centralized regulatory agency.

As their preferences are identical, there is nothing to be gained from the flexibility associated with the independent solution. In what follows, we consider the more realistic situation in which countries may be different.

5. Incentives to Form a Regulatory Union

Financial systems, banking markets, and institutions are typically heterogeneous across countries. It follows that the standards set by independent and competing national regulators are likely to be asymmetric as well. Similarly, a central regulator with the ability to discriminate across countries would probably choose to apply different standards to each country. However, we argue that a supranational regulatory agency would find it politically infeasible to apply different standards across countries under its jurisdiction. Because of this constraint, when countries are heterogeneous, the establishment of centralized bank regulation entails losses that could dominate any gains from internalizing the externalities discussed in the previous section. In what follows we investigate the conditions under which countries endogenously choose to form a regulatory union. First, we analyze the simple case in which there are only two countries that, because of the absence of significant financial links with others, can be considered in isolation from the rest of the world. Second, we discuss some further issues that arise when more than two countries need to be taken into account.

5.1 The Two-Country Case

We start by dropping the assumption that both countries are identical and instead allow the regulator in each country to place a different weight on bank profits relative to stability. Without loss of generality, assume that $\alpha_1 > \alpha_2$, so that we can think of country 1's regulator as being more captured. We assume also the following standard regularity conditions, which imply that each regulator's reaction function is decreasing in the capital requirement set by its competitor (see Dixit, 1986, for further discussion):

$$\left| \frac{\frac{\partial^2 U^i}{\partial k_i \partial k_j}}{\frac{\partial^2 U^i}{\partial k_i^2}} \right| < 1 \quad \text{for } i, j = 1, 2, \quad i \neq j. \tag{13.12}$$

We state sufficient conditions for Eq. (12) to hold in the Appendix. A restriction that the weight each regulator places on bank profitability, α_1, be sufficiently small is sufficient for this regularity condition to hold. Although such restriction is not necessary for condition (12) to hold, it suggests that our model best suits settings such that all countries involved have fairly well-developed prudential regulatory systems; i.e., all regulators put substantial emphasis on systemic stability. We can now state the following result, where, as in the previous section, k_1^* and k_2^* are the capital adequacy standards chosen in equilibrium by competing (independent) regulators.

Proposition 2: *Under condition* (12), $\alpha_i > \alpha_j$ *implies* $k_i^* < k_j^*$.

Proof: See the appendix.

The intuition for this result is straightforward. Since capital requirements are costly, a regulator that places a greater emphasis on bank profits will choose a lower capital requirement than one that places a relatively greater emphasis on banking system stability. Because asymmetric regulators would choose unequal standards under independent regulation (i.e., $k_i^* \neq k_j^*$), the question arises as to whether there exists a common level of required capital, k, such that, were it imposed, both individual regulators would be made better off. If such a common level of regulation exists, the Pareto improvement achieved by its imposition would imply that each individual regulator should find it in his or her own interest to cede authority to a centralized agency. Looking for a Pareto improvement allows us to ignore the design of the objective function for the centralized regulator by focusing on instances in which individual regulators would find it individually optimal to relinquish their authority.

The following proposition demonstrates that the answer to this question is not entirely straightforward, and establishes that centralizing regulation must raise regulatory standards even for the case with asymmetric countries.

Proposition 3: *There exists no common capital adequacy ratio* $k < \max\{k_1^*, k_2^*\}$ *that is preferred by both regulators to the outcome under independent regulation.*

Proof: Assume without loss of generality that $\alpha_1 > \alpha_2$, or $k_1^* < k_2^*$. Define the reaction function $\widehat{k}_i(k_j)$ as $\widehat{k}_i = \arg\max_k U^i(k, k_j)$, so that $k_i^* = \widehat{k}_i(k_j^*)$. By the envelope theorem, we know that

$$\frac{\mathrm{d}U^i(\widehat{k}_i(k_j), k_j)}{\mathrm{d}k_j} = \left.\frac{\partial U^i(k_i, k_j)}{\partial k_j}\right|_{k_i = \widehat{k}_i(k_j)} > 0. \tag{13.13}$$

Now, consider $k = k_2^*$. By (13), we have $U^2(k_2^*, k_2^*) > U^2(k_2^*, k_1^*)$. However, by definition $U^1(k_2^*, k_2^*) < U^1(k_1^*, k_2^*)$, so that a uniform regulation with $k = k_2^*$ would not be accepted by regulator 1. Furthermore, because of (13), for any $k < k_2^*$, we have $U^1(k, k) < U^1(\widehat{k}_1(k), k) < U^1(k_1^*, k_2^*)$. Therefore no $k \in [0, k_2^*]$ will be preferred by regulator 1 over the Nash solution. □

This result merits some discussion, as it calls into question the possibility, and the ease, of obtaining a centralized solution. The proposition states that in order for each country's regulator to be better off under centralized regulation, the capital adequacy ratio chosen by the central regulator must be greater than the ratio that either regulator would choose independently. The intuition for this result is as follows. Although with independent regulators capital adequacy standards are too low relative to what would be jointly optimal, they nevertheless represent optimal responses to each competing regulator's choice. If a country-level regulator is to relinquish its authority and, hence, its ability to set standards optimally given its competitor's choice, it must be compensated by an increase in the capital requirement for its competitor's banks. In other words, a necessary condition for a centralized regulator to emerge endogenously as an agreement between the independent regulators is that the new common regulatory standards represent an increase for both countries.

The proposition does not imply, however, that the solution reached if national-level regulators were forced to relinquish control to a centralized agency would necessarily lead to a higher common regulatory standard. For instance, if external pressure were imposed to form a centralized regulator with an objective function that averaged out the concerns of each country, such an outcome involves a tendency toward an intermediate standard. However, a move in this direction would likely be opposed by the national regulators of at least one of the countries, as the proposition demonstrates that in order for each independent regulator to find it individually optimal to relinquish control, the agreement would have to specify an increase in the standards for the competing country. In what follows, we analyze under what conditions such a higher (common) level of regulation exists. In other words, we study when the creation of a centralized regulator is likely to result from the negotiations between the regulators in the competing countries.

One immediate consequence of the previous result is that, were the independent regulators to switch to a centralized solution, one country would necessarily have to increase its standards more than the other. This insight leads to the following lemma, which is useful for our main result below.

Lemma 1: *For any common capital adequacy ratio k such that* $U^1(k, k) > U^1(k_1^*, k_2^*)$, *we have* $U^2(k, k) > U^2(k_2^*, k_1^*)$.

Proof: See the appendix.

This lemma implies that any level of common regulation preferred to the independent solution by regulator 1 would also be preferred by regulator 2. Since regulation in country 1 is lower than in country 2, any move to a common standard will imply a larger increase in the standard for country 1 than for country 2. Therefore, if country 1 finds such an increase in regulation acceptable, so will country 2.

An important consequence of the previous lemma is that it establishes a necessary and sufficient condition for the emergence of a central regulator to be feasible, namely that there exist a capital requirement that, if imposed uniformly across countries, makes regulator 1 better off than in the independent solution. Formally, the condition requires that

$$\max_k U^1(k, k) \geq U^1(k_1^*, k_2^*). \tag{13.14}$$

The net maximum benefit to regulator 1 from choosing to merge in a unified regulatory agency can be written as $U^1(\widetilde{k}, \widetilde{k}) - U^1(k_1^*, k_2^*)$, where $\widetilde{k} = \arg\max_k(U^1(k, k)$. Lemma 1 thus allows us to abstract from the choice of an objective function for the centralized regulator and focus directly on this net benefit function for one single regulator. If this condition is satisfied, centralizing regulation will yield a Pareto improvement and therefore will be a mutually agreeable outcome. By Proposition 3, we can also restrict our attention to values of $\widetilde{k} > k_2^*$, since otherwise the net benefit to regulator 1 will be negative. To simplify notation in what follows, we use the variable s to represent a measure of the difference between the regulators' objective functions, so that $\alpha_2 = \alpha_1 - s$. We can now prove that only countries with sufficiently similar objective functions will be able to reach an agreement on a regulatory union.

Proposition 4: *For any* α_1, *there exists an* $\widehat{s} \in (0, \alpha_1)$ *such that* $U^1(\widetilde{k}, \widetilde{k}) - U^1(k_1^*, k_2^*) \geq 0$ *if* $s \leq \widehat{s}$, *and* $U^1(\widetilde{k}, \widetilde{k}) - U^1(k_1^*, k_2^*) < 0$ *otherwise.*

Proof: See the appendix.

This proposition states that, while similar countries may benefit from having a centralized regulator, countries that are more dissimilar will be unable to find a common level of regulation preferred by both regulators to what obtains in the independent solution. When countries are very different, optimal regulation may in fact call for unequal standards to address country-specific concerns. Since centralizing regulation eliminates the ability to impose heterogeneous regulatory standards in each country, asymmetry across countries makes it more difficult to improve upon the independent solution for all regulators.

To provide some intuition, suppose that the weight the regulator in country 1 places on financial stability is much lower than that placed by country 2. In that case, the increase in country 1's capital requirement needed to satisfy the regulator in country 2 would have a very large (and negative) effect on bank profits in country 1. As the differences between countries magnify, the cost of this loss of flexibility increases, with the consequence that only countries that are relatively symmetric find it beneficial to form a regulatory union. Only if the differences between countries are not too large can regulators find mutually agreeable regulatory standards such that the benefits of coordination outweigh the loss of flexibility of imposing uniform regulation across countries. Specifically, the proposition shows that there is a maximal difference $\widehat{s} = \alpha_1 - \alpha_2$ between countries such that centralized regulation is preferable to maintaining independence.

5.2 The Multiple-Country Case

In the previous section, we analyze the conditions under which two countries operating in isolation choose to form a regulatory union. However, countries are likely to have financial links with more than one counterparty and should take into account the effects stemming from those links when considering a regulatory union with a subset of their financial partners. We therefore extend the analysis to consider how the incentives to form a regulatory union between two countries change when other countries are taken into account.

The study of the multiple-country case is relevant for a number of reasons. Regulatory unions, such as ones that could emerge across countries in Europe, typically involve a large number of jurisdictions. The degree of heterogeneity and the political problems associated with the regulatory union are likely increasing in the number of participating countries, making the regulatory union less likely to arise when there are more than two countries. Hence, it is important to determine whether the formation of a regulatory union among a subset of countries makes it more or less likely that countries outside the union will subsequently choose to join. Second, it is important to understand whether a subset of countries that would otherwise choose to form a regulatory union may be helped or hindered in this endeavor by the existence of financial links with other countries. In what follows, we discuss both of these issues.

Proposition 5: *Suppose there are N symmetric countries, $N-1$ of which are joined in a regulatory union, with the remaining country not part of the union. Then there is always an $\bar{N} > 0$ such that, if $N \geq \bar{N}$, the country currently outside the union will prefer not to join the union. Moreover, this country will choose a lower capital adequacy ratio than that chosen by the other $N-1$ countries that are part of the union.*

Proof: See the appendix.

This proposition shows that a regulatory union among a subset of countries will not necessarily constitute a "pole of attraction" for other countries to join. On the contrary, it may be the case that countries left out will find their incentives to coordinate with members of the union reduced. The intuition behind this result is the following. When a subset of countries form a regulatory union, they increase their, now common, capital adequacy ratio. Countries left out of the union benefit from the positive spillover associated with the union's increased regulatory requirement without having to pay a cost in terms of lost independence and tighter regulation themselves. In other words, a country that remains outside the union is able to free-ride on the increased standards established for the countries in the union. As the number of countries within the union rises, the marginal increase in standards from adding one more country decreases. This implies that the benefit for a new member of joining the union also decreases. Hence, countries outside the regulatory union that would have found it desirable to coordinate their regulation with some of the countries in the union when they all operated independently, may find it optimal to remain on the outside once a partial union is formed.

It is important to note that Proposition 5 applies to situations in which a full union among all the countries would be feasible if all countries simultaneously agreed to join, since in our model symmetric countries can always reap the benefits of centralizing regulation without bearing any of the costs associated with the loss of independence. As such, the proposition points out that following an approach of partial centralization may not be the best path towards eventually achieving full centralization.

Our second question is addressed in the following proposition.

Proposition 6: *Consider any two asymmetric countries,* 1 *and* 2, *with* $\alpha_1 > \alpha_2$, *that would find it optimal to join into a regulatory union in the absence of financial links with other countries. Then there exists an* $\tilde{N}$ *such that, if* $N \geq \tilde{N}$ *symmetric countries have established financial links with countries* 1 *and* 2, *these two countries will choose not to form the (partial) regulatory union.*

Proof: See the appendix.

The intuition for this result is the following. In the previous section we show that, in a two-country world, a condition for a regulatory union to be acceptable for both countries involved is that the capital adequacy ratio chosen under the union be higher than the highest ratio chosen under independence. However, in the presence of multiple countries, if there are countries that do not participate in the union, an increase in the capital adequacy ratio, by constraining banks' abilities to grant loans, makes banks in the participating countries less competitive relative to banks in countries outside the union. This reduces banks' profits and consequently also the benefits from forming a union relative to the case in which the countries considering centralization are not financially integrated with the rest. When a sufficient number of other countries have ties with countries 1 and 2, the net benefit from coordination is outweighed by the costs associated with increases in each country's standards. It is therefore the presence of the other countries outside of the union that makes the partial union infeasible. Indeed, since asymmetric regulators find it costly to merge into a regulatory union, the existence of other countries not themselves part of the regulatory union may also prevent the formation of a union among countries that, although not identical, would find it mutually beneficial to increase regulatory coordination if they were operating in isolation.

6. Generalizations

Throughout the paper, we maintain fixed a number of assumptions related to the form of regulation, the possibility for banks to obtain deposits in addition to granting loans abroad, and the exogenous return offered on deposit contracts. We discuss here some implications of varying these assumptions.

6.1 Home Versus Host Country Regulation

In our model, we impose "home country regulation," in that a bank's home country (i.e., the locality in which the bank is chartered) regulates all of the bank's activities, including its lending activities abroad. This framework accurately describes the current regulatory environment in a number of markets, most notably the European Union, for the case of bank branches. Moreover, this form of regulation is consistent with our assumption that while banks collect deposits only in their home country, they can extend loans either at home or abroad. From the viewpoint of prudential regulation, the design of regulation is primarily geared towards protecting depositors who, because of various free-rider issues, may have neither the ability nor the incentive to monitor a bank's activities (see, e.g., Dewatripont and Tirole, 1994, for elaboration). Our results demonstrate that the externality associated with regulation, and the ensuing trade-off between centralization and independence, arises even when banks engage in no cross-border activities other than lending.

However, this is not the only possibility for the regulation of banks from countries or states that are members of a political or economic union. An alternative is that banks be subject to "host country regulation," meaning that domestic regulators have authority over all banks operating in their jurisdiction. This would imply that the foreign activities of domestic banks would be regulated by the foreign regulator, and vice versa for the domestic subsidiaries of foreign banks. However, as argued above, the results presented so far stem purely from a domestic regulator's failure to internalize the positive externality abroad associated with capital requirements placed at home. Therefore, so long as there is not a one-to-one matching between a domestic bank's foreign loans and foreign-raised deposits and capital, our analysis should continue to apply. Furthermore, to the extent that a foreign entity has full control of the subsidiary, its capitalization will enter into the determination of the subsidiary's monitoring/risk profile choice; i.e., regulators should be concerned with the health and proper supervision of their foreign banks' parent companies.

The case for which our analysis does not directly apply is one such that banks are legally obligated to form a completely separately capitalized subsidiary in order to enter and lend in foreign markets. In that case, regulatory constraints placed on a bank in one country will have no direct impact on other countries in which that bank operates. Nevertheless, it is likely that, despite having no explicit financial obligations across borders, international banks may have reputational considerations that lead to them to bail out affiliated failing institutions abroad. If these kinds of linkages exist across the balance sheets of the parent institution and its subsidiaries, we expect that the issues raised above would continue to be of relevance. Furthermore, the health and proper supervision of the parent bank is of direct relevance for the risk-taking behavior of the subsidiary if the parent company retains full managerial control. Consider, as an extreme example, the case of a parent company with zero capital of its own that finances an equity participation in the subsidiary by borrowing funds. Then, to the extent that such a parent company has control of the subsidiary, the subsidiary's own capital requirement will have no impact on its risk-taking decisions. The existence of this problem is implicitly acknowledged by the Basel Committee, which has emphasized that bank regulators should be concerned with the proper capitalization and supervision of foreign banks owning subsidiaries operating in their countries.[9]

6.2 Alternative Regulatory Objectives

We have focused our attention on the case of pure "prudential regulation," where bank regulators are concerned first and foremost about minimizing the risk of failure of their depository institutions, while allowing for the possibility that the regulator may be captured by the banks it oversees. This would be the case if, for instance, a regulator's primary mandate were to minimize the expected payout rate of the deposit insurance fund, as is by and large the case for institutions such as the FDIC in the U.S. and for some of the regulators in the E.U.[10] Since in this model the expected payout of the deposit insurance fund is $(1 - q_i)L_i(1 - k_i)$, the payout rate is just $1 - q_i$. Minimizing this rate is equivalent to maximizing the loan repayment probability q_i, which coincides with the regulatory objective function described earlier.

There is also, however, the possibility that from a welfare-maximizing point of view, a social planner would be concerned with fostering lending competition and increasing the quantity of credit available in the economy. In practice this function is often divorced from prudential regulation and is the purview of monetary and competition policies, as prudential regulatory instruments are not often seen as particularly good tools for stimulating lending activity. However, in principle, a government could set up an entity with a mandate to balance out this objective along with the others specified previously. Using the notation of our model, this could be accomplished by setting the regulator's objective function to be

$$U^i = \alpha_i^\pi \Pi_i + \alpha_i^q q_i + \alpha_i^L L, \tag{13.15}$$

where L is the total quantity of loans supplied to domestic borrowers, and $\alpha_i^\pi + \alpha_i^q + \alpha_i^L = 1$ represent the weights regulator i places on bank profitability, banking system stability, and loan quantity, respectively. Our model is robust to this specification for sufficiently low values of α_i^L, so that the regulator's primary concern is not the promotion of competition in lending. If α_i^L is very large, however, the regulator in country i may in fact benefit from lax regulation abroad, since it encourages loose lending practices and increases the supply of credit. Nevertheless, this increase in foreign lending reduces domestic banking system stability as well as bank profitability. A domestic regulator that is overly concerned with promoting competition may therefore reduce regulatory standards in order to encourage lending, at the expense of profitability and stability.

6.3 Endogenizing the Deposit Rate

So far we assumed that the deposit rate, δ, is exogenously given, which corresponds to the case in which there is full deposit insurance in the economy so that depositors offer a perfectly elastic supply of deposits at the given rate. In the absence of complete deposit insurance, rational depositors would anticipate the risk-taking behavior of banks. Since monitoring is increasing in the bank's capital, the deposit rate would become a

[9]See, for example, the Bank for International Settlements publication "Minimum Standards for the Supervision of International Banking Groups and their Cross-Border Establishments," July 1992. Available at http://www.bis.org.

[10]We thank seminar participants at the FDIC for clarifying the role of this institution in prudential regulation.

decreasing function of the capital requirements. This introduces an additional channel through which regulation affects bank monitoring and profits. By reducing δ, an increase in the capital requirement has an additional positive effect on monitoring, since $\mathrm{d}\widehat{q}_i/\mathrm{d}k_i = \partial\widehat{q}_i/\partial k_i + (\partial\widehat{q}_i/\partial\delta)\partial\delta/\partial k_i$, with $\partial\widehat{q}_i/\partial\delta < 0$ and $\partial\delta/\partial k_i \leq 0$ when depositors are sensitive to bank risk. Furthermore, the reduction in the deposit rate, while not eliminating it entirely, limits the negative effect on bank profitability of tighter regulation.[11] At the same time, the externality associated with regulation abroad remains prevalent, since $\mathrm{d}\widehat{\Pi}_i/\mathrm{d}k_j = \partial\widehat{\Pi}_i/\partial k_j + (\partial\widehat{\Pi}_i/\partial\delta)\partial\delta/\partial k_j$, and $\partial\delta/\partial k_j \leq 0$ since an increase in k_j increases domestic monitoring (q_i), leading to a reduction in δ. This implies that $\mathrm{d}\widehat{\Pi}_i/\mathrm{d}k_j > 0$, as before. A similar argument can be applied to show that $\mathrm{d}\widehat{q}_i/\mathrm{d}k_j = \partial\widehat{q}_i/\partial k_j + (\partial\widehat{q}_i/\partial\delta)\partial\delta/\partial k_j > 0$.

It is worthwhile to also discuss issues that may arise from imperfect competition among banks in the deposit market. While in our model we formally assume that in each country there is only one bank, it is clear that similar results hold if there are multiple competing banks. In this case, competition for (scarce) deposits will drive the deposit rate up, so that the deposit rate becomes a function of bank regulation to the extent that such regulation affects competition. In recent work analyzing imperfect competition on the deposit market, Repullo (2004) shows that the costs of an increase in capital requirements get passed on to depositors, so that the regulatory effect of a capital requirement is enhanced relative to a situation such that deposit rates are fixed. Matutes and Vives (2000) find a similar result and argue that asset-side restrictions may be necessary when bank risk is not perfectly observable by depositors. The general finding in this literature is that limited liability for banks continues to play a role in determining banks' investment strategies, implying that there is a role for regulation even when the return on deposits is set competitively.

7. Conclusions

This paper shows that competition among regulators reduces regulatory standards relative to a centralized solution, and that a regulatory union is more likely to be beneficial for more homogeneous countries. In addition, the paper shows that the formation of partial regulatory unions may be hindered by the presence of financially integrated "third countries," and that such unions, once formed, may prevent the creation of more comprehensive ones. The implications of this paper are relevant for regulatory policy in an increasingly integrated world.

A question that has not been analyzed, however, is whether a regulatory union is actually likely to emerge even if one is feasible. The analysis in the paper focuses on a situation in which centralizing regulatory policy leads to a Pareto improvement. However, what is ignored is that the formation of a central regulatory agency would probably be the outcome of negotiation among all the relevant parties, particularly the individual regulators. Our analysis shows that this is an important issue, since we demonstrate that in order for centralized regulation to be Pareto improving, it must raise the level of regulation of all banking systems involved. We expect that the inherent tensions of a negotiated outcome could push the centralized institution to choose a level of regulation somewhere between the levels that would be chosen by independent regulators. Even if the outcome could be

[11] Sinn (2001) argues that international depositors would not be able to fully price the differences in regulation across countries. Tighter regulatory standards would then still have a negative effect on bank profits. This would also be true in our model as long as depositors do not overreact to increases in regulatory standards by lowering δ to more than compensate for the increase in k_i.

successfully negotiated, it is still possible that after the centralized regulator is formed there might be strong pressure put on it to choose a moderate level of regulation. For example, there may be pressure to form a centralized regulator that assigns a weight $\bar{\alpha} = (\alpha_1 + \alpha_2)/2$ to bank profits. There may then be situations in which the level of regulation chosen by this centralized regulator is below k_2^*, even if a level exists greater than k_2^* that would make both countries better off. The exploration of this issue is beyond the scope of this paper.

The analysis in this paper can be extended in a number of directions. One natural extension is to allow banks to change the location of their headquarters, and hence, implicitly allow them to choose their regulator. Under those circumstances, the race-to-the-bottom effect of competition described in this paper would be even stronger as regulators would compete to prevent banks from leaving their regulatory domain. An issue also not treated in the present paper is that of the existence of costs associated with the move towards a centralized regulatory regime. Example of these transition costs are, for example, the loss of country-specific information and expertise once a centralized regulator is imposed (see, e.g., Holthausen and Roende, 2002). A recent paper by Kahn and Santos (2003) argues that having separate institutions for deposit insurance and lender of last resort functions may create an incentive for them to hide information from each other. While similar concerns are likely to arise in this context, the analysis of this issue is beyond the scope of this paper and is left for future research.

Appendix A. Proofs

We start by establishing some results concerning the bank's (maximized) profit function, as well as the monitoring objective of bank regulation. First, since $\widehat{q}_i = (R_i(\widehat{L}_i, \widehat{L}_j) - (1 - k_i)\delta)/2c$ (we ignore throughout the boundary condition), its derivative with respect to k_i is

$$\frac{\mathrm{d}\widehat{q}_i}{\mathrm{d}k_i} = \frac{(\mathrm{d}R_i/\mathrm{d}L_i)\mathrm{d}\widehat{L}_i/\mathrm{d}k_i + \delta}{2c} = \frac{(1/2)\mathrm{E}/k_i^2 + \delta}{2c} > 0. \tag{13.16}$$

The second derivative is

$$\frac{\mathrm{d}^2\widehat{q}_i}{\mathrm{d}k_i^2} = \frac{-(\mathrm{d}^2R_i/\mathrm{d}L_i^2)(\mathrm{E}/k_i^2)^2 + (\mathrm{d}R_i/\mathrm{d}L_i)2\mathrm{E}/k_i^3}{2c}. \tag{13.17}$$

Since in equilibrium $R_i = A - \frac{1}{2}L_i - \frac{1}{2}\theta L_j$, we see that $\mathrm{d}^2R_i/\mathrm{d}L_i^2 = 0$ and it follows that $\widehat{q}_i$ is increasing and concave in k_i, i.e., $\mathrm{d}^2\widehat{q}_i/\mathrm{d}k_i^2 = -(1/2c)\mathrm{E}/k_i^3 < 0$. We also have

$$\frac{\mathrm{d}\widehat{q}_i}{\mathrm{d}k_j} = \frac{(\mathrm{d}R_i/\mathrm{d}L_j)\mathrm{d}\widehat{L}_j/\mathrm{d}k_j}{2c} = \frac{1}{2c}\frac{\theta}{2}\frac{\mathrm{E}}{k_j^2} > 0. \tag{13.18}$$

The fact that capital requirements are a binding constraint on loan quantities means that the derivative of profits with respect to L_i must be weakly positive,

$$\frac{\mathrm{d}\Pi_i}{\mathrm{d}L_i} = \widehat{q}_i[R_i(L_i, L_j) - (1 - k_i)\delta] + \widehat{q}_i\frac{\mathrm{d}R_i}{\mathrm{d}L_i}L_i - \rho k_i - c\widehat{q}_i^2 \geq 0. \tag{13.19}$$

Let us focus on equilibrium profits, $\widehat{\Pi}_i = \widehat{q}_i[R_i(\widehat{L}_i, \widehat{L}_j) - (1-k_i)\delta]\widehat{L}_i - \rho \mathrm{E} - c\widehat{q}_i^2\widehat{L}_i$. The derivative of $\widehat{\Pi}_i$ with respect to the capital requirement is

$$\frac{\mathrm{d}\widehat{\Pi}_i}{\mathrm{d}k_i} = \frac{\partial \widehat{\Pi}_i}{\partial k_i} + \frac{\partial \widehat{\Pi}_i}{\partial L_i}\frac{\mathrm{d}\widehat{L}_i}{\mathrm{d}k_i} + \frac{\partial \widehat{\Pi}_i}{\partial q_i}\frac{\mathrm{d}q_i}{\mathrm{d}k_i}, \tag{13.20}$$

where the last term is zero because of the envelope theorem, the first term is negative as long as capital is more expensive than deposits ($\rho > \delta$), and the middle term is nonpositive by (19), implying that $\mathrm{d}\widehat{\Pi}_i/\mathrm{d}k_i < 0$.

The derivative of profits with respect to the other country's capital requirement, k_j, is

$$\frac{\mathrm{d}\widehat{\Pi}_i}{\mathrm{d}k_j} = \widehat{q}_i\frac{\partial R_i}{\partial L_j}\frac{\partial \widehat{L}_j}{\partial k_j}\widehat{L}_i = \widehat{q}_i\frac{\theta}{2}\frac{\mathrm{E}}{k_j^2}\frac{\mathrm{E}}{k_i} > 0, \tag{13.21}$$

so that bank i benefits from an increase in the capital requirement for bank j.

A.1. Regularity Condition

We restate the standard regularity condition as

$$\left|\frac{\frac{\partial^2 U^i}{\partial k_i \partial k_j}}{\frac{\partial^2 U^i}{\partial k_i^2}}\right| < 1 \quad \text{for } i,j = 1,2, \quad i \neq j. \tag{13.22}$$

Because of the linearity of R_i, $\partial^2\widehat{q}_i/\partial k_i \partial k_j = 0$. We can then rewrite (22) as

$$\left|\frac{\alpha_i \frac{\partial^2 \widehat{\Pi}_i}{\partial k_i \partial k_j}}{\alpha_i \frac{\partial^2 \widehat{\Pi}_i}{\partial k_i^2} + (1-\alpha_i)\xi \frac{\partial^2 \widehat{q}_i}{\partial k_i^2}}\right| < 1 \quad \text{for} \quad i,j = 1,2, \quad i \neq j. \tag{13.23}$$

Now, define $\widetilde{L}_i = \min\{\mathrm{E}/k_i, \widehat{L}_i\}$, where $\widehat{L}_i = \max\{L_i : \partial \Pi_i/\partial L_i = 0\}$. From this, one can see that independent of α_i, there is no benefit to the regulator of choosing a k_i lower than the one implied by this relation, since a lower capital requirement will not lead to greater lending. Denote the lowest possible k_i consistent with $\partial \Pi_i/\partial L_i \geq 0$ as $\underline{k}_i$. This establishes that the capital requirement chosen by each regulator bounded strictly away from zero. Now consider that

$$\frac{\partial^2 \widehat{\Pi}_i}{\partial k_i \partial k_j} = \frac{1}{8}\theta \mathrm{E}^2 \frac{2\mathrm{E}k_j - 2(A-\delta)k_i k_j + \theta \mathrm{E} k_i}{k_i^3 k_j^3 c}, \qquad \frac{\partial^2 \widehat{q}_i}{\partial k_i^2} = -\frac{1}{2c}\frac{\mathrm{E}}{k_i^3}$$

and

$$\frac{\partial^2 \Pi_i}{\partial k_i^2} = \frac{1}{8}\mathrm{E}\frac{4\mathrm{E}k_i k_j(-\theta k_i - 3k_j)(A-\delta) - 4k_i^2 k_j^2(\mathrm{E}\delta - (\delta - A)^2) + \mathrm{E}^2(6\theta k_i k_j + 6k_j^2 + \theta^2 k_i^2)}{k_i^5 k_j^2 c}$$

Therefore, Eq. (22) can be rewritten as

$$\left| \frac{\alpha_i \theta E \frac{2\mathrm{E}k_j - 2(A-\delta)k_i k_j + \theta \mathrm{E} k_i}{8k_j^3 c}}{\alpha_i \left(\frac{4\mathrm{E}k_i k_j(-\theta k_i - 3k_j)(A-\delta) - 4k_i^2 k_j^2 (\mathrm{E}\delta - (\delta - A)^2) + \mathrm{E}^2 (6\theta k_i k_j + 6k_j^2 + \theta^2 k_i^2)}{8k_i^2 k_j^2 c} \right) - (1-\alpha_i)\xi 1/2c} \right| < 1. \quad (13.24)$$

From the above, one sees that, for any parameter values, since $k_j \geq \underline{k}_j > 0$, there is always an α_i small enough such that (22) is satisfied for any value of k_i.

Proof of Proposition 1: The set of first-order conditions (FOC) for the case of independent national regulators, Eq. (10), is (note that we ignore the subscripts for each country, since the objective functions are symmetric)

$$\alpha \frac{\mathrm{d}\widehat{\Pi}(k_i, k_j)}{\mathrm{d}k_i} + (1-\alpha)\xi \frac{\mathrm{d}\widehat{q}(k_i, k_j)}{\mathrm{d}k_i} = 0 \quad (13.25)$$

and

$$\alpha \frac{\mathrm{d}\widehat{\Pi}(k_j, k_i)}{\mathrm{d}k_j} + (1-\alpha)\xi \frac{\mathrm{d}\widehat{q}(k_j, k_i)}{\mathrm{d}k_j} = 0. \quad (13.26)$$

The solution to this maximization problem defines a Nash equilibrium of the game between competing regulators, and constitutes a pair (k_i^*, k_j^*) satisfying these two equations simultaneously. Since the countries are symmetric, an equilibrium exists with $k_i^* = k_j^*$. We focus on this case.

The case of the central regulator is given as follows. The FOC for Eq. (11) is

$$\alpha \left(\frac{\mathrm{d}\widehat{\Pi}(k_i, k_j)}{\mathrm{d}k_i} + \frac{\mathrm{d}\widehat{\Pi}(k_i, k_j)}{\mathrm{d}k_j} \right) + (1-\alpha)\xi \left(\frac{\mathrm{d}\widehat{q}(k_i, k_j)}{\mathrm{d}k_i} + \frac{\mathrm{d}\widehat{q}(k_i, k_j)}{\mathrm{d}k_j} \right) = 0. \quad (13.27)$$

Along with the constraint that $k_i = k_j$, the solution to this problem yields a regulatory standard k^*.

Compare now the solutions to the two problems. If we substitute the solution of the Nash game between independent regulators, the pair (k_i^*, k_j^*), into the first-order conditions for the central regulator, Eq. (27), and rearrange slightly, we obtain with a slight abuse of notation

$$\left[\alpha \frac{\mathrm{d}\widehat{\Pi}(k_i^*, k_j^*)}{\mathrm{d}k_i} + (1-\alpha)\xi \frac{\mathrm{d}\widehat{q}(k_i^*, k_j^*)}{\mathrm{d}k_i} \right] + \alpha \frac{\mathrm{d}\widehat{\Pi}(k_i^*, k_j^*)}{\mathrm{d}k_j} + (1-\alpha)\xi \frac{\mathrm{d}\widehat{q}(k_i^*, k_j^*)}{\mathrm{d}k_j}. \quad (13.28)$$

The first term in expression (28) is zero as it is identical to the first-order condition for national regulator i when it chooses regulatory standards independently. That leaves only the two last terms, which are better expressed as

$$\left. \frac{\mathrm{d}\widehat{\Pi}(k_i, k_j)}{\mathrm{d}k_j} \right|_{k_i^*, k_j^*} \quad \textit{and} \quad \left. \frac{\mathrm{d}\widehat{q}(k_i, k_j)}{\mathrm{d}k_j} \right|_{k_i^*, k_j^*}$$

However, we have already shown these terms to be positive, meaning that expression (27) evaluated at (k_i^*, k_j^*) is positive. This implies that $k^* > k_i^*, k_j^*$, or in other words, we need a higher regulatory standard in order to satisfy expression (27). □

Proof of Proposition 2: Start from a symmetric equilibrium with $\alpha_1 = \alpha_2$ and $k_1^* = k_2^*$, and consider a mean-preserving spread over α so that $\alpha_1 = \alpha + \frac{\omega}{2}$ and $\alpha_2 = \alpha - \frac{\omega}{2}$. We need to show that $\mathrm{d}(k_1^* - k_2^*)/\mathrm{d}\omega < 0$. Define

$$a_i = \frac{\partial^2 U^i}{\partial k_i^2}; \quad b_i = \frac{\partial^2 U^i}{\partial k_i \partial k_j}; \quad \mu_\alpha^i = \frac{\partial^2 U^i}{\partial k_i \partial \alpha_i}. \tag{13.29}$$

Note that a_i and μ_α^i are both negative, while the sign of b_i can be either positive or negative and b_i determines the slope of the reaction functions. Totally differentiating the first-order conditions and rearranging, we have

$$\begin{bmatrix} a_1 & b_1 \\ a_2 & b_2 \end{bmatrix} \begin{bmatrix} \mathrm{d}k_1^* \\ \mathrm{d}k_2^* \end{bmatrix} = -\begin{bmatrix} \mu_\alpha^1 \frac{\partial \alpha_1}{\partial \omega} d\omega \\ \mu_\alpha^2 \frac{\partial \alpha_2}{\partial \omega} d\omega \end{bmatrix}. \tag{13.30}$$

Solving gives

$$\begin{bmatrix} \mathrm{d}k_1^* \\ \mathrm{d}k_2^* \end{bmatrix} = \frac{1}{\Delta} \begin{bmatrix} -a_2 & b_1 \\ b_2 & -a_1 \end{bmatrix} \begin{bmatrix} \mu_\alpha^1 \mathrm{d}\omega \\ -\mu_\alpha^2 \mathrm{d}\omega \end{bmatrix}, \tag{13.31}$$

where Δ is the determinant of the matrix. Now, we can write

$$\frac{\mathrm{d}(k_1^* - k_2^*)}{\mathrm{d}\omega} = -\frac{1}{\Delta}[(a_2 + b_2)\mu_\alpha^1 + (a_1 + b_1)\mu_\alpha^2]. \tag{13.32}$$

Condition (12) implies $\Delta > 0$, and together with $a_1 < 0, a_2 < 0$ implies that $a_i + b_i < 0$. Then, as $\mu_\alpha^1 < 0$, $\mu_\alpha^2 < 0$, we have $\mathrm{d}(k_1^* - k_2^*)/\mathrm{d}\omega < 0$. □

Proof of Lemma 1: Assume $U^1(k,k) > U^1(k_1^*, k_2^*)$. As $k_1^* < k_2^*$, by the envelope theorem we know that $U^1(k_1^*, k_2^*) > U^1(\widehat{k}(k_1^*), k_1^*)$, and by definition $U^1(\widehat{k}(k_1^*), k_1^*) > U^1(k_2^*, k_1^*)$, where $\widehat{k}(\cdot)$ is as defined in Proposition 3. Hence, we can write

$$U^1(k,k) - U^1(k_2^*, k_1^*) = \alpha_1[\widehat{\Pi}(k,k) - \widehat{\Pi}(k_2^*, k_1^*)] + (1-\alpha_1)\xi[\widehat{q}(k,k) - \widehat{q}(k_2^*, k_1^*)] > 0 \tag{13.33}$$

As $k > k_2^*$ (by Proposition 3), we know that the second term, $\widehat{q}(k,k) - \widehat{q}(k_2^*, k_1^*)$, has to be positive. Given $\alpha_1 > \alpha_2$, the equivalent expression with α_2 instead of α_1 must also be positive, since we put more weight on the component we know is positive. Therefore $U^2(k,k) > U^2(k_2^*, k_1^*)$. □

Proof of Proposition 4: We begin by focusing on the benefit to integration for the regulator in country 1, $U^1(\widetilde{k}, \widetilde{k}) - U^1(k_1^*, k_2^*)$, and seeing how this changes with s, where $\alpha_2 = \alpha_1 - s$. We therefore focus on

$$\frac{\mathrm{d}[U^1(\widetilde{k}, \widetilde{k}) - U^1(k_1^*, k_2^*)]}{\mathrm{d}s}. \tag{13.34}$$

This can be written as (the subscripts on the utility functions refer to the first derivative with respect to that argument)

$$U_1^1\frac{\partial\widetilde{k}}{\partial s}+U_2^1\frac{\partial\widetilde{k}}{\partial s}+\left.\frac{\partial U^1}{\partial s}\right|_{\widetilde{k},\widetilde{k}}-U_1^1\frac{\mathrm{d}k_1^*}{\mathrm{d}s}-U_2^1\frac{\mathrm{d}k_2^*}{\mathrm{d}s}-\left.\frac{\partial U^1}{\partial s}\right|_{k_1^*,k_2^*}. \tag{13.35}$$

Applying the envelope theorem, this reduces to

$$\left.\frac{\partial U^1}{\partial s}\right|_{\widetilde{k},\widetilde{k}}-U_2^1\frac{\mathrm{d}k_2^*}{\mathrm{d}s}-\left.\frac{\partial U^1}{\partial s}\right|_{k_1^*,k_2^*}. \tag{13.36}$$

Now, note that since $U^1=\alpha_1\widehat{\Pi}+(1-\alpha_1)\xi q$ and $U^2=(\alpha_1-s)\widehat{\Pi}+(1-\alpha_1+s)\xi q$, we have

$$\left.\frac{\partial U^1}{\partial s}\right|_{\widetilde{k},\widetilde{k}}=0 \quad \text{and} \quad \left.\frac{\partial U^1}{\partial s}\right|_{k_1^*,k_2^*}=0.$$

This implies that

$$\frac{\mathrm{d}[U^1(\widetilde{k},\widetilde{k})-U^1(k_1^*,k_2^*)]}{\mathrm{d}s}=-U_2^1\frac{\mathrm{d}k_2^*}{\mathrm{d}s}. \tag{13.37}$$

To show that this expression is negative, note that U_2^1 is clearly positive, since $U_2^1=\alpha_1(\partial\widehat{\Pi}/\partial k_2)+(1-\alpha_1)\xi(\partial\widehat{q}/\partial k_2)$. Second, $\mathrm{d}k_2^*/\mathrm{d}s$ is nonnegative given the regularity condition for the equilibrium, which implies that the regulator should (weakly) increase the level of regulation if the weight placed on banking system stability increases ($\mathrm{d}k_2^*/\mathrm{d}s$ is strictly negative if $k_2^*<1$). Therefore,

$$\frac{\mathrm{d}[U^1(\widetilde{k},\widetilde{k})-U^1(k_1^*,k_2^*)]}{\mathrm{d}s}=-U_2^1\frac{\mathrm{d}k_2^*}{\mathrm{d}s}<0,$$

which demonstrates that the benefit from integrating is decreasing in the difference between the two countries, and that if $U^1(\widetilde{k},\widetilde{k})-U^1(k_1^*,k_2^*)=0$ for any difference $\hat{s}$ between the countries, it will be negative for any larger value of s; $\hat{s}$ therefore represents the maximal difference between the countries, for a given α_1.

To show that such an $\hat{s}$ exists, note that for $s = 0$, it is always true that $U^1(\widetilde{k},\widetilde{k})-U^1(k_1^*,k_2^*)>0$ because of Proposition 1. At the same time, it is also clear that, for any $\varepsilon>0$, there is some value of $s,\tilde{s}$, such that, for $\alpha_2=\alpha_1-\tilde{s}$, regulator 2 chooses $k_2^*=1-\varepsilon$ since regulator 2 places greater weight on financial system stability. As $\varepsilon\to 0, \tilde{s}\to\alpha_1-\underline{\alpha}$ (i.e., $\alpha_2\to\underline{\alpha}$), and it is clear that regulator 1 prefers to remain independent instead of increasing its level of regulation since k_2^* cannot be raised sufficiently to compensate regulator 1, i.e., $U^1(\widetilde{k},\widetilde{k})-U^1(k_1^*,k_2^*)<0$. By continuity, an $\hat{s}<\alpha_1$ such that $U^1(\widetilde{k},\widetilde{k})-U^1(k_1^*,k_2^*)=0$ must exist. □

Proof of Proposition 5: Suppose there are N symmetric countries. Keeping constant the degree of financial integration, for each bank the return on loans depends on the loan quantity it grants and on the average loan quantity granted by other countries' banks,

$$R_i\left(\frac{\mathrm{E}}{k_i}, \frac{1}{N-1}\sum_{j\neq i}^{N-1}\frac{\mathrm{E}}{k_j}\right). \tag{13.38}$$

Suppose that $N-1$ of the N symmetric countries participate in a regulatory union, and one country, country 1, does not. For $i \neq 1$, the regulator of this partial union maximizes the utility of a representative country in the union:

$$\max_k \alpha\left\{\widehat{q}_i[R(N)-(1-k)\delta]\frac{\mathrm{E}}{k} - \rho\mathrm{E} - c\frac{\mathrm{E}}{k}\widehat{q}_i^2\right\} + (1-\alpha)\xi\widehat{q}_i, \tag{13.39}$$

where

$$R(N) = R\left(\frac{\mathrm{E}}{k}, \frac{1}{N-1}\sum_{j=1}^{N-2}\frac{\mathrm{E}}{k} + \frac{1}{N-1}\frac{\mathrm{E}}{k_1}\right) \quad \text{and} \quad \widehat{q}_i = \frac{R(N)-(1-k)\delta}{2c}.$$

Since banks maximize profits with respect to q, we can write

$$\frac{\mathrm{d}\widehat{\Pi}_i}{\mathrm{d}k} = \frac{\partial\widehat{\Pi}_i}{\partial k} + \frac{\partial\widehat{\Pi}_i}{\partial R}\frac{\mathrm{d}R(N)}{\mathrm{d}k}, \tag{13.40}$$

since the remaining term, $(\partial\widehat{\Pi}_i/\partial q_i)\mathrm{d}\widehat{q}_i/\mathrm{d}k$, equals zero because of the envelope theorem. Note that

$$\frac{\partial\widehat{\Pi}_i}{\partial k} = \widehat{q}_i\delta\frac{\mathrm{E}}{k} - \frac{\mathrm{E}}{k^2}\left\{\widehat{q}_i[R(N)-(1-k)\delta]\frac{\mathrm{E}}{k} - c\frac{\mathrm{E}}{k}\widehat{q}_i^2\right\} \tag{13.41}$$

and $\partial\widehat{\Pi}_i/\partial R = \widehat{q}_i(\mathrm{E}/k)$. Using the definition of $\widehat{q}_i$, we know that $\mathrm{d}\widehat{q}_i/\mathrm{d}k = \frac{\delta}{2c} + \frac{\mathrm{d}R/\mathrm{d}k}{2c}$.

Define R'_{own} to be the partial derivative of the return function with respect to its first argument (the regulation in the home country), and R'_{other} to be the partial derivative of the return function with respect to its second argument (the average regulation in countries other than home). Then, for any given N, we have for the regulator of the partial union

$$\frac{\mathrm{d}R(N)}{\mathrm{d}k} = -\frac{\mathrm{E}}{k^2}R'_{\text{own}} - \frac{N-2}{N-1}\frac{\mathrm{E}}{k^2}R'_{\text{other}}. \tag{13.42}$$

This means that for any pair (k, k_1) we have

$$\lim_{N\to\infty}\frac{\mathrm{d}R(N)}{\mathrm{d}k} = -\frac{\mathrm{E}}{k^2}R'_{\text{own}} - \frac{\mathrm{E}}{k_i^2}R'_{\text{other}}. \tag{13.43}$$

It is now easy to see that (43) implies that the first-order condition for the regulator of the partial union

$$\alpha\left[\frac{\partial\widehat{\Pi}_i}{\partial k} + \frac{\partial\widehat{\Pi}_i}{\partial R}\frac{\mathrm{d}R}{\mathrm{d}k}\right] + (1-\alpha)\xi\left(\frac{\delta}{2c} + \frac{\mathrm{d}R/\mathrm{d}k}{2c}\right) = 0, \tag{13.44}$$

whose solution is $\widehat{k}_{\text{partial}}$, converges to that for a centralized regulator for all N countries. It follows that $\lim_{N\to\infty}\widehat{k}_{\text{partial}}=\widehat{k}$.

The first-order condition for the regulator of the sole country outside the union is

$$\alpha\left[\frac{\partial\widehat{\Pi}_1}{\partial k_1}+\frac{\partial\widehat{\Pi}_1}{\partial R_1}\frac{\mathrm{d}R_1}{\mathrm{d}k_1}\right]+(1-\alpha)\xi\left(\frac{\delta}{2c}+\frac{\mathrm{d}R_1/\mathrm{d}k_1}{2c}\right)=0, \tag{13.45}$$

where

$$\frac{\partial\widehat{\Pi}_1}{\partial k_1}=\widehat{q}_1\delta\frac{\mathrm{E}}{k_1}-\frac{\mathrm{E}}{k_1^2}\left\{\widehat{q}_1[R_1(N)-(1-k_1)\delta]\frac{\mathrm{E}}{k_1}-c\frac{\mathrm{E}}{k_1}\widehat{q}_1^2\right\} \tag{13.46}$$

and

$$R_1(N)=R\left(\frac{\mathrm{E}}{k_1},\frac{1}{N-1}\sum_{j=2}^{N}\frac{\mathrm{E}}{k_j}\right). \tag{13.47}$$

This means that we have

$$\lim_{N\to\infty}\frac{\mathrm{d}R_1(N)}{\mathrm{d}k_1}=-R'_{\text{own}}\frac{\mathrm{E}}{k_1^2}. \tag{13.48}$$

Then, since $R'_{\text{own}}<0$ and $R'_{\text{other}}<0$, we have that at $k_1=\widehat{k}$,

$$\frac{\partial\widehat{\Pi}_1}{\partial k_1}=\frac{\partial\widehat{\Pi}_i}{\partial k};\quad R_1(N)=R(N);\quad \frac{\mathrm{d}R_1(N)}{\mathrm{d}k_1}<\frac{\mathrm{d}R(N)}{\mathrm{d}k}, \tag{13.49}$$

which implies that (45) is negative at $k_1=\widehat{k}$, so that the equilibrium, as $N\to\infty$; is characterized by the pair$(\widehat{k}_1,\widehat{k})$, with $\widehat{k}_1<\widehat{k}$.

Because of the externalities, any $\widetilde{k}$ such that $U^1(\widetilde{k},\widetilde{k},\ldots,\widetilde{k})>U^1(\widehat{k}_1,\widehat{k},\ldots,\widehat{k})$ would also have to satisfy $\widetilde{k}>\widehat{k}$. However, since $\widehat{k}$ is by definition the level of regulation that maximizes the utility of any given country's regulator conditionally on imposing uniform regulation across all countries, there cannot exist a $\widetilde{k}$ that satisfies this condition. Since we have just shown that $U^1(\widehat{k}_1,\widehat{k},\ldots,\widehat{k})>U^1(\widehat{k},\widehat{k},\ldots,\widehat{k})$ at the limit, there cannot exist any level of regulation at which the independent country is willing to join the partial regulatory union.

Finally, note that since $U^1(\widehat{k}_1,\widehat{k},\ldots,\widehat{k})>U^1(\widehat{k},\widehat{k},\ldots,\widehat{k})$, there must exist some $Z>0$ such that $U^1(\widehat{k}_1,\widehat{k},\ldots,\widehat{k})-U^1(\widehat{k},\widehat{k},\ldots,\widehat{k})\geq Z>0$. Fix $\widehat{k}_1$. Since U^1 is continuous in all its variables, $\exists$ some $\delta>0$ such that $U^1(\widehat{k}_1,\widehat{k}-\delta,\ldots,\widehat{k}-\delta)-U^1(\widehat{k},\widehat{k},\ldots,\widehat{k})\geq Z/2>0$. This tells us that there must be some level of regulation for all other countries but the first, given by $\widehat{k}-\delta$, such that country 1 still does not want to join the union if the increase in regulation will be only by the amount δ, in order to get everyone up to $\widehat{k}$. However, since $\lim_{N-\infty}\widehat{k}_{\text{partial}}=\widehat{k}$, there exists some $N'>0$ such that for all $n>N'$, $\widehat{k}_{\text{partial}}\geq\widehat{k}-\delta$. Therefore, this proves that for all $n>N'$, $U^1(\widehat{k}_1,\widehat{k}_{\text{partial}},\ldots,\widehat{k}_{\text{partial}})-U^1(\widehat{k},\widehat{k},\ldots,\widehat{k})>0$, which demonstrates that given country 1 can do strictly better by staying out of the union and regulating by an amount $\widehat{k}_1$, a fortiori it must be able to do at least as well by regulating optimally. This establishes our result. □

Proof of Proposition 6: As posited, suppose that there are two countries 1 and 2, with $\alpha_1 > \alpha_2$, for which their respective regulators would choose to centralize their regulation in the absence of financial links with other countries. This implies that $U^1(\widetilde{k},\widetilde{k}) - U^1(k_1^*, k_2^*) > 0$. Now, suppose that, as in Proposition 5, financial links develop with N additional countries, 3 to $N+2$, all of which are symmetric: $\alpha_j = \alpha$ for $j = 3, \ldots, N+2$. Since these countries are all symmetric, we focus on the equilibrium in which their regulators all choose a symmetric level of regulation, denoted by k_N^*. Focus now on bank 1. As in Proposition 5, the return for bank 1 on its loans depends on the loan quantity it grants and on the average loan quantity granted by the banks chartered in other countries,

$$R_1\left(\frac{\mathrm{E}}{k_1}, \frac{1}{N+1}\frac{\mathrm{E}}{k_2} + \frac{1}{N+1}\sum_{j=3}^{N+1}\frac{\mathrm{E}}{k_j}\right). \tag{13.50}$$

In equilibrium this becomes

$$R_1\left(\frac{\mathrm{E}}{k_1^*(N)}, \frac{1}{N+1}\frac{\mathrm{E}}{k_2^*(N)} + \frac{N}{N+1}\frac{\mathrm{E}}{k_N^*}\right), \tag{13.51}$$

where $k_i^*(N), i = 1, 2$, is defined always as the

$$\arg\max_{k_i} U^i\left(k_i, \frac{1}{N+1}\sum_{j\neq i}^{N+1}\frac{\mathrm{E}}{k_j^*}\right),$$

and k_N^* is defined above as the

$$\arg\max_{k_n} R_n\left(\frac{\mathrm{E}}{k_n}, \frac{1}{N+1}\frac{\mathrm{E}}{k_1^*} + \frac{1}{N+1}\frac{\mathrm{E}}{k_2^*} + \frac{N-1}{N+1}\frac{\mathrm{E}}{k_N^*}\right).$$

As in the previous result, for any k_1,

$$\lim_{N\to\infty} R_1\left(\frac{\mathrm{E}}{k_1}, \frac{1}{N+1}\frac{\mathrm{E}}{k_2^*} + \frac{N}{N+1}\frac{\mathrm{E}}{k_N^*}\right) = R_1\left(\frac{\mathrm{E}}{k_1}, \frac{\mathrm{E}}{k_N^*}\right).$$

This implies that $\lim_{N\to\infty} \partial R_1/\partial k_2 = 0$, which also implies that $\lim_{N\to\infty} \partial\widehat{\Pi}_1/\partial k_2 = \lim_{N\to\infty} \partial\widehat{q}_1/\partial k_2 = 0$. However, it is still true that $\partial\widehat{\Pi}_1/\partial k_1 < 0$ and $\partial\widehat{q}_1/\partial k_1 > 0$ for all N. Therefore, while the benefit to integrating for country 1 goes to zero (since the effect of increasing the capital requirement for country 2 becomes negligible), the cost associated with any loss of independence remains strictly positive.

The final step is to show that in the limit integration still implies a strict loss of independence (and therefore a cost) to country 1. Note that since the weight of country 2's loans on the average loan quantity goes to zero, and the total loans granted by any country is finite, we have that $\lim_{N\to\infty} U^1(k_1, k_2, k_N, \ldots, k_N) = U^1(k_1, k_N, \ldots, k_N)$. A similar result holds for country 2: $\lim_{N\to\infty} U^2(k_2, k_1, k_N, \ldots, k_N) = U^2(k_2, k_N, \ldots, k_N)$. It is now clear that since $\alpha_1 > \alpha_2$, it must be that $\lim_{N\to\infty} k_1^*(N) < \lim_{N\to\infty} k_2^*(N)$. Since any unilateral increase in k_1 makes country 1 strictly worse off, and there is no increase in k_2 that can compensate country 1 for that loss, the regulator for country 1 would not like to join into a regulatory union with country 2. □

References

Acharya, V., 2003. Is the international convergence of capital adequacy regulation desirable? Journal of Finance 58, 2745–2781.

Almazan, A., 2002. A model of competition in banking: bank capital vs. expertise. Journal of Financial Intermediation 11, 87–121.

Besanko, D., Kanatas, G., 1993. Credit market equilibrium with bank monitoring and moral hazard. Review of Financial Studies 6, 213–232.

Besanko, D., Kanatas, G., 1996. The regulation of bank capital: do capital standards promote safety? Journal of Financial Intermediation 5, 160–183.

Bhattacharya, S., Thakor, A., 1993. Contemporary banking theory. Journal of Financial Intermediation 3, 2–50.

Calem, P., Rob, R., 1999. The impact of capital-based regulation on bank risk-taking. Journal of Financial Intermediation 8, 317–352.

Chen, Z., Knez, P., 1995. Measurement of market integration and arbitrage. Review of Financial Studies 8, 287–325.

Dermine, J., 1991. The regulation of financial services in the EC: centralization or national autonomy? New York University Salomon Brothers Center Working Paper: S-91-31, June.

Dewatripont, M., Tirole, J., 1994. The Prudential Regulation of Banks. MIT Press, Cambridge, MA.

Dixit, A., 1986. Comparative statics for oligopoly. International Economic Review 27, 107–122.

Gehrig, T., 1998. Competing markets. European Economic Review 42, 277–310.

Gorton, G., Winton, A., 2000. Liquidity provision, bank capital, and the macroeconomy. Unpublished working paper. University of Minnesota.

Hellmann, T., Murdock, K., Stiglitz, J., 2000. Liberalization, more hazard in banking, and prudential regulation: are capital requirements enough? American Economic Review 90, 147–165.

Holthausen, C., Roende, T., 2002. Cooperation in international banking supervision: a political economy approach. Unpublished working paper. European Central Bank.

John, K., Saunders, A., Senbet, L., 2000. A theory of bank regulation and management compensation. Review of Financial Studies 13, 95–125.

Kahn, C., Santos, J., 2003. Allocating bank regulatory powers: lender of last resort, deposit insurance, and supervision. Unpublished working paper. University of Illinois.

Kane, E., 1984. Regulatory structure in futures markets: jurisdictional competition among the SEC, the CFTC, and other agencies. NBER Working Paper No. 1331.

Kane, E., 1990. Principal agent problems in S&L salvage. Journal of Finance 45, 755–764.

Laffont, J.-J., Martimort, D., 1999. Separation of regulators against collusive behavior. RAND Journal of Economics 30, 232–262.

Matutes, C., Vives, X., 2000. Imperfect competition, risk taking, and regulation in banking. European Economic Review 44, 1–34.

Oates, W., 1996. The Economics of Environmental Regulation. Edward Elgar Press, UK.

Peek, J., Rosengren, E., 1997. The international transmission of financial shocks: the case of Japan. American Economic Review 87, 495–505.

Peek, J., Rosengren, E., 2000. Collateral damage: effects of the Japanese bank crisis on real activity in the United States. American Economic Review 90, 30–45.

Prati, A., Schinasi, G., 1999. Financial stability in European economic and monetary union. Princeton Studies in International Finance, Princeton University, NJ.

Repullo, R., 2004. Capital requirements, market power, and risk-taking in banking. Journal of Financial Intermediation 13, 156–182.

Rochet, J.C., 1992. Capital requirements and the behavior of commercial banks. European Economic Review 36, 1137–1178.

Santos, J., 2001. Bank capital regulation in contemporary banking theory: a review of the literature. Financial Markets, Institutions and Instruments 10, 41–84.

Santos, T., Scheinkman, J., 2000. Competition among exchanges. Quarterly Journal of Economics 116, 1027–1061.

Sinn, H.W., 2001. Risk taking, limited liability, and the competition of bank regulators. NBER Working Paper No. 8669.

Stein, J., 1998. An adverse selection model of bank asset and liability management with implications for the transmission of monetary policy. RAND Journal of Economics 29, 466–486.

Thakor, A., 1996. Capital requirements, monetary policy, and aggregate bank lending: theory and empirical evidence. Journal of Finance 51, 279–324.
Vives, X., 2000. Central banks and supervision. Unpublished working paper. Institut d'Analisi Economica.
Vives, X., 2001. Restructuring financial regulation in the European monetary union. Journal of Financial Services Research 19, 57–82.
Wagster, J., 1996. Impact of the 1988 Basel accord on international banks. Journal of Finance 51, 495–505.
White, L., 1993. International regulation of securities markets: harmonization or competition? Unpublished working paper EC-93-26. New York University.
White, L., 1994. On the international harmonization of bank regulation. Oxford Review of Economic Policy 10, 94–105.

III MONEY, LIQUIDITY CRISES AND ASSET PRICES

14 Money in a Theory of Banking

Douglas W. Diamond and Raghuram G. Rajan

What is the connection between money, banks, and aggregate credit? When can expansionary monetary policy lead to expanded bank credit? And when can monetary policy help avert bank failures? These are the questions that motivate this paper.

We start with a "real" model where all contracts are denominated in goods. A bank is an intermediary, which has special skills that enable it to lend to firms that are hard to collect from. The bank finances these loans by issuing demandable claims. In Diamond and Rajan (2001), we show why such an arrangement allows banks to fund potentially long-term projects while allowing investors to consume when needed.

Unfortunately, demandable claims expose the banking system to real shocks that create a mismatch between the production of consumption goods and the real amount promised to the depositors. Even if the shortage of consumption goods, also termed a real "liquidity shortage," is merely due to delay in production and not because of any reduction in the production possibilities of the economy, it can be amplified by the banking system. Banks will cut short long-term projects, that is, curtail credit. Banks may fail even if depositors have the most optimistic beliefs possible (unlike, say, in models like that of Diamond and Philip Dybvig, 1983).

All this is shown in an economy where all contracts, including demand deposits, are denominated in goods. The repayment on deposits is assumed fixed over the next instant and, because of difficulties in contracting, cannot be an explicit function of realizations of individual bank states or detailed aggregate conditions. In practice, however, bank deposits and loans typically promise to repay money, not goods—though deposits are denominated in foreign currencies in some countries, which essentially makes them real from the perspective of that country's citizens. What would happen if deposit contracts were instead *nominal*, that is, denominated and repayable in domestic currency? Would the system smooth real shocks?

To examine this, we focus on two sources of value for money. First, money, and any maturing government liability, is a claim on the government and may have intrinsic value from the ability of citizens to pay taxes with it. Second, money, specifically currency, facilitates transactions; some goods may be sold only for cash as in cash-in-advance models (see Robert Clower, 1967; Robert Lucas, Jr., and Nancy Stokey, 1987). Examples are illegal goods such as drugs, services that are sold in transactions where the seller seeks to keep his identity hidden from tax authorities, or goods encountered serendipitously where the relative cost of establishing a credit transaction may be too high. Depending on circumstances, the "fiscal" value of money may exceed or be dominated by its "transactions" value.

Suppose now that banks issue nominal deposits. To the extent that the real value of a unit of money falls when the current aggregate supply of goods is low, deposits denominated in money offer banks a natural hedge by adjusting effective real demand to supply. And there are reasons why this might happen—the present value of taxes on production falls if production is delayed, so the fiscal value of money falls. Similarly, it is plausible that transactions fall when aggregate production is delayed, so the transactions value of money could also fall. If the quantities of currency and bonds are fixed, the real value required to be paid out on nominal deposits will then fall in consonance with an adverse shock to the supply of goods, reducing the real liquidity shortage and its effects on, and via, the banking system.

However, perfect state contingent adjustment of liquidity demand using nominal deposit contracts is a fairly special idealization. More generally, the transactions value of money may have large variation that is independent of aggregate production.[1] If so, banks that issue nominal demandable deposits are particularly vulnerable: if cash goods are temporarily cheap (for example, because the supply of money is low relative to available cash goods), banks will be forced to increase interest rates offered on demandable deposits to keep depositors from withdrawing. In turn, this will increase the real repayment obligations of the banks, potentially even causing bank failures. When the value of money is not "well behaved," far from reducing aggregate real liquidity demand when aggregate supply falls, nominal deposits may actually increase it, exacerbating real liquidity shortages, and reducing credit.

Monetary intervention could play a useful role here by making the value of money correspond better to aggregate real liquidity conditions. By increasing the money supply available for transactions when the transactions demand is high (and by committing to provide monetary support in the future when needed), the monetary authority offsets aberrant monetary or real shocks and keeps the price level stable. This limits depositor incentives to withdraw and the future real repayment obligations of banks. Banks, then, will respond by continuing, rather than curtailing, credit to long-term projects, thus increasing aggregate economic activity.

Our view of the monetary transmission mechanism could then be termed a version of the *bank lending channel view* (see Ben S. Bernanke and Mark Gertler, 1995, or Anil Kashyap and Jeremy Stein, 1997, for comprehensive surveys) but with a difference. According to the traditional lending channel view, monetary policy affects bank loan supply, which in turn affects aggregate economic activity. Three assumptions have been thought to be key to the centrality of banks in the transmission process: (a) binding reserve requirements tie the issuance of bank demand deposits to the availability of reserves; (b) banks cannot substitute between demand deposits and other forms of finance easily, so they have to cut down on lending when the central bank curtails reserves; (c) client firms cannot substitute between bank loans and other forms of finance, so they have to cut down on economic activity.

The concern with the traditional view of the bank lending channel is that, as reserve requirements have been eliminated for almost all bank liabilities except demand deposits, the argument that banks will find it difficult or expensive to raise alternative forms of

[1] If illegal goods and informal services require cash in advance, there is no reason they should be positively correlated with aggregate formal production. In fact, if more workers lose formal employment and enter the informal sector, there could be a case for arguing for negative correlation between aggregate production and cash transactions. Similarly, if a temporary downturn prompts asset sales, a negative correlation could again emerge.

financing to demand deposits becomes less persuasive. See, for example, the critique by Cristina D. Romer and David H. Romer (1990), although Stein (1998) argues that demand deposits are still special because they are insured. But there does seem to be strong evidence that monetary policy has effects on bank loan supply (Kashyap et al., 1993; Sydney Ludvigson, 1998), has greater effect on banks at times when their balance sheets look worse (Michael Gibson, 1997), and has the greatest effect on the policies of the smallest and least liquid banks (Kashyap and Stein, 2000).

In contrast to traditional models of the lending channel, our model does not rely on reserve requirements or on deposit insurance, or even on sticky prices. An expansionary open market operation (buying bonds with money) increases financial liquidity and decreases the real value banks must pay in the future to retain deposits in the present, which alleviates the real liquidity demands on banks, which then allows them to fund more long-term projects to fruition. These effects will be most pronounced for constrained banks in bad times. Thus it is perhaps best to term ours the *liquidity* version of the lending channel of transmission.

The paper is organized as follows. In Section I, we describe the framework. In Section II, we describe the problems with real deposit contracts and the circumstances under which nominal contracts can improve upon them. In Section III, we introduce money and examine how aggregate activity and bank credit are affected by shortages of real and financial liquidity. In Section IV, we examine how monetary policy is transmitted in our model. In Section V, we examine robustness, after which we conclude.

I. The Framework

A. Agents, Assets, Endowments, Preferences, Technology

Consider an economy with four types of risk-neutral agents (investors, entrepreneurs, bankers, and dealers), a date when contracts are written, and five future dates: 0, 1, 2, 3, and 4. Dates 1 and 3 are event rather than calendar dates and are best assumed close in calendar time to dates 2 and 4, respectively.

There are goods, and financial assets consisting of cash and government bonds. Only investors are initially endowed with resources. Each investor has one unit of good, M_0 of cash, and B_2 face value of government bonds maturing at date 2 (a list of symbols follows in the Appendix).[2] When the bonds mature, the government extinguishes them by repaying their face value in new money or issuing fresh bonds maturing at date 4.

Investors are impatient in that their utility is only the sum of consumption on, or before, date 2. Because all consumption on or before date 2 is perfectly substitutable, we will refer to all such consumption as *early* consumption. All other agents also get equal utility from consumption after date 2 (*late* consumption), so their utility is the sum of early and late consumption. The impatience of investors limits the response of consumption demand to interest rates (equivalently, it limits the substitutability of consumption across time), which is needed for liquidity to matter.

Each entrepreneur has a project, which requires the investment of a unit of good before date 0. It produces C in goods at date 2 if the project is *early* or C at date 4 if the project is delayed and produces *late*. Alternatively, goods can be stored at a gross real return of 1.

[2]Because we have three calendar dates in the model, 0, 2, and 4, a bond maturing at date 2 is a one-period (short-term) bond. We do not consider long-term bonds in this paper.

We assume that there is a shortage of endowments of goods initially relative to projects that can be invested in. Let the gross real interest rate between date j and date k be r_{jk} and the gross nominal interest rate be i_{jk}.

B. Projects and the Nontransferability of Skills

The primary friction underlying the model is that those with specific skills cannot commit to using their human capital on behalf of others, that is, they cannot commit to repay all the value they generate to outsiders. Creditors will lend only to the extent that they can compel borrowers to repay—either by threatening to seize the borrower's assets and generate value with them or by committing to harm the borrower if the borrower defaults.

Specifically, since entrepreneurs have no endowments, they need to borrow to invest. Each entrepreneur has access to a banker who has, or can acquire during the course of lending, knowledge about an alternative, but less effective, way to run the project. The banker's specific knowledge allows him to (make the credible threats that will enable him to) collect γC from an entrepreneur whose project just matures. No one else has the knowledge to collect from the entrepreneur. Because the entrepreneur's skills are critical to the project, the project is illiquid in that the entrepreneur can pay at most γC of the C that he generates.

Regardless of whether a project is early or late, the banker can also *restructure* the project at any time to yield c in early consumption goods—intuitively, restructuring implies stopping half-finished projects and salvaging all possible goods from them. We assume $c < 1 < \gamma C < C$.

Since no one other than the bank has the specific skills to collect from the entrepreneur, the loan to the entrepreneur is also illiquid in that the banker will get less than γC if he has to sell the loan before the project matures. Any buyer will realize that the banker will extract a future rent for collecting the loan, and the buyer will reduce the price he pays for the loan accordingly. In fact, bank loans are so dependent on the banker's specific skills for collection that the banker prefers restructuring projects to selling them.[3] The illiquidity of both projects and bank loans stems from the inalienability of human capital (see Oliver Hart and John Moore, 1994).

Given the shortage of endowment relative to projects, competition will force the select few entrepreneurs who get a loan to promise to repay the maximum possible on demand, γC, to obtain the loan. This simplifying assumption is relaxed later.

C. Financing Banks

Since bankers have no resources initially, they have to raise them from investors. But investors have no collection skills (and, consequently, bank loans are worthless in their hands), so how do banks commit to repaying investors? By issuing demand deposits! In our previous work (Diamond and Rajan, 2000, 2001), we argued that the demandable nature of deposit contracts introduces a collective action problem for depositors which makes them run to demand repayment whenever they anticipate the banker cannot, or will not, pay the promised amount. Runs destroy the banker's rents. Because depositors are committed to harming the banker if he reneges on his promise to pay, the banker will repay the promised amount on deposits whenever he can.

[3] See Diamond and Rajan (2005) for the easily satisfied conditions that lead to this outcome.

Deposit financing introduces rigidity into the bank's required repayments. Ex ante, this enables the banker to commit to repay if he can (that is, avoid strategic defaults by passing through whatever he collects to depositors). However, it exposes the bank to destructive runs if he truly cannot pay (it makes nonstrategic default more costly): when depositors demand repayment before projects have matured and the bank does not have the means of payment, it will be forced to restructure projects to get c immediately instead of allowing them to mature and generate γC.

All banks face a perfectly competitive deposit market where deposits flow freely to any bank that can credibly repay the market clearing rate of return.

D. Uncertainty

Each bank faces an identical pool of entrepreneurs before date 0. At date 0, the state s is realized and the banks become differentiated. A bank could turn out to be type G with all entrepreneurs having early projects or type B with $\alpha^{B,s} < 1$ entrepreneurs with early projects. The fraction of banks of type G in state s is $\theta^{G,s}$. In what follows, we will suppress the dependence on the state for notational convenience. Also, instead of introducing the whole model at one go, we will introduce the essential features of the "real" model, leaving the details of money for later.

E. Timing

Before Date 0. Investors deposit goods in competitive banks in return for claims that make them better off in expectation than storage.[4] Let us start by assuming that banks issue real deposits, that is, each bank offers to repay d_0 early consumption goods (or claims of equivalent value) on demand for the resources they get from each identical investor. Banks lend the goods to entrepreneurs in return for a promise to repay γC on demand. Entrepreneurs invest the goods in projects. There is a competitive market for deposits, bonds, and goods at each date.

Date 0. Uncertainty is resolved: everyone learns which entrepreneur is early and who is late, and thus what fraction α^i of a bank i's project portfolio is early. Depositors withdraw or renew. If they renew, they get $d_2 = d_0 * r_{02} = d_0$ (because everyone is indifferent between consumption at date 0 and at date 2 and no real investments between those dates offer a higher return, r_{02} is 1). We assume that depositors in a given bank run at date 0 only if they anticipate it cannot survive at date 2 given its realized distribution of projects and given the market clearing interest rate that will prevail at date 2. In other words, we do not consider panics where depositors run at date 0 only because they think other depositors will run, regardless of date-2 fundamentals—we allow collective action problems but not coordination failures.[5] A run will force the bank first to pay out all the goods it has, and then restructure late projects, and finally early ones, to generate the goods needed to pay depositors.

[4]While we have made assumptions here forcing the investor to lend via the bank, we show in Diamond and Rajan (2001) that banks and their fragile liability structures arise endogenously to facilitate the flow of credit from investors with uncertain consumption needs to entrepreneurs who have hard-to-pledge cash flows.

[5]Put another way, while we assume that each depositor expects the others in the same bank to choose a withdrawal that is an individual best response to others' actions (so we assume noncooperative actions where individual incentives may not lead each depositor to maximize the welfare of the whole), they all agree to choose the set of Nash actions that make them best off.

Date 2. Entrepreneurs with early projects will produce C and repay the bank γC. This leaves them with $(1-\gamma)C$ to invest as they choose. If no run has occurred, the bank decides how to deal with each late project—whether to restructure it if proceeds are needed before date 4 or get more long-run value by rescheduling the loan payment from date 2 to date 4 and keeping the project as a going concern. The bank obtains repayments from early entrepreneurs, proceeds from restructured late projects, and raises new funds by issuing deposits to early entrepreneurs and other bankers with surplus. It repays depositors d_2 out of all these resources.

Date 4. Late entrepreneurs repay banks and banks repay date-2 depositors. Entrepreneurs and bankers consume.

II. Aggregate Liquidity Shortages and Bank Credit

In the normal course, banks can repay initial investors by borrowing from entrepreneurs and other banks that are flush with resources at date 2. But if aggregate production is significantly delayed (that is, the fraction of B-type banks, $(1-\theta^G)$, or their fraction of late projects, $(1-\alpha^B)$, increases), the liability structure of banks causes them to multiply the temporary delay, through bank credit contraction and bank failures, into a longer-term, and more widespread, adverse shock to production. We will sketch why this may be the case, then introduce a role for money.

A. Banks' Maximization Problem after Uncertainty Is Revealed

It will be convenient to work on a per-project (or, equivalently, per-investor) basis. It is easy to show that if banks lend any of the real goods they obtain before date 0 to entrepreneurs because the expected return on lending even for a single project dominates the return on storage, they will lend all of them and not store at all (see Diamond and Rajan, 2005).

The B-type banker has the following decision problem: what fraction of late projects does he restructure at date 0 to maximize his consumption while constrained by the necessity to pay off all bank claimants? Let the B-type banker restructure μ^B of his late projects (since all of a G-type banker's projects are early, $\mu^G = 0$). His maximization problem *if the bank is expected to survive* after uncertainty is revealed at date 0 is

$$\max_{\mu^B \varepsilon [0,1]} \left\{ \text{Real value of bank's financial assets} \right.$$
$$\left. + \left[\alpha^B \gamma C + \mu^B (1-\alpha^B) c + (1-\mu^B)(1-\alpha^B)\frac{\gamma C}{r_{24}} \right] \right\}. \qquad (14.1)$$

For the bank to be solvent requires

$$\text{Real value of financial assets}$$
$$+ \left[\alpha^B \gamma C + \mu^B (1-\alpha^B) c + (1-\mu^B)(1-\alpha^B)\frac{\gamma C}{r_{24}} \right] \geq d_2. \qquad (14.2)$$

Condition (2) is simply that the real amount the banker raises should be enough to pay outstanding deposits. On the left-hand side of (2), the real value of the bank's financial assets is the value of the bank's money and bond holdings in terms of date-2 goods—we will derive expressions for these shortly. The term in square brackets is the value in date-2 consumption goods that the B-type banker obtains from his project loans. The first term is the amount repaid by the α^B early entrepreneurs whose projects mature at date 2. The second term is the amount obtained by restructuring late projects. The third term is the amount the bank can raise in new deposits against late projects that are allowed to continue without interruption until date 4. Note that r_{24}, the gross real interest rate banks offer on deposits between dates 2 and 4, need not be 1 (unlike r_{02}), because initial investors prefer date-2 consumption over date-4 consumption.

The banker wants to maximize the present value of his total consumption, which is the residual amount he has left after paying initial depositors d_2. Since d_2 is a constant, the banker's objective is simply to maximize the real present value of all his assets, the left-hand side of (2). The solution to the banker's problem is

Lemma 1: *Let $R = \gamma C/c$. The banker will restructure no late projects if $r_{24} < R$, be indifferent between continuing and restructuring late projects if $r_{24} = R$, and prefer restructuring all late projects if $r_{24} > R$.*

Essentially, R is the implied real rate of return foregone in restructuring late projects, hence the lemma stems from comparing the return with the opportunity or market real rate of return, r_{24}.

As for other agents, the entrepreneur produces in due course if his project is not restructured by the bank. If he produces, he repays the bank. Early entrepreneurs deposit their residual goods (of $(1-\gamma)C$) in the B bank at date 2 if it can credibly promise to repay $r_{24} \geq 1$, or they store otherwise. G bankers do likewise with the value left after repaying their depositors.

B. Equilibrium Condition and Aggregate Credit

Since initial investors can express their purchasing power only with their claims on the bank, the demand for consumption at date 2 is their (real) deposit claim on the bank. Thus, market clearing implies the demand for real liquidity (that is, for date-2 goods) is less than the supply, so

$$d_2 \leq \text{Goods available for consumption on or before date 2} \qquad (14.3)$$

where we will derive a specific expression for the right-hand side shortly. Because demand deposits are real and investors are unwilling to substitute future consumption, goods prices at date 2 will not affect demand. Since all initial goods are invested in the bank, which further invests in projects, the supply of date-2 real consumption goods can come only from early projects or from restructured late projects. More supply can come only from more restructuring, so the only price that can adjust to clear the market is the real interest rate, r_{24}, which determines banks' incentives to restructure late projects.

The real side of our model should now be fairly clear. The adverse shocks in our model are merely delays in the timing of production—adverse shocks to total production would only exacerbate the problems. Even though the total production possibilities of the economy over dates 2 and 4 do not change with increases in late projects, the amount of consumption goods available at date 2 (aggregate real liquidity) falls. Given an excess of demand over supply for liquidity, the real interest rate will rise, increasing supply as banks restructure more late projects until the market clears.[6] The number of projects funded to maturity falls. We will expand on this shortly.

III. Money and Banking

We now introduce a role for money. Not only will this help us flesh out the date-2 real value of financial assets in (1) and (2), it will also let us determine the real value of nominal deposits and show when they can serve as a hedge.

We focus on two natural sources of value for money. First, money can serve as a store of value; we introduce this into our finite horizon economy by assuming that money (and any maturing government liability) can be used to pay future taxes. This generates a demand for nominal claims which we shall call the *fiscal* demand. Second, currency facilitates certain transactions that by their very nature are unexpected, opportunistic, small-volume, or worth concealing so that the use of formal credit is ruled out. This is the *transactions* demand for money. Both demands will be important in understanding the link between money and banking.

A. Transactions Demand

Start first with the transactions demand. Dealers, whom we referred to earlier but did not describe, receive an endowment of a perishable good, which can be sold for cash only (to fix ideas, the good is their labor, and they do not report income to the tax authorities so they accept only cash). "Early" dealers obtain an endowment q_1 of this *cash* good at date 1 while "late" dealers obtain q_3 at date 3 (recall that all quantities are per unit of initial project financed). One unit of this cash good is a perfect substitute for one unit of the production good. Unlike the cash good, both deposits and cash can be used to pay for the production good.

To introduce a motive for trade, we assume that no one can consume his own endowment or production. All trades require payment one period ahead in cash or deposits. This means that in order to consume a cash good that is produced at date j, the buyer has to pay cash to the seller at date $j - 1$. If he wants to consume a production good, he *also* has the option of writing a check to the seller at date $j - 1$, which will clear against the funds he has on deposit at date j. The seller can use the cash or deposit he receives at date j to buy goods for consumption at date $j + 1$. This payment-in-advance constraint also applies to sales of bonds (to be described) and restructured loans. Finally, if a bank issues deposits (in exchange for cash, bonds, or loans) at date j, they can be used to initiate transactions at date j. Let P_{jk} denote the price in date-j cash of a unit of date-k consumption. For example, a transaction for date-4 goods initiated at date 3 in cash at price P_{34} yields the seller P_{34}

[6]In this model without bank capital and only one type of project, the interest rate will jump to R as soon as restructuring is needed. In a more continuous model with capital or heterogeneous projects, the interest rate moves smoothly up.

Before date 0
Banks offer interest rates on deposits and issue deposits for bonds and cash, entrepreneurs receive loans (in bank claims), and entrepreneurs buy goods from initial investors with bank claims.
Date 0
State of nature is realized. Depositors withdraw cash to buy cash goods (if no more expensive than produced goods) or to hold as an asset. If a bank faces withdrawals exceeding its cash, it sells bonds and restructured loans for date-1 delivery to meet withdrawal (similarly on all future dates).
Date 1
Cash goods sold at 0 delivered (similarly on all future dates). Cash from date-0 good sales available to seller to deposit or spend (similarly on all future dates). Cash from date-0 bank asset sales available for depositor to spend (similarly on all future dates). Early entrepreneurs sell produced goods for deposits or cash.
Date 2
Early entrepreneurs repay loans with deposits or cash. Early entrepreneurs pay taxes with cash from sales and withdrawn bank deposits. Government repays maturing bonds in currency and issues new bonds. Cash is withdrawn to buy date-3 cash goods or to hold as an asset.
Date 3
Cash goods sold at date 2 delivered. Late entrepreneurs sell goods for bank claims and cash.
Date 4
Late entrepreneurs repay bank with currency and deposits. Banks repay remaining net deposits in currency. Government repays maturing bonds in currency. All currency goes to pay taxes.

Figure 14.1. Time Line of Transactions

units of cash at date 4. Figure 14.1 shows the timing of the transactions described in the next few paragraphs.

B. The Fiscal Demand

The government taxes sales of produced goods at the rate t. To maintain consistency with the expressions derived thus far, assume that the production quantities specified earlier are aftertax, so total nominal taxes due on a project that matures at date j are $[tC/(1-t)]P_{j-1,j}$. Because cash goods may lie outside the formal economy, we assume they are not taxed—nothing significant depends on this. Taxes are due at the time of production and are payable in cash or through a check on a deposit (with the bank then transferring the cash to the government).

The odd-numbered dates, 1 and 3, simply make payment and settlement explicit. Since date 3 is close to date 4, we allow actions at date 4 to be committed to at date 3, so late entrepreneurs can borrow deposits at date 3 against what they will have at date 4 after repaying the bank loan ($= (1-\gamma)CP_{34}$). They can use the resulting deposits at date 3 to purchase goods for consumption at date 4. Similarly, the banker can also issue himself deposits at date 3 against his date-4 rents. This saves us the need to introduce another date to clear purchases initiated at date 4.

C. Money and Prices

Since cash goods and produced goods offer equivalent consumption on the dates agents want to consume, their relative prices will constrain the nominal interest rate deposits have to pay to prevent depositors arbitraging between cash and deposits. This is important in what follows.

Assume no new money or bonds are issued after date 2, so at date 4 there are M_2 units of money and bonds maturing into B_4 units of cash. Cash at this date is useful only to pay taxes, so it will be accepted in payment for produced goods because the seller wants to use them to pay taxes. Let $X_4 (= (1-\theta^G)(1-\alpha)(1-\mu^B)C)$ be the quantity of goods produced and sold for date-4 delivery. The nominal sales (all sales, including those paid with deposits) are $P_{34}X_4$, nominal tax owed is $tP_{34}X_4$, and the total supply of cash at date 4 is $M_2 + B_4$.[7] As a result,

$$P_{34} = \frac{M_2 + B_4}{tX_4}. \tag{14.4}$$

Intuitively, an examination of the government's balance sheet suggests if tax rates (and government spending) do not change, but aggregate taxable output falls, the real value of government revenues falls, and so must the real value of its nominal liabilities. Prices must, therefore, increase (see Charles W. Calomiris, 1988; John Cochrane, 2005; Michael Woodford, 1995).

At date 2, the purchase of q_3 of cash goods can be initiated with the outstanding date-2 cash, M_2. Since agents who get utility from consumption after date 2 are indifferent between consumption at date 3 or date 4, a holder of date-2 cash will spend it at date 2 or 3 depending on where he can purchase greater consumption. So the real value of the money stock at date 2 will be the larger of its purchasing power in buying cash goods for delivery at date 3, or the value of holding it to purchase produced goods at date 3 for delivery at date 4. The purchasing power of the money stock is $max\{q_3, M_2tX_4/(M_2 + B_4)\}$ where the second term is the quantity of produced goods the current money stock can purchase at date 3 for delivery at date 4 ($= M_2/P_{34}$).[8] As a result, if P_{24} is the price of date-4 consumption in date-2 cash, the date-2 real value of the money stock is

$$\frac{M_2}{P_{24}} = max\left\{q_3, \frac{M_2}{(M_2 + B_4)}tX_4\right\}$$

or, equivalently:

$$P_{24} = \frac{M_2}{max\left\{q_3, \frac{M_2}{(M_2+B_4)}tX_4\right\}} = min\left\{\frac{M_2}{q_3}, P_{34}\right\}.$$

Comparing the two terms within the curly brackets in the expression for M_2/P_{24}, we see that when $q_3 > M_2tX_4/(M_2 + B_4)$, the transactions demand dominates in that money is valued more for its role in paying for transactions at date 2 (it has a liquidity premium)

[7] Implicit in this is that the price of produced goods in assignable date-4 deposits (what one could term P_{44}) is the same as its price in date-3 cash. Equivalently, the gross nominal interest rate on bonds and deposits between dates 3 and 4, i_{34}, equals 1. Suppose not, and the rate banks paid on deposits were higher than 1. Then everyone would deposit their cash in banks and use deposits to buy goods. But for any bank to hold cash, the rate on deposits should be 1, or the bank would use any excess cash to pay down deposits. Similarly, for banks to hold cash and bonds, the rates of return on them should be equal. So the nominal rate, i_{34}, is 1, and cash, deposits, and bonds pay the same rate, as they will on all dates that cash has no special value. This also explains why i_{12} equals 1.

[8] Another way to see this is that so long as the price of cash goods for transactions initiated at date 2 is below the price of produced goods at date 3, money will be fully used up in buying cash goods. But once there is enough money such that the price of cash goods equals the price of produced goods, any money left over after buying cash goods will be used as a store of value until it can be used for purchasing produced goods at date 3. Therefore, money will effectively be valued in terms of its date-3 purchasing power. This is the intuition behind the max function.

than as a store of value. Since a depositor can withdraw cash on date 2 to make payments, for someone to leave their money in the bank, deposits must offer a gross nominal interest rate of $i_{23} = P_{34}/P_{24} = q_3/[M_2tX_4/(M_2 + B_4)] > 1$, and this is also the nominal rate on bonds (because banks can trade bonds with each other in a competitive market). Importantly, the quantity of currency at date 2 changes the relative price of cash goods and produced goods and thus influences the nominal interest rate, the opportunity cost of holding money.

Folding back to earlier periods, one can similarly derive the value of all nominal claims, cash, and bonds. All nominal bond prices on date j of bonds maturing on date k are given by $b_{jk} = B_k/i_{jk}$. Proposition 1 gives the equilibrium price levels and nominal interest rates for all dates, given real interest rates and real tax collections.

Proposition 1: *The price levels on each date are given by:*

$$P_{34} = \frac{M_2 + B_4}{tX_4}, \quad P_{24} = min\left\{\frac{M_2}{q_3}, P_{34}\right\},$$

$$P_{12} = \frac{M_0 + B_2}{tX_2 + \frac{\left(M_2 + \frac{B_4}{i_{24}}\right)}{r_{24}P_{24}}},$$

$$P_{02} = \frac{M_0}{max\left\{q_1, \frac{M_0}{P_{12}}\right\}} = min\left\{\frac{M_0}{q_1}, P_{12}\right\}.$$

Nominal interest rates are given by:

$$i_{01} = \frac{P_{12}}{P_{02}}, \quad i_{12} = 1,$$

$$i_{23} = i_{24} = \frac{P_{34}}{P_{24}}, \quad i_{34} = 1.$$

Proof: See Appendix.

D. Revisiting the Real Model

Augmenting the basic model with cash goods, prices, and the opportunity for depositors to withdraw cash to buy cash goods at dates 0 and 2 does not change the banker's maximization problem ((1) s.t. (2)). We substitute the date-2 real value of the bank's financial assets, $M_0/P_{02} + B_2/P_{12}$, into those expressions (intuitively, money can buy goods at price P_{02}, and deposits against maturing bonds can buy them at P_{12}).

Also, the total (pre-tax) supply of real liquidity—the goods available for consumption on or before date 2 in (3)—is $q_1 + [1/(1-t)][\theta^G C + (1-\theta^G)(\alpha^B C + (1-\alpha^B)\mu^B c)]$. This should be (weakly) greater than the real value of deposits, d_2, to satisfy the demand for real liquidity. We show in the Appendix that (3) is also the market clearing condition.

Now that we have the framework in place, we describe some comparative statics of the model with real deposits when the total supply of consumption goods is not enough to meet the total demand without some restructuring by B-type banks. We focus on both *total credit*, which is the fraction of projects that retain credit to maturity,

$\theta^G + (1-\theta^G)\{\alpha^B + (1-\alpha^B)(1-\mu^B)\}$, and the *fraction of late projects continued*, $(1-\mu^B)$. We have:

Proposition 2: *For a given real level of deposits issued before date 0, if both types of banks survive and there is an aggregate liquidity shortage such that the B-type banks have to restructure a positive fraction of their late projects (that is* $q_1 + \{\theta^G[C/(1-t)+(1-\theta^G)\alpha^B[C/(1-t)]\} < d_2$*), then:*

(i) *Total credit and the fraction of late projects continued increase in the fraction of G-type banks,* θ^G;

(ii) *Total credit and the fraction of late projects continued increase in the fraction of projects of B-type banks that are early,* α^B;

(iii) *For a given* θ^G *and* α^B*, total credit and the fraction of late projects continued decrease in the outstanding level of real deposits,* d_2.

Proof: See Appendix.

The proposition indicates that a decrease in the intrinsic supply of real liquidity (early goods) via a decrease in either θ^G and α^B, or an increase in demand (an increase in d_2), leads to a curtailment in credit. Essentially, in a situation of aggregate liquidity shortage, banks are squeezed between a rock (nonnegotiable deposits) and a hard place (hard-to-sell loans). They survive only by calling loans and restructuring projects. Ironically, when aggregate liquidity is plentiful, the same features of demand deposits commit the bank to collect, enabling it to issue new deposits against late projects and thus meet the individual liquidity needs of depositors and borrowers.

E. Bank Failures

If the liquidity shortage is severe enough, there are two reasons banks with real deposits can fail. First, there can be insufficient aggregate output to allow all deposits to be repaid even if all late loans are called and projects restructured. Second, it is possible that B-type banks are insolvent at the real interest rate that must prevail for banks to have incentives to call in loans and force projects to be restructured.

Recall that if a bank is expected to fail, depositors run and demand payment immediately on the revelation of uncertainty at date 0. Since projects pay at date 2 at the earliest, and since the bank obtains more from restructuring than from selling the illiquid project loans to satisfy depositor demands at date 0, all projects of a failing bank are restructured, including the early ones that would pay off at date 2. Failure is inefficient because early projects could have produced C in a timely manner to satisfy early consumption needs, but now produce only c. The specificity of bank relationships means that bank failures can cause a persistent drop in real activity, as in Bernanke (1983). The collective action problem inherent in demand deposits is now destructive, for it forces the costly production of consumption goods at a time when they are not really needed.

When bank contracts are real, the real interest rate, r_{24}, is the only price that can adjust to clear markets. The system may have insufficient degrees of freedom to adjust to an adverse shock without the stark consequences we have documented—major changes in credit and possibly bank failures. This real model is not without practical interest—when a country's banking system has deposits denominated in foreign exchange (or if the country were on the gold standard), it is as if the banks issue real deposits. But our primary purpose is to make clear that credit contraction and failure are essentially real phenomena and occur when the bank is squeezed between nonrenegotiable demand deposits and a limited production of consumption goods.

If fully state-contingent deposit contracts were available, where the real face value of each deposit depended on the individual bank's situation and the aggregate state of nature, then the banking system would produce a given amount of liquidity (expected date-2 consumption) at the minimum cost of foregone future (date-4) consumption. The outcomes with such contracts are easily characterized. First, early projects should never be restructured because the cost of providing liquidity increases with no offsetting benefit. A necessary and sufficient condition for avoiding restructuring of early projects is that there be no runs. Second, the minimum number of late projects should be restructured, in order just to meet the consumption needs of investors; none should be restructured if goods are to be stored, or consumed by those who are willing to consume late. This condition will also be met if there are no runs. Last, in order to minimize the date-4 cost of a given amount of expected date-2 consumption, if late projects must be restructured in some states of nature, then the contingent deposit payment in all other states should at least be all of the return from the early projects.

Explicit and full state contingency may not be possible for the usual technological and institutional reasons. The real interest rate, with just two values in our model, offers limited additional contingency even if observable and verifiable. Deposits could be made implicitly contingent, however, by denominating them in cash, so that their real value can fluctuate with the price level. If the price level rises with production delays, the real payout on deposits will fall, reducing liquidity demand. Nominal deposits will thus offer a hedge against the consequences of aggregate shortages. Because banks are of heterogeneous types ex post, automatic movements in the state contingent value of money cannot possibly replicate complete state contingent contracts, but they can be "contingent enough" to hedge the banking system as a whole against runs.

In what follows, we describe conditions under which nominal deposits can hedge the banking system as a whole against real shocks. But we go on to show that it also exposes the system to monetary shocks. This then suggests a role for monetary policy: to smooth over such monetary shocks (which may have real roots). Not only does our model then highlight a distinctive channel for the transmission of monetary policy, it also suggests that an objective of monetary policy is to ensure that a banking system with nominal deposits is not destabilized.

F. Nominal Deposits as a Hedge against Aggregate Liquidity Shortages

Instead of real deposits, let banks have nominal deposits outstanding at date 0, which let the depositor withdraw δ_0 units of cash on demand. Deposits will return the nominal rate, i_{02}, if rolled over until date 2, so they will pay $\delta_2 = \delta_0 * i_{02}$.

Fiscal Demand Dominates. First consider a situation where the fiscal demand dominates—for example, when there is plenty of money relative to cash goods (most simply, if there exist no cash goods), so at the margin money is valued only for its role in paying taxes. It is easy to see from Proposition 1 that

$$P_{02} = P_{12} = \frac{M_0 + B_2}{t\left[X_2 + \frac{X_4}{r_{24}}\right]}. \tag{14.5}$$

Prices are inversely proportional to the present value of taxes, which is a constant function of discounted production. Now nominal deposits serve as a hedge; intuitively, the real date-2 payment they entail adjusts via the price level to be a fixed fraction of the present value of total output. If the bank's assets are also a fixed fraction of the present value of total output, repayment, if feasible for any realization of output, will always be feasible both in terms of aggregate liquidity and bank solvency.

To see this, consider a "representative" bank, with $\alpha^i = \bar{\alpha} = \theta^G * 1 + (1-\theta^G) * \alpha^B$—for instance, if we imagine that all banks are merged into one. Net of what they can buy with their financial assets, banks have to find additional real goods at date 2 of $\delta_0/P_{02} - [M_0/P_{02} + B_2/P_{12}] = [\delta_2 - (M_0+B_2)][tX_2 + tX_4/r_{24}]/(M_0+B_2)$ to pay off their depositors, where P_{02} and P_{12} are from (5) and $\delta_2 = \delta_0 * i_{02} = \delta_0$ because $i_{02} = 1$ when the transaction demand is dominated.

The banking system's ability to pay depositors on date 2 is increasing in the fraction of projects that are early. If all projects are early, then $\alpha^B = 1, X_2 = C/(1-t), X_4 = 0$, and the bank collects γC on its loans. For the bank to be able to repay when all projects are early, we require that $\gamma C \geq [\delta_2 - (M_0 + B_2)][tC/(1-t)]/(M_0 + B_2)$, or simply that

$$\frac{\delta_2 - (M_0 + B_2)}{M_0 + B_2}\frac{t}{(1-t)} \leq \gamma < 1. \tag{14.6}$$

Interestingly, once there is some α^B at which the representative bank survives, we can show the representative bank will never fail, no matter what the aggregate liquidity shock, that is, no matter what the aggregate $\bar{\alpha}$. To see this, note that for the bank to be solvent, we require

$$\bar{\alpha}\gamma C + (1-\bar{\alpha})\left[\bar{\mu}c + (1-\bar{\mu})\frac{\gamma C}{r_{24}}\right] \geq \frac{\delta_2 - (M_0 + B_2)}{P_{02}} = \frac{\delta_2 - (M_0 + B_2)}{M_0 + B_2}\left(tX_2 + \frac{tX_4}{r_{24}}\right)$$

where the left-hand side of the inequality is the date-2 value of the representative bank's real assets based on the aggregate amount of restructuring, $\bar{\mu}$. Expanding the right-hand side,

$$\bar{\alpha}\gamma C + (1-\bar{\alpha})\left[\bar{\mu}c + (1-\bar{\mu})\frac{\gamma C}{r_{24}}\right]$$
$$\geq \frac{\delta_2 - (M_0 + B_2)}{M_0 + B_2}\frac{t}{1-t}\left\{\bar{\alpha}C + (1-\bar{\alpha})\left[\bar{\mu}c + (1-\bar{\mu})\frac{C}{r_{24}}\right]\right\}.$$

Given (6), this is certainly true for $\bar{\mu} = 1$. Since there is at least one feasible level of restructuring that leaves the bank solvent (and arguing similarly, also liquid[9]), the bank will not fail because it will select a $\bar{\mu} \in [0, 1]$ such that it is solvent and liquid. Nominal deposits can eliminate the inefficient restructuring of late projects caused by runs.

Proposition 3: *If the fiscal demand determines the value of money, the bank issues nominal deposits, and there is some $\bar{\alpha}$ such that the representative bank survives, then the representative bank will not fail no matter what the actual realization of $\bar{\alpha}$.*

[9]In order for the bank to be liquid when all projects are early, it must be that $[C/(1-t)] + q_1 > \delta_2/P_{02} = \delta_2 * [t/(1-t)]C/(M_0 + B_2)$ or $t\delta_2/(M_0 + B_2) \leq \{1 + (1-t)q_1/C\}$. If there are no cash goods, this condition is sufficient to ensure that the banking system is liquid regardless of $\bar{\alpha}$ when all late projects are restructured, for it ensures that $\bar{\alpha}C/(1-t) + (1-\bar{\alpha})c/(1-t) > \delta_2/P_{02} = \delta_2 * [t/(1-t)](\bar{\alpha}C + (1-\bar{\alpha})c)/(M_0 + B_2)$.

We do require some conditions. First, each bank's loan portfolio has to be representative of aggregate economic activity, that is, bank portfolios should be similar. If not, then banks with low α^i can fail, even when they have issued nominal deposits. Of course, given our results that prices adjust to aggregate liquidity, there exists a set of cross subsidies from high-α banks to low-α banks that will keep all the banks alive. These cross subsidies may not be privately rational for a healthy bank but may be in the collective interest.

Second, for the fiscal demand to provide a value of nominal claims that is proportional to the discounted value of real production, taxation should also be proportional to aggregate production (for example, a linear sales tax).

A Well-Behaved Dominant Transactions Demand. All this was derived in the context of a dominant fiscal demand for money. We can obtain a similar result to Proposition 3 if the transactions demand were "well" behaved (there are no nominal shocks). If the quantities of cash goods are positively linearly related to the quantities of produced goods—if when the real economy flourishes, so does the illegal economy—then $q_1 = \phi X_2$ and $q_2 = \phi X_4$ for $\phi > 0$, and the price level again adjusts to offset real liquidity shocks. We will then have $P_{24} = M_2/X_4\, max\{\phi, tM_2/(M_2 + B_4)\}$ and

$$\frac{M_0}{P_{02}} = max\left\{\phi X_2, \frac{M_0}{(M_0+B_2)}[tX_2 + \frac{1}{r_{24}} max\left\{\phi X_4 + \frac{B_4}{(M_2+B_4)} tX_4, tX_4\right\}\right\}.$$

This is bilinear in X_2 and X_4. If the fiscal demand is small (t close to zero), then the date 0 price level is $P_{02} = M_0/\phi\ max\{X_2, [M_0/(M_0 + B_2)]X_4/r_{24}\}$. Following the logic above, this is a case where a nominal deposit contract with a fixed money supply again provides a good automatic hedge against aggregate liquidity shocks.[10]

The transaction demand for money is well behaved here because the ratio of means of payment to the quantity of goods to be purchased is always the same for both cash and noncash goods. The nominal interest rate is a constant. It is similar to what would occur if deposits as well as cash could be used for the cash goods (and currency and deposits were perfect substitutes). In that case, the gross nominal interest rate would be fixed at one, only the total quantity of currency plus deposits would matter, and a version of the quantity theory of money would apply.

In our model with a dominant fiscal value or a "well-behaved" transactions demand, a banking system that issues nominal deposits has built state contingency into its deposit liabilities even though the state of real liquidity may not be directly contracted on. Why, then, would any banking system issue real deposits and risk meltdowns? To see why, let us turn to a less well-behaved transactions demand for money, where instead of nominal deposits serving as a hedge, they may destabilize the banking system.

G. Nominal Deposits and Shocks to Transactions Demand

Let the quantity of cash goods at date 1, q_1, no longer be a constant fraction of date-2 production. Let the transactions demand dominate, implying the value of money is set by

[10] David Skeie (2004) presents a model combining elements from this paper, from Diamond and Dybvig (1983), and Franklin Allan and Gale (1998), which extends our result that nominal deposits can serve as an automatic hedge. He shows that they hedge against other types of shocks or coordination failures between depositors when all banks have identical portfolios. The hedging follows from the quantity theory of money, rather than a fiscal demand for money.

its value in purchasing cash goods. At date 0, depositors can withdraw up to δ_0 in cash to buy the cash good, but they can also roll over their deposit at the prevailing nominal rate, i_{02}. Since banks set the nominal rate $i_{02} = i_{01}*1 = P_{12}/P_{02}$ to make depositors indifferent between withdrawing cash to buy cash goods at date 0 and paying with deposits for delivery at date 2, it must be that the real deposit value a bank has to pay out at date 2 is

$$\frac{\delta_2}{P_{12}} = \frac{\delta_0 * i_{02}}{P_{12}} = \frac{\delta_0 * \frac{P_{12}}{P_{02}}}{P_{12}} = \frac{\delta_0}{P_{02}}.$$

Now, instead of the real value of deposits being determined by the price of date-2-produced goods, the real value is determined by the price of cash goods at date 0. But this price may have no relationship to aggregate real liquidity conditions (largely determined by the production of date-2 goods) in the economy. Instead, it will depend on the quantity of money (financial liquidity) relative to available cash goods. For example, when M_0 is not too large or q_1 is high, $P_{02} = M_0/q_1$. We substitute $d_2 = \delta_0 q_1/M_0$ in (2) to get the bank's solvency condition.

Intuitively, when depositors are promised a fixed amount of cash on demand rather than a fixed real value, the real claim they must be promised at date 2 to leave their money in depends on the real value of withdrawing cash *anytime* earlier. In our model, the only outside opportunity they have is to buy cash goods, so if the price of cash goods is low, the real burden of deposit claims on banks becomes very high. Moreover, the real burden of repayment is now a function of the ex ante contracted level of nominal deposits, the quantity of cash goods available for purchase at date 0, and the money supply, M_0, none of which are necessarily sensitive to aggregate liquidity.

If these shocks to money demand due to transactions in cash goods are sufficiently large, the banking system may be worse off issuing nominal demand deposits. In the worst case, q_1, is not constant but has a negative correlation with $\bar{\alpha}$ (for example if the illegal economy expands when the legal economy is anticipated to slow), the real deposit burden on banks issuing nominal deposits will be high precisely when they have the least resources to pay. By contrast, the repayment burden, if real deposits had been issued, would be constant across states, and this will result in lower bank failures. An example may be useful in bringing all this together.

H. Example

Let the realized fraction of banks of type G be $\theta^G = 0.3$ and those of type B be 0.7. Let $\alpha^B = 0.25$, $c = 0.8$, $C = 1.6$, $\gamma = 0.8$, $t = 0.15$. Let $M_0 = 0.2$, $B_2 = 0.4$, $q_1 = 0.3$. Plugging in values, the real interest rate that will induce banks to restructure projects is $R = 1.2$. Let the level of outstanding real deposits per unit invested in the bank at date 0 be $d_0 = 1.3$.

In the absence of any restructuring, the total supply of goods for early consumption is just $q_1 + [1/(1-t)][\theta^G C + (1-\theta^G)\alpha^B C] = 1.19$. But outstanding deposits are 1.3, so at least some late projects have to be restructured to meet the liquidity demand. This implies that the real interest rate r_{24} must rise to 1.2 to provide incentives to restructure, and that B-type banks must restructure a fraction of the late projects equal to $\mu^B = 0.779$ for aggregate liquidity supply to equal the aggregate liquidity demand of 1.3 (solving $q_1 + [1/(1-t)][\theta^G C + (1-\theta^G)\{\alpha^B C + (1-\alpha^B)\mu^B c)] = 1.3$).

If α^B falls to 0.115, aggregate liquidity, $q_1 + [1/(1-t)][\theta^G C + (1-\theta^G)(\alpha^B C + (1-\alpha^B)c)]$, is below 1.3 even if all late projects are restructured. Depositors will run at date 0, and all B-type bank projects are restructured, including early ones.

Now consider nominal deposits. Let the level of nominal deposits be $\delta_0 = 0.8667$. With $M_0 = 0.2$ and $q_1 = 0.3$, the date 0 price of a unit of date-2 consumption of produced goods is $P_{02} = M_0/q_1 = 0.66$, the real value of required deposit payments is $d_2 = \delta_0/P_{02} = 1.3$, and the outcomes are the same as with real deposits of this amount; no banks fail and $\mu^B = 0.779$.

Now, if there is a money demand shock because available cash goods, q_1, go up to 0.32, P_{02} falls to 0.625 and the real deposit repayment rises to 1.39, B-type banks fail. By contrast, when banks have issued real deposits, an increase in q_1 only increases the available goods for date-2 consumption without increasing the real deposit burden. As a result, available credit increases, and restructuring is reduced. In sum, then, when the transactions demand dominates and does not fluctuate in lock-step with aggregate production, banks that issue nominal deposits can be extremely vulnerable to money demand shocks if monetary policy simply keeps the supply of money and bonds fixed.

I. Discussion

When a bank offers nominal deposit contracts, its real repayment burden depends on the value of moving into cash at each instant. We have modeled one reason this value could rise—too little money in the system can depress the price of cash goods and make cash transactions extremely lucrative—but there are others. Nominal deposits make the bank highly susceptible to fleeting opportunities available in the cash market (or, equivalently, other exogenous changes in the money demand function). This indicates the desirability of policies to offset temporary shocks to money demand that are unrelated to total output.

Important prior work has noted that unaccommodated shocks to money demand can cause "panics" when banks issue nominal liabilities (see Bruce Champ et al., 1996). There are two particularly important differences in our paper. First, the demand for money in Champ et al. (1996) comes from easily identified "movers" who demand it inelastically to carry it as a store of value to another location. This implies that if there are too many movers, relative price changes cannot deter them from withdrawing currency, and the constant quantity of currency is shared pro rata among movers. The reduced value obtained by those who withdraw implies that depositors who do not move do not want to withdraw, and do not have to be paid to stay in. By contrast, in our model, all depositors face the outside opportunity that causes them to want to withdraw. Given that demand for currency is elastic, the potential currency drain, or more generally, potential conversions of deposits to other uses (or even currencies), raises the rate that the bank has to pay. Even if the actual currency "drain" is small, bank health can be impaired.

The second difference follows from the first: a panic in their model is simply a loss of reserves from banks. No banks actually fail as a result of high demand for cash because withdrawers are rationed pro rata. The critical feature in our model, by contrast, is that a high transaction demand for cash translates into a higher payout on all deposits, which can affect aggregate credit and, in extremis, impair the solvency of the bank. Thus not only will there be a premium on cash during panics, but also banks will fail, as the historic evidence indeed suggests.

IV. Monetary Policy and Its Channels of Transmission

Thus far, we have examined what happens when the quantities of money and bonds are fixed and endogenous price-level adjustments cause the real value of nominal deposits to vary. If, however, the endogenous adjustments do not serve to stabilize the system, monetary policy, by changing the quantities of money and bonds, can influence the price levels and, thereby, the real obligations of banks, and thus cause a better match between the aggregate liquidity demand and supply. If a monetary policy that prevented inefficient bank failure could be committed to, it could be seen as part of the optimal contract described in Section IIIE.

A. Effects of Policy Changes

Given real parameters α^B and θ^G, bank solvency, liquidity, and credit decisions will be determined by the required real repayment on deposits at date 2. Both the date-0 price level (for cash goods), P_{02}, and the date-1 price level, P_{12}, are critical here. If P_{02} is very low relative to P_{12} because of a shortage of money relative to cash goods, the real quantity depositors can get by withdrawing at date 0 goes up. In order to prevent all depositors from withdrawing, the bank will have to pay depositors a nominal interest rate that equalizes the real goods they can purchase by withdrawing at date 0 and the real goods they can purchase by writing checks at date 1 (since the gross real rate is 1 between these dates, they will then be indifferent between the two choices). But this means that when cash is at a premium, the date-0 price of cash goods determines the required date-2 real payout of the bank. The way to reduce the real obligations of the bank is then to raise the date-0 price by increasing the supply of money, M_0. Open market operations that exchange money for bonds at date 0 will be effective in this case and lead to lower future real rates (r_{24}), greater credit, and more solvent banks.

It may seem at odds with reality that expansionary open market operations work by increasing the price of goods immediately. One can, however, think of the price level for early consumption as the quantity-weighted average of the price of cash and noncash goods for date-2 consumption. In the limit where the quantity of cash goods is very small, such an open market operation has almost no effect on inflation of the price of early consumption, but still changes the nominal rate of interest. In general, open market operations affect both inflation and nominal rates of interest, and work by reducing the value of liquidity.

Of course, once there is enough money supply such that net nominal interest rates are driven to zero ($P_{02} = P_{12}$), open market operations are no longer effective because the price level P_{02} is determined by the sum of money and bonds and not by money alone. Put another way, money no longer has a liquidity premium because cash goods are no longer cheaper than produced goods, the nominal interest rate is zero, and money and bonds are equivalent so exchanging one for the other has no effect. Even so, the government can still affect credit by printing more money or bonds and transferring them to agents (a "helicopter drop") to inflate prices (alternatively, one could think about a credible reduction in the tax rate), thus reducing the real liabilities of the banking system. We examine the mechanics of all this in what follows.

B. The Liquidity Channel of Transmission of Monetary Policy

To see the channel working, consider an open market repurchase conducted by the monetary authority, which has the effect of increasing the date-0 money supply to $M_0 + \Delta$ and reducing the face value of outstanding date-2 bonds to $B_2 - i_{02}\Delta$ where Δ is a small number.

To focus on the pure effect of the open market operation, let no other exogenous parameter be changed at this or other dates. The open market repurchase takes place after initial contracts are negotiated and projects initiated, and is executed so that banks have the added money at date 0. So long as $i_{02} > 1$, the effect of an increase in money will be to increase the price of cash goods $P_{02}(= [M_0 + \Delta]/q_1)$. This will lower the real value that the bank must pay at date 2 to retain its nominal deposits to $d_2 = \delta_0 q_1/(M_0 + \Delta)$ (and lower both the nominal rate i_{02} and the premium on cash).

Proposition 4: *If both types of banks survive without intervention, then so long as the gross nominal interest rate exceeds 1 and some late projects are being restructured, an open market repurchase of bonds with money at date 0 reduces the nominal interest rate, increases total credit, and reduces the fraction of late projects restructured.*

Proof: See Appendix.

Corollary 1: (*i*) *Open market operations may be effective but no longer feasible if the outstanding stock of bonds is fully bought back and the gross nominal interest rates still exceeds one.* (*ii*) *Further open market operations are ineffective if gross nominal interest rates fall to one.* (*iii*) *In either case, if late projects are being restructured, an unrequited transfer of money or bonds from the government to agents will increase total credit and reduce the fraction of late projects restructured, with a dollar of money being more effective than a dollar of bonds when the nominal interest rate exceeds 1.*

Proof: Available on the AER Web site at http://www.e-aer.org/data/mar06_app_20030982.pdf.

One could ask if all situations of liquidity shortage can be alleviated by nominal deposits and state contingent monetary policy, so long as the ex ante expected return constraint of depositors is satisfied. The answer is yes, for the price level at all dates can be driven up arbitrarily high, and the demand for liquidity made arbitrarily low simply by flooding the market with enough money and bonds. In fact, the banking system will continue all late projects if the real value of deposits is driven below the minimum of (i) the amount of liquidity available to a B-type bank when no late project is restructured and (ii) the real value of the B-type bank when no late project is restructured and the real rate r_{24} is 1. After this point, further monetary expansion will have no effect on real activity.

C. Example Continued

Consider again our base case example with $\alpha^B = 0.25$ and nominal deposits of $\delta = 0.9333$. If the money supply is fixed at 0.2, the B-type banks fail (implying that all B-type bank projects are restructured). A small increase in the money supply to 0.207 effected by buying down the quantity of outstanding bonds from 0.4 to 0.375 (see the proof of Corollary 1 for formulae) reduces the real value B-type banks must pay out at date 2. This allows the B-type banks to be just solvent at the real interest rate that provides incentives for restructuring ($r_{24} = R = 1.2$), and they restructure a fraction 0.26 of their late projects but can also see all early projects to maturity. So a small open market operation has a large effect on real activity. If the money supply at date 0 is increased to 0.234 by buying down bonds from 0.4 to 0.314, the B-type banks survive without restructuring any projects ($\mu^B = 0$) and the date-2 real interest rate r_{24} falls to one.

D. Financial Contagion

Our simple model of money allows us to see the effects of alternative assumptions easily. For instance, suppose depositors who run on a bank will not accept deposits on other banks but will take only money (for instance, because they need time to verify the quality of the bank they will deposit in). Bank failures can now be contagious through their effect on monetary conditions.

To see this, suppose that B-type banks are not expected to meet their nominal deposit obligations at date 2 and fail. Then they will be run immediately at date 0. They will pay out their cash reserves to depositors, but once they run out, they will have to sell assets. If the only asset that their depositors will accept is cash, all bank assets must be sold for cash (and not for deposits in other banks). These transactions will lock up cash, leaving less cash to buy cash goods. The cash good price will fall further to

$$P_{02} = \frac{M_0}{q_1 + \theta^B(c + B_2)} \tag{14.7}$$

where the denominator in (7) now also includes the value of restructured loans and bonds that the B-type banks sell. At this "fire-sale" price, the purchase of cash goods becomes even more lucrative and forces the G-type banks to pay a yet higher rate to keep their depositors from moving to cash.[11] Given the higher payout to deposits at date 2, these G-type banks could also fail if their value falls below δ_0/P_{02}. This resembles the contagious bank failures described by Milton Friedman and Anna J. Schwarz (1963). Depositors run on banks, forcing banks to sell more assets for cash, which renders the money supply inadequate for the quantum of real activity, forcing a further drop in the price level, still greater incentive to withdraw, and still more bank failures.

E. Notes

Finally, a few notes. First, we do not need reserve requirements, capital requirements, or deposit insurance for monetary expansion to have real effects. Moreover, it is not necessary to fool the public or even surprise it. A fully anticipated preannounced plan involving more appropriate state contingent monetary accommodation than another preannounced plan can lead to greater credit today and credit and output in the future. As a stark example, consider a change in policy that prevents bank failures by reducing the real deposit burden by a small amount; this change will increase the ex ante expected return on deposits, as well as credit and output.

Second, because a significant portion of bank liabilities is convertible on demand, banks are susceptible to temporary spikes in the transactions demand for money. By contrast, financial intermediaries with longer maturity liabilities are affected only if a substantial fraction of their liabilities mature together at a time of high transactions demand or shortage of liquidity supply. A financial intermediary with longer-term liabilities that are diversified across maturities will be much less affected by fluctuations in monetary conditions, and they will be less central channels to the conduit of monetary policy.

Third, we have modeled the temporary shock as one to money demand, coming from a surge in supply of cash goods. It could equally well come from a direct increase in the

[11] Note that it is the increase in the interest rate required to keep money from being withdrawn, rather than the price drop of the assets sold in the fire sale (see Diamond, 1997) which is the source of the problem.

demand for cash (for instance, a flight to cash) or from temporary fluctuations in the supply of money.

Finally, more traditional channels through which an exchange of money for bonds can affect the real activity of banks can also be seen in this model. For example, because demand deposits are special—even when uninsured—any kind of reserve requirement on demand deposits will immediately make banks a channel of transmission (also see Stein, 1998). Similarly, if firms have future revenues that are fixed in nominal terms, then a shortage of money can push up the nominal interest rate, reduce their net worth, and thus reduce lending (see Bernanke and Gertler, 1989).

V. Evidence and Robustness

A. Empirical Implications

The model has four important implications.

A Shortage of Real Liquidity Supply Relative to Real Liquidity Demand Causes Bank Fragility. One obvious situation where the demand and supply of liquidity could be mismatched is when neither is under the direct control of monetary authorities and market clearing price adjustments do not insulate banks from liquidity shocks—for example, when the banking system predominantly has foreign currency deposits. One would expect, *ceteris paribus*, a "dollarized" banking system to be more fragile and to have greater deposit volatility than one with domestic currency deposits. Gianni de Nicolo et al. (2003) find this to be the case. Banks in "dollarized" economies are, on average, more fragile: they are closer to default as measured by their Z-score or the ratio of nonperforming loans to total loans. Deposit growth is also more volatile in these countries. An obvious caveat is that more fragile banking systems are more likely to issue foreign currency liabilities, and the authors use instrumental variables to correct for this.

An example of an adverse liquidity supply shock in such countries is a cessation of external capital inflows. There is a strong correlation between such a "sudden stop" to a country, the extent of dollarization of the country's banking system, and the prevalence of banking crises (see Inter-American Development Bank (IADB), 2004).

Finally, one example of a dramatic change in the value of money is a devaluation. In Argentina, by end 2000, an increasingly cash-strapped government with substantial debt service in dollars was tapping into the same dollar pool as the banking system, which had significant dollar liabilities of its own (see Rajan and Ioannis Tokatlidis, 2004, for details). As the recognition dawned that the dollar pool might not be enough at current exchange rates to service all the debt and a devaluation was likely, a domestic currency deposit run started on the banks—the current value of withdrawals (and conversion into goods or dollars) was greater than anticipated future value. Interestingly, dollar deposits were initially more stable, though eventually the knowledge that the dollar shortage would render all banks insolvent caused a more general run.

Unaccommodated Temporary Increases in the Demand for Money Will Cause Banking System Fragility. Reinhold Mueller (1997, p. 326), in his history of the Venetian money market, describes how the sailing of the trading galleys was fixed for July and August. Naturally, this was a time of enormously high transactions demand for money, as merchants strove to buy the goods and bullion to stock the ships. Interestingly, nominal interest rates were very high during this time, causing tremendous pressure on the banks and concentrating bank failures around this time. Soon after the galleys sailed, rates collapsed and pressure eased on the surviving banks.

A Money Supply That Responds Quickly and Elastically to an Increased Demand for Money Will Mitigate Panics and Bank Failures. Champ et al. (1996) examine interest rates and strains on the banking system during periods of "crop moving" in the period 1880–1910 across two systems: the United States, where all U.S. currency was either a direct liability of the U.S. government or banknotes backed by government bonds and, therefore, relatively inelastic; and Canada, where chartered banks were free to issue notes against their general assets. The authors find the greater seasonal variation of Canadian currency (with a peak during the autumn crop moving) was associated with much smoother interest rates. Currency fluctuated less in the United States, resulting in greater fluctuations in interest rates, peaking around the crop-moving period. The banking panics of 1893 and 1907 in the United States indeed occurred during the crop-moving season.

Changes in Monetary Policy Should Most Affect the Lending Decisions of the Least Liquid and Least Creditworthy Banks (low α). Kashyap and Stein (2000) find that the effect of monetary policy on lending is indeed stronger for banks with less liquid balance sheets, that is, banks with lower ratios of securities to assets. Moreover, this effect is primarily due to the smallest (and thus least diversified) banks in their sample.

Other implications are less central. For instance, nominal deposits lend stability only if the monetary authority can be relied upon to be appropriately state contingent. However, if they do not have the necessary acumen or credibility, or have conflicting goals, nominal deposits are destabilizing. This implies that countries with histories of weak monetary management are likely to prefer real deposits (for example, through deposit dollarization) despite the attendant risks because the alternative could be worse (also see Douglas Gale and Xavier Vives, 2002; Olivier Jeanne, 2003; Ricardo Caballero and Arvind Krishnamurthy, 2003). De Nicolo et al. (2003) find that countries with weak institutions, high inflation, and high volatility of inflation "dollarize" more, but have more financial depth (M2/GDP) than similar countries that do not.

B. Alternative Assumptions: Sticky Prices

The pattern of response of aggregate output to monetary expansion has been well studied in the United States (see, for example, Bernanke and Gertler, 1995). One fact that is at odds with our model is that prices do not adjust rapidly. While we think the fact that our model does not require sticky prices to obtain monetary transmission is a virtue, we need to ask how we could get transmission if prices were indeed sticky. It turns out that a simple extension is sufficient.

Consider a very simple search model where dealers first post prices at the beginning of the period and buyers search for a seller. If the price cannot vary with supply or demand changes, goods must be rationed. Assume the probability of a buyer meeting a dealer is an increasing function of the ratio of supply of cash goods to demand at the posted price, P_{02}. The nominal supply of goods at date 0 is $q_1 P_{02}$ and the nominal demand is the total amount of cash withdrawn at date 0 by depositors. An open market operation that increases the amount of cash that can be withdrawn by depositors will decrease the probability of each withdrawer finding a dealer. As this probability decreases, the return from withdrawing cash falls toward the return of holding cash to buy goods one period later, and the nominal interest rate on bank deposits between dates 0 and 1 will fall. The real payout burden on deposits at date 2 falls with an expansionary open market operation, much as in the case of flexible prices. While sticky prices prevent the real price level from changing immediately with changes in monetary policy, an immediate increase in the supply of money will reduce the real value of withdrawing to make an immediate purchase.

C. Alternative Assumptions: Nominal Loans

We have discussed real loans thus far, with nominal or real deposits. This is consistent with the assumption that resources are in short supply so the borrowing entrepreneur promises to pay out the maximum possible ex ante by agreeing to an extremely high nominal repayment on demand. As a result, actual repayments on project loans are renegotiated down to the underlying real collateral value of assets. By contrast, bank deposits are enforced through the threat of collective action, so their nominal face value matters, regardless of how high it is.

It is, however, interesting to discuss whether the system stabilizes automatically through the price level if the nominal repayment on the project loan, L, were set at a level that did not exceed the collateral value of underlying project assets (e.g., $L < CP_{jk}$). We have:

Proposition 5: *If the fiscal demand for money dominates and project loans are always nominal, then:*

(*i*) *If deposits are also nominal, the representative bank will never fail at any $\bar{\alpha}$ if it is solvent and liquid at some $\bar{\alpha}'$.*
(*ii*) *If deposits are real, the representative bank becomes (weakly) less solvent as $\bar{\alpha}$ falls. Even if it is solvent at an $\bar{\alpha}'$, it can fail at some $\bar{\alpha} < \bar{\alpha}'$.*

Proof: See Appendix.

When financial assets are all nominal and effectively have the same maturity, changes in the price level have no effect on a bank's nominal solvency and cannot push a bank from solvency to insolvency (or vice versa). Price level changes will, however, change the real value of deposits and influence the real excess demand for liquidity. So long as there is a binding liquidity constraint, policy-induced increases in the price level will reduce the excess liquidity demand and will increase aggregate credit.

When loans are nominal but deposits are real, an increase in the price level reduces the value of the bank's assets without affecting liabilities. Since, *ceteris paribus*, a fall in the economy-wide fraction of early projects, $\bar{\alpha}$, (weakly) increases the price level, it can impair solvency. Automatic changes in the price level do not stabilize the banking system when it has this kind of asset-liability mismatch.

D. Alternative Assumption: Capital

For simplicity, banks in our model do not issue capital. Clearly, capital can buffer some of the effects of liquidity shortages but it will also reduce the ability of the bank to commit to pay depositors. An optimal capital structure will typically have the bank issuing a significant proportion of its capital structure in deposits (see Diamond and Rajan, 2000) and, as we show in the working paper version of this paper, liquidity shortages are still possible and all our results continue to hold. The issuance of capital (or heterogeneity in project returns) will, however, result in a much smoother and plausible path of real interest rates, r_{24}.[12]

VI. Conclusion

Starting with the problem that banks are vulnerable to real liquidity shortages, we show that they may be able to mitigate this by issuing nominal deposits. Because bank deposits can be converted on demand to money, however, this leaves them exposed to fluctuations in monetary conditions. This suggests a "liquidity" channel of transmission of monetary policy and a role for monetary authorities in smoothing these conditions, even in a world without many of the traditional assumed frictions. Our model suggests why policy would work largely through banks.

There is ample scope for future work in expanding our simple model. For example, we have examined only purchases with currency as the opportunity that causes strains on the banking system. More generally, any opportunities that require immediate nominal liquidity would strain the system, and these deserve exploration. Also, our model ties the health of the banking system to monetary and fiscal policies. We have only touched on monetary policy and have not explored fiscal policy (e.g., changes in the tax rate) at all. Also, we have made a number of strong assumptions to simplify our analysis. The effect of relaxing some assumptions is easy to see. For example, initial investors cannot substitute at all for consumption between dates. If they are willing to postpone consumption once the interest rate rises enough, the destructive effects of liquidity shortages will be capped. Similarly, allowing cash goods to be taxed will simply change the form of the fiscal demand for money. But the effects of relaxing others are harder to anticipate. For instance, we do not have long dated bonds, nor do we incorporate concerns about monetary policy credibility or fiscal performance. Relaxing each of these is a realistic and potentially interesting extension that suggests scope for future work.

References

Allen, Franklin and Gale, Douglas. "Optimal Financial Crises." *Journal of Finance*, 1998, *53*(4), pp. 1245–84.

Bernanke, Ben S. "Non-Monetary Effects of the Financial Crisis in the Propagation of the Great Depression." *American Economic Review*, 1983, *73*(3), pp. 257–76.

Bernanke, Ben S. and Gertler, Mark. "Agency Costs, Net Worth, and Business Fluctuations." *American Economic Review*, 1989, *79*(1), pp. 14–31.

Bernanke, Ben S. and Gertler, Mark. "Inside the Black Box: The Credit Channel of Monetary Policy Transmission." *Journal of Economic Perspectives*, 1995, *9*(4), pp. 27–48.

Caballero, Ricardo J. and Krishnamurthy, Arvind. "Excessive Dollar Debt: Financial Development and Underinsurance." *Journal of Finance*, 2003, *58*(2), pp. 867–94.

Calomiris, Charles W. "Institutional Failure, Monetary Scarcity, and the Depreciation of the Continental." *Journal of Economic History*, 1988, *48*(1), pp. 47–68.

[12]So long as all bank liabilities are held for liquidity purposes, bank capital also introduces an additional channel through which an exchange of money for outstanding bonds can expand credit. In particular, through such an open market operation, the government captures the liquidity premium that would otherwise go to traders, and thus reduces the real value of government liabilities held on bank balance sheets. The reduced value of bank financial assets will translate into a lower value of bank liabilities (deposits plus capital) and hence a lower aggregate liquidity demand.

Champ, Bruce; Smith, Bruce D. and Williamson, Stephen D. "Currency Elasticity and Banking Panics: Theory and Evidence." *Canadian Journal of Economics*, 1996, *29*(4), pp. 828–64.

Clower, Robert W. "A Reconsideration of the Microfoundations of Monetary Theory." *Western Economic Journal*, 1967, *6*(1), pp. 1–8.

Cochrane, John. "Money as Stock." *Journal of Monetary Economics*, 2005, *52*(3), pp. 501–28.

De Nicolo, Gianni; Honohan, Patrick and Ize, Alain. "Dollarization of the Banking System: Good or Bad?" International Monetary Fund, IMF Working Papers: No. 03/146, 2003.

Diamond, Douglas W. "Liquidity, Banks, and Markets." *Journal of Political Economy*, 1997, *105*(5), pp. 928–56.

Diamond, Douglas W. and Dybvig, Philip H. "Bank Runs, Deposit Insurance, and Liquidity." *Journal of Political Economy*, 1983, *91*(3), pp. 401–19.

Diamond, Douglas W. and Rajan, Raghuram G. "A Theory of Bank Capital." *Journal of Finance*, 2000, *55*(6), pp. 2431–65.

Diamond, Douglas W. and Rajan, Raghuram G. "Liquidity Risk, Liquidity Creation, and Financial Fragility: A Theory of Banking." *Journal of Political Economy*, 2001, *109*(2), pp. 287–327.

Diamond, Douglas W. and Rajan, Raghuram G. "Liquidity Shortages and Banking Crises." *Journal of Finance*, 2005, *60*(2), pp. 615–47.

Friedman, Milton and Schwartz, Anna J. *A monetary history of the United States 1867–1960*. Princeton: Princeton University Press, 1963.

Gale, Douglas W. and Vives, Xavier. "Dollarization, Bailouts, and the Stability of the Banking System." *Quarterly Journal of Economics*, 2002, *117*(2), pp. 467–502.

Gibson, Michael S. "More Evidence on the Link between Bank Health and Investment in Japan." *Journal of the Japanese and International Economies*, 1997, *11*(3), pp. 296–310.

Hart, Oliver and Moore, John. "A Theory of Debt Based on the Inalienability of Human Capital." *Quarterly Journal of Economics*, 1994, *109*(4), pp. 841–79.

Inter-American Development Bank. *Unlocking Credit: The Quest for Deep and Stable Bank Lending*. Washington, DC: Inter-American Development Bank, 2004.

Jeanne, Olivier. "Why Do Emerging Economies Borrow in Foreign Currency?" International Monetary Fund, IMF Working Papers: No. 03/177, 2003.

Kashyap, Anil K. and Stein, Jeremy C. "The Role of Banks in Monetary Policy: A Survey with Implications for the European Monetary Union." *Federal Reserve Bank of Chicago Economic Perspectives*, 1997, *21*(5), pp. 2–18.

Kashyap, Anil K. and Stein, Jeremy C. "What Do a Million Observations on Banks Say about the Transmission of Monetary Policy?" *American Economic Review*, 2000, *90*(3), pp. 407–28.

Kashyap, Anil K.; Stein, Jeremy C. and Wilcox, David W. "Monetary Policy and Credit Conditions: Evidence from the Composition of External Finance." *American Economic Review*, 1993, *83*(1), pp. 78–98.

Lucas, Robert E., Jr. and Stokey, Nancy L. "Money and Interest in a Cash-in-Advance Economy." *Econometrica*, 1987, *55*(3), pp. 491–513.

Ludvigson, Sydney. "The Channel of Monetary Transmission to Demand: Evidence from the Market for Automobile Credit." *Journal of Money, Credit and Banking*, 1998, *30*(3), pp. 365–83.

Mueller, Reinhold. *Money and banking in Mediaeval and Renaissance Venice: Volume II—The Venetian money market: Banks, panics and the public debt 1200–1500*. Baltimore: Johns Hopkins University Press, 1997.

Rajan, Raghuram G. and Tokatlidis, Ioannis. "Dollar Shortages and Crises." *International Journal of Central Banking*, 2005, *1*(2).

Romer, Christina D. and Romer, David H. "New Evidence on the Monetary Transmission Mechanism." *Brookings Papers on Economic Activity*, 1990, *0*(1), pp. 149–98.

Skeie, David R. "Money and Modem Bank Runs." Society for Economic Dynamics, 2004 Meeting Paper Series: No. 785, 2004.

Stein, Jeremy C. "An Adverse-Selection Model of Bank Asset and Liability Management with Implications for the Transmission of Monetary Policy." *RAND Journal of Economics*, 1998, *29*(3), pp. 466–86.

Woodford, Michael. "Price-Level Determinacy without Control of a Monetary Aggregate." *Carnegie-Rochester Conference Series on Public Policy*, 1995, *43*(0), pp. 1–46.

Appendix

List of Symbols

C	(After-tax value of) goods produced by entrepreneur with project on maturity
γ	Fraction of entrepreneur's production that can be produced by bank
c	(After-tax value of) goods that can be produced by anyone if the project is restructured
q_j	Cash goods for sale on date $j(j = 1, 3)$
$\theta^{G,s}$	Fraction of G-type banks in state s
$\alpha^{B,s}$	Fraction of early projects in the portfolio of B-type banks (for G-type banks, this is 1)
$\bar{\alpha}$	Fraction of early projects in the portfolio of the representative bank
μ^B	Fraction of late projects restructured by B-type banks (G-type banks have no late projects to restructure)
$\bar{\mu}$	Fraction of late projects restructured by the representative bank
X_t	Total taxable goods produced on date $t(t = 2, 4)$
d_j	Face vale of real deposits due on date j
δ_j	Face vale of nominal deposits due on date j
M_j	Quantity of money available to make purchases on date j
B_j	Face value of bonds (repaying in money) maturing on date j
b_{jk}	Cash value on date j of bond maturing on date k
r_{jk}	Real interest rate between date j and date k
i_{jk}	Nominal interest rate between date j and date k
$R(=\gamma C/c)$	Real interest rate necessary to give B-type banks an incentive to restructure late projects
P_{jk}	The price in date i cash for a unit of date j consumption
t	Tax rate on produced goods

Proof of Proposition 1: We derived the price levels and interest rates after date 2 in the text. To determine the price level at dates prior to date 2, we have to determine the real value of all government liabilities at date 2. Since we already know the value of the money stock, we now determine the value of outstanding bonds.

Let the date-2 value in cash of bonds maturing to pay B_4 at date 4 be b_{24}. Then, because of the competitive market for bonds,

$$b_{24} = \frac{B_4}{i_{24}} = \frac{B_4}{i_{23} * 1} = \frac{B_4}{max\left\{1, \frac{q_3}{\left[\frac{M_2}{(M_2+B_4)}tX_4\right]}\right\}} = B_4 min\left\{1, \frac{tX_4}{q_3}\left(\frac{M_2}{M_2+B_4}\right)\right\}.$$

The real value (in date-4 consumption) of government liabilities leaving date 2 then is:[13]

$$\frac{M_2 + b_{24}}{P_{24}} = \frac{M_2 + B_4 min\left\{1, \frac{tX_4}{q_3}\left(\frac{M_2}{M_2+B_4}\right)\right\}}{P_{24}}$$

[13]To simplify the expressions, we substitute for P_{24} and use $min[1, tX_4M_2/q_3(M_2 + B_4)] = tX_4M_2/[q_3(M_2 + B_4)]$ and $max[q_3, M_2tX_4/(M_2 + B_4)) = q_3$ when the nominal interest rate exceeds 1.

$$= max\left\{q_3 + \frac{B_4}{(M_2 + B_4)}tX_4, tX_4\right\}.$$

The quantity of money and bonds outstanding between dates 0 to 2 is constant at M_0 and B_2, respectively (we will later allow monetary policy to alter these quantities). At date 2, the existing money stock and new money repaid on maturing date-2 bonds can be used to pay date-2 taxes as well as "buy" M_2 and B_4. The value of maturing bonds and money in units of date-2 consumption goods purchased at date 1 is $(M_0 + B_2)/P_{12} = tX_2 + (1/r_{24})max\{q_3 + [B_4/(M_2 + B_4)]tX_4, tX_4\}$ where we use the real interest rate to transform units of date-4 consumption into units of date-2 consumption. Substituting values, we can transform this into the expression for P_{12} in the proposition. At date 0, cash of M_0 can be used to purchase cash goods q_1 at date 1. So its real value in terms of date-2 consumption is given by $M_0/P_{02} = max\{q_1, M_0/P_{12}\}$. Again, if $q_1 > M_0/P_{12}$, money is valued for its transaction services and the nominal interest rate paid by deposits and bonds from date 0 to 1 is $i_{01} = q_1/(M_0/P_{12}) = P_{12}/P_{02} > 1$.

Sketch That (3) Is the Market-Clearing Condition

The claim follows because (i) deposits are also claims to bonds and money (which together are worth the value of taxes and cash goods), and (ii) goods are stored when there is excess supply. To see this, take the simple case where some late projects have to be restructured to meet aggregate liquidity demand, there are no cash goods, and aggregate bank assets just equal deposits. Since the real interest rate exceeds 1, there will be no storage. Now

$$d_2 = \frac{M_0 + B_2}{P_{12}} + \theta^G \gamma C + (1 - \theta^G)\left[\alpha^B \gamma C + \mu^B(1 - \alpha^B)c + (1 - \mu^B)(1 - \alpha^B)\frac{\gamma C}{r_{24}}\right].$$

We know from Proposition 1 that

$$\frac{M_0 + B_2}{P_{12}} = \theta^G \frac{C}{1 - t} + \frac{(1 - \theta^G)}{(1 - t)}\left[\alpha^B C + \mu^B(1 - \alpha^B)c + (1 - \mu^B)(1 - \alpha^B)\frac{C}{r_{24}}\right].$$

Substituting this in the expression for d_2 and rearranging, we get

$$d_2 = \frac{1}{(1-t)}[\theta^G C + (1-\theta^G)(\alpha^B C + (1-\alpha^B)\mu^B c)] - \theta^G(1-\gamma)C - (1-\theta^G)(1-\gamma)\alpha^B C$$
$$+ (1-\theta^G)(1-\mu^B)(1-\alpha^B)\frac{\gamma C}{r_{24}} + \frac{t}{(1-t)}(1-\theta^G)(1-\mu^B)(1-\alpha^B)\frac{C}{r_{24}}.$$

On the right-hand side, the second term and third term are the (negative of) goods left with early entrepreneurs (of *G*-type and *B*-type banks, respectively) after repaying their banks. The fourth term is the value deposited in the *B*-type bank and the last term is the value of future claims on the government that are sold at date 2 ($= tX_4/r_{24} = (M_2 + B_2)/(r_{24}P_{24})$). For the early goods market to clear, the value of future claims sold to early entrepreneurs should equal their holdings of early goods. So the terms on the second line of the right-hand side sum to zero, leaving the condition on the first line that deposits should equal the pre-tax value of early goods produced, which is (3).

Proof of Proposition 2: The aggregate liquidity market clearing condition is: $q_1 + [1/(1-t)]\,[\theta^G C + (1-\theta^G)(\alpha^B C + (1-\alpha^B)\mu^B c)] = d_2$. This implies $\mu^B = [(d_2 - q_1)(1-t) - C(\theta^G + \alpha^B)(1-\theta^G))]/[c(1-\alpha^B)(1-\theta^G)]$. As a result,

$$\frac{\partial \mu^B}{\partial \theta^G} = -\frac{C-(d_2-q_1)(1-t)}{c(1-\alpha^B)(1-\theta^G)^2} < 0 \quad \text{and} \quad \frac{\partial \mu^B}{\partial \alpha^B} = -\frac{C-(d_2-q_1)(1-t)}{c(1-\alpha^B)^2(1-\theta^G)} < 0.$$

These are negative because $C-(d_2-q_1)(1-t) > 0$, which follows because if banks are to avoid failure there must be sufficient liquidity to pay deposits in the best possible case, where all banks are of G-type (which requires that $[(C/(1-t)] + q_1 > d_2)$. Of projects that are late, fewer are restructured (more are continued, $1-\mu^B$ increases) when there is more aggregate liquidity. In addition, more aggregate liquidity increases the total credit $\theta^G + (1-\theta^G)\{\alpha^B + (1-\alpha^B)(1-\mu^B)\}$ because it is directly increasing in θ^G and α^B, and $1-\mu^B$ is increasing in them. Finally, $\partial\mu^B/\partial d_2 = (1-t)/[c(1-\alpha^B)(1-\theta^G)] > 0$. An increase in real deposits requires increased restructuring; this decreases total credit and the fraction of late projects that are continued.

Proof of Proposition 4: When net nominal interest rates are positive, we have the real payout on deposits at date 2, $d_2 = \delta_0 q_1/M_0$. Clearly, this falls as M_0 increases. We showed in the proof of Proposition 2 that a fall in d_2 increases $(1-\mu^B)$, the amount of credit extended at date 2 by the B-type banks, or $\partial\mu^B/\partial d_2 > 0$, and therefore $\partial(1-\mu^B)/\partial M_0|_{M_0+B_2=Const} > 0$.

Proof of Proposition 5: (i) Suppose the nominal face value of a project loan is always L. This means that even when the project is late and the loan is restructured, the entrepreneur repays only L and keeps the residual of $P_{02}c - L$. Suppose also that the representative bank is solvent and liquid when $\bar{\alpha} = 1$. Because it is solvent, $L \geq \delta_2 (= \delta_0)$. Then it is solvent at any other $\bar{\alpha}$. To see this, note that for any realization $\bar{\alpha}$, the bank is solvent if $\bar{\alpha}(L/P_{02}) + (1-\bar{\alpha})\mu(L/P_{02}) + (1-\bar{\alpha})(1-\mu)L * i/r_{24}P_{24} \geq \delta_2/P_{02}$, where i is the nominal interest rate at which the project loan is rolled over for late projects. But the inequality holds if we set $\mu = 1$ because $L \geq \delta_2$. Since there is some μ at which the bank is solvent, and the banker can always choose it rather than be run, the bank will always be solvent. Since the liquidity condition does not depend on the actual repayment to the bank, the argument in footnote 9 is valid even for nominal loans. So if the representative bank is solvent and liquid at some $\bar{\alpha}'$, it is solvent and liquid at any $\bar{\alpha}$.

(ii) Sketch: Since the number of late projects, the fraction restructured, and the real interest rate r_{24} all (weakly) increase as $\bar{\alpha}$ falls, the price level $P_{02} = P_{12} = (M_0 + B_2)/t[X_2 + (X_4/r_{24})]$ will increase. Now the solvency of the bank hinges on the rate i at which loan repayments on late projects are rolled over. Regardless of the precise bargaining process, a plausible assumption is that the value in date-2 consumption goods of the required payment on a continued loan does not increase as the value in date-2 consumption goods of a restructured loan falls. As $\bar{\alpha}$ falls, not only are more projects restructured but also the value in date-2 consumption goods of current nominal loan repayments of L will decrease because P_{02} increases (and hence, so (weakly) will the value in date-2 consumption goods of continued loans), as will the value of the financial assets on the bank's balance sheet. When the deposit repayments are fixed in real terms, the representative bank becomes weakly less solvent.

15 Liquidity and Asset Prices

Nobuhiro Kiyotaki and John Moore[1]

1. Introduction

The quantity of liquid assets (broad money) and the value of fixed assets (such as capital and real estate) fluctuate considerably over the business cycle. Standard asset-pricing models with a representative agent do not pay much attention to monetary matters, nor are they very successful in explaining large procyclical movements in asset prices (at least not with standard utility functions). Beside the volatility of asset prices, there are well-known puzzles in the asset-pricing literature, such as the low risk-free rate puzzle and the equity premium puzzle—puzzles that presume that the underlying economy is nonmonetary.[2] But these puzzles can be related to a traditional question in monetary economics: Why do people hold money, even though the rate of return is low and often dominated by the return on other assets? This article develops a canonical model of a monetary economy, in order to examine the interaction between the circulation of liquid assets, resource allocation, and asset prices.

We broadly define liquid assets, or monetary assets, as any asset that can be readily sold in the market and can be held by a number of people in succession before maturity. When an asset circulates among many people as a means of short-term saving (liquidity), it also serves as a medium of exchange (money): People hold it not for its maturity value, but for its exchange value. Thus we will use liquid asset and monetary asset interchangeably. We ask in what environment is the circulation of monetary assets essential for the smooth running of the economy. Here, we contrast broad monetary assets with other assets solely in terms of their liquidity; how quickly they can be sold in the market. That is, in this article, all assets are real; a broad liquid asset is not denominated in cash, and we ignore the issue of fiat money and inflation.[3]

[1]This article is a development of the Lawrence R. Klein lecture delivered by the first author in April 2002 at Osaka University. We thank Ed Green, Bengt Holmstrom, Narayana Kocherlakota, Neil Wallace, and especially our discussant at the 25th anniversary conference, Mike Woodford, and an anonymous referee for their comments. We also thank Dave Donaldson for his excellent research help. Please address correspondence to: Nobuhiro Kiyotaki, Department of Economics, London School of Economics, Houghton Street, London WC2A 2AE, United Kingdom. E-mail: *n.kiyotaki@lse.ac.uk*.

[2]See Mehra and Prescott (1985), Weil (1989), Campbell et al. (1997), and Campbell (1999).

[3]In a companion paper (Kiyotaki and Moore, 2001), we consider an economy in which the only liquid asset is cash, and we address the determination of the nominal price level. In some popular monetary frameworks,

In order to analyze the role of liquid assets for resource allocation, we consider an economy in which output is produced from two types of asset, capital and land. Capital stock can be accumulated through productive investment, whereas the supply of land is fixed. We depart from a standard model of a stochastic production economy with a representative agent (a real business cycle model) in two respects. First, we assume that only a fraction of agents have a productive investment opportunity to accumulate capital stock at each point in time, even though agents are equally likely to find investment opportunities in the future. We also assume that there is no insurance contingent on the arrival of an investment opportunity. Thus, the economy must transfer purchasing power through financial markets from those who do not have a productive investment opportunity to those who do.[4] The second departure is that, at the time of productive investment, people can sell only a fraction of their capital stock (or equivalently, a claim to the future returns from capital stock). Thus capital stock is an asset with limited liquidity. Investing people may, therefore, face binding liquidity constraints. One interpretation of our model is that the productive investment opportunities disappear so quickly that investing agents do not have enough time to raise funds against their entire capital holding, nor to process an insurance claim, in order to finance new investment. In contrast, land is a liquid asset, and people can raise funds against their entire land holdings at the time of investment.[5]

We show that the circulation of the liquid asset is essential for resource allocation—i.e., the economy is "monetary"—if each agent rarely has a productive investment opportunity, if investing agents can sell only a small fraction of capital, and if the income share of land is small relative to capital. In the monetary economy, people with investment opportunities are liquidity constrained in the equilibrium. Also, there is a liquidity premium: a gap in the expected rates of returns between the illiquid asset (capital) and the liquid asset (land). The expected rate of return on the liquid asset is lower than the time preference rate. These phenomena are closely related. If people anticipate a binding liquidity constraint at the time of investment, they will hold the liquid asset in their portfolios even if its expected rate of return is dominated by that of the illiquid asset, and even if it is lower than their time preference rate, because the liquid asset is more valuable for financing the down payment

such as the cash-in-advance model or the dynamic sticky-price model, the circulation of monetary assets is not indispensable for efficient resource allocation. Other monetary frameworks, overlapping-generations models and random-matching models, do explain why the circulation of money improves efficiency. However, these models are not easy to apply to an economy with well-developed financial markets. Perhaps the closest ancestors of this article are Townsend (1987) and Townsend and Wallace (1987). Although our model does not start from as fundamental assumptions as theirs, our framework is closer to standard business cycle models.

[4]A large part of the asset-pricing literature with credit constraints uses an endowment economy, in which the focus is on risk sharing for households who face idiosyncratic utility shocks or income shocks (Cochrane, 2001). Here, we consider a production economy in which the role of financial markets is to transfer resources to those agents who have a productive investment opportunity. Holmstrom and Tirole (2001) develop a liquidity-based asset-pricing model of a three-period production economy with financial intermediaries in which the arrival of an investment opportunity is contractible. Our analysis largely abstracts from financial intermediation and contingent contracting of this kind in order to concentrate on the dynamic general equilibrium effects. Our framework is perhaps more comparable to a standard asset-pricing model, given that, in our economy, agents are identical ex ante, risk averse, and infinitely lived.

[5]In reality, land (or a claim to the future returns on land) is often less liquid than capital. The term "land" in this article may be taken to represent the productive assets of old and well-established sectors of the economy. Such sectors consist of publicly traded firms; their stock market is well organized and their productive assets are relatively constant. In contrast, the term "capital" might represent the productive assets of new and dynamic sectors of the economy, comprising less-established businesses.

for investment than the illiquid asset. That is, the liquidity constraint for investing agents, the liquidity premium, and the low return on the liquid asset are all equilibrium features of the monetary economy.

In a standard asset price model, an asset price is the expected present value of dividends, where dividends are either exogenous (as in an endowment economy model) or determined in equilibrium without feedback from the asset price itself (as in a real business cycle model). In contrast, in a monetary economy, there is a two-way interaction between asset prices and aggregate quantities. As in the standard framework, the higher future expected dividends are, the higher are asset prices. But, at the same time, the higher are asset prices, the more liquidity there is, which helps transfer resources from those who save to those who invest, thus encouraging aggregate investment and future production. This two-way interaction helps us explain large fluctuations in asset prices and aggregate output.

In the later part of the article, we extend our basic model. We introduce labor as a factor of production and workers as a new group of agents. Workers do not have productive investment opportunities, nor can they borrow against their future wage income. We show that, when the economy is monetary, the workers do not save, while entrepreneurs save using both the liquid asset and the illiquid asset. The difference in savings behavior between workers and entrepreneurs stems from the difference in their respective future investment opportunities: workers, who never invest, do not save because of the low rates of return on assets relative to the time preference rate, whereas entrepreneurs, anticipating binding liquidity constraints, save using assets despite the low rates of return in order to finance the down payment for their future investment. It is not because they have different preferences.

Although our framework does not have nominal assets or nominal price stickiness and the modeling strategy is close to real business-cycle theory, the behavior of our model has some Keynesian features: The circulation of liquid assets plays an essential role in transferring resources from those who save to those who invest (as emphasized in Keynes, 1937); there is an intimate interaction between the goods and asset markets (as in the formulations by Hicks, 1937; Tobin, 1969); and the main savers are not workers but entrepreneurs, including entrepreneurial households (as in Kaldor, 1955–56; Pasinetti, 1962). The main difference from traditional Keynesian approaches is that we systematically deduce these characteristics of a monetary economy from a dynamic general equilibrium model with liquidity constraints.

2. Basic Model

Consider a discrete-time economy with one homogeneous output. There is a continuum of infinitely lived agents with population size of unity. The utility of an agent at date 0 is described by

$$V_0 = E_0\left[\sum_{t=0}^{\infty} \beta^t \ln c_t\right] \tag{15.1}$$

where c_t is his or her consumption at date t, $\beta \in (0, 1)$ is the constant discount factor, $\ln x$ is the natural logarithm of x, and $E_0[x]$ is the expected value of x conditional on information at date 0.

The individual agent produces output from two types of homogeneous asset, capital stock and land, according to a constant returns to scale production function:

$$y_t = a_t k_t'^{\alpha} \ell_t^{1-\alpha}, \quad 0 < \alpha < 1 \tag{15.2}$$

where y_t is output, k_t' is capital stock, and ℓ_t is land used for production. The variable $a_t > 0$ is aggregate productivity, which is common to all individuals. We assume that the aggregate productivity follows a stationary Markov process that fluctuates exogenously in the neighborhood of some constant level. The individual agents own capital and land, and can freely rent capital and land for production in a perfectly competitive rental market. The capital stock depreciates at a constant rate $1 - \lambda \in (0, 1)$. The total supply of land is fixed at L.

Each agent meets an opportunity to invest in capital with probability Π in each period. The arrival of the investment opportunity is independent across periods and across agents. When an agent has a productive investment opportunity, he can convert goods into capital one for one instantaneously.

In order to finance investment, the agent can sell his land and capital holdings, in exchange for goods. But, crucially, the transfer of ownership of capital is not instantaneous; delivery is overnight. This delay opens the door to a potential moral hazard problem. After receiving goods from an agreed sale of capital (in the evening before the overnight transfer of ownership), the agent can abscond and start a new life the next day with a fresh identity and clear record. We assume that he cannot take all his capital with him, though; he can steal at most a fraction $1 - \theta \in (0, 1)$. To ensure that sales agreements are honored, they must be incentive compatible. Hence an investing agent can credibly sell at most a fraction θ of the capital he holds before investment. Equally, he can sell only a fraction θ of the new capital he produces from the investment. The exogenous parameter θ can be thought of as a measure of the liquidity of capital.[6] Note that if θ were to equal unity, then, because the agent could not abscond with any capital, there would be no moral hazard problem, and in effect capital would be perfectly liquid. The transfer of ownership of land is also overnight, but we assume that agents cannot abscond with any land, so that land (or a claim to the future rental income on land) is a liquid asset, which serves as money in our model.

One way to think of the parameter θ is that it reflects how quickly an agent must exploit an investment opportunity once he meets one. The opportunity disappears the next day (although with probability Π he will meet another), and, therefore, he does not have much time to sell capital. In principle he could eventually disinvest his entire capital holding by selling off a fraction θ every period, but this would be too late.

We assume that the arrival of an investment opportunity is not contractible, so that an agent cannot arrange contingent insurance. Again, we are thinking of an environment in which, by the time an insurance company has verified that the agent does indeed have an investment opportunity, the opportunity is gone.[7]

[6] There are other justifications for why capital, or claims secured against capital, may not be perfectly liquid. For example, it may take time to inspect the capital or to verify the authenticity of a claim, in which case θ would be a proxy for the speed of verification. Or there may be different qualities of capital, and buyers may be less informed than sellers so that there is adverse selection in the secondhand market.

[7] Self-reporting insurance arrangements as in Diamond and Dybvig (1983) are not incentive compatible here, because we assume that an insurance company cannot monitor individual transactions in financial markets (Jacklin, 1987; Cole and Kocherlakota, 2001). We will not consider the possibility of insurance payments being made after the investment opportunity has gone, because this kind of insurance is not very useful for improving resource allocation; we expect our main findings are robust to allowing for delayed insurance payments.

Let p_t be price of land, let q_t be the price of capital installed, and let r_t^K and r_t^L be the rental prices of capital and land—all in terms of goods, the numeraire. The flow-of-funds constraint of an agent at date t is

$$\begin{aligned} c_t + i_t + q_t(k_{t+1} - i_t - \lambda k_t) + p_t(m_{t+1} - m_t) \\ = r_t^K k_t + r_t^L m_t + \left(y_t - r_t^K k_t' - r_t^L \ell_t\right) \end{aligned} \tag{15.3}$$

where i_t is investment, m_t and k_t are land and capital owned before investment, and ℓ_t and k_t' are land and capital used for production. The left-hand side is expenditure on consumption and investment plus the net purchase of capital and land. The right-hand side is rental income from capital and land plus the profit from production of goods. Because the agent can rent capital and land for goods production, his usage need not match his capital and land ownership. The constraints governing his ownership of capital and land are

$$k_{t+1} \geq (1 - \theta)(\lambda k_t + i_t) \tag{15.4}$$

$$m_{t+1} \geq 0 \tag{15.5}$$

Inequality (4) says that, since the agent cannot sell more than a fraction θ of his existing (depreciated) stock λk_t or of his new capital i_t, he has to retain at least a fraction $1 - \theta$. Inequality (5) says that he cannot short sell land. Taken together, these inequalities constitute the agent's liquidity constraints.[8]

We will see that the aggregate state of the economy, s_t, is summarized by the aggregate capital stock, K_t, and the aggregate productivity, a_t; $s_t = (K_t, a_t)$. Competitive equilibrium is described as price functions $p_t = p(s_t)$, $q_t = q(s_t)$, $r_t^K = r^K(s_t)$, and $r_t^L = r^L(s_t)$, and quantities of consumption, investment, output, and ownership and usage of capital and land, $(c_t, i_t, y_t, k_t, m_t, k_t', \ell_t)$, such that (i) individual agents choose rules of consumption, investment, asset portfolio, and production to maximize their utility subject to the flow-of-funds constraints (3) and the liquidity constraints (4) and (5), taking the price functions as given; (ii) the sum of the individual capital holdings equals the aggregate capital stock K_t; (iii) the sum of the individual land holdings equals the total land supply L; (iv) aggregate consumption and investment equals aggregate output; and (v) the rental markets for capital and land clear.

The decision by an individual agent of how many goods to produce is straightforward. He chooses output and usage of capital and land to maximize his profit, $y_t - r_t^K k_t' - r_t^L \ell_t$, subject to the production function. Profit is maximized when the marginal products of capital and land equal their rental prices. Maximized profit is zero, so as to be consistent with competitive equilibrium with positive production. That is,

$$r_t^K = \alpha y_t / k_t' \quad \text{and} \quad r_t^L = (1 - \alpha) y_t / \ell_t \tag{15.6}$$

Thus, when the agent does not have an opportunity to invest in capital stock, the flow of funds constraint (3) can be written as

$$c_t^n + q_t k_{t+1}^n + p_t m_{t+1}^n = (r_t^K + \lambda q_t) k_t + (r_t^L + p_t) m_t \equiv b_t^n \tag{15.7}$$

[8] Strictly speaking, to avoid the possibility that the agent might abscond, leaving behind his land plus a fraction θ of his capital, we need to place a lower bound on a combination of k_{t+1} and m_{t+1}: A linear combination of (4) and (5) must hold. But, whenever an agent is credit constrained in equilibrium, (4) and (5) both bind, so nothing is lost by imposing them as separate inequality constraints.

where the superscript n represents an agent without an investment opportunity and b_t is his total wealth.

When the agent has an opportunity to invest at date t, he has two ways of acquiring capital in Equation (3): one through investment at his production cost of unity and the other through the market at the price q_t. If $q_t < 1$, the agent will not invest. The agent is indifferent if $q_t = 1$. Thus, his flow-of-funds constraint is the same as (7) if the agent has an investment opportunity, but $q_t \leq 1$. On the other hand, if $q_t > 1$, the agent will invest and sell as much capital as he can, subject to the constraint (4). Such an agent is liquidity constrained because his investment is limited by his available funds. The investment choice is similar to Tobin's q theory (Tobin, 1969). Tobin's q may exceed unity here, because at each date only a small fraction (Π) of agents have the opportunity to invest in capital stock and they are liquidity constrained. When $q_t > 1$, the flow-of-funds constraint (3) of an investing agent, given that (4) binds, can be written as

$$c_t^i + \frac{1-\theta q_t}{1-\theta} k_{t+1}^i + p_t m_{t+1}^i = \left(r_t^K + \lambda\right) k_t + \left(r_t^L + p_t\right) m_t \equiv b_t^i \tag{15.8}$$

where the superscript i represents an agent with an investment opportunity that is strictly profitable. Think of $[(1-\theta q_t)/(1-\theta)]$ as the cost of investment with maximum leverage: Because the agent sells the maximum fraction θ of each unit of new capital, he needs to finance only the down payment $(1-\theta q_t)$ from his own funds in order to retain the residual fraction $1-\theta$. Capital in total wealth on the right-hand side is valued at the replacement cost λk_t rather than at the market value $q_t \lambda k_t$, given that the agent is unable to sell as much capital as he would wish in the market. Thus, when the agent has an investment opportunity at date t, the rate of return on capital from the last period is $[(r_t^K + \lambda)/q_{t-1}]$ rather than $[(r_t^K + \lambda q_t)/q_{t-1}]$.

In what follows, we concentrate on the case where Tobin's q exceeds unity so that the liquidity constraint is binding for the investing agents; we will later derive the condition that guarantees $q_t > 1$.

When an agent does not have an investment opportunity at date t, he chooses between consumption and saving in order to maximize his expected utility. The marginal utility of consumption must be equal to the expected marginal benefit of acquiring capital and land:

$$\frac{1}{c_t^n} = \frac{1}{q_t} \beta E_t \left(\Pi \frac{r_{t+1}^K + \lambda}{c_{t+1}^{ni}} + (1-\Pi) \frac{r_{t+1}^K + \lambda q_{t+1}}{c_{t+1}^{nn}} \right) \tag{15.9a}$$

$$\frac{1}{c_t^n} = \frac{1}{p_t} \beta E_t \left(\Pi \frac{r_{t+1}^L + p_{t+1}}{c_{t+1}^{ni}} + (1-\Pi) \frac{r_{t+1}^L + p_{t+1}}{c_{t+1}^{nn}} \right) \tag{15.9b}$$

where c_{t+1}^{ni}(resp. c_{t+1}^{nn}) is the date $t+1$ consumption of the agent, who does not have an investment opportunity at date t, if he turns out to have an investment opportunity at date $t+1$ (resp. if he still doesn't have an investment opportunity at date $t+1$). Because utility is the logarithm of consumption, marginal utility is the inverse of consumption on the left-hand sides of the above equations. On the right-hand side of Equation (9a), the agent can acquire $(1/q_t)$ units of capital by giving up one unit of consumption at date t. With probability Π, the agent has an investment opportunity at date $t+1$, and the return on capital becomes $r_{t+1}^K + \lambda$ with a marginal utility of $(1/c_{t+1}^{ni})$. With probability $1-\Pi$, the agent does not have an investment opportunity at date $t+1$, and the return on capital is

$r_{t+1}^K + \lambda q_{t+1}$ with a marginal utility of $(1/c_{t+1}^{nn})$. On the right-hand side of Equation (9b), the return on land is always equal to $r_{t+1}^L + p_{t+1}$, given that land is liquid.[9]

When an agent has an investment opportunity at date t, he chooses between consumption and investment with maximum leverage:

$$\frac{1}{c_t^i} = \frac{1-\theta}{1-\theta q_t}\beta E_t\left(\Pi\frac{r_{t+1}^K + \lambda}{c_{t+1}^{ii}} + (1-\Pi)\frac{r_{t+1}^K + \lambda q_{t+1}}{c_{t+1}^{in}}\right) \tag{15.10}$$

where c_{t+1}^{ii}(resp. c_{t+1}^{in}) is the date $t+1$ consumption of the agent, who has an investment opportunity at date t, if he turns out also to have an investment opportunity at date $t+1$ (resp. if he doesn't have an investment opportunity at date $t+1$). In Equation (10), the agent can acquire $(1-\theta)/(1-\theta q_t)$ units of capital by giving up one unit of consumption with maximum leverage. The investing agent will not hold any land, if the marginal cost of acquiring land exceeds the marginal benefit:

$$\frac{1}{c_t^i} > \frac{1}{p_t}\beta E_t\left(\Pi\frac{r_{t+1}^L + p_{t+1}}{c_{t+1}^{ii}} + (1-\Pi)\frac{r_{t+1}^L + p_{t+1}}{c_{t+1}^{in}}\right) \tag{15.11}$$

Later, we will verify that inequality (11) holds.

From Equations (7)–(11), we can show that

$$c_t^n = (1-\beta)b_t^n \tag{15.12a}$$

$$c_t^i = (1-\beta)b_t^i \tag{15.12b}$$

$$m_{t+1}^i = 0 \tag{15.13a}$$

$$(1-\theta q_t)i_t = \left(r_t^K + \theta\lambda q_t\right)k_t + \left(r_t^L + p_t\right)m_t - c_t^i \tag{15.13b}$$

$$(1-\Pi)E_t\left(\frac{\frac{r_{t+1}^K+\lambda q_{t+1}}{q_t} - \frac{r_{t+1}^L+p_{t+1}}{p_t}}{\left(r_{t+1}^K + \lambda q_{t+1}\right)k_{t+1}^n + \left(r_{t+1}^L + p_{t+1}\right)m_{t+1}^n}\right)$$

$$= \Pi E_t\left(\frac{\frac{r_{t+1}^L+p_{t+1}}{p_t} - \frac{r_{t+1}^K+\lambda}{q_t}}{\left(r_{t+1}^K + \lambda\right)k_{t+1}^n + \left(r_{t+1}^L + p_{t+1}\right)m_{t+1}^n}\right) \tag{15.14}$$

In Equations (12a) and (12b), consumption is proportional to the total wealth.[10] In Equations (13a) and (13b), the investing agent holds no land and uses all his funds after consumption to finance downpayment for investment. Equation (14) describes the portfolio decision of the agent who does not have an investment opportunity at date t, which is derived from (9). The numerator in the bracket on the left-hand side represents how much the rate of return on

[9]On a day immediately after investment, an agent holds only capital stock and no land. Then, even if he no longer has an investment opportunity, (4) may be binding, in which case Equation (9a) becomes an inequality. In examining the aggregate economy, we will ignore this because the proportion of such agents is small when Π is not large. For most of our comparative static and dynamic analysis, we use the continuous-time approximation, where we can show that the effects of such agents on the aggregate economy is infinitesimal.

[10]The logarithmic utility in (1) is isomorphic to a Cobb–Douglas utility function, where the expenditure share of present consumption is constant and equal to $1/(1+\beta+\beta^2+\cdots) = 1-\beta$.

capital exceeds that of land if there is no investment opportunity at date $t+1$ (which happens with probability $1-\Pi$). Because marginal utility equals the inverse of consumption (which is proportional to total wealth from (12a)), the left-hand side is the expected advantage of capital over land in terms of utility (times a constant $1-\beta$), if there is no investment opportunity in the next period. The right-hand side is the expected advantage of land over capital when the agent meets an investment opportunity in the next period (which happens with probability Π).

Since the arrival of the productive investment opportunity is independent across agents, we can aggregate the individuals' investment functions (13b):

$$(1-\theta q_t)I_t = \Pi\left(\left(r_t^K+\theta\lambda q_t\right)K_t+(r_t^L+p_t)L-(1-\beta)\left[\left(r_t^K+\lambda\right)K_t+\left(r_t^L+p_t\right)L\right]\right) \tag{15.15}$$

where I_t is aggregate investment. Equation (15) shows that when investing agents are liquidity constrained, aggregate investment is an increasing function of capital price and land price. This two-way interaction between aggregate investment and asset prices is an important propagation channel for the effects of shocks on aggregate output.[11] The aggregate capital stock evolves over time as

$$K_{t+1} = I_t + \lambda K_t \tag{15.16}$$

Market-clearing condition for capital holdings implies

$$K_{t+1} = (1-\theta)(I_t+\Pi\lambda K_t)+K_{t+1}^n \tag{15.17}$$

where K_{t+1}^n is the aggregate date $t+1$ capital holdings of the agents who did not have an investment opportunity at date t. The first term on the right-hand side is the aggregate capital holdings of the agents who do have an investment opportunity and who face the binding liquidity constraint (4), which is a $1-\theta$ fraction of new capital (I_t) and capital held from the previous period ($\Pi\lambda K_t$).

Through the competitive rental markets for capital and land, both the marginal products are equalized across producers. Thus aggregate output Y_t is a function of aggregate capital stock:

$$Y_t = a_t K_t^{\alpha} L^{1-\alpha} \tag{15.18}$$

In these rental markets, prices equal marginal products:

$$r_t^K = \alpha Y_t/K_t \tag{15.19a}$$

$$r_t^L = (1-\alpha)Y_t/L \tag{15.19b}$$

Aggregating the individuals' consumption and investment, we have the goods-market-clearing condition:

$$Y_t = I_t + (1-\beta)\left(\left[r_t^K+\Pi\lambda+(1-\Pi)\lambda q_t\right]K_t+\left(r_t^L+p_t\right)L\right) \tag{15.20}$$

[11]There is a similar two-way interaction in our earlier article, (Kiyotaki and Moore, 1997), but there the mechanism relied on the fact that debt could not be indexed to asset prices. There is no such ad hoc restriction here.

All the land is held by the agents who do not have an investment opportunity. Their portfolio behavior (14) is now

$$(1-\Pi)E_t\left(\frac{\frac{r^K_{t+1}+\lambda q_{t+1}}{q_t}-\frac{r^L_{t+1}+p_{t+1}}{p_t}}{\left(r^K_{t+1}+\lambda q_{t+1}\right)K^n_{t+1}+\left(r^L_{t+1}+p_{t+1}\right)L}\right)$$

$$=\Pi E_t\left(\frac{\frac{r^L_{t+1}+p_{t+1}}{p_t}-\frac{r^K_{t+1}+\lambda}{q_t}}{\left(r^K_{t+1}+\lambda\right)K^n_{t+1}+\left(r^L_{t+1}+p_{t+1}\right)L}\right) \tag{15.21}$$

A competitive equilibrium of our economy in the aggregate is described recursively as prices (p_t, q_t, r_t^L, r_t^K) and aggregate quantities $(I_t, K_{t+1}, K^n_{t+1}, Y_t)$, all as functions of the aggregate state (K_t, a_t), which satisfy (15)–(21), together with an exogenous evolution of aggregate productivity a_t.

It is worth remarking that our model is almost as simple as standard asset-pricing models of a production economy, real business cycle models, and IS-LM models. The main difference from standard asset-pricing models (such as Merton, 1975; Brock, 1982) is the portfolio behavior, which takes into account the illiquidity of capital in financing investment, Equation (21). Our model differs from standard real business cycle models (such as Kydland and Prescott, 1982) because we have a two-way interaction between asset prices and aggregate quantities. In a typical real business cycle model, quantities are determined first, before deriving implied prices. In this aspect, our model is closer to traditional IS-LM models (in particular to Tobin, 1969, where q is the key variable linking goods market equilibrium and asset market equilibrium). Our framework, however, differs substantively (beyond modeling strategy) because, while IS-LM compares cash and interest-bearing assets in determining the nominal interest rate, we draw a contrast between broad liquid assets and illiquid assets in determining the liquidity premium.[12]

Before analyzing dynamics in the next section, let us examine the steady-state equilibrium for constant aggregate productivity, $a_t \equiv a$. In steady state, capital stock is constant so that $I = (1-\lambda)K$, and

$$(1-\theta q)(1-\lambda)K = \Pi((r^K+\theta\lambda q)K + (r^L+p)L - (1-\beta)[(r^K+\lambda)K + (r^L+p)L]) \tag{15.22a}$$

$$aK^\alpha L^{1-\alpha} = (1-\lambda)K + (1-\beta)([r^K + \Pi\lambda + (1-\Pi)\lambda q]K + (r^L+p)L) \tag{15.22b}$$

$$\frac{r^K+\lambda q}{q} - \frac{r^L+p}{p} = \Pi\lambda\frac{q-1}{q}\left\{1+\left(\frac{r^L+p}{p}-\frac{r^K+\lambda}{q}\right)\left(\frac{qK^n}{(r^K+\lambda)K^n+(r^L+p)L}\right)\right\} \tag{15.22c}$$

$$r^L = (1-\alpha)aK^\alpha L^{-\alpha} \tag{15.22d}$$

[12] In this respect, we are close to Keynes (1937), who defines "money" broadly as liquid assets, including Treasury bills.

$$r^K = \alpha a K^{\alpha-1} L^{1-\alpha} \tag{15.22e}$$

$$K^n = [1 - (1-\theta)(1 - \lambda + \lambda\Pi)]K \tag{15.22f}$$

From these conditions, we can show the following proposition:

Proposition 1: *Suppose that the parameters of the economy satisfy:*

$$\theta < \theta^* \equiv 1 - \frac{\Pi}{1 - \lambda + \Pi\lambda}\left(1 + \frac{1-\alpha}{\alpha}\frac{1-\beta\lambda}{1-\beta}\right) \qquad \text{(Assumption 1)}$$

Then, in the steady-state equilibrium

(i) *Tobin's q exceeds* 1, *so that investing agents are liquidity constrained;*
(ii) $\frac{r^L}{p} < \frac{r^K}{q} - (1-\lambda) < \frac{1-\beta}{\beta}$;
(iii) $K < K^*$, *where K^* is the capital stock in the first-best steady state, which solves* $\alpha a (K^*)^{\alpha-1} L^{1-\alpha} = (1/\beta) - \lambda$;
(iv) *investing agents do not hold land at the end of the period,* $m^i_{t+1} = 0$.

Proof: See Part A of the Appendix.

Assumption 1 requires that the fraction of capital that agents can sell in order to finance their investment is smaller than some critical level θ^*. The value of θ^* is a decreasing function both of the arrival rate of investment opportunities, Π, and of the ratio of the land value to capital in a first-best allocation, $(\frac{1-\alpha}{1-\beta})/(\frac{\alpha}{1-\beta\lambda})$. Thus, Proposition 1(i) says that investing agents are liquidity constrained if and only if capital is sufficiently illiquid in relation to the arrival rate of investment opportunities and the ratio of land value to capital. Proposition 1(ii) says that the rate of return on the liquid asset, land, is dominated by the rate of return on the illiquid asset, capital, which in turn is smaller than the time preference rate. The gap between the rates of returns on illiquid and liquid assets may be called the liquidity premium, which arises if and only if investing agents are liquidity constrained. From (22c), the magnitude of the liquidity premium is roughly equal to $\Pi(q-1)$, which can be substantial.[13] Proposition 1(iii) says that there is underinvestment relative to the first-best allocation if the investing agents' liquidity constraints are binding: Not enough resources are transferred from savers to investors. All of these features—liquidity constraints, liquidity premium, low liquid asset return, underinvestment—are features of a "monetary economy," in which the circulation of a liquid asset is essential for the smooth running of the economy.

The reverse of Proposition 1 is also true. Suppose that $\theta \geq \theta^*$. Then the steady-state equilibrium is the first-best allocation. Tobin's q equals 1 and the investing agents are not liquidity constrained. The rates of returns on capital and land are both equal to the time preference rate. (Incidentally, notice that if $\theta > (1-\Pi) \times (1-\lambda)/(1-\lambda+\Pi\lambda)$ the economy achieves first-best even if the liquid asset, land, is unimportant for production, $\alpha \cong 1$. In this case, the economy ceases to be monetary in the sense that the circulation of a liquid asset is no longer necessary for an efficient allocation.)

[13]For example, if Tobin's q is 5% above 1 and each agent has an investment opportunity once every 2 years on average, then the liquidity premium is 2.5% at an annual rate.

3. Dynamics

We now examine the dynamics of the economy with stochastic fluctuations in aggregate productivity a_t. Let us assume that a_t follows a two-point Markov process:

$$a_t = \text{either } a(1+\Delta_a), \quad \text{or} \quad a(1-\Delta_a), \text{ where } \Delta_a \in (0, 1) \text{ is small} \tag{15.23}$$

and the arrival of the productivity changes follows a Poisson process with arrival rate $\bar{\eta}$.

There are two ways to investigate the dynamics. One is to calibrate the recursive equilibrium system, $(p_t, q_t, r_t^L, r_t^K, I_t, Y_t, K_{t+1}, K_{t+1}^n)$, as functions of the aggregate state (K_t, a_t), that satisfies Equations (15)–(21).

The other way is to use analytical methods, in a continuous-time approximation. Let the length of a period be Δ instead of 1, and define the continuous-time parameters ρ, δ, π and η that satisfy

$$\beta = e^{-\rho\Delta}, \quad \lambda = e^{-\delta\Delta}, \quad \Pi = 1 - e^{-\pi\Delta}, \quad \bar{\eta} = 1 - e^{-\eta\Delta} \tag{15.24}$$

The parameter ρ is time preference rate, δ is depreciation rate, π is the Poisson arrival rate of an investment opportunity for each agent, and η is the arrival rate of an aggregate productivity shock. We assume that Assumption 1 holds with strict inequality in the continuous time limit, so that investing agents are always liquidity constrained in the neighborhood of the steady-state equilibrium:

$$\theta < \tilde{\theta}^* \equiv 1 - \frac{\pi}{\pi+\delta}\left(1 + \frac{1-\alpha}{\alpha}\frac{\rho+\delta}{\rho}\right) \tag{Assumption 1$'$}$$

We also assume that the arrival rate of an investment opportunity is greater than the depreciation rate:

$$\pi > \delta \tag{Assumption 2}$$

Assumption 2 is a mild condition. For example, if the depreciation rate is 10% a year, the arrival rate of investment opportunity for each agent is more frequent than once every 10 years.

Define I_t and Y_t as the investment and output rates. Let r_t^K and r_t^L be the rental prices of capital and land per unit of time. Take the limit of the aggregate equilibrium as Δ goes to 0. Then we have

$$(1-\theta q_t)I_t = \pi(\theta q_t K_t + p_t L) \tag{15.25}$$

$$\dot{K}_t = I_t - \delta K_t \tag{15.26}$$

$$K_t^n = K_t \tag{15.27}$$

$$Y_t = I_t + \rho(q_t K_t + p_t L) \tag{15.28}$$

$$\frac{r_t^K}{q_t} - \delta - \frac{r_t^L}{p_t} + \lim_{dt\to 0} E_t\left(\frac{1}{dt}\left(\frac{q_{t+dt}}{q_t} - \frac{p_{t+dt}}{p_t}\right)\frac{q_t K_t + p_t L}{q_{t+dt}K_t + p_{t+dt}L}\right)$$
$$= \pi\left(1 - \frac{1}{q_t}\right)\frac{q_t K_t + p_t L}{K_t + p_t L} \tag{15.29}$$

Equations (18) and (19) are unchanged except that a_t is aggregate productivity per unit of time. In Equation (25), the investing agents use maximum sales of capital and land to finance the downpayment of investment. Because the fraction of agents who invest in an infinitesimal period $[t, t+dt]$ is equal to $\pi\ dt$ (which is infinitesimal), effectively all the capital stock is owned by the agents who do not have an investment opportunity in Equation (27). The left-hand side of (29) is the liquidity premium: the difference between the expected rates of return on capital and land, taking into account risk aversion. The right-hand side is the expected "capital loss" on illiquid capital if an investment opportunity arrives. When the agent has an investment opportunity (with arrival rate π), the implied value of capital falls from q_t to 1, and the holder suffers from the capital loss of $1-(1/q_t)$. (Liquid land does not suffer such a capital loss.) This is adjusted by the marginal rate of substitution between consumption with an investment opportunity and consumption without an opportunity. As a check, in Part C of the Appendix we lay out a model of a continuous time economy in order to derive the above equations directly, instead of taking a limit of the discrete time economy.

Because it is easier to analyze the model in intensive form, let us define $i_t = I_t/K_t$ (i_t is now the investment rate, not investment by an individual agent), $v_t = P_t/K_t$ (ratio of land value to capital), and $x_t = Y_t/K_t$ (ratio of output to capital). Equations (25), (26), (18), (28), and (29), respectively, become

$$(1-\theta q_t)i_t = \pi(\theta q_t + v_t) \tag{15.30}$$

$$\dot{K}_t/K_t = i_t - \delta \tag{15.31}$$

$$x_t = a_t K_t^{\alpha-1} L^{1-\alpha} = i_t + \rho(q_t + v_t) \tag{15.32}$$

$$\left[\frac{\alpha}{q_t} - \frac{1-\alpha}{v_t}\right] x_t - i_t + \lim_{dt\to 0} E_t\left(\frac{1}{dt}\left(\frac{q_{t+dt}}{q_t} - \frac{v_{t+dt}}{v_t}\right)\frac{q_t+v_t}{q_{t+dt}+v_{t+dt}}\right)$$
$$= \pi\frac{q_t-1}{q_t}\frac{q_t+v_t}{1+v_t} \tag{15.33}$$

We now examine a linearized dynamic system in the neighborhood of the steady state. Using $\hat{x}_t$ to denote the proportional deviation of variable x_t from the steady-state value x, i.e., $\hat{x}_t \equiv (x_t - x)/x$, we can postulate the endogenous variables as functions of the state variables:

$$\hat{i}_t = \phi\hat{K}_t + \psi\hat{a}_t \tag{15.34a}$$

$$\hat{v}_t = \phi_v\hat{K}_t + \psi_v\hat{a}_t \tag{15.34b}$$

$$\hat{q}_t = \phi_q\hat{K}_t + \psi_q\hat{a}_t \tag{15.34c}$$

From (23), (24), (31), and (32),

$$d\hat{x}_t = d\hat{a}_t - (1-\alpha)\delta\hat{i}_t dt \tag{15.35}$$

Equation (35) says that the proportional change of the output/capital ratio in an infinitesimal period $[t, t+dt]$ is equal to the proportional change in productivity (if the productivity shock occurs) plus the effect on capital accumulation through investment.

In Part B of the Appendix, we show that there is a unique negative ϕ that satisfies saddle-point stability of the dynamic system. (If ϕ were positive, the growth rate of capital stock would be an increasing function of capital stock, which would make the economy unstable.) Part B of the Appendix also shows

$$\psi > 0 \quad (15.36)$$

$$\psi_v < 0 \quad (15.37)$$

Inequality (36) implies that the investment rate (I_t/K_t) is an increasing function of aggregate productivity. Inequality (37) implies that the ratio of land value to capital stock is a decreasing function of capital stock, even though the total land values may increase with capital stock.

The stochastic process of asset prices and aggregate quantities are described by the recursive rules (34) together with the evolution of aggregate productivity (23) and (24). It is surprisingly difficult to derive the signs of the other values, ϕ_v, ϕ_q, and ψ_q, in (34) generally. But, for reasonable parameters, Figure 15.1 summarizes the typical fluctuations of aggregate quantities and prices.

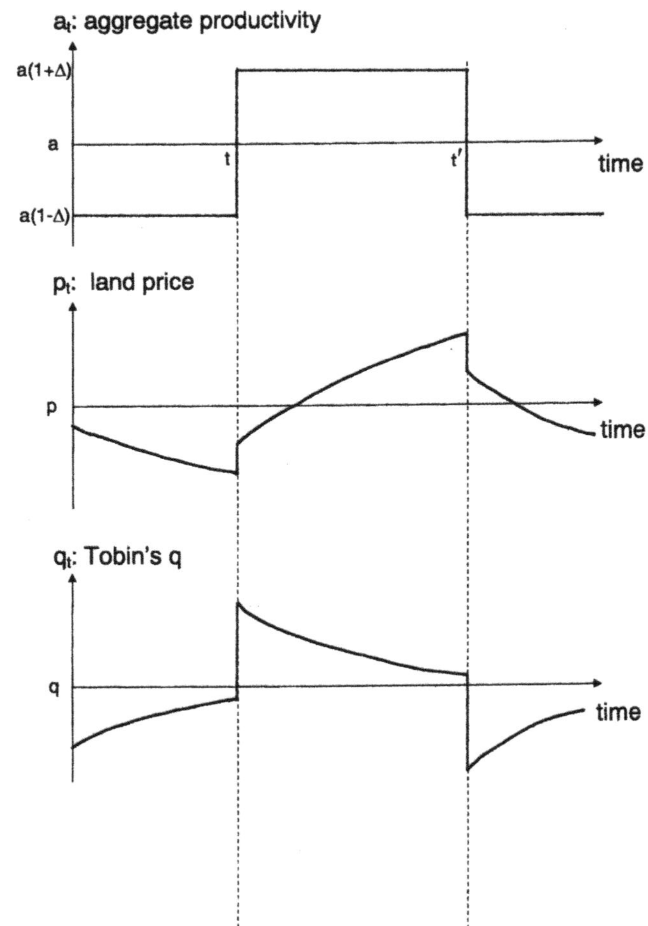

Figure 15.1. Response to productivity shocks. (*Continued*)

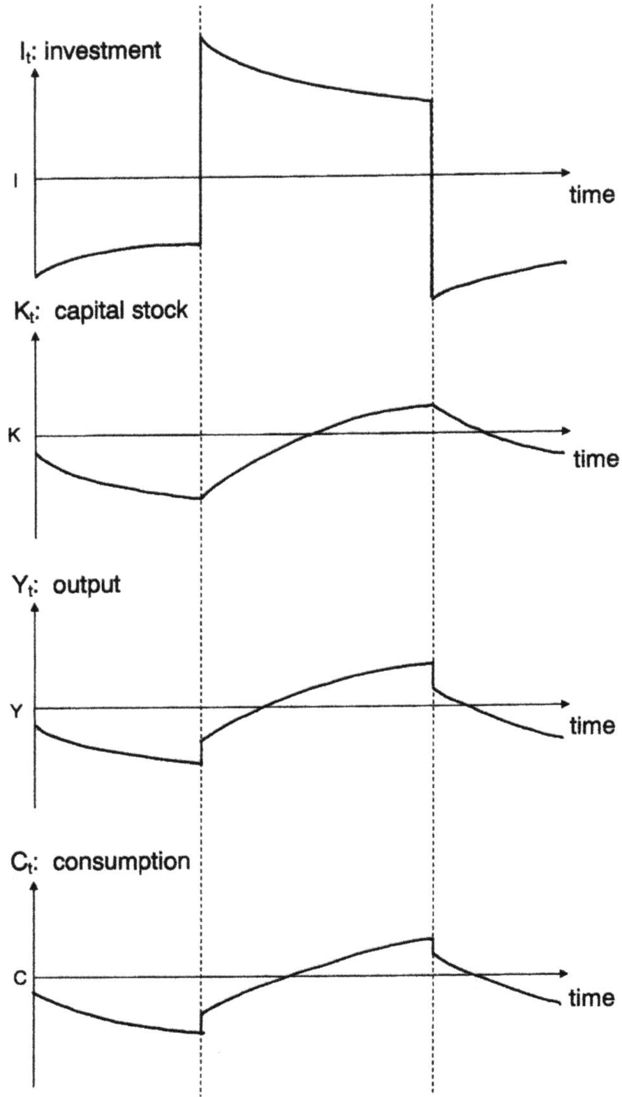

Figure 15.1. Continued

When the productivity rises to a higher level at date t, such a change is considered good news, even if people anticipate occasional changes of the productivity. The prices of capital and land rise discontinuously. Investment increases vigorously, because the investing entrepreneurs can raise more funds against land and capital. Output and consumption also increase but, proportionately, not as much as investment. After date t, capital stock starts accumulating with the increased investment. With capital accumulation, output, consumption, and land price further increase. On the other hand, Tobin's q starts falling to a normal level as the liquidity constraint loosens with the capital accumulation—that is, until a negative productivity shock arrives and the above dynamics reverse.

For applications to asset pricing, it is perhaps more natural to suppose that aggregate productivity follows a geometric Brownian motion, instead of a two-point Markov process:

$$da_t = \sigma a_t dz_t \tag{15.38}$$

where z_t is a Wiener process and $\sigma > 0$ is the standard deviation of the innovation in aggregate productivity. Such an economy can be seen as the economy of Merton (1975), but with limited liquidity of capital stock. With this stochastic process of productivity, we no longer can presume that the investing agents are always liquidity constrained. Depending on the state of the economy, the investing agents may invest up to the maximum, may invest without a liquidity constraint, or may not invest at all. In Part C of the Appendix, we derive some preliminary results for such an economy.

4. Workers

We now introduce workers into the basic model from Section 2. Suppose that output is produced from homogeneous capital, land, and labor, according to the aggregate production function

$$Y_t' = a_t' K_t^{\alpha'} L_t^{\gamma'} N_t^{1-\alpha'-\gamma'}, \quad \alpha', \gamma', 1-\alpha'-\gamma' > 0 \tag{15.39}$$

where Y_t', is aggregate output, K_t is capital, L_t is land, and N_t is labor. Suppose also that there is a continuum of a new group of people, called workers, with a population size of unity. The workers supply labor, but they never have investment opportunities. The utility of a worker at date 0 is described by

$$E_0\left(\sum_{t=0}^{\infty} \beta^t u\left(c_t - \frac{\omega}{1+\nu} N_t^{1+\nu}\right)\right), \quad \nu, \omega > 0 \tag{15.40}$$

where c_t is consumption, N_t is labor supplied, and $u(\cdot)$ is an instantaneous utility function satisfying $u' > 0$, $u'' < 0$, $u'(0) = \infty$ and $u'(\infty) = 0$. We assume that the workers cannot borrow against their future wage income. Let the agents described in the basic model, those who do meet investment opportunities, be called entrepreneurs.

There is a competitive labor market in which the producing entrepreneurs hire labor. The real wage rate, w_t, equals both the marginal product of labor and the marginal disutility of labor

$$(1-\alpha'-\gamma') a_t' K_t^{\alpha'} L_t^{\gamma'} N_t^{-(\alpha'+\gamma')} = w_t = \omega N_t^{\nu} \tag{15.41}$$

Define the gross profit of entrepreneurs, Y_t, as the aggregate output minus the aggregate wage for the workers. Then from (39), we have

$$Y_t \equiv Y_t' - w_t N_t = a_t (K_t^{\alpha} L^{1-\alpha})^{\frac{(\alpha'+\gamma')(1+\nu)}{\alpha'+\gamma'+\nu}} \tag{15.42}$$

where

$$\alpha \equiv \frac{\alpha'}{\alpha'+\gamma'} \quad \text{and} \quad a_t \equiv (\alpha'+\gamma')\left(\frac{1-\alpha'-\gamma'}{\omega}\right)^{\frac{1-\alpha'-\gamma'}{\alpha'+\gamma'+\nu}} a_t'^{\frac{1+\nu}{\alpha'+\gamma'+\nu}}$$

Note that because there is no income effect in the labor supply of workers, we have been able to write down the gross profit function as a function of capital and land. And since the marginal disutility of labor is an increasing function of labor ($\nu > 0$), the gross profit function has decreasing returns to scale in capital and land, i.e., $(\alpha' + \gamma')(1 + \nu)/(\alpha' + \gamma' + \nu) < 1$. Think of α as the income share of capital in gross profit, and $1 - \alpha$ as the share of land. Note that from the entrepreneur's perspective, this economy is the same as that in the basic model without workers.

As in Section 3, let us suppose that the aggregate productivity shock a_t follows the two-point Markov process (23), where the shock Δ_a is small, so that we are in a neighborhood of steady state. The interesting case is where liquidity constraints bind—we later derive the condition that guarantees this—with the implication that the equilibrium rates of return on land and capital are both lower than the time preference rate.

Because the returns on assets are low, the workers will not save at all, i.e., they always consume their entire wage income. (This is provided the arrival of an aggregate productivity switch is not so frequent that there is a large incentive to smooth consumption.) Notice that workers save nothing not because they are myopic or irrational, but rather because they do not expect any future investment opportunities and the rates of return on land and capital are lower than their time preference rate. Remember that the workers' time preference rate is the same as the entrepreneurs'. The feature that entrepreneurs save whereas workers do not is common in the Keynesian literature, e.g., Kaldor (1955–56) and Pasinetti (1962). The difference between our model and this traditional literature is that we derive differences in saving patterns as the equilibrium outcome of a liquidity-contained economy, rather than making ad hoc assumptions about differences in propensities to save.

In the goods market, aggregate output is the sum of investment and consumption by entrepreneurs and workers. Because the consumption of workers equals their wage income, goods-market clearing is equivalent to the condition that the gross profit (aggregate output minus wage income) equals investment and entrepreneurs' consumption:

$$Y_t = I_t + (1 - \beta)\left(\left[r_t^K + \pi\lambda + (1 - \pi)\lambda q_t\right] K_t + (r_t^L + p_t)L\right) \tag{15.43}$$

This equation is same as the goods-market-clearing condition from the basic model, Equation (20), except that Y_t represents gross profit rather than aggregate output. Moreover, given that workers neither save nor hold assets, the entrepreneurs hold all the assets, so the asset-market-clearing condition is unchanged from Section 2. That is, competitive equilibrium is described recursively by $(p_t, q_t, r_t^L, r_t^K, I_t, Y_t, K_{t+1})$ as functions of aggregate states (K_t, a_t) that satisfy Equations (15)–(17), (19), (21), (42), and (43). Proposition 1 still holds: Assumption 1 continues to be the condition for the liquidity constraint to be binding in the neighborhood of the steady state.

Arguably, we may have gone too far in predicting that workers do not save at all. In reality, workers do hold some liquid assets (money), albeit they may not hold illiquid assets. How can this be explained? One way might be to suppose that the aggregate productivity shock Δ_a were larger, or that instead of a Poisson arrival there were continuous shocks (as in geometric Brownian motion), in which cases, as in a buffer stock model, workers would save in order to smooth their consumption, despite the low returns on assets (see Bewley, 1977, 1980, 1983; Carroll, 1992; Deaton, 1992). However, in the usual buffer stock model there is only one means of saving. By itself, this would not necessarily explain why workers choose to save holding mainly liquid assets.

Alternatively, we can extend our model to give workers (small) investment opportunities of their own. Consider the continuous-time version of our model from Section 3.

Suppose that each worker suffers a "health" shock according to a Poisson process with arrival rate ε. Following a shock, a worker has to spend ζ goods instantaneously in order to maintain his human capital. There is then a time interval T during which he is immune from shocks, where the equilibrium wage greatly exceeds ζ/T. Thereafter, times revert to normal, i.e., the worker faces the possibility of a further shock, again with arrival rate ε. Shocks cannot be contracted on, so workers can only insure themselves through saving. We restrict attention to the case where ε and ζ are sufficiently small that the economy continues to be monetary, under Assumption 1′.

Then we can show that, (i) in normal times, a worker holds liquid assets worth ζ, which he sells to meet a shock when it arrives; (ii) following the shock, during the period of immunity, he steadily accumulates a liquid asset holding that is worth ζ by the end of the interval T; and (iii) the worker never holds the illiquid asset. Intuitively, the worker need not save more than ζ units of the liquid asset, given that its rate of return (and that of the illiquid asset) is below his time preference rate. And he does not save in the illiquid asset, even though it yields a higher expected return than the liquid asset, because

$$\frac{1}{\theta}\left\{\rho+\delta-E_t\left[\frac{r_t^K dt+dq_t}{q_t dt}\right]\right\}>\rho-E_t\left[\frac{r_t^L dt+dp_t}{p_t dt}\right] \tag{15.44}$$

Inequality (44) says that the opportunity cost of holding $1/\theta$ units of capital is greater than the opportunity cost of holding one unit of land (remember that the agent can sell only a fraction θ of capital in order to meet the cost ζ of the shock). In Part A of the Appendix, we prove (44) holds in the neighborhood of steady state, if the economy is monetary.

The contrast between the entrepreneurs' savings behavior and the workers' savings behavior throws up another feature of a monetary economy: An agent's portfolio choice depends upon his future investment opportunities. If people were not anticipating liquidity constraints, their savings portfolios would not be sensitive to their future investment needs. But, in a monetary economy, liquidity constraints are expected to bind, and the nature of future investment affects the extent to which people keep their savings liquid. On the one hand, entrepreneurs save substantial amounts of both liquid and illiquid assets, because their future investment opportunities are large (constant returns to scale) and arrive steadily (Poisson). On the other hand, workers save only a small amount of liquid assets, because their investment needs are small (fixed size) and interspersed (a minimum interval T between each).[14]

5. Individual Persistence in Investment Opportunities

So far, we have assumed that the arrival rate of an investment opportunity is the same for every entrepreneur in every period. In effect, each date the identity of investing entrepreneurs and saving entrepreneurs is completely reshuffled. As we have seen, this greatly simplifies aggregation: Aggregate quantities and prices are functions of just two state variables, aggregate capital stock and aggregate productivity. At the aggregate level, then, the distribution of wealth (between those who invest and those who save) does not matter.

[14] If the workers were expecting large investments in the future, say buying a house or paying for their children's college education, then they would save substantial amounts. In national income accounts, when households build houses it counts as investment, entrepreneurial activity. We might think of households with large investments as entrepreneurs instead of workers.

In this section, we sketch out an extension of the basic model from Section 2 in which distribution matters—although aggregation is still kept relatively simple.

Let us introduce individual persistence in investment opportunities. That is, if an agent has an investment opportunity in period t, he is more likely to have one in period $t+1$ as well. Now the model has an interesting new twist: There is an interaction between investment and the wealth distribution between savers and investors.[15]

More specifically, we assume that this period's arrival rate of an investment opportunity for those who invested last period is Π^i, whereas the rate for those who didn't invest is Π^n, and

$$\Pi^i > \Pi^n > 0 \qquad \text{(Assumption 3)}$$

Now the equilibrium depends on not only aggregate capital K_t and aggregate productivity a_t, but also on the total capital stock held by those who invested last period, K_t^i, versus the stock held by those who didn't invest, $K_t^n = K_t - K_t^i$. The equilibrium Equations (15)–(21) are modified to

$$\begin{aligned}(1-\theta q_t)I_t &= \Pi^i\left(\left(r_t^K+\theta\lambda q_t\right)K_t^i-(1-\beta)\left(r_t^K+\lambda\right)K_t^i\right)+\Pi^n\left(\left(r_t^K+\theta\lambda q_t\right)K_t^n\right.\\ &\quad \left.+\left(r_t^L+p_t\right)L-(1-\beta)\cdot\left[\left(r_t^K+\lambda\right)K_t^n+\left(r_t^L+p_t\right)L\right]\right)\\ &= \left[r_t^K+\theta\lambda q_t-(1-\beta)\lambda\right]\left((\Pi^i-\Pi^n)K_t^i+\Pi^n K_t\right)+\beta\left(r_t^L+p_t\right)\Pi^n L \qquad (15.45)\\ Y_t &= I_t+(1-\beta)\left(\left[r_t^K+\Pi^n\lambda+(1-\Pi^n)\lambda q_t\right]K_t\right.\\ &\quad \left.+\left(r_t^L+p_t\right)L-(\Pi^i-\Pi^n)\lambda(q_t-1)K_t^i\right) \qquad (15.46)\\ K_{t+1}^i &= (1-\theta)\left(I_t+\Pi^n\lambda K_t+(\Pi^i-\Pi^n)\lambda K_t^i\right) \qquad (15.47)\end{aligned}$$

$$\begin{aligned}&(1-\Pi^n)E_t\left(\frac{\frac{r_{t+1}^K+\lambda q_{t+1}}{q_t}-\frac{r_{t+1}^L+p_{t+1}}{p_t}}{\left(r_{t+1}^K+\lambda q_{t+1}\right)\left(K_{t+1}-K_{t+1}^i\right)+\left(r_{t+1}^L+p_{t+1}\right)L}\right)\\ &= \Pi^n E_t\left(\frac{\frac{r_{t+1}^L+p_{t+1}}{p_t}-\frac{r_{t+1}^K+\lambda}{q_t}}{\left(r_{t+1}^K+\lambda\right)\left(K_{t+1}-K_{t+1}^i\right)+\left(r_{t+1}^L+p_{t+1}\right)L}\right) \qquad (15.48)\end{aligned}$$

together with (16), (18), and (19). Competitive equilibrium is described by $(p_t, q_t, r_t^K, r_t^L, I_t, K_{t+1}, K_{t+1}^i, Y_t)$ as functions of the aggregate state (K_t, K_t^i, a_t). From (45) and (46), we notice that investment and saving are functions of the capital stock held by the previously investing agents, K_t^i. The economy tends to exhibit more persistence because we have K_t^i as an additional state variable through which the effects of this period persist to the next period.

[15]This has been emphasized in, for example, Bernanke and Gertler (1989), Kiyotaki and Moore (1997), and Bernanke et al. (1999).

Appendix

A. Proof of Propositions

Proof of Proposition 1: Define $x \equiv Y/K = a(L/K)^{1-\alpha}$, $v \equiv pL/K$, and $\xi \equiv K^n/K = \lambda(1-\Pi)+\theta(1-\lambda+\lambda\Pi) \in (0,1)$. From (22), we get

$$(1-\theta q)(1-\lambda) = \Pi[\beta x + \theta\lambda q - (1-\beta)\lambda + \beta v] \tag{15.A.1a}$$

$$\beta x = 1-\lambda+\lambda\Pi(1-\beta)+(1-\beta)(1-\Pi)\lambda q + (1-\beta)v \tag{15.A.1b}$$

$$\left(\frac{\alpha}{q}-\frac{1-\alpha}{v}\right)x-(1-\lambda) = \Pi\lambda\frac{q-1}{q}\frac{(1-\alpha)x+v}{v} \times \frac{\xi q+v}{\xi(\alpha x+\lambda)+(1-\alpha)x+v} \tag{15.A.1c}$$

Then we have

$$x = x(q;\theta) = \frac{1}{\Pi\beta}((1-\beta+\Pi\beta)[1-\lambda+\lambda\Pi(1-\beta)] + (1-\beta)[\lambda\beta\Pi(1-\Pi)-(1-\lambda+\lambda\Pi)\theta]q) \tag{15.A.2a}$$

$$v = v(q;\theta) = \frac{1}{\Pi}((1-\Pi)[1-\lambda+\lambda\Pi(1-\beta)] - [\lambda\Pi(1-\beta)(1-\Pi)+(1-\lambda+\lambda\Pi)\theta]q) \tag{15.A.2b}$$

$$F(q;\theta) \equiv 1-\lambda+\frac{(1-\alpha)x}{v}-\frac{\alpha x}{q}+\Pi\lambda\frac{q-1}{q}\left(1+\xi q\frac{\frac{(1-\alpha)x}{v}+1-\frac{\alpha x+\lambda}{q}}{(\alpha\xi+1-\alpha)x+\lambda\xi+v}\right) = 0 \tag{15.A.2c}$$

Part 1(i): From (22c) in the text, we have that the second term in the large bracket of the right-hand side (RHS) of (A.2c) is positive. From (A.2a) and (A.2b), it follows that $\delta v(q;\theta)/\partial q < 0$, $\partial[x(q;\theta)/q]/\partial q < 0$, $\partial[x(q;\theta)/v(q;\theta)]/\partial q > 0$, and

$$\frac{\partial}{\partial q}[(\alpha\xi+1-\alpha)x(q;\theta)+\lambda\xi+v(q;\theta)] < 0$$

Therefore, F is an increasing function of q. And hence there is a unique q, which is larger than 1 if and only if $F(1;\theta) < 0$. Because F is an increasing function of θ, $F(1;\theta) < 0$ if and only if Assumption 1 holds. ■

Part 1(ii): From the optimal portfolio condition (22c), the return on land is dominated by that on capital, $(r^L+p)/p < (r^K+\lambda q)/q$, if and only if q exceeds unity, or Assumption 1 holds. Also, the left-hand side (LHS) of (A.1c) can be written as

$$\text{LHS of (A.1c)} = \left(\alpha\frac{x}{q}+\lambda-\frac{1}{\beta}\right)\left(1+\frac{q}{v}\right)+\frac{1}{\beta}-1-\frac{1}{v}\left(x+q\left(\lambda-\frac{1}{\beta}\right)\right)$$

$$= \left(\alpha\frac{x}{q}+\lambda-\frac{1}{\beta}\right)\left(1+\frac{q}{v}\right)+(q-1)\frac{1-\lambda+\lambda\Pi(1-\beta)}{\beta v}, \quad \text{(from 15.A.1b)}$$

Thus, because the RHS of (A.1c) is an increasing function of q and $\xi < 1$, a sufficient condition for $(r^K + \lambda q)/q < 1/\beta$ is

$$\Pi\lambda\frac{v+(1-\alpha)x}{q}\frac{q+v}{x+\lambda+v} < \frac{1-\lambda+\lambda\Pi(1-\beta)}{\beta} \quad \text{or}$$

$$\frac{\lambda\beta\Pi[1+(v/q)]}{1-\lambda+\lambda\Pi(1-\beta)} < \frac{x+\lambda+v}{v+(1-\alpha)x} \tag{15.A.3}$$

From (A.2a) and (A.2b), we know that the RHS of (A.3) is an increasing function of q and that the LHS of (A.3) is a decreasing function of q. Hence a sufficient condition for (A.3) is

$$\left.\frac{\lambda\beta\Pi[1+(v/q)]}{1-\lambda+\lambda\Pi(1-\beta)}\right|_{q=1} < \left.\frac{x+\lambda+v}{v+(1-\alpha)x}\right|_{q=1} \quad \text{or}$$

$$\frac{\lambda\beta(1-\lambda+\lambda\Pi)(1-\theta)}{1-\lambda+\lambda\Pi-\lambda\Pi\beta} < \frac{(1-\lambda+\lambda\Pi)(1-\theta)}{(1-\lambda+\lambda\Pi)(1-\theta)-\lambda\Pi\beta-\Pi\beta\alpha x}$$

But, this holds for any $x > 0$, which implies $(r^K + \lambda q)/q < 1/\beta$. ■

Part 1(iii): From (A.1c):

$$\begin{aligned}\text{LHS of (A.1c)} &= \left(\alpha x+\lambda-\frac{1}{\beta}\right)\left(1+\frac{1}{v}\right)-\frac{x}{v}+\left(\frac{1}{\beta}-\lambda\right)\frac{1}{v}+\frac{1}{\beta}-1-ax\left(1-\frac{1}{q}\right)\\ &= \left(\alpha x+\lambda-\frac{1}{\beta}\right)\left(1+\frac{1}{v}\right)-(q-1)\frac{(1-\beta)(1-\Pi)\lambda}{\beta v}-\alpha x\frac{q-1}{q},\end{aligned}$$

(from (A.1b))

But, RHS of (A.1c) > 0. Together with $q > 1$, we have $r^K + \lambda > 1/\beta$. ■

Part 1(iv): We know $m^i_{t+1} = 0$ iff (11) is true. From (8), (12), and (13b)

$$c^{ii}_{t+1} = (1-\beta)\left(r^K_{t+1}+\lambda\right)k^i_{t+1} = (1-\beta)\left(r^K_{t+1}+\lambda\right)\frac{1-\theta}{1-\theta q_t}\beta b^i_t$$

$$c^{in}_{t+1} = (1-\beta)\left(r^K_{t+1}+\lambda q_{t+1}\right)k^i_{t+1} = (1-\beta)\left(r^K_{t+1}+\lambda q_{t+1}\right)\frac{1-\theta}{1-\theta q_t}\beta b^i_t$$

Thus, together with (12b), the inequality (11) in the steady-state is equivalent to

$$1 > \left(1+\frac{r^L}{p}\right)\frac{1-\theta q}{1-\theta}\left(\frac{\Pi}{r^K+\lambda}+\frac{1-\Pi}{r^K+\lambda q}\right) \quad \text{or}$$

$$\begin{aligned}&\left(1+\frac{r^L}{p}\right)\frac{1-\theta q}{1-\theta q}\left(1+\frac{\Pi\lambda(q-1)}{r^K+\lambda} < \frac{r^K+\lambda q}{q}\right)\\ &= \left(1+\frac{r^L}{p}\right)\left(1+\Pi\lambda\frac{q-1}{q}\frac{qK^n+pL}{(r^K+\lambda)K^n+(r^L+p)L}\right),\end{aligned}$$

(from (15.22c))

This is equivalent to

$$1 > \Pi\lambda\frac{1-\theta q}{r^K+\lambda} - \Pi\lambda(1-\theta)\frac{qK^n + pL}{(r^K+\lambda)K^n + (r^L+p)L}$$

But, this is true because the first term in RHS is smaller than 1. ■

Proof of Inequality (44): The inequality (44) holds in the neighborhood of the steady-state equilibrium if and only if

$$\theta\left(\rho-(1-\alpha)\frac{x}{v}\right) < \rho+\delta-\alpha\frac{x}{q} \tag{15.44'}$$

From (30)–(33), the steady-state conditions for the continuous-time model are $i = \delta$ and

$$(1-\theta q)\delta = \pi(\theta q + v) \tag{15.A.4a}$$

$$x = \delta + \rho(q+v) \tag{15.A.4b}$$

$$\frac{\alpha}{q}x - \delta - \frac{1-\alpha}{v}x = \pi\frac{q-1}{q}\frac{q+v}{1+v} \tag{15.A.4c}$$

The LHS of (A.4c) can be written as $(\frac{\alpha}{q}x-\delta-\rho)\frac{q+v}{v}+\delta\frac{q-1}{v}$. Thus from (A.4c) and (A.4a), we obtain

$$\rho+\delta-\frac{\alpha}{q}x = \frac{q-1}{q+v}\left(\delta-\pi v\frac{q+v}{q(1+v)}\right) = \frac{q-1}{q(1+v)}\left(\delta(q-1)\frac{v}{q+v}+(\pi+\delta)\theta q\right)$$

Then, again from (A.4c), we also obtain

$$\rho-\frac{1-\alpha}{v}x = \rho+\delta-\frac{\alpha}{q}x+\pi\frac{q-1}{q}\frac{q+v}{1+v}$$

Thus, condition (44′) is equivalent to

$$\begin{aligned} 0 &< (1-\theta)\frac{q-1}{q(1+v)}\left(\delta(q-1)\frac{v}{q+v}+(\pi+\delta)\theta q\right) - \theta\pi\frac{q-1}{q}\frac{q+v}{1+v} \\ &= \frac{q-1}{q(1+v)}\left((1-\theta)\delta(q-1)\frac{v}{q+v}+\theta\delta(q-1)\right), \qquad \text{(using (15.A.4a))} \end{aligned}$$

But, the last expression is positive by $q > 1$. ■

B. Derivation of Local Dynamics

From (A.4), the steady-state of the continuous-time version of the model is

$$x = \frac{1}{\pi}((\pi + \rho)\delta + [\pi - \theta(\pi + \delta)]\rho q) \tag{15.A.5a}$$

$$v = \frac{1}{\pi}(\delta - \theta(\pi + \delta)q) \tag{15.A.5b}$$

$$\begin{aligned}&\left(\frac{\alpha}{\pi q} - \frac{1-\alpha}{\delta - \theta(\pi+\delta)q}\right)((\pi + \rho)\delta + [\pi - \theta(\pi + \delta)]\rho q)\\ &- \delta - \pi\frac{q-1}{q}\left(1 + \frac{\pi(q-1)}{(\pi+\delta)(1-\theta q)}\right)\\ &\equiv \tilde{F}(q, \theta) = 0\end{aligned} \tag{15.B.1c}$$

From (B.1c), we learn that $\tilde{F}(q, \theta)$ is a decreasing function of q and θ, and that $\tilde{F}(q, \theta) = 0$ has a solution $q > 1$ if and only if Assumption 1′ satisfies, i.e.,

$$\theta < \tilde{\theta}^* \equiv \frac{1}{\pi + \delta}\left(\delta - \pi\frac{1-\alpha}{\alpha}\frac{\rho + \delta}{\rho}\right)$$

Assumption 1′ is the continuous-time version of Assumption 1 in the text, which we will assume in the following argument.

From (34),

$$\lim_{dt \to 0} E_t\left(\frac{1}{dt}\left(\frac{q_{t+dt}}{q_t} - \frac{v_{t+dt}}{v_t}\right)\frac{q_t + v_t}{q_{t+dt} + v_{t+dt}}\right) = (\phi_q - \phi_v)\delta\hat{i}_t + (\psi_q - \psi_v)\eta(-2\hat{a}_t)$$

The first term on the RHS is the difference in the rate of capital gains between capital and land due to capital accumulation. The second term is the difference in the expected rates of capital gains associated with the productivity change, noting that the arrival rate of the change is η and that the proportional size of the change ($d\hat{a}_t$) is equal to $-2\hat{a}_t$ by (23) and (24). Thus linearizing (30), (32), and (33) around the steady state, we have

$$(1 - \theta q)\delta\hat{i}_t = \pi v\hat{v}_t + \theta(\pi + \delta)q\hat{q}_t \tag{15.B.2}$$

$$x\hat{x}_t = \delta\hat{i}_t + \rho v\hat{v}_t + \rho q\hat{q}_t \tag{15.B.3}$$

$$0 = G_x\hat{x}_t + G_q\hat{q}_t + G_v\hat{v}_t - (1 + \phi_v - \phi_q)\delta\hat{i}_t - 2\eta(\psi_q - \psi_v)\hat{a}_t \tag{15.B.4}$$

where

$$G_x \equiv \left(\frac{\alpha}{q} - \frac{1-\alpha}{v}\right)x,\ G_q \equiv -\left(\frac{\alpha}{q}x + \frac{1}{q}\frac{v + q^2}{v+1}\right), \quad \text{and}$$

$$G_v \equiv \left[\frac{1-\alpha}{v}x + \pi\frac{v}{q}\left[\frac{q-1}{v+1}\right]^2\right]$$

Substituting (34) and (35) into (B.2), (B.3), and (B.4), these equations must hold for any $\hat{K}_t$ and $\hat{a}_t$. Thus we have six unknowns variables ($\phi, \phi_q, \phi_v, \psi, \psi_q, \psi_v$), which satisfy six equations: equating the coefficients of $\hat{K}_t$ and $\hat{a}_t$ in each of (B.2), (B.3), and (B.4).

Solving (B.2), (B.3) for $\hat{v}_t$ and $\hat{q}_t$ with respect to $\hat{i}_t$ and $\hat{x}_t$, we have

$$\begin{pmatrix} \hat{v}_t \\ \hat{q}_t \end{pmatrix} = \frac{1}{d} \begin{pmatrix} [\rho(1-\theta q)+\theta(\pi+\delta)]\delta q & -\theta(\pi+\delta)qx \\ -[\rho(1-\theta q)+\pi]\delta v & \pi v x \end{pmatrix} \begin{pmatrix} \hat{i}_t \\ \hat{x}_t \end{pmatrix}$$
$$\equiv \begin{pmatrix} D_{vi} & D_{vx} \\ D_{qi} & D_{qx} \end{pmatrix} \begin{pmatrix} \hat{i}_t \\ \hat{x} \end{pmatrix}, \quad \text{where } d \equiv [\pi - \theta(\pi+\delta)]\rho q v \tag{15.B.5}$$

From (34), (35), and (B.5), we learn

$$\begin{pmatrix} \phi_v(\phi) & \psi_v(\psi) \\ \phi_q(\phi) & \psi_q(\psi) \end{pmatrix} = \begin{pmatrix} D_{vi} & D_{vx} \\ D_{qi} & D_{qx} \end{pmatrix} \begin{pmatrix} \phi & \psi \\ -(1-\alpha) & 1 \end{pmatrix} \tag{15.B.6}$$

Substituting (B.5) and (B.6) into (B.4), we have two equations for the coefficients of $\hat{K}_t$ and $\hat{a}_t$

$$0 = -(1-\alpha)G_x - [1+\phi_v(\phi) - \phi_q(\phi)]\delta\phi + G_q\phi_q(\phi) + G_v\phi_v(\phi)$$
$$\equiv \Phi(\phi) \equiv \Phi_2\phi^2 + \Phi_1\phi + \Phi_0 \tag{15.B.7}$$
$$0 = G_x - [1+\phi_v(\phi) - \phi_q(\phi)]\delta\psi - 2\eta[\psi_q(\psi) - \psi_v(\psi)] + G_q\psi_q(\psi) + G_v\psi_v(\psi)$$
$$\equiv \Psi(\psi,\phi) \equiv \Psi_1(\phi)\psi + \Psi_0 \tag{15.B.8}$$

From (B.7), we learn that $\Phi(\phi) = 0$ is a quadratic equation in ϕ with

$$\Phi_2 = -\delta(D_{vi} - D_{qi}) = \frac{\delta^2}{d}[\delta\theta q + x(1-\theta q)] \tag{15.B.9a}$$

$$\Phi_0 = -(1-\alpha)[G_x + G_q D_{qx} + G_v D_{vx}] \tag{15.B.9b}$$

Under Assumptions 2, $d \equiv [\pi - \theta(\pi+\delta)]\rho q v > 0$ and thus $\Phi_2 < 0$. Also, because we have $D_{qx} > 1$ and $G_x + G_q < 0$ and $G_v D_{vx} < 0$, we have $\Phi_0 > 0$. Therefore, there is a unique ϕ that satisfies the saddle-point stability condition $\phi < 0$. Also, from (B.6) and (B.8), we see that $\Psi(\psi, \phi) = 0$ is a linear equation in ψ with

$$\Psi_0 = G_x + G_q D_{qx} + G_v D_{vx} - 2\eta(D_{qx} - D_{vx}) \tag{15.B.10a}$$

and

$$\Psi_1 = -\delta[1+\phi_v(\phi) - \phi_q(\phi)] - 2\eta(D_{qi} - D_{vi}) + G_q D_{qi} + G_v D_{vi} \tag{15.B.10b}$$

Using the same argument that we used for Φ_0, we learn $\Psi_0 < 0$. Also using (B.7), we can rewrite (B.10b) as

$$\Psi_1 = -\frac{\Phi_0}{\phi} - 2\eta(D_{qi} - D_{vi})$$

Because $\phi < 0$ and $D_{qi} - D_{vi} < 0$, we obtain $\Psi_1 > 0$. Therefore, $\psi > 0$, from (B.8). Again from (B.5), (B.6), (B.7), and (B.8), we can derive the property (37) in the text.

C. Continuous-Time Formulation of the Agent's Behavior

Here we describe the individual agent's behavior using a continuous-time formulation. The agent's utility is given by

$$V_0 = E_0 \left[\int_0^{\infty} \ln c_t e^{-\rho t} dt \right] \tag{15.C.1}$$

where c_t is the consumption rate at date t, ρ is a constant time preference rate. The individual agent can produce according to production function (2), where y_t is output per unit of time. The aggregate productivity a_t follows the continuous-time two-point Markov process (23) and (24). The depreciation rate of capital is δ.

Each agent meets an opportunity to invest in capital according to a Poisson process with arrival rate π. At the time of the investment, the agent can sell up to a fraction θ of the capital held before the investment plus a fraction θ of the newly invested capital. Also the agent cannot short sell land. Thus the flow-of-funds constraint of the investing agent is

$$(1 - \theta q_t) i_t \leq p_t m_t + \theta q_t k_t \tag{15.C.2}$$

where i_t is investment, m_t is land, and k_t is capital owned before the investment. Let b_t be the total assets of the individual:

$$b_t = p_t m_t + q_t k_t \tag{15.C.3}$$

If the agent has a productive investment opportunity at date t, he can choose whether or not to invest the maximum amount subject to the flow-of-funds constraint. After maximal investment, the agent has sold all his land, and holds a fraction $1 - \theta$ of the capital he held previously plus a fraction $1 - \theta$ of his newly invested capital. Thus, from (C.2), his total assets after the investment are

$$\begin{aligned} b_{t+dt} &= \text{Max}(q_t(1-\theta)(k_t + i_t), b_t) \\ &= \text{Max}\left(\frac{(1-\theta)q_t}{1-\theta q_t}(p_t m_t + k_t), b_t \right) \end{aligned} \tag{15.C.4}$$

Let r_t^L be the rental price of land and r_t^K be the profit per unit of capital, each per unit of time. Then the accumulation of total assets of the agent between dates t and $t + dt$ is

$$\begin{aligned} db_t = {} & \left(r_t^L dt + dp_t\right) m_t + \left(r_t^K dt + dq_t\right) k_t - c_t dt \\ & + \text{Max}\left(\frac{(1-\theta)q_t}{1-\theta q_t}(p_t m_t + k_t) - b_t, \quad 0 \right) dM_t \end{aligned} \tag{15.C.5}$$

where $dM_t = 1$ if the agent has an investment opportunity at date t and $dM_t = 0$ otherwise.

In the following, we concentrate on the case in which Tobin's q exceeds unity so that the credit constraint is binding for the investing agents. Let $V(b, s)$ be the value function of an individual with total assets b when the aggregate state is $s = (K, a)$. Then the Bellman equation is

$$\rho V(b, s) = \underset{c,m,k}{\text{Max}} \left\{ \ln c + V_b(b, s)[(r^L + \dot{p})m + (r^K + \dot{q})k - c]_{da=0} \right.$$
$$+ \pi \left[V\left(\frac{(1-\theta)q}{1-\theta q}(pm + k), s \right) - V(b, s) \right]$$
$$\left. + \eta [V(p(s')m + q(s')k, s') - V(b, s)]_{da \neq 0} \right\} \tag{15.C.6}$$

subject to (C.3) and (C.5), where s is the aggregate state at date t and s' is the state at date $t + dt$. The first line in the RHS is the utility of consumption and the value of saving when there is no switch in aggregate productivity. With the same productivity, there is no discontinuous jump in the asset prices and $\dot{x}$ denotes $\frac{dx}{dt}$. The second line is the expected gain in the value with the arrival of a productive investment opportunity, corresponding to Equation (C.4). The last term is the capital gains associated with a switch of the aggregate productivity. The first-order conditions for consumption and portfolio choice are

$$\frac{1}{c} = V_b(b, s) \tag{15.C.7}$$

$$V_b(b, s) \left[\frac{r^L + \dot{p}}{p} - \frac{r^K + \dot{q}}{q} \right]_{da_t = 0} + \eta V_b(p(s')m + q(s')k, s') \left[\frac{p(s')}{p} - \frac{q(s')}{q} \right]_{da_t \neq 0}$$
$$+ \pi V_b \left(\left(\frac{(1-\theta)q}{1-\theta q} \right) (pm + k), s \right) \frac{(1-\theta)q}{1-\theta q} \left(1 - \frac{1}{q} \right) = 0 \tag{15.C.8}$$

Equation (C.7) says that the marginal utility of consumption must be equal to the marginal value of assets. Equation (C.8) says that the expected rates of return on liquid land and illiquid capital should be equal in terms of utility for an optimal portfolio. In particular, the second line is the expected return from financing the downpayment of investment, in which the rate of return on illiquid capital is $(1/q_t)$ times as much as the rate of return on liquid land. Hence we have

$$V(b_t, s_t) = \tilde{V}(s_t) + \frac{1}{\rho} \ln b_t \tag{15.C.9}$$

$$c_t = \rho b_t \tag{15.C.10}$$

$$\left[\frac{r_t^L}{p_t} - \frac{r_t^K}{q_t} \right] + \pi \frac{q_t - 1}{q_t} \frac{p_t m_t + q_t k_t}{p_t m_t + k_t} + \left[\frac{\dot{p}_t}{p_t} - \frac{\dot{q}_t}{q_t} \right]_{da_t = 0}$$
$$+ \eta \left[\left(\frac{p_{t+dt}}{p_t} - \frac{q_{t+dt}}{q_t} \right) \frac{p_t m_t + q_t k_t}{p_{t+dt} m_t + q_{t+dt} k_t} \right]_{da_t \neq 0} = 0 \tag{15.C.11}$$

Because the instantaneous utility function is the logarithm of the consumption rate, the value function is a log-linear function of total assets in Equation (C.3).

In aggregate, since between dates t and $t + dt$ exactly a fraction $\pi\, dt$ of agents invest with binding flow-of-funds constraint (C.2), we get (25). From (C.10), goods market equilibrium is given by (28). And from (C.11) with (27), asset market equilibrium is given by (29). This confirms that the formulation in the text, as a limit of the discrete time model, is consistent with the continuous-time formulation.

Next in this Appendix, we lay out the basic model with an aggregate productivity shock that follows the geometric Brownian motion (38). We first guess that the aggregate output/capital ratio $x_t = a_t K_t^{\alpha-1} L^{1-\alpha}$ and the aggregate productivity a_t summarize the aggregate state of nature. We also guess that the land price/capital ratio, capital price, and investment rate are functions of x_t only:

$$v_t = v(x_t), \quad q_t = q(x_t), \quad \text{and} \quad i_t = i(x_t) \tag{15.C.12}$$

Next we derive the equilibrium conditions that these functions must satisfy, and then we verify that our initial guess was correct.

Using Ito's lemma with (31) and (32), we have

$$\frac{dx_t}{x_t} = (\alpha - 1)[i(x_t) - \delta]dt + \sigma dz_t \tag{15.C.13}$$

Write down the rates of returns on land and capital as

$$\frac{r^L dt + dp}{p} = \frac{(1-\alpha)x\,dt + dv(x)}{v(x)} + [i(x) - \delta]dt \equiv r^p(x)dt + \omega^p(x)dz \tag{15.C.14a}$$

$$\frac{(r^K - \delta q)dt + dq}{q} = \frac{\alpha x\,dt + dq(x)}{q(x)} - \delta dt \equiv r^q(x)dt + \omega^q(x)dz \tag{15.C.14b}$$

Let b_t be the total assets as in (C.3) and let h_t be the share of liquid assets in the portfolio, $h_t \equiv p_t m_t / b_t$. Then the budget constraint of the agent (C.5) is

$$\begin{aligned} db_t = {} & \left(\left[h_t r_t^p + (1-h_t) r_t^q\right] b_t - c_t\right) dt + \left[h_t \omega_t^p + (1-h_t)\omega_t^q\right] b_t dz_t \\ & + \text{Max}\left(\frac{1-\theta}{1-\theta q_t}(1 - h_t + h_t q_t) b_t - b_t, 0\right) dM_t \end{aligned} \tag{15.C.15}$$

The Bellman equation of an agent is

$$\begin{aligned} \rho V(b_t, x_t) = {} & \underset{c_t, h_t}{\text{Max}} \left\{ \ln c_t + V_b(b_t, x_t)\left(\left[h_t r_t^p + (1-h_t) r_t^q\right] b_t - c_t\right) \right. \\ & + \frac{1}{2} V_{bb}(b_t, x_t)\left[h_t \omega_t^p + (1-h_t)\omega_t^q\right]^2 b_t^2 \\ & \left. + \pi \text{Max}\left[V\left(\frac{1-\theta}{1-\theta q_t}(1 - h_t + h_t q_t) b_t, x_t\right) - V(b_t, x_t), 0\right] \right\} \end{aligned} \tag{15.C.16}$$

The optimal investment rule is the same as Tobin's q theory of investment, as in the text. From the first-order conditions, we get the optimal consumption rule and optimal portfolio rule:

$$c_t = \rho b_t \tag{15.C.17}$$

$$r_t^p - r_t^q - \left(\omega_t^p - \omega_t^q\right)\left[h_t \omega_t^p + (1-h_t)\omega_t^q\right] + \pi \frac{\text{Max}(q_t - 1, 0)}{1 - h_t + h_t q_t} = 0 \tag{15.C.18}$$

These are very similar to consumption and portfolio rules (C.10) and (C.11), except for the effect of risk due to the difference in the stochastic process of aggregate productivity.

From (C.18), we see that the optimal share of liquid assets is

$$h_t = h\left(r_t^p - r_t^q, q_t, \pi, \omega_t^p, \omega_t^q\right), \quad \text{where}$$
$$h_{(r^p - r^q)} > 0, \quad h_q \geq 0, \quad h_\pi \geq 0, \quad h_{\omega^p} < 0, \quad h_{\omega^q} > 0 \tag{15.C.19}$$

The difference from standard portfolio theory is that the liquid asset ratio is a weakly increasing function of Tobin's q and the arrival rate of a productive investment opportunity.

Now we can combine the individuals' behavior with the market-clearing conditions to define equilibrium as price functions $v(x)$, $q(x)$ and investment rate $i(x)$ that satisfy

$$[1 - \theta q(x)]i(x) \leq \pi[v(x) + \theta q(x)], \quad \text{where}$$
$$\begin{cases} = \text{holds}, & \text{if } q(x) > 1 \\ \leq \text{holds}, & \text{if } q(x) = 1 \\ i(y) = 0, & \text{if } q(x) < 1 \end{cases} \tag{15.C.20}$$

$$x = i(x) + \rho[v(x) + q(x)] \tag{15.C.21}$$

$$[r^p(x) - r^q(x)] - [\omega^p(x) - \omega^q(x)]\frac{v(x)\omega^p(x) + q(x)\omega^q(x)}{v(x) + q(x)}$$
$$+ \pi\frac{\text{Max}[q(x) - 1, 0]}{q(x)}\frac{v(x) + q(x)}{v(x) + 1} = 0 \tag{15.C.22}$$

where the returns characteristics $r^p(x)$, $r^q(x)$, $\omega^p(x)$, and $\omega^q(x)$ are defined in (C.14). The stochastic process of a_t and x_t follow (38) and (C.13). Equation (C.20) describes the behavior of aggregate investment. Equation (C.21) describes the goods market equilibrium, and (C.22) describes the asset market equilibrium. In (C.22), the first term is the difference of the expected rates of return on the liquid asset and illiquid capital, the second is the effect of risk aversion, and the last is the expected advantage of the liquid asset over illiquid capital for financing productive investment. This last term distinguishes our model from a standard capital asset-pricing model. All the above equilibrium conditions are functions of the output/capital ratio x_t only, and aggregate productivity together with the output/capital ratio are sufficient statistics for the aggregate state of the economy. Our initial conjecture was correct.

This system is not much more complicated than a real business cycle model, or Merton (1975). Thus, in principle we can simulate the above system to examine its dynamics. Alternatively, if $v(x)$ and $q(x)$ were three-times differentiable, we would know from Ito's Lemma that

$$r^p(x) = \frac{(1-\alpha)x}{v(x)} + \left(1 + \frac{xv'(x)}{v(x)}(\alpha - 1)\right)[i(x) - \delta] + \frac{1}{2}\sigma^2\frac{x^2v''(x)}{v(x)}$$

$$r^q(x) = \frac{\alpha x}{q(x)} - \delta + \frac{xq'(x)}{q(x)}(\alpha - 1)[i(x) - \delta] + \frac{1}{2}\sigma^2\frac{x^2q''(x)}{q(x)}$$

$$\omega^p(x) = \sigma\frac{xv'(x)}{v(x)}$$

$$\omega^q(x) = \sigma\frac{xq'(x)}{q(x)}$$

However, such a property may not hold here, because the pattern of investment differs qualitatively depending on the value of $q(x)$—unless the liquidity constraint is always binding. But, here it is not guaranteed that the liquidity constraint does always bind, given that aggregate productivity follows a Brownian motion. Obviously, more study is needed before we fully understand this economy.

References

BERNANKE, B. S., AND M. GERTLER, "Agency Costs, Net Worth, and Business Fluctuations," *American Economic Review* 79 (1989), 14–31.

——, ——, AND S. GILCHRIST, "Financial Accelerator in a Quantitative Business Cycle Framework," in J. B. Taylor and M. Woodford, eds., *Handbook of Macroeconomics*, Vol. 1c (Amsterdam: North Holland, 1999).

BEWLEY, T., "The Permanent Income Hypothesis: A Theoretical Foundation," *Journal of Economic Theory* 16 (1977), 252–92.

——, "The Optimum Quantity of Money," in J. Kareken and N. Wallace, eds., *Models of Monetary Economies* (Minneapolis: Federal Reserve Bank of Minneapolis, 1980).

——, "A Difficulty with the Optimum Quantity of Money," *Econometrica* 51 (1983), 1485–504.

BROCK, W. A., "Asset Prices in a Production Economy," in J. J. McCall, ed., *The Economics of Information and Uncertainty* (Chicago: University of Chicago Press, 1982).

CAMPBELL, J. Y., "Asset Prices, Consumption, and the Business Cycle," in J.B. Taylor and M. Woodford, eds., *Handbook of Macroeconomics*, Vol. 1c (Amsterdam: North Holland, 1999).

——, A. W. LO, AND A. C. MACKINLAY, *The Econometrics of Financial Markets* (Princeton, NJ: Princeton University Press, 1997).

CARROLL, C. D., "The Buffer Stock Theory of Saving: Some Macroeconomic Evidence," *Brookings Papers on Economic Activity* 2 (1992), 61–135.

COCHRANE, J. H., *Asset Pricing* (Princeton, NJ: Princeton University Press, 2001).

COLE, H. L., AND N. R. KOCHERLAKOTA, "Efficient Allocations with Hidden Income and Storage," *Review of Economic Studies* 68 (2001), 523–42.

DEATON, A. S., *Understanding Consumption* (Oxford: Oxford University Press, 1992).

DIAMOND, D, AND P. DYBVIG, "Bank Runs, Deposit Insurance, and Liquidity," *Journal of Political Economy* 91 (1983), 401–19.

HICKS, J. R., "Mr. Hicks and the 'Classics'; A Suggested Interpretation," *Econometrica* 5 (1937), 147–59.

HOLMSTROM, B., AND J. TIROLE, "LAPM: A Liquidity-Based Asset Pricing Model," *Journal of Finance* 56 (2001), 1837–67.

JACKLIN, C. J., "Demand Deposits, Trading Restrictions and Risk Sharing," in E. Prescott and N. Wallace, eds., *Contractual Arrangements for Intertemporal Trade* (Minneapolis: University of Minnesota Press, 1987).

KALDOR, N., "Alternative Theories of Distribution," *Review of Economic Studies* 23 (1955–56), 83–100.

KEYNES, J. M., *The General Theory of Employment, Interest and Money* (London: Macmillan, 1937).

KIYOTAKI, N., AND J. MOORE, "Credit Cycles," *Journal of Political Economy* 105 (1997), 211–48.

——, AND ——, "Liquidity, Business Cycles, and Monetary Policy," Working paper, London School of Economics, 2001.

KYDLAND, F. AND E. C. PRESCOTT, "Time to Build and Aggregate Fluctuations," *Econometrica* 50 (1982), 1345–71.

MEHRA, R., AND E. C. PRESCOTT, "The Equity Premium Puzzle," *Journal of Monetary Economics* 15 (1985), 145–61.

MERTON, R. C., "An Asymptotic Theory of Growth under Uncertainty," *Review of Economic Studies* 42 (1975), 375–93.

PASINETTI, L., "Rate of Profit and Income Distribution in Relation to the Rate of Economic Growth," *Review of Economic Studies* 23 (1962), 83–100.

TOBIN, J., "A General Equilibrium Approach to Monetary Theory," *Journal of Money, Credit and Banking* 1 (1969), 15–29.

TOWNSEND, R., "Asset Return Anomalies in a Monetary Economy," *Journal of Economic Theory* 41 (1987), 219–47.

——, AND N. WALLACE, "Circulating Private Debt: An Example with Coordination Problem," in E. C. Prescott and N. Wallace, eds., *Contractual Arrangements for Intertemporal Trade* (Minneapolis: University of Minnesota Press, 1987).

WEIL, P., "The Equity Premium Puzzle and the Risk-Free Rate Puzzle," *Journal of Monetary Economics* 24 (1989), 401–21.

16 Collateral Constraints in a Monetary Economy

Juan Carlos Cordoba and Marla Ripoll

1. Introduction

The extent and mechanism by which monetary policy affects real economic activity over business cycles has been a long-standing question in macroeconomics. Different mechanisms that explain the propagation of money shocks have been proposed. These include sticky prices, wage contracting, monetary misperceptions, and limited participation.[1] Another mechanism that has received special attention in recent years is credit-market imperfections. In particular, the agency-cost model of Bernanke and Gertler (1989) has been extended to monetary environments to analyze how fluctuations in borrowers' net worth can contribute to the amplification and persistence of exogenous money shocks to the economy: for example, Fuerst (1995), Bernanke, Gertler, and Gilchrist (1999), and Carlstrom and Fuerst (2001).[2]

In contrast with these agency-cost models, little attention has been devoted to analyzing monetary economies in which agents face endogenous credit limits determined by the value of collateralized assets. The environment we have in mind is one in which lenders cannot force borrowers to repay their debts unless debts are secured. Using real-economy models, Kiyotaki and Moore (1997), Kiyotaki (1998), and Kocherlakota (2000), among others, have shown that collateral constraints may be a powerful mechanism of amplification and persistence of real shocks.[3] These papers show that if debts must be fully secured by collateral (say land) and if the collateral is also an input in production, then a small shock to the economy can be significantly amplified. For instance, a small negative shock that

[1] See Cooley and Hansen (1998) for an illustration of the role of monetary shocks in the equilibrium business cycle theory.

[2] Credit-market imperfections in these models emerge from asymmetric information and costly state verification. In this framework, entrepreneurs borrow to pay the amount of the factor bill that is not covered by their net worth. Lenders must pay a monitoring cost in order to observe the entrepreneur's project outcome. If an entrepreneur has little net worth invested in the project, monitoring costs increase because there is larger divergence between the interests of the entrepreneur and the lender, and so the premium for external financing is larger. With procyclical net worth, periods of low output are associated with higher monitoring costs and a higher external finance premium. This mechanism amplifies the effects of external shocks on production and investment.

[3] Scheinkman and Weiss (1986) also study the effects of borrowing contraints in the presence of uninsurable risk. They simulate a lump-sum monetary injection that changes the distribution of assets across agents.

reduces the net worth of credit-constrained firms forces them to curtail their investment in land. Land prices and output fall because credit-constrained firms are by nature more productive in the use of land. The fall in the value of the collateral further reduces the debt capacity of constrained firms, causing additional declines in investment, land prices, and output.

This paper studies the potential role of collateral constraints as a transmission mechanism of monetary shocks. We do this by introducing a cash-in-advance constraint for consumption and investment in the real-economy model of Kiyotaki and Moore (1997). We exploit the simplicity of this framework to study monetary injections carried out via open-market operations—in contrast with the less realistic but simpler "helicopter drops" employed by many monetary models. Due to the presence of credit-market imperfections, the exact path of the money supply is important in determining the real effects of open-market operations. We choose a parsimonious type of monetary path that avoids changes in long-run inflation and fiscal variables. Thus, current monetary expansions must be offset by future monetary contractions to avoid changes in inflation or unstable government bond paths. As in real-economy models, the price of the collateral plays a central role in generating large and persistent effects of exogenous shocks. Moreover, the response of the nominal interest rate also becomes critical in determining the effects of shocks.[4]

The main finding of this paper is that a monetary shock can generate persistent movements in aggregate output, the amplitude of which depends on whether or not debt contracts are indexed. In particular, if indexed contracts cannot be written, then unanticipated money shocks can trigger large output fluctuations. In this case an unanticipated money expansion triggers an economic boom, whereas unanticipated money contractions generate depressions. The basic mechanism at work is the Fisher effect, according to which unexpected debt deflation (even if small) redistributes resources from borrowers to lenders. In our model, because of the existence of collateral constraints, this Fisher effect can amplify output fluctuations significantly. In contrast, if contracts are indexed then output amplification is smaller and, moreover, it is possible for money expansions to generate downturns in output. This occurs because—even though indexed contracts prevent any redistribution of resources from lenders to borrowers—the inflationary tax reduces borrowers' net worth.

Unanticipated shocks may induce default and renegotiation if the value of debts exceed the collateral value ex post. The possibility of renegotiation can generate asymmetric business cycles, since default may occur during depressions but not during booms. We find that, if contracts are nonindexed, then an unanticipated monetary contraction reduces the value of the collateral and hence may induce default and renegotiation, depending on the timing of the shock. Renegotiation benefits borrowers and prevents a larger output downturn; that is, renegotiation can substantially reduce the responses of output to shocks.

A third property of the model is that monetary shocks trigger highly persistent dampening cycles rather than smoothly declining deviations. This occurs due to the interplay between the cash-in-advance and collateral constraints. In particular, investment in the cash-in-advance constraint is analogous to a "time to build" or an "adjustment cost" restriction. As a result, the full impact of a shock that increases net worth is delayed because, with a binding cash-in-advance constraint, collateral can only be accumulated gradually.

[4] In Kiyotaki and Moore (1997) and Kocherlakota (2000), the equilibrium interest rate is constant.

The cyclical dynamics of the model is consistent with the hump-shaped pattern of output response to monetary shocks that has been observed in the data.[5]

Finally, the model also generates endogenous limited participation in the government bonds market because, in equilibrium, collateral constraints are binding only for a set of agents. This implies that only unconstrained agents hold government bonds and participate in open-market operations. In this context, the propagation of the money shock is nontrivial because agents differ not only in whether or not they are credit constrained but also in their productivity.

The remainder of the paper is organized as follows. Section 2 presents the model and characterizes the steady state. In Section 3 we discuss the dynamics of the model in response to a monetary shock. The dynamic structure of the model can be summarized by a nonhomogeneous second-order difference equation in the distribution of capital across agents. We parameterize the model and provide a numerical illustration of the dynamics in Section 4, and Section 5 concludes. Technical details omitted in the text are presented in several appendices.

2. The Model

The model for this heterogeneous-agent economy is an extension of the framework of Kiyotaki and Moore (1997). We keep the main features of their model and introduce money using a cash-in-advance constraint. There are two goods in this economy: a durable asset (capital) and a nondurable commodity (output). We focus on the effects of monetary shocks on the distribution of capital across agents and abstract from capital accumulation. Capital is available in an aggregate fixed amount $\overline{K}$.

There are two types of private agents in this economy. They are both risk-neutral, but they operate different technologies and have distinct discount factors. As will become clear in what follows, around the steady state the more patient agents become lenders while the impatient agents become borrowers. To abbreviate, let us refer to the two types of agents as borrowers and lenders. Both types of agents face a cash-in-advance (CIA) constraint and a collateral constraint. Finally, in this economy the government's only role is controlling money supply through open-market operations.

Events in this model occur as follows. Production takes place overnight. A household can default on its debt by escaping with the production and money balances overnight and leaving its installed capital behind. Early in the morning, lenders seize the capital of the defaulting households. No default occurs during the day, because movers can be easily detected and their output, capital, and money balances can be seized. We assume that there are different "types of capital", so that lenders cannot directly use seized capital and instead must sell it and then buy their correct capital "type." As in other CIA models, we also assume that households value the different "types" of output produced by other households.

Assume that there are two members per household who carry out different activities: "shoppers" and "producers." Households enter each period with money balances stored from the previous period, output that was produced overnight, and capital holdings (if any). During the day, all markets are opened simultaneously. Shoppers leave early in the morning with their money balances to make transactions in both the capital and goods markets.

[5]See Bernanke, Gertler, and Gilchrist (1999), as well as Carlstrom and Fuerst (2001).

They can buy or sell capital, and they buy goods. We assume that in each period shoppers can make only one transaction in the capital market—that is, they can either buy or sell capital, but they do not have "enough time" to both buy and sell. One may suppose that buying and selling capital goods takes more time or is "more involved" than buying and selling consumption goods. This assumption, together with the existence of different types of capital, prevents default from becoming a cheaper way of acquiring capital.[6]

Finally, "producers" stay at home, selling the production and making transactions in the money and bonds markets. In particular, producers pay outstanding debts using the revenues from output sales made during the day. Financial transactions must satisfy a standard budget constraint for the producer as well as a collateral constraint. Monetary interventions occur via open-market operations. In particular, the government can expand and contract the money supply only by buying or selling bonds. These open-market operations take place after shoppers have left for the day.

The assumed market arrangement means that cash is required for trading capital and consumption goods but not for financial transactions. Producers can pay outstanding debts with cash generated during the day, or (equivalently) they can pay directly with goods. The important point is that it is not necessary to accumulate cash in advance in order to carry out financial transactions. We could alternatively restrict financial transactions to be cash-based (as in, e.g., Freeman 1996 and Aiyagari, Braun, and Eckstein 1998). In this case, monetary shocks could have a direct impact on financial markets. Our research strategy is to keep separate the financial and monetary elements of the model in order to focus on the effects of nominal versus indexed financial contracts (i.e., the Fisher effect).

2.1 Lenders

The mass of lenders in the economy is n. Lenders differ from borrowers in their production technology and preferences. Lenders use a strictly concave technology, and they are more patient than borrowers. Their production function is given by $y_t = G(k'_{t-1})$, where $G' > 0$, $G'' < 0$, $G'(0) = \infty$, and k'_{t-1}, is their capital stock at the end of the last period. Lenders choose sequences of consumption $\{x'_t\}$, capital holdings $\{k'_t\}$, nominal money balances $\{m_t^{d\prime}\}$, bonds holdings $\{b'_t\}$, and government bonds purchases $\{h'_t\}$ in order to solve the following problem for given sequences of output prices $\{p_t\}$, nominal interest rates $\{R_t\}$, and nominal capital prices $\{q_t^n\}$:

$$\max \sum_{t=0}^{\infty} \beta'^t x'_t$$

$$\text{subject to} \quad q_t^n(k'_t - k'_{t-1}) + p_t x'_t = m_{t-1}^{d\prime}, \tag{16.1}$$

$$m_t^{d\prime} + R_t b'_{t-1} + h'_t = p_t G(k'_{t-1}) + b'_t + R_t h'_{t-1}, \tag{16.2}$$

where the prime denotes a lender's decision variable.[7] We define the nominal rate R_t as the interest rate paid at t on loans made at $t-1$. Equation (1) is the CIA constraint. Money is

[6] In other words, by restricting the number of transactions in the capital market, we prevent lenders from selling seized capital and then buying new capital immediatly thereafter. This would make default a cheaper way to acquire capital because no cash accumulated from the previous period would be required.

[7] In order to avoid introducing more notation, we have assumed that the constraints are binding, as will be the case in equilibrium.

required for both consumption $p_t x'_t$ and investment $q^n_t(k'_t - k'_{t-1})$. Equation (2) is the budget constraint. The revenues collected through output sales $p_t G(k'_{t-1})$, new bonds issued b'_t, and the proceeds from government bond holdings $R_t h'_{t-1}$ must be enough to accumulate new money balances $m^{d\prime}_t$, pay outstanding debt obligations $R_t b'_{t-1}$, and purchase government bonds h'_t.

Let $\beta'^t \Omega_t$ be the Lagrange multiplier associated with the CIA constraint and $\beta'^t \Lambda_t$ the one for the budget constraint. Then the first-order optimality conditions for the preceding problem are given by[8]

$$x'_t : 1 = \Omega_t p_t,$$

$$m^{d\prime}_t : \Lambda_t = \beta' \Omega_{t+1},$$

$$b'_t, h'_t : \Lambda_t = \beta' R_{t+1} \Lambda_{t+1},$$

$$k'_t : q^n_t \Omega_t - \beta' q^n_{t+1} \Omega_{t+1} = \beta' \Lambda_{t+1} p_{t+1} G'(k'_t).$$

Let the real price of capital be $q_t \equiv q^n_t / p_t$. From the optimality conditions just given it is easy to obtain expressions for the nominal interest rate and the users' cost of capital for the lenders $u' \equiv q_t - \beta' q_{t+1}$:

$$R_t = \frac{1+\pi_t}{\beta'}; \tag{16.3}$$

$$u'_t = \frac{\beta'^2}{1+\pi_{t+1}} G'(k'_t). \tag{16.4}$$

Here $\pi_t = (p_{t+1} - p_t)/p_t$ is the inflation between t and $t+1$. Equation (4) states that lenders equate their users' cost with the present value of the marginal product of capital. Since in equilibrium these agents are not credit constrained, the users' cost is simply the difference between the cost q_t of buying capital today and the discounted value $\beta' q_{t+1}$ of selling capital tomorrow. Notice that the lenders' users' cost is not affected by inflation because the proceeds of selling the capital can be consumed or invested immediately, without requiring a previous accumulation of cash. In contrast, the marginal product of capital must be discounted by $\beta'^2/(1+\pi_{t+1})$, since output must be exchanged for money before it can be consumed. This means that the investor must wait two periods and pay the inflation tax before consuming the returns of the investment.

2.2 Borrowers

The measure of borrowers is normalized to unity. Their technology is given by the production function $y_t = (a+c)k_{t-1}$. They choose sequences of consumption $\{x_t\}$, capital holdings $\{k_t\}$, nominal money balances $\{m^d_t\}$, privately issued bonds $\{b_t\}$, and government bonds purchases $\{h_t\}$ in order to solve the following problem for given sequences of output prices, nominal capital prices, nominal interest rates, and nominal rates on government

[8] These are the first-order conditions for interior solutions; assumptions detailed later guarantee their attainment.

bonds:

$$\max \sum_{t=0}^{\infty} \beta^t x_t$$

$$\text{subject to} \quad q_t^n(k_t - k_{t-1}) + p_t x_t = m_{t-1}^d, \tag{16.5}$$

$$m_t^d + R_t b_{t-1} + h_t = (a + c)p_t k_{t-1} + b_t + R_t h_{t-1}, \tag{16.6}$$

$$R_{t+1} b_t \leq q_{t+1}^n k_t. \tag{16.7}$$

In addition to the CIA and budget constraints, borrowers face the collateral constraint given by equation (7). Borrowing can only take place up to the point at which the principal plus interest $R_{t+1}b_t$, is secured by the market value $q_{t+1}^n k_t$ of the capital owned by the household. Notice that money cannot be used as collateral.[9] Lenders also face a collateral constraint, but we did not write it explicitly. Around the steady state, this constraint is not binding under the following assumption.[10]

Assumption 1: $\beta' > \beta$.

It is also assumed that only the fraction a of the output is tradable between borrowers and lenders. The fraction c can be traded only among borrowers, and it can be interpreted as a subsistence minimum consumption. We refer to this fraction as nontradable output. The purpose of the assumption is to avoid situations in which borrowers continuously postpone consumption.[11]

In Appendix A we prove that, around a zero-inflation steady state the borrower's optimal plan is: to consume only the nontradable fraction of output ($x_t = ck_{t-1}$), to borrow up to the limit imposed by the collateral constraint, and to invest all remaining resources. This implies that borrowers do not purchase government bonds (i.e., $h_t = 0$) and that the CIA constraint is binding. Notice that, since borrowers do not hold government bonds whereas lenders do, this model generates endogenous limited participation in this market. These results hold under the following additional assumption.

Assumption 2:

$$\frac{c}{a} > \frac{1-\beta}{\beta^2}\frac{2-\beta-\beta'}{1-\beta'}.$$

[9] Money is not collateral because the borrower can hide it, or escape with it "overnight," whereas it is not possible for the borrower to either hide or escape with installed capital. The fact that money is not collateral reduces the debt-to-asset ratio in our model and weakens the leverage effect. This is analogous to the role that noncollateralizable trees play in Section III of Kiyotaki and Moore (1997). We thank an anonymous referee for drawing this to our attention.

[10] As in Kiyotaki and Moore (1997), under Assumption 1 there is no steady-state equilibrium in which the collateral constraint for *borrowers* is not binding. This is not true if $\beta \geq \beta'$.

[11] Kiyotaki and Moore (1997) introduce a similar assumption. As will be explained below, due to the linearity of preferences, borrowers would like to continuosly postpone consumption in exchange for investment. This is avoided by introducing a nontradable fraction of output, which we think of as subsistence minimum consumption. Notice that money is required to buy nontradable output because this type of output can be traded among borrowers. One may view this as households that can produce (say) fruit of a particular color only, even though they value fruits of all colors.

This condition is easy to satisfy if the discount factors are close to unity.[12] We can use equations (5)–(7) to obtain

$$k_t = \frac{1}{u_t}\left[(a+q_t)k_{t-1} + \frac{m^d_{t-1}}{p_t} - R_t\frac{b_{t-1}}{p_t} - \frac{m^d_t}{p_t}\right]. \tag{16.8}$$

Borrowers' net worth consists of their assets net of debt repayments. In equation (8) real net worth corresponds to the term $(a + q_t)k_{t-1} + m^d_{t-1}/p_t - R_t(b_{t-1}/p_t)$, that is, the value of tradable output and capital held from the previous period, plus the real money balances brought from the previous period, all net of debt repayments. Finally, the users' cost of capital for borrowers u_t is given by

$$u_t \equiv q_t - \frac{1+\pi_t}{R_{t+1}}q_{t+1}, \tag{16.9}$$

where borrowers discount the future value of the capital at the nominal interest rate R_{t+1} because, as will become clear, in equilibrium borrowers need to borrow in order to buy capital.

2.3 Government

The government controls the money supply in this economy through open-market operations (OMOs), which take place in the bonds market. Let H^s_t be the nominal supply of government-issued bonds. The stock M^s_t of money supply in this economy is given by

$$M^s_t = M^s_{t-1} - H^s_t + R_t H^s_{t-1}, \tag{16.10}$$

where

$$H^s_t = \tau H^s_{t-1}, \quad \tau \geq 0, \tag{16.11}$$

so that at time t the government withdraws an amount τH^s_{t-1} of money and injects $R_t H^s_{t-1}$ back into the economy. Two comments are in order. First, we choose a simple law of motion for government bonds H^s_t. This simplicity is convenient for the purpose of analyzing the effects of a money shock. Observe that in the wake of this shock, unless $\tau < 1$ for all t, government bonds may exhibit an explosive path. To avoid this, any money expansion through OMOs must be eventually followed by a "policy reversal" or "sterilization" that guarantees convergence back to the steady state. In particular, the size of τ determines the speed at which such a monetary contraction takes place. In the analysis here we shall consider τ very close to 1 in order to simulate a very slow policy reversal. Since credit markets are imperfect in this economy, real effects of monetary shocks may depend on the path of government debt. Although we choose a parsimonious law of motion for H^s_t, we will also discuss the role of τ's size in our results as well as other paths for government debt.

[12] In this case, $(2 - \beta - \beta')/(1 - \beta')$ is some constant near 2 and $(1 - \beta)/\beta^2$ is close to zero. Further, in the proposed equilibrium, c/a is the ratio between the marginal propensity to consume and the marginal propensity to save for borrowers, which can be assumed to be bounded away from zero.

Second, notice that we do not consider a rebate of the inflationary tax. Since some agents face corner solutions, such a rebate cannot be lump-sum in general. For example, simple helicopter drops redistribute wealth and affect agents' decisions. Since here we want to focus on the effects of the "pure monetary shock," we do not include any rebates in the model. Tax rebates may, in fact, reinforce the results of the paper.[13]

2.4 Aggregate Resource Constraints

Let $K_t, K_t', B_t, B_t', H_t, H_t', M_t^d$, and $M_t^{d\prime}$ be the aggregate variables corresponding to the lowercase individual variables. There are five markets in the model: consumption goods, capital, money, private bonds, and public bonds. By Walras' Law, one needs only to consider four of them. The equilibrium conditions to clear the last four markets are

$$M_t^s = M_t^d + M_t^{d\prime} = m_t^d + nm_t^{d\prime},$$
$$B_t = b_t = -B_t' = -nb_t',$$
$$\overline{K} = K_t + K_t' = k_t + nk_t',$$

and, since $H_t = 0$,

$$H_t' = nh_t' = H_t^s.$$

Using these market-clearing conditions along with equations (2) and (6), we obtain

$$M_t^s + H_t^s - R_t H_{t-1}^s \equiv M_{t-1}^s = p_t \left[(a+c)K_{t-1} + nG\left(\frac{\overline{K} - K_{t-1}}{n} \right) \right], \tag{16.12}$$

which is just the quantity equation. Notice that this equation implies that prices at time t are not affected by the money supply at time t but rather by the money supply at $t-1$. This is a consequence of the cash-in-advance constraint. Notice also that p_t is completely determined by choices made at $t-1$, since both K_{t-1} and M_{t-1}^s are determined at $t-1$.

2.5 Steady State

Define a steady state in which all real variables are constant and all nominal variables grow at the constant rate π, which is the steady-state growth rate of money supply. From equations (10) and (11) it follows that $\pi = \tau - 1$ if $\tau \geq 1$ and $\pi = 0$ if $\tau < 1$.

Next, it is easy to see that the steady-state users' cost of capital for lenders and borrowers is the same: $u = u' = q(1-\beta')$. Further, since under the proposed equilibrium the collateral constraint (7) binds for the borrowers, we can use R, u'. and the budget constraint of these agents (6) to obtain: $u = a + c - M^d/pK^*$, where K^* is the borrowers' steady-state

[13]The intuition for this result is simple. Suppose the economy starts off at the steady state and there is a money expansion. Assume that borrowers were to receive a money transfer that compensates them for the inflationary tax in an amount higher than their optimal consumption level. This may happen, for example, with helicopter drops. In this case, borrowers will buy capital with the extra resources and next-period output will increase. This reinforces our results because (as will be shown later), in general, monetary expansions generate booms.

capital level. Next, using the CIA constraint (5) yields: $M^d/p = cK^*(1+\pi)$; that is, borrowers' real money balances exactly cover their consumption adjusted by inflation.

Combining the last two expressions we obtain $u = a - \pi c$. Notice that, if $\pi = 0$, then we obtain the intuitive results that $M^d/p = cK^*$ and $u' = u = a$. This last equation means that, in a steady state with no money growth, the users' cost equals the tradable marginal product of capital.

Finally, using equation (4), we obtain an implicit solution K^*:

$$G'\left(\frac{\overline{K} - K^*}{n}\right) = \frac{1+\pi}{\beta'^2}(a - \pi c). \tag{16.13}$$

Along with Assumption 2, equation (13) implies that, in equilibrium, borrowers have higher marginal products of capital than do lenders. The following proposition summarizes the main features of the steady state.

Proposition 1: *Under Assumptions 1 and 2:*

(1) *if $G'(\overline{K}/n) < (1+\pi)(a-\pi c)/\beta'^2$ then there exists a unique steady state;*
(2) *$\partial K^*/\partial\pi \neq 0$ for $(1+2\pi)c \neq a$, so that inflation affects the steady-state output Y^*.*

***Proof*:** The existence of a unique steady-state level K^* is guaranteed by the properties of the production function $G(\cdot)$. It is easy to see that the left-hand side of Equation (13) is continuous and strictly increasing in K, while the right-hand side is a constant. If

$$G'\left(\frac{\overline{K}}{n}\right) < \frac{1+\pi}{\beta'^2}(a - \pi c),$$

then the left- and right-hand sides cross only once. Figure 16.1 illustrates the determination of the steady state. The second property follows easily. □

It is interesting to note that, in the long run, money is not superneutral (as indicated by Proposition 1) even though aggregate capital is constant. It is well known that money is not superneutral if investment enters in the CIA constraint, because inflation acts as a tax on capital accumulation (Abel 1985). However, aggregate capital is constant in our model, so the standard result does not apply. The nonsuperneutrality arises because inflation acts as a tax for all agents, but at the margin it affects borrowers and lenders differently. Higher inflation decreases the marginal cost of investing for both types; that is, it decreases the users' cost of capital. For a given K^*, borrowers' net worths decrease with higher inflation because they must demand more money in order to sustain their consumption, cK^*. Moreover, since borrowers are credit constrained, they are in a corner solution. In contrast, lenders have an interior solution, and since u has decreased, their marginal benefit of investing must decrease, which can happen only if lenders' capital holdings $\overline{K} - K^*$ increase. Thus, because of the asymmetric effect of inflation on constrained and unconstrained agents, money is not superneutral.[14]

[14] If the borrowers' propensity to consume $c/(a+c)$ is larger than 0.5 then higher inflation reduces output, a result consistent with Abel (1985). However, if money is injected via helicopter drops rather than via OMOs, higher steady-state inflation may have the opposite effect; i.e., higher π implies larger K^* and larger Y^*. This occurs if

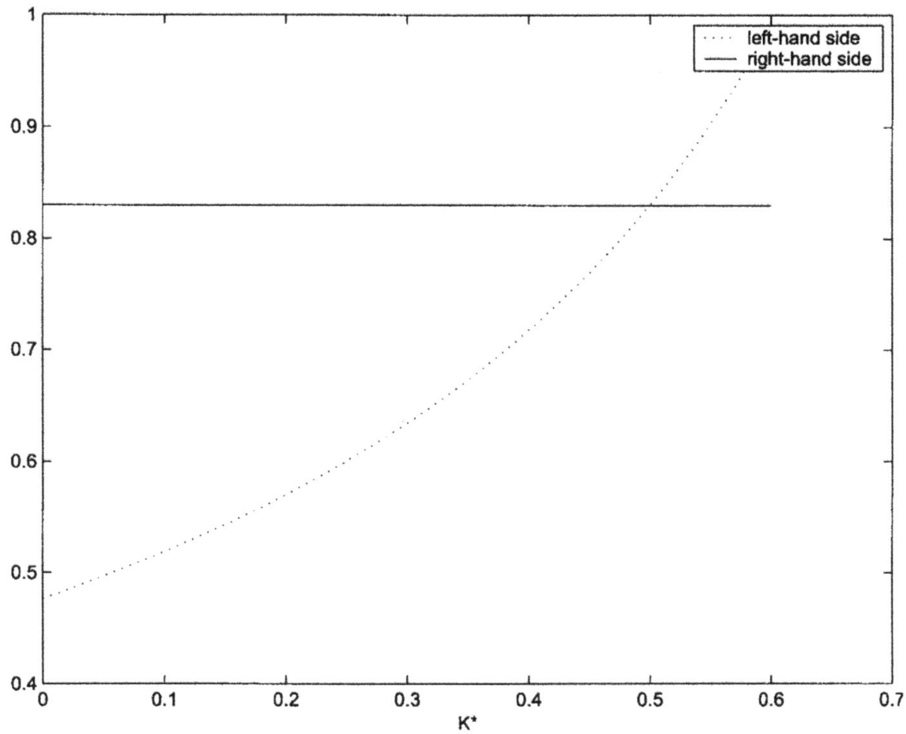

Figure 16.1. Steady-state distribution of capital.

3. Dynamics

To simplify the analysis, we present the dynamics of the model only around the steady state and assume zero steady-state inflation, $\pi = 0$. The solution for the case $\pi > 0$ is summarized in Appendix E. We also assume that β' is close to 1. This occurs, for example, if the length of the periods is small. This assumption allows as to obtain some sharp analytical results, but numerical simulations confirm that the main results hold even if β' is far from 1. Let $g_t \equiv M_t^s/M_{t-1}^s$ (i.e., g_t is 1 plus the growth rate of money supply) and $v_t = p_{t+1}/p_t$ (i.e., v_t is 1 plus the inflation rate). Thus, in the steady state, $g = v = 1 + \pi$. In general, let $\hat{x}_t = (x_t - x^*)/x^*$ denote the rate of deviation of a variable x from its steady-state value.

Assume that the economy starts off at the steady state and that an unexpected increase in the growth rate of money $\varepsilon > 0$ occurs at $t = 0$; that is, $\hat{g}_0 = \varepsilon$. Since the monetary expansion occurs through OMOs, H_0 decreases below its steady-state level ($\widehat{H}_0 < 0$). According to our law of motion for government bonds, $H_t^s = \tau H_{t-1}^s$, and H_t gradually returns to zero in order to avoid changes in the long-term inflation rate. Thus, the money expansion at $t = 0$ is followed by a monetary contraction—that is, by a "sterilization policy".

borrowers receive a fraction of the transfer higher than their steady-state consumption share, $\alpha \equiv cK^*/Y^*$. In this case, borrowers are overcompensated for the inflationary tax and, as a result, they can afford to buy additional capital with the extra resources. In addition, inflation increases the marginal cost of investing u, but lenders are particularly hurt because they face an interior solution.

In particular, the size of $\tau < 1$ determines the speed at which such monetary contraction takes place.

Let the ratio of government debt to money be $d_t \equiv H_t^s/M_t^s$. Using the law of motion of money supply and bonds, one can obtain the following path of money growth:[15]

$$\hat{g}_0 = -\partial d_0,$$
$$\hat{g}_t = -(R-\tau)\tau^{t-1}\hat{g}_0.$$

Notice that this path is fully determined by the exogenous initial shock, and it converges to zero at a rate determined by the size of τ. In particular, a larger τ implies a smoother sterilization of the initial monetary expansion. In what follows we will assume a τ very close to unity in order to simulate a very slow monetary contraction.[16]

To complete the characterization of the dynamics of the model, we need to solve for the paths of $\hat{v}_t$, $\hat{q}_t$, and $\widehat{K}_t$. Linearizing equation (12) yields

$$\hat{v}_t = \hat{g}_t - \rho(\widehat{K}_t - \widehat{K}_{t-1}),$$

where $\rho = (a + c - G')K^*/(M^s/p)$. Notice that prices at $t = 0$ do not change, because both output and the money supply used for transactions in the goods market are predetermined. Next, linearizing equation (4) yields

$$\hat{q}_t - \beta'\hat{q}_{t+1} = (1-\beta')\left(\frac{1}{\eta} - \rho\right)\widehat{K}_t + (1-\beta')\rho\widehat{K}_{t+1} - (1-\beta')\hat{g}_{t+1}, \tag{16.14}$$

where $1/\eta = -G''K^*/(nG') > 0$.[17] Equation (14) describes the forward-looking nature of capital prices; that is, the price of capital at $t = 0$ depends on the full path of capital distributions across types.

Finally, using the three preceding expressions as well as the linearized versions of Equations (5)–(7), it is easy to show that $\widehat{K}_t$ satisfies the following nonhomogeneous second-order difference equation for $t \geq 2$:

$$\theta_0\widehat{K}_t = \theta_1\widehat{K}_{t-1} + \theta_2\widehat{K}_{t-2} + \mu_0\tau^{t-2}\hat{g}_0, \tag{16.15}$$

where $\theta_0, \theta_1, \theta_2$, and μ_0 are constants that depend on steady-state variables (see Appendix B). It can be shown that, for β' close to 1, these constants are given

[15] Here, because $d = 0$ we compute the absolute deviations of the government debt/money ratio ∂d_0 instead of the percentage deviations from the steady state. The first expresion follows from linearizing the stationary version of the equation $M_0^s = M_{-1}^s - H_0^s$. For $t \geq 1$, combine the law of motion for H_t^s and M_t^s, transform variables to render them stationary, and linearize to obtain $\hat{g}_t = (R-\tau)\partial d_{t-1}$. Next, use the law of motion of government debt to obtain $\partial d_t = \tau\partial d_{t-1} = \tau^t\partial d_0$, which together with the previous expression implies that $\hat{g}_t = (R-\tau)\tau^{t-1}\partial d_0 = -(R-\tau)\tau^{t-1}\hat{g}_0$.

[16] When there is a monetary expansion at $t = 0$ and τ is very close to 1 the money contraction at $t = 1$ is very small. Ideally, for a more "realistic" scenario one could have a more persistent money expansion, eventually followed by a contraction. In the context of our simple model, since we analyze a one-time money expansion, using τ close to unity means that most of the subsequent money contraction occurs several periods after the money expansion.

[17] The term $1/\eta$ can be rewritten as $1/\eta = [-(G''(\overline{K} - K^*)/n)/G']K^*/(\overline{K} - K^*)$, and it can be interpreted as a measure of the elasticity of the marginal product of borrowers' capital weighted by the ratio of borrowers' to lenders' capital in the steady state.

by $\theta_0 = 1 - \rho > 0$, $\theta_1 \approx 2\theta_0$, $\theta_2 \approx -\theta_0$, and $\mu_0 \approx -(1-\tau)^2$. This last term reflects that a money injection at $t = 0$ generates a negative trend in K_t as a result of the sterilization that takes place after the injection.

Equation (15) summarizes the equilibrium dynamics of the model. It can be shown that $\widehat{K}_t$ exhibits persistent and dampening cycles, as captured by the following proposition.

Proposition 2: *For β' sufficiently close to* 1 *and for $\pi = 0$,*

(1) *the general solution to* (15) *is*

$$\widehat{K}_t = Ar^t \cos(\omega t - \phi) + A_\tau \tau^t \hat{g}_0, \tag{16.16}$$

where A and ϕ are constants, $r = \sqrt{-\theta_2/\theta_0}$, $\omega = \cos^{-1}((\theta_1/\theta_0)/2r)$, and $A_\tau = \mu_0/(\theta_0\tau^2 - \theta_1\tau - \theta 2)$;[18]

(2) *r is close to but less than,* 1, *and w is close to but larger than* 0.

***Proof*:** See Appendix B. □

Corollary 1: *$\widehat{K}_t$ exhibits persistent and dampening cycles.*

The cyclical dynamics of the model are consistent with the hump-shaped pattern of output response to shocks that has been observed in the data. In order to develop some intuition for the cycles, it is useful to rewrite the dynamics in terms of the two state variables of the model: the borrowers' capital stock K_{t-1} and their real money balances M^r_{t-1}. These real balances are defined as $M^r_{t-1} \equiv M^d_{t-1}/p_t$. Notice that M^r_{t-1} is predetermined at time t because both nominal balances M^d_{t-1} and prices are predetermined.[19] Using Equation (15) and the linearized version of (5), we can write a dynamic system that has the following sign pattern for β' close to 1:[20]

$$\begin{bmatrix} \widehat{M}^r_t \\ \widehat{K}_t \end{bmatrix} = \begin{bmatrix} + & - \\ + & + \end{bmatrix} \begin{bmatrix} \widehat{M}^r_{t-1} \\ \widehat{K}_{t-1} \end{bmatrix}.$$

Here the borrowers' capital holdings $\widehat{K}_{t-1}$ act as a "predator," and their real money holdings $\widehat{M}^r_{t-1}$ act as "prey." A rise in M^r_{t-1} allows borrowers to purchase more capital ($\partial K_t/\partial M^r_{t-1} > 0$). However, a rise in K_{t-1} means that borrowers have a greater debt overhang at date t, which restricts their ability to expand $M^r_t (\partial M^r_t/\partial K_{t-1} < 0)$. In other words, capital is a predator because—as a result of the binding collateral constraint—capital is linked strongly to debt. In turn, money acts as the prey, because higher debt payments restrict borrowers' ability to demand cash in order to buy more capital next period.[21,22]

[18]Note that $\lim_{\beta' \to 1} A_\tau = -1/(1-\rho)$.

[19]See the quantity equation (12).

[20]It can be shown that the elements of the 2 × 2 matrix are given by: $a_{11} = -(1 - c/q) + \theta_1/\theta_0$; $a_{12} = (q/c)(\theta_2/\theta_0) + (1 - q/c)[(1 - c/q) - \theta_1/\theta_0]$; $a_{21} = c/q$; and $a_{22} = 1 - c/q$.

[21]The predator–prey analogy is not as clear as in Section III of Kiyotaki and Moore (1997), where they decouple the system in terms of capital (prey) and debt (predator). We cannot decouple the system in those terms because aggregate capital and debt are strongly linked when the borrowing constraint is binding for all borrowers.

[22]The matricial representation shown above makes apparent that our monetary model does not exhibit indeterminacy. We have two initial conditions that can be used to solve for A and ϕ in equation (16).

The existence of dampening cycles rather than monotonic dynamics occurs in this model because of the interplay between the CIA and collateral constraints. In particular, the full impact of a shock that increases net worth is delayed in this model because, with a binding CIA constraint, collateral can be accumulated only gradually. In other words, the CIA constraint on investment acts as a "time to build" constraint for capital. This constraint delays the reaction of the economy to shocks in a way that is similar to adjustment-costs models, which are well known to generate cyclical responses. We demonstrate this formally in Appendix C, where we show that a model without investment in the CIA constraint but with a time-to-build restriction exhibits cyclical dynamics similar to the one described in Proposition 2.[23]

To fully characterize the equilibrium solution summarized in equation (15), we require two additional conditions on the trajectory of $\widehat{K}_t$. We first show that $\widehat{K}_0 = 0$ (or $K_0 = K^*$). To see this, consider the borrower's CIA constraint at time 0,

$$q_0^n(k_0 - k^*) + p_0 x_0 \leq m_{-1}^d.$$

Notice that m_{-1}^d was chosen the period before the shock in order to buy consumption goods; that is, $m_{-1}^d = p_0^e ck^*$, where p_0^e denotes the expected price at time 0. In addition, we have already shown (in Appendix A) that around the steady state it is optimal to set $x_t = ck_{t-1}$. Therefore, the preceding equation can be rewritten as

$$q_0^n(k_0 - k^*) \leq (p_0^e - p_0)ck^*.$$

Moreover, according to the quantity equation (12), p_0 depends only on M_{-1}^s and K^* so that $p_0^e = p_0$. In particular, the monetary injection does not affect time-0 prices because the injection occurs in the bonds market, not in the goods market. As a result, k_0 must satisfy $q_0^n k_0 \leq q_0^n k^*$. Finally, we have already shown (in Appendix A) that it is optimal for borrowers to invest all resources around the steady state. Thus, $k_0 = k^*$ and $K_0 = K^*$.

Since $\widehat{K}_0 = 0$, it follows that the equilibrium path can be completely characterized in terms of $\widehat{K}_1$. Given $\widehat{K}_1$ and $\widehat{K}_0 = 0$, one can use equation (16) evaluated at $t = 0$ and $t = 1$ to solve for A and ϕ. The solution is

$$A = \frac{\widehat{K}_1 - A_\tau \tau \hat{g}_0}{\cos(\omega - \phi)} \quad \text{and} \quad \cos(\phi) = -\frac{A_\tau \hat{g}_0}{A}.$$

We now solve for $\widehat{K}_1$ following a monetary shock at $t = 0$. For this purpose, combine (5), (6), and (7) to obtain

$$q_1(K_1 - K_0) + cK_0 = \frac{a + c}{1 + \pi_0} K_{-1} + \frac{1}{1 + \pi_0} \frac{B_0}{p_0} - \frac{R_0}{(1 + \pi_0)(1 + \pi_{-1})} \frac{B_{-1}}{p_{-1}}, \tag{16.17}$$

[23]The fact that it is the time-to-build feature of the CIA that lies behind the cyclical dynamics allows us to draw a parallel between our model and Section III of Kiyotaki and Moore (1997), where noncollateralizable "trees" are introduced. In their model with trees, cyclical dynamics emerge from the fact that, in each period, only a fraction of the farmers have an investment opportunity. In a way, investors are exogenously constrained because they must "wait" for the arrival of the investment opportunity. In our model, investors are constrained by the CIA because they must "wait" until they collect the cash before they can buy capital.

Furthermore, in Section III of Kiyotaki and Moore (1997), the existence of noncollateralizable trees by itself does not generate cyclical dynamics; it only dampens the reaction of quantities relative to the price of land. Similarly, in our model, the fact that money is a noncollateralizable asset is not the explanation for cycles; it simply generates a weakening of the leverage effect by reducing the debt-to-asset ratio.

where B_{-1}/p_{-1} is the aggregate steady-state level of debt in real terms and where K_{-1} corresponds to the borrowers' steady-state capital level.

We consider two relevant cases at this point, nonindexed (or nominal) versus indexed debt contracts. The difference between these two is that, under indexed contracts, borrowers must compensate lenders for any unexpected inflation. Thus, debt repayments at time 0 are immune to inflation π_0, that is, $R_0 B_{-1} = [(1+\pi_0)/\beta']B_{-1}$. In contrast, under nominal financial contracts, unexpected inflation/deflation produces a redistribution of wealth between debtors and creditors, as emphasized by Fisher (1933).

The focus of this paper is the transmission of money shocks in the presence of nominal financial contracts, the Fisher effect, and indexation. If contracts are indexed, then borrowers' nominal liabilities are proportional to the price level. Here, we do not consider fully state-contingent contracts under which these liabilities can be any function of the price level, and the collateral constraint will be set state-by-state.[24]

3.1 Nominal Contracts

When debt contracts are nominal or nonindexed, R_0 in (17) is simply the steady-state nominal interest rate $R = 1/\beta'$. Linearizing (17) in this case yields

$$\widehat{K}_1 = \frac{1}{1-\beta'\rho}[\beta'\hat{q}_1 + (2 - r^h - \beta'\tau)\varepsilon]. \tag{16.18}$$

In order to solve for $\widehat{K}_1$ we must first solve for $\hat{q}_1$, which in turn depends on the full sequence $\{\widehat{K}_t\}$. Solving equation (14) forward yields a solution for $\hat{q}_1$, as shown in Appendix D. The expression that relates $\hat{q}_1$ to $\widehat{K}_1$ is algebraically complicated.

We can use equation (18) to gain some intuition on the real effects of a monetary expansion $\varepsilon > 0$ under nonindexed contracts. Suppose initially that the real price of capital remains unchanged after the monetary shock, so that $\hat{q}_1 = 0$. In this case, the real effects of the shock depend on the size of τ. Specifically, if $\tau < \bar{\tau} \equiv (1/\beta')(2 - r^h)$, then K_1 (and also Y_2) move in the same direction as the monetary shock. This condition is satisfied when β' is close to 1 because in that case $\bar{\tau}$ is close to 2. Finally, this change in the distribution of capital toward the more productive agents induces an increase in the price of capital, $\hat{q}_1 > 0$, which reinforces the initial effect of the shock. Therefore, a monetary expansion under nonindexed debt contracts induces a redistribution of capital toward borrowers and also increases output.

3.2 Indexed Contracts

As we have indicated, if debt contracts are indexed then $R_0 = (1+\pi_0)/\beta'$. In this case, linearization of equation (17) yields

$$\widehat{K}_1 = \frac{1}{1-\beta'\rho}[\beta'\hat{q}_1 + (1 - r^h - \beta'\tau)\varepsilon]. \tag{16.19}$$

Equation (19) is very similar to (18), except that now we have a smaller coefficient for ε. This smaller coefficient has two important implications. First, the real effects of the

[24]We thank an anonymous referee for pointing this out to us. We analyze the effects of nominal versus indexed contracts without asking which of the two types of contracts would emerge as optimal. For optimal state-contingent contracts in simple nonmonetary economies see Krishnamurthy (2003) and Lorenzoni (2003).

money shock will be smaller than in the case of nonindexed debt contracts; that is, the redistribution of capital as well as the output amplification are smaller. Second, in contrast with the case of nonindexed debt contracts, a monetary expansion may now produce an output downturn rather than a boom. To see why, assume for a moment that $\hat{q}_1 = 0$. In that case, the real effects of the shock again depend on the size of τ. If $\tau < \bar{\tau} \equiv (1/\beta')(1 - r^h)$, then the monetary expansion will increase output. But for β' close to 1, $\bar{\tau}$ is close to 1. Thus, it may be possible to find $\tau > \bar{\tau}$ such that the monetary expansion generates a downturn.

To better highlight the mechanisms behind this result, it is useful to rewrite equation (17) as

$$q_1(K_1 - K_0) + cK_0 = \frac{a+c}{1+\pi_0}K_{-1} + \frac{\beta' q_1 K_0}{1+\pi_1} - \frac{R_0}{(1+\pi_0)(1+\pi_{-1})}\frac{B_{-1}}{p_{-1}}, \qquad (16.20)$$

where the left-hand side represents consumption and investment in $t = 1$, while the right-hand side captures the real balances brought from period $t = 0$. In particular: The first term on the right-hand side denotes output sales; the second term is new debt contracted in $t = 0$; and the third term is the repayment for debt contracted in $t = -1$. Notice that consumption in $t = 1$ is fixed because K_0 remains at the steady-state level. Thus, the only way borrowers can increase their investment in capital K_1 is if the right-hand side of the equation is larger than its steady-state value.

First, observe that under indexed debt contracts, since $R_0 = (1 + \pi_0)/\beta'$ it follows that the last term on the right-hand side does not change with the money expansion—it remains at its steady-state value. This implies that lenders do not transfer any wealth to borrowers via interest-rate repayments in the period of the shock.

Second, due to the monetary expansion $\hat{g}_0 > 0$, the level of prices in $t = 1$ increases, so that π_0 increases ($\hat{v}_0 > 0$). This hurts borrowers because the first term on the right-hand side, $[(a + c)/(1 + \pi_0)]K_{-1}$, decreases. Thus, the only way borrowers could increase K_1 is if the second term on the right-hand side, $\beta' q_1 K_0/(1 + \pi_1)$, increases by more than the decrease in $[(a + c)/(1 + \pi_0)]K_{-1}$. In general, π_1 decreases ($\hat{v}_1 < 0$) because of the policy reversal (i.e., the money contraction that follows the expansion). However, for τ sufficiently close to 1 (the case in which the money contraction in $t = 1$ is very small), the drop in π_1 is so small that $\beta' q_1 K_0/(1 + \pi_1)$ increases very little. In this case, borrowers decrease K_1 and the money expansion causes a downturn. In summary, the only way a monetary expansion can generate an increase in output when debt contracts are indexed is when this expansion is quickly reverted by a monetary contraction (i.e., small τ).

Finally, notice that, when debt is nonindexed, the third term on the right-hand side of (20) decreases with respect to the steady state, since π_0 increases due to the money expansion. What this means is that there is a transfer of wealth from creditors to debtors, which ultimately allows borrowers to increase K_1 and generate an output expansion.

3.3 Default and Asymmetric Business Cycles

Until now, we have assumed that the shock arrives in the morning, when it is too late to escape. Borrowers thus never have incentives to repudiate their debt contracts in the face of a shock because lenders could seize their capital, production, and money. Consider now what would happen if the shock is known when borrowers still have a chance to escape. For example, the government announces—after all markets are closed for the day—that an open-market operation will take place the next day. In this case, if the value of the collateral is expected to fall below the value of the debt, then borrowers could find it optimal to escape overnight. Alternatively, borrowers could renegotiate their debt down to the market value of the collateral. It turns out that if such renegotiation is possible then our model can generate asymmetric business cycles. In particular, if contracts are nonindexed and if there is a monetary contraction, then borrowers have incentives to renegotiate their debt and the output downturn is smoother.

The intuition for this result is as follows. If contracts are nonindexed, then the interest rate that borrowers pay is the steady-state rate. If there is a money contraction, this steady-state rate will be higher than the equilibrium rate due to deflation. Thus, borrowers' net worth is reduced, as well as their capital holdings. This, in turn, triggers a decrease in the price of capital. In this case, borrowers have incentives to repudiate their debts and pay back just the market value of the collateral. The fact that borrowers end up paying back less makes the output downturn less severe. Notice that, in contrast, if there is a monetary expansion, then borrowers will have no incentive to repudiate and renegotiate their debts. This is so because, in this case, the price of capital increases while the nominal interest rate remains at its steady-state value.[25]

Analytically, when debt is renegotiated, debt repayments R_0B_{-1}/p_{-1} are equal to the market value q_0K_{-1} of the collateral. Linearizing Equation (17) in this case yields

$$\widehat{K}_1 = \frac{1}{1-\beta'\rho}[\beta'\hat{q}_1 - \hat{q}_0 + (2 - r^h - \beta'\tau)\varepsilon],$$

which holds for both the indexed and nonindexed debt cases. It turns out that, when debt is renegotiated, the solution for $\widehat{K}_1$ can be simply written as[26]

$$\widehat{K}_1 = \frac{1}{\theta_0}[(1 - r^h) - (1 - 2\beta')(R - \tau)]\hat{g}_0. \tag{16.21}$$

Since this expression is algebraically simple, we can use it to analyze whether—following the monetary contraction in period $t = 0$—we then have $\widehat{K}_1 < 0$ and so $\widehat{Y}_2 < 0$. Further, if $\widehat{K}_2 < \widehat{K}_1$ then, since the model exhibits persistent dampening cycles, we should observe a downturn in the economic activity as borrowers' capital level decreases. Proposition 3 summarizes the conditions under which these results hold. Let $\alpha \equiv cK^*/Y^* < 1$ be the fraction of steady-state output consumed by the borrowers.

Proposition 3: *Let β' be sufficiently close to* 1 *and $\pi = 0$. Then:*

(1) *Following a decrease in the money growth rate $\varepsilon < 0$ at $t = 0$, borrowers decrease their capital holdings in period $t = 1$ (i.e., $\widehat{K}_1 < 0$). Furthermore, the lower is τ, the larger is $|\widehat{K}_1|$.*

[25] If debt contracts are indexed, renegotiation occurs depending on how interest payments change compared to the change in the price of the collateral. For instance, suppose τ is small enough that a monetary expansion triggers an increase in output. Then, if the nominal interest rate increases by more than the increase in the price of capital, borrowers will have incentives to renegotiate.

[26] Under renegotiation, the solution for $\widehat{K}_1$ is the same as that implied by the nonhomogeneous second-order differential equation for $t = 1$ and $\widehat{K}_0 = 0$.

(2) *If τ is sufficiently close to 1, then $\widehat{K}_2 < \widehat{K}_1$; if $\tau \to 0$, then a sufficient condition for $\widehat{K}_2 < \widehat{K}_1$ is that $\alpha < 1/3$.*

Proof: (1) If $\beta' \to 1$ then $\rho \to \alpha$ and $r^h \to 0$. Hence, $\theta_0 \to (1-\alpha)$. Thus, when $\beta' \to 1$ from equation (21) we have $\widehat{K}_1 \to [(2-\tau)/(1-\alpha)\hat{g}_0$, and since $\tau < 1$ and $\hat{g}_0 < 0$ it follows that $\widehat{K}_1 < 0$. Observe that the more slowly government debt returns to the steady state (i.e., the larger is τ), the lower is the multiplier of monetary policy in the first period.

(2) From equation (15) we have $\widehat{K}_2 = (\theta_1/\theta_0)\widehat{K}_1 + (\mu_0/\theta_0)\hat{g}_0$. When $\beta' \to 1$ we have that $R \to 1$ and so $\mu_0 \to -(1-\tau)^2$; therefore,

$$\widehat{K}_2 \to \frac{1}{1-\alpha}\left[\frac{2-\tau}{1-\alpha} - (1-\tau)^2\right]\hat{g}_0.$$

If $\tau \to 1$, then $\widehat{K}_2 \to [1/(1-\alpha)]\widehat{K}_1$ and so $\widehat{K}_2 < \widehat{K}_1$. On the other hand, if $\tau \to 0$ then $\widehat{K}_2 \to [1/(1-\alpha) - 1/2]\widehat{K}_1$, so that $\widehat{K}_2 < \widehat{K}_1$ if $\alpha < 1/3$. □

Part (2) in Proposition 3 indicates the role of τ in strengthening the real effects of a monetary contraction. In fact, when the sterilization policy is smooth (i.e., when τ is large), borrowers further decrease their capital stock at $t = 2$. This implies that they would be able to borrow less against their collateral, and their capital holdings will decrease for a number of periods after the shock. This occurs because, when the sterilization is smooth, the government expands the money supply in small amounts during several periods and so the nominal interest rate remains above the steady state (i.e., $\widehat{R}_t > 0$) for a longer time. In contrast, when the monetary contraction is reversed quickly (i.e., when $\tau \to 0$), this dynamic pattern for capital may not necessarily hold unless further conditions are imposed.

4. Simulations

To illustrate the magnitude and persistence of monetary shocks in this economy, we assign values to the parameters of the economy and simulate the effects of a 1% change in the growth rate of money at $t = 0$. The only purpose here is to illustrate the dynamics generated by our model, not to calibrate our stylized model. As such, the quantitative results presented here are not to be taken literally. We choose the parameters of the model to satisfy the assumptions imposed. We set $\beta' = 0.995$ in order to simulate a time period equal to a month. Note that β' is sufficiently close to 1, in accordance with the proofs already presented.

We normalize to unity the total stock of capital. The production technology for lenders is $G(K) = B(\overline{K} - K)^\gamma$, where B is also normalized to unity and $\gamma = 0.2$. We set $n = 3$, which implies that in this economy only 25% of the agents are constrained. Finally, we choose $c = 1/2$ and a such that lenders hold 50% of the total capital in steady state.

Figure 16.2 displays the effects of an unanticipated increase of 1% in the growth rate of money when $\pi = 0, \tau = 0.9$, and debt contracts are nonindexed. The figure shows percentage deviations from steady-state values. Since τ is large, the subsequent money contraction is smooth and government bonds go back gradually to their steady-state value $H^s = 0$. As is shown in the graph, this policy generates ample and persistent dampening cycles. The cycle starts with an increase in borrowers' capital holdings, as

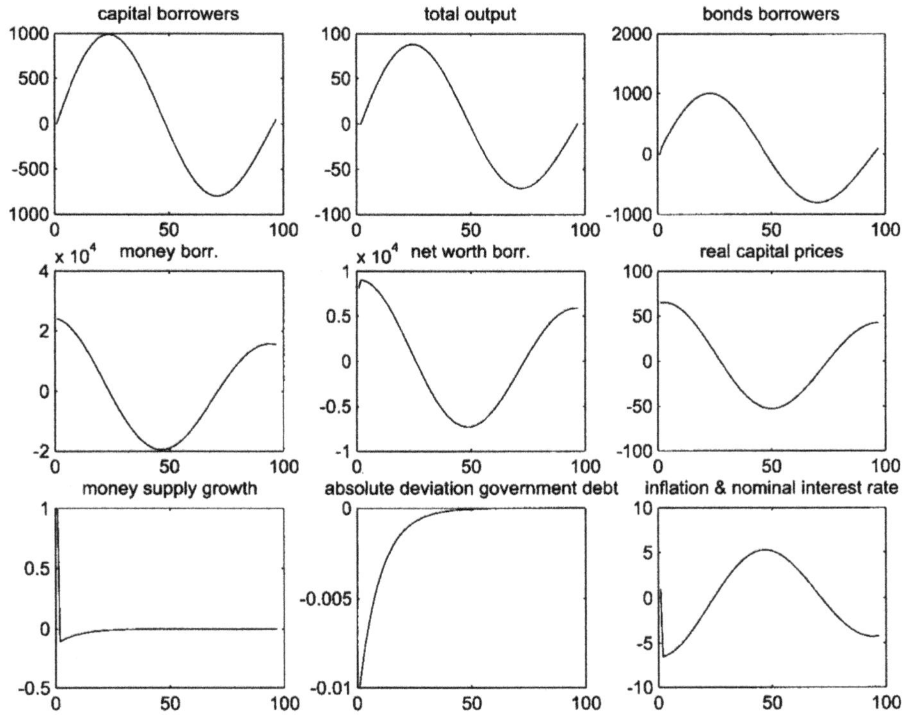

Figure 16.2. A 1% unexpected money expansion at $t = 0$ with nonindexed debt.

well as an increase in output. The peak of the cycle is reached about 25 months after the shock, when output is around 80% above the steady state. Of course, this quantitative result is unrealistically large and is due to nonstandard assumptions of the model, such as linear utility and linear production function for borrowers. What lies behind such large amplification is the redistribution of wealth from lenders to borrowers due to the nominal nature of the debt contract. In the figure, since the collateral constraint binds, real borrowers' debt mimics the behavior of capital.

These results emerge from the combination of two mechanisms that affect both sides of the collateral constraint: One is the asset-price effect, and the other is the interest-rate effect. First, in the period of the shock there is an increase of about 60% in the real price of capital which increases the value of the collateral for a number of periods. This increase in the asset price comes from the fact that, in order to clear the capital market, the users' cost for lenders must increase. Notice that the real price of capital is above the steady state for 25 months, which is exactly the time at which capital and bonds reach their peaks. Second, the nominal interest rate is at its steady-state value in the period of the shock, but it then decreases below the steady state.

Finally, borrowers' money demand and net worth mimic the pattern of capital prices: they are above the steady state while borrowers are investing and below the steady state when borrowers disinvest. Thus, in this model, disinvestment temporarily reduces liquidity needs. Notice that borrowers' net worth increases in the period of the shock because the value of capital increases and also because unexpected inflation under nonindexed contracts reduces real debt repayments.

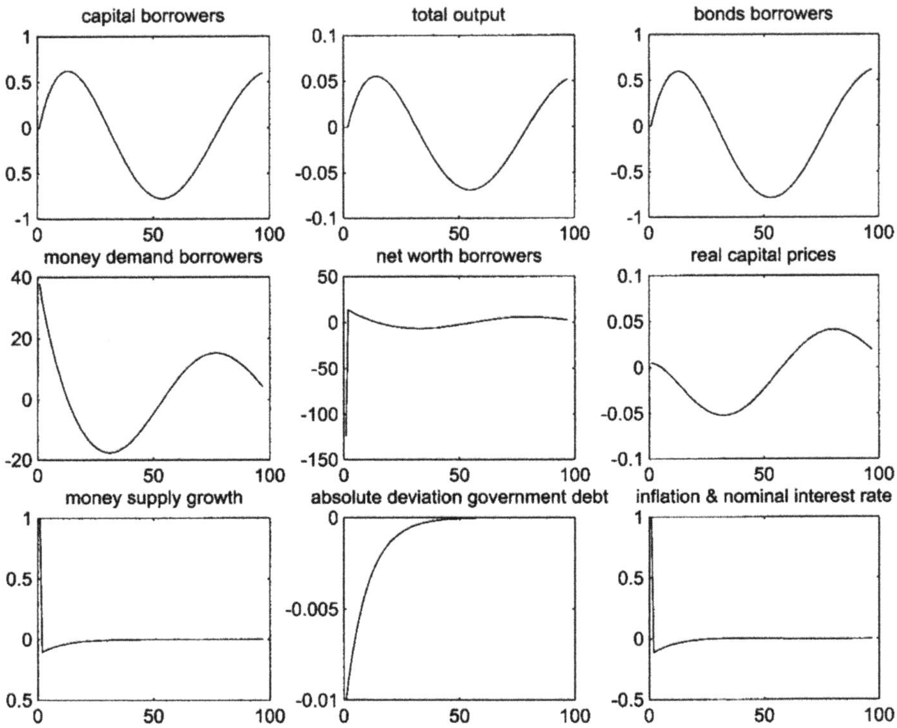

Figure 16.3. A 1% unexpected money expansion at $t = 0$ with indexed debt.

Figure 16.3 displays the effects of an unanticipated increase of 1% in the growth rate of money when $\pi = 0$, $\tau = 0.9$, and debt contracts are indexed. The most striking feature of Figure 16.3 is that the real effects of the money shock under indexed contracts are small when compared to those obtained in Figure 16.2. This highlights the difference between nominal and indexed contracts. When debt is indexed, there is no redistribution of wealth from less-productive lenders to more-productive borrowers. Moreover, the asset-price effect under indexed contracts is very small. Net worth decreases dramatically in the period of the shock because unexpected inflation under fully indexed contracts increases debt repayments.[27]

Finally, Figure 16.4 illustrates the case in which debt renegotiation takes place. It displays the effects of a decrease of 1% in the growth rate of money when $\pi = 0$, $\tau = 0.9$, and debt is nonindexed. In this case, the model still exhibits persistence, and the amplitude of the effects is much smaller than those observed in Figure 16.2. Notice that output reaches a trough of about -1.5%. Renegotiation avoids a deep economic downturn because it partially protects borrowers from deflation. In fact, in the period of the shock, net worth remains at its steady-state value because borrowers are able to renegotiate debt payments down to the market value of collateral.

[27]Although it is not clear from Figure 16.3, borrowers' net worth also cycles around the steady state. In this case, since there is indexation of contracts, deviations from the steady state are small compared with the substantial decrease in net worth observed in the period of the shock.

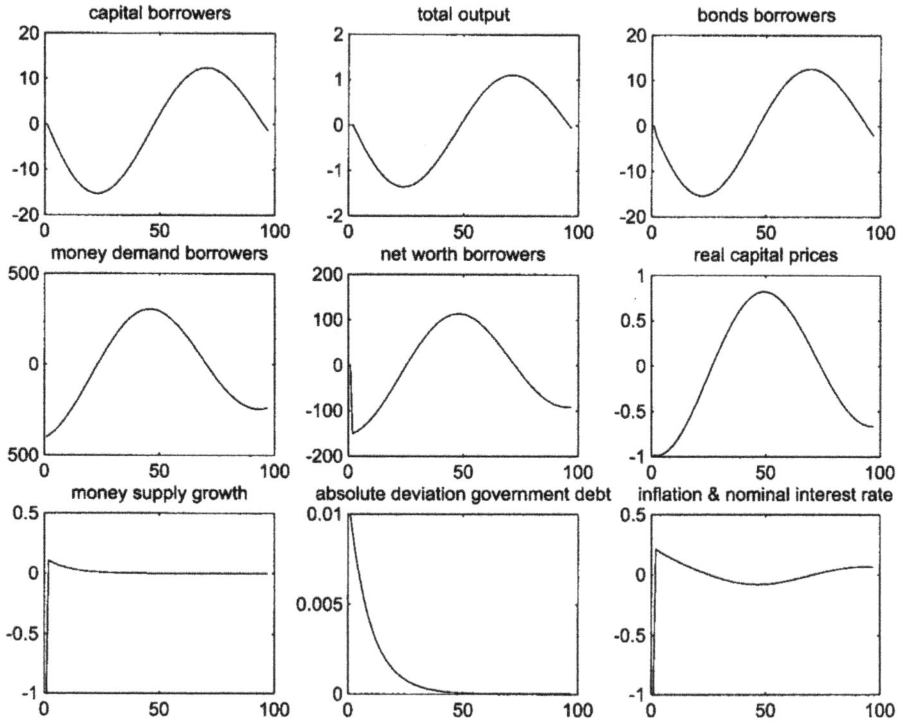

Figure 16.4. A 1% unexpected money contraction at $t = 0$ with debt renegotiation.

5. Concluding Comments

This paper analyzes the propagation of monetary shocks by combining collateral and cash-in-advance constraints in a world where changes in the money supply occur via open-market operations. We find that an unanticipated monetary injection generates persistent movements in aggregate output, the amplitude of which depends upon whether debt contracts are nominal or indexed. In general, output fluctuations are larger if only nominal contracts exist. Due to the interaction between the cash-in-advance and collateral constraints, monetary shocks trigger a highly persistent dampening cycle rather than a smoothly declining deviation.

The model is sufficiently simple to provide insights on how collateral constraints work in a monetary economy. Since the model is highly stylized, future work can involve the following extensions. First, both the utility and production functions may be modified to a more standard concave specification. This would be particularly important if the mechanisms described here were to be carefully quantified and compared with data. Second, in order to avoid excess response in nominal prices, other frictions besides collateral constraints would need to be introduced. Finally, the model has not been carefully calibrated to assess its ability to match the data. A careful calibration exercise is beyond the scope of this paper and is left for future research.

In summary, what we learn from the simple, stylized model analyzed here is that collateral constraints—in combination with cash-in-advance constraints—constitute a potential mechanism that can transform small monetary shocks into persistent output fluctuations.

Appendix A: Proof of Optimal Solution for Borrowers

We need to prove the claim that a borrower's optimal plan is to consume only the nontradable fraction of output (i.e., $x_t = cK_{t-1}$), to borrow up to the limit, and to invest all remaining resources. Toward this end, we compare the utility achieved under the different alternative plans. The first plan is to follow the proposed investment path; alternatively, borrowers can consume or save. For these last two alternatives, we consider only single deviations from the investment path at date $t = 0$.[28]

Consider the borrower's marginal utility of investing p_0 dollars, given that all aggregate variables remain unchanged at their steady-state levels. For simplicity, let $\pi = 0$. In steady state we have $R = 1/\beta'$ and $q = a/(1-\beta')$. Therefore, for given prices and aggregate variables at their steady-state levels, equations (5)–(7) can be rewritten as

$$qk_t + (c-q)k_{t-1} = \frac{m_{t-1}^d}{p_{t-1}}, \tag{16.A.1}$$

$$\frac{b_t}{p_t} = q\beta' k_t, \tag{16.A.2}$$

$$\frac{m_t^d}{p_t} = (a+c)k_{t-1} + \frac{b_t}{p_t} - R\frac{b_{t-1}}{p_{t-1}}. \tag{16.A.3}$$

Substituting the borrowing constraint into the budget constraint, we have

$$\frac{m_t^d}{p_t} = (a+c-q)k_{t-1} + q\beta' k_t. \tag{16.A.4}$$

Substituting $(A.4)$ into $(A.1)$ and solving for k_t then yields

$$k_t = \left[\beta' + 1 - \frac{c}{q}\right]k_{t-1} + \left[\frac{a+c}{q} - 1\right]k_{t-2}. \tag{16.A.5}$$

From the steady-state value of q, we have that

$$\left(\beta' + 1 - \frac{c}{q}\right) = 2 - (1-\beta') - \frac{c}{q} = 2 - \frac{a+c}{q} = 2 - r^h.$$

Let $r^h \equiv (a+c)/q$. Then we can rewrite $(A.5)$ as

$$k_t = (2-r^h)k_{t-1} + (r^h - 1)k_{t-2}. \tag{16.A.6}$$

It is easy to check that the roots of the associated characteristic polynomial are 1 and $1 - r^h$. Therefore, k_t can be expressed as

$$k_t = A_1 + A_2(1-r^h)^t, \tag{16.A.7}$$

where the constants A_1 and A_1 need to be determined. Under the proposed guess, the optimal strategy for borrowers is to use the extra p_0 dollars to invest in capital. With this amount, the

[28]Following the logic of Kiyotaki and Moore (1997), "we appeal to the principle of unimprovability," which states that—in order to prove that our proposed strategy of investing all the extra p_0 dollars is optimal—we need only consider single deviations from this plan at date $t = 0$.

borrower can buy $k_0 = 1/q$ units of capital at $t = 0$. This allows him to borrow $q\beta' k_0 = \beta'$ additional units of output.[29] At $t = 1$, consumption increases by ck_0 units so that, from the additional resources, $\beta' - c/q$ can be used to buy capital. Therefore, investment is given by $k_1 - k_0 = (\beta' - c/q)/q$, so that $k_1 = k_0(\beta' - c/q + 1)$. With these two initial values (k_0, k_1), the constants A_1 and A_2 can be determined as

$$A_1 = \frac{1}{r^h}[k_1 - (1 - r^h)k_0] \quad \text{and} \quad A_2 = \frac{k_0 - k_1}{r^h}.$$

Utility under the investment path is given by

$$\begin{aligned} U^{inv} &= \beta c \sum_{t=0}^{\infty} \beta^t k_t = \beta c \sum_{t=0}^{\infty} \beta^t [A_1 + A_2(1 - r^h)^t] \\ &= cA_1 \frac{\beta}{1 - \beta} + cA_2 \frac{\beta}{1 - \beta(1 - r^h)} \\ &= \frac{c}{q} \frac{\beta}{1 - \beta} \frac{\beta}{1 - \beta(1 - r^h)}. \end{aligned}$$

To show that higher utility is attained in the investment path than in the consumption path, we need to find conditions under which

$$\frac{c}{q} \frac{\beta}{1 - \beta} \frac{\beta}{1 - \beta(1 - r^h)} > 1.$$

We can transform this expression to obtain

$$\frac{c}{a} > \frac{(1 - \beta)}{\beta} \frac{(1 - \beta)}{(1 - \beta')} + (1 - \beta)\frac{a + c}{a}.$$

Since $(1 - \beta)/\beta < (1 - \beta)/\beta^2$, it follows that a sufficient condition for the utility from the investment path being higher is

$$\frac{c}{a} > \frac{(1 - \beta)}{\beta^2} \left[\frac{(1 - \beta)}{(1 - \beta')} + 1 \right],$$

which corresponds to Assumption 2 in the text.

To complete the proof we need to show that higher utility is attained in the investment path than in the savings path. Borrowers can save the p_0 dollars and use the return R to commence a strategy of maximum leveraged investment from date $t = 1$ onward. Then, all we need to show is that the returns from saving p_0 dollars in period $t = 0$ are lower than

[29] Note that p_0 dollars are equivalent to one unit of output at $t = 0$ prices. Also, by borrowing extra $b_0 = \beta'$, the agent can demand extra β' real money balances in the third subperiod of $t = 0$ in order to buy additional capital in the first subperiod of $t = 1$.

the returns from investing at $t = 0$. Since $\beta' > \beta$ by Assumption 1, using Assumption 2 we can easily show that $\beta' > a/(a+c)$. Thus,

$$1 + r^h = 1 + \frac{a+c}{q} = 1 + \frac{(a+c)(1-\beta')}{a} > 1 + \frac{1-\beta'}{\beta'} = \frac{1}{\beta'} = R.$$

Therefore, $1 + r^h > R$, which guarantees that the investment path yields more utility than the alternative savings path. This completes the proof that the proposed solution is an equilibrium. We have presented an analytical proof for $\pi = 0$. For $\pi \neq 0$, it is not possible to provide an analytical proof. However, for all the numerical simulations in the text, we have verified by computer that the decision rules for the borrower are optimal.

Appendix B: Proof of Proposition 2

Let $\pi = 0$, so that in steady state $u = a$. Equation (15) reads

$$\theta_0 \widehat{K}_t = \theta_1 \widehat{K}_{t-1} + \theta_2 \widehat{K}_{t-2} + \mu_0 \tau^{t-2} \hat{g}_0, \tag{16.B.1}$$

where

$$\begin{aligned}
\theta_0 &= 1 + (1-2\beta')\rho, \\
\theta_1 &= (1-r^h)(1-\rho) + 1 + (1-2\beta')\rho - (1-\beta')\frac{1}{\eta}, \\
\theta_2 &= -(1-r^h)(1-\rho), \\
\mu_0 &= -(R-\tau)[(1-2\beta')\tau + (1-r^h)].
\end{aligned}$$

Since the particular solution for equation $(B.1)$ is

$$\widehat{K}_p = \frac{\mu_0 \hat{g}_0 \tau^t}{\theta_0 \tau^2 - \theta_1 \tau - \theta_2},$$

it follows that the general solution is given by

$$\widehat{K}_t = A_1 \lambda_1^t + A_2 \lambda_2^t + A_\tau \tau^t \hat{g}_0. \tag{16.B.2}$$

Here $A_\tau = \mu_0/(\theta_0 \tau^2 - \theta_1 \tau - \theta_2)$ is a constant, and the eigenvalues λ_1 and λ_2 satisfy $\lambda_1 \lambda_2 = -\theta_2/\theta_0$ and $\lambda_1 + \lambda_2 = \theta_1/\theta_0$. Finally, solutions for the constants A_1 and A_2 can be obtained from $\widehat{K}_1 = A_1 \lambda_1 + A_2 \lambda_2 + A_\tau \tau \hat{g}_0$ and $\widehat{K}_0 = A_1 + A_2 + A_\tau \hat{g}_0$.

B.1. Cycles

The dynamic properties of equation (B.1) depend on the eigenvalues associated with the homogeneous difference equation $\theta_0\widehat{K}_t = \theta_1\widehat{K}_{t-1} + \theta_2\widehat{K}_{t-2}$, which are given by

$$\lambda_1, \lambda_2 = \frac{\theta_1 \pm \sqrt{\theta_1^2 + 4\theta_0\theta_2}}{2\theta_0}.$$

The necessary and sufficient condition for cycles is $\theta_1^2 + 4\theta_0\theta_2 < 0$. Note that θ_1 can be rewritten as

$$\theta_1 = \theta_0 - \theta_2 - (1-\beta')\frac{1}{\eta}. \tag{16.B.3}$$

Adding and subtracting proper terms, θ_2 can be rewritten as

$$\theta_2 = \xi(\beta') - \theta_0, \tag{16.B.4}$$

where

$$\begin{aligned}\xi(\beta') &\equiv 2\rho(1-\beta') + r^h(1-\rho)\\ &= (1-\beta')\left(2\rho + \frac{a+c}{a}(1-\rho)\right) > 0.\end{aligned}$$

From (B.3) and (B.4), θ_1 can be written as

$$\theta_1 = 2\theta_0 - \zeta(\beta'), \tag{16.B.5}$$

where

$$\begin{aligned}\xi(\beta') &\equiv (1-\beta')\left(2\rho + \frac{a+c}{a}(1-\rho) + \frac{1}{\eta}\right)\\ &< (1-\beta')\left[\max\left\{2, \frac{a+c}{a}\right\} + \frac{1}{\eta}\right].\end{aligned}$$

Finally, from (B.3) and (B.4), $\lim_{\beta'\to 1}\theta_2 = \theta_0$ and $\lim_{\beta'\to 1}\theta_1 = 2\theta_0$.

B.2. Proof of Proposition 3

To show that the model exhibits cycles for β' sufficiently large, it needs to be proven that $\theta_1^2 + 4\theta_0\theta_2 < 0$. Use ($B$.4) and ($B$.5) to get

$$\begin{aligned}\theta_1^2 + 4\theta_0\theta_2 &= (2\theta_0 - \zeta(\beta'))^2 - 4[\theta_0 - \xi(\beta')]\theta_0\\ &< -4\theta_0(1-\beta')\frac{1}{\eta} + (1-\beta')^2\left[\max\left\{2, \frac{a+c}{a}\right\} + \frac{1}{\eta}\right]^2.\end{aligned}$$

Note that

$$\lim_{\beta'\to 1} \frac{1}{\eta} = -\frac{G''((\overline{K} - K^1)/n)K^1}{nG'((\overline{K} - K^1)/n)} > 0,$$

where K^1 is the solution of (13) for $\beta' = 1$ and $\pi = 0$. Therefore, the second term in the last expression approaches zero faster than the first term as $\beta' \to 1$. Note that θ_0/η remains bounded above, since θ_0 approaches $1 - \alpha^N(K^1) > 0$ and since $1/\eta$ approaches a constant greater than zero. Thus, for β' large enough, the first term dominates and the expression is negative.

It is also useful to state solution (B.2) in its polar representation

$$\widehat{K}_t = Ar^t \cos(\omega t + \phi) + A_\tau \tau^t,$$

where A and ϕ are constants that can be determined from the initial conditions and where

$$r = \sqrt{-\theta_2/\theta_0},$$

$$\omega = \cos^{-1}\left(\frac{\theta_1/\theta_0}{2r}\right).$$

Stability is guaranteed if the modulo r is less than 1, a result that follows from (B.5) for large β'. In addition, r is close to 1 when β' is close to 1. Thus, the difference equation displays persistent dampening cycles.

Appendix C: Cash in Advance in Investment as Time-to-Build Capital

We devise a model that generates a cyclical response (like the one described in Proposition 2) if investment is not in the CIA constraint and there is a time-to-build constraint for capital accumulation. We proceed in two steps: first, we show that changes in capital prices are fundamental in obtaining cyclical dynamics but that changes in interest rates are not. This result allows us to abstract from changes in the nominal interest rate.[30] Second, we solve the model just proposed.

Step 1. Equation (A.6) shows that when prices (the nominal interest rate and capital prices) are constant, cyclical dynamics cannot emerge in our model. Next, if capital prices are kept fixed and interest rates are allowed to adjust, then (A.6) is transformed to

$$\widehat{K}_t = (1 + \phi)\widehat{K}_{t-1} - \phi\widehat{K}_{t-2},$$

where $\phi \equiv (1 - r^h)(1 - \rho)/(1 - \beta'\rho)$. Again, cyclical dynamics cannot emerge in this case because the associated roots are 1 and ϕ.

[30] If the interest rate is allowed to adjust then similar results hold, but we can only verify them numerically.

In contrast, if the interest rate is kept fixed and capital prices are allowed to adjust, it can be shown that the dynamics of the model are described by

$$\widehat{K}_t = (2 - r^h - \epsilon)\widehat{K}_{t-1} + (r^h - 1)\widehat{K}_{t-2},$$

where $\epsilon \equiv (1 - \beta')/\eta$; the associated roots are given by

$$\left(1 - \frac{r^h + \epsilon}{2}\right) \pm \frac{1}{2}\sqrt{(r^h + \epsilon)^2 - 4\epsilon}.$$

For β' sufficiently large, ϵ and r^h are close to zero and the term in the square root is negative, giving rise to cyclical dynamics. Since, in addition, the real part of the roots is less than 1, the model exhibits dampening oscillations. It can also be shown that, for β' sufficiently large, the general equilibrium equation for capital behaves in the same way as the partial equilibrium equation with fixed interest rates. In conclusion, since changes in the interest rate play no role in generating the cyclical behavior of the model, we abstract from them in what follows.

Step 2. Consider the following model, in which: (a) investment does not enter the CIA constraint and (b) in order to introduce some time to build, capital for period $t + 1$ is decided at time t. The CIA and budget constraints for lenders in this model are given by

$$p_t x'_t \leq m^{d\prime}_{t-1},$$

$$m^{d\prime}_t + R_t b'_{t-1} + h'_t + q^n_t(k'_{t+1} - k'_t) \leq p_t G(k'_{t-1}) + b'_t + R_t h'_{t-1},$$

which imply the equilibrium nominal interest rate

$$R_t = \frac{p_{t+1}}{\beta' p_t} \equiv \frac{1 + \pi_t}{\beta'}$$

and a users' cost for lenders given by

$$u'_t \equiv \frac{q_t}{1 + \pi_t} - \beta' \frac{q_{t+1}}{1 + \pi_{t+1}} = \beta'^2 \frac{1}{1 + \pi_{t+2}} G'(k'_{t+1}).$$

Similarly, for borrowers the CIA, budget, and collateral constraints are (respectively) given by

$$p_t x_t \leq m^d_{t-1},$$

$$m^d_t + R_t b_{t-1} + q^n_t(k_{t+1} - k_t) + h_t \leq (a + c)p_t k_{t-1} + b_t + R_t h_{t-1},$$

$$R_{t+1} b_t \leq q^n_{t+1} k_t.$$

These equations (along with optimality conditions) imply that

$$k_{t+1} = (1 + \pi_t)\left[\beta' \frac{q_{t+1}}{q_t} \frac{1}{1 + \pi_{t+1}} - \frac{c}{q_t} + \frac{1}{1 + \pi_t}\right] k_t + \left[\frac{a + c}{q_t} - 1\right] k_{t-1}.$$

It can be shown that, for fixed interest rates, the linearized version of the foregoing equation is given by[31]

$$\widehat{K}_t = \frac{2 - r^h}{1 + \epsilon}\widehat{K}_{t-1} + \frac{r^h - 1}{1 + \epsilon}\widehat{K}_{t-2},$$

whose associated roots are

$$\frac{2 - r^h}{2(1 + \epsilon)} \pm \frac{1}{2(1 + \epsilon)}\sqrt{(r^h)^2 - 4\epsilon(1 - r^h)};$$

since $r^h \to 0$ as $\beta \to 1$, it follows that the term in the square root is negative and we have cyclical dynamics as desired.

Appendix D: Forward-Looking Solution for Asset Prices

This appendix gives the solution for $\hat{q}_0$ and $\pi = 0$. Equation (14) reads

$$\hat{q}_t - \beta'\hat{q}_{t+1} = (1 - \beta')\left(\frac{1}{\eta} - \rho\right)\widehat{K}_t + (1 - \beta')\rho\widehat{K}_{t+1} - (1 - \beta')\,\hat{g}_{t+1};$$

from this we iterate forward, using the transversality condition $\hat{q}_\infty = 0$ to rule out bubbles in the price of capital, and so obtain

$$\begin{aligned}\frac{\hat{q}_0}{1 - \beta'} &= \sum_{j=0}^{\infty} \beta'^j \left[\left(\frac{1}{\eta} - \rho\right)\widehat{K}_j + \rho\widehat{K}_{j+1} - \hat{g}_{j+1}\right] \\ &= \left(\frac{1}{\eta} - \rho\right)\widehat{K}_0 + \sum_{j=0}^{\infty} \beta'^j \left(\beta'\left(\frac{1}{\eta} - \rho\right) + \rho\right)\widehat{K}_{j+1} - \sum_{j=0}^{\infty} \beta'^j \hat{g}_{j+1}.\end{aligned}$$

Using the solution for the nonhomogeneous second-order difference equation (B.1), we have

$$\begin{aligned}\frac{\hat{q}_0}{1 - \beta'} &= \left(\frac{1}{\eta} - \rho\right)\widehat{K}_0 + \left(\beta'\left(\frac{1}{\eta} - \rho\right) + \rho\right) \\ &\quad \times \sum_{j=0}^{\infty} \beta'^j \left(A_1\lambda_1^{j+1} + A_2\lambda_2^{j+1} + A_\tau \tau^{j+1}\hat{g}_0\right) + (R - \tau)\hat{g}_0 \sum_{j=0}^{\infty} \beta'^j \tau^j,\end{aligned}$$

[31] If interest rates are allowed to adjust, then the linearized dynamic equation would be an AR(3) rather than an AR(2). Since analytical results are more complicated with an AR(3), we have verified numerically that cyclical dynamics also obtain in this case.

which after some algebra yields

$$\frac{\hat{q}_0}{(1-\beta')} = \left(\frac{1}{\eta}-\rho\right)\widehat{K}_0 + \left(\beta'\left(\frac{1}{\eta}-\rho\right)+\rho\right)\frac{(\lambda_1 A_1+\lambda_2 A_2)-\beta'\lambda_1\lambda_2(A_1+A_2)}{1-\beta'(\lambda_1+\lambda_2)+\beta'^2\lambda_2\lambda_2} + \left(\beta'\left(\frac{1}{\eta}-\rho\right)+\rho\right)\frac{\tau A_\tau \hat{g}_0}{1-\beta'\tau}+\frac{(R-\tau)\hat{g}_0}{1-\beta'\tau}.$$

Finally, using $\widehat{K}_0 = 0$ and the properties of λ_1, λ_2, and $\widehat{K}_1$ from Appendix B, we obtain (after some algebra)

$$\frac{\hat{q}_0}{1-\beta'} = \frac{(\beta'(1/\eta-\rho)+\rho)\theta_0}{\theta_0-\beta'\theta_1-\beta'^2\theta_2}\widehat{K}_1 + \frac{(R-\tau)\hat{g}_0}{1-\beta'\tau} + \left(\beta'\left(\frac{1}{\eta}-\rho\right)+\rho\right)\left[\frac{\tau}{1-\beta'\tau}-\frac{(\theta_0\tau+\beta'\theta_2)}{\theta_0-\beta'\theta_1-\beta'^2\theta_2}\right]A_\tau \hat{g}_0,$$

which solves for $\hat{q}_0$ as a function of $\widehat{K}_1$. Also, the following equation relates $\hat{q}_0$, $\hat{q}_1$, and $\widehat{K}_1$:

$$\hat{q}_0 = \beta'\hat{q}_1 + (1-\beta')\rho^\pi \widehat{K}_1 + (1-\beta')(R-\tau)\hat{g}_0.$$

Appendix E: Solution for Nonzero Inflation

If the steady-state inflation is not zero ($\pi > 0$) then our simple rule—that following a money shock at $t = 0$ we can guarantee convergence of d_t back to the steady state by imposing $\tau < 1$—no longer holds. Recall that, since $H_t^s = \tau H_{t-1}^s$ and since $H^s = 0$ when $\pi = 0$, it follows that $\tau < 1$ is enough to guarantee that H_t^s eventually converges to zero. In contrast, this is not the case when $\pi > 0$, for then $d > 0$. Thus, when $\pi > 0$, the "sterilization" policy needs to be changed.

In particular, assume that the economy starts off in the steady state and, at time $t = 0$, there is an unexpected increase in growth rate of money $\varepsilon > 0$; that is, $\hat{g}_0 = \varepsilon/(1+\pi)$. In this case, the government chooses a period $t = T$ such that, from T on, the growth rate of money supply is zero (i.e., $\hat{g}_t = 0$) for $t \geq T$. What this implies is that, for $t \geq T$, the law of motion of $\hat{d}_t$ is given by[32]

$$\hat{d}_t = \frac{1}{\beta'}\widehat{R}_t + \frac{1}{\beta'}\hat{d}_{t-1},$$

which is clearly unstable because $\beta' < 1$. Iterating this equation forward and imposing the transversality condition that $\hat{d}_\infty = 0$, we obtain that $\hat{d}_{T-1}$ must satisfy

$$\hat{d}_{T-1} = -\sum_{\tau=0}^{\infty}\beta'^\tau \widehat{R}_{\tau+T}$$

[32]This equation is the linearized version of the law of motion of the money supply when $\hat{g}_t = 0$.

in order to guarantee convergence back to the steady state. Moreover, since our law of motion of the money supply yields

$$\hat{g}_{T-1} = -\frac{d}{1+d}\hat{d}_{T-1} + \frac{d}{\beta'(1+d)}\widehat{R}_{T-1} + \frac{d}{\beta'(1+d)}\hat{d}_{T-2},$$

so it follows that $\hat{g}_{T-1}$ depends on $\hat{d}_{T-1}$. In summary, when the government chooses a period T such that $\hat{g}_T = 0$, it must also choose $\hat{g}_{T-1}$ to satisfy the transversality condition. Furthermore, for periods $1 \leq t < T-2$ we allow the government to choose any exogenous law of motion for $\hat{g}_t \leq 0$—that is, any rule by which the monetary expansion at time $t = 0$ is reverted. For instance, a natural choice would be a gradual money contraction up to period $T-2$ and a choice of $\hat{g}_{T-1}$ that satisfies the transversality condition.

When $\pi > 0$, the dynamics of capital are described by

$$\theta_0^\pi \widehat{K}_t = \theta_1^\pi \widehat{K}_{t-1} + \theta_2^\pi \widehat{K}_{t-2} \frac{1}{1+\pi}[(1-2\beta')\hat{g}_t + (1-r^h)\hat{g}_{t-1}],$$

where

$$\theta_0^\pi = 1 + (1-2\beta')\frac{\rho}{1+\pi},$$

$$\theta_1^\pi = \frac{(1-r^h)(1-\rho)}{1+\pi} + 1 + (1-2\beta')\frac{\rho}{1+\pi} - \frac{1-\beta'}{\eta(1+\pi)},$$

$$\theta_2^\pi = -\frac{(1-r^h)(1-\rho)}{1+\pi}.$$

Using the dynamic equation of capital, the transversality condition for government debt, the law of motion of money supply, and the forward-looking solution for capital prices, it is possible to construct a system of five equations in five unknowns: $\widehat{K}_{T-1}$, $\hat{q}_{T-2}$, $\hat{q}_{T-1}$, $\hat{d}_{T-1}$, and $\hat{g}_{T-1}$. Because this system is a function of the past values $\widehat{K}_{T-3}$, $\widehat{K}_{T-2}$, and $\hat{d}_{T-2}$, an iterative procedure that starts with a guess for $\widehat{K}_1$ must be implemented in order to find the solution.

References

Abel, Andrew (1985). "Dynamic Behavior of Capital Accumulation in a Cash-in-Advance Model." *Journal of Monetary Economics*, 16, 55–71.

Aiyagari, S. Rao., R. Anton Braun, and Zvi Eckstein (1998). 'Transaction Services, Inflation, and Welfare." *Journal of Political Economy*, 106, 1274–1301.

Bernanke, Ben and Mark Gertler (1989). "Agency Costs, Net Worth, and Business Fluctuations." *American Economic Review*, 79, 14–31.

Bernanke, Ben, Mark Gertler, and Simon Gilchrist (1999). "The Financial Accelarator in a Quantitative Business Cycle Framework." In *Handbook of Macroeconomics*, Vol. 1, edited by John B. Taylor and Michael Woodford. Elsevier, New York.

Carlstrom, Charles and Timothy Fuerst (2001). "Monetary Shocks, Agency Costs and Business Cycles." *Carnegie-Rochester Public Policy Conference*, 54, 1–27.

Cooley, Thomas and Gary Hansen (1998). "The Role of Monetary Shocks in Equilibrium Business Cycle Theory: Three Examples." *European Economic Review*, 42, 605–617.

Fisher, Irwin (1933). "The Debt-Deflation Theory of Great Depressions." *Econometrica*, 1, 337–357.

Freeman, Scott (1996). "The Payments System, Liquidity, and Rediscounting." *American Economic Review*, 86, 1126–1138.

Fuerst, Timothy (1995). "Monetary and Financial Interactions in the Business Cycles." *Journal of Money, Credit and Banking*, 27(4 part 2), 1321–1338.

Kiyotaki, Nobuhiro (1998). "Credit and Business Cycles." *Japanese Economic Review*, 49, 18–35.

Kiyotaki, Nobuhiro and John Moore (1997). "Credit Cycles." *Journal of Political Economy*, 105, 211–248.

Kocherlakota, Narayana (2000). "Creating Business Cycles through Credit Constraints." *Federal Reserve Bank of Minneapolis Quarterly Review*, 24, 2–10.

Krishnamurthy, Arvind (2003). "Collateral Constraints and the Amplification Mechanism." *Journal of Economic Theory*, 111, 277–292.

Lorenzoni, Guido (2003). "The Cost of Credit Booms." Working paper, Department of Economics, Princeton University.

Scheinkman, Jose and Laurence Weiss (1986). "Borrowing Constraints and Aggregate Economic Activity." *Econometrica*, 54, 23–46.

17 Inefficient Credit Booms

Guido Lorenzoni

1. Introduction

In the past two decades, both developed and emerging economies have experienced episodes of rapid credit expansion followed, in some cases, by a financial crisis with a collapse in asset prices, credit, and investment.[1] This experience has led policy makers to be increasingly wary of credit booms and to propose various preventive measures to reduce the probability and/or the depth of a potential crisis.[2] However, relatively little theoretical work has analysed the reasons why a credit boom may be inefficient from an *ex ante* perspective and whether any intervention is warranted. If the private sector correctly perceives the risk of a negative aggregate shock, it will incorporate this risk in its optimal decisions. If agents still decide to borrow heavily during the boom, it means that the expected gains from increased investment today more than compensate for the expected costs of financial distress in future. Therefore, to assess the need for policy intervention, one needs to understand how, and under what conditions, this private calculation leads to inefficient decisions at the social level. In this paper, I address this question focusing on a pecuniary externality which arises from the combination of financial constraints with a competitive market for real assets. I analyse constrained efficiency by considering a planner who faces the same constraints faced by the private economy and asking whether a reduction in borrowing *ex ante* can lead to a Pareto improvement. My main result is that excessive borrowing can arise in equilibrium and that it is associated to an excessive contraction in investment and asset prices if the crisis takes place.

The paper develops a three-period model of investment with financial frictions. In the first period, entrepreneurs with limited internal funds borrow and invest in some productive asset (real estate, machinery, equipment, etc.). In the second period, their revenues are subject to an aggregate shock, which can take two values, good and bad. When the bad shock hits, they face operational losses. Given their limited access to outside funds, they need to sell part of the assets to finance these losses. Assets are sold on a competitive market where they are absorbed by a traditional sector, which makes a less productive use of them. Each entrepreneur has access to state-contingent debt contracts: he can decide both

[1] For the main stylized facts on boom–bust cycles, see Gourinchas *et al.* (2001), Borio and Lowe (2002), Bordo and Jeanne (2002), Tornell and Westermann (2002), and Ranciere *et al.* (2003).

[2] See Borio (2003) and references therein.

how much to borrow in the first period and how much to repay in different states of the world in the following periods. By investing more in the first period, the entrepreneur earns higher revenues if the good shock is realized but faces larger losses if the bad shock hits. Entrepreneurs are fully rational and correctly perceive the risks and rewards associated to different financial decisions. However, since they are atomistic, they do not take into account the general equilibrium effect of asset sales on prices. This is the pecuniary externality at the basis of my inefficiency result. By reducing aggregate investment *ex ante*, a planner can reduce the size of the asset sales in the bad state. This increases asset prices, leading to a reallocation of funds from the traditional sector, who is buying assets, to the entrepreneurial sector, who is selling them. Due to the presence of financial frictions, this reallocation leads to an aggregate welfare gain, which is not internalized by private agents.

Many accounts of recent financial crises have emphasized the interaction between asset prices and financial distress in the corporate and financial sectors. As an example, take the case of the banking sector in Thailand prior to the crisis of 1997. In the first half of the 1990s, Thai banks increased their investment in real estate, both directly, through loans to property developers and, indirectly, through loans to finance companies which had extensive investment in real estate. When the crisis erupted, the fall in real estate prices eroded the value of the assets held by the banks, as loans, backed by real estate guarantees, started going into default. This prompted a cut back in lending, which, in turn, led to a further reduction in the demand for real estate and a further drop in real estate prices. In these circumstances, the large supply of recently developed real estate, fuelled by bank lending during the boom, contributed to the severe collapse in prices during the crisis.[3] This is the type of mechanism I model in this paper. To capture the essence of the argument, I do not model explicitly financial intermediation and I concentrate on a setup where financially constrained agents invest directly in real assets.

Current policy debates mention a number of reasons why a credit boom might be inefficient: irrational optimism of the borrowers, moral hazard caused by the expectation of a bailout, inefficient delays in the treatment of information, and some negative externality by which higher borrowing of some agents may increase "systemic risk". Of these arguments, only the first two have been fully developed in the literature.[4] This paper attempts to formalize the "systemic risk" argument, focusing on a pecuniary externality working through asset prices. The idea of focusing on the general equilibrium feedback between financial distress and asset prices goes back to Shleifer and Vishny (1992) and Kiyotaki and Moore (1997). The role of asset "fire sales" during recent episodes of financial crisis has been emphasized by Krugman (1998). Systematic evidence on fire sales is presented in Pulvino (1998) and Aguiar and Gopinath (2005).

The fundamental source of inefficiency in this paper is in financial frictions, both on the borrowers' (entrepreneurs) and on the lenders' (consumers) side. In particular, my model assumes that both entrepreneurs and consumers have limited ability to commit to future repayments. Lack of commitment on the entrepreneurs' side implies that they have limited access to external finance. Lack of commitment on the consumers' side limits the entrepreneurs' ability to insure *ex ante* against aggregate liquidity shocks, as in Holmstrom

[3]See Herring and Wachter (1999) for a narrative of the boom–bust cycle in Thailand. See Watanabe (2007) for an empirical estimate of the effect of losses on real estate investment on banks' lending in Japan.

[4]The literature on optimal monetary policy has analysed economies where an investment boom is driven by an irrational fad or "bubble"; see Cecchetti *et al.* (2000), Bernanke and Gertler (2001), and Dupor (2002). For the moral hazard argument applied to recent crises, see McKinnon and Pill (1996), Corsetti *et al.* (1999), and Schneider and Tornell (2004).

and Tirole (1998). As I will show in Section 4, the combination of these two imperfections drives the inefficiency result.

The paper is related to the large literature on the role of financial frictions in the amplification and propagation of macroeconomic shocks.[5] Existing papers have compared the equilibrium arising in models with financial constraints with a first-best benchmark in which no financial constraints are present. The main contribution of this paper is to study welfare from a second-best perspective and to identify the possibility of over-borrowing. The closer precedent to the model presented is Krishnamurthy (2003), who develops a model à la Kiyotaki and Moore (1997) with state-contingent contracts. He uses the model to argue that in presence of state-contingent contracts, the degree of amplification is smaller than in the case of non-state-contingent debt.[6] Gertler (1992) offers an early analysis of multi-period financial contracts in an environment with agency costs, aggregate shocks, and state-contingent contracts. The analysis of state-contingent debt is also related to the literature on hedging in the presence of financial constraints. In particular, Froot *et al.* (1993) make the case that firms with access to costly external finance and with a concave technology should hedge cash flow shocks. In my model, firms have a constant return to scale technology. However, a similar motive for hedging aggregate cash flow shocks arises in general equilibrium. Since asset prices drop when aggregate entrepreneurial wealth is low, that increases the rate of return on investing in the bad state and induces entrepreneurs to transfer financial resources to that state.

From a methodological standpoint, the idea that the competitive equilibrium in economies with endogenous borrowing constraints can be constrained inefficient goes back to Kehoe and Levine (1993). They show that in an economy with limited enforcement, the first welfare theorem holds when there is only one good but fails to hold with more than one good.[7] In the second case, private contracts fail to internalize their effect on equilibrium prices, and, in turn, these prices affect the financial constraints. This paper shows that pecuniary externalities of this type provide a useful framework to study credit booms. Recent contributions that use constrained efficiency analysis to study the role of preventive policies in financial markets include Caballero and Krishnamurthy (2001, 2003), Lorenzoni (2001), Allen and Gale (2004), Gai *et al.* (2005), and Farhi *et al.* (2007).

A recent paper by Bordo and Jeanne (2002) approaches credit booms from a point of view similar to the one taken here, focusing on the trade-off between high investment *ex ante* and financial distress *ex post*. They consider an economy with sticky prices and show that if the firms are highly leveraged when a negative shock hits, this causes a sharper reduction in investment and output. In this environment, they study the effect of preventive monetary policy, which can help to reduce firms' leverage *ex ante*.

The paper is organized as follows. In Section 2, I introduce the model. In Section 3, I characterize the competitive equilibrium. Section 4 contains the welfare analysis and a discussion of policy implications. Section 5 concludes. All the proofs are in the appendix.

[5]See Bernanke and Gertler (1989), Lamont (1995), Carlstrom and Fuerst (1997), Acemoglu and Zilibotti (1997), Aghion *et al.* (1999), Schneider and Tornell (2004), Rampini (2004), Cooley *et al.* (2004), Guerrieri and Lorenzoni (2007), and references in Bernanke *et al.* (2001).

[6]"Fire sales" of assets are not present in his model, that is entrepreneurial investment is always positive. Therefore, my conjecture is that over-borrowing cannot arise in that setup, although the equilibrium is not constrained efficient.

[7]In turn, this result is related to the inefficiency result in economies with incomplete markets; Geanakoplos and Polemarchakis (1986).

2. The Model

There are three periods, 0, 1, and 2, and two groups of agents of equal mass, consumers and entrepreneurs. There are two goods, a perishable consumption good and a capital good. Consumption goods can be turned into capital goods one for one at any point in time, but the opposite is not feasible.

Consumers are risk neutral with preferences represented by the utility function $E[c_0 + c_1 + c_2]$ and receive a constant endowment e of consumption goods in each period. Entrepreneurs are also risk neutral but only consume in period 2. Their preferences are given by $E[c_2^e]$. They begin life with an endowment n of consumption goods and receive no further endowment in the following periods. Moreover, they have access to the following technology. In period 0, they choose the level of investment k_0. In period 1, this investment yields $a_s k_0$ units of consumption good, with $a_s > 0$. The productivity of investment at date 1, a_s, is random and depends on the aggregate state s, which takes the values l and h (low and high) with probabilities π_l and π_h. In period 1 the capital k_0 requires maintenance in order to remain productive. Maintenance costs are equal to γ units of consumption goods per unit of capital. If γ is not paid, capital is scrapped, that is it fully depreciates. Entrepreneurs choose the fraction of capital they want to keep productive, denoted by $\chi_s \in [0, 1]$. Hence, $\chi_s k_0$ is the undepreciated part of the capital stock, and total maintenance costs are equal to $\gamma \chi_s k_0$. At the end of period 1, entrepreneurs choose the capital stock for next period, k_{1s}, by making the net investment $k_{1s} - \chi_s k_0$. The capital stock k_{1s} produces Ak_{1s} units of consumption goods in period 2, with $A > 1$. Capital fully depreciates at the end of period 2.

Each consumer owns a firm in the "traditional sector". Firms in the traditional sector invest capital k_{1s}^T in period 1 to produce consumption goods in period 2. The technology of the traditional sector is represented by the production function $F(k_{1s}^T)$. The function $F(\cdot)$ is increasing, strictly concave, and twice differentiable and satisfies the following properties: $F(0) = 0$, $F'(0) = 1$, and $F'(k_{1s}^T)$ is bounded below, with lower bound $\underline{q}$.

The goods and capital markets are competitive. The price of capital in period 1 is denoted by q_s. For simplicity, I assume that the economy begins with no capital, so the price of capital is one in period 0, as long as some investment takes place. On the other hand, the price of capital is zero in period 2 since that is the final date.

2.1 Financial Contracts with Limited Commitment

At date 0, entrepreneurs offer financial contracts to consumers. A financial contract specifies a loan d_0 at date 0 from the consumer to the entrepreneur and state-contingent payments d_{1s} and d_{2s} from the entrepreneur to the consumer in periods 1 and 2, respectively, for each state s.

In period 0, the entrepreneur can invest his initial wealth plus the amount borrowed from the consumer,

$$k_0 \leq n + d_0.$$

In period 1, the entrepreneur's cash flow is equal to current revenues minus maintenance costs. Part of these funds are used to pay d_{1s} to the consumer; the rest goes to finance current investment. The budget constraint is then

$$q_s(k_{1s} - \chi_s k_0) \leq a_s k_0 - \gamma \chi_s k_0 - d_{1s}.$$

Finally, in period 2, the entrepreneur can consume the final revenues net of debt repayments,

$$c^e_{2s} \leq Ak_{1s} - d_{2s}.$$

The consumer's budget constraints are easily derived. If he accepts the contract, his expected utility is

$$e - d_0 + \sum_s \pi_s(e + d_{1s} - q_s k^T_{1s} + e + d_{2s} + F(k^T_{1s})), \tag{17.1}$$

while if he does not accept, it is

$$e + \sum_s \pi_s(e - q_s k^T_{1s} + e + F(k^T_{1s})).$$

I will assume throughout the paper that e is sufficiently large that the non-negativity constraints for c_0, c_{1s}, and c_{2s} are never binding.[8] The consumer's participation constraint is then given by

$$d_0 \leq \sum_s \pi_s(d_{1s} + d_{2s}).$$

Financial contracts are subject to a form of limited commitment both on the entrepreneur's and on the consumer's side. Consider first the entrepreneur. In periods 1 and 2, he chooses whether or not to make the contractual payments d_{1s} and d_{2s}, respectively. If he fails to pay, he gets to make a take-it-or-leave-it offer to the consumer regarding current and future payments. If the consumer rejects the offer, the firm is liquidated. When the firm is liquidated, a fraction $(1 - \theta)$ of the firm's current profits is lost, where θ is a scalar in (0, 1). The rest of the profits and the firm's capital stock go to the consumer. Therefore, if liquidation occurs in period 1, the consumer receives the revenue $\theta a_s k_0$ and the capital stock k_0. The latter can be either scrapped or sold on the asset market after paying the maintenance costs.[9] Given that the price of capital is q_s, the consumer will pay the maintenance costs as long as $q_s - \gamma > 0$. Therefore, the net value of a liquidated firm in period 1 is $(\theta a_s + (q_s - \gamma)_+)k_0$. From now on, the notation $(\cdot)_+$ will be used to denote the non-negative part of a variable, for example $(q_s - \gamma)_+ \equiv max\{q_s - \gamma, 0\}$. In period 2, the value of a liquidated firm is simply θAk_{1s}. Since state-contingent contracts are available, I can, without loss of generality,

[8]Given the assumptions made below, a sufficient condition for this is

$$e > \frac{1}{1 - \sum_s \pi_s(\theta a_s + 1 - \gamma)} n.$$

This ensures that the consumer is constrained in neither period 0, when choosing whether to accept the financial contract, nor in period 1, when choosing how much to invest in the traditional sector.

[9]The consumer might also use some of this capital in his traditional firm. Since there is a competitive market for capital, this option is irrelevant. Note also that in the event of a default, the entrepreneur has no incentive to pay the maintenance cost.

restrict attention to contracts where default and renegotiation never happen in equilibrium. The entrepreneur will never default if and only if the following inequalities are satisfied:

$$d_{1s} + d_{2s} \leq (\theta a_s + (q_s - \gamma)+)k_0, \tag{17.2}$$

$$d_{2s} \leq \theta A k_{1s}, \tag{17.3}$$

for $s = l, h$. A natural interpretation of these constraints is that the liquidation value of the firm acts as collateral for the financial obligations of the entrepreneur.

The consumer can always walk away from a financial contract, and his current and future income cannot be seized. Then, the consumer no-default conditions are

$$d_{1s} + d_{2s} \geq 0, \tag{17.4}$$

$$d_{2s} \geq 0, \tag{17.5}$$

for $s = l, h$. Note that the revenue of the traditional sector, $F(k_{1s}^T)$, cannot be used as collateral in financial contracts.

For simplicity, I consider only bilateral financial contracts involving one entrepreneur and one consumer, which, in the current environment, is without loss of generality. In particular, cross-holdings of financial securities across entrepreneurs are irrelevant, given that there is only aggregate uncertainty.[10]

Three additional assumptions will be useful in the analysis. First, I assume that the liquidation value of entrepreneurial firms is sufficiently small.

Assumption 1: *The parameter θ is small enough that the following inequalities hold:*

$$\sum_s \pi_s(\theta a_s + 1 - \gamma) < 1,$$

$$\theta A < 1.$$

This will imply that investment cannot be fully financed with outside funds either in period 0 or in period 1. Second, I impose some restrictions on the shocks a_l and a_h and on the maintenance cost γ.

Assumption 2: *The values of a_l and a_h are such that*

$$(1 - \theta)a_h + \theta A - 1 > 0,$$

$$a_l + \theta A - \gamma < 0.$$

The maintenance cost γ satisfies $\gamma < \underline{q}$.

The first two conditions will be used to show that entrepreneurs' investment is positive in the high state and negative in the low state. The last condition allows me to rule out scrapping of capital in equilibrium. Finally, the next assumption simplifies the analysis by ruling out multiple equilibria in the asset market at date 1.

Assumption 3: *The function $(F'(k^T) - \theta A)k^T$ is increasing in k^T.*

[10]See Holmstrom and Tirole (1998) for a thorough discussion of this issue in a related model.

2.2 Equilibrium Definition

The entrepreneur's individual problem is to choose a financial contract, investment, and consumption levels so as to maximize expected utility subject to the budget constraints, the consumer's participation constraint, and the no-default constraints introduced above. The consumer's problem is to choose which financial contract to accept, if any, and, then, set consumption and investment in the traditional firm so as to maximize expected utility subject to the budget constraints. Both the entrepreneur and the consumer take as given the vector of asset prices $\{q_s\}$.

A symmetric competitive equilibrium is given by a vector of asset prices $\{q_s\}$, a financial contract $\langle d_0, \{d_{1s}, d_{2s}\}\rangle$, investment, and consumption decisions for the entrepreneur k_0 and $\{\chi_{1s}, k_{1s}, c^e_{2s}\}$ and investment and consumption decisions for the consumer c_0 and $\{k^T_{1s}, c_{1s}, c_{2s}\}$, such that entrepreneurs' and consumers' behaviour are optimal, and goods and capital markets clear in all periods and states.

3. Equilibrium

In this section, I give a characterization of the equilibrium. First, I will look at the optimal borrowing and investment decisions of the entrepreneur for given asset prices $\{q_s\}$. Next, I will show how the entrepreneurs' aggregate behaviour affects the asset prices which clear the capital market in period 1. Finally, I will put the two pieces together and show how equilibrium borrowing and investment are determined. It is useful, however, to begin with a preliminary result regarding the capital market in period 1.

Lemma 1: *In equilibrium, asset prices are characterized by the conditions*

$$q_s = F'(k^T_{1s}),$$
$$k^T_{1s} = (k_0 - k_{1s})_+,$$

for $s = l, h$, *and no scrapping occurs in equilibrium,* $\chi_s = 1$ *for* $s = l, h$.

From this lemma, it follows that two cases are possible in period 1 capital market. In the first case, the price of capital is one, the traditional sector chooses zero investment (recall that $F'(0) = 1$), and the entrepreneurial sector makes positive investment $k_{1s} - k_0 > 0$. This investment is done by transforming consumption goods into capital goods. In the second case, the price of capital is smaller than one, no consumption goods are transformed into capital, and the entrepreneurial sector sells capital to the traditional sector. In this case, market clearing requires $k^T_{1s} = k_0 - k_{1s}$, and optimality for firms in the traditional sector requires $q_s = F'(k^T_{1s})$.

This result implies that equilibrium asset prices are bounded

$$\underline{q} \leq q_s \leq 1. \tag{17.6}$$

Since $\underline{q} > \gamma$ by Assumption 2, this also implies that $q_s - \gamma > 0$, which rules out scrapping of capital in equilibrium. Both properties will help in the characterization of optimal financial contracts.

3.1 Optimal Financial Contracts

Since scrapping is never optimal, I simplify the notation by defining net profits per unit of capital

$$x_s = a_s - \gamma.$$

Moreover, I describe the financial contract in terms of the net present value of promised repayments per unit of capital, which are given by[11]

$$b_{1s} = \frac{d_{1s} + d_{2s}}{k_0}$$

and

$$b_{2s} = \frac{d_{2s}}{k_{1s}}.$$

The entrepreneur's problem can be written in the following form. The entrepreneur chooses the financial contract $\langle d_0, \{b_{1s}, b_{2s}\}\rangle$ and the investment levels k_0 and $\{k_{1s}\}$ to maximize

$$\sum_s \pi_s (A - b_{2s}) k_{1s} \tag{17.7}$$

subject to the budget constraints,

$$k_0 \leq n + d_0, \tag{17.8}$$

$$q_s k_{1s} \leq (q_s + x_s - b_{1s}) k_0 + b_{2s} k_{1s} \quad \text{for } s = l, h, \tag{17.9}$$

the no-default constraints,

$$0 \leq b_{1s} \leq \theta a_s + q_s - \gamma \quad \text{for } s = l, h, \tag{17.10}$$

$$0 \leq b_{2s} \leq \theta A \quad \text{for } s = l, h, \tag{17.11}$$

the consumer participation constraint,

$$d_0 \leq \sum_s \pi_s b_{1s} k_0, \tag{17.12}$$

and non-negativity constraints for k_0 and k_{1s}. The following lemma gives a characterization of optimal financial contracts.

[11]In the proof of Lemma 2, I show that the optimal values of k_0 and k_{1s} are positive, so these ratios are well defined.

Lemma 2: *Given a vector of equilibrium prices* $\{q_s\}_{s=l,h,}$ *an individually optimal financial contract satisfies the conditions:*

$$b_{1s} = 0 \qquad \text{if } z_0 < z_{1s}, \tag{17.13a}$$

$$b_{1s} \in [0, \theta a_s + q_s - \gamma] \quad \text{if } z_0 = z_{1s}, \tag{17.13b}$$

$$b_{1s} = \theta a_s + q_s - \gamma \qquad \text{if } z_0 > z_{1s}, \tag{17.13c}$$

$$b_{2s} = \theta A,$$

for $s = l, h$, *where*

$$z_{1s} = \frac{(1-\theta)A}{q_s - \theta A} \tag{17.14}$$

and

$$z_0 = \frac{\sum_s \pi_s z_{1s}(q_s + x_s - b_{1s})}{1 - \sum_s \pi_s b_{1s}}. \tag{17.15}$$

The variables z_{1s} and z_0 defined in (14) and (15), respectively, are the Lagrange multipliers on the budget constraints at dates 0 and 1; they represent the *rates of return on entrepreneurial wealth* in periods 0 and 1.[12] Since they play an important role in the analysis to follow, let me provide some intuition for them. When investing in period 1, the entrepreneur can buy capital at the price q_s and finance this investment by borrowing θA per unit of capital. One dollar of internal funds can thus be leveraged by a factor of $1/(q_s - \theta A)$. At date 2, this investment gives A per unit of capital, of which θA is paid to consumers. Therefore, the marginal return on internal funds available in period 1 is $z_{1s} = (1-\theta)A/(q_s - \theta A)$. Going back to period 0, one extra dollar of internal funds at date 0 can be leveraged by a factor of $1/(1 - \sum_s \pi_s b_{1s})$ and the capital invested gives a random net payoff of $q_s + x_s - b_{1s}$ in period 1. This net payoff can then be reinvested at the rate of return z_{1s}. Averaging across states gives equation (15).

The choice of the repayment ratios $\{b_{1s}\}$ depends on the comparison of rates of return on internal funds in periods 0 and 1 state by state. Suppose the entrepreneur increases his borrowing in period 0 by π_s dollars by promising \$1 in period 1 in state s. The increase in funds available at date 0 increases the entrepreneur's utility by $\pi_s z_0$, while the decrease in funds available at date 1 decreases the entrepreneur's utility by z_{1s} with probability π_s. Comparing these marginal effects shows that as long as $z_0 > z_{1s}$, the entrepreneur will increase his promised repayments in state s up to the point where $b_{1s} = \theta a_s + q_s - \gamma$. If, instead, $z_0 < z_{1s}$, the entrepreneur will decrease his promised repayments until $b_{1s} = 0$. An interior choice for b_{1s} will only arise if $z_0 = z_{1s}$.

The choice of the repayments in period 2 is much simpler. The marginal utility of entrepreneurial wealth is always equal to one in period 2 since at that point, the entrepreneur can only consume. Given that $z_{1s} > 1$ in all states, this implies that the entrepreneur always commits to maximum repayments in period 2, $b_{2s} = \theta A$, in order to maximize investment in period 1.

The argument above shows that the optimal financial contract depends on the prices q_s through their effect on the rates of return z_{1s} and z_0. In turn, the prices q_s depend on the

[12]More precisely, z_{1s} is the Lagrange multiplier normalized by the probability π_s.

contracts chosen by the entrepreneurs since they determine how much capital they sell on date 1. I will now look at this relation before turning to general equilibrium.

3.2 Asset Prices

Consider the asset market in period 1 taking as given the financial contract chosen by the entrepreneurs. Net investment by the entrepreneurs is

$$k_{1s} - k_0 = \frac{x_s + \theta A - b_{1s}}{q_s - \theta A} k_0, \tag{17.16}$$

for $s = l, h$. This expression comes from rearranging (9) and using the result that the financial constraint is always binding in period 2 (from Lemma 2). It is not difficult to show that in the high state, the R.H.S. of (16) is positive and so is investment. The opposite happens in the low state.[13] Then, Lemma 1 implies that $q_h = 1$ and $q_l < 1$. Therefore, let me focus on the determination of the asset price in the low state.

In the low state, the entrepreneurial firm is facing net losses since $x_l k_0 < 0$. Due to the collateral constraint, the firm has limited ability to borrow against future income. If it tried to keep the existing capital stock unchanged, its borrowing capacity would be insufficient to cover current losses since $b_{2l}k_0 \leq \theta A k_0 < -x_l k_0$ (the first inequality follows from no default and the second from Assumption 2). Moreover, the firm has limited ability to buy insurance *ex ante* due to consumers' limited commitment, $b_{1l} \geq 0$. The only remaining option to cover the firm's losses is to sell part of the capital stock. To induce the traditional sector to absorb this capital, the price of capital has to fall below 1.

Figure 17.1 gives a graphical illustration of the equilibrium in the low state for given values of k_0 and b_{1l}. Curve S plots the entrepreneurs' supply of capital as a function of q_l. For completeness, the figure includes the regions where $q_l \geq A$ and $q_l \leq \gamma$, although such prices never arise in equilibrium. When $\gamma < q_l < A$, the entrepreneurs' behaviour is captured by (16) and the supply of capital is given by $-(x_l + \theta A - b_{1l})k_0/(q_l - \theta A)$. Note that in this region, the supply is decreasing in q_l: a price increase allows entrepreneurs

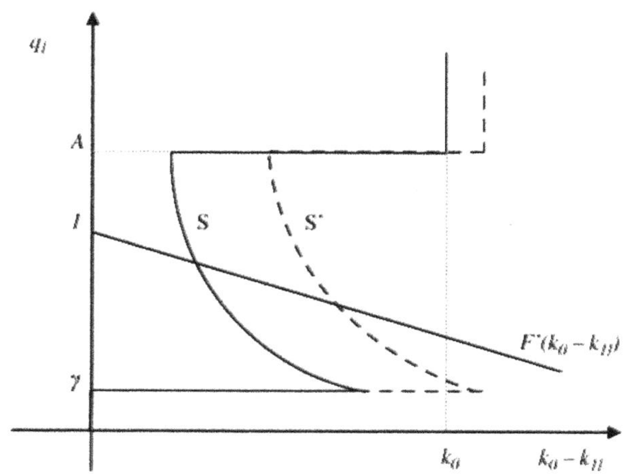

Figure 17.1 Asset market equilibrium.

[13] See Lemma A2 in the appendix.

to sell a smaller amount of capital to cover their losses.[14] When q_l goes above A, entrepreneurial investment becomes unprofitable and entrepreneurs sell all the capital stock k_0. Finally, when q_l goes below γ, scrapping is optimal and entrepreneurial capital is destroyed. In the same figure, I plot the traditional sector demand for capital, described by the condition $q_l = F'(k_0 - k_{1l})$. The equilibrium is determined at the point where the two curves meet.

Figure 17.1 can be used to show the relation between the financial contract and the asset price q_l. The choice of $\{b_{1s}\}$ affects the equilibrium price in two ways. An increase in either b_{1l} or b_{1h} increases the capital stock at date 0, given by

$$k_0 = \frac{1}{1 - \sum_s \pi_s b_{1s}} n,$$

and thus increases entrepreneurial losses in the low state. Moreover, an increase in b_{1l} directly increases repayments in the low state. Both channels lead to an increase in $-(x_l + \theta A - b_{1l})k_0$ and to a fall in the equilibrium asset price. This mechanism is illustrated by the curve S' in Figure 17.1, which shows the effect of an increase in borrowing, leading to a rightward shift of the entrepreneurs' supply and to a lower equilibrium price.

3.3 Equilibrium Hedging

Putting together entrepreneurs' optimality and the equilibrium determination of asset prices, I can show that an equilibrium exists and I can characterize the equilibrium financial contract. From now on, I will use the superscript CE to denote equilibrium values.

Proposition 1: *There exists a unique symmetric competitive equilibrium. In equilibrium, asset prices satisfy*

$$q_l^{\text{CE}} < q_h^{\text{CE}} = 1.$$

Depending on parameters, the equilibrium financial contract is of one of the following types:

1. $0 \leq b_{1h}^{\text{CE}} < \theta a_h + 1 - \gamma$ *and* $b_{1l}^{\text{CE}} = 0$;
2. $b_{lh}^{\text{CE}} = \theta a_h + 1 - \gamma$ *and* $b_{1l}^{\text{CE}} = 0$;
3. $b_{1h}^{\text{CE}} = \theta a_h + 1 - \gamma$ *and* $0 \leq b_{1l}^{\text{CE}} \leq \theta a_l + q_l^{\text{CE}} - \gamma$.

This proposition shows that there is a "pecking order" of repayments in different aggregate states. Entrepreneurs must first exhaust their borrowing capacity in the high state (setting $b_{1h} = \theta a_h + 1 - \gamma$) before they start borrowing against revenue in the low state (setting $b_{1l} > 0$). In the low state, the entrepreneurs are poor and the demand for assets is low. The associated fall in asset prices increases z_{1l} and induces entrepreneurs, *ex ante*, to reduce their promised repayments in that state. In equilibria of types 1 and 2, this

[14]The fact that the supply is decreasing has two implications: it magnifies the effect of entrepreneurial losses on asset prices and it opens the door to multiple equilibria. The amplification is important because it increases the quantitative relevance of the pecuniary externality discussed in Section 4. Multiplicity is ruled out in this paper by virtue of Assumption 3. Gai *et al.* (2006) study the implications of a similar model focusing on the case where multiple equilibria are possible.

incentive is sufficiently strong that entrepreneurs keep their promised repayments to zero in the low state. In equilibria of type 3, instead, the benefits from hedging are dominated by the return on investment at date 0. In this case, entrepreneurs decide to offer positive repayments also in the low state in order to raise more capital at date 0.

The general principle behind this result is that endogenous movements in asset prices determine the entrepreneurs' incentive to hedge aggregate shocks. In Section 4, I will show that the social benefits of this hedging are, in general, different from the private benefits.

3.4 A Graphical Illustration

An implication of Proposition 1 is mat the equilibrium financial contract can be summarized by the variable $\rho \equiv \sum_s \pi_s b_{1s}$ capturing the ratio of outside borrowing to total capital invested at date 0. For low levels of ρ, all the borrowing is against revenue in the high state, while if ρ is greater than the cutoff $\hat{\rho} \equiv \pi_h(\theta a_h + 1 - \gamma)$, the entrepreneurs also borrow against revenue in the low state. To illustrate the determination of the equilibrium financial contract, in Figure 17.2, I plot the relation between ρ and the rates of return on

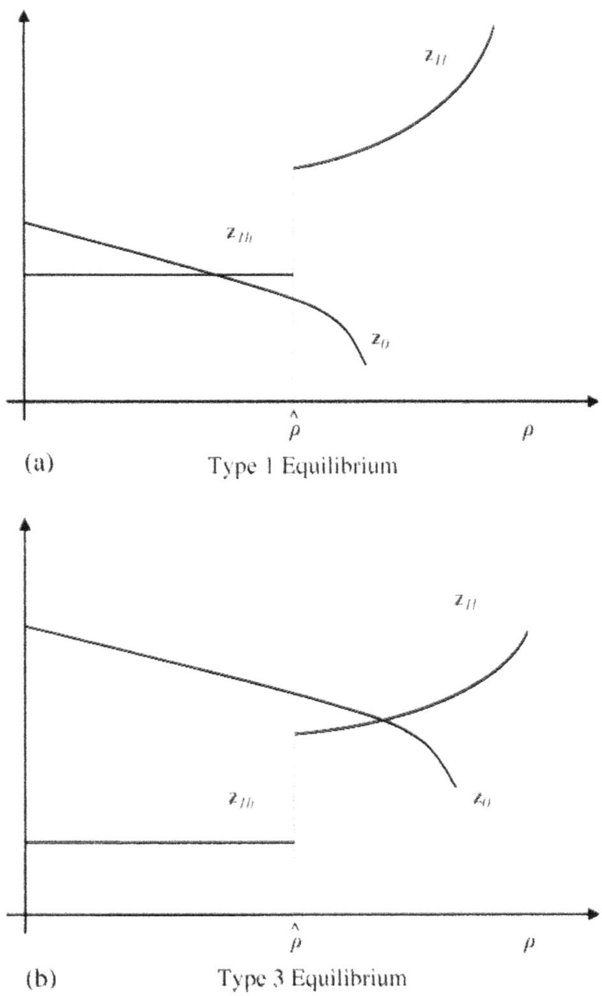

Figure 17.2 The borrowing ratio ρ and the rates of return on entrepreneurial wealth.

entrepreneurial wealth z_0 and z_{1s}. For each value of ρ, I derive the corresponding values of the state-contingent payments $\{b_{1s}\}$ and the equilibrium asset prices, proceeding as in Section 3.2. Given these asset prices, I derive the corresponding values of z_0 and z_{1s}, as in Section 3.1, and look for an optimal financial contract. Note that when $\rho < \hat{\rho}$, the entrepreneur is choosing an interior solution for b_{1h}. In this case, the relevant marginal trade-off is between investing more at date 0 and investing in the high state at date 1. On the other hand, when $\rho > \hat{\rho}$, the trade-off is between investing at date 0 and investing in the low state at date 1. Hence, in the first region, I plot z_{1h} as the relevant *ex post* rate of return, while in the second region, I plot z_{1l}. The *ex ante* return is always equal to z_0.

Consider now how an increase in borrowing changes the returns to entrepreneurial wealth in periods 0 and 1. As ρ increases, the price of capital q_l falls. This tends to reduce the *ex ante* return on entrepreneurial wealth, z_0, given that entrepreneurs face bigger expected capital losses in period 1.[15] At the same time, the *ex post* return on entrepreneurial wealth tends to increase for two reasons. First, if ρ crosses the cutoff $\hat{\rho}$, there is a discrete upward jump in the rate of return since $z_{1l} > z_{1h}$. Furthermore, once above $\hat{\rho}$, the rate of return z_{1l} keeps increasing. As q_l falls, an extra dollar available in the low state earns a higher return between periods 1 and 2. The equilibrium is determined at the point where the two rates of return are equalized, except in the cases where the entrepreneur is against a corner for both b_{1l} and b_{1h}. Figure 17.2(a) and (b) illustrates two cases of interior equilibria. In the first case, the equilibrium is of type 1 and $z_{1h} = z_0$; in the second, the equilibrium is of type 3 and $z_{1l} = z_0$.

4. Welfare

Let me now turn to efficiency. Consider a planner who, at date 0, can choose the financial contract $\langle d_0, \{d_{1s}\}, \{d_{2s}\}\rangle$. The planner faces the same constraints as the private economy, in particular: (i) the financial contract is subject to default and renegotiation and (ii) the allocation of used capital in period 1 is determined on an anonymous spot market. The only difference between the planner and the individual entrepreneur is that the planner takes into account the relation between the financial contract and the equilibrium price on the capital market. That is, instead of taking $\{q_s\}$ as given, the planner's problem includes the constraints

$$q_s = F'\left(k_{1s}^T\right), \tag{17.17}$$

$$k_{1s}^T = (k_0 - k_{1s})_+. \tag{17.18}$$

As in the previous section, I will describe a financial contract in terms of the initial loan d_0 and the repayments per unit of capital $\{b_{1s}, b_{2s}\}$. The Pareto frontier is defined by the following planner's problem. Fix a given utility level for the consumers $\bar{U}$. The planner chooses $\langle d_0, \{b_{1s}, b_{2s}\}\rangle$, k_0, and $\{k_{1s}\}$ to maximize the entrepreneurs' expected utility (7), subject to the budget constraints (8)–(9), the no-default constraints (10)–(11), the constraints (17)–(18), and a constraint on consumers' expected utility, which takes the place of the

[15]Note that, in general, the relation between ρ and z_0 is not necessarily monotone, given that equation (15) also includes z_{1l}. However, the difference $z_{1s} - z_0$ is locally monotone in ρ around any equilibrium, which ensures that the equilibrium is unique. See the proof of Proposition 1 for the detailed derivations behind this statement and for analytical derivations which mirror the graphical presentation in this section.

consumers' participation constraint,

$$3e - d_0 + \sum_s \pi_s b_{1s} k_0 + \sum_s \pi_s (F(k_{1s}^T) - q_s k_{1s}^T) \geq \bar{U}. \tag{17.19}$$

Since asset prices also determine the profits of the traditional sector, this is taken into account when writing constraint (19).

Let me first show that the only substantial difference between this problem and the problem of the individual entrepreneur is, indeed, the endogeneity of asset prices. Suppose asset prices are set at their competitive equilibrium level, that is replace (17)–(18) with $q_s = q_s^{\mathrm{CE}}$. Set also $\bar{U}$ at its equilibrium level, denoted by U^{CE}. Then, it would be optimal for the planner to choose k_{1s}^T to maximize $F(k_{1s}^T) - q_s^{\mathrm{CE}} k_{1s}^T$, so as to relax constraint (19), and thus choose $k_{1s}^T = k_{1s}^{T,\mathrm{CE}}$. Since $U^{\mathrm{CE}} = 3e + \sum_s \pi_s (F(k_{1s}^{T,\mathrm{CE}}) - q_s^{\mathrm{CE}} k_{1s}^{T,\mathrm{CE}})$, it follows that (19) could be replaced by (12). Since (17) and (18) are no longer present, the planner's problem would then be identical to the individual problem, and the competitive financial contract would be optimal.[16]

I now go back to the original formulation of the planner's problem. In order for that problem to be well defined, $\bar{U}$ cannot be too large or the constraint set may be empty. Let me assume that this is the case, and let me also assume that $\bar{U}$ is such that the entrepreneur gets positive utility. As in the previous section, I will ignore the non-negativity constraints for consumers' consumption, assuming that e is sufficiently large.

The following proposition gives a characterization of a constrained-efficient allocation, which is denoted by an asterisk.

Proposition 2: *Suppose the value of $\bar{U}$ is such that the entrepreneur can achieve positive utility. Then, a socially optimal allocation satisfies the following conditions. Asset prices satisfy*

$$q_l^* < q_h^* = 1,$$

and promised repayments satisfy

$$\begin{aligned}
b_{1s}^* &= 0 & &\text{if } \lambda^* < z_{1s}^*, \\
b_{1s}^* &\in [0, \theta a_s + q_s^* - \gamma] & &\text{if } \lambda^* = z_{1s}^*, \\
b_{1s}^* &= \theta a_s + q_s^* - \gamma & &\text{if } \lambda^* > z_{1s}^*, \\
b_{2s}^* &= \theta A,
\end{aligned}$$

for $s = l, h$, where λ^* is the Lagrange multiplier on constraint (19) and

$$z_{1s}^* = \frac{(1-\theta)A}{q_s^* - \theta A}. \tag{17.20}$$

The value of λ^* satisfies

$$\lambda^* \leq z_0^* = \frac{\sum_s \pi_s z_{1s}^* (q_s^* + x_s - b_{1s}^*)}{1 - \sum_s \pi_s b_{1s}^*}, \tag{17.21}$$

which holds as a strict inequality if $z_0^* \neq z_{1l}^*$.

[16] Kehoe and Levine (1993) call this property "conditional constrained efficiency".

The characterization of the financial contract parallels the result in Lemma 2. As in the individual problem, the planner chooses the promised repayments in each state comparing the marginal return on entrepreneurial wealth in periods 0 and 1. The social return on entrepreneurial wealth in period 1, z^*_{1s}, is identical to the private rate of return, as can be seen comparing (14) and (20). However, the social rate of return in period 0 is now captured by λ^*. Inequality (21) shows that λ^* is smaller than or equal to the corresponding expression for the private rate of return.

4.1 Over-Borrowing

Let me now use this characterization to show that over-borrowing can arise in equilibrium. Recall that $\rho = \sum_s \pi_s b_{1s}$ is the ratio between the net present value of promised repayments and the capital invested at date 0, introduced in Section 3.4. Thanks to Proposition 2, a socially optimal financial contract can be fully characterized by the ratio ρ, as it was the case for the competitive equilibrium contract. Therefore, I can focus on the comparison of ρ^* and ρ^{CE}. To prove the next proposition, it is convenient to introduce a slightly stronger version of Assumption 3.[17]

Assumption 4: *The function F satisfies the following condition*

$$F'(k^T) - \theta A + \eta F''(k^T)k^T > 0,$$

where $\eta \equiv (1 - \pi_h(\theta a_h + 1 - \gamma) - \pi_l(x_l + \theta A))/(1 - \sum_s \pi_s(\theta a_s + 1 - \gamma))$.

This condition is sufficient to show that when the planner increases the borrowing ratio ρ, this increases the sales of used capital by entrepreneurs in the low state. Under Assumptions 1, 2, and 4, the following proposition shows that under-borrowing never arises in equilibrium and over-borrowing arises if the equilibrium is of type 1.

Proposition 3: *(Over-borrowing) Let* $\bar{U} = U^{CE}$*, then a constrained-efficient financial contract satisfies* $\rho^* \leq \rho^{CE}$*. The inequality is strict if the equilibrium is of type 1.*

This result is due to the presence of a pecuniary externality: the financial decisions of the entrepreneurs affect the equilibrium price on the capital market in period 1, and this price affects the allocation of wealth between entrepreneurs and consumers. To clarify why this leads to a welfare loss, consider the following experiment. Suppose the equilibrium is of type 1 and suppose entrepreneurs and consumers get together in period 0 and coordinate to reduce entrepreneurial investment in the initial period by $dk_0 < 0$, by reducing b_{1h}. Since $z_0 = z_{1h}$, the direct effect of this change on the entrepreneurs' utility is 0. However, in general equilibrium, this change implies a reduced supply of used capital and a higher asset price in the low state, $dq_l > 0$. Since entrepreneurs are sellers of capital in that state, an increase in the asset price increases entrepreneurial wealth by $(k_0 - k_{1l})dq_l$ dollars. At the same time, by the envelope theorem, $(k_0 - k_{1l})dq_l$ corresponds to the reduction in profits for firms in the traditional sector. Suppose the entrepreneurs compensate the consumers for this profit loss by giving them $\pi_l(k_0 - k_{1l})dq_l$ at date 0. The marginal cost of this transfer is $z_0\pi_l(k_0 - k_{1l})dq_l$ since z_0 is the entrepreneurs' marginal utility of funds. The expected

[17] Assumption 4 is stronger because $\eta > 1$. Note that $\lim_{\pi_l \to 0} \eta = 1$, so the two assumptions tend to be equivalent for low values of π_l.

marginal benefit associated to the increase in asset prices at date 1 is $\pi_l z_{1l}(k_0 - k_{1l})dq_l$. The net effect of this local perturbation on the entrepreneurs' utility is

$$\pi_l(z_{1l} - z_0)(k_0 - k_{1l})dq_l, \tag{17.22}$$

which is positive since $z_{1l} > z_{1h} = z_0$ and $dq_l > 0$. This gives a Pareto improvement, as consumers are indifferent and entrepreneurs are better off.

4.2 A Graphical Illustration

Figure 17.3 is analogous to Figure 17.2 for the case of the planner. Proposition 2 shows that the socially optimal contract satisfies the same pecking order identified for equilibrium contracts. Therefore, also in this case, it is possible to represent the optimal financial contract in terms of the borrowing ratio ρ. For each level of ρ, I plot the corresponding values of z_{1s} and z_0 capturing the private benefits from *ex ante* and *ex post* investment. As in Figure 17.2, I plot z_{1h} when $\rho < \hat{\rho}$ and z_{1l} when $\rho > \hat{\rho}$. In the same picture, I use a dashed line to plot λ, the social benefits on entrepreneurial investment at date 0. As shown in Proposition 2, the social benefits from investment at date 1 coincide with the private benefits and are captured by z_{1s}.

The difference between the private and the social benefits of *ex ante* investment, z_0 and λ, is due to the pecuniary externality discussed above. An increase in borrowing has the effect of reducing q_l and thus reallocating funds from entrepreneurs to consumers at date 1. The welfare effect of this reallocation is given by (22). Therefore, the difference between λ and z_0 has the same sign as $z_0 - z_{1l}$. In panel (a), the graph of λ is below that of z_0, given that z_{1l} is above z_0 for the whole range of ρ. In panel (b), instead, the graph of λ crosses that of z_0 at the point where $z_{1l} - z_0 = 0$. In the case depicted in panel (a), this implies that at the competitive equilibrium, $\lambda < z_{1h}$. Therefore, a reduction in borrowing leads to a Pareto improvement. In the case depicted in panel (b), instead, the competitive equilibrium arises precisely when $z_{1l} = z_0$, so there is no room for a Pareto improvement.

The latter argument suggests that equilibria of type 3 are constrained efficient. This is indeed the case in specific examples, such as the one depicted in panel (b). However, due to the non-concavity of the planner's problem, the result cannot be established in general.

4.3 Sources of Inefficiency

The two imperfections introduced in the model are limited commitment on the entrepreneurs' and on the consumers' side. Both are at the roots of the inefficiency result. If I removed the entrepreneurs' commitment problem, by setting $\theta = 1$, the economy would reach a first-best allocation where all the consumption goods in periods 0 and 1 are devoted to investment.[18] In this case, not surprisingly, there is no inefficiency. Limited commitment on the consumers' side plays a subtler role. Consider the case of an equilibrium of type 1 where equation (22) is positive since $z_{1l} > z_0$. In this case, the reduction in borrowing is beneficial because the *ex post* value of funds to the entrepreneurs is larger than their value *ex ante*. This can only happen if the entrepreneur has limited ability to transfer resources between period 0 and period 1 (in state l). In the model, this happens because the constraint $b_{1l} \geq 0$ is binding, so the entrepreneurs are not allowed to buy more insurance against the low state.

[18] Note that, in this case, the non-negativity constraint for consumers' consumption is binding. See the appendix for the formal analysis of this case.

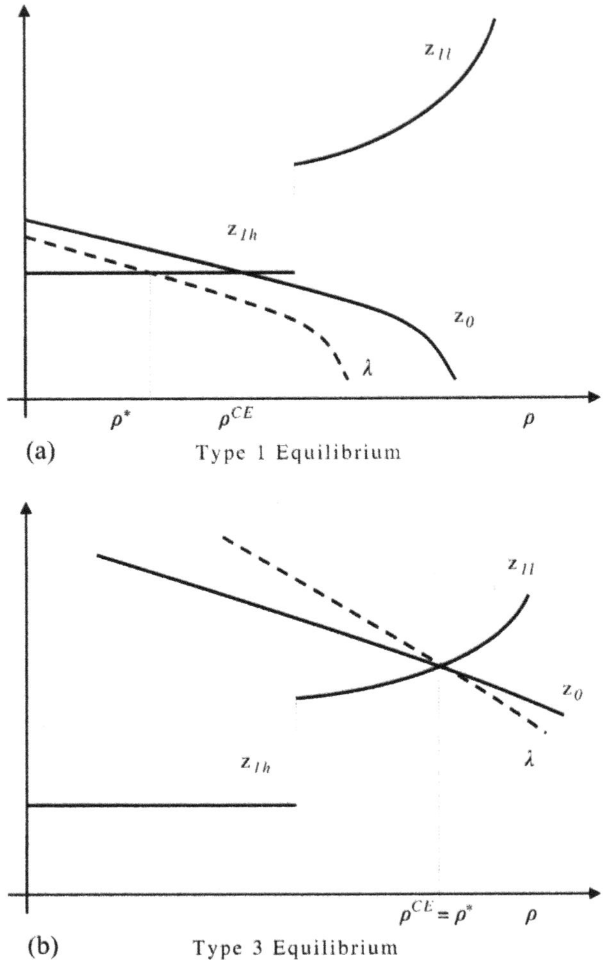

Figure 17.3 The borrowing ratio ρ and the private and social returns to entrepreneurial investment.

A coordinated reduction in borrowing, as described in Section 4.1, allows the entrepreneurs to partially circumvent the problem. Borrowing less *ex ante* leads to an increase in asset prices in the low state, and thus, it is an indirect way for entrepreneurs to transfer resources to the low state. This argument suggests that the pecuniary externality identified here will also be relevant in other environments where the entrepreneurs have difficulty channelling resources to the low state, for example in models with full commitment on the consumers' side but without state-contingent debt.

It is useful to remark that in this framework, the inefficiency is not due to fact that the price q_l affects the collateral available to entrepreneurs. As just noticed, the pecuniary externality identified matters when the constraint $b_{1l} \geq 0$ is binding. In that case, the collateral constraint $b_{1l} \leq \theta a_l + q_l - \gamma$ is slack and the fact that an increase in q_l increases the entrepreneur's borrowing capacity at date 0 is irrelevant for entrepreneurs. Asset prices matter here because they determine the asset side of entrepreneurs' balance sheets, not because of their effects on their capacity to borrow. In a model with endogenous asset prices in period 2, it would be possible to study the effect of asset prices on borrowing capacity in period 1 and to study a "collateral channel" different from the asset price channel discussed here.

As a final observation, note that constraint (19), with $\bar{U} = U^{CE}$, ensures that consumers are as well off at a constrained-efficient allocation as at the competitive allocation. One may ask, though, whether there should be an additional constraint to ensure that consumers participate voluntarily to the financial contract $\langle d_0^*, \{b_{1s}^*, b_{2s}^*\}\rangle$, that is a constraint of the form $d_0^* \leq \sum \pi_s b_{1s}^*$. In the analysis so far, I have left this constraint aside, to simplify the exposition, but it can be shown that the constraint is not binding at a constrained-efficient allocation. The proof of this claim is in the online appendix (Lemma 8).

4.4 Remarks on Policy

Regulatory interventions that impose minimum capitalization on financial firms are widespread in industrialized economies, and often, their introduction is justified based on the idea that excessive leverage in the financial sector may bring about an increase in "systemic risk". The model presented here gives a welfare-based rationale to this idea. When the equilibrium is inefficient, policies that restrict borrowing *ex ante* can restore constrained efficiency. For example, the planner can impose a capital requirement of the form $\nu k_0 \leq n$, which imposes that a minimum fraction ν of the firm's assets is financed with insiders' capital. Given that both the planner's optimum and the entrepreneur's optimum follow the same "pecking order", a restriction of this type is sufficient to ensure that the efficient financial contract $\{b_{1s}^*\}$ is chosen.[19]

Proposition 4: *Given a constrained-efficient allocation, there is a capital requirement ν and a transfer τ_0 from entrepreneurs to consumers such that the corresponding equilibrium is constrained efficient.*

An open question is how capital requirements should be calibrated for investments with different risky profiles. Existing capital requirements are usually based on the riskiness of the individual investment using some measure of "value at risk". The framework of this paper can be extended to analyse models with different types of investment. In particular, one can consider a model where the cash flows x_s of different investments have different exposure to the aggregate shock. In that case, the investments with a larger pecuniary externality are those which are more correlated with the aggregate shock since they are the ones that contribute more to a drop in asset prices in the event of a bad shock. This points to the idea of optimal capital requirements that depend on macroeconomic correlations and not just on measures of individual risk. In particular, it might be desirable that investments with higher correlation with macroeconomic conditions be subject to tighter requirements.[20]

5. Conclusions

The policy debate on financial supervision and regulation has been recently shifting towards a "macroprudential" approach (Borio, 2003). According to this approach, the regulator should be concerned most of all about the aggregate consequences of financial instability, and the main source of instability is identified in the common exposure to macroeconomic risks across financial institutions. The present paper provides at the same time a warning and

[19] The proof of the next proposition is in the online appendix.

[20] See Borio (2003, p. 10) for a discussion of recent policy proposals that go in this direction.

a justification for this approach. The warning is that aggregate volatility and some degree of financial fragility are unavoidable in the presence of financial constraints and that a reduction in financial fragility can only be achieved at the cost of reducing investment *ex ante*. Defining the objective of the regulator only in terms of reducing volatility, and disregarding the productive effects of capital accumulation, may be misleading. On the other hand, the welfare analysis in this paper provides a justification for a macroprudential approach. In a framework with financial constraints, private agents may underestimate the damage associated to a contraction in their wealth, and therefore, policies that limit their losses in a crisis may be welfare improving.

In practice, capital requirements are imposed on a specific class of firms, typically on commercial banks and financial intermediaries. To have a fully fledged theory of capital requirements would require an explicit model of financial intermediation. If entrepreneurial firms, which are more financially constrained, are also more reliant on bank credit, capital requirements on banks can help to stabilize the balance sheet of the firms that need it most. The analysis of capital requirements in an explicit framework with intermediation remains a topic for future research.

The model presented shows that over-borrowing is a possibility. However, it also shows that in some equilibria (*e.g.* the equilibrium illustrated in panel (b) of Figure 17.3), the gains from *ex ante* investment are sufficiently large that both the private economy and the planner choose the same high level of borrowing. Therefore, the presence and the severity of over-borrowing in specific episodes become an empirical issue. In particular, the model indicates that some relevant quantitative questions that should be addressed are how much the presence of financial distress contributes to the fall in asset prices during financial crises and how much that contributes to the propagation of financial distress across the economy.

Let me conclude with some remarks on the notion of constrained efficiency used in this paper. The social planner introduced here is constrained to take as given both the limited commitment problem in financial contracts and the fact that asset prices are determined in a spot market. The point of this exercise is both theoretical and practical. First, it is useful to consider a restrictive notion of constrained efficiency to identify minimal conditions under which a planner can improve upon the competitive allocation. Second, it is interesting to focus on policy interventions that impose restrictions on financial contracts since they seem close to regulatory policies already in place. However, this environment naturally suggests that interventions in different markets (*e.g.*, the asset market) can have important interactions with the equilibrium financial structure. Extensions of the welfare analysis to the case where the planner can intervene directly in the asset market are left to future research. This type of extensions will be of particular interest when one turns to monetary versions of the model and studies its implications for optimal monetary policy.[21]

Finally, one could allow the planner to directly intervene to relax the limited commitment constraints. In particular, Holmstrom and Tirole (1998) argue that the supply of public liquidity can alleviate the lack of commitment on the consumers' side. The government can issue state-contingent bonds in period 0 and tax consumers in period 1 to repay these bonds. Let the tax on consumers be denoted by τ_s. Then, a model with public liquidity is formally equivalent to the model presented here if the consumers' no-default constraint in period 1 is replaced by $d_{1s} + d_{2s} \geq -\tau_s$. This policy allows entrepreneurs to buy more insurance against the low state by holding state-contingent government bonds. By setting

[21] Recent papers on optimal monetary policy in economies with financial frictions include Iacoviello (2005) and Faia and Monacelli (2007).

a sufficiently high value for τ_s, the government is able to replicate the equilibrium of an economy with full commitment on the consumers' side. As argued above, in Section 4.3, this would eliminate the pecuniary externality identified in this paper. Clearly, there are a number of reasons why liquidity creation by the government may be costly and imperfect (*e.g*. the distortionary effects of taxation). In all these cases, the possibility of excessive borrowing remains open.

Appendix

Proof of Lemma 1: The consumer chooses $k_{1s}^T \geq 0$ to maximize expected utility, given by (1), that is to maximize $F(k_{1s}^T) - q_s k_{1s}^T$. Recall that F is strictly concave and $F'(0) = 1$. Therefore, if $q_s \geq 1$, optimal investment is $k_{1s}^T = 0$, while if $q_s < 1$, k_{1s}^T is positive and satisfies the first-order condition $F'(k_{1s}^T) = q_s$.

Recall that consumption goods can be turned into capital goods one for one but not the converse. This has two implications. First, by arbitrage, the price of capital must satisfy $q_s \leq 1$. Second, aggregate investment must be non-negative,

$$k_{1s}^T + k_{1s} - \chi_s k_0 \geq 0.$$

If aggregate investment is positive, then, by arbitrage, the price of capital must be $q_s = 1$. In this case, optimality for the traditional sector gives $k_{1s}^T = 0$, and thus, investment by entrepreneurs must be positive, $k_{1s} - \chi_s k_0 > 0$. If, instead, aggregate investment is zero, then we have $k_{1s}^T = \chi_s k_0 - k_{1s}$. In this case, optimality for the traditional sector implies that either $k_{1s}^T = 0$ and $q_s = 1$ or $k_{1s}^T > 0$ and $q_s < 1$. The following conditions hold in all the cases considered:

$$q_s = F'(k_{1s}^T), \tag{17.23}$$

$$k_{1s}^T = (\chi_s k_0 - k_{1s})_+. \tag{17.24}$$

Recall that $\underline{q}$ is the lower bound for $F'(k_{1s}^T)$ and, due to Assumption 2, $\underline{q} - \gamma$ is positive. These two facts imply that $q_s \geq \underline{q} > \gamma$. If any entrepreneur is scrapping capital in period 1, it is always a profitable deviation to pay the maintenance cost γ and sell the capital. Therefore, no scrapping takes place in equilibrium, $\chi_s = 1$. Substituting $\chi_s = 1$ in (24) completes the proof. ||

The following is a useful additional result which will be used in the equilibrium characterization.

Lemma A1: *The equilibrium price of capital satisfies*

$$q_s - \theta A > 0, \tag{17.25}$$

for each s.

Proof: If $k_{1s}^T = 0$, then $q_s = 1$ and the result follows immediately from Assumption 1. If instead $k_{1s}^T > 0$, Assumption 3 implies that $(F'(k_{1s}^T) - \theta A)k_{1s}^T > (F'(0) - \theta A)0 = 0$. Since $q_s = F'(k_{1s}^T)$, inequality (25) follows. ||

Proof of Lemma 2: Consider the problem of maximizing (7) subject to (8)–(12) and non-negativity constraints for k_0 and $\{k_{1s}\}$. Given the bounds for equilibrium prices (6) and (25) and given Assumption 1, it is possible to show that the constraint set is non-empty and compact; hence, a solution exists.

Consider the entrepreneur's problem defined in terms of the original variables $\{d_{1s}, d_{2s}\}$. It can be shown that the problem stated above (in terms of $\{b_{1s}, b_{2s}\}$) is equivalent to the original problem. That is, for any $\langle d_0, \{d_{1s}, d_{2s}\}\rangle$ and $\langle k_0, \{k_{1s}\}\rangle$ in the feasible set of the original problem, there is a $\langle d_0, \{b_{1s}, b_{2s}\}\rangle$ and $\langle k_0, \{k_{1s}\}\rangle$ in the feasible set of the transformed problem, which achieves the same payoff; the converse is also true. These statements are obvious when $k_0 > 0$ and $k_{1s} > 0$ for all s. When $k_0 = 0$ or $k_{1s} = 0$ for some s, they rely on the following facts: (i) $k_0 = 0$, (2), and (4) imply $d_{1s} + d_{2s} = 0$ and (ii) $k_{1s} = 0$, (3), and (5) imply $d_{2s} = 0$.

Let me replace (8) and (12) with the constraint

$$k_0 \leq n + \sum_s \pi_s b_{1s} k_0. \tag{17.26}$$

It is easy to show that if (26) is satisfied, there exists a d_0 such that both (8) and (12) are satisfied.

Let z_0 and $\pi_s z_{1s}$ denote the Lagrange multipliers associated, respectively, to (26) and (9). An optimum is characterized by the following first-order conditions:

$$-z_0 + z_0 \sum\nolimits_s \pi_s b_{1s} + \sum\nolimits_s \pi_s z_{1s}(q_s + x_s - b_{1s}) \leq 0, \tag{17.27}$$

$$\pi_s(A - b_{2s}) - \pi_s z_{1s}(q_s - b_{2s}) \leq 0, \tag{17.28}$$

which must hold with strict equality if, respectively, $k_0 > 0$ or $k_{1s} > 0$,

$$\text{if } \pi_s z_0 k_0 - \pi_s z_{1s} k_0 < 0, \quad \text{then } b_{1s} = 0, \tag{17.29a}$$

$$\text{if } \pi_s z_0 k_0 - \pi_s z_{1s} k_0 = 0, \quad \text{then } b_{1s} \in [0, \theta a_s + q_s - \gamma], \tag{17.29b}$$

$$\text{if } \pi_s z_0 k_0 - \pi_s z_{1s} k_0 > 0, \quad \text{then } b_{1s} = \theta a_s + q_s - \gamma], \tag{17.29c}$$

$$\text{if } \pi_s z_{1s} k_{1s} - \pi_s k_{1s} < 0, \quad \text{then } b_{2s} = 0, \tag{17.30a}$$

$$\text{if } \pi_s z_{1s} k_{1s} - \pi_s k_{1s} = 0, \quad \text{then } b_{2s} \in [0, \theta A], \tag{17.30b}$$

$$\text{if } \pi_s z_{1s} k_{1s} - \pi_s k_{1s} > 0, \quad \text{then } b_{2s} = \theta A. \tag{17.30c}$$

Lemma A1 and no default imply that $q_s > \theta A \geq b_{2s}$. Condition (6) and $A > 1$ imply $A > q_s$. Then, (28) gives

$$z_{1s} \geq \frac{A - b_{2s}}{q_s - b_{2s}} > 1,$$

for all s. Using condition (30c), I get $b_{2s} = \theta A$ for $s = l, h$. Moreover, since $z_{1s} > 0$, the constraint (9) is binding and

$$k_{1s} = \frac{q_s + x_s - b_{1s}}{q_s - \theta A} k_0. \tag{17.31}$$

Rearranging condition (27), I get

$$z_0 \geq \frac{\sum_s \pi_s z_{1s}(q_s + x_s - b_{1s})}{1 - \sum_s \pi_s b_{1s}},$$

where $z_{1s} > 0$, $q_s + x_s - b_{1s} > 0$ from (10) and $\theta < 1$, and $\sum_s \pi_s b_{1s} < 1$ from (10) and Assumption 1. Therefore, $z_0 > 0$, which implies that constraint (26) is binding and $k_0 = n + \sum_s \pi_s b_{1s} k_0 \geq n > 0$. This implies that (27) holds as an equality and gives (15). Then, (31) implies that $k_{1s} > 0$, which, in turn, shows that (28) holds as an equality, giving (14). Finally, conditions (29a)–(29c) give (13a)–(13c) in the lemma. ||

Proof of Proposition 1: The proof is split in three lemmas. I first prove the characterization part and then existence and uniqueness.

Lemma A2: *In any symmetric equilibrium, $q_h = 1 > q_l$ and the financial contract is of one of the types 1–3 defined in Proposition 1.*

Proof: First, let me prove that the prices satisfy $q_h = 1 > q_l$. Rewrite the budget constraint (9) as

$$(q_s - \theta A)(k_{1s} - k_0) = (x_s + \theta A - b_{1s})k_0.$$

Lemma A1 implies that $q_s - \theta A > 0$. Given that $k_0 > 0$, as shown in Lemma 2, to prove the statement regarding asset prices, it is sufficient to prove that $x_h + \theta A - b_{1h} > 0$ and $x_l + \theta A - b_{1l} < 0$, so that entrepreneurs' investment is positive in h and negative in l. To prove the first inequality, note that the no-default constraint, $b_{1h} \leq \theta a_h + q_h - \gamma$, and inequality (6) imply

$$x_h + \theta A - b_{1h} \geq (1 - \theta)a_h + \theta A - 1 > 0,$$

where the second inequality follows from Assumption 2. To prove the second inequality, note that $x_l + \theta A - b_{1l} \leq x_l + \theta A < 0$ follows from the consumers' no-default constraint and Assumption 2.

Having proved that $q_h = 1 > q_l$, it follows that

$$z_{1h} = \frac{(1 - \theta)A}{1 - \theta A} < \frac{(1 - \theta)A}{q_l - \theta A} = z_{1l}.$$

Therefore, one of the following three cases applies (1) $z_0 \leq z_{1h} < z_{1l}$, (2) $z_{1h} < z_0 < z_{1l}$, and (3) $z_{1h} < z_{1l} \leq z_0$. Applying Lemma 2, these three cases give the equilibrium financial contracts of types 1–3. ||

This characterization implies that the equilibrium financial contract takes the form

$$b_{1l} = \frac{1}{\pi_l} \max\{\rho - \hat{\rho}, 0\}, \tag{17.32}$$

$$b_{1h} = \frac{1}{\pi_h} \min\{\rho, \hat{\rho}\}, \tag{17.33}$$

for some parameter $\rho \geq 0$, where $\hat{\rho} \equiv \pi_h(\theta a_h + 1 - \gamma)$. That is, the equilibrium financial contract is fully characterized by ρ. Note that, by construction, $\rho = \sum_s \pi_s b_{1s}$, that is the parameter ρ captures the ratio of outside borrowing to total capital invested at date 0.

The next lemma contains useful results on the relation between ρ and the equilibrium price q_l. The proof is relatively mechanical and is relegated to the online appendix.

Lemma A3: *There is an upper bound* $\bar{\rho}$ *such that the contract* $\{b_{1s}\}$ *given by (32)–(33) is consistent with no default if and only if* $\rho \in [0, \bar{\rho}]$. *For each* $\rho \in [0, \bar{\rho}]$, *there is a unique equilibrium in the low-state capital market. The associated equilibrium price is given by the function* $q_l = Q(\rho)$, *which is continuous and decreasing, and is differentiable except at* $\rho = \hat{\rho}$.

I can now prove existence and uniqueness.

Lemma A4: *There exists a unique symmetric competitive equilibrium.*

Proof: *Step 1*: First, I will define a function $\zeta : [0, \bar{\rho}] \to \mathbb{R}$. For each ρ, let b_{1l} and b_{1h} be given by (32) and (33) and let $q_h = 1$ and $q_l = Q(\rho)$. Substitute in (14) and (15) to obtain $\{z_{1s}\}$ and z_0, and let

$$\zeta(\rho) \equiv \begin{cases} z_{1h} - z_0 & \text{if } \rho \in [0, \hat{\rho}] \\ z_{1l} - z_0 & \text{if } \rho \in (\hat{\rho}, \bar{\rho}] \end{cases}.$$

The function ζ is continuous and differentiable except at $\hat{\rho}$. Note that ζ corresponds to the difference between z_{1s} and z_0 plotted in Figure 17.2.

Step 2: The function ζ satisfies two properties. First, it satisfies $\zeta(\hat{\rho}) < \lim_{\rho \to \hat{\rho}} {+\zeta(\rho)}$. This follows from the inequality $z_{1h} < z_{1l}$, which can be proved for any $\rho \in [0, \bar{\rho}]$ proceeding as in the proof of Lemma A2. Second, if $\zeta(\rho) = 0$ and ζ is differentiable at ρ, then $\zeta'(\rho) > 0$. To prove this claim, consider first the case $\rho < \hat{\rho}$. In this case, some algebra shows that

$$\zeta'(\rho) = \frac{1}{1 - \sum \pi_s b_{1s}} \left(\pi_l z_{1l} \frac{x_l + \theta A - b_{1l}}{q_l - \theta A} Q'(\rho) + \zeta(\rho) \right)$$

(detailed derivations are in the online appendix). The last expression is positive given that $x_l + \theta A - b_{1l} < 0$ (see the proof of Lemma A2), $Q'(\rho) < 0$ (from Lemma A3), and $\zeta(\rho) = 0$. If $\rho > \hat{\rho}$, then

$$\zeta'(\rho) = -\frac{z_{1l}}{q_l - \theta A} Q'(\rho) + \frac{1}{1 - \sum_s \pi_s b_{1s}} \left(\pi_l z_{1l} \frac{x_l + \theta A - b_{1l}}{q_l - \theta A} Q'(\rho) + \zeta(\rho) \right),$$

which is also positive.

Step 3: Summarizing the properties derived in step 2: ζ is continuous except at $\hat{\rho}$, where it has an upward jump, and, if it crosses the horizontal axis, it is locally increasing at the point of crossing. These properties imply that there exists one and only one $\rho^{\mathrm{CE}} \in [0, \bar{\rho}]$ which satisfies one of the following conditions: (i) $\rho^{CE} = 0$ and $\zeta(0) \geq 0$; (ii) $\rho^{\mathrm{CE}} \in (0, \hat{\rho})$ and $\zeta(\rho^{CE}) = 0$; (iii) $\rho^{\mathrm{CE}} = \hat{\rho}$ and $\zeta(\hat{\rho}) \leq 0 \leq \lim_{\rho \to \hat{\rho}} {+\zeta(\rho)}$; (iv) $\rho^{\mathrm{CE}} \in (\hat{\rho}, \bar{\rho})$ and $\zeta(\rho^{CE}) = 0$; and (v) $\rho^{\mathrm{CE}} = \bar{\rho}$ and $\zeta(\bar{\rho}) \leq 0$. For each of these cases, it is possible to construct a competitive equilibrium. For example, case (ii) gives $b_{1l}^{\mathrm{CE}} = 0$, $b_{1h}^{\mathrm{CE}} = \rho^{\mathrm{CE}}/\pi_h$, and $z_{1l}^{\text{CE}} > z_{1h}^{\text{CE}} = z_0^{\text{CE}}$, showing that the entrepreneur's optimality conditions derived in Lemma 2 are satisfied. All remaining equilibrium conditions are satisfied by construction.

Step 4: To prove uniqueness, note that the characterization in Lemma A2 implies that if $\rho^{\text{CE}} = \sum \pi_s b_{1s}^{\text{CE}}$ and $\{b_{1s}^{\text{CE}}\}$ is the equilibrium contract, then ρ^{CE} must satisfy one of the conditions (i)–(v) described in step 3. ||

The following is a corollary of Lemma A4, which will be useful in the welfare analysis. It follows immediately from step 3 of the proof.

Corollary A1: *Let ζ be the function defined in the proof of Lemma A4 and let ρ^{CE} be the equilibrium level of ρ. Then, $\zeta(\rho) > 0$ for all $\rho > \rho^{CE}$.*

Proof of Proposition 2: Define the function G

$$G(y) = \begin{cases} F(y) & \text{if } y \geq 0 \\ y & \text{if } y < 0 \end{cases}.$$

Since $F'(0) = 1$, this function is differentiable. The planner's problem can then be written as follows:

$$\max_{k_0, \{k_{1s}, b_{1s}, b_{2s}\}_{s=l,h}} \sum_s \pi_s (A - b_{2s}) k_{1s}$$

subject to

$$n + 3e - \bar{U} - k_0 + \sum_s \pi_s b_{1s} k_0 + \sum_s \pi_s (G(k_0 - k_{1s}) - G'(k_0 - k_{1s})(k_0 - k_{1s})) \geq 0, \ (\lambda)$$

$$G'(k_0 - k_{1s})(k_0 - k_{1s}) + (x_s - b_{1s}) k_0 + b_{2s} k_{1s} \geq 0, \quad (\pi_s \mu_s)$$

$$0 \leq b_{1s} \leq \theta a_s + G'(k_0 - k_{1s}) - \gamma, \quad (\pi_s \nu_s)$$

$$0 \leq b_{2s} \leq \theta A,$$

$$k_{1s}, k_0 \geq 0.$$

In parentheses, I report the Lagrange multipliers corresponding to the first three sets of constraints. The multiplier ν_s refers to the inequality $b_{1s} \leq \theta a_s + G'(k_0 - k_{1s}) - \gamma$. I will write $G_s'^*$ for $G'(k_0^* - k_{1s}^*)$ and $G_s''^*$ for $G''(k_0^* - k_{1s}^*)$. As in the case of the entrepreneur's problem, the planner's problem can be stated in terms of the variables $\{b_{1s}\}$ and $\{b_{2s}\}$, even if k_0 or $\{k_{1s}\}$ is zero (see the proof of Lemma 2). The rest of the proof is split in several steps.

Step 1: I derive the Kuhn–Tucker necessary first-order conditions for an optimum. First, the optimality conditions for k_0 and k_{1s},

$$\lambda \left(\sum_s \pi_s [b_{1s}^* - G_s''^* (k_0^* - k_{1s}^*)] - 1 \right) + \sum_s \pi_s \mu_s [x_s + G_s'^* - b_{1s}^* + G_s''^* (k_0^* - k_{1s}^*)]$$
$$+ \sum_s \pi_s \nu_s G_s''^* \leq 0, \qquad (17.34)$$

and

$$\pi_s(A - b_{2s}^*) + \lambda\pi_s G_s''^*(k_0^* - k_{1s}^*) + \pi_s\mu_s(b_{2s}^* - G_s'^* - G_s''^*(k_0^* - k_{1s}^*)) - \pi_s\nu_s G_s''^* \leq 0, \tag{17.35}$$

which must hold with strict equality if, respectively, $k_0 > 0$ or $k_{1s} > 0$. The conditions for b_{1s} and b_{2s} give

$$\text{if } \pi_s\lambda k_0^* - \pi_s\mu_s k_0^* < 0, \quad \text{then } \nu_s = 0 \text{ and } b_{1s}^* = 0, \tag{17.36a}$$

$$\text{if } \pi_s\lambda k_0^* - \pi_s\mu_s k_0^* = 0, \quad \text{then } \nu_s = 0 \text{ and } b_{1s}^* \in [0, \theta a_s + G_s'^* - \gamma], \tag{17.36b}$$

$$\text{if } \pi_s\lambda k_0^* - \pi_s\mu_s k_0^* > 0, \quad \text{then } \nu_s = (\lambda - \mu_s)k_0^* \text{ and } b_{1s}^* = \theta a_s + G_s'^* - \gamma, \tag{17.36c}$$

$$\text{if } \pi_s\mu_s k_{1s}^* - \pi_s k_{1s}^* < 0, \quad \text{then } b_{2s}^* = 0, \tag{17.37a}$$

$$\text{if } \pi_s\mu_s k_{1s}^* - \pi_s k_{1s}^* = 0, \quad \text{then } b_{2s}^* \in [0, \theta A], \tag{17.37b}$$

$$\text{if } \pi_s\mu_s k_{1s}^* - \pi_s k_{1s}^* > 0, \quad \text{then } b_{2s}^* = \theta A. \tag{17.37c}$$

Step 2: Using the conditions above, I show that, at an optimum, $\mu_s > 1$ and $b_{2s}^* = \theta A$ for $s = l, h$, $q_l^* < q_h^* = 1$, and $k_0^* > 0$ and $k_{1s}^* > 0$ for $s = l, h$. First, note that conditions (36a)–(36c) imply that

$$\nu_s = (\lambda - \mu_s) + k_0^* \tag{17.38}$$

Lemma A1 and no-default in period 2 imply that $G_s'^* - b_{2s}^* > 0$. Then, condition (35) can be rewritten as:

$$\mu_s \geq \frac{A - b_{2s}^*}{G_s'^* - b_{2s}^*} + \frac{(\lambda - \mu_s)G_s''^*(k_0^* - k_{1s}^*) - (\lambda - \mu_s) + G_s''^* k_0^*}{G_s'^* - b_{2s}^*}. \tag{17.39}$$

Let me show that the expression $(\lambda - \mu_s)G_s''^*(k_0^* - k_{1s}^*) - (\lambda - \mu_s) + G_s''^* k_0^*$ is always non-negative. If $\lambda \leq \mu_s$, this expression is equal to $(\lambda - \mu_s)G_s''^*(k_0^* - k_{1s}^*) \geq 0$, where the inequality follows because either $k_0^* - k_{1s}^* > 0$ and $G_s''^* < 0$ or $k_0^* - k_{1s}^* \leq 0$ and $G_s''^* = 0$. If $\lambda > \mu_s$, this expression is equal to $-(\lambda - \mu_s)G_s''^* k_{1s}^* \geq 0$. Therefore, (39) implies that

$$\mu_s \geq \frac{A - b_{2s}^*}{G_s'^* - b_{2s}^*} > 1,$$

where the second inequality follows since $A > 1 \geq G_s'^*$. Condition (37c) then implies that $b_{2s}^* = \theta A$. Since $\mu_s > 0$, the budget constraint is binding in period 1 and

$$k_{1s}^* = \frac{G_s'^* + x_s - b_{1s}}{G_s'^* - \theta A} k_0^*. \tag{17.40}$$

Proceeding as in the proof of Lemma A2, I can show that $k_{1h}^* - k_0^* > 0$ and $k_{1l}^* - k_0^* < 0$, implying that $q_h^* = G_h'^* = 1$, $q_l^* = G_l'^* < 1$, and $G_h''^* = 0$. Moreover, I can show that k_0^* and k_{1s}^* are positive. First, note that if $k_0^* = 0$, then (40) implies that the entrepreneur's utility is zero, contradicting the assumption that it is positive. Second, $k_0^* > 0$ and (40) imply that $k_{1s}^* > 0$.

Step 3: Next, I show that $\mu_s > \lambda$ iff $z_{1s}^* > \lambda$. This, together with conditions (36a)–(36c), gives the characterization of $\{b_{1s}^*\}$ in the proposition. Since $k_{1s}^* > 0$ (from step 2), (35) and (39) hold as equalities. Suppose that $\lambda \leq \mu_s$. Then, given the definition of z_{1s}^*, subtracting λ on both sides of (39) and rearranging give

$$(\mu_s - \lambda)\frac{G_s'^* - \theta A + G_s''^*(k_0^* - k_{1s}^*)}{G_s'^* - \theta A} = z_{1s}^* - \lambda.$$

Assumption 3 implies that $G_s'^* - \theta A + G_s''^*(k_0^* - k_{1s}^*) > 0$. Therefore, $\mu_s - \lambda$ has the same sign as $z_{1s}^* - \lambda$. Suppose, instead, that $\lambda > \mu_s$. Then, I obtain

$$(\mu_s - \lambda)\frac{G_s'^* - \theta A + G_s''^* k_{1s}^*}{G_s'^* - \theta A} = z_{1s}^* - \lambda,$$

and, given that $G_s''^* \leq 0$, $\mu_s - \lambda$ inherits the sign of $z_{1s}^* - \lambda$ also in this case.

Step 4: Finally, I prove inequality (21). Since $k_0^* > 0$ (from step 2), (34) must hold as an equality. Using (38) to substitute for v_s gives

$$\lambda\left(1 - \sum_s \pi_s b_{1s}^*\right) = \sum_s \pi_s \mu_s (x_s + G_s'^* - b_{1s}^*)$$
$$- \sum_s \pi_s [(\lambda - \mu_s) G_s''^*(k_0^* - k_{1s}^*) - (\lambda - \mu_s) + G_s''^* k_0^*].$$

Substituting (39) (as an equality), using $q_s^* = G_s'^*$, $G_h''^* = 0$ (from step 3), and the definitions of z_{1s}^* and z_0^* give

$$(\lambda - z_0^*)\left(1 - \sum_s \pi_s b_{1s}^*\right) = \pi_l\left[(\lambda - \mu_l) G_l''^*(k_0^* - k_{1l}^*) - (\lambda - \mu_l) + G_l'' k_0^*\right]\frac{x_l + \theta A - b_{1l}^*}{G_l^* - \theta A}. \tag{17.41}$$

In step 3, I have shown that $(\lambda - \mu_l)G_l''^*(k_0^* - k_{1l}^*) - (\lambda - \mu_l) + G_l'' k_0^* \geq 0$, and it is easy to show that the inequality is strict whenever $\lambda \neq \mu_l$ (note that $k_0^* - k_{1l}^* < 0$). Since $x_l + \theta A - b_{1l}^* < 0$ and $1 - \sum_s \pi_s b_{1s}^* > 0$, it follows that $\lambda < z_0^*$ except if $\lambda = \mu_l$, in which case $\lambda = z_0^*$. This completes the proof. ||

Proof of Proposition 3: I will proceed by contradiction, assume that $\rho^* > \rho^{CE}$, and show that this leads to a violation of the optimality conditions of the planner's problem. Note that when $\bar{U} = U^{\text{CE}}$, the entrepreneurs must achieve positive utility at the social optimum (since they do so at the competitive equilibrium and the competitive allocation is feasible). So Proposition 2 applies.

Step 1: I first define the values $\hat{z}_0$ and $\hat{z}_{1s}$, which will be used below. Let $\hat{q}_h$ and $\hat{q}_l$ denote the prices which would arise in competitive equilibrium if the entrepreneurs were to choose $\{b_{1s}^*\}$ instead of $\{b_{1s}^{\text{CE}}\}$. That is, $\hat{q}_h = 1$ and $\hat{q}_l = Q(\rho^*)$, where $Q(\cdot)$ is the function defined in Lemma A3. Let $\hat{z}_0$ and $\hat{z}_{1s}$ denote the values of z_0 and z_{1s} obtained by substituting $\{b_{1s}^*\}$ and $\{\hat{q}_{1s}\}$ in (14) and (15). Note that substituting $\{b_{1s}^*\}$ and $\{q_{1s}^*\}$ in (14) and (15) gives z_0^* and z_{1s}^*.

Step 2: I now derive some inequalities regarding $\hat{z}_0$ and $\hat{z}_{1s}$. It is possible to show that $\rho^* > \rho^{CE}$ implies $q_l^* \leq \hat{q}_l$. The proof of this result is relatively cumbersome and is relegated to the online appendix (Lemma 7). This is where Assumption 4 is used. This result immediately implies that $\hat{z}_{1l} \leq z_{1l}^*$. Moreover, $q_h^* = \hat{q}_h = 1$ implies that $\hat{z}_{1h} = z_{1h}^*$. Finally, I want to show that $\hat{z}_0 \geq z_0^*$. To prove this inequality, it is sufficient to show that (15) defines an increasing function in q_l, which follows from differentiating (15) with respect to q_l and using the fact that $x_l + \theta A - b_{1l} < 0$.

Step 3: Define the state s' as follows: $s' = h$ if $0 < \rho^* \leq \hat{\rho}$ and $s' = l$ if $\rho^* > \hat{\rho}(\rho^* = 0$ is not possible since $\rho^* > \rho^{CE} \geq 0$ by hypothesis). The construction in step 1 implies that

$$\hat{z}_{1s'} - \hat{z}_0 = \zeta(\rho^*),$$

where $\zeta(\cdot)$ is the function defined in Lemma A4 . Since $\rho^* > \rho^{CE}$, Corollary A1 implies that $\zeta(\rho^*) > 0$. Finally, Proposition 2 shows that $\lambda^* \leq z_0^*$. Putting together these two inequalities and those derived in step 2 gives

$$z_{1s'}^* - \lambda^* \geq z_{1s'}^* - z_0^* \geq \hat{z}_{1s'} - \hat{z}_0 > 0.$$

Note that the definition of the state s' implies that $b_{1s'}^* > 0$. The inequalities $b_{1s'}^* > 0$ and $z_{1s'}^* - \lambda^* > 0$ violate the planner's optimality conditions derived in Proposition 2. This completes the argument.

Finally, I turn to the last statement of the proposition. Suppose that the equilibrium is of type 1, and suppose, by contradiction, that $\rho^* \geq \rho^{CE}$. Then, steps analogous to the ones above lead to the chain of inequalities:

$$z_{1s'}^* - \lambda^* > z_{1s'}^* - z_0^* \geq \hat{z}_{1s'} - \hat{z}_0 \geq 0,$$

where the first inequality is now strict because of Proposition 2. Again, I obtain a contradiction. ||

References

ACEMOGLU, D. and ZILIBOTTI, F. (1997), "Was Prometheus Unbound by Chance? Risk, Diversification, and Growth", *Journal of Political Economy*, **105** (4), 709–751.

AGHION, P., BANERJEE, A. and PIKETTY, T. (1999), "Dualism and Macroeconomic Volatility", *Quarterly Journal of Economics*, **114** (4), 1359–1397.

AGUIAR, M. and GOPINATH, G. (2005), "Fire-Sale FDI and Liquidity Crises", *Review of Economics and Statistics*, **87** (3), 439–452.

ALLEN, F. and GALE, D. (2004), "Financial Intermediaries and Markets", *Econometrica*, **72**, 1023–1061.

BERNANKE, B. and GERTLER, M. (1989), "Agency Costs, Net Worth, and Business Fluctuations", *American Economic Review*, **79** (1), 14–31.

BERNANKE, B. and GERTLER, M. (2001), "Should Central Banks Respond to Movements in Asset Prices?", *American Economic Review*, **91** (2), 253–257.

BERNANKE, B., GERTLER, M. and GILCHRIST, S. (2001), "The Financial Accelerator in a Quantitative Business Cycle Framework", in J. Taylor and M. Woodford (eds.), *Handbook of Macroeconomics*, Vol. 15 (Amsterdam: North Holland) 1341–1393.

BORDO, M. D. and JEANNE, O. (2002), "Monetary Policy and Asset Prices: Does 'Benign Neglect' Make Sense?", *International Finance*, **5** (2), 139–164.

BORIO, C. (2003), "Towards a Macroprudential Framework for Bank Supervision and Regulation?" (Bank for International Settlements Working Paper No. 128).

BORIO, C. and LOWE, P. (2002), "Asset Prices, Financial and Monetary Stability: Exploring the Nexus" (Bank for International Settlements Working Paper No. 114).
CABALLERO, R. J. and KRISHNAMURTHY, A. (2001), "International and Domestic Collateral Constraints in a Model of Emerging Market Crisis", *Journal of Monetary Economics*, **48** (3), 513–548.
CABALLERO, R. J. and KRISHNAMURTHY, A. (2003), "Excessive Dollar Debt: Financial Development and Underinsurance", *Journal of Finance*, **58** (2), 867–894.
CAPRIO, G., KLINGEBIEL, D., LAEVEN, L. and NOGUERA, G. (2005), "Banking Crisis Database", in P. Honohan and L. Laeven (eds.), *Systemic Financial Crises* (Cambridge, New York: Cambridge University Press) 307–340.
CARLSTROM, C. T. and FUERST, T. (1997), "Agency Costs, Net Worth, and Business Fluctuations: A Computable General Equilibrium Analysis", *American Economic Review*, **87** (5), 893–910.
CECCHETTI, S., GENBERG, H., LIPSKY, J. and WADHWANI, S. (2000), "Asset Prices and Central Bank Policy" (International Center for Monetary and Banking Studies Report No. 2).
COOLEY, T., MARIMON, R. and QUADRINI, V. (2004), "Aggregate Consequences of Limited Contract Enforceability", *Journal of Political Economy*, **111** (4), 817–847.
CORSETTI, G., PESENTI, P. and ROUBINI, N. (1999), "Paper Tigers? A Model of the Asian Crisis", *European Economic Review*, **43** (7), 1211–1236.
DUPOR, B. (2002), "The Natural Rate of Q", *American Economic Review*, **92** (2), 96–101.
FAIA, E., and MONACELLI, T. (2007), "Optimal Interest Rate Rules, Asset Prices and Credit Frictions", *Journal of Economic Dynamics and Control*, **31** (10), 3228–3254.
FARHI, E., GOLOSOV, M., and TSYVINSKI, A. (2007), "A Theory of Liquidity and Regulation of Financial Intermediation" (Mimeo, MIT).
FROOT, K. A., SCHARFSTEIN, D. S. and STEIN, J. C. (1993), "Risk Management: Coordinating Corporate Investment and Financing Policies", *Journal of Finance*, **48**, 1629–1658.
GAI, P., KAPADIA, S., MILLARD, S. and PEREZ, A. (2006), "Financial Innovation, Macroeconomic Stability and Systemic Crises" (Mimeo, Bank of England).
GAI, P., KONDOR, P. and VAUSE, N. (2005), "Procyclicality, Collateral Values and Financial Stability" (Bank of England Working Paper No. 304).
GEANAKOPLOS, J. and POLEMARCHAKIS, H. M. (1986), "Existence, Regularity, and Constrained Suboptimality of Competitive Allocations When the Asset Market Is Incomplete", in W. Heller, R. Starr and D. Starret (eds.) *Uncertainty, Information, and Communication: Essays in Honor of K. J. Arrow*, Vol. III (Cambridge, New York: Cambridge University Press) 65–96.
GERTLER, M. (1992), "Financial Capacity and Output Fluctuations in an Economy with Multi-Period Financial Relationships", *Review of Economic Studies*, **59**, 455–472.
GOURINCHAS, P.-O., VALDES, R. and LANDERRETCHE, O. (2001), "Lending Booms: Latin America and the World", *Economia*, **1** (2), 47–100.
GUERRIERI, V. and LORENZONI, G. (2007), "Liquidity and Trading Dynamics" (Mimeo, MIT).
HERRING, R. J. and WACHTER, S. (1999), "Real Estate Booms and Banking Busts: An International Perspective" (Group of 30 Occasional Paper No. 58).
HOLMSTROM, B. and TIROLE, J. (1998), "Private and Public Supply of Liquidity", *Journal of Political Economy*, **106** (1), 1–40.
IACOVIELLO, M. (2005), "House Prices, Borrowing Constraints and Monetary Policy in the Business Cycle", *American Economic Review*, **95** (3), 739–764.
KEHOE, T. and LEVINE, D. K. (1993), "Debt-Constrained Asset Markets", *Review of Economic Studies*, **60**, 865–888.
KIYOTAKI, N. and MOORE, J. (1997), "Credit Cycles", *Journal of Political Economy*, **105** (2), 211–248.
KRISHNAMURTHY, A. (2003), "Collateral Constraints and the Amplification Mechanism", *Journal of Economic Theory*, **111** (2), 277–292.
KRUGMAN, P. (1998), "Fire-Sale FDI" (Manuscript, NBER Conference on Capital Flows to Emerging Markets).
LAMONT, O. (1995), "Corporate-Debt Overhang and Macroeconomic Expectations", *American Economic Review*, **85** (5), 1106–1117.
LORENZONI, G. (2001), "Excess Interest Rate Volatility in an Intermediated Economy" (PhD Thesis (Chapter 1), MIT).

McKINNON, R., and PILL, H. (1996), "Credible Liberalizations and International Capital Flows: The Overborrowing Syndrome", in T. Ito and A. Krueger (eds.) *Financial Deregulation and Integration in East Asia* (Chicago: Chicago University Press) 7–50.
PULVINO, T. (1998), "Do Asset Fire Sales Exist? An Empirical Investigation of Commercial Aircraft Transactions", *Journal of Finance*, **53**, 939–978.
RAMPINI, A. (2004), "Entrepreneurial Activity, Risk, and the Business Cycle", *Journal of Monetary Economics*, **51**, 555–573.
RANCIERE, R., TORNELL, A. and WESTERMANN, F. (2003), "Crises and Growth: A Re-Evaluation" (NBER Working Paper No. 10073).
SCHNEIDER, M. and TORNELL, A. (2004), "Balance Sheet Effects, Bailout Guarantees and Financial Crises", *Review of Economic Studies*, **71** (3), 883–913.
SHLEIFER, A. and VISHNY, R. W. (1992), "Liquidation Values and Debt Capacity", *Journal of Finance*, **47** (4), 1343–1366.
TORNELL, A. and WESTERMANN, F. (2002), "Boom-Bust Cycles in Middle Income Countries: Facts and Explanation", *International Monetary Fund Staff Papers*, **49**, 111–155.
WATANABE, W. (2007), "Prudential Regulation and the Credit Crunch: Evidence from Japan", *Journal of Money, Credit and Banking*, **39**, 639–665.

IV CONTAGION EFFECTS IN FINANCIAL CRISES

18 Financial Contagion through Capital Connections: A Model of the Origin and Spread of Bank Panics

Amil Dasgupta

1. Introduction

A commonly held view of financial crises is that they begin locally—in some region, country, or institution—and subsequently "spread" elsewhere. This process of spread is often referred to as "contagion." What might justify contagion in a rational economy? There are (at least) two broad classes of explanations.

The first class of explanations posits that the adverse information that precipitates a crisis in one institution also implies adverse information about the other. This view emphasizes correlations in underlying value across institutions and Bayesian learning by rational agents.[1] For example, a currency crisis in Thailand may be driven by adverse information about underlying asset values in Southeast Asia, which can then apply to other countries in the region.

A second type of explanation begins with the observation that financial institutions are often linked to each other through direct portfolio or balance sheet connections. For example, entrepreneurs are linked to capitalists through credit relationships and banks are known to hold interbank deposits. While such balance sheet connections may seem to be desirable ex ante, during a crisis the failure of one institution can have direct negative payoff effects upon stakeholders of institutions with which it is linked.[2]

In this paper, we present a model of financial contagion that formalizes this latter view. We focus on a particular (but particularly important) type of financial institution: commercial banks. Throughout history, banks have cross-held deposits (for clearance, regulatory and insurance reasons), and thus the failure of some banks had direct consequences on others through capital linkages. Contagious bank failure is particularly complex because it involves an underlying coordination problem among depositors of each bank. Even weak banks may not fail if very few depositors withdraw their money early, while strong banks may fail if many depositors withdraw early. The existence of multiple equilibria (Diamond and Dybvig 1983) makes it difficult to examine even individual bank failures, which then compounds the difficulty of isolating contagious effects in many bank settings. Using and extending some recent developments in the theory of equilibrium

[1] See, for example, Chen (1999) or Acharya and Yorulmazer (2002).

[2] See, for example, Kiyotaki and Moore (1997) or Allen and Gale (2000).

selection in coordination games (Morris and Shin 2003), we present a model of an economy with multiple banks where the probability of failure of individual banks, and of systemic crises, is uniquely determined. This then permits us to identify contagion precisely and examine its properties.

The model presented here is too stylized to be a realistic depiction of any particular set of financial crises. While it may have some stylized similarities to aspects of episodes both in history (e.g., the pre–World War I panics of the National Banking Era in the United States) and in current times (e.g., recent episodes of volatility in Latin America and East Asia), our purpose is to provide further theoretical grounding for the existence of financial contagion in equilibrium and to show that it may occur with positive probability in banking systems. To motivate the model, however, it is useful at the outset to briefly describe the broad stylized features of the former group of financial crises mentioned previously.

The defining characteristics of the National Banking System were laid out in the National Banking Act of 1864. This act prohibited interstate branching of banks and established a system of reserve pyramiding under which country banks could hold reserves in designated reserve city banks, which in turn could hold reserves in New York. Thus, throughout this period, the reserve cities (including New York) directly or indirectly held the deposits of many country banks.

There were five major banking panics during the National Banking Era prior to the Great Depression. They occurred in 1873, 1884, 1890, 1893, and 1907. With the exception of 1893, these panics began in New York and subsequently spread to the interior of the country. The work of Calomiris and Gorton (1991), Wicker (2000), and others indicates that the panics usually began with local shocks to assets in New York. This was typically followed by suspension of payments by New York banks, followed by suspensions in banks at various parts of the country. In 1907, for example, the panic was started by an unsuccessful attempt to corner the copper market by a group of speculators who were associated with several trust companies in New York. When news of this speculative failure became public in October, there were runs on Knickerbocker Trust Company. This was followed by runs on the National Bank of North America and on other institutions thought to be directly or indirectly linked to the copper speculators, and then by a widespread panic. Sprague (1910, p. 259) points out: "Everywhere the banks suddenly found themselves confronted with demands for money by frightened depositors ... Country banks drew money from city banks and all banks throughout the country demanded the return of funds deposited or on loan in New York." Finally, the panic that began with a localized asset shock in New York led to suspensions through much of the country.

To summarize, two very broad stylized features of the National Banking System panics were as follows.

1. Panics originated due to local asset-side shocks. They were inherently dynamic, starting in New York and spreading to the interior of the country.
2. While other factors may also play a role, panics appeared to diffuse nationally through the correspondent network, from debtor New York banks to creditor banks in the interior.

Both of these stylized features emerge as equilibrium outcomes in our model, which we now proceed to describe.

1.1 Summary of Model and Results

We consider an economy with three periods and two regions. Each region has a representative bank. Each bank has access to a (common) liquid riskless asset and a local illiquid risky asset. The risky assets pay a higher expected return than the riskless asset if held to maturity, but they pay less than par value if liquidated early. The returns on the risky assets are revealed in the last period and are increasing functions of regional economic fundamentals.

There are two groups of risk-averse depositors, one in each region, each of whom lives three periods. The depositors receive uninsurable private liquidity shocks: they may need to consume in the interim period with positive probability. The total level of liquidity demand in the economy is fixed, but there may be (negatively correlated) regionally aggregate liquidity flucuations in the interim period. The two banks insure against such regional liquidity shocks by exchanging deposits in the initial period. Consumer and interbank deposits take the form of demand deposit contracts.

In the interim period, regional liquidity shocks are realized first and become publicly known. The bank facing high liquidity demand withdraws its interbank deposit. This creates an interim asymmetry among the two banks: one bank is now a net debtor to the other. Later in the same period, the depositors of a randomly chosen bank receive some information about the state of fundamentals in their region. This updates their beliefs about eventual returns on bank deposits and thus leads them to consider whether to leave their deposits in the bank or to withdraw. This may result in runs on that bank. The depositors of the other bank are able to observe the proportion of the customers of the first bank who withdraw their deposits prematurely. They are then able to obtain information about the fundamentals of their own region and choose whether to withdraw their deposits from their own bank.

As we have noted, the choices made by depositors at each bank involve a coordination problem: they may wish to withdraw their deposits if they believe that enough other depositors will do the same, leading to a run on the bank. This leads to multiple equilibria when payoffs to depositors are common knowledge. In our setting, however, the information available about economic fundamentals in either region is imperfect. Depositors receive private but correlated signals about the potential future returns on their deposits. The level of correlation can be arbitrarily high. However, even small asymmetries in the information received by depositors can lead to substantial strategic uncertainty—that is, uncertainty about the actions of other depositors (who condition their behavior on their own private signals). The presence of such strategic uncertainty prevents depositors from coordinating their actions with arbitrary precision and thus greatly reduces the set of potential equilibrium outcomes for a given level of economic fundamentals. Accordingly, and in contrast to the usual multiplicity of equilibria that arise in the classic bank-run models in the tradition of Diamond and Dybvig (1983), the game between our depositors is characterized by a unique threshold in regional economic fundamentals below which each bank will fail (Proposition 1) due to a run by depositors.[3] Bank failure thus depends upon the release of adverse information about local asset returns. The probability of failure is determined endogenously.

Given the interim debtor–creditor relationship between the regional banks, the emergence of adverse information about asset returns in one region can have broader consequences, causing instability in other regions. In our central result, we show that contagion arises in equilibrium: that is, there are regions of fundamentals in which one bank fails if and only if the other bank fails (Proposition 2). Conditional on the failure of a debtor bank, a creditor bank fails for a wider range of its own fundamentals than

[3]The equilibrium selection mechanism and the role of strategic uncertainty is discussed in detail in Section 3.

if the debtor bank survived. Contagion thus flows from debtors to creditors and spreads along the channels of interbank deposits. We also present a comparative statics result to demonstrate that the incidence of contagion is increasing in the size of interbank deposit holdings (Proposition 3).

Interbank deposits thus enable banks to hedge regional liquidity shocks but expose them to the risk of contagion. Should banks hold interbank deposits? Our framework enables us to consider the optimal level of interconnectedness within banking systems. We illustrate the conditions under which banks would want to hold maximal levels of interbank deposits. More importantly, when bank runs are relatively frequent, we show that only *partial* cross-holdings of deposits may be optimal (Remark 1). Thus, the existence of contagion prevents banks from insuring each other perfectly against liquidity risk via the cross-holding of deposits. When the probability of bank failure is high, banks may also find it optimal to hold excess reserves as liquidity buffers against depositor runs. Our model suggests that such unstable banking systems may be characterized by lower levels of optimal interconnectedness and higher excess liquidity buffers than their stable counterparts. Thus it is precisely in stable banking systems that the rare event of bank failure induces the most significant contagious consequences (Remark 2).

1.2 Related Literature

Our paper is connected with a diverse literature. We apply the equilibrium selection techniques summarized in Morris and Shin (2003). These are discussed further in Section 3. Goldstein and Pauzner (2004a) were the first to apply these techniques to the analysis of bank runs. They investigate the probability of bank runs in a single-bank setting, whereas we are interested in the problem of contagion with multiple banks. Rochet and Vives (2004) also analyze bank runs using similar techniques but do not concern themselves with the problem of contagion. Goldstein and Pauzner (2004b), like us, examine contagion of self-fulfilling crises, but their mechanism for contagion (through common lenders) is different from ours. A related mechanism—based upon a wealth effect—can be found in Kyle and Xiong (2001). Lagunoff and Schreft (2001) study contagion in an economy where the set of available projects, each with a minimum funding requirement, is characterized by overlapping groups of common lenders. When idiosyncratic shocks close down a given project, lenders to that project may optimally reallocate their portfolios. This, in turn, affects lenders who shared other projects with them. Kiyotaki and Moore (1997) explore the method by which contagion flows through credit chains among lenders and entrepreneurs. Their model shares with ours the feature that balance sheet connections are the channels for contagion, but does not concern itself with coordination problems. Rochet and Tirole (1996) examine correlated bank failures via monitoring: the failure of one bank is assumed to mean that other banks have not been monitored and thus triggers multiple collapses. Freixas, Parigi, and Rochet (2000) consider the role of a lender of last resort in a complete information framework where the presence of systemic risk arises from interbank connections. These connections are motivated by the fact that consumers are uncertain about where they need to consume. Fragility arises because there may be multiple self-fulfilling equilibrium actions for consumers at each location.

The paper that is closest to ours in theme is by Allen and Gale (2000). Their purpose is to model contagion as an equilibrium phenomenon in a many-bank setting. While our model thus shares features with Allen and Gale's, there are important differences. Contagion is assumed to occur with zero probability in Allen and Gale's model. Thus they do not consider the optimal systemic level of interbank deposit holdings. We are able to determine the probability of contagion in equilibrium and thus can show that full insurance against liquidity shocks via interbank deposits is not always optimal. In addition, our models differ in the source of bank failure. In Allen and Gale's work the source for bank failure is excess liquidity demand. In our model banks fail due to local shocks to bank assets that generate runs by depositors.

The rest of the paper is organized as follows. In Section 2 we present the model. In Section 3 we prove the existence and uniqueness of equilibrium. Section 4 contains our central result and the related comparative static. The optimal level of interbank deposit holdings is illustrated in Section 5. Section 6 concludes.

2. The Model

2.1 *Regional Liquidity Shocks*

We consider an economy with two nonoverlapping regions, A and B. There are three time periods $t = 0, 1, 2$. The regions are populated by distinct continuums of weakly risk-averse agents with utility functions $u(\cdot)[u'(\cdot) > 0, u''(\cdot) \leq 0]$ who each live for three periods. Each agent has an endowment of 1 unit. Agents face private (uninsurable) liquidity shocks: they need to consume either in Period 1 (impatient) or in Period 2 (patient). In the aggregate, there is no uncertainty about liquidity in the economy: there is exactly a proportion $w \in (0, 1)$ of agents who require early liquidity. However, individual regions experience (regionally) aggregate liquidity shocks of size $x > 0$. In particular, there are two states of the world: $\lambda = A$ or $\lambda = B$, corresponding to the cases where Region A and Region B (respectively) have high early liquidity demands. Since aggregate liquidity is constant, regional liquidity shocks are negatively correlated. The State λ is realized and publicly known immediately at the beginning of Period 1. States A and B occur with equal probability.

2.2 *Banks, Demand Deposits, and Interbank Insurance*

We consider two representative competitive banks that lie in two regions of the economy. There are two classes of assets: a safe and liquid storage technology with a low (unit) gross rate of return; and a risky, illiquid asset with high expected return but with costs to premature liquidation. The storage technology is common to both banks. One unit stored at time t produces one unit at time $t + 1$. In addition, Region i's bank also has access to risky illiquid technology R_i, with returns given by

$$R_i(t) = \begin{cases} r \in (\underline{r}, 1) & \text{when } t = 1 \\ R(\theta_i) & \text{when } t = 2, \text{ where } \theta_i \text{ is distributed uniformly on } [L, U], \end{cases}$$

Table 18.1 Regional liquidity shocks

	A	B
$\lambda = A$	$w + x$	$w - x$
$\lambda = B$	$w - x$	$w + x$

where t is the time of liquidation, $R(\cdot)$ is any increasing function, and $\underline{r} \geq 1/2$. The parameter θ_i indexes some underlying "fundamentals" related to the bank's assets, which determine the level of the bank's asset returns. These fundamentals θ_i are independent and identically distributed for $i = A, B$. We assume that $E_\theta i[u(R(\theta_i))] \geq u(1)$, that is, the risky asset pays a higher expected return if held until Period 2. Agents cannot directly invest in the risky asset, and begin their lives with their endowments deposited in the bank of their region.[4]

Banks are constrained to offer depositors demand deposit contracts. These contracts offer conversion of deposits into cash at par on demand in Period 1 conditional on sufficient cash being available. If, however, sufficient cash is not available, then the contract specifies that the bank will divide up evenly what cash it can generate by liquidating its portfolio amongst the depositors who demand early withdrawal. At this point of time, the bank goes out of business. For those depositors who choose to remain in the bank until Period 2, the bank promises to pay a stochastic amount, that is contingent upon the returns on the bank's assets, the proportion of early withdrawals, and payouts to any senior liabilities.

The two banks face aggregate demand shocks in Period 1, in keeping with the regionally aggregate liquidity shocks outlined before. However, since these aggregate regional liquidity shocks are negatively correlated, banks insure against these by holding interbank deposits. In particular, we assume that banks hold cash reserves equal to w, the average level of liquidity demand in the economy, and insure against regional liquidity shocks by holding interbank deposits of size $D \in [0, x]$ with the other bank. Given the cash holdings of the banks and given the timing of the model, it is easy to see that interbank deposits of size larger than x will not be desirable to banks. Thus, in this symmetric scheme, banks exchange deposits of size D and distribute their net wealth of 1, putting w in cash and $1 - w$ in long-term investment projects. We thus fix banks' portfolios ex ante. However, we relax this restriction in Section 5.

At the beginning of Period 1, the state A or B is realized, and the bank in the region with high liquidity demand receives a payment of D from the bank in the other region (before individual depositors can claim money from the bank). In Period 2, the debtor bank must pay both its own residual customers and its interbank claim to the creditor bank. We assume that the creditor bank is paid first and that patient depositors share the remainder. The assumed priority order for clearing at $t = 2$ is innocuous: giving interbank payments priority minimizes contagion at the cost of increasing the probability of bank runs in debtor institutions. Since the goal of this exercise is to show that contagion is an essential element of interconnected banking systems, this assumption actually works against us. Changing the relative seniority of interbank debt would lead to qualitatively similar results.

To fix ideas, it is helpful to consider an example. Suppose that only impatient agents withdraw money in Period 1 and that $D = x$. In addition, suppose State A is realized, so that Region A has a higher immediate liquidity shock. Upon the realization of the state, Bank A immediately receives from Bank B its deposit of x, so that Bank A now has $w + x$ in cash, which matches the amount of withdrawals it faces. Similarly, Bank B now has $w - x$ in cash, which is precisely the demand it faces in Period 1. Bank A now owes Bank B the amount $xR(\theta_A)$ and owes its own customers $(1 - w - x)R(\theta_A)$. But it has exactly $(1 - w)$ invested in the illiquid asset $R(\theta_A)$, so its proceeds in Period 2 are

[4]We are thus not considering participation. However, in the examples computed later, it is easy to see that participation in the banking system is indeed optimal.

$(1 - w)R(\theta_A)$, which is exactly the sum of its liabilities. Similarly, promises and earnings clear for Bank B.

2.3 Information and Timing

In Period 1, nature selects at random (and with equal probability) one of the sets of depositors to receive information about their bank and to act. Information is received in the form of private signals about the underlying fundamentals of their bank. Suppose Region i is selected first. Depositor j of Region i receives signal $\theta_{j,i} = \theta_i + \epsilon_{j,i}$, where $\epsilon_{j,i}$ are distributed uniformly in the population on $[-\epsilon, \epsilon]$. Shortly thereafter, depositors of the other bank (in region $-i$) receive information about their own bank and can then act themselves. The information structure is symmetric. Depositor j of Region $-i$ receives signal $\theta_{j,-i} = \theta_{-i} + \epsilon_{j,-i}$, where $\epsilon_{j,-i}$ are distributed uniformly in the population on $[-\epsilon, \epsilon]$. It is important to note that, before choosing, the depositors who move second learn what happened in the first bank. Thus, the timing of this game can be described in itemized form as follows.

1. Period 0
   Interbank deposits are initiated.
2. Period 1
   (*a*) State A or B is realized.
   (*b*) Period 1 interbank claims settle.
   (*c*) Depositors in Bank i receive information and choose actions.
   (*d*) Depositors of Bank i who demand early withdrawal are paid.
   (*e*) Depositors in Bank $-i$ receive information and choose actions.
   (*f*) Depositors in Bank $-i$ who demand early withdrawal are paid.
3. Period 2
   (*a*) Period 2 interbank claims settle.
   (*b*) Residual depositor claims on the two banks settle.

2.4 Depositor Payoffs and Interbank Payments

We are now ready to write down the payoffs to depositors in this game. In Period 1, depositors choose whether to demand conversion of their deposits into cash at par (withdraw) or to retain their deposits with the bank (remain). Impatient depositors can only consume in Period 1. They will therefore always withdraw. However, the patient depositors face a nontrivial decision problem. We explicate their payoffs next.

Recall that in Period 1, one bank will be a debtor and one bank will be a creditor. Thus, without loss of generality, we can label the payoff matrices for the patient depositors of the two banks as those of the debtor bank and the creditor bank respectively.

Begin by considering the debtor bank—that is, the bank that experienced a high liquidity shock in Period 1. There is a mass $1 - (w + x)$ of patient agents in the debtor region. Let n_d represent the proportion of the patient depositors who choose to withdraw in Period 1. If n_d of the patient depositors withdraw then, since impatient agents (of measure $w + x$) always withdraw in Period 1, total demand for cash in Period 1 is $(w + x)+n_d(1 - (w + x))$. The bank had w in cash and received D in cash from the creditor bank at the beginning of Period 1 (and hence became a debtor to the creditor bank). Thus, its total cash holdings are $w + D$. If demand for cash exceeds $w + D$, the bank can obtain more cash by liquidating its long assets. It has $1 - w$ invested in the long asset, from which it can generate $(1 - w)r$

in cash in Period 1. Thus, observe that if $[w+x]+(1-[w+x])n_d \geq [w+D]+(1-w)r$, that is, if

$$n_d \geq \frac{(1-w)r+D-x}{1-(w+x)} \tag{18.1}$$

then the debtor bank becomes insolvent and goes out of business in Period 1, and in the process divides up the proceeds of its liquidated asset portfolio equally among its claimants in Period 1. However, if the bank remains solvent in Period 1, then it must first settle its debt of $DR(\theta_i)$ to the creditor bank (because interbank deposits have seniority, within each period, to regular demand deposits). In order to pay early demands by patient agents in Period 1, the debtor bank had to liquidate $[(1-w-x)n_d+(x-D)]/r$ of the illiquid asset in Period 1. Its original investment in the long asset was $1-w$. The remaining proceeds are $(1-w-[(1-(w+x))n_d+(x-D)]/r)\,R(\theta_i)$. As long as

$$\left(1-w-\frac{(1-(w+x))n_d+(x-D)}{r}\right)R(\theta_i) > DR(\theta_i)$$

that is, $n_d < [(1-w)r+(D-x)-rD]/(1-w-x)$, the debtor bank pays $DR(\theta_i)$ to the creditor bank in Period 2, and then divides up the remainder equally among those depositors who chose to remain in the bank. This means that each patient depositor who chooses to remain receives

$$\frac{1-w-\frac{(1-(w+x))n_d+(x-D)}{r}-D}{(1-w-x)(1-n_d)}R(\theta_i).$$

However, if $n_d \geq [(1-w)r+(D-x)-rD]/(1-w-x)$, then residual depositors receive nothing, and the creditor bank receives (by seniority)

$$\left(1-w-\frac{(1-(w+x))n_d+(x-D)}{r}\right)R(\theta_i).$$

Thus, the Period-2 payments on the interbank deposits from the debtor to the creditor bank can be written as

$$g(\theta_i,n_d)=\begin{cases} DR(\theta_i) & \text{if } n_d<\frac{(1-w)r+(D-x)-rD}{1-w-x}, \\ \left(1-w-\frac{(1-(w+x))n_d+(x-D)}{r}\right)R(\theta_i) & \text{if } \frac{(1-w)r+(D-x)-rD}{1-w-x}\leq n_d<\frac{(1-w)r+(D-x)}{1-(w+x)}, \\ 0 & \text{if } n_d\geq\frac{(1-w)r+(D-x)}{1-(w-x)}. \end{cases}$$

Correspondingly, the payoffs to the patient depositors, if they withdraw, are given by

$$u_w(\theta_i,n_d)=\begin{cases} u[1] & \text{if } n_d<\frac{(1-w)r+(D-x)}{1-(w+x)}, \\ u\left[\frac{(w+D)+(1-w)r}{(w+x)+(1-(w+x))n_d}\right] & \text{if } n_d\geq\frac{(1-w)r+(D-x)}{1-(w+x)}; \end{cases}$$

and if they remain, by

$$u_R(\theta_i, n_d) = \begin{cases} u\left[\dfrac{1-w-\frac{(1-(w+x))n_d+(x-D)}{r}-D}{(1-w-x)(1-n_d)}R(\theta_i)\right] & \text{if } n_d < \dfrac{(1-w)r+(D-x)-rD}{1-w-x)}, \\ u[0] & \text{if } n_d \geq \dfrac{(1-w)r+(D-x)-rD}{1-w-x}. \end{cases}$$

The specific form of $t = 2$ payments to depositors is a consequence of the assumption of perfectly competitive banks that make zero profits. This is a convenient simplification, but is not necessary for the results that follow. Given the liquidation discount on bank assets, a broad class of contracts that promise redemption at par on deposits at $t = 1$ would lead to a coordination problem among depositors and thus to similar qualitative results. The creditor bank's payoffs are complicated by the fact that they depend on the condition of the debtor bank. If the debtor bank were to become insolvent in Period 1 (i.e., Condition (1) holds), then the creditor bank receives no money from the debtor bank in Period 2, and so must divide up a smaller pool of proceeds among its residual claimants. However, regardless of the condition of the debtor bank, the creditor bank may itself be run out of business. Let n_c denote the proportion of the patient depositors of the creditor bank who choose to withdraw in Period 1. Observe that if

$$n_c \geq \frac{(1-w)r + (x-D)}{1-(w-x)} \tag{18.2}$$

then the creditor bank will become insolvent. It is thus possible for the creditor bank to become insolvent while the debtor bank remains solvent. In the simplest possible interpretation of bankruptcy laws, we assume that in this event the proceeds from the debtor bank will be divided equally among all the depositors of the creditor bank. The payoffs to depositors of the creditor bank are then:

$$u_W(\theta_i, n_c) = \begin{cases} u[1] & \text{if } n_c < \dfrac{(1-w)r+(x-D)}{1-(w-x)}, \\ u\left[\dfrac{(w-D)+(1-w)r}{(w-x)+(1-(w-x))n_c} + g(\theta_{-i}, n_d)\right] & \text{if } n_c \geq \dfrac{(1-w)r+(x-D)}{1-(w-x)}; \end{cases}$$

$$u_R(\theta_i, n_c) = \begin{cases} u\left[\dfrac{(x-D)-(1-w+x)n_c+(1-w)R(\theta_i)+g(\theta_{-i},n_d)}{(1-n_c)(1-w+x)}\right] & \text{if } n_c < \dfrac{x-D}{1-w+x}, \\ u\left[\dfrac{(1-w)-\frac{D-x+n_c(1-(w-x))}{r}R(\theta_i)+g(\theta_{-i},n_d)}{(1-n_c)(1-(w-x))}\right] & \text{if } \dfrac{x-D}{1-w+x} \leq n_c < \dfrac{(1-w)r+(x-D)}{1-(w-x)}, \\ u[g(\theta_{-i}, n_d)] & \text{if } n_c \geq \dfrac{(1-w)r+(x-D)}{1-(w-x)}. \end{cases}$$

2.5 A Note on the Payoffs

It is worth discussing some assumptions implicit in the payoffs. The payoffs are written under the assumption that, should the debtor bank's depositors choose to run, the creditor bank cannot "preempt" them by withdrawing its deposit before the run takes place. This is a reasonable assumption, since our bank runs are induced by local news about local asset shocks and are short-lived events. For example, rumors of speculation in the New York money market are likely to be known in New York before they are known in the interior of the country. In addition, relaxing this assumption will not change the qualitative nature of the results. All that is necessary for the results below is that the creditor bank lose part of its deposit in the event of a run on the debtor bank. This would always be the case except in the unrealistic scenario where the creditor bank knew before local depositors at the debtor bank of local news regarding asset returns.

We have also assumed here that payoffs to debtor bank depositors are independent of events in the creditor bank. This simplifies the analysis substantially. The content of this assumption is twofold. First, it means that the debtor bank always pays its interbank claim in Period 2 (if it survives) regardless of whether or not the creditor bank survives. The failure of the creditor bank implies, by definition, that there are residual claimants and hence it is reasonable for them to be paid from residual assets available at $t = 2$.[5] The second implication of the assumption has substance. We are implicitly abstracting from a different interlinkage: if the creditor bank experiences a run at $t = 1$, it may be possible for the creditor bank to liquidate its interbank holdings in the debtor bank in Period 1. This could generate contagion from the creditor bank to the debtor bank, in addition to the form of contagion (from debtors to creditors) identified in the remainder of the paper.[6] We argue in Section 4 (and illustrate in Appendix B) that such contagion from creditors to debtors is likely to be of a much smaller magnitude than contagion in the opposite direction. Thus, our assumption, while restrictive, enables us to isolate the more relevant form of contagion.

2.6 Notation

We label the entire game Γ. For $i = c, d$, we label the realization of Γ in which the depositors of Bank i are chosen to act first by Γ_i. Within each Γ_i there are two stage games. We denote the first stage games by $\Gamma_{i,1}$. We denote the second-stage game by $\Gamma_{j,k}$, where $j = c, d$ denotes the bank whose depositors make their choices second, and $k = S, F$ denotes whether the bank in the first stage game survived or failed. For example, in the game Γ_d, the stage game $\Gamma_{d,1}$ involves depositors at the debtor bank. This is followed by the stage game $\Gamma_{c,S}$, or $\Gamma_{c,F}$ among depositors of the creditor bank, depending on whether the debtor bank survived or failed at Stage 1.

The structure of the game is common knowledge among participants. We look for symmetric Bayesian–Nash equilbria of this game.

3. Equilibrium

In order to cleanly characterize the equilibrium set we make the following assumptions.

Assumption 1 (Lower dominance): For each depositor of each bank in each stage game $\Gamma_{i,j}$ for $i \in \{c, d\}$ and $j \in \{1, 2\}$, if $\theta_{i,j} < \theta$ (where $\theta \geq L + 2\epsilon$) then it is strictly dominant to withdraw.

[5]If debtor banks did not pay depositors of failed creditor banks, then creditor failure would benefit debtors. This would not conflict with the debtor-to-creditor contagion results that follow. The banks' preferences for interbank deposits identified in Section 5 are also qualitatively unchanged: debtor banks find them all the more useful, while to creditor banks they are riskier.

[6]I am grateful to Elu von Thadden for pointing this out.

In other words, if depositors knew that the bank's returns were going to be sufficiently close to its lowest possible level, it would then be strictly dominant to withdraw. This is an extremely weak assumption that emerges essentially endogenously from the payoffs of the game. In addition, since we are principally concerned with the case where $\epsilon \to 0$, the region $[L, \theta]$, which we shall term the "lower dominance region", can have vanishing measure.

Assumption 2 (Upper dominance): For each depositor of each bank in each stage game $\Gamma_{i,j}$ for $i \in \{c, d)$ and $j \in \{1, 2\}$, if $\theta_{i,j} > \bar{\theta}$ (where $\bar{\theta} \leq U - 2\epsilon$) then it is strictly dominant to remain.

In other words, if depositors knew that the bank's returns were going to be sufficiently close to its highest possible level, it would then be strictly dominant to remain. Again, this region, $[\bar{\theta}, U]$, which we call the "upper dominance region", can also be as small as we like for $\epsilon \to 0$. This is also a weak assumption. Though we do not explicitly model it, we can support it by a number of explanations. For example, we could assume that for very high θ, the risky asset in each region pays a premium over cash even in Period 1; that is, the early liquidation payoff r is a function of θ: $r(\theta) < 1$ for $\theta < \bar{\theta}$ but $r(\theta) > 1$ for $\theta \geq \bar{\theta}$. It is also worth emphasizing that the equilibria computed next will exist even without this assumption. However, in that case, there may also be other equilibria.

We also wish to ensure that the game does not become trivial outside the dominance regions. Thus, we insist that even in the region with high liquidity demand, there are some patient depositors ($w + x < 1$), and that in the complementary region there are some impatient ones ($w - x > 0$). Further, we wish to guarantee that, for $\theta \in (\theta, \bar{\theta})$, it is possible for banks to fail due to actions by depositors. Inspection of the preceding payoffs shows that this can be achieved by imposing the condition that $x < (1 - r)(1 - w)$. Finally, we wish these three conditions to hold simultaneously, which we guarantee as follows.

Assumption 3: $x < \min[w, (1 - r)(1 - w)]$.

We begin our equilibrium analysis by establishing some intuition for the benchmark case with complete information. With complete information, the signals received by agents are identical to the actual fundamentals. If θ is in a dominance region, the game has a trivial outcome. However, given Assumption 3, for $\theta \in (\underline{\theta}, \bar{\theta})$, the analysis is more complex. How depositors behave in these states depends crucially on what they believe others are going to do. For any given θ in this intermediate region, if patient depositors believe that other patient depositors will leave their deposits in the bank, then it is optimal for them to do the same. On the other hand, if they believe that a sufficient number of other patient depositors will withdraw prematurely, then it is optimal for them to withdraw, too. Thus, a given level of intermediate returns observed by a patient depositor can lead to two distinct "self-fulfilling" outcomes, corresponding to the survival and failure of banks. Such multiplicity was formally modeled for banks in the seminal paper of Diamond and Dybvig (1983).

It is clear from this discussion that outcomes in banking models depend not only on agents' beliefs about fundamentals but also on their beliefs about other agents' actions (and thus, in turn, their beliefs). With complete information, agents have common knowledge of the fundamentals of their bank and complete certainty regarding the actions of other agents in equilibrium. Such strategic certainty enables perfect coordination of actions and beliefs by agents, thus removing the link between fundamentals and outcomes and resulting in multiplicity. The presence of asymmetric information introduces strategic uncertainty and thus reduces the ability of agents to precisely coordinate on arbitrary actions and beliefs. In addition, the existence of dominance regions also imposes additional structure over beliefs. In the presence of dominance regions, the actions of agents with very extreme signals are deterministic, which influences the beliefs of agents with similar but less extreme signals and thus, in turn, the beliefs of all agents.

These ideas were first formalized in the context of coordination games by Carlsson and van Damme (1993) and have since been widely applied and generalized (for a survey, see Morris and Shin 2003). Our work belongs to this literature, with one important difference. These papers consider games of strategic complementarities: the excess payoff to taking some action must always be increasing in the number of other agents taking the same action. In our model, when a bank survives, the actions of agents are indeed strategic complements. However, if a bank fails, actions become strategic substitutes. This is because, in the event of failure, the payoff to withdrawing from a bank diminishes in the number of other agents who also withdraw. There is a finite pool of resources to be divided up among those who choose to run. We are nevertheless able to show that, in our model, there is a unique Bayesian–Nash equilibrium. This equilibrium is characterized by monotone strategies: strategies under which agents choose to remain in the bank if and only if their private information $\theta_{i,j}$ is above some threshold. Thus, each monotone strategy is characterized by a threshold. Symmetric equilibria in such strategies are called monotone equilibria or threshold equilibria. The stage game among the depositors of each bank in the dynamic game is characterized by one such equilibrium threshold, which in turn implies a unique set of thresholds for the dynamic game.

Proposition 1: *There is a unique equilibrium in* Γ. *In* Γ_c *it is characterized by the triple* $(\theta^*_{c,1}, \theta^*_{d,S}, \theta^*_{d,F})$. *In* Γ_d *it is characterized by the triple* $(\theta^*_{d,1}, \theta^*_{c,F}, \theta^*_{c,S})$, *where* $\theta^*_{d,S} = \theta^*_{d,F} = \theta^*_{d,1}$.

Here $\theta^*_{i,j}$ is the threshold for Game $\Gamma_{i,j}$ according to the notation introduced before. We now sketch the argument and provide intuition for this result. It is simplest to begin by showing the existence of equilibria in monotone strategies in the static stage games. We illustrate this proof for only one of the static coordination games: The coordination game of the debtor bank's patient depositors. The proofs for the other games are similar.

For the purposes of this proof, denote by θ the underlying fundamentals of the bank concerned and by θ_i the signal received by Agent i. Upon receiving signal θ_i, the agent must decide whether to remain or withdraw. The quantity she is interested in is the expected payoff difference between withdrawing and remaining. Suppose all other agents were following threshold strategies with threshold θ^*. Conditional upon receiving signal θ_i, the agent knows that fundamentals lie between $\theta_i - \epsilon$, and $\theta_i + \epsilon$, and has uniform beliefs over this interval. Hence, for any θ, the agent believes that a proportion

$$n(\theta, \theta^*) = \begin{cases} 1 & \text{if } \theta \leq \theta^* - \epsilon, \\ \frac{1}{2} + \frac{\theta^* - \theta}{2\epsilon} & \text{if } \theta^* - \epsilon < \theta < \theta^* + \epsilon, \\ 0 & \text{if } \theta \geq \theta^* + \epsilon \end{cases}$$

of agents will withdraw from the bank. For a particular (θ, θ^*), the payoff premium to remaining is given by

$$\pi(\theta, n) = \begin{cases} u[0] - u\left[\frac{w+D+(1-w)r}{w+x+(1-w-x)n}\right] & \text{if } \frac{(1-w)r+(D-x)}{1-w-x} \leq n \leq 1, \\ u[0] - u[1] & \text{if } \frac{(1-w)r+(D-x)-rD}{1-w-x} \leq n \leq \frac{(1-w)r+(D-x)}{1-w-x}, \\ u\left[\frac{1-w-\frac{(1-(w+x))n+(x-D)}{r}-D}{(1-w-x)(1-n)}R(\theta_i)\right] - u[1] & \text{if } 0 \leq n \leq \frac{(1-w)r+(D-x)-rD}{1-w-x}. \end{cases}$$

Thus, the quantity of interest to the agent is

$$\Pi(\theta_i, \theta^*) = \int_{\theta_i-\epsilon}^{\theta_i+\epsilon} \pi(\theta, n(\theta, \theta^*))d\theta$$

θ^* is a monotone equilibrium if the following hold:

(a) $\Pi(\theta^*, \theta^*) = 0$;
(b) $\Pi(\theta_i, \theta^*) > 0$ if $\theta_i > \theta^*$;
(c) $\Pi(\theta_i, \theta^*) < 0$ if $\theta_i < \theta^*$.

Observe that the existence of upper and lower dominance regions implies that $\Pi(\theta^*)$ is negative for sufficiently low θ^* and positive for sufficiently high θ^*. Thus, it must cross the θ^* axis somewhere. This establishes condition (a).

To prove (b) and (c) observe that changing θ_i while holding θ^* constant only changes the bounds of integration in $\Pi(\cdot)$. In particular, notice that $\pi(\theta, n) < 0$ for $\theta \leq \theta^* - \epsilon$ and $\pi(\theta, n) > 0$ for $\theta \geq \theta^* + \epsilon$. Since $\Pi(\theta^*, \theta^*) = 0$, the positive and negative parts of the integral exactly offset each other. Increasing θ_i above θ^* increases the positive part of the integral and reduces the negative part, thus making $\Pi(\cdot)$ strictly positive. By the same token, reducing θ_i below θ^* makes $\Pi(\cdot)$ strictly negative. Thus we have established conditions (b) and (c), and this completes the argument for existence.

Given existence, it is not difficult to show, as we do in the appendix, that $\Pi(\theta^*, \theta^*)$ is monotone in θ^*, and thus there is exactly one equilibrium in monotone strategies. This result holds quite generally. Morris and Shin (2003) show that, in the absence of strategic complementarities, as long as the payoffs satisfy a single crossing property and the information structure satisfies a monotone likelihood ratio property, there exists a unique equilibrium in monotone strategies. With uniform noise, we can show an additional result: there are no other equilibria in more complex nonmonotone strategies. The proof technique used to show this result builds on the work of Goldstein and Pauzner (2004a), extending their arguments to our more complex payoffs. It is given in the Appendix.

We have thus argued that in each of the stage static coordination games, there is a unique Bayesian–Nash equilibrium. What does this imply about equilibria in the dynamic game? The debtor bank's depositor payoffs are unaffected by the actions and payoffs of other agents, and thus the debtor bank's depositors' switching threshold is uniquely determined without reference to the actions of depositors of the creditor bank. Therefore $\theta^*_{d,S} = \theta^*_{d,F} = \theta^*_{d,1}$. It is easy to see that correponding to each possible threshold for the debtor bank, the switching thresholds for the creditor bank's depositors are uniquely determined. Thus, there is a unique equilibrium in the dynamic game.

We conclude this section with an interpretation of this result. For simplicity, consider the case where the bank's fundamentals are almost public (i.e., $\epsilon \to 0$). In this case, all agents receive essentially the same signal. Let θ^* be the threshold corresponding to the monotone strategies used by the agents in the unique equilibrium for this bank's depositors' game. If the bank's fundamentals are low, that is, if $\theta < \theta^*$, then essentially all depositors will receive signals below their threshold and will choose to withdraw their deposits. This will cause the bank to fail. In contrast, if $\theta > \theta^*$, no depositors will withdraw and the bank will survive. Thus, we can reinterpret the switching thresholds of a bank's depositors as the failure thresholds of the banks themselves. In this model, therefore, banks fail due to the (correct) anticipation of adverse returns to their portfolios. Since regional fundamentals are independent, bank failure is therefore driven by local shocks to assets. However, we shall see that even such local shocks to bank assets can, via interbank deposits, have wider consequences.

4. Contagion

Contagion emerges as a natural equilibrium property of this game. In the context of bank runs, the most natural concept of contagion is as follows. Consider any two banks, *i* and *j*, within a banking system. Banks *i* and *j* each have some probability of failure independent of what happens in other banks. Thus, even if Bank *i* does not fail, Bank *j* may fail for some realized level of adverse information about it. However, if Bank *i* fails, this may create an adverse effect on Bank *j*. Now, Bank *j* may fail for a larger range of information about itself. Thus, we say that the failure of Bank *i* has a contagious effect on Bank *j* if, conditional on the failure of Bank *i*, Bank *j* fails with higher probability than it would have had Bank *i* not failed. Formally, we can define this as follows.

Definition 1 (Contagion): Consider a pair of banks, *i* and *j*, whose asset returns are indexed by θ_i and θ_j. Let $\theta^*_{j,F}$ and $\theta^*_{j,S}$ denote the failure threshold of Bank *j* conditional on the failure and survival (respectively) of Bank *i*. We say that the failure of Bank *i* contagiously affects Bank *j* if the region of fundamentals $[\theta^*_{j,S}, \theta^*_{j,F}]$ has positive measure.

Having thus defined contagion, we are ready to state a central result of this paper.

Proposition 2 (Contagion): *In the game where depositors of the debtor bank act first, the failure of the debtor bank contagiously affects the creditor bank. In other words, there exists a region of fundamentals* $[\theta^*_{c,S}, \theta^*_{c,F}]$ *in which the creditor bank fails if and only if the debtor bank fails.*

The proof is in the Appendix.

The proposition states that, in the unique equilibrium of our model, the failure of debtor institutions adversely affects the prospects of creditor institutions and thus, ceteris paribus, makes it likelier that the creditor will fail. This is because the failure of the debtor bank reduces the assets of the creditor bank. Rational depositors, knowing this, will be more likely to run on the creditor bank in the event of the failure of the debtor bank. Conditional upon the failure of a bank, this result also characterizes which other banks, ceteris paribus, are likelier to face runs.

It is apparent that, under the particular payoff structure imposed here, there is no contagion from creditors to debtors in this model. In a more general model, the failure of a creditor institution could contagiously affect the debtor if, in the process of facing a run from its own depositors, the creditor bank withdraws its deposit from the debtor bank in Period 1. However, it is easy to see that such contagion would be of smaller order than the debtor-to-creditor contagion identified in the preceding result. The reason is straightforward. The incentive for any given depositor to withdraw from a bank is decreasing in the extent of available resources in Period 2. The complete failure of the debtor bank in Period 1 causes the creditor bank's depositors to lose an amount $DR(\theta)$ at $t = 2$. Consider instead the losses to the depositors of the debtor bank if the creditor bank failed due to a run, in the process prematurely liquidating its deposit of size D in the debtor bank. If the creditor bank had been unaffected by a run, the debtor bank would have owed the creditor bank $DR(\theta)$ at $t = 2$. However, in case of the premature withdrawal of funds by the creditor bank, the debtor no longer has to pay an interbank claim in Period 2, but the early withdrawal of D in Period 1 (which must be funded by premature liquidation of the illiquid asset) costs its depositors total resources of $(D/r)R(\theta)$ at $t = 2$. Thus, losses due to the failure of the creditor to the depositors of the debtor are: $(D/r - D)R(\theta)$, which is strictly smaller than the losses to depositors of the creditor bank due to the failure of the debtor when $r > 1/2$. In Appendix B, we compute the payoffs of the debtor bank conditional on the failure of the creditor bank in the case where the latter may prematurely withdraw its deposits from the former. We compare the contagion thus caused to the contagion identified above. While a full analytical comparison proves intractable, numerical computations show that, for reasonable values of the early liquidation payoff r, debtor-to-creditor contagion is substantially larger than contagion in the reverse direction.

Finally, we demonstrate a natural comparative statics result.

Proposition 3: *The extent of contagion $\theta^*_{c,F} - \theta^*_{c,S}$ is increasing in the size of interbank deposit holdings D.*

The proof is in the Appendix. The interpretation is straightforward. Contagion flows from debtors to creditors through the channels of interbank deposits. The larger the interbank deposits, the larger the "pipe" through which the contagious effect can flow. This is a testable implication of our model.

5. Should Banks Hold Interbank Deposits?

We have shown that, when banks cross-hold deposits to hedge against regional liquidity shocks, the failure of one bank may contagiously affect the other. Thus, in deciding the amount of interbank deposit holdings, banks trade off the benefit of insuring liquidity shocks against the cost of exposing themselves to the risk of contagion. We have demonstrated that, for a given set of parameters of our stylized banking system (w, x, r, U, L), and for each choice of $D \in [0, x]$, there is a unique equilibrium with an associated level of social welfare. This makes it possible to determine the optimal interbank deposit amount by maximizing ex ante social welfare.

Upon inspection of the defining equations for the failure thresholds of banks it is clear that θ^*_d and $\theta^*_{c,F}$ are defined locally with no reference to L or U, the bounds of the fundamentals. In turn, $\theta^*_{c,1}$ and $\theta^*_{c,S}$ are decreasing in U (holding L fixed). This is because for a given θ^*_d, the higher is U, the higher is the expected interbank payment received by patient depositors of the creditor bank if they wait until $t = 2$, and thus the lower are incentives to withdraw. Clearly, then, as U becomes larger (holding L fixed), the banking system becomes stable and the relative probability of failure of any bank diminishes. Intuition would suggest that it should then be optimal for banks to fully insure ex ante against liquidity shocks. Figures 18.1 and 18.2 present examples to support this intuition.

We consider risk-neutral depositors when bank runs are rare: $L = 0$, $U = 30$. We set the following parameter values: $r = 0.7$ and $R(\theta) = \sqrt{\theta}$, and consider the limiting case where noise vanishes (ϵ is set to 10^{-3}). Figure 18.1 considers the case in which $w = 0.3$ and $x = w/2$; Figure 18.2 considers $w = 0.5$ and $x = w/4$. On each horizontal axis we plot the ratio of interbank deposits (D) to the size of regional liquidity shocks (x). The vertical axis shows the ex ante welfare corresponding to the chosen level of D/x. The top and bottom locii represent the ex ante welfare of banks under the hypothetical assumption that they know whether they will be interim debtors or creditors (i.e., receive high or low idiosyncratic regional shocks in Period 1). Since the two regions receive idiosyncratic liquidity shocks with equal probability in the model, the ex ante welfare locus is simply the arithmetic average of these two locii.

Interbank holdings are always beneficial for the debtor bank. They protect the debtor against liquidity shocks but do not come at the cost of contagion risk. Thus, welfare for the debtor bank is always increasing in D. In the presence of contagion risk, this may not be the case for the creditor bank. It must trade off the benefits of holding interbank deposits (higher returns compared to cash when repaid) against the costs (losses due to debtor failure). However, when bank runs are rare (as in this example), contagion risk is negligible and thus creditor bank welfare is also increasing in D. Since both welfare locii are increasing, ex ante welfare is maximized at maximal interbank deposit holdings.

Our framework allows us to illustrate a further result: that banks may sometimes find it optimal not to insure fully against regional liquidity shocks. While interbank deposits are

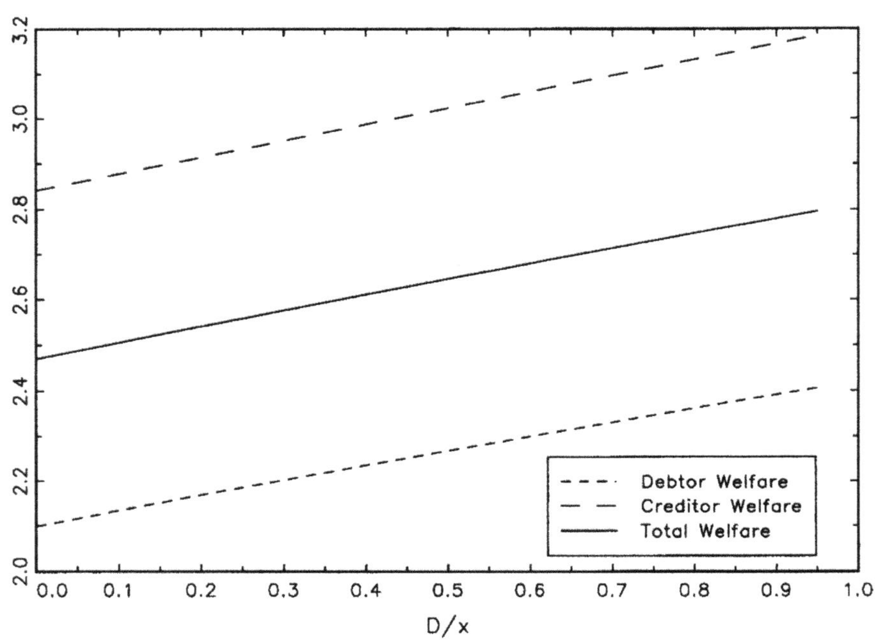

Figure 18.1. Bank runs rare ($U = 30, L = 0$): $w = 0.3, x = 0.5w$.

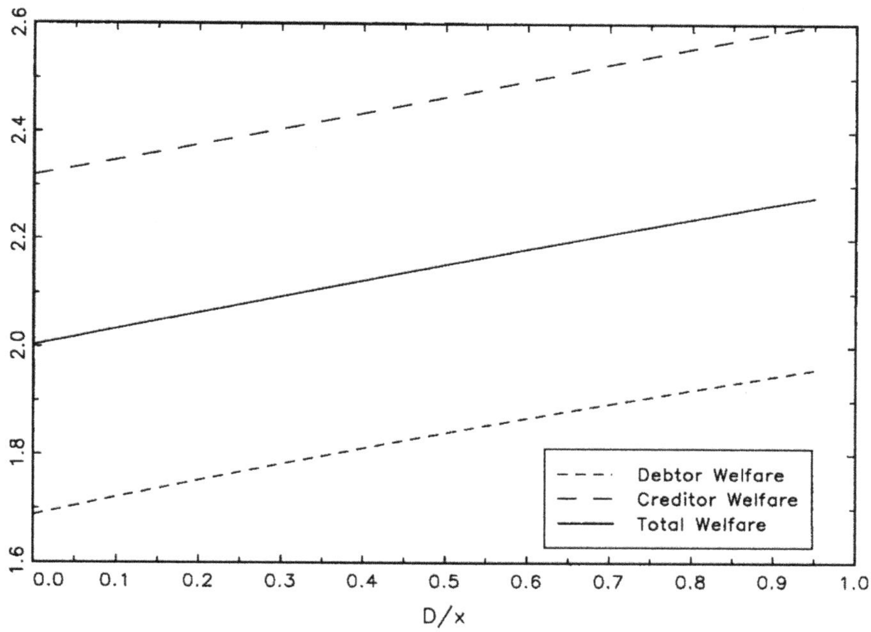

Figure 18.2. Bank runs rare ($U = 30, L = 0$): $w = 0.5, x = 0.25w$.

always better for the interim debtor bank, they are not unambiguously beneficial for the creditor bank, since they expose it to contagion risk. When bank runs are less uncommon, this potential risk can affect choices. Since banks assign positive probability to being the interim creditor, they may find it optimal to insure incompletely against regional liquidity variations when bank failures are likely. Figures 18.3 and 18.4 illustrate this point.

By setting $U = 10$, we now substantially increase the relative likelihood of bank runs and recompute ex ante social welfare. Here, as before, debtor welfare is increasing in D. However, creditor welfare is decreasing in D. The aggregate effect leads to a nonmonotone ex ante welfare function. Thus, banks will find it optimal not to insure completely against liquidity demand shocks. We may summarize as follows.

Remark 1: When the banking system is relatively unstable, it is not optimal for banks to insure completely against regional liquidity shocks using interbank deposit holdings.

It is thus clear that, in relatively unstable banking systems, interbank deposits alone cannot eliminate liquidity risk due to regional variations in cash demand. Even if banks had the ability to insure completely against such shocks via interbank deposits, they would choose not to do so.

The preceding discussion suggests that stable and unstable banking systems will have different levels of optimal interconnectedness. In deriving this conclusion, we have up until now abstracted from the issue of portfolio choice for banks: corresponding to different levels of interbank deposit holdings, banks may choose to hold excess liquid reserves (larger than w) to protect themselves against liquidity risk. As we shall argue next, it is not difficult to see that incorporating such "idle reserve" holdings will reinforce our conclusions above. The reason is that interbank deposits and idle reserves are substitutes. They both insure the

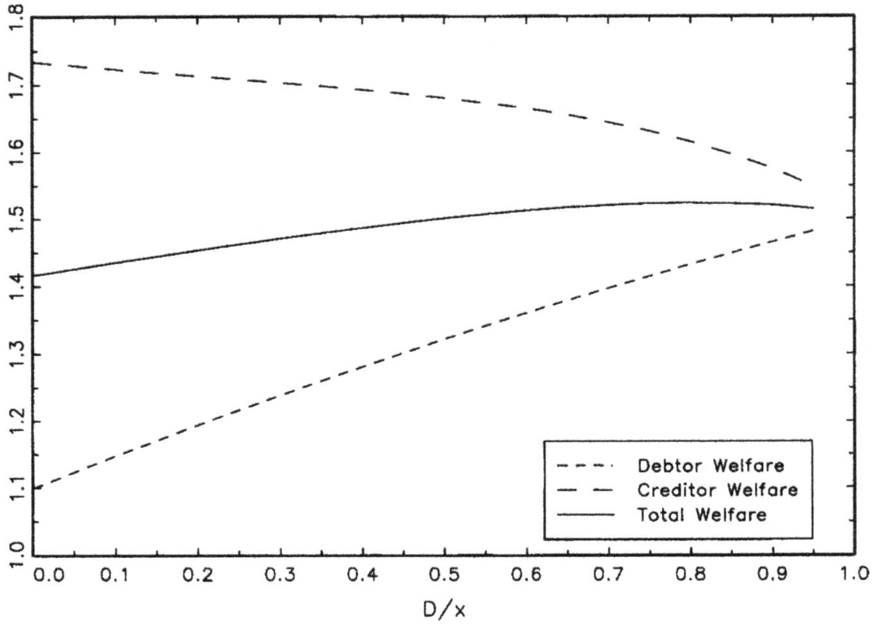

Figure 18.3. Bank runs likely ($U = 10, L = 0$): $w = 0.3, x = 0.5w$.

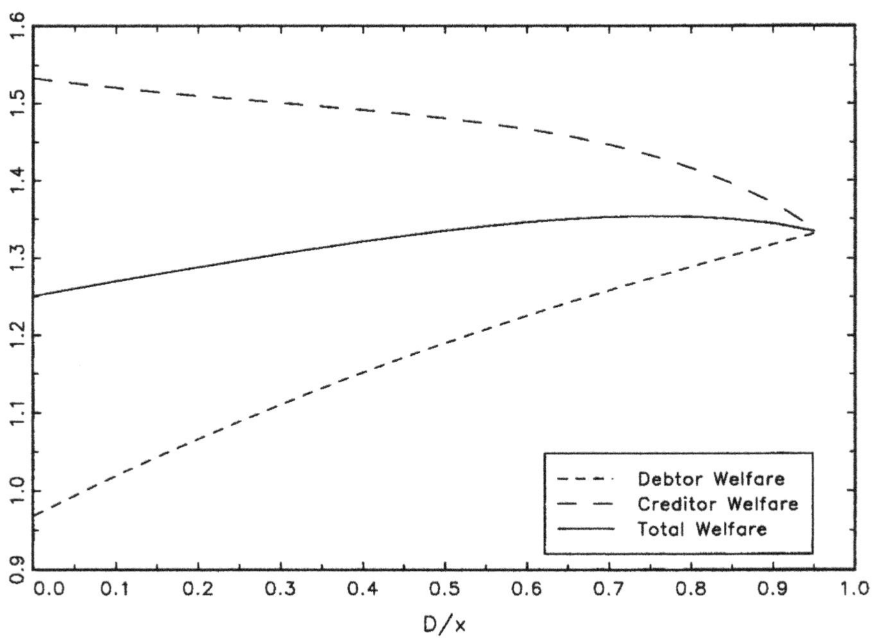

Figure 18.4. Bank runs likely ($U = 10, L = 0$): $w = 0.5, x = 0.25w$.

bank against excess liquidity demand. They are both costly. Idle reserves come with the direct cost of lowered returns to depositors. Interbank deposits come with the indirect cost of potential contagion.

When bank runs are rare (as in the scenario depicted in Figures 18.1 and 18.2), interbank deposits are clearly preferable to idle reserves. We can numerically solve the model to account for endogenous choice of idle reserves. To be precise, for each level of interbank deposits, we can solve for the ex ante socially optimal level of idle reserves (l) for $D + l \leq x$, thus allowing banks to complement low interbank deposit holdings by high idle reserves. We then compute social welfare for such optimal (D, l) pairs.[7] Our computations confirm this intuition: even when idle reserves are chosen endogenously, if bank runs are sufficiently rare, then banks will optimally use full interbank deposit holdings to insure against liquidity shocks and will avoid holding idle reserves. Therefore, allowing for idle reserves does not change Figures 18.1 and 18.2. Such reserves are most costly precisely in stable banking systems characterized by high returns to bank assets.

However, when bank runs are more common, the situation changes. Consider, for example, the scenario depicted in Figures 18.3 and 18.4. In this case, U is low and thus interbank deposits are more risky ex ante. At the same time, since returns from illiquid investments are lower, idle reserves are less costly. Thus, inuition suggests that banks may optimally complement interbank deposits by idle reserves. Simulations of the model for the parameters of Figures 18.3 and 18.4 where idle reserves are selected optimally ex ante, confirm this intuition. These results are presented in Figures 18.5 and 18.6.

To obtain some intuition for Figures 18.5 and 18.6, observe that when the creditor bank is able to complement risky interbank deposits by a buffer of idle reserves, it is welfare enhancing (up to a point) to exchange deposits. However, very high levels of interbank deposits are still too risky. The optimum is attained at a lower level of interbank deposits than in the case without idle reserves. This means that, in unstable banking systems, banks would ex ante not only complement their interbank holdings with idle reserve buffers, but these buffers (to some extent) also substitute for cross-held deposits. Thus, taking the bank's choices of idle reserves into account accentuates the difference between stable and unstable banking systems discussed earlier.

In this context, it is worth making an additional point. Our discussion to date suggests that in relatively unstable banking systems, banks will optimally choose lower levels of interconnectedness and also will hold idle reserves to protect themselves. This suggests that even though bank failures are more common in unstable systems by definition, contagious effects in such systems will be of moderate magnitude. However, when banks fail (with low probability) in relatively stable banking systems, contagion, though rare, will be severe: Institutions will be highly interconnected in equilibrium, and banks will not have taken precautionary measures in the form of idle reserves to protect themselves. To summarize:

Remark 2: Contagion is much less common in stable banking systems than in unstable ones. However, in the unlikely instance of bank failure within a relatively stable system, contagion is most severe, since banks have optimally chosen higher levels of interconnectedness ex ante, and have optimally not held liquidity buffers in the form of idle reserves.

[7] The model is intractable for the unconstrained case where we allow $D + l > x$. However, since there will always be a trade-off between D and l, we believe that the conclusions will not be qualitatively different.

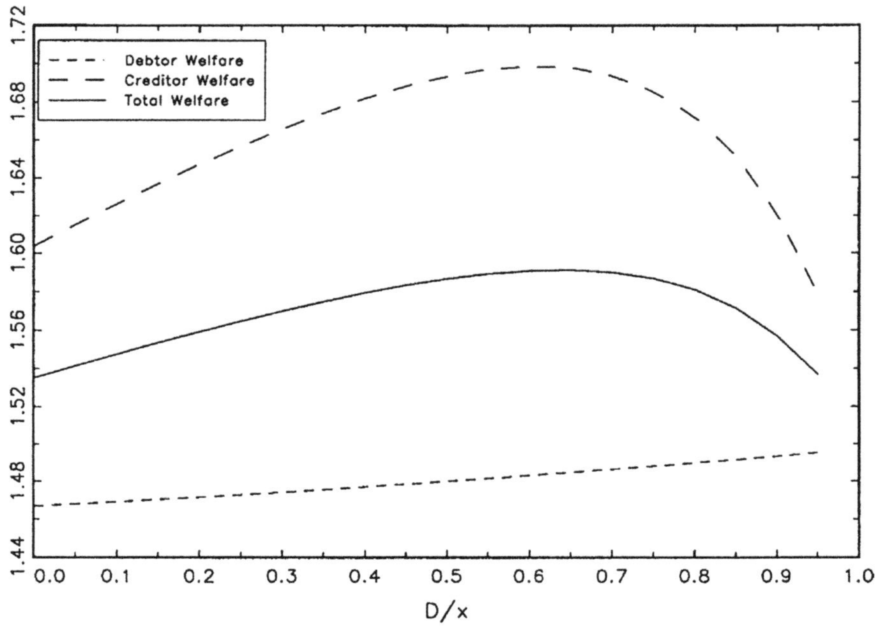

Figure 18.5. Welfare with endogenous reserves ($U = 10, L = 0$): $w = 0.3, x = 0.5w$.

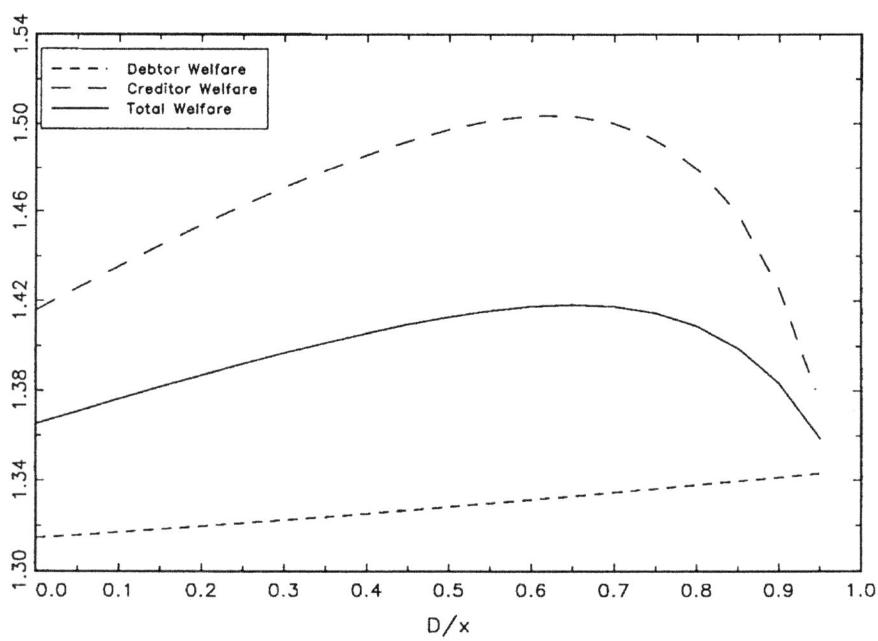

Figure 18.6. Welfare with endogenous reserves ($U = 10, L = 0$): $w = 0.5, x = 0.25w$).

6. Conclusion

The existence of contagion in the real world is a much debated issue, both in the context of banking systems and more generally (see Gorton and Winton 2002 and Dungey et al. 2003 for a survey of the literature). In the context of this debate, this paper makes two contributions. First, we argue theoretically that contagion may occur with positive probability in a banking system as a result of balance sheet connections across institutions. Such contagion does not require any aggregate excess demand for liquidity in the system and is purely a spread of local asset-side disturbances. Second, we show that the positive probability of such contagion prevents banks from perfectly insuring each other against liquidity risk via the cross-holding of deposits.

We conclude with a few thoughts on the robustness of these results and on potential extensions. Our model extends naturally to more than two regions. With more than two regions, holding aggregate liquidity constant, there would be some level of negative correlation across regional liquidity demands. This would create, as before, the incentive to insure against regional liquidity demand shocks using interbank deposits and, as a consequence, interim debtor–creditor relationships among banks. The only substantive difference would be one of algebraic complexity.

Adding aggregate liquidity shocks to our model would create a second source of bank failure without changing the internal structure of interbank deposits and contagion. With large aggregate liquidity shocks, banks may fail simply because there is just not enough money in the system to meet all claims in Period 1 even in the absence of expectations-based runs. We limit our attention to economies with constant aggregate liquidity demand and show that contagion occurs even in such economies.

Our analysis abstracts from informational contagion. We assume that fundamentals in the two regions are independent, and thus eliminate any conclusions that agents in one region can draw about their own bank from the observed failure or survival of a bank in a different region. Introducing correlations among assets across the regions of our economy would introduce learning into our model and a second source of contagion, enriching the analysis. Incorporating learning into a model similar to ours, building on recent theoretical work (e.g., Dasgupta 2002) on coordination games with social learning, is a natural direction for future research.

Appendix A: Proofs

A.1. Unique Equilibrium in Monotone Strategies

Again, we prove this only for the coordination game of the patient depositors of the debtor bank, and extend by symmetry to all other games. By a slight abuse of notation, we write $\Pi(\theta^*) = \Pi(\theta^*, \theta^*)$. We shall show that $\Pi(\theta^*)$ is monotone in θ^*. Write

$$n^d = \frac{(1-w)r + (D-x)}{1-w-x}.$$

Note that if $n(\theta, \theta^*) < n^d$, then $\theta > \theta^* + \epsilon(1 - 2n^d)$. Thus, we can express $\Pi(\cdot)$, as a sum of integrals over θ, with limits of integration given by functions of θ^*, following the piecewise definition of $\pi(\theta, n)$ above. Since the limits of integration are always linear with slope 1 in θ^*, integrating over constant terms gives us final products that are independent of θ^*. Thus, we can rewrite $\Pi(\cdot)$ as

$$\int_{\theta^*+\epsilon(1-2r)}^{\theta^*+\epsilon} f(\theta,\theta^*)d\theta - \int_{\theta^*-\epsilon}^{\theta^*+\epsilon(1-2n^d)} g(\theta,\theta^*)d\theta + K,$$

where K proxies for the terms that do not involve θ^*, and

$$f(\theta,\theta^*) = u\left[\frac{1-w-\frac{(1-(w+x))n_d+(x-D)}{r}-D}{(1-w-x)(1-n_d)}R(\theta)\right]$$

and

$$g(\theta,\theta^*) = u\left[\frac{w+D+(1-w)r}{w+x+(1-w-x)n(\theta,\theta^*)}\right].$$

Holding other parameters constant, we differentiate with respect to θ^*:

$$\frac{d}{d\theta^*}\Pi(\theta^*) = \frac{d}{d\theta^*}\int_{\theta^*+\epsilon(1-2r)}^{\theta^*+\epsilon} f(\theta,\theta^*)d\theta - \frac{d}{d\theta^*}\int_{\theta^*-\epsilon}^{\theta^*+\epsilon(1-2n^d)} g(\theta,\theta^*)d\theta.$$

Since the limits of integration in each case are linear in θ^*, their derivatives are simply unity, and thus, differentiating under the integral yields:

$$\begin{aligned}\frac{d}{d\theta^*}\int_{\theta^*+\epsilon(1-2r)}^{\theta^*+\epsilon} f(\theta,\theta^*)d\theta =& f(\theta^*+\epsilon,\theta^*) - f(\theta^*+\epsilon(1-2r),\theta^*)\\ &+\int_{\theta^*+\epsilon(1-2r)}^{\theta^*+\epsilon}\frac{d}{d\theta^*}f(\theta,\theta^*)d\theta.\end{aligned}$$

We can rewrite this as

$$\begin{aligned}\frac{d}{d\theta^*}\int_{\theta^*+\epsilon(1-2r)}^{\theta^*+\epsilon} f(\theta,\theta^*)d\theta =& \int_{\theta^*+\epsilon(1-2r)}^{\theta^*+\epsilon}\frac{d}{d\theta}f(\theta,\theta^*)d\theta\\ &+\int_{\theta^*+\epsilon(1-2r)}^{\theta^*+\epsilon}\frac{d}{d\theta^*}f(\theta,\theta^*)d\theta.\end{aligned}$$

Similarly,

$$\begin{aligned}\frac{d}{d\theta^*}\int_{\theta^*-\epsilon}^{\theta^*+\epsilon(1-2n^d)} g(\theta,\theta^*)d\theta =& \int_{\theta^*-\epsilon}^{\theta^*+\epsilon(1-2n^d)}\frac{d}{d\theta}g(\theta,\theta^*)d\theta\\ &+\int_{\theta^*-\epsilon}^{\theta^*+\epsilon(1-2n^d)}\frac{d}{d\theta^*}g(\theta,\theta^*)d\theta.\end{aligned}$$

Now, we observe that (i) $f(\theta,\ \theta^*)$ decreases in $n(\theta,\ \theta^*)$, (ii) $g(\theta,\ \theta^*)$ decreases in $n(\theta,\theta^*)$, (iii) $n(\theta,\theta^*)$ increases in θ^*, $(iv) n(\theta,\theta^*)$ decreases in θ, $(v)|dn(\theta,\theta^*)/d\theta| = |dn(\theta,\theta^*)/d\theta^*|$, since θ and θ^* enter $n(\theta,\ \theta^*)$ symmetrically, and (vi) $R(\theta)$ increases in θ, but is unaffected by θ^*. Together (i) and (iii) imply that $f(\theta,\ \theta^*)$ decreases in θ^*, while (i) and (iv) imply that $f(\theta, \theta^*)$ increases in θ; (i) together with (iii)–(vi) imply that $|df(\theta, \theta^*)/d\theta| = |df(\theta, \theta^*)|d\theta^*|$. Thus,

$$\frac{d}{d\theta^*}\int_{\theta^*+\epsilon(1-2r)}^{\theta^*+\epsilon} f(\theta, \theta^*)d\theta > 0$$

Similarly, (ii) and (iii) imply that $g(\theta, \theta^*)$ decreases in θ^*, while (ii) and (iv) imply that $g(\theta, \theta^*)$ increases in θ. Together (ii), (iii), and (v) imply that $|dg(\theta, \theta^*)/d\theta| = |dg(\theta, \theta^*)/d\theta^*|$. Thus,

$$\frac{d}{d\theta^*}\int_{\theta^*-\epsilon}^{\theta^*+\epsilon(1-2n^d)} g(\theta, \theta^*)d\theta = 0$$

In the net, we have just shown that $\Pi(\cdot)$ is strictly increasing in θ^*. Thus, there is only one value of θ^* that solves $\Pi(\theta^*, \theta^*) = 0$. □

A.2. No Nonmonotone Equilibria

We present the proof for the static coordination game for the debtor bank's patient depositors. The proofs for all other static games are similar. We first establish a series of lemmas.

Lemma 1: *Let $n(\theta)$ be any feasible belief about the number of patient depositors who choose to run when the state is θ. Then $dn(\theta)/d\theta \in [-1/2\epsilon, 1/2\epsilon]$*

Proof: At state θ, the possible realizations of signals lie in $[\theta - \epsilon, \theta + \epsilon]$. Let $p(\theta_i)$ denote the beliefs of Agent i about the mass of patient agents who shall run when she receives signal θ_i. Then, for this agent:

$$n(\theta) = \int_{\theta-\epsilon}^{\theta+\epsilon} p(\theta_i)\frac{1}{2\epsilon}d\theta_i$$

Differentiating relative to θ, we have:

$$\frac{dn(\theta)}{d\theta} = \frac{1}{2\epsilon}[p(\theta + \epsilon) - p(0 - \epsilon)].$$

Since $p(\cdot) \in [0, 1]$, the result follows. □

Lemma 2: *Assume that $0 < \theta_T - \theta_B \leq 2\epsilon$ and that for all $\theta \in [\theta_B, \theta_T]\hat{\theta}(\theta) < \theta_B$ and $n(\theta) \geq (\theta_T - \theta)/2\epsilon$.*

$$\textit{If} \int_{\theta_B}^{\theta_T} \pi\left(\theta, \frac{\theta_T - \theta}{2\epsilon}\right) d\theta \geq 0$$

$$\textit{then} \int_{\theta_B}^{\theta_T} \pi\left(\theta, \frac{\theta_T - \theta}{2\epsilon}\right) d\theta > \int_{\theta_B}^{\theta_T} \pi(\hat{\theta}(\theta),\ n(\theta))d\theta.$$

Proof: As we have seen above

$$\pi(\theta, n) = \begin{cases} u[0] - u\left[\frac{w+D+(1-w)r}{w+x+(1-w-x)n(\theta,\theta^*)}\right] & \text{if } \frac{(1-w)r+(D-x)}{1-w-x} \leq n \leq 1 \\ u[0] - u[1] & \text{if } \frac{(1-w)r+(D-x)-rD}{1-w-x} \leq n \\ & \leq \frac{(1-w)r+(D-x)}{1-w-x}. \\ u\left[\frac{1-w-\frac{(1-(w+x)n_d+(x-D)}{r}-D}{(1-w-x)(1-n_d)}R(\theta_i)\right] - u[1] & \text{if } 0 \leq n \leq \frac{(1-w)r+(D-x)-rD}{1-w-x} \end{cases}.$$

Notice the following:

1. If $[(1-w)r+(D-x)]/(1-w-x) \leq n \leq 1$, then $\partial\pi(\theta, n)/\partial\theta = 0$ and $\partial\pi(\theta, n)/\partial n > 0$. Call this the (strategic) "substitutes" range of $\pi(\cdot, \cdot)$.
2. If $[(1-w)r+(D-x)-rD]/(1-w-x) \leq n \leq [(1-w)r+(D-x)]/(1-w-x)$, then $\partial\pi(\theta, n)/\partial\theta = 0$ and $\partial\pi(\theta, n)/\partial n = 0$. Call this the "flat" range of $\pi(\cdot, \cdot)$
3. If $0 \leq n \leq [(1-w)r+(D-x)-rD]/(1-w-x)$, then $\partial\pi(\theta, n)/\partial\theta > 0$ and $\partial\pi(\theta, n)/\partial n < 0$. Call this the (strategic) "complements" range of $\pi(\cdot, \cdot)$.
4. $\pi(\cdot, \cdot)$ is always negative in the "substitutes" or "flat" ranges. The maximum value it can attain in this range is $u[0] - u[w+D+(1-w)r] < 0$.

Now, suppose $\pi(\theta, (\theta_T - \theta)/2\epsilon > 0$ for all $\theta \in [\theta_B, \theta_T]$. Then the result follows trivially because $\pi(\theta, (\theta_T - \theta)/2\epsilon) \geq \pi(\hat{\theta}(\theta), n(\theta))$ for all θ under these circumstances. To see why, notice that since $n(\theta) \geq (\theta_T - \theta)/2\epsilon$, $\pi(\hat{\theta}(\theta), n(\theta))$ can either fall in the "complements" range, in which case it is smaller than $\pi(\theta, (\theta_T - \theta)/2\epsilon)$ by (3) above, or it can fall in the "flat" or "supplements" range, in which case it is smaller by (4).

Suppose now that $\pi(\theta, (\theta_T - \theta)/2\epsilon) > 0$ for some θ and $\pi(\theta, (\theta_T - \theta)/2\epsilon) < 0$ for some other θ in $[\theta_B, \theta_T]$. Since $(\theta_T - \theta)/2\epsilon$ is monotone in θ, there is exactly one point, call it θ_1 at which $\pi(\theta, (\theta_T - \theta)/2\epsilon) = 0$. Let

$$\theta_2 = \inf\{\theta \in [\theta_B, \theta_T] : \pi(\hat{\theta}(\theta), n(\theta)) = 0\}.$$

Now we shall show that

$$\int_{\theta_B}^{\theta_1} \pi(\theta, \frac{\theta_T - \theta}{2\epsilon})d\theta \geq \int_{\theta_B}^{\theta_2} (\hat{\theta}(\theta), n(\theta))d\theta. \tag{18.A.1}$$

To establish this, we first prove two claims.

Claim 1: $\pi(\hat{\theta}(\theta), n(\theta)) < 0 \quad \forall\theta \in [\theta_B, \theta_2)$.

Proof: Consider $\theta < \min[\theta_1, \theta_2]$. For such θ, $\pi(\theta, (\theta_T - \theta)/2\epsilon) < 0$. The various possibilities are as follows, where $n^D = [(1-w)r+(D-x)-rD]/(1-w-x)$:

1. $(\theta_T - \theta)/2\epsilon > n^D$. This implies that $n(\theta) > n^D$. Thus, $\pi(\hat{\theta}(\theta), n(\theta))$ is in the "flat" or "substitutes" range, and is negative.
2. $(\theta_T - \theta)/2\epsilon \leq n^D$. Now, either $n(\theta) > n^D$, in which the case the above comment applies, or $n(\theta) \leq n^D$, in which case we are in the "complements" range, and hence $\pi(\hat{\theta}(\theta), n(\theta)) \leq \pi(\theta, (\theta_T - \theta)/2\epsilon) < 0$.

Thus, if $\min[\theta_1, \theta_2]=\theta_2$ then the claim is proved. If $\min[\theta_1, \theta_2] < \theta_2$, then suppose there exist $\theta \in [\min[\theta_1, \theta_2], \theta_2]$ such that $\pi(\hat{\theta}(\theta), n(\theta)) \geq 0$. But then by continuity, we can find a point $\theta_3 < \theta_2$ such that $\pi(\hat{\theta}(\theta_3), n(\theta_3)) = 0$, a contradiction. This completes the proof of claim.

Claim 2: $\quad n(\theta_2) < (\theta_T - \theta_1)/2\epsilon.$

Proof: At θ_1,

$$u\left[\frac{1-w-\frac{(1-(w+x))\frac{\theta_T-\theta}{2\epsilon}+(x-D)}{r}-D}{(1-w-x)(1-\frac{\theta_T-\theta}{2\epsilon})}R(\theta)\right] = u[1].$$

At θ_2,

$$u\left[\frac{1-w-\frac{(1-(w+x))n(\theta)+(x-D)}{r}-D}{(1-w-x)(1-n(\theta))}R(\hat{\theta}(\theta))\right] = u[1].$$

Since $\hat{\theta}(\theta_2) < \theta_1$, it must be the case that $n(\theta_2)$ is smaller than $(\theta_T - \theta_1)/2\epsilon$ to compensate. This completes the proof of Claim 2.

Now we shall use Claims 1 and 2 to demonstrate inequality $(A.1)$. Denote $m(\theta) = (\theta_T - \theta)/2\epsilon$. By a change of variables:

$$\int_{\theta_B}^{\theta_1} \pi(\theta, m(\theta))d\theta = \int_{m(\theta_1)}^{(\theta_B)} \pi(\theta(m), m)\left|\frac{\partial\theta}{\partial m}\right|dm$$

$$\int_{\theta_B}^{\theta_2} \pi(\hat{\theta}(\theta), n(\theta))d\theta = \int_{\min\{n(\theta):\theta\in[\theta_B,\theta_2]\}}^{\max\{n(\theta):\theta\in[\theta_B,\theta_2]\}} \pi(\hat{\theta}(\theta(n)), n)\left|\frac{\partial\theta}{\partial n}\right|dn$$

$$+\int_{\theta:\partial\theta/\partial n=0} \pi(\hat{\theta}(\theta(n)), n)d\theta.$$

The second integral is smaller, because it is computed over a range that is larger (by Claim 2), because $|\partial\theta/\partial n| \geq |\partial\theta/\partial m|$ (by Lemma 1), and because $\pi(\cdot, \cdot)$ is negative in the range considered (by Claim 1). This establishes $(A.1)$.

Since $m(\theta)$ declines faster than $n(\theta)$, and since $n(\theta_2) < m(\theta_1)$, we know that $\theta_2 > \theta_1$. Thus,

$$\int_{\theta_1}^{\theta_T} \pi(\theta, m(\theta))d\theta \geq \int_{\theta_2}^{\theta_T} \pi(\theta, m(\theta))d\theta > \int_{\theta_2}^{\theta_T} \pi(\hat{\theta}(\theta), n(\theta))d\theta. \qquad (18A.2)$$

We combine inequalities $(A.1)$ and $(A.2)$ to conclude the proof of the lemma. □

By the existence of the upper and lower dominance regions, we know that for any feasible beliefs n over the actions of other agents, there exists at least one point θ^* such that $\Pi(\theta^*, n) = 0$. If there is only one such point, it must be true that $\Pi(\theta_i, n) > 0$ for all $\theta_i > \theta^*$, and $\Pi(\theta_i, n) < 0$ for all $\theta_i < \theta^*$. But in that case there would be only one equilibrium, and it would be a monotone equilibrium with threshold θ^*. Thus, if we could show that under any feasible beliefs n over the actions of other agents, there can be only one point θ^* such that $\Pi(\theta^*, n) = 0$, then we would be able to establish the nonexistence of nonmonotone equilibria. We now proceed to do so.

Let $\theta_H = \sup\{\theta_i : \Pi(\theta_i, n) \leq 0\}$. By continuity, $\Pi(\theta_H, n) = 0$, and it is easy to see that $d\Pi(\theta_H, n(\theta))/d\theta_B = \pi(\theta_H + \epsilon, n(\theta_H + \epsilon)) - \pi(\theta_H - \epsilon, n(\theta_H - \epsilon))$. By definition of θ_H, $n(\theta_H + \epsilon) = 0$, and thus $n(\theta_H - \epsilon) \geq n(\theta_H + \epsilon)$. Then, it is easy to see that $d\Pi(\theta_H, n(\theta))/d\theta_B > 0$. There must exist a region immediately to the left of θ_H where $\Pi < 0$. If this is a threshold equilibrium, then this region is $[L, \theta_H]$. To the contrary suppose this region is smaller. Let $\theta_L = sup\{\theta_i : \theta_i < \theta_H, \Pi(\theta_i, n) \geq 0\}$. By continuity, $\Pi(\theta_L, n) = 0$.

Consider the case when $\theta_H - \theta_L < 2\epsilon$.[8] Then

$$\theta_L - \epsilon < \theta_L < \theta_H - \epsilon < \theta_L + \epsilon < \theta_H < \theta_H + \epsilon$$

Thus, eliminating the common parts of the two integrals, we can write

$$\Pi(\theta_H, n) - \Pi(\theta_L, n) = \int_{\theta_L+\epsilon}^{\theta_H+\epsilon} \pi(\theta, n(\theta))d\theta - \int_{\theta_L-\epsilon}^{\theta_H-\epsilon} \pi(\theta, n(\theta))d\theta.$$

Now by a change of variables $\hat{\theta} = \theta - 2\epsilon$, we can rewrite this as:

$$\Pi(\theta_H, n) - \Pi(\theta_L, n) = \int_{\theta_L+\epsilon}^{\theta_H+\epsilon} \pi(\theta, n(\theta))d\theta - \int_{\theta_L+\epsilon}^{\theta_H+\epsilon} \pi(\hat{\theta}, n(\hat{\theta}))d\theta.$$

Claim 3:

(i) *For* $\theta \in [\theta_L + \epsilon, \theta_H + \epsilon]$, $n(\theta) = (\theta_H + \epsilon - \theta)/2\epsilon$.
(ii) $n(\theta_H - \epsilon) \geq n(\theta_L + \epsilon)$

Proof: For $\theta \in [\theta_L + \epsilon, \infty]$, we have $n(\theta) = Pr(\theta_i \leq \theta_H|\theta)$. This is because if $\theta \in [\theta_L + \epsilon, \infty]$ then $\theta_i \in (\theta_L, \infty)$ and the only θ_i for which $\Pi(\theta_i) < 0$ lie in (θ_L, θ_H). Thus, in particular, for $\theta \in [\theta_L + \epsilon, \theta_H + \epsilon]$, $n(\theta) = \mathrm{pr}(\theta_i \leq \theta_H|\theta) = (\theta_H - \theta + \epsilon)/2\epsilon$. This proves part (i) of Claim 3.

Using the above, $n(\theta_L + \epsilon) = (\theta_H + \epsilon - \theta_L - \epsilon)/2\epsilon = (\theta_H - \theta_L)/2\epsilon$. For $\theta \in (-\infty, \theta_H - \epsilon)$, by an argument parallel to the above, $n(\theta) \geq \Pr(\theta_i > \theta_L|\theta)$. The inequality arises because while $\Pi(\theta_i)$ is definitely negative between θ_L and θ_H, it can also be negative elsewhere. Thus, $n(\theta_H - \epsilon) \geq \Pr(\theta_i \geq \theta_L|\theta_H - \epsilon) = (\theta_H - \theta_L)/2\epsilon$. Therefore, $n(\theta_H - \epsilon) \geq (\theta_H - \theta_L)/2\epsilon = n(\theta_L + \epsilon)$. This proves part (ii) of Claim 3.

Given Claim 3,

$$\begin{aligned}\int_{\theta_L+\epsilon}^{\theta_H+\epsilon} \pi(\theta, n(\theta))d\theta &= \int_{\theta_L+\epsilon}^{\theta_H+\epsilon} \pi\left(\theta, \frac{\theta_H + \epsilon - \theta}{2\epsilon}\right) d\theta \\ &= \int_{\theta_B}^{\theta_T} \pi\left(\theta, \frac{\theta_T - \theta}{2\epsilon}\right) d\theta,\end{aligned}$$

where $\theta_B = \theta_L + \epsilon$, and $\theta_T = \theta_H + \epsilon$. It is easy to see that $\int_{\theta_B}^{\theta_T} \pi(\theta, (\theta_T - \theta)/2\epsilon)d\theta \geq 0$. Furthermore, note that when $\theta = \theta_L + \epsilon, \hat{\theta} = \theta_H - \epsilon$, so that we know, from the second part

[8] The complementary case has an essentially identical but simpler proof, and is omitted.

of the claim that at the bottom end of the integral, $n(\hat{\theta}) \geq n(\theta)$. Thus, because $(\theta_T - \theta)/2\epsilon$ decreases at the fastest feasible rate, we can now say, for all $\theta \in [\theta_B, \theta_T]$, $n(\hat{\theta}) \geq (\theta_T - \theta)/2\epsilon$. Finally, note that $\hat{\theta} < \theta$ throughout the bound of intergration. Thus we can now directly apply Lemma 2 to claim that $\Pi(\theta_H, n) - \Pi(\theta_L, n) > 0$, a contradiction, since under our hypotheses $\Pi(\theta_H, n) = \Pi(\theta_L, n) = 0$. □

Proof of Proposition 2: To prove this result, we begin by writing down the threshold equation for the coordination game among depositors at the creditor bank conditional on the failure of the debtor bank. First, we write $n_1^c = (x - D)/(1 - w + x)$, and $n_2^c = [(1 - w)r + x - D]/(1 - w + x)$. Let $l_1 = 1 - 2n_1^c$, and $l_2 = 1 - 2n_2^c$. Finally, for brevity, we let $m = 1 - w + x$, and suppress the arguments of $n(\theta, \theta^*)$. Then, the threshold equation for patient depositors of the creditor bank conditional upon the failure of the debtor bank can be written as $L_f(\theta^*) = R_f(\theta^*)$, where

$$L_f(\theta^*) = \int_{\theta^*+\epsilon l_1}^{\theta^*+\epsilon l_2} u\left[\frac{1 - w - \frac{x-D+nm}{r}}{(1-n)m} R(\theta)\right] d\theta$$

$$+ \int_{\theta^*+\epsilon l_2}^{\theta^*+\epsilon} u\left[\frac{(x - D) - mn + (1 - w)R(\theta)}{(1-n)m}\right] d\theta$$

$$R_f(\theta^*) = \int_{\theta^*-\epsilon}^{\theta^*+\epsilon l_1} \left(u\left[\frac{w - D + (1 - w)r}{w - x + mn}\right] - u[0]\right) d\theta + K_1,$$

where $K_1 = \int_{\theta^*+\epsilon l_1}^{\theta^*+\epsilon} u[1]d\theta$. We know by our previous results that there is a unique $\theta^*_{c,F}$ that solves this equation. Now, we write down the corresponding threshold equation for the depositors of the creditor bank conditional upon the survival of the debtor bank as $L_s(\theta^*) = R_s(\theta^*)$, where

$$L_s(\theta^*) = \int_{\theta^*+\epsilon l_1}^{\theta^*+\epsilon l_2} u\left[\frac{(1 - w - \frac{x-D+nm}{r})R(\theta) + g}{(1-n)m}\right] d\theta$$

$$+ \int_{\theta^*+\epsilon l_2}^{\theta^*+\epsilon} u\left[\frac{(x - D) - mn + (1 - w)R(\theta) + g}{(1-n)m}\right] d\theta$$

$$R_s(\theta^*) = \int_{\theta^*-\epsilon}^{\theta^*+\epsilon l_1} \left(u\left[\frac{w - D + (1 - w)r}{w - x + mn} + g\right] - u[g]\right) d\theta + K_1$$

and K_1 is as before. Observe that since $g > 0$, it follows that $L_s(\theta^*) > L_f(\theta^*)$ for all θ^*. Since $u(\cdot)$ is a concave function, $u(x + y) - u(y) \leq u(x) - u(0)$, for all $x, y > 0$. Thus, $R_s(\theta^*) \leq R_f(\theta^*)$ for all θ^*. In particular, this means that

$$L_s(\theta^*_{c,F}) > R_s(\theta^*_{c,F})$$

that is, $\theta^*_{c,F} \neq \theta^*_{c,S}$. Now, observe that by analogy to the proof of unique equilibrium in monotone strategies we know that $L_s(\theta^*)$ is increasing in θ^*, while $R_s(\theta^*)$ is invariant with θ^*. Thus, in order to make the indifference equations hold, we need to reduce θ^* below $\theta^*_{c,F}$, and thus, we have just shown that $\theta^*_{c,S} < \theta^*_{c,F}$. □

Proof of Proposition 3: We refer to the proof of the previous proposition for notation. Clearly, $\theta^*_{c,S}$ is defined by

$$G_s(\theta^*) = L_s(\theta^*) - R_s(\theta^*) = 0,$$

while $\theta^*_{c,F}$ is defined by

$$G_f(\theta^*) = L_f(\theta^*) - R_f(\theta^*) = 0.$$

By analogy to the proof of earlier results, we note that G_s and G_f are both strictly increasing in θ^*. Also, note that when $g(\cdot) > 0$, it is strictly increasing in D.

We know that $L_s(\theta^*) > L_f(\theta^*)$ for all θ^*. Since $u' > 0$, the difference between the two is increasing in $g(\cdot)$ which, in turn, is increasing in D. We also know that $R_s(\theta^*) < R_f(\theta^*)$ because u is concave, and thus $u(x+y) - u(y) \leq u(x) - u(0)$, for all $x, y > 0$. Define $d(y) = u(x+y) - u(y)$, and note that $d'(y) \leq 0$. Thus, the difference between $R_s(\theta^*)$ and $R_f(\theta^*)$ is also weakly decreasing in g, and therefore in D. Thus,

$$G_s(\theta^*) > G_f(\theta^*) \text{ for all } \theta^*$$

and

$$G_s(\theta^*) - G_f(\theta^*) \text{ is increasing in } D \text{ for all } \theta^*.$$

Thus, the difference between the zeros of G_s and G_f is increasing in D. □

Appendix B: Creditor-to-Debtor Contagion

We now consider the more general setting in which the creditor bank, when faced with a run in Period 1, can prematurely liquidate its holdings in the debtor bank at $t = 1$. Suppose the creditor bank has failed and has (in the process) withdrawn its interbank deposit in the debtor. What are payoffs to the depositors of the debtor bank in this case? The demand for cash at the debtor bank in Period 1 from its own depositors is $w + x + (1 - w - x)n_d$, where n_d, as before, is the proportion of patient depositors who run. The amount of cash available, after the early withdrawal of D by the creditor bank is $w + (1 - w)r$. Thus, if $n_d \geq [(1 - w)r - x]/(1 - w - x)$, the debtor bank fails; otherwise, it survives. However, if it survives, it no longer has an interbank liability to pay to the creditor bank or its residual claimants. In order to pay the cash demands in Period 1, the debtor bank had to liquidate $[w + x + (1 - w - x)n_d - w]/r$ units of the illiquid asset. The remaining proceeds are available solely to its depositors who chose to leave their money in the bank. Thus, payoffs to the depositors are:

$$u_W(\theta_i, n_d) = \begin{cases} u[1] & \text{if } n_d < \frac{(1-w)r-x}{1-(w+x)}, \\ u\left[\frac{w+(1-w)r}{(w+x)+(1-(w+x))n_d}\right] & \text{if } n_d \geq \frac{(1-w)r-x}{1-(w+x)}; \end{cases}$$

$$u_R(\theta_i, n_d) = \begin{cases} u\left[\frac{1-w-\frac{(1-(w+x))n_d+x}{r}}{(1-w-x)(1-n_d)} R(\theta_i)\right] & \text{if } n_d < \frac{(1-w)r-x}{1-(w+x)}, \\ u[0] & \text{if } n_d \geq \frac{(1-w)r-x}{1-(w+x)}. \end{cases}$$

Table 18.B.1. Bank runs relatively likely: $U = 10$

D/x	$\theta^*_{d,S}$	$\theta^*_{d,F}$	C → D Contagion	$\theta^*_{c,S}$	$\theta^*_{c,F}$	D → C Contagion
0.2	6.46	7.14	11%	2.03	2.77	36%
0.4	5.84	7.14	22%	2.01	3.61	79%
0.6	5.26	7.14	36%	2.10	4.77	127%
0.8	**4.73**	**7.14**	**51%**	**2.34**	**6.47**	**175%**
1.0	4.36	7.14	64%	2.68	8.27	209%

Table 18.B.2. Bank runs very unlikely: $U = 30$

D/x	$\theta^*_{d,S}$	$\theta^*_{d,F}$	C → D Contagion	$\theta^*_{c,S}$	$\theta^*_{c,F}$	D → C Contagion
0.2	6.46	7.14	11%	1.73	2.77	60%
0.4	5.83	7.14	22%	1.42	3.61	155%
0.6	5.26	7.14	35%	1.19	4.77	302%
0.8	4.73	7.14	51%	1.04	6.47	520%
1.0	**4.36**	**7.14**	**64%**	**0.99**	**8.27**	**731%**

Using these payoffs, we can now compute the failure threshold of the debtor bank conditional on the prior failure of the creditor bank ($\theta^*_{d,F}$). In addition, from the analysis in the paper, we are able to compute the failure threshold of the debtor bank conditional on the survival of the creditor bank ($\theta^*_{d,S}$). The proportionate difference between these measures is the creditor-to-debtor contagion in this economy. The proportionate difference between $\theta^*_{c,F}$ and $\theta^*_{c,S}$ as defined in the paper measures the debtor-to-creditor contagion in this economy. While an analytical comparison of these two proportionate differences is intractable, we can compute and compare the differences numerically. We present in Tables 18.B.1 and 18.B.2 the computations for the two cases identified in the simulations given in Section 5, for the same assumptions on parameter values ($w = 0.3, x = w/2, L = 0, R(\theta) = \sqrt{\theta}$). The specific parameter values do not affect the qualitative properties of our analysis.

The boldface entries in each table correspond to the optimal level of interbank deposit holdings, as shown in Section 5. Inspection of the tables makes it clear that contagion from debtors to creditors is much larger in magnitude than contagion in the reverse direction. It is worth noting that all thresholds except for $\theta^*_{c,S}$ (the threshold of the creditor bank conditional on the survival of the debtor bank) are the same across the two tables. This is not a coincidence: it is because the other thresholds are defined locally and so do not depend on the value of U. The value of U affects $\theta^*_{c,S}$ because, conditional on the survival of the debtor bank, the creditor bank receives an interbank payment in Period 2 from the debtor bank. The higher is U, the higher is the payment it receives and thus the lower is its failure threshold, for a given level of D.

References

Acharya, Viral and Tanju Yorulmazer (2002). "Information Contagion and Inter-Bank Correlation in a Theory of Systemic Risk." Working paper, London Business School.

Allen, Franklin and Douglas Gale (2000). "Financial Contagion." *Journal of Political Economy*, 108, 1–33.

Calomiris, Charles and Gary Gorton (1991). "The Origins of Banking Panics: Models, Facts, and Bank Regulation." In *Financial Markets and Financial Crises*, edited by Glenn Hubbard. University of Chicago Press.

Carlsson, Hans and Eric van Damme (1993). "Global Games and Equilibrium Selection." *Econometrica*, 61, 989–1018.

Chen, Yehning (1999). "Banking Panics: The Role of the First-Come, First-Served Rule and Information Externalities." *Journal of Political Economy*, 107, 946–968.

Dasgupta, Amil (2002). "Coordination, Learning, and Delay." Financial Markets Group Discussion Paper No. 435, London School of Economics.

Diamond, Douglas and Philip Dybvig (1983). "Bank Runs, Deposit Insurance, and Liquidity." *Journal of Political Economy*, 91, 401–419.

Dungey, Mardi, Renée Fry, Brenda González-Hermosillo, and Vance Martin (2003). "Empirical Modelling of Contagion: A Review of Methodologies." Working paper, Australian National University.

Freixas, Xavier, Bruno Parigi, and Jean-Charles Rochet (2000). "Systemic Risk, Interbank Relations, and Liquidity Provision by the Central Bank." *Journal of Money, Credit and Banking*, 32, 611–638.

Goldstein, Itay and Ady Pauzner (2004a). "Demand Deposit Contracts and the Probability of Bank Runs." *Journal of Finance*, 60(3), 2005, p. 1293–1327

Goldstein, Itay and Ady Pauzner (2004b). "Contagion of Self-Fulfilling Financial Crises Due to Diversification of Investment Portfolios." *Journal of Economic Theory*, 199, 2004, p. 151–183.

Gorton, Gary and Andrew Winton (2002). "Financial Intermediation." In *Handbook of the Economics of Finance*, edited by George Constantinides, Milton Harris, and René Stulz. North-Holland, Amsterdam.

Kiyotaki, Nobuhiro and John Moore (1997). "Credit Chains." Working paper, London School of Economics.

Kyle, Albert and Wei Xiong (2001). "Contagion as a Wealth Effect." *Journal of Finance*, 56, 1401–1440.

Lagunoff, Roger and Stacey Schreft (2001). "A Model of Financial Fragility." *Journal of Economic Theory*, 99, 220–264.

Morris, Stephen and Hyun Shin (2003). "Global Games: Theory and Applications." In *Advances in Economics and Econometrics*, edited by Mathias Dewatripont, Lars Hansen, and Stephen Turnovsky. Cambridge University Press.

Rochet, Jean-Charles and Jean Tirole (1996). "Interbank Lending and Systemic Risk." *Journal of Money, Credit and Banking*, 28, 733–762.

Rochet, Jean-Charles and Xavier Vives (2004). "Coordination Failures and the Lender of Last Resort." *Journal of the European Economic Association*, 2, 1116–1148.

Sprague, O. M. W. (1910). *History of Crises under the National Banking System.* Government Printing Office, Washington, DC.

Wicker, Elmus (2000). *Banking Panics of the Gilded Age.* Cambridge University Press.

19 Information Contagion and Bank Herding

Viral V. Acharya and Tanju Yorulmazer

In this paper, we show that the likelihood of information contagion can induce even profit-maximizing bank owners to herd with other banks. Banks have an incentive to herd so as to minimize the information spillover from bad news about other banks on their borrowing costs and in turn on their future profits.

In our model, there are two periods and two banks with access to risky loans and deposits that are borrowed from risk-averse depositors. The returns on each bank's loans consist of a systematic component, say a common factor driving loan returns such as an aggregate or an industry cycle, and an idiosyncratic component. The ex ante structure of each bank's loan returns, specifically, their exposure to systematic and idiosyncratic factors, is common knowledge; the ex post performance of each bank's loan returns is also publicly observed. However, the exact realization of systematic and idiosyncratic components is not observed by the economic agents. Ex ante, banks choose whether to lend to similar industries and thereby maintain a high level of interbank correlation, or to lend to different industries. If banks lend to similar industries, their lending margins are eroded relative to the margins they earn upon lending to different industries.

The poor performance of each bank conveys potential bad news about the common factor affecting loan returns. Similarly, the good performance of each bank is good news about the common factor. Depositors rationally update priors about the prospects of their bank based on the information received about not only their bank's returns but also of the other bank. In particular, depositors require a higher promised rate on their deposits if the other bank has performed poorly compared to the state in which both banks have done well. This is an information spillover of one bank's poor performance on the other bank's borrowing costs.[1] Indeed, if the future profitability of loans is low, the bank that performed

[1]Empirical evidence on the information spillover from bank failures on other banks' borrowing costs is plenty: Carron (1982) shows that the Franklin National failure in New York (and perhaps also the Herstatt failure in Germany) in mid-1974 led to an increase in the quarterly average spread between U.S. jumbo certificates of deposits (CDs) and 3-month Treasury bills by a factor of at least six. Cooperman, Lee, and Wolfe (1992) examine the effect of the 1985 Ohio Deposit Insurance crisis on the pricing of retail 6-month CDs for a sample of 69 federally insured Ohio banks and savings and loans. The results indicate a significant unexpected rise in weekly CD prices for less solvent Ohio depository institutions (lasting approximately 7 weeks). Jayanti and Whyte (1996) estimate statistically significant increases in the average CD rates—at constant Treasury bill reference rates—for both UK and Canadian banks after the Continental Illinois failure in the United States in May 1984. Finally, Saunders (1987) acknowledges that the average spread between 3-month Eurodollar deposits and T-bills doubled

well may not be able to pay the borrowing rate when one bank performs poorly though it can pay this rate when both banks perform well. Hence, we interpret this spillover as an information contagion.

We argue that in order to minimize the impact of such information contagion on profits, banks alter their ex-ante investment choices. The increase in cost of borrowing for a bank when the other bank has performed poorly relative to when this other bank has done well is greater when bank loan returns have less commonality. Formally, let r_i^{HH}, r_i^{HL}, and r_i^{LL} denote, respectively, the costs of borrowing when both banks perform well, only one bank performs well, and both banks perform poorly with $i \in \{s, d\}$ denoting whether banks invested in the same industry or in different industries (with r_s^{HL} not defined in the model as banks are perfectly correlated when they invest in the same industry). Then, it can be shown that (Proposition 1):

$$r_d^{HH} < r_s^{HH} < r_d^{HL} = r_d^{LH} < r_s^{LL} < r_d^{LL}. \quad (19.1)$$

The intuition for this result is that when banks invest in the same industry, their returns are perfectly correlated and banks' performance will be identical. Hence, observing the other bank's performance will reveal no additional information about a given bank. Thus, when banks invest in the same industry, joint good (poor) performance is not as good (bad) news about the common systematic risk factor as in the case where banks invest in different industries. Given this relationship between costs of borrowing in different future states and under different investment choices, the expected borrowing cost of banks is minimized by investing in the same industry. This result holds as long as depositors are risk-averse.

Counteracting this herding force is the erosion of lending margins from investing in similar industries. As long as the effect of competition on bank margins is not too severe, the above intuition prevails: banks herd—that is, they choose correlated investments—over a robust set of parameter values for the future profitability of the corporate sector (Proposition 2). Incentives to herd by lending to a common industry are thus stronger if there is a high concentration amongst banks in lending to that industry, or, if that industry has experienced a positive technology shock reducing the rate at which returns-to-scale diminish. Such herding can lead to productive inefficiency as banks may bypass profitable projects in other industries of the economy.

Section 1 discusses the related literature. Section 2 presents the model. Section 3 analyzes the model and delivers the results on herding. Section 4 discusses the robustness of our results. Section 5 concludes.

1. Related Literature

The empirical studies on bank contagion test whether bad news, such as a bank failure, the announcement of an unexpected increase in loan-loss reserves, bank seasoned stock issue announcements, and so on adversely affect other banks.[2] These studies have found evidence

during the Continental Illinois problem in April and May 1984. An even stronger effect was visible in the average monthly domestic (U.S.) risk premium, as measured by the difference between 3-month CD rates and 3-month T-bill rates, which more than tripled during April and May 1984.

[2]If the effect is negative, the empirical literature calls it the "contagion effect." The overall finding is that the contagion effect is stronger for highly leveraged firms (banks being typically more levered than other industries) and is stronger for firms with similar cash flows. If the effect is positive, it is termed the "competitive effect."

of contagion using a variety of indicators: intertemporal correlation of bank failures (Hasan and Dwyer 1994, Schoenmaker 1996), bank debt risk premiums (Carron 1982, Saunders 1987, Cooperman, Lee, and Wolfe 1992, Jayanti and Whyte 1996), deposit flows (Saunders 1987, Saunders and Wilson 1996, Schumacher 2000), survival times (Calomiris and Mason 1997,2003), and stock price reactions (Aharony and Swary 1983, Swary 1986, Slovin, Sushka, and Polonchek 1992, 1999, Lang and Stulz 1992, to cite a few). This evidence is consistent with the channel of information spillover across banks that drives our results.

Our model of information contagion is close to the models of Chen (1999) and Kodres and Pritsker (2002). Chen builds a model with multiple banks with interim revelation of information about the performance of some banks. With Bayesian-updating depositors, a sufficient number of interim bank failures results in pessimistic expectations about the general state of the economy, and leads to runs on the remaining banks. In contrast, in our model the information spillover shows up in increased borrowing rates (and potentially also in bank failures)—an aspect that relates better to the empirical evidence. Kodres and Pritsker allow for alternative channels for contagion and show that contagion can occur between markets due to cross-market rebalancing even in the absence of correlated information and liquidity shocks. Neither of these papers models the endogenous choice of correlation of banks' investments.

Our paper is closest in spirit to Acharya (2001), who examines the choice of ex ante inter-bank correlation in response to pecuniary externalities that arise upon bank failures, and Acharya and Yorulmazer (2007, 2008) who investigate a similar problem but in response to "too-many-to-fail" regulatory guarantees. The channel of information spillover that we examine complements these channels.

Finally, our paper is related to the vast literature on herding. In this literature, herding is often an outcome of sequential decisions, with the decision of one agent conveying information about some underlying economic variable to the next set of decision-makers.In Scharfstein and Stein (1990), for example, herding behavior is driven by managerial concerns for reputation ("sharing the blame" when there is joint underperformance) and involves sequential investments. Herding, however, need not always be the outcome of such an informational cascade. It can also arise from a coordination game. In our paper, herding is a simultaneous ex ante decision of banks to coordinate correlated investments. In this sense, our modeling approach is similar to Rajan (1994) who also considers herding based on managerial reputation considerations but models coordination in the announcement of losses by short-termist bank managers. We view our channel of herding under which even profit-maximizing bank owners have incentives to herd as being complementary also to these reputation-based channels.

2. Model

There are two banks in the economy, bank A and bank B, and three dates, $t = 0, 1, 2$. The timeline in Figure 19.1 details the sequence of events in the economy. There is a single consumption good at each date. Each bank can borrow from a continuum of depositors of measure 1. Depositors consume their each-period payoff (say, ω). We assume the following:

The intuition is that demand for the surviving competitors' products (deposits, in the case of banks) can increase. Overall, this effect is found to be stronger when the industry is less competitive, that is, more concentrated.

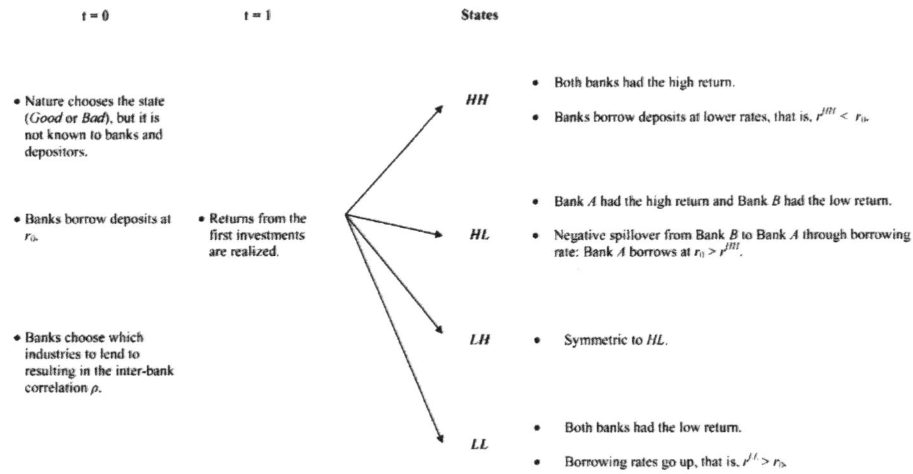

Figure 19.1. Timeline of the Model.

(Al): Depositors have risk-averse time-additive utility $u(\omega)$, with $u'(\omega) > 0$, $u''(\omega) < 0$, $\forall \omega > 0$. By way of normalization, we assume that $u(0) = 0$, and we denote $u(1)$ by $\bar{u}$

Depositors have one unit of the consumption good at t =0 and t =1. Bank owners are risk neutral and also consume their each-period payoff. All agents have access to a storage technology that transforms one unit of the consumption good at date t to one unit at date $t+1$. In each period, that is, at dates $t = 0$ and $t = 1$, depositors choose to keep their good in storage or to invest it in their bank. We assume the following:

(A2): Deposits take the form of a simple debt contract with maturity of one period. In particular, the promised deposit rate is not contingent on realized bank returns, which are assumed to be observable but non-verifiable.

(A3): Banks are monopolists in the deposit markets they operate. This can arise due to the costs associated with changing banks that unsophisticated depositors incur, such as switching and searching costs.[3]

Banks choose to invest the borrowed goods in storage or in a risky asset. The risky asset is to be thought of as a portfolio of loans to firms in the corporate sector. The performance of a bank's loan portfolio is determined by the random output of its borrowers and is denoted by $\tilde{R}_t$: either the output is high and there is correspondingly a high return on the bank portfolio, denoted by Rt, or the output is low, in which case the return on bank's loan portfolio is low, denoted by L_t. We assume the following:

(A4): The low return from the first period investment is equal to 1, that is, $L_0 = 1$. And the low return from the second period investment is equal to 0, that is, $L_1 = 0$.

Hence, from the depositors' point of view, deposits in the first period are riskless.

[3]Data collected on current account switching behavior from the Financial Research Survey of the National Opinion Poll for the United Kingdom imply that a representative current account holder would only change banks every 91 years (Gondat-Larralde and Nier 2006).

The return on bank investments depends on a systematic component, a common factor affecting loan returns, and an idiosyncratic component. We refer to the common factor as the overall state of the economy, which can be good (G) or bad (B), recognizing that it represents more broadly any common component of loan returns (such as a sector-specific or a regional component) that is not perfectly observable.[4] The state of the economy is assumed to persist for both periods of the economy. The prior probability that the state is G for the risky asset is p. Even if the overall state of the economy is good (bad), the return can still be low (high) due to the idiosyncratic component. The probability of a high return on bank investments when the state is good is $q \in (1/2, 1)$: when the state is good, it is more likely, although not certain, that the return will be high. The probability that the return is high when the state is Bad is $(1 - q)$. Therefore, the probability distributions of returns in different states are symmetric. For simplicity, we also assume the following:

(A5): Conditional on the state of the economy, the realizations of returns in the first and second period are independent.

Furthermore, we allow the promised returns on bank loans to vary over time.

The possible states at date 1, denoted by j, are given as follows: HH: both banks had the high return; $HL(LH)$: bank $A(B)$ had the high return, while bank $B(A)$ had the low return; and LL: both banks had the low return.

2.1 Correlation of Bank Returns

Banks can choose the level of correlation between the returns from their respective investments by choosing the composition of loans that compose their respective portfolios. We will refer to this correlation as "inter-bank correlation" and denote it as ρ.[5]

We model banks' choice of correlation in a simple way. There are two possible industries in which banks can invest, denoted as 1 and 2. Bank $A(B)$ can lend to firms A_1 and $A_2(B_1$ and $B_2)$ in industries 1 and 2, respectively. If in equilibrium banks choose to lend to firms in the same industry, specifically they either lend to A_1 and B_1, or they lend to A_2 and B_2, then their returns are assumed to be perfectly correlated ($\rho = 1$). However, if they choose different industries, then their returns are less than perfectly correlated, say independent ($\rho = 0$). Let $E(\pi_i)$ be the expected profit for a bank when banks invest in the same industry ($i = s$) or in different industries ($i = d$). Hence, in a Nash equilibrium, if banks invest in the same industry, then they receive $E(\pi_s)$, whereas if they invest in different industries, that is, in (A_1, B_2) or (A_2, B_1), then they receive $E(\pi_d)$. In the Nash equilibrium, banks invest in the same industry if $E(\pi_s) > E(\pi_d)$, and invest in different industries otherwise. Thus, for the same level of inter-bank correlation, the identity of the industries banks invest in does not matter in terms of bank returns. In other words, while there may be multiple Nash equilibria that correspond to the same level of inter-bank correlation, they are payoff equivalent. In turn, it is sufficient to concentrate analysis on the inter-bank correlation ρ, rather than on the identity of individual industries for banks' choice.

[4]This opaqueness about the bank balance sheet and realized returns is critical to our model. Given that a proportion of bank loans is in fact to small-and medium-sized firms, usually unrated by rating agencies, we believe the assumption that such an unobservable common factor exists is a reasonable one.

[5]In order to focus exclusively on the choice of inter-bank correlation, we abstract from the much-studied issue of the banks' choice of the scale of their loan portfolios and their absolute level of risk. This abstraction is common to several papers in this literature including the ones on herding due to managerial reputation considerations.

When banks operate in the same industries, they compete with each other for corporate loans and drive each other's profit margins down. We model this in the following simple way:

(A6): The return on a bank's investment when the return is high is $(\theta(\rho)R_t)$, where $\theta(\rho)$ captures the effect of competition on bank returns.[6] When $\rho = 0$, banks invest in different industries and do not face any competition, that is, $\theta(0) = 1$. And, when banks invest in the same industry, that is, when $\rho = 1, \theta(1) = (1 - \delta)$, where $\delta[0, 1]$.

We can provide a micro-foundation for competition in the lending market in the following way. Suppose that when banks operate in different industries, they are monopolists in the markets they operate in, whereas when they operate in the same industry, they compete as Cournot duopolists. [7] In this case, we can show that, when the return is high, the profit of each bank when they operate in different industries, that is, when they are monopolists, is equal to 9/4 times the profit of each bank when they invest in the same industry, that is, when they are Cournot duopolists. This, in turn, gives us $\delta = \left(\frac{5(R_t-1)}{9R_t}\right)$.

In our model banks choose which industries to invest in for both of their investments, that is, at $t = 0$ and $t = 1$. Later on we show that it is never optimal to invest in the same industry at $t = 1$.

3. Analysis

While the choice of interbank correlation is determined by backward induction, it is easier for sake of exposition to first examine the investment problem at date 0.

3.1 First Investment Problem (Date 0)

Recall that deposits in this period are riskless. Thus, banks can attract deposits by offering depositors the risk-free rate of 1. However, when the return is low, bank pays all the proceeds back to depositors and makes a profit equal to 0.[8] Thus, the expected payoff to the bank at date 0 from its first-period investment, $E(\pi_1, i)$, where $i = s$ when they invest in the same industry and $i = d$ when they invest in different industries, is

$$E(\pi_1, i) = \alpha_0[\theta(\rho)R_0 - 1], \tag{19.2}$$

where α_0 is the probability of having the high return from the first investment and is given as: $\alpha_0 = [pq + (1 - p)(l - q)]$.

Note that this first-period expected payoff is decreasing in the interbank correlation.

3.2 Second Investment Problem (Date 1)

Recall our simplifying assumption that realizations of returns in the first and second periods are independent, conditional on the state of the economy. Since there is a systematic

[6]We assume that when the return is low, the investment is liquidated, there is a separate market for liquidating these investments and the liquidation value does not depend on the interbank correlation. Hence, when the return is low, banks get a return of L_t for $\rho \in \{0, 1\}$.

[7]A detailed analysis of this case as well as the proofs for our propositions are available from the authors.

[8]We assume that $(1 - \delta)R_0 > 1$, as otherwise the problem at hand is rendered uninteresting.

component in the probabilities of returns which persists for both periods, the banks' return from their first investments is relevant information and depositors rationally update their beliefs in response to this information.

However, the extent of information revealed to the depositors depends on whether banks have invested in the same or different industries at $t = 0$. Next, we analyze each case separately. Before doing so, we would like to introduce the following notation. Let $P_i(G|j)$ and $P_i(B|j)$ and represent the posterior probabilities of the overall state of the economy being good (G) and bad (B), respectively, when the industries banks invest in at $t = 0$ are denoted by $i \in \{s, d\}$, and the states at $t = 1$ being denoted by $j \in \{HH, HL, LH, LL\}$.

Same industry ($i = s$) *at* $t = 0$. Note that when banks invest in the same industry at $t = 0$, their returns are perfectly correlated, that is, either both banks have the high return (HH) or both have the low return (LL). Using this, depositors update the probabilities about the overall state of the economy to obtain

$$P_s(G|HH) = \frac{pq}{pq + (1-p)(1-q)} \quad \text{and} \quad P_s(B|HH) = \frac{(1-p)(1-q)}{pq + (1-p)(1-q)} \tag{19.3}$$

$$P_s(G|LL) = \frac{p(1-q)}{p(1-q) + (1-p)q} \quad \text{and} \quad P_s(B|LL) = \frac{(1-p)q}{p(1-q) + (1-p)q} \tag{19.4}$$

Using these posterior probabilities for the state of the economy, depositors calculate the probability of a high return for their bank in the second period, denoted as α_i^j, as

$$\alpha_s^{HH} = \frac{pq^2 + (1-p)(1-q)^2}{pq + (1-p)(1-q)} \quad \text{and} \quad \alpha_s^{LL} = \frac{q(1-q)}{p(1-q) + (1-p)q} \tag{19.5}$$

By the individual rationality of depositors, we obtain that $r_s^{HH} = u^{-1}(\bar{u}/\alpha_s^{HH})$ and $r_s^{LL} = u^{-1}(\bar{u}/\alpha_s^{LL})$. Note that the borrowing rates (r_i^j), and hence the expected borrowing cost, at $t = 1$ depend on the information revealed by banks' performances from the first period investments, which, in turn, depend on the correlation in banks' investments in the first period. However, the borrowing rates at $t = 1$ do not depend on banks' choice of correlation at $t = 1$. Furthermore, if banks invest in the same industry at $t = 1$, they drive down their returns by (δR_1). Hence, banks never invest in the same industry at $t = 1$,

The payoff to each bank at date 2 from the second-period investment, denoted by $\pi_{2,i}^j$, is thus given by

$$\pi_{2,s}^j = \begin{cases} R_1 - r_s^{HH} & \text{if } j = HH \text{ and } \tilde{R}_1 = R_1 \text{ and } R_1 > r_s^{HH} \\ R_1 - r_s^{LL} & \text{if } j = LL \text{ and } \tilde{R}_1 = R_1 \text{ and } R_1 > r_s^{LL} \\ 0 & \text{otherwise.} \end{cases} \tag{19.6}$$

Different industries ($i = d$) *at* $t = 0$. With the information of the returns of both banks in the first period, depositors can update the probabilities about the overall state of the economy, to obtain

$$P_d(G\,|\,HH) = \frac{pq^2}{pq^2 + (1-p)(1-q)^2} \quad \text{and} \quad P_d(B\,|\,HH) = \frac{(1-p)(1-q)^2}{pq^2 + (1-p)(1-q)^2}, \tag{19.7}$$

$$P_d(G\,|\,LL) = \frac{p(1-q)^2}{p(1-q^2) + (1-p)q^2} \quad \text{and} \quad P_d(B|\,LL) = \frac{(1-p)q^2}{p(1-q^2) + (1-p)q^2}, \tag{19.8}$$

$$P_d(G\,|\,HL) = P_d(G\,|\,LH) = p \quad \text{and} \quad P_d(B\,|\,HL) = P_d(B\,|\,LH) = (1-p). \tag{19.9}$$

Using these posterior probabilities about the state of the economy, depositors can calculate the probability of a high return for their bank in the second period as

$$\alpha_d^{HH} = \frac{pq^3 + (1-p)(1-q)^3}{pq^2 + (1-p)(1-q)^2} \text{ and } \alpha_d^{HL} = \alpha_d^{HL} = \alpha_0, \tag{19.10}$$

$$\alpha_d^{LL} = \frac{pq(1-q)^2 + (1-p)q^2(1-q)}{p + (1-q)^2(1-p)q^2} \tag{19.11}$$

By the individual rationality of depositors, we obtain that $r_d^{HH} = u^{-1}(\bar{u}/\alpha_d^{HH})$,$r_d^{HL} = r_d^{HL} = u^{-1}(\bar{u}/\alpha_d^{HL})$ and $r_d^{LL} = u^{-1}(\bar{u}/\alpha_d^{LL})$. Thus, the payoff to each bank at date 2 from the second period investment, denoted as $\pi_{2,d}^{j}$ is given by

$$\pi_{2,d}^{j} = \begin{cases} R_1 - r_d^{HH} & \text{if } j = HH \text{ and } \tilde{R}_1 = R_1 \text{ and } R_1 > r_d^{HH} \\ R_1 - r_d^{HL} & \text{if } j = HL\,(LH) \text{ and } \tilde{R}_1 = R_1 \text{ and } R_1 > r_d^{HL} \\ R_1 - r_d^{LL} & \text{if } j = LL \text{ and } \tilde{R}_1 = R_1 \text{ and } R_1 > r_d^{LL} \\ 0 & \text{otherwise.} \end{cases} \tag{19.12}$$

Note that if $R_1 < r_s^{HH}$ in equation (6), or $R_1 < r_d^{HH}$ is equation (12), then it is individually rational for depositors not to lend their goods to banks. Storage is preferred to deposits, since the highest return on loans is insufficient to compensate depositors for the risk of bank failure. We consider all such possible cases in our analysis.

3.3 Information Spillover

We can now characterize the spillover from the realization of a return for one bank on the other bank. In particular, the bank that had the high return has a higher cost of borrowing when the other bank has the low return, relative to the state where both banks had the high return (*HH*)[9] This is a negative spillover resulting from a bank's poor performance. This spillover tends to reduce the profits of banks in states where they have high returns but their

[9]Under our assumed two-point return distribution for each bank, the information spillover arises precisely when a bank has the low return. With a continuous return distribution, any combination of realizations of bank profits leads to rational updating by depositors and the overall spillover remains qualitatively similar. The bank with superior performance always suffers some information spillover due to the relatively inferior performance of the other bank. To summarize, date 1 in our model could simply be considered an "information event" that leads to rational updating by depositors. The resulting revision of borrowing costs would affect bank profits as long as banks require additional financing.

peers have low returns. The result is an "information contagion."[10] In fact, if the profitability of the surviving bank's investments (level of promised return on loans $R1$) is low enough, the increased borrowing cost can render the surviving bank unviable: depositors "run" on the bank in response to other bank's low return since it is better for them to invest in storage than to lend to their bank. Conversely, the good performance of a bank results in a positive spillover on the other bank by lowering its cost of borrowing.

Proposition 1 (Information Spillover): *$\forall p \in (0, 1)$ and $q \in (1/2,1)$, we have*

$$r_d^{HH} < r_s^{HH} < r_d^{HL} = r_d^{LH} < r_s^{LL} < r_d^{LL}. \qquad (19.13)$$

Note that the return depositors demand in state *HH (LL)* increases (decreases) as the correlation in banks' investments increases. The reason for this is the following: when banks are perfectly correlated, $\rho = 1$, banks' performance will be identical and observing the other bank's performance will reveal no additional information about a given bank.

Proposition 1 suggests that if a period of good news for the banking sector in general is followed by bad news for a few banks, then other banks' profits and values could fall due to an increase in borrowing costs. Much empirical evidence exists to support such rational updating by depositors and the resulting information spillover on bank values and borrowing costs.[11] It is worthwhile to point out that what is crucial for our analysis is that bank profits fall as a result of information updating. While in our model profits fall due to an increase in the cost of borrowing deposits, this could arise more generally due to an increase in the cost of issuing subordinated debt and/or equity. This observation is crucial once the possibility of deposit insurance is considered. We discuss this in more detail in Section 4.

Before exploring the consequences of such information contagion for the endogenous choice of inter-bank correlation at date 0, the following computation of the expected payoff of banks from their second-period investment is required. The ex-ante expected second-period return of bank *A* (and by symmetry, of bank *B*) is given by

$$\begin{aligned} E(\pi_{2,i}) = {} & P_i(R_1, HH)[R_1 - r_i^{HH}]^+ + P_i(R_1, HL)[R_1 - r_i^{HL}]^+ \\ & + Pi(R_1, LH)[R_1 - r_i^{LH}]^+ + P_i(R_1, LL)[R_1 - r_i^{LL}]^+, \end{aligned} \qquad (19.14)$$

where the expressions, $P_i(R_1, HH)$, $P_i(R_1, HL)$, $Pi(R_1, LH)$ and $P_i(R_1, LL)$represent, respectively, the joint probabilities of having the high return from the second investment and having states *HH, HL, LH,* and *LL* from the first investments, when banks invest in the same ($i = s$) and different industries ($i = d$) at $t = 0$.

[10]It is plausible that banks increase their lending rates when faced by an increased borrowing cost. However, this would ration those bank borrowers with project returns that are lower than the lending rate offered by the bank. Providing that a bank cannot undo completely the decrease in its profits from increased borrowing rates by increasing its lending rates, this result on information contagion holds. We consider this scenario reasonable, given the typical diminishing returns-to-scale faced by banks on lending side.

[11]See footnote 1 and the references in Section 1. In addition, Rajan (1994) examines the effects of an announcement on December 15, 1989, that Bank of New England was hurt from the poor performance of the real estate sector and that it would boost its reserves to cover bad loans. He documents significant negative abnormal returns (−2.4%) for all banks, and that the effect was stronger for banks with headquarters in New England (−8%). Both of these features are consistent with the analysis of our model. He also documents significant negative abnormal returns for the real estate firms in general, whereas the negative effect is stronger for real estate firms with holdings in New England. This suggests that the information revealed by the announcement was rationally taken into account by investors in their updating process.

3.4 Choice of Inter-Bank Correlation

In this section, we show that under some conditions banks choose to be perfectly correlated at date 0 in response to the anticipated information spillover at date 1.

Note that, at $t = 1$, banks always choose to invest in different industries. Hence, the objective of each bank is to choose whether to invest in same ($i = s$) or different ($i = d$) industries at $t = 0$ to maximize

$$\max_{i \in \{s,d\}} E(\pi_{1,i}) + E(\pi_{2,i}).$$

This choice implies inter-bank correlation $\rho = 1$ for $i = s$ and $\rho = 0$ for $i = d$ for the first period investment. Note that E $(\pi_{1,i})$ equals $[\alpha_0(\theta(\rho)R_0 - 1)]$ and $E(\pi_{2,i})$is given by equation (14). This maximization yields the following result on ex ante herding by banks.

Proposition 2: *If banks are not viable in state HH when they invest in the same industry, that is, for $R_1 < r_s^{HH}$ banks invest in different industries. In all other cases, there exist threshold values of δ such that, when δ is above that threshold, banks invest in different industries and when S is below that threshold, banks invest in the same industry.*

If competition among banks in lending to a common set of industries does not erode their lending margins too rapidly, then herding occurs over a robust set of parameter values. Below, we provide an intuitive explanation of our result based on the special case where $\delta = 0$, that is, when competition does not have any effect on bank loan returns, and where banks are viable in all states at $t = 1$, that is, $R_1 \geq r_d^{LL}$.

Since there is no competition in this special case, $E(\pi_{1,i})$ is independent of p. Thus, banks concentrate on the second-period profits and choose to be perfectly correlated provided $E(\pi_{2,s}) > E(\pi_{2,d})$. Next, we show that for the economy studied thus far, this condition always holds. In particular, the expected cost of attracting depositors in the second period is minimized when banks are perfectly correlated.

The expected second-period profit, given in equation (14), is effectively the expected return on bank loans minus the expected borrowing cost in the second period. Note that whether banks invest in the same or different industries, the probability of having the high return R_1 from the second investment is given as

$$P_i(R_1) = P_i(R_1, HH) + P_i(R_1, HL) + P_i(R_1, LH) + P_i(R_1, LL) = \alpha_0. \tag{19.15}$$

Thus, interbank correlation affects bank profits only through the expected borrowing cost. For sake of argument, suppose that depositors are risk neutral with the utility function $u(w) = w$. In this case, we can calculate the expected borrowing cost $E(r_i)$ as

$$E(r_i) = \sum_j P_i(R_1, j) \cdot (1/\alpha_i^j), \tag{19.16}$$

where $\alpha_i^j = P_i(R_1 | j) = \frac{P_i(R_1, j)}{P_i(j)}$ represents the conditional probability of having the high return R_1 from the second investment in state $j \in \{HH, HL, LH, LL\}$. Using the conditional probabilities α_i^j, we can show that

$$E(r_i) = \sum_j P_i(R_1, j) \left(\frac{P_i(j)}{P_i(R_1, j)} \right) = P_i(HH) + P_i(HL) + P_i(LH) + P_i(LL). \tag{19.17}$$

Furthermore, we have

$$P_d(HH) + P_d(HL) = P_d(H) = P_s(HH) = P_s(H). \quad (19.18)$$

Also note that we have $P_s(R_1, HH) = P_d(R_1, HH) + P_d(R_1, HL)$. Thus, when depositors are risk neutral, by equation (18), the expected borrowing cost at $t = 1$ when a bank has the high return (H) from the first investment is the same when they invest in the same or in different industries. In other words, the probability distribution f_d^H that assigns probability $(\frac{P_d(R_1,HH)}{P_s(R_1,HH)})$to $r_d^{HH} = (1/\alpha_d^{HH})$ and probability $(\frac{P_d(R_t,HL)}{P_s(R_1,HH)})$ to $r_d^{HL} = (1/\alpha_d^{HL})$ can be shown to be a mean-preserving spread of the probability distribution f_s^H that assigns probability $1(= \frac{P_s(R_1,HH)}{P_s(R_1,HH)} to\, r_s^{HH} = (1/\alpha_s^{HH})$.

Now, consider the risk aversion of depositors. If depositors are risk averse, then $v(= u^{-1})$ is a convex function and we obtain

$$E(r_i) = \sum_j P_i(R_1, j) \cdot v(\bar{u}/\alpha_i^j). \quad (19.19)$$

Thus, by second-order stochastic dominance and the convexity of u, we have

$$p_d(R_1, HH) \cdot v(\bar{u}/\alpha_d^{HH}) + P_d(R_1, HL) \cdot v(\bar{u}/\alpha_d^{HL}) > P_s(R_1, HH) \cdot v(\bar{u}/\alpha_s^{HH}). \quad (19.20)$$

The same result can be shown to hold for the case of low returns. Hence, as long as depositors are risk averse (Assumption 1), expected borrowing cost is higher when banks invest in different industries. Thus, in the special case of no competition ($\delta = 0$), banks herd and invest in the same industry.

In the general case where competition among banks reduce their profit margins, the benefit of lower expected borrowing costs from investing in the same industry can be eroded by lower profit margins. Hence, there is a critical level of δ, denoted by δ^*, such that when competition reduces profit margins severely, that is, when $\delta > \delta^*$, banks invest in different industries whereas when competition is not very severe, that is, when $\delta \leq \delta^*$, banks herd.

Hence, incentives to herd by lending to a common industry are stronger if there is a high concentration amongst banks in lending to that industry, or, if that industry has experienced a positive technology shock reducing the rate at which returns-to-scale diminish. In turn, such herding can lead to productive inefficiency as banks may bypass profitable projects in other industries of the economy.

4. Robustness

In this section, we discuss the robustness of our results to relaxing various assumptions, considering deposit insurance and uninsured bank funding, and allowing for alternative ways of bank herding such as creating inter-bank linkages and making syndicated loans.

4.1 Deposit Insurance and Uninsured Bank Funding

If banks are funded only by insured deposits, then their cost of borrowing would be rendered insensitive to fluctuations in banks' health. In turn, information spillover of the sort we described would be irrelevant. Formally, suppose a proportion $y \in [0, 1]$ of bank deposits are insured and the rest are uninsured deposits. Then, if the bank performs well, depositors receive the promised return of r, whereas if the bank performs poorly, depositors receive y units from the deposit insurance fund. It is straightforward to show that as the proportion of insured deposits y increases, the sensitivity of the promised deposit rate r to the probability of success α decreases. This, in turn, weakens the effect of information spillover.

The provision of deposit insurance is only partial in most countries. Some countries do not have deposit insurance (e.g., Australia, New Zealand, and Malaysia) while the coverage is limited in almost all countries that have insurance schemes (e.g., in the United States, deposits are insured up to \$100 000, and in the United Kingdom, up to £20,000).[12]As long as deposits are not fully insured and banks do access sizable quantities of uninsured deposits and other uninsured forms of capital (such as subordinated debt), our results continue to hold. For example, in the United States, the proportion of funding that is FDIC-insured is only 31% and 62% for large and small banks, respectively, illustrating the importance of uninsured forms of bank funding.[13] Increasingly, banks have employed uninsured subordinated debt as a form of funding whose interest rates respond to information pertaining to the bank's health. Empirical studies have documented a significant correlation between bank-specific risks and secondary-market subordinated debt spreads, especially in the post-FDICIA period in the United States starting in 1991.[14] Recognition of such risk-sensitive marginal sources of bank funding implies that poor performance of a bank affects other banks' cost of borrowing even in the presence of partial deposit insurance.

4.2 Alternative Ways of Herding

While lending to similar industries is one way for banks to increase the correlation in their returns, there are also other approaches that may not lead to erosion of profit margins as in the case of lending. First, banks could bet on systematic risk factors such as interest rate risk through choosing from a range of products such as mortgages and interest rate derivatives. That is, banks could specialize within a class of risk exposures to achieve a trade off between incentives to correlate and to differentiate. Second, banks can lend to a

[12]As Jayanti and Whyte (1996) note in their study of UK and Canadian banks after the Continental Illinois failure: "In reality, however, deposit insurance schemes vary across countries in terms of, inter alia, the extent of coverage (maximum amount per deposit or per customer), scope of coverage (whether foreign banks and foreign offices of domestic banks are covered), the types of deposits covered (whether residents' and non-residents' deposits and foreign currency deposits are covered), and premium structure (flat premium or risk-based premium). Furthermore, absence of an explicit deposit insurance scheme may result in a contagion effect. In all the countries where deposit insurance is in existence, ceilings on the amount of deposits insured are imposed. Thus, although the presence of deposit insurance reduces fear of loss by insured depositors, the uninsured depositors may still incur losses in the event of a bank failure. The market's perception of the extent to which uninsured depositors are likely to suffer losses may significantly influence the market reaction [to bank failures]."

[13]See, for example, the presentation by George Pennacchi, University of Illinois at Urbana Champaign, at www.business.uiuc.edu/gpennacc/f461n02.ppt.

[14]See, for example, Covitz, Hancock, and Kwast (2004) for the period 1985–87 and Jagtiani, Kaufman, and Lemieux (2000), DeYoung et al. (2001), Hancock and Kwast (2001), and Morgan and Stiroh (2001) for the post-FDICIA period. Moreover, the National Depositor Preference Act of 1993 lowered the liquidation standing of bank subordinated debt, which had a positive effect on the subordinated debt market's sensitivity to bank-specific risks. Furthermore, Morgan and Stiroh (1999), using data for the 1993–98 period, found that the relationship between issuance bond spreads and bond ratings was about the same for banks as it was for other corporate firms.

similar set of customers and get exposed to similar risks without erosion of profit margins by participating in syndicated loans to a common set of borrowers.[15]

4.3 Bankruptcy and Flight to Quality

In this model, we assumed that the low return from the first-period investment is equal to 1, that is, $L_0 = 1$. Hence, banks do not fail at $t = 1$ and always have the chance to make the second-period investment. In an unabridged version of this paper, we relax this assumption and allow for lower values for L_0 so that banks can go bankrupt at $t = 1$, in which case, they are closed and cannot take the second-period investment. In that case, depositors of the failed bank can migrate to the surviving bank, if there is any. This increases the benefit for banks from surviving when other banks fail and, in turn, strengthens incentives for differentiation.

4.4 Origins of Banking Crises

The literature on the origins of banking crises provide strong empirical evidence for the fact that bank failures result from shocks to the asset side of banks' balance sheet, which is consistent with the predictions of our model. In many instances, bank failures are related to the current condition of the economy or the particular sectors banks operate in, which affect the asset side of banks' balance sheets. Gorton (1988) conducts an empirical analysis using U.S. data from the late 19th and early 20th centuries and finds a close relation between the occurrence of banking panics and the overall state of the economy. Calomiris and Gorton (1991) use a larger set of data and find similar evidence. Furthermore, consistent with the predictions of our model, we observe from the empirical literature that bank failures and periods of tranquillity cluster over time. Grossman (1993), Hasan and Dwyer (1994), and Schoenmaker (1996) analyze data from the U.S. Free Banking Era (1837–63) and provide evidence of intertemporal clustering of bank failures.

5. Conclusion

This paper showed that the likelihood of information contagion can induce profit-maximizing bank owners to herd with other banks. Our model provides a way to jointly study various aspects of systemic risk, the risk that banks may fail together. While most studies of systemic risk and financial fragility are concerned with the ex post effects of bank failures and losses, our paper demonstrates that analyzing the ex ante response of banks to these effects may be important. The extent of herding can be considered the ex ante aspect of systemic risk: it affects the likelihood of joint failure of banks but also affects and is affected by the extent of information contagion, which can be considered the ex post aspect of systemic risk. The lack of exhaustive empirical evidence on the extent of bank herding, its causes, and the nature of its variation over the business cycle suggest that further investigation of these issues is warranted to improve our understanding of systemic risk in financial sectors. We view our channel of herding under which even profit-maximizing bank owners have incentives to herd as being complementary to other herding channels. Differentiating between these various channels of herding (reputational,

[15]See Jain and Gupta (1987) for a discussion of the role of syndicated loans for bank herding during the emergining market debt crisis in the early 1980s.

regulatory, or information-based) are open theoretical and empirical questions for future research.

Literature Cited

Acharya, Viral. (2001) "A Theory of Systemic Risk and Design of Prudential Bank Regulation." Working Paper, London Business School.

Acharya, Viral, and Tanju Yorulmazer. (2007) "Too-Many-To-Fail: An Analysis of Time-Inconsistency in Bank Closure Policies." *Journal of Financial Intermediation*, 16, 1–31.

Acharya, Viral, and Tanju Yorulmazer. (2008) "Cash-in-the-Market Pricing and Optimal Resolution of Bank Failures." *Review of Financial Studies*, 21(6), 2705–42.

Aharony, Joseph, and Itzhak Swary. (1983) "Contagion Effects of Bank Failures: Evidence from Capital Markets." *Journal of Business*, 56, 305–17.

Calomiris, Charles, and Gary Gorton. (1991) "The Origins of Banking Panics: Models, Facts, and Bank Regulation." In *Financial Markets and Financial Crises*, edited by G. Hubbard, pp. 109–73. Chicago, IL: The University of Chicago Press.

Calomiris, Charles, and Joseph Mason. (1997) "Contagion and Bank Failures During the Great Depression: The June 1932 Chicago Banking Panic." *American Economic Review*, 87, 863–83.

Calomiris, Charles, and Joseph Mason. (2003) "Consequences of U.S. Bank Distress During the Depression." *American Economic Review*, 93, 937–47.

Carron, Andrew. (1982) "Financial Crises: Recent Experience in U.S. and International Markets." *Brookings Papers on Economic Activity*, 2, 395–118.

Chen, Yehning. (1999) "Banking Panics: The Role of the First-Come, First-Served Rule and Information Externalities." *Journal of Political Economy*, 107, 946–68.

Cooperman, Elizabeth, Winson Lee, and Glenn Wolfe. (1992) "The 1985 Ohio Thrift Crisis, the FSLIC's Solvency and Rate Contagion for Retail CDs." *Journal of Finance*, 47, 919–41.

Covitz, Daniel, Diana Hancock, and Myron Kwast. (2004) "A Reconsideration of the Risk Sensitivity of U.S. Banking Organization Subordinated Debt Spreads: A Sample Selection Approach." *Federal Reserve Bank of New York Economic Policy Review, September*, 73–95.

DeYoung, Robert, Mark Flannery, William Lang, and Sorin Sorescu. (2001) "The Information Content of Bank Exam Ratings and Subordinated Debt Prices." *Journal of Money, Credit and Banking*, 33, 900–25.

Gondat-Larralde, Celine, and Erlend Nier. (2006) "Switching Costs in the Market for Personal Accounts: Some Evidence for the United Kingdom." *Bank of England Working Paper* No. 292.

Gorton, Gary. (1988) "Banking Panics and Business Cycles." *Oxford Economic Papers*, 40, 751–81.

Grossman, Richard. (1993) "The Macroeconomic Consequences of Bank Failures under the National Banking System." *Explorations in Economic History*, 30, 294–320.

Hancock, Diana, and Myron Kwast. (2001) "Using Subordinated Debt to Monitor Bank Holding Companies: Is It Feasible?" *Journal of Financial Services Research*, 20, 147–87.

Hasan, Iftekhar, and Gerald Dwyer. (1994) "Bank Runs in the Free Banking Period." *Journal of Money, Credit and Banking*, 26, 271–88.

Jagtiani, Julapa, George Kaufman, and Catherine Lemieux. (2000) "Do Markets Discipline Banks and Bank Holding Companies? Evidence from Debt Pricing." *Federal Reserve Bank of Chicago Emerging Issues Series*, No: S&R-99-3R, June.

Jain, Arvind, and Satyadev Gupta. (1987) "Some Evidence on 'Herding' Behavior of U.S. Banks." *Journal of Money, Credit and Banking*, 19, 78–89.

Jayanti, S V, and Ann Marie Whyte. (1996) "Global Contagion Effects of the Continental Illinois Failure." *Journal of International Financial Markets, Institutions and Money*, 6, 87–99.

Kodres, Laura, and Matthew Pritsker. (2002) "A Rational Expectations Model of Financial Contagion." *Journal of Finance*, 57, 769–99.

Lang, Larry, and Rene Stulz. (1992) "Contagion and Competitive Intra-Industry Effects of Bankruptcy Announcements." *Journal of Financial Economics*, 32, 45–60.

Morgan, Donald, and Kevin J. Stiroh. (1999) "Bond Market Discipline of Banks: Is the Market Tough Enough?" *Federal Reserve Bank of New York Staff Reports*, 95.

Morgan, Donald, and Kevin J. Stiroh. (2001) "Market Discipline of Banks: The Asset Test." *Journal of Financial Services Research*, 20, 195–208.

Rajan, Raghuram. (1994) "Why Bank Credit Policies Fluctuate: A Theory and Some Evidence." *Quarterly Journal of Economics*, 109, 399–442.
Saunders, Anthony. (1987) "The Interbank Market, Contagion Effects and International Financial Crises." *In Threats to International Financial Stability*, edited by R. Portes and A.K. Swoboda, pp. 196–232. New York: Cambridge University Press.
Saunders, Anthony, and Berry Wilson. (1996) "Contagious Bank Runs: Evidence from the 1929–1933 Period." *Journal of Financial Intermediation*, 5, 409–23.
Scharfstein, David, and Jeremy Stein. (1990) "Herd Behavior and Investment." *American Economic Review*, 80, 465–79.
Schoenmaker, Dirk. (1996) "Contagion Risk in Banking." LSE. Financial Markets Group Discussion Paper No. 239, *London: London School of Economics*.
Schumacher, Liliana. (2000) "Bank Runs and Currency Run in a System without a Safety Net: Argentina and the 'Tequila' Shock." *Journal of Monetary Economics*, 46, 257–77.
Slovin, Myron, Marie Sushka, and John Polonchek. (1992) "Information Externalities of Seasoned Equity Issues: Difference between Banks and Industrial Firms." *Journal of Financial Economics*, 32, 87–101.
Slovin, Myron, Marie Sushka, and John Polonchek. (1999) "An Analysis of Contagion and Competitive Effects at Commercial Banks." *Journal of Financial Economics*, 54, 197–225.
Swary, Itzhak. (1986) "Stock Market Reaction to Regulatory Action in the Continental Illinois Crisis." *Journal of Business*, 59, 451–73.

20 Cash in-the-Market Pricing and Optimal Resolution of Bank Failures

Viral V. Acharya and Tanju Yorulmazer

Empirical evidence on the resolution of bank failures suggests that regulatory actions taken in response to banking problems vary significantly. Kasa and Spiegel (1999) and Santomero and Hoffman (1999) document that these actions appear to depend on whether the problems arise from idiosyncratic reasons specific to particular institutions or from aggregate reasons with potential threats to the whole system. Hoggarth, Reidhill, and Sinclair (2004) also study resolution policies adopted in 33 banking crises over the world during 1977–2002. They find that when faced with individual bank failures, authorities have usually sought a private-sector resolution where the losses have not been passed onto taxpayers. However, during systemic crises, liquidity support from central banks and blanket government guarantees have been granted, usually at a cost to the budget; bank liquidations have been rare and creditors have rarely made losses.

We argue in this article that such variation arises from the fact that resolution options open for an isolated bank failure are different from those available for systemic failures. When only a few banks fail, these banks can be acquired by surviving banks. However, for a large number of failures, the liquidity of surviving banks enables them to acquire all failed banks only at fire-sale prices, an effect akin to the industry-equilibrium hypothesis of Shleifer and Vishny (1992). The resulting "cash-in-the-market" pricing, as in Allen and Gale (1994, 1998), makes it more likely that investors outside the banking sector, who are liquidity-endowed but potentially not the most efficient users of these assets, end up purchasing some failed banks' assets. Thus, there are "too many (banks) to liquidate" and regulatory intervention in the form of bailing out some banks may be optimal in order to avoid allocation inefficiencies.

The ex-post optimal bailout policy may, however, be suboptimal from an ex-ante standpoint since it induces banks to herd, for example, by lending to similar industries or betting on common risks such as interest and mortgage rates, in order to increase the likelihood of being bailed out. This increases the ex-ante likelihood of experiencing systemic crises. Can other regulatory policies mitigate this time-inconsistency problem? We show that the answer is yes. We propose a novel liquidity provision policy that subsidizes surviving banks for the purchase of failed banks. This policy can be designed to be ex-post equivalent to the bailout policy, and yet gives banks incentives to differentiate ex-ante, rather than to herd.

In this article, we build a framework wherein the ex-ante and the ex-post optimal regulatory policies and the cash-in-the-market pricing are endogenously derived. We consider a two-period model with n banks, a regulator, and outside investors who can purchase banking assets were they to be liquidated. Allowing for an arbitrary number of banks enables us to explore the richness of the cash-in-the-market price function.

The regulator adopts policies to resolve bank failures with the objective of maximizing the total output of the banking sector net of any costs associated with the adopted policies. We consider the following policies: failed banks may be sold to surviving banks and outsiders at market-clearing prices; failed banks may be bailed out, in which case their owners are allowed to continue operating the banks; and finally, the regulator may also provide liquidity, essentially a grant or a subsidy, to various players—failed banks, surviving banks, and outsiders. For simplicity, we assume that deposits are fully insured (at least in the first period). The immediacy of funds required for deposit insurance and for the liquidity granted during failure resolution, net of proceeds from bank sales, entails fiscal costs for the regulator.

Three central assumptions drive our results: (i) banks have limited liquidity— in particular, we assume that surviving banks only have their first-period profits to acquire failed banks' assets; (ii) banks are more efficient users of banking assets than outsiders as long as bank owners take good projects; and (iii) there is a possibility of moral hazard in that bank owners derive private benefits from bad projects; hence, banks take good projects only if bank owners retain a large enough share of bank profits.

Banks whose return from first-period investment is low are in default. Surviving banks, if any, use their first-period profits to purchase failed banks' assets. Up to a critical number of failures, surviving banks' liquidity is enough to purchase all failed banks' assets at the "fundamental" price: surviving banks compete for these assets and their surplus is eroded to zero. Beyond this critical number of failures, additional assets cannot be absorbed by the available liquidity of surviving banks at the fundamental price. Thus, the market-clearing price declines with each additional failure. Under assumption (ii), outsiders enter the market only when the price declines sufficiently. Since outsiders are not as efficient as surviving banks in using these assets, this results in an allocation inefficiency.

The regulator decides whether to let surviving banks and outsiders purchase failed banks' assets, or to intervene. We first consider intervention in the form of bailing out failed banks. In a bailout, a failed bank is allowed to operate under its existing owners. Bailouts are thus associated with an opportunity cost: the regulator incurs a higher fiscal cost to pay off insured deposits since no proceeds are collected through bank sales. Since bailouts are costly, the regulator does not intervene as long as all failed banks are acquired by surviving banks. However, when asset prices decline sufficiently, it is optimal for the regulator to prevent sales to outsiders by bailing out banks as long as the fiscal cost of a bailout is lower than the misallocation cost.

With limited outsider funds, once the number of failures is sufficiently large, total liquidity of surviving banks and outsiders is not enough to clear the market for bank sales at the threshold value of outsiders. Thus, there is a further decline in the market-clearing price as the number of failures increases. Additional bailouts do not entail any opportunity cost as proceeds from bank sales always equal total liquidity in the market. Hence, the regulator bails out failed banks until prices are sustained at the threshold value of outsiders. Crucially, there is always a welfare loss when the number of failures is high—either fiscal cost from bailouts or misallocation cost from liquidation to outsiders.

We show that liquidity provision of a specific form to the surviving banks is ex-post equivalent in welfare terms to this bailout policy.[1] Intuitively, bailouts are ex-post optimal when the price falls sufficiently to elicit participation of outsiders in asset purchase. The lack of sufficient liquidity with efficient users—the surviving banks—is the primary cause for this price drop. Hence, assisting surviving banks in purchasing failed banks by granting them sufficient liquidity can ensure that the price never falls enough to draw outsiders into the market, thereby eliminating the allocation inefficiency. We show that the minimum amount of liquidity provision required to achieve this entails the same fiscal cost as the ex-post optimal bailout policy.

Next, we compare these two policies from an ex-ante standpoint in a setting where banks choose to differentiate or herd. Each bank invests either in a common industry or in a bank-specific industry. This decision affects the correlation of bank returns and the likelihood that banks fail together. Ex ante, the regulator wishes to implement a low correlation between banks' investments to minimize the likelihood that many banks fail, and simultaneously implement resolution policies that are ex-post optimal. The regulator can achieve this by employing the bailout policy, only if it can commit to sufficiently diluting the share of bank owners when they are bailed out. By doing so, the bailout subsidy becomes small enough that banks prefer to differentiate and capture the surplus from buying assets at cash-in-the-market prices. However, assumption (iii) implies that such a dilution may not always be feasible. If moral hazard due to private benefits is sufficiently severe, then excessive dilution of a bank's equity leads bank owners to choose bad projects, generating continuation values that are worse than liquidation values. In this case, a low correlation can only be implemented by committing to liquidate a large number of failed banks. But, in general, this is ex-post inefficient and lacks commitment. We show that this time-inconsistency problem leads to inefficient herding when the likelihood of bank failure is sufficiently high.

From an ex-ante standpoint, the liquidity provision policy dominates bailouts. Subsidizing surviving banks in acquiring failed banks increases the anticipated surplus and strengthens incentives to differentiate. Thus, relative to the bailout policy, the liquidity provision policy can implement a low correlation over a wider range of the severity of the moral hazard problem due to private benefits. To summarize, the important policy implication of our analysis is that assisting surviving banks rather than the troubled ones can ameliorate the commitment problem in optimal resolution of bank failures.[2]

Our article is related to the banking literature that has focused on optimal bank closure policies. Mailath and Mester (1994) and Freixas (1999) discuss the time-inconsistency of closure policy in a single-bank model. Penati and Protopapadakis (1988) assume that the regulator provides insurance to uninsured depositors when the number of bank failures is large, and show that this leads banks to invest inefficiently in common markets so as to attract deposits at a lower cost. Mitchell (1997) extends the "signal-jamming" model of Rajan (1994) to show that if the regulator bails out banks when they fail together, then banks coordinate on disclosing their losses and delay classifying bad loans by rolling them over.

Closest to our article is the work of Perotti and Suarez (2002), Cordella and Yeyati (2003), and Gorton and Huang (2004). Perotti and Suarez consider a dynamic model where

[1] It is suboptimal in our model to grant liquidity to outsiders or to a bank that is bailed out.

[2] This liquidity provision policy has similarities as well as differences with the much-studied lender-of-last-resort (LOLR) policy of providing liquidity to banks that are in distress. Like the LOLR policy, the liquidity provision policy aims at resolving problems arising from illiquidity, However, unlike the LOLR policy, liquidity is provided to *surviving* banks to assist them in purchasing failed banks. Furthermore, unlike the LOLR policy, the liquidity provision policy is in the form of a grant.

selling failed banks to surviving banks, by reducing competition, increases the charter-value of surviving banks and gives banks ex-ante incentives to stay solvent. The liquidity provision policy we propose is similar in spirit to this policy since it raises anticipated surplus for banks from surviving and gives banks incentives to differentiate. Similarly, Cordella and Yeyati (2003) show that the regulator, by bailing out banks during systemic crises, can increase the charter value of banks, which induces banks to manage their risk prudently. In their model, systemic crises occur because of adverse macroeconomic shocks that are exogenous, whereas in our article, systemic crises arise endogenously as a result of banks' overinvestment in particular industries.[3] Gorton and Huang (2004) also analyze the optimal resolution of bank failures and focus on the risk-taking incentives of banks. An important difference between our analysis and theirs is that we assume a cost to the regulator in providing funds to the banking sector with immediacy. Gorton and Huang assume that since such funding can be recovered through taxes in the future, there are no costs of immediacy. As a result, our setup gives rise to the time-inconsistency of regulatory policies that does not arise in their model.

Finally, some of the ideas presented in this article are related to the analysis in Acharya (2001) and Acharya and Yorulmazer (2007). In our opinion, the strongest differentiating point of the current article is its modeling generality in allowing for an arbitrary number of banks and endogenously deriving the cash-in-the-market pricing. This lends the model an element of richness that we have exploited to provide an in-depth normative analysis of the various options available to regulators to resolve and restructure failed banks.[4]

The remainder of the article is structured as follows. Sections 1–3 present the model and its analysis. Section 4 provides empirical evidence supporting the model's assumptions and results. Section 5 concludes. Proofs not contained in the text are contained in the Appendix.

1. Model

The benchmark model is outlined in Figure 20.1. We consider an economy with three dates, $t = 0, 1, 2$, n banks, bank owners, depositors, outside investors, and a regulator. Each bank borrows from a continuum of depositors of measure 1. Bank owners and depositors are risk-neutral and obtain a time-additive utility u_t, where u_t is the expected payoff at time t. Depositors receive a unit of endowment at dates 0 and 1, and have access to a reservation investment opportunity that gives them a utility of 1 per unit of investment. In each period, that is at dates 0 and 1, depositors choose to invest their good in this reservation opportunity or in their bank.

Deposits take the form of a simple debt contract with maturity of one period. In particular, the promised deposit rate is not contingent on investment decisions of the bank or on its

[3]While direct exposure to the common risks analyzed in our article is one reason banks may fail together, interbank linkages may also lead to joint failures since these linkages may lead to the problems of one bank being transmitted to other banks in a contagion-type phenomenon, as analyzed by Rochet and Tirole (1996), Allen and Gale (2000), and Kahn and Santos (2005). In a different contagion model, Diamond and Rajan (2005) show that a bank failure can cause aggregate liquidity shortages. They show that liquidity and solvency problems interact in a complex manner and are difficult to distinguish ex-post. They do not analyze implications of such effects for the ex-ante investment choice of banks.

[4]Acharya and Yorulmazer (2007), for example, consider a two-bank model, which focuses on comparing the too-big-to-fail problems with the too-many-to-fail problem, and show that herding incentives are stronger for small banks than for large banks. They do not consider the liquidity provision role of the regulator in subsidizing purchases of failed banks by surviving banks—a novel policy implication of this article.

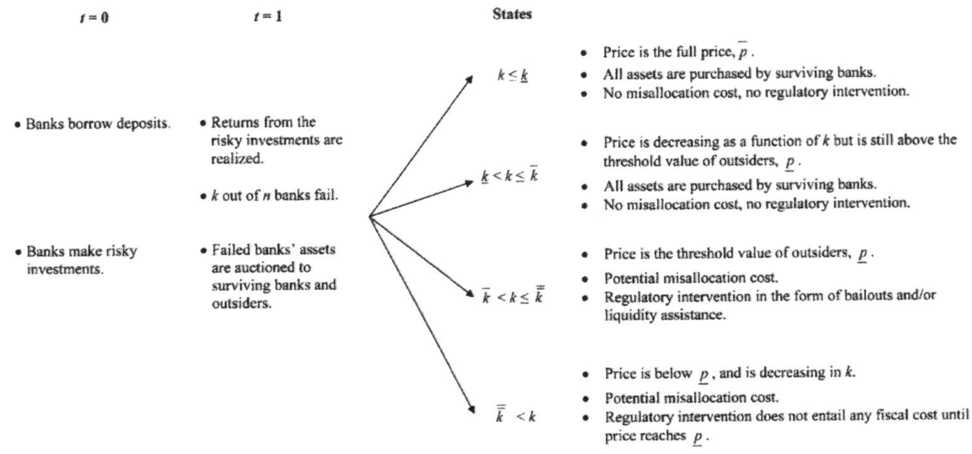

Figure 20.1. Timeline of the model.

realized returns. In order to keep the model simple and yet capture the fact that there are limits to equity financing (e.g., due to asymmetric information as in Myers and Majluf, 1984), we do not consider any bank financing other than deposits.

Banks require one unit of funds to invest in a risky technology, which is to be thought of as a portfolio of loans to firms in the corporate sector. The performance of the corporate sector determines its random output at date $t+1$. We assume that all firms a bank has lent to can either repay fully the borrowed bank loans or they default. In the case of a default, we assume for simplicity that there is no repayment. Suppose R_t is the promised return on a bank loan at time t and we denote the random repayment on this loan as $\tilde{R}_t$, $\tilde{R}_t, \in \{0, R_t\}$. The probability that the return from these loans is high in period t is denoted by α_t. We assume that the returns in the two periods are independent and allow the probability, as well as the level of the high return, to be different in the two periods. This helps isolate their effect on our results.

There is potential moral hazard at the individual bank level. If bank owners choose a bad project, then when the return is high, they do not generate R_t but only $(R_t - \bar{\Delta})$ and enjoy a nonpecuniary benefit of $B < \bar{\Delta}$. Therefore, appropriate incentives have to be provided to bank owners to choose the good project. We denote the share of bank owners as θ. If r_t is the cost of borrowing deposits, then the incentive-compatibility constraint is

$$\alpha_t[\theta(R_t - r_t)] \geq \alpha_t[\theta((R_t - \bar{\Delta}) - r_t) + B]. \quad \text{(IC)} \tag{20.1}$$

We have assumed that the promised deposit rate r_t can be paid when the investment has a high return irrespective of whether the project is good or bad. The (IC) constraint implies that bank owners need a minimum share of $\bar{\theta} = B/\bar{\Delta}$ to choose the good project.[5] We assume that at $t = 0$, the entire share of the bank profits belongs to the bank owners, and therefore, moral hazard is not a concern at the beginning.

[5]See Hart and Moore (1994) and Holmstrom and Tirole (1998) for models with similar features. Also, for detailed evidence on large inside ownership of banks around the world and their role in alleviating moral hazard problems, see Caprio, Laeven, and Levine (2005).

In addition, there are risk-neutral outside investors who have limited funds amounting to ω to purchase banking assets were these assets to be sold. Outsiders are inefficient users of banking assets relative to bank owners, provided bank owners take good projects. This can be considered a metaphor for some form of expertise or "learning-by-doing" effect in making and administering loans. It is also a simple way of introducing barriers to entry into the banking sector. Formally, we assume that outsiders cannot generate R_t in the high state but only $(R_t - \Delta)$. Thus, when banking assets are sold to outsiders, there may be a social welfare loss due to a misallocation of the assets. We also assume that $\bar{\Delta} > \Delta$ so that outsiders can generate more than what the banks can generate from bad projects. The notion that outsiders may not be able to use banking assets as efficiently as the existing bank owners is akin to the notion of *asset-specificity*, first introduced in the corporate-finance literature by Williamson (1988) and Shleifer and Vishny (1992). This literature suggests that firms, whose assets tend to be *specific*, that is, whose assets cannot be readily redeployed by firms outside of the industry, are likely to experience lower liquidation values or "fire-sale" discounts in cash auctions for asset sales, especially when firms within an industry get simultaneously into financial distress.[6]

Finally, there is a regulator who employs policies such as sale of failed banks' assets, bailouts, and provision of liquidity with the objective of maximizing the total output of the banking sector net of any costs associated with these policy options. These policies are rationally anticipated by banks and depositors. Below we describe these policies informally. The formal description follows in the model analysis.

We assume that deposits are fully insured in the first period. The provision of immediate funds to pay off failed deposits, net of any proceeds from the sale of failed banks' assets, entails fiscal costs for the regulator (assumed to be exogenous to the model). These fiscal costs can be linked to a variety of sources: (i) distortionary effects of tax increases required to fund deposit insurance and bailouts and (ii) the likely effect of huge government deficits on the country's exchange rate, manifested in the fact that banking crises and currency crises have often occurred as "twins" in many countries (especially, in emerging market countries). Ultimately, the fiscal cost we have in mind is one of immediacy: government expenditures and inflows during the regular course of events are smooth, relative to the potentially rapid growth of liabilities, such as deposit-insurance funds, costs of bank bailouts, and liquidity provision, etc.[7] Note that the second period is the last period in our model and there is no further investment opportunity. As a result, our analysis is not affected by whether deposits are insured for the second period or not.

[6]There is strong empirical support for this idea in the corporate-finance literature, for example, in Pulvino (1998) for the airline industry, and in Acharya, Bharath, and Srinivasan (2007) for all defaulted firms in the USA over the period 1981 to 1999 (see also Berger, Ofek, and Swary, 1996; Stromberg, 2000). In the evidence of such specificity for banks and financial institutions, James (1991) studies the losses from bank failures in the USA during the period 1985 through mid-year 1988, and documents that "there is significant going concern value that is preserved if the failed bank is sold to another bank (a "live bank" transaction) but is lost if the failed bank is liquidated by the Federal Deposit Insurance Corporation (FDIC)."

[7]See, for example, the discussion on fiscal costs associated with banking crises in Calomiris (1998). Also, see Dell'Ariccia, Detragiache, and Rajan (2007) for an analysis of the effect of banking crises on real economic activity. Hoggarth, Reis, and Saporta (2001) find that the cumulative output losses have amounted to a whopping 15–20% of annual GDP in the banking crises of the past 25 years. Caprio and Klingebiel (1996) argue that the bailout of the thrift industry cost $180 billion (3.2% of GDP) in the USA in the late 1980s. They also document that the estimated cost of bailouts was 16.8% for Spain, 6.4% for Sweden, and 8% for Finland. Honohan and Klingebiel (2000) find that countries spent 12.8% of their GDP to clean up their banking systems, whereas Claessens, Djankov, and Klingebiel (1999) set the cost at 15–50% of GDP.

If the bank return from the first-period investment is high, then the bank operates for one more period and makes the second-period investment. For a bank to continue operating, it needs to pay its old depositors r_0, and it needs an additional one unit of funds for the second investment. A failed bank cannot generate the needed funds, $(1 + r_0)$, from its depositors at $t = 1$: Its depositors are endowed with only one unit at $t = 1$. Thus, if the return is low, then the bank is in default. We assume that surviving banks (if any) use their first-period profits (and the liquidity provided by the regulator, if any) to purchase failed banks' assets. The regulator decides whether to let surviving banks and/or outsiders purchase failed banks' assets or to intervene and bail out some or all of the failed banks, and whether to grant liquidity to the surviving banks for purchasing assets.[8] Proceeds from the sale of failed banks reduce the net costs of providing deposit insurance. Hence, bailouts are associated with an opportunity cost for the regulator. In a bailout, the regulator may dilute the equity share of bank owners. In liquidity provision policy, the regulator simply transfers liquidity to surviving banks without it being returned in the future. Therefore, provision of liquidity also increases the net costs of providing deposit insurance. These costs are a part of the regulator's objective function.

Depending on the first period returns, say k out of n banks fail. Since banks are identical at $t = 0$, we denote the possible states at $t = 1$ with k.

2. Analysis from an Ex-Post Standpoint

We analyze the model proceeding backwards from the second period to the first period. The deposit rate at t is denoted by r_t and we assume throughout that $R_t > r_t$.

The surviving banks operate for another period at $t = 1$. The probability of having the high return in the second period is equal to α_1 for all banks. As this is the last period, there is no further investment opportunity and the expected payoff to a bank from its second-period investment, $E(\pi_2)$, is equal to $[\alpha_1(R_1 - r_1)]$.

An important possibility is that surviving banks and outsiders may purchase failed banks. Next, we investigate the sale of failed banks' assets and the resulting liquidation values when there are no bailouts or liquidity provision.

2.1 Asset Sales and Liquidation Values

In examining the sale of failed banks' assets, several interesting issues arise. First, surviving banks and outsiders may compete with each other if there are enough resources with them to acquire all failed banks' assets. Second, unless the game for asset sales is specified with reasonable restrictions, an abundance of equilibria arises. To keep the analysis tractable and, at the same time, reasonable, we make the following assumptions:

(i) The regulator pools all failed banks' assets and auctions them to surviving banks and outsiders. Assets of a failed bank can be acquired partially, and the purchasing bank can access the same portion ("branches") of the failed bank's depositors. This assumption of partial sales is motivated by the literature on share auctions (Wilson, 1979) and simplifies the analysis substantially.

[8] Note that given the relative expertise of banks compared to outsiders, it is never optimal to provide liquidity to outsiders. Also, there is no benefit of providing liquidity to a bailed-out bank.

(ii) We denote the surviving banks as $i \in \{1, 2, \ldots, (n-k)\}$ and the outsiders as $i = 0$. Each surviving bank and outsiders submit a schedule $y_i(p) \in [0, k]$ for the amount of assets they are willing to purchase at the price p at which a unit of the banking asset (inclusive of associated deposits) is being auctioned.

(iii) We assume that surviving banks cannot raise additional financing. Hence, the resources available with each surviving bank for purchasing failed banks' assets, denoted by l, equal the first-period profits, $(R_0 - r_0)$.

(iv) The regulator cannot price-discriminate in the auction.

(v) The regulator determines the auction price p to maximize the expected output of the banking sector, subject to the market-clearing condition $\sum_{i=0}^{n-k} y_i(p) \leq k$. Given the allocation inefficiency from sales to outsiders, if surviving banks and outsiders pay the same price, the regulator optimally allocates the maximum possible amount to surviving banks.

(vi) We focus on the symmetric outcome where all surviving banks submit the same schedule, that is, $y_i(p) = y(p)$ for all $i \in \{1, 2, \ldots, (n-k)\}$.

First, we derive the demand schedule for surviving banks. Let $\bar{p} \equiv [\alpha_i(R_1 - r_1)]$, which is the expected second-period profit $E(\pi_2)$ to a surviving bank from the risky asset. The expected profit to a surviving bank from the asset purchase can be calculated as $y(p)[\bar{p} - p]$. The surviving bank wishes to maximize these profits subject to the budget constraint $y(p) \cdot p \leq l$. Hence, for $p < \bar{p}$, surviving banks are willing to purchase the maximum amount of assets using their resources so that their optimal demand schedule is $y(p) = (l/p)$. And, for $p > \bar{p}$, the demand is $y(p) = 0$, and for $p = \bar{p}$, $y(p)$ is indeterminate.[9]

We can derive the demand schedule for outsiders in a similar way. Note that outsiders can generate only $(R_1 - \Delta)$ in the high state. Let $\underline{p} \equiv [\alpha_1((R_t - \Delta) - r_1)] = [\bar{p} - \alpha_1 \Delta]$ be the expected second-period profit for outsiders from owning the risky asset. For $p < \underline{p}$, outsiders are willing to supply all their funds for the asset purchase and their optimal demand schedule is $y_0(p) = (\omega/p)$. For $p > \underline{p}$, the demand is $y_0(p) = 0$, and for $p = \underline{p}$, $y_0(p)$ is indeterminate.

Next, we analyze how the regulator optimally allocates the assets and the price function that results (see Figure 20.2). Note that, in the absence of financial constraints, the efficient outcome is to sell all assets to surviving banks. However, surviving banks may not be able to pay the threshold price of $\underline{p}$ for all assets. If prices fall further, these assets become profitable for outsiders and they enter the auction.

The regulator cannot set $p > \bar{p}$ since in this case we have $y(p) = y_0(p) = 0$. If $p \leq \bar{p}$, and the number of failed banks k is sufficiently small, then surviving banks have enough funds to pay the full price $\bar{p}$ for all assets. Specifically, for $k \leq \underline{k}$, where:

$$\underline{k} = \text{floor}\left(\frac{nl}{l + \bar{p}}\right), \tag{20.2}$$

floor (z) being the largest integer smaller than or equal to z, the regulator sets the auction price at $p^* = \bar{p}$. At this price, surviving banks are indifferent between any quantity of assets purchased. Hence, the regulator can allocate a share $y(p^*) = k/(n-k)$ to each surviving bank.

[9] A formal derivation of the surviving banks' demand schedule that takes into account the correlation structure of assets is available upon request.

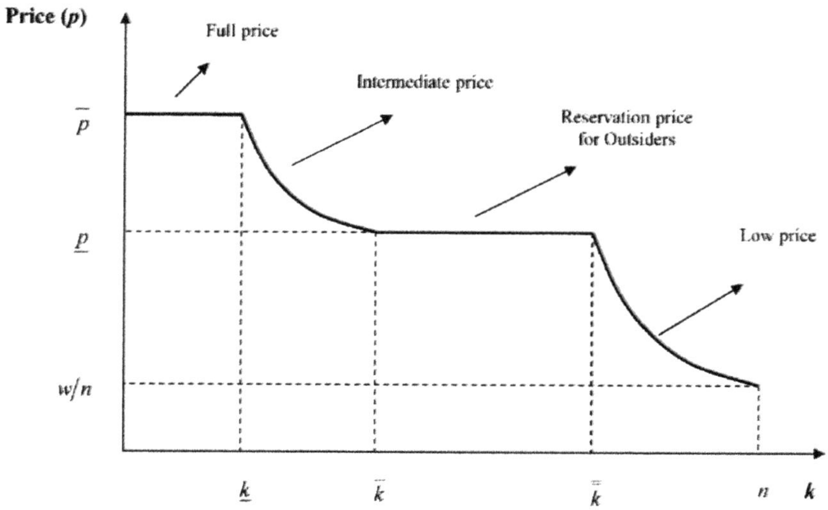

Figure 20.2. Price without bailouts and liquidity provision.

For $k > \underline{k}$, surviving banks cannot pay the full price for all assets but until a critical value $\bar{k}$, they can still pay at least the threshold value of $\underline{p}$, below which outsiders have a positive demand. Formally, for $k \in \{\underline{k} + 1, \ldots, \bar{k}\}$, where

$$\bar{k} = \text{floor}\left(\frac{nl}{l + \underline{p}}\right), \tag{20.3}$$

the regulator sets the price at $p^* = ((n - k)l/k)$, and again, all assets are acquired by surviving banks. In this region, surviving banks use all available funds and the price falls as the number of failures increases, an effect akin to the cash-in-the-market pricing in Allen and Gale (1994, 1998) and the industry-equilibrium hypothesis of Shleifer and Vishny (1992).

For $k > \bar{k}$, surviving banks cannot pay the threshold price of $\underline{p}$ for all assets, and outsiders have a positive demand and are willing to supply their funds for asset purchase. With the injection of outsider funds, prices can be sustained at $\underline{p}$ until some critical number of failures $\bar{\bar{k}} \geq \bar{k}$. However, for $k > \bar{\bar{k}}$, even the injection of outsiders' funds is not enough to sustain the price at $\underline{p}$. Formally, for $k \in \{\bar{k} + 1, \ldots, \bar{\bar{k}}\}$, where

$$\bar{\bar{k}} = \text{floor}\left(\frac{nl + w}{l + \underline{p}}\right), \tag{20.4}$$

the regulator sets the price at $p^* = \underline{p}$. At this price, outsiders are indifferent between any quantity of assets purchased. Hence, the regulator can allocate a share of $y(\underline{p}) = (l/\underline{p})$ to each surviving bank, and the rest, $y_0(\underline{p}) = (k - (n - k)l/\underline{p})$, to outsiders.

And for $k > \bar{\bar{k}}$, the price is again strictly decreasing in k and is given by $p^*(k) = (((n - k)l + w)/k)$, with $y(p^*) = (l/p^*)$ and $y_0(p^*) = (w/p^*)$.

The resulting price function is downward-sloping in the number of failed banks, k, in two separate regions. In the first downward-sloping region, outsiders have not yet entered the market and there is cash-in-the-market pricing given the limited liquidity of surviving banks. In the second downward-sloping region, even the liquidity of outsiders is not enough to sustain the price at p and there is cash-in-the-market pricing given the limited liquidity of the *entire* set of market players bidding for assets. This price function is formally stated below.

Proposition 1: *In the absence of bailout and liquidity provision policies, the price of failed banks' assets as a function of the number of failed banks is as follows:*

$$p^*(k) = \begin{cases} \bar{p} & \text{for} \quad k \leq \underline{k}, \\ \frac{(n-k)l}{k} & \text{for} \quad k \in \{\underline{k}+1, \ldots, \bar{k}\}, \\ \underline{p} & \text{for} \quad k \in \{\bar{k}+1, \ldots, \bar{\bar{k}}\}, \\ \frac{[(n-k)l]+w}{k} & \text{for} \quad k > \bar{\bar{k}}. \end{cases} \tag{20.5}$$

Note that by assumption (iii), surviving banks cannot raise additional financing from outsiders. In an extension in the unabridged version of the article, we relax this assumption and show that our results are robust to allowing surviving banks to issue equity to outsiders.[10]

2.2 Bailouts

To summarize the result from previous analysis, when the number of bank failures is sufficiently small, $k \leq \bar{k}$, all assets are purchased by surviving banks. Since this entails no misallocation cost, the regulator does not have an incentive to intervene ex-post. In contrast, if $k > \bar{k}$, then some of these assets are purchased by outsiders who are not the most efficient users. Hence, it may be optimal for the regulator to bail out some banks (we analyze the liquidity provision policy later). In particular, the regulator compares the misallocation cost resulting from asset sales to outsiders with the cost of bailing out failed banks. Since the misallocation cost is constant, equal to $(\bar{p} - \underline{p}) = (\alpha_1 \Delta)$ per unit of failed banks' assets, the regulator bails out failed banks as long as the marginal cost of a bailout is less than this misallocation cost.

Note that for a failed bank to continue operating at $t = 1$, it needs a total of $(r_0 + 1)$ units. Since available deposits for a bank amount to only one unit (the endowment of its depositors), the bank cannot operate unless the regulator injects r_0. Under our assumption of full deposit insurance, the regulator does inject r_0, so that a bailout is equivalent to the regulator granting permission to a failed bank's owners to operate one more period.

[10] In this case we have two markets: one for the assets of failed banks and one for the shares of surviving banks. When the number of failures is large ($k > \bar{\bar{k}}$), the price of assets falls below the threshold value of outsiders, p. Since purchasing assets at such prices becomes profitable for outsiders, in equilibrium they must be compensated for purchasing shares in surviving banks. As a result, the share price of surviving banks also falls below the fundamental value, $\bar{p}$. In other words, surviving banks can raise equity financing only at a discount. The resulting dilution limits their ability to raise such financing and purchase more assets. Thus, limited funds within the whole system and the resulting cash-in-the-market pricing affects not only the price of failed banks' assets but also the price of shares of surviving banks.

In order to analyze the regulator's decision to bail out or liquidate failed banks, we make the following assumptions:

(i) The regulator incurs a fiscal cost of $f(c)$ when it injects c units of funds with immediacy into the banking sector. We assume that this cost function is strictly increasing and convex (possibly linear): $f' > 0$ and $f'' \geq 0$.

(ii) If the regulator decides not to bail out a failed bank, the existing depositors are paid r_0 through deposit insurance and the failed bank's assets are sold at the market-clearing price. Thus, if the regulator bails out b of the k failed banks, the fiscal cost incurred is $f(kr_0 - (k-b) \cdot p^*(k-b))$, where proceeds from sale of the remaining $(k-b)$ banks are $[(k-b) \cdot p^*(k-b)]$. The crucial difference between bailouts and asset sales from an ex-post standpoint is that proceeds from asset sales lower the fiscal cost, whereas bailouts produce no such proceeds. Hence, bailouts entail an opportunity cost to the regulator in fiscal terms.

(iii) The regulator can take an equity share β in the bailed-out bank(s). Expost, such dilution of a bailed-out bank's equity is merely a transfer from the bank owners to the regulator. However, as argued before, if the regulator takes a share β that is greater than $\left(1-\bar{\theta}\right)$, then bank owners are left with a share of less $\bar{\theta}$ so that they choose the bad project. Since sales to outsiders generate a higher payoff compared to that from a bailed-out bank that chooses a bad project $\left(\bar{\Delta} > \Delta\right)$, the regulator never takes a share greater than $\left(1-\bar{\theta}\right)$. As the value of this stake will be realized in the future, it is assumed not to affect the cost of providing deposit insurance with immediacy.

We characterize the optimal bailout policy under these assumptions. As argued before, the regulator never intervenes when $k \leq \bar{k}$. When $k \in \left\{\bar{k}+1, \ldots, \bar{\bar{k}}\right\}$, the price for assets is $\underline{p}$ and the marginal cost of bailing out the bth bank is:

$$g(k,b) = f(kr_0 - (k-b)\underline{p}) - f(kr_0 - (k-b+1)\underline{p}). \tag{20.6}$$

Since $f(\cdot)$ is convex, this marginal cost is weakly increasing in b. Hence, there is a maximum number of banks, denoted by $\bar{b}(k)$, up to which the bailout costs are smaller than misallocation costs. Formally, $\bar{b}(k)$ satisfies the following conditions:

$$g\left(k,\bar{b}\right) \leq \alpha_1 \Delta < g\left(k,\bar{b}+1\right). \tag{20.7}$$

The maximum number of banks that can be acquired by surviving banks is $(n-k)y(\underline{p})$, where $y(\underline{p}) = l/\underline{p}$. Thus, the regulator bails out $b^*(k) = \min\{\bar{b}(k), [k-(n-k)y(\underline{p})]\}$ banks.

Finally, when $k > \bar{\bar{k}}$, all funds with surviving banks and outsiders, a total of $[(n-k)l + w]$, are collected through asset sales. Hence, if the regulator decides to bail out a bank, proceeds from sales are not affected and bailouts do not lead to any incremental fiscal cost. Thus, the regulator first bails out $\hat{b}(k)$ banks, where $\hat{b}(k)$ is the maximum number of bailouts such that the regulator can collect all available liquidity in the system, $[(n-k)l + w]$, by selling the remaining $[k-\hat{b}(k)]$ banks. With $\hat{b}(k)$ bailouts, the price for the remaining $[k-\hat{b}(k)]$ assets never falls below $\underline{p}$ (see Figure 20.3). Formally, $[(n-k)l + w] = (k-\hat{b}(k))\underline{p}$, which gives

$$\hat{b}(k) = \left[k - \frac{(n-k)l + w}{\underline{p}}\right]. \tag{20.8}$$

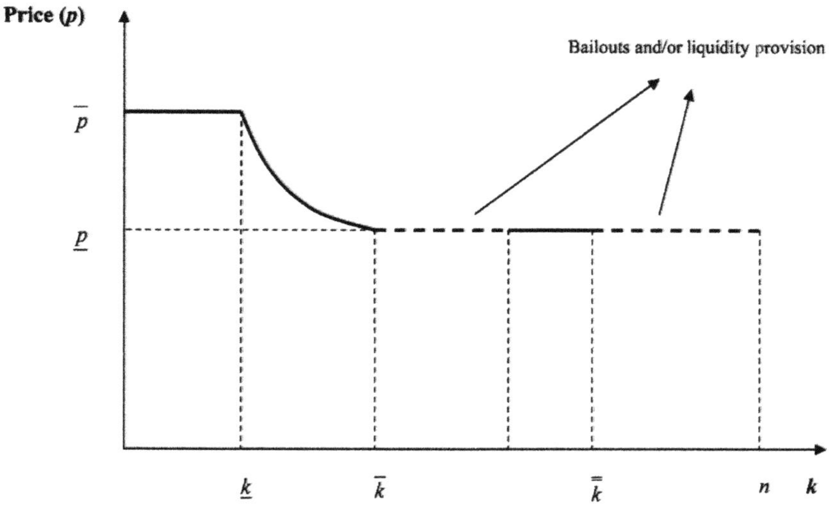

Figure 20.3. Price with bailouts and/or liquidity provision.

An additional bailout beyond $\hat{b}$(k) decreases the proceeds from asset sales by p. Hence, the regulator's decision to bail out additional banks is similar to that for the case where $k \in \{\bar{k}+1, \ldots, \bar{\bar{k}}\}$. In particular, the regulator bails out a total of $[\hat{b}(k) + \bar{\bar{b}}(k)]$ banks, until the marginal bailout cost exceeds the misallocation cost. Thus, $\bar{\bar{b}}(k)$ is given by the conditions

$$h(k, \bar{\bar{b}}) \leq \alpha_1 \Delta < h(k, \bar{\bar{b}}+1), \tag{20.9}$$

where

$$h(k, \bar{\bar{b}}) = f(kr_o - ((k - \hat{b}(k)) - \bar{\bar{b}})\underline{p}) - f(kr_o - ((k - \hat{b}(k)) - \bar{\bar{b}}+1)\underline{p}). \tag{20.10}$$

Note that $[((k - \hat{b}(k)) - \bar{\bar{b}})\underline{p}]$ are the proceeds the regulator receives from asset sales.

To summarize, the regulator's optimal bailout policy b*(k) is such that[11]

$$b^*(k) = \left\{ \begin{array}{ll} \min\left\{\bar{b}(k), \left[k - (n-k)y(\underline{p})\right]\right\} & \text{for } k \in \left\{\bar{k}+1, \ldots, \bar{\bar{k}}\right\}, \\ \min\left\{\hat{b}(k) + \bar{\bar{b}}(k), \left[k - (n-k)y(\underline{p})\right]\right\} & \text{for } k > \bar{\bar{k}} \end{array} \right\} \tag{20.11}$$

Banks are chosen randomly between the three options of being sold to surviving banks, bailed out, or liquidated to outsiders, and the regulator takes a share of β in all bailed-out banks.

[11]The general behavior of the bailout policy $b^*(k)$ is illustrated in Figure 20.4. The bailout policy $b^*(k)$ is not always monotone increasing in k since the marginal cost of bailout, $g(k, b)$, is strictly increasing in k when the fiscal cost function is strictly convex: with more bank failures, the fiscal cost is higher, and given the convexity of this cost function, the opportunity cost of bailouts becomes greater. In other words, $\bar{b}$(k) is decreasing in k when the cost function is convex. A similar argument applies to the marginal cost, $b(k, \bar{\bar{b}})$.

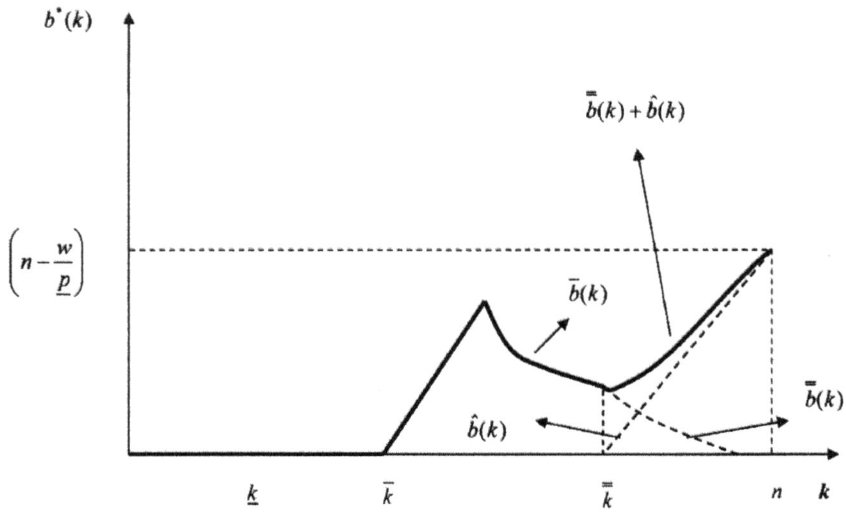

Figure 20.4. Number of bailouts as a function of the number of failures with convex fiscal cost.

To summarize, when $k \leq \bar{k}$, surviving banks purchase all failed banks' assets and the regulator does not intervene. When $k > \bar{k}$, the regulator bails out $b^*(k)$ failed banks, given by conditions in Equations (7), (9), and (11). This optimal bailout policy has the intuitive property that, in states with a large number of bank failures, there are "too many (banks) to liquidate" and the regulator is forced to bail out some failed banks. In particular, irrespective of the fiscal cost function, it is always optimal to bail out up to $\hat{b}(k)$ banks in the region of high bank failures, $k > \bar{\bar{k}}$. Bailouts in this region entail no opportunity costs for the regulator but help avoid misallocation costs. With bailouts, the price never falls below the reservation price of outsiders, p.

In order to derive and explōit a closed-form expression for the optimal bailout policy, we consider a linear cost function: $f(c) = Fc, F > 0$. One analytical advantage of the linear fiscal cost function is that the bailout policy $b^*(k)$ is always monotone increasing (Figure 20.5). Specifically, if the cost parameter F is sufficiently small, then surviving banks acquire as many failed banks as they can and the remaining failed banks (if any) are bailed out, that is, $b^*(k) = [k - ((n-k)l/\underline{p})]$, for $k > \bar{k}$ Otherwise, $b^*(k) = \hat{b}(k)$, for only $k > \bar{\bar{k}}$. This bailout policy is formally statēd below.

Proposition 2: *With a linear fiscal cost function $f(c) = Fc$, the regulator bails out $b^*(k)$ of the k failed banks when $k > \bar{k}$, where $b^*(k)$ is defined as follows:*

$$\text{(i) } \textit{When } F \leq \frac{\alpha_1 \Delta}{\underline{p}},\ b^*(k) = \left[k - \frac{(n-k)l}{\underline{p}}\right]. \tag{20.12}$$

$$\text{(ii) } \textit{When } F > \frac{\alpha_1 \Delta}{\underline{p}},\ b^*(k) = \begin{cases} 0 & \textit{for } k \in \{\bar{k}+1, \ldots, \bar{\bar{k}}\}, \\ \hat{b}(k) & \textit{for } k > \bar{\bar{k}}, \end{cases} \tag{20.13}$$

with $\hat{b}(k)$ given by Equation (8).

Note that the number of bailed-out banks increases linearly in the number of failed banks k with a slope of $[1 + (l/\underline{p})]$, which is greater than one. The reason is that as more banks

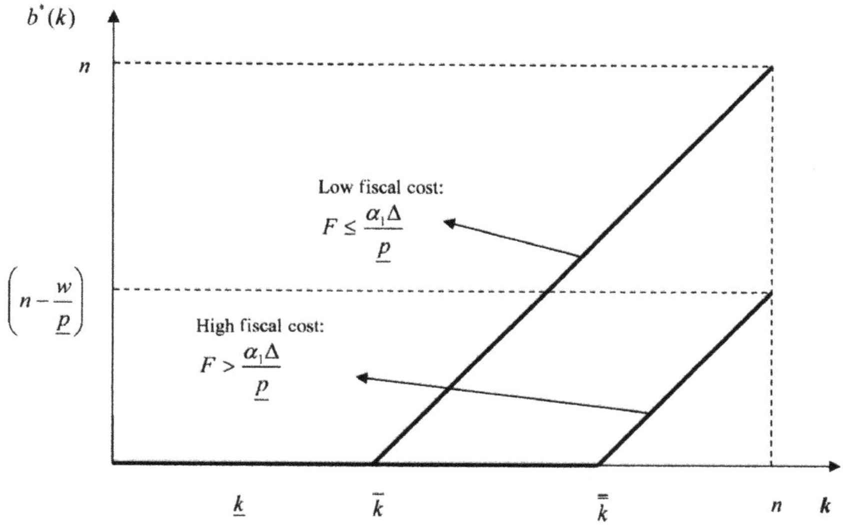

Figure 20.5. Number of bailouts as a function of number of failures with linear fiscal cost.

fail, not only do assets to be sold increase but also total available liquidity with surviving banks decreases. Hence, an additional bank failure increases the quantity of assets that cannot be acquired by surviving banks by more than one. By implication, as more banks fail, the probability of being bailed out $(b^*(k)/k)$ increases as well (at a rate of l/p): as more banks fail, not only the number of bailed-out banks but also the likelihood of being bailed-out increases. We interpret this result as a stronger form of the too-many-to-fail problem.

2.3 Liquidity Provision

While the regulator can use bailouts to prevent allocation inefficiency resulting from sales to outsiders, the regulator can also employ other policies. We consider one such policy of assisting surviving banks for asset purchases wherein the regulator grants liquidity to these banks without it being returned in the future. Since surviving banks are efficient users, this policy can also prevent misallocation of assets. We show below that a specific form of the liquidity provision policy and the ex-post optimal bailout policy result in the same level of ex-post social welfare.

There are two cases to consider: first, when $k \in \{\bar{k}+1, \ldots, \bar{\bar{k}}\}$, and second when $k > \bar{\bar{k}}$.

Note that for $k \in \{\bar{k}+1, \ldots, \bar{\bar{k}}\}$, the participation of outsiders in the auction ensures that the price stays at p (see Figure 20.2). Thus, bailing out a bank increases the total funds needed by the regulator to resolve bank failures by p. Alternatively, the regulator can grant p units of funds to surviving banks to assist their asset purchase. Hence, both liquidity provision and bailout policies increase the funds needed by the regulator by p and both policies prevent the misallocation cost of $(\alpha_1 \Delta)$. Thus, from an ex-post welfare standpoint, bailouts and liquidity provision to surviving banks are equivalent.

Formally, when the regulator employs the ex-post optimal bailout policy for $k \in \{\bar{k}+1, \ldots, \bar{\bar{k}}\}$, $b^*(k)$ banks are bailed out, where $b^*(k)$ is given by Equation (11).

The proceeds from asset sales equal $[(k - b^*(k))\underline{p}]$ and outsiders acquire $[k - ((n - k)l/\underline{p}) - b^*(k)]$ units of assets. Hence, we can write the social welfare cost as:

$$C_b(k) = f\left(kr_o - \left[(k - b^*(k))\underline{p}\right]\right) + \left[k - \frac{(n-k)l}{\underline{p}} - b^*(k)\right](\alpha_1 \Delta). \tag{20.14}$$

Suppose instead that the regulator grants a total of $[b^*(k)\underline{p}]$ units of liquidity to surviving banks so that they can altogether acquire $[((n - k)l/\underline{p}) - b^*(\bar{k})]$ units of assets. Then, all assets are sold at a price of p, resulting in total proceeds of kp. Outsiders acquire $[k - ((n - k)l/\underline{p}) - b^*(k)]$ units of assets, so that we can write the social welfare cost as

$$c_1(k) = f\left(\left[kr_o + b^*(k)\underline{p}\right] - k\underline{p}\right) + \left[k - \frac{(n-k)l}{\underline{p}} - b^*(k)\right](\alpha_1 \Delta), \tag{20.15}$$

which equals $C_b(k)$ in Equation (14), the welfare cost under the bailout policy.

For the second case, recall from the discussion of bailouts that for $k > \bar{\bar{k}}$, bailing out up to $\hat{b}(k)$ banks does not give rise to any incremental fiscal cost. Thus, the regulator first bails out $\hat{b}(k)$ failed banks, so that the price for remaining $[k - \hat{b}(k)]$ assets is $\underline{p}$. Thus, the regulator requires $[kr_0 - (k - \hat{b}(k))\underline{p}]$ units of funds for deposit insurance.

Suppose, instead, that the regulator provides $[\hat{b}(k)\underline{p}]$ units of liquidity to surviving banks. With these additional funds, surviving banks have a total liquidity of $[(n - k)l + \hat{b}(k)p]$, and with outsider funds of w, this is just enough to keep the price at $\underline{p}$. Thus, surviving banks can acquire the $\hat{b}(k)$ failed banks that would have been bailed out and the regulator collects (kp) units from asset sales. Thus, funds needed by the regulator equal $[(kr_o + \hat{b}(k)\underline{p}) - k\underline{p}]$, which is identical to the funds needed under the bailout policy.

Once $\hat{b}(k)$ banks have been sold, the total amount of liquidity in the whole system is sufficient to sustain the price for the sale of remaining $[k - \hat{b}(k)]$ banks at p, whereby an additional bailout or liquidity provision decreases the proceeds from asset sales by $\underline{P}$. Hence the regulator's decision is similar to that for the case where $k \in \{\bar{k} + 1, \ldots, \bar{\bar{k}}\}$. Therefore, as argued above, we can show that the liquidity provision policy and the ex-post optimal bailout policy result in the same level of ex-post social welfare.

To summarize, consider a liquidity provision policy of granting $\hat{l}(k)$ units of liquidity to each surviving bank for assistance in asset purchase, where:

$$\hat{l}(k) = \begin{cases} 0 & \text{for } k \leq \bar{k}, \\ \frac{b^*(k)\underline{p}}{(n-k)} & \text{for } k \in \{\bar{k} + 1, \ldots, n - 1\}, \\ 0 & \text{for } k = n, \end{cases} \tag{20.16}$$

and $b^*(k)$ is the ex-post optimal bailout policy characterized in Equation (11).[12] Then, we obtain the following formal proposition.

Proposition 3: *The ex-post optimal bailout policy characterized in Equation (11), and the liquidity provision policy in Equation (16) result in the same level of ex-post social welfare.*

[12]This liquidity provision policy can be shown to be equivalent to a form of price-discrimination, where the regulator charges different prices to surviving banks and outsiders in the auction for asset sales.

3. Analysis from an Ex-Ante Standpoint

Having shown that the regulator is indifferent between the bailout and liquidity provision policies from an ex-post standpoint, we next analyze the ex-ante optimality of these policies. We allow banks to choose the level of correlation in their investments (so-called the interbank correlation, denoted by ρ), analyze the incentives different regulatory policies create for this choice, and compare the resulting social welfare from an ex-ante standpoint. For the remainder of the article, we use the linear fiscal cost function $f(c) = Fc$.

At $t = 0$, banks choose the composition of loans in their portfolios. There is a common industry that all banks can access and there are n other industries, one for each bank, such that only bank i can access industry i (region, set of customers, etc.). To focus on the effect of interbank correlation, we assume that the returns to all industries are independent and identically distributed. That is, the return from industry i, denoted by $\tilde{R}_{it}$ takes the values $\tilde{R}_{it} \in \{0, R_t\}$, where the probability of having the high return R_t is given by α_t and $i \in \{1, 2, \ldots, n\}$ denotes the bank-specific industries, whereas $i = c$ denotes the common industry. Banks choose whether to invest one unit in the bank-specific industry ($x_i = 0$) or in the common industry ($x_i = 1$). The vector of choices $(x_1, \ldots, x_n)$ determines the joint probability distribution of bank returns. We focus on the joint choice of banks and hence denote x_i's simply as x.

If banks lend to different industries ($x = 0$), then their returns are independent ($\rho = 0$). In this case, we obtain a binomial distribution for the number of bank failures:

$$\Pr(k) = C(n, k)\alpha_0^{n-k}(1 - \alpha_0)^k \quad \text{for } k \in \{0, 1, \ldots, n\}, \tag{20.17}$$

where $C(n, k)$ is the number of combinations of k objects from a total of n. However, if banks choose the common industry ($x = 1$), then their returns are perfectly correlated ($\rho = 1$). In this case, they all survive with probability α_0, that is, $\Pr(0) = \alpha_0$, or they all fail with probability $(1 - \alpha_0)$, that is, $\Pr(n) = (1 - \alpha_0)$.

Next, we analyze the choice of interbank correlation under different regulatory policies.

3.1 Interbank Correlation Under Bailout Policy

We first consider the ex-post optimal bailout policy. We show that the choice of interbank correlation depends on the expected profit from the purchase of failed banks' assets when they survive and the expected subsidy from bailouts when they fail. In Proposition 4, we formally state the conditions under which banks choose to invest in the common industry.

The objective of each bank is to choose the level of interbank correlation ρ at date 0 that maximizes $[E(\pi_1(\rho)) + E(\pi_2(\rho))]$, where discounting has been ignored since it does not qualitatively affect the results. The expected payoff from the first-period investment, $E(\pi_1)$ equals $[\alpha_0(R_0 - r_0)]$, which does not depend on interbank correlation. Hence, banks only take into account the second-period profits, $E(\pi_2)$, while choosing ρ.

If banks invest in the same industry and the return is low, then all banks fail and the regulator bails out (randomly picked) $b^*(n)$ of them taking an equity stake of β in the bailed-out banks. Thus, the expected profit from the second-period investment is given as

$$E(\pi_2(1)) = \alpha_0\, E(\pi_2) + (1 - \alpha_0)\left(\frac{b^*(n)}{n}\right)(1 - \beta)\, E(\pi 2). \tag{20.18}$$

If banks invest in idiosyncratic industries, then using the price function in Figure 20.3, we can see that when only a few banks fail, $k \leq \underline{k}$, surviving banks pay full price for the acquired assets. Thus, banks profit from asset purchase only in states that exhibit cash-in-the-market pricing, that is, when $k \leq \underline{k}$. For $k \in \{\underline{k}+1, \ldots, \bar{k}]$, each surviving bank captures a surplus from asset purchase that equals:

$$y(p^*).[\bar{p} - p^*] = \frac{k}{(n-k)} \cdot \left(\bar{p} - \frac{(n-k)l}{k}\right). \tag{20.19}$$

Note that for $k \leq \bar{k}$, all failed banks are purchased by surviving banks and bank owners of failed banks have no continuation payoffs.

For $k \leq \bar{k}$, the regulator bails out some of the failed banks and the remaining banks are sold at $\underline{p}$. As a result, failed banks receive a bailout subsidy equal to

$$\varphi(k) = \left(\frac{b^*(k)}{k}\right).(1-\beta)E(\pi_2), \tag{20.20}$$

and the surplus per unit of asset purchased is $(\bar{p} - \underline{p}) = (\alpha_1 \Delta)$, so that each surviving bank captures a surplus equal to $[(l/\underline{p}) \cdot (\alpha_1 \Delta)]$. However, surviving banks do not receive any *additional* benefit as k increases (including for $k > \bar{\bar{k}}$), as all their funds are used to purchase assets at price $\underline{p}$.

Given this analysis, we can calculate $E(\pi_2(0))$, which has returns from investments, asset purchases, and bailouts in different states in the second period [see Equation (25) in the Appendix]. Comparing this to $E(\pi_2(1))$ in Equation (18), we obtain the following result.

Proposition 4: *Under the ex-post optimal bailout policy (characterized in Proposition 2), there exists a critical threshold* $\beta^* \in (0, 1)$ *such that*

(i) *if the continuation moral hazard is severe, that is,* $(1-\bar{\theta}) < \beta^*$, *then the regulator takes an equity stake of* β *in the bailed-out bank(s), such that,* $\beta \leq (1-\bar{\theta}) < \beta^*$, *and banks invest in the common industry.*

(ii) *if* $(1-\bar{\theta}) \geq \beta^*$, *then the regulator takes an equity stake* β, *such that* $\beta^* \leq \beta \leq (1-\bar{\theta})$, *and banks invest in different industries.*

This result is in contrast to the case with no bailouts. Without bailouts, failed banks receive no subsidy from the regulator, whereas surviving banks capture some surplus through asset purchase at discounted prices. Hence, without bailouts, banks choose the low correlation. In summary, bailouts lower the ex-post allocation inefficiency but give banks incentives to herd, since bailouts occur only when a sufficiently large number of banks have failed. The presence of moral hazard implies that the regulator cannot always dilute the equity stake of bailed-out banks up to a level that induces banks to invest in different industries.

Intuitively, as w decreases, the second cash-in-the-market region becomes larger ($\bar{\bar{k}}$ decreases). Thus, the region over which $\hat{b}(k)$ banks are always bailed out increases (see Proposition 2). This increases the bailout subsidy when many banks fail and aggravates incentives to herd. Furthermore, β^* is decreasing in w: as w decreases, the regulator must hold a larger share in bailed-out banks to induce low correlation, and, in turn, herding incentives prevail over a larger range of the continuation moral-hazard parameter $\bar{\theta}$.

This leads to the interesting conclusion that the herding incentives of banks are likely to be more pronounced in economies where banking crises are accompanied by lower aggregate wealth. Also, the too-many-to-fail (or too-many-to-liquidate) problem and the induced herding are likely to be more prevalent in economies where the governance of banks is poor: when agency problems such as fraud by bank owners are more severe, banks hold greater equity stakes (high $\bar{\theta}$) for incentive reasons (Caprio, Laeven, and Levine, 2005).

3.2 Interbank Correlation with Liquidity Provision

Under the liquidity provision policy, the expected profit for banks when they invest in different industries can be calculated as in the case of bailout policy. We do not repeat the derivation but highlight the important differences.[13]

On the one hand, when the regulator follows the liquidity provision policy, surviving banks acquire a larger proportion of assets. In particular, for $k > \bar{k}$, they acquire $b^*(k)$ bailed-out banks so that each surviving bank acquires $[b^*(k)/(n-k)]$ additional units of assets. This gives each surviving bank an extra surplus of

$$\gamma(k) = \left(\frac{b^*(k)}{n-k}\right)\bar{p} \tag{20.21}$$

from asset purchase, relative to the case with bailouts.

On the other hand, under the liquidity provision policy, there are no bailouts (unless all banks fail), whereas under the bailout policy, a failed bank is bailed out with probability $(b^*(k)/k)$, giving rise to a bailout subsidy that is given by $\phi(k)$, for $k > \bar{k}$ [see Equation (20)].

Proposition 5 characterizes the choice of interbank correlation under the liquidity provision policy.

Proposition 5: *Under the liquidity provision policy characterized in Equation (16), there exists a critical threshold $\beta_l^* \in (0, 1)$, such that*

(i) *if the continuation moral hazard is severe, that is, $(1-\bar{\theta}) < \beta_l^*$, then the regulator takes an equity stake of P in the bailed-out bank(s), such that $\beta \leq (1-\bar{\theta}) < \beta_l^*$, and banks invest in the common industry.*
(ii) *if $(1-\bar{\theta}) \geq \beta_l^*$, then the regulator takes an equity stake β, such that $\beta_l^* \leq \beta \leq (1-\bar{\theta})$, and banks invest in different industries.*

This result is qualitatively similar to the result in Proposition 4 with the bailout policy. However, outsiders' funds w have a different effect on herding incentives when the regulator employs the liquidity provision policy. Intuitively, for efficient allocation of assets, it is desirable to have as much liquidity with surviving banks as possible relative to the liquidity with outsiders. Recall that as outsider funds w decrease, the second cash-in-the-market region becomes larger ($\bar{\bar{k}}$ decreases). Thus, the region over which the regulator provides liquidity to surviving banks widens. This increases the expected surplus surviving banks make from asset purchase and mitigates bank incentives to herd. Formally, β_l^* is decreasing in w: as w decreases, $E(\gamma)$ increases and the regulator can induce a low ex-ante correlation amongst banks by holding a smaller share in bailed-out banks. In turn, herding incentives can be mitigated over a larger range of the continuation moral-hazard parameter $\bar{\theta}$.

[13] See Equation (29) in the Appendix for the whole expression. Note that when all banks fail ($k = n$), there is no surviving bank to acquire assets and the regulator follows the ex-post optimal bailout policy. As a result, the expected profit for banks when they invest in the common industry ($x = 1$) is the same under liquidity provision and bailout policies, and is given is Equation (18).

3.3 Welfare Analysis

Having derived the choice of interbank correlation under different regulatory policies, we now analyze ex-ante welfare under this choice. We start with the bailout policy.

Let $E(\Pi_t(\rho))$ be the expected output of the banking sector at date t, net of liquidation and bailout costs. If banks invest in the same industry, then with probability α_0, all n banks have the high return, so that $E(\Pi_1(1)) = n\alpha_0 R_0$. However, if they invest in different industries, then with probability $\Pr(k) = C(n,k)\alpha_0^{(n-k)}(1-\alpha_0)^k$, k banks have the low return and the remaining $(n-k)$ banks have the high return. Thus,

$$E(\Pi_1(0)) = R_0 \sum_{k=0}^{n} (n-k)\Pr(k) = R_0 \left[n - \sum_{k=0}^{n} k\Pr(k) \right]. \tag{20.22}$$

Note that $\left[\sum_{k=0}^{n} k\Pr(k)\right]$ is the expected number of failed banks and is equal to $[(1-\alpha_0)n]$ for the binomial distribution, so that $E(\Pi_1(0)) = E(\Pi_1(1)) = n\alpha_0 R_0$. thus, total expected output in the first period is independent of the choice of interbank correlation.

In the second period, the number of banks that survive depends on the outcome of the first-period investments and the regulator's action. If banks invest in the same industry, then with probability α_0, they all succeed; with probability $(1-\alpha_0)$, they all fail, $b^*(n)$ of them are bailed out by the regulator at a fiscal cost of $f(nr_0 - (n - b^*(n))\underline{p})$, and the remaining $(n - b^*(n))$ failed banks are sold to outsiders resulting in a misallocation cost of $[(n - b^*(n))(\alpha_1\Delta)]$. Thus,

$$E(\Pi_2(1)) = n(\alpha_1 R_1) - (1-\alpha_0)[f(nr_0 - (n - b^*(n))\underline{p}) + (n - b^*(n))(\alpha_1\Delta)]. \tag{20.23}$$

If banks invest in different industries, then from Proposition 2, we know that for $k > \bar{k}$, $b^*(k)]$ banks are bailed out, $(n-k)$ surviving banks buy $((n-k)l/\underline{p})$ assets, and the remaining $[k - ((n-k)l/\underline{p}) - b^*(k)]$ banks are sold to outsiders. This gives

$$\begin{aligned} E(\Pi_2(0)) = n(\alpha_1 R_1) &- \sum_{k=1}^{\bar{k}} \Pr(k)\ f(kr_0 - k\cdot p^*(k)) \\ &- \sum_{k=\bar{k}+1}^{n} \Pr(k)\ f(kr_0 - (k - b^*(k))\underline{p}) \\ &- (\alpha_1\Delta)\cdot \sum_{k=\bar{k}+1}^{n} \Pr(k)\left[k - \left(\frac{(n-k)l}{\underline{p}} + b^*(k) \right) \right]. \end{aligned} \tag{20.24}$$

The last term in the RHS represents the expected misallocation cost. The second and third terms represent the fiscal cost for small and large number of bank failures, respectively.

From a welfare standpoint, the optimal level of correlation is $\rho = 0$ when $E(\Pi_2(0)) > E(\Pi_2(1))$. Hence, we compare $E(\Pi_2(1))$ in Equation (23) and $E(\Pi_2(0))$ in Equation (24) term by term. First, we compare the misallocation cost in these two cases. The number of assets purchased by outsiders (weakly) increases in the number of failures. Therefore the misallocation cost is maximum when all n banks fail. When banks choose the high correlation, the probability that they all fail is $(1-\alpha_0)$, whereas when they choose the low correlation, there is a positive misallocation cost with probability of at most $\left[\sum_{k=\bar{k}+1}^{n} \Pr(k)\right]$.

Thus, $(1-\alpha_0) \geq \left[\sum_{k=\bar{k}+1}^{n} \Pr(k)\right]$ is a sufficient condition for the expected misallocation cost to be higher when banks' returns are perfectly correlated.

Next, we show that the expected fiscal cost of deposit insurance net of proceeds from asset sales is strictly greater if banks choose the high correlation. Recall that the expected number of bank failures is equal to $[(1-\alpha_0)n]$ for both levels of correlation. Hence, the expected amount of funds needed for deposit insurance is $[(1-\alpha_0)nr_0]$ in both cases. However, when banks choose the high correlation, if all banks fail, then the regulator collects only $\underline{p}$ per unit of assets from outsiders. In contrast, if banks choose the low correlation, then up to an intermediate number of failures, $\bar{k}$, surviving banks are able to pay a price that is higher than $\underline{p}$. Thus, expected proceeds from asset sales are greater when banks choose the low correlation. Thus, $(1-\alpha_0) \geq \left[\sum_{k=\bar{k}+1}^{n} \Pr(k)\right]$ is in fact a sufficient condition for low correlation to dominate high correlation. For example, if $\bar{k} \geq n/2$ (a condition that simplifies to $l \geq \underline{p}$), then $\alpha_0 < 1/2$ is sufficient to suggest that the socially optimal level of correlation is $\rho = 0$. Hence, we obtain the following formal result.

Proposition 6: *For all α_0, such that $\alpha_0 < (\sum_{k=0}^{\bar{k}} \Pr(k))$, the expected total output of the banking sector at date 0 (net of any anticipated costs of liquidations and bailouts) is maximized when banks operate in different industries, that is, when $\rho = 0$.*

We showed that when the likelihood of bank failures is sufficiently high, social welfare is maximized when banks invest in different industries. Thus, the regulator may wish to implement "hard" closure policies, such as liquidating a sufficient number of banks, in order to create incentives for banks to choose the low correlation.[14] These policies may, however, lack commitment. For example, conditional upon a large number of failures, liquidation of banks may not be credible if bailout costs are smaller than liquidation costs. The regulator can also induce low interbank correlation by diluting the equity share of bailed-out banks (see Proposition 4). However, this may also lack commitment ex-post: if the minimum dilution required to induce low correlation is sufficiently large, then such dilution may have adverse consequences for continuation moral hazard and banks may choose bad projects. We formalize this trade-off below. In particular, we characterize the ex-ante optimal bailout policy assuming that the regulator can commit to its implementation and examine when this policy is not subgame perfect and thus time-inconsistent.

If the regulator commits not to bail out more than a threshold number of banks, then banks may choose to invest in different industries. Thus, we focus on a bailout policy $\tilde{b}^*(k) = \min\{b^*(k), \tilde{b}\}$, where $\tilde{b}$ is the maximum number of bank bailouts that implements the low correlation (see Figure 20.6).[15] Since it is optimal ex post to bail out more than $\tilde{b}$ banks, it suffices to concentrate the analysis on $\tilde{b}^*(k)$ among the set of bailout strategies that implements the low correlation.[16]

It is optimal for the regulator to commit to not bailing out more than $\tilde{b}$ banks if and only if the expected output of the banking industry in this case is higher compared to the case where the regulator follows the ex-post optimal bailout policy and banks choose the

[14]We assume that the regulator cannot write contracts that "force" banks to adopt specific investment choices, that is, the regulator cannot impose regulation that is explicitly contingent on interbank correlation.

[15]A policy that never bails out banks ($\tilde{b} = 0$) implements the low correlation. Hence, $\tilde{b}$ is well defined.

[16]This analysis is interesting only when the ex-post optimal bailout $b^*(k)$ induces banks to choose the high correlation. In other cases, the regulator can implement a low correlation using the ex-post optimal closure policy and we would not observe time-inconsistency in the regulatory actions.

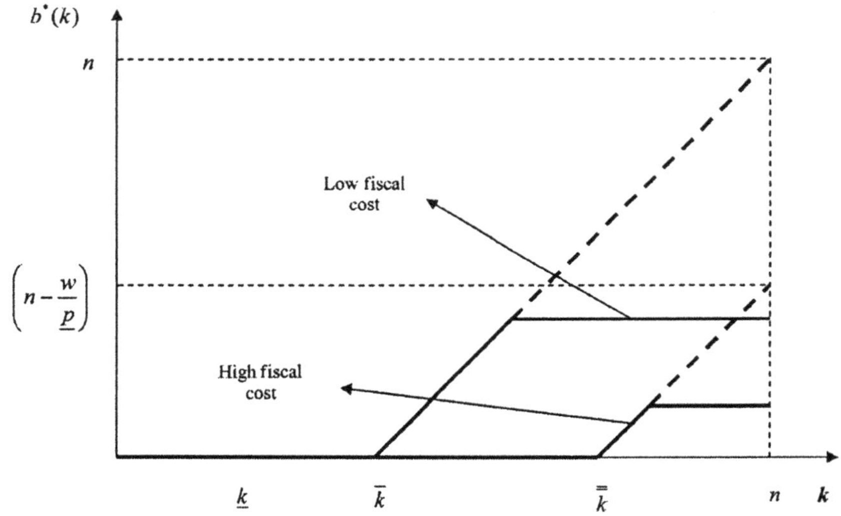

Figure 20.6. Bailout strategy that implements low correlation.

high correlation. The trade-off is simple: ex-post, the regulator cares only about continuation payoffs in states where $k > \bar{k}$, whereas ex ante, the regulator is willing to give up some of these payoffs in order to induce better incentives for banks to be less correlated. This gives us the following proposition, which shows that the time-inconsistency of ex-ante optimal policy arises when the likelihood of bank failures, $(1 - \alpha_0)$. is sufficiently high.[17]

Proposition 7: *For all α_0, such that $\alpha_0 \leq [1 - (\lambda(\underline{p}/\tilde{p}^*(n)) \sum_{k=\bar{k}+1}^{n} \Pr(k))]$, where $\lambda =$ $\max\{[(\alpha_{1\Delta})/(F\,\underline{p})], 1\}$, if the regulator can credibly commit to a bailout strategy ex-ante, then it is optimal to commit to the strategy $\tilde{b}^*(k) = \min\{b^*(k), \tilde{b}\}$, where $\tilde{b}$ is the maximum number of bank bailouts that implements the low correlation and $b^*(k)$ is defined in Equation (12).*

It is possible that the regulator can mitigate this time-inconsistency problem using the liquidity provision policy characterized in Equation (16), which achieves the same level of ex-post social welfare as the ex-post optimal bailout policy. With liquidity grant, the surviving banks' surplus from asset purchase increases. Thus, to mitigate herding incentives, the regulator may not have to resort to excessive liquidation in states where banking crises are systemic. To illustrate this, we show that under the liquidity provision policy, the regulator can implement low correlation over a wider range of parameter values.

Recall that under the liquidity provision policy, surviving banks receive an additional surplus of $\gamma(k)$ given by Equation (21), but there are no bailouts. Under the ex-post optimal bailout policy, a failed bank receives an expected bailout subsidy of $\phi(k)$, as given in Equation (20). Hence, the condition $\gamma(k) > \phi(k)$ for all $k > \bar{k}$ is sufficient to show that the expected surplus for banks from asset purchases outweighs the expected loss of bailout subsidy. In particular, if this condition holds, then the regulator can implement low

[17]The proof for this Proposition is available upon request.

correlation under the liquidity provision policy by taking a smaller stake in the bailed-out banks, that is, $\beta_l^* \leq \beta^*$. Proposition 8 states a sufficient condition for this result to hold.

Proposition 8: For $l \geq \underline{p}$, *we have* $\beta_l^* < \beta^*$.

First, $l \geq \underline{p}$ is only a sufficient condition which guarantees that $\gamma(k) > \phi(k)$ for all $k > \bar{k}$. Herding incentives are in fact mitigated under the liquidity provision policy over a larger range of parameter values. Second, the condition $l \geq \underline{p}$ simplifies to $\bar{k} \geq n/2$, a condition under which it is socially optimal to have low interbank correlation for all $\alpha_0 < 1/2$. Furthermore, $\gamma(k)$ increases faster in the number of failures k than $\phi(k)$. Hence, $\gamma(\bar{k}) > \phi(\bar{k})$, is sufficient to obtain $\gamma(k) > \phi(k)$ for all $k > \bar{k}$. And the condition $l \geq \underline{p}$ simply guarantees that. To summarize, assisting surviving banks by granting them liquidity to purchase failed banks is an ex-post optimal policy that dominates the bailout policy from an ex-ante standpoint.

4. Empirical Support and Robustness

In this section, we discuss how our article relates to the resolution of bank failures in practice and also provide empirical support for the assumptions and results of our model.

4.1 Resolution of Bank Failures

One of our main results is that in states with a small number of bank failures ($k \leq \bar{k}$), the regulator should let surviving banks acquire failed banks, whereas with a larger number of failures ($k > \bar{k}$), it may be optimal for the regulator to intervene. In particular, we allowed the regulator to employ a variety of policy options including bailouts, sales to surviving banks with and without liquidity assistance, and finally, sales to outsiders.

These policies broadly cover the spectrum of options regulators employ in practice to resolve bank failures. The report by the Basel Committee on Banking Supervision (BCBS) (2002) provides a detailed discussion. We provide a brief summary. At one end of the spectrum, regulators seek a private-sector resolution first, where the troubled bank is sold to another healthy institution without any government assistance. These arrangements are typically called "Merger and Acquisition" (M&A) agreements.

However, during systemic crises, such private-sector resolution is not always feasible and regulators employ other policies, which are broadly classified as "Purchase and Assumption"(P&A) agreements with surviving banks. Such P&A agreements are generally enhanced by government guarantees to attract buyers. For example, if the whole bank is purchased, then the acquirer may receive a government payment covering the difference between the market value of assets and liabilities. If only some deposits are purchased, the acquirer may be given the option of purchasing any of the others and get their pick of bank assets. Furthermore, P&A agreements typically include some form of a put option, whereby the government promises to buy back the assets at a stated percentage of value within a specified time frame, and often also include a contractual profit or loss-sharing agreement. And, at the other end of the spectrum, banks are kept open through an injection of capital, which corresponds to bailouts in our article. Goodhart and Schoenmaker (1995) provide a cross-country survey of 104 bank failures in 24 different countries during the 1980s and early 1990s that corroborates this summary. They show that liquidation of failed banks has not been the rule but the exception. While 31 of the 104 banks were liquidated, 22 were bailed out using a rescue package and 49 were taken over by other banks. Hawkins and Turner (1999, Table 12, p. 40) document evidence on the resolution methods used during the banking crises in the 1980s and 1990s for 23 countries. They show that in 20 of these countries, government capital injection was used as one of the resolution policies; in 20 countries, domestic bank mergers were employed; and, troubled banks were taken over by foreign banks in 9 countries.

Santomero and Hoffman (1999) discuss the US Thrift Crisis, banking crises in Norway, Sweden, and Finland, and the Credit Lyonnais experience in France. They document that liquidation of banking assets has not been a preferred strategy during systemic crises since fire-sale prices, large bid-ask spreads, and the virtual lack of bids are common elements of a mass liquidation. Furthermore, they report that during systemic crises, it has been costly for regulators to close down a significant portion of the banking system due to issues relating to investment disruption and consumer confidence. Kasa and Spiegel (1999) use bank closure data for the USA for the period 1992 through 1997 and provide similar evidence. They compare an *absolute* closure rule, which closes banks when their asset/liability ratios fall below a given threshold with a *relative* closure rule, which closes banks when this ratio falls sufficiently below the industry average. A direct implication of the relative closure rule is forbearance when the banking industry as a whole performs poorly. They find strong evidence that US bank closures were based on relative performance during this period.

Finally, Brown and Dinc (2006) analyze failures among large banks in 21 major emerging markets in the 1990s and show that the government decision to close or take over a failing bank depends on the financial health of other banks in that country. In particular, intervention is delayed if other banks are also weak. They show that this too-many-to-fail effect is robust to controlling for bank-level characteristics, macroeconomic factors, political factors such as electoral cycle and potential IMF pressure, as well as worldwide time-specific factors.

4.2 Evidence on Herding

We modeled herding by banks as coordination in lending to similar firms or sectors of the economy. This coordination is a rational choice of banks given the trade-off between surplus from differentiation and herding. This form of herding is different from irrational herding, reputation-based herding, or herding resulting from informational externalities.[18]

In practice, there are countervailing effects such as competition in loan margins, which make herding less attractive (Winton, 2000; and Acharya, Hasan, and Saunders, 2006). Though our model does not allow for competition in lending, it does consider one countervailing effect on herding incentives: when banks survive, they acquire failed banks at discounted prices. This feature of our model leads to precise implications for when we should expect herding incentives to dominate. In particular, herding incentives are stronger when the likelihood of bank defaults is high (Proposition 7). Thus, the question of whether banks herd or not, and in which states, is ultimately an empirical one.

Hence, we provide evidence supportive of our modeling approach and results, and also document that banks correlate their portfolios in several other ways that are less likely to erode profit margins.

[18] See the survey by Devenow and Welch (1996) for a detailed discussion of various forms of herding.

In evidence that studies correlation of different banks' assets measured through the correlation of their equity returns, Luengnaruemitchai and Wilcox (2004) find that during the period 1976–2001, banks in the U.S. chose market and asset betas that clustered together more when the banking sector was troubled, in terms of banks having low capital ratios. They find a lower standard deviation of bank betas in such times. Their interpretation of this finding is one of herding by banks to seek "safety in similarity": "[Banks] more tightly mimicked each other during troubled times." In troubled times, banks would be concerned more about regulatory bailouts, as implied by our model.

A number of studies have analyzed herding by employing evidence from the over-exposure of banks to emerging market economies before the debt crisis of 1982–1984. Guttentag and Herring (1984), for example, discuss three potential explanations. While their first two explanations are related to the bounded rationality of banks, the only rational explanation they consider is that too-many-to-fail guarantees created incentives for banks to get over-exposed to risks in these countries. They suggest that deposit insurance, existence of lender-of-last-resort facilities, as well as official support for debtor countries from the IMF gave banks the impression that they would be protected against risks. They also suggest that by herding and keeping concentrations in line with each other, banks made sure that any problem that occurred would be a system-wide problem, not just the problem of an individual institution. Banks reasoned that this in turn would make it harder for the regulatory authorities to blame or discriminate against individual institutions and would induce governments to take actions to prevent the adverse consequences of a system-wide banking crisis.

While directly investing in similar industries is one way for banks to increase the correlation of their returns, there are also other approaches. First, banks could bet on systematic risk factors such as interest-rate risk through choosing from a range of products such as mortgages and interest-rate derivatives. That is, banks could specialize within a class of risk exposures to achieve a trade off between incentives to correlate and to differentiate. Second, banks can achieve high levels of default correlation through interbank lending since this leads to the problems of one bank being transmitted to other banks in a contagion-type phenomenon, which indirectly increases the likelihood of bailout of the problem bank.

Another interesting alternative for banks to get exposed to similar risks without erosion of profit margins is to participate in syndicated loans to common set of borrowers (as in the debt crises of 1980s for less developed countries and the extension of telecom loans in late 1990s). Through syndication, banks can ensure that they are more likely to receive regulatory subsidies when loans perform poorly, affecting all syndicate members. Adams (1991, Chapter 10) argues that before the emerging market debt crisis, banks comforted themselves by herding, thinking that as long as all banks made similar loans, any crisis would be system-wide and would force governments to bail out those countries in trouble.[19] She also argues that syndicated loans acted as an important vehicle for herding and hundreds of billions of dollars in loans were syndicated between 1970 and 1982. On a similar point, Jain and Gupta (1987) also discuss the role of syndicated loans for bank herding during the emerging market debt crisis.

[19]According to Pedro-Pablo Kuczynski, a former World Bank official, Peruvian cabinet minister, and later an investment banker with First Boston Corporation, "Bank preferred to lend to the public sector, not for ideological reasons but because government guarantees eliminated commercial risk."

5. Conclusion

In this article, we developed a theoretical framework with an arbitrary number of banks wherein liquidity effects in the market for asset sales lead to welfare costs during systemic crises, which is conducive to a comprehensive normative analysis of regulatory options to resolve bank failures.

The framework is flexible and tractable to provide a foundation for examining several other aspects of financial crises and their resolution. For example, surviving banks are financially constrained in our model and use their first-period profits for asset purchase. It would be interesting to extend the model to endogenize banks' choice of available funds for asset purchase, in particular, by allowing banks to choose ex-ante a portfolio of liquid and illiquid assets. Such an extension can shed light on the relative levels of socially and privately optimal liquidity choices of banks, and how they respond to regulatory policies. Repullo (2005), for instance, argues that the traditional lender-of-last-resort policies (without penalty rates on borrowers) can lead to smaller liquidity buffers in the banking system. Interestingly, the liquidity provision policy proposed in our article does not suffer from this problem: banks receive liquidity under this policy when they survive and not when they are in trouble.

Appendix

Proof of Proposition 4: For $k \leq \bar{k}$, no bank is bailed out, all assets are purchased by surviving banks (capturing a surplus of $[(k/(n-k))E(\pi_2) - l]$), and a failed bank's expected second period profit is equal to zero. For $k > \bar{k}$, $b^*(k)$ banks are bailed out, where $b^*(k)$ is given in Proposition 2. The expected continuation payoff for a bailed-out bank is $(1-\beta)E(\pi_2)$, where β is the regulator's share, and each surviving bank captures a surplus of $[(l/\underline{p})(\alpha_1\Delta)]$.

If banks choose $x = 0$, their returns are independent and we have a binomial distribution for the number of failures, k. We can write banks' expected profit $E(\pi_2(0))$ as

$$= \alpha_0 \left[E(\pi_2) + \sum_{j=\underline{k}+1}^{\bar{k}} \left[P(j) \left[\left(\frac{j}{n-j} \right) E(\pi_2) - l \right] \right] \right]$$
$$+ \alpha_0 \left[\sum_{j=\bar{k}+1}^{n-1} \left[P(j) \left(\frac{l(\alpha_1\Delta)}{\underline{p}} \right) \right] \right]$$
$$+ (1-\alpha_0) \left[\sum_{j=\bar{k}}^{n-1} \left[P(j) \left(\frac{b^*(j+1)}{j+1} \right) (1-\beta) E(\pi_2) \right] \right], \qquad (20.25)$$

where j is the number of failures among the remaining $(n-1)$ banks and $P(j)$ is the corresponding probability for this event, when we exclude the bank that we calculate the expected profit for. For the binomial distribution, we have that $P(j) = C(n-1, j)\,\alpha_0^{n-1-j}(1-\alpha_0)^j$.

If banks choose $x = 1$, they are perfectly correlated and their expected return is

$$E(\pi_2(1)) = \alpha_0 E(\pi_2) + (1 - \alpha_0)\left(\frac{b^*(n)}{n}\right)(1 - \beta) E(\pi_2). \tag{20.26}$$

Next, we derive the critical equity share, denoted by β^*, which if taken by the regulator in each bailed-out bank, then banks would choose not to invest in the common industry.

Note that, banks choose $x = 1$ if and only if $E(\pi_2(1)) - E(\pi_2(0)) > 0$. Let $d(\beta) = \left[E(\pi_2(1)) - E(\pi_2(0))\right]$, where

$$d(\beta) = (1 - \alpha_0)(1 - \beta)E(\pi_2)\left[\frac{b^*(n)}{n} - \sum_{j=\bar{k}}^{n-1}\left[P(j)\left(\frac{b^*(j+1)}{j+1}\right)\right]\right]$$
$$- \alpha_0\left[\sum_{j=\underline{k}+1}^{\bar{k}}\left[p(j)\left(\frac{(j)}{n-j}\right)E(\pi_2) - l\right]\right]$$
$$+ \left[\sum_{j=\bar{k}+1}^{n-1}\left[p(j)\left(\frac{l(\alpha_1 \Delta)}{\underline{p}}\right)\right]\right]. \tag{20.27}$$

Note that only the first term depends on β. Also, note that $(b^*(k)/k)$ is increasing in k. Hence, $(b^*(n)/n) > (b^*(k)/k)$ for all $k \in \{0, \ldots, n-1\}$ and we have $\partial d/\partial\beta < 0$. Thus, there exists a unique β^*, such that $\left[E(\pi_2(1)) - E(\pi_2(0))\right] > 0$ if and only if $\beta < \beta^*$, where

$$\beta^* = 1 - \left[\frac{\alpha_0\left(\sum_{j=\underline{k}+1}^{\bar{k}}\left[p(j)\left[\left(\frac{j}{n-j}\right)E(\pi_2) - l\right]\right] + \sum_{j=\bar{k}+1}^{n-1}\left[p(j)\left(\frac{l(\alpha_1\Delta)}{\underline{p}}\right)\right]\right)}{(1 - \alpha_0)E(\pi_2)\left[\frac{b^*(n)}{n} - \sum_{j=\bar{k}}^{n-1}\left[p(j)\left(\frac{b^*(j+1)}{j+1}\right)\right]\right]}\right]. \tag{20.28}$$

For $\beta^* \leq 0$, banks always choose $x = 0$. For $\beta^* > 0$, banks choose $x = 1$ when $\beta < \beta^*$, otherwise, they choose $x = 0$.

Note, however, that the regulator will ex-post never take a share β that exceeds $(1 - \bar{\theta})$: it is better to liquidate the bank than to have it run inefficiently by bank owners due to poor provision of incentives. Thus, if $(1 - \bar{\theta}) < \beta^*$, then the regulator's share β is smaller than β^* in the subgame perfect equilibrium, and banks choose $x = 1$. If $(1 - \bar{\theta}) \geq \beta^*$, then the regulator takes a share β between β^* and $(1 - \bar{\theta})$ and this induces banks to choose $x = 0$.

Also, note that with the linear cost function, $(b^*(k)/k)$ is increasing in k, whereby the denominator in the last term in Equation (27) is positive, and, in turn, $\beta^* < 1$ always. ◇

Proof of Proposition 5: Note that, under the liquidity provision policy characterized in Equation (16), for $k > \bar{k}$, each surviving bank can acquire $[(l/\underline{p}) + (b^*(k)/(n-k))]$ units of failed banks' assets, where $b^*(k)$ is given by the ex-post optimal bailout policy.

Hence, if banks choose $x = 0$, we can write each bank's expected profit $E\left(\pi_2^l(0)\right)$ as

$$= \alpha_0\left[E(\pi_2) + \sum_{j=\underline{k}+1}^{\bar{k}}\left[P(j)\left[\left(\frac{j}{(n-j)}\right)\bar{p} - l\right]\right]\right.$$

$$+ \alpha_0\left[\sum_{j=\bar{k}+1}^{n-1}\left[P(j)\left[\left(\frac{l}{\underline{p}} + \frac{b^*(j)}{(n-j)}\right)\bar{p} - l\right]\right]\right]$$

$$+ (1-\alpha_0)^n\left(\frac{b^*(n)}{n}\right)(1-\beta)E(\pi_2), \tag{20.29}$$

where j is the number of failures among the remaining $(n - 1)$ banks and $P(j)$ is the corresponding probability for this event, when we exclude the bank that we calculate the expected profit for.

If banks choose $x = 1$, they are perfectly correlated and their expected return is

$$E(\pi_2^l(1)) = \alpha_0 E(\pi_2) + (1-\alpha_0)\left(\frac{b^*(n)}{n}\right)(1-\beta)E(\pi_2) \tag{20.30}$$

Note that, banks choose $x = 1$ and only if $E(\pi_2(1)) > E(\pi_2(0))$. Let $d_t(\beta) = [E(\pi_2(1)) - E(\pi_2(0))]$, where:

$$d_t(\beta) = (1-\alpha_0)(1-(1-\alpha_0)^{n-1})\left(\frac{b^*(n)}{n}\right)(1-\beta)E(\pi_2)$$

$$-\alpha_0\left[\sum_{j=\underline{k}+1}^{\bar{k}}\left[P(j)\left[\left(\frac{j}{(n-j)}\right)\bar{p} - l\right]\right] + \sum_{j=\bar{k}+1}^{n-1}\left[P(j)\left[\left(\frac{l}{\underline{p}} + \frac{b^*(j)}{(n-j)}\right)\bar{p} - l\right]\right]\right]. \tag{20.31}$$

Note that only the first term depends on β and we have $\partial d_l/\partial\beta < 0$. Thus, $E(\pi_2(1)) - E(\pi_2(0)) > 0$ if and only if $\beta < \beta_l^*$ where

$$\beta_l^* = 1 - \left[\frac{\alpha_0\left[\sum_{j=\underline{k}+1}^{\bar{k}}\left[P(j)\left[\left(\frac{j}{n-j}\right)E(\pi_2) - l\right]\right] + \sum_{j=\bar{k}+1}^{n-1}\left[P(j)\left[\left(\frac{l}{\underline{p}} + \frac{b^*(j)}{(n-j)}\right)\bar{p} - l\right]\right]\right]}{(1-\alpha_0)(1-(1-\alpha_0)^{n-1})\left(\frac{b^*(n)}{n}\right)E(\pi_2)}\right]. \tag{20.32}$$

For $\beta_l^* > 0$, banks choose $x = 1$ when $\beta < \beta_l^*$, otherwise, they choose $x = 0$.

Note, however, that the regulator will ex-post never take a share β that exceeds $(1 - \bar{\theta})$: it is better to liquidate the bank than to have it be run inefficiently by bank owners due to the poor provision of incentives. Thus, if $(1 - \bar{\theta}) < \beta_l^*$, then the regulator's share β is smaller than β_l^* in the subgame perfect equilibrium, and banks choose $x = 1$. If $(1 - \bar{\theta}) \geq \beta_l^*$, then the regulator takes a share β between β_l^* and $(1 - \bar{\theta})$ and this induces banks to choose $x = 0$.

Note that the denominator in the last term in the above expression for β_l^* is positive, and, in turn, $\beta_l^* < 1$ always. For $\beta_l^* \leq 0$, banks always choose $x = 0$.

Proof of Proposition 6: The socially optimal level of correlation is $\rho = 0$ when $E(\Pi_2(0)) > E(\Pi_2(1))$. With the linear fiscal cost function $f(c) = Fc$, we have

$$E(\Pi_2(1)) = n(\alpha_1 R_1) - \underbrace{(1-\alpha_0)\left[nFr_0\right]}_{\text{expected cost of insurance}} + F\underbrace{(1-\alpha_0)\left[(n-b^*(n))\underline{p}\right]}_{\text{expected recovery from asset sales}}$$

$$+\underbrace{(1-\alpha_0)\left[(n-b^*(n))(\alpha_1\Delta)\right],}_{\text{expected misallocation cost}} \tag{20.33}$$

$$E(\Pi_2(0)) = n(\alpha_1 R_1) - \underbrace{\sum_{k=1}^{n}\Pr(k)k(Fr_o)}_{\text{expected cost of insurance}}$$

$$-\underbrace{\sum_{k=\bar{k}+1}^{n}\Pr(k)\left(k - \frac{(n-k)l}{\underline{p}} - b^*(k)\right)[\alpha_1\Delta]}_{\text{expected misallocation cost}}$$

$$+F\left[\underbrace{\sum_{k=1}^{\bar{k}}\Pr(k)(k\cdot p^*(k)) + \sum_{k=\bar{k}+1}^{n}\Pr(k)\left((k-b^*(k))\underline{p}\right)}_{\text{expected recovery from asset sales}}\right]. \tag{20.34}$$

For $E(\Pi_2(0))$, we can write the expected cost of insurance as $(1-\alpha_0)n\,Fr_0$. Note that this term is common in $E(\Pi_2(1))$ and $E(\Pi_2(0))$.

Note that $p^*(k) > \underline{p}$ for $k = 1, \ldots, \bar{k}$ and we can show that the expected recovery from asset sales when $p = 0$ is greater than

$$\underline{p}\left[\sum_{k=1}^{n}\Pr(k)k - \sum_{k=\bar{k}+1}^{n}\Pr(k)b^*(k)\right]. \tag{20.35}$$

If $(1-\alpha_0) \geq \left[\sum_{k=\bar{k}+1}^{n}\Pr(k)\right]$, then the above expression is greater than the expected funds recovered from asset sales when $\rho = 1$, which is equal to $\left((1-\alpha_0)(n-b^*(n))\underline{p}\right)$.

Note that, using Equations (12) and (13), we can show that the number of failed banks' assets that are sold to outsiders (weakly) increases in k. Thus, $[k - ((n-k)l/\underline{p}) - b^*(k)] \leq (n - b^*(n))$ for all $k = \bar{k}+1, \ldots, n-1$, and these two expressions are equal when $k = n$. Again, if $(1-\alpha_0) \geq \left[\sum_{k=\bar{k}+1}^{n}\Pr(k)\right]$, the expected cost of misallocation of failed banks' assets is greater when $\rho = 1$.

Thus, if $(1-\alpha_0) \geq \left[\sum_{k=\bar{k}+1}^{n}\Pr(k)\right]$ which can also be written as $\alpha_0 < [\sum_{k=0}^{\bar{k}}\Pr(k)]$, then $E(\Pi_2(0)) > E(\Pi_2(1))$ and the socially optimal level of correlation is $\rho = 0$.

Proof of Proposition 8: Recall from the proofs of Propositions 4 and 5 that:

$$d(\beta) = \left[E\left(\pi_2(1)\right) - E\left(\pi_2(0)\right)\right] \text{ and}$$
$$d_1(\beta) = \left[E\left(\pi_2^1(1)\right) - E\left(\pi_2^1(0)\right)\right].$$

Let $D(\beta) = d(\beta) - d_l(\beta)$. Note that under both the bailout and liquidity provision policies, the expected return for banks from investing in the common industry is the same, that is, $E\left(\pi_2^l(1)\right) = E\left(\pi_2(1)\right)$. Hence, we have

$$D(\beta) = E\left(\pi_2^l(0)\right) - E\left(\pi_2(0)\right).$$

Recall that $\partial d/\partial\beta < 0$ and $\partial d_1/\partial\beta < 0$. Hence $D(\beta) \geq 0$ for all β, implies that $\beta_l^* \leq \beta^*$.

Next, we find a sufficient condition under which $D(\beta) \geq 0$

We have $D(\beta) = E\left(\pi_2^l(0)\right) - E\left(\pi_2(0)\right)$ given as

$$= \alpha_0 \left[\sum_{j=\bar{k}+1}^{n-1} \left[p(j)\left[\left(\frac{b^*(j)}{n-j}\right)\bar{p}\right]\right]\right]$$
$$- (1-\alpha_0)\left[\sum_{j=\bar{k}}^{n-2} \left[P(j)\left(\frac{b^*(j+1)}{j+1}\right)(1-\beta)\bar{p}\right]\right], \tag{20.36}$$

where j is the number of failures among the remaining $(n-1)$ banks and $P(j)$ is the corresponding probability, when we exclude the bank that we calculate the expected profit for. Note that we can write this as

$$= \sum_{k=\bar{k}+1}^{n-1} \left[\Pr(k)\left[\underbrace{\left(\frac{b^*(k)}{n-k}\right)\bar{p}}_{=\gamma(k)}\right]\right] - \left[\sum_{j=\bar{k}+1}^{n-1} \left[\Pr(k)\left[\underbrace{\left(\frac{b^*(k)}{k}\right)(1-\beta)\bar{p}}_{\phi(k)}\right]\right]\right] \tag{20.37}$$

$$= \sum_{k=\bar{k}+1}^{n-1} \left[\Pr(k)\left[\left(\gamma(k) - \phi(k)\right)\right]\right], \tag{20.38}$$

where $\Pr(k)$ is the probability of having k failed banks out of the n banks. The benefit from the liquidity provision policy, which is denoted by $\gamma(k)$, arises from the extra units of failed banking assets a surviving bank can purchase. The cost of the liquidity provision policy, denoted by $\phi(k)$, is basically the forgone bailout subsidy.

Hence, a sufficient condition for $\left[E\left(\pi_2^l(0)\right) - E\left(\pi_2(0)\right)\right] \geq 0$ is $[\gamma(k) - \phi(k)] \geq 0$ for all $k \in \{\bar{k}+1, \ldots, n-1\}$. We have

$$\gamma(k) - \phi(k) = \left[\left(\frac{b^*(k)}{(n-k)}\right) - \left(\frac{b^*(k)}{k}\right)(1-\beta)\right]\bar{p} \tag{20.39}$$

$$= b^*(k)\bar{p}\left[\left(\frac{k-(n-k)(1-\beta)}{(n-k)k}\right)\right]. \tag{20.40}$$

Note that $[\gamma(k) - \phi(k)]$ is increasing in k. Hence, if $[\gamma(\bar{k}+1) - \phi(\bar{k}+1)] \geq 0$, then $[\gamma(k) - \phi(k)] \geq 0$ for all $k \in \{\bar{k}+1, \ldots, n-1\}$. Thus,

$$(\bar{k}+1) - (n - (\bar{k}+1))(1-\beta) \leq 0,$$

is a sufficient condition for $[E(\pi_2^1(0)) - E(\pi_2(0))] \leq 0$.

Also, note that $(\bar{k}+1) \geq (nl/(l+\underline{p}))$ from the expression for $\bar{k}$ from Equation (3). And note that the expression in Equation (41) is increasing in the number of failed banks, so that the inequality in Equation (41) is satisfied for $(\bar{k}+1)$ if it is satisfied for $(nl/(l+\underline{p}))$. Hence, we can show that the condition in Equation (41) is satisfied when

$$l - (1-\beta)\underline{p} \geq 0.$$

Hence, for $(1-\beta) \leq (l/\underline{p})$, we have $\gamma(k) \leq \phi(k)$, for all $k > \bar{k}$. A sufficient condition for this to hold for all $\beta \in [0, 1]$ is $l \geq \underline{p}$. This guarantees that the expected profit from choosing idiosyncratic industries is higher when the regulator uses the liquidity provision policy instead of the ex-post optimal bailout policy. Hence, for $l \geq \underline{p}$, the regulator can induce banks to choose the low correlation for a wider range of parameter values when the liquidity provision policy is used, that is, $\beta_l^* \leq \beta^*$. ◇

References

Acharya, V. 2001. A Theory of Systemic Risk and Design of Prudential Bank Regulation, Working Paper, New York University and London Business School.

Acharya, V., S. Bharath, and A. Srinivasan. 2007. Does Industry-Wide Distress Affect Defaulted Firms? Evidence from Creditor Recoveries. *Journal of Financial Economics* 85:787–821.

Acharya, V., I. Hasan, and A. Saunders. 2006. Should Banks be Diversified? Evidence from Individual Bank Portfolios. *Journal of Business* 79:1355–412.

Acharya, V., and T. Yorulmazer. 2007. Too Many to Fail—An Analysis of Time-Inconsistency in Bank Closure Policies. *Journal of Financial Intermediation* 16:1–31.

Adams, P. 1991. *Odious Debts: Loose Lending, Corruption and the Third World's Environmental Legacy*. Toronto, Canada: Probe International.

Allen, F., and D. Gale. 1994. Limited Market Participation and Volatility of Asset Prices. *American Economic Review* 84:933–55.

Allen, F., and D. Gale. 1998. Optimal Financial Crises. *Journal of Finance* 53:1245–84.

Allen, F., and D. Gale. 2000. Financial Contagion. *Journal of Political Economy* 108:1–33.

Berger, P., E. Ofek, and I. Swary. 1996. Investor Valuation of the Abandonment Option. *Journal of Financial Economics* 42:257–87.

BCBS. 2002. Supervisory Guidance on Dealing with Weak Banks. Report of the Task Force on Dealing with Weak Banks, BIS, March.

Brown, C., and S. Dinc. 2006. Too Many to Fail? Evidence of Regulatory Reluctance in Bank Failures When the Banking Sector is Weak, Working Paper, University of Michigan.

Calomiris, C. W. 1998. Blueprints for a Global Financial Architecture, Reform Proposals, IMF.

Caprio, G., and D. Klingebiel. 1996. Bank Insolvencies: Cross Country Experience, World Bank, Policy Research Working Paper No. 1620.

Caprio, G., L. Laeven, and R. Levine. 2005. Governance and Bank Valuation, Working Paper, Brown University.

Claessens, S., S. Djankov, and D. Klingebiel. 1999. Financial Restructuring in East Asia: Halfway There? World Bank, Financial Sector Discussion Paper No. 3.

Cordella, T., and E. L. Yeyati. 2003. Bank Bailouts: Moral Hazard vs. Value Effect. *Journal of Financial Intermediation* 12:300–30.

Dell'Ariccia, G., E. Detragiache, and R. Rajan. 2008. The Real Effect of Banking Crises. *Journal of Financial Intermediation*, 17: 89–112.

Devenow, A., and I. Welch. 1996. Rational Herding in Financial Economics. *European Economic Review*, 40:603–15.
Diamond, D., and R. Rajan. 2005. Liquidity Shortages and Banking Crises. *Journal of Finance*, 60, 615–47.
Freixas, X. 1999. Optimal Bailout Policy, Conditionality and Constructive Ambiguity, LSE Financial Markets Group, Discussion Paper No. 237.
Goodhart, C., and D. Schoenmaker. 1995. Should the Functions of Monetary Policy and Banking Supervision be Separated? *Oxford Economic Papers* 47:539–60.
Gorton, G., and L. Huang. 2004. Liquidity, Efficiency, and Bank Bailouts. *American Economic Review* 94:455–83.
Guttentag, J., and R. Herring. 1984. Commercial Bank Lending to Developing Countries: From Overlending to Underlending to Structural Reform, in G. Smith and J. T. Cuddington (eds), *International Debt and the Developing Countries*. Washington, DC: World Bank 129–50.
Hart, O., and J. Moore. 1994. A Theory of Debt Based on the Inalienability of Human Capital. *Quarterly Journal of Economics* 109:841–79.
Hawkins, J., and P. Turner. 1999. Bank Restructuring in Practice: An Overview, BIS Policy Papers No. 6, 6–105.
Hoggarth, G., J. Reidhill, and P. Sinclair. 2004. On the Resolution of Banking Crises: Theory and Evidence, Bank of England Working Paper No. 229.
Hoggarth, G., R. Reis, and V. Saporta. 2001. Cost of Banking Instability: Some Empirical Evidence. *Journal of Banking and Finance*. 26:825–55.
Holmstrom, B., and J. Tirole. 1998. Private and Public Supply of Liquidity. *Journal of Political Economy* 106:1–40.
Honohan, P., and D. Klingebiel. 2000. Controlling Fiscal Costs of Bank Crises, World Bank Working Paper No. 2441.
Jain, A. K., and S. Gupta. 1987. Some Evidence on 'Herding' Behavior of U.S. Banks. *Journal of Money, Credit and Banking*. 19:78–89.
James, C. 1991. The Losses Realized in Bank Failures. *Journal of Finance*, 46:1223–42.
Kahn, C, and J. A. C. Santos. 2005. Endogenous Financial Fragility and Bank Regulation, Working Paper, Federal Reserve Bank of New York.
Kasa, K., and M. Spiegel. 1999. The Role of Relative Performance in Bank Closure Decisions, Working Paper, Federal Reserve Bank of San Francisco.
Luengnaruemitchai, P., and J. A. Wilcox. 2004. Procyclicality, Banks' Reporting Discretion, and 'Safety in Similarity,' in B. E. Gup (ed)., *The New Basel Accord*. Oklahoma City, OK: South-Western Publishing, 151–75.
Mailath, G., and L. Mester. 1994. A Positive Analysis of Bank Closure. *Journal of Financial Intermediation* 3:272–99.
Mitchell, J. 1997. Strategic Creditor Passivity, Bank Rescues, and Too Many to Fail, CEPR Working Paper No. 1780.
Myers, S., and N. Majluf. 1984. Corporate Financing and Investment When Firms Have Information Shareholders Do Not Have. *Journal of Financial Economics* 13:187–221.
Penati, A., and A. Protopapadakis. 1988. The Effect of Implicit Deposit Insurance on Banks' Portfolio Choices, with an Application to International 'Overexposure'. *Journal of Monetary Economics* 21:107–26.
Perotti, E., and J. Suarez. 2002. Last Bank Standing: What do I Gain If You Fail? *European Economic Review* 46:1599–1622.
Pulvino, T. C. 1998. Do Asset Fire Sales Exist: An Empirical Investigation of Commercial Aircraft Sale Transactions. *Journal of Finance* 53:939–78.
Rajan, R. 1994. Why Bank Credit Policies Fluctuate: A Theory and Some Evidence. *Quarterly Journal of Economics* 109:399–442.
Repullo, R. 2005. Liquidity, Risk Taking, and the Lender of Last Resort. *International Journal of Central Banking* 2:47–80.
Rochet, J. C, and J. Tirole. 1996. Interbank Lending and Systemic Risk. *Journal of Money, Credit and Banking*. 28:733–62.
Santomero, A., and P. Hoffman. 1999. Problem Bank Resolution: Evaluating the Options, Working Paper, University of Pennsylvania.
Shleifer, A., and R. Vishny. 1992. Liquidation Values and Debt Capacity: A Market Equilibrium Approach. *Journal of Finance* 47:1343–66.

Stromberg, P. 2000. Conflicts of Interest and Market Illiquidity in Bankruptcy Auctions: Theory and Tests. *Journal of Finance* 55:2641–92.
Williamson, O. E. 1988. Corporate Finance and Corporate Governance. *Journal of Finance* 43, 567–92.
Wilson, R. 1979. Auctions of Shares. *Quarterly Journal of Economics* 93:675–89.
Winton, A. 2000. Don't Put All Your Eggs in One Basket? Diversification and Specialization in Lending, Working Paper, University of Minnesota.

21 Credit Risk Transfer and Contagion

Franklin Allen and Elena Carletti

1. Introduction

It is often argued that financial innovation in the form of creating new instruments and opening up new markets is desirable because it creates opportunities for diversification and potentially promotes liquidity. Although this argument appears to be a powerful one, practical experience of financial liberalization such as the introduction of new instruments and the creation of new markets has not always been positive, particularly in emerging markets. Such changes have often led to financial crises.

This paper is concerned with credit risk transfer. This has existed for many years, but recent innovations such as credit derivatives have increased the amount that it occurs. Table 21.1 (BIS, 2003) shows the size of credit risk transfer markets using various instruments from 1995 to 2002. It can be seen that the use of all types of credit risk transfer has increased substantially. The growth has been particularly rapid in credit derivatives and collateralized debt obligations. Studies by the British Bankers Association (BBA, 2002) and Fitch Ratings (2003) indicate that banks are the major participants both as buyers and sellers in the markets for credit risk transfer. Overall banks are net buyers and insurance companies are net sellers.

We show how financial innovation in the form of new credit risk transfer instruments can lead to beneficial diversification in some circumstances but to a fall in welfare through the creation of contagion in others. This argument is developed in a model with a banking sector and an insurance sector based on Allen and Gale (2005a). Both sectors are competitive and can buy risk-free short and long assets. The difference between the two sectors is that banks can make risky loans to firms, while insurance companies insure another group of firms whose assets may be damaged. Also, banks raise funds in the form of deposits and capital, while insurance companies have as funds only the premiums they receive from the firms they insure.

We start by considering the case where all banks face the same demand for liquidity from their depositors. When both sectors are autarkic so they operate without links, banks and insurance companies hold different assets and only the insurance sector is subject to systemic risk. If the return on the risk-free long asset is low compared to the return on the risky loans, banks invest in the short term asset to repay their early depositors and in risky loans. Insurance companies offer partial insurance, and invest the premiums they initially receive in the short asset. Since there is aggregate risk in the insurance sector,

Table 21.1 Size of credit risk transfer markets (in billions of US $)

Instruments	**1995**	**1996**	**1997**	**1998**	**1999**	**2000**	**2001**	**2002**
Loan trading (turnover)								
US market	34	40	61	78	79	102	118	117[a]
(Loan Pricing Corporation)								
Credit derivatives (outstanding)								
BIS triennial survey				108			693	
US OCC[b]				144	287	426	395	492[c]
British Bankers Association			180	350	586	893	1189	1952[d]
Risk Magazine						810	1398	
ISDA							919	1600[d]
Asset-backed securities								
US market (outstanding)	315	403	517	684	816	947	1114	1258[f]
(Bond Market Association)[e]								
European market (issuance)								
(Moody's)[g]					68	80	134	50[h]
Australian market (outstanding)	7	10	15	19	27	33	38	54
(Australian Bureau of Statistics)								
Collateralized debt obligations								
US market (outstanding)	1	1	19	48	85	125	167	232[f]
(BondMarket Association)								
European market (issuance)								
(Moody's)					42	71	114	70[h]
Total bank credit(outstanding)[j]	23,424	23,576	23,309	26,018	26,904	27,221	27,442	29,435[i]
IMF								
Corporate debt securities[k] (outstanding)	3241	3373	3444	4042	4584	4939	5233	5505[i]
BIS								

[a] First three quarters of 2002, annualized.
[b] Holdings of US commercial banks.
[c] Second Quarter of 2002.
[d] Forecast for 2002.
[e] Excluding CBOs/CDOs.
[f] September 2002.
[g] ABSs and MBSs.
[h] First half of 2002.
[i] June 2002.
[j] Domestic and international credit to non-bank borrowers (United States, United Kingdom, Japan, Canada, Euro area).
[k] Debt securities issued in international and domestic markets, non-financial corporates.

insurance companies may not be able to repair all damaged assets and so go bankrupt. This systemic risk is benign in the sense that there are no deadweight costs associated with it.

In the case where all banks face the same demands for liquidity from their depositors, credit risk transfer between the banking and insurance sectors is beneficial. Specifically, it allows the risk the two sectors face to be shared without creating contagion because the two sectors still hold different assets. As in autarky, banks invest in the short asset and in risky loans. By contrast, insurance companies now also hold the long asset to facilitate their ability to transfer risks; and they are forced to liquidate it when the firms they are insuring have high losses. The price they receive for the long asset is very low to ensure there are adequate incentives for providing liquidity to the market. This implies that insurance companies may still not be able to pay all firms with damaged assets and go bankrupt. Importantly though, this low price does not affect the banking sector because banks do not use the long asset. Credit risk transfer is then desirable because its only effect is to allow diversification of risk between the banking and the insurance sectors.

The effect of introducing the credit risk transfer differs when banks face idiosyncratic liquidity risk. In this case, some banks have a large number of early consumers who withdraw at the intermediate date and other banks have a large number of late consumers who withdraw at the final date. Banks can hedge this risk by holding the risk-free long asset and trading it in a liquid market. If a bank has a large number of early consumers, it can sell the long asset to banks with a large number of late consumers. Since there is assumed to be no aggregate liquidity risk, in the autarkic equilibrium only insurance companies face systemic risk. As before, they invest the premiums they receive in the short asset, and go bankrupt when the firms they insure experience high losses. The banking sector experiences no crises and banks hedge their idiosyncratic liquidity risk using the market for long term assets.

However, since banks now hold the long term asset, introducing credit risk transfer can be damaging because of the possibility of contagion. The insurance sector again uses the long asset to allow it to undertake its credit risk transfers effectively. When insurance companies face a shock where their losses are high, they will be forced to liquidate the long asset. This liquidation forces down the price. The reason is that there is "cash in the market pricing". The buyers optimally use all of their liquidity and sellers supply all of their holdings. The price is the ratio of the two. If the quantity sold goes up, the price goes down. This fall in price now affects the banking industry as banks are using the long asset to hedge their idiosyncratic liquidity risk. There is then the possibility of damaging contagion of systemic risk to the banking sector. Although taking prices as given it is optimal to engage in credit risk transfer, the equilibrium with credit risk transfer can be Pareto worse than the autarkic equilibrium. The systemic risk is costly since banks' loans cannot be liquidated for a positive amount and the contagion interferes with the risk sharing between banks with different proportions of early and late consumers through the interbank market.

There is a small but growing literature on credit risk transfer. The first strand of this literature considers the impact of credit risk transfer on the allocation of resources when there is asymmetric information. Morrison (2005) shows that a market for credit derivatives can destroy the signalling role of bank debt and lead to an overall reduction in welfare as a result. He suggests that disclosure requirements for credit derivatives can help offset this effect. Nicolo and Pelizzon (2004) show that if there are banks with different abilities to screen borrowers, then good banks can signal their type using first-to-default basket contracts that are often used in practice. These involve a payment to the protection buyer if any of a basket of assets defaults. Only protection sellers with very good screening abilities will be prepared to use such contracts. Chiesa (2004) considers a situation where banks have a comparative advantage in evaluating and monitoring risks but limited risk bearing capacity. Credit risk transfer improves efficiency by allowing the monitored debt of large firms to be transferred to the market while banks can use their limited risk bearing capacity for loans to small businesses. Arping (2004) considers the change in lender and borrower incentives when credit risk is transferred. He shows that lenders will be more willing to call loans but will be less willing to provide monitoring effort. Effective incentives can be provided by designing the maturity structure of credit protection appropriately. Parlour and Plantin (2005) consider the effect of credit risk transfer on relationship banking. Banks can receive proprietary information about loan quality or can have a shock to their discount factor. Either can cause them to try to transfer the risk and this creates an adverse selection problem. Parlour and Plantin identify when credit risk transfer markets arise and whether this is efficient. In contrast to these papers, our paper focuses on the situation where there is symmetric information and shows how credit risk transfer can improve the allocation of resources through better risk sharing across sectors.

The second part of the literature focuses on the stability aspects of credit risk transfer. Wagner and Marsh (2004) consider the transfer of risk between banking and non-banking sectors. They find that the transfer of risk out of a relatively fragile banking sector leads to an improvement in stability. Wagner (2005a) develops a model where credit risk transfer improves the liquidity of bank assets. However, this can increase the probability of crises by increasing the risks that banks are prepared to take. Wagner (2005b) shows that the increased portfolio diversification possibilities introduced by credit risk transfer can increase the probability of liquidity-based crises. The reason is that the increased diversification leads banks to reduce the amount of liquid assets they hold and increase the amount of risky assets. In contrast to these contributions, in our paper the focus is on idiosyncratic liquidity shocks and their interaction with credit risk transfer in creating contagion between banking and insurance systems.

The paper also contributes to the literature on financial innovation. Hart (1975) shows that with incomplete markets, the introduction of a new market can lead to a Pareto reduction in welfare. Since then a number of authors have shown that financial innovation can be bad for welfare (see, e.g., Newbery and Stiglitz, 1984; Allen and Gale, 1990; Elul, 1995; and Cass and Citanna, 1998). The most closely related paper in this context is Duffee and Zhou (2001). They show that credit risk transfer can cause the collapse of other risk sharing mechanisms such as the loan-sale market, and this can result in a reduction in welfare. The credit risk transfer market attracts some participants from the loan-sale market and this worsens the adverse selection problem in the latter to such an extent that it collapses. In contrast, our paper shows that credit risk transfer can cause contagion and the spread in systemic risk makes everybody worse off.

The rest of the paper proceeds as follows. Section 2 develops a model with a banking and an insurance sector. Section 3 shows how credit risk transfer can improve welfare relative to the autarkic equilibrium through better risk sharing. Section 4 describes the detrimental effect of credit risk transfer when banks are subject to idiosyncratic liquidity shocks. Section 5 contains concluding remarks.

2. The Model

The model is based on the analyses of crises and systemic risk in Allen and Gale (1998, 2000a–c, 2004a, b, 2005b) and Gale (2003, 2004), and particularly in Allen and Gale (2005a). A standard model of intermediation is extended by adding an insurance sector. Since the risks faced by the insurance sector are not perfectly correlated with the risks faced by the banking sector, there is scope for diversification. This is the basic motive for credit risk transfer.

There are three dates $t = 0, 1, 2$ and a single, all-purpose good that can be used for consumption or investment at each date. There are two sectors in the financial system, the banking sector and the insurance sector. Each sector consists of a large number of competitive firms and the lines of business of banks and insurance companies do not overlap. This is a strong assumption but a necessary one, since the combination of insurance and intermediation activities in a single financial institution would obviate the need for credit risk transfer outside the institution.

There are two securities, one *short* and one *long*. The short security is represented by a storage technology: one unit at date t produces one unit at date $t + 1$. The long security is represented by a constant-returns-to-scale investment technology that takes two periods to mature: one unit invested in the long security at date 0 produces $R > 1$ units of the good at date 2 (and nothing at date 1). These securities represent the investment opportunities that banks and insurance companies have in common. In practice there are many such securities, for example, government and other bonds.

In addition to the short and long securities, banks and insurance companies have distinct direct investment opportunities. Banks can make loans to firms which succeed with probability β. More precisely, each firm borrows one unit at date 0 and invests in a risky venture that produces B_H units of the good at date 2 if successful and B_L if unsuccessful. There is assumed to be an infinite supply of such firms, so that banks take all the surplus on the loan market.

Banks raise funds from depositors, who have one unit of the good at date 0 and none at dates 1 and 2. Depositors are uncertain of their preferences: with probability λ they are *early consumers*, who only value the good at date 1 and with probability $1 - \lambda$ they are *late consumers*, who only value the good at date 2. Uncertainty about time preferences generates a preference for liquidity and a role for the intermediaries as providers of liquidity insurance. The utility of consumption is represented by the function $U(c)$ with the usual properties. We normalize the number of consumers to 1. Since banks compete to raise deposits, they choose the contracts they offer to maximize depositors' expected utility. If they failed to do so, another bank could step in and offer a better contract to attract away all their customers.

Insurance companies sell insurance to a large number of firms, whose measure is normalized to one. Each firm has one unit of endowment at date 0 and owns an asset that produces A units of the good at date 2. With probability α the asset suffers some damage at date 1. Unless this damage is repaired, at a cost of γ, the asset becomes worthless and will produce nothing at date 2. Thus, firms can decide to buy insurance against the probability of incurring the damage in exchange for a premium at date 0. The insurance companies collect the premiums and invest them in the short security at date 0 in order to pay the firms' damages at date 1. The owners of the firms consume at date 2 and have a utility function $V(C)$ with the usual properties. Similarly to the banks, the insurance companies operate in competitive markets and thus maximize the expected utility of the owners of the firms. If they did not do this, another firm would enter and attract away all their customers.

Finally, we introduce a class of risk neutral investors who can provide capital to the insurance and banking sectors. Investors have a large (unbounded) amount of the good W_0 as endowment at date 0 and nothing at dates 1 and 2. They provide capital to the intermediary through the contract $e = (e_0, e_1, e_2)$, where $e_0 \geq 0$ denotes an investor's supply of capital at date $t = 0$, and $e_t \geq 0$ denotes consumption at dates $t = 1, 2$. Although investors are risk neutral, we assume that their consumption must be non-negative at each date. Otherwise, they could absorb all risk and provide unlimited liquidity. The investors' utility function is then defined as

$$u(e_0, e_1, e_2) = \rho W_0 - \rho e_0 + e_1 + e_2,$$

where the constant ρ is the investors' opportunity cost of funds. This can represent their time preference or their alternative investment opportunities that are not available to the other agents in the model. We assume $\rho > R$ so that it is not worthwhile for investors to just invest in assets at date 0. This has two important implications. First, since investors have a large endowment at date 0 and the capital market is competitive, there will be excess supply of capital and they will just earn their opportunity cost. Secondly, the fact that investors have no endowment (and non-negative consumption) at dates 1 and 2 implies that their capital must be converted into assets in order to provide risk sharing at dates 1 and 2.

For the purposes of illustrating the scope for diversification, the structure of uncertainty is one that allows for some diversification and some aggregate risk. This is achieved by assuming that the proportions of successful firms for the banking sector and of damaged firms for the insurance sector equal the probabilities β and α, respectively, and that these probabilities are themselves random. In particular, β and α take two values each, β_H and β_L and α_H and α_L. Note also that β and α are independent so that we have four possible states, (β_H, α_H), (β_H, α_L), (β_L, α_H), (β_L, α_L) . We denote them simply as *HH, HL, LH,* and *LL*, respectively. This simple structure is enough to illustrate the main points, and nothing would change with a more general structure. All uncertainty is resolved at the beginning of date 1. Banks discover whether loans will pay off or not at date 2. Depositors learn whether they are early or late consumers. Insurance companies learn which firms have damaged assets.

3. Beneficial Credit Risk Transfer

The purpose of this section is to show that credit risk transfer can be beneficial as it allows risk sharing across sectors. This is demonstrated using numerical examples. The first case considered is when the banking sector and the insurance sector are autarkic and operate separately.

3.1 The Autarkic Banking Sector

The return on the long asset is $R = 1.25$. Depositors become early consumers with probability $\lambda = 0.5$ and have utility function $U(c) = Ln(c)$. Loans pay off $B_H = 1.75$ with probability $\beta_H = 1$ in state H, which occurs with probability 0.7; and $B_L = 0.75$ with probability $1 - \beta_L = 1$ in state L, which occurs with probability 0.3. The expected payoff on loans is then $0.7 \times 1.75 + 0.3 \times 0.75 = 1.45$.

No capital In order to understand the role of capital in the model, it is helpful to start with the case where there is no capital. Since banks are competitive, they choose the contracts they offer to maximize depositors' expected utility. At date 0 banks choose how to split their 1 unit of deposits investing x units in the short term asset, y units in the long asset, and z units in loans. Since ex ante all banks are identical, they choose x, y, and z to solve the following problem:

$$\text{Max} \quad 0.5U(c_1) + 0.5[0.7U(c_{2H}) + 0.3U(c_{2L})] \tag{21.1}$$

s.t.

$$x + y + z = 1, \tag{21.2}$$

$$c_1 = \frac{x}{0.5}, \tag{21.3}$$

$$c_{2H} = \frac{yR + zB_H}{0.5}, \tag{21.4}$$

$$c_{2L} = \frac{yR + zB_L}{0.5}. \tag{21.5}$$

Each bank has 1 unit of depositors and 0.5 of them become early consumers. The first term in the objective function represents the utility $U(c_1)$ of the 0.5 early consumers. The bank uses the proceeds of the short term asset to provide them with a level of consumption $c_1 = x/0.5$. The second term represents the 0.5 depositors who become late consumers. With probability 0.7 the banks' loans pay off B_H and the late consumers receive consumption $c_{2H} = (yR + zB_H)/0.5$. With probability 0.3 the banks' loans pay off B_L and the late consumers receive consumption $c_{2L} = (yR + zB_H)/0.5$. The constraint (2) is the budget constraint at date 0.

It can be shown using direct numerical hill-climbing techniques that the optimal solution in this case is

$$x = 0.5, \quad y = 0, \quad z = 0.5,$$
$$c_1 = 1, \quad c_{2H} = 1.75, \quad c_{2L} = 0.75,$$
$$EU = 0.153.$$

Banks use the short term asset to provide consumption to the early consumers. It is not worth them using the long asset. The expected return of 1.45 on loans is sufficiently greater than the return of 1.25 on the long asset that banks put nothing in the latter. Note also that the late consumers have an expected consumption at date 2 equal to $Ec_2 = 0.7c_{2H} + 0.3c_{2L} = 1.45$. As we will see shortly, this will be lower when we introduce capital.

With capital Next consider what happens when there are investors who can make an amount of capital e_0 available to the banks. Their opportunity cost for providing this equity capital is $\rho = 1.5$. Since investors are indifferent between consumption at date 1 and date 2, it is optimal to set $e_1 = 0$, invest e_0 in the long asset or loans, and make a payout e_2 at date 2 to investors.

Banks' optimization problem is the same as before except now the budget constraint at date 0 is

$$x + y + z = 1 + e_0, \tag{21.6}$$

rather than (2). This reflects the fact that, in addition to the depositors' endowment of 1, banks can now also invest the investors' contribution of e_0. Banks have to pay e_2 at date 2 to investors to compensate for supplying the capital. It is best to make this payment in state H when loans pay off B_H and depositors' marginal utility of consumption is lowest. Thus, (4) is replaced by

$$c_{2H} = \frac{yR + zB_H - e_2}{0.5}. \tag{21.7}$$

In order for the risk neutral investors to be willing to supply the capital, e_0, they must receive an expected payoff equal to their opportunity cost $e_0\rho$. Since e_2 is paid when state H occurs, which happens 0.7 of the time, it is necessary that

$$e_0\rho = 0.7e_2. \tag{21.8}$$

The optimal solution in this case is

$$x = 0.5, \quad y = 0, \quad z = 0.818, \quad e_0 = 0.318, \quad e_2 = 0.682,$$
$$c_1 = 1, \quad c_{2H} = 1.5, \quad c_{2L} = 1.227,$$
$$EU = 0.173.$$

Comparing this to the previous optimum without capital allows us to see the role of capital. The providers of capital are risk neutral. They only receive a payment e_2 when banks' loans pay off $B_H = 1.75$. In return for this payment, investors provide capital of $e_0 = 0.318$, and banks use this to make more loans. Again it is not worth banks investing anything in the long asset because its payoff is too low compared to the expected payoff of the loans. Overall, capital allows banks to reduce the variance of the payments to depositors in the second period. Instead of $c_{2H} = 1.75$, and $c_{2L} = 0.75$ without capital, depositors now receive $c_{2H} = 1.5$, and $c_{2L} = 1.227$. In effect, the late consuming depositors are sharing risk with the investors. This risk sharing comes at a cost, however. The opportunity cost of the investors providing the capital is $\rho = 1.5$, which is greater than the expected return on loans of 1.45. The expected consumption $Ec_2 = 0.7c_{2H} + 0.3c_{2L}$ of the late consuming depositors is thus reduced from 1.45 to 1.418. Their expected utility, though, is increased from 0.153 to 0.173. The fact that the opportunity cost of the capital provided by the investors is above the return on loans means that capital is costly and is only used for partial rather than complete risk sharing.

3.2 The Autarkic Insurance Sector

The insurance sector is considered next on its own. For simplicity, we consider here the case where there is no market for liquidating the long asset. It can be shown (see below), however, that at the equilibrium prices that would ensure a supply of liquidity, the autarkic equilibrium in the insurance sector would be unaltered if such a market was included.

As explained above, insurance companies offer insurance to firms against the probability that their assets are damaged at date 1 and need to be repaired in order to produce A at date 2. In our example, the probability of such damage is $\alpha_H = 0.5$ in state H, which occurs with probability 0.9, and $\alpha_L = 1$ in state L, which occurs with probability 0.1. Assets produce $A = 1.35$ at date 2 and repairing them when damaged costs $\gamma = 1$ at date 1. The utility function of the owners of the firm is $V(c) = Ln(c)$.

The insurance industry is competitive so the insurance companies do not earn any profits. Similarly to the banks, they maximize the expected utility of the owners of the firms they insure. They can offer partial or full insurance to firms. If they offer partial insurance, they charge a premium equal to 0.5 at date 0 to the firms so that the latter still have another 0.5 of their initial endowment to invest. Firms will find it optimal to invest this 0.5 in the long asset rather than the short asset since their owners do not consume until date 2. In order to have funds to repair the damaged assets, insurance companies must invest in the short asset so that they have liquidity at date 1. In state H they need funds $\alpha_H\gamma = 0.5$ at date 1 for claims to repair the damaged assets so they put $X = 0.5$ in the short asset and $Y = 0$ in the long asset. This means they have funds of 0.5 at date 1 and can pay all the claims to repair the damaged assets. With insurance the firms' assets will pay off A for sure in this state. Given this and the fact that the firms' owners invest 0.5 in the long asset, their consumption in state H is $C_{2H} = A + 0.5R = 1.975$. In state L the insurance companies receive claims of $\alpha_L\gamma = 1$. They do not have sufficient funds to pay these so they go bankrupt. With partial insurance there is thus systemic risk in the insurance industry. When insurance companies go bankrupt, their assets are distributed equally among the claimants. The firms receive 0.5 from the insurance companies' liquidation of the short term assets, but cannot repair their assets so these produce nothing. The consumption of the owners of the firms is therefore $C_{2L} = 0.5 + 0.5R = 1.125$. Their expected utility with partial insurance is then

$$EV_{\text{partial}} = 0.9V(A + 0.5R) + 0.1V(0.5 + 0.5R) = 0.624.$$

If the insurance companies offered full insurance, they would charge 1 at date 0. They would invest all of this in the short term asset and could meet all of their claims in both states. Now, however, the firms' owners would have nothing left over at date 0 and would hold no investments of their own. In state H the insurance companies would only use 0.5 of their assets at date 1 to repair their customers' machines and would have 0.5 left over. Since the industry is competitive they would pay this out to the insured firms. Hence $C_{2H} = A + 0.5 = 1.85$. In state L all the insurance companies' funds are used to repair their customers' machines and $C_{2L} = A$. In this case the expected utility of the firms' owners would be

$$EV_{\text{full}} = 0.9V(A + 0.5) + 0.1V(A) = 0.584.$$

Partial insurance is thus superior to full insurance. It can readily be checked that partial insurance is also better for the firms than self insurance. Thus the optimal scheme for the insurance industry is to partially insure firms and offer the owners of the firms an expected consumption at date 2 equal to $EC_2 = 0.9C_{2H} + 0.1C_{2L} = 1.890$. The firms put the remaining part of their endowment in the long asset. There is no point in the insurance company holding the long asset because there is no market for it when they go bankrupt. If a market is included as explained below, then it will still not be optimal for the insurance companies to hold the long asset because there is a liquidation cost while if the firms hold it directly there is none.

There is no role for capital in the insurance sector so their capital is $E_0 = 0$. Capital providers charge a premium to cover their opportunity cost $p = 1.5$. Their funds would have to be invested in the short asset since it is not optimal to hold any long assets. There are already potentially enough funds from customers for insurance companies to hold more of the short asset but it is not efficient to do so. There is a small probability of a large loss and it is not worth holding enough short assets to guard against this contingency given the high opportunity cost of holding short assets. If the short assets are funded by capital and there is a premium to be paid for the capital it is even less efficient. Capital will not be used in the insurance industry unless there are regulations forcing this.

3.3 *Credit Risk Transfer*

In the previous sections the banking and insurance sectors have been considered in isolation. We now consider them together, and introduce the possibility for the long term asset to be liquidated in a market at date 1. Since the risks in the two sectors are independent, we have four possible states for the probabilities β and α, which we describe as *HH, HL, LH* and *LL*. The payoffs in these four states are given in Table 21.2.

It can be seen that the late consuming depositors have different payoffs in states *HH* and *HL* compared to states *LH* and *LL*. Similarly the payoffs to the owners of the firms being insured are different in states *HH* and *LH* as compared to *HL* and *LL*. These differences

Table 21.2

State	Bank loans	Late depositors	Insurance claims (%)	Firms	Probability
HH	1.75	1.5	50	1.975	$0.7 \times 0.9 = 0.63$
HL	1.75	1.5	100	1.125	$0.7 \times 0.1 = 0.07$
LH	0.75	1.227	50	1.975	$0.3 \times 0.9 = 0.27$
LL	0.75	1.227	100	1.125	$0.3 \times 0.1 = 0.03$

mean that there is potential for risk sharing between the two groups. Credit risk transfer between the two sectors represents one way of achieving this risk sharing.

For simplicity the focus is on a particularly simple form of risk transfer. Banks make a payment τ_{HL} to the insurance companies in state *HL*; and the insurance companies make a payment τ_{LH} to the banks in state *LH*. Notice that markets are still not complete with this credit risk transfer. For simplicity it is assumed that the banks' depositors obtain the surplus from the credit risk transfer. The insurance companies will compete to provide the credit risk transfer that maximizes the utility of the banks' depositors at the lowest cost to themselves. In equilibrium they will obtain their reservation utility, which is what they would receive in autarky.

How can such transfers be funded? In state *HL* banks' loans pay off B_H so they have a large amount of funds and can simply transfer some of these to the insurance companies. Banks still maximize the expected utility of depositors (1) subject to the constraints (6) and (8). The only difference is that now they have to pay τ_{HL} in state *HL* to the insurance companies, and receive τ_{LH} in state *LH*. Thus, the per capita consumption of late consumers in these two states becomes

$$c_{2HL} = \frac{yR + zB_H - \tau_{HL} - e_2}{0.5},$$

$$c_{2LH} = \frac{yR + zB_L + \tau_{LH}}{0.5}.$$

The problem is more complex for the insurance companies. In state *LH* the owners of the firms that insure their assets with the insurance companies have plenty of funds. However, the companies themselves do not. They are only holding enough to meet claims at date 1 in states *HH* and *LH*. In order for them to be able to make a payout on the credit risk transfer to the banks at date 2 in state *LH* they must hold extra assets. They must charge the firms more initially and the firms will consequently have to reduce their holdings of the long asset. If the insurance companies hold the short asset there is an opportunity cost of $R - 1$ in all states. Let the transfer from the banks to the insurance companies in state *HL* be τ_{HL}, and the amount invested in the short asset to fund the transfer from the insurance companies to the banks in state *LH* be $\sigma_{LH} = \tau_{LH}$. The opportunity cost in each state is $\sigma_{LH}(R - 1)$. The expected utility of the insured firms' owners, which is ultimately the objective function of the insurance companies, is equal with partial insurance to

$$\begin{aligned} EV_{\text{short}} &= 0.63V(A + \sigma_{LH} + (0.5 - \sigma_{LH})R) \\ &\quad + 0.07V(0.5 + \sigma_{LH} + \tau_{HL} + (0.5 - \sigma_{LH})R) \\ &\quad + 0.27V(A + (0.5 - \sigma_{LH})R) + 0.03V(0.5 + \sigma_{LH} + (0.5 - \sigma_{LH})R). \end{aligned}$$

To see this, note that the firms pay an insurance premium $0.5 + \sigma_{HL}$ to the insurance companies who invest it in the short asset. The firms then invest the amount that remains after they have paid the insurance premium, $(0.5 - \sigma_{LH})$, in the long asset, and this pays off $(0.5 - \sigma_{LH})R$ in every state. In state *HH*, which occurs with probability 0.63, all the machines that are damaged are repaired using 0.5 of the proceeds from the short asset. The firms receive *A* from their machines. There are no credit risk payments so the insurance companies pay the proceeds of their investment in the short asset, σ_{LH}, out to the firms (since the insurance market is competitive). In state *HL*, which occurs with probability 0.07, the insurance companies have all their customers claim and go bankrupt. They are unable to repair any machines and distribute the $0.5 + \sigma_{LH}$ that was invested in the short asset to their customers. They receive a credit risk transfer payment of τ_{HL} from the banks which they also pay out to their customers. In state *LH*, which occurs with probability 0.27, everything is the same as in state *HH*, except that the insurance companies must pay out $\tau_{LH} = \sigma_{LH}$ as a credit risk transfer payment to the banks instead of to their customers. Finally in state *LL*, which occurs with probability 0.03, everything is the same as in state *HL* except there is no payment from the banks.

It turns out that in the example considered it is not possible to keep the insurance companies at their reservation level of utility $EV = 0.624$ and make the banks better off if the insurance companies fund the credit risk transfer with the short asset. This is the case for all feasible values of τ_{LH} and τ_{HL} and the corresponding optimal choices by banks and insurance companies. The opportunity cost in each state, $\sigma_{LH}(R - 1)$, from investing in the short asset rather than in the long asset is simply too large for credit risk transfer to be worthwhile.

If instead of investing σ_{LH} in the short asset, the insurance companies invest ℓ_{LH} in the long asset so $\tau_{LH} = \ell_{LH}$R, there would not be an opportunity cost $\ell_{LH}\{R - 1)$ in every state. On the other hand, however, there is a cost in states *HL* and *LL*, when the insurance companies go bankrupt and must sell the ℓ_{LH} long asset at date 1 for a price $P_{HL} = P_{LL} = P_{IL}$. The expected utility of the insured firms' owners in this case is

$$\begin{aligned} EV_{\text{long}} &= 0.63V(A + \ell_{LH}R + (0.5 - \ell_{LH})R)) \\ &\quad + 0.07V(0.5 + \ell_{LH}P_{IL} + \tau_{HL} + (0.5 - \ell_{LH})R) \\ &\quad + 0.27V(A + (0.5 - \ell_{LH})R)) + 0.03V(0.5 + \ell_{LH}P_{IL} + (0.5 - \ell_{LH})R). \end{aligned}$$

Now the firms pay an insurance premium $0.5 + \ell_{HL}$ to the insurance companies who invest $X = 0.5$ in the short asset and $Y = \ell_{HL}$ in the long asset. The firms then invest the assets that remain after they have paid the insurance premium, $(0.5 - \ell_{LH})$, in the long asset, and this pays off $(0.5 - \ell_{LH})R$ in every state. In state *HH*, all the machines that are damaged are repaired using the 0.5 from the short asset. The firms receive *A* from their machines. There are no credit risk payments so the insurance companies pay the proceeds of their investment in the long asset, $\ell_{LH}R$, out to the firms. In state *HL*, the insurance companies have all their customers claim and go bankrupt. They are unable to repair the assets and distribute the 0.5 that was invested in the short asset together with the $\ell_{LH}P_{IL}$ they get from liquidating their holdings of the long asset to their customers. They receive a credit risk transfer payment of τ_{LH} from the banks which they also pay out to their customers. In state *LH*, everything is the same as in state *HH*, except that the insurance companies must pay out $\tau_{LH} = \ell_{LH}R$ as a credit risk transfer payment to the banks instead of to their customers. Finally, in state *LL*, everything is the same as in state *HL* except there is no payment from the banks.

In order to find the optimal credit risk transfer in this case, it is first necessary to find P_{IL}. The first issue to consider is that somebody must supply liquidity to this market. In other words, some agents must hold the short asset between dates 0 and 1 in order to have the funds to purchase the long asset that the insurance companies supply to the market when they go bankrupt in states *HL* and *LL*. If nobody held liquidity, then there would be nobody on the other side of the market and the price of the long asset would fall to zero at date 1. This would not be an equilibrium though, because by holding a very small amount of cash somebody would be able to enter and buy up all the supplied long asset and make a large profit.

In our framework, the group supplying liquidity is the investors who provide the capital to the banks. In order to be willing to hold this liquidity, they must be able to recoup their opportunity cost. Since in states *HH* and *LH* when there is no liquidation of assets they end up holding the short asset throughout, they must make a significant profit in states *HL* and *LL* when the insurance companies go bankrupt. In other words, the price of the long asset must be low in these states.

To find the price P_{IL} that allows investors to just recover their opportunity cost $\rho = 1.5$, suppose they invest 1 in the short term asset at date 0. As mentioned, in states *HH* and *LH*, which occur with total probability 0.9, they will hold the short term asset throughout and receive 1 at date 2. In states *HL* and *LL*, which occur with total probability 0.1, investors will be able to buy $1/P_{IL}$ of the long asset at date 1 and receive $(1/P_{IL}) \times R = (1/P_{IL}) \times 1.25$ at date 2. The price P_{IL} must then satisfy

$$0.9 \times 1 + 0.1 \times \frac{1}{P_{IL}} \times 1.25 = 1.5,$$

so that

$$P_{IL} = 0.208.$$

We also need to find the price of the long asset $P_{HH} = P_{LH} = P_{IH}$ at date 1 in states *HH* and *LH*. This is simply equal to

$$P_{IH} = R = 1.25.$$

The reason for this is straightforward. In states *HH* and *LH* there is no bankruptcy and no sale of assets. A price equal to *R* ensures that the investors will hold cash and the insurance companies will hold the long asset between dates 1 and 2 so markets will clear. If $P_{IH} < R$ the investors would want to buy the long asset since it would provide a higher return than cash. If $P_{IH} > R$ the insurance companies would sell the long asset and hold cash until date 2. The only price at which both the long asset and cash will be held between dates 1 and 2, which is necessary for equilibrium, is $P_{IH} = R$.

Given this pricing of the long asset it can be shown that the optimal values for the transfers and ℓ_{LH} are

$$\tau_{HL} = 0.17, \quad \ell_{LH} = 0.037, \quad \tau_{LH} = \ell_{LH}R = 0.046.$$

When the insurance companies go bankrupt in states *HL* and *LL*, they are forced to liquidate the 0.037 of the long asset they hold to finance the credit risk transfer. In order

Table 21.3

Banks	Autarky	CRT	Insurance	Autarky	CRT
c_1	1	1			
c_{2HH}	1.5	1.541	C_{2HH}	1.975	1.975
c_{2HL}	1.5	1.211	C_{2HL}	1.125	1.251
c_{2LH}	1.227	1.241	C_{2LH}	1.975	1.929
c_{2LL}	1.227	1.149	C_{2LL}	1.125	1.086
Ec_2	1.418	1.425	EC_2	1.890	1.885
x	0.5	0.5	X	0.5	0.5
y	0	0	$Y = \ell_{LH}$	0	0.037
z	0.818	0.766	Insurance	Partial	Partial
e_0	0.318	0.266	E_0	0	0
EU	0.173	0.174	EV	0.624	0.624

for the market to clear at $P_{IL} = 0.208$, the investors must hold $0.037 \times 0.208 = 0.008$ in the short asset.

Table 21.3 gives the full equilibrium with credit risk transfer and also includes the full equilibrium with autarky for the purpose of comparison. It can be seen that the overall effect of credit risk transfer in this case is to make a Pareto improvement in welfare. Credit risk transfer represents a way of sharing risk between the sectors. It is an alternative to bank capital. Since bank capital is a relatively expensive way of sharing risk because of investors' high opportunity cost, the effect of credit risk transfer is to lower the amount of capital banks use. With autarky banks use 0.318 unit of capital, while with credit risk transfer they reduce this to 0.266 and consequently reduce their loans by a corresponding amount. The reduction in the use of relatively expensive capital means the expected consumption of late consumers goes from 1.418 to 1.425. The improvement in risk sharing allows depositors' expected utility to go from 0.173 to 0.174 while the insurance companies' customers, the firms, remain at 0.624.

One important aspect of this equilibrium is that banks do not use the long asset at all. It does not have a high enough return relative to loans to make it worth investing in. This means that when insurance companies liquidate the asset at a low price when they go bankrupt, there is no contagion to the banking sector.

Figure 21.1 summarizes the operation of the financial system in the autarky and with beneficial credit risk transfer. Banks always raise funds from depositors and investors and invest in the short term asset and loans. Firms with damageable assets at date 1 buy partial insurance from the insurance companies. In exchange for this insurance, firms pay a premium at date 0 and invest the rest of their initial endowment in the long asset. In the autarky equilibrium, the insurance companies invest the premiums they receive in the short asset, and use the proceeds to meet claims at date 1. Since returns to the short asset are technologically determined, there are no links between the two sectors. Neither banks nor insurance companies find it worthwhile to use the long asset so the dotted lines in the figure are not operational.

The introduction of credit risk transfer modifies the working of the financial system. To facilitate their ability to make a payout to the bank at date 2, insurance companies also start to invest in the long asset, as the line with short dashes in Figure 21.1 indicates. Banks choose not to invest in the long asset and the line with long dashes between the bank sector and the market for the long asset is not operative. There is no contagion between the insurance sector and the banking sector, and credit risk transfer is beneficial.

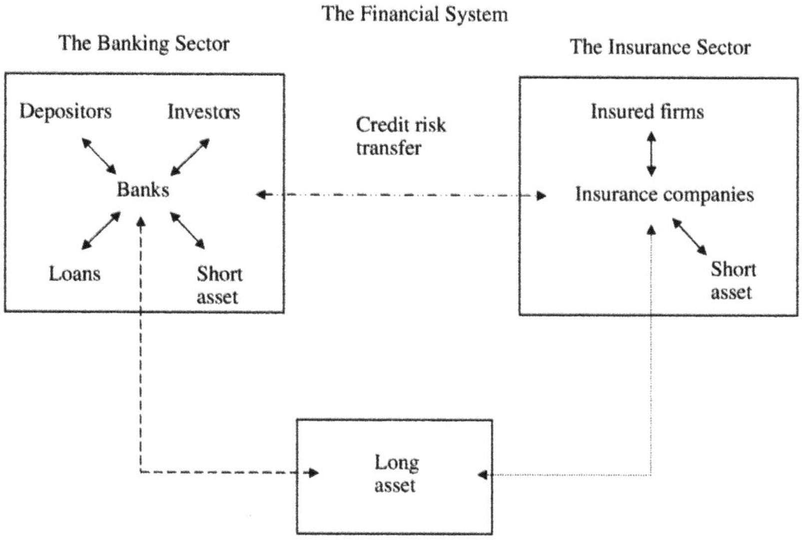

Figure 21.1. The financial system.

4. Detrimental Credit Risk Transfer

So far credit risk transfer has been beneficial because the two sectors hold different assets and there is no contagion to the banking sector when the insurance companies go bankrupt. However, if for some reason banks also start to hold the long term asset, then there is potentially a problem. Banks would be affected by the bankruptcy of the insurance sector and their solvency might be threatened. In terms of Fig. 1 the line with long dashes between the banking sector and the long asset now becomes relevant.

To see how this can happen, we assume that, instead of all facing the same risk, banks are subject to idiosyncratic liquidity risk. With probability 0.5 the proportion of their customers that are early consumers is λ_i, $i = 1, 2$, and the proportion of late consumers is $1 - \lambda_i$ with $\lambda_1 > \lambda_2$. There is no aggregate uncertainty so $0.5\lambda_1 + 0.5\lambda_2 = \lambda$. For simplicity, we assume $\lambda_1 = 1$, $\lambda_2 = 0$, so these shocks are extreme. Either all of a bank's depositors are early consumers or they are all late consumers. Furthermore, the liquidity risk that banks face is independent of the risk from the payoffs on their loans.

In this new framework, banks hold the long term asset and credit risk transfer can reduce welfare. As before, the insurance companies are forced to liquidate their holdings of the long asset at a low price when they go bankrupt. This now also implies a reduction in the price of the long asset which banks use to hedge their liquidity risk. The banks that are selling the long asset receive a lower amount and are unable to pay their depositors. Within the equilibrium taking prices as given, it is optimal for banks and insurance companies to undertake credit risk transfer. Nevertheless, comparing this equilibrium with the autarkic one with no credit risk transfer, banks are worse off and insurance companies are indifferent.

Note that the insurance sector is not affected by the introduction of idiosyncratic liquidity shocks for banks. Thus, the autarkic equilibrium in the insurance sector is the same as in Section 3.2. We first analyze the new operation of the autarkic banking sector, and consider what happens when credit risk transfer is introduced.

4.1 The Autarkic Banking Sector with Idiosyncratic Liquidity Shocks

We focus here on how the idiosyncratic liquidity shocks affect the banking sector in autarky. It is initially assumed as a benchmark that there is no interbank market to allow banks to share liquidity risk and no capital for banks. In this case banks only use the short asset. Then we introduce an interbank market for the long asset which allows banks to hedge the risk associated with the idiosyncratic liquidity shocks they face, and we show banks start to use the long asset. Finally, we introduce capital and show how this also helps the idiosyncratic liquidity risk to be shared. We maintain throughout the assumption that loans cannot be liquidated.

No interbank market or bank capital We initially suppose there is no interbank market so banks cannot sell the long asset, and there is no capital so $e_0 = 0$.

As before, banks maximize depositors' expected utility so they choose to invest x in the short asset, y in the long asset and z in loans to solve the following problem:

$$\begin{aligned}
\text{Max} \quad & 0.5U(c_1) + 0.5[0.7U(c_{2H}) + 0.3U(c_{2L})] \\
\text{s.t.} \quad & \text{(2) and} \\
& c_1 = \frac{x}{1}, \\
& c_{2H} = \frac{x + yR + zB_H}{1}, \\
& c_{2L} = \frac{x + yR + zB_L}{1}.
\end{aligned}$$

The objective function is the same as in (1). The constraints are the per capita consumption of early consumers and of late consumers in states H and L. Note that they differ from the case of uniform liquidity shocks. In aggregate there is always 1 unit of depositors. Of these, 0.5 turn out to be early consumers and 0.5 are late consumers. A fraction 0.5 of the banks has all their depositors be early consumers and the remaining 0.5 have all their depositors be late consumers. The measure of the banks with early consumers and the measure of the early consumers are the same so each bank perceives that it has either all depositors be early consumers with probability 0.5 or all late consumers with probability 0.5. Since there is no interbank market, banks have no opportunity for trade once the state is determined at date 1. They can only use the assets they have at hand to repay depositors. This implies banks can only give depositors $c_1 = x/1$ from the short asset when they are all early consumers. When all depositors are late consumers, loans pay off $B_H (B_L)$ in states $H(L)$ and consumers receive $c_{2H} = x + yR + zB_H (c_{2L} = x + yR + zB_L)$.

The solution to the optimization problem is

$$\begin{aligned}
& x = l, \quad y = z = 0, \\
& c_1 = c_{2H} = c_{2L} = 1, \\
& EU = 0.
\end{aligned}$$

For the particular parameter values of the example, the payoffs on the long asset and the loans are not sufficient to compensate for the fact that they are wasted when all the depositors withdraw early. The reason the long asset and loans are wasted is there are no markets to liquidate them. As a result, the optimal solution is for banks to only use the short asset.

An interbank market but no bank capital We next introduce the possibility for banks to sell the long asset on an interbank market at date 1 if they need to. Suppose the price of the long asset in state i is P_i where $i = H, L$. Then banks having all early consuming depositors sell their holdings of the long asset to obtain yP_i to pay out to their depositors; while banks with all depositors being late consumers buy x/P_i of the long asset. This implies each bank solves the following problem at date 0:

$$\text{Max} \quad 0.5[0.7U(c_{1H}) + 0.3U(c_{1L})] + 0.5[0.7U(c_{2H}) + 0.3U(c_{2L})] \tag{21.9}$$

$$\text{s.t.} \quad (2) \text{ and}$$

$$c_{1i} = x + yP_i \quad \text{for } i = H, L, \tag{21.10}$$

$$c_{2i} = \left(\frac{x}{P_i} + y\right) R + zB_i \quad \text{for } i = H, L. \tag{21.11}$$

The first term in the objective function represents the 0.5 probability that a bank's depositors are all early consumers. With probability 0.7 (0.3) the bank's holdings of the long asset, y, can be sold for P_H (P_L) and depositors receive $c_{1H} = x + yP_H(c_{1L} = x + yP_L)$. Loans are wasted because there is no market for them. The second term in the objective function represents the 0.5 probability that all the bank's depositors are late consumers. In this case the bank uses its holdings of the short asset, x, to purchase x/P_i of the long asset to add to its existing holdings of y. In addition depositors receive the payoffs of the bank's loans zB_i. Thus with probability 0.7 (0.3) the late depositors receive $c_{2H} = ((x/P_H)+y)R+zB_H(c_{2L} = ((x/P_L) + y)R + zB_L)$.

Since the proceeds from loans are wasted when all depositors turn out to be early consumers, banks do not find it worthwhile to hold loans. It is only worth using the long asset and $z = 0$. This implies also that banks' portfolios do not bear any risk and $P_H = P_L = P$. The only equilibrium price is

$$P = 1.$$

To see this note that if $P < 1$ all banks would prefer the short asset between dates 0 and 1 and those with late depositors would attempt to buy the long asset at date 1. But this cannot be an equilibrium. There would be no supply of the long asset at date 1 because all banks held the short asset between 0 and 1. Similarly if $P > 1$, all banks would hold the long asset between dates 0 and 1, and the banks with early consumers would attempt to sell their holdings at date 1. There would then be no demand so $P > 1$ cannot be an equilibrium price.

Given this pricing of the long asset, the optimal solution to the bank's problem is

$$x = y = 0.5, \quad z = 0,$$

$$c_1 = 1, \quad c_{2H} = c_{2L} = 1.25,$$

$$EU = 0.112.$$

The fact that the long asset can be sold in an interbank market means that banks can use it to hedge their liquidity risk. If all their depositors are early consumers, banks sell their holdings of the long asset and use the proceeds together with their holdings of the short asset to pay their depositors. Any holdings of loans would be wasted so they do not find it worth holding these. If all their depositors turn out to be late consumers, banks buy the long asset and thus supply liquidity to the market.

An interbank market and bank capital We now analyze the autarkic equilibrium of the banking sector when there is an interbank market for liquidating the long asset and investors are willing to provide capital. Introducing capital now has two effects. As when banks have uniform liquidity risks, capital allows late consuming depositors to share some risk with investors and have higher expected utility. In addition to this though, capital now prevents the waste of a bank's loans when all their depositors want to consume early. Because they are risk neutral, investors provide e_0 of capital to the banks in return for total expected payoffs that are equivalent. These payoffs consist of the payoffs from the loans when there are all early consumers and a payoff e_2 in state $i = H$ when there are all late consumers.

The bank's problem is to maximize (9) subject to (6), (10), (11) with $i = L$, and

$$c_{2H} = \left(\frac{x}{P_H} + y\right) R + zB_H - e_2, \tag{21.12}$$

$$\rho e_0 = 0.5[0.7(zB_H) + 0.3(zB_L)] + 0.5 \times 0.7 \times e_2. \tag{21.13}$$

This problem is the same as in the case without capital except for the budget constraint (2) being replaced with (6), which has capital included, and two further constraints. The first one, (12), is the per capita consumption of late consuming depositors, and it differs from (11) with $i = H$ because it now allows for the payment e_2 to the investors providing capital. The second constraint, (13), is the investors' participation constraint. To understand it, recall that each bank faces a probability 0.5 that all its depositors become early consumers and a probability 0.5 of having all late consuming depositors. In the former case, the bank gives the proceeds of its loans to the investors. Thus, investors receive payments $zB_H(zB_L)$ with (conditional) probability 0.7 (0.3), as the first terms on the right-hand side of the constraint show. When all depositors are instead late consumers, the bank gives a payment $0.7 \times e_2$ to the providers of capital as 0.7 is the (conditional) probability that loans pay off B_H and the providers of capital are paid e_2.

In this case the optimal solution is $P = 1$ as before and

$$x = y = 0.459, \quad z = 0.160, \quad e_0 = 0.077, \quad e_2 = 0,$$
$$c_1 = 0.917, \quad c_{2H} = 1.427, \quad c_{2L} = 1.267,$$
$$EU = 0.117.$$

Differently from the optimal solution without capital, it is now worth investing in loans. The reason is that the investors receive the payoffs when the banks customers are early consumers and are willing to provide capital as a result. Thus, loans are no longer wasted and their returns are high enough to induce banks to hold them.

4.2 Credit Risk Transfer

Now that we have considered the banking sector in autarky, we can analyze the effects of credit risk transfer when banks face idiosyncratic liquidity risks. The insurance sector

Table 21.4

State	Bank loans	Late depositors	Insurance claims (%)	Firms	Probability
HH	1.75	1.427	50	1.975	0.63
HL	1.75	1.427	100	1.125	0.07
LH	0.75	1.267	50	1.975	0.27
LL	0.75	1.267	100	1.125	0.03

remains the same as before. Given the risks in the two sectors are independent, we have again four possible states with the payoffs shown in Table 21.4.

As before we focus on credit risk transfer where banks pay τ_{HL} to insurance companies in state *HL*, and insurance companies transfer τ_{LH} to banks in state *LH*. As before, it is assumed that banks gain the surplus created by the credit risk transfer.

We first consider whether, taking prices as given at the same levels as in the autarkic solution, it is worth introducing credit risk transfer. With $P = 1$ in all states as above, the optimal credit risk transfer has $\tau_{HL} = 0.26$. The insurance companies invest $\ell_{LH} = 0.075$ in the long asset and make a payment $\tau_{LH} = 0.094$. Depositors increase their expected utility to $EU = 0.119$, and the firms' owners have the same expected utility of $EV = 0.624$ as in autarky. Thus, credit risk transfer is perceived to increase welfare. This, however, cannot be an equilibrium. The insurance companies invest in the long asset to fund the transfer to the banks in state *LH*. In states *HL* and *LL* they go bankrupt when the machines of all the firms they insure get damaged. They are forced to liquidate the long asset, and markets no longer clear at $P = 1$.

We next solve for the equilibrium with credit risk transfer. The most important feature of this equilibrium is that there is contagion from the insurance sector to the banking sector. The bankrupt insurance companies are forced to sell the long asset in states *HL* and *LL*. These forced sales drive down the price of the long asset. As a result, the banks that have early consumers and are selling their holdings of the long asset to satisfy their liquidity needs are adversely affected. They can no longer meet their commitments to the early consumers and also go bankrupt. As we shall see, this leads to a Pareto reduction in welfare. The first reason for this is that banks are unable to liquidate their loans because there is no market for them. The second is that the bankrupt banks lose out to the solvent ones, and this reallocation involves inefficient risk sharing.

Banks in this case solve the following optimization problem:

$$\begin{aligned}\text{Max}\quad & 0.5[0.9U(c_{1IH}) + 0.1U(c_{1IL})] \\ & \quad + 0.5[0.63U(c_{2HH}) + 0.07U(c_{2HL}) + 0.27U(c_{2LH}) + 0.03U(c_{2LL})] \\ \text{s.t.}\quad & (6), \\ & \rho e_0 = 0.5 \times 0.9 \times z(0.7B_H + 0.3B_L) + 0.5 \times 0.27 \times \ell_{LH} \times R + 0.5 \times 0.63 \times e_2, \end{aligned} \tag{21.14}$$

$$\begin{aligned} c_{1IH} &= x + yP_{IH}, \\ c_{1IL} &= x + yP_{IL}, \\ c_{2HH} &= \left(\frac{x}{P_{IH}} + y\right) R + zB_H - e_2, \end{aligned}$$

$$c_{2HL} = \left(\frac{x}{P_{IL}} + y\right) R + zB_H - \tau_{HL} - e_2,$$

$$c_{2LH} = \left(\frac{x}{P_{IH}} + y\right) R + \tau_{LH} + zB_L,$$

$$c_{2LL} = \left(\frac{x}{P_{IL}} + y\right) R + zB_L.$$

The objective function of the bank can be understood as follows. Each bank has a 0.5 chance of having all early consuming depositors. The insurance industry is in state $H(L)$ with probability 0.9 (0.1). Banks provide consumption to early consumers $c_{1HH} = c_{1LH} = c_{1IH}(c_{1HL} = c_{1LL} = c_{1IL})$ using their holding x of the short asset and by selling the long asset y for $P_{IH}(P_{IL})$ so that in total they offer $c_{1IH} = x + yP_{IH}(c_{1IL} = x + yP_{IL})$. When banks have all late consuming depositors, which occurs also with probability 0.5, depositors' payoffs depend on the state of both the banking and the insurance sectors. In state *HH*, which occurs with probability 0.63, these banks use their holding of the short asset to purchase x/P_{IH} of the long asset at date 1 so the total return from the long asset is $((x/P_{IH}) + y)R$. They receive zB_H from their loans and pay out e_2 to shareholders. The same happens in state *HL*, which occurs with probability 0.07, except that the price for buying the long asset is P_{IL} instead of P_{IH} and banks pay τ_{HL} to the insurance companies as part of the credit risk transfer. In state *LH*, which occurs with probability 0.27, the main difference is that banks receive τ_{LH} from the insurance companies as part of the credit risk transfer. In state *LL*, which occurs with probability 0.03, there is no credit risk transfer payment so late consuming depositors just consume the returns from the long asset and the loans.

The other constraints, (6) and (14), are the usual budget constraint at date 0 with capital and the investors' participation constraint. In the latter, the first term, $0.5 \times 0.9 \times z(0.7B_H + 0.3B_L)$, represents the expected payoff investors receive when the bank has early consumers and the investors receive the proceeds from the loans. The reason for the 0.9 is that this only happens when the bank remains solvent. The remaining 0.1 of the time the bank goes bankrupt and the loans are worth zero because there is no market for liquidating them. The second term, $0.5 \times 0.27 \times \ell_{LH} \times R$, is the expected payoff to investors when the bank has all early consumers and receives a credit risk transfer from the insurance companies in state *LH*. The final term, $0.5 \times 0.63 \times e_2$, is the payment to the investors in state *HH*.

The method of finding the equilibrium now differs slightly from the previous cases. In particular, we now have to find the equilibrium prices and the solution to the maximization problem simultaneously rather than sequentially. The reason is that there is "cash in the market pricing" in the market for the long asset (see Allen and Gale, 2005b). The buyers of assets find it optimal to use all of their liquidity and the sellers supply all of their long assets so the price is simply the ratio of the liquidity to the amount of the long asset. To calculate it, we then need to know the total liquidity and supply of the long asset in each state, and therefore the optimal values for the transfers and the investments of both banks and insurance companies.

The optimal values for the transfers and ℓ_{LH} are

$$\tau_{HL} = 0.192, \quad \ell_{LH} = 0.053, \quad \tau_{LH} = 0.066.$$

Given these values, Table 21.5 reports the full optimal solution for both banks and insurance companies with credit risk transfer and in autarky for the purpose of comparison.

Table 21.5

Banks	Autarky	CRT	Insurance	Autarky	CRT
c_{1lH}	0.917	0.979			
c_{1lL}	0.917	0.892			
c_{2HH}	1.427	1.308	C_{2HH}	1.975	1.975
c_{2HL}	1.427	1.057	C_{2HL}	1.125	1.294
c_{2LH}	1.267	1.326	C_{2LH}	1.975	1.909
c_{2LL}	1.267	1.392	C_{2LL}	1.125	1.102
Ec_2	1.379	1.297	EC_2	1.890	1.883
x	0.459	0.489	X	0.5	0.5
y	0.459	0.489	$Y = \ell_{LH}$	0	0.053
z	0.160	0.049	Insurance	Partial	Partial
e_0	0.077	0.027	E_0	0	0
e_2	0	0			
EU	0.117	0.114	EV	0.624	0.624

The values of x, y and ℓ_{LH} determine the functioning of the market for the long asset. Since $x = y = 0.489$ and $\ell_{LH} = 0.053$, the 0.5 banks that have late consumers have liquidity $0.5 \times 0.489 = 0.245$ at date 1, while the 0.5 banks that have early consumers have $0.5 \times 0.459 = 0.245$ of the long asset to sell. In states *HH* and *LH* insurance companies do not liquidate their long asset and the equilibrium price is simply

$$P_{lH} = 1.$$

In states *HL* and *LL*, in addition to the banks with early consuming depositors, the bankrupt insurance companies sell 0.053 of the long asset, thus increasing the supply in the market and reducing the price. The market clearing price in states *HL* and *LL* is then given by

$$P_{lL} = \frac{0.245}{0.245 + 0.053} = 0.823.$$

This price is too high to make it worthwhile for investors to provide liquidity to the market as in the case where banks face uniform liquidity shocks, but at the same time it is low enough to also make banks with early consuming depositors go bankrupt in states *HL* and *LL*.

As a result, the equilibrium with credit risk transfer can be Pareto worse than autarky. As Table 21.5 shows, the customers of insurance companies obtain the same expected utility of 0.624 in both cases. Banks' depositors obtain 0.117 in autarky and only 0.114 with credit risk transfer. Within the latter equilibrium, taking prices as given, banks' depositors will only obtain expected utility of 0.107 if they do not engage in credit risk transfer so it is definitely worth them undertaking it. Depositors are worse off with credit risk transfer because of the inefficient liquidation of the long asset due to the contagion and the poor risk sharing between banks with early consumers and banks with late consumers. The banks with early consumers go bankrupt and are forced to sell their long asset cheaply. The banks with late consumers make a profit from buying the long asset cheaply. This is bad from an ex ante point of view because the early consumers have the lowest consumption and they are the ones losing out.

Fig.21.1 illustrates the key point of the equilibrium with credit risk transfer when banks face idiosyncratic liquidity risk. Without credit risk transfer only banks hold the long asset and they trade it on the interbank market to hedge against liquidity risk. The introduction of credit risk transfer induces the insurance companies to use the long asset as well. This means the two sectors are linked through the market as the dotted lines to the long asset market indicate. The fall in prices caused by the liquidation of insurance companies' long assets result in contagion to the banking sector. The banks that are forced to liquidate their long assets to meet their liquidity needs go bankrupt.

5. Concluding Remarks

This paper has shown that credit risk transfer can be beneficial because it improves risk sharing. However, it can also induce contagion and lead to a Pareto reduction in welfare. Financial innovation can thus have somewhat unexpected results. It is necessary to consider all the systemic effects when deciding whether or not it is beneficial.

The examples presented in this paper were developed in the context of banking and insurance. Despite the recent rapid growth in credit risk transfer shown in Table 1, a comparison of the outstanding amounts of credit risk transfer instruments with the total outstanding amounts of bank credit and corporate debt securities shows that they remain small in relative terms. Although credit risk transfer may not pose a systemic problem at the moment, it may do in the future as it continues to grow in importance. Perhaps more important is that this kind of analysis is applicable in many different contexts. The interaction of incomplete markets and the role of liquidity in asset pricing are the key factors for the contagion across sectors. These elements can occur in the context of many financial institutions. Hedge funds have become increasingly important in many markets. They potentially provide a conduit for contagion across many illiquid markets.

We have assumed very simple contractual forms in the insurance industry. More complex contractual forms such as incorporating junior and senior policyholders to allow some claims to be met in the bad state would improve the allocation of resources. However, provided it is not possible to contract around bankruptcy completely, similar results to ours should still hold.

This paper has focused on the private provision of liquidity in markets and has not analyzed the role of central banks in liquidity provision. In markets with limited participation it is likely that central banks will have problems injecting liquidity into the financial system that will reach the required markets and prevent the kind of contagion considered here. The justification used by the Federal Reserve Bank of New York for their intervention in arranging a private sector bailout of Long Term Capital Management in 1998 explicitly used this rationale. The issue of what the precise role of central banks in this kind of situations should be is an interesting question for future research.

References

Allen, F., Gale, D., 1990. Incomplete markets and incentives to set up an options exchange. In: Polemarchakis, H. (Ed.), Geneva Papers on Risk and Insurance Theory, vol. 15, pp. 7–46 (special issue entitled "The Allocation of Risk with Incomplete Asset Markets").

Allen, F., Gale, D., 1998. Optimal financial crises. Journal of Finance 53, 1245–1284.

Allen, F., Gale, D., 2000a. Financial contagion. Journal of Political Economy 108, 1–33.

Allen, F., Gale, D., 2000b. Optimal currency crises. Carnegie-Rochester Conference Series on Public Policy 53, 177–230.

Allen, F., Gale, D., 2000c. Comparing Financial Systems. MIT Press, Cambridge, MA.

Allen, F., Gale, D., 2004a. Financial intermediaries and markets. Econometrica 72, 1023–1061.

Allen, F., Gale, D., 2004b. Financial fragility, liquidity, and asset prices. Journal of the European Economic Association 2, 1015–1048.

Allen, F., Gale, D., 2006. Systemic risk and regulation. In: Carey, M., Stulz, R. (Eds.), Risks of Financial Institutions, NBER, 341–375.

Allen, F., Gale, D., 2005b. From cash-in-the-market pricing to financial fragility. Journal of the European Economic Association 3, 535–546.

Arping, S., 2004. Credit protection and lending relationships. Working paper, University of Amsterdam.

BBA, 2002. Credit Derivatives Report, British Bankers Association.

BIS, 2003. Committee on the Global Financial System. Credit Risk Transfer. Bank for International Settlements, Basel, Switzerland.

Cass, D., Citanna, A., 1998. Pareto improving financial innovation in incomplete markets. Economic Theory 11, 467–494.

Chiesa, G., 2004. Risk transfer, lending capacity and real investment activity. Working paper, Department of Economics, University of Bologna.

Duffee, G., Zhou, C., 2001. Credit derivatives in banking: useful tools for managing risk? Journal of Monetary Economics 48, 25–54.

Elul, R., 1995. Financial innovation in incomplete markets economies with several consumption goods. Journal of Economic Theory 65, 43–78.

Fitch Ratings, 2003. Global Credit Derivatives: Risk Management or Risk? <www.fitchratings.com>, March 10, 2003.

Gale, D., 2003. Financial regulation in a changing environment. In: Courchene, T., Neave, E. (Eds.), Framing Financial Structure in an Information Environment. Kingston, Ontario, John Deutsch Institute for the Study of Economic Policy, Queen's University.

Gale, D., 2004. Notes on optimal capital regulation. In: St-Amant, P., Wilkins, C. (Eds.), The Evolving Financial System and Public Policy. Bank of Canada, Ottawa.

Hart, O., 1975. On the optimality of equilibrium when market structure is incomplete. Journal of Economic Theory 11, 418–433.

Morrison, A., 2005. Credit derivatives, disintermediation and investment decisions. Journal of Business, 78, 621–647.

Newbery, D., Stiglitz, J., 1984. Pareto inferior trade. Review of Economic Studies 51, 1–12.

Nicolo, A., Pelizzon, L., 2004. Credit derivatives: capital requirements and strategic contracting. Working paper, Department of Economics, University of Padua.

Parlour, C., Plantin, G., 2005. Credit risk transfer. Working paper, Tepper School of Business, Carnegie Mellon University.

Wagner, W., 2005a. The liquidity of bank assets and banking stability. Working paper, Cambridge Endowment for Research in Finance, University of Cambridge.

Wagner, W., 2005b. Interbank diversification, liquidity shortages and banking crises. Working paper, Cambridge Endowment for Research in Finance, University of Cambridge.

Wagner, W., Marsh, I., 2004. Credit risk transfer and financial sector stability. Working paper, Cambridge Endowment for Research in Finance, University of Cambridge.

22 Estimating Bilateral Exposures in the German Interbank Market: Is There a Danger of Contagion?

Christian Upper and Andreas Worms

1. Introduction

Credit risk associated with interbank lending may lead to domino effects, where the failure of a bank results in the failure of other banks even if the latter are not directly affected by the initial shock. Recent work in economic theory shows that this risk of contagion depends on the precise pattern of interbank linkages. For example, in the model of Allen and Gale (2000) banks hold deposits with banks of other regions in order to insure against liquidity shocks in their own region. Here a 'region' should not necessarily be interpreted in geographical terms but could, in principle, refer to any grouping of banks. If a bank is hit by a shock, it tries to meet its liquidity need by drawing on its deposits at other banks before liquidating long-term assets. This pecking order follows from the assumption that the premature liquidation of long-dated assets is costly, for example, because otherwise profitable real investment projects would have to be abandoned or long-term lending relationships interrupted.

On the aggregate, the interbank market can only redistribute liquidity but does not create liquidity of its own. While this may not be a problem if the overall liquidity need is lower than the total holdings of liquid assets, it may give rise to contagion if the opposite is true. Instead of liquidating their long-term assets in response to a liquidity shock, banks withdraw their deposits at other banks, thus spreading the liquidity shortage throughout the financial system. The possibility of contagion depends strongly on the precise structure of interbank claims. Contagion is less likely to occur in what Allen and Gale term a 'complete structure of claims', in which every bank has symmetric linkages with all other banks in the economy (see Figure 22.1). 'Incomplete structures', where banks have links only to a few neighbouring institutions (see Figure 22.2 for an extreme example), are shown to be much more fragile.

In a related paper by Freixas et al. (2000), interbank lending arises not from consumers' uncertainty about *when* to consume (as in Allen and Gale) but about *where* to consume. Their model may be interpreted as a payment system, where interbank credit lines are used to reduce the overall amount of liquid (but costly) reserves. In their setting, contagion may occur even if all banks are solvent. If the depositors in a sufficiently large number of banks believe that they will not obtain payment at the bank of their destination, it is optimal for them to withdraw their deposits. Since this forces banks to liquidate their investments, it triggers a run where all other depositors withdraw their deposits and the banking system reaches a gridlock. Besides contagion driven by non-banks' behaviour, the authors also consider the impact an insolvent bank has on the banking system. They find

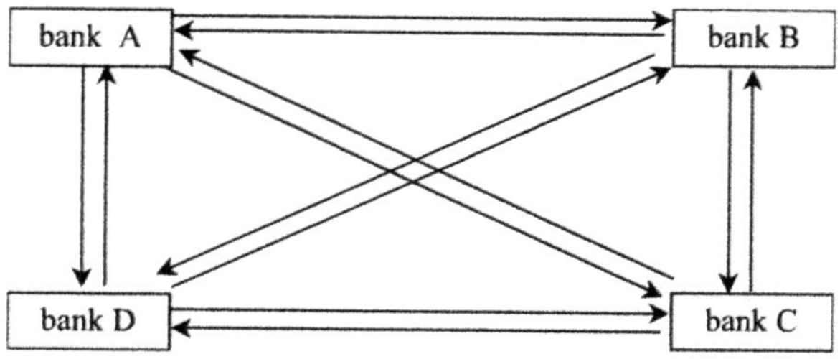

Figure 22.1 'Complete market structure' according to Allen and Gale (2000).

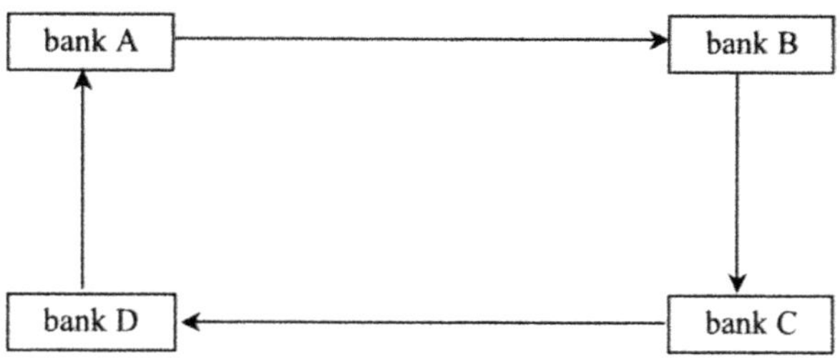

Figure 22.2 'Incomplete market structure' according to Allen and Gale (2000).

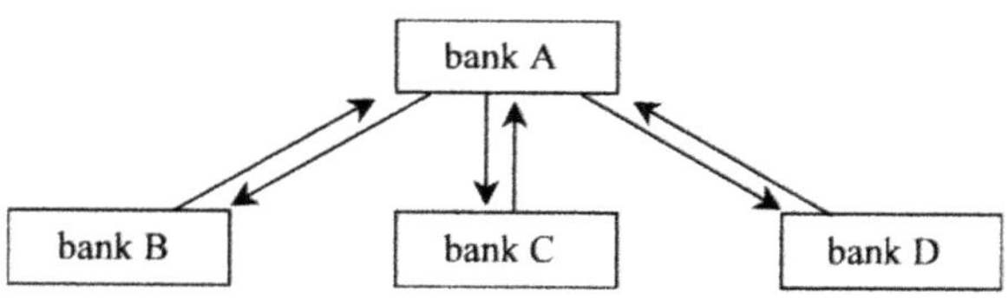

Figure 22.3 Money centre bank according to Freixas et al. (2000).

that interbank connections generally enhance the resiliency (i.e. the ability to withstand shocks) of the financial system. Interbank credit lines provide an implicit subsidy to the insolvent bank, which is able to spread part of its losses to other banks. As in Allen and Gale, a 'complete structure of claims' reduces the risk of contagion, while 'incomplete structures', or 'credit chains' (like the one in Figure 22.2) increase the fragility of the system.

A third case considered by Freixas et al. is that of a money centre bank, where the institutions on the periphery are linked to the bank at the centre but not to each other (Figure 22.3). They find that for some parameter values the failure of a bank on the periphery will not trigger the breakdown of other institutions while the failure of the money centre bank would. They do not provide any general results, though.[1]

Unfortunately, very little is known about how the actual structure of bilateral exposures affects the danger of contagion as banks do not have to disclose their counterparts. The only exception we are aware of is the paper by Blavarg and Nimander (2002), who use data on the counterparts of the four major Swedish banks.[2] They find that the failure of a large

[1] Rochet and Tirole (1996) and Aghion et al. (2000) consider the incentives to bail out failing banks by providing interbank loans. The absence of a bailout could be due to a weak financial position of the banking system and thus serves as a signal triggering a bank run. They do not say much about how the precise direction of interbank linkages affects the possibility of contagion.

[2] In contrast to Germany or the U.S., the Swedish banking system is very concentrated, with the top four institutions accounting for more than 80% of all assets (Blavarg and Nimander, 2002).

Swedish bank could push the tier 1 capital of the other three banks below 4% (the level at which supervisors would normally close the banks), provided that recoveries of assets are close to zero. The failure of the largest foreign exchange counterparty could have even stronger effects.

Given the absence of data on counterparty loan exposures,[3] researchers interested in interbank lending either have to limit the analysis to particular market segments for which information is available, or use some kind of identifying assumptions to estimate bilateral exposures.[4] Furfine (2003) adopts the former approach and uses settlement data to compute bilateral exposures in the U.S. federal funds market. He finds that even in his worst-case scenario (failure of the most significant bank and a loss given default of 40% [5]) only between two and six other banks fail, accounting for less than 0.8% of total bank assets. No contagion occurs at all if the loss rate is 5%—such as the one estimated by Kaufman (1994) for Continental Illinois. The results have to be interpreted with care, however, since the federal funds market accounts for only 10–20% of total interbank exposures in the United States, although its share is likely to be higher if only uncollateralised positions are considered.

The present paper follows the second line of research and estimates a matrix of bilateral credit relationships from bank balance sheet data. In contrast to studies based on settlement data, this permits us to cover total interbank lending rather than only overnight lending. This is particularly relevant for Germany, where about half of all lending between banks is long-term.[6] This advantage comes at a cost, however. Owing to the fact that we do not have complete information on the individual counterparties in the interbank business, we need to make assumptions on the distribution of bank i's interbank loans and deposits over the other banks. We assume that interbank lending is as widely dispersed as possible, given the observed distribution of loans and deposits. This is likely to bias our estimates against the hypothesis of finding contagion, although it may lead to an overstatement of the number of institutions affected if contagion does take place.

Our paper is closely related to those of Sheldon and Maurer (1998) and of Elsinger et al. (2003). Sheldon and Maurer estimate a matrix of interbank loans for Switzerland by maximising entropy.[7] They come to the conclusion that the interbank loan structure that existed among Swiss banks posed little threat to the stability of the Swiss banking system in the period under consideration. Elsinger et al. embed a similar matrix of interbank credit relationships estimated from Austrian data in a risk management model and explore the effects of macroeconomic shocks. In their paper, 94% of all default events in their simulations were directly due to exposures to non-banks, and only 6% involved contagion in the interbank market, which suggests that the risk of domino effects caused by macroeconomic shocks is very small.

Our work differs from these two papers in several respects. First of all, our approach is much more disaggregated than those adopted in these two papers and uses all the partitioning available in our data. By contrast, for computational reasons, Sheldon and Maurer aggregate the individual banks into 12 categories and estimate the linkages between these categories.

[3]In some countries, credit registers also cover large exposures in the interbank market. Unfortunately, to the best of our knowledge these data are not available to researchers.

[4]Another strand of the literature focuses on contagion in the payment system. See, for example, Humphrey (1986) and Angelini et al. (1996).

[5]The 40% loss rate corresponds to the typical loss on assets of a failing bank estimated by James (1991).

[6]We focus only on direct lending relationships and do not capture exposures arising in the payment or security settlement systems or exposures due to the cross-holding of securities.

[7]They also estimate the probability of failure, and thus the likelihood of contagion, which we ignore.

Elsinger et al. use bank-level data that contain information on the bilateral linkages between certain types of institutions, for example, Austrian savings and cooperative banks and their respective head institutions, as well as total exposures. We use the same kind of information, but in addition have a breakdown of interbank lending by maturity, which considerably increases the efficiency of the estimates. More specifically, we estimate separate matrices for (i) loans of savings banks to their regional giro institutions, (ii) loans of giro institutions to affiliated savings banks, (iii) loans of cooperative banks to cooperative central banks, (iv) loans of cooperative central banks to cooperative banks, and (v) the remaining interbank loans and deposits of all banks, each for five maturity categories. We thus obtain 25 separate matrices for a given point in time, one for each counterparty/maturity class. We then add up these 25 matrices to form a system-wide matrix of interbank credit exposures. Since banks tend to be active only in a few maturity segments at any given point in time, this disaggregated approach considerably reduces the number of possible counterparties in each of the separate matrices, allowing us to spread the exposures over a much smaller number of institutions than would otherwise be the case. Owing to these zero restrictions, our estimate is more accurate than a matrix estimated with figures for the aggregate exposures of every bank.

Despite the assumption that loans are spread among potential counterparts as evenly as possible given the data, we find that interbank lending is relatively concentrated. As has already been pointed out, the theoretical literature suggests that this could make contagion a real possibility. We assess this danger by letting every bank go bankrupt one at a time and computing the effect of this failure on the other banks. The simulations show that the vast majority of banks could fail without significant knock-on effects on other banks due to interbank credit exposures. Although domino effects are rare, they could occur. In the worst case, the failure of a single bank could trigger a chain that ends with the bankruptcy of almost 15% of the banking system in terms of assets. If we ignore safety mechanisms such as the institutional guarantees in the savings and cooperative bank sector, the results are even more pronounced. It has to be borne in mind, however, that our analysis takes the initial shocks leading to contagion as given. We are therefore unable to attach probabilities to our scenarios.

It is important to stress that our analysis concentrates exclusively on contagion due to credit exposures in the interbank market. We do not capture exposures arising in the payment or security settlement systems or exposures due to the cross-holding of securities—not because they are unimportant but because we have no data on them. Moreover, we assume that the bank failure triggering contagion is unexpected and that the pattern of interbank lending remains invariant during the process of contagion. The latter assumption is less strict than it may seem at first sight, since domino effects may take place over a very short period of time, leaving banks little room for manoeuvre. We thus rule out other channels of contagion such as bank runs, which have commanded the attention of much of the theoretical literature and have dominated the discussion on banking regulation. We believe that this omission is justified not only for methodological reasons in that it permits us to isolate one specific channel of contagion. Contagion due to bank runs by non-bank depositors in the wake of the breakdown of a single institution is highly unlikely in Germany, where virtually all deposits by non-financial institutions are insured.[8] The type of contagion we analyse hinges less on the behavioural interdependence of the respective parties and more on interdependence owing to interbank linkages. In this sense, it can be labelled as being mechanical.

[8]A detailed description of the guarantee schemes is contained in Deutsche Bundesbank (1992) and (2000b).

The paper is structured as follows. After a description of the dataset we present the estimation methodology. This is followed by a discussion of the structure of the German banking system in general and the interbank market in particular. In Section 5, we estimate the danger of contagion in the German interbank market, leaving aside for a moment the existence of a safety net. We find that, in this case, contagion may lead to the breakdown of a large part of the German banking system. Having done this, we measure the importance of the safety net in place in Germany designed to prevent such scenarios. Our findings suggest that these institutions dramatically reduce, but do not eliminate, the danger of contagion. The final section presents conclusions.

2. Description of the data

The analysis is based on balance sheets, which all German banks and German branches of foreign banks have to submit to the Bundesbank every month. In their submissions, banks have to state whether their counterpart in the interbank market is a domestic or a foreign bank, a building society (*Bausparkasse*), or the Bundesbank. Savings banks and cooperative banks also have to identify lending to giro institutions (*Landesbanken*) and cooperative central banks, respectively (and vice versa). In addition, all banks have to break down their interbank business into five maturity categories (listed in Table 22.1).[9] Assets and liabilities denominated in foreign currencies were converted into DM (before 1999) or euro (afterwards) at the current market exchange rate. For our estimations, we consider the balance sheets from end-December 1998. After this date, the number of maturity categories was reduced to effectively three in the wake of the EMU harmonisation of the banking statistics. Since the precision of our estimation procedure crucially depends on the number of maturity brackets, the estimates for the period after 1998 should be considered exclusively as robustness checks.

In order to obtain a closed system where, in principle, all interbank loans and deposits add up to zero, we only consider lending between domestic banks, i.e. we exclude all business with building societies, the Bundesbank and foreign banks.[10] As can be seen in Table 22.1, 71% of all interbank assets and 63% of liabilities are with domestic banks. The share of domestic counterparts is highest for savings banks (assets: 93%, liabilities: 85%) and cooperative banks (assets: 97%, liabilities: 87%) and lowest for commercial banks (assets: 42%, liabilities: 37%). The Landesbanken and cooperative central banks fall somewhere in between.

Table 22.1 also shows the maturity structure of domestic interbank lending. What is striking is that more than one-half of the interbank lending takes place at maturities of four years or more. However, this share varies widely across bank type: whereas long-run interbank liabilities are very important for savings banks (92%) and for cooperative

[9]Deposits from banks are actually broken down into six categories, which we consolidate into five in order to make them comparable with the lending side.

[10]In practice, discrepancies between assets and liabilities do arise. They are particularly acute for overnight loans and deposits, where the latter consistently exceed the former in the order of 10-15%. For this reason, the individual asset positions were scaled so that their sum matches that of the liability positions within the same maturity category. Errors in the data are a likely source of the discrepancies between assets and liabilities. The database has been checked for consistency (for example, all positions on the balance sheet have to satisfy an adding-up constraint), but entries in the wrong category remain a possibility. Provisions, which can be deducted from the corresponding asset position, are another possible source of discrepancy. Nevertheless, it is hard to believe that provisions in the domestic interbank market account for a substantial proportion of the discrepancy.

Table 22.1 Interbank assets and liabilities by maturity and broad bank categories (end December 1998)

		Share of dom. interbank lending in total interbank lending[a]	Maturities[b]				
			1 day	> 1 day and < 3 months	≥ 3 months and ≤ 1 year	> 1 year and < 4 years	≥ 4 years
All banks	Liabilities	62.8	11.7	13.2	14.5	5.6	55.0
	Assets	70.8	10.6	14.1	17.2	5.6	52.5
Commercial banks	Liabilities	37.2	21.1	18.0	21.3	3.4	36.2
	Assets	42.1	22.3	30.3	27.1	5.3	14.9
Savings banks' sector	Liabilities	65.2	9.6	19.0	17.3	8.6	45.5
Landesbanken	Assets	73.0	4.6	7.7	15.7	4.3	67.7
Savings banks	Liabilities	84.8	2.7	2.2	2.0	1.5	91.5
	Assets	92.9	20.7	38.5	28.7	3.2	8.8
Cooperative sector	Liabilities	75.1	26.5	20.5	14.3	10.8	27.8
	Assets	78.9	9.7	5.7	18.5	5.6	60.5
Central banks	Liabilities	86.8	3.5	1.7	1.8	1.2	91.7
Coop. bank	Assets	96.8	28.9	27.4	20.4	11.8	11.5
Other banks	Liabilities	84.3	7.0	9.3	18.9	5.9	58.9
	Assets	86.6	2.9	4.5	5.1	7.4	80.0

[a]Domestic assets and liabilities vis-à-vis all banks excluding building societies and the Bundesbank divided by total interbank assets and liabilities.
[b]Domestic assets and liabilities vis-à-vis all banks excluding building societies and the Bundesbank only.

banks (92%), they are less important for commercial banks (36%), *Landesbanken* (46%) and cooperative central banks (28%). The picture differs considerably when it comes to interbank assets: here, only 9% (savings banks) and 12% (cooperative banks) of interbank loans have a maturity of at least 4 years. For the *Landesbanken* and the cooperative central banks the corresponding figures are 68% and 61%, respectively. On the whole, Table 22.1 shows that the interbank market consists of far more than just the exchange of liquidity on a day-to-day basis. For the assessment of the danger of contagion, it is therefore not sufficient to consider just these short-run relationships. It is also—and especially—necessary to take into account the longer-term assets and liabilities.

3. Estimation methodology

The lending relationships in the interbank market can be represented by the following $N \times N$ matrix:

$$\boldsymbol{X} = \begin{bmatrix} x_{11} & \cdots & x_{1j} & \cdots & x_{1N} \\ \vdots & \ddots & \vdots & \iddots & \vdots \\ x_{i1} & \cdots & x_{ij} & \cdots & x_{iN} \\ \vdots & \iddots & \vdots & \ddots & \vdots \\ x_{N1} & \cdots & x_{Nj} & \cdots & x_{NN} \end{bmatrix} \begin{matrix} \Sigma_i \\ a_1 \\ \vdots \\ a_i \\ \vdots \\ a_N \end{matrix}$$

$$\Sigma_j \quad l_1 \quad \cdots \quad l_j \quad \cdots \quad l_N \tag{22.1}$$

where x_{ij} is the credit exposure of bank i vis-à-vis bank j and N is the number of banks. We cannot observe the bilateral exposures but we do know the sum of each bank's interbank loans and deposits,

$$a_i = \sum_j x_{ij} \quad \text{and} \quad l_j = \sum_i x_{ij}, \tag{22.2}$$

respectively. This information does not suffice to identify the elements of X, so we are left with $N^2 - 2N$ unknowns. If we want to estimate the bilateral exposures, we have to make assumptions on how banks spread their interbank lending.

With the appropriate standardisation, we can interpret the a's and l's as realisations of the marginal distributions $f(a)$ and $f(l)$, and the x's as realisations of their joint distribution, $f(a, l)$. If $f(a)$ and $f(l)$ are independent, then $x_{ij} = a_i l_j$. In the terminology of information theory, this amounts to maximising the entropy of $\boldsymbol{X}$. The assumption of independence implies that interbank loans and deposits are spread over banks as equally as is consistent with the observed marginal distributions. It may thus be interpreted as an analogue to Allen and Gale's (2000) 'complete structure of claims', where banks symmetrically hold claims on all other banks in the economy, conditioned on the size-structure of the banks (see Figure 22.1).

There are many reasons to believe that independence is a rather poor description of reality. For example, we are ruling out relationship lending, which may be an important feature of the interbank market.[11] Nevertheless, since we have to make identification assumptions, our aim should be to deviate as little as possible from the information in our data. Furthermore, by assuming independence we probably reduce the likelihood of contagion, although we may increase the number of institutions affected if contagion does occur.

The independence matrix $\boldsymbol{X}$ in (1) has the unappealing feature that the maximisation of entropy creates elements on the main diagonal that are non-zero if a bank is both lender and borrower. In this case, using $\boldsymbol{X}$ to compute bilateral exposures would amount to assuming that banks lend to themselves. This problem does not necessarily disappear as the number of banks increases if interbank lending or borrowing is relatively concentrated. We therefore need to modify the independence assumption by setting $x_{ij} = 0$ for $i = j$.[12]

$$X^* = \left[\begin{array}{ccccc} 0 & \cdots & x^*_{1j} & \cdots & x^*_{1N} \\ \vdots & \ddots & \vdots & \cdot^{\cdot^{\cdot}} & \vdots \\ x^*_{i1} & \cdots & 0 & \cdots & x^*_{iN} \\ \vdots & \cdot^{\cdot^{\cdot}} & \vdots & \ddots & \vdots \\ x^*_{N1} & \cdots & x^*_{Nj} & \cdots & 0 \end{array}\right] \begin{array}{c} \Sigma_i \\ a_1 \\ \vdots \\ a_i \\ \vdots \\ a_N \end{array}$$
$$\begin{array}{cccccc} \Sigma_j & l_1 & \cdots & l_j & \cdots & l_N \end{array} \tag{22.1*}$$

This should be done by departing from the assumption of independence as little as possible. More formally, this means that we have to minimise the relative entropy of X^* with respect

[11] Cocco et al. (2003) show that interbank lending relationships are important in the money market.

[12] Setting the elements on the diagonal equal to zero also reduces the number of coefficients to be estimated to $N^2 - 3N$ by imposing more structure on X.

to a matrix $\boldsymbol{X}$ with elements $x_{ij} = a_i l_j$ for $i \neq j$ and zero for $i = j$:

$$\min_{x^*} x^{*\prime} \in \frac{x^*}{x}$$
$$\text{s.t.} \quad x \geq 0 \quad \text{and} \quad \boldsymbol{A}x = \left[a', l\right]', \qquad (22.3)$$

where $\boldsymbol{x}^*$ and $\boldsymbol{x}(N^2 - N) \times 1$ vectors containing the off-diagonal elements of X^* and $\boldsymbol{X}$, respectively, a and l are the marginals, and $\boldsymbol{A}$ is a matrix containing the adding-up restrictions (2). Since the objective function is strictly concave, programme (3) yields a unique solution for the structure of interbank lending $\boldsymbol{X}^*$. Programme (3) is solved numerically with the RAS algorithm that is commonly used in computing input-output tables.[13]

4. The structure of the German interbank market

As was mentioned above, our data contain information on interbank lending and borrowing in each of five maturity categories for

(1) deposits and loans from savings banks to regional giro institutions *(Landesbanken)*,
(2) deposits and loans from regional giro institutions *(Landesbanken)* to savings banks,
(3) deposits and loans from cooperative banks to cooperative central banks,
(4) deposits and loans from cooperative central banks to cooperative banks, and
(5) all interbank loans and deposits that do not belong to (1)–(4).

This permits us to compute a total of 25 matrices of bilateral exposures, which add up to give the total amount of interbank exposures. We use this added-up matrix to test for the possibility of contagion. For (1)–(4), we can compute interbank exposures using the independence matrix $\boldsymbol{X}$(Eq.(1)) because no bank appears as both lender and depositor. Where banks do appear on both sides, in (5), we use the RAS algorithm.[14]

Table 22.2 shows the exposures of the average bank within a given category in the interbank market.[15] What is particularly striking is the large share of the head institutions at the base level. 75% of the interbank deposits at savings are held by *Landesbanken*, who also receive 81% of their loans. Cooperative central account for 82% of the deposits at and 94% of the loans of cooperative banks. There are almost no deposits held between banks on the base level of the same giro system (savings banks: 0.5%, cooperative banks: 0.2%) and across the two giro systems (savings banks at cooperatives: 0.3%, cooperatives at savings banks: 0.3%).

Table 22.2 points to the existence of two relatively closed systems, where lower-tier banks (which include most savings banks and all cooperative banks) have very few direct

[13] See Blien and Graef (1991). In a previous version of the paper we used a different algorithm which yielded the same results.

[14] We also estimated a matrix on the basis of aggregated (over counterpart and maturity) interbank assets and liabilities only. This matrix has the unappealing characteristic that all banks hold virtually the same portfolio, the only difference being that they do not lend to themselves. The scope for contagion thus becomes a function of the ratio of interbank assets to capital multiplied by the loss rate and little else. In the terminology of Allen and Gale (2000), such a matrix would correspond to a 'complete structure of claims'.

[15] The figures are not comparable with those from the consolidated balance sheet of each group presented in Deutsche Bundesbank (2000a).

Table 22.2 Exposures in the German Interbank Market: Interbank assets and liabilities (average % share of banks by categories, end-December 1998)

Interbank assets/liabilities		**Commercial bank**	**Savings banks' sector**		**Cooperative sector**		**Other banks**
			Landes-banken	**Savings banks**	**Central banks**	**Cooper-atives**	
All banks	Liabilities	5.1	20.3	0.9	58.2	0.5	15.0
	Assets	7.6	19.0	1.3	67.1	0.4	4.7
Commercial banks	Liabilities	31.7	24.6	5.3	6.2	2.2	30.0
	Assets	43.1	23.0	2.9	10.3	1.3	19.5
Savings bank's sector	Liabilities	18.6	21.5	19.2	4.1	1.6	35.0
	Assets	18.4	19.7	35.6	5.0	1.7	19.7
Landesbanken	Liabilities	2.8	75.2	0.5	0.5	0.3	20.7
Savings banks	Assets	8.3	81.0	1.8	1.9	0.4	6.5
Cooperative sector	Liabilities	10.0	10.7	1.8	1.4	59.0	17.0
	Assets	17.5	15.6	1.8	3.2	49.8	12.0
Central banks	Liabilities	1.9	5.1	0.3	81.7	0.2	10.8
	Assets	1.8	1.8	0.5	94.2	0.1	1.5
Cooperatives							
Other banks	Liabilities	18.6	27.6	4.0	4.1	1.6	44.2
	Assets	25.9	27.6	10.4	8.5	2.7	24.9

Linkages *within* a giro system are shaded in grey.

linkages to banks of other categories except those with the respective head institutions and deposits from other banks, which comprise mainly mortgage and development banks (e.g. KfW). About half of these deposits represent credit lines that serve to refinance development loans. The upper tier consists of the commercial banks, a small number of savings banks (around 10), the *Landesbanken* and cooperative central banks plus a variety of other banks. Instead of focused relationships with a small number of head institutions, banks belonging to the upper tier entertain lending relationships with a variety of other banks belonging to the same tier, including those of other categories. As a consequence, in the upper tier the pattern of interbank exposures is much closer to a 'complete structure of claims' than that in the lower tier.

The two-tier structure of the interbank market in Germany depicted in Figure 22.4 differs considerably from the stylised structures considered in the theoretical literature, although it shows some parallels with the money centre structure studied in Freixas et al. (see Figure 22.3). It is not clear a priori whether such a structure leads to a significantly higher danger of contagion compared with the complete structure as indicated by the baseline matrix. The subsequent estimations will deal with this question.

5. Estimating the danger of contagion in the absence of the safety net

We estimate the scope for contagion by letting banks go bankrupt one at a time and measuring the number of banks that fail owing to their direct or indirect exposure to the failing bank.

In our simulations, the failure of bank *i* triggers the failure of bank *j* if $\theta x_{ij} > c_j$, where θ is the loss rate, x_{ji} is *j's* gross exposure to *i*, and c_j is *j's* book capital. Contagion need

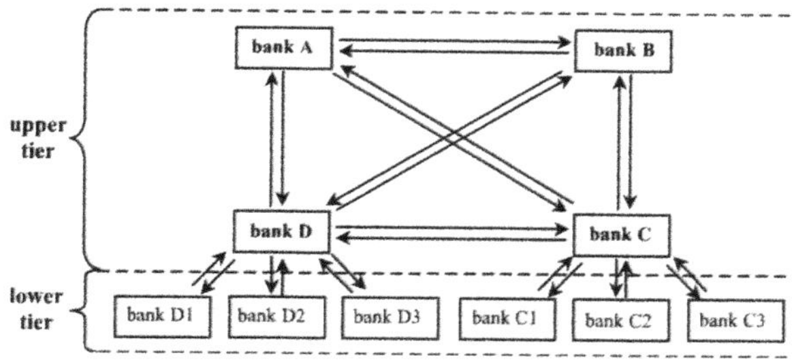

Figure 22.4 Two-tier structure of the German interbank market.

Table 22.3 Interbank lending and capital, by broad banking category (end-December 1998)

	All banks	Commercial banks	Savings banks' sector		Cooperative sector		Other banks
			Landes-banken	Savings banks	Central banks	Cooperative banks	
No of banks	3246	331	13	594	4	2256	48
of which with dom.interbank loans > cap	2758	228	13	432	4	2043	38
dom.interbank loans/capital	2.96	4.64	13.73	1.95	14.39	2.69	12.94

not be confined to such first-round effects, however. Instead, the failure of a single bank can potentially trigger a whole chain of subsequent failures (the domino effect) even if the initial impact is relatively weak. For example, suppose that bank j fails owing to its exposure to bank i. This will cause the breakdown of bank k if its exposure to banks i and j multiplied by the loss rate exceeds its capital, i.e. if $\theta(x_{ki} + x_{kj}) > C_k$. This line of argument also applies to higher orders.

The focus on gross exposures stems from the fact that German bankruptcy law stipulates that offsetting claims—unless explicitly earmarked as collateral—enter the asset pool from which all claims are satisfied in accordance with their seniority. We also consider whether bilateral netting arrangements would have any impact on the scope for contagion, although we have reservations about their feasibility.

The assumption that banks fail only after having exhausted their book capital does not correspond to normal regulatory practice, where banks are closed as soon as their *risk-weighted* capital falls below a certain threshold (usually around 4%). We believe that preventive closure is unrealistic in the context of the scenarios analysed in the paper as contagion may occur over very short time spans, which precludes regulatory action.

A necessary condition for contagion to occur is that the volume of a bank's interbank loans exceeds its capital. As can be seen from Table 22.3, this is generally the case. Of the 3246 banks that existed in Germany at the end of 1998, 2758 (85%) had domestic interbank loans in excess of their capital. The average ratio of domestic interbank loans to capital was just below 3, although this was driven by the large number of small cooperative banks in our sample which tend to hold relatively few interbank assets. The corresponding figures for the *Landesbanken*, cooperative central banks and other banks are well above 10. This suggests that there could be scope for domino effects.

Perhaps the key parameter in determining whether or not contagion is possible is the loss ratio θ, which refers to the share of assets that cannot be recovered in the case of bankruptcy. Unfortunately, the choice of θ is by no means obvious. There is little systematic evidence for countries other than the United States, where the average loss realised in bank failures in the mid-1980s was 30% of the book value of the bank's assets. In addition, creditors had to bear administrative and legal costs of a further 10% (James, 1991).[16] The average loss incurred by holders of bonds issued by US commercial banks that defaulted between 1971 and 1995 was even higher at about 70% (Altman and Kishore, 1996).

It is not clear how much guidance these figures can give us. They refer to mostly small banks which failed in completely different circumstances than those analysed here. It has been argued that the losses incurred owing to the unexpected failure of individual banks are much lower. For example, Kaufman (1994) estimates that the creditor banks of Continental Illinois—a bank with large interbank operations that failed owing to its exposure to Latin America—would have suffered a loss of only 5% had it not been bailed out by the Fed. Other cases point in a different direction, however. When BCCI failed in the early 1990s, creditors at first expected losses of up to 90%, but ended up recovering more than half of their deposits—albeit many years after the failure.[17] Creditor banks of Herstatt, a German bank that was an important player in the interbank market, have so far received 72% of their assets, with the liquidation of the bank continuing to drag on even a quarter of a century after its closure in 1974.[18] The uncertainty about eventual recoveries, combined with the time it takes for creditors to get their money, show that it may not be the actual losses borne by the creditor banks that matter. Instead, it is the expected losses at the moment of failure that determine the extent to which the exposure to the failing bank has to be written down and hence whether the creditor bank becomes technically insolvent or not. We therefore cannot rule out high values for θ.[19]

The loss rate also depends on the availability of collateral, for example, in repos. Unfortunately, our data do not provide information on the share of collateralised positions. It was only in 1999—after the end of our sample period and after the major structural change of European Monetary Union—that the monthly balance sheet statistic was amended to include interbank repos. Unfortunately, the size of these positions cannot be matched to the individual maturity or counterparty categories, which form the basis of our estimates. However, in the summer of 2000, repos accounted for no more than 6.2% of all interbank lending. Moreover, anecdotal evidence suggests that these are mostly with foreign banks. We therefore believe that the possible dampening effect of collateral on the danger of contagion in Germany is negligible.

Another major determinant of θ is the seniority of interbank claims vis-à-vis other creditors. Deposits are junior to bankruptcy costs, taxes and, at least to some extent, wage payments. Unfortunately, it is not possible to make any statement about how the seniority of deposits by banks compares with those by non-banks as contractual arrangements vary from case to case. Given the difficulties in determining the appropriate loss rate, we test for the possibility of contagion using a broad range of values for θ, which we assume to

[16]This cost represents the discount of the market value of the failed bank's assets relative to their book value.

[17]Financial Times, 8 July 1998.

[18]Frankfurter Allgemeine Zeitung, 26 June 1999.

[19]There are several cases where regulators have been lenient in forcing banks to write down assets even though hardly anybody seriously expected their value to recover. Examples are U.S. banks in the wake of the Mexican debt moratorium in 1982 and Japanese banks in the 1990s.

Table 22.4 Incidence of contagion in the absence of any safety net (based on end-December 1998 matrix)

		loss ratio θ=					
		0.75	**0.50**	**0.40**	**0.25**	**0.10**	**0.05**
Average number of banks affected	Gross exp.	**30.3**	**22.2**	**20.0**	**18.0**	**17.0**	**17.0**
	Netting	*16.6*	*14.2*	*14.1*	*13.3*	*13.3*	*13.3*
% of total assets of banking system affected on average	Gross exp.	**0.85**	**0.66**	**0.58**	**0.30**	**0.26**	**0.25**
	Netting	*0.46*	*0.23*	*0.23*	*0.20*	*0.20*	*0.20*
Maximum number of banks affected	Gross exp.	**2444**	**1740**	**115**	**31**	**19**	**18**
	Netting	*275*	*85*	*54*	*23*	*18*	*17*
Maximum share of total assets affected	Gross exp.	**76.3**	**61.6**	**5.0**	**0.75**	**0.57**	**0.30**
	Netting	*8.2*	*1.1*	*0.9*	*0.57*	*0.30*	*0.25*

be constant across banks. Endogenising θ would, taken together, be at least as arbitrary as assuming a fixed loss ratio in the first place.[20]

The results of the simulations are presented in Table 22.4. The figures in bold refer to contagion due to gross exposures exceeding capital (our preferred scenario), and the figures in italics to the case of bilateral netting. At this stage, we do not explicitly take into account any institutional safeguards present in the German system, which may affect the possibility of contagion, although they may in part be reflected in the bilateral lending matrix $\boldsymbol{X}$. In the absence of a safety net, contagion always occurs irrespective of whether netting is feasible and no matter which loss rate we choose, although the choice of θ determines how many banks are affected on average. There are 17 commercial banks which fail, irrespective of which bank is the first to break down. However, we should not overvalue this result. Firstly, the banks in question are relatively small, accounting for only 1/4 percentage point of the total assets of the banking system. Secondly, the fact that 10 of them always break down in the first round, that is due to the immediate impact, suggests that this, rather than being a description of reality, is more a reflection of our assumption that interbank exposures are as equally spread as is consistent with the data. We would expect that small banks are much more likely to concentrate their lending on a small number of counterparties, which would preclude the same bank always breaking down in the first round.

While the finding that contagion always occurs may be an artifact of our methodology and should not be taken too seriously, the other results are more interesting. Without netting and with a relatively high loss ratio of 75%, the maximum number of bank failures caused by domino effects (the 'worst case')[21] is 2444. This means that 88% of the institutions where contagion is a possibility, because domestic interbank loans exceed

[20]Elsinger et al. (2003) endogenise θ by assuming that interbank liabilities are junior to non-bank deposits and abstract from taxes and wage payments. We believe that these assumptions do not provide a good characterization of the German interbank market. Elsinger et al.'s simulations yield loss ratios ranging from virtually zero to almost one, with a median of 34%. In their baseline scenario, they assume that no assets are destroyed in bank failures. Assuming bankruptcy costs of 10%, which is in line with the estimate of James (1991), raises the maximum number of contagious defaults by a factor of ten.

[21]Alternatively, the worst case could be defined in terms of assets lost. In our simulations, the two cases coincide.

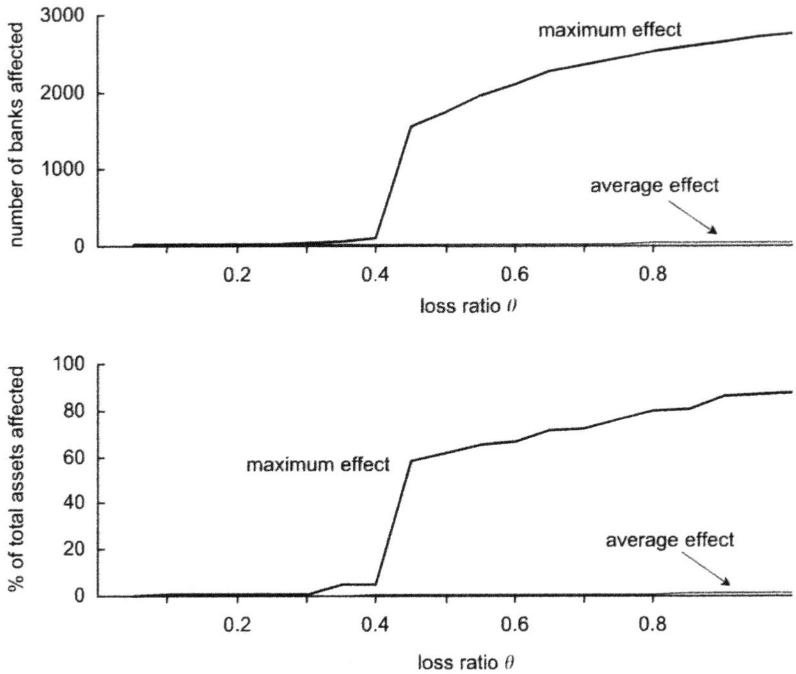

Figure 22.5. Loss ratio and the severity of contagion in the absence of the safety net (no netting).

capital, are affected. As is to be expected, the number of breakdowns increases with the loss rate. This increase is not linear, however. Figure 22.5 shows that there is a jump in the severity of contagion if the loss ratio exceeds 40%. This points to the existence of a critical range of θ: if θ is smaller than 0.40 even in the worst case the effects on contagion are rather small. With a loss ratio larger than 0.45, the increase in the damage caused by contagion again seems to be rather moderate. But, if θ lies between 0.40 and 0.45, the loss of assets due to contagion is very sensitive to changes in θ.

Bilateral netting could reduce the scope for contagion considerably. For instance, for $\theta = 0.75$, the maximum number of banks affected by contagion falls from 2444 in the absence of netting to 275. The discontinuity observable in Figure 22.5 does not disappear, but shifts to the right, from around $\theta = 0.5$ to 0.7, and becomes less pronounced.

Figure 22.6 plots the spreading of contagion over time.[22] The number of banks that fail in the worst case (without netting) are plotted on the vertical axis (note the different scales and the fact that the worst case may refer to different banks for different loss ratios), and the round of failure on the horizontal axis. For small θ's or if claims are netted—that is, when the severity of contagion is limited even in the worst possible case—the bulk of banks fail in the first-round, with some minor second and, possibly, third-round effects. For $\theta > 40\%$, the path of contagion is very different. Although the first-round effects are only slightly larger than before, they do not peter out but at some point reach a critical mass that leads to the collapse of much of the banking system. Intuitively, a higher θ has the potential to

[22]Here we equate 'time' and 'rounds'.

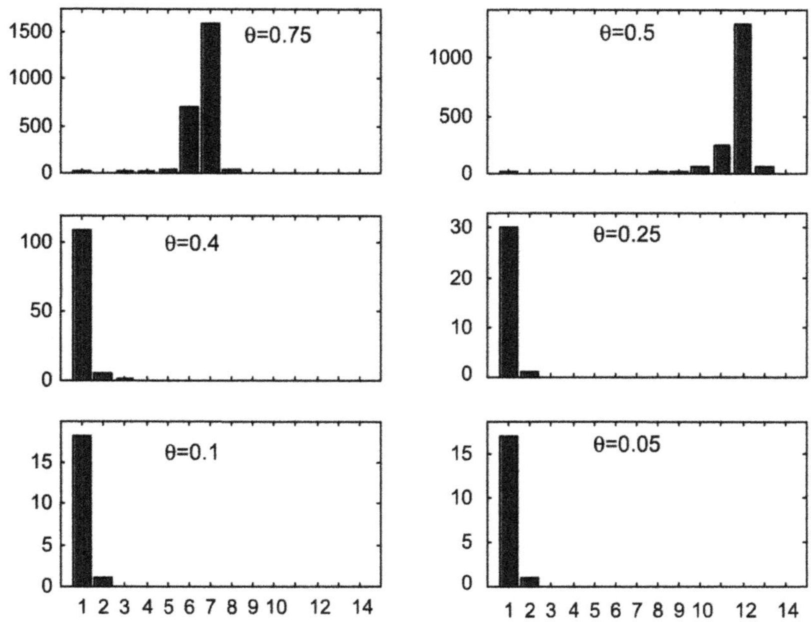

Figure 22.6. Number of banks affected in round $r = \ldots$ (worst case in the absence of the safety net, no netting).

increase the build-up of pressure in the system. At some point, a critical mass of losses is reached at which the bulk of the system fails.[23]

However, widespread contagion is rare even for high θ's. In most cases, the initial shock leads to the breakdown of a number of banks, which in turn causes a smaller number of further failures. Then the process stops. This, together with the high values of θ necessary to cause prolonged chains of failures, is one of the reasons why Furfine (2003) does not obtain higher than second-round effects.[24]

This switching in the time pattern of contagion has major implications for the regulation of banks and the design of institutional safeguards. It shows that it may be possible to stop the most severe scenarios with relatively low costs at an early stage, i.e. before the dramatic wave of bank failures sets in. It must nevertheless be kept in mind that the rounds on the horizontal axis of Figure 22.5 are not comparable to discrete time periods in the usual sense. In principle, domino effects take place instantaneously. In practice, it may take some time before banks realise the losses they have incurred but, even so, late rounds can occur a very short time after the initial shock. This means that there may be virtually no possibility for a regulator to react to a process once it has started.

Table 22.5 shows the contagion effects by bank category of the initial shock for the loss rates of 0.50 and 0.10, respectively. As one would expect, failures of savings banks or cooperative banks have very little impact on other banks. Even in the case of a loss rate of 0.50, the damage would remain below 1% of total assets. The largest contagion effects

[23]This shift in the time profile of contagion is related to the assumption that the loss rate is constant. It should be less likely if losses incurred in higher rounds are lower than those in the early stages of contagion.

[24]The other reasons are Furfine's focus on a single—albeit important—segment of the interbank market and, possibly, the different structures of the U.S. and German banking systems.

Table 22.5 Incidence of contagion in the absence of the safety net, by bank categories (based on end-December 1998 full information matrix)

	loss rate $\theta =$	Max. no. of failures (worst case) in brackets: % of total assets		Mean no. of failures (normal case) in brackets: % of total assets		Average % share in total interbank loans
		In $r = 1$	sum $r > 1$	In $r = 1$	sum $r > 1$	
Commercial banks	0.50	22 (0.61)	18 (0.58)	13.9 (0.22)	6.2 (0.36)	
	0.10	17 (0.25)	15 (0.25)	13.9 (0.22)	3.1 (0.04)	16.0
Savings banks' sector Landesbanken	0.50	20 (0.75)	1720 (60.17)	17.9 (0.37)	268.4 (9.51)	30.0
	0.10	17 (0.25)	0 (0.00)	17.0 (0.25)	0.0 (0.00)	
Savings banks	0.50	17 (0.25)	18 (0.58)	11.8 (0.21)	8.2 (0.37)	7.7
	0.10	17 (0.25)	15 (0.25)	11.8 (0.21)	5.2 (0.05)	
Cooperative sector Central banks	0.50	195 (1.56)	1545 (60.06)	57.6 (0.54)	312.2 (12.28)	7.8
	0.10	18 (0.30)	1 (0.27)	17.2 (0.26)	0.2 (0.05)	
Cooperatives	0.50	17 (0.25)	18 (0.58)	9.3 (0.17)	10.7 (0.41)	
	0.10	17 (0.25)	15 (0.25)	9.3 (0.17)	7.7 (0.08)	7.0
Other banks	0.50	25 (3.6)	1715 (56.95)	15.8 (0.32)	40.6 (1.52)	31.5
	0.10	17 (0.25)	15 (0.25)	15.5 (0.24)	1.5 (0.02)	

occur if a head institution of one of the giro systems or a large development bank fails. With $\theta = 50\%$, the failure of a *Landesbank* could trigger the failure of up to 1740 banks and more than 60% of total assets. On average, 286 banks are affected, corresponding to 10% of total assets. The effects of the failure of a cooperative central banks are similar. Again 1740 banks—or more than 60% of the banking system in terms of assets—would fail in the worst case, and 370 banks (13% of total assets) on average. These results are compatible with the implications derived theoretically by Freixas et al. (2000) on the basis of their money centre bank model.

What is striking is the limited effect of a failure of a commercial bank (the category that includes the large banks). Even in the worst case, it would only cause a loss of 40 banks or 1.2% of total assets. This may in part be due to the fact that a large proportion of the interbank claims of large commercial banks are on foreign banks, which are not included in our simulation exercise. Another reason might be that, owing to the absence of detailed information on intra-group lending, the independence assumption is stronger for commercial banks than it is for savings or cooperative banks or their respective head institutions.

In order to check whether our results depend on the particular choice of time period, we repeat the simulations for January 2002. For reasons of space, the results are not presented here but are available from the authors upon request. As described in Section 4, interbank assets and liabilities are broken down into three maturity categories, instead of five for the period before 1999. Given that this reduces the precision of the estimates, this exercise should be viewed as a robustness check only. Having said this, the 2002/1 estimates confirm the findings obtained for 1998/12. For θ=0.75, two-thirds of the banking system are affected by contagion in the worst case.[25] The discontinuity in schedule, relating the loss ratio to the severity of contagion, shifts somewhat to the right, but does not disappear. This suggests, firstly, that the pattern of interbank linkages in Germany has not changed significantly since the introduction of the euro, and, secondly, that our findings do not depend on the particular month chosen for the analysis.

6. Banking supervision, regulation and the safety net

The preceding analysis ignored the existence of a safety net which may limit the probability of our scenarios. In particular, as will become clear below, the safety mechanisms that are in place in Germany are designed to prevent the failure of *Landesbanken* and cooperative central banks. The worst-case scenarios identified in the previous section are therefore virtually impossible. In the present section, we address this omission and extend our analysis to incorporate the safeguards present in the German system. We limit ourselves to the case of gross exposures, both because we deem this to be more realistic and because there is not much scope for contagion even in the absence of a safety net if netting arrangements are in place.

Prudential supervision limits the danger of contagion in a number of ways. Firstly, banking supervision aims at reducing the incidence of failures by encouraging banks to behave more prudently. In our model, this corresponds to a reduction in the probability of a shock (i.e. the initial failure of a bank) occurring in the first place. Secondly, if banks do fail, swift action by the regulator could ensure that banks are liquidated before the losses become too large. This would be reflected by a low loss ratio θ. Finally, banking regulation may limit the exposures of banks to any single debtor or group of debtors, which in turn reduces the scope for contagion. For example, in Germany, bank loans to a single debtor should, in principle, not exceed 25% of the capital of the creditor, although interbank loans are partly exempted. For the purpose of our paper, such regulations are reflected in the pattern of interbank exposures.

While prudential supervision does play an important role in reducing the risk of contagion ex ante, it cannot stop this process once it is under way. In this case, two additional mechanisms could step in. The first is the Liko-Bank, a bank owned by the banking system with participation by the Bundesbank, which exists solely to provide liquidity to illiquid but solvent banks. Since our focus is on contagion due to insolvency, the Liko-Bank need not concern us here.

The second mechanism in place is the insurance of interbank deposits. Deposit insurance can halt contagion through credit exposures in the interbank market—as opposed to contagion through bank runs—only if it covers deposits by banks as well as deposits by non-banks. The statutory deposit insurance applies to non-bank deposits only (Deutsche

[25]The worst case were triggered by the failure of the same institutions as before.

Bundesbank, 2000b), whereas for savings and cooperative banks, including their respective head institutions, this is supplemented by "institutional guarantees". Both the savings banks' and cooperative banks' associations operate funds backed up by mutual guarantees which serve to recapitalise member institutions in the event they become insolvent.[26] In addition to the guarantee fund, savings banks are also explicitly guaranteed by the relevant local or regional government.[27] There are also a (small) number of public banks implicitly guaranteed by the federal government.[28]

We incorporate these safeguards into our analysis by assuming that

- savings banks never fail,
- public banks guaranteed by the federal government never fail, and
- cooperative banks never fail in the first round and hence never trigger contagion. In further rounds, they only fail if the exposure of the aggregate cooperative sector to the banks failed in previous rounds exceeds its aggregate capital. This is equivalent to assuming unlimited cross-guarantees and may thus overstate the solidarity between the individual banks of this group. As a consequence, either no cooperative bank fails or the cooperative sector as a whole, including the cooperative central banks, breaks down.[29]

Since in the previous section we found that the largest effects were caused by a breakdown of a development bank or a head institution of the savings or the cooperative sector, we should expect much lower contagion once we incorporate the existing safeguard mechanisms. The fact that during the past half century the stability of the German banking *system* has never been called into question despite a number of bank failures may be seen as an indication that the existing banking supervision and safety mechanisms have worked well in the past. This effectiveness is well confirmed by our results presented in Figure 22.7.

We find that contagion is much more limited in scope but remains a possibility even if we incorporate safety mechanisms into our analysis. As before, we find that the maximum percentage of assets affected remains relatively flat for loss ratios below 40% but increases for higher values. For θ's in excess of 75%, about 100 banks may be affected in the worst case of contagion. This corresponds to 15% of the banking system in terms of assets, which is considerably below the corresponding values of up to 80% if one ignores the safety mechanisms. In particular, we find that the cooperative system never fails, even for the highest θ's

When interpreting our results, it has to be borne in mind that we do not say anything about the *efficiency* of safety nets, since we do not incorporate their direct and indirect costs.

7. Summary and Conclusions

Credit risk associated with interbank lending may lead to domino effects, where the failure of one bank results in the failure of other banks not directly affected by the initial shock. Recent work in economic theory shows that this risk of contagion depends on

[26] In order to alleviate moral hazard problems, failed cooperative banks usually lose their independence and are merged with stronger banks, which obtain support from the guarantee fund.

[27] These state guarantees are being phased out starting in 2005.

[28] For example, the Kreditanstalt für Wiederaufbau (KfW).

[29] The charter of the safety fund for cooperative banks stipulates that each bank has to provide guarantees amounting to 60% of its statutory credit provisions. This is in addition to the contributions to the deposit guarantee fund, which covers non-bank deposits.

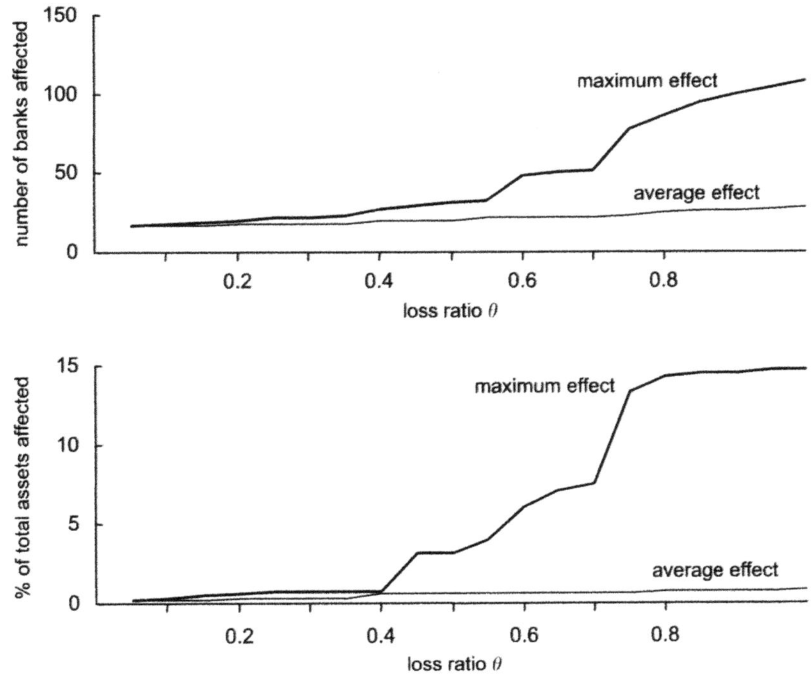

Figure 22.7. Loss ratio and the severity of contagion in the case of a perfect safety net (no netting).

the precise pattern of interbank linkages. We use balance sheet information to estimate matrices of bilateral credit relationships for the German banking system by maximising entropy. This is equivalent to assuming that banks spread their interbank lending as evenly as possible, given the data. Although this assumption is at odds with the notion that credit screening is costly, assuming a more concentrated structure would be at least as arbitrary. Moreover, more concentrated structures may lower the threshold of contagion, although we cannot assess by how much. In contrast to commercial datasets, our data cover the entire banking system, so all domestic interbank loans and deposits add up to zero in principle. In their submissions to the Bundesbank, which provide the basis of our analysis, banks have to provide a detailed breakdown of their interbank assets and liabilities, showing maturity categories and whether or not the counterparty is a head institution of the giro system to which the bank in question belongs. This permits us to estimate a matrix of bilateral credit exposures for each maturity and banking group, thus imposing much more structure on the problem than would be possible with aggregate interbank loans and deposits alone. The estimated system-wide matrix differs considerably from a matrix estimated from aggregate exposures across all maturities and banking groups alone.

We find that interbank lending in Germany is characterised by a two-tier structure. The first tier consists of most savings banks and virtually all cooperative banks, which transact mainly with the *Landesbanken* and cooperative central banks. The second tier consists of the head institutions of the two giro systems, the commercial banks and the other banks.

Our results suggest that domino effects through interbank credit exposures are possible,[30] although we have nothing to say about the probability of the shock that brings them about.[31] While the danger of contagion is normally confined to a limited number of relatively small banks, bank failures that affect a sizeable part of the banking system remain a possibility even if we explicitly take into account safety mechanisms like the institutional guarantees for savings banks and cooperative banks. In the absence of such mechanisms, the effects of the breakdown of a single bank could potentially be very strong indeed. This cannot be taken as a statement on the desirability of these mechanisms or a system with publicly owned banks, however, as we do not consider the incentive effects or other important aspects they are associated with. Neverthless, the results confirms that the existing safety nets significantly reduce the danger of contagion.

Not surprisingly, the danger of contagion crucially depends on the losses experienced by the creditor bank in the case of insolvency of the debtor bank. We find that large-scale contagion can in any case only occur if the loss rate on interbank loans exceeds a value of approximately 40%. This value is equal to the average loss rate including bankruptcy costs that has been observed for a sample of bank failures in the United States in the 1980s and therefore does not appear to be unreasonably high.

Our findings have major implications for banking regulation. The regulator can minimise the danger of contagion in a number of ways. Firstly, it can reduce the probability of the initial shock which could trigger contagion by encouraging banks to behave more prudently. Secondly, if a bank does fail, the regulator should ensure a quick and orderly liquidation before the ratio of losses to assets becomes too large. And finally, banking regulation can limit the exposures of banks to individual debtors.

References

Aghion, P., Bolton, P., Dewatripont, M., 2000. Contagious bank failures in a free banking system. European Economic Review 44, 713–718.

Allen, F., Gale, D., 2000. Financial contagion. Journal of Political Economy 108 (1), 1–33.

Altman, E., Kishore, V., 1996. Almost everything you wanted to know about recoveries on defaulted bonds.Financial Analysts Journal 52 (6), 57–64.

Angelini, P., Mariesca, G., Russo, D., 1996. Systemic risk in the netting system. Journal of Banking and Finance 20, 853–868.

Blavarg, M., Nimander, P., 2002. Inter-bank exposures and systemic risk, Sveriges Riksbank. Economic Review 2, 19–45.

Blien, U., Graef, F., 1991. Entropieoptimierungsverfahren in der empirischen Wirtschaftsforschung (Entropy optimization in empirical economic research). Jahrbuch fur Nationalökonomie und Statistik 208 (4), 399–413.

Cocco, J.F., Gomes, F.J., Martins, N.C., 2003. Lending relationships in the Interbank market, Mimeo.

Deutsche Bundesbank, 1992. Deposit protection schemes in the Federal Republic of Germany. Monthly Report, July, pp. 28–36.

Deutsche Bundesbank, 2000a. Longer-term trend in German credit institutions' interbank operations. Monthly Report, January, pp. 49–68.

Deutsche Bundesbank, 2000b. Deposit protection and investor compensation in Germany. Monthly Report, July, pp. 29–45.

[30]Contagion could also arise from linkages in the payment system or exposures from securities or derivatives. However, given the available data, testing for these other channels of contagion would require a set of very strong assumptions which would limit the clarity of the results.

[31]We do not consider other channels for contagion, such as runs by non-banks.

Elsinger, H., Lehar, A., Summer, M., 2003. Risk assessment for banking systems, Oesterreichische Nationalbank, Working Paper 79.
Freixas, X., Parigi, B., Rochet, J.C., 2000. Systemic risk, Interbank relations and liquidity provision by the Central Bank. Journal of Money, Credit, and Banking 32 (3) (Part 2), 611–638.
Furfine, C.H., 2003. Interbank exposures: Quantifying the risk of contagion. Journal of Money, Credit, and Banking 35 (1), 111–128.
Humphrey, D.B., 1986. Payments finality and the risk of settlement failure. In: Saunders, A., White, L.J. (Eds.), Technology and the Regulation of Financial Markets: Securities, Futures and Banking. Lexington Books, Lexington, MA.
James, C, 1991. The losses realized in bank failures. Journal of Finance 46, 1223–1242.
Kaufman, G.G., 1994. Bank contagion: A review of the theory and evidence. Journal of Financial Services Research 8, 123–150.
Rochet, J.-C, Tirole, J., 1996. Interbank lending and systemic risk. Journal of Money, Credit, and Banking 28, 733–762.
Sheldon, G., Maurer, M., 1998. Interbank lending and systemic risk: An empirical analysis for Switzerland. Swiss Journal of Economics and Statistics 134 (4.2), 685–704.

V FINANCIAL CRISES AND CURRENCY CRISES

23 Asset Market Linkages in Crisis Periods

Philipp Hartmann, Stefan Straetmans, and Casper de Vries

I. Introduction

Do different financial markets crash jointly, or is a fall of one a gain for another? The answer to this question is crucial for our view on the stability of international financial markets and any systemic risk related to these markets. The more markets crash simultaneously, the more in danger are even large banks that hold widely diversified trading portfolios, possibly also threatening the payment and settlement process. The number of markets affected by a crisis situation may also determine the severity of any real effects that might follow. Recent financial crises in emerging market economies have again drawn attention to these issues. Market participants, policymakers, and academics frequently point to the perceived occurrence of contagion, witness terminology like the "Asian flu." Others highlight joint shocks and macroeconomic fluctuations, triggering simultaneous crises in several markets or countries.

The phenomenon of financial-market crises spilling over to other countries was first systematically studied by Morgenstern (1959, ch. X).[1] He examined the effects of 23 stock market panics on foreign markets and explicitly referred to the "statistical extremes" of the stock market movements. The more recent econometric literature uses correlation analysis, often based on ARCH-type models. This literature asks whether stock-market comovements become stronger during crashes than in noncrash times. It also investigates the direction of international spillovers. Representative articles of this literature are King and Wadwhani (1990), Hamao, Masulis, and Ng (1990), Malliaris and Urrutia (1992), Lin, Engle, and Ito (1994), and Susmel and Engle (1994). There is also some empirical work on whether currency crises are contagious, notably in Eichengreen, Rose, and Wyplosz, (1996), Sachs, Tornell, and Velasco (1996), and Kaminsky and Reinhart (2000). However, there is very little work on bond market spillovers.[2]

[1]We thank Charles Goodhart for pointing us to this historical reference.

[2]We know of only two studies that systematically address international bond-market spillovers in volatile periods, namely Borio and McCauley (1996) and Domanski and Kremer (2000). In contrast with recent advances in the theoretical analysis of (for example) bank contagion, there are surprisingly few theoretical attempts to explicitly model crisis linkages between different securities markets. The published literature comprises King and Wadhwani (1990), Calvo and Mendoza (2000), Kodres and Pritsker (2002), and Kyle and Xiong (2001). For a comprehensive survey of the contagion literature, see de Bandt and Hartmann (2000).

The present paper adds a new perspective to the linkages between asset markets, by studying comovements between different types of assets and by using a novel methodology. In contrast to the existing literature, we do not only study the connection between, say, different stock markets during times of stress; we explicitly focus on the linkages between stock and government bond markets. Thus, apart from studying phenomena like contagion or joint crashes of stocks, we look into phenomena such as *flight to quality*, by which we mean a crash in stock markets accompanied by a boom in government bond markets. Extreme cross-asset linkages are important for the analysis of international financial stability, for they have a hearing on the overall, or *systemic*, reach that contagion or joint crashes can have. We are not aware of any other hard quantitative examination of cross-asset crisis linkages, including the flight-to-quality phenomenon.

The methodological novelty is that we do not use conditional correlation analysis. We directly measure and report the expected number of market crashes conditional on the event that at least one market crashes. Studies which rely on conditional correlation analysis usually do report the amount of correlation, but stop short of reporting the information that has more direct economic meaning. In our opinion, the correlation measure is only an intermediate step in obtaining a measure such as the likelihood of a crash spillover. The conditional correlation, moreover, is strongly predisposed toward the multivariate normal distribution. As our empirical analyis below shows, however, the multivariate normal dramatically underestimates the frequency of extreme market spillovers. Boyer, Gibson, and Loretan (1997) demonstrate for the bivariate normal that the conditional correlation measure varies considerably with the conditioning sets.[3] In addition, this variation can easily be shown to be different for different classes of multivariate distributions; worse, the conditional crash correlation can be 0 even if there is a high spillover probability. For all these reasons, we do not regard the statistical concept of correlation as an unambiguous measure of the economic interdependence between markets during times of stress.

This paper instead characterizes the return linkages between asset markets in periods of crisis by a measure from statistical extreme-value analysis that captures the dependence structure of multivariate distributions far away from the center. It turns out that this limiting dependence measure can be described by a single function that exists under fairly general conditions. In contrast to correlation-based approaches toward measuring market linkages, the probability law of the joint return process can be left unspecified, because we use a nonparametric estimator for the limiting dependence function. From these nonparametric estimates of the limiting dependence function we derive estimates for the expected number of market crashes (or the probability of a simultaneous crash) given that at least one market crashes. Thus market linkages in crisis periods are measured directly in the economically relevant money metric and associated probabilities, and we do not make the detour via correlations.

The methodology is then used to analyze the linkages within and between equity and bond markets in the G-5 industrial countries in times of market turmoil.[4] Our results indicate small but nonnegligible cross-asset market linkages in times of stress. The strongest

[3]Forbes and Rigobon (2002) show a similar conditional correlation bias in the context of the linear regression model and propose a correction for it.

[4]Related analyses for a single type of contract have recently been carried out on foreign exchange data by Straetmans (1998) and Starica (1999), and on major stock markets by Straetmans (2000), Longin and Solnik (2001) and Poon, Rockinger, and Tawn (2001). For analyse of stock market comovements using regime-switching volatility models, see Ramchand and Susmel (1998). For studies of regular noncrisis cross-asset interdependence, see, for example, Longin and Solnik (1995), Fleming, Kirby, and Ostdiek (1998). or Bodart and Reding (1999).

extreme linkages are between different national equity markets, and the flight-to-quality phenomenon is approximately as frequent as simultaneous crashes of stock and bond markets. Whereas single bond or stock market crashes are relatively rare events happening once or twice a human lifetime, the conditional probabilities of having a crash (or boom) in a market given that one occurred in another market are quite high. Interestingly, cross-border linkages are not weaker than domestic linkages. Whereas these results confirm that in the era of free capital flows and globalization, surveillance of financial market stability cannot stop at national borders, they also suggest that there are some limits to how widely contagion can spread.

The paper is organized as follows. The next section introduces our nonparametric asymptotic tail dependence measure for extreme financial market comovements. Section III presents the way in which this extreme linkage measure can be estimated in two steps, a univariate one and a bivariate one. Some related testing techniques are discussed in section IV Section V contains the results from applying this approach to weekly G-5 country stock and bond market returns. The empirical analysis follows the two steps described in section III, first comparing extreme returns in stock and bond markets and then detailing national cross-asset linkages, cross-border linkages within the same asset class, and finally cross-border cross-asset linkages. Conclusions are drawn in section VI. Four appendices provide details about the derivation of a test statistic for extreme dependence, the small-sample properties of the tests used in the main body of the paper, the small-sample properties of our extreme linkage measure, and the data employed.

II. Extreme Linkages: Probability Theory

Suppose one is interested in measuring the expected number of market crashes given that at least one market crashes (or booms, as in the flight-to-quality case). This measure reflects how many markets are on average drawn down when one market crashes. Consider the case of two markets with random returns X and Y. Let x and y be the quantiles (or *thresholds*) above which we speak of a market boom or crash (in case of a loss). To study market crashes we adopt the convention of taking the negative of a return, so that we can study all extreme evens in the first quadrant. Let κ stand for the number of markets with extreme returns. Our extreme linkage indicator is the conditional expectation $E[\kappa|\kappa \geq 1]$. From elementary probability theory (starting from the standard definition of conditional probability) we have that

$$\frac{P\{X > x,\ Y \leq y\} + P\{X \leq x,\ Y > y\} + 2P\{X > x, Y > y\}}{P\{X > x, Y > y\}}$$

$$= E[\kappa|\kappa \geq 1] = \frac{P\{X > x\} + P\{Y > y\}}{P\{X > x\, or\, Y > y\}}, \tag{23.1}$$

with $P\{X > x \text{ or } Y > y\} = 1 - P\{X \leq x, Y \leq y\}$. Notice also that $E[\kappa|\kappa \geq 1] = P\{\kappa = 2|\kappa \geq 1\} + 1$, so that an alternative interpretation of our extreme linkage indicator is in terms of (1 plus) the conditional probability that both markets crash given that at least one market crashes for higher dimensions than two $E[\kappa|\kappa \geq 1]$ is still equal to the ratio of the sum of the marginal excess probabilities divided by the joint failure probability. The measure $P[\kappa = 2|\kappa \geq 1]$ is however not as easily extended to higher dimensions.

The question is how $E[\kappa|\kappa \geq 1]$ can be calculated in practice. Within the framework of the multivariate normal distribution this would be a trivial exercise, because only the first two moments have to be estimated. In the introduction we argued, however, that the framework of the multivariate normal and the associated correlation structure may not be suitable for analyzing extreme linkages between asset markets. To be able to break away from specific distributional assumptions, we investigate $E[\kappa|\kappa \geq 1]$ when the conditioning quantiles x and y become very large. To this end, define the upper quantile functions for the returns X and Y respectively as

$$Q_1(tu) = (1 - F_1)^{-1}(tu),$$
$$Q_2(tv) = (1 - F_2)^{-1}(tv), \tag{23.2}$$

for some small but positive values u, v and a scaling parameter t. Choose u, v. and t such that tu and tv are smaller than 1 and thus interpretable as excess probabilities. Moreover, set $Q_1(tu) = x$ and $Q_2(tv) = y$, which are the original crash levels from equation (1) that we are interested in. In other words, we have inverted the cdf so as to work out the asymptotic equivalent of out linkage measure in terms of the (small) probabilities of having very extreme returns. This will prove convenient below for bringing out some nice properties of the measure.

Upon substituting the above quantile functions into equation (1), one obtains the following asymptotic equivalent for that equation;

$$\begin{aligned}\lim_{t\to 0} & E\left[\kappa|\kappa \geq 1\right] \\ &= \lim_{t\to +0} \frac{t^{-1}P\left\{X > Q_1(tu)\right\} + t^{-1}P\left\{Y > Q_2(tv)\right\}}{t^{-1}\left[1 - P\left\{X \leq Q_1(tu),\ Y \leq Q_2(tv)\right\}\right]} \\ &= \frac{u+v}{l(u,v)}\end{aligned} \tag{23.3}$$

The result of letting t converge to 0 is that the excess probabilities tu, tv also tend to 0, and hence the quantiles become very large. Thus equation (3) says that very far from the origin our linkage indicator is asymptotically equal to the sum of the marginal probabilities divided by a limit function $l(u, v)$. The function $l(u, v)$ in the denominator in equation (3) is the so-called *stable tail dependence function* (STDF) and was introduced by Huang (1992), Multivariate extreme value theory deals with existence conditions, properties, and estimators for this function; see Huang (1992) or de Haan and de Ronde (1998).[5] The curvature of $l(u, v)$completely determines the dependence structure between $X$and Y in the tail area. Basic properties of $l(u, v)$ are its linear homogeneity and the inequality

$$\max(u, v) \leq l(u, v) \leq u + v. \tag{23.4}$$

Equality holds on the left-hand side if X and Y are completely dependent in the tail area, whereas it holds on the right-hand side if X and Y are independent in the tail area. Note that independence means that for all Q_1 and Q_2

$$P\{X < Q_1, Y < Q_2\} = P\{X < Q_1\}P\{Y < Q_2\}, \tag{23.5}$$

[5]The limit function exists if the joint external returns from X and Y lie in the domain of attraction of a multivariate extreme-value distribution.

whereas tail independence only requires this factorization to hold asymptotically. Thus it may well be that nonextreme return pairs are dependent although their extremes are asymptotically independent. The bivariate normal distribution with $\rho \in (-1,\ 1)$ and $\rho \neq 0$ constitutes such a case, for example.

The linear homogeneity of $l(u, v)$ implies that all contour lines exhibit the same shape toward the origin. Thus it suffices to plot the *unit* contour line in order to get a full graphical representation of dependence in the bivariate tail. Moreover, the combined properties of $l(u, v)$ imply that the unit contour line is concave toward the origin, ending at $(1, 0)$ and $(0, 1)$ and being fully contained in the uniform rectangular. For illustrative purposes consider the bivariate cdf

$$F(x, y) = \exp\left[-\left(x^{-1[l-d]} + y^{-1[l-d]}\right)^{1-d}\right]$$

$$0 \leq d < 1, \quad x, y \in [0,\ \infty],$$

with marginal Frechet distributions (see, for example, Gumbel, 1958). Upon taking the limit in the denominator of equation (3), the STDF of this distribution boils down to

$$l(u, v) = \left(u^{1(l-d)} + v^{1(l-d)}\right)^{1-d},$$

The dependence parameter d determines the degree of tail dependence between X and Y. Figure 23.1 plots unit contour lines (the asymptotic marginal probabilities on the axes are normalized to $u,\ v \in [0, 1]$) for this pair of random variables for different values of d. The lower bound of asymptotic independence is hit when $d = 0$, and the unit contour line coincides with the uniform rectangular (complete asymptotic dependence) when d approaches 1.

The STDF relates marginal and joint probabilities as follows. First define the excess probabilities $p_1 = P\{X > x\}$, $p_2 = P\{Y > y\}$ and $P_{12} = 1 - P\{X \leq x,\ Y \leq y\}$, for ease of reference. Exploiting the homogeneity property, one can easily show that the bivariate excess probability p_{12} and the marginal probabilities p_1 and p_2 are related via the STDF. For sufficiently small $t > 0$,

$$l(u, v) \approx t^{-1}\left[1 - P\left\{X \leq Q_1(tu),\ Y \leq Q_2(tv)\right\}\right], \tag{23.6}$$

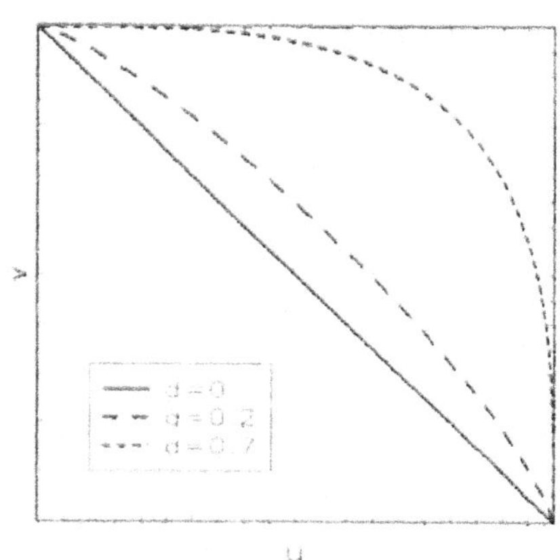

Figure 23.1 Unit Contour Lines of the Bivariate Gumbel Distribution Function
Note: The variables on the axes interpretable as asymptotic excess probabilities; see equation (6). The linear homogeneity of $l(u, v)$ implies that a single unit contour line $l(u, v) = 1$ visually characterizes the tail dependence structure for each value of the dependence parameter d. The solid line corresponds with full asymptotic independence, whereas the dashed lies reflect increasing dependence in the tails.

Choose $tu = p_1$ and $tv = p_2$, so that $l(u, v) = l(t^{-1}p_1, t^{-1}p_2)$. Use the linear homogeneity of the STDF to write $tl(t^{-1}p_1, t^{-1}p_2) = l(p_1, p_2)$. Hence, for small values of p_1 and p_2, approximately,

$$l(p_1, p_2) \approx p_{12}, \tag{23.7}$$

Thus the joint probability p_{12} only depends on the marginal probabilities p_1 and p_2 and the dependence function $l(\cdot, \cdot)$. The linkage measure can thus be expressed as

$$E[\kappa|\kappa \geq 1] = \frac{p_1 + p_2}{p_{12}} \approx \frac{p_1 + p_2}{l(p_1, p_2)}. \tag{23.8}$$

Assume for example that $p_1 = p_2 = p$. Then, approximately,

$$E[\kappa|\kappa \geq 1] \approx \frac{2p}{l(p, p)} = \frac{2}{l(1, 1)}. \tag{23.9}$$

If both returns are completely dependent in the tails, that is, $l(1, 1) = \max(1, 1)$, then $E[\kappa|\kappa \geq 1] \approx 2$ and the markets cocrash with certainty. But without extreme comovements in the two markets, $E[\kappa|\kappa \geq 1] \approx 1$, because $l(1, 1) = 2$.

III. Extreme Linkages: Estimation

The conditional expectation (1) is estimated by a two-step estimation procedure. In the first step one estimates the marginal extreme quantile cum probability combinations (p_1, p_2). In the second step one imputes these univariate probability estimates into an estimator for the tail dependence function $l(\cdot, \cdot)$ in order to obtain an estimator for p_{12}. The estimation procedure therefore essentially exploits equation (7).

Univariate excess probability estimation uses the stylized fact that asset return distributions exhibit heavy tails. Loosely speaking, this implies that the excess probability as a function of the corresponding quantile can be approximately described by a power law. The defining characteristic of these distributions is the property of regular variation at infinity,

$$\lim_{q \to \infty} \frac{1 - F(qx)}{1 - F(q)} = x^{-a}, \quad x > 0, \ \alpha > 0 \tag{23.10}$$

From this property it directly follows that such distributions (for example, the Student t) have bounded moments only up to α, where α is known as the tail index. In contrast, distributions with exponentially decaying tails or with finite endpoints have all moments bounded.

Univariate excess probabilities for fat-tailed marginals can be estimated by using the semiparametric probability estimator from de Haan et al. (1994):

$$\hat{P}_q = \frac{m}{n}\left(\frac{X_n - m, n}{q}\right)^{\alpha}, \tag{23.11}$$

where the *tail cutoff point* $X_{n-m,n}$ is the $(n - m)^{\text{th}}$ ascending order statistic (or, loosely speaking, the mth smallest return) from a sample of size n such that $\lim[1/m(n)] = 0$

but $m = 0(n)$, and where the extreme (probability quantile) combination $(\hat{p}_p, q)$ is such that $q > X_{n-m,n}$.[6] An important aspect of the estimator $\hat{p}_q$ is that it can extend the empirical distribution function outside the domain of the sample by means of its asymptotic Pareto tail from equation (10). The estimator (11) is conditional upon the tail index α. We estimate the tail index by means of the popular Hill (1975) estimator:

$$\bar{\gamma} = \frac{1}{m} \sum_{j=0}^{m-1} \ln \left(\frac{X_{n-j,n}}{X_{n-m,n}} \right), \tag{23.12}$$

where m has the same value and interpretation as in equation (11) and $\hat{\alpha} = l/\hat{\gamma}$ stands for the estimated tail index. Further details are provided in Jansen and de Vries (1991) and the recent monograph by Embrechts, Klüppelberg, and Mikosch (1997).

The estimation of the *bivariate* excess probability p_{12} either requires adopting a specific functional form for the STDF, as in Longin and Solnik (2001), or proceeding semiparametrically. Because there does not exist a unique parametrization for the STDF, we pursue a *semiparametric* estimation method based on the highest order statistics. Let $t = k/n$ in equation (6), such that $\lim[l/k(n)] = 0$, but $k = 0(n)$. (The role of the nuisance parameter k corresponds to that of m in the univariate estimation step.) Because the marginal probability estimates are available from the univariate step, we can also replace (u, v) by $(\hat{p}_1, \hat{p}_2)$:

$$l(\hat{p}_1, \hat{p}_2) = \lim_{n \to \infty} \frac{n}{k} P \left\{ X \geq Q_1 \left(\frac{k\hat{p}_1}{n} \right) \text{ or } Y \geq Q_2 \left(\frac{k\hat{p}_2}{n} \right) \right\}. \tag{23.13}$$

In order to turn this expression into an estimator for $l(\cdot, \cdot)$, we replace $P\{\cdot\}$, $Q_1(\cdot)$, and $Q_2(\cdot)$ by their empirical counterparts, so that approximately

$$\hat{l}(\hat{p}_1, \hat{p}_2) \approx \frac{n}{k} \frac{l}{n} \sum_{l=1}^{n} \mathbf{1} \left\{ X_1 > X_{n-[k\hat{p}_1],n} \text{ or } Y_i > Y_{n-[k\hat{p}_2]n} \right\}, \tag{23.14}$$

where $\mathbf{1}$ denotes the indicator function and where $[x]$ is the integer satisfying $x \leq [x] < x + 1$. So, loosely speaking, the estimator of l boils down to counting the instants at which one or both of the markets experience an extreme return within a given sample period.

Because the marginal probability arguments of the STDF are typically smaller than the reciprocal of the sample size n, the empirical probability measure (14) is not operational. However, one can increase the number of excesses by scaling up the marginal probabilities in equation (14) by a factor $\lambda > 1$ and exploiting the linear homogeneity property $\hat{l}(\hat{p}_1, \hat{p}_2) \approx \lambda^{-1}\hat{l}(\lambda\hat{p}_1, \lambda\hat{p}_2)$.[7] Huang (1992) proposed to transform the marginal probability

[6] In financial risk management the scaling parameter q is usually referred to as the "value at risk (VaR)," and it is often used in a reversed fashion: what is the VaR $\hat{q}_p$, for a given probability p?

[7] Appendix C provides a discussion of the approximate character of linear homogeneity in finite samples. More specifically, it is shown that the finite-sample character of the estimator $\hat{l}$ together with the inward shift of the quantiles on assuming homogeneity creates an upward bias in the extreme linkage estimates for E. This bias may be empirically relevant in small samples.

pair $(\hat{p}_1, \hat{p}_2)$ to polar coordinates $(\hat{r}\cos\hat{\phi}, \hat{r}\sin\hat{\phi})$ such that $\lambda = 1/\hat{r}$.[8] The polar coordinate representation of the empirical measure (14) is

$$\hat{p}_{12} \approx \hat{r}\hat{l}(\cos\hat{\phi}, \sin\hat{\phi})$$
$$= \frac{1}{k}\hat{r}\sum_{i=l}^{n} \mathbf{1}\left(X_t > X_{n-[k\cos\hat{\phi}]n} \text{ or } Y_i > Y_{n-[k\sin\hat{\phi}],n}\right). \tag{23.15}$$

This estimator evaluates l on the unit circle, which is convenient in that it is based on a larger set of observations than equation (14). Notice that this procedure of counting coexceedances is easily applicable in higher dimensions. An estimator for the expected number of simultaneous crashes $E[\kappa|\kappa \geq 1]$ directly follows if one replaces p_1, p_2, and p_{l2} in equation (8) by their respective estimators in equations (11), (12), and (15):

$$\hat{E}[\kappa|\kappa \geq 1] = \frac{\cos\hat{\phi} + \sin\hat{\phi}}{\hat{l}(\cos\hat{\phi}, \sin\hat{\phi})}. \tag{23.16}$$

The entire estimation procedure thus depends on three estimators (11), (12), and (15) that are easy to calculate. Conditional on the proper choice of the nuisance parameters m and k, the three estimators are asymptotically normally distributed. Goldie and Smith (1987) and Huang (1992) propose to pick m and k in a range that minimizes the respective asymptotic mean squared errors (MSEs).[9] Consequently, minimizing the sample MSE is the appropriate selection criterion. In small samples best practice is to plot the estimators as a function of the threshold, that is, $\hat{\gamma} = \hat{\gamma}(m)$ and $\hat{l} = \hat{l}(k)$, and to select m and k in the region over which the estimators tend to be constant. [10]

IV. Extreme Linkages: Hypothesis Testing

The asymptotic normality of the estimators enables some straightforward hypothesis testing. Hall (1982) showed for $m/n \to 0$ as $m, n \to \infty$ that the statistic $\sqrt{m}[\hat{\gamma}(m)/\gamma - 1]$ is asymptotically standard normally distributed. A test for the equality of tail indices can thus be based on the following T-statistic:

$$T = \frac{\hat{\gamma}_1(m_1) - \hat{\gamma}_2(m_2)}{\sigma\left[\hat{\gamma}_1(m_1) - \hat{\gamma}_2(m_2)\right]}, \tag{23.17}$$

which converges to a standard normal distribution in large samples. The denominator's standard deviation is calculated as the standard deviation of the bootstrapped difference

[8] Consistent estimators for the angle and radius are provided by $\hat{\phi} = \arctan(\hat{p}_2/\hat{p}_1)$ and $\hat{r} = \sqrt{\hat{P}_1^2 + \hat{P}_2^2}$ respectively.

[9] If the value chosen for m or k is too small, then the respective estimate is inefficient, because not enough observations are used. If it is too large, then one incurs a bias, because the interior of the distribution is measured rather than the tails. For a given sample there exists an intermediate range of values for which bias squared and variance vanish at the same rate, but outside this range one of the two parts dominates and the asymptotic MSE is higher.

[10] Plots are available from the authors upon request. See, for example, Embrechts et al. (1997) and de Haan and de Ronde (1998) for this widespread practice in small samples.

$\hat{\gamma}_1 - \hat{\gamma}_2$ (we chose the number of bootstraps equal to 600). Small-sample properties of tail index estimators are studied in (for example) Dekkers and de Haan (1989).

Huang (1992) has proven the asymptotic normality of the estimator (15) for $k/n \to 0$ as $k, n \to \infty$. We use this to compare the amount of extreme dependence across different return quadrants. For a pair of stock and bond markets, we can test whether a cocrash (for example, through contagion) is more likely than flight to quality from stocks into bonds or vice versa by calculating the following Z-statistic:

$$Z = \frac{\hat{l}_{\mathrm{CO}}(k_1) - \hat{l}_{\mathrm{FTQ}}(k_2)}{\sigma\left[\hat{l}_{\mathrm{CO}}(k_1) - \hat{l}_{\mathrm{FTQ}}(k_2)\right]}, \tag{23.18}$$

which has a standard normal distribution in large samples. The denominator's standard deviation is calculated as the standard deviation of the bootstrapped difference $\hat{l}_{\mathrm{CO}} - \hat{l}_{\mathrm{FTQ}}$ (again with the number of bootstraps set equal to 600).[11] In equation (18) the subscripts CO and FTQ on the STDF estimates refer to stock cum bond market cocrashes and stock market crashes cum bond market booms (flight to quality), respectively.

It is also of interest to *pretest* for the presence of asymptotic dependence in specific market pairs. Peng (1999) proposes a testing procedure that starts from a general second-order expansion for $l(u, v)$ in finite samples:

$$l(u, v) \approx u + v - c(u, v)t^{1/\eta - 1}\left[1 + O(t^{\beta})\right], \quad \eta \in (0, 1],\ \beta > 0. \tag{23.19}$$

The value of the tail dependence coefficient η governs whether extremal returns are asymptotically dependent or not. The function $c(u, v)$ is a concavity term that is retained far into the bivariate tail ($t \to 0$) only if the exponent $\eta = 1$, indicating asymptotic dependence. If the joint distribution is asymptotically independent, then $\eta < 1$. For example, in case of independence, $\eta = \frac{1}{2}$ and $c(u, v) = uv$, so that $l(u, v) \approx u + v - uvt$ [and hence as $t \to 0$, $l(u, v) = u + v$ asymptotically]. A heuristic derivation of an estimator $\hat{\eta}$ for the tail dependence coefficient is provided in appendix A. This estimator enables one to test the $H_0 : \eta = 1$ (asymptotic dependence) against the $H_1 : \eta < 1$ (asymptotic independence) by means of the statistic

$$w = \frac{\hat{\eta} - 1}{\sigma(\hat{\eta})} \tag{23.20}$$

which is asymptotically normally distributed under H_0. The asymptotic standard error $\sigma(\hat{\eta})$ can be expressed in terms of the limiting dependence function and its partial derivatives (see Peng, 1999).

Because only a fraction of our original data set enters the estimators and test statistics for extreme dependence patterns, we investigated the small-sample properties of the tools developed. In appendix B we describe Monte Carlo simulations to discuss the small-sample behavior of both the Z-statistic and the W-statistic. The results show that the left-tail critical values for Z lie reasonably close to their limiting values, whereas we find some evidence for size distortions in W. However, if one uses the small-sample critical values instead of

[11] The tail dependence function is evaluated at (1,1) along the 45-degree line for convenience.

their asymptotically normal counterparts, the empirical section's test results for asymptotic dependence hardly change. As for the small sample power of W, it might be low if η is close to 1 under the alternative hypothesis of asymptotic independence.[12] Heffernan (2001), however, shows that a majority of parametric models with asymptotically independent tails exhibit a tail dependence parameter η equal to $\frac{1}{2}$, making the local alternatives problem relatively unlikely to occur.

Regardless whether the data are asymptotically independent or not, in the end we are interested in the accuracy of the linkage measure $E[\kappa|\kappa \geq 1]$ evaluated for large but finite crash levels. Appendix C contains both analytical results and Monte Carlo evidence on the small-sample bias in the linkage estimator. We report simulation results on this bias for three data-generating processes: independent normal data, bivariate normal data that are asymptotically independent but exhibit nonzero correlation, and bivariate Pareto data that exhibit asymptotic dependence. It transpires that for the sample sizes we are working with and at the typical correlation level in our data, the estimates of the linkage measure provide a conservative upper bound for extreme market spillovers. Moreover, the bias seems more severe if the data are asymptotically independent. The simulations also show that with a data set 10 times larger than the current one, the bias disappears almost completely.

To conclude, from both the power and the size study of the W-test and from the performance of the linkage measure in small samples we infer that the results for the true data reported below provide an upper bound on the amount of extreme linkage between different financial markets. As we will argue below, the upper bound interpretation will make some of our results even stronger.

V. Extreme Linkages: Results for G-5 Countries

In this section we evaluate the extent of extreme comovements within and between stock and bond markets. The data consist of 663 (nonoverlapping) weekly stock and government bond returns for the G-5 market indices over the period 1987 to 1999. A detailed description of the data is given in appendix D. We start with the univariate stock and bond market extremes, eyeballing first indications for their joint occurrence. Then we turn to the systematic application of our extreme linkage measure and the tests of extreme dependence patterns.

A. Extreme Returns in Stock and Bond Markets

In the univariate step, we report tail index and quantile-probability estimates on the basis of equations (12) and (11). Table 23.1 contains information on the magnitude and timing of the most extreme in-sample events for stocks (panel A) and bonds (panel B). The table also gives the estimates of the tail index α and the accompanying tail probabilities conditioned on different quantile levels. Within both panels we further distinguish between the upper and the lower tails of the univariate return distributions in order to take into account possible asymmetries.[13]

[12] For example, take the case of the bivariate normal with correlation coefficient ρ. In this case $\eta = (1 + \rho)/2$, $\rho \in (-1, 1)$.

[13] For reasons of space the nuisance parameters m on which the Hill estimator and the tail probability estimates are conditioned are omitted from the table. The values, which varied between 10 and 50, are available from Table 23.1 of the underlying working paper (Hartmann, Straetmans, & de Vries, 2001).

Table 23.1 Minima, maxima, Tail Index and Univariate Tail Probability Estimates for Weekly G-5 Asset Returns (1987–1999)

A. Stocks								
	Left Tail				Right Tail			
			$P(X < -q)$				$P(X > q)$	
Country	**Min (%)**	$\hat{\alpha}$	**−15%**	**−20%**	**max(%)**	$\hat{\alpha}$	**15%**	**20%**
GE	−13.81 (10/2/98)	3.32	0.05013	0.01926	11.57 (10/16/98)	4.68	0.00591	0.00153
FR	−11.12 (10/23/87)	3.24	0.03320	0.01308	9.61 (10/16/98)	5.68	0.00202	0.00039
UK	−24.83 (10/23/87)	3.76	0.01129	0.00382	8.19 (9/18/92)	4.54	0.00340	0.00090
US	−13.60 (10/23/87)	2.33	0.05009	0.02559	7.25 (10/16/98)	5.56	0.00086	0.00017
JP	−13.32 (10/23/87)	3.07	0.05337	0.02209	11.18 (8/21/92)	4.61	0.01495	0.00397

B. Bonds								
	Left Tail				Right Tail			
			$P(X < -q)$				$P(X > q)$	
Country	**Min (%)**	$\hat{\alpha}$	**−6%**	**−8%**	**max (%)**	$\hat{\alpha}$	**6%**	**8%**
GE	−6.61 (12/30/94)	5.39	0.06564	0.01393	3.77 (1/9/98)	5.57	0.00749	0.00151
FR	−5.14 (10/28/94)	6.01	0.03202	0.00568	5.21 (10/23/87)	5.58	0.00568	0.00114
UK	−6.35 (10/9/98)	3.91	0.03412	0.01109	4.81 (4/10/92)	4.46	0.02771	0.00767
US	−5.41 (5/15/87)	3.45	0.08996	0.03301	9.77 (10/23/87)	3.72	0.04323	0.01480
JP	−5.08 (12/25/98)	4.58	0.03497	0.00936	4.30 (11/6/87)	2.84	0.05164	0.02277

Note: $\hat{\alpha}$ is the reciprocal of the Hill estimator in equation (12). Marginal probabilities P are conditioned on extreme stock and bond market return quantiles near the historical sample boundaries and are calculated using equation (11). Weekly prices were sampled on Fridays.

From the table we see that extreme losses are generally much higher for stock indices than for government bond indices. Moreover the historical extremes point toward asymmetries in stock index returns: the (absolute) extreme loss returns consistently exceed the maximum positive returns.[14] When comparing the entries for stock and bond markets, the timing of the extreme events, as recorded in parentheses, suggests the presence of cocrashes and flight-to-quality effects during periods of market turbulence. Indeed, all stock markets covered, except for Germany's, reached historically low returns in the week of Black

[14]On Friday, October 16, 1987 the UK stock market remained closed due to a hurricane. Therefore, the weekly return in the UK for the period around Black Monday is calculated from Thursday to Friday, not from Friday to Friday. As a result the figure of a 25% fall (much higher than for the four other countries) might somewhat overstate the London crash in relative terms.

Monday. As an aside, the table also shows that three stock markets (FR, GE, US) exhibited parallel record gains as a consequence of a major rebound in mid October 1998 following the Russian and LTCM crises, and two stock markets (JP, UK) exhibited comparable record gains around the September 1992 European currency crisis.[15] The casual extreme linkage evidence is less clear for the bond markets. For example, none of the largest bond index corrections occurred during the February-to-June 1994 fixed-income market turmoil, and only the United Kingdom experienced a record slump in the aftermath of the LTCM crisis. The October 1987 rallies in the French and U.S. bond markets (and perhaps also the Japanese rally two weeks later) are suggestive of a flight-to-quality effect from stocks into government bonds.

We turn to the remaining columns in Table 23.1. The left-tail index estimates are highest for the bond returns, indicating thinner lower tails than for the stocks. This reflects the more limited downside risk of government-bond investments. Moreover, and in contrast to the bond series, the point estimates $\hat{\alpha}$ for the left tail of the stock index series are lower than their right-tail counterparts. This is consistent with the observed asymmetry between the minimum and maximum stock returns reported in the left part of the table and also squares well with the results reported by Longin and Solnik (2001). Using the T-test as defined in equation (17), we formally tested for equality of tail indices across lower and upper tails and across assets. It turned out that only in the French and U.S. stock markets are the larger sizes of left tails statistically significant in our sample. And again, only for France is the left stock market tail significantly thicker than the left bond market tail. In almost all other cases the null hypothesis of equal tail indices could not be rejected.[16]

The economic issue of interest, both for the general assessment of financial market stability and for financial institutions' risk management, is the likelihood of the extreme returns as reflected by the tail probabilities. The reported probabilities are expressed over a yearly time horizon by multiplying the weekly probability estimates from equation (11) by a factor of 52. First, note that the excess probabilities are conditioned on different quantiles for stocks and bonds with an eye toward the historical minima and maxima displayed in table 23.1. One reason why conditioning crash levels ate deliberately chosen to be in the vicinity of the historical extremes is to get a feeling for the probability of worst-case losses over a longer period of time such as a year in our case. Another reason, perhaps even more important for policymakers, is that there can be little doubt that such extremes constitute severe securities market crisis situations.

An interpretation of the loss levels in the table is as follows. For example, the entry 0.02559 for the left tail of the U.S. stock index implies that a 20% weekly crash on average happens once per $1/0.02559 \approx 39$ years (a 15% decline, a figure closer to the one for the week of the 1987 stock market crash, would happen approximately every 20 years). In U.S.

[15]The October 1998 stock market rallies occurred in an environment of high uncertainty and volatility in international financial markets. They seem to be directly related to the U.S. Fed's emergency interest rate cut on October 15. On that day the Federal Open Market Committee decided to reduce both the Fed funds target rate and the discount rate by 25 basis points (see Federal Reserve Board, 1998a). This action surprised markets, because it happened by means of an FOMC telephone conference between the scheduled meetings of September 29 and November 17 (see Federal Reserve Board, 1998b, conference call). Three weeks before, the Federal Reserve Bank of New York had coordinated a private-sector bailout of the Long-Term Capital Management hedge fund (see Greenspan, 1998). During the same period exchange rates also experienced historical jumps, notably in the form of an unprecedented yen appreciation (see Hartmann, Straetmans, & de Vries, 2003, table 23.1).

[16]Further details on test results are reported in the underlying working paper (Hartmann et al., 2001, appendix 1) and are available on request.

government bond markets a weekly decline of 8% is expected to occur approximately once per 30 years (and a 6% decline—close to the historical negative extreme in table 23.1—once every 11 years). In other words, such crashes are rare events, but not so uncommon as one might believe. Compare these estimates with a normal-distribution-based estimate, which predicts weekly crashes in U.S. common stock of 20% or more to happen only once per 31.5×10^{20} years!

B. Extreme Comovements Within and Between Stock and Bond Markets

In the bivariate step we first look separately at extreme linkages between G-5 stock markets and between G-5 bond markets (table 23.2); then we consider domestic and international cross-asset market linkages (table 23.3). Both tables contain the W-pretest on asymptotic dependence [equation (20)], the correlation coefficient ρ, and the estimated linkage measure [equation (16)]. The linkage estimates ate conditioned on the same extreme stock and bond return quantiles as in table 23.1 (see the discussion of their levels in the previous section). Displaying two crash levels for each asset class allow for some sensitivity analysis. Also, the quantile pairs on which the linkage estimates are conditioned in tables 23.2 and 23.3 are chosen so that the corresponding univariate excess probabilities (table 23.1) are of similar order of magnitude and equation (9) approximately applies.

Table 23.2 reports estimation and testing results on extreme linkages within the same asset class (across borders). First, the W-test never rejects the null of asymptotic dependence at the 5% significance level for either of the two asset categories. Appendix B suggests some caution when testing asymptotic dependence in small samples, particularly regarding the use of asymptotic (normal) critical values. However, when using the small-sample critical values for the W-test in table 23.2 (and also in table 23.3 below), hardly any of the test results change. Second, the extreme linkage estimates are only marginally altered when shifting the conditioning quantiles further outward. Also, with the exception of the continental European country pair GE-FR, which exhibits the most highly interlinked stock

Table 23.2 Cross-Border Extreme Linkages within Stock and Bond Markets (1987–1999)

	Stocks				Bonds			
			E				E	
Pair	W	ρ	**−15%**	**−20%**	W	ρ	**−6%**	**−8%**
GE-FR	0.601	0.686	1.283	1.263	−0.251	0.600	1.194	1.164
GE-UK	−0.457	0.575	1.149	1.130	−0.859	0.438	1.124	1.109
GE-US	−1.206	0.470	1.140	1.148	−0.466	0.291	1.075	1.090
GE-JP	−0.437	0.314	1.205	1.216	−1.307	0.198	1.041	1.051
FR-UK	−1.131	0.589	1.220	1.208	−0.758	0.491	1.071	1.085
FR-US	−1.156	0.497	1.175	1.201	−1.059	0.363	1.077	1.049
FR-JP	−1.159	0.322	1.148	1.142	−0.691	0.129	1.030	1.023
UK-US	−1.404	0.546	1.135	1.079	−0.512	0.425	1.075	1.100
UK-JP	−1.370	0.361	1.071	1.057	−1.340	0.184	1.094	1.104
US-JP	−0.888	0.328	1.104	1.119	−0.876	0.164	1.079	1.079

Note: W refers to Peng's asymptotic dependence test in equation (20). The extreme linkage measure E is conditioned on extreme quantiles near the historical sample boundaries and is estimated using equation (16). Unconditioned (full-sample) correlation estimates are reported for comparison.

Table 23.3 Domestic and International Extreme Stock-Bond Linkages: Cocrashes versus Flight to Quality (1987–1999)

A. Domestic

	Test Statistics			Linkage Estimates				
					E_{CO}		E_{FTQ}	
Country	W_{CO}	W_{FTQ}	Z	ρ	**(−20; −6)**	**(−20; −8)**	**(−20; 6)**	**(−20; 8)**
GE	−0.881	−0.265	0.311	0.190	1.034	1.027	1.061	1.034
FR	−0.906	−0.974	−1.753	0.248	1.069	1.115	1.050	1.055
UK	−0.740	−0.463	−3.992*	0.217	1.040	1.059	1.057	1.073
US	−0.658	−0.906	−0.432	0.235	1.030	1.052	1.059	1.046
JP	−0.719	−1.376	0.099	0.051	1.061	1.092	1.036	1.050

B. Cross-Border

	Test Statistics			Linkage Estimates				
					E_{CO}		E_{FTQ}	
Pair	W_{CO}	W_{FTQ}	Z	ρ	**(−20; −6)**	**(−20; −8)**	**(−20; −6)**	**(−20; 8)**
GE-FR	−2.452*	−0.681	—	0.187	1.114	1.093	1.071	1.057
FR-GE	0.468	−0.534	−0.310	0.172	1.050	1.039	1.044	1.039
GE-UK	−1.271	−1.031	0.000	0.079	1.035	1.078	1.087	1.059
UK-GE	−0.362	−0.437	0.810	0.083	1.022	1.053	1.062	1.052
GE-US	−1.445	−0.314	−0.914	0.015	1.023	1.035	1.078	1.079
US-GE	−0.490	0	0.600	0.122	1.044	1.060	1.056	1.057
GE-JP	−0.450	−0.416	0.277	−0.056	1.045	1.096	1.090	1.068
JP-GE	−0.413	−0.861	0.683	−0.000	1.038	1.014	1.028	1.031
FR-UK	−1.107	0	−0.367	0.165	1.076	1.052	1.065	1.080
UK-FR	−1.013	−0.269	−0.874	0.102	1.049	1.068	1.068	1.051
FR-US	−0.473	−1.459	0.831	0.101	1.030	1.080	1.030	1.077
US-FR	−0.795	−0.939	0.718	0.097	1.033	1.028	1.028	1.030
FR-JP	−0.498	−0.891	1.000	−0.007	1.055	1.041	1.047	1.083
JP-FR	−1.269	−1.334	−0.467	0.021	1.043	1.038	1.026	1.036
UK-US	−0.681	−0.285	0.663	−0.055	1.021	1.025	1.058	1.083
US-UK	−0.456	−0.721	1.267	0.141	1.024	1.038	1.052	1.052
UK-JP	−0.855	−0.270	0.778	−0.015	1.018	1.016	1.048	1.080
JP-UK	−0.706	−0.640	−0.925	0.042	1.048	1.049	1.041	1.032
US-JP	−0.244	−0.744	0.516	0.068	1.088	1.069	1.058	1.080
JP-US	−1.426	−0.496	−2.118*	−0.011	1.034	1.050	1.070	1.033

Note: The pairs in panel B consist of a stock market (first country in each pair) and a bond market (second country in each pair), implying that one has to consider two stock-bond pairs for each pair of countries. Columns 1 and 2 report the W-test for the presence of stock-bond cocrashes (third data quadrant) or flight to quality (second data quadrant), respectively. The Z-statistic in column 3 reflects whether the difference between stock-bond contagion and flight to quality is statistically significant. *denotes statistical rejections at the 1% significance level. Columns 5–6 and 7–8 contain extremal linkage estimates reflecting the frequency of stock-bond cocrashes or flight to quality, respectively. The conditioning quantile pairs (expressed in percentages) are chosen in the vicinity of the historical sample boundaries.

and bond markets, no clear geographical patterns of crisis linkages can be discerned. Most strikingly, however, and regardless of the conditioning quantile pairs, extreme cross-border linkages at the lower tail are stronger within stock markets than within bond markets. For example, for the pair consisting of Germany (GE) and the United States (US), only 1 out of $6(\approx -1/0.148)$ stock crashes is expected to be a 20% cocrash. However, only 1 out of $13(\approx 1/0.075)$ bond crashes in the United States or Germany is expected to be a 6% cocrash.

To illustrate this in yet another way, we plot estimated contour lines for stock and bond tail dependence between Germany and Japan in figure 23.2 (the figure illustrates an empirical semiparametric application of the STDF introduced in section II, whereas figure 23.1 provided a theoretical illustration for a given parametric distribution). As a benchmark for comparison the linear contour line corresponding to asymptotic independence is also entered in the figure. The estimated contour lines reveal a degree of limiting dependence that is clearly higher for stock market pairs than for bond market pairs. The bond market contour lies close to the asymptotic independence benchmark case but is still significantly nonlinear (cf. the results in table 23.2 on significant asymptotic dependence between pairs of bond market returns). Note that the greater propensity of stock markets to extreme comovements than that of government bond markets is not an artifact created by the choice of conditioning quantiles, for the stock market quantiles are not less extreme compared to historical stock market experience than the bond market quantiles compared to bond market experience.

One may be tempted to interpret the potential for stock and bond cocrashes in Table 23.2 as small. However, compared to the unconditional univariate probability of experiencing a crash in a specific market (table 23.1), the (conditional) probability of having a crash in this market given that there is already one in another market is markedly higher. This illustrates the relevance of phenomena like contagion or joint crises as a consequence of a common shock. In other words, although severe securities market crises seem to be fairly rare events if one predicts them without using price information from other markets, it is not that unlikely for crashes to occur jointly once one market is hit by a crisis. Nevertheless, the spillover probabilities estimated do not appear very high in absolute terms either, rarely exceeding 20%. This means that whereas contagion or joint securities market crashes are of practical likelihood, they do not seem to be prevalent among the G-5 countries. This point

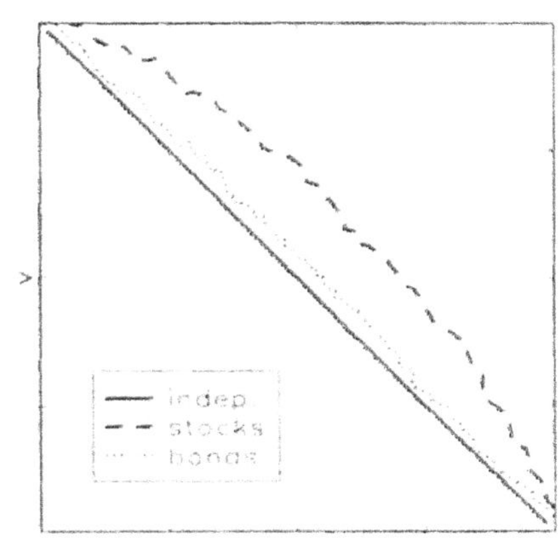

Figure 23.2 Estimated unit contour lines for stock and bond pairs (Germany, Japan).
Note: The eatimator (14) is used to estimate unit contour lines (the dotted and dashed lines) by letting the angle ϕ vary over the first quadrant. The dashed and dotted lines represent the limiting dependance structure for the German-Japanese pair of stock markets and the German-Japanese pair of bond markets, respectively. The solid straight line corresponds with asymptotic independence and is included for comparison.

may be further strengthened by noting the potential for an upward bias in the linkage estimator for small samples (see section IV and appendix C).

Finally, we also included full-sample correlations as a traditional linkage measure in table 23.2. One might easily interpret these as suggesting even higher linkages, but that is rather illusory. Suppose one applied the bivariate normal distribution to assess the extreme stock-stock and bond-bond market linkages, say, between France and Germany, the two most financially interlinked economies in table 23.2 (using the sample variances and correlations, with only the latter shown in the table). One would find that codependence is absent for stock markets in both countries at the 20% level. In fact, we only find codependence for crash magnitudes of 15% or lower (1 out of 228 stock crashes is then expected to be a cocrash). As for bonds, an 8% crash is expected to spread in only 1 out of 1,667 cases. Hence, the multivariate normal massively underrates extreme financial market linkages.[17]

Table 23.3 contains estimation and testing results on extreme linkages across asset classes, allowing for comparisons of stock-bond cocrash probabilities with the flight-to-quality phenomenon (the probability that a bond market booms, given that a stock market crashes). The table is further divided in two panels. The upper one (panel A) gives the results for stock-bond market linkages within a specific G-5 country, and the lower one (panel B) details international stock-bond market linkages between the G-5 countries. In the lower panel we adopt the convention that the first country mentioned has the stock market crash and the second country the bond market crash or boom. This allows us to treat the country pairs in panel B asymmetrically in terms of conditioning. This refinement enables us to look below at a new phenomenon, namely safe-haven behavior by investors.

The two left side columns show results for the W-test of asymptotic dependence in the lower tails (W_{CO}) and between the lower and the upper tails (W_{FTQ}) using equation (20). The pretest statistics do not indicate a rejection of asymptotic dependence for most asset market pairs. Only for the GE-FR pair in row 6 is the hypothesis of asymptotic cocrashes between German stocks and French bonds rejected at the 5% level (but not for French stocks and German bonds, as shown in the row below). In other words, for most pairs of G-5 countries our data display statistically significant interdependence among financial markets during periods of crisis.

Given that there is asymptotic dependence both between the losses on stocks and bonds and between stock losses and gains in the bond markets, it is of some interest to test for the equality of the two effects using the Z-test from equation (18) in column 3.[18] The test shows that cocrashes dominate flight to quality in only 2 out of 25 cases (in both cases at the 1% significance level; see the two asterisks in the Z column). For all other countries and market pairs the two effects are not significantly different from each other. On the other hand, the stock-bond correlations in table 23.3 are in most cases positive, which may be read as suggesting that cocrashes dominate flight-to-quality phenomena. This apparent difference between correlations and our extreme-events approach illustrates

[17]Due to the risk of biased correlation coefficients when conditioning on different ranges of the return distribution's support (Boyer et al., 1997: Forbes & Rigobon. 2002) and due to the extreme quantiles needed for calculating our conditional linkage indicator, we report the regular correlation coefficient for the whole distribution rather than conditional correlations in tables 23.2 and 23.3. All probabilities displayed in the text are derived from bivariate normals using these unconditional correlations.

[18]The Z-test value for the GE-FR pair is omitted from table 23.3, because its limit distribution is degenerate under asymptotic independence.

that full-sample correlations are unreliable as indicators for the direction of extreme co-movements. One interpretation of these results on extreme cross-asset linkages (in particular the nonnegligible occurrence of FTQ) is that capital fleeing one market has to go somewhere else. This puts some bounds on how far contagious financial market crashes can reach.

The remaining columns report estimates of the conditionally expected number of simultaneous crashes in stocks and bonds (E_{CO}) and for flight to quality from stocks into bonds (E_{FTQ}). Apart from the now asymmetric conditioning, the extreme linkage results can be interpreted in the same manner as in the previous table. For example, for the pair consisting of France (FR) and the United Kingdom (UK) we expect that roughly 1 out of 20($\approx 1/0.052$) stock crashes at the 20% level in France will coincide with an 8% decline in U.K. bonds. However, flight to quality from stocks into government bonds seems more likely for this country pair, because on average 1 out of 12.5($\approx 1/0.080$) French stock crashes of 20% are expected to coincide with a U.K. bond market boom of 8%. For the reverse case (UK-FR) the figures mean that joint crashes in U.K. stocks and French bonds are more likely than a U.K. stock crash accompanied by a flight to quality into French bonds (6.8% > 5.1%). Just as in the previous table, the estimated extreme market linkage indicators are only slightly altered upon changing the conditioning quantile pairs.

In general, however, the expected values for cocrashes and flight-to-quality phenomena are found to be comparable in magnitude, that is, $E_{\text{FTQ}} \approx E_{\text{CO}}$, as already suggested by the Z-tests. Comparing the extreme linkage results in table 23.3 with the figures in table 23.2, we see that the linkage measures across different assets tend to be lower than those for linkages across bond markets, so that roughly the following ordering emanates from the data: $E_{\text{CO}}^{\text{SS}} > E_{\text{CO}}^{\text{BB}} > E_{\text{CO}}^{\text{SB}}$.[19]

The patterns for extreme cross-border linkages in table 23.3 (panel B) are surprisingly similar to within-country linkages (panel A). National borders do not seem to limit the degree of contagion or flight to quality, which illustrates well a potential disadvantage of international financial market integration from the perspective of domestic financial market stability. Also, it is very hard to disentangle any clear geographical patterns (for example, related to distance). For example, the three European countries FR, GE, UK do not seem to have systematically stronger extreme linkages with each other than with US or JP.

However, there is some evidence of safe-haven behavior. To see this compare the flight-to-quality effects for the country pairs involving the United States in the two cases XX-US and US-XX (XX = FR, GE, JP, or UK). For example, the probability that a government bond market rally in the United States coincides with a stock market crash in France is 7.7% (FR-US), whereas the reverse case in which the French bond market booms in case of a U.S. equity market crash (US-FR) has only a 3.0% probability. This relationship also holds for Germany and the United Kingdom (Japan being the only exception). It shows the historical role of U.S. government securities and the dollar as a safe haven for European investors.

[19]The extreme linkage results in tables 23.2 and 23.3 also have implications for portfolio VaR estimations very far into the tails of financial market return distributions. This is because the degree of extremal dependence determines the potential for diversifying risk. For a given low significance level, the VaR levels of pure stock portfolios will usually be higher than those of mixed (stock bond) portfolios, whereas one may expect those of pure bond portfolios to take on an intermediate position. For readers interested in the details of the implications of our work for risk management these results are available upon request.

VI. Conclusions

The linkages between asset markets in periods of crisis are characterized by their asymptotic tail dependence. From this measure we derive nonparametric estimates for the expected number of market crashes given that at least one market crashes. This novel approach does not rely on a specific probability law for the returns, and therefore has the distinct advantage over the often used conditional correlation measure that it cannot distort the view of the extreme spillover likelihood. Thus the approach in this paper bypasses the indirect method of computing a correlation and subsequently inferring the probability of loss, by directly calculating the economically relevant measure.

A first result for the G-5 countries from the univariate analysis is that stock market crashes on the order of a 20% weekly loss and government bond market crashes on the order of an 8% weekly loss are rare events, but nevertheless do happen once or twice per lifetime. Turning to the bivariate results, we found that stock markets experience a cocrash in approximately one out of five to eight crashes. This number is lower for bond markets, and tends to be still less for a cocrash between a stock and a bond market.

Nevertheless, returns of different G-5 securities markets seem to be statistically dependent during crises. In particular, following up on the upper bound 20% ballpark estimate for a cocrash between stock markets, given that for the United States, for example, a crash happens only approximately once every 40 years and considering that bond market or cross-asset cocrashes tend to happen less frequently, one may conclude that a widespread securities market meltdown in the main industrialized countries happens much less than once every 200 years. Also, the frequency of such phenomena among G-5 countries is much higher than what a normal-distribution-based analysis would lead one to believe. On the other hand, the flight-to-quality phenomenon is about as common as the cocrash of a bond and a stock market, highlighting some limits to the propagation of financial market crises across asset classes. And finally, whereas the likelihood that a securities market crisis reaches a certain breadth is of significant magnitude, it does not seem large in absolute terms. This point is even further strengthened by our finding that in small samples our linkage measure may have a bias that leads to an overestimation of the probability of extreme financial market spillovers. So, one implication of our analysis is that securities market contagion (a severe crisis in one market spilling over to another market) cannot be a prevalent phenomenon among G-5 countries. Overall, our results seem to be in line with some very recent literature arguing for other reasons that the financial market contagion phenomenon may have been overestimated in the earlier literature on financial market crises (see, for example, Forbes & Rigobon, 2002). This should not lead policymakers into complacency, for the next crisis might still be broad and be associated with contagion.

In line with free capital flows and financial integration between G-5 countries, national borders do not seem to matter very much. From the perspective of domestic financial stability this might sometimes be regarded as the downside of such integration, suggesting that the surveillance of financial market stability cannot stop at national borders.

References

Bodart, V., and P. Reding, "Exchange Rate Regime, Volatility and International Correlations on Bond and Stock Markets," *Journal of international Money and Finance* 18 (1999), 133–151.

Borio, C. E. V., and R. N. McCauley, "The Economics of Recent Bond Yield Volatility," BIS economic papers no. 45 (Basel, 1996).

Boyer. B., M. Gibson, and M. Loretan, "Pitfalls in Tests for Changes in Correlation," Board of Governors of the Federal Reserve System, international finance discussion paper no. 5–97 (Washington, 1997).

Calvo, G. A., and E. G. Mendoza, "Rational Contagion and the Globalization of Securities Markets," *Journal of International Economics* 51 (2000), 79–113.

de Bandt, O., and P. Hartmann, "Systematic Risk: A Survey," ECB working paper no. 35 (European Central Bank, Frankfurt, 2000).

de Haan, L., and J. de Ronde, "Sea and Wind: Multivariate Extremes at Work," *Extremes* 1 (1998), 7–45.

de Haan, L., D. W. Jansen, K. Koedijk, and C. G. de Vries, "Safety First Portfolio Selection, Extreme Value Theory and Long Run Asset Risks," in J. Galambos (Ed.), *Proceedings from a Conference on Extreme Value Theory and Applications* (Kluwer Press, 1994).

Dekkers, A. L. M., and L. de Haan. "On the Estimation of the Extreme-Value Index and Large Quantile Estimation," *Annals of Statistics* 17 (1989), 1795–1832.

Domanski, D., and M. Kremer, "The Dynamics of International Asset Price Linkages and Their Effects on German Stock and Bond Markets," in *International Financial Markets and the Implications for Monetary and Financial stability*, BIS conference papers no. 8, (Bank for International Settlements, Basel, 2000).

Eichengreen, B., A. Rose, and C. Wyplosz, "Contagious Currency Crises: First Tests," *Scandinavian Journal of Economics* 98 (1996), 463–484.

Embrechts, P., C. Klüppelberg, and T. Mikosch, *Modelling Extremal Events* (Berlin: Springer-Verlag, 1997).

Federal Reserve Board, "Press Release" (Washington. October 15, 1998a).

—— "Minutes of the Federal Open Market Committee" (Washington, September 29, 1998b).

Fleming, J., C. Kirby, and B. Ostdiek, "Information and Volatility Linkages in the Stock, Bond and Money Markets," *Journal of Financial Economics* 49 (1998), 111–137.

Forbes, K., and R. Rigobon, "No Contagion, Only Interdependence: Measuring Stock Market Co-movements." *journal of finance* 57 (2002), 2223–2261.

Goldie, C. M., and R. H. Smith, "Slow Variation with Remainder: Theory and Applications," *Quarterly Journal of Mathematics (Oxford 2nd Series)* 38 (1987), 45–71.

Greenspan, A., "Testimony of Chairman Alan Greenspan. Private-Sector Refinancing of the Large Hedge Fund Long-Term Capital Management, before the Committee on Banking and Financial Services, U.S. House of Representatives" (Washington. October 1, 1998).

Gumbel, E. J., *Statistics of Extremes*, 2nd ed. (New York: Columbia University Press, 1958).

Hall, P., "On Some Simple Estimates of an Exponent of Regular Variation," *Journal of the Royal Statistical Society, Series B*, 42 (1982), 37–42.

Hamao, Y., R. W. Masulis and V. Ng, "Correlations in Price Changes and Volatility across International Stock Markets," *Review of Financial Studies* 3 (1990), 281–307.

Hartmann. P., S. Straetmans, and C. G. de Vries, "Asset Market Linkages in Crisis Periods." ECB working paper no. 71 (European Central Bank. Frankfurt. July 2001), www.ecb.eu/pub/pdf/scpwps/ecbwp071.pdf

—— "A Global Perspective on Extreme Currency Linkages," in W. C. Hunter, G. G. Kaufman, and M. Pomerleano (Eds,). *Asset Price Bubbles: Implications for Monetary Regulatory and International policies* (Cambridge, MA: MIT Press, 2003).

Heffernan, J. E., "A Directory of Coefficients of Tail Dependence." *Extremes* 3 (2001), 279–290.

Hill, B. M., "A Simple General Approach to Inference about the Tail of a Distribution." *The Annals of Statistics* 3 (1975), 1163–1173,

Huang, Xin, "Statistics of Bivariate Extreme Values," Tinbergen Institute Research Series, PhD thesis no. 22 (Erasmus University, Rotterdam, 1992).

Jansen, D. W., and C. G. de Vries, "On the Frequency of Large Stock Returns: Putting Booms and Busts into Perspective," *The Review of Economics and Statistics*, 73 (1991), 19–24.

Kaminsky, G. I., and C. M. Reinhart, "On Crises, Contagion and Confusion," *Journal of International Economics* 51 (2000), 145–168.

King, M., and S. Wadhwani, "Transmission of Volatility Between Stock Markets," *Review of Financial Studies* 3 (1990), 5-33.

Kodres. L. E., and M. Pritsker. "A Rational Expectations Model of Financial Contagion," *Journal of Finance* 57 (2002), 768–799.

Kyle, A. S., and W. Xiong, "Contagion as a Wealth Effect." *Journal of Finance* (Papers and Proceedings) 56 (2001), 1401–1440.

Lin, W. L., R. Engle, and T. Ito, "Do Bulls and Bears Move Across Borders? International Transmission of Stock Returns and Volatility," *Review of Financial Studies* 7 (1994), 507–538.
Longin, F., and B. Solnik. "Is the Correlation in International Equity Returns Constant: 1960–1990?" *Journal of International Money and Finance* 14 (1995), 3–26.
—— "Extreme Correlation of International Equity Markets," *Journal of Finance* 56 (2001), 649–676.
Malliaris, A. G., and J. L. Urrutia, "The International Crash of October 1987: Causality Tests," *Journal of Financial and Quantitative Analysis* 27 (1992), 353–363.
Morgenstern, O., *International Financial Transactions and the Business Cycle* (Princeton, NJ: Princeton University Press, 1959).
Peng, L., "Estimation of the Coefficient of Tail Dependence in Bivariate Extremes," *Statistics & Probability Letters* 43 (1999), 399–409.
Poon, S. H., M. Rockinger, and J. Tawn, "New Extreme-Value Dependence Measures and Finance Applications," CEPR discussion paper no. 2762 (London, 2001).
Ramchand, L., and R. Susmel, "Volatility and Cross Correlation across Major Stock Markets." *Journal of Empirical Finance* 5 (1998), 397–416.
Sachs, J., A. Tornell, and A. Velasco, "Financial Crises in Emerging Markets: The Lessons from 1995," *Brookings Papers on Economic Activity* 1 (1996), 147–198.
Starica, C., "Multivariate Extremes for Models with Constant Conditional Correlations," *Journal of Empirical Finance* 6 (1999), 515–553.
Straetmans, S., "Extreme Financial Returns and their Comovements," Tinbergen Institute research series PhD thesis no. 181 (Rotterdam: Erasmus University, 1998).
—— "Extremal Spill-overs in Equity Markets," in P. Embrechts (Ed.), *Extremes and Integrated Risk Management* (London: Risk Books, 2000).
Susmel, R., and R. F. Engle, "Hourly Volatility Spillovers between International Equity Markets," *Journal of International Money and Finance* 13 (1994), 3–25.

Appendix A

Derivation of the Tail Dependence Coefficient

In this appendix we provide a heuristic derivation of the tail dependence coefficient η used in the Peng test introduced in section IV. Equation (19) implies for $k, n \to \infty$ and $\tau = k/n \to 0$

$$\frac{P\left\{X > Q_1\left(2k/n\right), Y > Q_2\left(2k/n\right)\right\}}{P\left\{X > Q_1\left(k/n\right), Y > Q_2\left(k/n\right)\right\}} \to 2^{1/\eta} \qquad (23.A.1)$$

Denote by $X_{i,n}$ and $Y_{i,n}$ the ith ascending order statistics of the two return series. To estimate η from the sample we may replace P, Q_1, and Q_2 in equation (A-1) by their empirical counterparts. Therefore write

$$C_n\left(k, k\right) = k^{-1} \sum_{i=1}^{n} \mathbf{1}\left\{X_i > X_{n-k,n} \text{ and } Y_i > Y_{n-k,n}\right\} \qquad (23.A.2)$$

and substitute equation (A-2) into (A-1), Taking logs renders

$$\hat{\eta} = \ln 2 / \ln\left(\frac{C_n\left(2k, 2k\right)}{C_n\left(k, k\right)}\right);$$

see Peng (1999), who also proved consistency and asymptotic normality of the estimator. Consequently the test statistic $W = \left(\hat{\eta} - 1\right)/\sigma\left(\hat{\eta}\right)$ converges to a standard normal distribution and can be used to test the null hypothesis of asymptotic dependence (H_0: $\eta = 1$) against the alternative hypothesis of asymptotic independence (H_1: $\eta < 1$).

Appendix B

Small-Sample Properties of Tests

In this appendix we study the small-sample properties of the Peng pretest for asymptotic dependence [equation (20)] and of the Z-test [equation (18)]. A Monte Carlo study of the size and power properties for W requires choosing data-generating processes for simulating return pairs under H_0 and H_1. As H_0 we choose the bivariate Pareto distribution on $[1, \infty) \times [1, \infty)$.

$$F(x, y) = 1 + (x + y - 1)^{-\alpha} - x^{-\alpha} - y^{-\alpha},$$

with correlation coefficient $\rho = 1/\alpha$ (α being the tail index). Note the close association between tail dependence and tail fatness in this distribution. Asymptotically independent data are drawn from either a bivariate normal or a bivariate Gumbel-Pareto distribution. The latter distribution is

$$G(x, y) = \left(1 - x^{-\alpha}\right)\left(1 - y^{-\alpha}\right)\left[1 + \gamma x^{-\alpha} y^{-\alpha}\right], \quad 0 \le \gamma \le 1,$$

with correlation coefficient

$$\rho = \frac{\alpha(\alpha - 2)}{(2\alpha - 1)^2}\gamma.$$

Like the bivariate Pareto, the Gumbel-Pareto distribution has Pareto-distributed marginals. But unlike the bivariate Pareto distribution, it is asymptotically independent, because the tail dependence coefficient η equals ½. Similarly, the bivariate normal distribution is asymptotically independent, because $\eta = (1 + \rho)/2$. Interestingly, for the normal case the tail dependence parameter varies with the correlation coefficient, but η is constant for the Gumbel-Pareto distribution. These distribution functions represent a sufficiently rich dependence structure to evaluate the W-test performance.

In table 23.B1 we report small-sample critical values for W under H_0 (bivariate Pareto distribution exhibiting asymptotic dependence) for different significance levels θ, degrees of tail dependence α, and the threshold choices k. The values for α and k are chosen in accordance with the correlations observed in our data and the thresholds employed in the empirical section, respectively.

The table suggests that one should be careful using the normal critical values of $-1.65(\theta = 5\%)$ and $-1.96(\theta = 2.5\%)$ for testing asymptotic dependence in small samples. Assuming that the empirical financial data are also bivariate-Pareto-distributed, we can check whether the W-values from the empirical section lie within the small-sample rejection areas from table 23.B1. More specifically, for each of the seventy asset pairs in tables 23.2 and 23.3 we selected the $\theta\%$ rejection are for values of α and k that most closely resemble their true values, that is, the estimated correlation and the threshold choice for each

Table 23.B.1. Small-Sample Critical Values of the W-Test for Bivariate Pareto Draws

	$W(\theta = 5\%)$			$W(\theta = 2.5\%)$		
α	$k = 25$	50	75	25	50	75
2	−0.875	−1.274	−1.631	−0.925	−1.326	−1.693
3	−0.822	−1.244	−1.628	−0.867	−1.289	−1.675
4	−0.770	−1.204	−1.600	−0.818	−1.250	−1.645

Note: Critical values are determined for Peng's W-test for testing asymptotic dependence. The small sample df of W is obtained by 10,000 Monte Carlo replications from the bivariate Pareto df. The critical values are conditioned on different values of the significance level θ, the tail index α, and the threshold k of the tail dependence function. The range of k is consistent with the threshold values used in the empirical application.

asset pair.[20] Despite the tendency for lower critical values shown in table 23.B1, we find that the empirical section's test results for asymptotic dependence hardly change.

Next we investigate the power properties of W. The simulation setup consists of three steps:

1. We draw samples of size $n = 663$ from the bivariate Pareto (H_0), the bivariate normal, and the bivariate Gumbel-Pareto (H_1) distribution and calculate η for the asymptotically dependent and independent samples. We then condition estimates of η on $k = 75$ and repeat this sampling scheme *rep* (= 10,000) times. This renders the small-sample distributions $\bar{\eta}\,(H_0)$ and $\bar{\eta}^{\text{ind}}\,(H_1)$.
2. We estimate the 5% quantile of $\bar{\eta}$ by the order statistic $\bar{\eta}_{i,rep}$ with $i/rep = 0.05$.
3. We evaluate the small-sample power:

$$P_{SS} = \frac{1}{rep} \sum_{j=1}^{rep} \mathbf{1}\left\{\bar{\eta}_{rep}^{\text{ind}} < \bar{\eta}_{i,rep}\right\}.$$

Table 23.B2 reports the power of W simulated by applying this procedure (for $k = 75$). The power clearly decreases in α, reflecting the degree of tail dependence for the null model (the stronger toil dependence under the null, the higher the power). Moreover the power under the Gurnbel-Pareto alternative is nearly unaffected by changes in ρ because $\eta = 0.5$, regardless of the correlation value. As for the power under the H_1 of normality, it decreases when η (and thus ρ) is increased. This implies that, for any given sample size and significance level, a normal alternative with dependence parameter η close to 1 can be found that is indistinguishable from the null model of asymptotic dependence, that is, the *local alternatives* problem. However. Heffernan (2001) shows that a large majority of parametric models with asymptotically independent tails are governed by a tail dependence parameter of ½. Thus, one might interpret the power results under the normal alternative as the worst case to be encountered.

We also investigated the small-sample critical behavior of the Z-statistic equation (18) by applying the above simulation setup. Table 23.B3 shows that small-sample critical values are again deviating from their asymptotic comterparts, but they are reasonably close to them for k-values of 50 or 75. Applying these altermative rejection regions to the Z-values

[20] Because of space considerations we did not report threshold choices for each of the seventy empirical return pairs in tables 23.2 and 23.3. They are available upon request.

Table 23.B2. Small-Sample Power of the W-Test

	H$_0$ (Bivariate Pareto)		
	$\alpha = 2$	3	4
	H$_1$ (Normal)		
$\rho = 0$	86.94	73.49	60.52
$\rho = 0.25$	61.53	37.59	21.88
$\rho = 0.5$	21.62	5.26	1.15
	H$_1$ (Gumbel-P)		
$\gamma = 0.5$	87.64	67.72	50.95
$\gamma = 0.9$	86.68	63.1	42.29

Note: The power of the W-test is determined under the null hypothesis of a bivariate Pareto df and under two different alternative hypotheses with asymptotically independent tails. The small-sample dfs of W under asymptotic dependence and asymptotic independence are derived from 10,000 Monte Carlo replications. The alternative models might exhibit some statistical dependence reflected by the parameters ρ and γ, but this dependence dies out very far into the tails. Further details on the power calculations are provided in the main text.

Table 23.B3. Small-Sample Critical Values of the Z-Test for Bivariate Pareto Draws

	$Z(\theta = 5\%)$			$Z(\theta = 2.5\%)$		
α	$k = 25$	50	75	25	50	75
2	−1.438	−1.500	−1.564	−1.716	−1.807	−1.872
3	−1.395	−1.534	−1.554	−1.670	−1.869	−1.813
4	−1.426	−1.571	−1.551	−1.700	−1.867	−1.853

Note: Critical values are determined for the Z-test in equation (18) for testing equality of the cocrash and flight-to-quality effects between stocks and bonds. The small sample df of Z is obtained by 10,000 Monte Carlo replications from the bivariate Pareto df. The critical values are presented for different values of the significance level θ, the tail index α and the threshold k of the tail dependence function.

in table 23.3 does not alter the test results. However, the Z-test may exhibit low power in small samples.

Appendix C

Small-Sample Properties of the Estimator

The linkage estimator (16) can be shown to constitute an upper bound on the true amount of comovement in the crisis area. We show this both analytically and by simulation. Let us start with the analytic argument. Assume symmetric and equal marginal distribution functions such that $P\{X > x\} = P\{Y > x\} = p$, where x is some crash level. The expected number of cocrashes in the crisis area (1) can now be rewritten as:

$$E_p = \frac{2}{p^{-1}P\left\{X > Q_1(p) \text{ or } Y > Q_2(p)\right\}} \rightarrow \frac{2}{l(1,1)} \quad \text{for} \quad p \rightarrow 0, \tag{23.C.1}$$

and where $l(1, 1)$ is defined as in equation (3). This limiting relationship suggests the following estimator for E_p:

$$\hat{E} = \frac{2}{\hat{l}(1,1)}, \tag{23.C.2}$$

With $\hat{l}(1,1) = k^{-1}\sum_{i=1}^{n} \mathbf{1}\left(X_i > X_{n-k,n} \text{ or } Y_i > Y_{n-k,n}\right)$ Notice the analogy with the proposed estimators in equations (15) and (16), the only difference being that we allowed for marginal asymmetry and inequality in the empirical section. It can now be shown that $\hat{E}$ exceeds E_p by applying Peng's finite-sample expansion for the bivariate tail (19) to the denominators of $\hat{E}$ and E_p.

To demonstrate this claim, note that the bivariate tail probability in the denominator of E_p is nested into Peng's expansion for $t = p$ and $u = v = 1$:

$$p^{-1} P\left\{X > Q_1(p) \text{ or } \gamma > Q_2(p)\right\} = 2 - c(1,1)p^{\frac{1}{\eta}-1}\left[1 + 0(p)^{\theta}\right], \tag{23.C.3}$$

Likewise we obtain a finite-sample expansion for $l(1,1)$ for $t = k/n$ and $u = v = 1$ in equation (19):

$$\hat{l}(1,1) = 2 - c(1,1)\left(\frac{k}{n}\right)^{\frac{1}{\eta}-1}\left[1 + 0\left(\frac{k}{n}\right)^{\theta}\right]. \tag{23.C.4}$$

The choice of p reflects the crisis area we are interested in. In the empirical application we typically condition on crash levels Q_1 and Q_2 at the sample boundary or beyond, which corresponds to significance levels smaller than the reciprocal of the sample size ($p \leq n^{-1}$). It then immediately follows that equation (C-4) exceeds (C-3). Notice also that the second-order expansions lie closer to each other when the bivariate tail exhibits asymptotic dependence ($\eta = 1$). The small-sample bias in the linkage estimator should thus be lower under asymptotic dependence than under asymptotic independence.

We performed a Monte Carlo study of the small-sample bias, using a bivariate normal distribution (asymptotically independent tails) and a bivariate Pareto distribution (asymptotically dependent tails) as data-generating processes. Estimated linkage measures are reported in Table 23.C1 for different sample sizes, threshold values k, and correlations ρ. The reported estimates are averages over 100 replications. Correlations and thresholds k are again chosen close to the observed correlations in the data and values of k used in the

Table 23.C1. Upward Bias in Linkage Estimators Bivariate Normal versus Bivariate Pareto

	n = 663				**n = 5,000**			
	Ext. $E[k]$				**Ext. $E[k]$**			
ρ	**k = 25**	**50**	**75**	**E_p**	**25**	**50**	**75**	**E_p**
				A. Bivariate Normal				
1/2	1.117	1.165	1.204	1.032	1.052	1.070	1.082	1.015
1/3	1.075	1.111	1.145	1.012	1.022	1.032	1.042	1.004
0	1.018	1.040	1.060	1.000	1.002	1.005	1.007	1.000
				B. Bivariate Pareto				
1/2	1.173	1.198	1.219	1.149	1.152	1.156	1.162	1.141
1/3	1.120	1.148	1.167	1.081	1.086	1.096	1.103	1.073

Note: The table reports estimated values (Est. E) and "true" analytic values (E_p) of the extreme linkage measure for the bivariate normal and bivariate Parteo dfs and for different samples sizes n and correlations p. Moreover, the linkage estimates are presented for different values of the threshold k. The conditioning qualities for the linkage estimates and analytic counterparts are chosen such that the corresponding marginal excess probabilities are equal to the inverse of the sample size, that is, exactly at the sample boundary.

empirical section. The theoretical linkage value E_p is also recorded and evaluated at the sample boundary ($p = n^{-1}$).

The values of the measure provide an upper bound for the amount of linkage E_p during crisis periods. The amount of upward bias is higher in Panel A, which is consistent with our analytical considerations on the bias. The difference between the asymptotically independent normal distribution and the bivariate Pareto distribution becomes apparent in the larger sample. For data sets 10 times larger than the current sample ($n = 663$), the normal-based linkage estimates start to approach 1 while the Pareto-based estimates retain their higher levels.

Appendix D

Data Description and Discussion

Data were obtained from Datastream, Inc. G-5 countries are listed in Tables 23.1, 23.2, and 23.3 with the following abbreviations: France (FR), Germany (GE), United Kingdom (UK), United States (US), Japan (JP). The stock data are Financial Times/Standard & Poors world price indices, whereas the bond data correspond to price indices on 10-year (all-traded) government bonds. We did not include corporate bond indices, because of our particular interest in the flight-to-quality phenomenon. Returns were calculated as log price differences, Friday to Friday, in local currency. The stock and bond returns are not compensated for dividends and coupon payments, respectively. The sample of daily raw data used started on February 27, 1987 and ended on November 18, 1999, which amounts to 663 weekly observations.

Weekly data have the advantage that one significantly reduces the typical time zone problems encountered with international data at the daily frequency. Moreover, they capture more sustained crash phenomena, which can be expected to have more significant effects on financial institutions and the real economy than one would usually pick up with daily returns. An even longer holding period was not possible, due to the limited length of the bond index data available to us. Of course, the two advantages of the use of weekly data mentioned above come at the cost of not being able to address explicitly intraday or daily short-run dynamics that could also help to understand crisis propagation mechanisms. Although that is outside the scope of the present paper, in future work we plan also to investigate the time structure of extreme financial market spillovers by studying the following intertemporal specification of our extreme linkage indicator: $P(X_t > x, Y_{t-k} > y)$ for $k > 0$.

24 Strategic Complementarities and the Twin Crises

Itay Goldstein

It is well known that strategic complementarities among economic agents may cause financial crises. According to banking-crises theory, due to the fact that banks finance long-term investments with short-term liabilities, an individual creditor is better off demanding early withdrawal if other creditors do so. This, in turn, may cause a panic among creditors, and may generate a bank run that cannot be explained by economic fundamentals alone (Diamond and Dybvig, 1983). Similarly, in currency-crises theory, the willingness of the government to maintain a fixed exchange rate regime decreases with the number of speculators that attack the currency. As a result, the incentive of an individual speculator to attack the currency increases with the number of speculators who do that, and, again, this might lead to a currency attack that is not justified by economic fundamentals (Obstfeld, 1996; Morris and Shin, 1998).

A common feature in all the papers mentioned above is that they look at one group of homogeneous agents – either creditors or speculators – and analyse the consequences of strategic complementarities among members of this group. An interesting case (that was not analysed in the literature) arises when strategic complementarities exist, not only within a group of creditors or within a group of speculators, but also between the two groups. By this, we mean that the incentive of creditors to run on the bank increases, not only with the number of creditors that run on the bank, but also with the number of speculators that attack the currency. Similarly, the incentive of speculators to attack the currency increases with the number of creditors that run on the bank as well as with the number of speculators that attack the currency.

We believe that such a pattern of strategic complementarities is quite realistic, and can result from some basic features that characterised small open emerging markets in the last two decades. In fact, this pattern was mentioned in two descriptive papers that documented recent financial crises in such markets.[1] In these economies, governments maintained fixed exchange rate regimes or narrow exchange rate bands, which were obviously vulnerable to speculative attacks. Domestic banks, in these markets, had a mismatch between foreign liabilities and domestic assets and were thus exposed to

[1] See Radelet and Sachs (1998) for the case of South East Asia in 1997 and Dornbusch *et al.* (1995) for the cases of Chile in 1982 and Mexico in 1994.

(and not hedged against) exchange-rate risks.[2] This basic set-up can generate strategic complementarities between foreign creditors and speculators. (In addition to the strategic complementarities among members of each group.)

Two effects account for these strategic complementarities. First, a currency attack that yields depreciation of the exchange rate reduces the value of banks' investments relative to the value of their liabilities. Knowing that, foreign creditors expect that banks will have fewer resources to pay their future liabilities and thus find it more profitable to take their money out immediately, i.e., to run on the bank. Second, when foreign creditors run on domestic banks and pull their money out of the economy, they indirectly reduce the amount of foreign reserves held by the government. Then, the government faces a higher cost of defending the currency and abandons the fixed exchange rate regime in more circumstances. This increases the incentive of speculators to attack the currency, as they know that the attack is more likely to succeed.

In this paper, we study a model with two types of agents: foreign creditors and speculators. Due to the features of emerging markets that were described above, our model has strategic complementarities between foreign creditors and speculators (in addition to strategic complementarities within each group). We study the implications that these strategic complementarities have for the realisation of both banking crises and currency crises and for the correlation between the two.

A major empirical motivation for this study is the recent evidence on the *twin crises* phenomenon documented by Kaminsky and Reinhart (1999). They show that many international financial crises that occurred during the 1980s and 1990s included both a massive devaluation and a collapse of the banking system. They find that macroeconomic variables at the root of both of these crises may explain some of the positive correlation between them, however, they also point to the existence of a vicious circle, in which banking and currency problems aggravated each other during that time.

In our model, due to strategic complementarities between speculators and creditors, an increase in the probability of one type of crisis generates an increase in the probability of the other type. This yields a vicious circle between the two types of crisis: a higher probability of bank runs leads to a higher probability of currency attacks, which, in turn, causes the probability of bank runs to increase even more. This vicious circle can continue on and on – generating higher probabilities of both crises.

Our model shows that in equilibrium, the vicious circle has two interesting effects. The first effect is a destabilising effect. There are states of nature, in which a banking crisis occurs just because creditors believe that a currency crisis is going to occur, and a currency crisis occurs just because speculators believe that a banking crisis is going to occur. In these cases, each crisis should not have occurred on its own, but both crises occur as a result of the complementarities between the banking sector and the currency market. The second effect is on the correlation between the two crises. Due to the vicious circle, both crises become strongly connected to each other and the result in many cases will be a perfect correlation between the two crises: either both crises occur or none of them does.

[2]As Krugman (1999) suggested, this exposure can be indirect. In such a case, the assets of the bank can be loans that are denominated in terms of the foreign currency but are extended to domestic firms. Then, depreciation can harm the balance sheets of the domestic firms, which are directly exposed to exchange rate risks. This will harm their solvency and lead to a reduction in the value of bank assets.

We analyse other empirical implications of the model and confront them with empirical findings of other recent studies on the twin crises phenomenon.[3] We focus on two issues: the frequency of twin crises relative to regular banking or currency crises, and the costs of twin crises. We show that in our model twin crises are expected to be more frequent in financially liberalised emerging markets than in industrial economies and in developing economies that are not financially liberalised. We also show that in emerging markets twin crises are expected to be more costly than regular banking and currency crises, but this is not necessarily the case in industrial countries. These implications are broadly consistent with the empirical evidence.

Our framework also yields some interesting policy implications. First, as the two crises are strongly connected, our model suggests that a useful way to reduce the probability of one type of crisis is to prevent the other crisis. Thus, an increase in the transaction cost that speculators have to bear when they attack the currency will directly reduce the probability of a currency attack and indirectly reduce the probability of a bank run. Similarly, higher commitment to maintain the fixed exchange rate regime, or lower short-term payoffs to investors will reduce the probabilities of both types of crises. Second, a 'Lender of Last Resort' regime might not achieve its goal of preventing bank runs. Thus, when the government acts as a Lender of Last Resort, it loses more reserves and increases the probability of a currency crisis. Then, since a currency crisis increases the probability of a banking crisis, the result of a Lender of Last Resort might be a higher probability of a banking crisis. As a result, other policy measures that do not affect the reserves of the government, such as an international Lender of Last Resort (IMF) or suspension of convertibility, may be preferable in the presence of spillovers between the banking sector and the currency market.

Because of strategic complementarities, in our model both banking crises and currency crises result from self-fulfilling beliefs. We think this is an important feature since the common view on many recent crises is that the state of the economy that preceded them was not sufficiently bad to justify a crisis without some economic agents believing that a crisis was indeed about to occur. However, unlike most models of self-fulfilling beliefs, our model has a unique equilibrium, in which the fundamentals of the economy uniquely determine whether crises are going to occur or not. This unique equilibrium enables us to derive predictions, which cannot be derived in standard models of self-fulfilling beliefs. Thus, it enables us to characterise endogenous probabilities of both types of crisis, demonstrate the vicious circle between the two crises, discuss the effect of strategic complementarities on the equilibrium outcomes and analyse policy measures that can affect the probabilities of crises.

The existence of unique equilibrium in our framework results from the assumption that agents do not have common knowledge about the fundamentals of the economy. Carlsson and van Damme (1993) were the first to show that non-common knowledge generates a unique equilibrium in models of strategic complementarities. Morris and Shin (1998) applied this argument in the context of currency attacks and Goldstein and Pauzner (2005) applied it in the context of bank runs. Our paper integrates the banking sector in Goldstein and Pauzner (2005) with the currency market in Morris and Shin (1998) and studies the twin crises phenomenon, which was not studied in any of these papers. Because of the existence of two groups of agents, the methodology used in our paper to study the equilibrium

[3] See Bordo *et al.* (2001), Eichengreen and Bordo (2002), Glick and Hutchison (2002), Hoggarth *et al.* (2002), and Hutchison and Noy (2004).

outcomes is different from the methodologies used by Goldstein and Pauzner and by Morris and Shin. Some of the theoretical tools we use here are based on the recent work of Frankel *et al.* (2003), who generalised the basic result of Carlsson and van Damme.[4]

To date, few models have addressed the relationship between currency crises and banking crises. The list includes: Allen and Gale (2000), Burnside *et al.* (2001*a*,*b*), Chang and Velasco (2000, 2001), Goldfajn and Valdes (1997), Miller (1996, 1998*a*) and Velasco (1987). Miller (1998*b*) and Marion (1999) provide short surveys. Our paper is different from these papers in three aspects: first, we analyse strategic complementarities between creditors and speculators, whereas the other papers do not look at the interaction between these two groups of agents. Second, we derive firm predictions in a framework of self-fulfilling beliefs. Third, we obtain new results on the occurrence of both types of crises in equilibrium and analyse new policy implications.

The remainder of this paper is organised as follows. Section 1 presents the basic model. In Section 2, we analyse the different types of strategic complementarities and demonstrate the vicious circle between the two crises. Section 3 presents the equilibrium outcomes. In Section 4, we study empirical implications. Section 5 discusses policy implications. Section 6 concludes. Proofs are relegated to the Appendix.

1. The Model

Our economy has a banking sector and a currency market. In the banking sector, a continuum [0,1] of foreign creditors holds claims in a commercial bank. Each creditor has to decide whether to demand her money from the bank immediately (i.e. to run on the bank) or to wait. In the currency market, a continuum $[0, A]$ of speculators holds units of the domestic currency peso. The exchange rate of the peso against the dollar (the foreign currency) is initially fixed at 1. The government is committed to maintaining this level of the exchange rate and is therefore willing to exchange pesos for dollars at that rate. Each speculator has to decide whether to demand such an exchange (i.e. to attack the domestic currency) or not. In case that many speculators attack the currency, the government might decide to break its commitment and to let the market determine the level of the exchange rate.

Agents from both groups are risk neutral and thus choose their actions so as to maximise their expected payoffs.[5] Each agent makes her decision after receiving a private signal about the state of the economy. (We assume that agents make their decisions simultaneously.) This state, which is denoted as θ and will be referred to as the *fundamentals of the economy*, affects the prospects of the bank and the prospects of the currency in the same direction. It can represent either the terms of trade or the level of productivity, as both of them – when they improve – strengthen the prospects of the domestic currency and those of the domestic bank.[6]

We assume that θ has the (improper) uniform prior over the real line. The value of θ is not publicly reported after it is realised. Instead, each agent from both groups receives a private

[4]The literature that followed Carlsson and van Damme (1993) is known as the global games literature. Other applications in this literature include Dasgupta (2004), Goldstein and Pauzner (2004) and Rochet and Vives (2004). For excellent surveys see Morris and Shin (2001, 2003).

[5]Because of the risk neutrality, some agents can belong to both groups and still maximise their expected payoffs from each activity without considering the payoff received from the other activity.

[6]The fact that we have a unique variable that affects both the banking sector and the currency market helps to simplify our model. This assumption does not account for our result of perfect correlation between banking crises and currency crises (See Section 3).

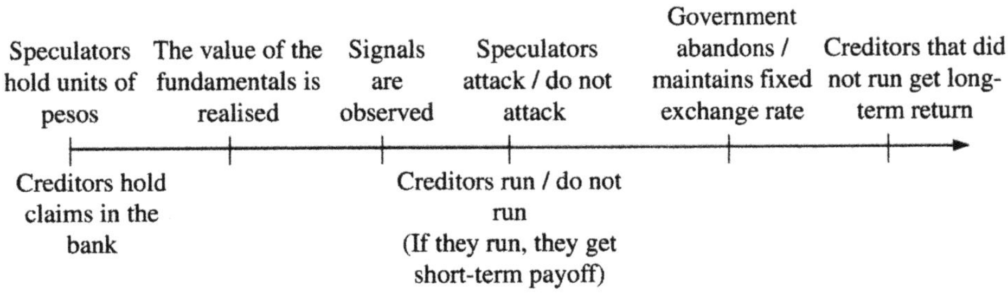

Figure 24.1. The Order of Events.

signal regarding the value of the fundamentals. More specifically, when θ is realised, agent i observes a signal $\theta_i = \theta + \sigma\epsilon_i$, where $\sigma > 0$ is a constant and the individual specific noise terms ϵ_i are independently distributed according to a smooth symmetric density function $g(\cdot)$ (the c.d.f. is denoted as $G(\cdot)$) with mean zero.[7]

Figure 24.1 depicts the order of events in the economy. We now turn to describe the banking sector and the currency market in more detail.

1.1 The Banking Sector

In the banking sector, there is one commercial bank and a continuum [0,1] of foreign creditors. Each creditor holds a claim of 1 dollar in the commercial bank. The bank invests the total sum of money in a local long-term asset. The gross return of the asset per each dollar of investment is either $R(\theta, n)$ pesos after maturity (that is, in the long term) or 1 peso in case of an early withdrawal (that is, in the short term). We assume that a portion α of the short-term return is obtained in dollars, and the rest $(1 - \alpha)$ is obtained in pesos. This may represent the ability of the bank to sell only a part of the liquidated investment abroad. We also assume that the long-term return R is an increasing function of the state θ, given that the asset is local. It is also a decreasing function of n, the proportion of the investment that is withdrawn early, due to an increasing return to scale on aggregate investment.[8]

The loan contract enables creditors to withdraw money from the bank either in the short term or in the long term. If they withdraw in the short term, creditors are promised a payment of 1 dollar, whereas if they withdraw in the long term, they are promised a payment of r_2 dollars; $r_2 > 1$. In order to serve creditors that wish to withdraw money in the short term, the bank has to liquidate a portion of the investment and to exchange the peso-return for dollars with the government (recall that creditors are promised to get their payments in dollars). The bank has to exchange $(1 - \alpha)$ pesos with the government per each unit of investment that he has to liquidate.

[7]Improper priors simplify the exposition by allowing us to concentrate on the updated beliefs of creditors and speculators conditional on their signals without taking into account the information contained in the prior distribution. Thus, our results can be seen as the limiting case as the information in the prior density goes to zero. They will go through with a proper prior as long as the information in the private signal is sufficiently more precise than the information in the prior distribution. See Hartigan (1983), Morris and Shin (2003, Section 2) and Corsetti *et al.* (2004) for more discussion on improper priors and their use in the global games literature.

[8]Here, increasing returns to scale are the source for strategic complementarities among creditors. We think this is a realistic assumption in the context of a small open emerging market. Such complementarities could also result from lack of liquidity in the short term (Diamond and Dybvig, 1983). See also footnote 9 for a related discussion.

Since the exchange rate is initially fixed at 1, creditors know that they can get 1 dollar from the bank if they withdraw immediately (in the short term). If they wait, however, the bank might not be able to pay them the promised r_2 dollars. This is because the dollar value of the banks' assets in the long term might be low due to a change in the exchange rate, a low level of the fundamentals, or a high proportion of agents who decided to withdraw early. In such a case, creditors that did not run in the short term will get control over the banks' assets in the long term. Thus, denoting the level of the exchange rate (i.e. the price of one peso in terms of dollars) in the long term as e, the long-term payoff of creditors will be $\widehat{R}(\theta, n, e)$ dollars, where:[9]

$$\widehat{R}(\theta, n, e) = \begin{cases} eR(\theta, n) & \text{if } eR(\theta, n) \leq r_2 \\ r_2 & \text{if } eR(\theta, n) \leq r_2 \end{cases}. \tag{24.1}$$

Clearly, $\widehat{R}(\theta, n, e)$ is an increasing function of the fundamentals of the economy and a decreasing function of the proportion n of creditors that withdraw early. Moreover, it is also an increasing function of the level of the exchange rate e, since in case of depreciation, the long-term value of the bank's asset in dollar terms will decrease.[10]

Each creditor has to decide whether to withdraw her money from the bank immediately (that is, to run on the bank) or to wait until the long term. Creditors will choose the action that yields a higher expected payoff. Clearly, the decision depends on what they believe other creditors and speculators are going to do.

We follow Morris and Shin (2003) and assume the existence of uniform dominance regions.[11] Specifically, there exist $\underline{\theta}_B, \overline{\theta}_B$ and $k_B > 0$, such that $R(\underline{\theta}_B, 0) = 1 - k_B$ and $R(\overline{\theta}_B, 1).f(\overline{\theta}_B) = 1 + k_B \cdot (f(\theta)$ is the market level of the exchange rate; it is defined in the next subsection.) Since e is equal to 1 or $f(\theta)$, and since $f(\theta) < 1$ (see below), we know that when the level of fundamentals is below $\underline{\theta}_B$, the long-term return is lower than the short-term return by at least k_B dollars for any possible behaviour of other creditors and speculators. Similarly, when the fundamentals are above $\overline{\theta}_B$, the long-term return is higher than the short-term return by at least k_B dollars.[12]

[9]Note that in our specification, banks do not fail in the short term as they always have enough resources to pay creditors who demand early withdrawal. Instead, the fact that many creditors demand early withdrawal might cause banks to fail in the long term. This specification follows Morris and Shin (2004). We chose this specification to simplify the exposition. Alternative specifications, where banks might fail also in the short term, are offered by Goldstein and Pauzner (2005) and by Rochet and Vives (2004), and follow Diamond and Dybvig (1983). Adopting one of these specifications in a model of twin crises will complicate the exposition without adding much economic content.

[10]Here, the positive effect of the exchange rate on the long-term payoff is a result of the assumption that the return of the asset is denominated in pesos. However, such an effect can exist even when the bank holds a local asset, whose value is denominated in dollars. See footnote 2.

[11]See assumption A4* in Morris and Shin (2003).

[12]The existence of $\underline{\theta}_B(\bar{\theta}_B)$ implies that there are signals that are low (high) enough such that it is a dominant action for a creditor to run on the bank (not to run on the bank). To see this, note that when the fundamentals are below $\underline{\theta}_B$, the difference between running on the bank and waiting is at least, k_B, while when the fundamentals are above $\underline{\theta}_B$, this difference must be above $1 - r_2$. Thus, running on the bank will be a dominant action when the posterior probability that the fundamentals are below θ_B is higher than $(r_2 - 1)/(k_B + r_2 - 1)$. This will happen when a creditor gets a signal $\underline{\theta}_i$ that satisfies $G[(\theta_i - \underline{\theta}_B)/\sigma] < k_B/(k_B + r_2 - 1)$. Since the distribution of signals has full support, and since $G(x)$ approaches 0 (1) as x approaches $-\infty(\infty)$, there are signals for which this condition holds. Similarly, waiting will be a dominant action when θ_i satisfies $G[(\theta_i - \overline{\theta}_B)/\sigma] > 1/(1 + k_B)$.

1.2 The Currency Market

The government is committed to maintain the domestic currency's exchange rate e at a fixed level of 1. The government will keep this commitment as long as the benefit from maintaining the fixed exchange rate exceeds the cost of doing that. If the government decides to abandon the fixed exchange rate, it will let the currency market determine the new level of the exchange rate. In such cases, e will equal $f(\theta)$, where f is an increasing function of the fundamentals (that is, the currency tends to appreciate when economic conditions improve). We assume that $f(\theta) < 1$ for every θ, that is, the government initially fixes the exchange rate at an over-appreciated level.

We denote the benefit that the government derives from maintaining the fixed exchange rate as υ. This benefit results from credibility that the government gains when it keeps its commitment. The cost of maintaining the fixed rate is denoted as c. We follow Obstfeld (1996) and Morris and Shin (1998) and assume that this cost depends positively on two parameters. The first is the macroeconomic misalignment that is generated by the fixed exchange rate regime. This misalignment is greater when the difference between the market level of the exchange rate and the fixed level of the exchange rate is higher. As a result, c is a decreasing function of θ. The second parameter that has a positive effect on c is the amount of foreign reserves that the government loses when it defends the exchange rate. This is because the government has some target level of reserves, which is essential in order to maintain the fixed exchange rate regime. When the difference between this target level and the actual level of reserves is higher, the cost of maintaining the regime becomes higher as well.

In our model, the demand for the foreign reserves of the government originates from two sources: the first is the bank that has to serve early withdrawals (recall that the bank does not have enough dollars to pay creditors in the short term, and thus it has to buy some dollars from the government), and the second is the speculators that attack the currency. We denote the proportion of speculators that attack the currency as m. We also know that the demand of the bank for foreign reserves in the short term is increasing in n (it equals $(1-\alpha)n$). Eventually, we get that $c = c(\theta, m, n)$, where $\partial c/\partial \theta < 0$, $\partial c/\partial m > 0$, and $\partial c/\partial n > 0$.

Then, the government will maintain the fixed exchange rate regime if and only if:

$$\upsilon - c(\theta, m, n) > 0. \tag{24.2}$$

That is, if and only if $m(\theta, n)$, which is the proportion of speculators that attack the currency at the level of fundamentals θ and the level of capital outflows n, is lower than $m^*(\theta, n)$, which is given by:

$$\upsilon - c[\theta, m^*(\theta, n), n] = 0. \tag{24.3}$$

Finally, the level of the exchange rate e will be determined by the following function:

$$e(\theta, m, n) = \begin{cases} 1 & \text{if } m < m^*(\theta, n) \\ f(\theta) & \text{if } m \geq m^*(\theta, n) \end{cases}. \tag{24.4}$$

Note that $m^*(\theta, n)$ is an increasing function of θ and a decreasing function of n. Thus, $e(\theta, m, n)$ is increasing in θ and decreasing in m and in n.

We now turn to describe the speculators. As we mentioned earlier, there is a continuum $[0, A]$ of speculators. Each speculator holds one unit of peso and has to decide whether to attack the currency or not. The net payoff of a speculator that attacks the currency in terms of dollars is given by:

$$a(\theta, m, n) = 1 - e(\theta, m, n) - t. \tag{24.5}$$

Here, the benefit from the attack in terms of dollars is $1 - e(\theta, m, n)$, which captures the change in the level of the exchange rate following the attack. This benefit is zero if the government maintains the fixed exchange rate regime, and positive otherwise. The cost of the attack in terms of dollars is $t > 0$. A speculator that does not attack the currency simply gets 0. Each speculator will choose the action that yields the highest expected payoff. (Again, the decision of speculators depends on their beliefs regarding the behaviour of other agents.)

We assume there exist $\underline{\theta}_C, \overline{\theta}_C$ and $k_C > 0$, such that $\underline{\theta}_C$ is the highest θ at which $c(\theta, 0, 0) \geq v$ and $1 - f(\theta) - t \geq k_C.\overline{\theta}_C$ is defined by $f(\overline{\theta}_C) = 1 - t + k_C$. Similar to the banking sector, $\underline{\theta}_C$ and $\overline{\theta}_C$ define uniform dominance regions.[13]

2. Strategic Complementarities and the Vicious Circle

Our model has two types of strategic complementarities. First, there are strategic complementarities within each group of agents. In the banking sector, due to the increasing returns to scale on the investment held by the bank, the incentive of each creditor to withdraw her money early is higher when more creditors withdraw early. In the currency market, since the cost of defending the currency increases when the government has fewer reserves left, the incentive of each speculator to attack the currency is higher when more speculators attack the currency.

Second, there are also strategic complementarities between the two groups of agents. Since the bank has a mismatch between foreign liabilities and domestic assets, its prospects will deteriorate when the probability of depreciation is higher. As a result, the incentive of creditors to run on the bank increases with the number of speculators that attack the currency. In the other direction, when foreign creditors demand early withdrawal, the bank has to exchange pesos for dollars with the government. This reduces the amount of reserves that the government has, and increases the incentive of speculators to attack the currency. The result of these strategic complementarities is that when speculators attack the currency, they 'effectively' also run on the bank, although they attack for different reasons. Similarly, when creditors run on the bank, they 'effectively' also attack the currency.

In this paper, we are interested mainly in the second type of strategic complementarities, that is, in the complementarities between the two groups. As we show below, this type of strategic complementarities generates a vicious circle between banking crises and currency crises. In the rest of this Section we analyse the strategies of agents in our model and show how their strategies lead to the vicious circle.

We start by looking at threshold strategies. Suppose that all speculators use the same threshold strategy: they all attack the currency if they observe a signal below θ_C and they do not attack if they observe a signal above θ_C. As we show in the Appendix, given these strategies, creditors will also coordinate on a threshold strategy: they will run on the bank if

[13] As in the banking case, we can show that it is a dominant action to attack the currency when θ_i satisfies $G[(\theta_i - \underline{\theta}_C)/\sigma] < k_C/(k_C + t)$, and that it is a dominant action not to attack when θ_i satisfies $G[(\theta_i - \underline{\theta}_C)/\sigma] > (1 - t)/(1 - t + k_C)$.

they observe a signal below θ_B and will not run if they observe a signal above θ_B. Moreover, as we also show in the Appendix, for each θ_c that characterises the behaviour of speculators, there is a unique θ_B that characterises the behaviour of creditors. As a result, we can define a function $\theta_B(\theta_c)$ that determines the threshold strategy played by creditors for each threshold strategy that is played by speculators.

We now turn to characterise this function. We know that under the belief that speculators act according to the threshold signal θ_C, creditors will coordinate on playing according to θ_B. Now, consider a creditor that observes the signal θ_B and believes that other creditors play a threshold strategy characterised by the signal θ_B, and that speculators play a threshold strategy characterised by θ_C. Due to continuity, this creditor will be indifferent between running and not running. Thus, observing this signal, the payoff she will get from running on the bank (1 dollar) is equal to the expected payoff from waiting until the long term. Given the structure of information, this yields the following equation:

$$\int_{-\infty}^{\infty}\left(\widehat{R}\left\{\theta, G\left(\frac{\theta_B-\theta}{\sigma}\right), e\left[\theta, G\left(\frac{\theta_C-\theta}{\sigma}\right), G\left(\frac{\theta_B-\theta}{\sigma}\right)\right]\right\}-1\right)\frac{1}{\sigma}g\left(\frac{\theta_B-\theta}{\sigma}\right)\mathrm{d}\theta=0. \tag{24.6}$$

Here, conditional on the signal θ_B, the posterior density over θ is $(1/\sigma)g[(\theta_B-\theta)/\sigma]$. Then, given the state θ, the proportion of creditors that run on the bank when they play a threshold strategy characterised by θ_B is $G[(\theta_B-\theta)/\sigma]$. Similarly, the proportion of speculators that attack the currency when they play a threshold strategy characterised by θ_C is $G[(\theta_C-\theta)/\sigma]$. Changing the variable of integration, we can get the following equation that implicitly characterises $\theta_B(\theta_C)$:

$$\int_0^1\left[\widehat{R}\left(\theta_B-G^{-1}(n)\sigma, n, e\left\{\theta_B-G^{-1}(n)\sigma, G\left[G^{-1}(n)+\frac{\theta_C-\theta_B}{\sigma}\right], n\right\}\right)-1\right]\mathrm{d}n=0. \tag{24.7}$$

Similarly, we define a function $\theta_C(\theta_B)$ that determines the threshold strategy played by speculators for each threshold strategy that is played by creditors. This function is implicitly characterised by the following equation:

$$\int_0^1 a\left\{\theta_C-G^{-1}(m)\sigma, m, G\left[G^{-1}(m)+\frac{\theta_B-\theta_C}{\sigma}\right]\right\}\mathrm{d}m=0. \tag{24.8}$$

Proposition 1 studies an important feature of the two functions: $\theta_B(\theta_C)$ and $\theta_C(\theta_B)$.

Proposition 1: *$\theta_B(\theta_C)$ is increasing in θ_C and $\theta_C(\theta_B)$ is increasing in θ_B.*

The implication of Proposition 1 is the following: when creditors believe that speculators attack the currency in more circumstances, they will run on the bank in more cases. Similarly, when speculators believe that creditors run on the bank in more circumstances, they will attack the currency more. This property is a result of the strategic complementarities between creditors and speculators. This property lays the ground for the vicious circle between banking crises and currency crises.

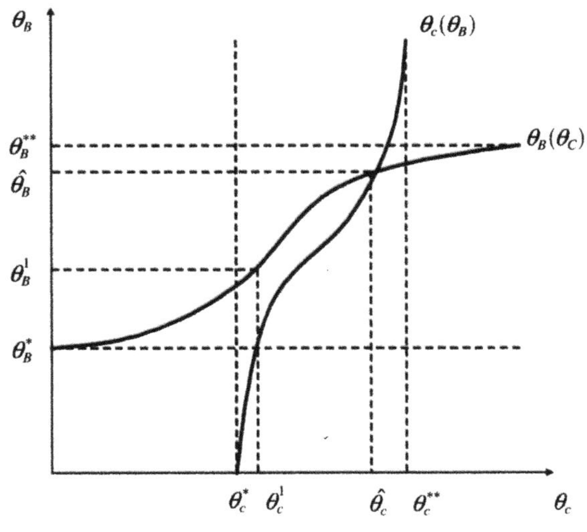

Figure 24.2 Threshold Strategies.

Before we turn to describe the vicious circle, we define four fundamental threshold signals that characterise the behaviour of agents under extreme beliefs: threshold θ_C^* characterises the behaviour of speculators when they believe that creditors never run on the bank, that is that $n = 0$. It is defined by the following equation: $\int_0^1 a\left[\theta_C^* - G^{-1}(m)\sigma, m, 0\right]\mathrm{d}m = 0$. Similarly, threshold θ_C^{**} characterises the behaviour of speculators when they believe that $n = 1$, threshold θ_B^* characterises the behaviour of creditors when they believe that $m = 0$, and threshold θ_B^{**} characterises the behaviour of creditors when they believe that $m = 1$. The equations that define θ_C^{**}, θ_B^* and θ_B^{**} are analogous to the equation that defines θ_C^*. Following Proposition 1, we know that $\theta_B^* < \theta_B^{**}$ and $\theta_C^* < \theta_C^{**}$.

In order to demonstrate the vicious circle between the two types of crises, we use Figure 24.2. As we see in the Figure, as θ_C becomes small, $\theta_B(\theta_C)$ converges to θ_B^*. This is because creditors become more and more positive that speculators will not attack the currency. Similarly, as θ_C becomes large, $\theta_B(\theta_C)$ converges to θ_B^{**}. As we showed in Proposition 1, overall, $\theta_B(\theta_C)$ increases in θ_C: as θ_C increases and more speculators attack the currency, the level of signal that makes creditors indifferent has to increase in order to compensate them for the higher probability of depreciation. The shape of $\theta_C(\theta_B)$ is analogous to that of $\theta_B(\theta_C)$.

Then, as the Figure shows, the vicious circle between the two crises goes as follows: suppose that creditors believe that $\theta_C = -\infty$; in this case, they will coordinate on a threshold signal: $\theta_B = \theta_B^*$. Then, given that $\theta_B = \theta_B^*$, speculators will act according to a higher threshold signal; this threshold signal is $\theta_C\ (\theta_B^*)$, which is denoted as θ_C^1 in the Figure. Now, creditors will have to update their beliefs about the behaviour of speculators. Given the new threshold signal that characterises the behaviour of speculators, creditors will now set θ_B to be equal to $\theta_B[\theta_C\ (\theta_B^*)]$, which is denoted as θ_B^1. This vicious circle, where both θ_B and θ_C are updated upwards will continue on and on. Eventually, as we show later, we will get to an equilibrium point $\{\hat{\theta}_B, \hat{\theta}_C\}$, where $\theta_C(\hat{\theta}_B) = \hat{\theta}_C$ and $\theta_B(\hat{\theta}_C) = \theta_B$. At this point, the process will stop.

To sum up, due to strategic complementarities between creditors and speculators, we observe a pattern where bank runs and currency attacks strengthen each other: when creditors believe that speculators will attack the currency with a higher probability, they will tend to run more on the bank. This, in turn, will cause speculators to attack the currency even more, and so on.

3. Equilibrium Outcomes and Correlation between Crises

We now turn to analyse the equilibrium outcome. As we noted above, a threshold equilibrium is characterised by two threshold signals $\hat{\theta}_B$ and $\hat{\theta}_C$ that satisfy the equations: $\theta_B(\hat{\theta}_C) = \hat{\theta}_B$ and $\theta_C(\hat{\theta}_B) = \hat{\theta}_C$ Analysing (7) and (8) that define $\theta_B(\theta_C)$ and $\theta_C(\theta_B)$, respectively, we can see that $\partial\theta_B(\theta_C)/\partial\theta_C < 1$ and $\partial\theta_C(\theta_B)/\partial\theta_B < 1$. This implies that there is exactly one pair $\{\hat{\theta}_B, \hat{\theta}_C\}$ that can form a threshold equilibrium.[14] We provide a formal proof for this point in the Appendix.

Moreover, as we also show in the Appendix, the equilibrium defined above is the only possible equilibrium in our model (i.e., our model does not have non-threshold equilibria). To prove this point we use the assumptions on dominance regions of the fundamentals. Importantly, the proof of uniqueness here is different from the one in most papers in the global games literature (Morris and Shin, 1998), since we have two groups of agents, and thus two threshold signals in equilibrium.[15]

Knowing the equilibrium strategies of agents, and taking account of the fact that we have two continuums of agents, we can calculate n and m for each realisation of θ. In order to get a simple characterisation, we focus on the case where σ approaches 0. In this case, the aggregate behaviour of agents in equilibrium is approximately the following: all creditors run on the bank if and only if θ is below $\hat{\theta}_B$ and all speculators attack the currency if and only if θ is below $\hat{\theta}_C$. Then, as noted by Corsetti *et al.* (2004), comparative statics on the prior probability of a bank run (currency attack) can be reduced to the behaviour of $\hat{\theta}_B(\hat{\theta}_C)$. Thus, this framework is convenient for deriving predictions on the probabilities of crises although we are using an improper prior.[16]

As it turns out, the equilibrium outcome depends on the configuration of the four threshold signals: $\theta_B^*, \theta_C^*, \theta_B^{**}$ and θ_C^{**}. Given Proposition 1, we know that $\theta_C^* < \theta_C^{**}$ and that $\theta_B^* < \theta_B^{**}$. Thus, there are only six possible configurations of the threshold signals.[17] These configurations are illustrated in Figure 24.3.

Suppose that $\theta_B^* < \theta_C^*$: if the effect of a currency crisis on the probability of a banking crisis is large enough such that $\theta_C^* < \theta_B^{**}$ (that is, one of the following configurations holds: $\theta_B^* < \theta_C^* < \theta_B^{**} < \theta_C^{**}$ *or* $\theta_B^* < \theta_C^* < \theta_C^{**} < \theta_B^{**}$), we will observe a strong form of interdependence. If, on the other hand, the effect of a currency crisis on the probability of a banking crisis is relatively weak such that $\theta_B^{**} < \theta_C^*$ (that is, $\theta_B^* < \theta_B^{**} < \theta_C^* < \theta_C^{**}$), we will observe a weak form of interdependence. Similarly, in the case where $\theta_C^* < \theta_B^*$, if the effect of a banking crisis on the probability of a currency crisis is large enough such that $\theta_B^* < \theta_C^{**}$, we will observe strong interdependence, whereas if the effect of a banking crisis on the probability of a currency crisis is relatively weak, we will observe weak interdependence.

Proposition 2 characterises the equilibrium outcome for one configuration that generates strong interdependence, and for one configuration that generates weak interdependence. The outcomes under all other four possible configurations are qualitatively similar to the

[14] I thank the referee for offering this intuition.

[15] Another property of our equilibrium is that it is the result of elimination of dominated strategies. Since this is not the focus of the paper, we do not prove this property.

[16] As Corsetti *et al.* (2004) note, when the signals received by agents are very precise relative to the information in the prior, a uniform prior over θ serves as a good approximation in generating the conditional beliefs of agents. Then, the equilibrium obtained under the uniform prior will be a good approximation to the true equilibrium. Thus, if we can say something about the state θ under which a crisis happens, then we may give an approximate answer to the *ex ante* probability of a crisis by evaluating the prior distribution $H(\theta)$ at this state.

[17] The configuration of the threshold signals is determined by the exogenous parameters and functions: t, v, $R(\cdot)$, $f(\cdot)$, and $c(\cdot)$. We ignore cases where two or more of these thresholds equal each other.

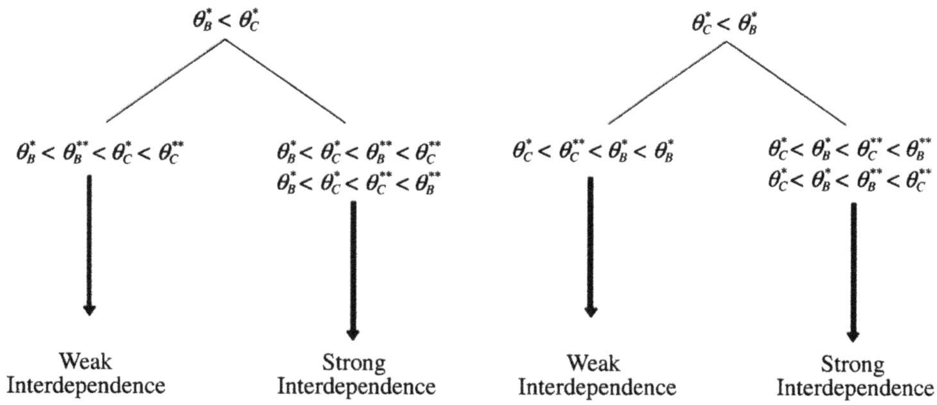

Figure 24.3. Possible Configurations of Threshold Signals.

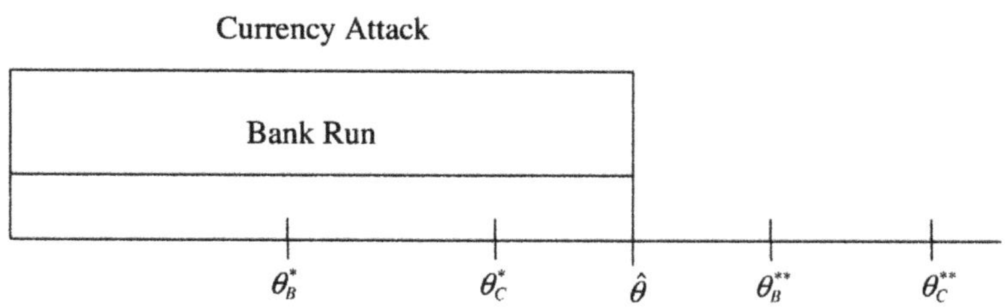

Figure 24.4. Strong Interdependence.

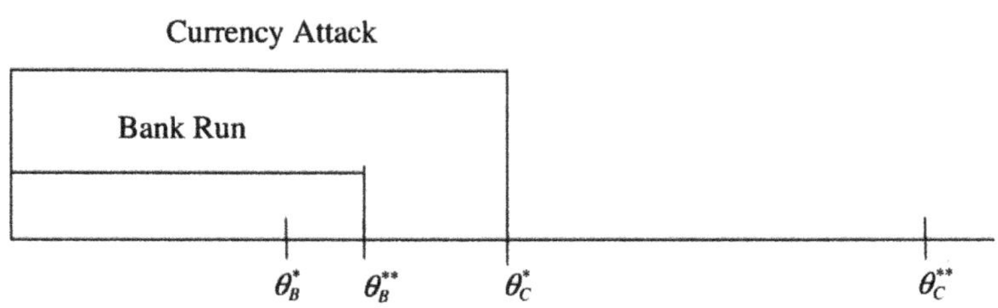

Figure 24.5. Weak Interdependence.

outcomes under one of the two configurations discussed in the Proposition. The Proposition demonstrates two interesting effects of the vicious circle: its effect on the correlation between the two crises and its destabilising effect on the economy. The equilibrium outcomes are also illustrated in Figure 24.4 (the case of strong interdependence) and in Figure 24.5 (the case of weak interdependence).

Proposition 2:

(*a*) *Equilibrium outcome in a case of strong interdependence:*
In the case where $\theta_B^* < \theta_C^* < \theta_B^{**} < \theta_C^{**}$ *and* σ *approaches 0:* $\hat{\theta}_B$ *and* $\hat{\theta}_C$ *converge to a single value* $\hat{\theta}$*, where* $\hat{\theta}$ *is between* θ_C^* *and* θ_B^{**}.

(*b*) *Equilibrium outcome in a case of weak interdependence:*
In the case where $\theta_B^* < \theta_B^{**} < \theta_C^* < \theta_C^{**}$ *and* σ *approaches 0:* $\hat{\theta}_B$ *converges to* θ_B^{**} *and* $\hat{\theta}_C$ *converges to* θ_C^*.

We now discuss the implications of the vicious circle in the case of strong interdependence. The first interesting implication of the vicious circle is its effect on the correlation between the two crises. As we can learn from Figure 24.4, the case of strong interdependence yields perfect correlation between banking crises and currency crises. Thus, in equilibrium, either both crises occur or neither of them does. This perfect correlation is a result of the vicious circle between the two types of crises: as a result of the strong spillovers between the two types of crises, both crises become strongly connected and always happen together.

It is important to note that the perfect correlation is not a result of the fact that both crises are affected by the same fundamentals (θ). Without the existence of spillovers between the two crises, a banking crisis would have occurred below θ_B^* and a currency crisis would have occurred below θ_C^*. While this case generates some positive correlation between the two crises, it does not yield a perfect correlation (since $\theta_B^* < \theta_C^*$). Thus, as Kaminsky and Reinhart (1999) observed in the data, there are two sources for the correlation between the two crises: the first is the common macroeconomic fundamentals behind the two crises, and the second is the vicious circle linking them. In our model, the first source generates some positive correlation between the two crises, while the other magnifies this correlation and makes it perfect.

The other interesting implication of the vicious circle is the destabilising effect that it has on the economy. As we can see from Figure 24.4, in the range of fundamentals between θ_C^* and $\hat{\theta}$, both crises occur. However, in this range, each crisis occurs just because agents believe that the other crisis is going to occur. To see this, note that this range is above θ_B^* and, thus, creditors that observe signals in this range will not run on the bank if they think that speculators are not going to attack the currency; similarly, since this range is above θ_C^*, speculators that observe signals in this range will attack only if they think that creditors are going to run on the bank. To sum up, in this range, each crisis should not have occurred on its own, however both crises occur just because of the strategic complementarities between speculators and creditors.

In the case of weak interdependence, the implications of the vicious circle are not as extreme as those in the case of strong interdependence. As we can see in Figure 24.5, in this case, bank runs occur if and only if the fundamentals are below θ_B^{**} and currency attacks occur if and only if the fundamentals are below θ_C^*. Thus, the correlation between the two crises is not perfect: there is a range of fundamentals where only a currency crisis occurs. (Note, however, that the correlation is still higher than what we would get without any spillovers.) Moreover, in the case of weak interdependence, there is no range of fundamentals where both crises occur just because of the vicious circle. Here, the vicious circle increases the probability of bank runs by increasing the threshold from θ_B^* to θ_B^{**} but does not affect the probability of currency attacks.

To sum up, the vicious circle between banking crises and currency crises increases the correlation between the two crises and affects the vulnerability of the economy to crises. This pattern is much more pronounced when we have a strong form of interdependence. We saw that this strong interdependence results from a strong effect of a currency crisis on the probability of a banking crisis or from a strong effect of a banking crisis on the probability of a currency crisis. In our model, these effects originate from the fact that local banks finance domestic investments with foreign liabilities. Thus, one would expect that economies that rely more on foreign liabilities will be more likely to have a strong form of interdependence. These economies are usually financially liberalised emerging markets. In the next Section we discuss some empirical implications of the model along these lines.

4. Empirical Implications

The strong correlation between banking crises and currency crises in our model is broadly consistent with the twin crises phenomenon documented by Kaminsky and Reinhart (1999). Since the phenomenon was first documented, the empirical literature on twin crises has grown and produced more related findings. In this Section we confront some implications of our model with some of the empirical findings in the literature. We analyse findings on two basic issues that were investigated in the empirical literature:

(*i*) How frequent are twin crises relative to regular banking crises (that is, banking crises that are not accompanied by currency crises) and regular currency crises (that is, currency crises that are not accompanied by banking crises)?

(*ii*) What are the costs generated by twin crises relative to the costs generated by regular banking or currency crises?

4.1 The Frequency of Twin Crises

The empirical literature has mostly found that the frequency of twin crises relative to regular banking or currency crises is high in financially liberalised emerging markets. This relative frequency is much lower in industrial economies or in developing economies that are not financially liberalised. This finding is the main conclusion of the study by Glick and Hutchison (2002) and it is also supported by Eichengreen and Bordo (2002) and Bordo *et al.* (2001). Kaminsky and Reinhart (1999) also point to the strong connection between financial liberalisation and the twin crises phenomenon. They conclude that during the 1970s, when financial markets were highly regulated, there was no apparent link between banking crises and currency crises but the two became closely entwined in the 1980s following the liberalisation of financial markets across many parts of the world.

Our model is consistent with these findings. In the model, two factors account for the correlation between banking crises and currency crises (which determines the frequency of twin crises). The first factor is the common fundamental θ, which affects the prospects of the bank and the prospects of the currency in the same direction. The second factor is the vicious circle between the two crises, according to which the occurrence of a banking crisis increases the likelihood of a currency crisis (θ_B has a positive effect on θ_C), and vice versa. In the model, the vicious circle is generated by the dependence of the country on foreign loans denominated in terms of the foreign currency. These loans lead to the currency mismatch that generates the effect of a currency crisis on the probability of a banking crisis, and they also lead to the loss of reserves that follows a banking crisis and affects the probability of a currency crisis.

Thus, when the country does not depend on these loans, the correlation between the two crises will be caused mostly by the common fundamental θ, and will be smaller. The dependence on loans denominated in foreign currency is typical to financially liberalised emerging markets. It is less typical to industrial economies and to developing economies that are not financially liberalised. Thus, in our model, financially liberalised emerging markets are expected to exhibit more twin crises.

For example, consider the case studied in part a of Proposition 2. A perfect correlation between banking crises and currency crises is obtained there as a result of the strong positive effect that the occurrence of one crisis has on the probability of the other crisis. This effect is a result of the dependence on foreign liabilities, which is typical to financially liberalised emerging markets. If this effect was weak, as in part *b* of Proposition 2, the correlation between the two crises would be smaller, and thus the frequency of twin crises relative to regular crises would be smaller.

4.2 The Costs of Twin Crises

Many researchers have analysed the costs of twin crises and compared them with the costs of regular banking crises or with the costs of regular currency crises. In most cases, twin crises have been shown to generate higher costs than either a regular banking crisis or a regular currency crisis. Kaminsky and Reinhart (1999), for example, show that, on average, the cost of bailout that follows a twin crisis (13.3% of GDP) is much higher than the cost that follows a regular banking crisis (5.1% of GDP). Similarly, in their sample, the loss of reserves that follows a twin crisis (25.4% of total reserves) is much higher than the loss of reserves that follows a regular currency crisis (8.3% of total reserves). Hoggarth *et al.* (2002) analysed the costs of twin crises and regular banking crises in terms of fiscal costs and output loss, and also found that twin crises are generally more costly than regular banking crises. Interestingly, they show that this pattern holds very strongly in emerging markets but not in developed economies.

Since a twin crisis involves a banking crisis and a currency crisis, an additional natural way to assess its severity is by comparing its costs with the sum of the costs of a regular banking crisis and those of a regular currency crisis. If the costs of a twin crisis are higher, it means that there are additional interactive effects associated with twin crises that damage the economy beyond the damage that is generated by regular banking and currency crises. Evidence provided by Eichengreen and Bordo (2002) suggest that in emerging markets, during the period 1973–97, the loss of output following a twin crisis was, on average, higher than the loss that followed a regular banking crisis plus the loss that followed a regular currency crisis. The case of industrial economies is different: there, on average, the costs of a twin crisis were not higher than the sum of the costs of a banking crisis and the costs of a currency crisis. Hutchison and Noy (2004), who looked at the same question, did not find any evidence to support the hypothesis that the occurrence of a twin crisis exerts an additional significant cost beyond the sum of the costs of each of the crises alone.

To address this issue in our model, we need to find a measure for the severity of a crisis. A natural measure for the severity of a banking crisis is n – the number of creditors that run on the bank. When n is higher, more long-term projects are being liquidated, and thus the loss of output is expected to be higher. Also, if the government bails out the bank, the fiscal costs associated with the bail out will be higher when more creditors run on the bank.[18] Similarly, a natural measure for the severity of a currency crisis is m – the number of speculators that attack the currency.

Then, according to Proposition 1, due to the vicious circle between banking crises and currency crises, for each level of θ, when more creditors run on the bank, more speculators will attack the currency, and vice versa. Thus, banking crises will be more severe when they are accompanied by currency crises, and vice versa. As a result, the costs generated by twin

[18] The case of a lender of last resort is studied in the next Section.

crises are expected to be higher than the costs of regular banking crises, the costs of regular currency crises, and the sum of the two. Importantly, in the model, this pattern is a result of the vicious circle between banking crises and currency crises. Thus, as we explained above, the pattern is more likely to hold in financially liberalised emerging markets. In developed countries, on the other hand, the occurrence of a currency crisis is not expected to affect the severity of a banking crisis, and vice versa, and thus the crises will not be more costly when they happen together. These results are consistent with the findings of Kaminsky and Reinhart (1999), Hoggarth *et al.* (2002) and Eichengreen and Bordo (2002).

4.3 The Causes of Twin Crises

In addition to the effect of financial liberalisation on the likelihood of twin crises, the empirical literature analysed other factors that affect the likelihood of these crises. For example: Eichengreen and Bordo (2002) found that the strength of the commitment to a fixed exchange rate regime has a negative effect on the likelihood of twin crises. Kaminsky and Reinhart (1999) found that low international reserves and expansion of bank credit have a positive effect on the likelihood of twin crises. These factors and others are consistent with our model. However, since these factors are not unique to the twin crises phenomenon, we do not discuss them here.

5. Policy Implications

The literature on financial crises has proposed many policy measures that may be able to reduce the likelihood of banking crises or currency crises. An interesting implication of our model is that, due to the spillovers between the banking sector and the currency market, the overall effect of such policy measures may be more complicated than their simple direct effect. Below, we discuss several standard policy measures that were proposed in the literature, and show how their implications change when the interaction between the banking sector and the currency market is taken into account. Methodologically, we distinguish between policy measures that have a direct effect on the probability of one crisis and those that have a direct effect on the probability of two crises. Throughout the discussion we preserve the basic set up, where the bank has a currency mismatch and the government is committed to a fixed exchange rate regime. While it is important to understand why this basic set up existed in so many emerging markets, this issue is beyond the scope of this paper.

5.1 Policy Measures with a Direct Effect on One Crisis – Transaction Costs

Due to the spillovers between the banking sector and the currency market, a basic implication of our model is that policy measures that are usually perceived as helpful in reducing the probability of currency crises can also reduce the probability of banking crises, and vice versa. This effect can be quite significant given the magnifying effect that the vicious circle has on the probabilities of both crises.

For example, we analyse the effect of t: the transaction cost that speculators have to bear in order to attack the currency. We define a function $\theta_C(\theta_B, t)$ that characterises the threshold signal that is played by speculators as a function of the threshold signal that is played by creditors and of the transaction cost. As we can learn from the characterisation of $\theta_C(\theta_B)$ in Section 2, $\theta_C(\theta_B, t)$ is increasing in θ_B and decreasing in t. Suppose that at the current level of t, t_0, the following configuration holds: $\theta_B(-\infty) < \theta_C(-\infty, t_0) < \theta_B(\infty) < \theta_C(\infty, t_0)$. (Note that θ_B depends only on θ_C and not on t.) Assume also that σ approaches 0. Then, as we show in part (*a*) of Proposition 2, both $\hat{\theta}_B$ and $\hat{\theta}_C$ will be between $\theta_C(-\infty, t_0)$ and $\theta_B(\infty)$.

Now, suppose that the government increases t to t_1, and as a result the threshold signals in the currency market decrease such that $\theta_C(-\infty, t_1) < \theta_C(\infty, t_1) < \theta_B(-\infty)$. Using arguments similar to the ones in Proposition 2, we can show that in this case, $\hat{\theta}_B = \theta_B(-\infty)$ and $\hat{\theta}_C = \theta_C(\infty, t_1)$. Thus, by increasing the transaction cost, the government can directly reduce the probability of a currency attack – as was already noted by Morris and Shin (1998) – and indirectly reduce the probability of a bank run.

Other policy measures that will directly reduce the probability of a currency attack and indirectly reduce the probability of a bank run include: strengthening the commitment to the fixed exchange rate regime (increasing ν), and increasing the amount of reserves held by the government (thus, changing the function $c(\cdot)$, such that a loss of reserves will have a smaller effect on the cost of defending the currency). Similarly, policy measures that have a direct effect on the probability of a bank run may indirectly reduce the probability of a currency attack. Such a policy measure could be a decrease in the payment that is promised to creditors in case of an early withdrawal.

5.2 Policy Measures with a Direct Effect on Two Crises – Lender of Last Resort

The analysis becomes more complicated when a policy measure has direct effects on the probabilities of both crises, especially if these effects are in opposite directions. Such a policy measure, which is often mentioned as a potential solution to the bank-run problem, is the 'Lender of Last Resort'. In our framework, due to its effect on the likelihood of currency attacks, the effect of this policy measure is ambiguous. We now turn to discuss this issue.

Under a regime of 'Lender of Last Resort' (LOLR), the government commits to lend money to the bank in case of a bank run. Then, the bank will be able to pay creditors that demand early withdrawal, without liquidating the long-term asset. In the bank-run literature, it is known that a LOLR can prevent bank runs.[19] This is because it eliminates the strategic complementarities among creditors. Thus, under a LOLR regime, each creditor knows that even if other creditors withdraw early, the bank will not have to liquidate any asset, and thus her long-term return is not going to be affected.

In our framework, however, when we take into account the effect of a LOLR on the exchange rate, and the effect of the exchange rate on the prospects of the bank, the issue of a LOLR becomes more complicated. First, note that since the liabilities of the bank are in dollars, a LOLR has to lend dollars to the bank in case of a bank run. This, in turn, generates a loss of reserves and an increase in the probability of depreciation. (Note that if the government does not act as a LOLR, there is an indirect loss of $(1 - \alpha)$ dollars of reserves per each creditor that runs on the bank. However, when the government acts as a LOLR, the loss of reserves will be 1 dollar per creditor.) Then, since depreciation generates a higher incentive to run on the bank, a LOLR might encourage creditors to run. The key point is that when we take into account the change in the exchange rate, a LOLR does not eliminate the complementarities among creditors, and as a result does not prevent panic-based bank runs. Thus, when more creditors run on the bank, the expected level of the

[19]For example, Rochet and Vives (2004).

exchange rate is lower, and the incentive of other creditors to run increases. As a result, panic-based bank runs are not prevented and their probability might even be higher under a LOLR regime.

In order to demonstrate this point in the simplest possible way, we simplify our framework, and preserve only the ingredients that are essential for the discussion on LOLR. Suppose that the gross return creditors get from the bank is either $R(\theta, n, e)$ dollars in the long term or 1 dollar in the short term. Here, θ represents the level of fundamentals, n represents the proportion of the asset that is liquidated in the short term, and e is the level of the exchange rate in the long term. In the spirit of our model, $\partial R/\partial\theta > 0$, $\partial R/\partial n < 0$, *and* $\partial R/\partial e > 0$. We assume that the bank can sell the asset at the short term for dollars (thus, $\alpha = 1$) and that the level of the exchange rate e depends only on the amount of reserves that the government loses, which is denoted as l. Then, $e = e(l)$, and $\partial e/\partial l < 0$. Suppose also that the only players besides the government and the bank are creditors that have to decide whether to withdraw early or not (we have a continuum [0,1] of creditors).[20] The structure of information remains the same and σ approaches 0. The government is losing reserves only if it acts as a LOLR. We analyse the equilibrium outcome with and without a LOLR.

Without a LOLR, a bank run does not cause any loss of reserves for the government, which means that $l = 0$. Strategic complementarities among creditors result from the increasing returns to scale on the investment of the bank. As in Section 3, one can show the existence of a unique threshold equilibrium, where a bank run will occur if and only if the level of the fundamentals is below θ_{NL}. Then, a creditor that observes θ_{NL} will be indifferent under the belief that the proportion of creditors who run is uniformly distributed between 0 and 1. This yields the following characterisation of θ_{NL} (for more details, see the derivation of $\theta_B(\theta_C)$ in Section 2):

$$\int_0^1 \left\{R\left[\theta_{NL}, x, e(0)\right] - 1\right\} \mathrm{d}x = 0. \tag{24.9}$$

With a LOLR, a bank run does not cause any liquidation of the asset but leads to depreciation that reduces the return in terms of dollars. Then, a bank run will occur if and only if the level of the fundamentals is below θ_L, where θ_L is characterised by:

$$\int_0^1 \left\{R\left[\theta_L, 0, e(x)\right] - 1\right\} \mathrm{d}x = 0. \tag{24.10}$$

From the above two equations, it is not clear whether the probability of a bank run is higher without LOLR or with LOLR. The answer depends on the derivatives of R with respect to n and e, and on the derivative of e with respect to l. Thus, if a loss of reserves is going to generate a huge depreciation and a sharp decrease in the real long-term return of the asset, then LOLR might increase the probability of a bank run.

The analysis suggests that before stating its willingness to act as a LOLR, the government should carefully assess the implications of this policy measure on the currency market.

[20]Here, we chose to ignore speculators and preserve only the basic interaction between the banking sector and the currency market. Adding speculators to the analysis will not change the results.

This is not merely because of the adverse effect that a LOLR has on the currency market, but mainly because of the feedback effect that this might have on the bank. As shown above, although a LOLR is meant to prevent bank runs, it might have an opposite effect when the interaction between the banking sector and the currency market is taken into account.

Thus, other policy measures to prevent bank runs may be preferred when a vicious circle between the banking sector and the currency market exists. An example for such a policy measure is suspension of convertibility. Here, when a bank run happens, the bank suspends liquidation of short-term liabilities. Then, creditors do not have a reason to run on the bank, as they know that long-term projects are not going to be liquidated. As we know from the bank run literature, suspension of convertibility may prevent bank runs, as it eliminates the strategic complementarities between creditors. In addition, when suspension of convertibility is announced, there should not be a direct effect on the probability of a currency attack. Thus, suspension of convertibility can directly reduce the probability of a bank run without generating any feedback effect that might eventually generate an increase in the probability of a bank run.

Another policy measure that can reduce the probability of a bank run without having any feedback effect through the currency market is an international LOLR. Here, an international lender (for example: the IMF) provides liquidity to the bank in case of a bank run, and thus there is no loss of reserves to the government. Thus, the existence of an international LOLR may be extremely important when individual countries are exposed to a vicious circle between the banking sector and the currency market.

To sum up, the analysis of LOLR demonstrates that before taking a policy measure against one type of crisis, the government should assess the effect that this policy measure has on the probability of the other type of crisis. There are other cases, in which this type of argument may be applied. For example, a policy measure that is often used against currency attacks is an increase in the interest rate that increases the cost of speculation, and reduces the likelihood of an attack. However, an increase in the interest rate also generates an adverse effect on the banking sector, as it makes creditors more eager to run, and thus increases the likelihood of a bank run.

6. Concluding Remarks

In this paper, we studied a model where strategic complementarities between creditors and speculators generate a vicious circle between banking crises and currency crises. This vicious circle magnifies the correlation between the two crises and destabilises the economy. We analysed empirical and policy implications that are unique to the case of interaction between the banking sector and the currency market, and showed that a Lender of Last Resort might not achieve its goal in such a framework.

In this paper, strategic complementarities between creditors and speculators are the result of foreign liabilities held by domestic banks. Thus, the paper shows that foreign capital might generate some undesirable outcomes. However, one should not conclude that foreign liabilities are not desirable. This is because there are several ways to prevent the vicious circle without reducing the amount of foreign liabilities.

First, if domestic banks avoid short-term debt contracts that enable creditors to withdraw a fixed amount of money in the short term, there would not be a problem of coordination among creditors, and as a result there would not be a vicious circle between banking and currency crises. Second, if banks hedged themselves against (direct or indirect) exchange rate risks, the positive impact of depreciation on the probability of a bank run would be prevented, and vicious circles would not be observed. Third, if governments avoided fixing the exchange rate at an over-appreciated level, speculators would not have an incentive to attack the domestic currency and the destabilising effect of depreciation on the banking system would be prevented.

An open question is why, in many recent events, short-term contracts were used, banks did not hedge themselves against exchange rate risks and governments held non-flexible exchange rate regimes. A potential explanation is that these features might be essential in the case of a small emerging market that is trying to raise capital from abroad. For example, short-term debt contracts could be a result of asymmetric information between foreign lenders and domestic borrowers; lack of hedging could reflect undeveloped financial markets; and non-flexible exchange rate regimes could originate from the need to provide some stability in order to attract foreign capital. However, this paper does not try to provide explanations for the existence of the above features. The purpose of this paper is rather to analyse their consequences.

References

Allen, F. and Gale, D. (2000). 'Optimal currency crises', *Carnegie Rochester Series on Public Policy*, vol. 53, pp. 177–230.

Bordo, M., Eichengreen, B., Klingebiel, D. and Martinez-Peria, S. M. (2001). 'Is the crisis problem growing more severe?', *Economic Policy*, vol. 24, pp. 51–82.

Burnside, C., Eichenbaum, M. and Rebelo, S. (2001a). 'Hedging and financial fragility in fixed exchange rate regimes', *European Economic Review*, vol. 45, pp. 1151–93.

Burnside, C., Eichenbaum, M. and Rebelo, S. (2001b). 'Prospective deficits and the Asian currency crises', *Journal of Political Economy*, vol. 109, pp. 1155–98.

Carlsson, H. and van Damme, E. (1993). 'Global games and equilibrium selection', *Econometrica*, vol. 61, pp. 989–1018.

Chang, R. and Velasco, A. (2000). 'Financial fragility and the exchange rate regime', *Journal of Economic Theory*, vol. 92, pp. 1–34.

Chang, R. and Velasco, A. (2001). 'A model of financial crises in emerging markets', *Quarterly Journal of Economics*, vol. 116, pp. 489–517.

Corsetti, G., Dasgupta, A., Morris, S. and Shin, H. S. (2004). 'Does one Soros make a difference? The role of a large trader in currency crises', *Review of Economic Studies*, vol. 71, pp. 87–114.

Dasgupta, A. (2004). 'Financial contagion through capital connections: a model of the origin and spread of bank panics', *Journal of the European Economic Association*, vol. 22, pp. 1049–84.

Diamond, D. W. and Dybvig, P. H. (1983). 'Bank runs, deposit insurance, and liquidity', *Journal of Political Economy*, vol. 91, pp. 401–19.

Dornbusch, R., Goldfajn, I. and Valdes, R.O. (1995). 'Currency crises and collapses', *Brookings Papers on Economic Activity*, vol. 2, pp. 219–70.

Eichengreen, B. and Bordo, M. (2002). 'Crises now and then: what lessons from the last era of financial globalisation?', NBER Working Paper no. 8716.

Frankel, D., Morris, S. and Pauzner, A. (2003). 'Equilibrium selection in global games with strategic complementarities', *Journal of Economic Theory*, vol. 108, pp. 1–44.

Glick, R. and Hutchison, M. M. (2002). 'Banking and currency crises: how common are twins?', unpublished manuscript, University of California, Santa Cruz.

Goldfajn, I. and Valdes, R. O. (1997). 'Capital flows and the twin crises: the role of liquidity', IMF Working paper no. 97–87.

Goldstein, I. and Pauzner, A. (2004). 'Contagion of self-fulfilling financial crises due to diversification of investment portfolios', *Journal of Economic Theory*, vol. 119, pp. 151–88.

Goldstein, I. and Pauzner, A. (2005). 'Demand deposit contracts and the probability of bank runs', *Journal of Finance*, vol. 60, pp. 1293–1327.

Hartigan, J. A. (1983). *Bayes Theory*, New York: Springer-Verlag.

Hoggarth, G., Reis, R. and Saporta, V. (2002). 'Costs of banking system instability: some empirical evidence', *Journal of Banking and Finance*, vol. 26, pp. 825–55.
Hutchison, M. M. and Noy, I. (2004). 'How bad are twins? Output costs of currency and banking crises', *Journal of Money, Credit and Banking*, vol. 37, pp. 725–52.
Kaminsky, G. L. and Reinhart, C. M. (1999). 'The twin crises: the causes of banking and balance-of-payments problems', *American Economic Review*, vol. 89, pp. 473–500.
Krugman, P. (1999). 'Balance sheets, the transfer problem, and financial crises', *International Tax and Public Finance*, vol. 6, pp. 459–72.
Marion, N. P. (1999). 'Some parallels between currency and banking crises', *International Tax and Public Finance*, vol. 6, pp. 473–90.
Miller, V. (1996). 'Speculative currency attacks with endogenously induced commercial bank crises', *Journal of International Money and Finance*, vol. 15, pp. 383–403.
Miller, V. (1998a). 'Domestic bank runs and speculative attacks on foreign currencies', *Journal of International Money and Finance*, vol. 17, pp. 331–8.
Miller, V. (1998b). 'The double drain with a cross-border twist: more on the relationship between banking and currency crises', *American Economic Review*, vol. 88, pp. 439–43.
Morris, S. and Shin, H. S. (1998). 'Unique equilibrium in a model of self-fulfilling currency attacks', *American Economic Review*, vol. 88, pp. 587–97.
Morris, S. and Shin, H. S. (2001). 'Rethinking multiple equilibria in macroeconomics', in *NBER Macroeconomics Annual 2000*, pp. 139–61. Cambridge: MIT Press.
Morris, S. and Shin, H. S. (2003). 'Global games: theory and applications', in (M. Dewatripont, L. Hansen and S. Turnovsky, eds), *Advances in Economics and Econometrics*, pp. 56–114. Cambridge: Cambridge University Press.
Morris, S. and Shin, H. S. (2004). 'Coordination risk and the price of debt', *European Economic Review*, vol. 48, pp. 133–53.
Obstfeld, M. (1996). 'Models of currency crises with self-fulfilling features', *European Economic Review*, vol. 40, pp. 1037–47.
Radelet, S. and Sachs, J. D. (1998). 'The East Asian financial crisis: diagnosis, remedies, prospects', *Brookings Papers on Economic Activity*, vol. 1, pp. 1–74.
Rochet, J. and Vives, X. (2004). 'Coordination failures and the lender of last resort: was Bagehot right after all?', *Journal of the European Economic Association*, vol. 2, pp. 1116–47.
Velasco, A. (1987). 'Financial crises and balance of payments crises', *Journal of Development Economics*, vol. 27, pp. 263–83.

25 Inefficient Foreign Borrowing: A Dual- and Common-Agency Perspective

Jean Tirole

The paper addresses a few familiar questions related to capital account liberalization: What makes a country attractive to foreign investors? Do countries borrow enough? Should one add some "sand in the wheels" of international capital markets, or, rather, should international diversification be further encouraged? And should incentives be provided to the private sector to avoid "dangerous forms of finance"?

Regarding level issues, the evidence overwhelmingly points in the direction of underborrowing. Almost all countries have small gross asset positions,[1] invest most of their equity portfolio at home,[2] and exhibit a high sensitivity of consumption to domestic production.[3] Thus, the potential benefits from capital account liberalization seem to have gone largely unreaped. Poor countries seem to borrow only a small fraction of what their development needs or cost advantages would vindicate, while rich countries hardly diversify their portfolios internationally. Standard attempts at explaining the home biases have proved unsatisfactory.[4]

On structure issues, a majoritarian view has emerged in the wake of the recent twin currency and banking crises. Commentaries have expressed much concern about a trilogy of dangerous forms of financial structures: debt finance,[5] short maturities, and foreign currency denomination of liabilities. In particular, a widespread consensus has developed in favor of encouraging equity portfolio and foreign direct investment and discouraging short-term capital inflows and of promoting better risk management so as to prevent large corporate exposures to a depreciation of the currency.

[1] Aart Kraay et al. (2000).

[2] Kenneth R. French and James M. Poterba (1991) estimate that over 90 percent of U.S. and Japanese financial portfolios are invested in domestic assets (the corresponding percentages are 89 percent for France and 85 percent for Germany).

[3] See Karen Lewis (1990). A related fact is that the cross-country correlation of consumptions is typically less than 0.5 and smaller than that of outputs.

[4] See Lewis (1999) for a review. These standard attempts consist in introducing (a) purchasing power parity failures, (b) nontraded wealth, (c) indirect diversification through domestic stocks of multinationals, and (d) costs associated to foreign portfolio investment.

[5] The debt finance bias is not specific to emerging markets, Kraay et al.'s (2000) estimates for industrial countries are that foreign equity assets and liabilities account for about 3.3 percent and 3.9 percent of wealth, respectively. The corresponding percentage on the loan side is approximately 11 percent.

Beneath the debates on borrowing level and structure lies an implicit assumption of a capital market failure. Somehow, capital account liberalization per se does not induce financial markets to generate the right economic signals. There is no arguing that short-term, dollar- denominated debt constitutes a poor hedge against liquidity and currency risks. (For an empirical analysis and a questioning of the causal link, see Enrica Detragiache and Antonio Spilimbergo, 2001.) But, presumably, borrowers design their financial structures to their own benefit, and one cannot presuppose that dangerous forms of debt constitute suboptimal liability structures.

This paper identifies and focuses on a specific market failure, stemming from a dual- and common-agency problem. In contract economics, dual agency, also called "moral hazard in teams," refers to a situation in which the welfare of a principal is affected by the combined actions of two agents. Common agency in contrast arises when a single agent's action affects the welfare of multiple principals. The paper's take is that, in a private lending arrangement, the investor's prospect of recouping his investment depends on the behavior of the borrower, with whom he contracts, and of the borrower's government, with whom he does not. That is, investor returns depend on government policy as well as the firm's managerial choices. This dual-agency problem translates into a common-agency one in which pairwise optimal contracts exert externalities on each other through their impact on country incentives: The government is a common agent of all firms (borrower-investor pairs), and its policy choice depends on a representative financial contract, but not, with a large number of private sector players, on the financial contract of any single firm.[6]

The model has three dates. Date 0 is the financing stage, in which borrowing levels and structures are specified by pairwise optimal contracts between foreign and domestic lenders and private sector companies. Domestic capital is limited, and thus the benefit from capital account liberalization is the firms' access to foreign capital (1 will occasionally invoke risk diversification as well). Profits accrue and are distributed according to contractual commitments at date 2.

The date-2 outcomes depend on a policy selected by the government at date 1. Following the international economics literature,[7] the government favors domestic interests over foreign ones. And, when arbitrating among domestic interests, it may either put equal weights on domestic constituencies' surpluses or engage in redistributive politics.

The government impacts the foreign investors' return through the exercise of its many control rights. A first set of control rights held by the government affects both domestic and foreign investors' returns as in the case of a change in corporate governance and bankruptcy laws or in the resources affected to their enforcement, or a change in tax and labor laws.[8] A second set of control rights affects the tradable-nontradable mix and international collateral. Foreigners are ultimately reimbursed in tradables. Any government policy that reduces the amount of tradable goods that can be returned to foreigners can exert a negative externality on foreign investors. Examples of government moral hazard with respect to the mix includes encouraging excessive investments in the non-tradable sector, most commonly in real estate, failing to sink export promoting investments, for example

[6]More generally, this common-agency externality exists as long as there are at least two private sector borrowers.

[7]See for example the terms-of-trade literature (Harry Johnson, 1954: Avinash Dixit. 1987: Kyle Bagwell and Robert Staiger, 2000).

[8]Another example is poor infrastructure management due to nepotism, clientelism or corruption. A more indirect impact operates through increases in public liabilities through regulatory forbearance and fiscal deficits, that affect the likely exercise of government control rights in the future.

investments in public infrastructure for tourism, depleting international reserves, failing to diversify exports, thus making repayment to foreigners riskier, and, when foreigners hold domestic currency denominated assests, failing to take steps that would reduce the risk of depreciation of the currency. All these behaviors reduce the return to foreign investors.[9]

The model embodies two possible sources of time inconsistency. First, as in the sovereign debt literature, domestic interests prevail over foreign ones which, if anticipated, result in scant or more expensive foreign borrowing.[10] Second, when domestic firms are subject to agency costs, the date-1 policy choice no longer internalizes the possibility that an investor-friendly course of action alleviates credit rationing and attracts capital.

Attempts to alleviate the cost of time inconsistency belong to two distinct categories. The first refers to the abandonment of sovereign rights and has received much attention in the literatures on trade (e.g., joining the World Trade Organization [WTO]) and central banking (e.g., making the central bank independent). The second addresses common agency and the resulting lack of coordination in foreign borrowing by altering private sector incentives. I focus on this latter and newer aspect.[11]

The paper first looks at aggregate borrowing. Section I studies whether and when partial capital account liberalization benefits countries in the presence or absence of credit rationing. While no strong case can be built on a priori grounds that countries over- or under borrow, the section identifies some factors that call for or against capital controls.

The paper then shifts attention to structure issues and analyzes whether and when equity portfolio investments and home biases and (Section II), longer maturities (Section III) and domestic currency denomination (Section IV) enhance borrowing countries' access to international lending. Section V summarizes and concludes.

A general theme of the analysis of borrowing structure is that dangerous forms of finance are also "policy resistant;" they make the government more accountable, ultimately to the benefit of the country. Encouraging foreign direct and equity portfolio investment and promoting international diversification do not encourage accountability. Some match between stakeholders and political constituencies must be achieved. Debt financing and small frictions inducing a home bias, therefore, should not be the object of widespread opprobrium, even though, as Section II shows, they will be encouraged by politicians eager to favor their corporate friends and then may have perverse consequences.

[9] To these must be added, of course, less subtle ways of reducing foreigners' returns, as when the Argentinian government pleases local firms through "peso-ification" of dollar debts.

Commentaries often downplay the role of moral hazard in recent crises, on the grounds that following a crisis incumbent politicians may lose office and that IMF programs further erode their power. There are two issues with this argument. First, excluding government moral hazard on the ground that no finance minister would voluntarily provoke a crises is like saying that fire insurance does not create moral hazard because homeowners do not usually set fire to their house once insured. The problem with governments and homeowners is not that they will set fire to their homes but rather that they will be less cautions at the margin. Governments will not take the actions that reduce the probability of a crisis ten years from now from 5 percent to, say, 1 percent, if they entail an immediate political cost.

Second, "government moral hazard" is usually given a narrow definition and related to the investors' expectation of a banking bailout. Actions that directly impact the value of foreign investors' assets are less likely to generate a backlash.

[10] To be certain, the U.S. government also impacts the return of investors in GM, Intel or a Silicon Valley startup. However, dual agency is much more relevant in a financially integrated economy than in a financially isolated economy, for two reasons: First, the government has much less incentive to defend the investors' interests when these investors do not vote or more generally have limited political leverage. Second, the government has many more degrees of freedom in the open economy context as it can impact the tradable-nontradable mix.

[11] The control rights implications are discussed from a corporate finance perspective in Tirole (2002).

Closely related insights apply to what Barry Eichengreen and Ricardo Hausmann (1999) call the original sin, referring to emerging markets' widespread practice of borrowing short and in foreign currency. Section III develops a general equilibrium model of independent interest, in which domestic firms optimally design the term structure of their liabilities in anticipation of future government policies and the government responds to these privately optimal, but uncoordinated financial structures when selecting a domestic-welfare maximizing policy. It shows that forcing private borrowers to tilt the maturity structure toward the long term reduces welfare. Section IV studies the choice of currency denomination and again shows that risk exposure is the flip side of policy resistance.

By focusing on a specific market failure (lack of coordination of private sector borrowing), the paper delivers strong results and sharp (though potentially controversial) policy prescriptions. While I view the particular market failure as important and the public policy effects as first order, I also acknowledge that a broader view embodying other well-grounded market failures is warranted. In this respect, the paper's analysis can be read from a different perspective, namely that of a complementarity between "corporate finance reform" and "government governance reform."[12] Public policies that counter dangerous forms of finance, such as taxes on short-term capital inflows or foreign currency borrowing[13] or the subsidization of foreign direct investment, have more appeal when the country's constitutional design, institutional features (such as the creation of pension funds), domestic politics, and residents' pattern of investment (home versus abroad) concur to put investor protection reasonably high on the rulers' priority list. Conversely, banning dangerous forms of finance is likely to be more costly when the government's commitment toward investors is weak. With this perspective, the reader can take along the highlighted effects without necessarily embracing all policy implications.

Related Literature. This paper builds on a number of disjoint literatures. Technically, it is most related to the literature on common agency with moral hazard, pioneered by Mark Pauly (1974) and B. Douglas Bernheim and Michael Whinston (1986). For example, Pauly's celebrated insight is that nonexclusive insurance contracts give rise to externalities between insurers who do not internalize the impact of the reduction in the insuree's care on the other insurers; this inefficiency is ultimately borne by the insuree who ends up overinsured.

Several research lines have emphasized the cost of the governments' time inconsistency problem in an international context. The literature on sovereign debt (Jeremy Bulow and Kenneth Rogoff, 1989a, b: Jonathan Eaton and Raquel Fernández, 1995), like this paper, emphasizes domestic preferences of governments. Bulow and Rogoff (1989b) show how creditor country governments may be gamed into contributing to rescheduling agreements. Kraay et al. (2000) argue that countries minimize their exposure to sovereign risk by keeping small net asset positions, and even small gross asset positions if transfers of ownership involve large transaction costs. Jeffrey Sachs (e.g., 1989) and others have argued that countries which high levels of sovereign debt are subject to debt overhang and invest too little because part of the benefits from this investment accrue to foreigners (which implies that the sovereign and foreign lenders can reach a Pareto improvement by renegotiation); Application I in Section II, subsection B, makes a similar point in the context of private sector borrowing and general public policies

[12] I am grateful to a referee for suggesting this interpretation.

[13] Assuming these taxes are effective in reaching their goal.

(although renegotiation is less credible in our context since individual borrower-lender pairs have no private incentive to renegotiate). In contrast with the sovereign debt literature, this paper emphasizes uncoordinated borrowing and its policy implications; it also takes a much broader view of "repudiation" as it applies to the exercise of all control rights held by governments; last, it focuses on rather different issues, such as original sin.

The international trade literature on time inconsistency and excessive protection (Staiger and Guido Tabellini, 1987; Kiminori Matsuyama, 1990; Aaron Tornell, 1991) is also relevant here; it for example shows that the socially optimal policy—free trade, say—is often time inconsistent and that the time-consistent policy frequently leads to (*ex ante*) excessive protection. Giovanni Maggi and Andrés Rodriguez Clare (1998) add capture-by-interest groups as in Gene Grossman and Elhanan Helpman (1994): politicians may want to commit to free trade (join the WTO) in order to avoid an *ex ante* misallocation of investment in favor of the sector that will receive protection *ex post*, even though this implies forgoing future contributions by interest groups.

My analysis also complements Tornell and Andres Velasco's (1992) and Velasco's (1996) modeling of capital flights, in which domestic residents decide how much to invest at home and abroad in the presence of domestic redistributive policies or increasing fiscal returns.[14] These contributions focus on capital flows from poor to rich countries: I focus on moral hazard by a borrowing rather than lending country. The implications accordingly differ. For example, the domestic residents' ability to invest abroad acts as a disciplining device in Tornell-Velasco, while a home bias tends to be beneficial in my analysis. Furthermore, a major concern of this paper is the impact of borrowing structure on government moral hazard, which requires modeling capital inflows and composition. Wolf Wagner (2001) shows how a home bias can reduce government moral hazard in a world in which investors want to diversity internationally, and governments tax their residents (for their own sake) in order to discourage them from competing to supply (investment) inputs that partly benefit foreign investors.

There are few corporate finance approaches to international finance. Mark Gertler and Rogoff (1990) is a notable exception. This paper however is primarily interested in the size of capital flows, and has no government moral hazard, and a fortiori no dual- and common-agency problem. Government moral hazard in contrast plays an important role in Olivier Jeanne's work (1999, 2000a, b, 2002). Jeanne shows that a lack of domestic monetary credibility may induce private borrowers to borrow in foreign currency. While foreign currency debt is dangerous in the event of bad shock, it reflects optimal risk management by firms conditional on the lack of domestic monetary credibility. This may arise because of the interaction between government's moral hazard and commitment and signaling problems at the level of entrepreneurs (Jeanne, 1999, 2000a) or bankruptcy costs (Jeanne, 2002).

Last, a number of themes developed in this paper are to some extent part of the "folk wisdom" in the international economics community, rather than related to a specific literature. Relative to this, the paper's contribution is two-fold. First, the corporate finance techniques and the dual- and common-agency formulation allow me to build a formal framework to validate the insights and identity their limits. Second, a formal model takes

[14]An earlier contribution to capital flights and increasing fiscal returns is Eaton (1987). In that paper, foreign lenders require a government guarantee on their loans (as the latter is the only entity able to enforce their contracts, say). Domestic residents have an incentive to invest their money abroad and thereby escape taxation if other residents also do, since then foreign lending and concomitant government guarantees increase. The process may result in multiple equilibria.

the folk wisdom in new directions, most notably by incorporating political economy considerations.

I. Inefficient Borrowing Level

A. Bare-Bones Framework

The bare-bones framework abstracts from the issues of domestic incidence and redistributive politics by focusing on entrepreneurs and foreign investors (so, it ignores domestic savings, and assumes that the incidence of government policy is entirely on firms and foreign investors).

A small country is populated by a large number (technically, a continuum of mass 1) of identical, risk neutral "entrepreneurs," who more generally stand for domestic firms or insiders. There is a single (tradable) good and three dates, $t = 0, 1, 2$.

Date 0: At the initial date, the representative entrepreneur borrows I_f from foreign investors. In exchange of I_f, the representative entrepreneur issues financial claims (debt, equity) on the date-2 proceeds of her firm.

The capital market is competitive. Investors are risk neutral and the world's rate of interest is normalized to zero. That is, domestic entrepreneurs can borrow as much as they want as long as their lenders break even on average.

Date 1: At date 1, the country's government chooses an action or policy $a \in \mathcal{A} \subseteq \mathbb{R}$. The policy is chosen so as to maximize the entrepreneurs' (*ex post*) welfare.

Date 2: The proceeds from investment accrue at the final date, date 2. The expected total surplus or value created by the investment is denoted $V(I_f, a)$ and embodies both the costs and benefits for entrepreneurs and foreign investors of the government's policy. Let $V_f(I_f, a)$ [smaller than $V(I_f, a)$] denote the foreigners' expected date-2 income from their financial claims.

Letting I_f^* and a^* denote the equilibrium investment and policy choice, the competitive capital market assumption implies that foreign investors just break even:

$$V_f(I_f^*, a^*) = I_f^*; \tag{25.1}$$

equivalently, the firms' net present value (NPV) is captured by the domestic entrepreneurs, who receive utility

$$U^* \equiv U(I_f^*, a^*) \equiv V(I_f^*, a^*) - I_f^*. \tag{25.2}$$

In the following, I will assume that objective functions have the required concavity properties and that choices are governed by first-order conditions. I will interpret the policy in the following way:

Assumption 1: *Policy a is an investor-friendly policy: In the relevant range*

$$\frac{\partial V_f}{\partial a} > 0.$$

For example, a higher policy choice may correspond to an improvement in the corporate governance legal framework or enforcement, to lower taxes on capital, to a more investor-friendly labor environment, or to a public investment in complementary infrastructure financed through taxes on domestic residents.[15]

B. Country Borrowing in the Absence of Agency Cost

Let us first assume that borrowing is not subject to any agency cost and so there is no credit rationing. The first-best investment I^{FB} and policy a^{FB} respectively equalize the marginal benefit and marginal cost of investment:[16]

$$\frac{\partial V}{\partial I_f}(I_f^{FB}, a^{FB}) = 1, \tag{25.3}$$

and maximize value:

$$\frac{\partial V}{\partial a}(I_f^{FB}, a^{FB}) = 0. \tag{25.4}$$

When selecting her investment level at date 0, the representative entrepreneur rationally anticipates and takes the government policy as given and thus solves

$$\max_{I_f} \left\{ V(I_f, a^*) - I_f \right\}$$

yielding an equilibrium value I_f^* equalizing marginal benefit and marginal cost of investment:

$$\frac{\partial V}{\partial I_f}(I_f^*, a^*) = 1. \tag{25.5}$$

At date 1, the government acts when the foreigners' investment I_f^* has already been committed; and so the government maximizes the entrepreneurs' *ex post* payoff, which is equal to the total pie minus what is returned to foreigners:

$$\max_a \left\{ V(I_f^*, a) - V_f(I_f^*, a) \right\}.$$

yielding

$$\frac{\partial V}{\partial a}(I_f^*, a^*) = \frac{\partial V_f}{\partial a}(I_f^*, a^*).$$

Unsurprisingly, the government underinvests—from an *ex ante* perspective—in the investor-friendly action ($\partial V/\partial a > 0$). An equilibrium is a pair (I_f^*, a^*) satisfying (5) and (6).

[15]"In the relevant range" refers to the fact that at some point, even V_f may end up decreasing as a increases. For example, an excessively harsh corporate governance environment may prevent managers from acting or may involve public expenditures that can only be financed by taxing foreign investors.

[16]To implement the first-best policy, the government need choose only a at date 0. As equation (25.5) below shows, the investment policy can then be left to the firms' discretion. The same remark holds for the second-best policy analyzed in Section I, subsection C. In contrast, I show that the government wants to control I_f when it is unable to commit to a.

As discussed in the introduction, the analysis from there on can either analyze external constraints[17] that alleviate the time inconsistency problem, as is done in the literature, or address the common-agency problem so as to alter the government's incentives. I focus on the latter. So, I ask, does the country borrow too much or too little from abroad? Suppose that, starting from laissez-faire, foreign borrowing can be encouraged (e.g., through subsidies) or restrained (e.g., through a capital control). Using the Envelope theorem, a small increase or decrease in the representative firm's investment has the following impact on the entrepreneur's welfare:

$$\frac{d}{dI_f}(V(I_f, a) - I_f) = \frac{\partial V}{\partial a}\frac{da^*}{dI_f},$$

where $a^*(I_f)$ is given by condition (6):

$$\frac{\partial V}{\partial a}(I_f, a^*(I_f)) = \frac{\partial V_f}{\partial a}(I_f, a^*(I_f)).$$

The right-hand side of (7) will be called the *commitment effect*. We then obtain the following simple result:

Proposition 1: *In the absence of credit rationing. a capital control (a reduction in I_f starting from the no-capital-control benchmark) raises welfare if and only if*

$$\frac{da^*}{dI_f} < 0 \Leftrightarrow \frac{\partial}{\partial a}\left(\frac{\partial V_f}{\partial I_f}\right) > \frac{\partial}{\partial a}\left(\frac{\partial V}{\partial I_f}\right).$$

While we would often expect less care to be exerted by the government as foreign investment and therefore foreign ownership in the country increase ($da^*/dI_f < 0$), it is equally easy to find circumstances under which, in the absence of credit rationing, a capital control lowers welfare. For example, if the policy is subject to increasing returns to scale,[18] as may be the case for some types of supporting infrastructure, a more massive capital inflow may actually result in a more investor-friendly outcome. Relatedly, suppose that here are increasing fiscal returns to scale as in Olivier Blanchard and Lawrence Summers (1987) and Velasco (1996); that is, the country must rely on capital taxes to fund an incompressible level of government expenditures. A capital control shrinks the tax base and raises per-unit capital taxes, with potentially detrimental effects (for example, a reduction in domestic savings, if these are introduced into the picture).[19] Before putting more structure on the model, let us look at the general impact of credit rationing.

C. Credit Rationing

Borrowing is usually subject to substantial agency costs. The study of the concomitant problem of credit rationing and of the various ways in which firms attempt to reduce its impact has spawned a large variety of models. Fortunately, these corporate finance models

[17] These can be seen as shrinking the government's choice set $\mathcal{A}$.

[18] In which case the first-order approach used here needs to be amended.

[19] I am grateful to Pierre-Olivier Gourinchas for providing this example.

have many common implications. For the purpose of this paper the common feature of interest is that borrowing is constrained by the maximal expected income that can be promised to investors. The latter is called the "pledgeable income" and (for an anticipated policy a^*) will be denoted $\overline{V}_f(I_f, a^*)$. In corporate finance models, $\partial \overline{V}_f / \partial I_f < 1$ for the equilibrium investment (for, if the pledgeable income increased faster than investment, investors would benefit from a higher investment level and so there would be no credit rationing!). Section II, subsection A, provides an illustration of the notion of pledgeable income.

In corporate finance, the unconstrained borrowing condition (5) is replaced by the twin conditions that firms borrow as much as they are able to:

$$I_f = \overline{V}_f(I_f, a^*). \tag{25.8}$$

and would like to borrow more if they could:

$$\frac{\partial V}{\partial I_f}(I_f, a^*) > 1. \tag{25.9}$$

How is our conclusion about country borrowing level affected? Because condition (6) is unaffected (taking $V_f = \overline{V}_f$),

$$\frac{d}{dI_f}(V(I_f, a) - I_f) = \left[\frac{\partial V}{\partial I_f} - 1\right] + \left[\frac{\partial V}{\partial a^*}\frac{da^*}{dI_f}\right]. \tag{25.10}$$

The second term on the right-hand side of equation (10) is the same commitment effect as in the absence of credit rationing. The difference relates to the first term. The Envelope theorem no longer applies, and a capital control implies a direct loss in net present value since $\partial V / \partial I_f > 1$.

It is also worth pointing out that under credit rationing the optimal commitment or second best policy no longer satisfies $\partial V / \partial a = 0$. Rather, this policy $\left(I_f^{SB}, a^{SB}\right)$ solves:

$$\max_{(I_f, a)} \left\{V(I_f, a) - I_f\right\}$$

s.t.

$$I_f = \overline{V}_f(I_f, a), \tag{25.11}$$

or

$$\frac{\partial V}{\partial a} = -\left(\frac{\partial V}{\partial I_f} - 1\right)\frac{dI_f}{da} < 0,$$

where $I_f(a)$ solves equation (11).

The time-consistent policy a^* (which satifies $\partial V / \partial a = \partial \overline{V}_f / \partial a > 0$) thus is doubly biased relative to the commitment policy a^{SB}. First, and as in the absence of credit rationing, it does not internalize the foreigners' welfare. Second, and a specificity of credit rationing, an investor-friendly policy helps attract capital, which motivates a distortion relative to the first-best rule (4). Once this capital is in place, though, the distortion is no longer needed, and the government has a diminished incentive to be investor friendly. This second effect would exist even if investors were domestic residents. Both effects point in the same direction: The policy is not investor friendly enough, and the cost of this distortion is ultimately borne by the country itself.[20]

Proposition 2: *Under credit rationing, a positive commitment benefit from a capital control, if it exists, may be offset by the direct NPV loss.*

Because credit rationing is pervasive in all economies, and especially in borrowing countries, the analysis suggests that beneficial attempts at addressing government moral hazard are more likely to act on the structure of borrowing than on its level.[21] We therefore turn to a more structured version of this general model to investigate such policies.

II. Inefficient Borrowing Structure

A. Framework

Let us now specialize the model and analyze externalities in the structure of borrowing agreements.

The representative entrepreneur is risk neutral, is protected by limited liability, has initial wealth A, and invests $I > A$. Domestic savings per entrepreneur are fixed at level $I_d \geq 0$. and, like foreign investments, demand an expected rate of return equal to 0.[22] The entrepreneur finances the shortfall from foreigners: $I - A - I_d = I_f$.

At date 2, a firm either succeeds and then yields RI, or fails, that is yields nothing. Only a fraction of income is pledgeable: Investors receive $rI \leq RI$ in case of success, while the entrepreneur appropriates $(R - r)I$. Neither gets anything in case of failure.

The probability of success is $p + \tau$, where τ is determined by the government after the investments are sunk. (So τ is the action a of the previous section.) Enhancing the probability of success of domestic firms by τ involves an increasing and strictly convex lump-sum cost $\gamma(\tau)$ per unit of investment. This cost is borne by domestic residents.[23] The assumption that the cost γ is proportional to investment is purely for analytical convenience. For example,

[20]In this bare-bones model, foreigners would have an incentive to lobby in favor of investor-friendly policies only at date 1. They would have an incentive to do so at date 0 if they already had some stake in the country at date 0.

Note further that even if international investors have no stake at date 0, investor-friendly measures in (or a better commitment by) a number of borrowing countries would raise the demand for capital and the world interest rate and ultimately benefit these investors.

[21]Policy intervention alternatively may relax the credit constraint, as in the case, considered in section II, subsection B, of an improvement in corporate governance.

[22]For example, there is an alternative storage technology with which the domestic investors can obtain a zero rate of return.

Even with fixed domestic savings, it might be the case that the amount invested at home not be inelastic because the domestic investors invest abroad. Note, though, that, unlike Tornell-Velasco (1992) and Velsaco (1996), we focus on borrowing countries. And so, provided that foreign investors are willing to lend to the country and (unlike in Eaton, 1987), domestic investors are not discriminated against relative to foreign investors, risk-neutral domestic investors have no strict incentive to invest abroad. Risk aversion and portfolio diversification, by contrast, provide incentives to invest abroad: see Application 2.

[23]It is straightforward to allow for taxes on foreigners' portfolio income. See also the discussion of capital inflow taxation below.

the theory would carry through if γ included a fixed component. The cost γ may be incurred by the firms' insiders—as in the case of a strengthening in corporate governance or more flexible labor laws—or by the population as a whole—as in the case of investments in infrastructure financed by taxation or a reduction in public expenditures. I will discuss incidence shortly.

For equilibrium value τ^*, the pledgeable income is

$$\overline{V} \equiv (p + \tau^*)rI,$$

and the entrepreneur's date-2 expected payoff

$$(p + \tau^*)(R - r)I.$$

Example: The wedge between the full value RI and the pledgeable part rI, which is a distinctive feature of corporate finance, can for example be derived from a classic moral hazard problem. Suppose that the entrepreneur can obtain private benefit BI, proportional to investment, by misbehaving (and no such benefit when behaving). The probability of success then falls from $(p + \tau^*)$ to $(q + \tau^*)$, where $q < p$. The incentive constraint then requires that the entrepreneur's stake, R_b, in success be substantial enough so as to deter misbehavior.

$$(p + \tau^*)R_b \geq (q + \tau^*)R_b + BI, \qquad \text{or}$$

$$R_b \geq \frac{BI}{p - q}.$$

Then

$$r \equiv R - \frac{B}{p - q}.$$

The fraction $B/[(p - q)R]$ measures the agency cost.

Incidence. The section proceeds in two steps. First, it assumes that the government chooses the date-1 policy so as to maximize domestic welfare. Then, it generalizes the analysis to redistributive politics by allowing the government to put different weights on entrepreneurs and domestic investors/consumers. While incidence does not affect the date-1 policy choice under domestic-welfare maximization, it impacts the date-0 investment; in particular, suppose that the date-1 cost of the policy is $x\gamma(\tau)I$ for entrepreneurs, and $(1 - x)\gamma(\tau)I$ for domestic investors/consumers.[24] Entrepreneurs, if they can secure funding, invest if $(p + \tau^*)R - 1 - x\gamma(\tau^*) > 0$. They do not internalize the general population's

[24]The *ex post* incidence coincides with the *ex ante* (date-0) incidence under our assumption that γ is lump-sum. If the cost were not lump-sum, then the *ex ante* incidence y would in general exceed the *ex post* incidence x; in particular, a tax on capital decided at date 1 but anticipated at date 0 would be passed through to entrepreneurs via an increase in the interest rate.

Note also that the fraction $x\gamma(\tau)I$ borne by entrepreneurs can be viewed either as a nonmonetary cost imposed on entrepreneurs or as a tax on entrepreneurial income that cannot be pledged to investors.

investment-support cost $(1-x)\gamma(\tau^*)I$. We will return to this point in Applications 3 and 4.[25]

B. Government Maximizes Domestic Welfare

For a given anticipation τ of the policy choice, the representative entrepreneur's investment is limited by the extent of pledgeable income:

$$I - A = \overline{V} = (p+\tau)rI.$$

Hence

$$I = I(\tau) = \frac{A}{I-(p+\tau)r}. \qquad (25.12)$$

[We will assume that $I > (p+\tau)r$ in the relevant range. That is, an extra unit of investment creates less than one unit of pledgeable income: otherwise investment would be infinite in this constant-return-to-scale model.]

Commitment Policy. The first-best optimal policy τ^{FB} solves:

$$\max_{\tau} \{(p+\tau)RI - \gamma(\tau)I\}, \quad \text{or} \quad \gamma'(\tau^{FB}) = R.$$

However, and as was pointed out in Section I, subsection C, the first-best policy is not the proper benchmark in the presence of credit rationing. The second-best commitment policy should aim not only at increasing *ex post* total surplus but also at *ex ante* attracting capital in a situation in which the latter is insufficient. The second-best policy τ^{SB} maximizes date-0 total surplus:

$$\max_{\tau} \{[(p+\tau)R - 1 - \gamma(\tau)]I(\tau)]\},$$

where $I(\tau)$ satisfies (12), Assuming that investment is socially desirable,[26] that is, $(p+\tau)R - I - \gamma > 0$, the second-best commitment policy satisfies

$$\gamma'(\tau^{SB}) > R.$$

Time-Consistent Policy. Consider now an equilibrium policy τ^*. That is, at date 0, economic agents correctly anticipate that the policy choice at date 1 will be τ^*, and so the investment level is $I(\tau^*)$. At date 1, the foreign investors' stake is, for actual policy choice τ,

$$V_f = \left(\frac{I_f}{I_d + I_f}\right)\overline{V} = \left(\frac{I_f}{I_d + I_f}\right)\left[(p+\tau)rI(\tau^*)\right].$$

[25]This point bears some resemblance with the "soft budget costraint" problem, under which a benevolent social planner may rescue distressed, but viable investments and possibly encourage *ex ante* investments with negative social value.

[26]This is necessarily the case if the incidence falls primarily on entrepreneurs (x close to 1).

At date 1, the government chooses τ so as to maximize domestic welfare $V - V_f$:

$$\max_{\tau} \left\{ \left[(p+\tau) \left[(R-r) + \left(\frac{I_d}{I_d + I_f} \right) r \right] - \gamma(\tau) \right] I(\tau^*) \right\},$$

and so

$$\gamma'(\tau^*) = R - \left(\frac{I_f}{I_d + I_f} \right) r. \tag{25.13}$$

As expected, firms are less profitable, the higher the foreigners' stake in the firms. An equilibrium is a pair (τ^*, I_f^*) satisfying (13) with $I_f = I_f^*$ and

$$I_f^* + I_d = \frac{(p+\tau^*)rA}{1-(p+\tau^*)r}.$$

I now derive a few implications of this analysis.

Application 1: Impact of Domestic Savings. The policy inefficiency decreases with the share of domestic savings. As domestic savings grow, foreign investment is crowded out and so τ^* increases: Domestic savings act as a shield for foreign investment. Policies favoring domestic savings through tax incentives, pension funds or privatization targeted to investors therefore have a positive impact on government behavior (although they may involve costs of their own) and may increase not only total investment, but also foreign investment.

A related idea can be found in Bruno Biais and Enrico Perotti's (2002) model of privatization. There, a government lacking commitment power over its future policy allocates sufficiently many shares to its constituency in order to commit not to follow an expropriation policy. The common thread is that the government may want to alter the distribution of financial assets in order to manipulate its own incentives.

Application 2: International Diversification. A closely related point can be made with respect to international risk sharing. Suppose that there is aggregate risk in the country—that is, the realizations of the dometic firms' profits are not independent. Suppose further that domestic savers, instead of being risk neutral, exhibit at least a tiny bit of risk aversion. Then provided there is no worldwide risk, the domestic investors' optimal portfolio choice is to put all their money abroad, and so

$$I_d = 0.$$

Governmental moral hazard is then extreme:

$$\gamma'(\tau^*) = R - r.$$

This illustration does not aim at realism—if anything portfolios exhibit a very strong home bias, the reasons for which have been extensively discussed.[27] Rather, it leads us

[27] See, e.g., Lewis (1999).

to a more general point: Keeping domestic investment at home benefits the country (and actually the world in our model, since foreign investors always break even) as long as the corresponding policies do not create a substantial misallocation of investment. Put differently, small frictions inducing a home bias raise welfare.

Application 3: Capital Controls. Let us return momentarily to the question posed in Section I regarding the efficient level of foreign borrowing. Consider for instance a unit tax t on capital inflows at date 0. The proceeds of this tax, $tI_f = t(I - I_d - A)$, are redistributed in a lump-sum fashion to domestic residents (and do not affect domestic savings, say). The tax on foreign borrowing raises the return to domestic savings by t. The representative entrepreneur's borrowing capacity is then given by

$$(1 + \tau)(1 - A) = (p + \tau^*)rI,$$

since foreigners and domestic savers then expect an average return equal to $1 + t$. Condition (13) still holds:

$$\gamma'(\tau^*) = R - \left(\frac{I_f}{I_d + I_f}\right) r.$$

However, foreign investment decreases with the tax on capital inflows despite a favorable disciplining effect on policy choice.[28] Domestic welfare is then

$$W = [(p + \tau^*)R - 1 - \gamma(\tau^*)]I(\tau^*, t).$$

The impact of the tax on capital inflows can be decomposed into two terms:

$$\frac{dW}{dt} = [(p + \tau^*)R - 1 - \gamma]\frac{dI}{dt} + [(R - \gamma')I]\frac{d\tau^*}{dt}.$$

The first term on the right-hand side of this equation is the counterpart of that in equation (10). If the entrepreneurs bear the full cost of the policy ($x = 1$), as in Section 1, then $(p + \tau^*)R - 1 - \gamma$ is unambiguously positive if there is investment and so the reduction in investment brought about by the tax has a negative welfare impact. This need not be the case if part of the incidence falls on the general population ($x < 1$). Investments may then be sunk, that have a negative NPV $\{(p + \tau^*)R < 1 + \gamma(\tau^*)\}$. We are arguably more interested in situations in which investment is socially desirable. The second term is the commitment effect: The capital control reduces foreign investment and disciplines the government, with positive welfare consequences. This commitment effect is negligible if the share of foreign investment is small;[29] then, the impact of a capital control is unambiguously negative provided that investment is socially desirable. For large levels of foreign investment, though,

[28] Suppose that I (and I_f) increases as t increases. Then τ^* decreases, and so does

$$I = \frac{A}{I - \frac{(p+\tau^*)r}{1+t}},$$

a contradiction.

[29] Since $\gamma' = R$ if $I_f = 0$.

the commitment effect may dominate the first effect and capital controls may then increase welfare.

Application 4: Debt-Equity Composition. Last, but not least, let us turn to the foreigners' mix between loans and equity investment. The basic two-outcome, no-income-in-case-of-failure framework made no distinction between debt and equity. A simple variation allows us to discuss debt and equity in an easy way. Suppose now that, for investment level I, the firm yields $R^F I \geq 0$ in case of failure. One can think of $R^F I$ as the (pledgeable) salvage value of assets, or collateral. Success, as earlier, yields an extra income RI, and so overall income

$$R^S I = (R + R^F)I.$$

Firms issue (*safe*) *debt* corresponding to the salvage value $R^F I$ of its assets, and the rest represents *equity* claims. It is easily seen that it is optimal for the entrepreneurs to own equity and no debt since this arrangement maximizes their incentives and they have no demand for insurance. Thus the entire debt is held by domestic and foreign investors. Let $[R^F + (p + \tau^*)r]I$ denote the pledgeable income.[30] The per-unit-of-investment value of debt is therefore $r^D = R^F$, and that of equity $(p + \tau^*)r^E = (p + \tau^*)r$. Foreigners hold fractions α_f^E and α_f^D of the domestic equity and debt. The break-even constraints are:

$$I_f = [\alpha_f^E (p + \tau^*) r^E + \alpha_f^D r^D] I$$

and

$$I_d = [(1 - \alpha_f^E)(p + \tau^*) r^E + (1 - \alpha_f^D) r^D] I.$$

Being risk neutral, both foreigners and domestic residents are indifferent as to the claim they hold. Thus, the overall break-even constraint,

$$I - A = [(p + \tau^*) r^E + r^D] I$$

is compatible with a continuum of possible foreign equity stakes.

But, while investors *individually* are indifferent as to which claim they hold, they *collectively* are not. Indeed, the government selects its policy at date 1 so as to solve:

$$\max_{\tau} \left\{ [(p + \tau)[(R - r) + \alpha_d^E r] - \gamma(\tau)] I(\tau^*) \right\}.$$

Thus, an increase in the foreigners' equity holdings/value at stake, or equivalently in α_f^E, reduces discipline and country welfare.[31]

[30] In the moral hazard illustration, again

$$r = R - \frac{B}{p - q}.$$

[31] For the now familiar reason the conclusion on country welfare hinges on the entrepreneurs' bearing enough of the cost γ.

Again, I wish to emphasize the broader implications of this analysis rather than its details. The investors' indifference between domestic debt and equity only offers analytical convenience and can be broken in several ways. For example, a favorable capital adequacy treatment encouraging foreign banks to hold debt or an implicit deposit insurance in domestic banks pushes toward a low α_f^E. Similarly, the resort to high-powered monitoring by domestic conglomerates encourages equity holdings by domestic residents. Conversely, investor risk aversion would encourage domestic investors to avoid the domestic stock market if there are country shocks.

The broad point is that *at the margin* the basic externality applies: When a foreigner substitutes equity for debt, he does not internalize the change in the government's incentives and therefore the domestic entrepreneurs' increase in the cost of funds. In this sense, the conclusion is robust to a more sophisticated description of portfolio allocation.[32]

The following proposition summarizes our analysis:

Proposition 3: *In comparison to the first-best government policy (for which the marginal cost of the policy is equal to its marginal benefit), the equilibrium policy under a domestic-welfare maximizing government is more investor-friendly under commitment, and less investor-friendly in the time-consistent solution. Furthermore, provided that most of the cost of the policy is borne by the productive sector, country-welfare increases when*

(*a*) *domestic savings increase and/or exhibit a stronger home bias,*
(*b*) *a capital control is relaxed, provided that foreign ownership is small,*
(*c*) *marginal incentives are provided to foreigners to hold debt rather than equity.*

C. Redistributive Politics

Suppose next that the government weighs domestic constituencies unequally. Namely, entrepreneurs receive weight k and non-entrepreneurs weight $1 - k$. For example, one would expect k to be large under "crony capitalism"; in contrast, $1 - k$ should increase with the creation of pension funds, which make the median voter more concerned about portfolio returns. For simplicity I make no distinction between domestic savers and the median voter, although such a distinction would be warranted in many applications (indeed, the point on pension funds I just made implicitly rests on such a distinction. Pension funds imply that the median voter has a higher portfolio stake).

I assume that the government is stable in that the weights do not change between dates 0 and 1. This calls for two comments. First, even more so than previously, outside judgments on the government's policy are hard to formulate. As we will see, the latter may have very unpalatable features, which raises the usual moral dilemma of whether the international community ought to adopt a paternalistic attitude vis-à-vis a democratically elected government.[33] Second, it would be interesting to study how the strategic choice of

[32]A caveat, though; Government moral hazard may also affect the value of debt, in contrast with our depiction. A reduced budget for the enforcement of property rights in bankruptcy processes reduces the value r^D obtained by debtholders in case of failure. A more general analysis thus trades off the negative impacts of an increase in foreign equity holdings and debt holdings on the two forms of moral hazard. The market allocation however has no reason to be efficient in that respect.

[33]Relatedly, Jeanne and Jeromin Zettelmeyer (2001) discuss the moral dilemma involved in some bailouts, that may allow domestic extortion while easing the overall pain of a crisis.

date-0 public policies affecting borrowing structure and level is affected by the possibility of government turnover.[34]

Under redistributive politics ($k \neq 1/2$), the incidence of the effort, $\gamma(\tau)I$, incurred to boost profitability impacts the date-1 choice. As described earlier, I assume that a fraction x of this cost is borne by entrepreneurs and a fraction $1 - x$ by domestic savers. Let us focus on the two polar cases:

(a) *Crony capitalism* ($k \simeq 1$). Under crony capitalism, the government cares solely about the welfare of entrepreneurs. For $k = 1$, its date-1 choice solves:

$$\max_{\tau} \{(p + \tau)(R - r) - x\gamma(\tau)\},$$

yielding

$$\gamma'(\tau^*) = \frac{R - r}{x}.$$

As expected, if only a small fraction x is borne by the entrepreneurs (one can think of severe austerity measures or labor laws imposed on the population), the high emphasis on profitability may result in policies that are more investor-friendly than even the second-best policy under domestic-welfare maximization.[35]

Turning now to date 0, the government internalizes

$$[(p + \tau^*)(R - r) - x\gamma(\tau^*)]I(\tau^*).$$

Because the date-1 policy is fixed, the government has no instrument to boost investment, which is its date-0 goal. It contents itself with laissez-faire,[36] yielding, for salvage value R^F per unit of investment, investment $I(\tau^*)$ given by:

$$I(\tau^*) - A = [R^F + (p + \tau^*)r]I(\tau^*).$$

Suppose next that k is close to, but smaller than 1. The date-1 policy choice then solves:

$$\max_{\tau} \left\{ k[(p + \tau)(R - r) - x\gamma(\tau)] + (1 - k) \left[(p + \tau) \left(\frac{I_d}{I_d + I_f} \right) r - (1 - x)\gamma(\tau) \right] \right\}.$$

At date 0, the government optimally forces domestic investors to (a) invest at home. and (b) invest in stocks. This date-0 policy raises τ^* and allows the government's entrepreneurial friends to borrow more.

[34]Along the lines of the pioneering work of Torsten Persson and Lars Svensson (1989), Guido Tabellini and Alberto Alesina (1990), and Philippe Aghion and Patrick Bolton (1991) in closed economy settings.

[35]This provides a formulation of the classical argument according to which implicit guarantees represent a policy distortion. Indeed, bailouts by domestic taxpayers are mathematically very similar to a high level of τ in a context in which x is small.

[36]The government would like to subsidize date-0 investment, but I have not allowed this instrument.

(b) *Median voter politics* ($k \approx 0$). Let us in contrast assume that entrepreneurs carry little weight in the government's objective function. When $k = 0$, the government's date-1 policy solves:

$$\max_{\tau} \left\{ (p+\tau)\left(\frac{I_d}{I_d + I_f}\right) r - (1-x)\gamma \right\},$$

yielding

$$\gamma'(\tau^*) = \frac{\left(\frac{I_d}{I_d+I_f}\right)}{1-x} r.$$

The policy choice is not investor-friendly if the burden falls mainly on savers (x small).

Full capital-account liberalization is never optimal under median-voter politics if $x < 1$. Domestic savers never gain anything on their savings, that compete against a perfectly elastic supply of foreign funds $[(p+\tau^*)(I_d/(I_d + I_f))rI = I_d)]$, and they bear the cost $(1-x)\gamma I$. As losers, domestic savers are better off with strict capital controls, and, if their government is unable to impose capital controls, with date-0 policies that encourage a high foreign equity stake in the country and a capital flight of domestic savings, so as to *ex post* minimize τ.

However, the government can at date 0 transform domestic savers into winners by capturing the entrepreneurs, rent through capital controls and taxes on capital inflows. Capital controls (forcing I_f down) provide domestic savers with a supernormal rate of return. Furthermore, if I_d is small, domestic savers do benefit from some capital inflows as long as these can be taxed with proceeds redistributed to domestic savers. Either way, domestic savers' conversion into winners may alter their attitude toward investor-friendly policies.

Proposition 4:

(*a*) *The government's policy may be more investor-friendly under crony capitalism than in the second best. Furthermore, crony capitalism leads to a* (*policy induced*) *home bias and to a* (*policy induced*) *composition tilted toward debt-holding by foreigners. And while these biases are beneficial when the government maximizes domestic welfare, they result in an excessive concern for profitability when austerity measures aimed at benefiting the government's entrepreneurial friends are mainly borne by the population at large.*

(*b*) *Median-voter politics lead to investor-unfriendly policies, and to resistance to capital-account liberalization.*

III. Maturity of Liabilities

A. Framework

I now analyze the possibility of a short-term bias in foreign borrowing. To do so, I need to employ a multistage financing framework in which firms optimally trade off the costs and benefits of short-term liabilities. Let us enrich the framework of Section II, subsection A, by adding an intermediate income and an intermediate liquidity shock. The

0		1	2
• Representative entrepreneur has wealth A, borrows $I - A$, invests I. • Financial contract: dI to be reimbursed at date 1, and, if firm continues at date 1 and succeeds at date 2, rI to be reimbursed at date 2.	Government selects policy τ.	• Income sI accrues; debt dI due. • Liquidity shock: ρI. • Market observes choice of τ. • Firm continues iff liquidity shock met.	• (If continues at date 1): profit RI (prob $p + \tau$) or 0 (prob $1 - (p+\tau)$). • Sharing of profit according to date-0 contract.

Figure 25.1. Timing.

intermediate income enables firms to reimburse some short-term debt while the intermediate shock introduces a liquidity-shortage cost of such debt. The timing is summarized in Figure 25.1.

The only new feature is the management of date-1 liquidity. The firm receives deterministic income sI, out of which short-term debt $dI \leq sI$, is repaid. Furthermore, the firm faces a liquidity shock: It must then spend an overrun expenditure equal to ρI in order to continue. It is liquidated and no surplus accrues to any party if it does not spend this money. The liquidity shock ρ is distributed (independently across firms) according to cumulative distribution $F(\rho)$ with density $f(\rho)$ on $[0, \infty]$. This distribution has a monotone hazard rate:

$$\frac{f(\rho)}{F(\rho)} \text{ is decreasing.}$$

The monotone hazard rate condition is satisfied by almost all familiar distributions[37] and will guarantee the concavity of the government's objective function.

If the firm continues, it delivers as earlier at date 2 and with probability $p + \tau$, profit RI, of which rI is pledgeable to investors.

I assume that the country bears cost $\gamma(\tau)I$ per continuing firm and that this cost (or the fraction borne by entrepreneurs) is viewed as a lump-sum cost by the entrepreneurs (none of these assumptions is important). I also abstract from the issue of domestic- versus foreign-borrowing composition by assuming away domestic savings ($I_d = 0$). This simplification implies that *in the absence of liquidity shocks*, a domestic-welfare maximizing government would choose $\tau = \hat{\tau}$, where

$$\gamma'(\hat{\tau}) = R - r.$$

[37] E.g., uniform, normal, logistic, chi-squared exponential, and Laplace.

Let us first solve for the representative firm's optimal liquidity management.[38] Introduce the following notation:

$$\rho_1 \equiv (p+\tau^*)R \quad \text{and} \quad \rho_0 \equiv (p+\tau^*)r.$$

In words, ρ_1 and ρ_0 are the expected date-2 value and pledgeable income per unit of investment when the policy is expected to be τ^* (the equilibrium policy).

Optimal liquidity management commands that the firm withstands the liquidity shock if and only if $\rho \leq \hat{\rho}$ for some threshold $\hat{\rho}$ to be determined. The representative entrepreneur's utility is equal to the NPV (ignoring the lumpsum cost of the policy):

$$U = \left[\left[s + F(\hat{\rho})\rho_1\right] - \left[1 + \int_0^{\rho} \rho f(\rho)\, dp\right]\right] I, \tag{25.14}$$

where the investment I is given by the investors' break-even constraint:

$$\left[s + F(\hat{\rho})\rho_0\right] I = (I - A) + \left(\int_0^{\rho} \rho f(\rho)\, dp\right) I. \tag{25.15}$$

Substituting I into U yields:

$$U = \frac{\rho_I - c(\hat{\rho})}{c(\hat{\rho}) - \rho_0} A,$$

where

$$c(\hat{\rho}) \equiv \frac{1 - s + \int_0^{\rho} \rho f(\rho)\, dp}{F(\hat{\rho})}$$

is the average cost of bringing investment to completion [a unit of investment costs on average $1 + \int_0^{\rho} \rho f(\rho) dp$, yields s at date 1, and is maintained until date 2 with probability $F(\hat{\rho})$]. Simple computations yield the optimal threshold $\hat{\rho} = \rho^*$:

$$\int_0^{\rho} F(\rho)\, dp = 1 - s \quad \text{and } c(\rho^*) = \rho^*.$$

It must be the case that $\rho^* > \rho_0$ (if for some value of $\hat{\rho}$, $c(\hat{\rho}) \leq \rho_0$, then the firm could borrow an infinite amount) and $\rho^* < \rho_1$(otherwise, no investment would be made).

This optimal liquidity management is implemented by issuing short-term debt level d^*I satisfying:[39]

$$\begin{aligned} p^* &= s - d^* + (p+\tau^*)r \\ &= s - d^* + p_0. \end{aligned} \tag{25.16}$$

To understand (16), note that the firm can at date 1 raise up to $(p+\tau^*)r$ by issuing new securities, thereby diluting incumbent claim-holders;[40] for, capital markets will never bring

[38]The analysis here follows that of Bengt Holmström and Tirole (1998).

[39]This assumes that the short-term income is large enough: $s \geq p^* - p_0$. Otherwise, the firms would need to hoard liquidity as described in Holmström-Tirole (1998). Similar insights could then be obtained with respect to this hoarded liquidity.

[40]These claimholders would be willing to be diluted in order to raise cash to meet the liquidity shock, since they receive nothing if the firm is liquidated.

more money at date 1 than what they will get back on average at date 2. The nondistributed liquidity $s - d^*$ is needed to cover the shortfall between p^* and p_0.[41] Note also that an increase in its short-term debt makes the firm more likely to default. The firm optimally arbitrates between scale (which calls for high short-term debt) and inefficiency from default (an effect that calls for low short-term debt).

Let us now turn to the government's choice of date-1 policy. An out-of-eqilibrium choice τ implies that firms that continue are those firms with shocks satisfying[42]

$$\rho \leq s - d^* + (p + \tau)r, \quad \text{or} \quad \rho \leq \rho^* + (\tau - \tau^*)r.$$

The fraction of firms that are not liquidated, $F(\rho^* + (\tau - \tau^*)r)$, increases with τ. An investor-friendly policy encourages foreign investors to refinance frail firms.

The government maximizes *ex post* domestic welfare:

$$\max_{\tau} \left\{ F(\rho^* + (\tau - \tau^*)r) \left[(p + \tau)(R - r) - \gamma(\tau) \right] \right\}.$$

The monotone hazard rate assumption implies that this objective function is concave. The first-order condition is:

$$\gamma'(\tau^*) = R - r + [(p + \tau^*)(R - r) - \gamma(\tau^*)] r \frac{f(\rho^*)}{F(\rho^*)}. \tag{25.17}$$

Compared with a situation without liquidity shocks, the government adopts a more investor-friendly policy so as to reduce liquidation.

Equation (17), together with the monotone hazard rate property, yields the main insight of this section. Consider a small increase in the short-term debt from the privately optimal value d^*. This amounts to an equal reduction in the threshold ρ^* for a given government policy. From (17), and using the monotone-hazard-rate property, the government partly offsets the shortage in liquidity through an increase in τ.

$$0 < \left| \frac{d(r\tau)}{d(d^*)} \right| < 1.$$

In words, domestic firms do not internalize the disciplining effect of an increase in the level of their short-term debt level on the government's policy. Short-term debt fragilizes firms and forces the government to help them secure refinancing. This increased discipline in turn generates two welfare benefits that are ultimately reaped by domestic entrepreneurs. First, it improves the date-1 policy choice τ^*, and therefore financing conditions for a given level of investment. Second, it increases borrowing capacity, which is valuable given the presence of credit rationing.

[41]Note that it is crucial for this section to employ a corporate finance rather than an Arrow-Debreu model. In the absence of agency cost, the firm would not face liquidity problems and so leverage would be irrelevant.

[42]This assertion is true only locally. If τ differs from τ^* so much that the right-hand side of this inequality exceeds p_1 or falls below p_0, the contract between financiers and the entrepreneur is renegotiated. But we are here interested in deriving the first order condition.

B. Contingent Debt

Issuing noncontingent short-term debt is *privately* optimal in the deterministic equilibrium of Section III, subsection A. Thus the previous analysis is indeed an equilibrium analysis. More generally, though, optimal short-term debt ought to be state-contingent so as to react to macroeconomic news accruing at date 1 (in practice this flexibility is provided for example by indexed debt or by preferred equity).

This sensitivity to macroeconomic conditions in turn impacts the government's incentives. The Appendix checks that the insights obtained in Section III, subsection A, still hold when firms more generally issue state-contingent short-term debt. The only difference is that state-contingent debt generates more policy discipline.

More precisely, when τ is random, the optimal refinancing decision is shown to be sensitive to prospects:

$$\rho^*(\tau) = (p + \tau)\hat{r},$$

where

$$\hat{r} = \frac{R + \mu r}{1 + \mu} \in (r, R)$$

(and μ is the shadow price of the financing constraint). Because $\hat{r} > r$ and the firm can raise only up to $(p + \tau)r$ by issuing new securities, the optimal short-term debt $d^*(\tau)$ is linearly decreasing in τ. Intuitively, improved prospects for date 2 boost not only the pledgeable income (as reflected by an increased access to refinancing), but also the nonpledgeable income, vindicating lower short-term obligations.

The randomness of τ can be endogenized for example by letting the marginal cost of the investor-friendly policy depend on the realization of a state of nature ε with continuous distribution with a large support:

$$\gamma(\tau) = \varepsilon\tau.$$

When the distribution of ε is close to a spike at date 0[43] (to make the analysis comparable to that of Section III, subsection A), then the date-1 government policy can be shown to converge to that given by

$$\gamma'(\tau^*) = R - r + \left[(p + \tau^*)(R - r) - \gamma(\tau^*)\right] \hat{r}\frac{f(p^*)}{F(p^*)}. \tag{25.18}$$

The only difference between (17) and (18) is that an investor-friendly policy rescues more firms when debt is state-contingent ($\hat{r} > r$). The insights of Section III, subsection A, carry over to contingent debt.

Proposition 5: *Suppose that the firms optimally trade off the cost and benefit of short-term debt, namely the increased probability of being illiquid and the enhanced borrowing capacity. A fixed level of short-term debt d^* is optimal when the private sector has perfect foresight about the government policy. By contrast, an (optimal) state-contingent*

[43] Keeping the support of the distribution constant.

government policy calls for a contingent debt contract $d^* = a - b\tau$, that takes advantages of new information about the firm's prospects. State-contingent debt makes the government policy more investor-friendly.

In either case, a small increase in the short-term debt from the privately optimal level raises country welfare.

IV. Liability Dollarization

A. Framework

To illustrate the impact of the choice of liability denomination in the simplest possible manner, let us ignore credit rationing.

The model is a real exchange rate one. There are two goods, a tradable good, valued by both domestic residents and foreigners, and a nontradable good, valued only by domestic residents.

As earlier, there are three periods, $t = 0, 1, 2$. Date 0 is the financing stage and date 2 the return period. Date 1 is the intermediate date at which the government chooses its policy. Foreigners' preferences value the date-0 and date-2 tradable goods equally (and so the world rate of interest is zero):

$$W^* = c_0^* + c_2^*,$$

where a "star" indicates a tradable good and "no star" a nontradable one. Domestic residents have utility from consumptions c_2 of nontradables, c_2^* of tradables, and g^* of public good (see below) equal to:

$$W = c_2 + u_2(c_2^*) + v(g^*)$$

where u_2 and v are strictly concave. (We could add date-0 consumption. This would not affect the results.)

We will let e_2 denote the date-2 price of tradables in terms on nontradables (note: a depreciation corresponds to an increase in e_2). The date-2 consumption function is given by

$$u_2'(c_2^*(e_2)) = e_2$$

The domestic consumption of tradables decreases as the exchange rate depreciates.

The representative domestic resident is an entrepreneur who transforms a tradable input I_f^* into a deterministic nontradable output $y(I_f^*)$ at date 2. The date-0 input I_f^* is borrowed from foreigners, as the entrepreneur is not endowed with tradables. The production function $y(I_f^*)$ is strictly concave and satisfies the Inada conditions.

The entrepreneur commits to reimbursing d_2^* in tradable goods and d_2 in nontradables. The amount d_2 will be paid directly from $y(I_f^*)$, and foreign investors will then need to convert it into tradables. In contrast, to reimburse d_2^*, it will be incumbent on the entrepreneur to convert nontradable production at the going exchange rate.

While the theory below is purely one of the real exchange rate, I will, by a substantial leap of faith, interpret the denomination of debt in the tradable good as one in foreign currency (dollars). Note, though, that a similar story could be told in a monetary model, in which "depreciation" would be replaced by "nominal devaluation."[44]

Last, I formalize the common concern that recipients of large capital inflows may use them to finance large fiscal deficits or consumption booms by assuming that the government selects at date 1 a level of public good $g^* \in [0, R^*]$ (so the discretionary action a is here g^*). The key assumption is that a higher level of public good comes at the expense of "country reserves." The total amount of uncommitted domestic (privately and publicly owned) tradables available for trade at date 2 is $R^* - g^*$. While one can think of R^* as the government's initial endowment of foreign reserves, R^* should be given a much broader interpretation; for example, an increase in g^* may come at the expense of new activities and production in another, export sector.

B. Analysis

Let us begin with a derivation of the time-inconsistent policy. The first-best policy maximizes the utility of the representative entrepreneur:

$$\max_{\{g^*, I_f^*\}} \left\{ y(I_f^*) + u_2(R^* - g^* - I_f^*) + v(g^*) \right\},$$

where use is made of the fact that the entrepreneur will have to reimburse, one way or the other, the borrowed amount in tradables. This yields:

$$y' = u_2' = v' = e_2.$$

Let us now turn to the time-consistent policy. Fixing (d_2^*, d_2), the date-2 exchange rate clears the market for tradables goods:

$$c_2^*(e_2) + d_2^* + \frac{d_2}{e_2} = R^* - g^*. \tag{25.19}$$

The exchange rate $e_2(g^*)$ is an increasing function of g^*. Note also that: $\left| \frac{dc_2^*(e_2(g^*))}{dg^*} \right| \leq 1$, with strict inequality unless $d_2 = 0$.

In words, it is only when foreign debt is denominated in tradables, that is when the foreigner's stake $V_f = d_2^* + (d_2/e_2)$ is insensitive to the exchange rate, that an increase in the public good is offset one-for-one by a reduction in consumption.

[44]The type of moral hazard formalized in this section, though, need not be viewed as the government's action of expanding the monetary base to deflate the nominal value of foreigners' domestic currency claims through inflation. As for example Eichengreen-Hausmann (1999) and Marcos Chamon (2001) note, many emerging markets have inflation indexed instruments; furthermore foreign currency borrowing applies even to countries with no recent history of high inflation. And so the problem is much deeper than that of surprise inflation.

Chamon (2001) develops a model of foreign currency denomination in the absence of government moral hazard, but in the presence of aggregate productivity shocks. Domestic entrepreneurs invest and produce tradables, and issue debt liabilities labeled in tradables or nontradables. Entrepreneurial risk aversion implies that debt denominated in nontradables offers a hedge against macroeconomic shocks; however, if the share of output that can be collected by foreigners in bad states of nature is assumed to grow with total face value (expressed in tradables), then denomination in tradables facilitates private borrowing. See Aghion et al. (2001) for a model of foreign currency borrowing in the presence of nominal rigidities.

At date 1, the government selects g^* so as to solve:

$$\max_{g^*} \left\{u_2(c_2^*(e_2(g^*))) + v(g^*)\right\},$$

which yields:

$$v' = u_2' \left|\frac{dc_2^*}{dg^*}\right|. \tag{25.20}$$

The time-inconsistent policy coincides with the time-consistent one if and only if foreign debt is fully denominated in tradables:

$$d_2 = 0.$$

The government overconsumes international reserves when part of the debt is labelled in nontradables. Forcing firms to engage in risk management reduces country welfare.

In this model, firms are *individually* indifferent as to the "currency" denomination of their liabilities. Of course, they would not be indifferent in richer models. For example, one could combine this analysis and that of Section III to look at optimal risk management when firms face liquidity shocks at the intermediate date.[45]

The general point, though, is that *at the margin* the firms do not label enough their liabilities in tradables, as they do not internalize the disciplining effect of the denomination on government policy.

Remark: The assumption that the foreigners have no value at risk under foreign currency denomination is of course extreme. In practice, they have value at risk not only because governments may renege and directly expropriate a fraction of foreign holdings (a strategy not allowed here), but also because some of this foreign currency denomination is fictitious. Typically, individual firms' profit is random and the collateral received by foreigners in case of failure may be nontradable, as in the case of real estate.

Proposition 6: *In the liability-denomination model, encouraging at the margin domestic entrepreneurs to hedge their currency risk reduces country welfare.*

C. Redistributive Politics

Let us conclude with a few thoughts about the redistributive politics of exchange rate policies. Relaxing the assumption that domestic residents are a single (entrepreneur/consumer) constituency, note that consumers and entrepreneurs may be hurt differently

[45] The prospect of a government bailout may also affect this choice. In Martin Schneider and Tornell (2001), domestic firms (or blanks) optimally denominate their foreign debt in tradables goods. That paper assumes that the government undertakes "systemic bailout," i.e., bailouts are granted only if a critical mass of firms default. Tradable-good debt denomination is a gamble that increases the probability of receiving the bailout subsidy: in effect, it increase the probability that the firm goes bankrupt when other firms also do (i.e., when the price of nontradables over tradables is low), and so the government grants a bailout. A bailout policy on the other hand helps the credit-constrained domestic firms to borrow more.

More generally, "original sin features" that are induced by the prospect of domestic bank bailout or by Basle criteria on the lending-banks side are probably better addressed by a proper prudential regulation of domestic and foreign banks than by a broader prohibition of the features.

by a depreciation. Suppose that the government puts weights k on entrepreneurs and $1 - k$ on consumers. Assuming that the leftover reserves $R^* - g^*$ are distributed fairly in the population, and letting $K \equiv 2(1 - k)$, the government solves at date 1:

$$\max_{g^*} \left\{K[y - (d_2 + d_2^* e_2)] + e_2[R^* - g^*] + [u(c_2^*) - e_2 c_2^*] + v(g^*)\right\},$$

where e_2 is still given by (19). This yields first-order condition:

$$v' = u_2' \left|\frac{dc_2^*}{dg^*}\right| + (K - 1)d_2^* \frac{de_2}{dg^*}. \tag{25.21}$$

Comparing (20) and (21), the incentive to consume reserves is now affected in two ways. First, and as in the absence of redistributive politics, if $d_2 > 0$, the reduced availability of tradables hurts foreigners as well as residents. This international burden sharing leads to an excessive depreciation from a date-0 viewpoint.

The second effect is specific to redistributive politics ($K \neq 1$). Public good provision depreciates the currency ($de_2/dg^* > 0$), raising the debt burden on entrepreneurs if $d_2^* > 0$. This effect induces the government to keep the currency appreciated if it favors entrepreneurs over consumers ($K > 1$) and to depreciate it further if the government favors consumers ($K < 1$).

The analysis provides theoretical ammunitions in support of Eichengreen and Hausmann's (1999) suggestion as to why original sin applies to all non-OECD countries while some developed countries are able to borrow in their own currencies. They propose that the latter countries "developed their domestic markets first, creating a political constituency that opposed opportunistic depreciation."

V. Concluding Remarks

An analysis of countries' lack of access to attractive levels and forms of financing must build on a description of why capital markets fail. This paper focuses on uncoordinated private sector borrowing. Borrowers and lenders have no individual incentive to internalize the impact of their private financing arrangement on country incentives; the resulting inefficiency is borne by the country itself. Three broad conclusions emerge:

(1) No strong case can be made on a priori grounds that countries over- or underborrow. Forces conducive to overinvestment include (a) a reduction in the quality of policy brought about by an increase in foreign ownership in the country, as well as two forces that are unrelated to international borrowing: (b) the incidence on domestic third parties of public policies supporting private sector borrowers, an incidence that (c) is exacerbated under crony capitalism. In contrast, (d) capital controls impose a substantial cost to the extent that firms are subject to credit rationing and therefore are deprived by controls of access to highly productive capital, and (e) median voter politics result in an insufficient internalization of the country's benefits from capital accounts liberalization.

(2) As to the form of liabilities, "dangerous forms of debt" cannot be presumed to be suboptimal for those who issue them. The analysis of the externalities involved in the choice of financial structure points at the flip side of risk exposure: dangerous forms of debt are also "policy resistant"; they make the government more accountable, ultimately to the benefit of the country. Encouraging foreign direct and equity portfolio investment

and promoting international diversification do not encourage accountability. Some match between stakeholders and political constituencies must be achieved. Debt financing and small frictions inducing a home bias therefore should not be the object of widespread opprobrium, even though they will be encouraged by politicians eager to favor their corporate friends and then may have perverse consequences.

The critique concerning short maturities can be analyzed in a multistage framework in which firms optimally trade off the cost (liquidity shortage) and benefit (better access to capital) of short-term liabilities. Short-term liabilities unambiguously improve policy-making by a domestic-welfare maximizing government; this "public good" is not internalized by firms, whose maturity structure is therefore tilted toward long-term borrowing. While further effects must be accounted for (see below), this shows that strong views concerning short-terminism in capital flows may not be warranted.

The third member of the vulnerability trilogy, foreign currency denominated liabilities, is subject to a similar conclusion. Again, at the margin, borrowers do not internalize the disciplining impact of such borrowing.

(3) One cannot assess a country's ability to borrow and terms of borrowing without accounting for internal politics. The conclusions are reinforced or weakened depending on whether the interests of foreigners are aligned or dissonant with those of dominant domestic interest groups.

Overall, a country's level and quality of access to international capital depends not only on its level of international collateral,[46] but also on a variety of institutional features such as the level of domestic savings, their location (home versus abroad), the extent of control rights held by political authorities, and the interests of dominant domestic political forces. These institutional features probably are part of the reason why the United States, in which the government has limited control rights and key political constituencies' interests are aligned with investors' interests (e.g., through the pension fund system), can borrow so much; and why many poor African countries, which have a much more pressing need for foreign capital but whose wealth is often appropriated by a small group and invested abroad, and whose leaders have substantial control over economic life, have almost no access to the international capital market. A systematic analysis transcending this anecdotal evidence and connecting institutional features and foreign burrowing would be very useful.

The paper focused on a common-agency externality through the impact of firms' financial structure on government behavior. One should not restrict analysis to this externality among borrowers. For example, firms may take socially insufficient precautions against distress if the social cost of unemployment is convex in the rate of unemployment or if a soft asset market leads to fire sales in downturns. Furthermore, I have not allowed for potential externalities. such as financial contagion externalities, among countries. Such externalities may lead to a qualification of some policy implications of the common-agency perspective;[47] as discussed in the introduction, the broader point made in this paper will then be the complementarity between "corporate finance reform" and "government governance reform."

[46]An aspect investigated thoroughly in the work of Ricardo Caballero and Arvind Krishnamurthy (1999. 2001a, b, c).

[47]Another objection to foreign currency denominated debt is that, in a pegged exchange rate regime, it makes it hard for countries to resort to devaluation in order to address a balance-of-payments crisis. For example, Anne Krueger (2000) advocates delinking financial and balance-of-payments crises by making foreign currency obligations incurred by domestic entities unenforceable in court or by having developed countries force their financial institutions to accept liabilities abroad only in local currencies.

Last, let me broaden the perspective. The paper took sovereign rights as given and looked at policies altering private sector behavior. A complementary approach, more in the tradition of the trade and central banking literatures, would focus on the devolution of sovereign rights.[48] Clearly, many of the control rights listed in the introduction cannot be transferred to foreign investors, who, in contrast with governments, are excessively preoccupied with profitability and would impose large welfare costs on the population. As suggested in Tirole (2002), corporate finance sheds some light on the tradeoffs in the allocation of control rights; but this allocation is a complex issue, that deserves a thorough treatment of its own.

Appendix: Contingent Debt

Noncontingent debt contracts were optimal in the context of Section III. More generally, though, contingent debt is an optimal reaction to a random environment. In particular, the threshold ρ^* of Section III, subsection A, ought to be contingent on the realization of policy τ, this in turn affects the choice of government policy. Let us check that the analysis of Section III, subsection A, is robust to contingent debt. To this purpose let us derive the optimal liquidity-management policy $\rho^*(\tau)$ when τ is random. Letting E_τ denote expectations with respect to τ, the generalizations of equations (14) and (15) are:

$$U = \left[[s + E_\tau[F(\hat{\rho}(\tau))\rho_1(\tau)]] - \left[1 + E_\tau \left[\int_0^{\hat{\rho}(\tau)} \rho f(\rho) d\rho \right] \right] \right] I \tag{25.A1}$$

and

$$[s + E_\tau[F(\hat{\rho}(\tau))\rho_0(\tau)]] = (1 - A) + E_\tau \left[\int_0^{\hat{\rho}(\tau)} \rho f(\rho) d\rho \right] I, \tag{25.A2}$$

where $\rho_1(\tau) \equiv (p + \tau)R$ and $\rho_0(\tau) \equiv (p + \tau)r$.

Proceeding through the same steps as in Section III, subsection A, the optimal state-contingent threshold satisfies:

$$\rho^*(\tau) = \frac{\rho_\tau(\tau) + \mu\rho_0(\tau)}{1 + \mu} \quad \text{with} \quad \mu > 1,$$

or

$$\rho^*(\tau) = (p + \tau) \left[\frac{R + \mu r}{1 + \mu} \right] \equiv \alpha + \tau\hat{r}$$

where $\hat{r} \equiv [R + \mu r]/[1 + \mu]$ and $\alpha \equiv p\hat{r}$.

[48] The devolution can take many forms, such as joining a multilateral organization, entering a monetary union or a free-trade agreement, and devolving authority for bankruptcy and corporate governance to independent courts.

Consequently, the sensitivity of the refinancing decision to prospects is higher than with noncontingent debt:

$$dp^*/d\tau = \hat{r} > r.$$

The optimal state-contingent debt is

$$d^*(\tau) = \hat{r} - (p+\tau)\left(\frac{R-r}{1+\mu}\right).$$

It decreases with the expected nonpledgeable income $(p+\tau)(R-r)$. [The increase in the value of the pledgeable income brought about by an increase in τ is addressed through date-1 market refinancing]. We can perform the same analysis as in Section III, subsection A, but with contingent debt. To introduce some noise and thereby justify contingent debt, suppose that the analyzed cost of the policy is

$$\gamma(\tau) + \varepsilon\tau;$$

the case treated in Section III, subsection A, is therefore the case in which the random variable ε (realized at date 1) converges to a spike at 0. At date 1 the government, knowing the realization of ε, solves:

$$\max_{\tau} \left\{F(p^*(\tau))\,[(p+\tau)(R-r) - [\gamma(\tau)+\varepsilon\tau]]\right\},$$

and so,

$$\gamma'(\tau(\varepsilon)) = R - r + [(\rho+\tau(\varepsilon))(R-r) - [\gamma(\tau(\varepsilon)) + \varepsilon\tau(\varepsilon)]]\frac{\hat{r}(\rho^*(\tau(\varepsilon)))}{F(\rho^*(\tau(\varepsilon)))} - \varepsilon.$$

For ε small, the only difference with (17) is that "r" is replaced by "$\hat{r}$." State-contingent debt creates more discipline. Last, one can perform the same exercise as in Section III, subsection A: a small uniform increase in the debt level (i e., a decrease in α) increases τ for each ε.

References

Aghion, Philippe; Bacchetta, Philippe and Banerjee, Abhijit. "A Corporate Balance-Sheet Approach to Currency Crises." Lausanne, Department D'Econometrie et d'Economie Politique (DEEP), Cahiers de Recherches Economiques No. 0114, 2001.

Aghion, Philippe and Bolton, Patrick. "Government Debt and the Risk of Default," in Rudiger Dornbusch and Mario Draghi. eds. *Public debt management: Theory and history.* Cambridge: Cambridge University Press, 1991.

Bagwell, Kyle and Staiger, Robert. "GATT-Think." Mimeo, Columbia University and University of Wisconsin, 2000.

Bernheim, B. Douglas and Whinston, Michael. "Common Agency." *Econometrica*, July 1986, *54*(4), pp. 923–42.

Biais, Brono and Perotti, Enrico. "Machiavellian Privatization," *American Economic Review.* March 2002, *92*(1), pp. 240–58.

Blanchard, Olivier and Summers, Lawrence. "Fiscal Increasing Returns, Hysteresis, Real Wages and Unemployment." *European Economic Review*, April 1987, *31*(3), pp. 543–60.

Bulow, Jeremy and Rogoff, Kenneth. "A Constant Recontracting Model of Sovereign Debt." *Journal of Political Economy*, February 1989a. *97*(1), pp. 155–78.

——. "Multilateral Negotiations for Rescheduling Developing Country Debt: A Bargaining Theoretic Framework." in Jacob Frenkel, Michael P. Dooley, and Peter Wickham. eds., *Analytical issues in debt.* Washington. DC: International Monetary Fund, 1989b, pp. 644–57.

Caballero, Ricardo and Krishnamurthy, Arvind. "Emerging Markets Crises: An Asset Markets Perspectives." Mimeo, Department of Economics, Massachusetts Institute of Technology, 1999.

——. "International and Domestic Collateral Constraints in a Model of Emerging Market Crises." *Journal of Monetory Economics*, December 2001a. *48*(3), pp. 513–48.

——. "Dollarization of Liabilities: Underinsurance and Domestic Finacial Development." Mimeo, Massachusetts Institute of Technology and Northwestern University, 2001b.

——. "International Liquidity Illusion; On the Risks of Sterilization." Mimeo, Massachusetts Institute of Technology and Northwestern University, 2001c.

Chamon, Marcos. "Why Can't Developing Countries Borrow from Abroad in Their Currency?" Mimeo, Harvard University, December 2001.

Detragiache, Enrica and Spilimbergo, Antonio. "Short Term Debt and Crises." Mimeo, International Monetary Fund working paper, 2001.

Dixit, Avinash. "Strategic Aspects of Trade Policy," in Truman F. Bewley. ed., *Advances in economic theory: Fifth World Congress of Econometric Society*, Cambridge: Cambridge University Press, 1987, pp. 329–62.

Eaton, Jonathan. "Public Debt Guarantees and Private Capital Flight." *World Bank Economic Review*. May 1987, *1*, pp. 377–95.

Eaton, Jonathan and Fernandez, Raquel. "Sovereign Debt," in Gene Grossman and Kenneth Rogoff. eds., *Handbook of international economics.* Vol. 3. Amsterdam: North Holland, 1995, pp. 2031–77.

Eichengreen, Barry and Hausmann, Ricardo. "Exchange Rates and Financial Fragility." National Bureau of Economic Research (Cambridge, MA) Working Paper No. 7418, 1999.

French, Kenneth R. and Poterba, James M. "Investor Diversification and International Equity Markets" *American Economic Review*, May 1991 (*Papers and Proceedings*). *81*(2), pp. 222–26.

Gertler, Mark and Rogoff, Kenneth. "North-South Lending and Endogenous Domestic Capital Market Inefficiencies." *Journal of Monetary Economies*, October 1990, *26*, pp. 245–66.

Grossman, Gene and Helpman, Elhanan. "Protection for Sale." *American Economic Review*, September 1994, *84*(4), pp. 833–50.

Holmström, Bengt and Tirole, Jean. "Private and Public Supply of Liquidity." *Journal of Political Economy.* February 1998, *106*(1), pp. 1–40.

——."Domestic and International Supply of Liquidity," *American Economic Review*, May 2002 (*Papers and Proceedings*), *92*(2), pp. 42–5.

Jeanne, Olivier. "Foreign Currency Debt and Signaling." Mimeo, International Monetary Fund, Washington. DC, 1999.

——. "Foreign Currency Debt and the Global Financial Architecture." *European Economic Review*, May 2000a (*Papers and Proceedings*), *44*(4–6), pp. 719–27.

——. "Debt Maturity and the Global Financial Architecture." Center for Economic Policy Research Working Paper No. 2520, 2000b.

—— "Why Do Emerging Markets Borrow in Foreign Currency." Mimeo, International Monetary Fund. Washington, DC. November 2002.

Jeanne, Olivier and Zettelmeyer, Jeromin. "International Bailouts, Moral Hazard and Conditionality." *Economic Policy*, October 2001, (33), pp. 409–32.

Johnson, Harry. "Optimum Tariffs and Retaliation." *Review of Economic Studies*, 1954, *21*(2), pp. 142–53.

Kraay, Aart; Loayza, Norman; Serven, Luis and Ventura, Jaume. "Country Portfolios." National Bureau of Economic Research (Cambridge, MA) Working Paper No. 7795, July 2000.

Krueger, Anne. "Conflicting Demands on the International Monetary Fund." *American Economic Review*, May 2000 (*Papers and Proceedings*), *90*(2), pp. 38–42.

Lewis, Karen. "Trying to Explain Home Bias in Equities and Consumption." *Journal of Economic Literature*, June 1999, *37*(2), pp. 571–608.

Maggi, Giovanni and Rodriguez-Clare, Andrés. "The Value of Trade Agreements in the Presence of Political Pressures." *Journal of Political Economy*, June 1998, *106*(3), pp. 574–601.

Matsuyama, Kiminori. "Perfect Equilibria in a Trade Liberalization Game." *American Economic Review*, June 1990, *80*(3), pp. 480–92.

Pauly, Mark. "Overinsurance and Public Provision of Insurance; The Roles of Moral Hazard and Adverse Selection." *Quarterly Journal of Economics*, February 1974, *88*(1), pp. 44–62.

Persson, Torsten and Svensson, Lars. "Why a Stubborn Conservative Would Run a Deficit Policy with Time-Inconsistent Preferences." *Quarterly Journal, of Economics*, May 1989, *104*(2), pp. 325–45.

Sachs, Jeffrey. "The Debt Overhang of Developing Countries," in Guillermo A. Calvo, Ronald Findlay, Pentti Kouri, and Jorge Braga de Macedo, eds., *Debt stabilization and development: Essays in memory of Carlos Diaz-Alejandro*. Oxford. Basil Blackwell, 1989.

Schneider, Martin and Tornell, Aaron. "Boom-Bust Cycles and the Balance Sheet Effect." Mimeo. University of California Los Angeles, 2001.

Staiger, Robert and Tabellini, Guido. "Discretionary Trade Policy and Excessive Protection." *American Economic Review*, December 1987, *77*(5), pp. 823–37.

Tabellini, Guido and Alesina, Alberto. "Voting on the Budget Deficit." *American Economic Review*, March 1990, *80*(1), pp. 37–49.

Tirole, Jean. *Financial crises, liquidity, and the international monetary system* (*Paolo Baffi Lecture on Money and Finance*) Princeton, NJ: Princeton University Press, 2002.

Tornell, Aaron. "Time Inconsistency of Protectionist Programs." *Quarterly Journal of Economics*, August 1991, *106*(3), pp. 963–74.

Tornell, Aaron and Velasco, Andres. "The Tragedy of the Commons and Eonomic Growth: Why Does Capital Flow from Poor to Rich Countries?" *Journal of Political Economy*, December 1992, *100*(6), pp. 1208–31.

Velasco, Andres. "Animal Spirits, Investments and International Capital Movements" *Journal of International Money and Finance*, April 1996, *15*(2), pp. 221–37.

Wagner, Wolf. "International Diversification, Governmental Incentives, and the Home Bias in Portfolio Investment." Mimeo, Tilburg University, 2001.

26 Exchange Rate Volatility and the Credit Channel in Emerging Markets: A Vertical Perspective

Ricardo Caballero and Arvind Krishnamurthy

Emerging markets can suffer severe contractions when capital inflows suddenly reverse ("sudden stops"). What is the right monetary policy response to this event? Answering this important question requires understanding the mechanisms through which monetary policy can affect sudden stops and their consequences. The main contribution of this paper is to rethink the workings of the credit channel in emerging market economies and to propose an alternative view that shifts the focus from credit channel and aggregate demand to insurance considerations.

Much of the recent literature on emerging markets crises highlights the limited financial development of these economies and the severe credit squeeze experienced by local firms during crises. From this structure, two opposing arguments are commonly made regarding optimal monetary policy. Extrapolating from developed economy credit channel analysis, some advocate an expansionary monetary policy to offset the effect of the credit squeeze during downturns. Others advocate a contractionary monetary policy and dogged defense of the exchange rate during crises. Proponents of the latter view do not disagree on the centrality of the credit channel mechanism, but argue that a depreciating exchange rate will have dramatic effects in the credit channel mechanism, through a deterioration in borrowers' balance sheets. The argument is that this effect is most likely to happen when the economy is dollarized and when inflation credibility is limited.[1]

The starting point of our analysis is the observation from Caballero and Krishnamurthy (2001) that credit constraints in emerging markets may exist both at the country level as well as the firm level. A firm may have limited collateral and therefore be constrained in borrowing from either domestic or foreign lenders. Or the country as a whole may have limited international collateral, and therefore domestic firms are constrained in borrowing from foreign investors.[2] Extrapolation from developed economy analysis misses this distinction because in developed economies the credit constraint plausibly exists only at the firm level. The distinction is important for thinking through the effects of monetary

[1]For both sides of the argument see, e.g., Furman and Stiglitz (1998); Aghion, Bacchetta, and Banerjee (2000); Cespedes, Chang, and Velasco (2000); Gertler, Gilchrist, and Natalucci (2001); Christiano, Gust, and Roldos (2004); and Calvo and Reinhart (2003).

[2]The importance of international collateral constraints for emerging markets was first identified in the sovereign debt literature (see, e.g., Eaton and Gersovitz 1981 or Bulow and Rogoff 1989).

policy because a sudden stop created by the reversal of capital inflows is predominantly about a binding international collateral constraint.

We argue that during mild crises, the distinction between domestic and international constraints is immaterial. Analysis of this case can be conducted in the standard credit channel framework. Much of the recent debate on monetary policy during crises implicitly assumes this to be the relevant scenario. As is stressed in the credit channel literature (e.g., Bernanke, Gertler, and Gilchrist 1999; Kiyotaki and Moore 1997), increasing the net worth of borrowers is the optimal response to a negative shock. Our analysis of this case reinforces the conclusions in the literature: there is some ambiguity regarding whether the optimal monetary policy is to raise or lower interest rates. It depends on the extent of liability dollarization and inflation credibility of the central bank.

The recipe of using monetary policy to increase the net worth of borrowers fails when the credit constraint exists at the country level. The reason is that monetary policy only regulates the borrowing of a domestic agent from a domestic lender. Thus, when the marginal lender is a foreign investor, monetary policy is ineffective because it does not alter the international collateral of the country.[3] We argue that this is the relevant case for emerging markets' crises.

Although monetary expansions have little effect on output during a severe crisis, they have important general equilibrium effects on asset prices. In *partial* equilibrium, it is still true that a monetary expansion raises firms' borrowing capacity by increasing their domestic liquidity. But in general equilibrium, the expansion just translates into a decline in the relative price of domestic liquidity vis-à-vis international liquidity, not in an expansion in international liquidity (i.e., it does not loosen the international constraint). We show that the fall in the price of domestic liquidity implies a *temporary* exchange rate depreciation during the crisis. In fact, the depreciation of the exchange rate is beyond the depreciation due to the standard interest parity mechanism. The depreciation does weaken balance sheets, as some have argued in the context of the credit channel. But it is not firm-level balance sheets that are to blame. The exchange rate depreciation is just the general equilibrium counterpart of the tight international constraint.

Our conclusions regarding the effects of monetary policy are independent of the dollarization of balance sheets. Monetary policy is impotent during crises whether or not dollarized balance sheets undo the beneficial effects of lowering interest rates. The reason, again, is that domestic dollarization just tightens constraints at the firm level; it does not alter the aggregate international collateral of the country.[4]

The second main theme of the paper concerns the insurance effects of monetary policy. Despite the apparent impotence of monetary policy during sudden stops, expectations regarding a particular monetary rule have important effects on the private sector's ex-ante decisions. The anticipation of monetary policy actions during crises affects agents' expectations of the relative price of domestic to international liquidity, which in turn affects the private sector's insurance decisions against sudden stops. If the private sector expects

[3]Though in very different terms, Dornbusch (2001) also expresses his uneasiness about the assumption that emerging economies with access to monetary policy can use it to boost activity. For example, in criticizing the standard view, he writes: "The loss of the lender of last resort [argument] is intriguing. This argument is based on the assumption that the central bank—rather than the treasury or the world capital market—is the appropriate lender . . . "

[4]Dollarization of *external* liabilities has some additional external insurance implications that we discuss later in this paper and, more thoroughly, in Caballero and Krishnamurthy (2003). This is not an issue for the analysis of this paper since we allow for state-contingent debt.

a dogged defense of the exchange rate, then it also expects a smaller decline of the value of domestic to international liquidity. Conversely, if it expects an expansionary monetary policy, then it expects a sharper decline in the relative price of domestic liquidity. The incentive to hoard international over domestic liquidity is more pronounced in the latter than in the former case. Importantly, hoarding more international liquidity is desirable when there are negative pecuniary externalities in the use of international liquidity, a feature that is inherent to economies with underdeveloped financial markets (see Caballero and Krishnamurthy 2001).

From this perspective, our argument connects with the literature on the virtues of flexible versus fixed exchange rate systems.[5] In our model, a flexible exchange rate system coupled with a countercyclical monetary policy provides better *insurance* incentives to the private sector than a policy of defending the exchange rate during sudden stops.[6] More generally, monetary policy and its constraints have (unintended) consequences for the private sector's insurance decisions with respect to sudden stops. Policies that exacerbate the (partial equilibrium) domestic credit squeeze during sudden stops, or constraints that limit the central bank's ability to relax domestic financial constraints, lead to ex-ante imprudent private sector actions.

In section 1 we present a model of market segmentation in which we draw a distinction between domestic and international liquidity. Section 2 describes the consequences of monetary policy in the segmented financial market. In particular, we show the oversensitivity of the exchange rate to monetary policy and the role of the exchange rate in endogenously aligning the extent of domestic credit squeeze with the limited international liquidity. In Section 3 we turn to the ex-ante consequences of monetary policy and its private insurance implications. We show that the strategy of tightening monetary policy during crises lowers the private return to taking preventive measures.

In section 4 we revisit the dollarization of liabilities argument, but now in the context of our dual-liquidity model. We show that the balance-sheet effect typically emphasized in this literature has no aggregate consequences in general equilibrium during the crisis. However, and following our argument above, there is a dynamic cost. Dollarization lowers the expected return on hoarding international liquidity and hence reduces the private sector incentives to take adequate precautions against sudden stops. In section 5 we highlight that not having the credibility or willingness to conduct a countercyclical monetary policy means that an insurance mechanism against crises is lost. Thus, one should look for alternative measures that induce the private sector to carry more international liquidity into crisis states. Examples of these measures include taxation of capital inflows, international liquidity requirements, and large sterilizations of capital inflows. While enacting these measures may be costly, they should be seen as yet another cost of having lost the ability to use monetary policy in an environment of recurrent external crises.

Section 6 shows that our main conclusions are robust to the relaxation of some of the main stylized assumptions of our model, such as the presence of a "diagonal" supply of funds or an alternative model of money. Section 7 concludes and is followed by a technical appendix.

[5]See, e.g., Edwards and Levy-Yeyati (2003) for evidence supporting the advantages of a flexible exchange rate in absorbing external shocks.

[6]Our mechanism is distinct (or in addition to) the standard free insurance argument in the moral hazard perspective of crises (see, e.g., Dooley 1999). We return to this comparison after developing our model.

1. A Model of External Crises

We study a three-date economy ($t = 0, 1, 2$) with a single (tradeable) good. Date 0 is a fully flexible planning period. Agents make investment and financing decisions at this date. At date 1 an external crisis may occur. We assume that there are two states of the world at date 1, $\omega \in \{b, g\}$, which occur with probabilities $\{\pi, 1 - \pi\}$. The crisis can occur only if the b-state realizes. At date 2 agents repay all debts and consume.

1.1 Private Sector

There is a unit measure of domestic firms. Each has access to a production technology. Building a plant of size k at date 0 requires a firm to invest $c(k)$—with $c(.) \geq 0$, $c' > 0$ and $c'' > 0$. The output from production depends on the shocks at date 1. There is a maximum of Ak output goods at date 2, but if negative shocks hit firms, then only ak ($a < A$) output goods may be produced. A more detailed description is given below.

Domestic firms have no resources at date 0. They must import capital goods and borrow from foreigners to finance their investment. Each firm is run by a domestic entrepreneur/manager who has risk-neutral preferences over date 2 consumption of the single good. Thus, financing and investment decisions are taken to maximize expected plant profits at date 2.

Domestic firms face significant financial constraints, and hence their financial net worth affects investment decisions. We assume that firms are endowed with ω units of international collateral, in the form of receivables arriving at date 2. Our central assumption is that only these receivables have collateral value to foreigners (e.g., prime exports).

We disregard explicit equilibrium default and assume that all financing is done via fully collateralized debt contracts. Moreover, we assume that the debt contracts are made fully contingent on the state at date 1. We relax this in section 4 when discussing dollarized external debt, since the problem of dollar debt is essentially one of liabilities that are too inflexible.

At date 0, when firms sign debt contracts with foreigners, the contracted repayments of f^{ω} must not exceed ω. Foreigners lend against this collateral at dates 0 and 1 at the rate i_0^* and i_1^* from period 0 to 1, and 1 to 2, respectively.

We also assume that domestic agents have some "domestic" assets that they can only trade to other domestic agents. First, we assume that the minimum date 2 output of ak can be pledged as collateral to other domestic agents. Second, we assume that agents are endowed with $\underline{M}$ units of domestic money (see below) that they can sell to other agents.

This modeling captures the distinction between domestic borrowing capacity and international borrowing capacity. We think of the domestic assets as "peso" assets, while the international collateral are "dollar" assets. Thus, changes in the exchange rate have an effect on the dollar value of domestic assets but not that of the international assets.

1.2 Credit Constraints During Crises

A crisis is a time when there is a shortage of resources available to finance investments. Formally, we model the external crisis by assuming that the demand for external resources rises in the b-state, while holding the international collateral fixed. An alternative (and more realistic) modeling of a shortage of external resources would be to assume that international collateral contracts during the crisis, while demand for external resources remains fixed.

The implications of these two modeling strategies are similar for our purposes, but our approach reduces the number of assumptions and equations required. In particular, we do not need to add an assumption of incomplete international insurance markets.[7]

In the g-state there are no shocks and investment is unaffected. Let us now turn to defining the shock in the b-state and explaining how it affects investments.

The plants of one-half of the firms receive a shock at date 1 that lowers output per plant from A to a. The shock only arrives in the b-state, but is idiosyncratic in that each firm receives the shock with probability 1/2. The productivity decline can be offset by reinvesting $\theta k(\theta \leq 1)$ goods, to give date 2 output of

$$\tilde{A}(\theta)k = (a + \theta\Delta)k \leq Ak \quad \text{where} \quad \Delta \equiv A - a,$$

so that $\tilde{A}(1) = A$. We assume that the return on reinvestment exceeds the international interest rate:

$$\Delta - 1 > i_1^*.$$

This means that firms will borrow as much as possible to finance reinvestment. A crisis occurs if firms are financially constrained at date 1, so that $\theta < 1$. We make parametric assumptions to ensure that this occurs in equilibrium only in the b-state (see the appendix).

A firm that receives a production shock is termed *distressed.* To cope with the shock, the firm first borrows directly from foreigners against its net international collateral of $\omega - f$. After this, it must turn for funds to the domestic firms that did not receive a shock (termed *intact*). As noted above, domestic agents accept the money held by distressed firms as payment. They also accept ak of the output from the firm's plants as collateral for any domestic debt. Thus the *domestic* (real) liquidity of firms entering date 1 (i.e., the date 2 goods that can be pledged to domestic agents) is

$$ak + \underline{M}/e_2 \tag{26.1}$$

where e_2 is the date 2 nominal exchange rate (also the price level).

Intact firms have no output at date 1 either, so they must borrow from foreigners if they are to finance the distressed firms. At the interest rate of i_1^*, they can borrow up to $\frac{\omega - f}{1+i_1^*}$ from foreigners.

Since at date 1 firms, in aggregate, can borrow from foreigners up to

$$\omega^n \equiv \frac{\omega - f}{1 + i_1^*}, \tag{26.2}$$

we refer to ω^n as the *international* liquidity of the country during the crisis.

[7] See Caballero and Krishnamurthy (2001) for the alternative approach. See Broner, Lorenzoni, and Schmukler (2003) for evidence that some of these international collateral shocks are due to shocks to specialist investors (in our framework, this is as if suddenly foreign lenders decide to reduce the share of ω that is part of international collateral).

1.3 Central Bank

The central bank has $\underline{M}$ units of money outstanding at date 0. At date 1, it may choose to inject $(M - \underline{M})$ more money into firms. We assume that this money is distributed as "helicopter" drops to firms and redeemed at date 2 with taxes collected by the government.

We do not provide a detailed description of the government's tax powers and its tax base. Instead we assume that the government collects T goods via nondistortionary taxation, and that these taxes do not come from firms. We think of these taxes as resources from a consumer sector that has a date 2 endowment of $y^c \geq T$. When it is effective, expansionary monetary policy transfers resources from consumers to the corporate sector.[8]

We assume that the central bank is credible in maintaining the date 2 price level at one, so that money injections do not lead to inflation. We relax this assumption in section 5 when we discuss inflation credibility. Thus, for now, the date 2 exchange rate is $e_2 = 1$.

Our model of the monetary transmission mechanism involves no monetary frictions, because our qualitative conclusions do not depend on the presence of these frictions and ignoring them simplifies the exposition. The domestic "peso" interest rate is zero in our environment and is unaffected by monetary policy. Therefore the usual channel (through the interest parity condition) by which monetary policy affects the exchange rate is absent in our model. Despite this, we show that in our model, monetary policy still affects the exchange rate. For this reason, we refer to the exchange rate movements induced by monetary policy as "overresponsive." Our results should be interpreted as *in addition* to those that arise from the movement in the peso rate and its effect through the interest parity condition. In section 6, we sketch a more standard model in which money provides a transaction service, thus confirming that our results are robust to this simplification.[9]

2. Monetary Policy, Exchange Rate Determination, and the Credit Channel

In this section we examine the equilibrium in the crisis state at date 1. Thus, for now, we take the date 0 investment decision of k and the financing decision of f as given. We study the case where credit constraints are binding in this crisis state, illustrating that the power of monetary policy to relax these constraints changes from mild (horizontal) to severe (vertical) crises.

All of the discussion in this section takes place after the bad state has realized at date 1 and the central bank has injected $(M - \underline{M})$ pesos in response. Figure 26.1 illustrates the timing of shocks and agents' decisions.

2.1 Mild and Severe Crises (Date 1)

At date 1, distressed firms need to borrow in order to finance their production shock. Their total net worth, measured in dollars, is $\frac{ak+M}{e_1}+\omega^n$. Clearly, as M rises, so does net worth, at least for a given e_1. The key question is whether e_1 depreciates with an expansionary

[8] See, e.g., Woodford (1990) and Holmstrom and Tirole (1998) for a similar assumption.

[9] The discussion in section 6 also clarifies exchange rate determination in our setup. When the peso interest rate is zero, e_1, which we refer to as the date 1 exchange rate, can also be interpreted as the forward exchange rate standing at date 1 for exchange at date 2. In section 6 we show that when the peso interest rate is nonzero, this ambiguity disappears and e_1 is the date 1 exchange rate.

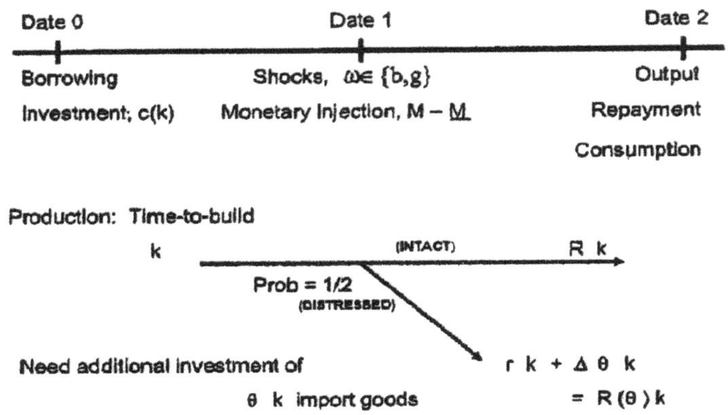

Figure 26.1. Timeline
Note: The figure presents the timing of investment, borrowing, and consumption decisions. Also pictured are the shocks affecting firms at date 1.

monetary policy and by how much. We argue that the answer to this question depends critically on the severity of the crisis. If the latter is severe, a monetary expansion is ineffective in raising output and leads to an exchange rate overreaction. This happens despite full inflation target credibility ($e_2 = 1$), as it reflects the fall in the real value of domestic collateral (i.e., not a monetary phenomenon).

Let us consider equilibrium at date 1. Distressed firms can borrow ω^n directly from foreign investors. Thereafter they must turn to other domestic agents to raise resources. Recall that intact firms can also borrow ω^n from foreign investors. Moreover, since they are willing to accept domestic money as payment as well as purchase debt claims backed by ak of collateral, they can also finance the production shock of the distressed firms.

There are two regions of interest. If

$$\frac{1}{2}\omega^n > \frac{1}{2}\frac{ak + M}{1 + i_1^*}, \tag{26.3}$$

then intact firms have sufficient access to foreign funds to satisfy demand from all distressed firms. We refer to this case as the horizontal region, because the supply of funds from intact firms is elastic at the margin.

The other case is when

$$\frac{1}{2}\omega^n > \frac{1}{2}\frac{ak + M}{1 + i_1^*},$$

while $\omega^n < k/2$. That is, intact firms have insufficient resources to satisfy demand from distressed firms. We refer to this case as the vertical region, because the supply of funds is inelastic at the margin.

2.2 Horizontal Region (Mild Crises): The Standard Credit Channel

Intact firms have portfolios that include domestic loans, money, and international collateral. Indifference requires that i_1^* be the interest rate on the domestic loans as well. The exchange rate can also be determined from this indifference condition. Since the return on holding money must be equal to $1 + i_1^*$, the exchange rate is

$$e_1 = 1 + i_1^*. \tag{26.4}$$

This equation is the interest parity condition, given that $e_2 = 1$ and that money provides no special transaction service (so the peso interest rate is zero). Note that the exchange rate is unresponsive to monetary injections.

Total reinvestment is determined by the total resources of individual distressed firms,

$$\theta^H k = \omega^n + \frac{ak + M}{e_1} = \frac{\omega - f + ak + M}{1 + i_1^*} < 2\omega^n, \quad \theta^H < 1, \tag{26.5}$$

where the superscript H denotes the horizontal equilibrium. The first inequality shows that the economy has not used all of its international liquidity, while $\theta^H < 1$ indicates that the economy is in a crisis: distressed firms are not able to meet their production shock fully because of their binding financial constraints.

As we mentioned above, we refer to this as the horizontal region, because the price of loans is not affected by their quantity. In principle, a distressed firm could continue borrowing at the given interest rate i_1^*, as long as its own financial constraint is relaxed.

We can see the effects of monetary injections from the preceding expressions. They operate though a credit channel à la Bernanke and Gertler (1995). From (5) we note that injecting money increases the resources of the distressed firms and increases their investment. From (4) we note that this policy has no effect on exchange rates in the horizontal region, so the monetary expansion is a powerful mechanism to raise the dollar value of distressed firms' collateral. It is possible that reintroducing the standard interest parity effect (which we have suppressed) will work against this conclusion. But as we show next, in the vertical region, we reach the unambiguous conclusion that the exchange rate effect will neutralize monetary expansions.

2.3 The Vertical Region (Severe Crises): Overresponsive Exchange Rate

In this region, the international supply of funds faced by emerging market economies during external crises is vertical (i.e., price inelastic). Since all investment at date 1 is eventually financed by foreigners, the stock of international liquidity is what determines investment in this region:

$$\theta^V k = 2\omega^n \tag{26.6}$$

where the superscript V stands for vertical equilibrium. Note that domestic collateral does not appear at all in this expression.

Consider the exchange rate next. Since intact firms borrow up to their maximum capacity from foreigners and hold portfolios only composed of domestic money and loans against domestic collateral, it must be that the return on holding domestic money exceeds i_1^*. That is,

$$e_1 > 1 + i_1^*,$$

and the date 1 exchange rate is depreciated.

Indifference between holding money and domestic loans implies that the (dollar) interest rate on loans against domestic collateral also rises above i_1^*. In equilibrium, loans collateralized by ω are made at rate i_1^*, while those collateralized by ak are made at a higher rate of i_1^d, where

$$i_1^d = e_1 - 1 > i_1^*.$$

Figure 26.2 represents the equilibrium determination of e_1. The vertical axis is the price, e_1, while the horizontal axis measures domestic reinvestment. For $e_1 = 1 + i_1^*$, intact firms elastically supply their international liquidity to distressed firms. However, at the point ω^n, intact firms run out of international liquidity, and the supply curve turns vertical. On the other side of the domestic financial market, distressed firms demand as much international liquidity as they can obtain as long as the exchange rate is less than or equal to Δ. However, they are constrained in their domestic borrowing by their holdings of money and domestic collateral. The demand for international liquidity turns downward at some point, and effective demand is $\frac{M+ak}{e_1}$. Figure 26.2 represents two cases: one equilibrium in the horizontal region (panel A) and one in the vertical case (panel B).

This figure illustrates how e_1 rises above $1 + i_1^*$ in the vertical region when international liquidity is scarce. Note also that e_1 can never exceed Δ, the marginal product of reinvestment for distressed firms. However, there is a large interval for demand within which e_1 lies strictly between $1 + i_1^*$ and Δ. In this case,

$$e_1 = \frac{M + ak}{\omega^n} > 1 + i_1^*. \tag{26.7}$$

We can see that monetary injections have a very different effect in the vertical than in the horizontal region. From (6), we note that injecting money has no effect on date 1 reinvestment. This is because the economy has a shortage of international liquidity, and reallocating domestic liquidity has no real (aggregate) effect.

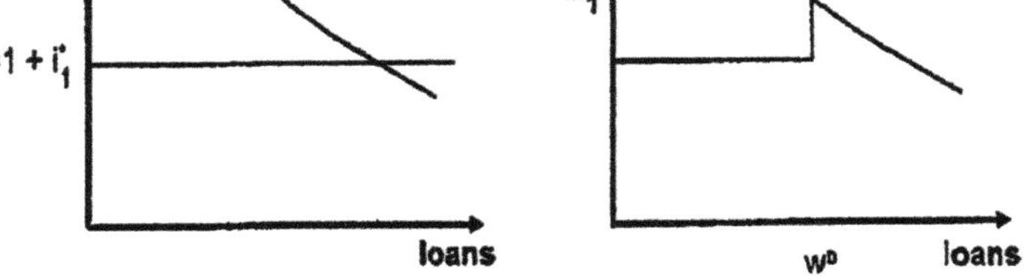

Figure 26.2. Equilibrium Exchange Rate
Note: The figure illustrates the equilibrium determination of e_1 in both the horizontal and vertical regions of the supply of international liquidity.

As before, the net worth of distressed firms is

$$\omega_n + \frac{ak + M}{e_1}.$$

That is, the credit channel is still active, and the net worth of distressed firms is what determines reinvestment at date 1. But the exchange rate now is *overresponsive* to monetary injections. Referring back to equation (7), we see that monetary injections are offset one-for-one by a depreciation in the exchange rate. Essentially, the exchange rate depreciates to ensure that the dollar net worth remains at a level consistent with the availability of external funds. This role of the exchange rate, captured in (7), is what is behind the monetary ineffectiveness result.

2.4 Discussion: The Credit Channel in Emerging Markets

Panels A and B in figure 26.3 summarize the differences between the horizontal and vertical views. In their downward sloping segments, demands are equal to $(ak + M)/e_1$.

In the horizontal case, the increase in domestic net worth of distressed firms caused by expanding monetary policy raises date 1 investment, leaving e_1 unaffected. In the vertical region, the same increase has *no effect* on equilibrium investment and only raises e_1.

We view the horizontal region as relevant for developed economies; ω is plentiful, and there is no distinction between domestic and international liquidity. It may also apply for emerging economies experiencing moderate contractions. The vertical region, on the other hand, seems to be a better description of the environment faced by emerging markets during severe external crises.

There are two points to emphasize from this analysis. First, it may be that other mechanisms overturn the result that injecting money is expansionary in the horizontal region (for example, debts may be dollarized, as we discuss shortly). But in the vertical region, we reach the unambiguous conclusion that injecting money is fully offset by the depreciation in the exchange rate.

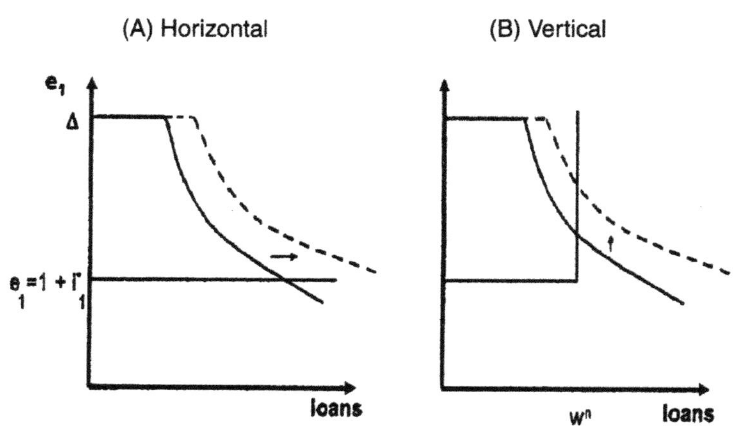

Figure 26.3. Domestic Liquidity Expansion
Note: The figure illustrates the effect of an expansion in domestic liquidity on the exchange rate, e_1, as well as the quantity of loans. The figure presents these effects in both the horizontal and vertical regions of the supply of international liquidity.

This leads to a second point. A researcher looking at the net worth of credit-constrained firms during a crisis will always conclude that the reason for monetary policy ineffectiveness is the deterioration in net worth triggered by the exchange rate depreciation—in particular, the dollarization of liabilities (more on this below). But this is *not* the right conclusion in the vertical region. The main credit constraint behind the crisis is an *aggregate* constraint, not a microeconomic one; the exchange rate depreciation is simply the equilibrium response to such restriction.

3. Underinsurance and Monetary Policy

Of course, all our claims so far are from the perspective of date 1 in the b-state, when ω^n is already given. But what is the impact of anticipated monetary policy in the event of a crisis on date 0 decisions? We turn to this discussion next.

We show that a central bank that is expected to contract money in the event of a vertical crisis at date 1 actually causes the private sector to alter date 0 decisions so as to arrive at date 1 with a smaller ω^n. By supporting the date 1 currency, the central bank causes the private sector to overborrow at date 0 and underinsure against the crisis. Conversely, expansionary monetary policy gives the private sector incentives to insure against the crisis and reduce date 0 borrowing.

3.1 Private Sector Date 0 Decisions and e_1^b

At date 0, the private sector decides how much to borrow from foreign investors and how much real investment to undertake. The borrowing contracts specify an amount loaned to a domestic firm and a repayment at date 2, f^ω, contingent on the date 1 (aggregate) state $\omega \in \{b, g\}$. Since the funds raised from this loan are used in date 0 investment, and since foreign investors are risk neutral, the date 0 budget constraint is

$$c(k) \leq \frac{1}{(1+i_0^*)(1+i_1^*)}\left((1-\pi)f^g + \pi f^b\right). \tag{26.8}$$

In the g-state at date 1, all firms make profits of

$$Ak + (\omega - f^g) + \underline{M}.$$

In the b-state, one-half of the firms are distressed and they make profits of

$$\left(\frac{ak+M}{e_1^b} + \frac{\omega - f^b}{1+i_1^*}\right)\Delta,$$

while the other half are intact and make profits of

$$Ak + (\omega - f^b)\frac{e_1^b}{1+i_1^*} + M.$$

Combining these expressions leads to the following problem for a firm at date 0:

PRIV:

$$\max_{k,f^g,f^b} \quad (1-\pi)(Ak+\omega-f^g+\underline{M})$$
$$+\pi\frac{1}{2}\left(\left(A+a\frac{\delta}{e_1^b}\right)k+(\Delta+e_1^b)\frac{\omega-f^b}{1+i_1^*}+\left(1+\frac{\Delta}{e_1^b}\right)M\right)$$
$$s.t. \quad f^g, f^b \leq \omega$$
$$c(k) \leq \frac{1}{(1+i_0^*)(1+i_1^*)}(\pi f^b+(1-\pi)f^g).$$

Our technical assumptions (see the appendix) guarantee that $f^g = \omega$ and $f^b < \omega$. The former holds as long as increasing investment in k at date 0 is more profitable than investment in international markets. And $f^b < \omega$ as long as saving some resources to absorb the production shocks at date 1 is more valuable than using all of those resources toward investment at date 0. It is apparent from the private program that e_1^b is the *only* equilibrium price that influences the date 0 decision. Let us study this connection more closely.

Since $f^g = \omega$, we simply need to consider the trade-off between increasing f^b and reducing k. At date 0, building a marginally larger plant increases (expected) date 2 profits by

$$(1-\pi)A+\pi\frac{1}{2}\left(A+a\frac{\Delta}{e_1^b}\right). \tag{26.9}$$

Building this larger plant requires the firm to raise an additional $c'(k)$ at date 0. The probability of a crisis is π, so in order to raise an additional $c'(k)$ at date 0, f^b must rise by

$$\frac{c'(k)(1+i_0^*)(1+i_1^*)}{\pi}.$$

The cost to the firm of raising f^b is that there are fewer resources to absorb the date 1 production shock. The fall in expected profits due to having fewer resources is

$$\pi\left(\frac{\Delta+e_1^b}{2(1+i_1^*)}\right)\frac{c'(k)(1+i_0^*)(1+i_1^*)}{\pi},$$

which can be simplified to

$$c'(k)(1+i_0^*)\left(\frac{\Delta+e_1^b}{2}\right). \tag{26.10}$$

The optimal choice of k by the private sector equalizes (9) and (10). We note two comparative statics and the conclusion that follows from them: (1) The benefit of building a larger plant size is decreasing in e_1^b; (2) The marginal cost of investing is increasing in e_1^b. For both reasons, k is decreasing with respect to e_1^b.[10]

The investment/financing decision at date 0 is really to create a (real) "peso" plant at the cost of having fewer "dollar" assets in the b-state. The reason for this is that the output from k can only be used as domestic collateral and hence is affected by the value of the exchange rate. On the other hand, to build the plant, the firm has to raise f^b, meaning that there is less international liquidity in the b-state.

Intuitively, the reason why e_1^b matters is that it changes the terms of this investment/financing decision. A more depreciated e_1^b gives firms less incentive to increase k and more incentive to decrease f. This is the reason that k is decreasing with respect to e_1^b.

3.2 Consumption Maximizing e_1^b

We now ask what level of the exchange rate, e_1^b, is required in order for the date 0 decisions to maximize (expected) aggregate consumption. We show that for $e_1^b < \Delta$, the private sector generally overborrows and overinvests relative to this benchmark.

Consider first the date 0 decisions of the private sector, (k, f^g, f^b), that maximize aggregate consumption. To arrive at this program, we simply substitute out the exchange rate of e_1^b from **PRIV**. If we substitute the market clearing condition for e_1^b from (7) into **PRIV** we find that

AGG:

$$\max_{k, f^g, f^b} \quad (1-\pi)(Ak + \omega - f^g) + \pi\left(\frac{\omega - f^b}{1+i_1^*}\Delta + \frac{A+a}{2}k\right)$$

$$s.t. \quad f^g, f^b \le \omega$$

$$c(k) \le \frac{1}{(1+i_0^*)(1+i_1^*)}(\pi f^b + (1-\pi)f^g).$$

The trade-off between increasing k versus f^b is very different here than in **PRIV**. The benefit of increasing plant size is

$$(1-\pi)A + \pi\frac{1}{2}(A+a).$$

For $e_1^b < \Delta$, this benefit is strictly lower than the private sector's computation. On the cost side, borrowing more to build this plant costs

$$c'(k)(1+i_0^*)\Delta.$$

For $e_1^b < \Delta$, the cost lies strictly above the private sector's computation.

We conclude that, if $e_1^b < \Delta$, then the private sector's date 0 decisions involve overborrowing and overinvesting.

[10] It is not e_1^b, per se, that matters in this trade-off, but $\frac{e_1^b}{e_2}$ (i.e., the expected future depreciation of the exchange rate) times one plus the i_1^p (the peso rate). Since we have set $e_2 = 1$ and $i_1^p = 0$, this point is obscured. We relax these assumptions later in the paper.

Intuitively, the cause of this date 0 overinvestment is that the private sector undervalues international liquidity in the b-state. At the aggregate level, resources in the b-state always generate a return of Δ from date 1 to date 2. On the other hand, firms see the cost of not having date 1 resources as proportional to e_1^b. As long as $e_1^b < \Delta$, the private sector's investment choices do not lead to maximization of date 2 expected aggregate consumption.

3.3 The Effect of Anticipated Monetary Policy

The previous result highlights a basic feature of the environment. Relative to the consumption-maximizing outcome, the private sector is always biased towards overborrowing and overinvesting. Thus we have a clear benchmark to evaluate policies that affect the exchange rate. In particular, the private sector's biases are exaggerated by a central bank that attempts to stabilize e_1^b. More generally, since the central bank can affect e_1^b with its choice of M, it can reduce this overborrowing problem through monetary policy. A straightforward argument establishes that if the private sector expects an increase in M if a crisis takes place at date 1, then k will be reduced at date 0 and expected date 2 consumption will rise.[11]

4. Dollarization of Liabilities

The credit channel literature in emerging markets has highlighted the role played by dollarization of domestic liabilities in magnifying the contraction. Indeed, even in our framework, a depreciated exchange rate deteriorates balance sheets by lowering the value of domestic assets relative to liabilities. But our framework qualifies the main conclusion from the literature: while dollarization may have the balance-sheet effect highlighted in that literature during mild crises (horizontal region), it does *not* during severe crises (vertical region).

At the firm level, it will seem that the problem is one of dollarized liabilities: firms are credit constrained, and the depreciated exchange rate will worsen balance sheets. But the relevant constraint is a shortage of aggregate international liquidity, not a firm-level balance sheet problem. That is, in a vertical crisis, the country faces a macroeconomic constraint, not a microeconomic one.[12]

However, for the insurance reasons we discussed in the previous section, dollarization is not innocuous. It will generally lead to private underinsurance. Let us discuss these dates 1 and 0 issues in turn.

4.1 Dollarization During Severe Crises: A Fallacy of Aggregation

In order to discuss domestic dollarization, we introduce a set of domestic consumers who lend to firms at date 0. For the purpose of this subsection, it is sufficient to start the analysis

[11]The argument is by contradiction. Suppose that increasing M causes k to rise. Then from market clearing at date 1, it must also cause e_1^b to rise. However, since k is a decreasing function of e_1^b, k must fall. This is a contradiction. Therefore, k is decreasing in M, and aggregate consumption is increasing in M.

[12]There can be distributional effects—i.e., from those that don't receive M to those that do, or from those with more dollarized liabilities to those with fewer liabilities—but these are likely to be subordinate to the aggregate constraint.

at date 1, given some preexisting debt. Suppose that firms arrive at the date 1 crisis state with some dollar-denominated debt, b^d, with domestic consumers. Thus, a distressed firm's investment is given as

$$\theta k = \omega^n + \frac{ak + M - e_1 b^d}{e_1}. \tag{26.11}$$

The literature emphasizes the fact that from (11) a depreciation reduces the dollar value of local assets ak and M, while it leaves unchanged the value of dollarized liabilities $e_1 b^d$. Moreover, since a monetary expansion depreciates the exchange rate, it may worsen balance sheets and, perversely, turn contractionary.

But, as we argue in section 2, this analysis does not consider that under severe crisis the main binding constraint is the lack of aggregate international liquidity. Thus, all these considerations of the effect of M on e_1, and hence on the domestic credit squeeze, are important for distributional issues (from more to less dollarized firms and consumers) but not for the aggregate. The exchange rate reacts to monetary policy precisely to cause a credit squeeze that equilibrates investment demand with the limited external supply. At the aggregate level, distressed firms' investment is still

$$\theta k = 2\omega^n. \tag{26.12}$$

Replacing (12) into (11) yields a new expression for the exchange rate as a function of M:

$$e_1^{b,d} = \frac{ak + M}{\omega^n + b^d}$$

where the $e_1^{b,d}$ stands for the equilibrium exchange rate with dollarized liabilities. This exchange rate expression needs to be contrasted with expression $e_1^{b,p}$ when domestic liabilities are denominated in pesos, b^p:

$$e_1^{b,p} = \frac{ak + M - b^p}{\omega^n}$$

From these two expressions, we can consider the effect of monetary expansions on the exchange rate in economies with different degrees of dollarization:

$$0 < e_1^{b,d}(M)' = \frac{1}{\omega^n + b^d} < \frac{1}{\omega^n} = e_1^{b,p}(M)'. \tag{26.13}$$

The first implication of this expression is that expanding money always depreciates the exchange rate. A central bank that is concerned with the balance sheet position of firms (as in [11]) will be inclined to contract money and support the exchange rate. But since during a vertical crisis, the important constraint is that of (12), the central bank will be *protecting the wrong margin.*

The second implication of (13) is that during severe crises the exchange rate in a dollarized economy will be *less* responsive to a monetary expansion than that of the nondollarized economy. This is a sort of *market-based fear of floating*, as it results from equilibrium considerations for a given monetary policy, and not from any additional caution that the central bank may choose to adopt when liabilities are dollarized. The reason for this result is precisely that a depreciation is more contractionary in a dollarized economy and, therefore, can more easily generate the domestic credit squeeze needed to reduce investment demand to levels compatible with the limited availability of international liquidity.

4.2 Underinsurance Effect of Dollarization

There is a more subtle effect of dollarization in our framework. A central bank at date 1 that is concerned with preserving the balance sheets of firms may, in the vertical region, choose to support the exchange rate. But boosting e_1^b causes firms to undervalue insuring against the b-state and set f^b higher. This follows from the underinsurance results of the previous section. In this sense, the negative effect of central bank support of the exchange rate is that external liabilities will become less contingent. In a model with richer options on the denomination of liabilities, this effect will lead to excessive dollarization of liabilities (see Caballero and Krishnamurthy 2003).[13]

That is, while we challenge the standard view that dollarization of liabilities is a key factor *during* severe crises, we argue that it is an important factor behind crises due to the negative effects it has on private agents' external *insurance* decisions.

4.3 Dollarization of External Liabilities

Before concluding this section, we should point out that there is a related but distinct issue—the dollarization of *external* liabilities. This refers to the fact that most emerging market external debt is not denominated in the issuing country's currency. If debt is denominated in a country's own currency, then the debt will be effectively contingent on aggregate outcomes. In practice, of course, unlike our theoretical assumptions, there is very little contingent debt issued by emerging markets. Thus, if developing economies could or would borrow abroad in their own currency, they would effectively obtain insurance from foreigners against events that depreciate their currency, such as the tightening of external financial constraints. The "original sin" literature in, e.g., Hausmann, Panizza, and Stein (2001) highlights reluctance on the supply side of that market, while Caballero and Krishnamurthy (2003) describe demand side problems behind the lack of contingency of external debt. In our current analysis, external dollarization simply means that there is less contingency in liabilities, so that f^b is higher and closer to f^g. As a result, the country will have less international liquidity in the crisis state. It is also worth noting that the problem of external liability dollarization is reinforced by the underinsurance effects of dollarization of domestic liabilities as discussed above.

Adding external liability dollarization to our problem is conceptually straightforward and makes the supply of international funds at date 1 effectively diagonal, but nothing substantive changes in our analysis. We discuss this extension in section 6.

5. Policy Constraints and Policy Options

In many instances, a central bank faces constraints that force it to support the exchange rate. Dollarization of domestic liabilities is one such instance (whether the market or the central bank determines this is not important for our argument here). Inflation credibility problems are another one. We begin this section with a discussion of inflation credibility, and then turn to alternative policy instruments when monetary policy is constrained to be procyclical or less countercyclical than desirable. There is an important difference in the

[13]This implication is supported by Bleakley and Cowan (2002), who find that in economies with fixed exchange rates, the match between the denomination of liabilities and that of revenues is weaker than in economies with flexible exchange rates.

costs of losing monetary policy during severe crises vis-à-vis doing so in mild ones. In the latter, as in the standard Mundell-Fleming context, the cost is that the central bank loses a countercyclical instrument to smooth fluctuations. In the former, on the other hand, the cost is mainly an "insurance" one. The central bank loses a relatively cheap instrument to induce the private sector to take adequate precautions against crises. In the standard framework, the natural response to the loss of monetary policy is to search for another countercyclical policy instrument (e.g., fiscal policy). In the vertical crisis environment, the natural response is to search for an alternative insurance mechanism. We discuss such alternatives in the second part of this section.

5.1 Limited Inflation Credibility

Limited inflation credibility has two effects in our environment. First, a central bank with a history of high inflation cannot afford the inflationary consequences of an exchange rate depreciation during a crisis. This is a common explanation for the apparent "fear of floating" of central banks in emerging economies (see, e.g., Calvo and Reinhart 2003). However, for the reasons we have outlined above, the anticipation of a contractionary monetary policy during a vertical crisis will exacerbate the private sector's underinsurance problem and thereby worsen the crisis.

A second problem caused by limited inflation credibility is that a central bank that expands monetary policy in a crisis will have a limited effect on real balances. That is, in our environment, a central bank does better by increasing real money balances during a crisis. However, a central bank with limited inflation credibility will create inflation with little effect on real money balances and thereby on the expected return from hoarding international liquidity. In order to see this, note that in all our derivations up to now we have assumed there is long-run inflation (price level) credibility, so that e_2 remains at one regardless of the monetary policy adopted at date 1. But suppose that whenever there is a depreciation during a crisis, some of it is expected to pass through into e_2.

To be concrete, suppose that e_2 (i.e., the date 2 price level) is an increasing function of $\frac{M}{\underline{M}}$, with $e_2(1) = 1$. In a vertical crisis, a distressed firm sells M units of money and ak of domestic collateral to raise funds for salvaging production. The intact firms lend ω^n against these assets. To an intact firm, the money is worth $1/e_2$, proportionately less than the ak of domestic collateral. Thus, let us define the return on lending international liquidity as

$$i_1^d = \frac{M/e_2 + ak}{\omega^n} - 1.$$

The return to an intact firm of purchasing money with international liquidity is just $\frac{e_1}{e_2} - 1$. Since this return must equal the return to lending against the domestic collateral of ak, we find that the interest parity condition is:

$$\frac{e_1}{e_2} - 1 = i_1^d.$$

For the case where $e_2 = 1$, we previously showed that the date 0 level of investment, k, is a decreasing function of e_1. We argued that supporting the currency at date 1 had the consequence of exacerbating the date 0 overinvestment problem of the private sector. Likewise, allowing e_1 to depreciate through an expansionary monetary policy reduced the overinvestment problem.

When e_2 is not fixed at one, a similar argument to that of section 3.1 establishes that k is a decreasing function of $\frac{e_1}{e_2}$. But since

$$\frac{e_1}{e_2} = \frac{M/e_2 + ak}{\omega^n},$$

the important term for policy purposes is the term involving real money balances (i.e., M/e_2). An expansionary monetary policy raises real balances only to

$$\frac{M}{e_2} < M.$$

Thus, a central bank with limited inflation credibility will have to resort to additional (and possibly very costly) mechanisms to induce adequate private sector insurance decisions. We turn to this discussion next.

5.2 Insurance Substitutes

The problem created by being unable to raise real balances is that the social-private spread, $\Delta - (1 + i_1^d)$, remains high. Thus, the return to hoarding international liquidity until date 1 remains undervalued, and private insurance decisions are distorted. As we argued in section 3, these considerations are unique to the vertical environment, because the insurance problem only arises if the aggregate international liquidity constraint binds.

There are two obvious ex-ante policy measures that can deal with the underinsurance problem: taxation of capital inflows during normal times (date 0) and international liquidity requirements at date 0. We now characterize the relationship between an ex-ante tax and i_1^d.

The first order condition in **AGG** is

$$c'(k^{AGG})(1 + i_0^*)\Delta = (1 - \pi)A + \pi\frac{1}{2}(A + a),$$

whereas for the private sector the condition sets (9) equal to (10) (with e_1 replaced by $1 + i_1^d$).

Aligning the date 0 private and consumption-maximizing incentives is a matter of choosing a tax/transfer policy. Suppose that the central bank levies a tax τ per unit of k, which is returned to firms in a lump sum fashion. Then the first order condition for the private sector becomes

$$c'(k)(1 + i_0^*)\frac{\Delta + 1 + i_1^d}{2} = (1 - \pi)A + \pi\frac{1}{2}\left(A + a\frac{\Delta}{1 + i_1^d}\right) - \tau.$$

Choosing τ to align the private and central-bank incentives yields that for any equilibrium level of $i_{1,\tau}^d$, the optimal tax solves

$$\tau(i_{1,\tau}^d) = \frac{1}{2}\left(\frac{a\pi}{1 + i_{1,\tau}^d} + c'(k^{AGG})(1 + i_0^*)\right)(\Delta - (1 + i_{1,\tau}^d)).$$

The tax is increasing in $\Delta - (1 + i_{1,\tau}^d)$. Thus, economies where the central bank cannot follow countercyclical monetary policy, and therefore $\Delta - (1 + i_1^d)$ remains high, may need to rely on capital controls to correct the underinsurance problem. Note that the same result could be achieved via a contingent liquidity requirement. The tax solution gives the private sector incentives to choose the efficient k, thus resulting in the efficient $\omega - f^b$. Alternatively, the central bank could mandate directly that each firm preserve international liquidity for the date 1 crisis state, so that the efficient level of $\omega - f^b$ is realized.

In practice, taxes come with their own sets of distortions: deadweight costs of taxation, costs of enforcement, evasion, etc. However, the important point to recognize is that, in the vertical environment, the cost of losing monetary policy is *not* being unable to manage aggregate demand or the extent of the domestic credit squeeze at date 1. Rather, the cost is the underinsurance by the private sector at date 0. In this sense, the cost of having to enforce capital controls may be seen as a direct cost of losing monetary policy.

6. Robustness: Peso Rates and Diagonal Supply

In this section, we show that our main conclusions are robust to modifications in two of the most stylized features of our model: the absence of a monetary friction and the absolute price inelasticity of the supply of funds during crises.

6.1 Peso Rates and Interest Parity Condition

Up to now we have simplified our analysis by removing all monetary frictions from the analysis, and therefore have set the domestic peso interest rate to zero. This simplifies exchange rate determination at date 1, but leaves us with an unusual model of money. Here we sketch a more standard model of money, in which money is special because it provides a transaction service.[14] Our substantive results remain unchanged, although now we recover the standard exchange rate effect via the interest parity condition in addition to the excess sensitivity result we discussed in the previous sections.

Let us return to the full inflation credibility case ($e_2 = 1$) and let us focus on the vertical region and the bad aggregate state.

At the end of date 1, the government has liabilities of B bonds and M units of money per capita. Each bond is redeemed at date 2 for one unit of money, and the government is credible in ensuring that the price level at date 2 is one. At date 1, money is the only domestically liquid asset. Neither claims against ak (corporate bonds) nor the government bonds are liquid. Thus, at date 1, distressed firms sell M units of money to the intact firms in exchange for ω^n units of international liquidity, which means that

$$e_1^b = \frac{M}{\omega^n}.$$

It is instructive to go through the steps that take us to this equation in order to disentangle the mechanisms through which money affects the exchange rate during severe crises in this economy.

We introduce a date 1^- in order to study peso interest rates and the effects of open market operations. At date 1^- the aggregate state of the world has been realized, but the identity

[14]See Diamond and Rajan (2001, 2003) and Lorenzoni (2001) for alternative models of money in liquidity-based frameworks.

of agents receiving the shock (distressed or intact) has not. Because of the latter, agents are all identical at 1^-.

At date 1^-, both the bond market and the money market are open to all agents. Entering date 1^-, the government has outstanding $\underline{B}$ bonds and $\underline{M}$ money. The government does an open market operation to purchase $(\underline{B} - B)$ bonds for $(M - \underline{M})$ money.

Let us consider the relative asset returns on bonds, money, and international liquidity at date 1^-.

One bond yields one unit of money at date 2 and costs $1/(1 + i_1^p)$ units of money at date 1^-, where i_1^p is the peso interest rate. One unit of money can be sold at date 1 to finance the liquidity shock if the agent is distressed. Money is sold for international liquidity at a price of $1/e_{1^-}$. Each unit of international liquidity yields Δ at date 2. Thus the expected return on holding money from date 1^- to date 2 is $0.5\ (\Delta/e_{1^-} + 1)$. As before, $(\Delta \geq e_{1^-}$, which means that the net return is positive. It immediately follows that indifference between holding money and bonds requires that

$$1 + i_1^p = \frac{1}{2}\left(\frac{\Delta}{e_{1^-}} + 1\right). \tag{26.14}$$

One unit of money also can be converted in the foreign exchange market into one unit of international liquidity, at the price of e_{1^-}. One unit of international liquidity either can be used in production at date 1 or sold to a distressed firm at date 1. The expected benefit of the unit of international liquidity is $\frac{1}{2}(\Delta + e_{1^-})$.Thus, the interest parity condition is

$$(1 + i_1^p)e_{1^-} = \frac{1}{2}(\Delta + e_{1^-}). \tag{26.15}$$

In the standard interest parity condition, the right-hand side of (15) is fixed, and a reduction in i_1^p must be offset by a depreciation in e_{1^-} to keep the left-hand side constant as well. But the depreciation in our vertical environment raises the return to the dollar-lender in the right-hand side of (15), which means that the left-hand side must rise, and this is achieved by a further depreciation in e_{1^-}. The latter is the excess sensitivity result we have discussed, and it results from the relaxation of the domestic credit squeeze caused by the monetary expansion.

Finally, combining (14) and (15), we can solve for the peso interest rate and the exchange rate as a function of monetary policy:

$$1 + i_1^p = \frac{1}{2}\left(\frac{\Delta}{M}\omega^n + 1\right)$$

$$e_{1^-} = \frac{M}{\omega^n}.$$

The latter is the expression we started this section with, and it summarizes the two channels through which money affects the exchange rate: interest parity and domestic credit squeeze.

Relative to our earlier model, it is the former (and standard) channel that is new. But neither channel can change the fact that international liquidity is fixed at date 1 and hence output cannot be affected by monetary policy:

$$C^V = \left(\frac{A + a}{2}\right)k + \omega^n\Delta + y^c.$$

And for date 0 decisions, it is only the *second* channel that matters, which is common to this and the model without monetary frictions.

6.2 "Diagonal" Supply

Let us now return to the model without monetary frictions, and continue to assume $e_2 = 1$. But rather than an inelastic supply of funds at date 1, let us consider instead a supply curve of the form

$$\omega^n s(e_1) \quad \text{where} \quad s(1) = 1, \quad s'(\cdot) > 0.$$

That is, the supply of international funds is "diagonal" as opposed to vertical.[15]

Equilibrium at date 1 is now

$$\frac{ak + M}{1 + i_1^d} = \omega^n s(e_1).$$

As in the pure vertical model, e_1 is increasing in M. However, consider the expression for total consumption at date 2. This is

$$C^V = \left(\frac{A + a}{2}\right) k + \omega^n s(e_1)\Delta + y^c,$$

which is now an increasing function of e_1 through the $s(\cdot)$ function. This implies that increasing M does have a contemporaneous effect on C^V.

Thus, from a date 1 perspective, the diagonal model has elements of both the horizontal model and the vertical model. As in the horizontal model, there is an aggregate demand channel/credit squeeze channel through which expanding money increases aggregate consumption. As in the vertical model, the money expansion depreciates the exchange rate beyond the standard interest parity effect.

Now, let us shift back to date 0. At this date, the firm contemplates borrowing some resources and increasing k, the size of the plant. As before, the shadow cost of the resources is increasing in e_1. A higher expected e_1 induces a firm to save some dollar resources until date 1, at which point these resources can always be lent to return $e_1 - 1$. Moreover, as long as $e_1 < \Delta$, the private sector's decisions will not be consumption maximizing. Thus, as in the vertical model, there is an insurance channel for monetary policy in the diagonal model. Expanding M at date 1 depreciates e_1. The anticipation of such depreciation makes the private sector reduce investment at date 0 and increase its insurance against the date 1 shock.

[15] The diagonal supply also captures the idea that depreciating the exchange rate increases exports and, if the export sector is an important part of international collateral, thereby expands supply. Christiano, Gust, and Roldos (2004) offer a related perspective on diagonal supply. In their model, imperfect liquidity substitution stems from imperfect input-substitution and from the fact that different inputs are paid in different currencies. The "diagonal" aspect of their model arises from the (limited) possibility of substituting tradables and nontradables inputs.

7. Final Remarks

The past decade has witnessed several episodes in which the sudden reversals of capital inflows triggers an emerging markets' crisis. These events have placed the risk of "sudden stops" as a central macroeconomic concern for emerging market economies. The main contribution of our paper is to illustrate how monetary policy affects financial constraints of firms during a sudden stop crisis and to highlight an *insurance* effect of monetary policy. Domestic monetary expansion relaxes individual financial constraints but is unable to relax the aggregate financial constraint faced by these economies during crises—it is the wrong kind of liquidity for such a purpose. However, while monetary policy is largely futile once the sudden stop has taken place, the anticipation of a particular reaction by the authority is important for private sector insurance decisions. A flexible exchange rate system, coupled with a countercyclical monetary policy, provides better *insurance* incentives to the private sector than a policy of defending the exchange rate during sudden stops.

Our insurance mechanism is distinct (or in addition to) the standard moral-hazard/free-insurance argument (see, e.g., Dooley 1999). In the latter argument, crises result from an implicit commitment by a local government or foreign institution to transfer resources to the imprudent borrower; a fixed exchange rate transfers reserves at submarket value (during crises) to the dollar-borrower or peso-investor. In our model, there is no direct transfer from the government. The monetary contraction implicit in the defense of the exchange rate lowers the domestic liquidity that borrowers can offer to dollar-lenders during the sudden stop, and in so doing, it lowers the effective return from *new* local dollar lending. By doing so, it affects the incentives to hoard international liquidity for crises.

More generally, monetary policy and its constraints have (unintended) consequences for the private sector's insurance decisions with respect to sudden stops. Policies that exacerbate the domestic credit squeeze during sudden stops, or constraints that limit the authorities' ability to relax domestic financial constraints, lead to socially imprudent private sector actions.

Our emphasis on dual liquidity and insurance has relevance for evaluation of other government policies. Proactively managing international reserves may result in benefits in our framework (see Caballero and Krishnamurthy 2004). Since international reserves are a form of international liquidity, and the private sector carries too little international liquidity into crises, the central bank has a role to play by carrying reserves in place of the private sector. Injecting reserves during a crisis relaxes the international financial constraint faced by the private sector and stabilizes the exchange rate. Relaxing the constraint is beneficial, but the effect on the private sector's own insurance incentives is not, for reasons akin to those we discussed in the context of monetary policy. Reserves management and monetary policy become complementary policy tools in this context. At the very least, the central bank ought to sterilize the forex intervention and possibly go beyond that in the monetary expansion in order to offset the perverse incentive effect of the reserves injection.

Of course, the insurance dimension we highlight in our analysis is not a substitute for conventional inflation credibility concerns. Quite the contrary, without inflation credibility, the central bank will be unable to let the exchange rate float and expand monetary policy during sudden stops, and may well be forced into tightening monetary policy. The anticipation of this behavior is very costly in our setting, precisely because it exacerbates the private sector's underinsurance problem. In other words, our insurance consideration *raises* the value of achieving medium-term inflation credibility.

Our stylized model is subject to many caveats. One worth mentioning in concluding is the lack of true dynamics. In reality, crises build up, going first through a horizontal phase in which domestic financial conditions tighten and external borrowing becomes gradually more expensive, then falling into a sharp vertical sudden-stop phase. A central question for policymakers in this context is how to conduct monetary policy at the early stages of the crisis, when supply is still horizontal but there is a concern that events may lead to a binding international liquidity constraint. At this stage, tightening monetary policy will destroy financially constrained projects but save international liquidity for the vertical event. We conjecture that this trade-off can be analyzed in terms similar to those we have used throughout: if the commitment to an aggressive countercyclical monetary policy in case of a vertical event is credible, then there is little need to tighten during the horizontal phase. But if the commitment is not credible or feasible, then the appropriate response is to tighten during the early phase in order to protect international liquidity, very much as taxing capital flows at date 0 was advisable in our simplified model when there were constraints on monetary policy during crises. In fact, the costs in terms of the additional financial distress imposed on the domestic private sector are, to a large extent, comparable to the costs of the ex-ante measures we already discussed.

Finally, while our analysis has focused on emerging markets, the underlying structure may be a starting point for other applications. Our model illustrates how a bottleneck may segment financial markets and create liquidity premia on assets. It shows how monetary policy affects and is affected by these bottlenecks. There are many other scenarios, such as liquidity traps and post-bubble-collapses, where similar ingredients appear worthy of consideration. We are currently exploring these applications.

Appendix

Financing Assumptions

The financial frictions of the model are embodied in the following two assumptions:

Assumption 1 (International Collateral): Foreigners lend to domestic firms only against the backing of ω. Domestic agents lend against ω, M, and ak.

Assumption 2 (Domestic Collateral): A domestic lender can only be sure that a firm will produce ak units of goods at date 2. Any excess production based on physical reinvestment at date 1 is neither observable nor verifiable.

One last assumption is required to rule out date 0 insurance arrangements that transfer resources from distressed firms to intact firms.

Assumption 3 (Nonobservability of Production Shock): The production shock at date 1 is idiosyncratic. The identity of firms receiving the shock is private information.

The mechanism design problem associated with these financing and informational constraints corresponds to the one in **AGG.** There is also a banking arrangement that, in principle, may get around the private information constraint, but this is very fragile.

Technical Assumptions

Consider next the technical assumptions on parameters that we have used. The program in **AGG** is

AGG:

$$\begin{aligned} \max_{k,f^g,f^b} \quad & (1-\pi)(Ak+\omega-f^g)+\pi\left(\frac{\omega-f^b}{1+i_1^*}\Delta+\frac{A+a}{2}k\right) \\ s.t. \quad & f^g, f^b \leq \omega \\ & c(k) \leq \frac{1}{(1+i_0^*)(1+i_1^*)}(\pi f^b+(1-\pi)f^g). \end{aligned}$$

First, we require that $\omega = f^g$ in this program, or that the return to investing domestically exceeds that of investing abroad.

Assumption 4 (High Investment Return):

$$(1-\pi)A+\pi\frac{A+a}{2} \geq c'\left(\frac{\omega}{(1+i_0^*)(1+i_1^*)}\right)(1+i_0^*)(1+i_1^*).$$

Second, we require that the solution features some insurance against the b-state, so that $f^b < \omega$

Assumption 5 (High Return to Insuring):

$$c'\left(\frac{\omega}{(1+i_0^*)(1+i_1^*)}\right)(1+i_0^*)\Delta \geq (1-\pi)A+\pi\frac{A+a}{2}.$$

These last two assumptions can both be met by choosing a large enough value for Δ.

We require that equilibrium, with no central bank intervention, places us in the vertical region, or

$$1+i_0^* < e_1 < \Delta$$

The first-order condition for the program in **PRIV** is

$$c'(k)(1+i_0^*)\frac{\Delta+e_1}{2} = (1-\pi)A+\pi\frac{1}{2}(A+a\frac{\Delta}{e_1}).$$

Denote the solution to this equation as $k(e_1)$. Then the largest value of k is attained when $e_1 = 1+i_1^*$, and the smallest value when $e_1 = \Delta$. Using this knowledge as well as the market clearing condition leads to:

Assumption 6 (Equilibrium in Vertical Region):

$$\frac{\pi(\underline{M}+ak(i_1^*))}{\omega-(1+i_0^*)(1+i_1^*)c(k(i_1^*))} < \frac{\Delta}{1+i_{1*}}$$

$$\frac{\pi(\underline{M}ak(\Delta-1))}{\omega-(1+i_0^*)(1+i_1^*)c(k(\Delta-1))} > 1$$

Finally, we have implicitly assumed that the maximum reinvestment constraint does not bind in the vertical equilibrium:

$$\frac{k}{2} > \frac{\omega - f^b}{1+i_1^*} = \frac{\omega - c(k)(1+i_0^*)(1+i_1^*)}{\pi(1+i_1^*)}$$

This can be rewritten as

$$e_1 = \frac{\pi(\underline{M} + ak)}{\omega - (1+i_0^*)(1+i_1^*)c(k)} > 2a.$$

This leads to:

Assumption 7 (Reinvestment Constraint Does Not Bind in V):

$$a < \frac{1+i_1^*}{2}$$

Dollarization of Domestic Liabilities

We sketch an extension to the model of section 6 in order to address dollarization of liabilities. As mentioned in section 5.2, this is one of the primary reasons that policymakers give for being unable to lower interest rates during a crisis.

Suppose that firms have debts of D dollars that have to be settled at date 1^-. These debts are owed to domestic consumers, so that they do not affect the international liquidity of the country. Then the total peso net worth of agents at date 1^-, before any open market operations, is

$$NW = \frac{B}{1+i_1^p} + \underline{M} + \frac{ak}{1+i_1^p} - De_{1^-} \tag{26.A1}$$

Now suppose that the government does an open market operation where it purchases bonds with money. Since this transaction is done at market prices, the net worth remains as in (Al).

The open market operation has two effects. First, it lowers i_1^p and thereby raises $\frac{ak}{1+i_1^p}$. Second, it raises e_{1^-} and thereby increases the debt burden of domestic firms. For a large enough value of D, it is clear that the second effect can overwhelm the first, so that peso net worth *falls* rather than rises with the open market operation.

The interesting case for our model is when, after the open market operation, $NW < M$. That is, the peso net worth of the firms is less than the aggregate amount of money in the domestic economy. In this case, firms will not be able to sell their assets at date 1^- to acquire all of M. Thus, the market clearing condition at date 1 becomes

$$1 + i_1^d = \frac{NW}{\omega^n}.$$

In this case, expansionary open market operations lower i_1^d rather than raise it, but still have no effect on output. At date 1, since expansionary open market operations depreciate the exchange rate, the central bank will raise interest rates. The reaction in this case is ex-ante optimal, since raising interest rates causes i_1^d to rise and leads to better insurance decisions by the private sector. However, the fact that the central bank's time inconsistency problem is attenuated when domestic liabilities are dollarized does not mean that the underinsurance problem has been resolved. Quite the contrary, time inconsistency has been reduced because the country has no access to monetary policy.

References

Aghion, Philippe, Philippe Bacchetta, and Abhijit Banerjee. 2000. "Currency Crises and Monetary Policy with Credit Constraints." Mimeo, Harvard University.

Bernanke, Ben, and Mark Gertler. 1995. "Inside the Black Box: The Credit Channel of Monetary Policy Transmission." *Journal of Economic Perspectives* 9 (Fall): 27-48.

Bernanke, Ben, Mark Gertler, and Simon Gilchrist. 1999. "The Financial Accelerator in a Quantitative Business Cycle Framework." *In Handbook of Macroeconomics*, Vol. 1C, ed. John B. Taylor and Michael Woodford. Elsevier Science.

Bleakley, Hoyt, and Kevin Cowan. 2002. "Corporate Dollar Debt and Depreciations: Much Ado About Nothing?" Working Paper 02–05, Federal Reserve Bank of Boston.

Broner, Fernando, Guido Lorenzoni, and Sergio Schmukler. 2003. "Why do Emerging Markets Borrow Short Term?" Mimeo.

Bulow, Jeremy, and Kenneth Rogoff. 1989. "A Constant Recontracting Model of Sovereign Debt." *Journal of Political Economy* 97 (1): 155–78.

Caballero, Ricardo J., and Arvind Krishnamurthy. 2001. "International and Domestic Collateral Constraints in a Model of Emerging Market Crises." *Journal of Monetary Economics* 48: 513–48.

Caballero, Ricardo J., and Arvind Krishnamurthy. 2003. "Excessive Dollar Debt: Underinsurance and Domestic Financial Underdevelopment." *Journal of Finance* 58 (2): 867–93.

Caballero, Ricardo J., and Arvind Krishnamurthy. 2004. "Smoothing Sudden Stops." *Journal of Economic Theory* 119 (1): 104–27.

Caballero, Ricardo J., and Arvind Krishnamurthy. 2005. "Inflation Targeting and Sudden Stops." In *The Inflation-Targeting Debate*, ed. Ben S. Bernanke and Michael Woodford. Chicago: University of Chicago Press.

Calvo, Guillermo A., and Carmen M. Reinhart. 2003. "Fear of Floating." *Quarterly Journal of Economics* 117 (2): 379–408.

Cespedes, Luis F., Robert Chang, and Andres Velasco. 2000. "Balance Sheets and Exchange Rate Policy." NBER Working Paper No. W7840 (August).

Christiano, Lawrence J., Christopher Gust, and Jorge Roldos. 2004. "Monetary Policy in a Financial Crisis." *Journal of Economic Theory* 119 (1): 64–103.

Diamond, Douglas W., and Raghuram G. Rajan. 2001. "Liquidity Shortages and Financial Crises." Mimeo, University of Chicago (June).

Diamond, Douglas W., and Raghuram G. Rajan. 2003. "Money in a Theory of Banking." NBER Working Paper No. 10070 (October).

Dooley, Michael. 1999. "Responses to Volatile Capital Flows: Controls, Asset-Liability Management and Architecture." World Bank Conference on Capital Flows, Financial Crises, and Policies (April).

Dornbusch, Rudiger. 1976. "Expectations and Exchange Rate Dynamics." *Journal of Political Economy* 84 (December).

Dornbusch, Rudiger. 2001. "Fewer Monies, Better Monies." NBER Working Paper No. 8324 (June).

Eaton, Jonathan, and Mark Gersovitz. 1981. "Debt with Potential Repudiation: Theory and Estimation." *Review of Economic Studies* 48: 289–309.

Edwards, Sebastian, and Eduardo Levy-Yeyati. 2003. "Flexible Exchange Rates as Shock Absorbers." NBER Working Paper No. 9867 (June).

Furman, Jason, and Joseph E. Stiglitz. 1998. "Economic Crises: Evidence and Insights from East Asia." *Brookings Papers of Economic Activity* 2.

Gertler, Mark, Simon Gilchrist, and Fabio M. Natalucci. 2001. "External Constraints on Monetary Policy and the Financial Accelerator." New York University Working Paper (February).

Hausmann, Ricardo, Ugo Panizza, and Ernesto Stein. 2001. "Why do countries float the way they float?" *Journal of Development Economics* 66 (2): 387–414.

Holmstrom, Bengt, and Jean Tirole. 1998. "Private and Public Supply of Liquidity." *Journal of Political Economy* 106 (1): 1–40.
Kiyotaki, Nobuhiro, and John Moore. 1997. "Credit Cycles." *Journal of Political Economy* 105 (2): 211–48.
Lorenzoni, Guido. 2001. "Interest Rate Stabilization and Monetary Control: A Reconciliation." Mimeo, Princeton University.
Woodford, Michael. 1990. "Public Debt as Private Liquidity." *American Economic Review, Papers and Proceedings* 80 (May): 382–88.

INDEX

Index

Note: Page numbers followed by "*f*" and "*t*" denote figures and tables, respectively.

www.ingramcontent.com/pod-product-compliance
Ingram Content Group UK Ltd.
Pitfield, Milton Keynes, MK11 3LW, UK
UKHW051224160926
475595UK00022B/164